THE LIFESPAN

FIFTH EDITION

GUY R. LEFRANÇOIS

University of Alberta

WADSWORTH PUBLISHING COMPANY

I(T)P® An International Thomson Publishing Company

Belmont • Albany • Bonn • Boston • Cincinnati • Detroit • London • Madrid • Melbourne •
Mexico City • New York • Paris • San Francisco • Singapore • Tokyo • Toronto • Washington

Education Editor	SABRA HORNE (P. 415)
Editorial Assistant	LOUISE MENDELSON
Developmental Editor	JOHN BERGEZ (P. 23)
Production Editor	ANGELA MANN (P. 402)
Managing Designer	ANDREW OGUS (P. 159)
Print Buyer	KAREN HUNT (P. 545)
Permissions Editor	JEANNE BOSSCHART
Art Editors	EMMA NASH AND CATHERINE LINBERG (P. 378)
Copy Editor	JENNIFER GORDON
Text and Cover Designer	CLOYCE WALL (P. XIV)
Dummier	ADRIANE BOSWORTH
Cover Illustration	ANDREW POWELL
Compositor	THOMPSON TYPE
Printer	VON HOFFMANN PRESS

FOR MORE INFORMATION,
CONTACT WADSWORTH PUBLISHING COMPANY:

Wadsworth Publishing Company
10 Davis Drive
Belmont, California 94002
USA

International Thomson Publishing Europe
Berkshire House 168-173
High Holborn
London, WC1V 7AA
England

Thomas Nelson Australia
102 Dodds Street
South Melbourne 3205
Victoria, Australia

Nelson Canada
1120 Birchmount Road
Scarborough, Ontario
Canada M1K 5G4

International Thomson Editores
Campos Eliseos 385, Piso 7
Col. Polanco
11560 México D.F. México

International Thomson Publishing GmbH
Königswinterer Strasse 418
53227 Bonn
Germany

International Thomson Publishing Asia
221 Henderson Road
#05-10 Henderson Building
Singapore 0315

International Thomson Publishing Japan
Hirakawacho Kyowa Building, 3F
2-2-1 Hirakawacho
Chiyoda-ku, Tokyo 102
Japan

Library of Congress Cataloging-in-Publication Data
Lefrançois, Guy R.
    The lifespan / Guy R. Lefrançois.—5th ed.
        p.   cm.
    Includes bibliographical references and index.
    ISBN 0-534-25482-9
    1. Developmental psychology.   I. Title.
BF713.L44   1995
155—dc20   95-17026

DEDICATED

TO MY GRANDPARENTS AND ALL THE OLD PEOPLE WITHOUT WHOM WE WOULD NOT BE HERE TODAY.

TO MY CHILDREN AND ALL THE YOUNG PEOPLE WITHOUT WHOM WE WILL NOT BE HERE TOMORROW.

Brief Contents

CONTENTS

PART ONE: THE BEGINNING

Know then thyself, presume not God to scan;
The proper study of Mankind is Man.

Alexander Pope,
Essays on Man

*The dwarf sees farther than the giant, when
he has the giant's shoulders to stand on.*

Samuel Taylor Coleridge,
The Friend

2 THEORIES OF LIFESPAN DEVELOPMENT   28

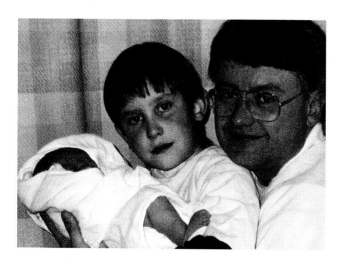

Sir Roger told them, with the air of a man who would not give his judgment rashly, that much might be said on both sides.

Joseph Addison,
The Spectator, Vol. 1

Nature is often hidden; sometimes overcome;
seldom extinguished.

Francis Bacon,
Of Nature in Man

4 PRENATAL DEVELOPMENT AND BIRTH   90

PART TWO: INFANCY

*I wish either my father or my mother, or indeed both of them,
as they were in duty both equally bound to it, had minded
what they were about when they begot me.*

Laurence Sterne,
Tristram Shandy

Language was not powerful enough to describe the infant phenomenon.

Charles Dickens,
Nicholas Nickleby

When the first baby laughed for the first time, the laugh broke into a thousand pieces and they all went skipping about, and that was the beginning of fairies.

James Matthew Barrie,
Peter Pan

PART THREE: EARLY CHILDHOOD

Go directly—see what she's doing, and tell her she mustn't.
Punch, 1872

Every time a child says "I don't believe in fairies," there is a little fairy somewhere that falls down dead.

James Matthew Barrie,
Peter Pan

8 SOCIAL DEVELOPMENT: EARLY CHILDHOOD 220

More than either, it [England] resembles a family, a rather stuffy Victorian family, with not many black sheep in it but with all its cupboards bursting with skeletons. It has rich relations who have to be kow-towed to and poor relations who are horribly sat upon, and there is a deep conspiracy about the source of the family income. It is a family in which the young are generally thwarted and most of the power is in the hands of irresponsible uncles and bedridden aunts. Still, it is a family.

George Orwell,
England, Your England

"I dare say you haven't had practice," said the Queen. "When I was your age, I always did it for half an hour a day. Why, sometimes I've believed as many as six impossible things before breakfast."

Lewis Carroll,
*Through the Looking-Glass
and What Alice Found There*

PART FOUR: MIDDLE CHILDHOOD

10 SOCIAL DEVELOPMENT: MIDDLE CHILDHOOD 282

PART FIVE: ADOLESCENCE

Everybody worships me, it's nauseating.

Noel Coward,
Present Laughter

12 SOCIAL DEVELOPMENT: ADOLESCENCE 342

Live as long as you may, the first twenty years are the longest half of your life.

Robert Southey,
The Doctor

We think so because other people think so,
Or because — or because —after all we do think so,
Or because, we were told so, and think we must think so,
Or because we once thought so, and think we still think so,
Or because having thought so, we think we will think so.

Henry Sidgwick,
Lines Composed in His Sleep

PART SIX: EARLY ADULTHOOD

13 PHYSICAL AND COGNITIVE DEVELOPMENT: EARLY ADULTHOOD 380

Give me chastity and continence, but not yet.
St. Augustine,
Confessions

PART SEVEN: MIDDLE ADULTHOOD

I am convinced digestion is the great secret of life.
Sydney Smith,
 in a letter to Arthur Kingslake

Happiness in marriage is entirely a matter of chance.

Jane Austen,
Northanger Abbey

16 Social Development: Middle Adulthood 468

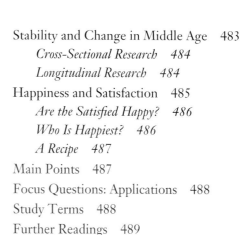

PART EIGHT: LATE ADULTHOOD

It is always the season for the old to learn.

Aeschylus,
Fragments

I keep looking back, as far as I can remember, and I can't think what it was like to feel young, really young.

John Osborne,
Look Back in Anger

18   SOCIAL DEVELOPMENT: LATE ADULTHOOD   518

So little done, so much to do!
Last words of Cecil John Rhodes

PART NINE: THE END

And come he slow or come he fast,
It is but Death who comes at last.
Sir Walter Scott,
Marmion

Topical Arrangement of Contents

A Visual Guide to The Lifespan, Fifth Edition

Dear Reader,

THE LIFESPAN is an academic text. Its purpose is to lay before you, in simple language, the concepts and preoccupations of lifespan developmental psychology, to present clearly and accurately the field's most compelling discoveries, controversies, puzzles, and promises. The substance of THE LIFESPAN is contemporary research in human development; its sources include psychology, biology, medicine, education, anthropology, philosophy, genetics, and demography; its function is to teach.

But teaching is more than just telling. It isn't enough simply to gather and organize the facts of a discipline and squeeze them between two covers. Good teaching also requires motivating, illustrating, explaining, relating, evaluating, maybe even inspiring.

THE LIFESPAN tries to be a good teacher. It illustrates and compares; sometimes it wonders; occasionally it is awed or puzzled or even frightened—although mostly it is hopeful. Sometimes it even pauses to tell tales about old people or infants, to intrigue with accounts of feral children or the misbehaviors of delinquent adolescents, to alarm with instances of social injustice or environmental atrocity, and to puzzle with accounts of life in other cultures.

On the following six pages, you will be guided through a number of important features designed to make THE LIFESPAN an effective learning experience, as well as some specific revisions to this Fifth Edition that reflect the most current interests in the study of human development.

FOCUS QUESTIONS

1. How might infants influence their caregivers?
2. Are infants born with certain personalities?
3. How important is early contact between parent and infant?
4. Is it better for mothers to stay home with their infants?
5. Is the nonaverage abnormal? What is exceptionality?

OUTLINE

This Chapter
Interactions in the Family Context
 Beyond the Dyad: A Model of Influences
Infant States
Temperament
 Types of Infant Temperament
 Classifying Temperament
 The Implications of Infant Temperament
 Cultural Context and Temperament
Infant Emotions
 Crying
 Smiling and Laughing
 Wariness and Fear
 Regulation of Emotions in Infancy
Early Attachment
 Stud
 Mo
 The
 Stag
 The
 Fath
Fear of S
 Fear
 Secu
 Long
Infant C
Parenting
 Cult
Early Ge
Exception
 Mot
 Epil
 Othe
 Auti
The Wh
Main Po
Focus Q
Study Te
Further

FOCUS QUESTIONS
introduce readers to the
chapter by identifying
some of the main ideas to
be covered.

FOCUS QUESTIONS

1. What is ageism? How does it affect the elderly?
2. How are lifespan and life expectancy different? Can either be changed?
3. What are some of the most common physical changes in late adulthood?
4. What are some of the most common intellectual changes in late adulthood?

OUTLINE

This Chapter
Ageism
 Examples of Ageism
 Social Treatment and Media Portrayal
 Child-Directed Speech
 Ageism and Other Negative Attitudes
Late Adulthood: Who and How Many?
 Dividing Up Old Age
 Changing Demographics
Lifespan and Life Expectancy
 Theories of Biological Aging
 Longevity in North America
 Longevity Elsewhere
 Models of Aging
Physical Changes
 Appearance
 Fitness and Exercise
 Health
 Sensory Changes
 Reaction Time and Attention Span
 Sexuality
Cognitive Changes
 Memory
 Intelligence
 Problem Finding and Intuition
 Learning in Adulthood

Wisdom
 Some Philosophical Conceptions
 Psychological Conceptions
The Implications of Physical and Cognitive Change
Main Points
Focus Questions: Applications
Study Terms
Further Readings

OUTLINES
indicate the order and
relationships of topics
within each chapter.

VIGNETTES
introduce the chapter
with a personal, relevant
story.

PHYSICAL AND
COGNITIVE DEVELOPMENT:
LATE ADULTHOOD

"You are old, Father William," the young man said,
"And your hair has become very white; and yet you incessantly stand on your head—
Do you think, at your age, it is right?"

LEWIS CARROLL
Alice in Wonderland

"Help me, Guy," she says.
"Prop me up in the corner
so's I don't fall down." I wrap my hands around her gray-socked ankles
and ease her feet back, planting one against either wall. My grandpa's coveralls, which she has put on not because she needs a work-out suit but
more to preserve her modesty, slip down past her bony knees, exposing
her blue-veined shanks.

CHAPTER 17

"Hey," I say, "I'll get the hammer and nail your feet smack to the wall so's
you don't fall down!" Gawd, what a sense of humor! But my grandmother
doesn't laugh; this is serious. Her *Digest* lies open on the table and I can
see the title of the article she had just read: "Shrink Your Varicose Veins!"
it promises, "And Increase Your Intelligence," the subtitle adds, as a less
consequential side benefit of standing on your head 10 minutes a day.

"Okay," says she, "beat it. I'll find my own way down." I look at her for a
minute, her inverted face framed by the thick green cushion under her
head, her features all upside-down slack, her wrinkles drooping unexpectedly toward her forehead. I can't tell whether she's smiling or grimacing
in pain, or whether it's just gravity pulling her lips in the wrong direction.

AT A GLANCE SECTIONS
consist of highly current
data and reflect some
important feature of life
in North America.

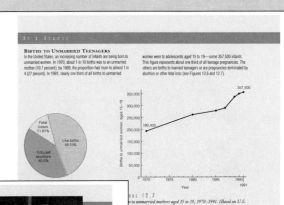

ACROSS CULTURES
boxed inserts in each
chapter depict sometimes
dramatically different
cultural contexts and
their impact on develop-
mental outcomes.

AT A GLANCE

BIRTHS TO UNMARRIED TEENAGERS
In the United States, an increasing number of infants are being born to unmarried women. In 1970, about 1 in 10 births was to an unmarried mother (10.7 percent); by 1989, the proportion had risen to almost 1 in 4 (27 percent). In 1991, nearly one third of all births to unmarried women were to adolescents aged 15 to 19—some 357,500 infants. This figure represents about one third of all teenage pregnancies. The others are births to married teenagers or are pregnancies terminated by abortion or other fetal loss (see Figures 12.6 and 12.7).

Fetal losses 11.81%
Live births 48.13%
Induced abortions 40.6%

... *to unmarried mothers aged 15 to 19, 1970–1991. (Based on U.S. ... of the Census, 1994, p. 80.)*

ACROSS CULTURES

BARUMBA OF THE MUNDUGUMOR
Barumba was born in the spectacular highlands of New Guinea, an island poised like some prehistoric bird above the continent of Australia. His father had spent the day strutting through the village, showing off his vest of brilliant orange, red, and green parrot feathers, his resplendent collar of green beetle shells, and his skirt of gorgeous plumes plucked from birds of paradise. He knew that if the others in the village looked at him in admiration, it would bode well for his first child.

Barumba's mother, too, had chosen to adorn herself for her first birth. Around both arms, she wore tightly woven, brightly colored armbands of orchid fibers. Around her neck hung the necklace of dog's teeth made for her by her mother; and below it, her favorite string of red nuts. And through her nostril she had the long leg bone of a wild guinea fowl.

The contractions were almost continuous now, and the mother knew it would be soon. Anxiously, she watched as the top of the head appeared, long black hair slicked down; now the ears, now the neck—yes! yes! yes!

"He will be a great artist," she yelled out in her excitement, and her husband crashed into the hut, beetle shells clanking, so that he too might see.

Sure enough, the infant's umbilical cord was wrapped around his neck. And, as the Mundugumor have known for centuries, only those infants whose umbilical cords are wound around their necks at birth stand any chance of becoming great artists. Amazingly, they are right.

"Hot dang!" said Barumba's father.

To Think About   We are a little like the Mundugumor, suggests Pogrebin (1980). We know, of course, that it's ridiculous to think that prenatal diagnosis has already spoiled the surprise). The simple anatomical fact of being boy or girl tells mother and father and all the significant others what to think and how to react. The knowledge that it's a "boy" or "girl" even colors the parents' perceptions. When Rubin, Provenzano, and Luria (1974) asked 30 parents to describe their day-old infants as they would to a relative or a close friend, without any hesitation they spoke of their alert, strong, well-coordinated, firm, and hardy sons. In contrast, they described their daughters as weaker, finer-featured, softer, less attentive, more delicate. Yet these parents, especially the fathers (who were most guilty of exaggerating the sex-appropriate characteristics of their sons), had scarcely had any opportunity to interact with and get to know their infants. And hospital records indicated clearly that these male and female infants were *indistinguishable* one from the other in terms of weight, muscle tone, activity, responsiveness, and so on.

But many parents waste little time making their new infants sexually distinct: They color the boy-infants blue, the girl-infants pink. Because of the connotations associated with these colors, they emphasize long-established

the position of the umbilical cord is of any consequence. Instead, we look for appendages between the legs of our infants. To a considerable extent, these tell us how to interact with them, what sorts of toys they are most likely to enjoy, what their personalities should be. And surprisingly often, our predictions are every bit as accurate as those of the Mundugumor! No?

sexual stereotypes. And in much the same way, the names parents give their infants reinforce their sometimes unconscious beliefs about male-female differences. Kasof (1993), for example, shows how male names (like John or Michael) are seen as more attractive, more intellectually competent, stronger. In contrast, many female names (like Edith) carry connotations of being less attractive, more old-fashioned, and less able. (See Across Cultures: "Barumba of the Mundugumor.")

EXCEPTIONALITY

The Lifespan is mainly about the physical, intellectual, and social development of the average person from conception until death. It is worth repeating, however, that this average person is simply a useful mathematical invention, that none of us is "average" in all ways. Instead, we are individuals, each different from every other. But there are so many of us—approaching 6 billion now—that to keep things clear and simple, psychology has to speak of the mythical average.

178   INFANCY

Teenage pregnancies are not restricted to any particular social, economic, religious, or ethnic group. However, in the United States, pregnancies are more common among black than white teenagers. In 1989, 23.1 percent of all births to black mothers were to teenagers; 10.7 percent of white births were to teenagers. For mothers of Hispanic origin, 16.7 percent of births were to teenage mothers (U.S. Bureau of the Census, 1994).

Teenage pregnancies are also more common in economically depressed areas (Donnelly & Voydanoff, 1991). Compared with married mothers of the same age, socioeconomic status, and religious background, unmarried teenage mothers often have lower educational and occupational status, more often come from broken homes, and have more difficulty with opposite-sex relationships (Danilewitz & Skuy, 1990).

Why?
The vast majority of teenage pregnancies are unplanned. Among reasons for the increasing rates of teenage pregnancy, note Black and DeBlassie (1985), are changes in so-

---

FLEXIBLE ORGANIZATION
Readers will find that the organization of this book is systematically chronological, encompassing four major divisions, each highlighted with a different second color: an introductory section (green: deals with methods, theories, genetics, and prenatal development) followed by sections on Growing Up (red: infancy through adolescence), Growing Together (blue: early and middle adulthood), and Growing Older (ochre: later adulthood). Nevertheless, chapters can be read independently rather than sequentially. Accordingly, it is relatively simple to rearrange chapters to conform to a topical approach using the detailed thematic table of contents found just before this visual guide.

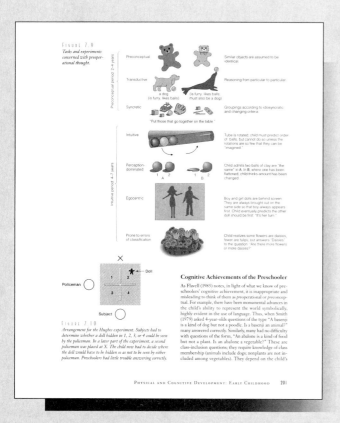

ILLUSTRATIONS

are used to reinforce a variety of text material (in the form of tables, charts, and graphs). Because subjects surrounding human development are often substantially data-driven, they can often be better understood when they are explained visually.

VIVID PHOTOS...
TIMELY EXAMPLES

that complement text discussions, are used to illustrate developmental concepts and theories and to reflect some of the realities of human development today.

END OF EACH CHAPTER

MAIN POINTS
provide an excellent means for quick review through brief synopses of the chapter's highlights.

FOCUS QUESTIONS: APPLICATIONS
restate the focus questions, found at the beginning of each chapter, into a wide variety of applied questions and projects, many requiring systematic observations of people as well as library research.

TERMS AND NAMES
appear boldfaced within the chapter and are listed alphabetically at the end of the chapter.

FURTHER READINGS
provide leads on up-to-date sources of information to assist with independent study or with research papers.

MAIN POINTS

The Newborn

1. A newborn is a primitive, self-driven little sensing machine designed to mature and grow physically in a pre-determined sequence and at a relatively predictable pace, programmed as an extraordinarily capable information-processing system, endowed with powerful gregarious tendencies and strong emotions, and pretuned to the development of language.

Health and Physical Growth

2. Human breast milk is infant-specific, easily digested, nourishing, useful in guarding against the possibility of diarrhea, and provides a degree of immunity to infant illnesses. Genital growth is minimal in infancy (until pubescence); lymphoid and neural growth occurs very rapidly; optimal brain development is profoundly influenced by nutrition (especially protein) and stimulation; and physical growth is relatively rapid (it slows through middle childhood and spurts again at adolescence).

Perceptual Development

6. Visual capacities (color, motion, depth) are well developed in the newborn. The infant's looking seems to be directed by rules that maximize information. Neonates are only slightly less sensitive than adults to sound intensity (loudness). They appear to recognize and prefer their mothers' voices at ages as young as 3 days. They prefer pleasant odors (such as vanilla) to those less pleasant (ammonia or raw fish) almost from birth. Similarly, they prefer the sweet to the bland, and they distinguish easily between sour and bitter tastes, and they appear to be sensitive to touch (and to pain), at least within a few hours of birth.

Cognitive Development

7. The neonate's memory is not as efficient, as powerful, or as long-term as that of older children or adults, but there is memory for smells and sights within days of birth. By the age of 3 months, infants actively search and show signs of recognition.

8. In Piaget's theory, adaptation (cognitive growth) results from the interplay of assimilation (responding in a habitual and preferred way based primarily on preexisting information and well-practiced capabilities) and accommodation (adapting behavior to some external characteristic or quality). Equilibration is the tendency to balance assimilation and accommodation. Other important factors in cognitive development are maturation, social interaction, and active experience. Piaget's six substages of the sensorimotor period are (1) exercising reflexes, (2) primary circular reactions, (3) secondary circular reactions, (4) purposeful coordinations, (5) tertiary circular reactions, and (6) mental representation.

9. There is increased frequency of simple infant behaviors like tongue protrusion following exposure to a model, even in very young infants. It is not entirely clear if deferred imitation is seen by the age of 9 to 12 months; it depends on the ability to represent mentally and to remember, and is therefore of considerable importance in cognitive development.

Language

10. Language involves the use of arbitrary speech sounds that have accepted meanings. It is characterized by displacement, meaningfulness, and productiveness. Its elements are phonology, semantics, syntax, and pragmatics.

PHYSICAL AND COGNITIVE DEVELOPMENT: INFANCY   153

FOCUS QUESTIONS: APPLICATIONS

1. What do children understand of death? And adolescents? And you?
   - How many examples of death denial and distancing can you find that relate to your cultural context? What sorts of arguments might you advance to support (or refute) the proposition that distancing and denying death is socially and psychologically healthy?

2. What are some possible stages of dying?
   - Why might it be inappropriate and unwise to assume that all dying is best described in terms of stages?

3. What is euthanasia? Is it legal?
   - Using current library resources, research the history of euthanasia in Holland, paying particular attention to the laws governing its application, and to alleged instances of violations of these laws.

4. How inevitable is grief following bereavement? Is it important to grieve?
   - Some theorists suggest that the value of grief work has been exaggerated. Can you find good evidence to support or contradict this belief?

STUDY TERMS

acceptance 548	denial 548	living will 553
active euthanasia 552	depression 548	mourning 544
anger 548	dying trajectories 549	palliative care 551
anticipatory grief 555	euthanasia 552	passive euthanasia 552
bargaining 548	grief 544	stages of dying 548
bereavement 544	hospice 551	
death 544	life trajectory 549	

FURTHER READINGS

A classic layperson's book on death and dying is the one by Kübler-Ross:

Kübler-Ross, E. (1969). *On death and dying.* New York: Macmillan.

Irish provides an enlightening look at how different cultures react to bereavement in:

The following is a useful guide intended specifically for those involved in helping children cope with death and dying:

Ward, B. (1993). *Good grief: Exploring feelings, loss, and death with under elevens: A holistic approach.* London: Jessica Kingsley.

DYING   557

---

3. What model of human memory is basic to current information-processing approaches?
   - Illustrate sensory, short-term, and long-term memory using examples from your own experiences.

4. What are the dimensions of intellectual exceptionality?
   - Write out a series of clearly documented arguments that might be used by one or the other side in a debate on the merits of mainstreaming.

STUDY TERMS

attention span 274	explicit memory 264	middle childhood 252
chunking 263	fat-free mass 252	nondeclarative memory 264
classes 260	fat mass 252	number 261
cognitive strategies 262	fluid abilities 268	obesity 254
compensation 258	general factor theory 267	operations 258
concrete operations 257	group intelligence tests 269	organizing 265
conservation 257	identity 258	otitis media 256
constructing knowledge 258	implicit memory 264	peak height velocity 253
contextual theory of intelligence 269	individual intelligence tests 269	preoperations 258
creativity 275	information-processing approach 261	rehearsing 264
crystallized abilities 268	intellectual giftedness 275	reliable 267
culture fair 271	intelligence 267	reversibility 258
declarative memory 264	knowledge base 262	scripts 263
developmental arithmetic disorder 274	learning disability 272	semantic memory 264
developmental reading disorder 274	locomotor skills 255	sensory memory 263
elaborating 265	long-term memory 263	seriation 261
episodic memory 264	mainstreaming 259	short-term (or working) memory 263
exceptionality 256	meaning-making 258	special abilities theory 267
	mental retardation 271	valid 267
	metacognition 262	

FURTHER READINGS

The following book is a highly readable and excellent analysis of cognitive development. It looks in detail both at Piaget's theory and at current work in information processing and metacognition:

Flavell, J. H. (1985). *Cognitive development.* Englewood Cliffs, NJ: Prentice-Hall.

A detailed look at research that explores children's memories is:

Nelson, C. A. (Ed.) (1993). *Memory and affect in development: The Minnesota Symposia on Child Psychology (Vol. 26).* Hillsdale, NJ: Erlbaum.

A clear and useful account of developmental disorders in infancy and childhood is:

Hooper, S. R., Hynd, G. W., & Mattison, R. E. (Eds.). (1992). *Developmental disorders: Diagnostic criteria and clinical assessment.* Hillsdale, NJ: Erlbaum.

A thorough look at physical and motor development in children is presented in:

Malina, R. M., & Bouchard, C. (1991). *Growth, maturation, and physical activity.* Champaign, IL: Human Kinetics Books.

A provocative and practical book dealing with the development of creativity, critical thinking, and problem-solving skills is:

Fisher, R. (1990). *Teaching children to think.* Oxford: Basil Blackwell.

PHYSICAL AND COGNITIVE DEVELOPMENT: MIDDLE CHILDHOOD   281

This Fifth Edition of THE LIFESPAN recognizes more clearly than its predecessors the extent to which contexts influence development and, therefore, affect our theories and our conclusions. A greater emphasis on the influence of culture can be seen through the Across Cultures inserts in every chapter as well as through a more careful examination of social interactions at every developmental level.

In addition, there has been a thorough updating of all topics—with more than 800 new references, the majority of which were published within the last two years. New or significantly expanded topics include sections on:

- Children's rights and the reliability of child witnesses
- Child abuse and adolescent recklessness
- Violence in society; violence in the family
- Ecological validity in developmental research
- Human sexuality; acquaintance rape; HIV infection
- Prenatal diagnosis and advances in genetic technology
- Changing patterns of work; love and mate selection
- Self-efficacy; gender stereotyping; the changing effects of divorce
- Adult health; menopause
- Poverty among the elderly; palliative care; and so on.

THE LIFESPAN deals with all of these concerns, and much more....

AVAILABLE TO INSTRUCTORS

An Instructor's Manual that includes chapter outlines/objectives, lists of terms and creative activities: role playing, essays, etc.; Test Items that include 3,000 multiple-choice, true/false, fill-in, essay, matching, and short answer questions (all test questions are available on disk for use with Macintosh, IBM, DOS, and Windows); Transparency Acetates of selected charts and artwork from the text; as well as free video rentals from Penn State University's Behavioral Sciences collection (ask your Wadsworth/ITP Higher Education sales rep for details).

FOR STUDENTS

A complete Student Resource Guide containing chapter summaries, plus a range of exercises and self-tests designed to help students gauge their progress and prepare for exams.

ACKNOWLEDGMENTS

THANK YOU . . .

After five editions, this text is heavily indebted to more people than can easily be listed here: editors from the old days, armies of production people, many dozens of reviewers, legions of students and their professors, squads of sales representatives and marketing people, even my old hunting dog, Zoe, who chewed up parts of an early version before I had learned to hide such things inside a computer. Without all of you, this book wouldn't be what it is. In fact, it would not even be. And so I thank you.

This most recent edition owes an enormous debt to a truly outstanding publishing team at Wadsworth. Among them:

Sabra Horne, Wadsworth editor, who brought new enthusiasm, creativity, and vigor to the project.

Angela Mann, production editor, who has again accomplished so well and so patiently each of the hundreds of sequenced and deadlined things that need to be done to make a book—after a thousand e-mail messages, countless faxes, and enough courier packages to bankrupt a small country.

Jennifer Gordon, copy editor, whose editing is as intelligent as any I have seen.

Andrew Ogus, managing designer, who contributed so much to the art and design of the book.

Tricia Schumacher, advertising project manager, who has a gift for visual guides.

Catherine Linberg, art editor, and the Wadsworth photo team with its dozens of photographers: Suzanne Astier, John Bergez, Kevin Berry, Adriane Bosworth, Pat Brewer, Roberta Broyer, Ann Butler, Laurie Campbell, Brandon Carson, Sandra Craig, Julie Davis, Carolyn Deacy, Jerilyn Emori, Jeanne Fleming, Karen Garrison, Sabra Horne, Karen Hunt, Robert Kauser, Debbie Kramer, Peseti Latu, Catherine Linberg, Carol Carreon Lombardi, Margrete Lyons, Angela Mann, Cecilia Mantecon, Emma Nash, Barbara Odone, Andrew Ogus, Jill Reinemann, Bill Ralph, Stephen Rapley, Mira Roytman, Nancy Spellman, Diane Tejo, Alan Venable, Pat Waldo, Tekla Weber, Amy Yates, and the subjects whose photos illustrate these pages.

Cloyce Wall, who created the design and the cover; Louise Mendelson, editorial assistant; Jeanne Bosschart, permissions editor; Karen Hunt, print buyer; John Bergez, developmental editor; Adriane Bosworth, dummier; Claire Masson, assistant editor; and Tom Tutko, who prepared the student resource guide, the test items, and the instructor's resource manual.

Reviewers Joan Jones, University of Wisconsin, Milwaukee; Robert Kiehl, Oral Roberts University; Karen Nelson, Austin College; Tony Williams, Marshall University; and Ruth Wilson, Idaho State University

There are still dozens of people to thank: Marie, who continues to be so understanding and supportive; the University of Alberta, which is such an excellent place to work and learn; students and professors in many parts of the world; friends and neighbors; my maternal grandmother; the many uncles, aunts, and cousins whose lives inspired some of my chapter introductions... To all of you, thank you.

In fact, now that I think of it, there is remarkably little in this book for which I can take complete credit. Unlike other more generous souls, I am not even willing to say that all the errors, omissions, subtle exaggerations, and blatant stupidities in it are mine. But some of them might be.

THE LIFESPAN

Forward, forward let us range,
Let the great world spin for ever down
the ringing grooves of change.

ALFRED LORD TENNYSON
Locksley Hall

THE BEGINNING

Change is what human development is all about—enormous, fantastic change. Change, yet continuity. First, we are a speck in a mother's womb, insignificant and microscopic; soon, a wailing infant, unfamiliar with the world, helpless and totally dependent; next, a burgeoning child exploring the mysteries of time and space, yet still awed by magic and enchanted by fairies; then, an adolescent practicing the secrets of love and logic, at once sophisticated and naive; now, an adult, vigorous and powerful, but no longer able to see elves and other mystical things; and before we know it, we ease into our last age. Through all these changes, our sense of who we are, of our *selves*, endures; thus is there continuity in the midst of constant change.

PART ONE

The four chapters in Part One, "The Beginning," are about the things we need to know to understand this change and continuity. The first and second chapters lay out the subject, its methods, its most important theories; the third explores complex gene–context interactions that account for change; and the fourth traces the course of prenatal human development.

There is much to consider if we are to understand ourselves in a world that "spins for ever down the ringing grooves of change."

STUDYING HUMAN DEVELOPMENT

*M*en fear Death as children fear to go in the dark; and as that natural
fear in children is increased with tales, so is the other.

FRANCIS BACON
Essays 2

In this childhood memory, I am only 6 or 7. I'm lying in

CHAPTER 1

bed with my older brother, Maurice, in the atticlike upstairs of our little house, which is smack in the woods of Northern Saskatchewan. It's winter, cold and dark as sin, and the chicken-feather comforter hasn't warmed up yet. There is still no electricity up there so the only light in our room is the orange glow from the kerosene lamp downstairs. It's not nearly enough light to see into any of the corners.

Then "Crowk!" there's another of those sudden, tearing noises and my heart lurches. I know they're just supposed to be nails letting go in the cold, at least that's what my dad said, but I listen real hard for a while just in case it's something else, which I'll know if it makes a different kind of noise. Maurice is listening too, I can tell, and for a minute, all I can hear is the wind pushing cold against the house. And then, I swear it, I hear a different sound, more like a groan or a sigh and I think, "Oh no, it's got to be a papoose this time for sure," which is what we call really bad witches in French.

"I hear one!" whispers Maurice. Me, I'm too scared to talk, but I think it's in the closet this time, which is what our cousin, Claude, told us. "That's where they hide," he said, "in closets or under beds. And they're bloody gonna eat you if they can."

I can hardly breathe, I'm so scared. And then Maurice says, "It's your turn," which I've been hoping he's forgotten, but he hasn't. So, shaking like a leaf, I get out of bed and snake around the wall toward the closet praying, "Gawd don't let there be one in there this time, please gawd wait until it's Maurice's turn to look."

"Under the bed," says Maurice. "I heard it under the bed." So now I bend down to peer under the bed, praying desperately, "Please gawd don't put a papoose under the bed tonight. Please gawd wait 'til it's Maurice's turn."

THIS TEXT

We're almost grown up now, Maurice and I. Our nighttime bedrooms are far quieter than they used to be,* and we've become very familiar with our closets. We no longer need to open their doors and look inside them before we sleep. We know there's nothing in our closets that's bloody gonna eat us while we sleep, don't we? Children don't always know that; they're less familiar with their closets.

That's a large part of growing up: becoming *familiar* with what's out there; sorting fact from fancy and magic from reality; discovering what is likely to eat us and what isn't; finding out what's in our closets. Describing how infants, children, adolescents—and even adults—become progressively more familiar with the world is a large part of what *The Lifespan* is about.

The text includes nine parts: The first consists of four introductory chapters (subject and methods of lifespan developmental psychology, main theories, gene-environment interaction, and prenatal development and birth); seven parts deal with physical, intellectual, and social change during infancy, childhood, adolescence, and adulthood; the final part looks at dying.

The text is also divided into four major sections, each highlighted by a different second color and prefaced by a color photo essay that captures the main themes of that section. The first is the introduction (green); the second deals with the growing up years (infancy through adolescence: red); the third, with our growing together years (early through middle adulthood: blue); and the last, with growing old (ochre) (see Table 1.1).

LIFESPAN DEVELOPMENTAL PSYCHOLOGY

Psychology† is a general term for the science that studies behavior and thinking. **Developmental psychology** is concerned specifically with changes that occur over time. Accordingly, **lifespan developmental psychology** is the discipline that studies changes that occur from concep-

*"It's your hearing that's shot," said my grandmother, adding meanly, "They're still there, you know."

†Boldfaced terms are defined in the Glossary at the end of the book. Terms are also listed in the Study Terms at the end of each chapter.

TABLE 1.1
Divisions of the Lifespan in This Text

Period/Part	Approximate Ages	Chapters
Introduction		
I. The Beginning	—	1. Studying Human Development
		2. Theories of Lifespan Development
		3. Gene–Context Interaction
		4. Prenatal Development and Birth
Growing Up		
II. Infancy	Birth to 2 years	5. Physical and Cognitive Development
		6. Social Development
III. Early Childhood	2 to 6–7 years	7. Physical and Cognitive Development
		8. Social Development
IV. Middle Childhood	6–7 to 11–12 years	9. Physical and Cognitive Development
		10. Social Development
V. Adolescence	11–12 to 19–20 years	11. Physical and Cognitive Development
		12. Social Development
Growing Together		
VI. Early Adulthood	20 to 40–45 years	13. Physical and Cognitive Development
		14. Social Development
VII. Middle Adulthood	40–45 to 65–70 years	15. Physical and Cognitive Development
		16. Social Development
Growing Old		
VIII. Late Adulthood	65–70 years onward	17. Physical and Cognitive Development
		18. Social Development
IX. The End	—	19. Dying

tion through adulthood and that looks at the processes and influences that account for these changes.

The Lifespan Perspective

Lifespan developmental psychology is a relatively new area of interest. During the century or so since the beginning of scientific psychology, most studies of human development have focused on infancy, childhood, and, to a lesser extent, adolescence. G. S. Hall, who published a major book on aging in 1922, is sometimes referred to as one of the founders of the study of aging. But even after the publication of Hall's book, the traditional view—one that focuses on the development of children rather than adults—continued to dominate psychological research. This traditional view is dramatically different from the contemporary **lifespan** view.

The traditional view of human development is, in some ways, quite simple. It holds that almost all important developmental changes occur between conception and adolescence, and that after adulthood is reached, little happens that might be of concern to a developmental psychologist. According to this view, adulthood is a lengthy period of little change eventually followed by the declines of old age.

Development Is Continuous

We now know that this traditional view of development is inaccurate and misleading. The more current lifespan view of development recognizes that important changes occur at all ages throughout the lifespan. In fact, as Lerner and his associates (1992) note, the lifespan view is rooted in the suggestion that the changes that occur in adulthood are similar in magnitude to those of earlier developmental periods. Hence the single most important characteristic of the lifespan view of human development is the recognition that both children and adults are developing organisms *throughout* life, that development does not stop with the beginning of adulthood.

Maturity Is Relative

Because development continues through adulthood, it cannot easily be described in terms of a predetermined final state. What is important to the developmental psychologist is not the state, which continues to change, so much as the process of change itself. People continually change, moving toward new states of readiness, new competencies. The infant who has just learned to recognize the meaning of the word *mother* is still a long way from a complete understanding of either words or mothers. Similarly, the 30-year-old who succeeds in resolving an emotional dilemma by finding someone to love may be far from having learned to solve other emotional problems. Thus maturity, like so many other states, is relative: We can be mature in certain areas but not in others. And even as we reach a state of relative maturity, we continue to change.

Change is what human development is about. Emphasis on the ongoing and never-ending processes of change—on the dynamism of the developmental process—is one of the distinguishing characteristics of the contemporary lifespan view of development.

Development Occurs in Context

The lifespan view of human development also recognizes the importance of the individual's context, or what is sometimes termed **ecology.** As a general term, *ecology* refers to the science that studies the relationship between organisms and their environment (*oikos* is the Greek word for "home"; the suffix *-logy* means "the study of"). As a more specialized term in developmental theory, *ecology* refers mainly to the social context in which behavior and development occur. Thus, ecological approaches to un-

derstanding and explaining development pay a great deal of attention to the individual's social environment, and to the changing relationships between the individual and the environment. As Kegan (1982) notes, the emphasis is no longer simply on how the child constructs the world but also on how the world constructs the child. And the adult.

Developmental Influences Are Bidirectional

"The emphasis in developmental contextualism," write Lerner and his associates (1992), "[is] on the bidirectional connections between the individual and the actual settings within which he or she lives" (p. 255). What this means is that developmental psychologists are interested not only in how the person is influenced by social context, but also in how the environment is influenced by the person—that is, they are interested in what is termed the **bidirectionality** of influences.

As will become increasingly apparent as you progress through this text, these beliefs are very important for contemporary lifespan developmental research. Among other things, they are reflected in a shifting of interest from the individual in isolation to the individual as part of a complex social system (ecological orientation). They also are apparent in increased attention to the ways in which the individual affects surrounding systems as well as the ways in which systems affect the individual. And, finally, they are evident in a shifting of our focus from describing states to investigating processes—that is, a shifting of concern from the static to the dynamic.

SOME DEFINITIONS IN DEVELOPMENT

Important concepts in the study of the lifespan include growth, maturation, and learning. Put another way, to develop is to grow, to mature, and to learn.

Growth ordinarily refers to physical changes such as increasing height or enlargement of the nose. The changes that define growth are primarily *quantitative*; they involve addition rather than transformation.

Maturation describes changes that are relatively independent of the environment and are closely related to heredity—such as the sexual changes of adolescence. In almost all aspects of human development, however, maturation and learning interact. Learning to walk, for example, requires not only that the child's physical strength and muscular coordination be sufficiently mature but also that there be opportunities to learn the various skills involved.

Learning is defined as relatively permanent changes that result from experiences (experiences like being stung by a bee or going to school) rather than simply from maturation or growth.

In summary, **development** describes the gradual, lifelong process whereby we adapt to our environment.

TABLE 1.2
Definitions in Human Development

Psychology	The science that studies human thought and behavior.
Developmental Psychology	Division of psychology concerned with changes that occur over time, and with the processes and influences that account for these changes.
Development Includes:	
Growth	Physical changes; primarily quantitative.
Maturation	Naturally unfolding changes, relatively independent of the environment (for example, pubescence—the changes of adolescence that lead to sexual maturity).
Learning	Relatively permanent changes in behavior that result from experience (rather than from maturation, fatigue, or drugs).

Because we adapt by growing, maturing, and learning, these are the basic aspects of development. (See Table 1.2 for a summary of these definitions.)

HISTORICAL SNAPSHOTS

Lifespan development is a recent area of psychological interest. Its most obvious roots can be found in the study of children. And the scientific study of children, too, is not very old. In fact, most of its development belongs to this century. At least some of the reasons for this long delay in the development of a science of child study have to do with attitudes toward children that appear to have been prevalent throughout much of human history. Some of these attitudes are reflected in the brief *historical snapshots* that follow.

Note at the outset that these historical snapshots are not always entirely accurate. There are few reliable records of what life might have been like for a child prior to what have sometimes been called the "print" cultures. When Ariès (1962) studied the lives of medieval children, he was forced to put together fragments from a variety of sources—16th- and 17th-century paintings, school and university regulations, and Doctor Heroard's description of the upbringing of the French king Louis XIII. The result is a fascinating but not entirely reliable account.

Snapshot 1: Child Rearing, Medieval Europe

In the Middle Ages, Ariès informs us, childhood did not exist as we know it—as is evident in the fact that early paintings often depicted children as miniature adults. True, early in the child's life there was a period of dependency during which the infant needed a parent or some other caregiver to survive. Sadly, many didn't survive. Ariès describes one scene in which a mother has just given

birth to her fifth child. She is depressed; there had not been enough food and clothing before. What will it be like now? The neighbor consoles her: "Before they are old enough to bother you," she says, "you will have lost half of them, or perhaps all of them" (Ariès, 1962, p. 38).

The implication clearly is that the children's dying is somehow preferable to the burden of caring for them. And the inference is that the mother is not strongly attached to the child; hence there is little need to worry that it might suffer or die. Thus this snapshot of medieval childhood reflects a cold, callous, unfeeling attitude toward children. We don't know for certain how accurate it is, but we do know that it omits exceptions, and as a result, it exaggerates—as do many historical accounts.

Snapshot 2: Begging in 18th-Century Europe

In the 18th and 19th centuries, written and printed records became more common as literacy slowly spread through the world. Accordingly, accounts of attitudes toward children are far more reliable than those for earlier periods. Sadly, in some ways, they are no less shocking. Laws and courts had not yet begun to grant children any rights or any protection. For example, in 1761, the British courts sentenced Anne Martin to two years in Newgate Prison. Her crime? She habitually poked out the eyes of the children she took begging with her; it increased their success—and hers. Aha, you say, the courts did offer some protection to children! True, but it was skimpy protection indeed. As Pinchbeck and Hewitt (1973) point out, Anne Martin's case was unusual in that the children whose eyes she removed were somebody else's. Had they been her own, it is likely that no one would have paid any attention. Parents could generally treat their own children any way they wanted.

The courts also were not above severely punishing children for infractions of laws. Siegel and White (1982)

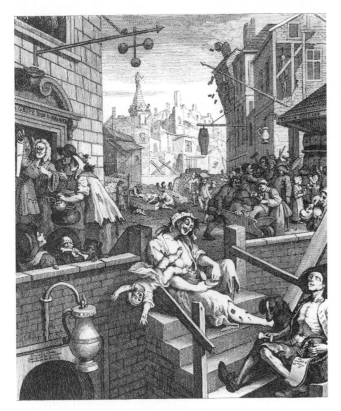

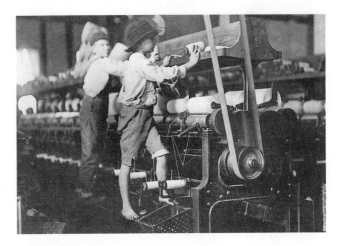

The scientific study of children is a relatively recent undertaking. Where infant mortality is high or where children are highly prized for their economic value, they are perhaps less likely to be loved and studied. Under those circumstances, they are also more likely to be exploited in child labor, as in this early 20th-century cotton mill in Georgia. Note the bare feet dangerously close to the turning spindles, and the completely exposed and unguarded belt and pulley system.

Contrasting attitudes toward children are reflected in 18th-century (William Hogarth, above) and 19th-century (Mary Cassatt, left) art.

report the case of a 7-year-old girl who stole a petticoat, surely not that terrible a crime. Still, she was brought to trial, convicted, sentenced—and hanged!

Snapshot 3: Child Abandonment, 18th Century

Eighteenth-century attitudes toward children are apparent not only in the ways courts treated them but also in the ways parents treated them. In the crowded slums of 18th-century European cities, thousands of parents bore children whom they promptly abandoned in the streets or on the doorsteps of churches and orphanages. Foundling homes were established throughout Europe to care for these children, but the majority died in infancy (before the age of 2). In fact, until the turn of that century, even if a child were not abandoned, chances of surviving until the age of 5 were less than one in two (Kessen, 1965). Bakwin (1949) cites evidence that, with few exceptions, children in infant homes (asylums) in the United States prior to 1915 died before the age of 2. Unfortunately, child abandonment, and even infanticide, are still not entirely uncommon (see Across Cultures: "Piyush Mittal's Sister").

Snapshot 4: Child Labor in the 19th Century

The 19th century brought some improvement in the status of children and a dramatic reduction in the number of abandonments. Unfortunately, these changes resulted less from increasing love and concern for children than from their economic value. At that time, for example, children

were widely used in British coal mines. Most of these mines were underground, and the tunnels that led to them were often no more than about 2 feet in height, poorly ventilated, and sometimes covered with 3 or 4 inches of water. Children were especially valuable in these mines because they were small enough to crawl through the tiny tunnels, dragging baskets loaded with coal behind them using a "girdle and chain."* The Seventh Earl of Shaftesbury (his name was Anthony Ashley Cooper) described the blisters and the wounds that resulted from this device, the injuries and diseases children suffered in the mines, the physical and mental abuse, the beatings. He begged the British House of Commons to pass a bill that would set age 13 as a minimum for male employment in the coal mines, and that would completely prohibit the employment of females underground. Following considerable debate, and in spite of strong opposition, a bill prohibiting females from working underground was passed. But the House was moved by the argument that children whose fathers were miners were more likely to profit from an education in the mines than from a "reading" education; boys could continue to work in the mines as long as they had reached the age of 10.

Conditions in North America were, in some instances, not very different from those in some parts of Europe. Large numbers of children were used in factories

---

*This device was a sturdy leather belt that was worn around the waist serving as a harness. At the front was a metal ring to which was fastened a heavy chain. The chain passed between the child's legs and was hooked onto the basket behind the child.

PIYUSH MITTAL'S SISTER

Piyush's sister's story is no different from that of thousands of other infant females born in northern India. It is a very short story. She was born into a proud but poor family of farmers, born into a culture where there is little demand for female labor, where females are not allowed to own property, where the cost of raising daughters is far higher than that of raising sons, and where there is also an intense preference for sons. And so when the newborn's mother saw that there was no appendage between the infant's legs, she shrugged in resignation.

There are different ways of killing an infant. One, quite common in the village of Piyush's parents, is to stuff rice into the newborn's mouth and nose and hold a pillow tight against its face until the struggles stop. In other villages, there is a distaste for violent measures, and the infant is simply "left to die from neglect and want of food" (Miller, 1981, p. 51). Piyush's mother used rice.

"Bury it," she said to Piyush tiredly, "so the dogs don't find it."

In parts of India, female infanticide has apparently long been common, although it became less visible after it was outlawed by the British in 1870. Even today, it is still practiced—as it is too, in parts of Japan, Pakistan, Bangladesh, China, and elsewhere. In these countries, says Grant (1992), more than a million female infants die each year *simply because they are female.* Many are aborted as fetuses following prenatal diagnosis to determine their sex.

There is tremendous discrimination against females in many of the world's less developed countries. "Employment rights, social security rights, legal rights, property rights, and even civil and political liberties," writes Grant (1992) "are all likely to depend upon the one, cruel chromosome" (p. 57). And access to education, too, is far more limited for females than for males.

To Think About   What are the probable implications of granting equal educational opportunity to girls in developing countries? How might this affect the care of children in these countries? Are Piyush's views of life and death, of male and female, likely to resemble yours?

and cotton mills, in fields and shops. But profound social and economic forces would soon change all that.

Snapshot 5: The Developing World Today

The 20th century, too, has its share of ignorance, of cruelty, of needless pain and suffering. Some 64 of the world's nations have under 5 mortality rates (abbreviated U5MR) greater than 71 per 1,000 children born alive—a rate many times higher than is common in developed countries (Grant, 1993). In Angola or Mozambique, for example, about 292 infants out of every 1,000 born alive die before the age of 5, a rate about 30 times higher than that of countries such as the United States or Canada (see At a Glance: "Infant Survival"). The United Nations reports that in developing countries almost 8 million children under 5 die each year from pneumonia, diarrheal dehydration, or vaccine-preventable diseases such as measles, tetanus, and whooping cough (Grant, 1993). Starvation adds significantly to this total, bringing it close to 13 million. That's more than 35,000 children under 5 dying every day, the majority of them from preventable causes (see Figures 1.2 and 1.3).

At a theoretical level, solutions for these social crimes are simple and technically possible: Vaccine-preventable diseases require immunization; nutrition-related suffering and dying can be alleviated through a redistribution of vast surpluses of food; and diarrheal infection can be lessened through sanitation, and its effects can be countered through oral rehydration therapy (ORT). (ORT involves an attempt to increase the infected child's fluid intake and to replace essential salts.) And the effects of each of these causes of infant and child death—vaccine-preventable diseases, diarrheal infection, and poor nutrition—can be lessened enormously through something as simple as breast-feeding.

Not surprisingly, one of the important factors in infant mortality is the mother's education. There is, according to Levine (1987), a growing consensus that female schooling can be a direct *cause* of reductions both in birthrate and in infant death. An analysis of information

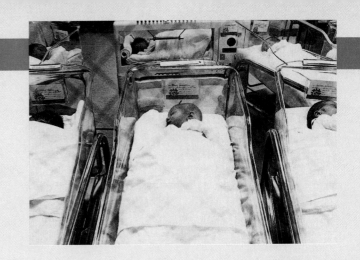

AGE DISTRIBUTION IN THE UNITED STATES

At the turn of this century in the United States, almost 100 of every 1,000 children died in infancy. But high infant mortality was compensated for by high birthrates so that parents more than replaced themselves. Now, infant mortality has been reduced to about 10 per 1,000, but since 1972, birthrates have been below replacement at between 14 and 16 per 1,000. However, the population continues to grow, largely as a result of increased life expectancy. In 1920, life expectancy in the United States was 54 years; it is now about 76. In 1992 in the United States there were about 20 million children under age 5 and about 14 million adults over age 75 (U.S. Bureau of the Census, 1994). By the year 2000, numbers should be approximately equal.

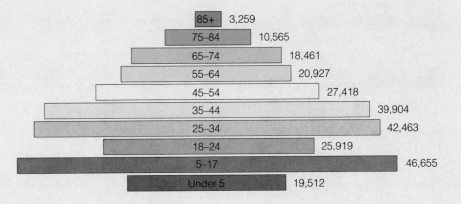

FIGURE 1.1
1992 U.S. population (in thousands) by age group. (Based on U.S. Bureau of the Census, 1994, p. 15.)

Age group	Population
85+	3,259
75–84	10,565
65–74	18,461
55–64	20,927
45–54	27,418
35–44	39,904
25–34	42,463
18–24	25,919
5–17	46,655
Under 5	19,512

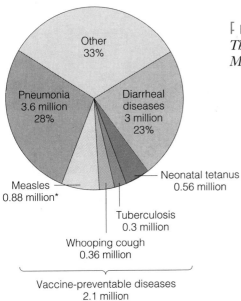

Other 33%

Pneumonia 3.6 million 28%

Diarrheal diseases 3 million 23%

Neonatal tetanus 0.56 million

Tuberculosis 0.3 million

Whooping cough 0.36 million

Measles 0.88 million*

Vaccine-preventable diseases 2.1 million 16%

*Including measles with diarrheal disease and measles with pneumonia

FIGURE 1.2
The main causes of the 12.9 million deaths of children under age 5 that occur each year. More than 60 percent are from preventable diseases. (From Grant, 1993, p. 6.)

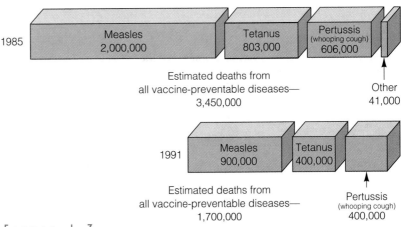

1985

Measles 2,000,000

Tetanus 803,000

Pertussis (whooping cough) 606,000

Estimated deaths from all vaccine-preventable diseases— 3,450,000

Other 41,000

1991

Measles 900,000

Tetanus 400,000

Estimated deaths from all vaccine-preventable diseases— 1,700,000

Pertussis (whooping cough) 400,000

FIGURE 1.3
Changes in estimated number of deaths in children under age 5 from vaccine-preventable diseases. (Based on UNICEF information in Grant, 1986, p. 3, and Grant, 1993, p. 5.)

INFANT SURVIVAL

In many parts of the nonindustrialized world, infant death exceeds 100 per 1,000 live births in the first year of life, a figure comparable to that for the United States at the turn of the century. Yet in some countries, such as Japan and Austria, under-1 infant mortality rates are less than 6 per 1,000. Deaths of children under age 5 number almost 13 million per year, reports Grant (1993). More than 60 percent of these can be pre-

vented at what he describes as "low cost"—about $25 billion (U.S.) per year. That, notes Grant, is about half of what is spent on cigarettes each year in Europe alone—and about 60 percent of what is spent on business entertainment in Japan or on beer in the United States. There is little doubt that education, vaccination, and improved health care could dramatically reduce infant mortality.

FIGURE 1.4

Under-5 mortality rates for selected countries (number of deaths per 1,000 live births for children under age 5). (Based on Grant, 1993, pp. 68–69.)

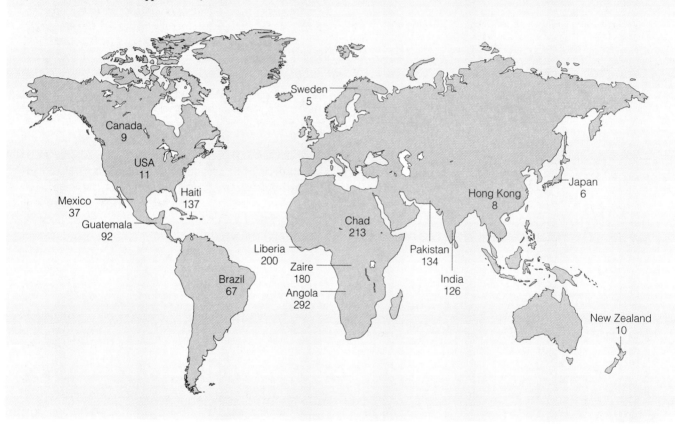

collected by the World Bank from some 99 different third world countries shows a very strong correlation between the proportion of a country's females enrolled in primary schools and infant mortality rates some 22 years later (Caldwell, 1986). These data reveal that even incomplete primary schooling often leads to smaller families and to the loss of fewer children, even where sanitation, nutrition, and medical care have not improved noticeably.

Snapshot 6: The Industrialized World

Obviously, not all children were murdered in the dark ages we call antiquity. Nor were all children abandoned through the Middle Ages—or ignored until they died and then were buried in the backyard or in the garden. The children of Europe's 18th and 19th centuries weren't all beaten into the coal mines, and North America's children weren't all driven into the cotton fields and the textile fac-

TABLE 1.3
*Six Historical Trends in the Treatment of Children**

Antiquity	Little evidence of strong parental attachment; occasional infanticide socially acceptable.
Middle Ages	Poverty and emotional indifference lead to widespread abandonment of infants; very high infant mortality rates.
Renaissance	Ambivalent attitude toward children.
18th Century	Industrialization contributes to widespread use of children as manual laborers in factories, mines, fields, shops.
19th Century	Child labor continues to flourish; beginnings of important medical and educational changes.
20th Century	Child-centered, especially in the industrialized world; concern with the rights and plights of children. But there are still many instances of abuse, starvation, exploitation, and unnecessary mortality.

* Note that although these trends and attitudes are descriptive of some cultures and of some families during the periods in question, they are sometimes not very general. Clearly, although infanticide might once have been acceptable under some circumstances, no society permitted all its infants to be killed. Similarly, even at the height of the period of child labor in the 18th century, there were many well-cared-for children who played and went to school and had carefree childhoods in loving homes.

SOURCE: Based in part on DeMause, 1975.

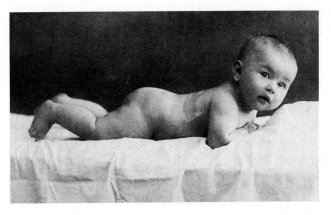

Childhood in the world's developed countries no longer brings a high probability of being abandoned on church steps or exploited in mines and factories. But it does bring an increasingly high probability of being cared for by strangers, even in infancy, and perhaps of having to adjust to the loss of a mother or a father for much of the time of growing up. Does this mean that infancy and childhood are more lonely and frightening?

tories. Even then, the majority of parents were probably loving and caring. Historical accounts often exaggerate.

In the industrialized world, we no longer abandon children for fear they will prove too much of an economic burden. Nor do we send them into mines and factories. The recognition of childhood as a distinct period, coupled with increasing industrialization and scientific advances, led to organized "child saving" movements, especially in the early 20th century. "For the first time in history," writes Culbertson (1991), "children were accorded basic rights as individuals to preservation of health and life, education, freedom from working in the adult labor force, and protection within the judicial system" (p. 8). (Children's rights are discussed in more detail later in this chapter.)

This does not mean that all is perfect with the Western industrialized world's children. There have been dramatic social changes in recent decades. For example, the percentage of never married 20- to 24-year-old women has more than doubled in the past three decades (from 30 in 1960 to 66.8 in 1993: U.S. Bureau of the Census, 1994). In addition, divorce rates have increased dramatically, so that at present about one quarter of all children live in a one-parent household. In about 85 percent of these families, the mother is the single parent (U.S. Bureau of the Census, 1994). Coupled with this, demographic (population) changes have resulted in smaller families, lower birthrates, larger numbers of childless couples, and a greater proportion of young adults (resulting from earlier

increases in birthrates) and of elderly people (resulting from medical advances). Another important change, the effects of which are discussed in detail in Chapter 10, is associated with the role of television in people's lives—and especially in the lives of children.

Some argue that the net effect of these changes is that current decades are less child-centered than had been anticipated. In fact, says Bullock (1993), childhood may be a terribly lonely and often frightening experience for many. Among other things, childhood in our times brings with it a high probability of being looked after by a series of strangers, most likely outside the child's home. It includes, as well, the probability of losing a father or a mother for much of the time of growing up—or at least of losing some of their interest and attention, and perhaps some of their affection as well. Childhood now brings the possibility of major readjustments if one or the other of the parents remarries, particularly if stepsiblings are brought into the family.

There was a time, not very long ago, when the things that most children feared were highly predictable: pain, death, spinach, darkness, and things that go bump in the night—or that hide in closets or under beds. Recent decades have added some new fears: concerns over whether or not parents will divorce, fears related to being left alone, fears associated with the likelihood of having to make new adjustments.

But lest this paint too bleak a picture, let me hasten to point out that the challenges and the changes of current decades don't overwhelm all children, and are not always a source of loneliness or despair. For many, they may be a challenge that results in strength rather than in weakness. Keep in mind, too, that these changes have little do with the lives of many children. (See Table 1.3 for a summary of historical trends in the treatment of children.)

CHILDREN'S RIGHTS

The brief, historical snapshots in the preceding section are included not so that you might be horrified at the inhumanity of your species—or proud of your apparent enlightenment. Rather, they are meant to illustrate how attitudes toward children reflect cultural and historical context—and how context influences development.

Historical Lack of Rights

Today's context—in at least some jurisdictions—emphasizes the rights that children have. It's a context that stands in sharp contrast to medieval times during which one of the sports by which the gentry amused themselves was that of **baby tossing.** Baby tossing was the practice of throwing infants from one gamesman to another, just for the sport of it. One of the unlucky babies used in this game was King Henry IV's infant brother who was killed when he fell while being tossed from window to window (DeMause, 1974). And in Massachusetts, as recently as 1646, parents did not have to put up with unruly offspring. A father whose son wouldn't listen to him, who was making his life miserable, could simply drag him before a magistrate and present his case. As long as the son was 16 or more, they'd put him to death (Westman, 1991)! That was the law.

Children's Rights Today

By the beginning of the 20th century, the absolute control that parents and various agencies had over the lives of children had been weakened considerably. Yet it was still possible for parents and teachers to get rid of troublesome children, often by committing them to mental institutions. Until recently, such children had little legal recourse. Now, however, parents no longer have absolute jurisdiction over their children. Increasingly, major court decisions favor children who feel they have been wronged.

Evidence of increasing concern with the rights of children is apparent not only in court decisions but also in the development of charters of children's rights. For example, a United Nations' convention on the rights of the child led to the formulation of an extensive charter of children's rights, which has now been signed by more than 135 of the world's nations (Bäckström, 1992; Balke, 1992). Among other things, this charter recognizes the child's right to:

- adequate medical care
- adequate nutrition
- affection, love, and understanding
- education
- the opportunity for play and recreation
- special care if required

- a peaceful environment
- the opportunity to develop individual abilities
- protection from abuse, neglect, and exploitation
- protection under the law
- freedom from discrimination based on race, sex, religious beliefs, and age

These are birthrights, says the National Committee for the Rights of the Child (Turgi, 1992). Sadly, however, they are not equally available to all children. (See Interactive Table 1.4.)

As Caldwell (1989) notes, the rights of children are geared toward providing optimal, growth-fostering conditions for them. In general, they are rights of *protection* rather than rights of *choice.* That is, children need to be protected from the dangers to which their immaturity exposes them, and their access to a growth-fostering environment needs to be safeguarded. Treating children as mini-adults is a misuse of the concept of children's rights, claims Saidla (1992). In many instances, children lack the maturity and the knowledge required for making the best choices in their own lives. Eleven-year-olds have the right to adequate nutrition, medical care, and education; but, understandably, they do not have the right to make all their own nutritional, educational, and medical choices.

This does not mean that children have no responsibilities. As Caldwell (1989) points out, society expects its children to assimilate dominant cultural values and eventually foster the continuation of the culture. In addition, society expects that its children will take advantage of the rights and opportunities provided for them—that they will mature and learn.

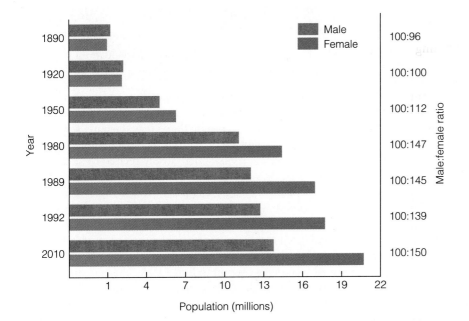

FIGURE 1.5

Changes in the U.S. population above age 65 since 1890. (Based on U.S. Department of Commerce, 1980, U.S. Bureau of the Census, 1991, p. 17, and U.S. Bureau of the Census, 1994, p. 14.)

STUDYING HUMAN DEVELOPMENT

The historical roots of the study of human development are closely linked with profound changes in our attitudes toward children as well as in our recognition that development is a lifelong process. In addition, current demographic changes, especially those associated with the aging of Western industrialized societies (largely as a result of reduced birthrates and increased longevity), have contributed to a shift in focus from the preadult years to the entire lifespan (see Figure 1.5).

Early Pioneers

Closely associated with the intellectual movements linked to changing attitudes toward children were such individuals as John Locke and Jean-Jacques Rousseau.

Locke

Locke (1699), writing in the late 17th century, argued that children are basically rational creatures whose minds are comparable to a blank slate (*tabula rasa*) upon which experience writes messages. Thus children are passive recipients of knowledge, information, and habits, and are highly responsive to rewards and punishments.

Rousseau

In contrast, Rousseau's child, immortalized in his book *Emile*, is active and inquiring. Furthermore, this child is not a "blank slate," neither good nor bad until the rewards and punishments of experience exert their influence, but innately good—a "noble savage." Rousseau (1762, 1911) insists that if children were allowed to de-

velop in their own fashion, untainted by the corruption and evil in the world, they would be undeniably good when grown: "God makes all things good; man meddles with them and they become evil."

Locke's and Rousseau's ideas have led to fundamentally different conceptions of childhood. Locke's description of the child as a passive creature, molded and shaped by the rewards and punishments of experience, has a close parallel in learning-theory descriptions of development (for example, the work of Skinner and Bandura, described in Chapter 2). Rousseau's view of an active, exploring child purposefully interacting with the environment is illustrated in the work of Jean Piaget (also described in Chapter 2).

Later Pioneers

Although the science of developmental psychology owes much to early "child philosophers" like Rousseau and Locke, its beginnings are usually attributed to the first *systematic* observations and written accounts of children. Preyer's detailed observations of his own children are generally considered among the first significant studies in child development (Preyer, 1888/1889), as is Darwin's (1877) biography of his son.

Hall

Hard on the heels of these two pioneers followed G. Stanley Hall (1891), the first president of the American Psychological Association, who was profoundly influenced by Darwin's theories of evolution. "**Ontogeny** recapitulates **phylogeny**," Hall informed his colleagues, summarizing in one short phrase his conviction that the development of an individual in a species parallels the evolution of the entire species. As evidence for this theory, Hall described the evolution of children's interests in games, noting how these seem to correspond to the evolution of human occupations and lifestyles. The child is, in sequence, interested in games corresponding to each of the following: tree-dwelling (for example, climbing on chairs and tables); living in caves (crawling into small spaces, making tiny shelters with old blankets); a pastoral existence (playing with animals); an agricultural life (tending flowers and plants); and finally industrialization (playing with vehicles).

Hall pioneered the use of the questionnaire for studying children. Often, he presented his questionnaires to adults, asking them to remember what they had felt and thought as children. And always, he summed, tabulated, averaged, and compared the results of his questionnaires, serving as an important pioneer in the application of scientific procedures in the study of human development.

Watson

Another pioneer of child psychology was John B. Watson, who introduced an experimental, learning-theory-based approach to the study of development. Following his influence, as well as B. F. Skinner's, this model dominated child study through the early part of the 20th century. It was a model that looked for the causes of developmental change among the rewards and punishments of the environment and viewed the child as the passive recipient of these influences.

RECURRING QUESTIONS

Several important questions have served as recurring themes in developmental psychology and guided much of its research and theorizing. The Locke–Rousseau question is one of them:

- Is it best to view the child as an active, exploring organism, discovering or inventing meaning for the world, as Rousseau argued? Or is it more useful to emphasize, as did Locke, the effects of rewards and punishments on a more passive recipient?

Most contemporary developmental psychologists do not adhere passionately to one or the other point of view as did Locke and Rousseau. However, the predominant current view is of an active, exploring child (Rousseau's view), while recognizing the importance of reward and punishment.

- What are the relative effects of genetics and of environments on the developmental process?

This question has been the source of one of the greatest controversies in psychology: the **nature–nurture controversy.** Extreme points of view maintain either that the environment is solely responsible for whatever we become (nurture) or that genetic background (nature) determines the outcome of development. Although neither of these

extreme positions is completely valid, the issue continues to be debated and is discussed in some detail in Chapter 3.

- Is development a continuous, relatively uninterrupted process, or does it consist of separate stages?

As for most of the recurring questions in lifespan development, there is no simple answer. **Stages** in developmental psychology are typically defined as separate, sequential steps in the evolution of abilities, understandings, or competencies, these steps being closely related to age. As we will see in the next chapter, many important developmental theories are stage theories (for example, Piaget or Freud). But as we will also see, it has been difficult to identify abilities or competencies that *invariably* develop in a fixed, predictable sequence, appearing at a predetermined age. We do not develop like caterpillars: cocoon to butterfly to egg to cocoon to butterfly, each stage undeniably different from the one preceding or following. Nevertheless, stage theories are useful in organizing the *facts* of human development and in helping us understand and talk about them.

- Is development invariably positive? Does all developmental change represent an improvement in abilities or other characteristics?

The answer seems clear: Age brings some obvious decline in certain physical characteristics such as strength, speed, and stamina, as well as in the functioning of senses such as vision and hearing (even as it brings inevitable death, which, at least in one sense, represents decline). But what is not clear is whether it is also accompanied by inevitable decline in intellectual functions such as remembering or solving problems. And if there is decline in these areas, how bad is it? Can it be avoided or lessened? As is discussed in some detail in Chapter 15, these questions are a source of controversy—not only because some of the answers are not particularly pleasant but also because they sometimes contradict our logic, our research, or our intuition.

METHODS OF STUDYING THE LIFESPAN

Observers of human development may focus on natural events, such as children playing in a park; they may collect information on less naturally occurring events, such as old people being interviewed; or they may collect *experimental* observations. In addition, lifespan research may be *longitudinal* (following the same subjects over a period of time) or *cross-sectional* (using a cross section of different subjects at one point in time). Note that these categories are not mutually exclusive. For example, a lifespan study might be experimental and longitudinal or cross-sectional simultaneously. Each of these approaches is described in the following sections.

TABLE 1.5
Naturalistic Observation in Developmental Research

Method	Description	Main Uses	Example
Diary description	Fairly regular (often daily or weekly) descriptions of important events and changes.	Detecting and understanding major changes and developmental sequences.	Investigator keeps detailed sequential record of child's speech.
Specimen description	Detailed description of sequences of behavior, detailing all aspects of behavior.	Studying individual children in depth; not restricted to only one or two predetermined characteristics.	Investigator videotapes sequences of woman's behavior for later analysis.
Time sampling	Behaviors are recorded intermittently during short but regular periods of time.	Detecting and assessing changes in specific behaviors over time.	Investigator records what prisoner is doing during 30-second spans, once every 30 minutes.
Event sampling	Specific behaviors (events) are recorded during the observational period and other behaviors are ignored.	Understanding the nature and frequency of specific behaviors (events).	Investigator notes each time child bangs her head on the wall.

SOURCE: Based in part on Wright, 1960.

Observation

Observation is the basis of all science. The study of the lifespan always begins with either naturalistic or nonnaturalistic observation.

Naturalistic Observation

Observations are termed **naturalistic** when people are observed without interference in natural rather than contrived situations—for example, on the playground or in school. Psychologists who observe children and write **diary descriptions** of their behavior are making use of naturalistic observation. Similarly, those who describe continuous sequences of behavior (**specimen descriptions**), specific behaviors only (**event sampling**), or behaviors during specified time intervals (**time sampling**) are using naturalistic observations (Wright, 1960; see also Table 1.5). In each of these naturalistic methods, the hope is that the observation will not affect the subject's behavior. In naturalistic observation, it is important that the investigator be a detached observer.

Time and event sampling are often used together. Time sampling specifies when observations will be made; event sampling specifies what will be observed. For example, if an investigator wanted to determine whether a new approach to teaching encourages student participation, a combination of time and event sampling would be appropriate. During specified intervals over a number of days (time sampling), the investigator would record instances of student participation (event sampling). Subsequently, observed participation before and after introduction of the new teaching method would be compared.

Nonnaturalistic Observation

In *nonnaturalistic observation*, the investigation affects the subject's behavior. Nonnaturalistic observations are some-times called *clinical* if they use interviews or questionnaires. If they attempt to manipulate or change the environment, they are termed *experimental*.

Experiments

Science's most powerful tool for gathering useful observations is the experiment. An **experiment** is distinguished from other observations in that it requires deliberately and systematically manipulating some aspect of a situation to detect and measure the effects of doing so. In an experiment, the observer controls certain **variables**—termed **independent**—to investigate their effect on other variables—termed **dependent**. For example, in an experiment designed to investigate the relationship between two teaching methods and the development of language skills, the experimenter can manipulate (control) the variable teaching method by arranging for the use of teaching method A with one group of students and teaching method B with a second group. In addition, if we are to have faith in the results of the experiment, subjects must be assigned to methods A or B *randomly* to guard against the possibility that students in one group might have some systematic advantage over students in the other.

In this illustration, teaching method is the independent variable; it is under the experimenter's control. Measures of the subjects' language skills are a dependent variable. The experimenter's **hypothesis** (scientific prediction) is that the independent variable (teaching method) will affect the dependent variable (language skills).

Experimental procedures often involve the use of experimental groups and control groups. **Experimental groups** are ordinarily made up of subjects who are treated in some special way. In this case, the goal is usually to discover whether the special treatment (independent variable) has a predictable effect on some outcome (dependent variable). To ensure that any changes in the dependent variable are due to the treatment, it is often necessary to use a second group—the **control** (or *no-treatment*) **group.** This second group must be as similar as possible to the experimental group in all relevant ways. The effect of the special treatment is then assessed by comparing the two groups with respect to some outcome (dependent variable) after the experimental group has been given the treatment.*

A careful, well-controlled experiment *that can be replicated* is science's only reliable method for discovering causes and effects. Experiments that cannot be replicated—that is, that lead to different conclusions on different occasions—tell us nothing about causes and effects. Science pays little attention to things that happen only once.

Unfortunately, there are many situations in psychological research in which a controlled experiment cannot be conducted—or would be highly unethical. For example, although it might be useful to randomly assign children to conditions of poverty (or war, or abuse) in order to determine what the impact of these conditions might be on their development, this can hardly be done. In many such cases, **correlational studies** might be used instead of experiments.

Correlational Studies

Many developmental studies proceed as follows: Researchers decide to investigate the sources (causes) of specific characteristics; people with these characteristics are identified; a comparison group *without* the same characteristics is found; an attempt is made to obtain historical information about the people in these two groups (home environment, presence or absence of a father, intelligence, similar characteristics in biological ancestors, and so on). Researchers then compare the two groups with respect to these historical variables. In the end, a relationship (correlation)† will be found to exist between specific historical variables and present characteristics, or no relationship will be found.

Through studies such as these, research has established relationships between variables such as poverty and delinquency, and between the personality characteristics of parents and those of children. Many such studies are described in this text. They are called *retrospective* studies because they try to establish relationships by looking backward at the person's history (*retro* means "backward") to see how factors in the individual's past affect present behavior.

One caution is extremely important here. One of the most common errors in the interpretation of research results stems from the apparently logical but false assumption that if two events are related (correlated), one causes the other. Some studies have demonstrated, for example, that children from disadvantaged homes (low socioeconomic level, low parental education, low academic aspirations, and so on) often do less well in school than children from more advantaged backgrounds. Does this mean that home background causes low or high achievement? No. At best, correlational studies show relationships or their absence; they do not establish causation. Thus, there is often a high positive correlation between the number of police officers in an area and rates of juvenile delinquency. Does this mean that police officers *cause* delinquency? No. It is more likely that both are related to a third factor—perhaps something as simple as population. Thus, with higher population there is more crime—and more policing (as well as more churches, more schools, more mothers, and so on). Hence correlation never establishes that something is necessarily the cause of something else. On the other hand, when two events are causally related, there *will* be a correlation between them. For this reason, correlational research can be extremely valuable for those who investigate human development, providing the results of such research are interpreted with caution.

Which Method?

In practice, the methods used by those who investigate development are determined by the questions they want to answer. Some questions can best be answered with one approach; others with another. And some questions, of course, lend themselves to more than one approach. If you are interested in knowing whether children have more affection for cats than for dogs, you might simply compare the number of children who have dogs with the number who have cats (naturalistic observation). Alternatively, you might ask a sample of children which they like best (interview technique). Or you might arrange for different children, alone and in groups, to meet different cats and dogs—also alone and in groups (experimental approach)—and assess their reactions (through simple visual observation or perhaps by measuring their heart rates and other physiological functions).

Notice that each of these approaches might lead to somewhat different answers for the same questions. Perhaps there are more cats than dogs in the homes of your subjects—many parents think cats are less demanding—but children really like dogs better. And maybe, even if they do like dogs better, more children would be afraid of dogs than of cats because strange dogs are more frightening than strange cats. It's important to keep in mind as you go through the studies described in this text that conclusions are sometimes partly a function of research methods; they might have been different had the investigation been conducted differently.

*This is only one of a large variety of experimental designs (arrangements) that are employed in psychological research. For others, see Ray (1993).

†A correlation is a statistical measure of relationship. It is usually expressed as a number ranging from +1.00 (a perfect *positive* relationship—as one variable increases, so does the other), through 0 (no relationship), to –1.00 (a perfect *inverse* relationship—as one variable increases, the other decreases).

The cross-sectional approach to studying changes through the lifespan compares different individuals across spans of years or even generations—of which there are four in the photo on the right. The longitudinal approach looks at the same individual at different periods of time. The person in the photo on the left is the great-grandmother in the photo on the right.

In many cases, the study of the lifespan involves a combination of methods rather than a single method. Experiments typically require observations. Hence, interviews and questionnaires are often part of an experiment.

Longitudinal and Cross-Sectional Studies

There are two broad approaches to the study of human development: the longitudinal and the cross-sectional. A **longitudinal study** observes the same subjects over a period of time; a **cross-sectional study** compares different subjects of different developmental levels at the same time. For example, there are two ways of investigating the different rules used in games played by 2-year-olds and 6-year-olds. One is to observe a group of 2-year-olds at play and four years later repeat the same procedure with the same children. This is the longitudinal approach, which, for this purpose, is more time-consuming than necessary. The same study might simply look at groups of 2- and 6-year-old children at the same time and compare them directly.

Advantages and Disadvantages

Cross-sectional and longitudinal approaches are both essential for studying human development. Each approach has its strengths, and each has weaknesses and limitations. For some questions, a longitudinal approach is best. As Bergman (1993) notes, longitudinal studies are essential for studying *individual* development. "[They] normally cannot for this purpose be replaced by other kinds of studies" (p. 217). If, for example, investigators wish to discover whether intelligence test scores for a given individual change with age or remain stable, they need to observe the same individual at different times. This question cannot be answered by a cross-sectional approach. Because it looks at each individual only once, a cross-sectional approach cannot give us information concerning changes that occur over time within a single individual. Put another way, cross-sectional research is insensitive to *intra-individual* change.

Longitudinal research has a number of disadvantages and limitations. Not only can it be very expensive and time-consuming, but also there is the possibility that instruments and methods may become outdated before the research is completed, or that some of the research questions will be answered in some other way. Often, a longitudinal investigation must be designed so that it can go beyond the lifetime of a single investigator (or team of investigators), especially if it is intended to examine most or all of the human lifespan. This is the case with the Terman study of giftedness that began in the early 1920s and continues today (Terman et al., 1925). This kind of longitudinal study encounters an additional problem: subject mortality. The death of subjects not only reduces the size of samples but may also bias the results. For example, if aggressive people die before those who are not aggressive, a longitudinal study might lead to the conclusion that people become less aggressive as they age.

Perhaps the most serious limitation of longitudinal studies is that their conclusions often depend on the assumption that currently valid measures will be equally valid later. This problem is illustrated in longitudinal studies of vocabulary growth or intelligence, for example,

TABLE 1.6
Methods of Studying Lifespan Development

Observation	The basis of all science. Observation is naturalistic when subjects are observed without interference in natural rather than contrived situations. Naturalistic observation may involve time or event sampling, diary descriptions, or specimen descriptions (see Table 1.5). Non-naturalistic observation may be clinical when it involves structured interviews or questionnaires.
Experiments	Science's most powerful means of gathering observations. They involve systematic attempts to manipulate the environment to observe what the effects of specific independent variables are on dependent variables.
Correlational Studies	Examinations of relationships among two or more variables. A correlation exists when changes in one variable are accompanied by systematic changes in another (for example, during childhood, increasing age is correlated positively with increasing strength). The existence of a correlation is necessary but *insufficient* for inferring causality.
Longitudinal Studies	Where the same subjects are followed over a period of time.
Cross-Sectional Studies	Where subjects of different ages are studied at one point in time.

where rapidly changing cultural conditions may significantly affect the appropriateness of the measures used.

Many of the problems associated with longitudinal research (for example, subject mortality, higher cost, greater time requirement, changing contexts in the lives of subjects) apply only to *longer*-term research. But not all longitudinal research is long-term. For example, longitudinal studies of infant development might span only weeks, or perhaps only days or hours. However, because human development spans a huge spread of years, much of our longitudinal research necessarily is long-term.

The main disadvantage of cross-sectional studies is that they do not tell the researcher anything about changes that occur *within* individuals. This is so because they do not compare the same children to themselves at different ages. Instead, they compare groups of *different* children—perhaps of different ages—to each other. Hence they are useful for providing information about differences among groups.

A second disadvantage of cross-sectional studies is that their conclusions often depend on the validity of the assumption that children at one age level now are comparable to children at that age level at another time. With respect to intelligence, for example, drastic improvements in educational experiences and perhaps in television fare can affect children sufficiently over time that measures of intelligence obtained at one time cannot easily be compared with measures obtained earlier. (See Table 1.6 for a summary of research methods.)

INTERVIEW

SUBJECT
Male, age 82; retired schoolteacher. (on children growing up)

It's a lot different for kids growing up now compared to my day. We didn't have TV, of course, which I think probably makes kids smarter . . . at least better informed. Kids know things now that we sure as heck never knew about. And they see things too, not always the best, because there's stuff on TV I wouldn't want my children to see. I think it's got to affect their morals and, for sure, their attitudes about all kinds of things.

Sources of Variation: Age, Time, and Cohort

Developmental research looks at how people change as they develop. What researchers are most interested in are changes that are related to age. However, research results are sometimes misleading because change in human behavior might also be due to one of two other factors. First, there may be influences related to the time of testing. Thus the same intelligence test given a decade before and decade after the appearance of television might reveal striking differences that are not age-related. Nesselroade and Baltes (1984) argue that for most developmental research, the effects of time of measurement are usually trivial.

Much more significant for the developmental researcher is the influence of the cohort (Schaie, 1983a). A **cohort** is a group of individuals who were born within the same range of time. The cohort of the decade of the 80s, for example, includes all those who were born from the beginning of 1980 to the end of 1989. A cohort is, therefore, of a specific size and composition initially and does not normally increase in size. Instead it becomes less numerous as members die, until it has completely disappeared. Its composition also changes gradually in important ways. For example, because men die at younger ages than women, the male:female ratio of a cohort usually changes over time. Similarly, racial composition might also change as a result of different mortality rates.

What is most important for the lifespan psychologist is that members of different cohorts may be subject to very different experiences as they develop. For example, cohort groups such as that of my grandmother date to the turn of this century and include people who were born into a world without radios, automobiles, televisions, or computers. These obvious cohort-related influences might be important in attempting to understand why an 80-year-old person in 1996 might be quite different from an 80-year-old in 2026 or in 1946. Less obvious cohort-related influences would also include changes in medical practices (including the general use of a variety of inoculations, for example), nutrition, recreation, work roles, morality, and so on. Because of these influences, cohorts might be very different in some important ways.

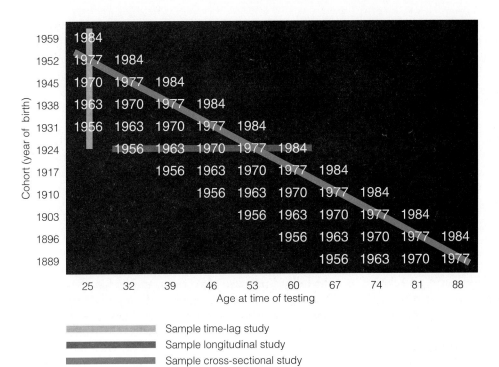

FIGURE 1.6
Schematic representation of the sequential design used in the Seattle Longitudinal Study. The years in the table indicate times of measurement. Vertical columns represent possible time-lag studies (different cohorts, different times of measurement, same age); horizontal rows represent longitudinal studies (the same cohort examined at up to five points in time); and diagonals represent cross-sectional studies (as many as nine cohorts examined at a single point in time). (Based on Schaie, 1965; 1983a; 1986.)

Sample time-lag study
Sample longitudinal study
Sample cross-sectional study

Separating the Effects of Age and Cohort

A serious problem in developmental research is that of separating the effects of age and cohort, which often become confounded in both longitudinal and cross-sectional research. Consider, for example, the apparently simple task of determining whether performance on intelligence tests changes with age. A cross-sectional approach would require administering intelligence tests to several different groups of subjects—say, a group of 20-year-olds and one of 70-year-olds—and comparing their performance. But what would it mean if differences were found among these groups—if, for example, 70-year-olds scored higher than 20-year-olds? Would it mean that intelligence increases with age or, at least, that 70-year-olds are more intelligent than 20-year-olds?

Perhaps not. The problem is that a cross-sectional design uses samples that, because they are of different ages at the same time, are by definition different cohorts. With a simple cross-sectional design there is no way to tell whether differences found between groups are related to their different ages, to the distinct experiences that might be associated with different cohorts, or to both.

Would a longitudinal design answer the question more accurately? Suppose that the same subjects were tested when they were 20 and again when they were 25, 30, and so on. Scores for each individual would then be compared across all age ranges. What if there were differences now? Could we confidently assert that these are related to age and that we have established that intelligence changes in such and such a way as individuals age? Again, perhaps not. One of the problems with longitudinal research is that only one cohort is used throughout the study. As a result, developmental changes identified in such research are not always universal. They might result from something specific to the history of the cohort; they might also be due to the time at which the testing occurred.

Sequential and Time-Lag Designs

One way of overcoming these important research problems is to use **sequential designs** (Schaie, 1965). This involves taking sequences of samples at different times of measurement. One well-known sequential design is the **time-lag study** in which different cohorts are compared at different times. For example, a time-lag study might compare 10-year-olds in 1997 with 10-year-olds in 1999, 2001, and 2003. Because these subjects are the same age when tested but were born in different years, they belong to different cohorts. Consequently, observed differences among the groups might reveal important cohort-related influences.

An Illustration

An excellent example of a sequential design is the 28-year longitudinal study conducted by Schaie and associates (see Figure 1.6). The study began in 1956 as a simple cross-sectional investigation of differences in intellectual functioning among groups of individuals ages 25 to 67. Schaie (1983b) soon realized that a cross-sectional design would not answer important questions about changes that occur within individuals. Accordingly, seven years later he retested as many of the original samples as he could and also selected a second series of samples ages 25 to 74 (those who had been 67 in 1956 were now 74). A third group was added seven years later (1970); this group included a sample of 81-year-olds because the oldest samples in the 1956 and 1963 samples were now 81. A fourth sample was added in 1977 and a fifth in 1984. Because samples were selected at seven-year intervals, subjects are grouped by cohort and by age in clusters seven years apart—that is, ages 25, 32, 39, 46, 53, 60, 67, 74, 81, and 88. Results of this study are discussed in Chapter 15.

CRITERIA FOR EVALUATING LIFESPAN RESEARCH

Truth in psychology, as in most disciplines, is relative rather than absolute. Conclusions derived from research are seldom flatly right or wrong; instead they are judged in terms of usefulness, clarity, logical consistency, and **generalizability.** Of all these criteria, perhaps generalizability is the most important. The value of conclusions that can't be generalized is highly limited.

Sampling

Researchers in psychology try to reach conclusions that are generalizable to entire populations—that is, to entire collections of individuals (or objects or situations) with similar characteristics. In most cases, the populations that are of interest to the researcher are too large to be investigated in their entirety. What the investigator does, instead, is select a sample from this larger population, carefully chosen to represent the entire population. It would be difficult, for example, to obtain valid information concerning the moral beliefs and behaviors of American children by observing a sample of subjects from San Francisco or Boston alone. If the results are to be generalized to the entire population, subjects should represent all major geographical areas in the nation. In addition, all nationalities, major religious groups, socioeconomic levels, occupations, and ages should be represented in proportions similar to the entire population. One of the simplest and most effective ways of ensuring that this is the case is to select subjects at random from the population.

Ecological and Cross-Cultural Validity

There is a large body of research that indicates that Japanese students perform better on measures of mathematics achievement than do American students (see, for example, Westbury et al., 1993). Several conclusions can be based on this observation: Japanese students are more intelligent—or at least more capable in mathematics; the Japanese school system is more effective than the American school system; or both.

Are these conclusions valid? No, says Westbury (1992), a more careful analysis of the data suggests that the Japanese mathematics curriculum fits the tests used in the study more closely than does the American curriculum. This gives Japanese students an unfair advantage. When students are compared only on what they have been taught, American students do about as well as the Japanese.*

A similar situation exists when comparing children from different cultures—or even when comparing children within single multicultural nations. We can never be certain that observed differences reflect real differences (in underlying capacities, for example) or whether they result from the influences of different ecologies—different environments. For example, the finding that Japanese (and Taiwanese) students do better than North American students in mathematics may also be due to a combination of the following facts, says Stevenson (see Coulter, 1993a): North American students spend about 20 hours per week with friends while Japanese and Taiwanese students spend closer to 10; more than three fourths of North American students but fewer than 40 percent of Asian students are dating; and 60 percent of North American students but only 20 percent of Asian students have jobs.

The fact that people from different cultures often perform differently on various tests and in different situations underlines the importance of asking: (1) whether the tests and assessment procedures we're using are suitable for different cultures, and (2) what the underlying causes of observed differences might be. Conclusions based on research conducted only with North American samples may not be valid in western Europe or in third world countries. Similarly, research conducted only with white middle-class subjects in North America should not be generalized to the entire population. Throughout this text, boxed inserts entitled "Across Cultures" are used to emphasize the extent to which we are products of our contexts, as well as the extent to which contexts can vary even within a single culture.

Memory

Studies of the ages at which girls experience their first menstrual period (**menarche**) have often had to rely on the memories of women for whom the event may not be entirely recent; investigations of the ages at which children first walk or talk sometimes base their conclusions on the memories of mothers. Unfortunately, human memory is far from perfect. Not only does it forget but it also distorts—sometimes in predictable ways, sometimes not.

---

*Not all researchers agree with Westbury's conclusions. Some, like Baker (1993), argue that even when American students are tested only on what they have been taught, they still do more poorly. Considerable controversy exists concerning whether there are real differences between American and Japanese children in mathematics achievement and what the reasons are for any such differences.

Those who study lifespan developmental changes are faced with the problem of separating the effects of time from those of the individual's cohort. Because of the vastly different historical periods in which they were born and raised, when the youngest members of this large extended family have lived as long as the oldest, they might be very different from them.

Honesty

Having to rely on the honesty of subjects is a serious problem with questionnaire and interview data, especially when highly personal areas are being researched. Comparisons of contemporary adolescent sexual behavior with behavior that was characteristic of adolescents several generations ago are typically unreliable primarily for this reason. Given prevailing attitudes toward sexual behavior, it is not unreasonable to suppose that today's adolescent may be more honest about sexual behavior than the adolescent of the 1930s might have been.

Experimenter Bias

Some research indicates that experimenters sometimes inadvertently bias the results of their experiments in the direction of their expectations. One effective way to guard against experimenter bias is the **double-blind procedure.** This requires simply that the experimenters and examiners, as well as subjects, not be aware of the expected outcomes of the research or of which subjects are experimental subjects and which are members of the control group.

Subject Bias

Subject bias may also have an effect on the outcome of an experiment. In a highly publicized experiment, two psychologists compared ways to increase productivity among workers in the Hawthorne plant of the Western Electric Company in Chicago (Roethlisberger & Dickson, 1939). In successive experiments, the workers were subjected to shorter and longer working periods, better and poorer lighting conditions, long and short periods of rest, work incentives such as bonuses, and other conditions. Under most of these conditions, productivity apparently increased. This observation led to the conclusion that if sub-jects are aware they are members of an experimental group, performance may improve simply because of that fact.

Although the "Hawthorne effect," as it is now called, is usually accepted as fact in social science research, its existence has not been well established—in spite of the experiments just described. Following a careful reexamination of these experiments and interviews with some of the people who were involved at that time, Rice (1982) found little evidence of a Hawthorne effect. He reports that productivity did not increase in many of the experiments but that later reports of the study usually concentrated on only experiments in which there was a marked improvement over the five-year course of the study.* It's ironic that the Hawthorne experiments, which were designed to demonstrate subject bias, might instead be an example of experimenter bias.

Some Special Problems

Problems involving inadequate sampling, memory distortions, questionable honesty, and experimenter or subject bias may affect research in all areas of psychology. In addition, lifespan research is faced with a handful of unique problems. One such problem, already mentioned, is that of comparing different cohorts. Many lifespan questions concern important changes that occur with advancing age or that follow major transitions. Identifying and investigating

---

*In this particular experiment, workers (all women) were paid according to the productivity of the entire group. Because there were only seven or eight women in the group, individual productivity would have a noticeable effect on the pay received by each woman. Accordingly, when several of the experimental group members proved to be slower than the average, the other women became unhappy; as a result, the slower workers were dropped from the group. Under these circumstances, is it any wonder that the experimental group's performance should improve?

**CHECKLIST FOR EVALUATING
DEVELOPMENTAL RESEARCH**

When you read lifespan research, you should ask yourself a number of questions in addition to "Are the research questions important, or are they merely trivial?" and "Do the answers really matter?" The following checklist can serve as a guide.

Sampling	Is the sample a good representation of the population to which the observations and conclusions are meant to apply?
Ecosystem	Is there something special or unique about the social, cultural, or historical context in which observations are made? Do the characteristics of the context *in interaction with* the characteristics of the individuals reduce the generalizability of the findings?
Memory	Does the investigation have to rely on human memories? Has the possibility of systematic or random distortion been taken into account?
Honesty	Does the validity of the observations depend on the honesty of subjects? Do they have a reason to distort facts, consciously or unconsciously?
Experimenter or Subject Bias	Is there a possibility that experimenter or subject expectations might have influenced observations?
Ethical Issues	Have the rights of all participants been considered and safeguarded?

these changes often require the comparison of different cohorts. It is often difficult to determine whether observed differences are due to changes that occur with age or simply reflect different cohort experiences.

A second problem specific to lifespan research is related to difficulties experienced in obtaining large, representative samples. Because most children are in schools for a large part of their childhood and are therefore easily accessible to researchers, this problem applies much less to them than it does to older subjects. In fact, approximately only 5 percent of the very old* are in retirement homes and other institutions for the aged. Unfortunately, this relatively small number of individuals serves as the subject group for an overwhelming majority of studies of the aged. Accordingly, investigators must be concerned about whether these subjects are actually representative of others not living in institutions. Also, they must always keep in mind that as people become older, they may become less representative. That is, there may be something special that allows 90-year-olds to live so long. Death does not always select at random.

The use of institutionalized individuals in psychological research poses an additional problem relating to research ethics. First, not all elderly people are capable of

*Although "very old" is uncomfortably vague, our studies and theories of aging have not yet provided us with terms that are specific and widely understood to discriminate among older age groups as the terms *neonate, infant, toddler, child,* and *adolescent* distinguish among those who are younger. In this context, the "very old" are over 80.

informed consent; second, there are sometimes subtle forms of coercion involved in research with those in institutions. Some might feel pressured into participating simply by being members of a group; others might volunteer to please their attendants or to ensure favorable treatment.

The use of children in psychological research also gives rise to ethical issues. These issues are addressed in the American Psychological Association's adoption of ethical principles to guide research with children (*Ethical Standards for Research with Children*, 1973). These principles recognize that research can be unethical when children are coerced into participating, when they are exposed to stress or other potentially damaging conditions, when their privacy is invaded, and so on. The principles specify not only that permission of parents but also permission of children must be obtained before conducting child research. Furthermore, consent must be "informed" in the sense that all are fully aware of any aspect of the research that might affect their willingness to participate. (See Interactive Table 1.7 for a checklist for evaluating developmental research.)

THE MYTHICAL AVERAGE

A word of caution is appropriate at this point. This book deals largely with so-called average individuals—with the normal processes of conception, fetal growth, birth, infancy, childhood, adolescence, adulthood, old age, and death. It describes typical behavior and characteristics throughout the lifespan, and it discusses theoretical explanations of normal patterns of development.

There Is No Average Child

But there is no average child, let alone adult! The concept is a convenient invention, a necessary creation if we are to speak coherently of human development. Bear in mind that each person is a unique individual, that each will differ from the average, and that no one theory will account for all behavior. We are incredibly more complex than any description provided by even the most complex of theories. A theory—and a book—can deal only with the objective details of human behavior, not with its essence.

There Is No Average Context

Just as there is no average child, there is no average environment—no average context. And context is fundamentally important in determining what we become. Being born in a wooden hut in the rain forests of the Amazon Basin must surely lead to a very different life than being delivered by a private doctor at a New York City medical center. Being raised in a war-ravaged country or in a peaceful and isolated village must surely shape children's lives in profound ways. But our world is changing remarkably rapidly. Most of our villages are no longer isolated. Telephones, computers, satellites, television, airplanes, transnational corporations—these bind us in a shrinking global village. "Today's realities," writes Greer (1991), "dictate that what happens in the rain forests of South America is as relevant to us as the unification of Germany. . . . In today's society, the economy of Japan affects the financial stability of the world. . . . Today's world has at last become the global village so long envisioned" (p. 198).

Global Environmental Change

"The universality of a child in need," Greer writes, "is perhaps the greatest unifier of all" (p. 199). But, unfortunately, there is another global unifier. It has to do with negative changes that affect our entire globe. Most of us have grown up believing that the world's bounties would never run out, that no matter what we did, nature would always clean up after us.

We were wrong. Some of the effects of human actions—burning fossil fuels, deforestation, emission of substances like carbon dioxide gas, methane, and chlorofluorocarbons (used mainly in refrigeration and air-conditioning and in electronics production)—are perhaps irreversible. These greenhouse gases increase the earth's temperature and deplete the ozone layer so that ultraviolet radiation is no longer effectively screened (Turner et al., 1991). Ultraviolet radiation damages our immune system, destroying its ability to fight infection and disease; it is also linked directly to skin cancer, the incidence of which has doubled in less than a decade (Pawlik, 1991). And the most vulnerable among us are the children. If we don't change our actions, the children of a future world may be driven indoors by the sun.

What does global environmental change have to do with psychology and with lifespan development? A great deal. Tomorrow's world is being shaped by global environmental change (Levy-Leboyer & Duron, 1991); environmental change results from human behavior, and human behavior is psychology's main concern.

Psychology's challenge, says Stern (1992), is to bring about changes in environmentally significant behaviors. We can respond in two ways: (1) We can take actions to prevent or slow negative change (like limiting deforestation and fuel consumption), or (2) we can respond by adapting to change (by developing ultraviolet screens and drought-resistant food-crops; or by staying indoors).

Or we can do absolutely nothing.

MAIN POINTS

This Text

1. *Lifespan developmental psychology* is concerned with understanding and explaining changes that occur between conception and death. *The Lifespan* is organized chronologically.

Lifespan Developmental Psychology

2. The contemporary lifespan view of development recognizes that change continues throughout the lifespan, that maturity is a relative and changing state, that it is important to consider the context (*ecology*) of human development, and that developmental influences are bidirectional.

Some Definitions in Development

3. Development, the total process by which individuals adapt to their environment, includes maturation (genetically programmed unfolding), growth (quantitative changes), and learning (changes due to experience).

Historical Snapshots

4. There is evidence that in medieval times the concept of childhood did not exist as we know it, that parent–child attachment was indifferent, and that infant mortality was very high. Through the 18th and 19th centuries, child labor flourished, and child-rearing practices were often harsh and cruel by current North American standards. The 20th century brought increasing concern with the social, physical, and intellectual welfare of children, especially in the industrialized world.

Children's Rights

5. The recognition of children's rights—a relatively recent international development—describes rights of protection and to growth-fostering conditions (rather than the more adult rights of choice).

Studying Human Development

6. Among early pioneers in the scientific study of human development were John Locke (*tabula rasa*) and Jean-Jacques Rousseau ("noble savage"). Later pioneers included Charles Darwin (child biography and evolution), G. Stanley Hall ("ontogeny recapitulates phylogeny"), and John B. Watson (we become what we are as a function of our experiences).

Recurring Questions

7. A recurring theme in studies of the lifespan are questions relating to the influence of heredity and environment: Which has more influence? Is development

continuous or does it progress in discrete stages? Is development primarily linear and is it characterized initially by increments, followed by inevitable decline in the later stages of life?

Methods of Studying the Lifespan

8. Observation is the basis of all science. Naturalistic observation occurs when individuals are observed without interference (diary descriptions, specimen descriptions, event sampling, and time sampling). Nonnaturalistic observations may be clinical (using questionnaires or interviews) or experimental (deliberately manipulating the environment). Experiments are useful for investigating cause-and-effect relationships, as are correlational studies (studies of relationships) that provide useful information about cause-and-effect relationships *but cannot prove causation.*

9. Longitudinal studies examine the same individuals at different periods in their lives; cross-sectional studies compare different individuals at the same time. Longitudinal studies may be more costly and time-consuming and may suffer from problems relating to subject (or experimenter) mortality and the eventual obsolescence of experimental methods and instruments. Cross-sectional studies are useful for comparing groups of different ages at one time but provide little information about intra-individual changes.

10. A cohort is a group of individuals born during a single timespan and often subject to a variety of unique influences that might account for important differences between them and members of other cohorts. Attempts to reduce the confounding of age and cohort in developmental research have led to *sequential* research designs—so called because they involve the selection of a sequence of samples. A time-lag study is a sequential design in which different cohorts are compared at different times with age held constant.

Criteria for Evaluating Lifespan Research

11. The validity and reliability of research results are subject to the influences of sample size and representativeness, ecological and cross-cultural validity, subject memory and honesty, experimenter and subject biases, and cohort-related experiences. There are also ethical issues to be considered in doing lifespan research.

The Mythical Average

12. The average individual is a conceptually useful invention but does not exist. Nor does the average context. Global environmental change presents a serious challenge for developmental psychologists—and for all humans.

FOCUS QUESTIONS: APPLICATIONS

1. What is the lifespan perspective of human development?
   - Describe and explain the four most important themes underlying the study of the lifespan.

2. How are growth, maturation, learning, and development related?
   - Define and give an example of each of these terms.

3. What are the most basic of children's rights?
   - Find at least one current example of a violation of children's rights described in your local newspaper.

4. What questions keep recurring in the study of human development?
   - What questions do you suppose you would ask if you were just undertaking your studies?

5. How do we study lifespan development?
   - List some of the questions you should ask yourself when evaluating the conclusions of developmental research.

STUDY TERMS

baby tossing   14

bidirectionality   7

cohort   20

control group   18

correlational studies   18

cross-sectional study   19

dependent variable   17

development   7

developmental psychology   6

FURTHER READINGS

The following book by Kegan is an intriguing, superbly written approach to human development. Its central theme is that we are "meaning-making organisms." Our lives are directed by behaviors that organize the world in meaningful ways, and that make us meaningful to others (as in "Hamlet *meant* a lot to Ophelia"):

Kegan, R. (1982). *The evolving self: Problem and process in human development.* Cambridge, MA: Harvard University Press.

Books by Belsky, Lerner, and Spanier, and by Bronfenbrenner are excellent examples of lifespan emphases on ecological (contextual) influences in development:

Belsky, J., Lerner, R. M., & Spanier, G. B. (1984). *The child in the family.* Reading, MA: Addison-Wesley.

Bronfenbrenner, U. (1979). *The ecology of human development: Experiments by nature and design.* Cambridge, MA: Harvard University Press.

Moving descriptions of changes in the status of children throughout history are provided by Ariès:

Ariès, P. (1962). *Centuries of childhood: A social history of family life* (R. Baldick, Trans.). New York: Knopf. (Originally published 1960.)

The following is a short book on science and its methods. It includes a number of useful suggestions for conducting experimental research as well as for writing research articles:

Ray, W. J. (1993). *Methods toward a science of behavior and experience* (4th ed.). Pacific Grove, CA: Brooks/Cole.

A booklet containing all the children's rights articles of the United Nations' Convention on the Rights of the Child can be obtained free from:

United Nations Children's Fund
UNICEF House, H-9F
United Nations Plaza
New York, NY 10017   (212) 326-7072

Not everyone believes that science is the only, or even the best, way of knowing. For a provocative and sometimes challenging view of science and our conception of reality, see:

Pearce, J. C. (1971). *The crack in the cosmic egg.* New York: Fawcett.

Theories of
Lifespan Development

"*N*ow what I want is facts. Teach these boys and girls nothing but Facts. Facts alone are wanted in life. Plant nothing else, and root out everything else. . . . Stick to Facts, Sir!"

CHARLES DICKENS
Hard Times

I'm standing on one side of the counter in Peltier's store; my dad and Mr. Peltier and Ricketts, the local policeman, are on the other side.

CHAPTER 2

"It wasn't me, and that's a fact," says I for about the tenth time. Innocence is sometimes a difficult thing to prove. "It wasn't," I say again, while waiting for a verdict that, I hope to gawd, isn't a wrong one because if it is, there'll be a punishment too. This time, again, I really am innocent. The fact is that it is Sylvia Tremblay who has drowned the three cats in a gunnysack into which she had dropped a cast-iron skillet stolen from Peltier's store. That the gunnysack came from the green shed behind my grandfather's barn is just about the only thing that links me to the crime.

"Maybe it's Sylvia again," says my dad. "Is it Sylvia?" asks the priest, throwing me into a terrible conflict. No one rats is our clear code of honor; but to lie to a priest . . . I can almost smell my soul frying. I shrug. It's only half a lie . . . maybe not even half, because what does a shrug mean anyway?

And then Sylvia comes into the store to buy something, which is bad luck for her, because now they point their accusations straight at her and I'm saved. "I didn't steal the cats," she insists. "They were just strays." Realizing that she has almost confessed, she quickly adds, "And I didn't drown them neither." But the pockets of her jacket, bulging with unused skillets, shout

out her guilt—well, not really *her* jacket because it has just recently come from Marie Boutin's aunt's coat rack. Her boots are from somewhere else.

Because it isn't the first time, they arrest her. Later, she stands in front of a judge and listens while they read a long list of the things she is supposed to have done. Her best friend, Cecile Watrin, stands next to her and holds her hand. Cecile's pockets are full of chocolate bars, which Sylvia gave her.

"These are facts," says the prosecutor when he finishes reading, smugly, clasping his hands tightly in anticipation. The judge weighs the facts for just a few moments before pronouncing his judgment. "The girl's a kleptomaniac," he says. "That's why she steals things."

THIS CHAPTER

The judge was dead wrong. Maybe Sylvia was a kleptomaniac, but that does not explain why she stole things. "Kleptomaniac" is just a label, a name. To assume that naming something explains it is a common error called the **nominal fallacy.** To explain behavior, we need more than the labels that the facts suggest.

The facts of developmental psychology are the observations we make—the replicable, objective observations

One of the measures of psychological theories is how useful they are in explaining observations considered important enough to need explaining—even when the observations relate to the thoughts and behaviors of people whose lives and experiences are as different as those of the Indiana Amish and the California surfer pictured here.

that are the basis of the discipline. But isolated facts do not necessarily lead to understanding; they don't often allow us to make predictions or to affect the outcomes of development. We need to go beyond facts; we need to build theories. That's what this chapter is about: theories that lifespan theorists have built to understand and explain their facts. Theories are what allow us to go *beyond* the facts.

This chapter deals with theories designed to explain normal and abnormal personality development (Freud and Erikson); theories intended to explain how we learn and how we respond to the consequences of our behaviors (conditioning and social-learning theories); theories that look at the development of mental capacities and processes (Piaget's cognitive theory; information-processing theory); theories concerned with the influences of culture and language on development (Vygotsky's sociocultural theories); and theories that look at the influences of biology on behavior (sociobiology and ethology). Each of these theories suggests different explanations for Sylvia Tremblay's behavior, and each might lead to a different kind of understanding.*

PSYCHOLOGICAL THEORIES

A **theory** is essentially a description and explanation of observations. A theory can be so specific and simple, says Kuhn (1970), that it attempts to explain only a single relationship. My grandfather's belief that drinking wild mint tea prevents colds is one such theory. The belief that kleptomaniacs are people whose left-handed mothers got pregnant on the night of a new moon in October is another. These types of beliefs are often labeled **naive theories** (or *commonsense theories*) (Wellman & Gelman, 1992).

*Even my grandmother's beliefs almost find justification in psychological theory. "It's in her blood," said she. "Her dad's brother's wife was just like that. And so's their dog."

Most of the theories that are important in the study of lifespan development are more general. They consist of collections of statements intended to organize and explain related observations. And most are based on more objective and systematic evidence than are naive theories.

Purposes of Theories

The purpose of theories is to explain. Explanation is important because if we can explain something, we might also be able to make predictions about it, and we might be able to control certain outcomes. If we can explain Sylvia's compulsion to steal, for example, we might have been able to predict it beforehand. And we might even have been able to eradicate this compulsion or change it into something else, like an urge to sing arias from Italian operas.

Not only do theories have a very practical aspect, they also are one of science's primary guides for doing research. In large part, it is a theory—sometimes crude, sometimes elegant and refined—that tells the researcher where to look for a cure for cancer, what the cure will look like when it is found, and how it might be used. In the same way, psychology's theories tell the researcher where and how to look for personality or cognitive change in the lifespan; they also indicate why it might be important to look for that change.

Evaluating Theories

Why, you might ask, must there be a variety of theories if a theory is simply an explanation of facts? One reason is that different theories may be used to explain quite different facts. And even the most general theories of development are not all based on the same observations. Theorists *select* observations that need to be explained. Furthermore, given the same set of observations, not all theorists will arrive at the same explanations. And, finally, fact (or truth) is just as elusive in developmental psychology as it is elsewhere. Our observations are often relative. Their accuracy is affected by the imprecision of our observation (or measurement); they often apply only in specific circumstances and sometimes for specific individuals; and they are colored by our beliefs and expectations.

We cannot easily determine whether a theory is right or wrong, say Wellman and Gelman (1992); but we can evaluate it in terms of its usefulness.

Characteristics of Good Theories
Thomas (1992) suggests several criteria that might be used to judge a theory. A theory is better, he says, if it (1) accurately reflects the facts, (2) is expressed in a clearly understandable way, (3) is useful for predicting future events as well as explaining past ones, (4) is applicable in a practical sense (that is, has real value for counselors, teachers, pediatricians, and so on), (5) is consistent within itself rather than self-contradictory, and (6) is not based on numerous assumptions (unproven beliefs).

A good theory should also be thought-provoking and should have *heuristic* value—that is, it should be useful in our quest for knowledge. It should lead to new ideas, new discoveries, or new applications. And it should provide satisfying explanations, says Thomas (1992).

MODELS IN LIFESPAN DEVELOPMENT

Imagine this problem: Your psychology instructor has brought into class a small thing inside a larger glass container. You don't know what this small thing is. Your task is to decide what the best way would be to discover all that you can about this thing. Think about the problem for a moment before reading on.

Is there enough information presented so that you can make some reasonably intelligent suggestions? Consider, now, what the nature of your suggestions might be had I written, "Your instructor has brought into class a small animal inside a glass cage," or "Your instructor has brought into class a small piece of machinery inside a glass box," or "Your instructor has brought into class a strange new fruit in a glass container." Why is the task of investigating the object so much easier in the last three cases? Simply because you have been presented with information that allows you to classify the object in terms of *something*, about whose properties and functioning you already know a great deal. You have, in your view of the world, a mental **model** of what animals, fruits, and machines are like.

In some important ways, psychologists investigating human development are in the same position as a student presented with this unknown thing. At first the investigators might not know what questions to ask. But if they could look at development in terms of something more familiar, many questions—and answers—might suggest themselves. In effect, that is the starting point of all systematic investigation. We begin with a metaphor—a comparison. We say, this is like that, and it might therefore work in the same way as that. The *that* serves as our model.

Machine–Organism Models

The early development of lifespan theories was strongly influenced by two basic models: the organismic and the mechanistic (Fischer & Silvern, 1985). A third model, the contextual, is rapidly becoming more influential.

The **organismic model** assumes that it is useful to view people as though they are like active organisms; the **mechanistic model** assumes that it is more useful to view people as though they are like machines. In the first instance, the model is primarily *active*; in the second, the model is *reactive*.

Models such as these are very important in the development of theory. In effect, they suggest what the theorist will investigate and what the resulting theory will look

TABLE 2.1
Three Basic Models in Developmental Psychology

	Organismic	Mechanistic	Contextual
Metaphor	A biological organism	A machine	A plastic—strong, resilient, but responsive
Perception of Person	Sees individual as active, self-directed	Sees individual as reactive, responsive to environment	Sees individual as active and reactive
Developmental Process	Tends toward final adult stage, describable in terms of adult thought structures (logical characteristics of adult thought)	Described in terms of learning and problem solving; no clearly described end goal	Involves universal principles influenced by the individual's specific social, historical, and personal context
Theories	Age-related stage theories emphasizing similarities of thought at each level	Theories emphasizing the continuity of development	Theories emphasizing the interaction of age, historical variables, important life events, culture, and other aspects of context
Emphasis	Attention to similarities	Attention to individual differences	Attention to similarities; recognition of context-related differences
Theorists	Jean Piaget; Sigmund Freud	Early behaviorism	Urie Bronfenbrenner; Richard M. Lerner; K. Warner Schaie; Gisela Labouvie-Vief; M. Basseches; also contemporary behaviorists

like. An organismic view (Piaget, for example) tends to see development as a process resulting from self-initiated activities and looks for regularities in behavior in order to understand the whole organism. In contrast, a more mechanistic view (early behaviorism, for example) sees development as a process resulting from reactions to external events and looks for the machinelike predictability that might result if we knew enough about how the machine reacts to external forces. Both the mechanistic and the organismic models emphasize *stages* that follow one another in predictable sequence.

A Contextual Model

But much of development is far less linear and predictable than simple stage theories might imply, says Steenbarger (1991). Development and behavior are profoundly influenced by the situations in which people find themselves. Put another way, human development reflects the influence of *context*. The **contextual** (or *ecological*) **model** emphasizes the role of society, culture, and family; it recognizes the importance of the historical period in which the individual develops, as well as the importance of events that are unique to the individual.

The contextual model shares characteristics of both the organismic and the mechanistic models. It is organismic in that it sees development as the product of organism–environment interaction and because it looks for universal principles that might be useful for describing development. It is mechanistic in that it is concerned with the influence of the environment on the developing organism. Its principal identifying feature, say Fisher and Lerner (1994), is the belief that "knowledge of an individual's biological, physical, interpersonal, cultural, and historical contexts is essential to an understanding of development" (p. 6).

The contextual or ecological model is exemplified in Bronfenbrenner's *ecological systems theory* and in Vygotsky's

social-cognitive theory, both of which are described later in this chapter. It is also the model that is most apparent throughout this text, which, with Bronfenbrenner, views lifespan development as the progressive adaptation of active, growing human beings to changing environments. Our emphasis is on understanding development as an interactive process involving individuals with different characteristics in a range of different contexts. Thus the emphasis on the importance of the family, school, peers, siblings, and other significant aspects of context. Thus, too, the emphasis on the importance of the social and interactive nature of the processes of development.

At this point, you might ask which of these models is correct. The answer is simple: The question is irrelevant. Models are simply metaphors—comparisons. You might as well ask whether "The moon was a ghostly galleon, tossed up on cloudy seas" is more accurate than "That orbed maiden with white fire laden / Whom mortals call the moon." Metaphors are apt and useful or they are clumsy and useless. We might judge our poetic metaphors in terms of the images and feelings they arouse; we can judge our scientific metaphors only in terms of their usefulness. (See Table 2.1 for a summary of these three metaphors.)

A PSYCHOANALYTIC APPROACH: FREUD

Psychoanalytic theory reflects an organismic model in *Sigmund Freud*'s basic assumption that the most important causes of human behavior and personality are unconscious forces within individuals. Freud believed that these forces, because they often lead to conflict between desires and conscience, are at the root of mental disorders. Hence therapists (psychoanalysts) can help restore mental health, argued Freud, by helping patients understand unconscious drives and resulting conflicts. Among the techniques that he found most useful for this—techniques that soon became part of standard psychoanalytic procedure—were free association; the analysis of dreams and of the unintended use of words and expressions (popularly referred to as *Freudian slips*), both of which were assumed to reflect unconscious desires or fears; hypnosis; and painstaking analysis of childhood experiences—especially those of a sexual or traumatic (intensely frightening) nature.

Although the principal usefulness of Freudian psychoanalytic theory has been for the treatment of mental disorder, much of the theory is developmental. While it's true that the most fundamental beliefs of psychoanalytic theory are no longer an important part of current developmental theories, they have had a profound influence on the thinking of later theorists. The following sections present an abbreviated account of this complex, sometimes bewildering, but always fascinating view of the development and machinations of human personality.

While going through these brief sections, keep in mind that Freud's theory reflects the Victorian era in which it was developed—an era that, by contemporary standards, was one of extreme sexual repression and masculine domination. These cultural factors greatly influenced Freud's theory and are reflected in the significance he attributed to sexual motives and behaviors and in the masculine orientation of the theory.

Basic Freudian Ideas

Among the most fundamental Freudian ideas is the notion that human behavior and development are motivated by two powerful tendencies: the urge to survive and the urge to procreate. Of these, the survival instinct is now only of secondary importance because it is not usually endangered by the environment. But because the urge to procreate is constantly discouraged and even prevented, sexuality is of tremendous importance in Freud's description of human development.

Sexuality is a very broad term in Freud's writings. It includes not only activities clearly associated with sex but also a wide range of other behaviors and feelings—affection and love, as well as actions such as eating, thumb-sucking, smoking, and others. Sexual urges are so important in Freud's system that they are given a special term—**libido.** The libido is the source of energy for sexual urges; accordingly, the urges themselves are referred to as *libidinal urges*. In Freud's theory, the satisfaction of sexual impulses need not always involve the sexual regions of the body.

Three Levels of Personality

According to Freud, human development occurs in three broad stages reflected in different aspects (or levels) of personality.

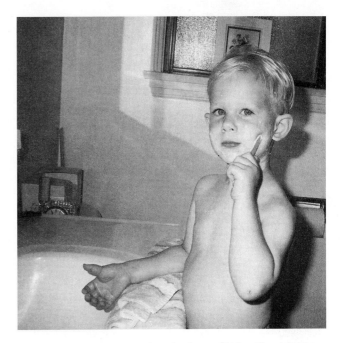

Freudian theory suggests that this boy will identify with his parents, especially with his father. But the shaving is only a trivial manifestation of identification. Far more important for this lad's development is that he will also adopt many of the values and beliefs of his parents.

Id

The Freudian infant is all instincts and *reflexes* (unlearned tendencies), a bundle of energy seeking, almost desperately, to satisfy urges that are based upon a need to survive and to procreate. These urges, labeled **id,** are a lifetime source of what Freud referred to as *psychic energy*, the urges and desires that account for behavior. An infant has no idea of what is possible or impossible, no sense of reality, no conscience, no internal moral rules that control behavior. The most powerful urge at this stage is to seek immediate satisfaction of impulses. A child who is hungry does not wait. *Now* is the time for the nipple and the sucking!

Ego

Almost from birth, the child's instinctual urges come into abrupt collision with reality. For example, the hunger urge (linked with survival) cannot always be satisfied immediately. The *reality* of the situation is that the mother is often busy elsewhere and the infant's satisfaction has to be delayed or denied. Similarly, the infant eventually discovers that defecation cannot occur at will, that parental demands sometimes conflict with personal impulses. This constant conflict between the id and reality develops the second level of personality, the **ego.**

In essence, the ego grows out of the infant's gradual realization of what is possible and what is not. It is the rational, intellectual level of human personality. It includes the realization that delaying gratification is often a desirable thing, that long-term goals sometimes require the denial of short-term goals. Although the id wants immediate

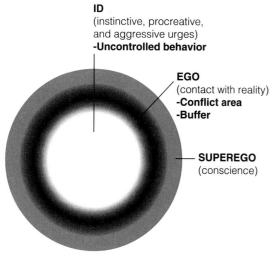

ID
(instinctive, procreative,
and aggressive urges)
-Uncontrolled behavior

EGO
(contact with reality)
-Conflict area
-Buffer

SUPEREGO
(conscience)

FIGURE 2.1

The Freudian conception of the three levels of personality: id, ego, and superego. The id, consisting of instinctual urges, develops first. The ego and the superego (conscience) develop later. In normal personality development, the ego acts as a buffer between the id and superego, which are in conflict with each other. Personality disorders may arise from unrestricted conflict when the ego fails to mediate successfully.

TABLE 2.2
Freud's Stages of Psychosexual Development

Stage	Approximate Ages	Characteristics
Oral	0 to 18 months	Sources of pleasure include sucking, biting, swallowing, playing with lips. Preoccupation with immediate gratification of impulses. Id is dominant.
Anal	18 months to 2–3 years	Sources of sexual gratification include expelling feces and urination, as well as retaining feces. Id and ego.
Phallic	2–3 to 6 years	Child becomes concerned with genitals. Source of sexual pleasure involves manipulating genitals. Period of Oedipus or Electra complex. Id, ego, and superego.
Latency	6 to 11 years	Loss of interest in sexual gratification. Identification with like-sexed parent. Id, ego, and superego.
Genital	11 and older	Concern with adult modes of sexual pleasure, barring fixations or regressions.

gratification, the ego channels these desires in the most profitable direction for the individual. Note that the levels of personality represented by the id and the ego are not in opposition. They work together toward the same goal: satisfying the needs and the urges of the individual.

Superego

In contrast, the third level of personality, the **superego,** sets itself up in opposition to the id and the ego. Like the ego, the superego develops from contact with reality, although it is more concerned with social than physical reality, and relates to the moral aspects of personality (to **conscience**). The development of the superego does not occur until early childhood. Freud assumed that it resulted principally from *identifying* with (trying to be like) parents, particularly the like-sexed parent. To *identify* in a Freudian sense is to adopt values, beliefs, and behaviors. By identifying with their parents, children learn the religious and cultural rules that govern their parents' behaviors, and these rules then become part of the child's superego. Because many religious rules, as well as many social and cultural rules, oppose the urges of the id, the superego and the id are generally in conflict. Freud assumed that this conflict accounts for much deviant behavior (see Figure 2.1).

Freud's Psychosexual Stages

Freud's account of the development of the three levels of personality is also a description of psychosexual development. In essence, **psychosexual development** consists of

stages that are distinguished by different objects and activities relating to satisfaction of urges during that stage. Hence the labels for each stage reflect changes in the areas of sexual satisfaction as the child matures.

The Oral Period

The **oral stage** lasts through infancy (approximately to the age of 18 months). It is characterized by the infant's preoccupation with the mouth and with sucking. During this first stage, the child's personality consists mainly of id. Children seek constantly to satisfy their urges and are incapable of deliberately delaying gratification.*

The Anal Period

Toward the end of the first year, the area of sexual gratification shifts gradually from the oral to the anal region. According to Freud, in the early part of the **anal stage** the child derives pleasure from bowel movements. Later in this stage the child acquires control of sphincter muscles and may then derive considerable pleasure from withholding bowel movements to increase anal sensation. Both of these behaviors oppose the mother's wishes. As a result of these conflicts, the child begins to develop an ego—a sense of reality, an awareness that some things are possible

---

*"That's where Robert got stuck," said my grandmother, displaying a remarkable talent for simplifying bizarre and complex things. Freud, too, believed that development sometimes gets "arrested" at an early stage, and that later maladjustments can occasionally be explained in this way.

INTERACTIVE TABLE 2.3

SOME FREUDIAN DEFENSE MECHANISMS

Defense mechanisms are irrational and sometimes unhealthy methods many people use to compensate for their inability to satisfy the demands of the id. They are invented by the ego as it attempts to establish peace between the id and the superego. Defense mechanisms are particularly important for understanding disturbed personalities, although they are not at all uncommon in the lives of those who have no clearly recognizable disturbances. It is only when people rely on them excessively that defense mechanisms become unhealthy. Can you think of an additional example of each defense mechanism?

Mechanism	Example
Displacement: Undesirable emotions are directed toward a different object.	A man who is angry at his wife kicks his dog.
Reaction formation: Behavior is the opposite of the individual's actual feelings.	A woman loves an unobtainable man and behaves as though she dislikes him.
Intellectualization: Behavior is stripped of its emotional meaning.	A mercenary who fears his enjoyment of his work is unhealthy convinces himself he is moved by duty and not by love of killing.
Projection: People attribute their own undesirable feelings or inclinations to others.	A man who is extremely jealous of a competitor believes it is the competitor who is jealous of him.
Denial: Reality is distorted to make it conform to the individual's wishes.	A heavy smoker is unable to give up the habit and decides that there is no substantial evidence linking nicotine with human diseases.
Repression: Unpleasant experiences are stored deep in the subconscious mind and become inaccessible to waking memory.	A child is sexually abused but remembers nothing of the experience.

while others are not, coupled with the ability to delay gratification to some extent.

The Phallic Stage

The third stage, which lasts roughly from ages 2 to 6, is labeled **phallic,** not only because the zone of sexuality has shifted from the anal to the genital region but also because the phallus (the male genital) is of primary importance in the sexuality of girls as well as boys. Whereas gratification had been obtained earlier by sucking or by expelling or withholding feces, children now often manipulate their genitalia (masturbate).

Normal development now takes the male child through the **Oedipus complex,** when his increasing awareness of the sexual meanings of his genital area leads him to desire his mother (and to wish unconsciously to replace his father). For girls ages 4 to 6 there is the **Electra complex,** in which a girl's sexual feelings for her father lead her to become jealous of her mother.

Sexual Latency

The resolution of the Oedipus complex marks the transition from the phallic stage to the period of sexual **latency** that follows. The period of latency (ages 6–11) is marked by a loss of sexual interest and a continued **identification** with the like-sexed parent (attempts to be like the object of identification in terms of beliefs and values). In this way, the child begins to develop a superego.

Genital Stage

Following this lengthy period of sexual neutrality, the child enters the stage of adult sexuality, the **genital stage** (at around age 11), and begins to establish the sorts of het-

erosexual attachments that characterize normal adult sexual relationships. Also during this last developmental stage, the superego (conscience), which has previously been rigid and almost tyrannical, normally becomes progressively more flexible with increasing maturity. (See Table 2.2 for a summary of Freud's stages of psychosexual development. See also Interactive Table 2.3 for a summary of an additional aspect of Freudian theory.)

Freud in Review

Hofer (1981) describes Freud's theory as one of the most comprehensive and influential of all human psychological theories. More than anyone else, Freud was responsible for making parents realize how important the experiences of the early years can be. Hence the theory has had a tremendous impact on our attitudes toward children and on child rearing. In addition, it has also had a profound influence on the development of other theories (for example, those of Erikson and Bowlby). However, many of Freud's students and followers have not accepted the theory entirely.

Freud paints a dark and somewhat cynical picture of human nature: In this system, primitive inherited forces over which we have no control drive us relentlessly to try to satisfy our sexual urges and bring us into repeated conflict with reality. Most of Freud's followers present a more optimistic view of human nature. And most give sexual urges a much less prominent role.

Freud's theory is clearly weak from a scientific point of view, based as it is on a limited number of observations collected by a single individual (Freud himself), and not subjected to any rigorous analysis. In addition, it uses difficult and important terms and concepts, such as *unconscious*, in confusing and ambiguous ways; it leads to contradictory predictions; and it places excessive emphasis on sexual and aggressive impulses (Rothstein, 1980). Also, much of what Freud initially thought about development applied primarily to male children, and to females only as a sometimes hasty and incomplete afterthought (Gilligan, 1982).

In spite of these criticisms, Freud's theorizing is an immensely rich basis for understanding human personality. In summarizing the contributions of psychoanalysis, Kegan (1982) notes that it remains the single most important guide for mental health practitioners in clinics and in hospitals. Ironically, however, its status in academic psychology is relatively minor. In contrast, theories such as Piaget's cognitivism are an ongoing source of debate and research in academic circles, but these theories have remarkably little influence on the application of psychology in the real world.

A PSYCHOSOCIAL APPROACH: ERIKSON

Of the theories inspired by Freud's psychoanalytic views, perhaps the most important for understanding lifespan human development is that proposed by *Erik Erikson* (1956, 1959, 1961, 1968). It draws heavily from Freud's work but also departs from it in important ways.

Recall that Freud's primary emphasis was on the role of sexuality (libido) and on the importance of conflicts involving id, ego, and superego in determining personality and mental health. In contrast, Erikson downplays the importance of sexuality and of psychodynamic conflicts. Instead he emphasizes the importance of the child's social environment. His theory is a theory of **psychosocial** rather than *psychosexual* development. It is more contextual than Freud's.

A second departure from Freudian theory is Erikson's emphasis on the role of the ego rather than the superego. As a result, the theory is more positively oriented, being concerned with the development of a healthy ego (of **identity,** in Erikson's terms) rather than with the resolution of powerful internal conflicts. Erikson's concern with the healthy personality is a third important difference between his work and that of Freud.

Psychosocial Stages

Erikson describes human development in eight stages, the first five of which span infancy, childhood, and adolescence; the last three describe adulthood. Each of Erikson's stages involves a basic conflict, brought about primarily by a need to adapt to the social environment. Resolution of this conflict results in the development of a sense of competence. Although Erikson's first five stages

One of the important achievements of the first two or three years, says Erik Erikson, is the development of a sense of autonomy. This achievement is linked with the realization that intentions can be acted out (thus, toys can be gotten by walking over to them—or sometimes just by pointing at them), and by imitation. (Note the toy the little girl has stuffed inside her shirt. Her mother was pregnant at the time.)

closely parallel Freud's psychosexual stages in terms of ages, his descriptions and his emphases are quite different. The stages are described briefly here; they are covered in more detail in Chapters 12, 14, 16, and 18.

Trust Versus Mistrust

One of the most basic components of a healthy personality is a sense of trust. This sense of trust toward oneself and toward others develops in the first year of life (Erikson, 1959). The infant is initially faced with a conflict between mistrust of a world about which little is known and an inclination to develop a trusting attitude toward that world. The most important person in the infant's life at this stage is the primary caregiver—usually the mother. Successful resolution of the conflict between **trust and mistrust** depends largely on the infant's relationship with this caregiver and on the gradual realization that the world is predictable, safe, and loving. According to Erikson, if the world is unpredictable and the caregiver rejecting, the infant may grow up to be mistrustful and anxious.

Autonomy Versus Shame and Doubt

Initially, infants do not deliberately act upon the world. Instead, they react to it. Sucking, for example, is not something the infant deliberately decides to do, but is something that occurs in the face of appropriate stimulation. During this second stage, corresponding to Freud's anal stage, children slowly begin to realize that they are the authors of their own actions. As they recognize that they can carry out some of the behaviors they intend, children develop a sense of autonomy. This autonomy, however, is threatened by children's inclination to avoid responsibility for their own actions, to go back to the comfort and security that characterized the first stage. If the child is to successfully resolve this conflict and develop a sense of autonomy, it is important that its parents encourage attempts to explore and provide opportunities for independence. Overprotectiveness can lead to doubt and uncertainty in dealing with the world later.

For Erikson, developmental progress involves resolving important conflicts by acquiring new competencies. In this second stage, children develop a sense of autonomy that surmounts earlier doubts and fears. But here, as in all areas of psychosocial conflict, the resolution is never quite complete. As Baltes and Silverberg (1994) note, the conflict between the need to be autonomous and the urge to remain dependent continues throughout the entire lifespan.

Initiative Versus Guilt

By the age of 4 or 5, children have resolved the crises of autonomy; in short, they have discovered that they are somebody. During the next stage, they must discover who it is that they are (Erikson, 1959). True to his Freudian orientation, Erikson assumes that children seek to discover who they are by attempting to be like their parents. During this stage, they establish a wider physical environment, made possible by their greater freedom of movement. Their sense of language becomes sufficiently advanced for them to be able to ask many questions and understand some of the answers; it also permits them to imagine all sorts of possibilities about themselves. With their increasing exploration of the environment, children need to develop a sense of initiative with respect to their behaviors. They are autonomous as well as responsible for initiating behavior.

Because the central process involved in resolving the **initiative versus guilt** conflict is one of identification, parents and the family continue to be the most important influences in the child's development. It is important for them to encourage the young child's sense of initiative and to nurture a sense of responsibility, claims Erikson.

Industry Versus Inferiority

The fourth developmental phase, corresponding to Freud's latency period, is marked by the child's increasing need to interact with and be accepted by peers. It now becomes crucial for children to discover that their selves, their identities, are significant, that they can do things—in short, that they are competent. Children now avail themselves of opportunities to learn things they think are important to their culture, hoping that by so doing they will become someone. Successful resolution of this stage's conflict depends largely on the responses of significant agencies—especially schools and teachers—to the child's efforts. Recognition and praise are especially important in developing a positive self-concept. If the child's work is continually demeaned, seldom praised, rarely rewarded, the outcome may well be a lasting sense of inferiority.

Identity Versus Identity Diffusion

Erikson's fifth developmental stage, corresponding to the beginning of Freud's genital period and dealing directly with the period ordinarily referred to as adolescence, involves the development of a sense of identity. Here, Erikson's emphasis on the ego becomes most evident. The development of a strong sense of identity implies the development of a strong ego—hence Erikson's expression *ego identity*. The crisis implicit in this stage concerns a conflict between a strong sense of self and the diffusion of **self-concepts.**

At a simple level, the formation of an identity appears to involve arriving at a notion not so much of who one is but rather of who one can be. The source of conflict resides in the various possibilities open to the child—possibilities that are magnified by the variety of models in the environment. Conflict and doubt over the choice of identity lead to what Erikson terms *identity diffusion*. It is as though adolescents are torn between early acceptance of a clearly defined self and the dissipation of their energies as they experiment with a variety of roles. The development of identity during adolescence is discussed in Chapter 12.

Adulthood

Erikson's description of development does not end with adolescence but continues through the entire lifespan. He describes three additional psychosocial conflicts that occur during adulthood and old age, and that require new competencies and adjustments. The first of these, *intimacy and solidarity versus isolation*, relates to the need to develop intimate relationships with others (as opposed to being isolated) and is particularly crucial for marital and parental roles. The second, *generativity versus self-absorption*, describes a need to assume social, work, and community responsibilities that will be beneficial to others (that will be generative), rather than remaining absorbed in the self. And the third, *integrity versus despair*, has to do with facing the inevitability of our own ends and realizing that life has meaning—that we should not despair because its end is imminent. The three Eriksonian stages that span adulthood

TABLE 2.4
Erikson's Psychosocial Stages

Erikson's Psychosocial Stage	Corresponding Freudian Psychosexual Stage	Principal Developmental Task	Important Influences for Positive Developmental Outcome
Trust vs. mistrust	Oral (0 to 18 months)	Developing sufficient trust in the world to explore it	Mother; warm, loving interaction
Autonomy vs. shame and doubt	Anal (18 months to 2–3 years)	Developing feeling of control over behavior; realizing that intentions can be acted out	Supportive parents; imitation
Initiative vs. guilt	Phallic (2–3 to 6 years)	Developing a sense of self through identification with parents and a sense of responsibility for own actions	Supportive parents; identification
Industry vs. inferiority	Latency (6 to 11 years)	Developing a sense of self-worth through interaction with peers	Schools, teachers; learning and education; encouragement
Identity vs. identity diffusion	Genital (11 years and older)	Developing a strong sense of identity—of ego (self); selecting among various potential selves	Peers and role models; social pressure
Intimacy vs. isolation	Genital (young adulthood)	Developing close relationships with others; achieving the intimacy required for marriage	Spouse, colleagues, partners, society
Generativity vs. self-absorption	Genital (adulthood)	Assuming responsible adult roles in the community; contributing; being worthwhile	Spouse, children, friends, colleagues, community
Integrity vs. despair	Genital (older adulthood)	Facing death; overcoming potential despair; coming to terms with the meaningfulness of life	Friends, relatives, children, spouse, community and religious support

SOURCE: Derived from *Identity and the Life Cycle* by Erik H. Erikson, by permission of W. W. Norton & Company, Inc. Copyright © 1980 by W. W. Norton & Company, Inc. Copyright © 1959 by International Universities Press, Inc.

are discussed in greater detail in Chapters 14, 16, and 18. (See Table 2.4 for a summary of Erikson's psychosocial stages.)

Erikson in Review

Erikson describes development in terms of a series of crises through which the individual progresses. Each of these crises involves a conflict between new abilities or attitudes and inclinations that oppose them. Resolution of conflicts results in the development of a sense of competence with respect to a specific capability that is primarily social (hence the label "psychosocial development"). The resolution of conflicts is never perfected during one developmental phase but continues through succeeding stages (hence the label "life cycle"). Perhaps the most crucial crisis involves the development of a strong sense of identity (hence the label "ego psychology").

Although Erikson assigns ages to each psychosocial stage, the ages do little more than indicate a general developmental sequence. This is particularly true during adulthood, when important social, physical, and emotional events such as retirement, children leaving home, illness, and death occur at widely varying ages and sometimes in a totally unpredictable sequence. Some of the important social and physical changes of childhood are far more predictable; hence, ages tied to the psychosocial crises of childhood are more accurate.

Erikson's theory, like Freud's, does not lend itself well to experimental validation. What Erikson's theory provides is a general framework for describing and interpreting some of the major changes that occur in the lifespan. Its usefulness rests largely in the insights that sometimes result from examining the lives of individuals within the context of the theory.

HAVIGHURST'S DEVELOPMENTAL TASKS

Robert Havighurst (1972, 1979), too, describes development in terms of a series of developmental tasks that need to be sequentially mastered. **Developmental tasks** are requirements that are placed on individuals by their societies and by themselves as they progress through life. As Havighurst (1972) put it, "A developmental task is a task which arises at or about a certain period in the life of the individual, successful achievement of which leads to his happiness and to success with later tasks, while failure leads to unhappiness in the individual, disapproval by the society, and difficulty with later tasks" (p. 2).

Developmental tasks begin with the simple and essential requirements of infancy, such as learning to eat, to walk, and to speak. They culminate in the requirements of old age, which include adjusting to changing physical strength and health, and the imminence of death. Thus, developmental tasks provide a rough but sometimes highly useful index of developmental maturity and adjustment *within a specific culture*. In a sense, they tell us

TABLE 2.5
Havighurst's Developmental Tasks

Period	Developmental Tasks	Period	Developmental Tasks
Infancy and early childhood (birth through preschool period)	1. Achieving physiological rhythms in sleeping and eating 2. Learning to take solid foods 3. Beginning to relate emotionally to parents and siblings 4. Learning to talk 5. Learning to control elimination of body wastes 6. Learning to walk 7. Learning to distinguish right from wrong 8. Learning sex differences and sexual modesty	Young adulthood	1. Courting and selecting a mate 2. Learning to live happily with partner 3. Starting a family and assuming parent role 4. Rearing children 5. Assuming home management responsibilities 6. Beginning career or occupation 7. Assuming appropriate civic responsibilities 8. Establishing a social network
Middle childhood (the elementary school period)	1. Learning skills necessary for physical games 2. Building a positive self-concept 3. Adopting an appropriate masculine or feminine role 4. Learning to get along with peers 5. Developing values, a sense of morality, a conscience 6. Becoming personally independent; weakening family ties 7. Developing basic reading, writing, and arithmetic skills 8. Developing an understanding of the self and the world	Middle adulthood	1. Assisting children in transition from home to world 2. Developing adult leisure activities 3. Relating to spouse as a person 4. Reaching adult social and civic responsibility 5. Maintaining satisfactory career performance 6. Adjusting to physiological changes of middle age 7. Adjusting to aging parents
Adolescence	1. Developing conceptual and problem-solving skills 2. Achieving mature relationships with male and female peers 3. Developing an ethical system to guide behavior 4. Striving toward socially responsible behavior 5. Accepting the changing physique and using the body effectively 6. Preparing for an economically viable career 7. Achieving emotional independence from parents 8. Preparing for marriage and family life	Old age	1. Adjusting to physical changes 2. Adjusting to retirement and to changes in income 3. Establishing satisfactory living arrangements 4. Learning to live with spouse in retirement 5. Adjusting to death of spouse 6. Forming affiliations with aging peers 7. Adopting flexible social roles

whether a child is ready for school, a young adult for marriage, an older adult for retirement (see Table 2.5).

BEHAVIORISTIC APPROACHES TO DEVELOPMENT

Freud's and Erikson's psychoanalytic approaches have a number of important things in common: (1) They are **developmental theories** in that they are concerned with changes that occur in individuals over time; (2) they are *stage theories* (development consists of progression through sequential stages); and (3) they make important assumptions concerning the biological (inherited) aspects of behavior and personality.

In contrast, behavioristic approaches (also called learning-theory approaches) make few assumptions about biological predispositions (and certainly none about *unconscious* forces); nor do they describe sequential stages of mounting capabilities and competencies (or, conversely, of declining abilities).

Basic Assumptions of Behavioristic Approaches

As the term implies, *behaviorism* focuses on the person's immediate behavior and on environmental forces that affect behavior. **Behavioristic theory** looks at relationships between experience and behavior and, consequently, makes extensive use of concepts such as reinforcement and punishment, which describe how behavior may be encouraged or discouraged.

Behaviorism reflects two basic assumptions: The most important is that behavior is reducible to responses or behaviors that can be observed, measured, and analyzed, and that can therefore be studied objectively; the second is that responses are affected by consequences such as reinforcement and punishment. Accordingly, one of the main goals of behavioristic theorists is to discover the rules that govern relationships between **stimuli** (conditions that lead to behavior) and **responses,** and to learn how responses can be controlled through the administration of **rewards** and punishments.

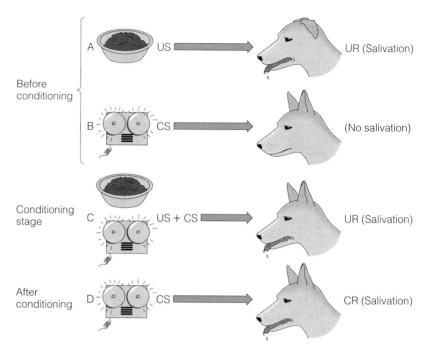

FIGURE 2.2

*Classical conditioning. In **A** an unconditioned stimulus leads to an unconditioned response; whereas in **B** a conditioning stimulus does not lead to the same response. In **C** the unconditioned stimulus is paired with the conditioning stimulus a number of times so that eventually the conditioning stimulus alone elicits the original response, as in **D**.*

Before conditioning

Conditioning stage

After conditioning

Underlying Model

Note that these are assumptions of the mechanistic model, which views the child as more passive than active. According to this model, the consequences of behavior—especially reinforcements and punishments—are among the most important factors in shaping the course of our development. In some ways, our behavior is like the functioning of a machine, the model asserts. If we understand how the machine works, we can predict its actions given sufficient knowledge of immediate circumstances. The goal of the behavioristic theorist is to understand the human machine so well that with sufficient knowledge of past functioning and of immediate circumstances, it would be possible to predict behavior accurately (and perhaps to control it as well).

The behavioristic approach is not only somewhat mechanistic, but is also contextual in its emphasis on the importance of environmental influences. The rewards and punishments that are the causes and consequences of behavior are, in fact, *context*.

Early Pioneers

The behavioristic approach was introduced into American psychology through the work of *John B. Watson* and *B. F. Skinner*, and led to a dramatic upheaval in psychology. Both theorists believed strongly in the importance of the environment (of context) as the principal force in shaping development, and both believed that development could be understood through an analysis of specific behaviors, the circumstances leading to them, and their consequences. Watson is associated with a learning theory based on a model of **classical conditioning;** Skinner developed a model of *operant conditioning*. **Conditioning** itself refers to a simple kind of learning whereby certain behaviors are affected by the environment, becoming more or less probable and predictable.

Classical Conditioning

While doing research with dogs, the Russian physiologist *Ivan Pavlov* (1927) noticed that the more experienced animals in his laboratory began to salivate when they saw their keeper approaching. Because none of the dogs had ever tasted the keeper, Pavlov reasoned that they were salivating not because they expected to eat him now but because they had formed an **association** between the sight of the keeper and the presentation of food. This observation led Pavlov to a series of investigations of a simple form of learning called *classical conditioning*. In the best known of these experiments, he paired a tone with food over a number of trials. Eventually the tone alone brought about salivation.

Basic Elements of Classical Conditioning

Psychology has its own language for the stimuli and responses involved in classical conditioning. The stimulus that is part of the original stimulus–response link is termed the **unconditioned stimulus** (US). Food is a US for Pavlov's dogs; it elicits a response without any new learning taking place. The stimulus that is originally neutral but comes to be effective through repeated pairing with the US is called the *conditioning* or **conditioned stimulus** (CS). The tone is an example of a CS. Eventually, this CS elicits responses similar to those originally made only for US. Corresponding responses are termed the **unconditioned response** (UR) or the **conditioned response** (CR), depending on whether they occur in response to the US or the CS. Thus, salivating in response to a buzzer is a CR. (See Figure 2.2.)

An Example: Little Albert

A well-known study demonstrating classical conditioning of emotional responses in children is reported by Watson

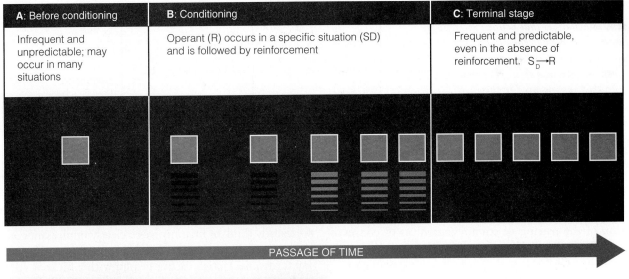

A: Before conditioning	**B**: Conditioning	**C**: Terminal stage
Infrequent and unpredictable; may occur in many situations	Operant (R) occurs in a specific situation (SD) and is followed by reinforcement	Frequent and predictable, even in the absence of reinforcement. $S_D \rightarrow R$

PASSAGE OF TIME

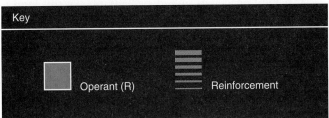

Key

Operant (R)   Reinforcement

FIGURE 2.3

Schematic model of operant conditioning. In **A** *the operant behavior alone is not rewarded. In* **B** *conditioning begins. The operant behavior takes place by chance; it is immediately reinforced. It occurs again, by chance or deliberately, and the reinforcement is repeated. As the timeline chart shows, repetition becomes more and more frequent as the learner catches on. Eventually, the operant behavior continues even without reinforcement at the terminal stage* **C**.

and Rayner (1920). Watson reasoned that because infants react with fear to loud noises, it should be possible to make them fear any other distinctive stimulus simply by pairing it often enough with a loud noise. In this case, the noise is an unconditioned stimulus because it elicits a fear response without any learning having taken place; the fear responses are unconditioned responses. The neutral stimulus that Watson and Rayner chose was a white rat. The subject was an 11-month-old infant named Albert.

At the beginning of the study, Little Albert showed no fear of the rat, instead playing with it as he sat on his mattress. But then Watson (or his assistant, Rosalie Rayner—the point is not clear from Watson's notes) pounded on a 3-foot long, 1-inch steel bar just behind Albert. Still, Little Albert didn't cry just yet, reaching instead for the rat again. And once more, someone pounded on the steel bar, this time frightening Albert enough so that he began to whimper. "On account of his disturbed condition," wrote Watson (1930), "no further tests were made for one week" (p. 160).

A week later, the procedure was repeated—the loud noise and the rat being paired a total of five more times. And now whenever Little Albert saw the rat, he began to cry and tried to crawl away. "Surely," claimed Watson (1930), "this is proof of the conditioned origin of a fear response. It yields an explanatory principle that will account for the enormous complexity in the emotional behavior of adults" (p. 161).

Although Watson and Rayner's experiment with Albert is more systematic and deliberate than most situations in which we acquire emotional responses, there are numerous examples of conditioned emotional responses in our daily lives. People who react with fear to the sound of a dentist's drill are not fearful because the *sound* of the drill has been responsible for any pain they have felt in the past. But the sound of the drill is a conditioned stimulus that has previously been associated with pain (an unconditioned response) and has thus acquired the capability of eliciting *conditioned emotional reactions* (termed CERs) associated with pain. There is considerable evidence that such emotional reactions do transfer from one situation to another.

Operant Conditioning

A classical conditioning model is sometimes useful for explaining the learning of simple behaviors that occur in response to specific stimuli. As Skinner (1953, 1957, 1961) notes, however, many human behaviors or responses are not **elicited** by any obvious stimuli but appear instead to be **emitted** by the organism, for whatever reason. In Skinner's terms, an emitted behavior is an **operant;** an elicited response is a **respondent.** Skinner's major work is an attempt to explain how operants are learned.

The simplest explanation of **operant conditioning** is that the *consequences* of a response determine how likely it is to be repeated. Behaviors that are reinforced tend to be repeated; those that are not reinforced (or that are punished) are less likely to occur again (see Figure 2.3). This

The four alternatives that define punishment and reinforcement, and a fifth where behavior has no apparent consequences, with examples. Were you ever punished or reinforced in these ways? Can you think of specific examples?

	Pleasant	Unpleasant	No consequences
Added to the situation	*Positive reinforcement:* Louella is given a jelly bean for being "good"	*Punishment:* Louella has her nose tweaked for being "bad"	*Extinction:* Louella's behavior has no apparent effects and is ignored
Removed from the situation	*Punishment:* Louella has her jelly beans taken away for being "bad"	*Negative reinforcement:* Louella's nose is released because she says "I'm sorry"	

is very different from saying that learning will occur as a function of the pairing of stimuli regardless of consequences. When Little Albert reacted with fear to the rat, it was not because his fear responses led to pleasant consequences but because the rat was paired with some other fear-producing situation.

Reinforcement

Whatever increases the probability of a response occurring is reinforcing. A **reinforcer** is the stimulus that reinforces; **reinforcement** is the effect of a reinforcer. Reinforcement can be positive or negative. Both increase the probability that a response will occur. The difference between the two is that **positive reinforcement** results from a reward being added to a situation after the behavior has occurred; **negative reinforcement** results from the removal of an unpleasant stimulus. In simpler terms, positive reinforcement involves a **reward** for behavior; negative reinforcement involves *relief* from something unpleasant.

Unfortunately, real-life situations are more complicated than this black-and-white terminology suggests. Subjective judgments such as "pleasant" and "unpleasant," although they make our understanding simpler, are misleading. Reinforcement and punishment have to do with *effects* rather than perceived pleasantness. Thus a parent or teacher who keeps "punishing" a child but who observes that the punished behavior becomes more rather than less frequent may well be reinforcing that behavior—or something (someone?) else is. Similarly, on occasion, a teacher's praise of a student's behavior will lead to a drastic reduction of that behavior. Reinforcement? No. By definition, this is **punishment.** The important point is that pleasantness and unpleasantness are subjective. In contrast, reinforcement and punishment are objective phenomena defined in terms of increases or decreases in the frequency of behavior.

Punishment

Both punishment and reinforcement are defined in terms of their effects. Whereas reinforcement, whether positive or negative, serves to make a response more likely, punishment does not.

In the same way as there are two types of reinforcement (positive and negative—or *reward* and *relief*), there

are also two distinct kinds of punishment. The kind that we usually think of first involves a clearly unpleasant consequence and is sometimes labeled "punishment I" or, in lay terms, *castigation*. Being beaten with a hickory stick or having one's hair pulled are examples of this kind of punishment.

The second kind of punishment, labeled "punishment II," involves taking away something that is pleasant (in lay terms, a *penalty*). Being prevented from watching television (what psychologists refer to as a *time-out procedure*) and having to give up something desirable, such as money or privileges (called *response–cost punishment*), are examples of this kind of punishment.

Another possibility, of course, is that a behavior will have no important consequences and will simply cease to be emitted (will be *extinguished*). Distinctions among the various kinds of reinforcement and punishment are illustrated in Interactive Figure 2.4. As the illustration makes clear, both may involve pleasant or unpleasant stimuli, but whether these stimuli are added to or removed from the situation determines their effect. It is worth repeating that reinforcement and punishment are defined by their effects.

Behavioristic Approaches in Review

Learning-theory explanations for human development emphasize the role of the environment in shaping our personalities and our behaviors. Unlike psychoanalytic approaches, they are not concerned with psychodynamic conflicts and other hidden causes of behavior; and unlike the more cognitive approaches, which we discuss next, they pay relatively little attention to concepts such as *understanding* and *knowing*. Instead, they focus on the role of reinforcement and punishment and on the extent to which behavior can be shaped by its consequences.

One of the main criticisms of these approaches is that they are poorly suited to explain what are referred to as *higher mental processes*—for example, thinking, feeling, analyzing, problem solving, evaluating, and so on. Their emphasis, and their principal usefulness, relates to actual behavior rather than to thinking and feeling.

A second criticism of behavioristic approaches is that to the extent that they emphasize the machinelike qualities of human functioning, they rob us of those capabili-

We are products of our surroundings—of our contexts. According to Bandura's social-learning theory, much of our behavior is a function of observing the behavior of others. Through observational learning (imitation), we not only learn specific behaviors (such as how to salute) but also acquire complex beliefs about right and wrong (such as notions about honor and duty and patriotism).

ties that we consider most human—our ability to think and imagine, and our ability to exercise significant personal control over our own behaviors. In brief, critics have claimed that in its attempts to reduce behavior to a handful of principles governing predictable relationships among stimuli and responses, behaviorism *dehumanizes* us.

Although these criticisms are valid for older, highly rigid interpretations of behaviorism, they are less pertinent for more current positions. For example, Bijou (1989) notes that whereas Watson's theory describes an essentially passive organism, contemporary behaviorism sees the individual "as always being in an interactive relationship with the environment" (p. 68). In his words, the individual is "adjustive" rather than simply reactive. Hence the environment is given a less important role in determining behavior. The causes of behavior, says Bijou, will be found not in the environment alone, but rather in all the factors that are involved in a person's interactions.

Behavioristic approaches to development are sometimes very useful not only for understanding developmental change, but also for controlling it. The deliberate application of conditioning principles to change behavior (termed **behavior modification**) has proven extremely useful both in the classroom and in psychotherapy.

SOCIAL-COGNITIVE THEORY

Elements from different theories can sometimes be combined to produce new theories, new insights, that go far beyond the original theories. A case in point is *Albert Bandura*'s theorizing, which combines elements of both behaviorism and cognitivism.

At one level, Bandura's (1977, 1986) is a behavioristic theory of imitation based on the assumption that much important learning involves models of various kinds that act as social influences on the child. At another level, it is a **cognitive theory** in that it recognizes the importance of our ability to think, to symbolize, to figure out cause-and-effect relationships, to anticipate the outcomes of behavior. There is no doubt, Bandura (1977) assures us, that reinforcement controls much of our behavior. But it does not control us blindly. Its effects depend largely on our awareness of the relationship between our behavior and its outcomes. Because reinforcement often occurs long after the behavior it follows—as happens, for example, when you study for an examination—it isn't reinforcement that is important so much as your ability to anticipate the consequences of behavior.

Bandura's social-learning theory is a theory of **observational learning** (or **imitation**). It is based on the assumption that a great deal of human learning and behavior is a function of observing and imitating the behavior of models, and that this learning can be explained largely through operant conditioning principles.

Manifestations of Observational Learning

The term *model* may refer to an actual, and perhaps very ordinary, person who does something, and whose behavior serves as a guide or perhaps an inspiration for somebody else. A model might also be **symbolic**. Symbolic models include books, oral or written instructions, pictures, mental images, cartoon or film characters, television programs, and so on. Bandura and Walters (1963) describe three different effects of imitation.

The Modeling Effect
The **modeling effect** is the learning of novel behavior through imitation. One example of the modeling effect is the learning of some aspects of language. That the rain forest people of the Cameroon speak their own language and not Chippewa is evidence that they model the language that surrounds them. (There is much more to language learning than simply imitation, however; see Chapters 5 and 7.)

The Inhibitory-Disinhibitory Effect
The effects of imitation are also found in the **inhibitory effect** (the suppression of deviant behavior) and the **disinhibitory effect** (the appearance of previously suppressed deviant behavior). These effects often result from seeing a model rewarded or punished for engaging in deviant behavior. As an illustration, consider the case of Ray, who is opposed to using drugs but whose friends have begun to use marijuana. The behavior is deviant by Ray's own standards, but the amount of reinforcement (in terms of social prestige, acceptance by the group, and so on) that others appear to get from smoking marijuana may *disinhibit* drug-using behavior. There is no new learning

STICKS AND STONES

Singapore, Malaysia: Michael Fay, an American teenager, tore down some street signs and vandalized some cars in Singapore. He was accused of vandalism, tried, convicted, sent to prison for four months, assessed a $2,215 U.S. fine—*and* given four lashes with a cane. In Singapore, caning is *mandatory* for offenses like rape, robbery, vandalism, and illegal immigration; for drug trafficking and armed robbery, the offender is executed (Bramham, 1994). Nor does caning just smart a little. In fact, says Bramham, it is administered by a martial arts expert using a moistened rattan pole. The offender is stripped, folded over a waist-high board, and his hands and ankles are bound together. The caner rears back and strikes hard enough to knock himself off balance and to split the skin open. The offender often loses consciousness, but the next blow will not come for another 3 minutes. The scarring will be permanent.

Mogadishu, Somalia: Abdulahi Weheliye Omar and his friend, Gelle Omar Ali, both 25, confessed to raping Maryan Hussein Amir, an 18-year-old girl. Under Islamic law, Gelle's crime was the least severe because he had never been married. So he was dragged into a public square and, surrounded by several hundred cheering people, was lashed 100 times and then dragged off unconscious. "The crowd laughed," writes Watson (1994). "The children laughed loudest, as if they were watching a circus clown" (p. A16).

Abdulahi was not so lucky because he had apparently been married once, although he vigorously denied this. His sentence: stoned to death. About 20 men were allowed to hurl the rocks. His victim asked whether she, too, might throw some rocks, but under the law, only men are allowed to join in. The rocks were about the size of softballs; a few were bigger chunks of concrete. Still, it was a full 20 minutes before Abdulahi died. "No one should feel sorry for Omar," said Sheik Ali Mohamed, "not after what he did" (p. A16).

To Research   In the past four years, Singapore has hanged 47 criminals (22 of them for drug trafficking), and has caned thousands. And in the United States, there have been increasingly insistent demands for tougher punishments, especially of young offenders. Research the proposition that a highly punitive context is less (or more) likely to prevent criminal behavior.

---

involved, as there is in modeling, but merely the disinhibition of previously suppressed behavior. If Ray later sees members of his peer group being punished (by law, parents, school authorities, or ill effects of the drug), he might stop using it—an example of the *inhibitory effect*. Again, no new learning is involved, but the change in behavior results from the influence of models (see Across Cultures: "Sticks and Stones").

The Eliciting Effect

The **eliciting effect** occurs when the model's behavior leads to *related* behavior in the learner that is not identical to that of the model's, but neither is it deviant nor novel. It is as though the model's behavior suggests some response to observers and therefore elicits that response. For example, a child "acting up" in school may elicit related but not identical misbehaviors among classmates. (See Interactive Table 2.6 for a summary of the effects of imitation.)

Self-Efficacy

Theories in psychology, as elsewhere, are not often static, unchanging things—unless the theorist has lost interest, moved on to other issues, or died. But even then, if the theory is at all compelling or important, there will be others who will chew at it, who will try to change its shape to fit new facts and to answer new questions.

Albert Bandura's theorizing is a case in point. His early ideas were based directly on a behavioristic orientation. Thus his imitation theory of social learning tried to explain the effects of modeling in terms of rewards and punishments. Increasingly, however, as Tudge and Winterhoff (1993) note, Bandura began to pay more attention to the learner's *cognitive* capacities. As a result, his theorizing gave an increasingly important role to the *informative* function of models. It is what the observer imagines and anticipates that is fundamentally important in learning through imitation.

Recently, Bandura's research and theorizing has taken yet another turn—one that is even more clearly cognitive and that is often referred to as *social cognitivism* (Bandura, 1981; 1986; Evans, 1989). It has to do with what is termed **self-referent thought**—thought that relates to our *selves*, our own mental processes. Among other things, self-referent thought deals with our estimates of our abilities, with our notions about how capable and how *effective* we are in our dealings with the world and with others. And a very specific term has been coined to describe our estimates of our effectiveness: **self-efficacy.**

Definition of Self-Efficacy
In a nutshell, efficacy signifies competence in dealing with the environment. The most *efficacious* people are those who can most effectively deal with a variety of situations even when these situations are ambiguous or highly stressful.

As a psychological concept, *self-efficacy* refers not so much to the skills required for the successful performance of a behavior, but more to the individual's beliefs about personal effectiveness. *Self-efficacy* refers to the judgments we make about how *efficacious* we are likely to be in given situations. Among the most important of all the different aspects of self-knowledge, Bandura insists, is our conception of personal efficacy.

Implications of Self-Efficacy Judgments
Among other things, our judgments about our personal effectiveness are extremely important determiners of what we do and don't do. In fact, in some situations, self-efficacy may be a better predictor of behavior than relevant skills are (Bandura, 1993). Under most circumstances, children—and adults—do not seek out and undertake activities in which they expect to perform badly. "Efficacy beliefs," says Bandura, "influence how people feel, think, motivate themselves, and behave." (1993, p. 118)

Judgments of personal efficacy affect not only our choices of activities and settings but also the amount of effort we are willing to expend when faced with difficulties. The stronger an individual's perceptions of efficacy, the more likely the individual is to persist and the greater the effort expended will be. But if notions of self-efficacy are not highly favorable, difficult activities may be abandoned after very little effort and time.

Finally, judgments of self-efficacy influence thoughts and emotions. Those whose estimate of their effectiveness is low are more likely to evaluate their behaviors negatively and to see themselves as being inadequate. Related to this, Cowen and associates (1991) found that children with the most favorable self-efficacy judgments were more resilient, more resistant to stress.

Sources of Efficacy Judgments
Judgments of personal efficacy, Bandura (1986) suggests, stem from several sources. First are the direct effects of behavior. Whether we succeed must surely have some effect on our estimates of how efficacious we are. However, the individual who is mostly successful does not invariably arrive at highly positive judgments of self-efficacy; nor does lack of success always correspond to negative judgments. As Weiner (1980) points out, success—or lack of success—can be attributed to a number of factors. Some of these, such as ability and effort, are under personal control and reflect directly on the efficacy of the individual. Others, such as luck or the difficulty of the task, are not under personal control and do not, therefore, have very direct implications for judgments of self-efficacy. Some individuals are prone to attribute the outcomes of their behaviors to factors over which they have control. Dweck (1975) refers to these people as *mastery-oriented*. Others are more likely to attribute their failures and successes to luck or to the task being too difficult or too easy (characterized by *helplessness* rather than by a mastery orientation; see Chapter 10).

A second influence on judgments of self-efficacy is *vicarious* (secondhand); it comes from observing the performance of others. Even as children, we judge how effective we are partly by comparing ourselves to others. The most informative comparisons we can make are those that involve others whose performance is similar to ours. A 12-year-old who demolishes his 6-year-old brother in a game of skill and intelligence learns very little about his personal effectiveness. Similarly, if he, in turn, is blown away by his father, he may not have learned much more—except, perhaps, a touch of humility.

A third source of influence on self-judgments, Bandura (1986) argues, is persuasion: "You can do it. We know you can. Sing for us. We love the way you sing." Persuasion, depending on the characteristics of the persuader and on the relationship between persuader and "persuadee," can sometimes change an individual's judgments of self-efficacy and lead that individual to attempt things that would not otherwise be attempted—or not to attempt them: "They're just flattering you. Please don't sing."

A fourth source of influence on judgments of self-efficacy is the person's **arousal** level. *Arousal* is a big word with many meanings. In this context, its most important

Sources of Information	Examples of Information That Might Lead Edna to Arrive at Positive Estimates of her Personal Efficacy
Enactive	She wins a scholarship to the Northern Alberta Institute of Technology.
Vicarious	She learns that Ronald studied hard but wasn't given a scholarship.
Persuasory	Her teacher tells her she should enroll in the advanced program for gifted learners.
Emotive	She was tense before her entrance exam, but felt exhilarated afterwards.

meaning is alertness or intensity of immediate emotional reaction. Whether arousal will have positive or negative effects on the individual's self-judgments may depend largely on experiences the individual has had in situations of high or low arousal. Some people find that moderately high arousal helps their performance; others react in the opposite way. For example, the fear that precedes speaking in public may be seen as helpful by some speakers and as highly negative by others.

In summary, there are four separate sources of influence that can affect the individual's judgments of self-efficacy. Bandura (1986) terms these *enactive* (based on the outcome of the individual's own actions); *vicarious* (based on comparisons between the person's performance and the performance of others); *persuasory* (the result of persuasion); and *emotive* (the result of arousal or emotion). (See Table 2.7.)

Development of Self-Efficacy

After watching Superman as a child, did you ever think you could put on a cape and actually fly? Many young children do. They don't have a very good notion of their personal capabilities. Their self-judgment, and their corresponding self-guidance, is less than perfect. As a result, without external controls, they would often be in danger of severely hurting themselves. Instead of imposing on themselves the internal self-judgment "*I* can't do that," they require the external judgment "*You* can't do that."

The sense of personal control over behavior that is essential for judgments of personal efficacy begins to develop very early in infancy. Some of its roots lie in the infant's discovery that looking at the mother makes her look back in return, that smiling or crying draws her attention, and that waving a hand makes her smile. Later, as infants start to move around freely, they begin to learn more about the *effects* of their behaviors—and also more about their *effectiveness* as "behavers." Language provides them with a means to analyze and think about themselves and a

means to symbolize and anticipate the consequences of their behaviors.

In the early stages, Bandura (1986) informs us, the most important source of information for the development of self-referential thought is the family. Soon, however, peers begin to increase in importance. Now the behavior of others, as well as their response to our behavior, is factored into our personal estimates of our efficacy. Eventually, schools, too, exert their powerful influences. Teachers tell us a great deal about how well—or how badly—we can do things. So, too, does the response of our classmates—and the response of our parents to the evidence we bring home of our worthwhileness in school, of our intelligence, of our ability to do the things that teachers require.

And so it continues throughout life. In adolescence, as well as through adulthood and into old age, we continue to face new tasks, new challenges. At every step, these challenges require new competencies and new behaviors—and new judgments of personal effectiveness.

Among the judgments of efficacy that are perhaps most important to us at all stages of life are those that have to do with our ability to capture the attention, the interest, the affection of others. As Kegan (1982) argues, we strive to *mean* something; we want people to pay attention to us, to like us, to want to be with us, to listen to us, to do things with us. Put another way, we need to feel that we are capable of eliciting these feelings in others—that we are *socially effective*. Hence the central role of self-efficacy judgments in our lives. And in our happiness.

Social-Cognitive Theory in Review

In some important ways, Bandura's social-cognitive theory bridges the gap between behavioristic theories, which try to explain development entirely in terms of observable, nonmentalistic events like stimuli and responses, and cognitive positions, which are mainly concerned with mental events. Thus the theory is based on the notion that certain social behaviors (notably imitative behaviors) are reinforced in various ways, and are therefore more likely to recur. At the same time, it recognizes the power of our ability to imagine the consequences of our actions. It is the child's *anticipation* of the taste of the ice cream that hurries her to the store, not just a blind reaction to external stimulation.

Bandura's theory is a striking example of how theories need not be static, unchanging things, of how they can change with new information and new beliefs. Thus his recent writings deal with self-efficacy and are concerned with how what we think, feel, and do is profoundly influenced by our judgments of our personal effectiveness.

Although the theory provides a useful way of looking at some aspects of development, and especially at social motivation, it is not a comprehensive theory meant to account for most of the important observations in human development—unlike the theory of Jean Piaget.

A Cognitive
Approach: Piaget

Psychoanalytic theorists are concerned primarily with personality development; behavioristic theorists emphasize behavior and its consequences; social-learning theorists are concerned with the influence of culture and experience; and a fourth group of theorists focuses on the intellectual (**cognitive**) development of children.

Cognition, my dictionary informs me, is the art or faculty of knowing. Cognitive theorists are concerned with how we know—that is, with how we obtain, process, and use information. The most widely cited and the most influential of all theories of cognitive development is *Piaget*'s (Stanton, 1993). Important aspects of his theory are introduced briefly in the following sections. More specific details of the theory, and the contributions of other approaches to cognitive development, are discussed in subsequent chapters that deal chronologically with intellectual development (Chapters 5, 7, 9, and 11).

Basic Piagetian Ideas

Because Piaget was trained as a biologist rather than a psychologist, it is not surprising that he began his study of children with two of the fundamental questions of biology: (1) What is it that enables organisms to adapt to their environments and survive? and (2) What is the most useful way of classifying living organisms? These biological questions can be rephrased and applied to the development of children: (1) What are the characteristics and capabilities of children that allow them to adapt to their environments? and (2) What is the most useful way of classifying or ordering child development? Piaget's answers for these two questions, developed over an extraordinarily prolific career spanning more than six decades (he died in 1980 at the age of 84), are the basis for his theory. One account indicates that before his death, he had published 478 articles and 52 books—another five articles and five books were published posthumously—for a total of more than 26,000 pages (Smith, 1993).

Assimilation and Accommodation Permit Adaptation
The newborn infant that Piaget describes is in many ways a helpless little organism, unaware that the world out there is real, with no storehouse of thoughts with which to reason, no capacity for intentional behaviors, no more than a few simple reflexes. But infants are much more than this. They are also remarkable little sensing machines that seem to be naturally predisposed to acquiring and processing a tremendous amount of information. They continually seek out and respond to stimulation. As a result, the sucking, reaching, grasping, and other reflexes that were present at birth become more complex, more coordinated, and, eventually, more purposeful. The process by which this occurs is **adaptation.** And to answer the first

of the biology questions as simply as possible, assimilation and accommodation are the processes that make adaptation possible.

Assimilation involves responding to situations in terms of activities or knowledge that have already been learned or that are present at birth. For example, an infant is born with the capability to suck—with a sucking **scheme,** in Piaget's terms (sometimes called *schema*, pluralized as *schemata*). The sucking scheme allows the infant to assimilate a nipple to the behavior of sucking. Similarly, a child who has learned the rules of addition can assimilate a problem such as 2 + 2 (can respond appropriately in terms of previous learning). Often, however, our understanding of the world is insufficient to deal with the present situation. The newborn's sucking scheme is adequate for ordinary nipples but does not work for fingers and toes; the preschooler's understanding of number is sufficient for keeping track of toys but is inadequate for impressing kindergarten teachers. Changes are required in information and behavior. These changes define **accommodation.** In short, assimilation involves reacting on the basis of previous learning and understanding; accommodation involves a change in understanding. The interplay of assimilation and accommodation leads to adaptation. (See Chapter 5 for a further illustration of these concepts.)

Development Can Be Ordered in Stages
The second of biology's questions asks what is the most useful way of organizing and classifying child development. Piaget's answer is found in his description of the stages through which each child passes. There are four major stages in this description, each marked by strikingly different perceptions of the world and by different adaptations to it. Each is the product of learning that occurred in earlier stages, and each is a preparation for the next stage.

Note that although Piaget's theory is most easily explained and understood in terms of stages, he nevertheless viewed development as a *continuous process* of successive changes. Development does not consist of abrupt, clearly recognizable changes like steps on a stairway; it is more like a gradual incline. Although cognitive development moves along relatively smoothly, it is useful, and simpler, to divide it into stages. Doing so allows us to compare behaviors and capabilities that are characteristic of different levels, and sometimes leads to discoveries about the processes underlying change. Note, too, that the ages Piaget assigned to each stage are simply average ranges reflecting the behaviors of upper-middle-class Swiss children through the middle of the 20th century. Children from different cultural contexts and with different characteristics sometimes pass through these stages much earlier or much later than Piaget's norms would suggest.

The Stages

Piaget's major stages are summarized very briefly here; they are discussed in more detail in Chapters 5, 7, 9, and 11.

For the sensorimotor infant, says Piaget, the world derives its meaning and its existence from the actions that can be performed on it. Thumbs, fingers, feet, anything around which the mouth will fit, is there to be chewed, sucked, and tasted. These actions, along with touching and looking, are the infant's means of exploring and knowing.

Sensorimotor Period

The first two years are labeled the **sensorimotor period** because during this period the child understands the world largely through immediate action and sensation. For the infant, the world exists *here and now.* It is real only when it is being acted upon and sensed. When the ball is not being chewed, looked at, or touched, it doesn't exist. Only toward the end of the second year do children finally realize that objects are permanent and have an identity of their own—that they continue to exist when they are out of sight. Also, toward the end of the first 2 years, the child begins to acquire language and progresses slowly from a sensorimotor to a more cognitive intelligence (see Chapter 5).

Preoperational Thinking

Following the acquisition of language, the child enters the period of **preoperational thought** (ages 2–7)—a period marked by an excessive reliance on perception rather than logic. For example, in one of Piaget's well-known *conservation* experiments, children are shown two identical glasses that contain equal amounts of water. The experi-

menter then pours the contents of one glass into a tall, thin tube—or into a low, flat dish. Do they still have the same amount, or does one now have more than the other? Preoperational children, relying on the appearance of the two containers, almost invariably think the tall tube has more because it is higher (or less because it is thinner)—or that the flat dish has more because it is "fatter" (or less because it is shorter). Even when they realize that the water could be poured back into the original container so that the two would then be equal, preoperational children continue to rely on perception (on actual appearance) rather than on reasoning (see Chapter 7 for more details).

Concrete Operations

The major acquisition of the next period of development is the ability to think operationally (ages 7–8 to 11–12). An **operation** is a thought—what Piaget called an internalized or *mental* action. Mental actions are governed by certain rules of logic. These rules permit the concrete-operations child to laugh at the ridiculous simplicity of a conservation problem. Of course there is the same amount of water in both containers, because none has been added or taken away, one misleading dimension is compensated for by the other (it is taller but thinner), and the act of pouring the water from one container to the other can be reversed to prove that nothing has changed. The concrete-operations child is capable of this kind of logic. But it is a logic that is tied to real, concrete objects and events. The child is still unable to reason logically about hypothetical situations or events and cannot go from the real to the merely possible or from the possible to the actual. Thought is bound to the real world, the concrete—hence the label **concrete operations** (see Chapter 9).

Formal Operations

The last stage of cognitive development—**formal operations**—is characterized by the ability to manipulate abstract ideas. During this stage, which begins around age 11 or 12 and ends at 14 or 15, the child's thought has the potential to become as logical as it will ever be. But the emphasis should be on the word *potential*. Many of us remain strangers to the deductive logic of formal operations throughout our lives. However, as Ricco (1993) argues, the logic of formal operations is a logic concerned with *hypothetical* states of affairs; for many of life's problems, other forms of logic—especially those dealing with meaning—are more appropriate. Piaget recognized this, and in some of his latest writings, he discussed a formal operations logic of meanings (see Piaget & Garcia, 1991). (See Table 2.8 for a summary of Piaget's stages of cognitive development.)

Piaget in Review

Development, says Piaget, is best described as the emergence of progressively more logical forms of thought that become increasingly effective in freeing children from the

TABLE 2.8
Piaget's Stages of Cognitive Development

Stage	Appropriate Age	Some Major Characteristics*
Sensorimotor	0 to 2 years	Intelligence in action
		World of the here and now
		No language, no thought, no notion of objective reality at beginning of stage
Preoperational	2 to 7 years	Egocentric thought
		Reason dominated by perception
		Intuitive rather than logical solutions
		Inability to conserve
Concrete operations	7–8 to 11–12 years	Ability to conserve
		Logic of classes and relations
		Understanding of numbers
		Thinking bound to concrete
		Development of reversibility in thought
Formal operations	11–12 to 14–15 years	Complete generality of thought
		Propositional thinking
		Ability to deal with the hypothetical
		Development of strong idealism

* Each of these characteristics is detailed in appropriate sections of Chapters 5, 7, 9, and 11.

present and allowing them to use powerful symbols to understand and to manipulate the environment. According to the theory, the major characteristics of thinking in each of the four developmental stages influence all aspects of children's understanding of the world, including their notions of space, time, number, reality, causality, and so on. It isn't so much that children discover some ready-made rules of logic that govern their understanding of the world; rather, they *invent* or *construct* these rules. Hence the current label **constructivism** to describe theories such as Piaget's (Smith, 1993). Constructivism is an important concept in educational theory and practice where the teacher's role is often seen as one of facilitating students' *construction* of knowledge (Cobb, 1994). As Driver and associates (1994) put it, "The view that knowledge cannot be transmitted but must be constructed by the mental activity of learners underpins contemporary perspectives" (p. 5).

Because Piaget's theory makes specific predictions about how children function intellectually at different ages, parts of it are relatively easy to evaluate objectively simply by testing the predictions. In general, research that has tried to do this confirms Piaget's initial findings with respect to the order of stages. However, this research also makes it clear that the ages at which different children reach specific stages can vary considerably.

Also, it appears that Piaget vastly underestimated the information-processing capabilities of infants and young children (Wellman & Gelman, 1992). However, this is due less to weaknesses in the theory than to Piaget's lack of instruments and procedures sensitive enough to detect the infant's cognitive capacities. For example, contemporary studies of infant responsiveness often use sophisticated instruments that measure changes in heart and respiration rates, movements of the eyeballs, changes in pupil size, brain-wave activity, and so on—all instruments not available to Piaget in the 1920s and 1930s.

Piaget's theory is also sometimes accused of having overestimated the importance of motor activity in the infant's cognitive development and of underestimating the importance of perception (Bullinger, 1985). Others criticize the theory because it says little about individual differences among children, about the factors that might account for those differences, or about what can be done to promote intellectual development. In addition, the theory's language and concepts are sometimes difficult, and it isn't always clear that terms such as *assimilation* and *accommodation* add significantly to our understanding of human behavior. In spite of these weaknesses, Piagetian theory has been the most dominant cognitive developmental theory of this century, and it continues to have a profound influence on current research and practice.

BIOLOGICAL AND ECOLOGICAL APPROACHES

Biological approaches to understanding human development stress the importance of innate, predetermined behavior patterns or tendencies. These approaches often stem from research conducted with animals, in which genetic influences are sometimes more readily apparent than they are among humans.

Ecological approaches emphasize the importance of the individual's context—hence the importance of the environment. But for contemporary ecological theorists, it is not so much the context as the interaction between the person's characteristics and specific characteristics of the environment that are important (Bronfenbrenner, 1989).

Ethology and Biological Attachment Theory

The importance of biology (of heredity) in determining animal behavior has long been accepted. I accept without question that my English setter is good at sniffing out certain potent-smelling birds precisely because she is an English setter. I would not expect the same behavior of Id, our rather useless, but aptly named, cat. Even if their early experiences had been identical, I still would not expect Id to enjoy walking at my heels or to drool at the prospect of a cold swim in a reedy pond. You see, we know that many of the behaviors and habits characteristic of nonhuman

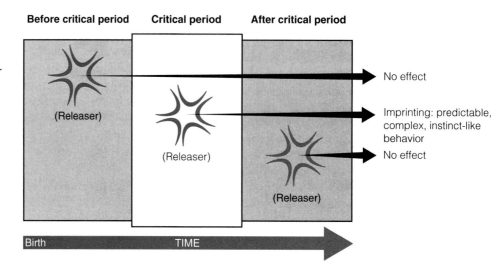

FIGURE 2.5

A model of imprinting. Under appropriate environmental conditions, exposure to a releaser during the critical period leads to imprinting, which is manifested in predictable behaviors in response to specific environmental conditions. Imprinting does not occur if a releaser is not present or if the releaser is presented too early or too late.

animal species are not acquired solely through experience. A moth does not fly into a flame because it has learned to do so; dead moths don't fly. We can therefore assume that the attraction light has for a moth, like the overpowering urge of a goose to go south or a salmon to swim up a specific river, is the result of inherited tendencies.

Are we, in at least some ways, like moths and salmon? If so, what are our flames? Our rivers?

Ethology

Ethologists (scientists whose principal concern is with studying behavior in natural situations) think that yes, we are a little like moths. And although the flames that entice us might be less obvious than those that draw the moth, they are perhaps no less powerful.

Lorenz's (1952) studies of imprinting in ducks and geese were among the first to draw parallels between inherited animal behavior and humans. **Imprinting** is the tendency of newly hatched geese (or chickens, ducks, and related birds) to follow the first moving object they see during a **critical period,** which occurs shortly after hatching. The period is *critical* because exposure to the same moving object (a *releaser*) before or after this period does not ordinarily result in the appearance of the same imprinted behavior (see Figure 2.5).

Imprinting among newly hatched birds clearly has survival value. The gosling's chances of survival are far better if it, along with all its fellow goslings, follows the mother goose. Of course, the gosling does not follow the mother because it is aware of a genetic relationship between this big bird and itself. It follows its mother simply because she happened to be the first moving object it saw during the critical few hours following hatching. Ethologists have repeatedly demonstrated that if some other object such as a balloon were to replace the mother goose, the young gosling would quite happily follow it instead. When Lorenz substituted himself for the mother goose, the young goslings followed him much as they would have their mother.

The critical period is all-important. Newly hatched geese or chickens that are not exposed to a moving object during this critical period fail to become imprinted and subsequently will not follow their mothers. Similarly, lambs that are removed from their mothers after birth and not brought back for a week or more do not ordinarily show any evidence of attachment to them. Perhaps even more striking, the mothers themselves do not appear to be attached to their kids under these circumstances and will sometimes butt them out of the way if they insist on coming too close (Thorpe, 1963).

Human Bonding

The search for imprinted behaviors among humans has not led to the discovery of behaviors as obvious as "following" among geese. Still, some theorists, such as *John Bowlby* (1979; 1980; 1982), believe that there are important links between the findings of ethologists and the development of attachment between mother and infant. Bowlby's research with young infants suggests we have a natural (inherited) tendency to form emotional bonds with our mothers or with some other permanent caregiver, during what Bowlby terms the **sensitive period.** Such bonds, Bowlby argues, would clearly have been important for the infant's survival in a less civilized age. The need for them is evident in the infant's attempts to maintain physical contact, to cling, and to stay in visual contact with the mother (Bowlby, 1969). It is also apparent in the effects of separating mother and infant—effects that are marked by "emotional distress and personality disturbance, including anxiety, anger, depression, and emotional detachment" (Bowlby, 1979, p. 127). (See Chapter 6 for a more detailed review of infant attachment research.)

Biology and Sociobiology

Bowlby is only one of a large number of theorists interested in applying knowledge of biology (and, more specifically, of genetics and evolution) to an understanding of

Development (or growth), says Vygotsky, requires that the demands of the environment be at an appropriate level for children—in his words, that they be within the zone of proximal development. Demands that are too trivial can be wasteful; those that are beyond a child's capabilities (say with peer or parental help) are ineffective.

human development and behavior. Some ethologically oriented scientists argue that science has neglected the role of heredity in determining many of the behaviors that we attribute to our environments and upbringing. Sometimes termed *behavioral biologists* or *sociobiologists*, their most striking and controversial belief is that human social behavior is the product of a lengthy evolutionary history—that it is therefore genetically based (Wilson, 1975; 1976). **Sociobiology** is defined as "the systematic study of the biological basis of all social behavior" (Wilson, 1975, p. 4). We are altruistic, sociobiologists argue, because helping others contributes to the group's survival. In much the same way as altruism might be explained by reference to the "selfishness" of genes (it is, after all, genetic material that survives), sociobiological theory can be used to explain maternal love, sexual mores, aggression, spitefulness—indeed, the entire range of human social behaviors.

Culture and Ecology

Ethologists (and sociobiologists) emphasize the importance of biological or genetic contributions to development; ecologically oriented theorists stress the importance of culture or context. However, the differences between

ethological and ecological positions frequently have more to do with different emphases than with different beliefs. Most theorists readily accept that both ecological (cultural or environmental) influences and biological tendencies are intimately involved in determining human development. Vygotsky and Bronfenbrenner present approaches that are, in some ways, a synthesis of the two orientations.

Vygotsky's Cultural-Historical Approach

By the age of 28, the Russian psychologist *L. S. Vygotsky* was a major force in Soviet psychology. Unfortunately, only 10 years later, he died of tuberculosis. Although that was 1934, many of his ideas, old as they may be, still seem fresh and important. Unfortunately, however, these ideas are not always entirely clear. As Nicolopoulou (1993) puts it, "Despite the fact that his writings are full of intuitions and illuminations, they are often sketchy and at times incomplete" (p. 7).

Vygotsky's Basic Ideas
Vygotsky's clearest and most important ideas provide a strong link between social factors—especially historical and cultural factors—and individual development (Tudge

& Winterhoff, 1993). As a result, three basic underlying themes run through Vygotsky's theorizing. One has to do with the centrality of culture in human development; a second deals with the functions of language; and a third relates to the developing child's relationship with the environment—a relationship Vygotsky described as the **zone of proximal development** (Kozulin, 1990).

Culture

Human development, claimed Vygotsky, is fundamentally different from the development of animals. Why? Because humans can use tools and symbols; as a result, they create *cultures*. And cultures have a vitality, a life of their own. They grow and change; and they exert a very powerful influence on their members. They determine the end result of competent development—the sorts of things that its members have to learn, the ways they should think, the things they are most likely to believe. As Bronfenbrenner (1989) puts it, we are not only culture producing, but culture-produced. Or, as Vygotsky (1986) notes, cultures permit humans to have a history, and perhaps a future as well.

The role of culture in human development is perhaps most evident in the distinction Vygotsky makes between *elementary* mental functions (which both humans and nonhuman animals have in common) and *higher* mental functions (which are exclusively human). Elementary functions are natural, unlearned capacities. They are evident in the newborn's ability to attend to sounds and to discriminate among them. They are apparent in the ability to remember the smell of the mother, or in the capacity to coo and gurgle, to scream and cry. In time, however, these elementary capacities are gradually transformed into higher mental functions—that is, they change from natural, unlearned functions to more sophisticated, learned behaviors and capacities. This transformation, which is absolutely fundamental to human development, is made possible through language.

The Role of Language

Language, after all, is what makes thinking possible, Vygotsky asserts. During the preverbal stage of development, the child's intelligence is much like that of, say, an ape. It is purely natural, purely practical—*elementary*, in other words. But language changes all that.

Vygotsky describes three forms of language that develop sequentially; each has different functions. The first, **social speech** (or external speech), is common until around the age of 3. The most primitive form of speech, its function is largely to control the behavior of others (as in "I want candy!") or to express simple concepts.

Egocentric speech dominates the child's life between ages 3 and approximately 7. This type of speech is a sort of bridge between the social speech of the preceding period and the more internal (inner) speech of the next period. Egocentric speech often serves to control the

TABLE 2.9
Vygotsky's Description of the Role of Language

Stage	Function
Social (external) speech (to age 3)	Controls the behavior of others; expresses simple thoughts and emotions
Egocentric speech (3 to 7)	Bridge between external and inner speech; serves to control own behavior, but spoken out loud
Inner speech (7 onward)	Self-talk; makes possible the direction of our thinking and our behavior; involved in all higher mental functioning

child's own behavior, but is frequently spoken out loud. For example, young children may talk to themselves as they are trying to do something: "Push. Okay, now turn. Turn. Turn . . . push . . ." **Inner speech** is our private self-talk—what James (1892) called our stream of consciousness. According to Vygotsky, inner speech is what makes thought possible. It is the basis of all higher mental functioning (see Table 2.9).

Zone of Proximal Development

Language, a cultural invention, is one of the most important ways in which the child's environmental context influences and shapes the course of development. For Vygotsky, development is a function of the interaction between culture and the child's basic biological capacities and maturational timetables. But, insisted Vygotsky, it is the environmental context (the culture) that is most important—not biological maturation (Valsiner, 1987). Development takes place when environmental opportunities and demands are appropriate for the child. In a sense, the environment instructs the child in the ways of development. But the instruction is effective only if the child's biological maturation and present developmental level are sufficiently advanced. For every child, says Vygotsky, there is a *zone of proximal growth*—a sort of potential for development (Belmont, 1989). Demands that are beyond this zone—in other words, that are beyond the child's capacities—are ineffective in promoting growth. Similarly, demands that are too simple are wasteful.

In summary, Vygotsky's developmental theory underscores the role of culture, and especially of its most important invention, language. The zone of proximal development—sort of a label for developmental potential—expresses Vygotsky's belief in the interdependence between the processes of child development and the resources that cultures provide. Another approach that also emphasizes the importance of context–person interaction is Bronfenbrenner's.

Bronfenbrenner's Ecological Systems Theory

One of the basic principles of *Bronfenbrenner's* **ecological systems theory** is that differences in intellectual performance between different groups are a function of interacting with different cultures (or subcultures) that are characterized by different types of cognitive processes. Hence a person's cognitive competence is always culturally relative. A very intelligent, well-adapted native of the Amazon jungle would not necessarily function very intelligently in downtown Chicago. But then a Chicago lawyer might quickly lose her bearings—and perhaps her marbles—in the Amazon jungle.

Bronfenbrenner refers to psychological, biological, and social systems as **open systems.** What this means is that their existence depends on *interaction* and that they are constantly subject to change as a function of interaction. The Piagetian infant, born with a small number of reflexes, adapts and changes as a function of interacting with the environment—in Piaget's terms, as a result of assimilating and accommodating. It is infant–environment interaction that results in the notion that objects are permanent, that symbols represent, that quantities can be added and subtracted, that a fine and elegant logic governs physics and chemistry.

Human Ecology

Bronfenbrenner refers to the interaction of the individual with the environment as the *ecology of human development* (also the title of his 1979 book). The cornerstone of his theory is the belief that human development consists of a series of ongoing changes (accommodations) in interactions between the person and the immediate context. Also of fundamental importance are the relationships that exist among different aspects of the contexts in which the individual interacts (Bronfenbrenner, 1989).

Not only are we influenced by our contexts, but we also influence them in turn. If infant Benjamin cries more than is expected, he may change some significant aspects of the environment with which he interacts. His mother may come running sooner than she otherwise would; his nurse might become more irritable, more impatient; his father might pay more, or less, attention to him; his siblings might openly resent his intrusion in the family; even the dog might be annoyed. And each of these changing aspects of context might, in turn, alter Benjamin's behavior. That his mother runs to soothe his cries might encourage his crying even more. But now, perhaps the mother senses what is happening and comes more slowly, more reluctantly, and again the interaction changes. Thus the mother's personality and her beliefs about child rearing interact with Benjamin's personality, and his behavior, in a constantly changing, *open ecological* system. There is always an interplay between the person's characteristics and those of the environment, says Bronfenbrenner: "The one cannot be defined without reference to the other" (p. 225). He also makes the point that some characteristics (termed *developmentally instigative*) are more important than others in influencing contexts. Temperament, size or appearance, age, sex, race, developmental handicaps, and many other factors tend to provoke important reactions—hence changes—in context. These, in turn, affect the individual.

Dimensions of Context

One of Bronfenbrenner's important contributions to the study of child development lies in his description of the contexts in which development occurs. The ecological system of which he speaks consists of interactions with four different levels of context. From nearest (most proximal) to most remote, these are the microsystem, the mesosystem, the exosystem, and the macrosystem.

- **Microsystem.** Interactions that occur at an immediate, face-to-face level define the microsystem. For the developing child, the most important aspects of the microsystem include patterns of behaviors, roles, and relationships within the home, the school, the peer group, the workplace, the playground, and so on. The interaction of Benjamin's crying with the behaviors of mother, father, siblings, and dog illustrates what is meant by a microsystem. Everybody in a microsystem influences everybody else.

- **Mesosystem.** In turn, microsystems may influence each other in important ways. For example, how Benjamin's mother treats him may be influenced by her interactions with his father. Perhaps she is less likely to be patient with her son if she has just had an argument with her husband. And how Benjamin interacts with his sister may also be negatively affected. Interactions between elements of the microsystem that include the developing person define what is meant by the mesosystem.

- **Exosystem.** All systems are part of other, larger systems. Thus, the home does not exist in isolation, but interacts with school, church, community, and so on. And how parents treat children may be profoundly influenced by schools, teachers, religious leaders, employers, friends. For example, interactions between Benjamin and his father may be influenced by the father's relationships with his colleagues or his fishing buddies. Interactions between an element of the microsystem that ordinarily includes the developing child and an element of the wider context that does not include the child define the exosystem.

- **Macrosystem.** All the interactive systems—micro, meso, and exo—that characterize cultures (or subcultures) define the macrosystem. Macrosystems are describable in terms of beliefs, values, customs, expected behaviors, social roles, status assignments, lifestyles, religions, and so on. In Bronfenbrenner's (1989) words, the macrosystem is "a societal blueprint

TABLE 2.10
*Levels of Context in Bronfenbrenner's
Ecological Systems Theory*

Level	Type of Interaction	Example
Microsystem	Child in immediate, face-to-face interaction	Mother singing to child
Mesosystem	Relationships between two or more microsystems	Mother and father interacting
Exosystem	Linkages and relationships between two or more settings, one of which does not include the child	Father's relationship with employer
Macrosystem	The totality of all other systems, evident in the beliefs, the options, the lifestyles, the values, the mores of a culture or subculture	Society's child-care legislation; expectations and requirements of culture

for a particular culture, subculture, or other broader social context" (p. 228). Macrosystems are identifiable in terms of such things as common beliefs, values, resources, goals, lifestyles, and ambitions.

Changes in macrosystems over time are sometimes very significant for the developing individual. For example, within the last few decades of this century, there have been profound changes in family employment patterns (from one to two wage-earners), in family structure (from two- to one-parent families), in child-rearing styles (from home-rearing to other child-care options), in age of marriage (from younger to older), in age of child-bearing (also from younger to older), in range of expected school attendance (from quasi-compulsory kindergarten to quasi-expected postsecondary education). Clearly, many of these macrosystem changes impact directly on the microsystems of which the child is a part—the family, the home, the school. (See Table 2.10.)

Biological and Ecological Approaches in Review

Biological approaches to understanding human development stress the role of genetics; ecological approaches emphasize the role of context. As is made clear in the next chapter, however, both are clearly important in human development. Nor can their influences easily be separated because their effects result from interactions between the two.

Ethology and Sociobiology

Ethologists and sociobiologists look for the causes of behavior among genetically determined (or genetically influenced) tendencies and capabilities. Some theorists argue that the recognition of genetic contributions to behavior, and to human social relationships, is critically important. These contributions, notes Wilson (1994), have often been ignored by psychology.

Sociobiological theory (also termed *behavioral biology*) assumes that all social behavior has a genetic basis. Not surprisingly, this assumption has provoked considerable controversy and reaction. Critics have been quick to point out that the theory is highly speculative and is based on a handful of assumptions that cannot easily be tested (Lyne & Howe, 1990). For example, the theory rests on the assumption that behaviors occur because they increase the genetic survival of a group (or the probability that genetic material will survive). How do we know this is so? Because the behavior occurred. Why did the behavior occur? Because it increases average genetic survival. This type of circular reasoning offers no hope of proof. To validate the theory, it would be necessary to establish the presence of "altruistic" genes, for example, by some means unrelated to the behaviors these genes are intended to explain. That has yet to be done.

This does not mean that genetics are therefore irrelevant to understanding human behavior. In fact, as is made clear in Chapter 3, our genes are fundamentally involved in everything we do. What it *does* mean is that science has not yet succeeded in showing that specific genes, or combinations of genes, directly cause specific individual behaviors. The basic error in interpreting sociobiological theory has to do with level of explanation. Evolutionary theory, the basis of sociobiology, explains variation at the level of groups with related genetic material (Boyles & Tilman, 1993). It can rarely predict individual behaviors.

A Cultural-Historical Approach

In one sense, Piaget's child is a solitary child, working alone to discover and create meaning. The driving force in Piaget's system is cognitive uncertainty and contradiction (*disequilibrium* is Piaget's term). In contrast, Bandura's child learns through social imitation; the driving force in his system is the child's need to learn through observation. And Vygotsky's theory underscores the role of culture, and especially of its most important invention, language. For Vygotsky, the driving force in development is found in the demands and requirements of the culture. As Tudge and Winterhoff (1993) note, Vygotsky believed that development is a social process assisted by adults and more competent peers.

Vygotsky's most important contribution to understanding development is his recognition of the importance of culture in shaping thought and behavior. And although the concepts of culture and language as determiners of development are perhaps too vague to be of immediate practical value to child-care specialists, teachers, or even psychologists, they are absolutely fundamental to our understanding of the complexity and variety of the human experience. In Bruner's (1986) words, Vygotsky serves as an "inspiration"—an inspiration that urges us to see more clearly that the *average* human beings of which our textbooks speak are always average *only in their culture*. It is largely to remind ourselves of this that in every chapter of this text, there are boxed inserts dealing with people from different cultures.

Ecological Systems Theory

Although most contemporary developmental theorists pay lip service to the importance of taking context, person, and interaction into account, many researchers continue to operate within more traditional models. Two such models have dominated much of our thinking and research. One, exemplified in Freud's theories, says that the causes of developmental change are to be found primarily *within* the individual; the other, evident in behavioristic approaches, insists that the individual's environment is a more important cause of change. It is, of course, the old nature–nurture debate (about which we say more in the next chapter).

The model that underlies our thinking is tremendously important to our research and our conclusions. The first model (Freud, for example) says that if Johnny turns out to be an unmanageable scoundrel, we should look for the cause and the explanation in his temperament and his personality characteristics; the second (behaviorism, for example) says we should look to his environment. Neither of these models says that we should look at how Johnny's characteristics influence his environment, and at how, in turn, his environment influences him. Neither insists that the cause is to be found in the progressive changes in the *interactions* that take place between Johnny and his alcoholic mother, his overworked and indifferent teachers, his peers (the microsystem). Neither suggests that the aborted love affair between Johnny's mother and his tee-ball coach is of consequence (the mesosystem). Neither is concerned with interactions that might have occurred between Johnny's mother and her employer leading to a reduction in her pay and chronic disgruntlement (the exosystem). Neither asks the researcher to look at how society's encouragement of the changing structure of the family impact on Johnny's well-being (the macrosystem). That they do not ask these questions is a weakness of some of our traditional approaches to understanding child development; that ecological systems theory does pose these questions is among its strengths.

But that is also among its weaknesses. Explanations based on ecological systems theory require careful analysis of an almost infinite number of highly complex interactions. Identifying these interactions, observing and quantifying them, sorting out relationships among them, teasing out reciprocal influences between individuals and their micro-, meso-, and exosystems, and determining how changing cultural values and options impinge on the individual—these are difficult tasks. But perhaps if we chew at them long enough, we may find that they are not impossible. Ecological systems theory at least suggests where we should begin.

HUMANISTIC APPROACHES

Had I spoken of Piaget or Freud, of Skinner or sociology, of ethology or ecology in my grandmother's kitchen, the old lady would have listened politely. She was always polite. But in the end, she would probably have said, "That's just theory. It's all very nice, but what about Frank?" Why Frank? Simply because he was a unique child—as we all were (or are). And although there is little doubt that Freud, Skinner, and Piaget might each have had something very intelligent, and perhaps even useful, to say about Frank's habits of stealing chicken eggs, writing poetry, and dancing little jigs in mudholes, they would have been hard pressed to convince my grandmother that they knew more about Frank than she did. My grandmother was a **humanist.**

Basic Concepts of Humanism

Humanistic psychologists are concerned with the uniqueness of the individual. A prevalent humanistic notion is that it is impossible to describe the environment, much less a person, in a truly meaningful way because the important features of the environment are particular to each individual. To understand the behavior of others, one must attempt to perceive the world as they see it—from the perspective of their knowledge, experiences, goals, and aspirations (Rogers, 1951). Such an orientation, sometimes labeled **phenomenology,** underscores again that the individual is unique rather than an average.

Because of their emphasis on the uniqueness of the individual, humanistic positions do not lend themselves easily to the formulation of specific theories that are widely applicable. But they do suggest an attitude toward people, and toward the process of developing, that is of tremendous potential value to those concerned with human welfare. Humanistic orientations tend to personalize (that is, to humanize) our attitudes toward others; they restore some of the dynamism of the developmental process that our more static and more complex theories might otherwise remove.

Maslow's Humanistic Theory

Perhaps the best known of humanistic psychologists is *Abraham Maslow* (1970), who was primarily concerned with the development of the healthy personality. Fundamental to his position is a belief that we are moved by two

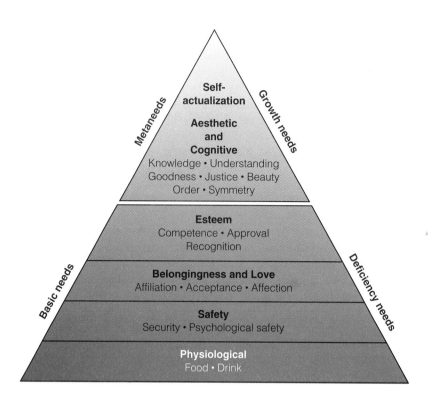

FIGURE 2.6
Maslow's hierarchy of needs.

systems of needs (Maslow, 1970). The **basic needs** are physiological (food, drink) and psychological (security, love, esteem). The **metaneeds** are higher-level needs. They manifest themselves in our desire to know, in our appreciation of truth and beauty, and in our tendencies toward growth and fulfillment (termed **self-actualization**) (see Figure 2.6). Alternately, these two groups of needs are sometimes termed *growth needs* (metaneeds) and *deficiency needs* (basic needs). The basic needs are called deficiency needs because when they are not satisfied, individuals engage in behaviors designed to remedy this lack of satisfaction. (For example, hunger represents a deficiency that can be satisfied by eating.) The metaneeds are called growth needs because activities that relate to them do not fulfill a lack but lead toward growth.

These needs are assumed to be hierarchically arranged in the sense that the metaneeds will not be attended to unless the basic needs are reasonably well satisfied. In other words, we pay attention to beauty, truth, and the development of our potential when we are no longer hungry and unloved (at least not terribly so). Put more simply, hunger for food is more compelling than hunger for knowledge. But keep studying—this is important.

Self-Actualization

Chief among Maslow's metaneeds, and most important for understanding human development, is *self-actualization*. By his own admission, the term is difficult to define (Maslow, 1970). He suggests that it is characterized by the absence of "neurosis, psychopathic personality, psychosis, or strong tendencies in these directions" (1970, p. 150). On the more positive side, he claims that self-actualized people "may be loosely described as [making] full use and exploitation of talents, capacities, potentialities, etc." (p. 150). And the reinforcement—the satisfaction associated with true self-actualization—comes from within rather than without. In contrast, satisfaction of lower-level needs, such as those associated with *esteem*, is associated with external sources of reinforcement (approval and recognition). Using this loose definition, Maslow searched among 3,000 college students and found only one person he considered to be actualized (although there were several dozen "potentials").

Humanism in Review

One way to look at self-actualization is as a process that guides the direction of development rather than as a state that we can attain. The view that children are directed by a need *to become* (to actualize) and that the process of actualization is essentially positive and self-directed presents a subtle but important contrast to the more mechanistic, more passive, and less inner-directed theories covered earlier in this chapter.

Critics have been quick to point out that humanism does not present a scientific theory in the sense that, for example, behaviorism does. Instead, it presents a general description of the human condition—a description that is

TABLE 2.11
Approaches to Developmental Theory

Approach	Representative Theorist	Major Assumptions (theoretical beliefs)	Key Terms
Psychoanalytic	Freud	Individual is motivated by instinctual urges that are primarily sexual and aggressive.	Id, ego, superego, psychosexual, fixation, regression
	Erikson	Child progresses through developmental stages by resolving conflicts that arise from a need to adapt to the sociocultural environment.	Competence, social environment, developmental tasks, psychosocial
Descriptive	Havighurst	Development consists of a series of culturally imposed tasks (competencies) imposed on the individual at different stages of the life cycle.	Developmental tasks, social requirements, social adaptation, maturity
Behavioristic	Watson, Skinner	Changes in behavior are a function of reinforcement and punishment.	Reinforcement, punishment, stimuli, responses
Social-Cognitive	Bandura	Observational learning leads to developmental change; our ability to symbolize and to anticipate the consequences of our behavior is fundamental as are our estimates of our self-efficacy.	Imitation, modeling, eliciting, inhibiting-disinhibiting, self-efficacy
Cognitive	Piaget	Child develops cognitive skills through active interaction with the environment.	Stages, assimilation, accommodation, adaptation, schema
Biological	Bowlby, Wilson	Social behaviors have a biological basis understandable in evolutionary terms. The formation of attachment bonds is one example.	Attachment bonds, biological fitness, survival value, altruistic genes, sensitive period
Ecological systems	Vygotsky, Bronfenbrenner	The ecology of development is the study of accommodations between a person and the environment (culture), taking the changing characteristics of each into account.	Culture, language, open systems, ecology, microsystem, mesosystem, exosystem, macrosystem
Humanistic	Maslow, Rogers	All individuals are unique but strive toward the fullest development of their potential.	Self, positive growth, metaneeds, basic needs, self-actualization

viewed by some as too vague and unreliable to contribute much to the development of psychology as a science. Humanists counter by pointing out that science is only one way of knowing, that there is value in the insights provided by more subjective approaches.

One of the most important contributions of the humanistic approach is its recognition of the importance of the self and its emphasis on the uniqueness of each child. Although humanistic theory does not address well the specifics of the developmental process, it might in the end serve to explain facts that are not easily accounted for by other theories.

A FINAL WORD ABOUT THEORIES

We began this chapter by insisting that facts and theories are not worlds apart in terms of "truthfulness"—that theories are intended as explanations of facts. From these explanations, scientists strive for understanding, for prediction, and sometimes for control.

Theories, we should remember, are inventions whose purpose is to simplify, to explain, sometimes to predict. They are never flatly wrong—or entirely correct. And, of course, they do not have to be accepted or rejected in their entirety. When Mahoney (1991) summarized the results of 15 surveys conducted between 1953 and 1988 to look at the theoretical beliefs of clinical psychologists, he found that through most of this period, the majority described themselves as "eclectic." That is, most preferred to combine features from more than one theoretical position rather than adhere strongly to a single orientation. Interestingly, early in the period, more clinical psychologists considered themselves followers of psychodynamic theory (Freud) than of any other theoretical position (almost half of all practicing psychologists). Even in 1988, while the most common theoretical orientation was eclectic, the psychodynamic orientation remained a strong second-place contender. Other orientations (cognitive, behavioristic, humanistic) are descriptive of much smaller numbers of clinical psychologists.

While the psychodynamic position continues to be very important in clinical psychology—cognitive orientations have become increasingly common in other areas of psychology, both in current theory and research as well as in educational applications. As so often happens, history will inform us later about the fruitfulness of these approaches. (See Table 2.11 for a summary of approaches to developmental theory discussed in this chapter.)

Psychological Theories

1. A theory is a collection of statements intended to organize and explain important observations. Theories are best evaluated in terms of usefulness rather than truthfulness. They should reflect "facts," be understandable, and be useful for predicting events as well as for explaining the past.

Models in Lifespan Development

2. Models are metaphors that underlie theories. The organismic model describes people as active, functioning biological organisms; the mechanistic view stresses the reactive, machinelike predictability of human functioning; the contextual model emphasizes the influence of historical variables, life events, and other aspects of context.

A Psychoanalytic Approach: Freud

3. Freud's theory is based on the assumption that among the most important causes of behavior are deep-seated, unconscious forces. The newborn child is all *libido* (instinctual urges), termed *id*, concerned solely with the gratification of primarily sexual urges. Conflict between the id and reality develops the *ego*, which tries to satisfy id urges within the constraints of reality. The *superego* (conscience) forms later and represents social and cultural taboos. Development involves progression through five stages (oral, anal, phallic, latency, and genital), each differentiated from the others primarily by the areas of the child's body that are the principal sources of sexual gratification at that time.

A Psychosocial Approach: Erikson

4. According to Erikson's *psychosocial* theory of development, the individual progresses through a series of stages characterized by basic conflicts, the resolution of which results in the appearance of new capabilities and attitudes: trust versus mistrust, autonomy versus shame and doubt, initiative versus guilt, industry versus inferiority, identity versus identity diffusion, intimacy versus isolation, generativity versus self-absorption, and integrity versus despair.

Havighurst's Developmental Tasks

5. Havighurst describes development in terms of a series of requirements that are placed on individuals by their society. These provide a rough index of developmental maturity.

Behavioristic Approaches to Development

6. Behavioristic (learning-theory) approaches focus on immediate behavior and on environmental forces that affect behavior. In classical conditioning, a conditioned stimulus, or CS (originally a neutral stimulus), is paired with an unconditioned stimulus, or US (a stimulus that reliably brings about a response termed an *unconditioned response*, or UR), until presentation of the CS by itself is sufficient to bring about the response (now termed a *conditioned response*, or CR). Operant conditioning changes the probability of a response occurring as a function of its consequences. Positive reinforcers increase the probability of a response as a function of being added to a situation; negative reinforcers have the same effect when they are taken away from a situation. Punishment (adding something unpleasant or removing something pleasant) unlike negative and positive reinforcement, does not ordinarily increase the probability of a response, but has the opposite effect.

Social-Cognitive Theory

7. Bandura's theory of observational learning, which depends on attending, remembering, reproducing what is observed, and motivation, explains socialization as a function of imitation. Observational learning may be evident in the learning of new responses (modeling effect), the suppression or reappearance of deviant behaviors (inhibitory-disinhibitory effect), and the emission of behaviors similar but not identical to that of the model (eliciting effect).

8. Self-referent thought has to do with our estimates of personal effectiveness and is important in determining the behaviors we undertake, the amount of effort we are willing to expend on a given task, and our feelings about ourselves. Judgments of *self-efficacy* derive from four sources: enactive (based on the outcome of our own behaviors), vicarious (based on comparisons between the self and similar others), persuasory (the result of persuading, cajoling, pleading, bribing by others), and emotive (the function of arousal or high emotion).

A Cognitive Approach: Piaget

9. Piaget's theory describes *cognitive* (intellectual) development in terms of adaptation resulting from interaction with the environment through using activities already in the child's repertoire (assimilation) and changing activities to conform to environmental demands (accommodation). The child's cognitive development is viewed as a sequential progression through four major stages:

sensorimotor (world of here and now; intelligence in action), preoperational (egocentric thought; perception-dominated; intuitive rather than logical), concrete operations (logical thought operations applied to real objects and events), and formal (propositional thinking; potentially logical thought; hypothetical, idealistic reasoning).

Biological and Ecological Approaches

10. Biological approaches to development look at the role of biology (heredity) in determining development and behavior; ecological approaches emphasize the importance of interaction in changing contexts; ethologists are biologically oriented scientists who study behavior in natural situations. Some theorists (like Bowlby) argue that the attachment bond that forms between caregivers and their infants is biologically based. Sociobiologists are concerned with the biological basis of social behavior and try to explain behaviors such as altruism and aggression in terms of their survival value for a related group of individuals.

11. Vygotsky's cultural-historical approach emphasizes the importance of culture and especially language. The *zone of proximal growth*, an expression of Vygotsky's belief in the interdependence of development and environment, is the child's potential for development in a given context. Bronfenbrenner's ecological systems theory looks at interactions and adaptations between the person and changing contexts at four levels: the microsystem (the child in face-to-face interaction), the mesosystem (interactions among contexts in the child's microsystem), the exosystem (interactions between one of the child's microsystem contexts and another context with which the child does not ordinarily interact), and the macrosystem (the totality of all cultural contexts relevant to the child's life).

Humanistic Approaches

12. Humanistic theory is concerned with individual uniqueness, the importance of the individual's point of view (phenomenology), and human potential (self-actualization). Maslow describes two motivational need systems: *deficiency* (basic) needs, which are psychological (esteem, love) and physical (food, drink); and *metaneeds* (growth needs) such as the need to *self-actualize*.

A Final Word About Theories

13. People are more complicated than this chapter might suggest, but they are easier to understand within the context of the more organized systems or theories provided here than within the context of our naive intuitions. Although theories are never entirely wrong or right, they can still be useful.

1. What purposes do theories serve?
    - Write out two or three clear and simple questions about human development for which a theory might suggest an answer.

2. What are the characteristics of a good theory?
    - List the criteria by which psychological theories might be evaluated.

3. What are the basic ideas underlying the theories of Freud? Erikson? Piaget? Skinner? Bandura? Sociobiology? Vygotsky? Bronfenbrenner?

    - Answer one or more of the questions you proposed in response to question 1, using each of these theories.

4. What is the most important thing each of these theories tells us about children?
    - Summarize each theory as completely and accurately as you can in a single sentence.

accommodation   47

adaptation   47

anal stage   34

arousal   45

assimilation   47

Bandura   43

basic needs   56

behavior modification   43

behavioristic theory   39

FURTHER READINGS

Theorists such as Freud, Erikson, and Piaget were often prolific and sometimes difficult writers. It is generally easier and perhaps more valuable to begin with secondary sources for information about their theories. The following are useful starting points:

Miller, P. H. (1993). *Theories of developmental psychology* (3rd ed.). New York: W. H. Freeman.

Thomas, R. M. (1992). *Comparing theories of child development* (3rd ed.). Belmont, CA: Wadsworth.

Wadsworth, B. J. (1989). *Piaget's theory of cognitive and affective development* (4th ed.). New York: Longman.

Research and theorizing based on Piaget's theory but taking into consideration new findings and beliefs in cognition and information processing—often termed *Neo-Piagetian* research—is discussed in:

Case, R. (Ed.). (1991). *The mind's staircase: Exploring the conceptual underpinnings of children's thought and knowledge.* Hillsdale, NJ: Erlbaum.

For a clear account of Vygotsky's life and theories, see:

Kozulin, A. (1990). *Vygotsky's psychology: A biography of ideas.* New York: Harvester Wheatsheaf.

More detailed information about Bronfenbrenner's eco-logical systems theory can be found either in Bronfen-brenner's own book or in the relevant chapter of the Vasta book:

Bronfenbrenner, U. (1979). *The ecology of human development*. Cambridge, MA: Harvard University Press.

Vasta, R. (Ed.). (1989). *Annals of child development* (Vol. 6). Greenwich, CT: JAI Press.

The first of the next two references is an excellent sum-mary of Bandura's social-cognitive theory. The second is a simple summary of his imitation-based theories:

Bandura, A. (1986). *Social foundations of thought and action: A social cognitive theory*. Englewood Cliffs, NJ: Prentice-Hall.

Bandura, A., & Walters, R. (1963). *Social learning and personality development*. New York: Holt, Rinehart & Winston.

Maslow's humanistic psychology is well explained in:

Maslow, A. H. (1970). *Motivation and personality* (2nd ed.). New York: Harper & Row.

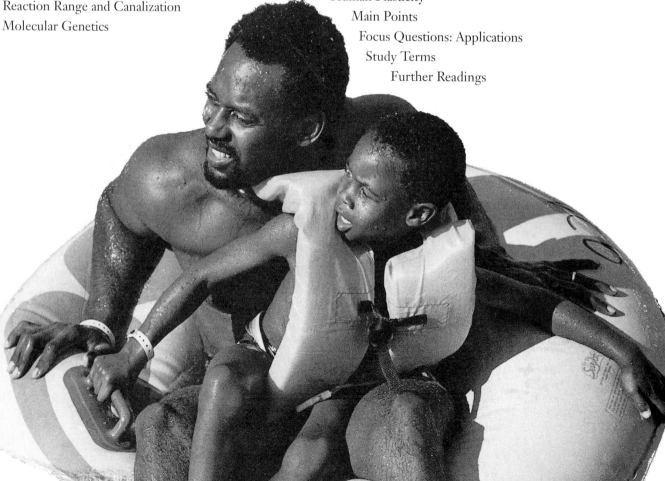

GENE–CONTEXT INTERACTION

*H*eredity philosophers should be interested in the portraits of Mr. Edison's parents.

LONDON DAILY NEWS, July 12, 1894, p. 6

The reason heredity philosophers should be interested in portraits of the famous Mr. Thomas Edison's parents is simply that Thomas bore his parents a stunning resemblance. Presumably from this resemblance, heredity philosophers could have drawn some useful conclusions.

CHAPTER 3

My grandmother, too, was a heredity philosopher, not because she commented on familial similarities or practiced her speculations on doubtful paternity cases, which is what other aspiring heredity philosophers did. Practice alone does not a heredity philosopher make; my grandmother had what many called *the gift*.

At age 4, I am hiding under the table, wondering how I can reach the cookie jar without being seen, which, it turns out, is not really difficult today because my grandmother's busy talking to my mother. "His father's a goat," she's saying. "Louis Watrin's father for sure is a goat, and mark my word, the way he carries on." Louis is an unusual guy; he's never been married; and he's never had a real job or actually worked much on his farm. All he does is keep a few goats and things. He spends most of his time visiting people, which is a diversion for farm wives whose husbands work so much.

"His father was definitely a goat," my grandmother says flatly, and Bango! the brilliance of her conclusion strikes me like a eureka experience. I have never known Louis Watrin's father, but if you look carefully at Louis, you definitely can see the source of my grandmother's insight. It isn't just the pointed beard, a clue that might be apparent to the most amateurish of heredity philosophers. It's a whole combination of features: the bright, dark eyes; the sudden way in which he moves his head up and to the side, holding it motionless for long moments while he scans the distance; the way he climbs porch steps, short footsteps alternating with little scampering bursts; his habit of nibbling at food. . . .

"Louis Watrin's father is a goat," I confide to Martin.

"Which one?" he asks.

"Which one what?"

"Which goat's the dad? Let's go see."

So Martin and I run over to Louis Watrin's place and look at the goats through the fence rails. At first, I think it might be the one with the broken horn. It has that Watrin look in its eye—that distant, knowing look that I am later to learn gives Louis much of his mystery and appeal.

"No way," says Martin. "That one's not old enough. It's got to be the bearded one."

Of course it has to be. After all, Louis Watrin most definitely had a beard.

THIS CHAPTER

Unfortunately, the situation with **heredity** and **environment** is not as simple as I thought it was at the age of 4. *Heredity philosophers* cannot simply look at parents and offspring to determine how genes and experiences shape developmental outcomes. Such an approach would offer little hope of solving the nature–nurture puzzle.

How does science begin to solve this puzzle? One argument runs something like this: For human characteristics that are determined mainly by genetic factors, changes in the environment should have little effect. By the same token, vastly different environments should have profound effects on characteristics that depend largely on nurture. Thus eye color should not change whether a person is reared by natives in the Amazon jungle, by Ihalmiuts in Greenland, or by Americans in Boston. But the individual's speech will be vastly different in each of these environments.

One way, then, of beginning to sort out and understand the interaction of heredity and environment is to look at individuals with similar genetic backgrounds—say, identical twins, whose genetic similarity is perfect. Investigators can examine the outcomes of the developmental

One way of beginning to unravel the complexities of gene–environment contributions to human development is to look at similarities and differences among individuals whose genetic backgrounds are absolutely identical—a situation that exists only for monozygotic (one-egg or identical) twins.

process when each member of the pair is raised in a highly similar environment (twins who are brought up in the same home) or in a highly different environment (twins who are reared apart). Another possibility is to look at fraternal twins, whose genetic similarity is about 50 percent—roughly that of any other pair of siblings—but whose environments might be nearly as similar as those of identical twins reared together. Still another alternative is to look at individuals who are adopted, and to compare them with their adoptive parents, their natural parents, their biological siblings, and their adoptive siblings. And another approach, of course, is to look at genetic material itself, to study its composition and map its organization. Examples of each of these approaches, together with the most important findings of this research, are summarized in this chapter.

GENE–CONTEXT INTERACTIONS

The nature–nurture question can be stated very simply: How do genes (nature) and context (nurture) interact to influence human development? Answering this question, however, is not so simple.

Feral Children

Among early attempts to shed light on nature–nurture interaction are fascinating accounts of children who have allegedly been abandoned in the wilds. Many of these chil-

VICTOR AND OTHER *ENFANTS SAUVAGES*

Aveyron, France: The story begins on a cold, blustery day in the fall of 1979 when a group of French peasants glimpse a naked boy runnng through the woods (Lane, 1977). They see him again the next day but don't succeed in capturing him until the following year. He is immediately brought to a village and put on display as *L'enfant sauvage d'Aveyron* (the wild boy of Aveyron). Within a few days, he escapes, but is eventually recaptured. People are fascinated by this wild creature—naked, speechless, and apparently in every way a wild animal. Itard, a famous physician, takes over the boy's care, convinced he can "civilize" him and teach him to speak. But in spite of Itard's efforts, Victor, as the boy is named, remains more wild than tame. He has little use for clothing, seems insensitive to heat or cold, sleeps as easily on the floor as anywhere, and carries out his toilet functions as the urge moves him. And he never does learn to speak.

Spanish Sahara, South Morocco: It was on one of his solitary journeys through one of the vast and largely unexplored deserts of Morocco that Jean-Claude Armen (1974) first saw the gazelles, a herd of sleek white forms leaping about the thorn-bushes and flowering tamarisks of a tiny oasis—and among them, a flash of jet-black hair "as a child with a bronzed and slender body darts from the same bush, throws himself at the unearthed roots, teeth first, peels them with clicks of his tongue, then cuts them up frantically with his incisors" (p. 29). It is the *gazelle-boy* of the Sahara. During the following weeks, Armen spends hours trying slowly, patiently, to approach the gazelles, and the boy. Finally one of the animals is brave enough to nuzzle and then lick his foot; it occurs to him that he should reciprocate, and so he licks her muzzle. Finally, the boy comes up and sniffs Armen's toes and then, "like two cats acknowledging each other," they move their noses toward each other and, suddenly, the boy licks Armen's nose—and Armen responds in the same manner. The ice is broken, and for the next several weeks Armen studies the boy, noting how his life seems perfectly balanced with that of the gazelles. He speculates that as an infant, the boy may have fallen from a camel traveling through the night, and that

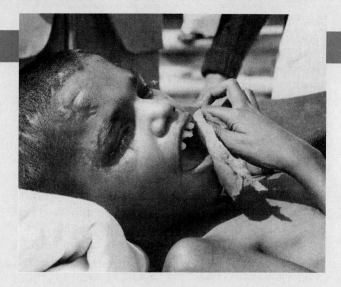

it happened that a female gazelle, perhaps having just lost her fawn, adopted him. And although the boy no longer fears Armen, he develops no special kinship with him. In the end, he wanders off with the gazelles on one of their migrations, and Armen cannot keep up. Several attempts are later made to find him using airplanes, but none succeed.

To Think About   There had been 53 wild children found in different parts of the world prior to the gazelle-boy, writes Armen. They show the remarkable adaptations of which humans are capable, and they emphasize the extent to which being human requires human experiences in early life. The other more scientific view is that this evidence is flimsy and unconvincing, that most of the feral children have traits in common with mentally retarded or brain-damaged children, which is maybe why they were abandoned in the first place (Dennis, 1951). What do you think? If the evidence *were* reliable, what might it teach us?

dren would, of course, have died. But some of them, legend and folklore inform us, were found by wild animals who took them into their lairs and dens and raised them as their own (hence the term **feral children,** meaning "wild children"). When recaptured, these children usually don't speak; instead, they run about on all fours, and growl or bark at people. Their wild behavior is strong evidence, Singh and Zingg (1942) argued, that the special qualities that make us human are not inherited, but have to be learned. (See Across Cultures: "Victor and Other *Enfants Sauvages*.")

But the evidence is not at all convincing, claimed Dennis (1951), because there is not a single fully documented case of a child having been raised by a wild animal.

Genie: A Modern-Day Wild Child

But there are other accounts of abandoned children that are more reliable. One is the story of a little girl, initially nameless but who later came to be known as Genie. Genie was not abandoned in the wilds, but in a small upstairs bedroom in her own home. Except for brief periods when she was still a toddler, Genie would not leave her room from the age of 20 months until she was almost 14—more than 12 years!

Curtiss (1977) describes how Genie's room was completely unfurnished save for a small crib covered with wire mesh, and an infant "potty." Genie was left completely alone in this room, day after day after day—alone and naked, with a sturdy leather harness strapped to her body and fastened to the potty so that she was forced to sit on it for hours. At night, she was sometimes simply left on the potty; other times she would be stuffed into a sleeping bag specially made to restrain her, much like a straightjacket, and placed inside the crib, imprisoned within the wire mesh. Now and again, someone, usually her father, would come in and feed her—almost always either baby food, soupy cereal, or a soft-boiled egg. Whoever fed her simply stuffed as much food as possible into her mouth; and if she spit some of it out, her face would be rubbed in it. If she whimpered or made some other noise, perhaps with her potty or her crib, her father would come in and beat her with a stick. No one was allowed to speak with her during feeding time, or to visit her at other times. Often the father would pretend he was a dog, barking and growling at Genie, and sometimes scratching her with his fingernails. If he just wanted to threaten her, he would stand outside her door and make his most vicious dog noises.

When Genie was 13 years old, following an especially violent fight with the father, the mother finally took her and left. Shortly after that, Genie was discovered, charges were filed against the parents, and Genie was brought into a hospital. Genie's father committed suicide on the day he was to be brought to trial. And although Genie made some progress, her language and social development remained far below normal. (See Chapter 7 for more details. See, also Curtiss, 1977, and Rymer, 1993).

Two Models of Gene–Context Relationships

Stories such as that of Genie and of other abandoned children are important for psychology because they provide evidence relevant to the heredity–environment (nature–nurture) issue. Whatever characteristics these children share with others who are brought up in more "normal" environments, we might assume to result from genetic influences; and whatever "human" characteristics they fail to develop, we can attribute to environmental forces. Thus we might begin to separate the relative contributions of each to our development.

But the issue is not quite so simple; nor is the answer. In fact, there have historically been at least two sorts of answers reflecting two different points of view: the *additive* and the *interactive*. The *additive* point of view assumes that the effects of heredity and environment are, in a sense, additive. That is, heredity accounts for a certain percentage of the variation in a characteristic, environment for the remainder. This is the model that has governed the work of early researchers. For example, Sternberg (1991) points out that in the 1960s, psychology accepted the reasoning that some children were more intelligent than others because they had inherited more "intelligence" from their parents.

By the 1980s, however, the additive model began to give way to the *interactive* model. Psychologists were now generally agreed that both heredity and environment are important, but not as isolated forces. Rather, it is the *interaction* between the two that is important (Gottlieb, 1992).

Interaction

Unfortunately, *interaction* is not a simple concept; and the results of interaction are not always highly predictable. Take something as simple as water and temperature. We know that water and temperature interact to form ice; but can we understand the hardness of ice, its taste, its effect on our skin solely by understanding temperature and water? And is it not true that steam also results from the interaction of water and temperature? The interaction becomes more complex, but it still appears linear and predictable: More heat equals steam; less heat equals ice. Even here, however, interaction is not quite so simple. With changes in air pressure, the interaction of water and temperature changes. Now an even higher or lower temperature is required for the same effect.

As with ice, temperature, and water, interaction among heredity, environment, and human behavior is not a simple additive affair. Relative contributions of heredity and environment might change with age, might be different in different environments, and might vary from one individual to another. Furthermore, quite apart from their interactive role in influencing developmental outcomes, genes and environment can influence each other directly (Lerner, 1991). What we know of evolution makes it clear, for example, that gene combinations that underlie *adaptive* behaviors are more likely to survive in our genetic pools; those that are *maladaptive* have a poorer chance of surviving. Thus does the environment influence genes.

The story of Genie provides one example of the complexity of gene–environment interaction specifically in the area of language development. Obviously, the acquisition of language is made possible by our genes. Not only have we been endowed with vocal cords, tongues, mouths, ears, brains, and other structures that make the production and the identification of speech sounds possible, but we also seem to be predisposed to acquire language early in our lives. Genie, who was not exposed to language during this sensitive early period (roughly, the early preschool years) had not learned to speak or to understand others. When she was later exposed to a normal language environment, as well as to direct language tuition, she managed to develop only a small vocabulary and to acquire a limited and uncertain grasp of simple language-production rules. As Rymer (1993) points out, her development of language was far from normal.

It is worth emphasizing again that both the characteristics of the person and those of the context need to be taken into account—as ecological-contextual theory makes clear. We look again at the relationship between person and context later in this chapter; first, a look at the mechanics of heredity.

THE MECHANICS OF HEREDITY

The mechanics of heredity are complex and sometimes bewildering, its marvels amazing. The mechanics can be simplified somewhat; the marvels are best left for saints and poets.

Conception

Human life begins with the joining of the mother's **ovum (egg cell)** and the father's **sperm cell.** For life to occur, this union is necessary; and because two people of opposite sexes are involved, it ordinarily requires a physical union between a male and a female as well—ordinarily, but not always. **Conception** is also possible with **artificial insemination,** a clinical procedure wherein the father's sperm is introduced directly into the mother (sometimes using anonymous donor sperm so that the identity of the biological father may never be clear).*

Another possibility is to insert an ovum from a female donor in a woman whose Fallopian tubes are blocked. Still another possibility is conception that occurs completely outside the mother's body, either in another woman's body or *in vitro* (literally, meaning "in glass"). The fertilized egg can then be implanted in the mother to develop as it normally would. Surrogate mothering, where one woman bears a child for another, is another possibility, as are fertility drugs—drugs whose effects are typically to stimulate the production of mature ova. In these cases, pregnancy typically comes about as a result of the male–female union to which we referred earlier in this section.

None of these procedures is a certain solution for all childless couples; and none is a cure for the causes of childlessness. But when successful, they do remove the symptom: childlessness.

Sex Cells
Mature women usually release a single mature ovum about once every 28 days (ordinarily between the 10th and the 18th day of their menstrual cycle). Sometimes two or more eggs are produced at once or a single fertilized egg divides, thus making possible multiple births.

*Artificial insemination of the mother is ordinarily a medical procedure. But an Associated Press report describes the case of an inventive woman who used a turkey baster to inseminate herself. She apparently administered herself a number of treatments, *and stood on her head for 30 minutes* after each. "I figured gravity couldn't hurt," said she ("Turkey Baster Used to Help Make Baby," 1993, p. 28). The report also states that the baster, sterilized in the kitchen dishwasher, cost only $2.95.

All of the woman's ova are present in her ovaries at birth—perhaps as many as a million of them. These are primitive and immature, and more than half of them atrophy before **puberty** (the beginning of sexual maturity). Of those that remain, approximately 400 will mature and be released between puberty and **menopause** (cessation of menstruation). In contrast, a man produces sperm at the rate of several billion a month (200 to 300 million every four days or so) and usually continues to produce them from puberty until death.

The ovum is the largest cell in the human body at approximately 0.15 millimeters in diameter—about half the size of each period (.) on this page. The sperm cell, by contrast, is one of the smallest cells in the body, 0.005 millimeters in diameter. What the sperm cell lacks in size is made up by the length of its tail—fully 12 times longer than the main part of the cell to which it is attached. It is this long tail that enables the sperm to swim toward the ovum.

Carriers of Heredity

The egg cell and the sperm cell, called **gametes,** are the immediate origins of new life. Not only do they give rise to the development of a new human, but they also carry the instructions or the blueprints that determine what that individual will inherit. **Genetics** is the science that studies heredity.

The complex field of genetics is among the fastest growing of all modern disciplines. To try to simplify it accurately in a few paragraphs, or a few pages, is somewhat presumptuous. But we have no choice; so we will strive for clarity and simplicity, if not completeness.

Proteins
The basis of all human life—the living, functioning cells of which we are composed—can be reduced to complicated molecules called **proteins.** These, in turn, are made up of different amino acids, of which there are 20 different known kinds (Emery & Mueller, 1992). A specific combination and sequence of amino acids determine the nature and function of the protein it makes up. The number of possible combinations is astronomical. Consider that the 26 letters that make up the alphabet by means of which you and I are now communicating allows us to generate new combinations of sentences, paragraphs, chapters, even books, virtually indefinitely.

DNA
The basis of life is proteins; the nature and function of proteins is determined by amino acid combinations and sequences. In turn, these combinations and sequences are determined by a special code contained in a substance called *deoxyribonucleic acid* or **DNA.** This substance consists mainly of four components, which are arranged in different sequences of pairs in a structure resembling what

FIGURE 3.1

DNA molecules are arranged in sequences of pairs in a spiraling, double-helix structure. Genes, labels for carriers of specific hereditary information, can be thought of as locations or addresses on a segment of the DNA molecule.

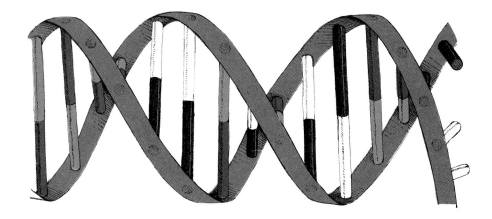

INTERACTIVE FIGURE 3.2

In this figure there is a clue to a fact of which Henry VIII was sadly ignorant as he beheaded a succession of wives for failing to give him a son. *Can you figure it out before continuing? Only the male sex cell, the sperm, can contain either an X or a Y sex chromosome; the ovum always contains only the X chromosome. Because an XY pairing determines that the offspring will be male (XX is female), the "failure" of Henry's wives to produce sons was really his fault.*

is termed a **double helix** (see Figure 3.1). In effect, this arrangement of DNA components is the blueprint or genetic code that determines our heredity.

Chromosomes

We have two kinds of cells in our body: sex cells (ova or sperm) and body cells (called somatic cells). All normal body cells contain identical genetic information. That is, all have the same assortment of DNA molecules—the same genetic code. These DNA molecules are located on rodlike structures called **chromosomes.** There are 23 pairs of these chromosomes in every human body cell. One member of each pair of chromosomes is inherited from our mothers and the other, from our fathers. In other words, we inherit 23 chromosomes from each of our parents for a total of 46 chromosomes. The division of body cells involves what is called **mitosis**—a process that results in genetically identical pairs of cells.

Unlike somatic cells, *mature* sex cells (sperm and ovum) each contain 23 chromosomes rather than 23 pairs. This is because the gametes (sex cells) result from a special kind of cell division termed **meiosis,** which results in daughter cells that have only half the number of chromosomes of the parent cell. And when chromosome pairs in the parent cell divide to form mature sperm (in males) or ova (in females), they do so randomly. That is, individual members of chromosome pairs wind up in any of a mindboggling number of different possible combinations. And because there are two parents involved, the total number of different individuals that can result from a single human

mating is some almost meaningless number larger than 60 *trillion.**

So should we be amazed that we are so much like our parents and siblings? Not really. You see, in these over 60 trillion theoretically possible combinations, there will be a vast amount of redundant information. And much of that redundant information is absolutely fundamental to our humanity. Among other things, it is expressed in the fact that most of us have a single head, two eyes, a brain with a marvelously developed cortex, limbs, digits, and on and on.

But genetics deals less with our sameness than with our variability. It is concerned with the chemistry and the biology that account for differences among individuals of the same species.

Sex Chromosomes

Of the 23 chromosomes contained in each sperm and each ovum, one, labeled the **sex chromosome,** determines whether the offspring will be male or female (the other 22 are called **autosomes**). As shown in Interactive Figure 3.2, the father produces two types of sperm, one type with a larger sex chromosome labeled X and one type with a smaller chromosome labeled Y. If the sperm that fertilizes the ovum contains an X chromosome, the offspring will

*And that does not even take into account that during meiosis segments of chromosomes sometimes "cross over" and exchange places, thereby increasing the number of possible combinations astronomically.

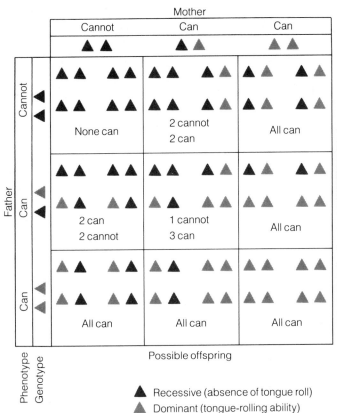

Can you roll your tongue as shown? If you can roll your tongue, would you be prepared to wager that either your mother or your father can also? Tongue-rolling ability is related to the presence of a dominant gene.

▲ Recessive (absence of tongue roll)
▲ Dominant (tongue-rolling ability)

be a girl; if the sperm cell contains a Y chromosome, the result will be a boy. Because the mother produces only X chromosomes, it is accurate to say that only the father's sperm can determine the sex of the offspring.

The ratio of males to females at birth is about 105 to 100 (U.S. Bureau of the Census, 1994). But males are more susceptible to various illnesses and diseases so that, by the age of 5, there are almost as many girls as boys. By age 75, women outnumber men about two to one.

Genes

The units of heredity carried by the chromosomes are called **genes.** Some of our 23 chromosomes contain between 50,000 and 100,000 genes; others, especially the sex chromosomes, contain far fewer (Friedman et al., 1992). These genes, either in pairs or in complex combinations of pairs, determine our potential for inherited characteristics.

Genetic Effects

There are, for example, pairs of genes that correspond to eye color, hair characteristics, and virtually every other physical characteristic of an individual. In addition, other combinations of genes appear to be related to personality characteristics such as intelligence—although the ways in which genes affect personality are not as obvious or as easily measured as the ways in which they affect physical characteristics.

Among many other characteristics known to be largely determined, or at least influenced, by genes are disorders, illnesses, and defects such as some forms of blindness and baldness, hemophilia, alcoholism, and Down syndrome. Some of these are discussed later in this chapter.

Gene Functioning

Genes are arranged in corresponding pairs on chromosomes, one gene being inherited from each parent. From studies of animals and plants (particularly fruit flies and peas), as well as from observations of humans and other animals, scientists have discovered that one of the pair may be *dominant* over the other. When a **dominant gene** is paired with a corresponding **recessive gene,** the characteristics corresponding to the dominant gene will appear in the individual. We know, for example, that the gene for normally pigmented skin is dominant over the gene for albinism (unpigmented skin). Hence an individual who inherits a gene for normal skin from one parent and one for albinism from the other will nevertheless have pigmented skin. A true albino (completely unpigmented skin) will have inherited a recessive gene for unpigmented skin from *each* parent. It follows as well that two albino parents will inevitably produce albino children. (See Interactive Figure 3.3 for an illustration of a characteristic related to the presence of a dominant gene.)

If human genetics were limited to the effects of single pairs of genes and their dominance or recessiveness, genetics would be far simpler. In fact, however, many

Phenotype is defined as the individual's manifested characteristics; genotype is the person's genetic makeup. But genotype can't always be inferred from phenotype. Thus, this infant's brown eyes are part of his phenotype; but the underlying genotype might be two genes for brown eyes or only one because the gene for brown eyes is ordinarily dominant over that for blue eyes.

characteristics are a function of an undetermined number of pairs of genes acting in combination. In addition, genes are seldom completely dominant or recessive under all circumstances. Some genes appear to be dominant over a specific gene but recessive with respect to another. Furthermore, the material of which genes consist (deoxyribonucleic acid, or DNA) occasionally undergoes *mutations*—changes that may be brought about through X-rays, chemicals such as mustard gas, some drugs, or other causes.

Genotype and Phenotype

Genetic makeup defines *genotype*; manifested characteristics are *phenotype*. That is, phenotype is what can be seen (color of hair, for example); in contrast, genotype is hidden and has to be inferred from phenotype or can sometimes be determined through an examination of the matter of which genes are composed.

For characteristics determined by recessive genes, it's possible to make accurate inferences about genotype; that is not the case for those determined by dominant genes. For example, the gene for brown eyes is normally dominant over that for blue eyes. Hence we can infer that individuals whose phenotype (manifested characteristics) include blue eyes must have two recessive genes for blue eyes (genotype). On the other hand, we can't be certain

about the genotype for brown-eyed individuals because they might have two dominant genes for brown eyes or a dominant gene for brown eyes and a recessive gene for blue eyes (see Figure 3.4).

The effects of genotype on phenotype are not quite as simple as the eye-color illustration implies. In fact, most human characteristics, including eye color, are usually the result of combinations of genes (polygenesis). The effects of polygenetic determination are not either-or (for example, either blue or brown), but include a whole range of possibilities. Thus it is that individuals are not simply blue- or brown-eyed, but can also have eyes that are green or hazel or blue-green, or a variety of other shades. In addition, some mutations (structural changes) of genes can change a normally recessive gene into a dominant gene (Offner, 1993).

Plomin (1987) summarizes the relationship between genotype and phenotype as follows:

- First, it is clear that genetic differences (genotype) lead to phenotypic differences. Blue-eyed parents are far more likely to produce blue-eyed offspring than are dark-eyed parents.

- Second, characteristics that are influenced by more than one gene tend not to be *dichotomous* (either-or) but are distributed in a manner that approximates what is referred to as the **normal curve** (a bell-shaped curve where the majority of cases cluster near the average, with fewer and fewer cases deviating farther and farther from the average). For example, height is influenced by genetic makeup. But most people aren't extremely tall or extremely short; instead, most are average, with the fewest numbers at the farthest extremes.

- Third, the environment also makes an important difference to manifested characteristics. Height reflects not only genetic influences but also environmental conditions such as nutrition and health.

Reaction Range and Canalization

The environment makes a great deal of difference for some things (like language learning); for others (like eye color) it makes little apparent difference. Characteristics that are less affected by environmental forces are said to be highly **canalized** (Waddington, 1975). Eye color is a highly canalized characteristic; it typically corresponds to genotype and is unaffected by experience. In contrast, many complex intellectual abilities (the ability to learn to speak several languages, for example) do not appear to be highly canalized but are highly affected by experience.

In evolutionary terms, canalization may be seen as a genetic tendency toward predictable regularity. This predictable regularity ensures that individuals of one species will be much more similar than dissimilar. For characteristics that are not highly canalized, phenotype may be very

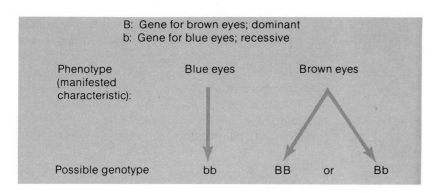

B: Gene for brown eyes; dominant
b: Gene for blue eyes; recessive

Phenotype (manifested characteristic):

Blue eyes — Brown eyes

Possible genotype — bb — BB or Bb

FIGURE 3.4

Phenotype (manifested characteristics) is influenced by genotype (genetic makeup). But genotype cannot always be inferred from phenotype. A brown-eyed person might have two genes for brown eyes or just one, with a recessive gene for blue eyes.

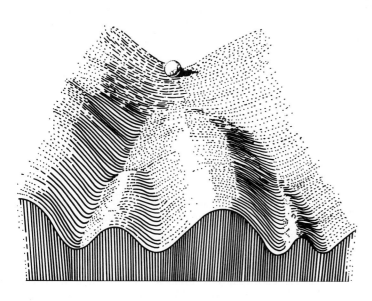

FIGURE 3.5

Waddington's epigenetic landscape, a graphic analogy depicting the interaction between environmental and genetic forces. Genetic forces are represented by the valleys and contours of the landscape; they make certain outcomes more probable than others. Environmental forces are represented by changes in the tilt of the landscape. (Based on Waddington, 1975.)

different from what might have been predicted on the basis of genetic makeup.

The Epigenetic Landscape

Waddington's (1975) *epigenetic landscape* is an analogy to illustrate the relationship of genetic and environmental forces in development (Figure 3.5). In this illustration, genetic forces are represented by the canals that run down the landscape; the tilt of the figure represents environmental forces; and the ball represents some characteristic of the developing organism. Where the ball ends up represents the final state of that characteristic.

The analogy makes several important points. First, changes in the environment (different tilts) can shift the ball's path and dramatically affect the final outcome; second, for highly canalized traits (deeper channels), far greater environmental forces (changes in tilt) will be needed to influence the final outcome; and third, subtle environmental forces are more likely to affect the course of development early (top of the figure) rather than late in development (bottom of the figure, where all channels are deeper).

Reaction Range

Even for highly canalized characteristics, phenotype (manifested characteristics) seldom results only from genetic influences, but is usually influenced by the environment as well. That is, **epigenesis,** the unfolding of genetically influenced characteristics, is brought about by the interaction of genes and environment. In a sense, it is as though genetic influences (genotypes) make possible a range of different outcomes, with some being more probable than others. This range of possible outcomes is termed *reaction range* (Gottesman, 1974).

The reaction range for a particular characteristic includes all the possible outcomes for that characteristic given variations in the nature and timing of environmental influences. Thus your genes at birth might have been such that your most probable adult height would be 6 feet (1.82 meters). But given exceptional nutrition and exercise (or the use of growth and performance-enhancing drugs), you might have ended up being 6 feet 8 inches tall (2.03 meters) and a star basketball player. Or, given inadequate nutrition and early ill-health, you might have ended up only 5 feet 6 inches (1.67 meters). Thus does the environment interact with genotype to determine which of the many possible outcomes—that is, which reaction from the range of all possible reactions—will be manifested. One of the important tasks of the psychologist is to determine the nature and timing of experiences that are most likely to have a beneficial influence on phenotype.

Molecular Genetics

Mendelian genetics, named after Gregor Mendel, the 19th-century monk who discovered the first secrets of genes, makes inferences about the dominance and recessiveness of genes largely by looking at the characteristics of parents and of offspring. In contrast, **molecular genetics** studies heredity by looking at the actual structure of genes. The techniques of molecular genetics make it possible to examine chromosomes directly, to look at sequences of DNA molecules, to identify their specific chemical components, and to locate chemical segments that correspond to genes. One way of doing this is to use certain *enzymes* that serve to cut through sequences of DNA (Wingerson, 1990). Where two individuals have identical DNA sequences, the length of the resulting fragments will be different; but if the sequences are different, the resulting fragments will be of different lengths (called *restriction fragment length polymorphisms,* or RFLPs). Thus RFLPs (pronounced "rifflips") allow geneticists to identify genes on specific chromosomes that are associated with the presence or absence of some observable characteristic. These genes are called **marker genes.** Marker genes are genes that are common to the general population; they are normally found in all individuals (Emery & Mueller, 1992).

Marker genes have now been discovered for all chromosomes. By 1992, more than 2,500 such genes had been assigned to specific locations on specific chromosomes (McKusick, 1992). Relatively recent discoveries include the gene for Huntington's disease (described later in this chapter) and a marker gene for a wide variety of human cancers (Offner, 1992; 1993).

Offner (1992) cautions that although the emphasis seems to be on identifying genes associated with diseases and defects, genes should not be seen merely as things that cause problems. In fact, our genes are complex sets of instructions for putting together *normal* human beings. The importance of studying defective genes, however, lies in the possibility of correcting those that are defective or, at the very least, of identifying their presence early—perhaps even before conception (Wills, 1993).

More than 95 percent of our genes still remain unmapped (Friedman et al., 1992). A massive federally funded genetics project is now underway in the United States. Its goal is eventually to provide a complete genetic map of the human being—a map of what is termed the **genome,** the complete set of genetic instructions contained in our cells (Bishop & Waldholz, 1990).

The implications of success in this endeavor are staggering. Correcting genetic defects might be possible, and so could accurately predicting the outcome of different gene pairings. What happens next? Does medicine play God? Do governments engineer genes to produce the kinds of people they want? Do chromosomal tests become mandatory? Do they become part of who we are, like our Social Security numbers?

GENETIC DEFECTS

"Genes are instructions for assembling an organism," says Offner (1993). "It is only when there is a mistake in these instructions that a genetic disease results" (p. 406). In most cases, the resulting disease is linked with *recessive* rather than *dominant* genes. The reason for this is simple: Abnormalities linked with a dominant gene are always manifested in all carriers and have much less chance of being passed on to offspring—especially if they lead to early death. In contrast, abnormalities linked to recessive genes are manifested only when the carrier inherits *two* related recessive genes. Thus, individuals who are carriers of a single recessive gene for some abnormality don't manifest the abnormality and are more likely to pass the gene on to their offspring—who will, likewise, not manifest the abnormality unless they inherit a *second* defective gene from the other parent.

Because related individuals (cousins, for example) have so many genes in common, they are more likely also to share defective genes. It is precisely for this reason that the risk of genetic disorders among the children of biologically related parents is so much higher than for children whose parents are not related. In contrast, if a person who is a carrier of a defective recessive gene mates with someone who does not carry the gene, there is only one chance in four that the offspring will inherit the gene and no chance that this offspring will manifest the disorder (because the gene is recessive). Thus continued matings among individuals who are not biologically related may, over a period of generations, eventually succeed in eradicating or greatly reducing the incidence of the recessive gene in question. By the same token, continued matings among family members might lead to a proliferation of the gene and a corresponding increase in the manifestation of the disorder it underlies (see At a Glance: "Hemophilia Among Royalty," and Figure 3.6).

Huntington's Disease

Most very serious or fatal genetic disorders are linked with recessive genes (otherwise all carriers would be affected and would either die before having children or would be aware of the risks involved and refrain from parenthood). One exception, however, is **Huntington's disease** (also

HEMOPHILIA AMONG ROYALTY

Hemophilia-A is a sex-linked recessive genetic disorder. Males who carry the recessive gene on their X chromosome are always affected: Their blood-clotting mechanisms don't work properly, and they run the risk of dying from untreated bruises, cuts, or internal bleeding. Females who carry the recessive gene on one X chromosome typically also have the normal *dominant* gene on the other X chromosome. Thus they don't suffer from the disease, but they can pass the defective gene on to their children. Many of the royal families of 19th-century Europe carried the gene. Queen Victoria of England was a carrier, and so were two of her daughters (Figure 3.6).

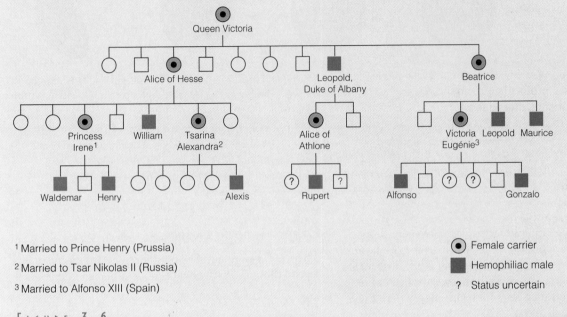

[1] Married to Prince Henry (Prussia)

[2] Married to Tsar Nikolas II (Russia)

[3] Married to Alfonso XIII (Spain)

FIGURE 3.6
Descendants of Queen Victoria, showing female carriers and affected males.

called Huntington's chorea), which is both fatal and associated with a dominant gene. The disorder is still present because it does not ordinarily manifest itself until the age of 30 or 40—after which it leads to rapid neurological deterioration and eventual death.

Until recently, there was no way of determining whether an individual carried the dominant gene for Huntington's disease so that a person whose parents or other relatives had cases of Huntington's could only wait to see whether the disease would eventually strike. Now, however, the gene has been identified, making it possible to determine relatively accurately the probability that an individual will be affected (Hayden, 1992). However, because Huntington's disease is fatal and incurable, many individuals who might be carriers of the gene prefer not to be screened. Jacopini and associates (1992) found that fewer than half of those who knew they were at risk intended to take advantage of the screening offered to them. Among the most common reasons for refusing to be tested are lack of treatment or cure, fear of losing health insurance, and inability to "undo" the knowledge (Quaid & Morris, 1993). However, as for other genetically based disorders, there exists the possibility of eventually being able to replace this defective DNA sequence with a normal gene.

Sickle-Cell Anemia

Sickle-cell anemia is a genetic disorder linked to a recessive gene. Approximately 10 percent of all blacks in the United States, and a much lower proportion of whites, carry the recessive gene for sickle-cell anemia (Thompson, Gil, & Abrams, 1992) (Figure 3.7). These 10 percent are **heterozygous** for this gene (having one normal and one abnormal gene); another 0.25 percent of the black population is **homozygous** (carrying two defective genes). Effects of the defective gene are clearly apparent in abnormally shaped red blood cells (sickle-shaped rather

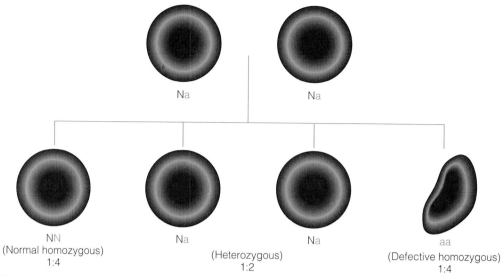

FIGURE 3.7

An illustration of recessive gene action in the determination of sickle-cell anemia. Parents are heterozygous; that is, they possess one normal (N) and one defective (a) gene, and will therefore not suffer from the disease. A child born to these parents will have one chance in four of not carrying the defective gene, one chance in two of being heterozygous, and one chance in four of possessing two defective genes and therefore suffering from sickle-cell anemia.

than circular), which multiply with lack of oxygen (Figure 3.8). Those who are homozygous for this gene often die in childhood or are severely ill throughout life. Those who are heterozygous are ordinarily healthy except in conditions of low oxygen such as at high altitudes, where they may become quite ill.

PKU

Phenylketonuria or **PKU** is a genetic defect associated with the presence of two recessive genes. It occurs throughout the world but is considerably more common among some ethnic groups such as the Gypsies of eastern Slovakia (Kalanin et al., 1994). In individuals suffering from this disease, the liver enzyme responsible for breaking down phenylalanine into usable substances is absent or inactive. Infants who inherit the two recessive genes for PKU appear normal at birth, but with the continued ingestion of phenylalanine (which makes up about 5 percent of the weight of protein), their nervous system deteriorates irreversibly, and they become increasingly mentally retarded (Costello et al., 1994). Fortunately, however, PKU is easily detected at birth, and its onset can be prevented by providing children with diets low in phenylalanine from infancy (Curtius, Endres, & Blau, 1994).

PKU is a striking example of a highly canalized tendency that is nevertheless subject to environmental influence. The disorder is clearly genetic, but in the absence of specific environmental influences (the ingestion of phenylalanine), the individual's phenotype will not reflect genotype.

Other Genetic Defects

There are a large number of other genetic defects; in fact several thousand have now been identified and catalogued.

Tay–Sachs Disease

Tay–Sachs disease, associated with a recessive gene, is an enzyme disorder that results in the brain's inability to break down certain fats. Eventually these build up, preventing neural transmission, and leading to the degeneration of brain cells. Affected individuals commonly die before the age of three. Tay–Sachs disease can be detected before birth but cannot yet be prevented or cured (Suzuki, 1994).

Muscular Dystrophy (MD)

A degenerative muscular disorder of which there are various forms, **muscular dystrophy (MD)** is often linked to a recessive gene or is multifactorial. It usually involves an inability to walk, and may lead to death. Some forms of MD (for example, *Duchenne* and *Becker MD*) can be detected in the fetus through genetic examination. In addition, parents can be tested to arrive at an estimate of the probability that their offspring will be affected (Kruyer et al., 1994).

Neural Tube Defects

Among the most common congenital malformations are **neural tube defects,** which occur at a rate of 1 for every 500 to 1,000 births (Miller et al., 1990). Neural tube defects may take the form of *spina bifida*, in which the spine remains open at the bottom, or of *anencephaly*, in which

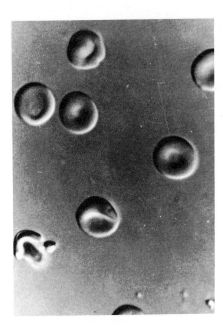

FIGURE 3.8
On the left, normal oxygenated red blood cells; on the right, sickle cells.

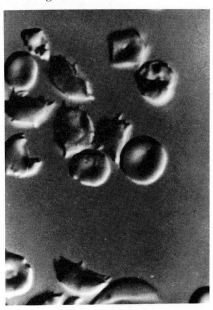

portions of the skull and brain are absent. Such defects often lead to severe retardation or death. Although genetically linked, the causes of these defects are multifactorial. They generally develop very early in pregnancy (as early as the first week), and can be detected by means of an **AFP test**—a standard test conducted at about the 13th week of pregnancy, which looks at the level of *alphafetoprotein* in the mother's blood. If this substance is present in concentrations higher than usual, further tests such as ultrasound or fetoscopy (described later) are performed to determine whether there is a neural tube defect. In some jurisdictions, AFP screening is routine or even mandatory (as are tests for PKU).

Diabetes Mellitus

Some forms of **diabetes,** an insulin deficiency disease, are associated with recessive genes, as well as with other factors. Children born to mothers with *diabetes mellitus* have a two to three times higher risk of birth defects. These can include limb deformities, cardiac problems, neural tube defects, and other problems (Friedman, 1992).

Nonmedical Conditions

In addition to the several thousand known medical conditions that are clearly genetically linked, there is increasing evidence of a genetic basis for at least some manifestations of emotional and behavioral problems such as alcoholism, depression, anorexia nervosa, infantile autism, and schizophrenia. For some of these conditions, specific marker genes have been located. However, their causes are usually multifactorial; accordingly, they are highly susceptible to environmental influence.

CHROMOSOMAL DISORDERS

Genetic defects are linked to specific recessive or dominant genes, or to a combination of genes; they may also be related to certain environmental conditions. **Chromosomal disorders,** on the other hand, are associated not with specific genes but with errors in chromosomes. Many of these errors result from improper divisions and recombinations during meiosis.

Down Syndrome

The most common chromosomal birth defect, **Down syndrome,** affects about 1 out of every 680 live births. About twice that many fetuses are affected by the condition, but approximately half result in spontaneous miscarriages during the first third of pregnancy (Dill & McGillivray, 1992).

Some children with Down syndrome have characteristic loose folds of skin over the corners of the eyes, producing an Oriental appearance; hence the now uncommon label "mongolism." Also, mental retardation is common among children with Down syndrome, and their language development is often retarded (Kumin, 1994). Not all children are equally affected.

Common Cause of Down Syndrome

Most cases of Down syndrome are due to failure of the 21st pair of chromosomes to separate during meiosis (termed *nondisjunction*). Hence the resulting gamete (sex cell) has an extra copy of the 21st chromosome (thus the alternative medical label *Trisomy 21*). When this gamete is

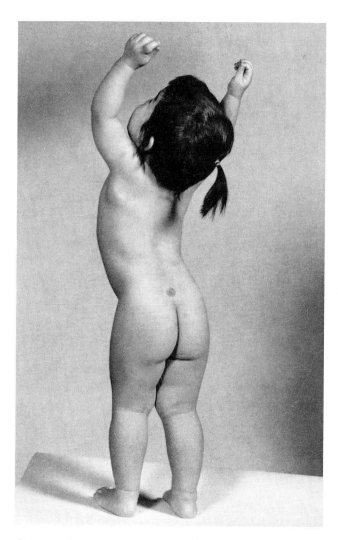

Down syndrome, the most common chromosomal birth defect, is closely related to parental age, and is often associated with mental retardation. But not all Down syndrome children are equally affected.

combined with the other gamete during fertilization, the zygote (fertilized egg) has an extra 21st chromosome.

Down Syndrome and Parental Age

Nondisjunction of the 21st chromosome is closely linked with the age of parents, and most often occurs during meiosis of the ovum rather than of the sperm. Thus, about 95 percent of Down syndrome cases are associated with the mother; the other 5 percent are associated with the father (Antonarakis, 1991). The probability of producing a child with Down syndrome is about 1 in 1,420 for women in their early twenties; it's close to 1 in 30 for women aged 45 (Dill & McGillivray, 1992; see Figure 3.9). Fathers aged 50 to 55 have a 20 to 30 percent greater chance of fathering children with Down syndrome.

Because medical science knows precisely what the genetic cause of Down syndrome is, it is possible to detect its presence in the fetus before birth. Procedures for doing so are discussed later in this chapter.

Abnormalities of the Sex Chromosomes

A number of chromosomal defects are linked to the sex chromosome. Some involve the absence of a chromosome; others, the presence of an extra chromosome.

Turner's Syndrome

Turner's syndrome affects 1 out of 2,500 female children (Dill & McGillivray, 1992) who are born with a missing sex chromosome (designated as 45, X or XO, rather than 46, XX; the "45" indicates the total number of chromosomes). Most such children are aborted spontaneously; those who do survive typically have underdeveloped secondary sexual characteristics, although this is not evident until puberty. Possible symptoms of the disorder include swelling in the extremities that disappears with age—leaving loose folds of skin (webbing) particularly in the neck region, fingers, and toes—and short stature. Mental ability is usually normal. Injections of the female sex hormone *estrogen* before puberty is sometimes helpful in bringing about greater sexual maturation, although Turner's syndrome females are sterile (Emery & Mueller, 1992).

Klinefelter's Syndrome

Klinefelter's syndrome involves the presence of an extra X chromosome in a male child (thus 47, XXY), and is considerably more common than Turner's syndrome (1 out of 1,000 males; Dill & McGillivray, 1992). It is marked by the presence of both male and female secondary sexual characteristics. Boys suffering from this disorder typically have small, undeveloped testicles, high-pitched voices, some breast development, and little or no facial hair after puberty. Therapy with the male sex hormone *testosterone* is often effective in improving the development of masculine characteristics and in increasing sex drive. Without therapy, many children suffering from Klinefelter's syndrome remain infertile throughout life. Also, incidence of schizophrenia is higher among Klinefelter's children (Friedman & McGillivray, 1992).

XYY Males

Males with an extra Y chromosome (47, XYY), sometimes referred to as "super males" because of the extra male chromosome, are characteristically tall; sometimes, they are also of lower than average intelligence. Some research evidence has linked this syndrome with criminality, but the conclusion remains tentative (Emery & Mueller, 1992). However, *XYY males* are often less mature and more impulsive than normal.

Fragile X Syndrome

Fragile X syndrome is the most common cause of *inherited* mental retardation and has, by many accounts, been greatly underestimated (Patel, 1994; Wiebe & Wiebe, 1994). Note that Down syndrome, which accounts for more cases of mental retardation, is not inherited in the sense that corresponding genes are transmitted from par-

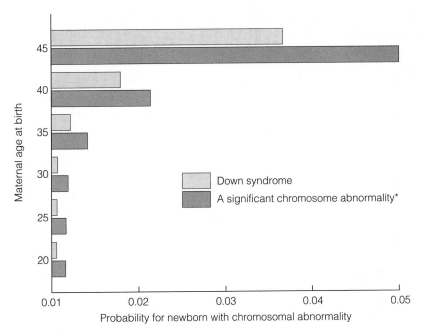

*Excludes unbalanced translocation and XXX

ents to children, but results instead from an abnormality in how chromosomes divide.

In fragile X syndrome, the X sex chromosome is abnormally compressed or even broken. Although the condition can also occur in females, it is far more common among males, and is one of the reasons why there are more mentally retarded males than females in the general population (Zigler & Hodapp, 1991). Interestingly, about 70 percent of females with fragile X syndrome are of normal intelligence; this is the case for only about 20 percent of affected males (Dill & McGillivray, 1992). In addition, about 12 percent of autistic children are fragile X (Wolf-Schein, 1992).

Unlike Down syndrome, in which mental retardation is typically apparent very early in life, fragile X individuals often manifest no symptoms of retardation until puberty (Silverstein & Johnston, 1990). Between the years of 10 and 15, however, there is frequently a marked decline in intellectual functioning, which becomes more severe with advancing age (Maes et al., 1994).

Other Sex-Linked Defects

The X chromosome is the site not only for genes related to fragile X syndrome but also for genes related to other defects such as night-blindness, baldness, and hemophilia. Each of these defects is associated with recessive genes; and each, like the fragile X syndrome, is far more common among males than females. Why? Simply because females who inherit the defective gene on one of their two X chromosomes often have the corresponding *normal* gene on the other chromosome. As a result, they are *carriers* of the defective gene but don't manifest the disorder because the gene is recessive. Males, on the other hand, have only one X chromosome; their other sex chromosome is a Y. In many cases, the normal dominant genes that would counter the effect of the recessive gene for one of these disorders is not present on the Y chromosome. Accordingly, males manifest conditions like hereditary baldness (and the fragile X syndrome) far more often than do females. Yet the gene is passed on from mother to son—not from father to son (because the father always passes on a Y chromosome to his sons, and the mother always passes on the X chromosome).

GENETIC RISK

Medical advances and improved nutrition have greatly reduced infections and nutritional deficiencies for which children are hospitalized, note Emery and Mueller (1992). Now, about 1 in 20 children admitted to hospitals suffer from problems that are at least partly genetic in origin.

For disorders that are linked directly to the presence or absence of known genes, it is sometimes possible to identify affected children before birth. For other disorders whose origins are only partly genetic or for which the genetic contributions are complex and not completely known, it is nevertheless often possible to determine the *probability* that a child will be affected.

Fetal Diagnosis

Fetal diagnosis is the assessment of the condition of the unborn. There are six principal techniques for fetal diagnosis.

Amniocentesis

In **amniocentesis** a hollow needle is inserted into the amniotic fluid surrounding the fetus, allowing the physician to obtain 15 to 20 ml of **amniotic fluid** that contains fetal cells. These can then be analyzed to reveal the absence of chromosomes or the presence of extra chromosomes, as well as the blood type of the fetus and the chemical composition of the amniotic fluid. Many diseases and defects that might affect the unborn child can thus be detected. Because the procedure involves a slight risk of infection and leads to miscarriages in from .5 to 1 percent of cases, it is commonly employed only in those cases where the pregnant woman is older and where there is a probability of fetal abnormality or other complications (Ryall et al., 1992). Amniocentesis is not usually performed until the 15th to 17th week of pregnancy.

One of the most common uses of amniocentesis has been for the detection of Trisomy 21 (Down syndrome). Because of the moderate risks associated with the procedure, and because incidence of Trisomy 21 increases dramatically with age (see Figure 3.9), the procedure is most commonly used when the mother is 35 or more, or when a younger mother is known to be at risk. However, because about 95 percent of pregnant women are under 35, initial screening by age alone misses about 80 percent of Down syndrome fetuses (Kloza, 1990).

Fortunately, there is now another way of screening women who are at higher risk of bearing a child with Down syndrome. Specifically, it has been discovered that the level of *alpha fetoprotein* (AFP) serum in the pregnant woman's blood is significantly lower than normal. (Recall that AFP levels are routinely assessed to detect the likelihood of neural tube defects, with higher than normal levels indicating a higher probability of problems.) Thus AFP tests can identify mothers of all ages who are at risk of bearing a child with Down syndrome (Rose et al., 1994).

Chorionic Villus Biopsy (CVS)

Chorion biopsy (*chorionic villus biopsy* or *CVS*) is a medical procedure for obtaining and examining fetal cells. In CVS, a plastic tube is inserted through the vagina (or a fine needle through the abdomen) to obtain a sample of the chorion (Liu, 1991). The chorion contains the same genetic information as the fetus. The advantage of a chorion biopsy over amniocentesis is that it can be performed as early as seven weeks after conception. Also, because it provides enough fetal cells, chromosomal examination can usually be performed the same day (Young, 1991). Amniocentesis, on the other hand, requires a two- to three-week period of tissue culture, and does not provide results until well into the second trimester of pregnancy. If the results lead to a decision to terminate the pregnancy, this can be accomplished more simply and more safely in the first trimester. Chorion biopsy procedures are somewhat more experimental than amniocentesis and carry a slightly higher risk of complications (de Saint-Hilaire, 1992).

Ultrasound

Ultrasound (sometimes called *sonogram*) provides computer-enhanced, sound-wave generated images of the fetus in "real time." It is among the least harmful and least invasive technique currently available, and is the method of choice for proving the presence of a living fetus. It is the most exact means for estimating fetal age, detecting the position of the fetus, discerning changes in fetal position, detecting multiple pregnancies, and identifying a variety of growth disorders and malformations. Ultrasound images make it possible to see the beginnings of fetal activity including behaviors such as thumb sucking; they also allow the physician to examine bone structure, to assess length of bones, to determine relationships among the size and growth of various bodily structures, and even to count fingers and toes. Ultrasound is always used with amniocentesis or CVS to guide the physician, but is not a substitute for these procedures because it cannot provide actual samples of fetal cells.

Fetoscopy

Fetoscopy is a surgical procedure that allows the physician to *see* the fetus. It is used mainly to obtain samples of tissues from the fetus itself, the most important being blood. Fetoscopy can furnish the physician with crucial information about the status of the fetus, especially when there is a possibility of disorders such as hemophilia. However, it carries higher risks than amniocentesis (about a 3 to 5 percent higher probability of miscarriage) (Emery & Mueller, 1992).

Radiography

Some inherited disorders and malformations can be diagnosed through *radiography*—that is, by means of X-rays of the fetus. However, because of the possibility that X-rays may harm the fetus, whenever possible, sonograms are used instead.

Preimplantation Diagnosis

All fetal diagnostic techniques we've considered so far can only be carried out after the fetus has begun to develop. However, it is now possible to determine the chromosomal structure of the fetus *before* the fertilized egg is implanted. One way of doing this is to remove the mature egg and fertilize it with the father's sperm (in vitro fertilization). The zygote is then allowed to multiply to the 8-cell stage, and a single cell is removed and examined for the presence of specific genetic disorders—all within a matter of hours. Removal of a single cell apparently does not affect later development. If no defects are found, the zygote can then be implanted in the uterus (Emery & Mueller, 1992). The great advantage of preimplantation diagnosis is that it can identify problems before a therapeutic abortion would otherwise be necessary. However, it is still limited to a handful of advanced, highly specialized medical centers.

TABLE 3.1
Probability of Some Common Genetic Defects

Genetic Defect	Incidence (per 100 Population)	Sex Ratio (M:F)	Normal Parents Having a Second Affected Child (%)	Affected Parent Having an Affected Child (%)	Affected Parent Having a Second Affected Child (%)
Asthma	3.0–4.0	1:1	10	26	—
Cerebral palsy	.2	3:2	1	—*	—
Cleft palate only	.04	2:3	2	7	15
Cleft lip and/or cleft palate	.1	3:2	4	4	10
Club foot	.1	2:1	3	3	10
Congenital heart disease (all types)	.5	1:1	1–4	1–4	10
Diabetes mellitus (juvenile, insulin-dependent)	.2	1:1	6	1–2	—
Dislocation of hip	.7	1:6	6	12	36
Epilepsy ("idiopathic")	.5	1:1	5	5	10
Hydrocephalus	.005	1:1	3	—	—
Manic-depressive psychosis	.4	2:3	10–15	10–15	—
Mental retardation (of unknown cause)	.3–.5	1:1	3–5	10	20
Profound childhood deafness	.1	1:1	10	8	—
Schizophrenia	1.0–2.0	1:1	10	16	—
Spina bifida (neural tube defect)	.3	2:3	5	4	—
Tracheo-esophageal fistula	.03	1:1	1	1	—

SOURCE: Adapted from *Elements of Medical Genetics* (8th ed.) by A. E. H. Emery & R. Mueller. Edinburgh and London: Churchill-Livingstone, 1992. Used by permission.

* — means no data.

Treating Genetic Disorders

Not all genetically based disorders are equally serious. Many can be treated and controlled; some can be cured. For example, the effects of PKU, as we saw, can be prevented through diet. And in the next chapter, we see how the effects of Rh incompatibility in the fetus, once a usually fatal condition, can be prevented through inoculation of the mother, or reversed through blood transfusions. For other conditions, it is sometimes possible to replace deficient enzymes, proteins, vitamins, or other substances (the use of insulin to control diabetes, for example). Similarly, various drugs or even surgery may be used to control and sometimes cure genetic disease (cancer, for example).

Emery and Mueller (1992) suggest that in addition to these medical treatments, there are several other *possible* though not yet *proven* treatments. One involves the use of clones (identical copies) of normal genes to replace those that are defective; another is the use of viruses or even of antibiotics to eradicate bacteria or other agents involved in the development of genetically linked diseases.

Genetic Counseling

Although fetal (and preimplantation) diagnosis, along with monitoring changes in the mother, provide powerful tools for detecting potential problems, there are many genetically based problems that medical science cannot determine with absolute certainty. In some cases, however, it's possible to assign a numerical value to the probability of a given outcome. When this occurs, parents and physicians may be faced with difficult decisions involving serious ethical questions. In these situations, genetic counseling offers a valuable service.

What Is Genetic Counseling?

Genetic counseling is a branch of medicine and of psychology that attempts to provide counsel to physicians and parents. Such counseling typically strives to assess the probability of a defect occurring, its likely seriousness, the extent to which it can be treated and even reversed, and the best courses of action to follow once a decision has been made about whether to have a child. In many instances, genetic counseling will take place before conception and might take into account the age and health of the mother as well as the presence of genetic abnormalities in ancestors or in siblings. In other cases, genetic counseling will occur after conception (see Table 3.1).

The Future in Genetics

Genetic counseling has traditionally been limited to advising prospective parents about the likelihood of their having a child with a given problem, and providing them with information about their options. And the options have typically consisted of deciding to try to conceive, or not to; or deciding to have a therapeutic abortion, or not to. It may be different in the very near future.

Rewriting Genetic Messages

We now appear to be on the threshold of a new age. Almost daily, there are new discoveries in genetics. We are now able to detect genetic weaknesses, as well as strengths, from the very earliest moments of life. Our mushrooming knowledge of cell biology at the molecular level is opening new doors into the vast and almost uncharted world of genetic engineering. Science is breaking the genetic code. It's learning to read the messages that direct the arrangements of the amino acids that, in turn, define the structure and function of the protein molecules that are the fundamental units of our biological lives. Science has begun to experiment with ways of altering genetic messages, of rewriting the code to enhance the possibilities implicit in our genes or to correct errors. Using recombinant DNA techniques, scientists can use bacteria to reproduce sequences of genetic material. The results include new medications, new refining and manufacturing processes, new products, even new lives.

Genetic Speculation

Pergament (1990) suggests that the following developments are possible, perhaps even highly probable, for the 21st century:

- By 2001 it will be possible to separate X- and Y-bearing sperm, to inactivate one or the other, and therefore to select the sex of the child prior to conception.

- By 2002, science will have discovered how to preserve mature ova that can then be banked and used for reproduction in future generations.[*]

- Using technologies of robotics, computers, and genetic engineering, by 2003 the analysis of chromosomes will be simple and accurate.

- The human genome will have been completely mapped by 2005 so that by 2010 it will be possible to analyze genetic makeup prior to implantation and, using in vitro fertilization, to ensure the genetic health of the zygote.

- By 2020, gene scanners will permit detailed analyses of all chromosomes, not only in the egg and sperm, but also in human tissue (kidneys, eyes, bladder, and so on) to detect anomalies and mutations.

- And by 2050, says Pergament, the artificial womb will have been perfected. Now it will be possible to take long-preserved ova and sperm, join them in vitro, and let the artificial womb take over.

*It happened before 2002. Ova can now be preserved, to be fertilized later.

Ethical Issues

There are ethical issues involved here—important ethical issues. Some have to do with the potential dangers of experiments that can, theoretically, produce new forms of life, the consequences of which cannot really be imagined because the nature of that life may be unknown before its creation. Other issues have to do with the morality of altering genetic codes, with the ethics of decisions relating to creating or ending life, with the legality and morality of surrogate mothering and artificial insemination, maybe even with the very definition of life. Responding to these concerns, a Canadian commission (the Royal Commission on Reproductive Technologies) has proposed 293 recommendations to govern genetic research and its applications (Kondro, 1992). The commission advocates jail sentences or fines for researchers trying to clone human embryos, produce human-animal hybrids, or sell human eggs, sperm, embryos, or fetal tissue ("Tough Curbs Urged for Reproductive Medicine," 1993). "This is not a medical policy but a social matter," explained Patricia Baird (1994), chair of the commission. "We must be careful not to commodify human beings, and commercialize human reproduction" ("Baird Sounds Off at Snell," 1994, p. 3).

Perhaps by 2050 these issues will have become more important than the science that gave them birth, and another new discipline will have arisen to deal with them. But we have not yet reached that stage, and we continue to struggle with questions whose answers are not at all clear. Although we know vastly more now than we did even 10 years ago, there is still much about our beginnings—and our ends—that we do not understand.

STUDYING GENE–CONTEXT INTERACTION

Genesis means beginning and unfolding. Our genes are aptly named: They are clearly our beginnings. And, in interaction with our contexts, they are also involved in guiding our development. "Genes do not by themselves produce structural or functional characteristics," says Lerner (1991, p. 27). Instead, they *interact* with context to produce change. The current emphasis in genetic research is on finding out how context and genes work together. Keep in mind that genetic and environmental forces do not compete; rather, they work together to increase the individual's adaptation (Lerner, 1993).

Galton's Conclusion

Family members share a wide range of genes and are therefore a good source of information about gene–context interaction. As Plomin (1987) points out, there is 100-percent genetic similarity between pairs of identical twins, approximately 50-percent similarity among siblings who share both parents, and somewhere around 25-percent similarity among stepsiblings who share only one parent.

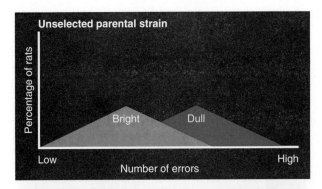

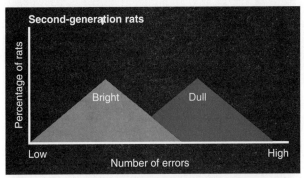

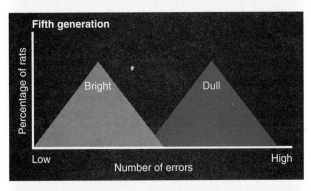

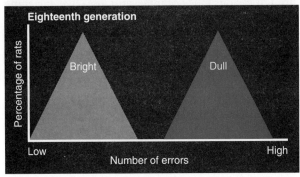

FIGURE 3.10
An approximate representation of Tryon's successful attempt to breed maze-bright and maze-dull rats. After 18 generations of selective breeding, the dullest rats among the bright group were now brighter than the smartest of the dull group. (Based on Tryon, 1940, p. 113.)

point. An environmentalist might argue, for example, that the reason these families produced outstanding scientists was simply that they provided children with environments conducive to the development of genius.

Animal Studies

Gene–environment interactions can sometimes be studied more easily with animals than with humans, not only because certain physiological measurements are sometimes possible with animals but not with humans (brain dissections, for example), but also because animal environments can be controlled far more completely than human environments. In addition, animal matings can be controlled precisely, and many generations can be produced and studied within a relatively short period of time. Not so with humans. But there are, of course, some serious limitations of animal studies, not the least of which is the difficulty of generalizing findings from animals to humans.

The classical study of genetic influence in rats is that of Tryon (1940), who began by having his rats learn a maze to test their intelligence. Fast learners were then mated with other fast learners, and slow learners were paired with other slow learners. After only 18 generations, there was no longer any overlap between the groups. The dullest rats among the bright group were now brighter than the smartest of the dull group, and vice versa (see Figure 3.10).

Other animal studies have demonstrated it is possible to breed different strains of the same species that are predictably different in some identifiable characteristic. For example, in only a few generations mice can be bred for aggression, emotionality, preference for alcohol, and other characteristics (see Cairns, Gariépy, & Hood, 1990). In much the same way, various "personality" characteristics have been developed in different breeds of dogs: fierceness and fighting ability in pit bull terriers, vigilance in German shepherds, obstinacy and contrariness in the Lefrançois hound.

Animal Studies of Gene–Context Interactions

But even in rats and dogs and other nonhuman animals, genetics by itself tells only part of the story. Consider, for example, the song thrush, which dearly loves to eat snails and which does so by grabbing the snail in its beak and smashing the shell against a rock by means of a rapid, sideways motion of its head, back and forth, back and forth (Weisfeld, 1982). This appears to be a genetically influenced behavior because the European blackbird, a close

The high degree of genetic relatedness among members of families is what led Francis Galton, Charles Darwin's cousin, to conclude that intelligence is largely hereditary. He had noticed that most of England's outstanding scientists came from a small number of families. As a result, he argued that parents should be selected for favorable genetic characteristics—a practice termed **eugenics.** Not very good research, surely. Even if Galton's observations were entirely accurate, they didn't prove his

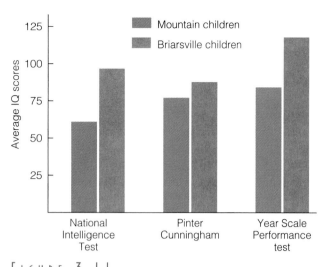

FIGURE 3.11
Comparisons between Mountain children and Briarsville children on some measures of intelligence.

Twins occur rarely in human births—approximately 1 in every 86 births. Identical twins are rarer—perhaps 1 in 300 or so births among caucasians and far fewer among the Chinese or Japanese. Twins provide researchers with an excellent opportunity to separate the effects of heredity and environment. Triplets, such as the Koralja trio, who are Jersey City policemen, are even rarer than twins.

relative of the song thrush that also eats snails, doesn't seem to be able to learn the same smash-the-snail's-shell* behavior. But it is also an environmentally influenced behavior because the young song thrush doesn't instinctively know how to smash a snail shell; it learns to do so largely by trial and error during a critical period early in its life. If it's not given an opportunity to learn during this critical period, it goes through life never knowing how to eat a snail properly, the way other song thrushes do it.

What investigations such as these illustrate most clearly is the complexity of gene–environment interaction, even for behaviors we might assume to be entirely genetically based. In addition, animal studies suggest that behaviors having important adaptive functions become more probable through succeeding generations. Because these behaviors have to do with biological adaptation and the survival and propagation of species, they are typically related to feeding, rest, defense, reproduction, or elimination (Weisfeld, 1982).

Genetically Determined Behaviors in Humans

Are there similar, genetically ordained behaviors among humans? Some researchers think so. These behaviors, they argue, are common to all members of the species—hence common to all human cultures. In addition, they occur in the absence of experiences that might otherwise explain their acquisition. Weisfeld (1982) suggests these genetically programmed behaviors might include such things as the infant's distress at being separated from the mother or other caregiver (more about this in Chapter 6); the tendency of mothers in all cultures to hold their infants on the left side, whether or not they are right-handed; various facial expressions that have identical

*Say that four times real fast. Then get back to your studying.

meanings everywhere (such as the human smile, which occurs in blind as well as in sighted infants); and human vocalizations, which are initially identical in deaf and in hearing infants.

Intervention Studies

Another way of studying gene–environment interactions is through various kinds of interventions—like enriching or depriving an individual's environment to see what the effects might be.

The Sherman and Key Study

An early study by Sherman and Key (1932) provides tentative evidence of the effects of a "natural" rather than experimental kind of intervention. The study compared the intelligence test scores of the *Mountain children* (from isolated families, no newspapers, magazines, or other forms of reading material, nor any consistent contact with the outside world) with a control group in a more typical environment (the *Briarsville children*). The Briarsville children had been exposed to conventional schooling and had access to the offerings of the wider culture through newspapers and so on. Results of the comparison are shown in Figure 3.11. Note that the Briarsville children performed significantly better than the Mountain children on all three measures of intellectual performance.

Sherman and Key argue that these differences reflect the effects of environmental characteristics. But that isn't the only explanation. We don't know, for example, whether the parents of these children were comparable in terms of

No. of Correlations	34	3	3	8	41	69	2	32	4	2	4	5	6	8	8	16
No. of Pairings	4,672	65	410	982	5,546	26,473	203	8,433	814	200	1,176	345	369	758	1,397	3,817
Median Correlation	.85	.67	.73	.475	.58	.45	.24	.385	.22	.35	.145	.29	.31	.19	.18	.365

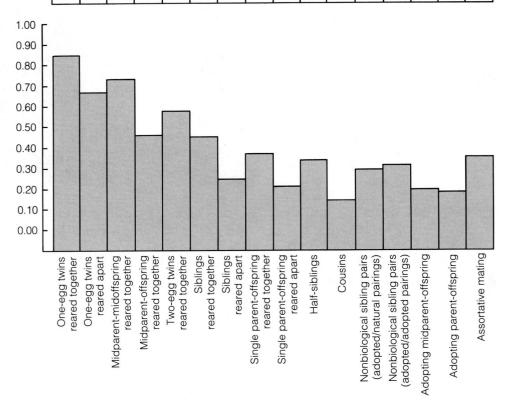

Figure 3.12

Median correlation coefficients for intelligence test scores from a large number of studies. The high correlation for identical twins shows the strong genetic basis of measured intelligence. The greater correlation for siblings or twins reared together compared with those reared apart supports the view that environmental forces are also important in determining similarity of intelligence test scores. (From T. J. Bouchard and M. McGue (1981). Familial studies of intelligence: A review, Science, 212, 1055–1059. © 1981 by the AAAS. Used by permission.)

intelligence; none were tested. Maybe the parents who chose to isolate themselves in the mountains were less intelligent than those who lived closer to the cultural mainstream. It's also possible that they were more intelligent.

Head Start as Intervention

There is an abundance of more recent and better controlled interventions. One example is Project Head Start, a massive, federally funded American program designed to alleviate, through intervention, some of the possible disadvantages of being born and raised in homes less advantaged economically, socially, and intellectually.

There have been more than 2,000 different Head Start programs (Zigler & Freedman, 1987). Many of these lasted only a few hours a day, and many did not expose children to systematic, well-thought-out experiences. In general, however, the evidence is that higher-quality programs are effective in increasing measured intelligence, and that children exposed to such programs often do better in subjects such as mathematics. In addition, there are usually improvements in more-difficult-to-measure areas such as social functioning (Zigler & Freedman, 1987).

Studies of Twins

"If I had any desire to lead a life of indolent ease," Stephen Jay Gould tells us, "I would wish to be an identical twin, separated at birth from my brother and raised in a different social class. We could hire ourselves out to a host of social scientists and practically name our fee. For we would be exceedingly rare representatives of the only really adequate natural experiment for separating genetic from environmental effects in humans" (1981, p. 234). Why is this so? Because identical twins are genetically identical; they result from the splitting of a single zygote, a fertilized ovum, into two genetically identical fertilized eggs (hence **monozygotic** or **identical twins**). The other type of twins results from the fertilization of two *different* egg cells by two *different* spermatozoa (hence **dizygotic** or **fraternal twins**). This is possible only when the mother produces more than one egg and results in twins who are no more alike genetically than ordinary **siblings.**

Unfortunately for research, the incidence of twins is relatively low—approximately 1 in every 86 births. Furthermore, identical twins are much rarer than fraternal twins—perhaps 1 in 300 births in North America. The precise causes of twin births are not known, although heredity appears to be a factor, because twins are found relatively frequently in some families and not at all in others. Also, older parents are more likely to have twins than are younger parents (Ernst & Angst, 1983).

Intelligence

Many studies of twins have looked at correlations for intelligence test scores. Recall from Chapter 1 that a correlation is a measure of relationship usually expressed in numbers ranging from 0 to plus or minus 1. A high *positive* correlation—say +0.75 to +1.00—means that if one twin has a low or high intelligence test score, the other is likely to have a correspondingly low or high score also. A high *negative* correlation—say, −0.75 to −1.00—means that a high score for one would be associated with a low score for the other.

In general, the median correlation for intelligence test scores for identical twins is above +0.80, whereas that for fraternal twins is below +0.60 (see Figure 3.12). If members of identical and fraternal twin pairs have had similar environments, these correlations may be interpreted as evidence that measured intelligence is influenced by heredity.

As Figure 3.12 also shows, with decreasing genetic similarity, there is a corresponding decrease in similarity between intelligence scores. Thus the correlation for cousins is less than that for twins. This, too, is evidence of the influence of heredity.

But these data also support the belief that contexts influence measured intelligence. Because most sets of identical twins have more similar environments than do cousins or siblings, the higher correlation between various intelligence measures for identical twins may be due at least in part to their more nearly identical environments. And the difference between identical twins reared together and those reared apart is additional evidence that environment influences development. Figure 3.12, for example, reports median correlations of +0.85 and +0.67 for intelligence test scores of identical twins raised together and apart, respectively. Because these twins are genetically identical, environmental forces are clearly important. It is also revealing that as identical twins grow up, their phe-

notypes (manifested characteristics) become less similar; but, of course, their genotypes remain identical. It seems that the interaction of these identical genotypes with somewhat different contexts leads to progressively more dissimilar developmental outcomes (McCartney, Bernieri, & Harris, 1990).

Personality

Twin studies also provide evidence that a host of personality characteristics are strongly influenced by genetic factors (Plomin, 1989). In an Australian survey of 3,810 pairs of adult identical and fraternal twins, for example, Martin and Jardine (1986) found high correlations for personality characteristics such as anxiety, depression, conservatism, and introversion/extroversion. Similar results have also been reported in a survey of American adult twins (Pogue-Geile & Rose, 1985).

Perhaps more striking is the finding that some mental disorders have a genetic basis. For example, Gottesman and Shields (1982) found that of 28 pairs of identical twins there was 42 percent concordance for schizophrenia—that is, 42 percent of all schizophrenic members of twin pairs had a schizophrenic twin. The concordance between members of fraternal twin pairs was only 9 percent, from a sample of 34 pairs.

Studies of adopted children and studies of mental disorders among related family members also confirm the finding that some forms of schizophrenia as well as manic-depression have a genetic component (Loehlin, Willerman, & Horn, 1988). Similarly, there appears to be little doubt that heredity is often involved in the onset of alcoholism. Not only are children of alcoholics about four times more likely to be alcoholics than are members of the general population, but studies of twins have found very high concordance rates for alcoholism (*high concordance* means that when one twin has a specific characteristic, the probability is high that the other will also have the characteristic). Also, certain racial groups appear to be more prone to alcoholism than others. This is partly explained by the fact that there appear to be detectable, biologically based differences between alcoholic-prone and "normal" individuals. Differences have been found with respect to certain liver enzymes involved in metabolizing alcohol (Emery & Mueller, 1992), and with respect to specific brain receptors that might be associated with responses to alcohol (Blum et al., 1990).

Adopted Children Studies

When it is possible to obtain information about biological as well as adoptive parents, and about natural and adopted children, adopted children studies permit a wide range of comparisons that make it easier to untangle the interaction of genes and context.

In the Texas Adoption Project, which began in 1973, investigators have access to data that include physical as well as cognitive measures of the adopted children's bio-

TABLE 3.2
IQ Correlations in the Texas Adoption Project

Correlation Pairing	Number of Pairs	Observed Correlations
Share genes only:		
Adopted child × biological mother	297	0.28
Share environment only:		
Adopted child × adopted mother	401	0.15
Adopted child × adoptive father	405	0.12
All unrelated children	266	0.18
Share genes and environment:		
Natural child × adoptive mother	143	0.21
Natural child × adoptive father	144	0.29
Natural child × natural child	40	0.33

SOURCE: From "The Texas Adoption Project," by J. M. Horn, 1983. *Child Development*, pp. 268–275. © 1983 by the Society for Research in Child Development, Inc. Reprinted by permission.

logical mothers (and sometimes fathers as well), in addition to similar measures for the children themselves, their adoptive parents, and other "natural" children in the adoptive home (Horn, 1983; Loehlin, 1985; Willerman, 1979). This makes it possible to compare relationships between adopted children and their biological mothers with those between the adopted children and their adoptive mothers. Furthermore, these relationships can also be compared with those that exist between the adoptive parents and their natural children. In other words, the design of this study makes it possible to look at correlations where the members of a pair have common genes but different environments (adopted children and their biological mothers); where members of a pair share an environment but are genetically unrelated (adopted children and their adoptive parents); and where there is some commonality with respect to both genes and the environment (adoptive parents and their natural children).

Some of the results of the Texas Adoption Project are summarized in Table 3.2. What is most striking about these findings is that the correlation between adopted children and their biological mothers is higher than that between the adopted children and their adoptive parents—a finding that has been replicated in other studies as well (Turkheimer, 1991). Also, the relationship between adopted children and their biological parents is about the same as that between adoptive parents and their own children although the adopted children are not raised by their own parents. Eysenck (Eysenck & Kamin, 1981) claims this is strong evidence that genetics is the principal determiner of variation in intelligence. It should be noted, however, that these correlations are very low; they do not, by themselves, account for very much variation in intelligence. But, as geneticists would be quick to point out, the degree of genetic relatedness between a child and a nat-

ural parent is not nearly as high as that between siblings, and even less than that between identical twins.

A FINAL LOOK AT GENE–CONTEXT INTERACTION

It seems clear that over the course of generations, environmental contexts exert a selective force on genes. We know, too, that the interaction of genes and environment affects behavior. It is perhaps not so obvious, but no less true, that genes can also influence environment.

Plomin and colleagues (1994) studied 93 nondivorced families in which there were identical twins, 98 families with fraternal twins, another 95 families with nontwin siblings, and other pairs of related and unrelated siblings in stepfamilies—a total of 707 families with 363 pairs of brothers and 344 pairs of sisters, all between 10 and 18. Principal measures used in the study were designed to assess important aspects of parent–child interaction such as *positivity* (warmth, support, rapport), *negativity* (frequency and intensity of disputes), and *control* (extent to which parent maintains ongoing awareness of children's activities). Similar measures of sibling interactions were also obtained, yielding a total of 18 separate measures of what might be termed *family context* or *family environment*.

The main objective of this study was to investigate the extent to which genetic factors might influence the child's family environment (as described by the 18 measures of family interactions used in the study). The reasoning is that if genes affect environment, measures for *monozygotic* twins should be more similar than those for *dizygotic* twins, which should be about the same as those for full siblings, both in nondivorced families and in stepfamilies; similarities of family environments for *full* siblings should, in turn, be higher than those for *half* siblings, which should be higher than those for *unrelated* siblings. Furthermore, the size of the differences among these groups should be predictable on the basis of the genetic similarity among them. Thus, the effect for monozygotic twins, who share 100 percent of their genes, should be twice that for dyzygotic twins and full siblings, whose genetic relatedness is 50 percent, and four times that for half siblings, who share only 25 percent of genes.

The results were as expected. For 15 of the 18 measures of family environment, there were significant genetic effects of about the magnitude that would be expected. What this means, in Plomin's (1994) words, is that "children are not passive receptacles for environmental influences—they select, modify, and even create their environments" (p. 32).

The close relationship between genetic influence and measures of environmental factors may come from two sources, Plomin (1987) explains. First, parental characteristics that are themselves genetically influenced might determine important aspects of a child's environment. For

FIGURE 3.13

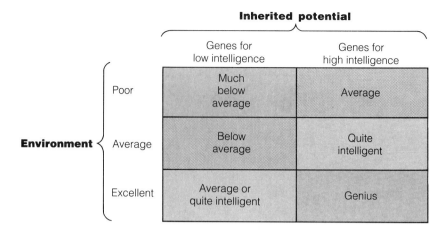

The Stern hypothesis, an example of gene–environment interaction. Individuals with different inherited potential for intellectual development can manifest a wide range of measured intelligence as a function of environmental influence.

example, high-IQ parents might provide more books for their children, might enroll them in a variety of courses, might take them on field trips, and so on. Second, children's characteristics that are genetically influenced might have a direct bearing on their environments. For example, parents might provide different experiences (hence different environments) for high-IQ children.

An Illustration of Gene–Context Interaction

Elder, Nguyen, and Caspi's (1985) analysis of the lives of 167 children who lived during the Great Depression (1930s) provides a dramatic example of how genes can affect the child's environment. The Depression was a time of severe economic hardships during which many fathers lost their jobs and their ability to look after their families. As a result, says Elder (1979), some fathers became more punitive and more exploitive; others became more rejecting and indifferent. These changes, notes Elder, were especially difficult for adolescents, whose relationships with parents changed in systematic ways (Elder et al., 1985). Boys' perceptions of the power and attractiveness of their fathers tended to decline, whereas their peers became more appealing. Interestingly, however, adolescent boys did not appear to suffer in terms of confidence, aspirations, and positive self-concept. In contrast, girls tended to lower their aspirations and their self-esteem, and to experience increased moodiness and unhappiness. These negative effects, claims Elder, were not linked so much to economic hardships as to the rejecting behavior of the fathers. And, in general, they were more serious for girls than for boys. But what is most striking is that the least attractive girls suffered most. In Elder, Nguyen, and Caspi's words, "If girls were unattractive, family hardship accentuated fathers' overly demanding, exploitive behavior . . . [but] only when girls were rated as unattractive" (p. 371). In fact, in some cases, economic hardship actually increased the extent to which fathers were warm and sup-

portive of their *attractive* daughters, sacrificing and going out of their way to provide for them.

Related to this, a large number of studies have found that on average, teachers judge physically attractive students to be more socially skillful, more likely to achieve, even more intelligent (Ritts, Patterson, & Tubbs, 1992).

The lesson to be learned from such studies is clear: If we are to understand the development and the lives of people, it is essential that we take into account the contexts in which they are born and live. In Bronfenbrenner's terms, we need to look at the *microsystem* (in the Elder study, the adolescent in interaction with father, mother, peers); the *mesosystem* (family interactions with school or with the adolescent's workplaces); the *exosystem* (the father's changed relationship with his work setting); and the *macrosystem* (the dramatic social and economic changes of the Great Depression). An ecological approach to understanding development emphasizes not only the importance of the interactions that define the child's context, but underscores as well the importance of the characteristics of individuals and settings in interaction. And it provides a framework for beginning to understand how characteristics that have a strong genetic basis (physical appearance or intelligence, for example), can influence interactions in systems that are also influenced by environmental factors (economic conditions, for example).

Human Plasticity

When Snyderman and Rothman (1987) questioned 1,020 American scholars, researchers, and theorists, they found that most believed that intelligence is inherited to a significant degree. But virtually all recognize that human characteristics are influenced by the interaction of genes and changing contexts.

Still, the old nurture–nature controversy—the question of whether certain traits are influenced primarily by heredity or only by the environment, and of how important each is—has not gone away completely. The persistence of this controversy, says Gottlieb (1992), "reflects an inadequate understanding of the relations among heredity, development, and evolution" (p. 137). It's a controversy sometimes fueled by the belief that we are—or at least should be—equal. And if we are equal, then it cannot be that Jill has an assortment of genes highly likely to lead to charm and intelligence and grace while Mikey starts his life with an assortment of genes that propel him blindly toward low intelligence or schizophrenia.

Or can it? Science suggests that yes, our genes are different, and yes, we have different probabilities of reaching certain outcomes. But science also tells us that genes, by themselves, determine little. They simply underlie potential, making some outcomes more probable than others. Even in the face of highly probable (highly canalized) outcomes, the human being is sufficiently *plastic* that environmental forces can lead to surprising and wonderful things.

That is the essence of Gottesman's (1974) concept of reaction range of which we spoke earlier. Reaction range is the range of possibilities implicit in our genes. It includes all the outcomes possible for any given characteristic, taking into account variations in the timing and nature of environmental influences. The concepts of *reaction range* and of human *plasticity* are simplified by Stern (1956) in what he calls the "rubber band hypothesis" (see Figure 3.13).

Simplified, the **rubber band hypothesis** compares intelligence to a rubber band. Some of us have short bands to begin with (limited inherited potential for intelligence); others have longer bands. Manifested intelligence is the eventual length of the band after it has been stretched by the environment. Some environments stretch bands a lot; others hardly stretch them at all. Longer bands, of course, stretch more easily than shorter bands.

Do highly demanding environments break bands? Do old bands become frayed and brittle? Do bands stretch more easily when new? Unfortunately, analogies are simply comparisons; they provide no answers for questions like these.

Gene–Context Interactions

1. The nature–nurture question asks about the interactions of genes and context that determine development. The older *additive* model assumed that genes contribute a certain percentage, and environment the remainder. The *interactive* model recognizes a more complex relationship between genes and environment, such that neither alone accounts for anything.

The Mechanics of Heredity

2. Conception, the beginning of life, requires the union of sperm and ovum. The bases of biological life are protein molecules made up of amino acids in complex arrangements determined by a special genetic code contained in sequences of deoxyribonucleic acid (DNA) molecules located on chromosomes. In the chromosomes are the carriers of heredity, the genes. Sex is determined by special chromosomes labeled X and Y (XX equals female; XY equals male; only the father produces a Y).

3. Genetic makeup is *genotype; phenotype* refers to manifested characteristics. Genes, in pairs or in combinations of pairs, interact with the environment to influence certain characteristics. In major gene determination, characteristics corresponding to *dominant* genes will be manifested in the individual except where two recessive genes are paired. Manifested characteristics that correspond closely to underlying genetic makeup are said to be highly *canalized. Reaction range* refers to the range of possibilities implicit in genotype. Waddington's epige-

netic landscape presents an analogy for understanding gene–environment interaction.

Genetic Defects

4. Molecular genetics, which looks at the structure and function of genes, has located a large number of *marker genes*—specific segments of DNA that are associated with some identifiable characteristic. Many genetic defects are associated with recessive genes and will therefore not be manifested unless the individual inherits the genes (or gene combinations) from both parents. Huntington's disease (a fatal neurological disorder) is caused by a dominant gene. Sickle-cell anemia (the reduced ability of red blood cells to obtain oxygen), PKU (an enzyme disorder that sometimes leads to mental retardation), Tay–Sachs disease (another enzyme disorder leading to brain degeneration and death), and some forms of muscular dystrophy (a degenerative muscular disorder), diabetes (a sugar-processing disorder), and neural tube defects are all examples of genetic disorders associated with recessive genes.

Chromosomal Disorders

5. Chromosomal disorders result from errors in chromosomes and include Down syndrome (Trisomy 21) and disorders associated with errors in sex chromosomes such as Turner's syndrome (linked to an absent sex chromosome); XYY syndrome (super males), affecting men only; Klinefelter's syndrome, affecting men with an extra X chromosome (XXY); and fragile X syndrome (a common cause of mental retardation especially among males).

Genetic Risk

6. Some genetic abnormalities and fetal diseases can be detected prior to birth by means of amniocentesis (analysis of amniotic fluid withdrawn through a needle), chorion biopsy (analysis of preplacental tissue), fetoscopy (a surgical procedure to obtain fetal blood or skin samples), ultrasound (use of sonar techniques to detect physical characteristics and movement), radiography (X-rays), or preimplantation diagnosis (analysis of zygote cells prior to implantation). Some genetic abnormalities and diseases can be treated or prevented; some can be detected before birth, or the risk of their occurrence can be estimated. There are some exciting and controversial possibilities in current genetics.

Studying Gene–Context Interaction

7. Animal studies, as well as intervention studies with children (like Sherman and Key's study or research on Project Head Start), indicate that the environment influ-ences characteristics such as intelligence. Twin studies and studies of adopted children corroborate these findings but also illustrate the importance of biology.

A Final Look at Gene–Context Interaction

8. Plomin and associates' study of mono- and fraternal twin pairs, as well as of siblings, stepsiblings, and nonrelated children, reveals that genes affect not only behavior but also environment (interactions in the family context, in this case). Elder's study of the differential impact of the Great Depression on the lives of attractive and less attractive girls also illustrates how biology (attractiveness) and the environment can interact to influence development.

It is useful to emphasize the plasticity of, rather than the limits implicit in, our genes. The Stern hypothesis that genetic endowment is like a rubber band that assumes its final length—the actual performance of an individual—as it interacts with the environment, stresses the plasticity of our genes.

FOCUS QUESTIONS: APPLICATIONS

1. What is the nature–nurture controversy about?
   - Outline some of the arguments that might be marshalled on either side of this controversy.

2. What are the most basic facts of heredity?
   - Explain, as you might to a 10th-grade student, what you know of the mechanics of conception and heredity.

3. What are some of the most common genetic defects?
   - Explain what sex-linked defects are and why they are typically more common among males than females.

4. What are some common chromosomal defects?
   - Describe several such defects, including two that are often linked with mental retardation.

5. How do genes and contexts interact to determine developmental outcomes?
   - Give a clear example of how genes might affect context, and another of how context might affect genes.

STUDY TERMS

additive 66

AFP test 75

amniocentesis 78

amniotic fluid 78

artificial insemination 67

autosomes 68

canalized 70

chorion biopsy 78

chromosomal disorders 75

chromosomes 68

conception 67

deoxyribonucleic acid 67

diabetes 75

dizygotic 83

DNA 67

dominant gene 69

double helix 68

Down syndrome 75

environment 64

epigenesis 71

eugenics 81

feral children 65

fetoscopy 78

fragile X syndrome 76

fraternal twins 83

gametes 67

genes 69

FURTHER READINGS

The following two books present a fascinating, and tragic, account of the life of Genie, an abandoned child. The first presents details of Genie's life before her eventual discovery at age 14; the second is an account of her later treatment and of the professional jealousies and bitterness that followed.

Curtiss, S. (1977). *Genie: A psycholinguistic study of a modern-day wild child.* New York: Academic Press.

Rymer, R. (1993). *Genie: A scientific tragedy.* New York: Harper Perennial.

A collection of articles that presents an insightful look at nature and nurture, at parent–child interaction, and at the plasticity and strengths of human beings is:

Tizard, B., & Varma, V. (Eds.). (1992). *Vulnerability and resilience in human development.* London: Jessica Kingsley.

For those interested in the details of heredity, see:

Emery, A. E., & Mueller, R. F. (1992). *Elements of medical genetics* (8th ed.). Edinburgh & London: Churchill Livingstone.

Friedman, J. M., Dill, F. J., Hayden, M. R., & McGillivray, B. C. (1992). *Genetics.* Baltimore: Williams & Wilkins.

Our genes are not simply limits; they are potential. They make possible our uniqueness and our flexibility. The following collection explores the potential implicit in our adaptability:

Gallagher, J. J., & Ramey, C. T. (Eds.). (1987). *The malleability of children.* Baltimore: Brookes.

1. What are the common probable and positive signs of pregnancy?
2. What is the normal sequence of prenatal development and birth?
3. What factors have the potential of being most harmful to the fetus? When?
4. What are the principal causes and implications of prematurity?

OUTLINE

PRENATAL
DEVELOPMENT AND BIRTH

"Who was your mother?"

"Never had none!" said the child, with another grin.

"Never had any mother? What do you mean? Where were you born?"

"Never was born!" persisted Topsy.

"Do you know who made you?"

"Nobody, as I knows on," said the child, with a short laugh. "I 'spect I grow'd."

HARRIET BEECHER STOWE
Uncle Tom's Cabin

We know, of course, that Topsy was wrong, that she # CHAPTER 4 didn't just "grow'd," that she had to have a mother. In Topsy's day, there was seldom any doubt about who the mother was—although there might occasionally have been some uncertainty about the father.

Things are no longer so clear-cut. In fact, under some circumstances they are so unclear that even the highest courts in the land are hard-pressed to determine maternity. Ironically, however, sophisticated DNA analyses can sometimes point unerringly to the father.

A case in point is that of one Ms. Anna M. Johnson, who agreed to bear a child for Mark and Crispina Calvert in exchange for $10,000 ("Court to Decide Right of Surrogate Mother," 1992). The Calverts later had a disagreement with the surrogate mother, and both parties sought legal custody of the child. The issue is complex: The child was conceived from Mark Calvert's sperm and Crispina Calvert's ovum; Ms. Johnson was then artificially inseminated with the fertilized ovum and bore the child to term. Who is the natural mother? Who is entitled to be the legal mother?

Not the surrogate mother, the California appellate court decided, agreeing with an earlier New Jersey Supreme Court ruling. Because surrogate mothers are not biologically related to the fetus, said the court, they cannot be considered either natural or legal mothers.

Where does that leave the growing numbers of single women who turn to artificial insemination to produce children, not as surrogate mothers but for themselves ("Babies Without Dads," 1992)? And what are the implications of childbearing at age 50, or even 60, as is now possible using a previously fertilized, donated ovum? A 60-year-old European woman recently gave birth to a baby girl ("Mom, 60, Delivers Healthy Girl," 1994). She had lied about her age so that her doctor would implant a zygote into her. The doctor claims he would otherwise have refused. "One has to set an age limit," said he. "I think age 50 is enough" (p. 18).

THIS CHAPTER

Sometimes **artificial insemination** involves donor sperm but uses the mother's ova, fertilized in the body or outside (in vitro). In such cases, the mother is also a biological parent. But in cases such as Ms. Johnson's and the 60-year-old mother, both sperm and ovum are donated, and the woman who carries the child serves as a host rather than a biological parent.

Whether **conception** is artificial or natural, however, the fetus usually develops in a highly predictable fashion. The function and structure of each of the body's cells is largely preordained by the genetic material in the 23 pairs of chromosomes in the fertilized egg. But even here, as in all of life, development is always subject to a variety of influences.

This chapter traces the normal course of prenatal development from conception through birth, looks at some of the factors that can affect the fetus, and describes childbirth.

DETECTING PREGNANCY

In the absence of chemical tests or a professional medical examination, there are few signs by which women can determine **pregnancy** with certainty before the later stages of **prenatal development.** However, there are a handful of tentative signs, none of which occur very early in pregnancy. Cessation of **menses** (menstruation) is not a certain sign of pregnancy because many other factors can cause it. Morning sickness, although it affects approximately two thirds of all pregnant women, does not ordi-

narily begin until about two weeks after the missed period and can easily be mistaken for some other ailment. Frequently during the early stages the breasts enlarge and become slightly painful, and the aureoles darken. Because these symptoms are highly subjective, they are quite unreliable. And movement of the fetus in the womb (termed **quickening**), is not usually noticed by the mother until the fourth or fifth month, and by then most women have realized for some time that they are pregnant.

In addition to these tentative signs of pregnancy, there are more *positive* symptoms such as the fetal heartbeat, which can be heard with the aid of a **stethoscope.** Similarly, fetal movements can be detected by feeling the abdomen or sometimes simply by observing it. X-rays and ultrasound are two other methods of ascertaining the presence of a fetus.

Several decades ago, the surest early medical test of pregnancy required the aid of a virgin animal such as a rabbit, frog, or mouse.* Fortunately for virgin rabbits and mice, who always had to be killed to complete the test, chemical pregnancy tests are now widely available, even in kit form for in-home use, and are very widely used. One study found that an average of five different pregnancy tests were performed for each confirmed pregnancy in a group of women, and that more than two thirds of these were purchased over the counter and performed at home (Voss, 1992). These tests detect changes in the woman's urine through a chemical reaction and are effective as early as two weeks after conception. Positive indications are highly reliable. Negative readings are less accurate, however, and should be followed by a second test a week or so later.

STAGES OF PRENATAL DEVELOPMENT

The **gestation period** (the time between conception and birth) for different species varies considerably: Cows take about as long as people; elephants need 600 days; dogs come to term in approximately 63 days, rabbits in 31, and chickens in 21.

The human gestation period is usually calculated in lunar months, each of which has 28 days—hence 10 lunar months or 280 days for pregnancy (counting from the *onset* of the last menstrual period). However, the actual gestation period is approximately 266 days because fertilization cannot usually occur until 12 to 14 days after the beginning of the menstrual period, which is when ovulation takes place.

The American College of Obstetrics and Gynecology has standardized the terminology used to describe prena-

*"What for?" harrumphed my grandmother. "Why the jiggers would anyone wanna get a rabbit killed for that unless you're gonna eat it. They'll find out soon enough if they're pregnant."

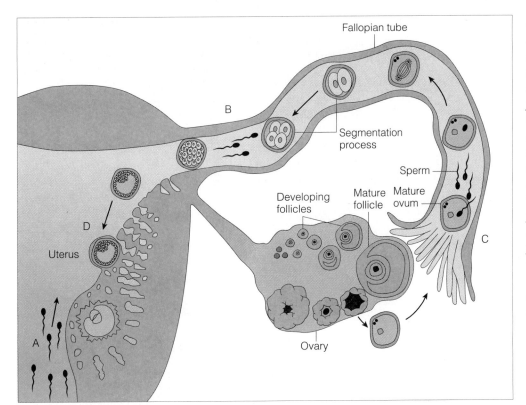

FIGURE 4.1

Fertilization and implantation. At **A,** *millions of sperm cells have entered the vagina and are finding their way into the uterus. At* **B,** *some of the spermatozoa are moving up the Fallopian tube (there is a similar tube on the other side) toward the ovum. At* **C,** *fertilization occurs. The fertilized ovum drifts down the tube, dividing and forming new cells as it goes, until it implants itself in the wall of the uterus (**D**) by the seventh or eighth day after fertilization.*

TABLE 4.1

Stages of Gestation (Prenatal Development)

Stage	Description
The Fertilized Ovum	Also termed the *germinal stage* or the period of the *zygote.* Begins at fertilization and ends with implantation of the zygote (fertilized egg) in the uterine wall about two weeks later. Still microscopic.
Embryo Stage	From end of second to end of eighth week of intrauterine development. During this stage most of the important morphological (pertaining to form) changes occur. *Teratogens* (influences that cause malformations and defects) are most influential during this period. At the end of this period, the embryo is close to 2 inches (4.5 cm) long and weighs about ⅟₁₆ ounce (19 grams).
Period of the Fetus	From the end of eighth week until birth. Accelerating growth curves toward the end of this period.

tal development by identifying three developmental stages with clear time boundaries (Table 4.1). The stage of the **fertilized ovum** or *zygote* (also called the **germinal stage**) begins at fertilization and ends two weeks later, shortly after implantation in the uterus. The **embryo stage** follows and terminates at the end of the eighth week. Finally, the **fetus stage** lasts from the end of the eighth week until the birth of the baby.

Stage of the Fertilized Ovum

Except in cases of in vitro conception, *fertilization* in the woman usually occurs in the **Fallopian tubes** that link the **ovaries** to the **uterus** (Figure 4.1). It results from the invasion of the tubes by millions of sperm cells, one of which succeeds in penetrating the outer covering of the ovum. Once a single sperm has penetrated the ovum's outer shell, the egg then becomes impenetrable to other sperm. From that moment a human child begins to form, but it will be approximately 266 days before this individual is finally born.

The fertilized ovum (zygote) is then carried toward the uterus by currents in the Fallopian tubes, a process requiring between five and nine days. Cell divisions occur during this time, so that the fertilized ovum, which initially consisted of the single cell resulting from the union of sperm and ovum, now contains about 125 cells (Handyside, 1991). Still, it is not much larger at the end of the first week than it was at the time of fertilization, mainly because the cells of which it consists are considerably smaller than they originally were—hardly surprising because the ovum has received no nourishment from any source other than itself.

About one week after fertilization, the ovum is ready to implant itself in the uterine wall. At this stage, many potential pregnancies terminate with implantation failure. For those that continue, the ovum facilitates implantation by secreting certain enzymes and producing tiny, tentaclelike growths (called *villi*) that implant themselves in

FIGURE 4.2

*Development during the stage of the fertilized ovum (**A:** 4 days after conception); the embryo (**B:** 32 days); and the fetus (**C** and **D:** 8.5 and 15 weeks respectively).*

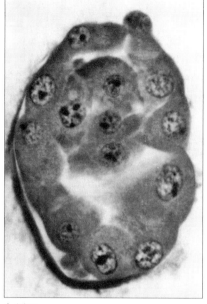

A 4 days

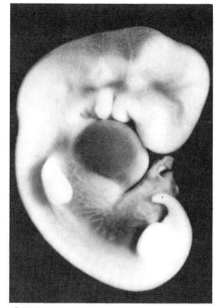

B 32 days

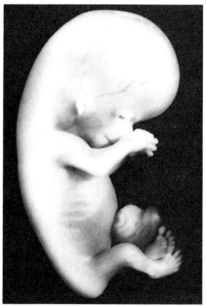

C 8½ post-ovulatory weeks

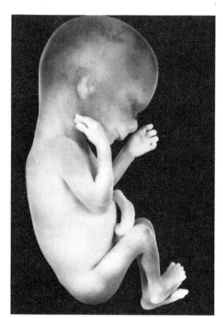

D 15 post-ovulatory weeks

the lining of the uterus to obtain nutrients from blood vessels. This is the beginning of the **placenta**—the organ that allows nutrients to pass to the fetus and waste materials to be removed while keeping the blood of the mother and the fetus separate. The placenta and the fetus will eventually be connected by the **umbilical cord,** a thick cord about 20 inches (50 cm) long, consisting of two arteries and one large vein. It is attached to the placenta at one end and to what will be the child's navel at the other. The umbilical cord contains no nerve cells, so that there is no connection between the mother's nervous system and that of the child **in utero** (in the uterus). Note that the placenta serves as a link between mother and fetus, whereas the umbilical cord links the fetus to the placenta.

The Embryo

The embryo stage, beginning at the end of the second week of pregnancy, follows implantation of the fertilized ovum in the wall of the uterus. The normal course of physiological development in the embryonic and fetal stage is highly predictable and regular (Figure 4.2).

At the beginning of this stage, the embryo is still only a fraction of an inch long and weighs much less than an ounce. Despite the size, not only has there been cell differentiation into future skin cells, nerves, bone, and other body tissue, but also the rudiments of eyes, ears, and nose have begun to appear. In addition, some of the internal organs are beginning to develop so that by the end of the

TABLE 4.2
*Prenatal Development According to Lunar Months**

Lunar Month	Weight	Length	Characteristics
1	Negligible	Negligible	Cell differentiation into those that will be bones, nerves, or other cells.
2	2/3 oz (19 g)	1½–2 in (3.8–5 cm)	All organs present; leg buds and external genitalia just appearing.
3	7/8 oz (25 g)	3 in (7.5 cm)	If aborted, will make primitive breathing movements and suck; bones forming, organs differentiated.
4	4 oz (114 g)	6 in (15 cm)	
5	11 oz (312 g)	10 in (25 cm)	Fetal movement (quickening); lanugo appears.
6	20 oz (568 g)	12 in (30 cm)	Heartbeat clearly discernible; eyelids present.
7	2.6 lb (1180 g)	15 in (38 cm)	
8	4 lb (1816 g)	16 in (41 cm)	All major changes have now occurred; development is largely a matter of increasing weight and length.
9	4.7 lb (2133 g)	17.5 in (44 cm)	
10	7.5 lb (3405 g)	20 in (50 cm)	

* Weight and length approximate.

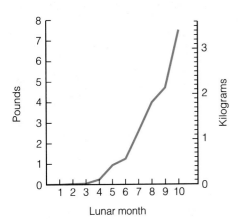 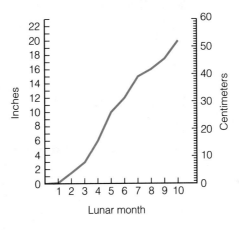

FIGURE 4.3
Approximate weight and length of the fetus at the end of each lunar month of prenatal development.

first lunar month, a primitive heart is already beating. By the end of the second lunar month, the embryo is between 1½ and 2 inches (3.8 and 5 cm) long and weighs close to two thirds of an ounce (19 gm). All the organs are now present, the whole mass has assumed the curled shape characteristic of the fetus, and the embryo is clearly recognizable as human. Arm and limb buds have appeared and begun to grow, resembling short, awkward paddles. External **genitalia** (sex organs) have also appeared.

The Fetus

By the end of the eighth week of pregnancy, which marks the beginning of the fetal period, the absolute mass of the fetus is still unimpressive. By the end of the third lunar month (10 weeks of pregnancy), it may reach a length of 3 inches (7.5 cm) but will still weigh less than an ounce (25 gm). The head of the fetus is one third of its entire length; this will have changed to one fourth by the end of the sixth lunar month and slightly less than that at birth (see Table 4.2 and Figure 4.3).

During the third month of pregnancy, the fetus is sufficiently developed that if it is aborted it will make breathing movements and will give evidence of a primitive **sucking reflex** and of the **Babinski reflex** (the infant's tendency to fan its toes when tickled on the soles of its feet) if stimulated appropriately.

During the fourth lunar month of pregnancy, the fetus grows to a length of 6 inches (15 cm) and weighs approximately 4 ounces (114 g). The bones have begun to form, all organs are clearly differentiated, and there may even be evidence of some intrauterine (within the uterus) movement.

By the fifth month, a downy covering (called **lanugo**) begins to grow over most of the fetus's body. This covering is usually shed during the seventh month but is occasionally still present at birth. The fetus weighs approximately 11 ounces (312 g) and may have reached a length of 10 inches (25 cm) by the end of the fifth lunar month.

Toward the end of the sixth month, it is possible to palpate (feel by touch) the baby through the mother's abdomen. The heartbeat, already discernible in the fifth month, is now much clearer. The eyelids have now separated so that the fetus can open and close its eyes. It is approximately a foot (30 cm) long and weighs close to 20 ounces (568 g). If born now in a modern hospital, it might survive with sophisticated care to compensate for the immaturity of its digestive and respiratory systems.

The fetus's growth in size and weight becomes more dramatic in the last few months of the fetal stage. Brain development is also particularly crucial during the last three months of pregnancy, as it will continue to be after birth, especially for the first two years of life. The unborn child's sensitivity to malnutrition is assumed to be related to neurological growth during the late stages of fetal development (Morgane et al., 1993). This sensitivity is sometimes evident in lower developmental scores during infancy and impaired mental functioning among children born to malnourished mothers.

Most of the physical changes that occur after the seventh month are quantitative (Table 4.2). It is now a matter of sheer physical growth: from 15 inches and 2.6 pounds in the seventh month (38 cm; 1180 g) to 16 inches and 4 pounds in the eighth (41 cm; 1816 g); from 17.5 inches and 4.7 pounds in the ninth (44 cm; 2133 g) to 20 inches and 7.5 pounds at the end of the tenth (50 cm; 3405 g).

Two terms that are sometimes used to describe the general pattern of fetal development are **proximodistal** (meaning, literally, "from near to far") and **cephalocaudal** ("from the head to the tail"). They refer to the fact that among the first aspects of the fetus to develop are the head and internal organs; the last are the limbs and digits.

FACTORS AFFECTING PRENATAL DEVELOPMENT

There are a wide range of influences that can enhance or impede the healthy development of the fetus. Influences that cause malformations and physical defects in the fetus include **teratogens** and **mutagens.** Teratogens affect the embryo or fetus directly and include various maternal illnesses, drugs, chemicals, and minerals. The term derives from *teras*, the Greek word for "monster." Note that the effects of teratogens are *not* passed on from one generation to another.

In contrast, the effects of mutagens may be transmitted from one generation to another because mutagens cause actual changes in genetic material that can then lead to malformations and defects. Radiation is a well-known mutagen. Thus, deafness caused by a mutated gene (re-

sulting from a mutagen like radiation, for example) may be passed on to offspring; deafness caused by a virus (such as the teratogenic virus *cytomegalovirus*) will not be.

Note that the effects of many teratogens often depend on a variety of factors, both environmental and genetic. That is, the occurrence and the severity of a defect associated with a particular teratogen are often determined by the fetus's genetic background and the timing of the influence, as well as the stresses that might result from the combined presence of other teratogens—not to mention the effects of other external positive influences. Accordingly, the effects of the same teratogen can vary widely from one fetus to another.

Prescription Drugs

Because it is clearly impossible to use human subjects in controlled investigations with chemical substances whose effects may be injurious to the fetus, our information about the effects of drugs on the fetus is often based on studies of animals or on human studies in poorly controlled situations. Generalizing from studies of animals to humans in the case of drugs presents an additional problem, because certain drugs have dramatically different effects on members of different animal species, as well as on children relative to adults (Friedman, 1992). Also, normal adult doses of a drug might well represent huge doses for a fetus weighing only ounces, particularly if the drug crosses the placental barrier easily.

Frequency of Drug Use
The frequency of drug use by pregnant women and the variety of drugs they consume is uncertain. In a U.S. study of 2752 mothers of infants *without major congenital malformations*, 68 percent claimed to have used at least one prescription or nonprescription drug during pregnancy (Rubin, Ferencz, & Loffredo, 1993). In a New Zealand study of 56,037 births between 1982 and 1989, 31 percent of mothers reported using *prescription* drugs during the first trimester (40 percent used alcohol and 29 percent smoked cigarettes) (Correy et al., 1992).

Some Teratogenic Medical Drugs
Among the better-known teratogenic drugs are *thalidomide*, which causes severe physical changes in the embryo; *quinine*, which is associated with congenital deafness; *barbiturates* and other painkillers that reduce the body's oxygen supply, resulting in varying degrees of brain damage; and various *anesthetics* that appear to cross the placental barrier easily and rapidly and cause depression of fetal respiration and decreased responsiveness in the infant (Brendt & Beckman, 1990).

Among nonprescription drugs that may also have negative effects on the fetus are *aspirin*, which may increase the tendency to bleed in both mother and fetus (Stock-

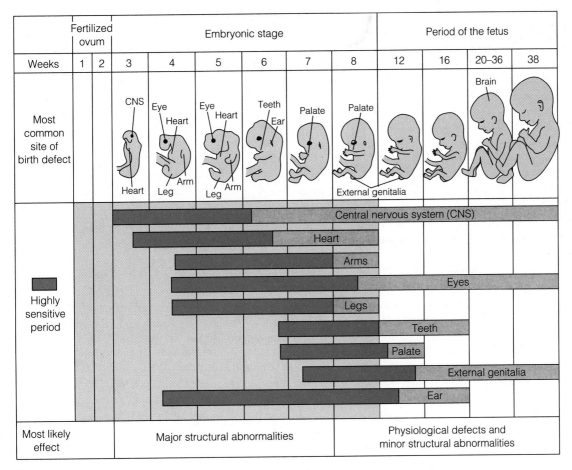

FIGURE 4.4

The most serious structural defects in prenatal development are most likely to occur in the first eight weeks, although teratogens can have serious consequences throughout gestation.

man, 1990) and which is clearly linked with physical deformities among experimental animals (Vorhees & Mollnow, 1987). Also, *megadoses of vitamins C, D, A, K, and B$_6$* have been linked with birth defects (Scher & Dix, 1983).

The prescription drugs mentioned in this section are only a few of the drugs that are known to be harmful to the fetus. There are many others that do not seem to have any immediate negative effects, but whose long-term effects are still unclear. *Diethylstilbestrol* (DES), for example, is a drug that was heavily prescribed through the 1940s and 1950s for women who were at risk for spontaneous abortions—and which is still prescribed in some parts of the world (Palmlund et al., 1993). Not until several decades later did medical researchers discover a link between DES use by pregnant women and vaginal cancer among girls subsequently born to these women. Because the effect occurs so long after taking the drug and because it is manifested in only a small percentage of the offspring, it is extremely difficult to detect. For this reason, many medical practitioners discourage the use of any prescription drugs by pregnant women unless absolutely necessary.

Importance of Timing

The most serious structural changes (physical deformities and abnormalities) associated with teratogens usually occur only during the embryonic stage of development. After this stage, the fetus's basic structure has already been formed and is not as vulnerable to external influences (see Figure 4.4). Also, the first two weeks after conception is thought to be highly resistant to the influence of teratogens—or if the embryo is affected, it is likely to be aborted (Friedman, 1992). In fact, about 30 to 40 percent of all potential pregnancies are lost before they are recognized—that is, in the first two weeks (Simpson, 1991).

Chemicals

There are now tens of thousands of chemicals currently in use in the world, and several thousand new ones are introduced each year. Although the majority of these are "contained" in one way or another—that is, they do not find their way into our air, our water, or our food—and are essentially harmless, others are not so benign. Large numbers of these chemicals are "endocrine-disrupting" and may have subtle, long-term consequences (Colborn, vom Saal, & Soto, 1993). Many tend to accumulate in body fat, and their negative effects can be transmitted to the fetus either directly or through the mother's milk. Other chemicals have more direct effects, sometimes causing serious fetal malformations or death.

One example of a highly toxic chemical is *methylmercury*, whose effects received worldwide attention following the births of a large number of severely deformed and retarded infants in Minimata Bay, Japan. The deformities were traced to the presence of high levels of mercury in the fish that inhabitants of this community consumed in great quantities; the mercury was, in this case, an industrial waste. The effects of mercury are now known as *Minimata disease.*

Another teratogenic group of chemicals whose effects are well known are the *polychlorinated biphenyls* (PCBs) and related chemicals such as *dioxin*, often used in manufacturing herbicides or insecticides. These chemicals appear to be associated with a higher incidence of miscarriage and with physical deformities (Jacobson & Jacobson, 1990). For example, following the leak of *methyl isocyanate* (used to manufacture pesticides) in Bhopal, India, the rate of spontaneous abortions quadrupled (Bajaj et al., 1993).

In addition to the chemicals known to be harmful to the fetus, there are many toxic chemicals whose effects on fetal development are unknown, although we know how they affect children and adults. *Lead* is one example. It is present in some fuel emissions, in some paints, in certain metal products, and elsewhere. It accumulates slowly in the body; and when it reaches sufficiently high concentrations, it can lead to serious physical and mental problems in children and adults (Weisskopf, 1987).

On a more reassuring note, although our highly industrialized environments are loaded with synthetic substances and potentially harmful chemicals, we have perhaps overemphasized their danger, says Tierney (1988). Fortunately, only relatively rarely are we exposed to them in sufficient doses or over a long enough period that they affect our health measurably—or become teratogens for the unborn.

Nicotine

The harmful effects of smoking on the smoker, and the effects of "sidestream" smoke on the nonsmoker, have been well documented. Some of its effects on the fetus also seem clear. Among its most consistent effects is a higher probability of placental problems, in which the placenta becomes detached from the uterine wall, often leading to fetal death or stillbirth, as well as significantly lower birthweight, which, in turn, is associated with a higher probability of subsequent complications. Nicotine use is linked with a higher risk of miscarriage and fetal death, and it is related

to a higher incidence of early childhood respiratory infections and diseases (Newman & Buka, 1991).

Although smoking during pregnancy has decreased since the 1960s, almost one third of pregnant women smoked in 1987 (Food and Nutrition Board, 1990). Twenty-nine percent of a sample of more than 56,000 New Zealand mothers smoked while pregnant.

Caffeine

The effects of caffeine on the human fetus do not appear to be very dramatic. Nevertheless, caffeine given to pregnant rats has been associated with birth defects in their offspring—but only in doses far larger than those ordinarily consumed by humans (Jacobson et al., 1985). Following a review of related research, Nehlig and Debry (1994) conclude that caffeine is not a human teratogen, although very high consumption might be toxic for the fetus. In addition, caffeine does not appear to change the composition of the mother's milk and may, in fact, serve to stimulate its production.

Alcohol

Alcohol consumption by pregnant women may be associated with premature birth and with various defects in their offspring.

Fetal Alcohol Syndrome
The most serious collection of alcohol-related effects in the newborn is labeled **fetal alcohol syndrome (FAS)**; less serious effects are termed *fetal alcohol effects*. The three major features of extreme FAS are facial malformations (low forehead, widely spaced eyes, a short nose and long upper lip, and absence of a marked infranasal depression), retarded physical growth, and central nervous system problems sometimes manifested in mental retardation. Less severe fetal alcohol effects might include learning impairment, attention deficits, behavior problems, and impaired language development (Newman & Buka, 1991).

Research on Maternal Drinking
With humans it is difficult to conduct the types of experiments that would allow researchers to separate the effects of alcohol from those of other factors, and to determine precisely what amounts of alcohol, and at what stage of development, will cause these effects. However, studies that have looked at FAS among animals have found that injections of ethanol in pregnant mice or rats readily produce what appears to be FAS in their offspring. Not only are these offspring less likely to be born alive but also many of them will display facial and skull deformations highly similar to those characteristic of FAS children. And a single exposure to a high dose of alcohol at a critical time is sufficient to harm the fetus significantly (Gavin et al., 1994).

The current consensus is that even in small amounts, alcohol may be harmful to the fetus, although it may not necessarily lead to fetal alcohol syndrome. For example, one study compared the effects of heavy drinking (four or more drinks a day) with the effects of more moderate drinking (two to four drinks a day) and with those of lighter drinking (fewer than two drinks a day) (Streissguth et al., 1980). Some of the symptoms associated with FAS were found in 19 percent of the children born to mothers in the first group, 11 percent of those in the second, and only 2 percent of those in the third.

How Much Can a Pregnant Woman Drink, and When?

The evidence is not all in, and the conclusions are still tentative. However, in summarizing the effects of alcohol on the developing fetus, Brendt and Beckman (1990) conclude that consuming six drinks or more of alcohol per day constitutes a high risk, but that fewer than two drinks per day is not likely to lead to fetal alcohol syndrome. As Newman and Buka (1991) point out, binge drinking may be especially harmful to the fetus in the early stages of pregnancy. Not surprisingly, an increasing number of medical practitioners recommend that pregnant women refrain completely from alcohol use. In Friedman's (1992) words, "No safe level of maternal drinking during pregnancy has been established" (p. 117).

Substance Abuse

As we saw, various prescription and nonprescription drugs used for medicinal purposes can harm the developing fetus; so can legal recreational drugs such as alcohol, nicotine, and caffeine. In addition, many illicit recreational drugs can also affect the fetus adversely.

Narcotics

Babies born to narcotics addicts are themselves addicted. These infants suffer a clearly recognizable withdrawal (labeled the **neonatal abstinence syndrome**). Its symptoms may include tremors, restlessness, hyperactive reflexes, high-pitched cries, vomiting, fevers, sweating, rapid respiration, seizures, and sometimes death (Fundaro et al., 1994). Often, these symptoms don't reach a peak until the infant is three or four days old, and may persist for up to six months. Some physicians recommend methadone maintenance in low doses for the mother during the later stages of pregnancy, and gradual weaning of the infant from methadone after birth. A study involving 223 infants born to drug-addicted mothers, many of whom were on methadone, found a close relationship between the magnitude of the mother's doses and the severity of the infant's abstinence syndrome (Fundaro et al., 1994).

Marijuana

There is some uncertainty about the effects of marijuana on infants (Food and Nutrition Board, 1990). Some studies suggest that the gestational period is somewhat shorter for heavy marijuana users (Zuckerman & Bresnahan, 1991). In addition, newborns whose mothers were regular heavy marijuana smokers exhibited more tremors and more intense startle reactions; and they were less responsive to a light directed at their eyes. However, tests of motor and cognitive functioning do not ordinarily reveal any differences between infants of marijuana users and nonusers (Fried, 1986). As a result, Friedman (1992) classifies marijuana as one of those drugs that has not been *proven* to be teratogenic in humans.

Cocaine

Marijuana was the drug of the 60s, claim Peters and Theorell (1991); heroin was the drug of the 70s; and cocaine (and "crack"*) became the drug of the 80s and 90s. Cocaine addiction is reportedly about 5 times higher than heroin addiction in the United States. Some reports claim it has reached "epidemic proportions" (Food and Nutrition Board, 1990). However, estimates of illegal drug use are seldom very reliable.

Once thought to be relatively harmless, cocaine is now considered not only highly addictive, but also potentially very harmful to the unborn. Like most mood-altering drugs, it crosses the placental barrier easily. And because it is fat-soluble, it remains in the placenta as well as in amniotic fluid where, notes Mullin (1992), the fetus ingests it over and over again. A dose of cocaine lasts about 48 hours in the adult; in the fetus it may last four or five days (Brody, 1988).

Infants born to cocaine and crack users manifest more startle reactions and more tremors than children of nonusers. They are also more likely to manifest disturbances in sleep patterns, feeding difficulties, diarrhea, fever, and increased irritability. On average, they are smaller and may show evidence of growth retardation—for example, delayed age of standing, pulling up to a sitting position, and developing visual and auditory orientation (Mullin, 1992). And not only are they more likely to be stillborn or to abort spontaneously (Rosenak et al., 1990), but they are about 10 times more likely to die of *sudden infant death syndrome* (SIDS, described in the next chapter) (Chasnoff, 1986/1987). There is evidence, too, that children of cocaine-addicted mothers are more likely to suffer emotional and physical abuse (Hawley, 1993).

There are now close to 1 million children who have been born to crack-addicted mothers, claims Hutchinson (1991). Because crack has been available since 1985, many

---

*Crack is easily manufactured from cocaine, is less expensive, and has far more intense and immediate effects than cocaine used more conventionally (see Chapter 12 for more information).

ANGEL ALDUS, BOARDER BABY

Angel Aldus (not her real name) was born to a cocaine-addicted mother in a county hospital. While in the early stages of labor, her mother was caught in a hospital washroom trying to inject cocaine. In another similar case in Minneapolis, a mother was charged and sentenced to more than two years in jail. "Your crime," said the judge, "is roughly akin to distributing cocaine in the schoolyard" (Logli, 1994, p.129).

Angel's mother wasn't charged. In fact, her mother left the hospital the moment she felt strong enough, and Angel never saw her again. Angel became one of 22,000 infants abandoned in her hospital crib in 1991—one of 22,000 so-called *boarder babies*. Like Angel, most boarder babies (about 75 percent) have been exposed to drugs prenatally.

Angel was subsequently adopted. But the damage had already been done. At age 4, she suffers from a variety of physical problems including cerebral palsy and bone deformities. Her adoptive mother writes: "My heart breaks for my little girl, who though physically disabled, is intellectually intact as she watches her siblings run and play. She, even at this young age, wonders why she cannot" (Logli, 1994, p. 127).

To Think About The economic and social costs of substance abuse by pregnant women are enormous. For example, fetal alcohol syndrome is the leading known cause of mental retardation in North America. Esti-

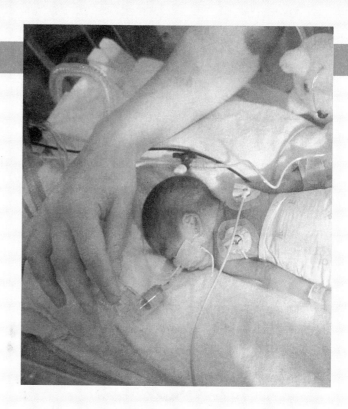

mates are that each year in the United States, more than 40,000 children are born with defects linked with their mother's use of alcohol. These defects are permanent.

of these children are now in school. The most seriously affected of them are, in Hutchinson's words, "a new breed, unlike other children with histories of drug exposure. They are in constant motion, disorganized, and very sensitive to stimuli. Crawling, standing, and walking take longer to develop. They are irritable and hard to please. It is hard for them to make friends. They respond less to the environment" (p. 31). (See Across Cultures: "Angel Aldus, Boarder Baby.")

Maternal Health

A wide range of diseases and infections are also known to affect the fetus. The best known is probably rubella (German measles); others are syphilis, gonorrhea, and poliomyelitis, each of which can cause mental deficiency, blindness, deafness, or miscarriage. Cretinism (subnormal mental development, undeveloped bones, a protruding abdomen, and rough, coarse skin) may be related to a thyroid malfunction in the mother or to an iodine deficiency in her diet. If the deficiency is not too extreme, it can sometimes be alleviated in the child through continuous medication after birth. And AIDS is a more recent, and lethal, threat to the fetus.

Diabetes

Diabetes is a maternal condition that can have serious consequences for the fetus. Before the discovery of insulin, fetal and maternal death were very high. Now, however, mortality rates among diabetic mothers are about the same as those among nonpregnant diabetic women. Management involves careful monitoring of mother and fetus to assess and control sugar levels (simple, self-monitoring procedures are available for in-home use) (Sparks, Jovanovic-Peterson, & Peterson, 1993). With timely diagnosis and proper medical management, fetal deaths are generally below 5 percent (Coustan, 1990). However, there is still a two to four times higher rate of birth defects among these infants. The most common defects include limb, heart, and neural tube defects (Friedman & McGillivray, 1992). Most of these birth defects result from influences that occur early in pregnancy. Hence the importance of careful monitoring from the outset.

Herpes

Herpes simplex 2 (vaginal and genital herpes) is the most common of all sexually transmitted diseases; it can have serious effects on the fetus, particularly if the mother's infection is active at the time of delivery. The probability of the infant's contracting the virus during birth is extremely high—40 to 60 percent (Eden et al., 1990). Because the newborn does not possess many of the immunities that are common among older children and adults, the herpes virus may attack the infant's internal organs, leading to visual or nervous system problems or death in as many as two thirds of all cases (Berland, 1991; Eden et al., 1990). As a result, infants born to mothers infected with the herpes virus are often delivered through cesarean section to prevent infection from occurring.

Another form of herpes virus, *cytomegalovirus*, affects the salivary glands and can also be passed on to the fetus during birth. It is one of the main *infectious* causes of mental retardation, and also an important cause of deafness.

Acquired Immunity Deficiency Syndrome

AIDS is another sexually transmitted disease that is of considerable current concern. First reported in the United States in 1981, the disease remains incurable and fatal. In 1992, there were more than 45,000 new cases of AIDS reported in the United States (U.S. Bureau of the Census, 1993). Estimates were that worldwide, more than 1 million women would be infected in 1993. And the prognosis is that virtually all will eventually die from resulting complications. By the year 2000, about 4 million women will have died ("AIDS Will Kill 4M Women by 2000: WHO," 1993.) And in the United States, in 1991 there were eight times more men than women diagnosed AIDS positive.

AIDS is transmitted through the exchange of body fluids, primarily through blood–blood exchange or through semen–blood exchange. Accordingly, transmission occurs mainly through anal intercourse (because of the thinness of rectal tissues that frequently tear during intercourse), through blood transfusions involving infected blood, and through the communal use of hypodermic syringes. Not surprisingly, AIDS is most common among homosexual males and among intravenous drug users (see Chapter 12 for more information).

Most infants and children with AIDS acquired it directly from their mothers through blood exchange in the uterus or during birth. The risk of transmission from infected mother to fetus ranges from 35 percent to 60 percent (Trofatter, 1990). Initially, prognosis for an infected newborn was poor, but with the combined use of AZT and antibiotics beginning soon after birth, about one third of infected children are surviving 8 to 10 years, or even longer ("AIDS Kids Beat Odds Against Survival," 1994).

Clearly, high-risk women (current or past intravenous drug users; those whose sexual partner(s) include bisexual males and/or men who have been or are intravenous drug users) should be tested for the AIDS antibody before considering pregnancy. (See At a Glance: "Pediatric AIDS Cases," and Figure 4.5, p. 102.)

Maternal Emotions and Stress

A once-common folk belief was that the mother's emotional states could be communicated directly to the child. If the pregnant woman worried too much, her child would be born with a frown; if she had a particularly traumatic experience, it would mark the infant, perhaps for life; if she was frightened by a rabbit, the result might be a child with a harelip.

Most of these beliefs about pregnancy are simply tales. Because there is no direct link between the mother's nervous system and that of the fetus, there is little possibility that the mother's emotional state or disorder could be communicated directly to the unborn child. However, because of the close relationship between the mother and the fetus, a number of investigators have pursued the idea that stimuli affecting *her* will also have some effect on the *child*, however indirect. One theory is that an anxious mother's chemical balance affects the child physiologically and therefore, indirectly, psychologically. However, given the fact that it is extremely difficult to measure emotional states accurately in both infant and mother, or to control other possible factors that might be associated with stress (like poverty, medical problems, inadequate diet), conclusive statements about the influence of maternal emotional state on the unborn are not warranted.

Older Mothers

The mother's age can also be related to the well-being of the fetus. We know, as was pointed out in Chapter 3, that the incidence of Trisomy 21 (Down syndrome) is about 40 times higher for women over 40 than for women aged 20 or 21. Fragile X syndrome is also more common with increasing maternal age, as are Klinefelter's syndrome and Trisomy 18 (associated with neural tube defects, congenital heart disease, growth retardation, and other problems).

However, given the availability of procedures (such as chorion biopsy or amniocentesis) that make it possible to determine the presence of a number of chromosomal abnormalities and other defects or diseases prenatally, increasing numbers of women, and men, are making the decision to have a family later. The greatest increase in fertility rates in recent years has been among women in their early thirties. About 13 percent of all births occur to women over the age of 35 (U.S. Bureau of the Census, 1994).

In spite of the association between the mother's age and some chromosomal abnormalities, modern health care makes it possible for many women to deliver healthy, full-term babies at ages that would have entailed much higher risk a few decades ago. In fact, when Spellacy, Miller, and Winegar (1986) compared outcomes for 511 pregnancies of women over 40 with more than 26,000 pregnancies of women between 20 and 30, they found that age posed little risk when factors such as cigarette smoking and maternal weight were taken into account.

PEDIATRIC AIDS CASES

AIDS is a fatal disease transmitted through the exchange of body fluids. Most cases of pediatric (childhood) AIDS are transmitted directly from mother to fetus. In later childhood, AIDS is acquired primarily through blood transfusions and is consequently rarer. With increasing sexual activity after adolescence, incidence of AIDS rises dramatically. Male AIDS cases outnumbered female AIDS cases by a factor of almost 10 to 1 in 1991.

FIGURE 4.5

Rising number of AIDS cases in the United States, 1983–1992. (From U.S. Bureau of the Census, 1993, p. 134, and 1994, p. 98.)

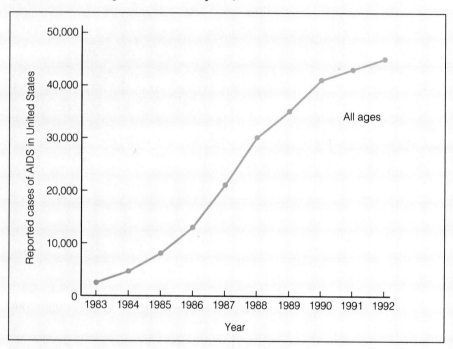

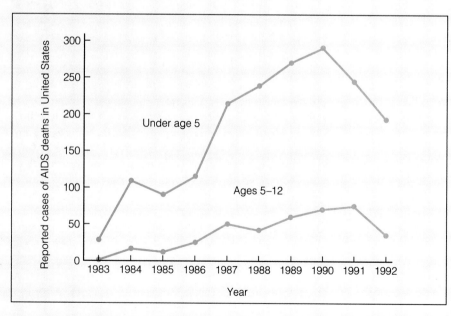

Infants in this high school infant center are among the approximately half-million children born to U.S. teenagers each year. Teenage mothers, half of whom are unmarried, account for 8 percent of all births in the country. When they receive the same medical attention and social support as older women, their children can fare as well.

Teenage Mothers

Births to teenage girls remain very high relative to the rest of the population—in spite of widespread sex education and sexual abstinence programs (Males, 1993b). In fact, in 1992, 8 percent of all births were to girls aged 15 to 19 (U.S. Bureau of the Census, 1994). And more than half of these were to unmarried teenage parents.

Children born to younger teenage mothers are often at a physical, emotional, and intellectual disadvantage relative to children born to older mothers. There are more miscarriages, premature births, and stillbirths among teenage mothers, and surviving infants are more often the targets of abuse and neglect. In one representative study, for example, Stier and colleagues (1993) compared children born to 219 mothers aged 18 or less with another group of 219 children whose mothers were 19 or more. There were about twice as many instances of physical abuse among children of younger mothers (12.8 percent of all children), and 50 percent more cases of retarded growth. In addition, about four times more of these children experienced changes in primary caregiver early in their lives—sometimes because of placement in foster care, sometimes because the mother left home.

As Buchholz and Korn-Bursztyn (1993) point out, however, much of this research fails to take into account the social circumstances of teenage parenthood—the poverty and the lack of social, educational, and medical assistance. It is not the age of the teenage parent that is the important factor as much as the greater financial, social, and emotional stressors she might face. All other things being equal, unless she is very young (below age 15), if a teenage mother and her infant receive the same medical attention and social support as an older mother, the health and developmental status of her infant will be normal. Unfortunately, however, all other things are not often equal for teenage mothers. (See Chapter 12 for a more detailed discussion of teenage pregnancy.)

Maternal Nutrition

Nutrition, claim Morgane and colleagues (1993), is the single most important external influence on the fetus and neonate.

Effects of Serious Malnutrition
Nutrition's importance is underlined by the consequences of serious malnutrition such as occurred during the

German siege of Leningrad in World War II. During this time, many Russians starved to death in bitterly cold, unheated homes—and birthrates dropped to about 13 percent of what they had previously been (Shanklin & Hoden, 1979). In addition to this dramatic decline in birthrates, there were also great increases in *amenorrhea* (cessation of menstruation, which, incidentally, is not uncommon among anorexic women), low levels of fertility, and an increase in miscarriages.

Effects of Less Serious Malnutrition

Investigating the effects of malnutrition is difficult because investigators can't always separate these effects from the effects of other factors that often accompany malnutrition (poor sanitation, poor medical care, drug use, and so on). In addition, malnutrition is seldom limited just to the period of prenatal development but usually continues into infancy and even childhood.

Studies with both animals and humans leave no doubt that malnutrition, especially protein deprivation, has negative effects on the developing brain. These effects, note Morgane and associates (1993), depend largely on the type and severity of the deprivation as well as its timing. Although some of the effects of malnutrition are reversible given adequate nourishment and stimulation after birth, long-term intellectual deficits may result from malnutrition that begins before birth and continues for some time afterward.

Nutritional Requirements During Pregnancy

During pregnancy, the mother's energy requirements change so that she now requires somewhere between 10 and 15 percent more calories. Accompanying metabolic changes include an increased synthesis of protein, which is important for the formation of the placenta and enlargement of the uterus; a reduction in carbohydrate consumption, the effect of which is to provide sufficient glucose for the fetus; and increased storage of fat to satisfy the mother's energy requirements (Chez & Chervenak, 1990).

Not only must the pregnant woman increase her protein intake, but there is also an increased need for important minerals (for example, calcium, magnesium, iron, and zinc) and vitamins (mainly B_6, D, and E). Recommended dietary allowances for pregnant women range from 25 to 50 percent above those for nonpregnant women (*Recommended Dietary Allowances*, 1980).

Research indicates that *average* intake of these nutrients is often less than recommended for American women (Food and Nutrition Board, 1990). Hence current medical advice emphasizes that *what* the woman eats is more important than *how much*. As noted, with respect to brain growth, protein appears to be among the most important ingredients of a good diet.

Optimal Weight Gain

Current medical advice contradicts the long-held belief that women should be careful to minimize weight gain during pregnancy. Infant mortality is often lower in countries where pregnant women gain significantly more weight than do pregnant women in the United States or Canada. Maternal weight gain leads to higher fetal weight and reduces the risk of illness and infection. Accordingly, doctors who once cautioned women to limit their weight gain to about 10 pounds now suggest that the optimal weight gain for a woman who begins pregnancy at an average weight is somewhere between 25 and 35 pounds (11.5 and 16 kg) (Chez & Chervenak, 1990); it is even higher for women who are initially underweight. For women who are initially overweight, recommended gains are correspondingly lower (15–25 lb; 7–11.5 kg) (Food and Nutrition Board, 1990). Total recommended weight gain for women carrying twins is 35 to 45 pounds (16–20.5 kg).

Unfortunately, this medical advice is most likely relevant to those least likely to be exposed to it and to those least able to take advantage of it. Malnutrition and starvation are seldom a deliberate choice. (See Table 4.3 for a description of some influences on the fetus.)

Social Class

The factor most closely related to premature births is social rather than medical. And premature birth is the greatest single cause of infant death. In addition, it is among the most direct causes of cerebral palsy and of various mental defects (prematurity is discussed in more detail later in this chapter).

Although social class does not explain anything by itself, the high correlation between low social class and higher incidence of premature birth suggests that the living conditions and associated emotional and health consequences of poverty may not be conducive to the production of healthy full-term babies (Baker & Mednick, 1984). There is little doubt that prenatal care of mothers who live in poverty is not often comparable to that afforded middle-class mothers—nor is postnatal health care. General diet, protein intake, and mineral and vitamin intake are frequently significantly inferior; and the effects of these factors are often the consequences of an infant's being born poor.

Rh(D) Immunization

There is a particular quality of blood in Rhesus monkeys that is often, but not always, present in human blood. Because this factor was first discovered in the Rhesus monkey, it is called the *Rh* (or Rhesus) *factor*. Individuals who have this factor are Rh-positive; those who don't are Rh-negative.

A specific component of the Rh blood group, labeled "D," is especially important for the pregnant mother and her fetus. Introduction of Rh(D)-positive blood into an individual who is Rh-negative leads to the formation of antibodies to counteract the D factor—a process termed *immunization* (Bowman, 1990). If these antibodies are

TABLE 4.3
Influences on the Fetus

Agent	Some Reported Effects or Associations
Alcohol	Fetal alcohol syndrome; intrauterine growth retardation; microcephaly; mental retardation
Diethylstilbestrol (DES)	Anomalies of cervix and uterus; higher risk of cervical cancer
Lithium carbonate	Heart and blood vessel defects; neural tube defects
Methylmercury	Minamata disease; cerebral palsy; microcephaly; mental retardation; blindness; death
Polychlorinated biphenyls	Cola-colored children; gum, nail, and groin pigmentation; can affect offspring for up to four years after maternal exposure
Radiation	Microcephaly; mental retardation; eye anomalies; visceral malformations
Street drugs	Fetal and pregnancy complications sometimes leading to death; no reported association with malformations
Tetracycline	Tooth and bone staining if exposed during last two thirds of pregnancy
Thalidomide	Limb reduction defects; anomalies of external ears, kidneys, and heart
Iodine deficiency	Hypothyroidism or goiter; neurological damage
Mechanical (constraint in womb)	Defects involving limb development and position; neural tube, lip, palate, or abdominal defects
Maternal starvation	Intrauterine growth retardation; central nervous system anomalies; fetal death
Diabetes	Malformations involving internal organs; caudal dysplasia
Rubella	Mental retardation; deafness; cardiovascular malformations; cataracts
Herpes simplex	Microcephaly; eye defects
Aspirin	Heavy use associated with lowered birthrate; no increase in malformation
Caffeine	Not likely to be a teratogen, although excess consumption may be toxic
Nicotine	Placental lesions; intrauterine growth retardation; increased mortality
Vitamin A	Urogenital anomalies associated with massive doses; ear malformations; neural tube defects; cleft palate; facial abnormalities
Vitamin D	Heart defects; facial malformation; mental retardation

source: Based on R. L. Brendt & D. A. Beckman. (1990). Teratology. In R. D. Eden, F. H. Boehm, & M. Haire (Eds.), *Assessment and care of the fetus: Physiological, clinical, and medicolegal principles* (Table 17-4, pp. 227–28). Norwalk, Conn.: Appleton & Lange. Reprinted by permission of the publisher.

then introduced into an individual with Rh(D)-positive blood, they attack that person's blood cells, causing a depletion of oxygen and, in the absence of medical intervention, death.

Unfortunately, this situation can occur in the fetus (termed *fetal erythroblastosis*) when the fetus has Rh(D)-positive blood and the mother is Rh-negative. Because the Rh factor is a dominant genetic trait, this situation will occur only when the father is Rh(D)-positive (and the mother Rh-negative). If blood from the fetus gets into the mother's bloodstream—termed *transplacental hemorrhage*—the mother's blood will begin to produce antibodies. These are usually not produced early enough or in sufficient quantities to affect the first child. Subsequent fetuses may be affected, however.

Transplacental hemorrhage occurs in approximately 50 percent of all pregnant women, either during pregnancy or immediately after birth (Knuppel & Angel, 1990). Hence, the chances of Rh(D) immunization are very high—if, of course, the mother is Rh-negative and the father Rh(D) positive. At one time, this condition was always fatal. Now, however, it is possible for the physician to monitor antibody levels in the mother's blood, determining when levels are high enough to endanger the fetus. At this point, there are several alternatives. If the fetus is sufficiently advanced (32 or 33 weeks, for example), labor might be induced or a cesarean delivery performed and the infant given a complete blood transfusion immediately (Bowman, 1990). If the fetus is not sufficiently advanced, a blood transfusion may be performed in utero.

Preventing Rh(D) Immunization

Fortunately, this type of medical intervention is not often necessary due to the development of the drug *Rhogam* (*Rh Immune Globulin* or *RhIG*) in 1968. Rhogam is blood that already contains *passive* antibodies that prevent the formation of additional antibodies.

It has become routine for all physicians to ascertain whether a pregnant woman is Rh-negative and whether she is at risk of immunization. Bowman (1990) suggests that husbands or partners of Rh-negative women should then be screened. If they too are Rh-negative, there is little chance of fetal erythroblastosis. However, because of the possibility of an extramarital conception, mothers who are Rh-negative and their fetuses should be monitored closely throughout pregnancy.

When an expecting mother is at risk of immunization (that is, she is Rh-negative and the father is Rh(D)-positive), Rhogam is sometimes administered during the

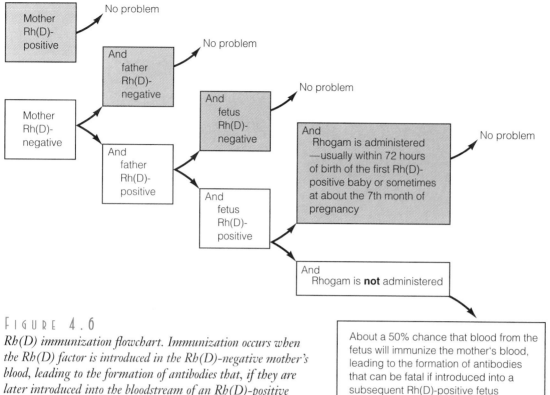

Mother Rh(D)-positive → No problem

Mother Rh(D)-negative →

And father Rh(D)-negative → No problem

And father Rh(D)-positive →

And fetus Rh(D)-negative → No problem

And fetus Rh(D)-positive →

And Rhogam is administered —usually within 72 hours of birth of the first Rh(D)-positive baby or sometimes at about the 7th month of pregnancy → No problem

And Rhogam is **not** administered →

About a 50% chance that blood from the fetus will immunize the mother's blood, leading to the formation of antibodies that can be fatal if introduced into a subsequent Rh(D)-positive fetus

Figure 4.6

Rh(D) immunization flowchart. Immunization occurs when the Rh(D) factor is introduced in the Rh(D)-negative mother's blood, leading to the formation of antibodies that, if they are later introduced into the bloodstream of an Rh(D)-positive fetus, attack the fetus's blood cells in a potentially fatal condition termed fetal erythroblastosis. *An injection of the drug Rhogam can prevent this from occurring.*

seventh month of gestation—or within no more than 72 hours of delivery, as soon as it has been determined that the fetus is Rh-positive, and that the mother is therefore at risk of Rh(D) immunization. Similarly, Rhogam should be administered in the event of the abortion or miscarriage of an Rh(D)-positive fetus if the mother is Rh-negative. The drug needs to be readministered after the termination of every Rh-positive pregnancy. (See Figure 4.6 for an Rh(D) immunization decision flowchart.)

CHILDBIRTH

In the United States, childbirth is something that happens almost 4 million times a year although fertility rates (proportion of women having children) have declined (U.S. Bureau of the Census, 1994). (See At a Glance: "Births and Deaths in the United States," and Table 4.4.)

In the world's developed countries, birth is largely a medical procedure, with doctors and other medical personnel working to ensure the safety and comfort of both newborn and mother. They have at their command techniques and procedures to induce labor, to accelerate it, to delay it, even to stop it if necessary. They can administer drugs to lessen the mother's pain, perform blood transfusions on the infant, or deliver through cesarean section.

Elsewhere and in earlier times, birth was a more natural process. It occurred in birthing huts, in fields, in forests, or, perhaps most often, in homes. Birth was sometimes a solitary experience; sometimes there were midwives, healers, or other attendants. In general, it was believed to be far simpler, shorter, and less painful than birth often is today. Goldsmith (1990) quotes a 19th-century traveler who had been trekking with the Guyana women of South America: "When on the march an Indian is taken with labor, she just steps aside, is delivered, wraps up the baby with the afterbirth and runs in haste after the others" (p. 22).

But we know too that "primitive" birth was (and is) often a tragic experience: Infant mortality was high, and the death of the mother too was not uncommon. A century ago, in most of the world including North America, more than 100 of every 1,000 infants died; that number has now been reduced by almost 90 percent (U.S. Bureau of the Census, 1994). The decline in infant mortality rates is due not only to medical advances, but also to improved sanitation and a consequent reduction in maternal and infant infections. Through the Middle Ages, high risk of death during childbirth (or of subsequent infections) made childbearing a relatively dangerous undertaking for mothers. Even as recently as 1960, of every 100,000 women giving birth in the United States, an average of 37

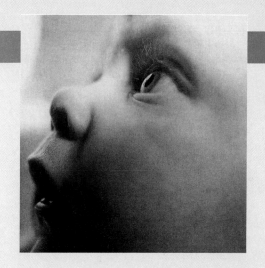

BIRTHS AND DEATHS IN THE UNITED STATES

In 1960, when the baby boom was nearing its peak, almost 4.3 million babies were born in the United States. And only 1.7 million people died, leaving a natural population increase of about 2.5 million. In spite of a substantial increase in total population—from 151 million in 1950 to 249 million in 1990—number of births have remained fairly constant at between 3.5 and 4 million since 1980. This means that the fertility rate (number of births per 1,000 population) has dropped—partly because of more effective contraception, and partly because of changed attitudes toward conception and childbearing.

TABLE 4.4

Births and Deaths in the United States, 1950–1991

	1950	1960	1970	1980	1990	1991
Live Births	3,632,000	4,258,000	3,731,000	3,612,000	4,158,000	4,111,000
Deaths	1,452,000	1,712,000	1,921,000	1,990,000	2,148,000	2,165,000
Natural Increase	2,180,000	2,546,000	1,810,000	1,622,000	2,010,000	1,946,000

SOURCE: Based on U.S. Bureau of the Census, 1994, p. 76.

died (75 percent of these were nonwhites). By 1990, maternal mortality rates had been cut by more than 75 percent (still twice as high for black as for white mothers). During the same period, infant and fetal death rates were more than halved (see At a Glance: "Maternal Deaths in the United States and Elsewhere," and Figures 4.7 and 4.8).

What Starts It

Surprisingly, what causes the childbirth process to begin remains almost as much of a mystery today as it has always been. Hippocrates, writing more than 400 years B.C., thought he knew. The child starts the whole process, he informed his readers. When the fetus has grown too big, there simply isn't enough nourishment available, so it becomes agitated—it kicks around and moves its arms, and it ruptures the membranes that hold it in. And then it forces its way out, head first because the head part is heavier than the bottom part (see Liggins, 1988).

Hippocrates was wrong, although there were many who believed his speculation right into the 18th century. We now know that fetuses that are dead may go through the process of labor—which would not be possible if they were responsible for initiating it.

There have been many other theories over the years; but, as Liggins (1988) concludes, we still don't have "the final chapter of the 2000-year-old search for the cause of labor" (p. 387). However, even though we don't know its cause, we do understand a lot about the process.

A Clinical View of Labor

Labor is the process whereby the fetus, the placenta, and other membranes are separated from the woman's body and expelled.

The onset of labor is usually gradual and may be described in three stages. That there are exceptions to the normal process has been substantiated by numerous fathers who were caught unawares, taxi drivers who drove too slowly, pilots who did not quite make it, and many others for whom nature would not wait. Although physicians can induce labor, as we saw, the precise natural cause of the beginning of labor remains unknown. Yet labor begins, more often than not, at the prescribed time.

Stage 1: Dilation

The first stage of labor is the longest, lasting an average of 12 hours but varying greatly in length. Generally, labor is longest and most difficult for the first delivery.

The first stage consists of initially mild contractions spaced quite far apart (like butterflies in my stomach, said one woman). Contractions become more painful, more

MATERNAL DEATHS IN THE UNITED STATES AND ELSEWHERE

Each year approximately 500,000 women die in childbirth, about 99 percent of them in the developing world. In addition, an estimated 100,000 die of unsafe abortions (Grant, 1993). There are three ways of attacking the problem, says Grant: (1) reduce unwanted pregnancies, many of which are higher risk; (2) prevent complications of pregnancy; and (3) provide medical assistance when there are complications.

FIGURE 4.7

Declining maternal mortality rates from delivery and complications of pregnancy and childbirth, 1960–1990. (Based on U.S. Bureau of the Census, 1993, p. 89.)

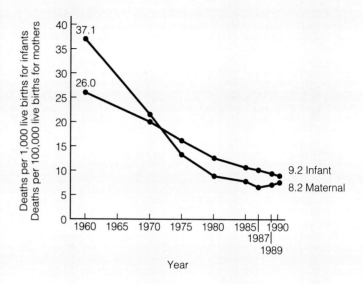

FIGURE 4.8

Maternal mortality rates for selected countries per 100,000 live births, 1980–1990. (Based on Grant, 1993, pp. 80–81.)

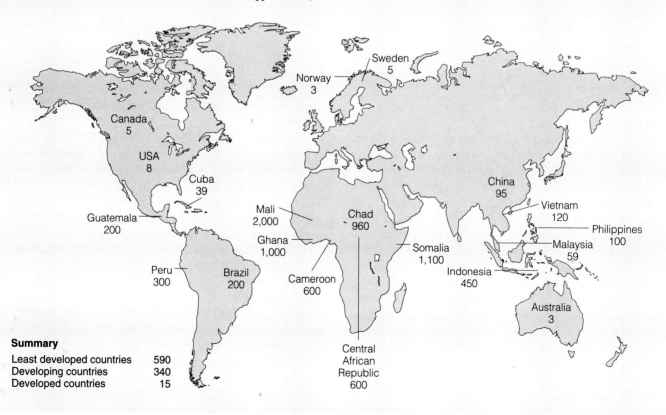

Summary

Least developed countries	590
Developing countries	340
Developed countries	15

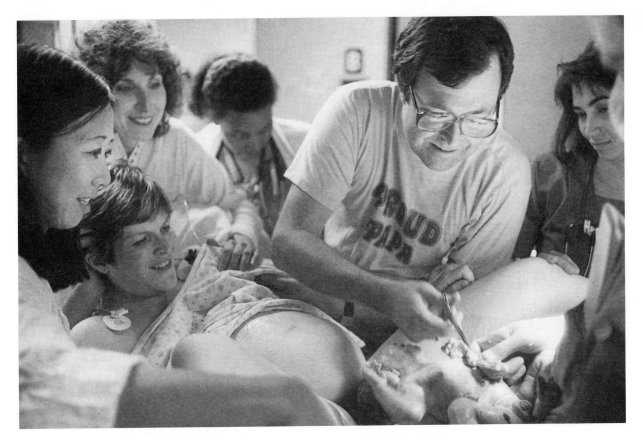

In North America, childbirth is increasingly occurring in more homelike environments, often with spouse, parents, and others present. And what used to be exclusively medical procedures—like cutting the umbilical cord on this twin—can sometimes be done even by the father.

frequent, and longer toward the end of the first stage of birth (like a bear cub in my guts, said another).

In the first stage, the **cervix** (the opening to the uterus) dilates to allow passage of the baby from the uterus, down through the birth canal, and eventually into the world. Contractions are involuntary and exert a downward pressure on the fetus as well as a distending force on the cervix. If the **amniotic sac** (the sac filled with amniotic fluid in which the fetus develops) is still intact, it absorbs much of the pressure in the early stages and transmits some of the force of the contractions to the neck of the cervix. However, if the sac has ruptured or bursts in the early stages of labor, the baby's head will rest directly on the pelvic structure and cervix, serving as a sort of wedge.

Stage 2: Delivery

The second stage of birth, *delivery*, begins when the cervix is sufficiently dilated. It starts with the baby's head emerging (in a normal delivery) at the cervical opening and ends with the birth of the child (Figure 4.9). The second stage usually lasts no more than an hour and often ends in a few minutes. The fetus ordinarily presents itself head first and can usually be born without the intervention of a physician. On occasion, however, complications arise that require some sort of intervention. For example,

the head of the fetus may be too large for the opening provided by the mother. In such a case the physician may make a small incision in the vaginal outlet (an **episiotomy**), which is sutured after the baby is born. Complications can also arise from abnormal **presentations** of the fetus: **breech** (buttocks first), **transverse** (crosswise), or a variety of other possible positions. Some of these can be corrected before birth by turning the fetus manually in the uterus (**version**). Sometimes the fetus is delivered just as it presents itself.

Stage 3: The Afterbirth

Toward the end of the delivery stage, the attending physician or nurse severs the neonate's umbilical cord; places silver nitrate or penicillin drops in its eyes to guard against gonococcal infection; and assures that its breathing, muscle tone, coloration, and reflexive activity are normal. Following this, the physician assists in the third and final stage of birth and evaluates the condition of the **neonate,** or newborn, perhaps by means of the Apgar scale (discussed later in this chapter).

In the third stage, the *afterbirth*—the placenta and other membranes—is expelled. This process usually takes less than 5 minutes and seldom more than 15. The physician examines the afterbirth carefully to ensure that all of

FIGURE 4.9
This cross section shows the normal, headfirst presentation and delivery of a baby.

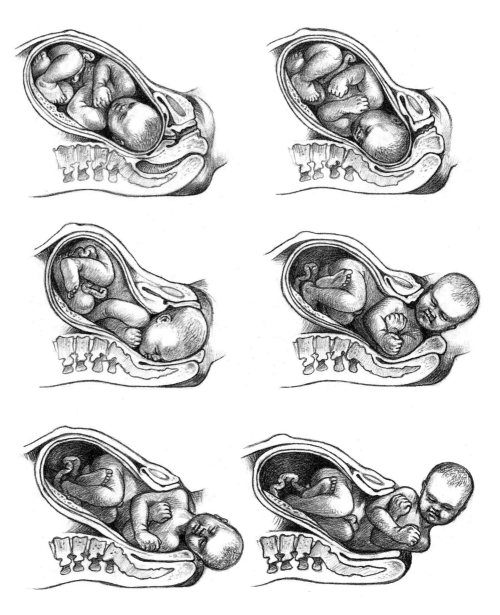

One of the advantages of birth in hospital family suites rather than in more conventional delivery rooms: the bonding of toddler and newborn.

it has been expelled. If it is incomplete, surgical procedures (frequently, **dilation and curettage,** or **D & C**—a scraping of the uterus) may be employed to remove remaining portions. At the end of the third stage of labor, the uterus should contract and remain contracted. It is sometimes necessary to massage the abdominal area or administer drugs to stimulate contraction and to guard against the danger of postpartum (afterbirth) hemorrhage.

Cesarean Delivery

In an increasing number of instances, medical intervention bypasses these three stages of birth through a **cesarean delivery**—almost one quarter of all births in the United States (U.S. Bureau of the Census, 1994) (See At a Glance: "U.S. Cesarean Deliveries," Figures 4.10 and 4.11.) In such cases, birth is accomplished by making an

U.S. CESAREAN DELIVERIES

Cesarean section deliveries have quadrupled in frequency since 1970. Not surprisingly, the highest rates are for older age groups. Cesarean deliveries have clearly saved the lives of many mothers and infants, but some critics argue that they are used too frequently. Although the procedure is routine and low risk, it entails a somewhat higher risk of infection, medical problems for the mother, and respiratory problems among infants.

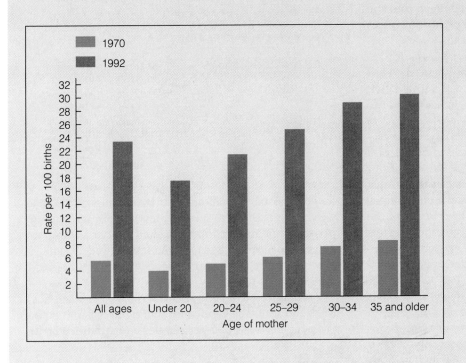

FIGURE 4.10

Changes in rate of cesareans by age, 1970–1992 (per 100 births). (From U.S. Bureau of the Census, 1994, p. 79.)

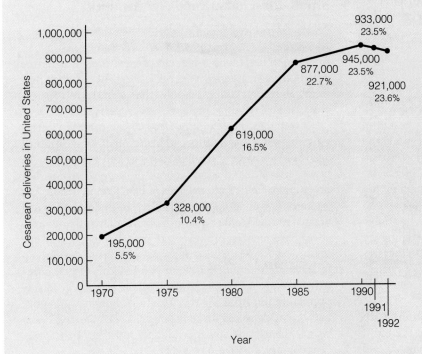

FIGURE 4.11

Cesarean deliveries in the United States, 1970–1992. (Percentages shown indicate the number of cesarean deliveries per 100 births.) (Based on U.S. Bureau of the Census, 1994, p. 79.)

incision in the mother's abdomen and uterus and removing the baby. Cesareans are most often indicated when the mother's labor fails to progress, when previous cesareans have been performed, when the fetus is in a breech presentation, or when the physician detects signs of fetal distress. *Epidural analgesia*, an injection of anesthetic frequently used to relieve childbirth pain, appears to increase the risk of insufficient cervical dilation leading to a cesarean delivery (Thorp et al., 1994).

Cesarean deliveries have clearly saved the lives of many mothers and infants and alleviated much pain and suffering; but the rapid increase in the proportion of cesarean births relative to nonsurgical births is a source of some concern. Although much of this increase clearly results from dramatic improvements in the physician's ability to monitor the fetus prior to birth and during labor, and is associated with higher fetal survival (Iffy et al., 1994), critics suggest that not all cesarean deliveries are necessary. Sperling and colleagues (1994) looked at reasons for cesarean births for *all* 1989 births in two Danish countries with very different rates of cesarean sections (8.3 percent and 15.2 percent). Their conclusion was that the greater use of cesarean deliveries in the one country could not be accounted for by differences in any of the conditions that ordinarily lead to a decision to perform a cesarean. Deciding factors seemed to be simply differences in obstetric practice as well as differences in maternal expectations and demands.

Lieberman (1987) reports that a number of hospitals have succeeded in dramatically reducing rates of cesarean deliveries without any increase in fetal or maternal problems. This is accomplished largely by reviewing the need for a cesarean delivery in cases where they might simply have been done routinely, as sometimes happens for breech births, twins, or patients who have had previous cesareans.

Classifications of Birth

The physical status of the child has traditionally been classified according to the length of time spent in gestation and by weight. A fetus born before the 20th week and weighing less than 500 grams (about 1 pound) is termed an **abortion** (sometimes called a *miscarriage*). A fetus delivered between the 20th and 28th week and weighing between 500 and 999 grams (between 1 and 2 pounds) is an **immature birth.** At one time, immature births invariably died; the majority still do, most of them from respiratory failure. But with modern medical procedures, an increasing number survive, some born as much as four months prematurely and weighing as little as 750 grams (1½ pounds) or less.

The birth of a baby between the 29th and the 36th weeks is called a **premature birth,** provided the child weighs between 1,000 and 2,499 grams (between 2 and

TABLE 4.5
Physical Status of Child at Birth

Classification by Gestation	Time	Average Weight
Abortion	Before 20th week	Less than 500 g (1 lb)
Immature birth	20th–28th week	500–999 g (1-2 lb)
Premature birth	29th–36th week	1,000–2,499 g (2–5½ lb)
Mature birth	37th–42nd week	Over 2,500 g (over 5 lb)
Postmature birth	After 42 weeks	—

Classification by Weight and Gestation	
SGA (small-for-gestational age)	10 percent less than average for infants of same gestational age
AGA (average-for-gestational age)	Within 10 percent of average weight for infants of same gestational age
LGA (large-for-gestational age)	10 percent more than average for infants of same gestational age

5½ pounds). Complications are more common if the child weighs less than 1,500 grams. A few decades ago, only 20 percent of premature infants in the 1,000 to 1,500-gram range (2 to 5½ pounds) survived. Now between 90 and 95 percent survive ("Preemies' Diet Seen Key to Progress," 1988).

A **mature birth** occurs between the 37th and the 42nd week and results in an infant weighing over 2,500 grams (5½ pounds). A late delivery is called a **postmature birth.**

Small-for-Gestational Age Infants

All newborns, regardless of whether they are premature, are also classified as *small-for-gestational age* (SGA) when they weigh less than 90 percent of newborns of the same gestational age; as *large-for-gestational age* (LGA) when they weigh above the 90th percentile (that is, in the top 10 percent); or as *average-for-gestational age* (AGA) (Table 4.5).

From a medical point of view, it's important to distinguish between prematurity and being small-for-gestational age (SGA) because the implications of being SGA may be more serious than the implications of being premature but not average-for-gestational age (AGA). The premature but average-for-gestational age infant has been developing at a normal rate and, unless very premature, may suffer no negative consequences. However, the small-for-gestational age infant, regardless of gestational age, has been developing less rapidly than normal. Palo and Erkkola (1993) compared 153 premature SGA infants with another 153 equally premature but AGA infants. The SGA infants were more likely to be delivered through emergency cesarean (82 percent of them) and had a much higher mortality rate (7 percent compared with 4.6 percent).

THE APGAR SCALE

When she was born, Carla Snipe snorted once, recalls her mother, then yelled about as loudly as anyone in the county ever had. Her color was as much red as pink, claims her mother, and she kicked out strongly enough that the nurse was hard-pressed to hang onto the still-slick infant. What would you guess Carla's Apgar score might have been?

Score	Heart Rate	Respiratory Effort	Muscle Tone	Color	Reflex Irritability
0	Absent	Absent	Flaccid, limp	Blue, pale	No response
1	Slow (less than 100)	Irregular, slow	Weak, inactive	Body pink, extremities blue	Grimace
2	Rapid (over 100)	Good, crying	Strong, active	Entirely pink	Coughing, sneezing, crying

Neonatal Scales

In almost all North American hospitals it is routine to evaluate the condition of a newborn by means of the *Apgar scale*. The scale, shown in Interactive Table 4.6, is almost self-explanatory. Infants receive scores according to whether each of the appropriate signs is present. Maximum score is 10; average score is usually 7 or better; a score of 4 or less indicates that the neonate must be given special care immediately. The Apgar evaluation is administered at least twice—at 1 minute after birth and at 5 minutes after birth (and sometimes at 10 minutes after birth). Five- and 10-minute scores are often higher than 1-minute scores.

A second important scale for assessing the condition of a newborn infant is the *Brazelton Neonatal Behavioral Assessment Scale* (NBAS) (Brazelton, 1973). Like the Apgar scale, it may be used to detect problems immediately after birth. In addition, it provides useful indicators of central nervous system maturity, as well as of social behavior. The Brazelton scale looks at a total of 26 specific behaviors in-

cluding reaction to light, cuddling, voices, and a pinprick; it also looks at the strength of various reflexes. The scale is especially useful in identifying infants who might be prone to later psychological problems. Brazelton (1990) suggests that use of the scale has done much to increase our understanding of infant developmental patterns and of their states of consciousness. It also provides physicians with information that might be important for them to share with parents. For example, parents of infants who are less responsive to cuddling and to other social stimulation could be alerted to this from the very beginning, and thus these parents could compensate by providing the infant with extra loving contact.

The Mother's Experience: Prepared Childbirth

The preceding discussion of the delivery of a human child is admittedly clinical and maybe a little like the antiseptic hospitals in which most North American babies are born; it doesn't uncover and transmit the magic and the mystery of the process. In an effort to recapture some of this mystery, I spoke with several women whose experience qualified them to make subjective comments more valid than those my imagination might supply.

"What's it like, having a baby?" I asked.

"It's a piece of cake," my first interviewee assured me in her characteristic, clichéd way. "It's as easy as rolling off a log."

"It hurts like #@*#!!" my second interviewee insisted in her usual profane manner. "It's a hell of a big log!"

Combining these impressions, an absolutely clear picture of the situation emerges.

The inexperienced mother sometimes approaches the event with some degree of apprehension; there is often some pain associated with childbirth. However, advocates of natural childbirth (also called *prepared* childbirth) claim that through a regimen of prenatal exercises and adequate

Having a baby is as easy as falling off a log.

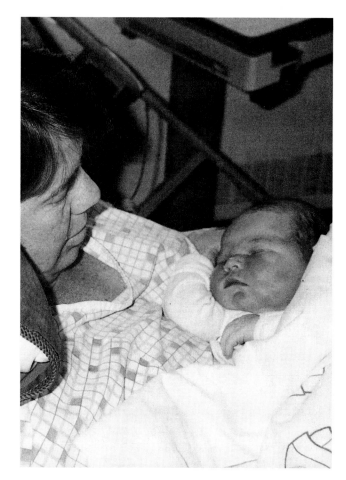

Birth means a staggering change in the infant's environment—from a dark, quiet, cushioned, temperature controlled world to a hectic world of changing smells, textures, sounds, temperatures, and movements. It also means enormous changes in the mother's world.

psychological preparations, many women experience relatively painless childbirths.

Natural childbirth, a phrase coined by a British physician, Grantly Dick-Read (1972), refers to the process of having a child without anesthetics. The Dick-Read process recommends relaxing exercises and psychological preparation for the arrival of the child, all directed toward delivery in which painkillers are unnecessary. Natural childbirth is based on the assumption that alleviating the fear of pain, together with training in relaxation, will result in less pain. Dick-Read's hypothesis has proved sound.

Lamaze and Leboyer Methods
Two popular methods of prepared childbirth are the Lamaze and the Leboyer techniques. The Lamaze method teaches expectant mothers a variety of breathing and relaxation exercises. These are practiced repeatedly, often with the assistance of the father or birth partner, until they become so habitual that they will be used almost "naturally" during the actual process of birth. The use of anesthetics during labor is less common among women who are thus prepared, and women's moods tend to be more positive during labor (Leventhal, Leventhal, & Shacham (1989).

The Leboyer method is concerned more with the delivery of the infant than with advance preparation of the mother. Leboyer's (1975) technique involves delivering the baby in a softly lit room, immersing the infant almost immediately in a lukewarm bath, and then placing the baby directly on the mother's abdomen. These procedures are designed to ease the infant's transition from the womb to the world; thus the need for soft lights, which do not contrast as harshly with the darkness of the womb as does conventional delivery room lighting, and for a lukewarm bath, which might feel something like amniotic fluid. Leboyer claims that his procedures eliminate much of the shock of birth and result in better-adjusted individuals. Critics suggest that birth in dimly lit surroundings might contribute to the physician's failing to notice important signs of distress or injury and that the dangers of infection are greater under these circumstances than they are when more conventional hospital practices are employed.

Hospitals or Homes: Doctors or Midwives
Not only are many mothers choosing to have their babies by natural means but many are also deciding *where* birth will occur. For some, home is that choice; for others, hospi-

tal birthing rooms—a homier and more comfortable alternative than a conventional operating or delivery room—or hospital family suites where father and other siblings can actually stay. Although most North American births still occur in hospitals, length of hospitalization is considerably shorter than it once was (often only a matter of hours).

Traditionally, in countries such as Britain, the majority of births were attended to by midwives rather than by physicians, a practice less common in North America (Sagov et al., 1984). However, with the medicalization of birth, the use of midwives has declined even in Europe and their role has changed. An increasing number of births are attended to by physicians; and where midwives are used, they are often part of a medical team. Their role on that team has also declined dramatically in importance (Robinson, 1989). In many cases, midwives are used primarily as receptionists or to do routine tasks like weighing pregnant women and taking urine samples.

Sedatives in Childbirth

For one mother, childbirth may be quite painful; for another mother, it may be a slightly painful, but intensely rewarding and satisfying experience. Although the amount of pain can be controlled to some extent with anesthetics, the intensity of the immediate emotional reward will also be dulled by the drugs. In addition, sedatives given to the mother may affect the infant. Children delivered without sedatives are frequently more alert, more responsive to the environment, and better able to cope with immediate environmental demands (Brazelton, Nugent, & Lester, 1987). In short, they may have a slight initial advantage, the long-range implications of which are unclear.

Postpartum Depression

As many as 10 percent of all women suffer from depression after giving birth (Campbell & Cohn, 1991). It isn't clear whether this **postpartum depression** is due to hormonal changes, to the effects of sedating drugs that might have been used in labor, to disruptions in lifestyle, or to other factors (Dalton, 1980). However, studies indicate that women who receive higher levels of social support (from friends and family, for example) are at lower risk for postpartum depression (Collins et al., 1993). Also, there is evidence that although postpartum depression is not different from other forms of depression, its symptoms tend to be relatively mild (Whiffen & Gotlib, 1993). Hence the prognosis for postpartum depression is excellent, with most cases improving quickly with time and disappearing completely within a year (Wolman et al., 1993).

The Child's Experience

How do children, the heroes of this text, react to the process of birth? From their point of view, birth must be an indifferent process: They cannot reason about it, can-

not compare it with other more or less pleasant states, can do nothing deliberately to alter it, and will not even remember it. But consider the incredibly dramatic difference that birth makes. Up to now, the child has been living in a completely friendly and supportive environment. Nourishment, getting oxygen, eliminating wastes—everything has been accomplished without effort. The uterus has been kept at exactly the right temperature, the danger of bacterial infection has been relatively insignificant, and there have been no psychological threats—we think. But at birth, the infant is suddenly exposed to new physiological and perhaps psychological dangers. Once mucus is cleared from the mouth and throat, the newborn must breathe unassisted for the first time. As soon as the umbilical cord ceases to pulsate, it is unceremoniously clipped an inch or two above the abdomen and tied off with a clamp. And the child is now completely alone—singularly dependent and helpless, to be sure, but no longer a biological parasite on the mother.

Dangers of Birth

Birth is not without danger for the newborn. Injuries, including brain damage, sometimes occur during birth, often resulting from the tremendous pressure exerted on the head during birth—especially if labor is long and if the amniotic sac has been broken early, in which case the head, in a normal presentation, has been repeatedly pressed against the slowly dilating cervix. In addition, the infant has to pass through an opening so small that deformation of the head often results. (For most infants the head usually assumes a more normal appearance within a few days.)

An additional source of pressure on the child's head may be **forceps,** clamplike instruments sometimes employed during delivery. Although the fetus can withstand considerable pressure on the head, the danger of such pressure is that it may rupture blood vessels and cause hemorrhaging. In severe cases, death may result; otherwise, brain damage may result because cranial hemorrhage can restrict the supply of oxygen to the brain.

Another possible danger is **anoxia,** a shortage of oxygen to the brain. Anoxia can result if the umbilical cord becomes lodged between the child's body and the birth canal, disrupting the flow of oxygen (referred to as **prolapsed cord**). Anoxia may be related to impaired neurological, psychological, and motor functioning associated with brain damage.

PREMATURITY

Prematurity is defined by a short gestation period (36 weeks or less) and low birthweight (small-for-gestational age, or SGA—less than 90 percent of average weight for term, usually less than 2,500 grams (5½ pounds). It is one

BIRTHWEIGHT AND PRENATAL INFLUENCES

Prematurity and low birthweight are among the most serious complications of birth. Low birthweight may contribute to infant death or general developmental retardation, including lower intelligence. Factors implicated in low birthweight include smoking and use of other drugs, mal-

nutrition, maternal age, socioeconomic status, and race. The relationship of age, social class, and race to low birthweight and prematurity is probably due primarily to other associated factors such as poorer nutrition and medical attention. In some of the world's least developed countries, such as Bangladesh, as many as half of all infants are born with low birthweight (under 2,500 grams); in Finland and Norway, only 4 percent of neonates are low birthweight. On average, 24 percent of infants in the least developed countries, 19 percent of infants in developing countries, and 6 percent of infants in developed countries weigh less than 2,500 grams at birth (Grant, 1993).

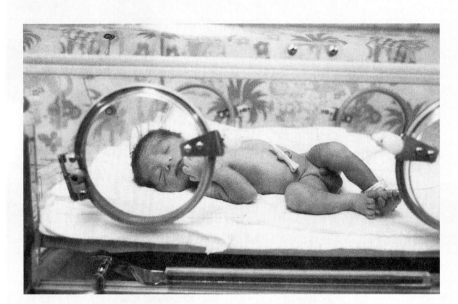

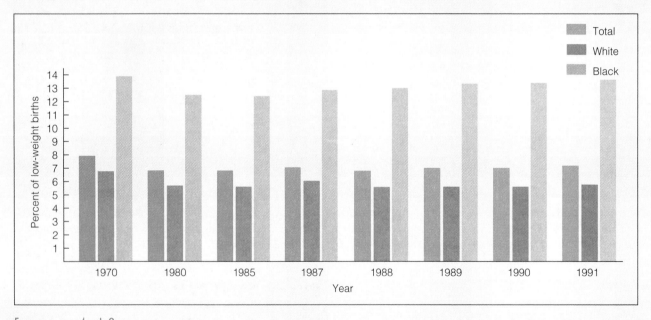

FIGURE 4.12

The relationship of race to low birthweight (less than or equal to 2,500 grams—5 pounds, 8 ounces—for 1970; less than 2,500 grams—5 pounds, 8 ounces—for 1980 through 1991). (From U.S. Bureau of the Census, 1994, p. 79.)

TABLE 4.7

Factors Associated with Higher Risk of Preterm Labor

Major Factors

Multiple gestation
DES exposure
Uterine anomaly
Cervix dilated more than 1 cm at 32 weeks
Two previous second-trimester abortions
Previous preterm delivery
Previous labor during preterm, with term delivery
Abdominal surgery during pregnancy
Uterine irritability

Minor Factors

Febrile (fever) illness
Bleeding after 12 weeks
More than 10 cigarettes per day
One previous second-trimester abortion
More than two previous first-trimester abortions

SOURCE: Based on R. H. Holbrook, Jr., R. K. Laros, Jr., & R. K. Creasy (1988), Evaluation of a risk-scoring system for prediction of preterm labor. *American Journal of Perinatology* 6, 62. Reprinted with permission of Thieme Medical Publishers, Inc.

of the more serious possible complications of birth, affecting approximately 10 percent of all infants born in the United States. Incidence of prematurity is considerably higher in some other countries (Grant, 1993).

Causes of Prematurity

We do not know the precise causes of premature delivery (Creasy, 1990). However, a number of factors are related to its occurrence. As we saw, these include poverty, malnutrition, age, smoking, and other drugs, all of which are implicated in other infant disadvantages. Note, however, that factors such as social class and race have no inherent explanatory value. Certainly, neither causes prematurity any more than they cause the environmental conditions of poverty, ill health, and lower social and economic opportunity with which they are often associated.

Other related factors include various illnesses in the mother while she is pregnant; gonorrhea is one such illness that is an important contributor to prematurity in many countries (Donders et al., 1993). In addition, infants from multiple births are more frequently premature than are infants from single births. Finally, a number of infants are preterm in the absence of any of these negative influences and in spite of excellent maternal care, nutrition, and health (see At a Glance: "Birthweight and Prenatal Influences," and Figure 4.12 and Table 4.7).

Effects of Prematurity

One of the most obvious possible effects of prematurity is death. Indeed, only a few decades ago the chances of death for a premature infant weighing between 2,000 and 2,500 grams (4½ and 5½ pounds) were approximately six times greater than for an infant weighing 3,000 grams (6 pounds, 10 ounces) or more. Now, however, the majority of premature infants weighing 2,000 grams (4½ pounds) or more survive. In fact, more than 90 percent of infants who weigh as little as 1,000 to 1,500 grams survive (Goldsmith, 1990). Most of these preterm infants spend the first two to three months of their lives in intensive care nurseries, often in *incubators* (also called *isolettes*). Chances of survival decrease 10 to 15 percent for each hundred grams below 1,000 (Goldsmith, 1990). However, half or more of those who weigh less than 1,250 grams suffer adverse consequences; one third or more suffer from *severe* physical or mental handicaps (Beckwith & Rodning, 1991). For research purposes, infants are sometimes classifed as *low birthweight* if they weigh less than 2,500 grams, *very low birthweight* if less than 1,500 grams, and *extremely low birthweight* when under 750 grams.

Hack and colleagues (1992; 1993) have been following a group of 249 very low birthweight infants (under 1,500 grams; about 3 pounds) through the first decade of their lives. Comparisons of these children with average birthweight controls reveal lower weight, height, and head circumference at age 8, significantly higher incidence of various illnesses and surgical procedures, and significantly poorer performance on most measures of intellectual functioning including intelligence, language, reading, mathematics, spelling, and motor abilities. A subgroup of these low birthweight infants who weighed less than 750 grams at birth (about 1½ pounds) were at even greater disadvantage. Almost 25 percent were mentally retarded, about half were in special education classes, 25 percent had vision problems, and 25 percent suffered from measurable hearing loss (Boodman, 1994.) These findings have now been confirmed in a number of other studies including one by Ross, Lipper, and Auld (1991), which found that 48 percent of a group of 88 children who weighed less than 1,500 grams at birth required special educational interventions at age 8—compared with 15 percent of the New York City public elementary school population of which they were part.

Other possible effects of prematurity and/or of prolonged hospitalization following birth include lower intelligence, a higher incidence of cerebral palsy, and general developmental retardation. These effects, of course, are not found among all preterm babies, and are progressively less likely for those infants who are least premature and who weigh the most at birth. For example, in studies of premature identical twins, the heaviest of the twins tends to have higher measures of intelligence (Churchill, 1965). Among preterm infants who weigh 2,000 or more grams, subsequent complications are relatively rare.

In view of these rather alarming findings, and given the highly likely relationship between nutrition and prematurity, probably a great deal can be done for unborn children and their mothers through programs of education, nutrition, and housing. But it should also be pointed out that not all premature infants suffer noticeable disadvantages relative to their mature peers.

Prevention of Prematurity

"We still aren't fully aware of all the events that occur to elicit this [birthing] reaction," says Dr. David Olson ("Shortening the Time Between the Bench and the Bedside," 1993, p. 4). If we were, he adds, we might be able to figure out how to prevent premature delivery. At present, all we can do is try to identify women who appear to be at greater risk. This can't be done with certainty because the precise causes of premature delivery are not usually known. However, it's possible to estimate degree of risk given knowledge of the woman's status with respect to the factors most often associated with prematurity—for example, previous preterm delivery, exposure to DES, the presence of more than one fetus, smoking, and uterine anomalies (see Table 4.7). It's also possible to monitor uterine activity and sometimes to detect an increase in activity prior to the onset of preterm labor.

There are a number of different approaches to preventing preterm labor, including bed rest, avoiding sexual intercourse, the use of antibiotics and other drugs, and suturing the cervix. None of these has been clearly proven to be effective, although there is some evidence that each might sometimes be helpful (Goldsmith, 1990).

Care of Premature Infants

Premature infants born in the 23rd to 25th week of pregnancy have a 50-percent survival rate; 85 percent of those born between the 26th and 28th week survive ("Shortening the Time Between the Bench and the Bedside," 1993). Nor is prematurity inevitably linked with physical, psychological, or neurological inferiority. With adequate care, many premature infants fare as well as full-term infants.

Nutrition and Medical Care

What are the dimensions of that care? First they include advances in medical knowledge and technology. Ventilators, for example, make possible the survival of infants whose hearts and lungs are not sufficiently developed to work on their own; so does intravenous feeding with what is termed *total parenteral nutrition* (TPN). The contents of this nutrition are especially important because they substitute for nutrients that the infant would ordinarily have received as a fetus. Certain fatty acids appear to be importantly involved in brain growth and neuron development during the last trimester of pregnancy—roughly the period of intrauterine growth that a 27-week preterm infant

would miss ("Preemies' Diet Seen Key to Progress," 1988). Accordingly, the premature infant's nutrition has to include these nutrients at the appropriate time and in the appropriate form. Not surprisingly, hospital care of premature infants is sometimes enormously expensive ("Shortening the Time Between the Bench and the Bedside," 1993).

Psychological Care

In addition to important medical advances in the care of premature infants, a tremendous amount of research in the last 20 years has looked at the possibility that at least some of the adverse psychological consequences of prematurity might be due to the lack of stimulation the preterm infant receives in an intensive care nursery—or, perhaps more accurately, the inappropriateness of the stimulation. Harrison (1985) summarized 24 studies that have looked at various forms of "supplemental" stimulation for preterm infants. Some investigated the effects of tactile stimulation (stroking; holding); others looked at auditory stimulation (taped recordings of a mother's voice, for example), vestibulary stimulation (oscillating hammock or waterbed), gustatory stimulation (pacifier), or a combination of different kinds of stimulation. In general, the studies support the conclusion that additional stimulation of preterm infants helps their development. Positive effects include greater weight gains, shorter hospital stays, greater responsiveness, and higher developmental scores on various measures. The evidence is clear that the traditional hands-off treatment once given most premature infants is not the best of all possible worlds for them.

A REASSURING NOTE

It is often very disturbing for nonmedical people to consult medical journals and textbooks in search of explanations for their various complaints. Inevitably, they discover that they have all the symptoms for some vicious infection or exotic disease. So if you happen to be pregnant at this moment or are contemplating pregnancy, or are otherwise involved in the business, you might find yourself a little apprehensive. I draw this to your attention only to emphasize that it really isn't that bad (pregnancy, that is). The intrauterine world of the unborn infant is less threatening and less dangerous than our world. Also, it is perhaps reassuring that nature often provides for spontaneous abortions when the embryo or the fetus would have been grossly abnormal. In fact, some 15 percent of recognized pregnancies result in spontaneous abortions, and more than half of these have chromosomal anomalies (Dill & McGillivray, 1992). In most cases, when the fetus comes to term, the probability that the child will be normal and healthy far outweighs the likelihood that it will suffer any of the defects or abnormalities described in this chapter.

Detecting Pregnancy

1. Early symptoms of pregnancy, such as cessation of menses, are uncertain, but simple chemical tests may be performed to detect changes in the woman's urine within a few weeks of conception. The gestation period for humans is 266 days (10 lunar months from the onset of the last menses).

Stages of Prenatal Development

2. Prenatal physiological development occurs in three stages: During the first two weeks, the *fertilized ovum* moves down the Fallopian tubes and embeds itself in the uterine wall; from week 2 to week 8, the *embryo* develops so that by the end of the eighth week, all the organs of the infant are present; from week 9 until birth, the *fetus* grows mainly in size and weight and neurologically.

Factors Affecting Prenatal Development

3. External influences that cause malformations and physical defects are labeled *teratogens. Mutagens* cause changes in genetic material. Effects of teratogens vary depending on genetic factors, the presence of other negative or positive influences, and their timing. Among teratogens are some prescription drugs (thalidomide or DES—linked with malformations and cancer); some chemicals (mercury—Minimata disease—and PCBs—linked with spontaneous abortions and physical deformities). Radiation can lead to spontaneous abortions and physical abnormalities.

4. Smoking cigarettes increases fetal heart rate and activity, and is associated with significant retardation of fetal growth, higher incidence of premature births, and higher risk of miscarriages and fetal death. Alcohol consumption may lead to fetal alcohol syndrome (FAS), symptoms of which may include mental retardation and characteristic cranial and facial malformations. Infants born to narcotic addicts are themselves usually addicted at birth; in severe cases, they may die. In addition, narcotics such as heroin and opium are associated with prematurity. Stimulants such as cocaine may also be associated with prematurity, lower birthweight, and developmental problems.

5. Various maternal diseases and infections such as rubella, syphilis, gonorrhea, and diabetes can lead to mental deficiency, blindness, deafness, or fetal death. Herpes can be transmitted to the fetus during birth and can lead to serious complications including death. AIDS can also be transmitted from mother to fetus (35–60 percent probability) and is fatal.

6. There is a higher probability of some chromosomal defects such as Down syndrome and fragile X syndrome

for older parents. Infants born to teenage mothers are at higher risk of physical, emotional, and intellectual disadvantage (more miscarriages, premature births, and stillbirths, and more emotional and physical abuse among those who survive—outcomes associated more with the social and medical circumstances of teenage parenthood than with the mother's age). Famine and malnutrition may lead to lower fertility rates and higher fetal mortality. Social class, because of related medical, nutritional, and drug use factors, is associated with a higher incidence of prematurity and other complications.

7. In the absence of medical intervention, mothers who are negative for the Rh blood factor, where the father is Rh-positive, would be at risk of giving birth to infants suffering from fetal erythroblastosis. This condition is routinely avoided in modern hospitals through use of the drug Rhogam.

Childbirth

8. Birth occurs in three stages: labor (dilation of the cervix, about 9–12 hours), the actual delivery (about 1 hour), and the afterbirth (the expulsion of the placenta and other membranes, several minutes). Cesarean deliveries have increased dramatically in recent years largely as a result of improved technology for fetal monitoring. Expected date of birth is 266 days after conception. Early deliveries are termed *premature* (before the 37th week). Newborns are also classified as small-for-gestational age (SGA) if they weigh 10 percent less than average newborns of the same gestational age. Newborns are routinely evaluated at birth by means of the Apgar scale—a scale that looks at their *A*ppearance (color), *P*ulse (heart rate), *G*rimace (reflex irritability), *A*ctivity (muscle tone), and *R*espiration (respiratory effort) (note the mnemonic, or memory, device).

9. Natural, or prepared, childbirth (Lamaze or Leboyer, for example) refers to the preparation for and process of having a child with little or no use of anesthetics. Birth poses two great dangers for the neonate: The first is cerebral hemorrhage, resulting from extreme pressures in the uterus or in the birth canal; the second is prolapse of the umbilical cord and shortage of oxygen.

Prematurity

10. Prematurity appears to be linked to social-class variables such as diet and poor medical attention, to the age of the mother, and to smoking. Its most apparent effects are the greater possibility of death, physical defects, hyperactivity, and impaired mental functioning. Medical advances have made it possible for more than 90 percent of premature infants weighing as little as 1,000–1,500

grams (½–⅔ pound) to survive. The severity of possible medical consequences of prematurity has been significantly ameliorated by medical advances. In addition, the psychological consequences of prematurity can be offset through increased tactile (stroking, cuddling), auditory, vestibulatory (rocking), gustatory (pacifier), or multimodal stimulation. Still, many premature infants suffer physical or mental handicaps.

1. What are the common probable and positive signs of pregnancy?
   - How can a physician (or mother) most easily ascertain pregnancy? What are some of the advantages of early detection?

2. What is the normal sequence of prenatal development and birth?
   - Describe the main features of the three main stages of intrauterine development, and of the three stages of birth.

3. What factors have the potential of being most harmful to the fetus? When?

- Distinguish between teratogens and mutagens. List several of the main classes of factors that can harm the fetus, and describe their possible effects.

4. What are the the principal causes and implications of prematurity?
   - Write a brief essay (a) looking at some of the possible implications of prematurity; or (b) examining some possible explanations for the relationship between social class and prematurity.

STUDY TERMS

abortion   112
afterbirth   109
AIDS   101
amniotic sac   109
anoxia   115
artificial insemination   92
Babinski reflex   95
breech presentation   109
cephalocaudal   96
cervix   109
cesarean delivery   110
conception   92
cytomegalovirus   101
delivery   109
diethylstilbestrol   97
dilation and curettage (D & C)   110
embryo stage   93
episiotomy   109

Fallopian tubes   93
fertilization   93
fertilized ovum   93
fetal alcohol syndrome   98
fetus stage   93
forceps   115
genitalia   95
germinal stage   93
gestation period   92
herpes   100
immature birth   120
in utero   94
labor   107
lanugo   95
mature birth   112
menses   92
mutagens   96
natural childbirth   114
neonatal abstinence syndrome   99

neonate   109
ovaries   93
placenta   94
postmature birth   112
postpartum depression   115
pregnancy   92
premature birth   112
prenatal development   92
prolapsed cord   115
proximodistal   96
quickening   92
stethoscope   92
sucking reflex   95
teratogens   96
transverse presentation   109
umbilical cord   94
uterus   93
version   109
zygote   93

The following is a provocative and straightforward look at childbirth and infant mortality in different parts of the world. It is updated yearly.

Grant, J. P. (1993). *The state of the world's children: 1993.* New York: Oxford University Press.

The following is a massive collection of detailed medical information on the factors that influence prenatal development (including drugs, diseases, and genes) and on the various medical interventions that are possible:

Eden, R. D., Boehm, F. H., & Haire, M. (Eds.). (1990). *Assessment and care of the fetus: Physiological, clinical, and medicolegal principles.* Norwalk, CT: Appleton & Lange.

Bellow's novel is an interesting change of pace from the usual fare of academic references. True, it's fiction, but it's also a chilling account of the potential dangers of lead in our environment:

Bellow, S. (1982). *The dean's December.* New York: Harper & Row.

The following is a highly practical and very informative book for prospective parents that not only describes what to expect in normal and higher-risk pregnancies, but also explores the various choices available to parents:

Lieberman, A. B. (1987). *Giving birth.* New York: St. Martin's Press.

Those interested in an account of birth in primitive tribes throughout the world might consult:

Goldsmith, J. (1990). *Childbirth wisdom: From the world's oldest societies.* Brookline, MA: East West Health Books.

The following is a detailed discussion of nutrition and weight gain for pregnant women:

Food and Nutrition Board. (1990). *Nutrition during pregnancy.* Washington, DC: National Academy Press.

"When I use a word," Humpty Dumpty said in a rather scornful tone, "it means just what I choose it to mean—neither more nor less."

LEWIS CARROLL
Alice Through the Looking-Glass

INFANCY

Infans means "without speech." Young infants are *infans:* They have no words upon which to hang meanings. Their meanings, Piaget tells us, are wrapped in sensation and perception. As we see in Chapters 5 and 6, they are meanings of the *here and now.* If the infant sees a bright red ball, the meaning of the ball is a circular redness—a sort of image on the mind's mirror. Or perhaps the ball's meaning is the peculiar, synthetic, rubbery taste of well-chewed balls; or the magic-aliveness of its skin against the palms or the cheeks; or the trajectory of its mysterious bouncing course down the stairs; or all these sensations and actions put together in a shapeless, happy kind of meaningfulness.

PART TWO

That's what *ball* means to the prelinguistic infant.

Later, the infant will discover—or perhaps invent—the actual word *ball.* And with experience and increasing sophistication, *ball* will come to mean much more than the "spherical or nearly spherical object" that my dictionary lists as its first definition. It will also come to mean any number of games played with such objects; the roundish part of something; a poorly thrown, off-base, spherical thing; a dance; a good time; to be especially "with it" as in "on the ball," and on and on.

But when *ball* is a fresh, young word, newly invented by the infant, it means, as Humpty Dumpty insists so scornfully, just what the infant chooses it to mean: a specific round object; the act of throwing anything; a request for mom or dad to do something amusing; a means of eliciting approval from some adult; and so on.

Ball is seldom just another four-letter word.

Physical and Cognitive Development: Infancy

*H*it shall be expedient that a noble mannes sonne, in his infancie, have with hym continually onely suche as may accustome hym by litle and litle to speake pure and elegant latin.

Elyot
Gov. I. v, 1531

CHAPTER 5

I, unfortunately, was not born a noble man's son, as my grandmother was fond of reminding me.* Nobody made sure that I would be accompanied through my infancy by someone who spoke only pure and elegant Latin. But, at a very young age, they did expose me to the local priest who, as priests generally did in those years, understood and perhaps even spoke a fair smattering of church Latin. I learned none of it.

My mother now informs me that what I did learn during my infancy was so unremarkable they decided to have me examined by Mr. Delisle. His expertise in judging the character and intelligence of dogs had led to his being widely consulted by parents whose children seemed not to be developing as expected. What saved me from the examination was that one of his dogs—perhaps embittered by a negative evaluation—had taken a savage bite out of his master's haunch, putting him out of commission for several of my most critical developmental weeks. Not entirely stupid, the dog did this in the absolute darkness of a moonless night while accompanied by all six of Delisle's other grown-up dogs. As a result, Mr. Delisle never knew who bit him and never got to pass formal judgment on the intelligence of his neighbor's 10-month-old who still didn't crawl.

---

*"We don't have no canopy above our beds," she would say, in the process using up most of the English words she knew. "The darn thing's *under* our beds."

Yes, it was the fact that I didn't crawl that concerned my parents—absolutely nothing else, I swear it. Nothing. Only the trivial fact that I never did crawl (although it's something I can now do as well as the next person). If I really needed to go somewhere, says my mother, I'd grab a couple of fistfuls of dog hair and just let the dog drag me around.

THIS CHAPTER

Should my parents have been concerned that I couldn't crawl? Would it have been wise and useful for them to look at tables and charts describing the normal and expected achievements of infancy so that they might compare my progress with that of the wonderful, and mysterious, average infant and take steps to correct my deviations before it was too late for me ever to be average? Do you suppose there's anything they could have done? Or should they have taken comfort from the fact that I spoke as early as expected (though only French in the beginning), that I eventually walked as straight a line as any toddler, that I fed myself with about as much dexterity, that, in the end, I even learned to dress myself—and left me alone as my grandmother advised?*

While this chapter doesn't answer all these questions as directly as my mother, and grandmother, might have wished, it does present tables and charts that describe the average infant's growth and behavior. It looks, as well, at motor and perceptual development, and at the infant's mind. The next chapter looks at social relationships and attachments during infancy, and at infant personality. These two chapters cover infancy, a period that lasts from the first few weeks of life to age 2.

THE NEWBORN

During the first two weeks of life, the newborn is often referred to as a **neonate.** Technically, the neonatal period lasts from birth (after which the infant initially loses weight) until birthweight has been regained.

What kind of creature is the newborn? What does it think, feel, sense? Of what is it capable? These are not easy questions to answer. In fact, it will take us the remainder of this chapter and most of the next to describe the answers that science—and sometimes good sense—have begun to provide. But let us start first with the bare bones of an answer.

Imagine that you have been asked to design an organism that begins life in as primitive a condition as a

neonate—that is, with as little physical and motor control as the infant has, and with as unsophisticated an understanding of self and world. Your task is to design this organism in such a way that within two years it can walk, talk, recognize its grandmother, ride a tricycle . . . yes, even crawl.

So what do you do? You program it for change. Because you're clever, you pay particular attention to change in three areas: biological, intellectual, and social. Biologically, you design a creature that is capable of converting foodstuffs into nutrients, and you program the effects of these nutrients into a sequence of biological growth and maturation that will, among other things, eventually lead to the organism's control of its movements.

Intellectually, you program your little organism to process an enormous amount of information even in the absence of any immediate and tangible reward (such as a cookie or a kiss) for doing so. You provide it with an information-processing system that is automatically geared to focus on the most informative aspects of the environment. Accordingly, your little organism reacts strongly to surprise and novelty; it searches out the unexpected; it develops ways of organizing the information it gathers; it is programmed to invent concepts and ideas.

Socially, you program into the organism a wide range of emotions to serve as motives for action. They drive the organism to seek relationships with other organisms of the same species, to be gregarious, to love, to strive to *mean* something to others and contribute to the survival of its species.

And one of the crowning achievements in your design of this creature is that you pretune it to attend to speech; you wire it so that it is capable of inventing language and building culture.

The infant is just such a creature, says Flavell (1985). To summarize: A newborn is a primitive, self-driven little sensing machine designed to mature and grow physically in a predetermined way, programmed as an extraordinarily capable information-processing system, endowed with powerful emotions and gregarious tendencies, and pretuned to speech and to the development of language.

HEALTH AND PHYSICAL GROWTH

Still, at birth newborns are almost completely helpless physically. They cannot ensure that their environments are neither too cold nor too warm; they cannot clean themselves; they have no protection against witches, wolves, or one-eyed cats. They can't even find food unless it's put under their very noses.

And then they suck. Sucking is one of those primitive reflexes present at birth in virtually all mammals.

*"Leave him alone," she reportedly said. "He's not a dog. I don't think."

Breast Versus Bottle

The sucking reflex is what ensures the infant's survival. It may seem strange, then, that, in Kessen's (1965) words, "the most persistent single note in the history of the child is the reluctance of mothers to suckle their babies" (p. 1).

The *breast-versus-bottle* battle has raged for many years. In the beginning, the breast side was fought by an army of physicians and philosophers, some of whom argued that breast-feeding was a child's natural right and the mother's duty. Besides, argued Copmenius (quoted in Kessen, 1965), infants pick up many things from their mother's milk, including values: "Who then, unless he be blind, does not see that babies imbibe, along with the alien milk of the foster mother, morals different from those of their parents?" (p. 3). (Does my early delinquency have to do with the morals of cows?)

The other army fighting this apparent battle were mothers who, for one reason or another, were reluctant to breast-feed their infants. Their arguments were generally more personal and more private, and their numbers varied through history, growing through certain decades, and lessening again through others.

Is there still a conflict—a breast-versus-bottle controversy? There probably is, although most mothers see the issue as largely a matter of personal choice. The choice is sometimes made on the basis of convenience. It is simply not convenient for many working mothers to breast-feed their infants. Or, it is not convenient for women who carry their infants on their backs, or take them to the fields, to also carry bottles with them—or to lead cows or goats around behind them.

At other times, the choice is made on the basis of current fashion. For example, through much of the early part of this century, breast-feeding declined in popularity in North America so that by the early 1970s, fewer than one in four mothers breast-fed their infants. But in the past several decades, breast-feeding has again increased in popularity. One survey reports that 83 percent of women in one Canadian city breast-fed their infants (Kuzyk, 1993). Throughout the rest of the world, the percentage of mothers who breast-feed their infants varies tremendously—from a low of 2 percent in Nigeria and Ghana to a high of 89 percent in Burundi and 70 percent in Uganda (Grant, 1993).

What do physicians (and philosophers?) now recommend? Pretty well what they have recommended all along: When possible, mothers should breast-feed their infants (Grant, 1993). But their reasons have changed over the years; they can now appeal to science. Mother's milk, science tells us, is the best of foods for most newborns. It contains just about the right combination of nutrients, the right proportion of fats and calories, the almost-perfect assortment of minerals and vitamins, and it is easier to digest than cow's milk, and less likely to lead to allergic reactions. Also, breast-feeding provides infants with a measure of immunity against infections and diseases, and especially against diarrhea, one of the principal causes of infant death in the developing world. Furthermore, it helps in population control because lactation (the production of milk) delays ovulation (from an average of 40 to 50 days after birth for mothers who don't breast-feed to an average of 30 to 40 weeks for those who do; Wang & Fraser, 1994). Accordingly, the World Health Organization strongly recommends advising women in developing countries to return to breast-feeding where this practice has been abandoned (see At a Glance: "Changes in Breast-Feeding Patterns in the United States," and Figure 5.1).

In spite of these compelling arguments, it would be misleading not to emphasize that in much of the industrialized world, where sanitation and nutrition are excellent, bottle-fed infants thrive every bit as well as those who are breast-fed. In addition, it is worth noting that breast milk is affected by what the mother eats as well as by any drugs she ingests or chemicals to which she is exposed (Byczkowski, Gearhart, & Fisher, 1994). Alcohol, nicotine, barbiturates, stimulants such as caffeine, sedatives, and prescription drugs can each have an effect on the infant (Spigset, 1994); and HIV infection can be transmitted by breast-feeding (Cutting, 1994). Clearly, under some circumstances, an infant might fare much better with a cow or a goat.

Human Growth

More than half a century ago, Scammon (in Malina & Bouchard, 1991) described four different aspects of human growth: genital (the development of sexual characteristics); neural (brain and nervous system); lymphoid (systems, like the lymph glands, tonsils, and appendix, involved in the child's immunities); and general (height and weight, for example). Each of these, as is shown in Figure 5.2, follows a characteristically different pattern of development.

Genital Growth

Genital growth, which involves the development of sexual characteristics, is neglible in infancy and through most of early and middle childhood. But, as shown in Figure 5.2, there is a dramatic spurt between ages 12 and 14 with the advent of **pubescence,** the series of changes that result in sexual maturity (see Chapter 11).

Lymphoid Growth

The **lymphoid system** refers to lymph tissues in the body such as in the lymph glands, the tonsils, and the thymus (located behind the top of the breastbone), and even in the intestine. The lymphoid system plays an important role in providing immunity and resisting infection. Note that this system develops very rapidly through childhood, peaking in early adolescence. Following adolescence, the tonsils and thymus shrink rapidly so that a normal adult has about half as much lymph tissue as a young adolescent.

CHANGES IN BREAST-FEEDING PATTERNS IN THE UNITED STATES

Through much of history, most philosophers, psychologists, religious leaders, physicians, and nurses have been in favor of breast-feeding; some mothers have not. Ultimately, the choice is a personal one. Breast-feeding may be especially important in developing countries where formulas are often overly diluted or are mixed with contaminated water, leading to malnutrition or to diarrheal dehydration and sometimes death. There has been a dramatic increase in breast-feeding in the United States in recent years, especially among more highly educated mothers.

FIGURE 5.1

Changes in breast-feeding patterns for U.S. women by race and education, 1970–1981. (From U.S. Bureau of the Census, 1988, p. 64.)

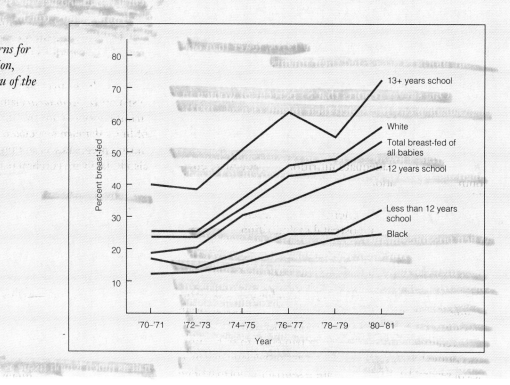

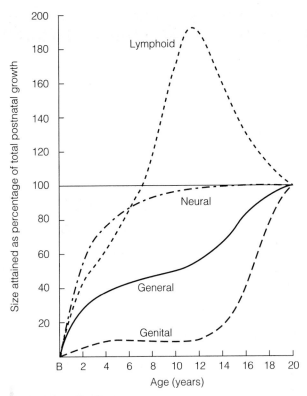

FIGURE 5.2

General growth curves in four areas of human development as described in Growth, Maturation and Physical Activity *(p. 9) by Robert M. Malina and Claude Bouchard, Champaign, IL: Human Kinetics Publishers. Copyright 1991 by Robert M. Malina and Claude Bouchard. Reprinted by permission. And from* The Measurement of Man, *J. A. Harris, et al., University of Minnesota Press, 1930, p. 193. Copyright © 1930 by the University of Minnesota. Reprinted by permission.*

Neural Development

The neonate's central nervous system is functionally immature at birth, but develops very rapidly early in infancy and is about 95 percent complete by age 7, as shown in Figure 5.2. Its optimal development is highly dependent upon two factors: adequate nutrition and adequate environmental stimulation. The infant's brain is most vulnerable to the effects of malnutrition prenatally (Crawford et al., 1993); it can also experience serious developmental retardation as a result of postnatal malnutrition. Especially dangerous is protein malnutrition that, claims Udani (1992), affects about 150 million children under age 5 worldwide. Among other things, severe lack of protein is associated with reduction in brain size, fewer connections among brain neurons, and changes in chemical brain transmitters. Malnutrition is also associated with lower birthweight; and low birthweight babies seem to be more susceptible to nutritional deficiencies (especially deficiencies of several fatty acids that are essential for normal brain

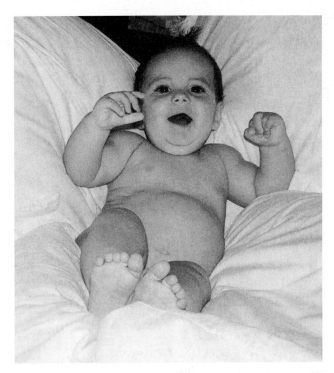

Rates of general physical growth, as well as of neural development, are higher during infancy than during any other subsequent period. Between birth and age 2, this infant will increase his weight by more than 270 percent—and his height by about 72 percent. If rate of change didn't slow down, the average 6-year-old would weigh nearly 400 pounds (182 kilograms) and be about 8.5 feet (2.6 meters) tall.

development, and that are consistently found in breast milk) (Crawford, 1993).

Although *severe* malnutrition can lead to poor mental development, the often-quoted conclusion that *moderate* malnutrition leads to lower IQ and retarded mental development is overstated and premature, claims Ricciuti (1991). The human brain does appear to be remarkably resistant to *permanent* damage resulting from moderate malnutrition—with the exception, notes DeLong (1993) of brain damage associated with iodine deficiency, which during pregnancy is an important cause of *cretinism* and is also linked with cerebral palsy and deafness.

The belief that the effects of malnutrition can be prevented or perhaps reversed through improved nutrition and various supplements is more a statement of social policy than of scientific fact, says Ricciuti (1991). Poor nutrition, Ricciuti explains, is only one facet of a collection of conditions that often accompany poverty—conditions such as poor sanitation, poor medical care, limited intellectual stimulation, and disease.

Physical Growth

Physical growth, as shown by the *general* curve in Scammon's representation (Figure 5.2), occurs in four stages: very rapid growth in infancy and early childhood; slower

FIGURE 5.3

Height at 50th percentile for U.S. infants, birth to 24 months. (Adapted from Health Department, Milwaukee, Wisconsin; based on data by H. C. Stuart and H. V. Meredith, prepared for use in the Children's Medical Center, Boston. Used by permission of the Milwaukee Health Department.)

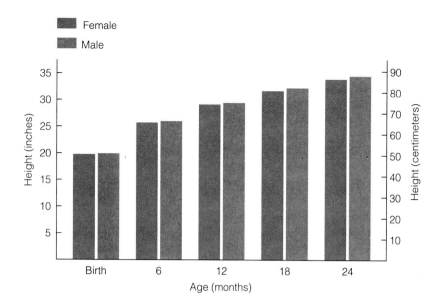

FIGURE 5.4

Weight at 50th percentile for U.S. infants, birth to 24 months. (Adapted from Health Department, Milwaukee, Wisconsin; based on data by H. C. Stuart and H. V. Meredith, prepared for use in the Children's Medical Center, Boston. Used by permission of the Milwaukee Health Department.)

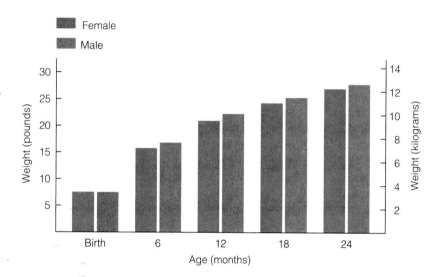

growth through middle childhood; a very rapid *growth spurt* in adolescence; slower growth ceasing in early adulthood.

Although physical growth in infancy is relatively predictable, because of different genetic programs and different nourishment, infants will not be exactly the same at all ages. Average physical development during infancy is shown in Figures 5.3 and 5.4. Note that these are median, or midpoint values—meaning that 50 percent of all infants of a given age are expected to be taller, and 50 percent will be shorter. Being some distance above or below the norms should not, by itself, be cause for alarm. Only when the infant is significantly above or below the average might there be cause for concern. Unfortunately, many of the world's children are significantly below the norm. Grant (1993) reports that almost half of all children in the least developed countries are moderately or severely underweight; half suffer from permanently stunted growth.

SUDDEN INFANT DEATH

Every year about 40,000 infants in the United States die before the age of 1, the majority from congenital anomalies, many of which are related to prematurity. For the remainder, the single leading cause of death is the mysterious **sudden infant death syndrome** (or SIDS, sometimes popularly referred to as "crib death" or "cot death")—mysterious because a diagnosis of sudden infant death syndrome is not really a diagnosis at all; it is an admission that cause of death is unknown (see At a Glance: "Causes of Infant Deaths in the United States," and Figure 5.5.)

What Is SIDS?

First formally defined in 1969, SIDS is simply "the sudden and unexpected death of an infant who has seemed well, or almost well, and whose death remains unexplained

CAUSES OF INFANT DEATHS IN THE UNITED STATES

Approximately 9 of every 1,000 infants born in the United States do not survive beyond age 1. About two thirds of these die during the first month, the majority from congenital anomalies (often associated with prematurity). For those who die later, the mysterious and largely unexplained condition, *sudden infant death syndrome* (SIDS), is the single most frequent cause of death. It accounted for almost 5,500 infant deaths in 1991 (U.S. Bureau of the Census, 1994).

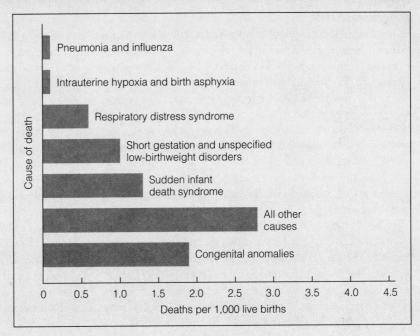

FIGURE 5.5

Some leading causes of death before the age of 1 in the United States, 1991. (Based on U.S. Bureau of the Census, 1994, p. 91.)

[later]" (Valdes-Dapena, 1991, p. 3). In spite of considerable ongoing research, SIDS can neither be predicted nor prevented.

Some Common Characteristics

Although the cause of SIDS is unknown, some SIDS victims share some characteristics. The most common of these, surprisingly, is age: SIDS occurs during a far narrower age span than almost all other diseases, seldom occurring during the first several weeks of life, peaking between 2 and 4 months, falling rapidly to age 6 months, and then declining more slowly. Fewer than 5 percent of SIDS deaths occur after age 1 (Hillman, 1991).

Other than age, there are a number of risk factors for SIDS. One is sex, with males accounting for about 60 percent of cases (Hillman, 1991). Another is sleep position: The evidence seems clear that infants who are put to sleep on their sides or on their backs are at far *lower* risk for SIDS than infants who sleep prone (Fleming, 1994). Research reported by Willinger, Hoffman, and Hartford (1994) indicates that countries where there has been a concerted attempt to advise parents to avoid placing their infants prone have experienced declines of up to 50 percent in SIDS rates.

SIDS and Neurological Immaturity

Why should this be? One line of speculation is that maturation of the brain may be delayed or abnormal in some SIDS victims (Kopp et al., 1994). Thus SIDS has sometimes been associated with *apnea*, a temporary paralysis or collapse of the throat muscles that prevents continued breathing and that generally causes the person to wake up. It is also sometimes associated with an abnormality in the diaphragm (Tennyson, Pereyra, & Becker, 1994). One suggestion is that SIDS may result from the infant's inability to *learn* the voluntary behaviors that eventually replace defensive breathing reflexes. "There is a critical at-risk period for all infants when reflexive defensive responses have faded, but voluntary defensive responses are not yet sufficiently strong," says Hunt (1991, p. 185). Young infants reflexively stick out their tongues when a piece of plastic is put over their mouths. If the object is not dislodged, they typically move their heads from side to side; and if that doesn't work, they swing their arms toward their faces. Eventually these behaviors are replaced by more voluntary behaviors. Perhaps the SIDS victim has not learned these voluntary behaviors because of behavioral or neurological problems linked with a slow-to-mature nervous system. And the infant lying prone may experience the added disadvantage of having the mouth and nose covered.

Preventing SIDS

Filiano and Kinney (1994) summarize the findings on SIDS in terms of what they term the *triple-risk model*. According to this model, SIDS results when *all three* of the following conditions occur simultaneously: (1) a vulnerable infant, perhaps neurologically immature; (2) a critical developmental period (mainly between 1½ and 4 months); and (3) some external stressor (which might include things like infant infections, temperature fluctuations, or parental smoking (see Fleming, 1994).

One approach to preventing SIDS is to provide parents of at-risk infants with monitors that sound an alarm when the infant stops breathing. Some of these infants can then be revived. But Ranney (1991) emphasizes that apnea is not involved in many cases of SIDS, and that a monitor cannot predict the occurrence of SIDS nor, of course, prevent it. The use of a monitor, suggests Ranney (1991), may add stress in an already stressful household especially when, as is not uncommon, the machine emits false alarms, further terrifying parents. At the same time, use of a monitor for at-risk children might reassure parents they are doing everything they can to ensure their child's survival.

In Conclusion

SIDS remains unexpected, unexplained, not preventable, and, by definition, fatal. It occurs throughout the world and appears to have existed many centuries ago although it would not easily have been recognized or considered important as long as infant mortality from other causes remained high (Valdes-Dapena, 1991). None of the factors sometimes associated with SIDS has been shown to *cause* it. Many SIDS victims are apparently thriving infants who seem to be completely normal and healthy, and who simply die, usually silently in their cribs at night. Small wonder that physicians and parents are baffled and that law-enforcement personnel are occasionally suspicious.

BEHAVIOR IN THE NEWBORN

Researching infancy presents some unique problems. Clearly, very young infants cannot be asked to interpret their own responses; nor can they be given instructions about how to behave in experimental situations. How, then, can the investigator determine whether the infant is curious, interested, bored, or confused? How do we know when and if learning has occurred?

The Orienting Response

Part of the answer lies in a group of sometimes almost imperceptible behaviors that have played a significant role in the development of experimental child psychology. These behaviors, collectively labeled the **orienting response,** are evident in our tendency (and that of other animals and birds) to respond to new stimulation by becoming more alert—that is, by attending or *orienting* to it. It is, as Berg and Berg (1987) put it, a "mechanism that enhances the processing of information in all sensory systems" (p. 268).

In animals such as dogs and cats, the orienting response is clear. On hearing a new sound, for example, a dog will pause, its ears may perk up and turn slightly toward the sound, and its whole attitude says, in effect, "What the *!$! was that?" Although the human infant may not respond so obviously, distinct and measurable changes nevertheless take place. These might include changes in pupil size, heart rate, conductivity of the skin to electricity (**galvanic skin response,** or **GSR,** also termed *electrodermal response*), and other physiological changes that are observable by using sensitive instruments. These in combination define the human orienting response.

The value of the orienting response to the child psychologist is that it can be used as an indication of attention, because it occurs only in response to novel stimulation to which the individual is then attending. It can also be used as an indication of learning, because it stops when the stimulation is no longer novel. In the same way, a dog might orient visibly when it first hears a cow in the distance, but will cease to do so when the sound has been identified. Such a decrease in the orienting reaction is termed *habituation*. Thus, even though infants cannot tell us whether "mother" sounds the same as "father," whether the color blue looks like red, or whether salt tastes like sugar, we can turn to the orienting response for answers to some of our questions.

Reflexes

Most of the behaviors in which the newborn first engages are reflexive—that is, they do not require learning and can easily be elicited by presenting the appropriate stimulus. Some of these reflexes, like the **sucking reflex,** are extremely important to survival. Another **vegetative reflex,** so called because these reflexes are nourishment-related, is the **head-turning reflex,** also called the **rooting reflex;** it can be elicited by stroking the baby's cheek or the corner of the mouth. Vegetative reflexes also include swallowing, hiccuping, sneezing, and vomiting.

A number of common motor reflexes in the newborn have no particular survival value now, but they might have been useful in some less "civilized" time. These include the startle reaction—or **Moro reflex**—which involves throwing out the arms and feet symmetrically and then pulling them back toward the center of the body. There is speculation that the Moro reflex might be important for infants whose mothers live or sleep in trees. If they suddenly fall but react by throwing out arms and legs, they might with luck catch a branch and save themselves. The Moro reflex is sometimes useful in diagnosing brain damage because in normal infants, these reflexes disappear with

SOME REFLEXIVE BEHAVIORS IN THE NEWBORN

If you have access to a newborn or young infant, it might be useful for you to provide appropriate stimulation to observe each of these reflexes. With older infants, you might carry out observations of gross and fine motor developments described in Table 5.2 on page 142.

Reflex	Stimulus	Response	Approximate Age of Appearance	Approximate Age of Disappearance
Sucking	Object in the mouth	Sucks	2–3 months in utero	Becomes voluntary during first year
Head-turning (rooting)	Stroking the cheek or the corner of the mouth	Turns head toward side from being stroked	Neonate	Becomes voluntary during first year
Swallowing	Food in the mouth	Swallows	Neonate	Becomes voluntary during first year
Sneezing	Irritation in the nasal passages	Sneezes	4–6 months in utero	Present in adult
Moro reflex	Sudden loud noise	Throws arms and legs out symmetrically	Neonate	3–4 months
Babinski reflex	Tickling the middle of the soles of the feet	Spreads and raises toes	Neonate	Diminishes by 1 month; disappears by 5–6 months
Toe grasp	Tickling the soles just below the toes	Curls toes around object	4–6 months in utero	Disappears by 9 months
Palmar grasp	Placing object in the infant's hand	Grasps object tightly	4–6 months in utero	Weak by 8 weeks; gone by 4–5 months
Swimming reflex	Infant horizontal, supported by abdomen	Coordinated swimming movements	8–9 months in utero	Disappears after 6 months
Tonic neck	Infant's head turned to one side	Arm and leg extend on that side, flex on opposite side	Late fetal period	Disappears after 4 months
Babkin	Object placed against both of infant's palms	Opens mouth, closes eyes, turns head to the side	Neonate	Disappears by 4 months
Stepping reflex	Infant vertical, feet lightly touching flat surface	Makes coordinated walking movements	8–9 months in utero	Disappears after 2–3 months

the development of the brain. As the infant develops control over motor actions, reflexes are inhibited (Mandich et al., 1994). However, the Moro reflex is often present later in life in people with impaired motor function.

Other reflexes that disappear in early infancy are the **Babinski reflex**—the typical fanning of the toes when tickled in the middle of the soles of the feet; the **palmar reflex** (grasping—also called the *Darwinian reflex*), which is sometimes sufficiently pronounced that the neonate can be raised completely off a bed when grasping an adult's finger in each hand; and the swimming and stepping reflexes, which occur when one holds the baby balanced on the stomach, or upright with the feet just touching a surface (see Interactive Table 5.1)

Although a reflex is, by definition, a simple, unlearned, and largely uncontrollable response to a specific set of circumstances, the infant's reflexive behaviors are not completely unmodifiable. Perhaps when the nipple is in the mouth, the infant cannot help sucking, but two things are noteworthy. First, very early the infant begins to exercise a degree of control over some of the circumstances that lead to reflexive behaviors. When the stomach is full, the infant may avert its head or purse its lips tightly, thus avoiding the stimulation that might lead to the sucking response.

Second, beginning very early in life, the infant is capable of modifying some reflexive responses, including sucking—perhaps changing the shape of the mouth or the placement of the tongue to increase the behavior's effectiveness (Widstrom & Thingstrom-Paulsson, 1993). The human organism—programmed to process information, to learn, to change—begins to change very early.

MOTOR DEVELOPMENT

The changes infants go through during the first two years of life, say Hazen and Lockman (1989), are more profound than any that will occur during the remainder of their lives. Within this brief period, initially helpless and completely dependent infants learn to move and to explore, to recognize recurring features of the world, to solve practical problems—and they also learn to represent symbolically and to communicate.

The infant's first movements appear to be largely uncoordinated and purposeless. However, researchers have discovered recurring patterns in these early movements. First, they appear to be cyclical. Beginning prenatally and continuing for about the first 4 months, the infant's spontaneous movements recur at relatively regular intervals,

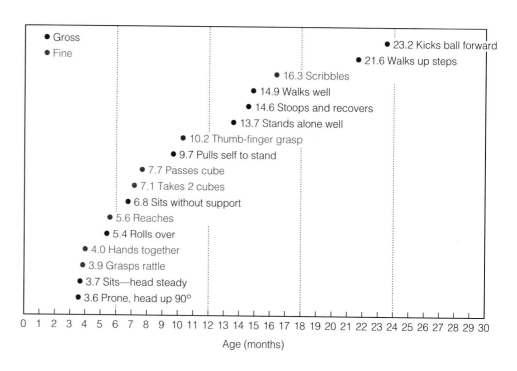

- Gross
- Fine

- 23.2 Kicks ball forward
- 21.6 Walks up steps
- 16.3 Scribbles
- 14.9 Walks well
- 14.6 Stoops and recovers
- 13.7 Stands alone well
- 10.2 Thumb-finger grasp
- 9.7 Pulls self to stand
- 7.7 Passes cube
- 7.1 Takes 2 cubes
- 6.8 Sits without support
- 5.6 Reaches
- 5.4 Rolls over
- 4.0 Hands together
- 3.9 Grasps rattle
- 3.7 Sits—head steady
- 3.6 Prone, head up 90°

0 1 2 3 4 5 6 7 8 9 10 11 12 13 14 15 16 17 18 19 20 21 22 23 24 25 26 27 28 29 30

Age (months)

At first, the only way of getting from A to B is in someone's arms—but then there is never a choice of B's. Learning to crawl not only opens up a wealth of new destinations, but also changes the visual perspective dramatically. Walking is even better.

spaced within minutes (Robertson, 1993a). This appears to be true for both waking and sleeping periods. At first, these **cyclic movements** are typically irregular and rapid, as well as asymmetrical (Grattan, DeVos, & Levy, 1992). That is, they involve various parts of the body (arms and legs) as well as either side (right or left) at different times. Rapid cyclic movements are typically followed by brief periods of quiescence. Later the movements become more coordinated and more symmetrical.

Some speculate that these cyclic movements are biologically important in that they provide a sort of built-in way of exercising muscle systems and of beginning to gain control over motor movements. At the same time, periods of quiescence between action provide an opportunity for the infant to interact with the environment. Thus, notes

Robertson (1993b), cyclic movements may regulate the infant's interactions. Interestingly, infant movements are typically suppressed during social interaction. In addition, the *movement* part of the cycle declines abruptly in strength at about 2 months as the infant begins to pay more attention to ongoing stimulation.

By the age of 4 months, cyclic motor movements decline and are eventually replaced by more deliberate, controlled movements. There is a close link between the development of control over physical actions and intellectual development. The infant's ability to manipulate and explore is what makes possible the discovery of the properties of physical objects, such as their permanence and their location in space. These discoveries, in turn, are related to the infant's growing ability to *reason* about objects, and to develop concepts (ideas) (Bushnell & Boudreau, 1993). Hence Piaget's (1954) term *sensorimotor* to describe development in the first two years of life.

The order in which children acquire motor skills is highly predictable, although the ages at which these skills appear can vary considerably. Tables of developmental **norms,** such as that represented by the Denver tests (Figure 5.6), are sometimes useful for assessing a child's progress. However, here as elsewhere, there is no *average* child.

Note that the normal sequence of motor development reflects the two developmental principles mentioned in Chapter 4 with respect to fetal development. First, development is *cephalocaudal* (proceeds from the head toward the feet). For example, infants can control eye movements and raise the head before acquiring control over the extremities. Second, it is *proximodistal* (proceeds in an inward–outward direction). That is, children acquire control over parts of the body closest to the center before they

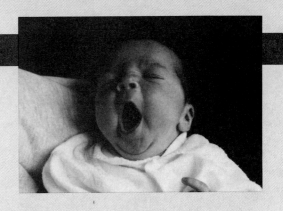

Infants as Subjects

Young infants, and especially newborns, are not always very good experimental subjects. When Fantz (1963) wanted to see how newborns react to visual stimulation, one of the most important conditions for selecting subjects was whether they kept their eyes open long enough to be shown the stimuli. And when Meltzoff and Moore (1989) investigated the newborn's ability to imitate, even though they chose 93 well-fed infants who showed no signs of hunger and who remained wide-eyed and alert for at least 5 minutes before the testing, only 40 completed the brief test session. The remainder fell asleep, cried, had spitting or choking fits, or, of all things, had a bowel movement!

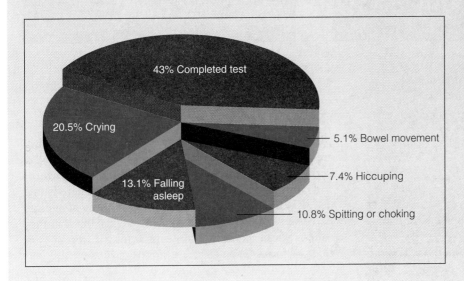

Figure 5.7

Difficulties in testing infants. Only 40 of 93 infants, ages 13.37–67.33 hours, completed an 8-minute test session. Testing had to be abandoned for the remaining 53 for the reasons shown. (Textual data from Meltzoff & Moore, 1989, pp. 954–962.)

can control the extremities. Thus, they can control gross motor movements before hand or finger movement (see Figure 5.6).

PERCEPTUAL DEVELOPMENT

The experience of human existence depends largely on our ability to make sense of the world and of ourselves. The struggle to discover what things are and what they mean begins in infancy and depends on three closely related processes: sensation, perception, and conceptualization.

Sensation is what happens when physical stimuli are translated into neural impulses that can then be transmitted to the brain and interpreted. Thus, sensation depends on the activity of one or more of our specialized sense organs—eyes, ears, and taste buds, for example.

In its simplest sense, **perception** is the brain's interpretation of sensation. Thus wavelengths corresponding to the color red affect our retinas in specific ways causing impulses that are transmitted to the part of our brain that deals with vision, causing us to *perceive* the color red. That

we can now *think* about the color red, compare it to other colors, or make some decision based on it is a function of the third process, **conceptualization.**

In brief, sensation is primarily a physiological process dependent on the senses (the effect of light waves on the retina of the eye); perception is the effect of sensation (the recognition that this is a red light); and conceptualization is a more cognitive, or intellectual, process (the realization that because this is a red light, I should stop).

Infant Vision

For years researchers incorrectly assumed newborns had poorly developed vision with little ability to detect form, patterns, or movements. One of the reasons for this relates to problems in doing research with preverbal infants. Now, however, researchers uses increasingly sensitive instruments to detect infant eye movements, visual preferences, and a range of other subtle changes in infant behavior (Friendly, 1993). But there are still difficulties with infant research (see At a Glance: "Infants as Subjects," and Figure 5.7).

FIGURE 5.8
This glass-covered "visual cliff" is used in studies of the infant's perception—and fear—of height. Interestingly, infants show little fear of heights until after they have learned to crawl.

Vision at Birth

Is the infant's world fuzzy and blurred or is it crisp and clear? Is it 20/20 or better—or worse? How can we find out?

Researchers, often using different methods and different criteria, don't always agree (see Norcia & Tyler, 1985). However, a number of important things seem clear. First, infants are far from blind at birth, although some of their visual world may be somewhat fuzzy and blurred. Second, there is a three- to fourfold improvement in the infant's visual acuity between birth and the age of 1 year (Aslin & Smith, 1988). In fact, by the age of 6 months, the infant's visual acuity may be close to that of a normal adult. And third, the newborn's visual accommodation is more limited than that of adults. It appears that newborns focus most accurately at a distance of approximately 12 inches (30 cm) (Banks, 1980). Significantly, that is about the distance of the mother's face when she is feeding the infant. This is one of the ways in which the neonate appears to be programmed to perceive important aspects of its environment; there are others.

Color and Movement

Although no one has determined exactly when color vision is first present in the infant, we do know that it is present by 2 to 4 months (Mercer, Courage, & Adams, 1991). By the age of 4 months, infants even show a preference for certain colors like pure reds and blues (Bornstein & Marks, 1982).

That newborns are sensitive to light intensity is shown by their **pupillary reflexes,** changes in the size of the pupil caused by changes in the brightness of visual stimulation. Also, their eye movements indicate that they are capable of visually following a slowly moving object within a few days of birth, and are sensitive to patterns and contours as early as 2 days after birth. There is evidence as well that infants less than 2 months of age can perceive high contrast contours (or edges), but that they cannot yet perceive relationships among different contours or forms (Pipp & Haith, 1984).

Depth Perception

In addition to perceiving color, movement, and form, and demonstrating preferences for these, young infants can also perceive depth. In Gibson and Walk's (1960) "visual cliff" studies, a heavy sheet of glass is positioned over a patterned surface; half of this surface is flush with the glass and half is some 3 feet lower. An adult standing or sitting on the glass can plainly see a drop or cliff where the patterned material falls away from the glass. So can infants, who, when they are old enough to crawl, typically refuse to cross the deep part, even when their mothers call them from the other side. Thus, perception of depth is present at least from the time that the infant can crawl (Figure 5.8). Interestingly, as Bertenthal and Campos (1990) report, infants who have not yet learned to crawl do *not* normally show much evidence of fear when lowered onto the deep side—that is, their heart rates do not accelerate significantly. Hence fear of falling is not entirely innate. These authors argue that through self-locomotion, infants develop the *visual-vestibular* sense essential to maintaining equilibrium (and related to fear of falling). In addition, locomotion requires them to develop skills of visual attention if they are to avoid colliding with objects; it allows them as well to learn about dangers associated with height, perhaps from parental reactions as they approach stairs or stand on chairs.

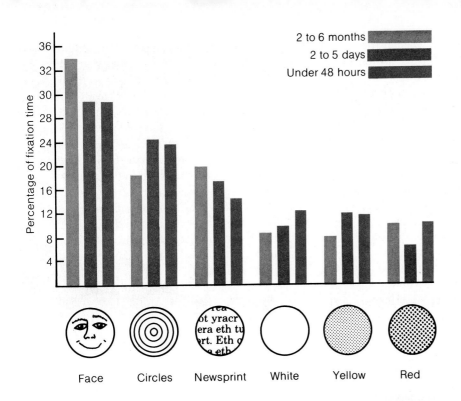

FIGURE 5.9
Relative duration (percentage of fixation time) of initial gaze of infants in successive and repeated presentations of six circular visual stimuli. The graph depicts infants' preference for the human face and the more complex stimuli. (Based on data in Fantz, 1963, pp. 296–297.)

Visual Preferences

As we saw, if looking at these colors longer is an indication of preference, very young infants prefer reds and blues. It's possible, but perhaps not likely, that they really don't prefer these colors at all, but are simply puzzled or intrigued by them.

Faces Versus Blanks

In a well-known study of infant visual preference, 18 infants, ranging in age from 10 hours to 5 days, were shown six circular stimulus patterns of varying complexity, the most complex being a human face and the least being an unpatterned circle (Fantz, 1963). Figure 5.9 shows the percentage of total time spent by subjects looking at each of the circles. That the face was looked at for significantly longer periods of time indicates not only that infants can discriminate among the various figures but also that they prefer faces—or perhaps that they prefer complexity.

Morton and Johnson (1991) also suggest that infants are born with some innate knowledge about faces that allows them to recognize and be attracted to them. There is evidence, for example, that by the second day of life they already prefer their mother's face. However, as Leon (1992) points out, studies of infant reactions to their mother's faces have generally provided the infant with the sound of the mother's voice and sometimes with her scent as well. So it isn't clear that infants actually prefer the *sight* of the mother rather than her scent or the sound of her voice.

Attractive Versus Ugly

Infants not only recognize faces, but seem to prefer certain kinds of faces over others—and that may be very important. When given a choice of attractive or unattractive dolls, they play with the attractive ones (Langlois,

Infants not only recognize faces, but seem to prefer those that are attractive. And what can be more attractive than yours truly in the old mirror, what?

Roggman, & Rieser-Danner, 1990). When confronted by an experimenter wearing either of two professionally constructed, highly realistic masks—one attractive and one unattractive—they withdraw from the attractively masked person far less and show more signs of positive emotions (Langlois et al., 1990). Even at the age of 6 months, infants seem to prefer faces judged attractive, whether the faces are male or female, young or old, black or white (Langlois et al., 1991).

Why? Perhaps, suggest Langlois and associates (1991), because attractiveness is a sort of facial "average-ness." Faces that are unusual may be interesting, but "average" faces are more clearly representative of the ideal human gene pool. Average, and therefore attractive, faces are less likely to carry genes that might be harmful. It is perhaps for this reason that faces created by averaging and digitizing facial features are judged highly attractive (Langlois & Roggman, 1990).

The significance of these observations is twofold. First, it had long been thought that attractiveness is a learned and culturally determined quality, and that young infants would not likely have been exposed to enough models or to enough value judgments to have developed preferences. But this does not appear to be the case. Second, if infants *prefer* attractive faces, where does that leave ugly parents or grandparents—or brothers and sisters? Or even strangers? Recall the Elder and colleagues' (1985) finding that attractive daughters were better treated by their fathers during the 1930s Depression (see Chapter 3). Are attractive fathers and mothers treated differently by their infants? Their children? If so, what might the implications be for the ecological systems defined by the family?

How Infants Look

Earlier in this chapter you were asked to consider the problem of taking something as primitive as a newborn and designing it so that it would become as sophisticated as a 2-year-old—and eventually a 12-year-old, a 42-year-old, a 92-year-old. In designing this little organism, we considered that, among other things, we would have to program it to become an extraordinarily capable information-processing system—a system tuned to notice and respond to the most important features of the environment, and predisposed, as well, to make sense of these features.

Does what we know about the infant's visual system conform to our design requirements? Haith (1980) says yes. The infant, he informs us, does not respond to the visual world in a simple, reflexive manner, response following stimulus in predictable mechanical fashion. Instead, infants behave as though preprogrammed to follow specific rules geared to maximizing information. After all, acquiring information is the purpose of looking.

Infants Look to See
So how do infants look? According to Haith's research, using infrared lights bounced off infant's corneas to reveal movements of their eyes, these are some of the important facts and what they mean:

First, contrary to what we might have expected, infants move their eyes even when there's no light, scanning the darkness in a highly controlled manner, using small movements appropriate for finding shadows, edges, spots. When viewing a uniformly lit but unpatterned field, their eye movements are broader, sweeping movements, suitable for discovering bolder contours. It seems clear that from birth, visual scanning patterns are not simply under the control of external stimuli (after all, scanning occurs in darkness as well as in light), but are internally controlled. It is as though the infant, true to our speculative design, is preprogrammed to obtain information.

Second, newborns actually *look* at stimuli, positioning their eyeballs so that a maximum amount of visual information falls on the *fovea*—the part of the retina that has the highest concentration of visual cells. It's as though the infant's scanning rules are designed to maximize stimulation—and, consequently, to maximize information.

Third, when the newborn looks at a simple stimulus (such as a vertical or a horizontal line), the eyes cross back and forth repeatedly over the edges of the stimulus. The effect is to maintain a high level of firing in the visual cells.

Haith concludes that there appears to be a single important principle that governs the newborn's visual activity: *maximize neural firing*. It's a built-in principle that assures that the newborn's visual activity will lead to the greatest possible amount of information—a vital feature for an organism that has to be an outstanding information-processing system.

Rules That Guide Infant Looking
This principle—*maximize neural firing*—is manifested in the rules that govern how babies look (Haith, 1980, p. 96):

- *Rule 1.* If awake and alert and light not too bright, open eyes.

- *Rule 2.* If in darkness, maintain a controlled, detailed search.

- *Rule 3.* If in light with no form, search for edges using broad, jerky sweeps of the field.

- *Rule 4.* If an edge is found, terminate the broad scan and stay in the general vicinity of that edge. Try to implement eye movements that cross the edge. If such eye movements are not possible in the region of the edge (as is the case for edges too distant from the center of the field), scan for other edges.

This view of the infant's visual perception as rule-governed and information-oriented rather than as stimulus-bound is a dramatic departure from psychology's traditional approach to these matters—a departure that is evident in many other areas of child study as well. This decade's infant—and child—is no longer merely a passive recipient of external influences, but has become active, exploring, information seeking. With regard to perception, Haith (1991) explains, we need to stop looking only at the infant's ability to sense and perceive; instead, we need to ask how perception contributes to the development of the infant's mind.

Hearing

Infant dogs, bears, cats—and many other animals—are deaf at birth; the human neonate is not. Instead, the ear is fully grown and potentially functional at about 26 weeks of gestation (Smith et al., 1990). In fact, most investigations indicate that neonates are only slightly less sensitive than adults to sound intensity (loudness).

Investigations of infant responsiveness to frequency (high or low pitch) have yielded somewhat inconsistent results partly because of the criteria employed, as well as because subjects of different ages have been used (Aslin, 1987). Studies of older infants usually show that sensitivity to higher frequencies increases with age (Trehub et al., 1991), and the general conclusion that infants (as opposed to newborns) are more sensitive to higher than to lower frequencies is widely accepted. Some researchers suggest that the common tendency of adults to raise the pitch of their voices when speaking to infants or young children is the result of an unconscious recognition of their greater sensitivity to higher frequencies.

Discriminating Voices

Infants as young as 3 days can not only discriminate among different voices but also seem to prefer the sound of the mother's voice. In a study where systematic changes in an infant's sucking were reinforced with the sound of a woman reading a book, the infant responded to the sound of its mother but not to that of other women (DeCasper & Fifer, 1980). DeCasper and Fifer argue that this doesn't mean that infants have learned to distinguish their mother's voice from that of other women in the space of a mere 3 days—or that they've developed a preference for it in the same period of time. They suggest, instead, that these findings are evidence that the fetus can hear sounds while in the uterus, can distinguish among them, and can also learn. In fact, studies with microphones inserted in the uterus indicate that the fetus is commonly exposed to sounds at a level of 70 or more decibels (Smith et al., 1990).* If DeCasper and Fifer's findings and interpretation are correct, they provide evidence of learning in utero (Aslin, Pisoni, & Jusczyk, 1983).

Smell, Taste, and Touch

Smell, explains Farbman (1994) is one of the most important senses for driving the behavior of earth's animal species. It should hardly be surprising that newborns are highly sensitive to odors, as well as to tastes and touch. In fact, there is evidence of fetal sensitivity to odors as early as 28 weeks after conception (Bartoshuk & Beauchamp,

*The human hearing threshold is 0 decibels; an ordinary conversation at 3 feet is at about 65 decibels; the noisiest spot at Niagara Falls is at around 75 decibels; with prolonged exposure, hearing damage can result at around 100 decibels. Smith and colleagues (1990) suggest that the fetus is exposed to far higher sound levels than had been anticipated.

1994). Also, animal studies indicate that when certain odors are introduced in the uterine fluid of pregnant animals, the behavior of their offspring is subsequently affected. Bartoshuk and Beauchamp speculate that it's possible that human infants begin to learn about the mother's diet and characteristic odors before they are born.

Within hours of birth, most infants turn their faces when exposed to a strong and unpleasant smell like ammonia. And their facial expressions are distinctly different when they are exposed to the smell of vanilla or of raw fish (Beauchamp, Cowart, & Schmidt, 1991).

In much the same way, they smack their lips when sweet things are placed on their tongues; and they pucker their mouths in response to sour tastes. In fact, even premature infants respond differently to sweet than to nonsweet tastes (Bartoshuk & Beauchamp, 1994). It seems that the ability to taste and smell is present at birth, and it does not depend on experience. Even at the age of a single day, infants can differentiate among solutions varying in type and concentration of sweetener. Almost invariably, they prefer sweet to plain water. And, contrary to what we might have been led to believe about the natural wisdom of the body, infants appear to have an innate liking for sweet things (Beauchamp et al., 1991).

The importance of the newborn's sensitivity to odors and tastes (and that of the fetus) lies in the possibility that certain behaviors and preferences may be learned at a very early age. Recall, for example, the study that indicated that at the age of 3 days, infants already seem to prefer the voices of their mothers to those of other women. A study by Porter and associates (1991) indicates the same might be true for certain smells associated with the mother. In this study, a group of 2-week-old infants were observed in a situation in which they had a choice of turning toward a clean, odor-free pad, or toward a pad worn on their mother's breast. In spite of the fact that these infants were bottle-fed, they typically spent more time turned toward the pad that carried the mother's odor.

Pain Sensitivity

Early investigations had concluded that the neonate is remarkably insensitive to much of the stimulation that children and adults would find quite painful (for example, McGraw, 1943). Circumcision doesn't really hurt boy babies, they assured us. But they (whoever *they* are) were probably at least partly wrong: Boy babies do holler when circumcised! And more recent research indicates that neonates of both sexes are sensitive to pain. McLaughlin and colleagues' (1993) survey of 352 physicians found that the vast majority now agree that newborns feel pain, and most use anesthetics for medical procedures with infants.

The State of the Neonate

Neonates are remarkably alert and well suited to their environments. They can hear, see, and smell; they can turn in the direction of food, suck, swallow, digest, and eliminate;

The infant's memory is not as powerful or well organized as yours or mine. It would be too much to expect that this child should remember the sounds that correspond to each key or should be able to organize them into a melody. But that she even recognizes the piano and remembers how to sit and pound its keys is no small feat either.

they can respond physically to a range of stimuli; and they can cry and vomit. Still, they are singularly helpless creatures who would surely die if the environment did not include an adult intimately concerned with their survival. There is much they need to learn, much with which they must become familiar, before they can stand on their own intellectual as well as physical feet.

COGNITIVE DEVELOPMENT

For a long time, Maya Pines (1966) tells us, psychology neglected the infant's mind, as if everyone assumed that babies didn't really have minds, or if they did, they wouldn't be very important at this stage of development. But our views have changed. "Babies are very competent," says Bower (1989). "They are set to use whatever information we give them" (p. ix).

As far back as 1920, Piaget had begun to map the course of the child's intellectual development. Piaget's story of the growth of children's minds tells of their growing awareness of the world in which they live and their discovery or invention of ways of interacting with this world. It is a complex and fascinating story, but it is not the whole story; there are other theories of cognitive development, other explanations of how we come to know. Some of these are termed *information-processing* approaches. They

look at what is involved in memory: deriving information, abstracting, sorting, organizing, analyzing, and retrieving, for example. We look at memory processes in infancy before we turn to Piaget's theory of cognitive development.

Infant Memory

If neonates are ever to reach the level of competence of the 2-year-old, there is a great deal that they must learn and remember: what is edible and what isn't; how to get from here to there; how to ask for things; how to hold a cup; how to get people's interest and attention; and much more.

The neonate's memory is not nearly as efficient and as powerful as yours or mine. Clearly, however, from the very beginning there must be some ability to learn and remember. This primitive ability will eventually develop into the type of memory that is characteristic of the 2-year-old, the 40-year-old, the 90-year-old.

Studying Infant Memory

One common way of investigating memory in very young infants is to use components of the orienting response described earlier. For example, researchers might look at the infant's response to the same photograph shown on two different occasions. If the infant remembers something about the photograph, heart rate would not be expected to change in the same way as it might when the infant is presented with a completely new photograph.

A second approach is simply to look at how long it takes for the infant to *habituate* (become accustomed) to a stimulus. Habituation might be revealed in patterns of eye movements (the infant stops looking at the stimulus) or, again, in changes in components of the orienting response, such as respiration or heart rate.

A third measure of infant memory involves the infant's behavior. For example, Sullivan and colleagues (1991) presented 1-day-old infants with a novel smell (a citrus odor; in this study, a conditioning stimulus) paired with stroking (a reinforcing stimulus) a total of 10 times, each for 30 seconds. Control babies received the stroking or the smell as well, but not the two paired. The next day all infants were given the odor for 30 seconds. Control infants responded indifferently; but those for whom the odor had been paired with stroking turned their heads toward the odor *even if they were asleep*. But a different odor produced no consistent response—strong evidence of learning (and memory) at the age of 1 day.

In another study, Swain, Zelazo, and Clifton (1993) had day-old newborns listen to a word, and monitored them as they turned their heads toward the sound. Within a short period of time, these infants habituated (learned) the word and stopped turning. One day later, half of these infants were again exposed to the same word; the other half heard a different word. Again, all infants initially oriented to the word, turning their heads toward it. But those who were exposed to the same word both days habituated significantly more rapidly than those who heard a new word—clear evidence that they remembered something of the word.

Still, evidence is that the infant's memory for most things appears to be of relatively short duration. For example, young infants who are conditioned to associate a puff of air with a tone, or a feeding schedule with a bell, may remember from one day to the next—or perhaps for 6 or 10 days. But without any reminders in the interim, all evidence of memory is likely to be gone within a few days (Rovee-Collier, 1987).

Developmental Phases in Infant Memory

Perlmutter (1980) describes three sequential phases in the development of infant memory. In the first, the infant's memory seems to be largely a matter of neurons firing when a new stimulus is presented and the firing stopping with habituation. As the infant becomes more familiar with the stimulus (that is, learns and remembers), the period before habituation becomes shorter.

The second phase, which begins at around 3 months, is related to the infant's growing ability to accomplish *intended* actions. Infants now actively look and search; they begin to reach, even to grasp; they explore; and they *recognize* things and people. Recognition is a sure sign of memory.

In the third phase, by the age of 8 or so months, infant memories have become much more like our own in that they are more abstract and more symbolic. They remember *classes* of things like fuzzy objects and big people and pets and building blocks and beets.

Our adult memories, and those of older children, are greatly helped by certain strategies, the most important of which are *organization*, *grouping*, and *elaboration*. Infants don't systematically use any of these strategies. But 2-year-old infants already have some notions about what memory is and understand mental-event terms like *remember*, *think*, *know*, and *pretend*. When asked to remember something, they *pay attention* and they *try* to remember. These, says Wellman (1988), are strategies in their own right.

There is a great distance between the immature memory of the week-old child who can demonstrate a vague recollection of a familiar smell or sound, and that of the 1-year-old who mistakenly yells "Dada" when he sees a stranger's familiar-looking back in the supermarket. There is also a vast distance between this 1-year-old's memory and the memory of the 12-year-old whose intellectual strategies permit mental feats of which the 1-year-old cannot yet even dream. (See Chapter 7 for more information about memory.)

Basic Piagetian Ideas

Of what can the 1-year-old dream? And the infant? Initially, perhaps not a great deal if, as Jean Piaget claims, the infant's world is truly a world of the *here and now*. If it is, in fact, a world that makes sense only when the infant looks at it, hears it, touches it, smells it, or tastes it, there might not be much with which to dream. This Piagetian infant does not have concepts in the sense that we think of them—no store of memories or hopes or dreams, no fund of information with which to think.

But what the neonate *has* are the sensory systems and the cognitive inclinations that make it into a self-reinforcing, information-processing organism. When Piaget describes the infant, he speaks of an organism that continually seeks out and responds to stimulation and that, by so doing, gradually builds up a repertoire of behaviors and capabilities—and, at the same time, *constructs* a representation of the world.

Assimilating and Accommodating

At first, behaviors are limited mainly to the simple reflexes with which the infant is born; but in time, these behaviors become more elaborate and more coordinated with one another as the infant adapts to the world. And the complementary processes that make **adaptation** possible are those of **assimilation** and **accommodation** (see Chapter 2).

To review briefly, assimilation and accommodation are highly active processes whereby the individual searches out, selects, and responds to information, the end result of which is the actual *construction* of knowledge. Imagine, for example, a young child walking on a wind-blown beach, stooping now and again to pick up pebbles and toss them onto the water. In Piaget's view, there is a **schema** involved here—a sort of mental or cognitive representation—that corresponds to the child's knowledge of the suitability of pebbles as objects to be thrown upon the waves, as well as other schemata that have to do with the activities involved in bending, retrieving, and throwing. The pebbles are, in a sense, being assimilated to appropriate schemata; they are understood and used in terms of the child's previous knowledge.

Imagine, now, that the child bends to retrieve another pebble but finds, instead, that she has picked up a stick. The stick is clearly not a pebble, and perhaps should not be responded to in the same way. But still, why not? The "throwing things on the big waves" schema is readily available, momentarily preferred. And so the stick too is assimilated to the throwing schema, and the child tries to hurl it toward the water. But the new object's heaviness is sudden and surprising, the child's throwing motion inadequate, and the stick falls again upon the sand. Now, when she picks it up again, she doesn't hurl it in quite the same way. Instead, she holds it in two hands tightly grasped with her pudgy fingers, and she pushes hard with her little legs as she throws. In Piaget's terms, she has accommodated to the characteristics of this object that make it different from the pebbles she has been throwing.

Equilibration

To assimilate, then, is to respond in terms of preexisting information; it often involves ignoring some aspects of the situation to make it conform to aspects of the mental system. In contrast, to accommodate is to respond to external

TABLE 5.2
Piaget's Four Factors That Shape Development

The Construction of Knowledge Depends On:	
Equilibration	The tendency to balance assimilation (responding in terms of previous learning) and accommodation (changing behavior in response to the environment).
Maturation	Genetic forces that do not determine behavior but are related to its sequential unfolding.
Active Experience	Interaction with real objects and events allow individual to discover things and to invent (construct) mental representations of the world.
Social Interaction	Interaction with people leads to the elaboration of ideas about things, people, and self.

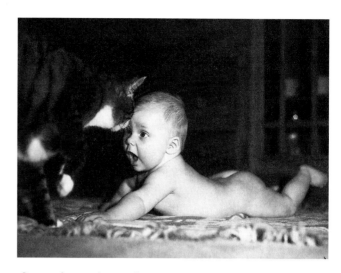

Our understanding and reasoning about the world demand that things be real, objective, substantive, independent. It would be more than a little confusing if our worlds, like that of this neophyte philosopher, disappeared from our minds with the mere closing of our eyes. Discovering the permanence of objects is one of the great achievements of early infancy.

characteristics and to make changes in the mental system as a result. One of the governing principles of mental activity, says Piaget, is a tendency toward **equilibration**—that is, a tendency toward maintaining a balance between accommodation and assimilation. At one extreme, if an infant always assimilated, never accommodated, there would be no change in schemata (mental structure), and no change in behavior. Everything would be assimilated to the sucking schema, the grasping schema, the looking schema (that is, everything would be sucked, or grasped, or simply looked at). Such a state of disequilibrium would result in little adaptation and little cognitive growth.

At the other extreme, if everything were accommodated to and not assimilated, schemata—and behavior—would be in a constant state of flux. Now the nipple would be sucked, now it would be chewed, now pinched, now swatted—again, an extreme state of disequilibrium resulting in little adaptation.

Factors That Shape Development

Equilibration, says Piaget, is one of the four forces that accounts for the *construction* of knowledge (Piaget, 1961). That is, it accounts for adaptation and cognitive growth throughout development. Another is *maturation*, a sort of biologically determined unfolding of potential. Maturation—or biology—does not determine cognitive growth but is related to the unfolding of potential. A third factor is *active experience*—the child's interaction with the world. The fourth is *social interaction*, which helps the child develop ideas about things and about people as well as about the self. These four factors—active experience, maturation, equilibration, and social interaction—are the cornerstones of Piaget's basic theory (see Table 5.2).

The Object Concept

The infant's world is a "blooming, buzzing mass of confusion," William James (1892) informed us more than a century ago. In those years, psychologists believed that the

neonate's senses didn't function at birth, or functioned very poorly, so that sensations like colors, sounds, smells, and tastes were all indistinct and blurred. As we saw earlier, they were wrong: Children see colors, movements, and shapes almost from birth; they can detect *and remember* odors; and they can hear even before they are born.

Still, James was at least partly right. Why? Because in the infant's *here and now* world, there are no permanent objects. The nipple exists when the infant sees, touches, or sucks it; when it can't be sensed, it doesn't exist. Imagine what the world would be like, suggest Wellman and Gelman (1992), if we thought objects disappeared and reappeared—that is, if we had no concept of *objective objects*. This *object concept*, they explain, is absolutely fundamental to our reasoning about the world, which demands that objects be real, out there, substantive, and independent of us. There is no "out there" for infants; they must discover the permanence and objectivity of objects for themselves. This discovery is one of the truly great achievements of infancy.

Discovering That Things Are Real

The processes by which infants discover that objects are real and permanent depend on experiencing and exploring the real world. When Stambak and associates (1989) videotaped young infants' responses to different objects such as nesting cups or hollow cubes or rods, they found that even very young infants organize their behaviors in systematic ways, as though actively exploring. Some subjects typically banged different objects with the rod; some explored the insides of the hollow cubes with their fingers or with their hands if the cubes were large enough. It's almost as if these infants had already invented questions and problems and were devising little experiments to find answers.

TABLE 5.3
Sensorimotor Development: The Six Substages

Substage and Approximate Age in Months	Principal Characteristics
1. Exercising reflexes (0–1)	Simple, unlearned behaviors (schemes) such as sucking and looking are practiced and become more deliberate.
2. Primary circular reactions (1–4)	Activities that center on the infant's body and that give rise to pleasant sensations are repeated (thumb-sucking, for example).
3. Secondary circular reactions (4–8)	Activities that do not center on the child's body but that lead to *interesting* sights or sounds are repeated (repeatedly moving a mobile, for example).
4. Purposeful coordinations (8–12)	Separate schemes become coordinated (such as the ability to look at an object and reach for it); recognition of familiar people and objects; primitive understanding of causality begins, implicit in the use of signs to anticipate events.
5. Tertiary circular reactions (12–18)	Repetition with variation (repeating a sound with a number of deliberate changes, for example) is experimented with.
6. Mental representation (18–24)	Transition between *sensorimotor* intelligence and a more *cognitive* intelligence; activity is internalized so that its consequences can be anticipated before its actual performance; language becomes increasingly important in cognitive development.

Not only does the exploration of objects by young infants become increasingly systematic with advancing age, but it also involves more varied activities. Initially, exploration is mainly visual or oral; later, it also becomes manual. By the age of 3 or 4 months, most infants use both hands and mouth to explore. And, increasingly, type of exploration depends more and more on the objects being explored: Some things are more easily understood, more meaningful, when held in both hands, licked, drooled on, and gummed emphatically.

Piaget's Classic Object Concept Study
To investigate the infant's understanding of objects, Piaget (1954) showed children an attractive object and then hid it from view. If the object exists only when infants perceive it, reasoned Piaget, they will make no effort to look for it when they can't see it *even if they actually saw it being hidden.* When children begin to look for an object they can no longer see, this is definite evidence that they can imagine it and therefore know it still exists.

Piaget found that in the earliest stage, children don't respond to the object once it is removed; next, they search for the object, but only in the place where they last saw it; and finally, they know that objects continue to exist, and they look for them in a variety of places. This final stage, claimed Piaget, occurs near the middle of the second year of life (about age 18 months).

Piaget Underestimated Infants
Some later investigations of the development of the object concept indicate that the age of acquisition is perhaps younger than Piaget suggests (Wellman & Gelman, 1992). For example, Bower (1989) used infants' orienting response to determine whether they had developed notions of object permanence. In one study, infants are shown a ball and then a screen is moved between the infant and the ball; a few seconds later, the screen is removed. On some trials, the ball has been taken away. When infants do not have object permanence, they should

not be surprised if the ball is gone. But they would be surprised to see it gone if they expected it to be there—in other words, if they had acquired notions of object permanence. Bower's main finding is that infants as young as 3 weeks of age seem to have some notion of object permanence, *providing the object is hidden from view for only a few seconds.* When the object is hidden for longer (15 seconds as opposed to 1½ seconds), infants at this age all show surprise when the ball is still present after the screen is removed. Similarly, Baillargeon (1987) found that infants as young as 3½ months seemed to have some primitive notions about the solidity of objects. When one object moved through a space that should have been occupied by another object, they seemed surprised.

It seems, then, that Piaget underestimated the age at which infants begin to develop notions of object permanence. Even 1-month-old infants appear to have a short-lived recollection of absent objects. And by the age of 3 or 4 months, they have begun to understand that objects are solid and stationary (Baillargeon, 1992). However, it will still be a long time before the 3-week-old infant deliberately searches for an object that has not been seen just recently (Bower, 1989).

Sensorimotor Development

Piaget believed that children's understanding of the world throughout most of infancy is determined by the activities they can perform on it and by their perceptions of it—hence his term *sensorimotor.* Piaget simplifies the infant's cognitive development during this period by dividing it into six substages, summarized in Table 5.3 and described below. Table 5.4 summarizes Piaget's stages of intellectual development from birth through adolescence.

Exercising Reflexes (Birth to 1 Month)
In Piaget's view, infants learn little that is new during the first month, instead spending much of their waking time exercising the abilities with which they are born (sucking,

TABLE 5.4
Piaget's Stages of Cognitive Development

Stage	Approximate Age	Some Major Characteristics
Sensorimotor	0–2 years	Motoric intelligence
		World of the here and now
		No language, no thought in early stages
		No notion of objective reality
Preoperational*	2–7 years	Egocentric thought
Preconceptual	2–4 years	Reason dominated by perception
Intuitive	4–7 years	Intuitive rather than logical solutions
		Inability to conserve
Concrete operations†	7 to 11–12 years	Ability to conserve
		Logic of classes and relations
		Understanding of number
		Thinking bound to concrete
		Development of reversibility in thought
Formal operations‡	11–12 to 14–15 years	Complete generality of thought
		Propositional thinking
		Ability to deal with the hypothetical
		Development of strong idealism

* Discussed in Chapter 7.

† Discussed in Chapter 9.

‡ Discussed in Chapter 11.

looking, grasping, and crying). But these activities have an important cognitive function (in addition to the obvious survival function of actions like sucking). By repeatedly performing these activities, the infant eventually develops control over them. By the end of the first month, infants are quite proficient at reaching and grasping, as well as at looking and sucking. However, they still have trouble putting different actions together to obtain a single goal. For example, infants presented with a visually appealing object can look at it but cannot reach toward it. Deliberately reaching and grasping is a complex activity dependent on the purposeful coordination of looking schemes, reaching schemes, and grasping schemes. This coordination is not usually apparent until the age of 3 to 5 months.

Primary Circular Reactions (1 to 4 Months)

Early in infancy, children engage in many highly repetitive behaviors (thumb-sucking, for example) called **primary circular reactions.** These are reflexive responses that serve as stimuli for their own repetition. For example, if the infant accidentally puts a hand or a finger into the

mouth, this triggers the sucking response, which results in the sensation of the hand in the mouth, which leads to a repetition of the response, which leads to a repetition of the sensation, which leads to a repetition of the response, and so on. This circle of action is called *primary* because it involves the infant's own body.

Secondary Circular Reactions (4 to 8 Months)

During the third substage, a new class of circular reactions appears. These deal with objects in the environment rather than only with the child's body, and are therefore called **secondary circular reactions.** Six-month-old infants engage in many secondary circular reactions, many of them resulting from accidentally doing something interesting or amusing that is then repeated again and again. By kicking, Piaget's young son caused a row of dolls dangling above his bassinet to dance. The boy stopped and watched the dolls. Eventually, he repeated the kicking, perhaps not *intending* to make the dolls move, but because they had stopped moving and no longer attracted his attention. But again they moved, and again he repeated the action so that, within a very short period of time, he was repeating the behavior over and over—a secondary circular reaction. This type of behavior, which Piaget described as *behavior designed to make interesting sights and sounds last,* is especially important because it signals the onset of *intention.* In Frye's (1991) words, these are behaviors in which infants "knowingly employ means to goals" (p. 15).

Purposeful Coordinations (8 to 12 Months)

The development of intention becomes even more apparent when, in the fourth substage, infants begin to coordinate previously unrelated behaviors to achieve a goal. They can now look at an object, reach for it, grasp it, and bring it to the mouth *with the intention* of sucking it. It is also during this substage that infants begin to recognize familiar objects and people—which explains why they may now become upset when a parent leaves or when a stranger appears (see Chapter 6).

Also, at about this time, the infant begins to use signs to *anticipate* events (Mom packing her briefcase is a sign she's leaving—and a signal to holler). Understanding that certain events are *signs* that some other event is likely to occur is closely related to an understanding of causality. For the young infant, whose logic is not always as perfect as yours or mine, the sign itself is often interpreted as the *cause.* A child who realizes that Mommy will be leaving when she packs her briefcase may believe that the cause of leaving is the packing of the briefcase—just as the cause of going to bed is taking a bath or putting on pajamas.

Tertiary Circular Reactions (12 to 18 Months)

In the fifth substage, children begin to modify their repetitive behaviors *deliberately* to see what the effects will be. Rayna, Sinclair, and Stambak (1989) observed this **tertiary circular reaction** in the behavior of a 15-month-old girl whose current preoccupation was with breaking objects. Breaking something often seemed to lead to a repetition of the behavior (hence a circular response), but with *deliberate* variation (hence *tertiary*; recall that primary and secondary reactions are repetitive with occasional *accidental* variations). For example, in one session, she picked up a ball of clay, scratched at it until a piece had come off, examined the piece, and then repeated the procedure several times, each time examining the clay on her finger. Next, she noticed a ball of cotton, picked it up, and pulled it into two halves; then she pulled one of the halves into two more pieces, and again, and again. Similarly, in another session, a 15-month-old boy who had been tearing apart bits of clay happened across a piece of spaghetti, pressed it to the floor, broke it, picked up the largest piece, broke it again, and repeated the process a number of times. Once finished, he attempted to break a short plastic stick, he tore a sheet of paper into tiny bits, and then he demolished a pipe cleaner.

The most important feature of tertiary circular reactions is that they are repetitive behaviors deliberately undertaken to see what their effects will be—that is, to explore.

Mental Representation (18 Months to 2 Years)
By the end of the sensorimotor period, infants are well on their way to making a transition from an action-based (motoric) intelligence to a progressively more *cognitive* intelligence. During this final substage of the sensorimotor period, infants demonstrate that they have begun to learn to represent objects and events *mentally*. As a result, they can now occasionally combine these representations to arrive at mental solutions for problems, and they are now able to anticipate the consequences of many of their activities before actually executing them. Their behavior is consequently no longer restricted to trial and error as it was previously. In Piaget's terms, it is as though the child can now begin to internalize (represent mentally) actions and their consequences without having to actually carry them out.

As an illustration of mental representation, Piaget describes his 22-month-old daughter's behavior when she was given a partly open matchbox containing a small thimble. Because the opening was too small for her to withdraw the thimble, she had to open the box first. A younger infant would simply grope at the box, attempting clumsily to remove the thimble. But Piaget's daughter appeared instead to be considering the problem, unconsciously opening and closing her mouth repeatedly as if mirroring her thoughts. Finally, she placed her finger directly into the box's partial opening, opened it, and removed the thimble.

The ability to conceptualize the environment is also reflected in infants' mushrooming language development, which, according to Piaget, is greatly facilitated by their imitative behavior.

Imitation in Infancy

In the earliest stages of imitation, infants are able to imitate objects, activities, or people that are immediately present. Stick your tongue out in front of a 3-month-old, and a tongue may be stuck right back out at you; open your mouth wide, or your eyes, and the infant might do the same.

Imitation in Very Young Infants
There is controversy over exactly when the ability to imitate first appears. Some researchers report that at a mere 2 weeks of age, infants already are able to imitate simple actions like sticking out the tongue or opening the mouth wide (for example, Meltzoff & Moore, 1989). Reissland (1988) claims to have detected imitation in the first hour after birth. His subjects were 12 awake and alert neonates; models bent over them, widening or pursing their lips as instructed. The results? Infants moved their lips in accordance with lip movements of the models significantly more often than at variance with them. Reissland concludes that the ability to imitate is already present at birth.

Some researchers do not agree that neonates are actually imitating when they stick out their tongue or purse their lips in apparent response to a model doing the same thing. Perhaps infants do not truly imitate these facial gestures, but instead simply manifest a generalized, almost reflexive response related mainly to feeding and released by the nearness of the model (Kaitz et al., 1988). It is possible, says Anisfeld (1991), that increased tongue protrusion *following* modeling occurs because tongue protrusion has been inhibited *during* modeling.

Meltzoff and Moore (1989) concede that although the evidence supports the conclusion that very young infants have a general ability to match certain adult behaviors, imitative behavior in the newborn is not completely automatic and easily triggered. In addition, many of the imitative behaviors of the very young infant do not continue when the model is no longer present. That is, the infant is initially capable of imitating only when the model is there or within a very short period of time thereafter. Piaget (1951) suggested that **deferred imitation**—the ability to imitate something or someone no longer present—is not likely to occur before the age of 9 to 12 months.

Imitation in Older Infants
Masur (1993) did a longitudinal study of 10 boys and 10 girls between 10 and 21 months of age, and found that imitation became increasingly common during this period. The second year of life, claims Masur, is a crucial period for the infant's burgeoning ability to represent mentally and to imitate. And although repetition of *familiar* repetitive behaviors like tongue protrusion might occur among very young infants, it isn't until the beginning of the second year that infants begin to imitate *novel* actions. The significance of this transition is that with the capacity to imitate new behaviors, an infant can now use imitation as

MPANDE, A ZULU CHILD

Mpande was born in a traditional "beehive hut" of woven grass and bent saplings. His mother's mattress, upon which he was delivered, was on a mat of straw laid on the hut's hard-polished clay and dung floor. The hut was near the center of the *kraal*, the cluster of huts that housed his parents and all his relatives—which was a good sign because it meant that Mpande's family's social position was important in the *kraal*.

Mpande's mother is a Zulu, a descendent of the ancient clan headed by the man named Zulu, later conquered and united by the great king, Shaka. As a child, he would hear the stories of Shaka's military skill, his zeal for conquest, his leadership. With his age-mates, he would crouch by the fire at night, listening to one of the grandmothers speak of these things. And he would hear the story, too, of how as Shaka's empire and his power grew, he became vain and boastful and so tyrannical that when his mother died, he had 7,000 people killed because their eyes were dry, which meant they did not mourn deeply enough. Only 10 years after he became king, two of Shaka's brothers killed him—and few mourned.

Mpande's mother was the second of his father's several wives, all of whom he would eventually learn to call "mother." And all the children of his mothers would be his brothers and sisters as well. As an infant, he would spend the days cradled on his mother's back, listening to her sing, while she scattered the seeds for mealies (maize), sorghum, watermelons, pumpkins, sugar cane, and sweet potatoes. Whenever he was hungry, she would give him her breast. Then he would sleep, reassured by her warmth and her voice, rocked by her movements as she hoed the ground and harvested the corn.

But Mpande's world is a rapidly changing one. Today, only a fraction of the South African Zulus are born and live in *kraals*. Many of the mothers no longer plant crops or make pottery and weave; even fewer of the fathers tend the cattle, which, for centuries, were the center of the

Zulu economy. Now many live in cities where large numbers of the men and boys work in the mines; and many of the women work in factories or weave and do beadwork or pottery to sell to tourists. There is little time now for sitting around the fire in the evening and listening to the old ones tell the stories of the people.

To Think About When we contrast our culture with another, we can highlight the extent to which we are products of our contexts. But very few cultures are homogeneous; within each, a tremendous variety of different experiences are possible. How many distinct and developmentally significant contexts can you identify in your own milieu?

(Based in part on Bleeker, 1986; Mack, 1980; and Ngubane, 1986.)

---

a powerful tool for new learning—and especially for learning language. In fact, Masur's (1993) research also indicates that there is a dramatic spurt in infants' imitation of novel words in the second half of year 2, and that this spurt is reflected in a sudden expansion of vocabulary.

The older infant's imitation is not limited to imitating and learning from adults, but is also evident in peer–peer imitation. Toddlers (older infants) imitating other toddlers is highly evident in child-care facilities. It has also been investigated by Hanna and Meltzoff (1993), who describe a series of experiments in which 14- to 18-month-old infants readily learned to imitate other "trained" toddlers. In addition, these toddlers demonstrated—in different settings and as much as 2 days later—that they remembered much of what they had learned through imitation.

Achievements of Imitation in Infancy

There are at least three different kinds of learning that imitation makes possible for infants, claim Hay, Stimson,

and Castle (1991). First, they learn about *places* by following people around, in much the same way that young kittens and other animals learn about places by following. When given the opportunity, infants readily follow their mothers in unfamiliar surroundings; often, too, they will follow strangers or a moving toy. Significantly, once they have followed a leader, they are more likely to go back and explore on their own.

Second, imitation facilitates certain *familiar social behaviors*, like sharing toys. When experimenters (or parents, or siblings) play "give and take" games with infants, infants are subsequently more likely to want to give toys to others.

And third, infants learn *new social behaviors* by observing them in others. And, among the most important of new behaviors that they learn at least partly through imitation are those that have to do with speaking and understanding a language. (See Across Cultures: "Mpande, a Zulu Child.")

LANGUAGE

In the beginning, the infant has no words—only cries. Words are simply more noises.

But for the 2-year-old, words are like magic spells that can transform the world. Words can make things appear and disappear; they can change tears into laughter; they have an almost palpable reality, like cats and colors.

And for teenagers and grown-ups, words have still other meanings and other functions. Among other things, words communicate feelings, ask and answer questions, affirm our meaningfulness to others, and theirs to us.

Communication

Despite its tremendous power, language is not essential for **communication** (the transmission of messages). Animals that don't have language can nevertheless communicate danger. Whitetail deer wave their tails; pronghorn antelope bristle their rump patches; ground squirrels whistle. Some of these signals communicate danger to other members of the same species.*

Communication between humans and other animals also occurs. An animal trainer who instructs his dog to roll over is communicating with the animal (at least when the dog obeys—and perhaps even when the dog does not obey). And the dog who walks to his empty dish, looks at his master, and then begins to growl is not only dangerous but is also communicating very effectively.

A Definition of Language

This communication, however, is a far cry from that made possible by language. The parrot who can say "Polly wants a cracker" is not only boringly conventional but is also probably incapable of saying "A cracker wants Polly, heh, heh" with the intention of conveying a different meaning. The parrot merely mimics. It cannot deliberately rearrange sounds according to established rules to say what it means. It does not know language.

Language is *the use of arbitrary sounds, with accepted referents, that can be arranged in sequences to convey different meanings.* This definition includes what Brown (1973) describes as the three essential characteristics of language: *displacement*, *meaning*, and *productiveness*.

Language involves displacement because it makes possible the representation of objects and events that are not immediate—that are *displaced*—in both time and space.

"The moon was a ghostly galleon," we can say, "tossed upon cloudy seas." Yet neither ghosts nor galleons, nor even moons nor seas need be where we can touch them or see them. Indeed, what you and I can speak of need not even exist.

One of the primary functions of language is the communication of *meaning*. Although **psycholinguists**—those who study the relationship between language and human functioning—do not always agree on the best definition for *meaning*, we in our ordinary conversations tend to agree much more than disagree. In fact, it is because you and I have similar meanings for words and sentences that we can communicate as we are now doing.

The third characteristic of language, *productiveness*, means that, given a handful of words, a set of mutually accepted rules about how they can be combined, and agreement about the significance of the various pauses, intonations, and other characteristics of speech, we can produce meanings forever. Language presents so many possibilities for meaningful combinations that almost every day of your life you will say something that no one else has ever said in exactly the same way. Language makes you creative.

Elements of Language

Linguists describe four basic components of language: phonology, semantics, syntax, and pragmatics. Each is essential for effective communication with language.

Phonology refers to the **phonemes,** or sounds, of a language. A phoneme is the simplest unit of language and is nothing more complex than a single sound such as that represented by a consonant or word. There are 45 phonemes in the English language.

Phonemes can be combined to form **morphemes,** which are the units of *meaning* (**semantics**) in language. Morphemes may be made up of sounds such as *ing* or *ed*—word endings that affect the meanings of words—or of whole words. Children cannot produce morphemes until they can first pronounce the phonemes. Simply making the sound is not enough; they must be able to make it when they intend to do so, and they must also be able to combine morphemes in meaningful combinations.

Organizing words into meaningful sentence units requires an intuitive knowledge of **syntax,** or grammar, the set of rules governing the combinations of words that will be meaningful and correct for the speakers of that language.

As children practice and master sounds (phonemes), meanings (semantics), and grammatical rules (syntax), they must also learn a large number of *unspoken* rules and conventions governing conversation. Put another way, they must learn the **pragmatics** of language. An implicit knowledge of pragmatics is what tells children when and how they should speak. It includes uncounted rules and practices governing manners of expression, intonation, accents, and all the other subtle variations that give different

---

*Some of these signals may also communicate to members of *other* species. For example, the flag-waving of the whitetail deer might not only signal danger to other deer, but might also serve as a signal to predators like wolves (Alcock, 1984). It says, in effect, "Ha, ha, I've seen you so forget it." And the wolf reads the signal. Because he knows he can't ordinarily catch a healthy deer in a prolonged chase, he lies down and licks his chops and dreams of sneaking up on other deer.

meanings to the same morphemes and that might vary appreciably from one context to another. For example, that parents use shorter sentences, speak in higher-pitched voices, and use more concrete names and fewer abstractions when speaking with young children than with other adults is a function of their knowledge of pragmatics.

Phonology, semantics, syntax, and pragmatics are the elements of language. Most of us acquired these elements in an amazingly painless, effective, and efficient way without really being conscious of what we were doing.

LANGUAGE DEVELOPMENT IN INFANTS

The transition from the first sounds of the neonate, the cries and the grunts, to the more controlled coos and gurgles, eventually to the babbling, finally to the word, is a fascinating and complex process that is not yet clearly understood.

Early studies of how infants acquire language were often concerned with counting their vocabularies and examining the difference between words they actually used (their **active vocabulary**) and words they didn't use but understood (their **passive vocabulary**). In the early stages of language learning, infants can usually understand many more words than they can use in their own speech. And before using words in speech, many also develop a wide range of communicative gestures (Bates et al., 1989).

Language learning may be divided into two broad stages: the *prespeech stage* and the *speech stage*. In the prespeech stage, which lasts until about age 1, meaningful speech sounds are gradually developed. In the speech stage, the child progresses from the first words to an increasingly sophisticated knowledge of grammar, and pragmatics, and conversation.

Achievements in the Prespeech Stage

During the prespeech stage, infants engage in three different speech-related behaviors: They cry (sometimes a great deal), coo, gurgle, and laugh; they develop a repertoire of gestures, many of which are intended to communicate desires; and they practice babbling—the production of single sounds (see Table 5.5).

The first year of infancy, the prespeech period, is marked by two critical achievements, explains Masur (1993). The first is marked by the appearance of the *intention* to communicate and is evident in signals and gestures that clearly have meaning for both infant and caregiver. Squirming and gazing intently at the milk bottle are pragmatic (effective) ways of saying to mama, "If I don't get that *!!$@ing bottle soon, I'm gonna holler!"

The second important achievement is the discovery of *symbols*—the discovery that things have names. This

TABLE 5.5

Age at Which Infants Demonstrate a Given Language Capability

Language Capability	Approximate Ages	
	50 Percent	90 Percent
Responds to bell		At birth
Laughs	1.9 mos.*	3.1 mos.
Squeals	1.7 mos.	4.3 mos.
Says "dada" or "mama," nonspecific	6.5 mos.	9.1 mos.
Imitates speech sounds	5.2 mos.	8.8 mos.
Says three words other than "mama," "dada"	13.6 mos.	18.0 mos.
Combines two different words	19.8 mos.	2.1 yrs.
Points to six named body parts	19.8 mos.	2.4 yrs.

* For example, 1.9 months equals 1 month and 27 days; 2.4 years equals 2 years and 4 months and 24 days.

SOURCE: From the revised *Denver II* by W. K. Frankenburg and J. B. Dodds, 1992. Denver Developmental Materials, Inc., Box 6919, Denver, CO 80206-0919. Reprinted by permission of the publisher.

discovery is reflected in the appearance of spontaneous, symbolic words at around the age of 1. This should not be confused with the simple ability to represent. As Mandler (1984) makes clear, there are two kinds of representation. *Simple representation* involves nothing more complex than memory. All that is in memory is represented. In this sense, the newborn's ability to suck involves representation. But this type of representation is a far cry from *symbolic representation*—the type of representation that defines semanticity (meaning) and that is essential for language. Symbolic representation begins with the infant's discovery that things can be named—can be symbolized with sounds. Ultimately, children learn to speak so they can communicate, Rice (1989) tells us. Thus they can achieve important social goals.

Language Origins

Research dealing with the origins of language has been particularly interested in the pragmatics and semantics of the infant's first gestures and sounds. Researchers believe that the ability to use and to understand words grows out of a complex series of interactions between infant and parents. These interactions, referred to collectively as the *language acquisition support system* (LASS) by Bruner (1983), involve things like learning how to make eye contact, how to direct attention through eye movements and gestures, and how to take turns.

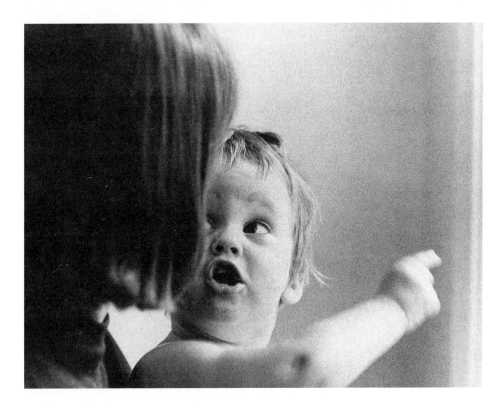

Language consists of sounds (phonology) that have meaning (semantics) when used according to certain grammatical rules (syntax) as well as practical rules (pragmatics). But communication involves far more than simply language. This toddler already possesses a wealth of nonverbal gestures that makes it far easier to say, "Mom, the cat's digging up your hibiscus again."

Turn-Taking

Knowing when and how to take turns is basic to adult conversation. When we have conversations, we wait for the signals that tell us it's our turn; and we give others their signals—well, most of us do; there are some who simply shout a little louder. Most of us have learned the rules that govern turn-taking without really knowing that we have learned them and without, in most cases, being able to verbalize them. Common turn-taking signals include an upward or downward change of pitch at the end of an utterance, the completion of a grammatical clause, a drawl on the last syllable, or the termination of a gesture.

Amazingly, children seem to have a relatively sophisticated awareness of turn-taking signals at very young ages. In one investigation, Mayer and Tronick (1985) videotaped 10 mothers and their infants in face-to-face interaction when the infants were 2, 3, and 5 months of age. Analyses of videotapes revealed that not only did infants rarely vocalize when their mothers were speaking, but they seemed to understand the mother's turn-taking signals. They responded not only to head and hand movements, but also to changes in intonation at the ends of utterances, to terminal drawls, and to the completion of grammatical clauses. Accordingly, they cooed and smiled mostly during the mother's pauses. Mothers, for their part, modified the number of turn-taking signals given depending on the child's responsiveness. Thus, even at the age of 2 months, infants and their mothers are already taking turns.

Gestures

Even before they have begun to use words, infants have typically developed a repertoire of gestures that are clearly meaningful for both infant and caregivers. One of the most common of these gestures, notes Bretherton (1991), is the *gaze*. Infants use looking not only to indicate what they want, but to direct other people's attention. And they typically alternate the gaze between the desired object and the person whose attention they are trying to direct, as if to confirm that the message is being received.

Other infant gestures include pointing, waving, reaching, and so on. Some of these are so common and so important, notes Locke (1992), that their absence may be an early warning of problems in language development. Similarly, problems with turn-taking in early infancy may also be a signal of language delays (Moseley, 1990).

First Sounds

Communicating through language depends on sounds— the ability of the infant to discriminate among them and the ability to produce them.

Sound Discrimination

Infants appear to be able to discriminate sounds at a very early age. Moffitt (1971) conducted an experiment in which the heart rates of 5- and 6-month-old infants were monitored while they were exposed to taped recordings of the sounds "bah" and "gah." Changes in heart rate whenever the sound changed indicated that these infants could tell the difference between them. More recent studies, using the same two syllables, indicate that infants require slightly louder sounds than adults to discriminate correctly, especially with noisy backgrounds (Nozza et al., 1990a; 1990b).

With language experience, infants' ability to discriminate reliably among difficult sounds like "sa" and "za" improves. However, if the sounds are not part of their language, they may experience difficulty discriminating among them even as adults—the sounds "la" and "ra" for a native Japanese speaker, for example (Miyawaki et al., 1975).

Sound Production

Discriminating among sounds is one aspect of early language learning; producing intended sounds is the other.

Infants as young as 3 weeks produce three kinds of sounds, reports Legerstee (1991). There are the longer, *melodic* sounds characterized by variable pitch; *vocalic* sounds, which are short, more nasal bursts characterized by relatively uniform pitch; and *emotional* sounds such as laughing, crying, and fussing.

One of the remarkable things about the infants' early sounds is that their emission is context-dependent. In a longitudinal investigation of eight infants, aged 3 to 25 weeks, Legerstee (1991) found that melodic sounds typically occur when mothers are conversing with their infants; that vocalic sounds are more common with unresponsive adults; and that emotional sounds occur far more often in contexts involving other people than in situations where the infant is interacting with an inanimate object such as a doll.

It was long believed that all the sounds of every language in the world are uttered in the **babbling** of an infant—even in the babbling of deaf infants. This belief leads directly to the conclusion that the ability to produce speech sounds is innate, a conclusion that does not appear to be entirely true. For example, although the first sounds uttered by deaf infants are very similar to those of hearing children, their later vocalizations are typically quite different. These first sounds, say Eilers and Oller (1988), are precursors to the form of babbling in which infants finally utter well-formed syllables with clearly articulated consonants and vowels—a stage that does not occur until some time between 7 and 10 months. Before then, infants make unarticulated noises: They goo, squeal, growl, whisper, and yell. And although it might be possible to discern many sounds that resemble those found in the world's 5,000 or so languages in these early infant sounds, their utterances remain unsystematic and do not obey the laws of syllables (requiring clarity and a complete vowel of adequate duration).

Infants' first sounds are "soft sounds," notes Bijou (1989), but eventually they gain control over their sound-producing apparatus. Also, they discover that producing sounds is fun, as is evident in the fact that contented infants may spend hours in solitary babbling without any prompting. As a result, by the age of 10 months, most hearing children babble clearly, systematically, and repetitively. Deaf children do not reach this stage until later. "It cannot be maintained," say Eilers & Oller (1988), "that babbling is independent of hearing" (p. 23).

That babbling is highly dependent on hearing is clear from a large number of studies that have looked at the babbling of infants exposed to different language environments. Blake and de Boysson-Bardies (1992) analyzed the babblings of three Canadian-English and three Parisian-French infants. Although their babbling was initially highly similar, after the age of 1, babbling patterns became predictably distinct. Similarly, a longitudinal study of a French and an American infant revealed progressive differences in babbling relating directly to the infant's language environment (Levitt & Utman, 1992). And comparisons of the babbling of French and Japanese infants show consistent increases in French-only sounds for the French infants corresponding with a rapid decline in French-only sounds for Japanese infants in the second year of life (Halle, de Boysson-Bardies, & Vihman, 1991).

While certain sounds do appear in the babbling of almost all infants, many other sounds are almost never heard even though they are an important part of some languages. The most common sounds that infants babble are the ones that are easiest given the anatomical structure of their vocal apparatus—consonants such as *b*, *d*, *w*, and *m* (described by linguists as *stop*, *glide*, or *nasal* consonants). Thus, words like *mama*, *papa*, and *dada* are among the simplest for virtually all infants. In fact, there are some who believe that "mama" and "papa" are common to an astounding number of the world's languages precisely because they are among the first systematic sounds infants babble. In many of these languages, says Ingram (1991), "'Mama' emerges as a general request for the fulfilment of some need, while 'papa' is a more descriptive term for parents" (p. 711).

The First Word

It is difficult to determine exactly when infants say their first word. Many infants repeat a sound such as "bah" many times before it becomes associated with an object. The point at which a sound like "bah" ceases to be a babble and become a word (*ball*, for example) is unclear but has usually occurred by the age of 1 year.

Not surprisingly, *mama* or *papa* is the first clearly recognizable word spoken by many infants. The appearance of the first word is rapidly followed by new words that the child practices incessantly. Most of an English-speaking child's first words are nouns: simple names for simple

TABLE 5.6
Stages in Children's Development of Grammar

Stage of Development	Nature of Development	Sample Utterances
1. Prespeech (before age 1)	Crying, cooing, babbling.	"Waaah," "dadadada."
2. Sentencelike word (holophrase) (by 1 year)	The word is combined with nonverbal cues (gestures and inflections).	"Mommy." (meaning: "Would you please come here, Mother?")
3. Two-word sentences (duos) (by 1½ years)	Modifiers are joined to topic words to form declarative, question, negative, and imperative structures.	"Pretty baby." (declarative) "Where Daddy?" (question) "No play." (negative) "More milk!" (imperative)
4. Multiple-word sentences (by 2 to 2½ years)	Both a subject and predicate are included in the sentence types. Grammatical morphemes are used to change meanings (*ing* or *ed,* for example).	"She's a pretty baby." (declarative) "Where Daddy is?" (question) "I no can play." (negative) "I want more milk!" (imperative) "I running." "I runned."
5. More complex grammatical changes and word categories (between 2½ and 4 years)	Elements are added, embedded, and permuted within sentences. Word classes (nouns, verbs, and prepositions) are subdivided. Clauses are put together.	"Read it, my book." (conjunction) "Where is Daddy?" (embedding) "I can't play." (permutation) "I would like *some* milk." (use of "some" with mass noun) "Take me *to* the store." (use of preposition of place)
6. Adultlike structures (after 4 years)	Complex structural distinctions made, as with "ask-tell" and "promise."	"Ask what time it is." "He promised to help her."

SOURCE: Based in part on Barbara S. Wood, *Children and communication: Verbal and nonverbal language development* (2nd ed.), ©1981, p. 142. Reprinted by permission of Prentice-Hall, Inc., Englewood Cliffs, New Jersey.

things—the simple things usually being objects or people that are part of the here and now: "dog," "mama," "banket" (blanket), "yefant" (elephant). Verbs, adjectives, adverbs, and prepositions are acquired primarily in the order listed, with the greatest difficulty usually being the use of pronouns, especially the pronoun *I* (Boyd, 1976).

But before learning words, infants have begun to show signs that they understand much more than they can say—words that will not be part of their active vocabulary for some time, as well as entire sentences. "Stick out your tongue," she is told by a proud parent, and she sticks out her tongue. "Show Daddy your hand," and she shows it. "Can you wink?" Sure can. Two eyes, though.

To simplify a complex process, the learning of language is described in this text in terms of six sequential stages (based on Wood, 1981). The first of these, just described, is the prespeech stage, which lasts until approximately age 1. It consists of the crying, the gooing, the babbling just described. The next two stages—that of the sentencelike word and the two-word sentence, are described in the following sections. The remaining three stages are detailed in Chapter 7 (see Table 5.6).

The Sentencelike Word (Holophrase)

Some time after the sixth month (usually around age 1) children utter their first meaningful word. This word's meaning is seldom limited to one event, action, or person but often means something that an adult would require an entire sentence to communicate; hence the term **holophrase.** Thus although most holophrases are nouns, they are not used simply for naming. When a child says "milk," she might mean, "There is the milk." She might also mean, "Give me some milk," "I'm thirsty," "I want you to hold me," "Go buy some milk," or "Are you going to do it to the cow again?"

Two-Word Sentences

Not surprisingly, the progression of speech development is from one word to two (roughly by the age of 18 months)—and later to more than two. There does not appear to be a three-word stage following this two-word stage, but rather a *multiword* stage where sentences range in length from two to perhaps five or more words.

Masur (1993) notes that there are three widely recognized general language-learning milestones in the first two years of life: The first is the acquisition of communicative gestures in the second half of year 1; the second is the appearance of the first words at about age 1; and the third is a dramatic vocabulary spurt at about 17 or 18 months. The appearance of two-word sentences coincides closely with this sudden acceleration in vocabulary growth.

Baby Talk

When they are first learning words, the range of syllables available to infants is limited. Many of their words are one- or two-syllable words, which often repeat the same

TABLE 5.7
Average Ages for Mental Development in Infants

Age (Months)	Mental Behavior Anticipated
0.2	Regards person momentarily, responding either to speech or to movements.
0.7	Eyes follow moving person.
0.7	Makes definite response to speaking voice.
1.5	Smiles or laughs in response to another person's speaking to and smiling at him or her.
2.0	Visually recognizes mother; expression changes when infant sees mother bending over to talk to him or her.
2.6	Manipulates red ring placed in child's hand or grasped by child.
3.8	Carries red ring to mouth during free play.
3.8	Inspects own hands.
4.1	Reaches for cube, even if not actually touching it.
5.1	Laughs or shows pleasure when held and played with.
5.8	Lifts cup with handle.
6.0	Looks for spoon that has fallen.
9.1	Responds to verbal request *not* accompanied by gesture.
12.0	Turns pages of book, even if effort is clumsy.
14.2	Says two words meaningfully (approximations all right if clear).
20.6	Puts two or more words denoting two concepts into one sentence or phrase.

SOURCE: Adapted from the *Bayley Scales of Infant Development*. Copyright © 1969 by The Psychological Corporation. Adapted and reproduced by permission. All rights reserved.

syllable in different combinations ("mommy," "daddy," "baby," "seepy" (sleepy), "horsy," "doggy"). Even when it is incorrect to do so, the child may repeat the syllable in a one-syllable word, as in "car car" or "kiss kiss."

In an attempt to communicate with children on their level, parents sometimes exaggerate the errors committed by their infants. The result is occasionally something like, "Wou my itsy bitsy witta baby come to momsy womsy?" But there is no evidence that parental (or grandparental) models of this type hamper the rapid and correct acquisition of language. In the early stages, the warmth of the interaction may be more important than the nature of the language employed.

Telegraphic Speech
The transition from holophrases to two-word sentences generally occurs at around 18 months and coincides with a period of increasingly rapid vocabulary growth. Speech at this stage is sometimes described as being *telegraphic* because it eliminates many parts of speech while still managing to convey meanings. "Dog allgone" is a two-word utterance "telegraphed" from the lengthier adult equivalent, "The dog is not in this location at this time."

Early Grammar
Whether precise grammatical functions can be accurately assigned to these two-word utterances is a matter of some debate. The functions of the words *fish* and *eat* in the two-word utterance "fish eat" are, in fact, dependent on the intended meaning. But because the child does not use number agreement (for example, "fish eats" to mean "the fish eats" and "fish eat" to mean "I eat fish") or order ("eat fish" versus "fish eat") to signal meaning, the psycholinguist can never be certain that children at this stage are aware of grammatical functions.

By the age of 2, infants have reached the point where they can name all the familiar objects and people in their environment. More than this, they can now combine words into meaningful sentencelike units. They can also use adjectives and adverbs, questions, and simple negatives and affirmatives; and they have begun to learn a variety of subtle and implicit rules governing intonation, inflection, and the conventions that guide conversations.

But there is much more yet to be learned; there remain three stages in our six-stage description of the sequence of language acquisition. The story of that sequence continues in Chapter 7.

FROM SENSATION TO REPRESENTATION

The term *sensorimotor* describes well the predominant relationship between infant and world; but it does not describe the most important cognitive achievements of the first two years of life—achievements that move the growing person from infancy to childhood. By definition, infants are no longer infants when they are no longer speechless.

Some of the achievements of infancy are apparent in Table 5.7. They include the realization of the independent existence and permanence of objects, a dawning understanding of cause-and-effect relationships, and the learning of language coupled with the effects this has on cognitive development. These achievements, together with children's recognition of their own identities—their selves—represent a dramatic transition from a quasi-animalistic existence to the world of thought and emotions as we know it. But although it is a dramatic transition, at least in its import, it is neither sudden nor startling. Those who follow the lives of individual children closely (and daily) never see the transition from sensorimotor intelligence to preoperational thought. It happens suddenly and irrevocably on the second birthday only in textbooks. Real life is less well organized.

The Newborn

1. A newborn is a primitive, self-driven little sensing machine designed to mature and grow physically in a predetermined sequence and at a relatively predictable pace, programmed as an extraordinarily capable information-processing system, endowed with powerful gregarious tendencies and strong emotions, and pretuned to the development of language.

Health and Physical Growth

2. Human breast milk is infant-specific, easily digested, nourishing, useful in guarding against the possibility of diarrhea, and provides a degree of immunity to infant illnesses. Genital growth is minimal in infancy (until pubescence); lymphoid and neural growth occurs very rapidly; optimal brain development is profoundly influenced by nutrition (especially protein) and stimulation; and physical growth is relatively rapid (it slows through middle childhood and spurts again at adolescence).

Sudden Infant Death

3. Sudden infant death syndrome (SIDS) accounts for the unexpected and largely inexplicable deaths of apparently healthy infants. It is more common among males, rarely occurs after the age of 6 months, and is sometimes associated with factors such as neurological immaturity, sleeping in a prone position, a mild upper-respiratory infection, apnea, lower Apgar scores, or other factors, none of which have been shown to cause SIDS.

Behavior in the Newborn

4. The orienting response (for example, changes in heart rate or respiration) is a useful measure of interest, attention, and learning in infants. The behavioral repertoire of the neonate consists largely of reflexes (for example, sucking, Moro, Babinski, palmar (grasping), swimming, stepping, swallowing, and sneezing). Many of these disappear with the development of the brain and the achievement of voluntary control over movements.

Motor Development

5. Infants engage in regular, cyclic motor activities. The development of motor skills seems to be governed by two principles: cephalocaudal (head to tail) and proximodistal (near to far).

Perceptual Development

6. Visual capacities (color, motion, depth) are well developed in the newborn. The infant's looking seems to be directed by rules that maximize information. Neonates are only slightly less sensitive than adults to sound intensity (loudness). They appear to recognize and prefer their mothers' voices at ages as young as 3 days. They prefer pleasant odors (such as vanilla) to those less pleasant (ammonia or raw fish) almost from birth. Similarly, they prefer the sweet to the bland, they distinguish easily between sour and bitter tastes, and they appear to be sensitive to touch (and to pain), at least within a few hours of birth.

Cognitive Development

7. The neonate's memory is not as efficient, as powerful, or as long-term as that of older children or adults, but there is memory for smells and sights within days of birth. By the age of 3 months, infants actively search and show signs of recognition.

8. In Piaget's theory, adaptation (cognitive growth) results from the interplay of assimilation (responding in a habitual and preferred way based primarily on preexisting information and well-practiced capabilities) and accommodation (adapting behavior to some external characteristic or quality). Equilibration is the tendency to balance assimilation and accommodation. Other important factors in cognitive development are maturation, social interaction, and active experience. Piaget's six substages of the sensorimotor period are (1) exercising reflexes, (2) primary circular reactions, (3) secondary circular reactions, (4) purposeful coordinations, (5) tertiary circular reactions, and (6) mental representation.

9. There is increased frequency of simple infant behaviors like tongue protrusion following exposure to a model, even in very young infants. It is not entirely clear that these are always imitative behaviors. Evidence of deferred imitation is seen by the age of 9 to 12 months; it depends on the ability to represent mentally and to remember, and is therefore of considerable importance in cognitive development.

Language

10. Language involves the use of arbitrary speech sounds that have accepted meanings. It is characterized by displacement, meaningfulness, and productiveness. Its elements are phonology, semantics, syntax, and pragmatics.

Language Development in Infants

11. Infants discriminate sounds at very young ages; also, they are able to produce many sounds in their babbling. Babbling becomes systematic by the age of 7 to 10 months. Linguistic experience eventually modifies the infant's ability to discriminate and to produce sounds. The ability to use and understand words grows out of a complex series of interactions between parents and young infants. Infants as young as 2 months have a relatively sophisticated awareness of the turn-taking signals used in conversation.

12. In the prespeech stage (first year of life), the infant coos, gurgles, cries, and babbles. Two important achievements of this stage are the development of the intention to communicate and the discovery that things have names. The first meaningful word appears around age 1, and is often sentencelike in nature (a holophrase). Two-word sentences (telegraphic, highly condensed) appear around the age of 18 months, at which time there is a spurt in vocabulary growth.

FOCUS QUESTIONS: APPLICATIONS

1. What are some of the advantages and disadvantages of breast-feeding?

- Organize a breast-feeding debate. Alternately, research and summarize arguments that might be used on one or the other side of this debate.

2. How might the neonate's behavioral repertoire be described?

- Arrange to demonstrate the most common infant reflexes with a newborn.

3. How do infants look?

- Describe the rules of infant visual perception, and their purpose.

4. Do infants think? What do they think?

- Outline and illustrate the principal characteristics of Piaget's sensorimotor period.

5. What is the basic sequence in language acquisition?

- Why are imitation theories of language acquisition not entirely adequate?

STUDY TERMS

accommodation 141

active vocabulary 148

adaptation 141

apnea 131

assimilation 141

babbling 150

Babinski reflex 133

breast-versus-bottle 127

communication 147

conceptualization 135

cyclic movements 134

deferred imitation 145

equilibration 142

galvanic skin response (GSR) 132

head-turning reflex 132

holophrase 151

language 147

lymphoid system 127

meaning 147

Moro reflex 132

morphemes 147

neonate 126

norms 134

object concept 142

orienting response 132

palmar reflex 133

passive vocabulary 148

perception 135

phonemes 147

phonology 147

physical growth 129

pragmatics 147

primary circular reactions 144

productiveness 147

psycholinguists 147

pubescence 127

pupillary reflexes 136

rooting reflex 132

schema 141

secondary circular reactions 144

semantics 147

sensation 135

sucking reflex 132

sudden infant death syndrome 130

syntax 147

tertiary circular reaction 144

vegetative reflex 132

The following two sources are simple, nontechnical descriptions of development in infancy. They offer many practical suggestions that might be useful for parents interested in understanding and promoting the intellectual development of their infants:

Devine, M. (1991). *Baby talk: The art of communicating with infants and toddlers.* New York: Plenum.

White, B. L. (1985). *The first three years of life* (rev. ed.). Englewood Cliffs, NJ: Prentice-Hall.

Guidelines and norms for monitoring physical growth in young children are detailed in:

Jelliffe, D. B., & Jelliffe, E. F. (1990). *Growth monitoring and promotion in young children: Guidelines for the selection of methods and training techniques.* New York: Oxford University Press.

The following collection presents a detailed and current overview of what is known about SIDS:

Corr, C. A., Fuller, H., Barnickol, C. A., & Corr, D. M. (Eds.). (1991). *Sudden Infant Death Syndrome: Who can help and how.* New York: Springer.

A clear and useful account of Piaget's theory is:

Wadsworth, B. J. (1989). *Piaget's theory of cognitive and affective development* (4th ed.). New York: Longman.

Bower's book is a stimulating explanation of how experience makes the rational infant even more competent:

Bower, T. G. R. (1989). *The rational infant: Learning in infancy.* New York: W. H. Freeman.

SOCIAL DEVELOPMENT: INFANCY

*T*he ancients classed individuals in one or other of four temperaments, founded on the hypothesis of four humours, . . . the red part [of the blood], phlegm, yellow, and black bile . . . Hence were derived the names of the sanguine, the phlegmatic, the choleric, and the melancholic temperaments.

A. WALKER
Beauty in Woman

They called my cousin Arthur "Little Art" through most of elementary school. Then puberty struck hard and Arthur became plain "Art." Now some people even call him Mister.

CHAPTER 6

But during his first year of life, and especially during the first six months of that first year, there were few around Arthur who felt kindly enough toward him to call him "Little Art"; the appellation seemed too sweet and gentle for an infant as cranky, plaintive, and loud as cousin Arthur. You see, Arthur was one of those infants who cried most of the time he wasn't feeding or sleeping. And even when he was feeding, he typically managed an assortment of cries in between suckles. The frustrating thing was that so unpredictable was their nature and timing that his mother, my poor aunt, could never figure out whether these were cries of hunger, expressions of disgust with his food, or just plain, genetically based cussedness. So, in the end, they sent for Mr. Delisle, who had gained considerable expertise in the analysis of human character largely as a result of vast experience in the assessment of canine dispositions.

Arthur was yelling when Mr. Delisle came in. "I see," he said at once, taking the pipe from his teeth. Perhaps he had already determined exactly what it was that was wrong with cousin Arthur; but to his credit, he didn't pronounce his judgment immediately. Instead, he picked the kid up, turned him this way and that, and poked him firmly in the belly with the stem of his pipe. Art, his puffy little face as red as Mr. Delisle's nose, immediately stopped crying as though momentarily stunned—and then doubled his volume.

"Not much you're going to be able to do about it," Mr. Delisle announced to my aunt, wiping the pipe stem on his sleeve before sticking the pipe back in his mouth.

"What is it?" she asked.

"His temperament," he said in that sidemouth delivery of his, teeth clamped firmly on the pipe. "He's got the choleric one. The yellow bile."

THIS CHAPTER

Mr. Delisle had taken a page from the book of the ancient Greeks, who thought those with a preponderance of yellow bile would be of choleric temperament, easily angered and quick to display it. It's an ancient book full of insight and poetry and folk wisdom. But science no longer considers its contribution to the analysis of human personality very useful.

This chapter deals with more current approaches to understanding and describing infant personality. It deals with predominant infant states, infant emotions, temperament, the development of attachments between infants and their caregivers, as well as with infant reactions to strangers and to separation from those to whom they are attached. It looks, too, at the care of young infants in contemporary societies, at current approaches to parenting and the effects these approaches might have on children, and at early influences on the development of gender roles. Finally, it looks at infants with characteristics different from those of the mythical average child—those with exceptionalities.

INTERACTIONS IN THE FAMILY CONTEXT

Our more current approaches to understanding the infant experience continue to recognize genetic contributions—although they also recognize that things are far more complex than the ancient Greeks' simple typology implied. At the same time, they pay increasing attention to the importance of the infant's interactions with parents, siblings, dogs, and so on.

Throughout much of child psychology's brief history, notes Ambert (1992), the principal emphasis has been on how parents affect their offspring. Now researchers have begun to recognize that how infants and children affect

parents' lives is extremely important. It is clear not only that infants and children affect their parents, but also that these influences are often instrumental in changing how parents, in turn, affect their children.

As an illustration, consider Marlis, an especially difficult infant, who cries a lot, refuses her mother's breast unpredictably, and soils her diaper at awkward times almost as if to say, "There, that'll teach ya!" Her mother, in turn, is easily annoyed, impatient, highly emotional, and given to temper tantrums. Brad, on the other hand, is an angel of a baby. He sleeps regularly, seldom cries, loves his mother's breast, and soils his diaper only at regular intervals and always very politely with an apologetic little grimace as if to say, "Phoo and Yuk! I sure hate to have to do that!" And Brad's mother is calm, enthusiastic, patient, and absolutely delighted with her infant.

In Bronfenbrenner's terms, the *ecology*—the interactions—will be very different in each of these two *microsystems*, reflecting distinct characteristics of infant and parent. A wide range of such characteristics are especially important influences on the infant's developmental context. Among these are the infant's temperament (the biological basis of personality), the sex of both parent and infant, and parental personality characteristics.

Beyond the Dyad: A Model of Influences

Discovering the nature of family interactions and their influences is not simple; interpreting them is even more difficult. Traditionally, the analysis has been of two-person, or *dyadic*, relationships: for example, mother–infant, father–infant, infant–sibling. This model, useful though it is, has one major shortcoming: It fails to take into consideration the far more complex nature of the majority of the families into which infants are born, as well as the great variety of indirect effects that parents and families can have on infants (White & Woollett, 1992). Newer approaches reflect the ecological or contextual model of which we spoke in Chapter 2.

The contextual model differs from the traditional dyadic model in a number of important ways. First, it emphasizes that in addition to the influence of mother and father on the infant, there is also the influence of the *family*—a social unit made up of husband and wife (as opposed to just father and mother) and characterized by a marital relationship. Second, the model suggests that many complex influences may be at play other than the obvious parent–infant links. Belsky (1981) refers to these as "second-order" effects. Some possible second-order effects include the influence that a father might have on a mother, which might then cause her to interact differently with the infant; the relationship that the mother has with the infant, which might influence the way the father interacts with the infant; the influence that the infant's arrival (or temperament) has on the marriage and the consequent

Families are very complex social units in which the characteristics and behaviors of each member can influence all other members. And sometimes crying is the best way of getting attention.

effects this might have on parenting—to name but a few effects. Note that these influences are what Bronfenbrenner (1989) terms the *meso-*, *exo-*, and *macrosystems*.

The contextual view underlines the dynamic and changing nature of family relationships, and their complexity. For example, family relationships can involve a variety of individuals like grandparents and other relatives. As Levitt, Guacci, and Coffman (1993) demonstrate, infants can form attachment relationships with these nonfamily members, as well as with other people who are initially strangers.

How Infants Influence Parents

What does research tell us about these relationships? Perhaps not as much as we would like to know, given that many of the results are still unclear or contradictory. But, as Ambert (1992) points out, there is a tremendous range of infant and child characteristics, and behaviors, that can have profound effects on parents. To list but a few of the more obvious, child *misbehaviors* and problems such as truancy, poor academic performance, illnesses, and juvenile delinquency might significantly affect parents' lives. In contrast, more positive child behaviors, for example, in academics or athletics, can also have profound effects on parents. Less obvious but perhaps no less important, there is evidence that the birth of an infant often changes the relationship between husband and wife (sometimes increasing stress and discord, sometimes having the opposite effect); that discordant and conflict-ridden marriages are sometimes related to the development of antisocial behavior in children; that highly supportive marital relationships are related to caregiving skills with young infants; that the birth of an infant can frequently make a good marriage better, although it is less likely to make a bad one good; and that among the key qualities of parenting reflected in

cognitive development and adjustment are sensitive mothering (attentiveness, warmth, responsiveness, and stimulation) and involved fathering (doing things with infants, including caregiving and playing) (Ambert, 1992).

But, as Belsky points out, we still know "very little about the direct influence of the child on marital relations and even less about the reverse process of influence" (1981, p. 17). The adoption of a contextual-ecological model that considers the family in addition to the mother and the father may increase our knowledge considerably.

INFANT STATES

Cousin Arthur cried a good deal of the time when he was an infant.* *Crying* was one of his predominant **infant states** (state is the general condition of the infant).

Wolff (1966), following a careful study of the behavior of infants, describes six distinct infant states: *regular sleep, irregular sleep, drowsiness, alert inactivity, alert activity,* and *crying* (these last two states are sometimes grouped together and termed *focused activity*) (see Interactive Figure 6.1).

Newborns vary consistently in the amount of time spent in each state, some sleeping more than half the day; others sleeping for only a few hours (Brown, 1964). Similarly, some cry as much as 40 percent of the time and others hardly at all. With increasing age, expected changes include a decline in the amount of time spent sleeping and an increase in alert activity.

Although the average neonate sleeps as much as 75 to 80 percent of the time, for most young infants periods of sleep are relatively short and are interspersed with many brief periods of wakefulness. It isn't clear whether infants dream while they sleep. However, an extremely high proportion of the infant's sleeping time (as much as 50 percent) is characterized by **rapid eye movement (REM) sleep**. And we do know that in children and adults, most dreams occur during REM sleep. Amount of REM sleep declines gradually during **infancy** (from birth to the age of 2). By the age of 2 years, approximately 25 percent of the infant's sleep is of the REM variety—very similar to that of an adult.

Note that the concept of *infant state* refers simply to the infant's condition of alertness. That is, infant state takes into account whether the infant is sleeping, drowsy, alert, or crying. As we saw, however, infants can differ markedly in the amount of time they characteristically spend in each of these states. Differences in predominant infant states may, in fact, reflect basic, genetically influenced differences in *temperament*.

---

*His wife believes that's why he now complains so much as a grown man. "It's his nature," she explains, strangely proud that her husband should have this kind of nature. "Maybe," says one of my other cousins, rather unkindly, "it's because she doesn't have a nature herself."

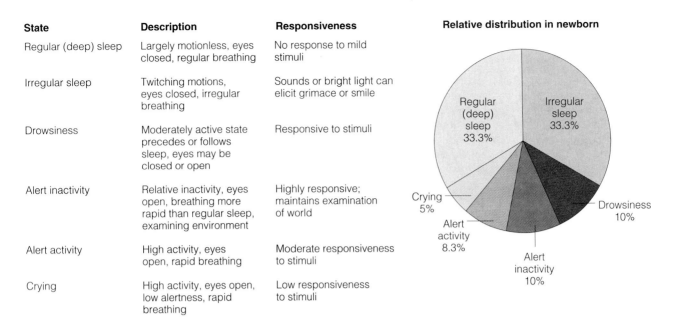

State	Description	Responsiveness
Regular (deep) sleep	Largely motionless, eyes closed, regular breathing	No response to mild stimuli
Irregular sleep	Twitching motions, eyes closed, irregular breathing	Sounds or bright light can elicit grimace or smile
Drowsiness	Moderately active state precedes or follows sleep, eyes may be closed or open	Responsive to stimuli
Alert inactivity	Relative inactivity, eyes open, breathing more rapid than regular sleep, examining environment	Highly responsive; maintains examination of world
Alert activity	High activity, eyes open, rapid breathing	Moderate responsiveness to stimuli
Crying	High activity, eyes open, low alertness, rapid breathing	Low responsiveness to stimuli

Relative distribution in newborn

- Regular (deep) sleep 33.3%
- Irregular sleep 33.3%
- Drowsiness 10%
- Alert inactivity 10%
- Alert activity 8.3%
- Crying 5%

I N T E R A C T I V E   F I G U R E 6.1

States reflecting infant's responsiveness to environment: Predominant states of the infant—that is, the infant's vigilance and wakefulness—vary a great deal from one infant to another. Some sleep more; others cry; some study their environments. If you have access to an infant, you might use one or more of the observation techniques described in Chapter 1 (diary description, time sampling, specimen description, or event sampling) to study infant states, and perhaps to compare two or more infants. (Based on information in Wolff, 1969).

TEMPERAMENT

Differences in the customary ways of reacting and behaving that differentiate adults from each other are generally referred to as *personality differences.* The term **personality** includes all of the abilities, predispositions, habits, and other characteristics that make each of us different from one another. A cluster of related characteristics is called a *trait* (Wiggins & Pincus, 1992).

When psychologists speak of differences among infants, they don't often use the term *personality* because it implies a degree of learning that has not yet had time to occur. Instead, psychologists speak of infant **temperament,** or characteristic emotional responses. Clusters of related temperament characteristics are termed *types.*

One important difference between temperament and personality is that temperament is assumed to have a primarily genetic basis whereas personality has developed through interaction with the environment (Chess & Thomas, 1989). Thus, Buss and Plomin (1985) define temperament as "inherited personality traits present in early childhood" (p. 84). That is, a child is born with a certain temperament rather than with a certain personality. Temperament is reflected in the prevailing states we described earlier (crying, for example).

Part of the reason for a very high current level of interest in infant temperament, suggests Kagan (1992), lies

This grandfather's personality includes all of the characteristics and tendencies that have resulted from a lifetime of experiences interacting with some early biological predispositions. Experience has had less time to shape the infant's customary ways of reacting and behaving—which are therefore labeled temperament rather than personality. Experiences such as sitting on grandpa's knee and blowing a magic whistle might do much to begin to shape this little boy's personality.

in research with animals that has found marked differences in the characteristics of different animals of the same species and breed—differences that appear to be genetically based, as are temperamental differences. For example, one dog may be highly timid; another from the same litter, bold and aggressive. Furthermore, recent advances in neuroscience suggest the possibility of identifying actual biological and chemical differences that might account for differences in temperament. However, as Kagan (1992) puts it, "Scientists have not yet discovered that physiology that is reliably and selectively linked to the [temperament]" (p. 994).

Types of Infant Temperament

In the pioneering and best-known investigation of infant temperament, the New York Longitudinal Study (NYLS), Thomas, Chess, and Birch (1968; 1970; Thomas & Chess, 1977; 1981) carefully observed 141 children from 85 highly educated, professional families, and interviewed their parents. They found that there are at least nine different characteristics that are easily observed in infants (particularly after the infant is 2 or 3 months of age) and on which they can be rated as being high, medium, or low (see Table 6.1). Furthermore, certain infants have remarkably similar patterns of characteristics giving rise to three distinct *types* of infant that parents seem to recognize readily. For example, *difficult* infants are characterized by irregularity (lack of rhythmicity) with respect to things such as eating, sleeping, and toilet functions; withdrawal from unfamiliar situations; slow adaptation to change; and intense as well as negative moods. In contrast, *easy* infants are characterized by high rhythmicity (regularity in eating, sleeping, and so on); high interest in novel situations;

high adaptability to change; and a preponderance of positive moods, as well as low or moderate intensity of reaction. And *slow-to-warm-up* infants are characterized by low activity level, high initial withdrawal from the unfamiliar; slow adaptation to change; and a somewhat negative mood, with moderate or low intensity of reaction. Of the original 141 children in the NYLS, 65 percent could be classified as belonging to one of these three temperament types (40 percent *easy;* 15 percent *difficult;* 10 percent *slow to warm up*); the remaining 35 percent displayed varying mixtures of the nine temperament characteristics (see Interactive Table 6.2).

TABLE 6.1
Nine Temperament Characteristics of Infants

1. Level and extent of motor activity
2. Rhythmicity (regularity of functions such as eating, sleeping, and eliminating)
3. Withdrawal or approach in new situations
4. Adaptability to changes in the environment
5. Sensitivity to stimuli
6. Intensity (energy level) of responses
7. General mood or disposition (cheerful, cranky, friendly, and so on)
8. Distractibility (how easily infant may be distracted from ongoing activities)
9. Attention span and persistence in ongoing activities

SOURCE: From "The Origin of Personality" by A. Thomas, S. Chess, and H. G. Birch, 1970, *Scientific American* 223, pp. 102–109.

INTERACTIVE TABLE 6.2

INFANT TEMPERAMENTS*

What sort of infant were you? Ask your mother, your father, a sibling, or someone else who can tell you. Do you see any relationship between who you are now and what you were like as an infant?

Temperament	Description	Approximate Percentage
Easy	Regularity in eating and sleeping (high rhythmicity); high approach tendencies in novel situations; high adaptability to change; preponderance of positive moods; low or moderate intensity of responses	40
Difficult	Irregularity in eating and sleeping (low rhythmicity); withdrawal in novel situations; slow adaptation to change; preponderance of negative moods; high intensity of reactions to stimulation	15
Slow to warm up	Low activity level; high initial withdrawal from the unfamiliar; slow adaptation to change; somewhat negative mood; moderate or low intensity of reaction to stimulation	10
Varying mixtures	Unclassified	35

* Thomas and Chess (1981) caution that these temperaments do not exhaust all possibilities. In addition, although it is sometimes convenient, as well as apparently logical, to classify infants in these ways, there are wide ranges of behaviors within each category. "Easy" children don't all react the same way to the same situations; nor do all "difficult" children. Note, too, that some 35 percent of all infants appear not to fit any of these categories.

SOURCE: Based on classifications used by Thomas, Chess, and Birch (1968; 1970; 1981) in the New York Longitudinal Study (NYLS).

Psychologists suggest that infants are born with biologically based tendencies to react one way more often than another. These tendencies are evident in the infant's temperament. These six urchins are only about half a year old, but already their personalities seem distinctly different.

Classifying Temperament

Infant temperament is evident primarily in the behavior of infants. However, classifications of temperament cannot always be accomplished by observing infants directly, which is a time-consuming and difficult task. More often, researchers rely on parental observation reported in specially designed questionnaires. For example, the *Early Infancy Temperament Questionnaire* developed by Medoff-Cooper, Carey, and McDevitt (1993), is designed for use with infants younger than 4 months of age; it is based on Thomas, Chess, and Birch's (1981) *Revised Infant Temperament Questionnaire*, which is more suitable for older infants.

There are also other ways of classifying infant temperament (see Bates, 1989). For example, Buss and Plomin (1985) classify infants on the basis of emotionality, activity, and sociability (termed the *EAS approach*). And Strelau (1989) suggests that temperamental differences might be assessed through physiological measures of the *excitability* of the nervous systems—that differences in physiological reactions such as brain-wave activity, heart rate, or motor responses may underly differences in temperament. For example, Stifter and Fox (1990) showed that measures of heart-rate variability are closely related to infant reactivity in the first year of life.

The Implications of Infant Temperament

Temperament may be defined as the infant's biologically based tendencies to react one way more often than another. Personality is an outgrowth of interaction between innate temperament and environmental influences (Carey, 1989). "An infant's temperament," say Kagan and Snid-

man (1991), "renders some outcomes very likely, some moderately likely, and some unlikely—although not impossible—depending on experience" (p. 856). As an example, the temperament they term *uninhibited to the unfamiliar*, characterized by a tendency to approach in strange situations, is likely to lead to spontaneous, fearless, outgoing youngsters. In contrast, infants who are markedly inhibited in the face of the unfamiliar are likely to continue to be timid at the age of 8 years. Similarly, in a long-term follow-up of infants in the Thomas and Chess (1981) study, researchers found that infants of difficult temperament were somewhat more likely to manifest problems requiring psychiatric attention. Note, however, that predictions of later problem behaviors on the basis of mothers classifying their infants as being of "difficult" temperament are often highly unreliable. For example, Oberklaid and associates (1993) found that maternal classifications predicted only 17.5 percent of children who had behavior problems in preschool—which is hardly more than the percentage of all preschoolers who had problems among this large group of 1,583 children (14 percent). In fact, in this study, sex (male) and socioeconomic status were better predictors than maternal ratings alone.

Implications for Parenting

Temperament does not mean, caution Kagan and Snidman (1991), that genetics inevitably determines our personalities—that our contexts are of no importance. In fact, knowing something of an infant's temperament may be very useful in allowing us to alter contexts in beneficial ways. Thomas, Chess, and Korn (1982) suggest, for example, that "easy" children, because of their high adaptabil-

They were real different when they were babies, you know. I mean Luke was a holy terror. Just about drove me crazy, always hollering for something or needing a change or falling out of his crib. He did that more than once. Wonder he didn't scramble his brains. And Chris, he was just about the opposite. Never cried or nothing unless he was real sick or hurt. Right through school, too, Chris—he never complained. Just done his work. But his brother, he was two years younger, Luke was . . . well, Luke, he complained, all right, and he got himself into trouble more times! Nothing serious, mind you. Just kid stuff. Never got kicked out of school or anything like that. . . .

Now? Well, I don't know. They're grown up. They're different all right. I mean Chris is more quiet and all, but Luke settled down a lot when he grew up. Marriage is what did it.

ity, will respond well to a variety of parenting styles (such as permissive or authoritarian). In contrast, a more difficult infant may require more careful parenting. Because these children adapt more slowly and respond less well to novelty and change, they require consistent and patient parents. Also, given their more intense and more negative moods, they are not likely to react well to highly authoritarian or highly permissive parents. Not surprisingly, researchers report that postive family relationships and contented parents are more often associated with highly rhythmic, "easy" infants than with those who are "difficult" (Wilson, Hall, & White, 1994). And it is probably not just a chance event that Mayberry and Affonso (1993) uncovered a number of studies that report a positive relationship between maternal postpartum depression and infant temperament, with excessive crying being most often identified as a contributing factor.

The contribution of temperament to the infant's development, and its relationship to the behavior of parents, presents yet another example of the extent to which parent–child influences are interactive (bidirectional) (Rothbart & Ahadi, 1994). Consider, for example, the case of Robert, an "easy" child. He adapts readily to change, smiles a lot, is rhythmic in feeding and sleeping routines, responds well to parents and to strangers, and, perhaps most important, appears to be happy. Parents react with pleasure to such a child, note Thomas and Chess (1981). They feel responsible for what Robert is; they think of themselves as wonderful parents. They smile and laugh as they tend to their little Robert, and he smiles right back at them. They gaze at each other and everything they say and do says, "You're wonderful!"

But Marlis does not smile so much, cries more, eats and sleeps irregularly, is timid in the face of the unfamiliar, and whines and fusses much of the time. Hence, her social progress seems slower than Robert's and the message her parents receive does not say, "You're wonderful, dear parent." Nope. Instead it says, "As a parent, you're just so-so," or worse yet, "As a parent, you ain't worth $%##@!"

Cultural Context and Temperament

Although temperament has a biological basis, it is constantly evolving as a result of child–context interaction. As Kagan (1992) notes, behaviors influenced by temperament are not immutable. In his words, "Membership in a temperamental category implies only a slight, initial bias for certain emotions and actions" (p. 994). Consequently, developmental outcomes are not always easy to predict. The infant who is initially difficult may become an adolescent whose charm, grace, and other good qualities make a mother blush with pride; and the one who is initially easy may, it's true, become a thoroughly reprehensible, no-good #@%^^&. Or worse.

DeVries and Sameroff (1984) point out that what is often important in influencing developmental outcomes is the *goodness-of-fit* between the infant's temperament and immediate context. For example, research indicates that it is often an advantage for an infant to be "easy" in North American contexts, and a disadvantage to be "difficult." However, in one study of the Masai in Africa, the opposite appeared to be the case, claims deVries (1989). There, six months after first being classified as "easy" or "difficult," the "difficult" infants seemed to have fared much better. In fact, mortality had been much higher among the "easy" infants. Why? One plausible explanation is that there had been a serious drought in the region, deVries explains, and many infants had died or suffered from malnutrition and disease. That the "difficult" infants had been least likely to die, speculates deVries, was probably because they yelled and hollered more when they were frustrated and hungry—and succeeded more often in being fed. Thus, a particular environmental characteristic "fit" better with the "difficult" temperament—a temperament that, under most circumstances in our culture, seldom "fits" as well as the "easy" temperament.

In Lerner and colleagues' (1986) terms, the most optimal situation, one where there is high *goodness-of-fit* between the infant and context, exists when external demands and expectations are compatible with the infant's basic temperament. Conversely, there is a poor fit when the infant's temperament is not in accord with environmental demands. For example, Marlis (who, you may recall, is a difficult infant) reacts loudly and impatiently to frustration. Her father is distressed and annoyed at this behavior because he expects and wants Marlis to be more like Robert. There is a poor fit here, and the result is conflict and strain in the relationship between Marlis and her father.

Difficult temperaments do not always lead to poor fit; nor does the easy temperament always result in high goodness-of-fit. Goodness-of-fit would be higher than expected, for example, if Marlis's father took pride in his daughter's lustiness, her independence, her aggressiveness. And if Robert's parents were concerned at how "easy" he is, afraid that he might not cope well in what they think is a dog-eat-dog world, goodness-of-fit between his temperament and his context might be unexpectedly poor. Here, as elsewhere, we need to consider the characteristics of the person *in interaction with* characteristics of the context.

INFANT EMOTIONS

"The emotions of one person cannot be directly perceived by another" notes Beckwith (1991, p. 78). This makes it especially difficult to investigate emotions among preverbal infants. Still, we can see infants smile and laugh, and we can hear them cry. And from these behaviors, we can make inferences about what they might be feeling.

Some psychologists, beginning with J. B. Watson (1914), have assumed that the infant is capable of reflexive emotional responses from birth. There are at least three such emotions, claimed Watson: *fear, rage,* and *love*. Because each of these is a reflex, each can therefore be elicited by a specific stimulus. Rage results from being confined or from having movements restricted; fear, from a loud noise or from being dropped suddenly; and love, from being stroked and fondled. Unfortunately, it isn't possible for psychologists to know for certain that the infant's responses to these stimuli is, in fact, what we think of as fear, rage, or love.

Another approach to studying emotions in infants is that of theorists such as Izard and Malatesta (1987), who base their conclusions on examinations of human facial expressions. These, they claim, reveal a number of distinct emotions including interest (or general excitement), joy, surprise, distress, anger, disgust, contempt, fear, shame, and guilt. They suggest as well that the facial expressions of infants indicate they may be capable of most of these feelings (Termine & Izard, 1988).

It is extremely difficult to separate such closely related emotions as joy and surprise (or distress, anger, and disgust—or shame and guilt). Accordingly, much of the research on infant emotions has looked at behaviors such as crying, smiling, and fear reactions. We look briefly at each of these before considering early infant attachments.

Crying

Infant crying, explains Pinyerd (1994) is one of the infant's main ways of communicating both physiological and psychological distress. However, not all infant cries are cries

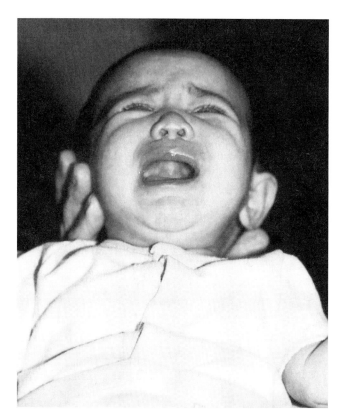

Many infants occasionally engage in rhythmic cries, angry cries, cries of pain, or cries of hunger, each of which most parents can identify and eliminate. But some infants also engage in more persistent cries, the causes of which are not always clear or controllable.

of pain. Furthermore, persistent and excessive infant crying, no matter what its cause, can be highly annoying for parents and siblings, and appears to be linked with higher incidence of postpartum depression (Mayberry & Affonso, 1993). Although crying related to hunger or pain can usually be eliminated, persistent crying, the cause of which is neither identifiable nor under the caregiver's control, may be more resistant to treatment. However, Wolke, Gray, and Meyer (1994) describe a number of specific infant-care approaches that are sometimes successful in reducing infant crying.

Kinds of Infant Cries

Crying that is excessive, persistent, or unusual in quality may be the earliest indication of a physiological problem, notes Pinyerd (1994); hence the importance of mothers and other caregivers being familiar with the infant's normal cries and their meanings.

Wolff (1969) described four common types of infant cries, the most frequent of which is called the *rhythmic* cry. It is the type of cry to which most infants eventually revert after initially engaging in another type of crying. Most experienced parents apparently recognize their infant's rhythmic cries and typically interpret them as meaning that there is nothing seriously wrong.

The *angry* cry is characterized by its protracted loudness and results from more air being forced through the vocal cords. It, too, does not fool an experienced caregiver.

A third distinguishable cry, says Wolff, is that of *pain*. The infant's pain cry is characterized by a long wail followed by a period of breath holding. Other highly useful facial indicators of infant pain include the *brow bulge* caused by the furrowing of the forehead, and a marked *nasolabial furrow*, the depression in the upper lip just below the nose (Rushforth & Levene, 1994).

Finally, there is the *hunger* cry. Gustafson and Harris (1990) report that most mothers respond quickly to hunger cries or to cries of pain and that they readily discriminate between the two—although most mothers seem to be more sensitive to the general distress level of the infant than to the cause of the distress. Interestingly, first-time parents tend to respond to infant crying sooner than parents who have more than one child (Donate-Bartfield & Passman, 1985). And mothers are more likely to be attentive than are fathers (Graham, 1993).

The meanings of an infant's cries are apparently not universal. Isabell and McKee (1980) observe that in many primitive cultures where the child is carried about constantly by the mother, mother–infant communication can occur through physical contact. In these cultures, there appears to be little need for the vocal signals of distress that we have come to expect from our infants. For instance, among South American Indian tribes in the northern Andes, infant crying is extremely rare and is invariably interpreted as a sign of illness. Why else would a warm, well-fed, and constantly embraced infant cry?

Smiling and Laughing

Smiling and *laughing* are central in parent–child interaction. From parents' smiles and strokes, infants learn that they are loved and important; and parents, too, look for smiles and other nonverbal gestures in their infants as evidence that they themselves are worthwhile and loved.

Smiling, a universal phenomenon among human cultures, is a fleeting response in the warm, well-fed infant and appears to occur as early as 2 to 12 hours after delivery (Wolff, 1963). This early smile involves the lower part of the face, not the upper cheeks and eyes, and is described as a reflex smile rather than as a true social smile. Interestingly, children born with no cerebral cortex (**anencephalic**), but with a functioning brain stem so that they survive for a few days after birth, also seem to be able to smile. Luyendijk and Treffers (1992) report that 78 percent of the time, impartial observers watching videotapes of the facial responses of four such children to being touched or having slight pressure applied to them, judged the responses as being smiles, grins, or laughter. This suggests that the neural mechanisms associated with early smiling are located in the brain stem, the most "primitive" of brain structures in an evolutionary sense.

Research leaves little doubt that smiles are highly reinforcing for young infants; it is almost as though the infants recognized the smiles' social significance at ages far too young to have learned them. For example, Kaplan, Fox, and Huckeby (1992) report a study in which month-old infants were conditioned to a tone using only a smiling face as a reinforcer. Interestingly, a neutral face was not nearly so effective.

In the weeks and months following birth, normal infants smile in response to an ever-widening range of sights and sounds. The social smile occurs first in response to a human voice (by the third week). By the age of 3½ months, infants smile more in response to familiar than unfamiliar faces (Gewirtz, 1965).

Gewirtz identified three stages in the development of smiling behavior. The first phase, spontaneous or reflex smiling, occurs in the absence of readily identifiable stimuli and is often, though perhaps incorrectly, attributed to gas pains. Social smiling, the second phase, takes place initially in response to auditory and visual stimuli that are social in nature—that is, related to other humans. Finally, the child displays the selective social smile, common among children and adults. It occurs in response to social stimuli that the child can identify as familiar. With the appearance of the selective social smile, infants smile less often in response to an unfamiliar voice or face and display more withdrawal behavior and other signs of anxiety in the presence of strangers. (More about stranger anxiety in a later section of this chapter.)

Hodapp and Mueller (1982) note that the development of smiling in infants follows the same general pattern as the development of crying. That is, the early development of these behaviors follows an internal to external progression. Whereas the first instances of smiling and crying are mainly responses to internal states—primarily gastric disturbances—within a short period of time, cognitive elements (such as are involved in recognizing a voice, a face, or an object) are clearly involved.

At about 4 months, infants begin to laugh in addition to smiling. At first, laughter is most likely to occur in response to physical stimulation such as tickling; later, infants laugh in response to more social and eventually more cognitive situations—seeing other children laughing, for example.

Although the function of laughter in infants has never been very clear, perhaps because it has not been investigated very much, Sroufe and Waters (1976) suggest that it probably serves to release tension. Fear, in contrast, signifies a continued building up of tension.

Wariness and Fear

Fear, argued Watson and Rayner (1920), is the infant's unlearned response to loud noises and sudden loss of support. Later, some infants come to fear a wide range of stimuli; others remain relatively unperturbed in the face of environmental changes.

Fear of heights appears to be almost universal in infants by the age of 13 to 18 months; fear of strangers is not ordinarily seen before the age of 6 months and becomes most common by 2 years. Other situations that may evoke fear in an infant typically involve some unexpected change. For example, a jack-in-the-box may be frightening; so might an experimenter or parent wearing a mask. In addition, separation from the mother is frightening for some infants. As Hinde (1983) notes, it seems that as certain objects and people become familiar, infants begin to react with fear to strangers and to unfamiliar objects.

In a detailed longitudinal study of fear, Bronson (1972) found that the most prevalent class of responses for 3- and 4-month-old infants is smiling rather than being uneasy or crying. By the age of 6½ months, however, there is increasing evidence of wariness; and by 9 months, evidence of *learned* fears. These findings are in agreement with many others, indicating that infants are not likely to display marked stranger anxiety until after the age of 6 months.

Interestingly, at all ages objects are far less potent than strangers in bringing about reactions of wariness or fear. By the age of 9 months, many of Bronson's infants had experienced fear reactions with strangers and seemed to have learned to associate specific features of a person with fear (beards or white smocks, for example). Similarly, wariness of novel objects was very rare before 9 months. Situations or objects that make loud noises or move suddenly are most likely to bring about fear reactions in infants (vacuum cleaners or a jack-in-the-box, for example).

Why Infants Are Sometimes Afraid

Why are infants sometimes wary and sometimes not? Bronson's research suggests the reason lies in innate temperament interacting with various experiences. The relationship of age to the development of fear may at least partly reflect the fact that certain experiences are unlikely or less frequent at earlier ages—also that the meanings of some experiences depend on the infant's level of understanding. Clearly, a stranger is not a stranger until a familiar person can be recognized as familiar.

But why should some strangers and some novel objects elicit fear? One plausible explanation is Hebb's (1966) suggestion that infants develop certain expectations about their world and that violation of these expectations (*incongruence* is Hebb's term) may lead to fear.

Regulation of Emotions in Infancy

When you or I find ourselves in a frightening situation, when our hearts race and our knees turn to jelly, we do something to control or *regulate* our emotions. Perhaps we play cognitive games with ourselves: We tell ourselves that we have nothing to be afraid of, that we are such wonderful surgeons or public speakers or students that we will perform marvelously. Or we change the situation so that it isn't frightening anymore, perhaps by avoiding it.

How Infants Control Their Emotions

There is a temptation to think that infants are not capable of this sort of control of emotions: that if they are frightened, all they can do is cry; and if they are delighted, then, like little robots, they must smile. We sometimes think of them as responding almost blindly to the stimulation that the world provides, willy-nilly, for them.

We are wrong; they are not nearly so helpless. Beginning very early in life, infants are capable of what Gianino and Tronick (1988) term *self-directed* and *other-directed regulatory behaviors*—behaviors designed to regulate, or control, their emotions.

As an example, Tronick (1989) describes a peek-a-boo game between a mother and her infant. In this little episode, the infant turns away from the mother just before the "peek" and begins to suck on his thumb, staring blankly into space. The mother sits back. Within a few seconds the infant turns to the mother, pulls out the thumb, and contorts his body; his expression is clearly interested. The mother smiles, moves closer, says "Oh, now you're back!" The infant smiles and crows. Shortly, he goes back to sucking his thumb. But again, after a few seconds, he turns to the mother once more and smiles.

The infant in this instance seems to be attempting to control the mother's behavior. This *other-directed regulatory behavior* is evident in how he turns back to the mother, how he crows and smiles, how he tries to make her do things that he finds exciting. In effect, by controlling her behavior, he is exercising control over his own emotions. And when things become too exciting, too emotional, he can regulate his emotions by turning away and distracting himself by sucking his thumb and by staring into space, a *self-directed regulatory behavior*.

EARLY ATTACHMENT

Tronick (1989) argues that the emotion-regulating behaviors of young infants not only control their emotions but are also evidence that the infants' behavior is *goal-directed*. And one of the important goals of all infants, and adults, is to form and maintain attachments.

Studying Attachment

Attachment is a powerful emotional bond, impossible for an infant to describe for us, and not easy to study because many of the experiments that might shed light on the area cannot be performed with humans. For this reason, infant monkeys have sometimes been used instead. (See At a Glance: "Mother-Deprived Monkeys," and Figure 6.2).

Measurements of infant attachment are always indirect. Investigators look at behaviors that are directed toward the object of attachment (crying, smiling, vocalizing, following, clinging, holding, and so on); they focus on the infant's reaction to strange situations and on physical contact between parents and infant; and they look at the infant's reaction to being separated from a parent.

MOTHER-DEPRIVED MONKEYS

Infant monkeys who are raised in isolation later experience serious developmental problems, often manifested in an inability to achieve sexual relations (Harlow, 1958; 1959). Female monkeys raised under such conditions, who then have infants of their own, will often reject them. But when the mothers of infant monkeys are replaced by a substitute, infants typically form a strong attachment to the substitute. Research that has compared infant monkeys' attachment to cloth-covered and wire mother-substitutes indicates that quality of physical contact is especially important for monkeys.

FIGURE 6.2

Amount of time spent by infant monkeys on cloth and wire surrogate mothers. The results show a strong preference for the cloth mother regardless of whether the infant was fed on the wire model or on the cloth model. (From Harry F. Harlow, Love in infant monkeys, Scientific American, *1959, 200, 68–74. Copyright 1959 by Scientific American, Inc. All rights reserved. Used by permission.)*

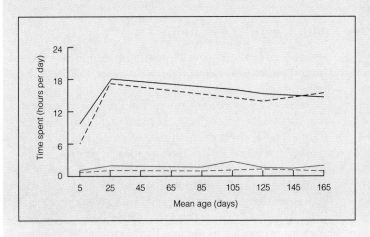

Cloth mother, infant fed on cloth mother

- - - Cloth mother, infant fed on wire mother

Wire mother, infant fed on cloth mother

- - - Wire mother, infant fed on wire mother

Ainsworth's Strange Situation

How do you determine whether, to whom, and how strongly an infant is attached? One way is Ainsworth and associates' (1978) **Strange Situation** procedure, a procedure often sequenced as follows (each event lasts approximately 3 minutes):

1. Mother and baby enter a room.
2. Mother puts baby down; stranger enters; speaks with mother; shows baby a toy; mother leaves.
3. If baby cries, stranger attempts to comfort; if baby is passive, stranger attempts to interest it in a toy.
4. Mother returns, pauses in doorway; stranger leaves; mother leaves.
5. Baby is alone.
6. Stranger comes back.
7. Mother returns; stranger leaves.

What the Strange Situation provides is a way of assessing attachment under stress. It permits researchers to determine the infant's anxiety or security in these circumstances. A large number of studies using the Ainsworth procedure with infants reveal attachment behaviors that sort themselves into four broad categories.

TYPES OF INFANT ATTACHMENT

In first grade, George Leroy used to get such severe stomach aches that he often had to be taken home to his mother. "He's always been like that," claimed his mother. "Why, when he was little, he used to raise a stink every time I had to leave him. And one time, when I come back from bowling or something, he up and heaved his potty at me, he was still so mad, and the dang thing was about . . . as heavy as a brick." According to Ainsworth's classification, what sort of attachment did George display toward his mother?

Attachment Classification	Common Behavior When Mother Leaves or Returns
Securely Attached	Uses mother as a base from which to explore; upset when she leaves but quickly soothed when she returns; greets her positively on return
Insecure-Avoidant	Rarely cries when mother leaves; ignores or actively avoids her when she returns, sometimes pushing her away or pointedly not looking at her
Insecure-Ambivalent	Very upset when mother leaves; often angry when she returns, sometimes pushing her away
Disorganized/Disoriented	Contradictory, disorganized reactions to separation and reunion; may cry for mother but run away when she returns, or approach her while looking away

SOURCE: Based in part on *Patterns of Attachment* by Ainsworth et al., 1978, Hillsdale, NJ: Erlbaum.

Securely attached infants are those who use the mother as a base for exploration—who go out freely and play in the room, but who often reestablish contact, either by looking at the mother, interacting verbally, or returning to her physically. When the mother leaves, these infants are upset and often stop their exploration. During the reunion episodes, they greet the mother warmly and try to reestablish physical contact or some sort of interaction with her. Securely attached infants manifest few, if any, negative reactions toward their mothers during reunion. If upset, they are easily soothed by the mother and return readily to play or exploration.

In contrast, *insecurely attached* infants (also termed *anxious-avoidant)* are those who display significant negative behavior toward the mother during reunion events. Some of these infants, the **insecure-avoidant** (also termed *anxious-avoidant*), either ignore the mother's reentrance or actively avoid contact with her—sometimes by looking away, sometimes by pushing her away physically. Interestingly, they rarely cry when the mother leaves.

A second group of insecurely attached infants, the **insecure-ambivalent,** are very upset when the mother leaves, their behavior being evidence of strong attachment. However, the mother's reappearance does not soothe their distress. Strangely, these infants sometimes display anger when the mother returns. The anger is sometimes very subtle; for example, they might push the mother away even when they appear to want to be held (hence the ambivalence).

A final group, originally termed *unclassified* by Ainsworth and associates (1978), is now often termed **disorganized/disoriented** (see, for example, Main & Cassidy, 1988). These infants typically display any of a range of disorganized or disoriented behaviors, such as crying for a parent at the door and then moving quickly away

when they hear the parent approaching; approaching the parent with the head turned away; or standing motionless with no clear reaction during the Strange Situation (see Interactive Table 6.3).

Mother–Infant Bonding

Attachment is a relatively general term that includes the host of positive emotions that link parents, children, and other people; *bonding* is a more specific and more biological term. Thus, **mother–infant bond** refers primarily to the very early, biologically based attachment that the mother develops for her infant. Attachment between mother and infant is both biologically and psychologically important. Biologically, the existence of a strong mother–infant bond serves to ensure that mother and infant will stay close to each other—a condition that, for most animals, is extremely important to the infant's survival. Hence it seems reasonable to suppose that there would be strong genetically based tendencies to establish such bonds.

Ethologists (those who study animal behavior in natural settings) inform us that yes, there are powerful preprogramed tendencies among many nonanimal species. They are evident in the fact that mothers and infants exposed to each other during a **critical period,** generally shortly after birth, typically "bond." In the absence of appropriate experiences during this critical period, bonding fails to occur. Theorists such as Bowlby (1958) and Klaus and Kennell (1983) argue that infants kept from their mothers at birth may fail to bond with them. They suggest, as well, that failure to establish a strong mother–infant bond is detrimental to the future adjustment and emotional health of the child, and may be related to such things as child abuse or "growth failure." Growth failure, or *failure to thrive* (FTT) (also called *maternal deprivation*

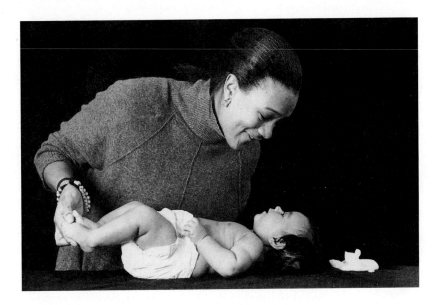

syndrome), is a condition in which an apparently normal infant fails to gain weight, falling to the bottom 3 percent of normal standards. Abramson (1991) reports significantly more expressions of negative emotion among these infants. In addition, the condition is marked by listlessness, loss of appetite, illness, and, in its more extreme manifestations, even death.

Bonding Mechanisms

It is likely that no emotional bond links the infant to its mother immediately at birth. A neonate taken from its mother and given to another will surely never know the difference unless, of course, the facts are disclosed later. But that a bond does form with the primary caregiver(s) is also clear. Wellman and Gelman (1992) point out that the infant has certain biological *preadaptations* that facilitate the development of this bond. These include perceptual biases such as the infant's built-in visual accommodation for a distance of approximately 8 to 10 inches (about the distance to the caregiver's face during feeding), the young infant's apparent preference for the human face, and a sensitivity and responsiveness to the human voice. They also include some reflexive response tendencies that seem especially designed for social interaction. Like the young of most mammals, for example, the human infant clings and turns and roots and sucks. One of the functions of these vegetative reflexes is surely to ensure that the infant obtains nourishment and survives. But more than this, feeding is among the first important social interactions between caregiver and infant. Almost invariably, feeding leads to the mutual gaze, which is highly significant in the development of attachment and which appears to be universal between mothers and infants in different cultures (Fogel, Toda, & Kawai, 1988).

Schaffer (1984) also suggests that certain biological rhythms are geared to social interaction. Some, like those expressed in the infant states of waking and sleeping, are modifiable and eventually become attuned to the mother's cycles of waking and sleeping. Others, like the rhythms apparent in *cyclical motor movements* (see Chapter 5), seem to contain many of the elements of a dialogue and may underly the learning of the turn-taking rules that are a fundamental part of conversations with language.

The Importance of Bonding

The existence of biological preadaptations that facilitate the formation of bonds between caregiver and infant may be evidence that powerful biological forces direct both mother and infant toward mutual attachment. This makes sense because attachment has important survival value—a value that would have been especially apparent at a time when physical survival was threatened by the "hissing serpents and dragons of Eden" (Sagan, 1977). One of the important functions of the infant's distress at being separated from the mother is that it serves to keep her close (Oatley & Jenkins, 1992)—and perhaps to protect the infant from wild beasts.

But now dragons and serpents no longer lurk so blatantly in our forests—or parking lots. But, say Klaus and Kennell (1976), there is nevertheless a critical period very early in our lives during which we *must* have contact with our mothers so that a bond may form. Bonding failure, they claim, can have serious negative consequences later.

The evidence? Klaus and associates (1972) randomly selected a group of 28 low-income mothers and allowed half of them extended contact with their infants immediately after birth (1 hour of the first 2 hours following birth), as well as 5 additional hours of contact with their infants on each of the first 3 days following birth. The remaining 14 mothers, serving as a control group, saw their infants regularly at feeding time in conformity with hospital routine (Klaus & Kennell, 1976). Interviews and observations one month later indicated that mothers in the extended-contact group were significantly more bonded to their infants, showed more concern for them, and

In the preattachment phase, infants seem predisposed for human interaction; in the attachment-in-the-making phase, they cry, look at, and smile to draw and hold attention; in the clear-cut-attachment phase, they can finally crawl over to the attachment object, climb on—and sometimes cling for dear life.

expressed considerably more interest in them. These mothers tended to cuddle their babies more, to engage in more verbal interaction with them, and to spend more time in mutual gazing.

It would be premature, however, to conclude that there is a critical period early in the lives of neonates during which contact with the mother (or perhaps some other important caregiver) is of absolutely fundamental importance. As Klaus and Kennell (1983) admit, "The human being is highly adaptable, and there are many fail-safe routes to attachment" (p. 50). Not surprisingly, a raft of subsequent studies has failed to demonstrate convincingly the existence of a critical period for mother–infant bonding (Goldberg, 1983; Schaffer, 1984). This does not mean, of course, that maternal deprivation or rejection are irrelevant. As we saw, they can lead to serious conditions like growth failure. However, the importance of a crucial few hours immediately after birth has not been clearly established.

Stages of Attachment

The *why* of infant attachment is clear: After all, the infant's very survival demands a solicitous caregiver. What better way to ensure that the caregiver will be there when needed than to program into the human gene pool powerful parent–infant attachment tendencies? However, nature does not program the attachment itself; it develops later. Nor do genes limit attachment to the biological mother or father.

Bowlby describes four phases in the infant's development of attachment. Through each phase, the infant's behavior seems to be guided by a single overriding principle: *keep the attachment object close.* And in most cases, that attachment object is the mother.

Preattachment

The *preattachment* phase spans the first few weeks of life, and is marked by the preadaptations that seem to predispose the infant for human interaction: things like their preference for the human voice and face, their movements in synchrony with adult speech, and their built-in visual accommodation for about the distance of the mother's face (Wellman & Gelman, 1992).

Attachment in the Making

During the second phase, *attachment in the making*, there is marked emphasis on behaviors that promote contact with important adults—for example, crying and smiling as well as sucking, rooting, clinging, looking at, and following with the eyes. The second phase culminates in clearly identifiable attachment during the second half of the first year of life. At this time, the infant manifests the "selective social smile"—the smile that occurs in recognition of familiar faces. At the same time, smiling in response to unfamiliar faces becomes less common.

Clear-Cut Attachment

Clear-cut attachment becomes evident with the infant's development of locomotor abilities. Now infants are able to attract the mother or father's attention not only by smiling, crying, reaching, and so on; they can also crawl over and grab a leg; they can climb up and wrap themselves around a neck; they can cling to the strings that hang from the rear of old aprons. In brief, they can indicate very clearly what (and whom) the objects of their attachment are.

Goal-Corrected Attachment

Some time in the second year, Bowlby informs us, the infant enters a phase of *goal-corrected attachment.* The infant has now developed notions of self and has begun to understand something of the point of view of others. Gradually, infants learn to make inferences about the effects of their behaviors, as well as about their parents' behavior; and they learn to affect the behavior of parents in ways more subtle than crying, smiling, yelling, or toddling over and grabbing hold. (See Table 6.4 for a summary of Bowlby's sequential phases.)

The Implications of Attachment Patterns

As we saw earlier, some infants are *securely attached* to their caregivers; others are more *insecure* or even *disorganized*. Among other things, securely attached infants are those who have achieved a good balance between the security of attachment and the ability to explore. Insecurely attached infants are more anxious, often about both their attachment and their exploration.

Patterns of attachment appear to reflect relatively stable qualities. For example, Main and Cassidy (1988) found infant attachments at the age of 1 to be highly predictable of attachment behaviors at the age of 6 years. However, stability is not the case when major changes occur in the in-

TABLE 6.4
Sequential Phases in the Development of Infant Attachment

Phase	Approximate Age	Important Behaviors
Preattachment	First month	Crying, smiling, rooting, clinging, sucking, looking at; movements synchronized with adult speech; discrimination of mother's voice
Attachment in the making	Into second half of first year	Singling out objects of primary attachment; selective social smile—directed more toward attachment objects or persons than toward the unfamiliar
Clear-cut attachment	Second half of first year	Continued use of behaviors designed to draw attention—smiling, crying, squirming; use of newly developed locomotor skills to approach attachment object or person
Goal-corrected attachment	Second year	Begins to adopt mother's point of view and to make inferences about mother's behavior; manipulation of mother's behavior in more subtle ways following gradual recognition of cause-and-effect relationships

SOURCE: Based on Bowlby, 1969.

fant's context such as somebody leaving or dying (Waters, Hay, & Richters, 1986). Similarly, infants who are maltreated often display marked instability of attachment, and are also more likely to be insecurely attached (Schneider-Rosen et al., 1985). Reassuringly, however, the more sensitive the new caregiver is, the more likely the infant is to form secure attachments (Howes & Segal, 1993).

There is increasing evidence that securely attached infants—who, as we noted, are in the majority in North American cultures—fare better in the long run (in these cultures). These infants are often more competent, better problem solvers, more independent, more curious, and perhaps more resilient. In one study, children who experienced high levels of support from their mothers—which is closely related to secure attachment—fared significantly better in kindergarten (Pianta & Ball, 1993). In contrast, insecurely attached infants are somewhat more likely to be overly dependent and to experience problems in school (see Collins & Gunnar, 1990).

Clearly, attachments are a function of interactions. Furthermore, the nature of these interactions, and their outcomes, will be influenced by the characteristics of both infant and caregiver (or other significant people in the child's context). Hence the importance of the family—and of the culture in which the family is embedded, because it, too, influences child-rearing practices and attitudes toward children. Our North American macrosystem is relatively child-centered: It emphasizes the rights of children, and it encourages parents to provide physically and psychologically safe environments. Not surprisingly, then, more than two thirds of infants appear to be securely attached (perhaps it should be surprising that as many as one third are not!).

Elsewhere in the world, cultures reflect different values, and sometimes child-rearing practices and attitudes toward children are quite different. In some of these cultures, insecurely attached infants are far more common than in North America (for example, West Germany, Japan, and Israel; see Sagi, Ijzendoorn, & Koren-Karie, 1991).

Whether parents should attempt to change their infants' predominant patterns of attachment—and indeed, whether they would be very effective in doing so—are important issues. Unfortunately, they are also very complex issues. What does seem clear is that all infants must be provided with an opportunity to develop attachments that will provide them with the security they need to engage in the exploration of a bewildering, exciting, and sometimes frightening world. Those opportunities are not always related solely to the presence of the mother. Grandparents, siblings, uncles, and aunts can also be important. So can fathers.

Fathers and Infant Attachment

Our traditional views of the family and of mother–father roles have typically focused on the importance of the mother in the early social development of the infant—and on the father's relative unimportance. Most of our developmental theorists (Freud, for example) argue that the father becomes important after the age of 2 or 3. Furthermore, many of these theorists have viewed the infant as largely incompetent—as passive and reflexive, as being moved by primitive physiological needs but seldom by a need to discover and to know. Little wonder that the father has not been seen as playing an important role.

Some of these traditional values are still the norm in many of the world's cultures. For example, Ho (1987) reports that in China, looking after the young is still largely a female function; the father's role is more that of a disciplinarian. There, traditional values stress filial devotion and respect—that is, children, and especially sons, are taught to respect and obey their fathers (and grandfathers). Recently, however, there appears to have been a dramatic decline in some of these filial values. At the same time, fathers have begun to involve themselves more in child rearing.

In North America, too, important changes are rapidly altering our conception of the father's role. These include

Infants form much the same sorts of attachment with fathers as with mothers—when given an opportunity to do so. That mothers have traditionally been the principal caregiver explains in large part the perception that they are more important in the lives of their infants.

an increasing number of "father-assisted" childbirths, in which the father has an opportunity to interact with the infant as early as does the mother. In addition, changing work patterns and changing male–female responsibilities in the home have done a great deal to change the role of the father with his infant. As Lamb (1987) notes, mothers continue to be extremely important to the infant, but they are not unique. Fathers and other caregivers are also tremendously important. In fact, considerable research indicates that newborns and young infants may form attachments almost as strong with fathers as with mothers (Collins & Gunnar, 1990). In addition, infants tend to form very similar attachments (secure or insecure, for example) with both parents (Fox, Kimmerly, & Schafer, 1991).

Fathers as Parents

In summarizing the research on father–infant attachment, Collins and Gunnar (1990) conclude that fathers are as competent and as important as mothers in a caregiving role. But there are some systematic differences between mother–infant and father–infant interactions. Fathers spend more time in play interactions with their infants; mothers spend more time in nurturant roles (feeding, bathing, changing). As a result, some infants—especially males—display more *affiliative* behaviors toward fathers

than toward mothers (Lamb, 1980). Affiliative behaviors are defined as behaviors that demonstrate a social relationship that stops short of being attachment. Evidence of **affiliation** includes smiling, looking at, laughing, and giving; evidence of attachment might include seeking to be close, clinging, wanting to be picked up, putting the head in the lap, snuggling, and so on. It appears that infants (especially males) begin to affiliate with their fathers at a very young age when they are given the opportunity to do so (Phares, 1992). And in an unfamiliar situation, the departure of both the father and the mother is followed by signs of distress, whereas the departure of a stranger leads to an increase in play behavior (Bridges, Connell, & Belsky, 1988).

What research has established is that the father is far from irrelevant in the early development of the infant. However, the mother typically has considerably more contact with young infants than does the father.

FEAR OF STRANGERS AND SEPARATION FROM PARENTS

One way of investigating parent–child attachment, as we saw, is Ainsworth's Strange Situation; it deals with the effects of very short-term separations and attempts to measure what is called *separation protest*. A second type of study looks at the consequences of longer-term separation, such as might result from divorce or the death of a parent. A third group of studies explores parent–child attachment by looking at the reactions of infants to strangers.

Fear of Strangers

Fear of strangers occurs in many infants, but not usually before the age of 6 to 9 months. It appears that once infants have become familiar with their environment, that is, once they have developed certain expectations of events that are most likely to occur, they may be uneasy and afraid when these events do not occur. A common early reaction to the unexpected, Shreeve (1991) explains, is *freezing* (not doing anything) and *mutism* (not saying anything). These responses are, in fact, common fear responses in young infants and children.

The belief that fear arises from the occurrence of the unexpected is sometimes labeled the **incongruity hypothesis** (Hebb, 1966). Infants who are in contact with the largest number of people (strangers and siblings) are less likely to manifest fear, react with the least amount of fear, and stop being afraid of strangers at an earlier age (Schaffer, 1966), providing support for this hypothesis. Infants exposed to many strangers at early ages will necessarily confront the "unexpected" less often than those whose early exposure to strangers is limited.

Additional corroboration of the incongruity hypothesis is provided by Kagan's (1976) investigations of the development of separation protest in four different cultural settings outside the United States: Ladino families in Guatemala; Indian families, also in Guatemala; Israeli kibbutzim infants; and Bushmen families in the Kalahari Desert. In all these groups, separation protest and fear of strangers was minimal prior to the age of 9 months, peaked between 12 and 15 months, and then declined. Kagan argues that the fact that separation anxiety becomes evident at about the same age in all infants is evidence that it is closely related to some maturational factors. He suggests that these factors are *cognitive* (related to mental processes, such as thinking and remembering) and that they relate specifically to the infant's ability to represent the parent's departure (or the stranger's appearance)—that is, to make inferences about its meaning and its consequences.

Separation Anxiety in Other Cultures

Child-rearing styles vary widely within North American cultures, and might have implications for the development of attachment behaviors and stranger anxiety. Jackson (1993), for example, points out that African-American child rearing makes far wider use of *multiple caregiving* than is the norm among white groups. As a result, African-American infants may develop quite different attachment patterns with primary caregivers. These cultural differences, says Jackson, need to be taken into consideration when designing infant-attachment studies.

Preventing Stranger Anxiety

Not all infants react the same way to the departure of a parent or the arrival of a stranger. As we saw, infants exposed to many strangers and siblings are less likely to be fearful of strangers. In one study, Jacobson and Wille (1984) studied the reactions of 93 children, aged 15 to 18 months, to brief periods of separation from their mothers. They found that previous separation experience was closely related to the amount of distress the children manifested, but the relationship was *curvilinear*. That is, distress did not increase in linear fashion with increasing separation experiences, but declined with moderate exposure to separation. Specifically, children who had experienced moderate amounts of maternal separation were best able to cope with the absence of their mothers; it was as though they had learned that the separation would only be temporary. Those who had experienced either very little or a great deal of separation were the most distressed—perhaps because they had had too little opportunity to learn about separation or because they had learned that separation would be frequent or prolonged.

One way of minimizing infant distress at being left with strangers, then, might be to ensure that the infant has frequent, short-term exposure to strangers (and siblings). In addition, the stranger's behavior may be critically important. For example, a study by Gunnar and colleagues (1992) looked at the effects of exposing infants to strangers for periods of 30 minutes (recall that the Ainsworth Strange Situation typically exposes infants to strangers for only about 3 minutes). They measured infant fear through the infant's behavior, as in the Ainsworth procedure, and also by looking at elevations of *cortisol* in the infant's saliva—a common measure of stress. They found that when caregivers were instructed to be warm and responsive and to interact with the infant, indications of anxiety were significantly lower than when caregivers were more distant (although not insensitive to the infant's distress). Not surprisingly, there is also evidence that mothers who are themselves attentive and interactive (rather than dismissing or preoccupied) are less likely to have highly fearful infants (Crowell & Feldman, 1991).

Trying to prepare young preschoolers in advance for an upcoming separation from the mother doesn't always work as intended. Adams and Passman (1983) had one group of mothers of 2- to 2½-year-old children discuss their upcoming departure for three days preceding the event; a second group did not prepare their children in advance. And, at the time of departure, some of these mothers in both groups provided a brief explanation of their departure and then either left immediately or lingered for 1 minute; others left as they normally would.

Amazingly, children who had not been prepared in advance showed *less* distress after the mother's departure than children whose mothers had discussed their departure during the previous three days. And those whose mothers did not linger after explaining they were leaving also showed less distress than those whose mothers lingered for 60 seconds. One possible explanation, argue Adams and Passman, is that the lengthy preparation actually teaches children to become alarmed. In the same way, lingering just prior to departure may teach the child that displaying anxiety might serve to delay the departure (Adams & Passman, 1981).

Security Blankets

A variety of inanimate objects such as blankets, teddy bears, and even thumbs, often called **transitional objects,** may also serve to reduce the fears of infants and young children. These objects are termed *transitional* because they become the focus of children's affection and attention while they are in transition between a state of high dependence on the parent and the development of a more independent self (Winnicott, 1971). According to this view, the development of self requires separation from the parent and *individuation*—the recognition of one's own individuality. The process of separating and becoming independent gives rise to anxiety; the blanket or the teddy bear serves to comfort the child.

No less than half of all middle-class American children show strong attachments to inanimate objects, report Passman and Halonen (1979), the two most common of which are, not surprisingly, the blanket and the pacifier. A large number also suck their thumbs, most often to fall asleep (Lee, 1992; Ozturk & Ozturk, 1990), but also as a refuge against fear and stress (Lookabaugh & Fu, 1992).

TABLE 6.5
Immediate Impact of Long-Term Mother–Child Separation on Infants, 3–16 Months

Impact	Percentage
No disturbances	15
Mild disturbances	36
Moderate disturbances	23
Severe disturbances	20
Extreme disturbances	6

SOURCE: Based on data provided by Yarrow & Goodwin, 1973.

TABLE 6.6
Severity of Reaction to Maternal Separation, According to Age

Age	Slight or No Reaction (percentage of infants)	Moderately Severe to Very Severe Reaction (percentage of infants)
Less than 3 months	100	0
3–4 months	60	40
4–5 months	28	72
6 months	9	91
9 months	0	100

SOURCE: Based on data provided by Yarrow & Goodwin, 1973.

In one study, Passman and Weisberg (1975) compared the effectiveness of mothers and blankets in reducing a child's anxiety in a strange situation. They found that as long as they had their blankets close by, children who were attached to their blankets played and explored as much and displayed no more anxiety than those who were not attached to blankets but whose mothers were present. In situations of higher stress (high arousal), however, the mother is more effective than a blanket in reducing anxiety (Passman & Adams, 1982). Lookabaugh and Fu (1992) also report that children who are attached to inanimate transitional objects, including their thumb, cope more effectively in stressful situations than children with no such attachment.

In North American cultures, attachment to blankets, teddy bears, pacifiers, and other inanimate objects seems to be normal in the sense that a majority of children manifest these attachments. But, some parents worry, is the child who is attached to these inanimate, nonsocial objects perhaps more insecure, less well adjusted, than the child whose attachments are more social?

Not likely, says Passman (1987). In a study of 108 preschoolers, he found little relationship between attachment to blankets and general fearfulness. "Blanket-attached children," he concludes, "are thus neither more insecure nor more secure than are others" (p. 829).

So if you are anxious and cannot bring your mother with you, do bring your blanket . . . or whatever.

Longer-Term Separation from Parents

Studies of the long-term effects of parent–infant separation sometimes look at children who have been adopted and therefore separated from their primary caregivers. Obviously, infants adopted soon after birth, before they have formed strong attachments with caregivers, are not likely to respond in the same way as older children. In fact, in one study of 70 adopted children, none showed even slight negative reactions before the age of 3 months; in contrast, all who were 9 months or more manifested mod-

erately or very severe negative reactions (Yarrow & Goodwin, 1973). In this study, only nine children were adopted before the age of 3 months, however; the remainder were placed at ages ranging from 3 to 16 months. Only 15 percent of all the children were completely free of all disturbances; the remainder showed disturbances of varying severity (see Tables 6.5 and 6.6). These disturbances were most obvious in the infant's sleeping schedule and were also evident in feeding behaviors, social reactions (withdrawal, for example), and emotional behavior (crying). Disruptions in social reactions included decreased social responsiveness, increased stranger anxiety, and specific disturbances in interactions with the new mother evident in feeding difficulties, colic, digestive upsets, and, most strikingly, physical rejection of the new mother or excessive clinging to her. In addition, developmental scores were lower in 56 percent of the cases following adoption.

We know that the permanent loss of a parent, as happens through death or sometimes through divorce, can have an adverse effect on many significant aspects of the infant's development. What about regular but temporary loss of parental contact, as happens in many forms of child care?

INFANT CARE

In 1975, fewer than one third of all U.S. women aged 18 to 44 were in the work force within one year of having a child; now more than half are. As a result, more than one out of every two North American preschool children is now in child care (U.S. Bureau of the Census, 1994; see At a Glance: "Working Mothers in the United States," and Figures 6.3 and 6.4). And, with increasing numbers of mothers going back to work within weeks of childbirth, the fastest-growing type of child-care facility is *infant care*. Given what we know about the importance of caregiver–infant interaction and attachment, questions relating to

WORKING MOTHERS IN THE UNITED STATES

Between 1960 and 1992, the percentage of married women in the work force doubled (from 30.5 percent to 59.3 percent). The number of married women in the work force who had given birth within the previous year and who lived with their husbands increased by about 50 percent between 1975 and 1992. By 1992, more than half of women with children under 1 *and husbands at home* worked. As a result, more infants than ever before are in some type of child care.

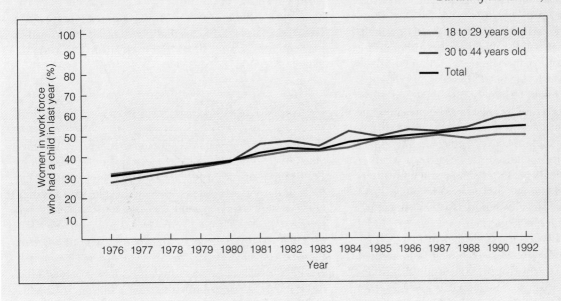

FIGURE 6.3

Increase in percentage of mothers who live with husbands and work outside the home. Note by comparison that growth in employment is far more modest for wives without minor children at home. (From U.S. Bureau of the Census, 1994, p. 402.)

FIGURE 6.4

Changes in percentages of women who enter the work force within one year of giving birth (1977–1979 data extrapolated). (From U.S. Bureau of the Census, 1994, p. 82.)

the effects of child care on the social, emotional, and intellectual development of infants become critically important. (See Chapter 8 for a discussion of the effects of child care on older children.)

Gamble and Zigler (1986) summarize a large body of research that has looked at the effects of child care on the infant's attachment to parents and on different aspects of social behavior. An important concern of this research has been to determine whether child care either can prevent the formation of parent–infant attachments or can serve to redirect that attachment toward a different caregiver. Reassuringly, all available evidence suggests not. Apparently, the infant's primary attachment to parents can be established in a wide variety of circumstances and is highly resistant to disruption. Konner (1982) reports that it occurs in societies as disparate as the !Kung, where infants are in immediate contact with their mothers 24 hours a day, and in the Israeli kibbutzim, where infants have contact with their mothers only for a short period each afternoon and on weekends.

Still, even though child care does not, in general, appear to disrupt parent–infant attachment bonds, some evidence suggests that the stress involved in repeated short-term separation from the mother might lead to the development of what Ainsworth termed *insecure* rather than *secure* attachment (Belsky & Rovine, 1988). Clarke-Stewart (1989) summarized more than a dozen studies that looked specifically at infant–mother attachment among infants in child care. She draws two principal conclusions: First, the evidence suggests a somewhat higher probability that child-care infants will avoid their mothers after separation—that they will be insecurely attached (36 percent of child-care infants as opposed to 29 percent for infants at home). Second, these children are sometimes less obedient later and may be more aggressive with their peers.

Clarke-Stewart cautions that the meaning of these findings is still unclear. For one thing, although the Ainsworth Strange Situation, which is typically used in all these studies, provides a very useful measure of attachment, its meaning and validity might be very different for children who are primarily at home with their mothers compared with those who are in child care part of the time. Whereas a stranger might be anxiety-provoking and might lead to one kind of behavior for the home-bound child, the day-care child might interpret the situation quite differently. In addition, we do not know whether slightly higher aggressiveness and independence are negative or whether they might even be marks of more rapid maturation—perhaps even an advantage. As Clarke-Stewart puts it, "We also know that infants and children in day care gain knowledge and self-confidence from their experience" (1989, p. 269). Here, as elsewhere, it is likely to depend on the individual child and the context in which the child interacts.

Bowman (1993) warns that the conclusion that infant day care might lead to anxious attachments is misleading.

Research on the effects of alternate forms of infant care has found no consistent negative effects of quality care. Nor does being looked after by someone else while parents work appear to disrupt parent-infant bonds.

It fails to take into account *quality* of day care. Where child care does have apparently detrimental effects on infants, these effects are often associated with *poorer-quality* child care. In contrast, high-quality child care is likely to have beneficial effects on most infants and older children. (See Chapter 8 for a discussion of the characteristics of high-quality child care.)

It is worth noting that most of the research in this area has focused on discovering the possible negative consequences of alternate forms of care for children—and has been largely unsuccessful in doing so. As Lerner and Abrams (1994) put it, "Research has not been able to clearly link maternal employment to any detriments in infant or toddler cognitive and intellectual development" (p. 178). The focus must now change, says Silverstein (1991). Instead of continuing to search for the negative consequences of mothers' working and of alternate child care, research should focus on documenting "the negative consequences of not providing high-quality, affordable day care" (p. 1025).

PARENTING IN INFANCY

In the same way as quality of infant care can have measurable effects on children, so too can quality of parenting. Following a review of research that has looked at the effects of parents on infants, Belsky, Lerner, and Spanier (1984) describe six important dimensions of parenting: *attentiveness, physical contact, verbal stimulation, material stimulation, responsive care,* and *restrictiveness*. The first five of these have positive effects on the infant's social, emotional, and intellectual well-being; the last is more negative. That is, parents who are attentive to their children (for exam-

Male and female characteristics stem from biology as well as from the countless gender-related messages that result from the behaviors and expectations of parents and siblings. Thus this young lad may already have begun to learn not only that video cameras are smooth black things, but also that men are more interested in electronics than are women.

ple, look at them more); who touch them, play with them, cradle and rock them; who speak to them and who provide them with objects to look at, to touch, to taste, to smell; and who are responsive to their cries and to their other signals of distress, amusement, interest, or amazement are more likely to have intellectually advanced and emotionally well-adjusted infants. Those who are restrictive in that they verbally and physically limit the infant's freedom to explore may, to some extent, influence their intellectual development negatively.

In summary, parents most likely to promote optimal cognitive development during infancy are those who serve as, or give the child access to, the greatest sources of stimulation (speaking, holding, touching, responding to, providing toys, and so on); those who are restrictive—that is, those who limit the amount of stimulation to which the infant is exposed—are likely to have an opposite effect. (See Chapter 8 for further discussion of parenting styles.)

Cultural Similarities

In general, children rate their mothers and fathers differently with respect to important dimensions of parenting such as warmth and control. In China, says Ho (1987), mothers look after children; fathers discipline them. Perhaps it isn't surprising that Berndt and associates (1993)

found that Chinese children (as well as children from Taiwan and Hong Kong) see their mothers as warmer and less controlling than fathers.

Interestingly, children in Western societies express very similar views of their parents (Collins & Russell, 1991). No matter how involved fathers are in child rearing, mothers are typically seen as more affectionate, warmer, and less strict. This is not surprising given that mothers are the ones who feed, wash, and clothe children—in other words, who nurture them (Hodapp & Mueller, 1982). In contrast, fathers play with them—or discipline them. Thus, even in these earliest parent–infant interactions, gender has begun to make a difference.

EARLY GENDER-ROLE INFLUENCES

Sex differences in attitudes and behaviors are evident in **gender roles** (or **sex roles**). A gender role is the particular combination of attitudes, behaviors, and personality characteristics that a culture considers appropriate for the individual's anatomical sex—in other words, that is considered masculine or feminine. **Gender typing** describes the processes by which boys and girls learn masculine and feminine roles.

To some extent, masculinity and femininity are clearly the products of genetically ordained physiological and hormonal differences between males and females; but the evidence makes it clear that this is only part of the story. In some cultures, behaviors that we might consider feminine are expected of men and are therefore masculine; at the same time, the aggressiveness and dominance that we think of as masculine characterize women (see Chapter 12 for more details). Clearly, cultures and families have a great deal to do with the eventual gender roles of their children.

When Does Gender Typing Begin?
The assigning of gender roles begins at the very beginning—or even before, when parents wonder, "Hey, should we take a chance and paint the room blue? But, shoot, it might be a girl! Maybe we'd better stay with something neutral, like desert tan, and we can add the blue or the pink later."*

When an infant is born, the attending physician or midwife doesn't say, "Holy jeepers, lady, it's a *baby!*" No. The key word is not *baby;* it's *boy* or *girl* (unless, of course,

---

*My aunt Eugenie, who had 10 kids, never had this problem: "I only had one room," she explains, "and it would have been a darn sight too expensive to repaint it each time." All 10 grew up with no apparent gender confusion.

BARUMBA OF THE MUNDUGUMOR

Barumba was born in the spectacular highlands of New Guinea, an island poised like some prehistoric bird above the continent of Australia. His father had spent the day strutting through the village, showing off his vest of brilliant orange, red, and green parrot feathers, his resplendent collar of green beetle shells, and his skirt of gorgeous plumes plucked from birds of paradise. He knew that if the others in the village looked at him in admiration, it would bode well for his first child.

Barumba's mother, too, had chosen to adorn herself for her first birth. Around both arms, she wore tightly woven, brightly colored armbands of orchid fibers. Around her neck hung the necklace of dog's teeth made for her by her mother; and below it, her favorite string of red nuts. And through her nostril she had the long leg bone of a wild guinea fowl.

The contractions were almost continuous now, and the mother knew it would be soon. Anxiously, she watched as the top of the head appeared, long black hair slicked down; now the ears, now the neck— yes! yes! yes!

"He will be a great artist," she yelled out in her excitement, and her husband crashed into the hut, beetle shells clanking, so that he too might see.

Sure enough, the infant's umbilical cord was wrapped around his neck. And, as the Mundugumor have known for centuries, only those infants whose umbilical cords are wound around their necks at birth stand any chance of becoming great artists. Amazingly, they are right.

"Hot dang!" said Barumba's father.

To Think About   We are a little like the Mundugumor, suggests Pogrebin (1980). We know, of course, that it's ridiculous to think that

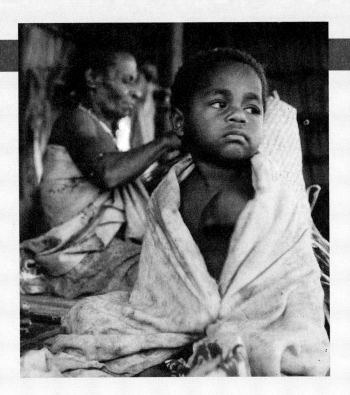

the position of the umbilical cord is of any consequence. Instead, we look for appendages between the legs of our infants. To a considerable extent, these tell us how to interact with them, what sorts of toys they are most likely to enjoy, what their personalities should be. And surprisingly often, our predictions are every bit as accurate as those of the Mundugumor! No?

prenatal diagnosis has already spoiled the surprise). The simple anatomical fact of being boy or girl tells mother and father and all the significant others what to think and how to react. The knowledge that it's a "boy" or "girl" even colors the parents' perceptions. When Rubin, Provenzano, and Luria (1974) asked 30 parents to describe their day-old infants as they would to a relative or a close friend, without any hesitation they spoke of their alert, strong, well-coordinated, firm, and hardy sons. In contrast, they described their daughters as weaker, finer-featured, softer, less attentive, more delicate. Yet these parents, especially the fathers (who were most guilty of exaggerating the sex-appropriate characteristics of their sons), had scarcely had any opportunity to interact with and get to know their infants. And hospital records indicated clearly that these male and female infants were *indistinguishable* one from the other in terms of weight, muscle tone, activity, responsiveness, and so on.

But many parents waste little time making their new infants sexually distinct: They color the boy-infants blue, the girl-infants pink. Because of the connotations associated with these colors, they emphasize long-established

sexual stereotypes. And in much the same way, the names parents give their infants reinforce their sometimes unconscious beliefs about male–female differences. Kasof (1993), for example, shows how male names (like John or Michael) are seen as more attractive, more intellectually competent, stronger. In contrast, many female names (like Edith) carry connotations of being less attractive, more old-fashioned, and less able. (See Across Cultures: "Barumba of the Mundugumor.")

EXCEPTIONALITY

The Lifespan is mainly about the physical, intellectual, and social development of the average person from conception until death. It is worth repeating, however, that this average person is simply a useful mathematical invention, that none of us is "average" in all ways. Instead, we are individuals, each different from every other. But there are so many of us—approaching 6 billion now—that to keep things clear and simple, psychology has to speak of the mythical average.

FIGURE 6.5
*The physical, social-
emotional, and intel-
lectual dimensions of
exceptionality.*

Normality

Physical

Visual impairment
Hearing impairment
Motor skill disorders
Other physical loss, injury,
  or disease

Superior athletic ability
Superior sensory ability

Social-Emotional

Autism
Schizophrenia
Hyperactivity
Conduct disorders
  (aggressiveness,
  delinquency, withdrawal,
  severe shyness)

Invulnerability
Leadership

Intellectual

Mild, moderate, severe,
  and profound retardation
Learning disabilities

Giftedness
Superior intellectual,
  creative, and
  motivational qualities

Still, we need to keep in mind that our average is a fiction and that the individual—Tara, Trevor, Tammy, Tommy—is our reality and our main concern. We need to keep in mind, too, that some of these individuals depart so dramatically from our average—are so *exceptional*—that they are worthy of study in their own right.

Exceptionality is a two-sided concept: There are, on the one hand, those who are exceptionally gifted; on the other, there are those who lack normal abilities and competence. Furthermore, exceptionality is found in each of the three major areas of human development: social, physical, and intellectual (see Figure 6.5).

Exceptionality is a two-sided concept: It includes those who lack normal skills and abilities as well as those who are socially, physically, or intellectual gifted. While handicaps are sometimes evident early in infancy, exceptional giftedness is often not immediately apparent. Thus, in spite of this father's dreams, there is yet little evidence that this small urchin will become the world's most gifted race-car driver—or that he will invent a lasting cure for some rapidly galloping disease.

TABLE 6.7
Categories of Cerebral Palsy (Classified by Body Functioning)

Ataxia	Manifested in balance problems and an uncertain walk. Affects approximately one out of four of those with cerebral palsy.
Spastic	Characterized by loss of control over voluntary muscles. Movements tend to be jerky and uncontrolled. Some symptoms in two out of five cerebral palsy victims.
Athetosis	Marked by trembling, drooling, facial gestures, and other involuntary and purposeless muscle activity (fluttering of the hands, for instance—in contrast with the rigid, jerky movements of spasticity). Often affects speech as well. Frequently found in combination with spasticity. Affects one out of five cerebral palsy individuals.
Tremor	Involves shaky movements, most often of the hands, sometimes visible only when the individual is voluntarily attempting to do something. Involves less extensive movement than athetosis or spasticity.
Rigidity	Caused by strong opposing tension of flexor and extensor muscles, resulting in fixed and rigid bodily postures (sometimes referred to as *lead pipe cerebral palsy*).
Mixed	Involves a combination of characteristics descriptive of one or more of the common classifications. Most cerebral palsy victims fall within this category, although the majority are described in terms of their most predominant characteristics.

* It should be stressed that the effects of cerebral palsy are sometimes so mild that they are undetectable. At other times, they are serious enough to cause death in infancy.

In this section, we deal briefly with some of the most common manifestations of physical and social-emotional exceptionality in infancy. In Chapter 9, we look at physical and at intellectual exceptionality in childhood; and in Chapter 10, we discuss social-emotional exceptionality.

Motor Skill Disorders

Not all children learn to walk or tie their shoes, or dance as expected; some experience *developmental delays* in acquiring motor skills.

Cerebral Palsy

Cerebral palsy, also labeled **significant developmental motor disability,** is a collection of symptoms (a syndrome) that includes motor problems and may also include psychological problems, convulsions, or behavior disorders (Dewey, 1993). It was originally known as *Little's disease* after the surgeon who first described it, but is, in fact, not a disease. It varies in severity from being so mild that it is virtually undetectable to being sufficiently serious that it is manifested in paralysis.

Cerebral palsy is most often a congenital disorder; that is, it is present at birth in more than two thirds of all cases. It is generally associated with brain damage, although the damage is often mild and nonspecific. Not surprisingly, it is far more common among highly premature infants. Hack and associates (1994) report that 9 percent of a group of infants who weighed less than 750 grams at birth had cerebral palsy; none of a comparable group born at full term did. Sometimes it results from *anoxia* (lack of oxygen during the birth process, or before or after birth). It can also result from maternal infection and disease, as

Many of the physical and motor problems of infancy and childhood are so mild as to be almost undetectable; others may be evident in paralysis. Some, like that of this little girl whose leg is about three inches shorter than the other, may require special devices or sometimes surgery. A positive self-image and acceptance by others are especially important for children with physical problems.

well as from postnatal brain injury sometimes resulting from diseases such as meningitis or encephalitis.

One of the most common symptoms of cerebral palsy is *spasticity* (inability to move voluntarily) in one or more limbs, or *dyskinesia* (abnormal movements) (see Table 6.7). Limb disorders in cerebral palsy may also be accompanied by disorders of facial movements (termed *orofacial praxis*), sometimes evident in inability to control facial expressions (Dewey, 1993). The motor impairments of cerebral palsy are sometimes sufficiently severe that it is difficult to assess the child's intellectual ability. As a result, it was often assumed that intellectual deficits were common among those suffering from cerebral palsy. However, more recent evidence suggests that fewer than half of cerebral palsy victims are mentally retarded (Erickson, 1987).

Physical therapy is sometimes effective in improving motor control and coordination of children with cerebral palsy (Pape et al., 1994). Also, electrical stimulation of certain muscle groups is sometimes effective (Hazelwood et al., 1994). In some cases, brain surgery is effective in decreasing spasticity (Kaufman et al., 1994).

Other Motor Skill Disorders

There are motor skill disorders that are not associated with brain damage or cerebral palsy. These are often evident in delayed development among children, many of whom also have other developmental disorders such as mental retardation, autism, or even attention deficit disorders (Deuel, 1992). They may be apparent in difficulties in *learning* motor tasks such as walking, running, skipping, tying shoes, and so on; they may also be apparent in difficulties in *carrying out* motor activities. A common label for these problems is **developmental coordination disorder.**

According to the *Diagnostic and Statistical Manual of Mental Disorders* (*DSM-III-R*) of the American Psychiatric Association, a *developmental coordination disorder* exists when (1) the person's performance of activities requiring motor coordination (such as crawling, walking, sitting, handwriting, sports) is markedly below what would be expected for the person's age, (2) the disturbance interferes with academic achievement or activities of daily living; and (3) the disturbance is not due to a known physical disorder (such as cerebral palsy) (American Psychiatric Association, 1987).

Epilepsy

Epilepsy is a seizure disorder whose origins are sometimes genetic and sometimes unknown. Seizures involve abnormal electrical activity in the brain. The more serious forms of epilepsy (sometimes termed *grand mal* as opposed to *petit mal*) can often be controlled with drugs. Petit mal seizures, which last between 1 and 30 seconds, are seen in a momentary "absentness" of the child and are often accompanied by rhythmic, fluttering movements of both eyelids. These seizures may occur very often and are sometimes interpreted by parents or teachers as a sign that the student is deliberately not paying attention. Medication can successfully prevent the occurrence of petit mal seizures in the majority of cases. In addition, in many cases medication can be discontinued with no further recurrence of seizures. Echenne and associates (1994) report that one form of infant epilepsy, termed *benign infantile epilepsy,* is associated with a dominant gene and can easily be controlled with antiepileptic drugs. The treatment typically lasts no more than 16 months and is effective in preventing further seizures.

Other Physical Problems

There are many other physical problems of infancy and childhood that sometimes require special services—diseases and conditions such as muscular dystrophy, cancer, asthma, diabetes, and the absence of one or more limbs, as well as paralysis, to name but a few. Some are congenital, some result from infections and diseases after birth, and others result from accidents of various kinds. Many cases are associated with serious emotional and social problems, which are often related to difficulties the child experiences in being accepted by others and in developing a positive self-concept. Hence a great deal of what special education programs, parents, and therapists can do for physically exceptional children relates to their emotional and social well-being.

Autism

Tim was an apparently normal, healthy child, the second child born to a couple in their early twenties. He was an "easy" infant who cried very little and who, in fact, appeared most contented when left alone. The mother later recalled that he didn't smile as a young infant and that he didn't appear to recognize her. Still, he progressed apparently normally through his first year, learned to walk at the young age of 9 months, displaying advanced motor development, seldom tripping or falling, as most toddlers do.

But at the age of 2, he had still not learned to speak. An examination showed his hearing to be normal. His parents hoped he would be a "late bloomer." But even at the age of 3, Tim still did not respond to his parents' speech. In addition, he had developed few social skills, and he engaged in unusual and repetitive behaviors—behaviors like spinning the wheels of his toy car or sitting and rocking his body endlessly.

Tim's condition is rare. It is what is labeled **autism,** a disorder described by the American Psychiatric Association (1987) as a **pervasive developmental disorder.** The causes of autism are unclear although some cases appear to be linked with a chromosome abnormality (Vostanis et al., 1994); others may be associated with defects or damage in the part of the brain called the *cerebellum* (Ciesielski & Knight, 1994).

Autistic disorder is apparent mainly in the infant's failure to develop normal communication skills. Its other features include a lack of normal responsiveness to other people, bizarre responses to aspects of the environment, and a pattern of developmental delays (Fong & Wilgosh, 1992). Also, some autistic children are self-destructive; others engage in destruction of other things (Hagopian, Fisher, & Legacy, 1994). Comparisons of videotapes of the first birthdays of 11 autistic infants with those of 11 normal children revealed a number of behavioral signs that seem to differentiate the two groups: These had to do with pointing, showing others different objects, looking at other people, and turning in response to hearing one's name (Osterling & Dawson, 1994).

Among the major symptoms of autism, the APA (1987), lists: (1) Severe and consistent impairment in social relationships (for example, inappropriate emotional responses, lack of awareness of feelings of others, abnormal social play, inability to make friends); (2) significant impairment in verbal and nonverbal communication (for example, absence of babbling, lack of facial expressiveness, absence of imaginative activity as in "make-believe" games, abnormal speech production, inability to initiate or maintain a conversation); and (3) markedly restricted range of interests and behaviors (for example, stereotyped movements like spinning or head banging, persistent preoccupation with parts of objects like repeatedly smelling or feeling something, serious distress over trivial changes in environment, unreasonable insistence on routines, and preoccupation with one activity).

Although the autistic disorder usually manifests itself before the age of 3, it sometimes develops later (Mesibov & Van Bourgondien, 1992). The most common treatment is to use tranquilizers and antipsychotic drugs. Although there is little evidence that they are very effective in alleviating the condition, they are useful in making patients more manageable. Psychotherapy (psychoanalysis, for example) has not proven very effective, although some forms of behavior therapy (based on conditioning theories described in Chapter 2) beginning early in the child's life and sustained over a long period of time are sometimes helpful (Hagopian et al., 1994). In general, the long-term prognosis for autistic children is not good, with only a very small percentage ever recovering sufficiently that they can be classed as "completely normal."

THE WHOLE INFANT

There is something frustrating about fragmenting the developing infant into such psychologically convenient categories as description of capabilities, physical development, motor development, social-emotional development, intellectual development, and so on. We lose the individual in the interminable and sometimes confused array of beliefs, findings, tentative conclusions, convincing arguments, and suggestions. The theoretical infant is a hypothetical average. And although many infants are very close to the hypothetical average child when they are 1 month old, fewer are still average at the age of 2 months, even fewer at the age of 6 months, and almost none by the age of 1 year. By the time the child becomes as old as you or I, the average individual will no longer exist but will appear only in the oversimplified theories of the social scientist or in the files of the market researcher who wants to know what the "average" person is wearing this spring.

Each person is an integrated whole, whose intellect, emotions, and physical being all interact; each part is inextricably linked with and dependent upon every other part of the living organism. However, if we attempt to describe a person in that way, the sheer complexity of the task might overwhelm us. And so we continue to speak of the isolated forces that affect human development as though they exist apart from the integrated, whole person. But it bears repeating that our divisions, although necessary, are artificial and sometimes misleading.

Interactions in the Family Context

1. Influence in infant–parent interactions is bidirectional and strongly affected by the characteristics of both parent and infant (the microsystem) as well as by the larger context.

Infant States

2. Infant states reflect basic individual differences very early in life. Common infant states include regular sleep, irregular sleep, drowsiness, alert inactivity, alert activity, and crying.

Temperament

3. Individual personality differences among infants define temperament, which is assumed to have a strong genetic basis. Three broad infant temperaments are difficult, easy, and "slow to warm up." In North America, "easy" may be an advantage. The infant's temperament may contribute to developmental outcomes by affecting how parents interact with it and how they feel about themselves as parents. Also "goodness-of-fit" between the infant's temperament and environmental demands may affect developmental outcome.

Infant Emotions

4. Infants' facial expressions and other behaviors reveal a number of distinct emotions, some of which are evident in infant crying (rhythmical, hunger, anger, and pain). The reflexive smile is often present only hours after birth; the social smile (often in response to a human voice) is uncommon before the age of 3 weeks; by 4 months, infants also laugh. Both crying and smiling progress from responses to internal stimuli to external stimuli. Fear responses occur most often in the face of the unexpected. Fear of strangers is not common before the age of 6 months and appears to be related to the infant's ability to distinguish between the familiar and the unfamiliar. Infant control over emotions may be through *other-directed regulatory behaviors* (smiling, for example) and *self-directed regulatory behaviors* (thumb-sucking, for example).

Early Attachment

5. Forming an attachment with a caregiver is one of the most important tasks of early infancy. (*Bonding* refers to the biologically based processes by which parents and infants form attachment links.) Ainsworth's Strange Situation procedure identifies *securely attached* infants (use mother as exploration base; upset when she leaves; react positively to her return); and *insecure-avoidant* (rarely cry when mother leaves; ignore or avoid her when she returns) or *insecure-ambivalent* (very upset when mother leaves; often angry when she returns). *Disorganized/ disoriented* infants display a range of disorganized behaviors (crying at the door but withdrawing when parent returns).

6. There appear to be powerful genetic tendencies toward the formation of caregiver–infant bonds (evident, for example, in infants' preference for the human voice and human face, as well as in response tendencies such as rooting and sucking reflexes). Infant attachment to the mother appears to be important to the healthy development and adjustment of the infant. Four sequential phases in the development of attachment are preattachment (first month); attachment in the making (into second half of first year: selective social smile); clear-cut attachment (after 6 months: use of motor skills to approach attachment object); and goal-corrected attachment (second year: more subtle manipulation of attachment person's behavior). Infants appear to become equally attached to their mothers and fathers when given the opportunity to do so.

Fear of Strangers and Separation from Parents

7. Fear of strangers is uncommon before 6 to 9 months and may result from *incongruity* between expectations and reality. Infants who have experience with siblings and strangers are less prone to stranger anxiety. Transitional objects such as blankets and teddy bears are sometimes effective in reducing anxiety in some stressful situations. Longer-term separation from the primary caregiver leads to disturbances in most infants after the age of 6 months.

Infant Care

8. High-quality infant care does not appear to disrupt parent–infant bonds or to prevent their formation and has no consistent negative effects.

Parenting in Infancy

9. Among important dimensions of parenting in infancy are attentiveness, physical contact, verbal stimulation, material stimulation, and responsive care—each of which has positive effects on the infant's social and intellectual development—and restrictiveness, the effects of which are more negative.

Early Gender-Role Influences

10. From the moment of birth, a subtle process of gender typing begins. Many mothers and fathers react differently to male and female children, interact with them differently, have different expectations of them, and perceive them differently.

Exceptionality

11. Exceptionality has both positive and negative dimensions, and may be evident in cerebral palsy, epilepsy, a variety of diseases, congenital physical problems, or physical problems resulting from accidents. Emotional exceptionality may be apparent in childhood-onset pervasive developmental disorders (like autism), which are rare but very serious early forms of emotional disorders.

1. How might infants influence their caregivers?
   - Do a single case study of an infant in an attempt to illustrate bidirectionality of parent–infant influence.

2. Are infants born with certain personalities?
   - Arrange to observe one or more infants. Systematically record evidence that might allow you to classify the infant(s) as easy, difficult, or "slow to warm up."

3. How important is early contact between parent and infant?

   - As a major project, review the bonding literature and evaluate its applicability to human infants.

4. Is it better for mothers to stay home with their infants?
   - Organize a debate around this question. Base your arguments on current research.

5. Is the nonaverage abnormal? What is exceptionality?
   - Summarize the dimensions of exceptionality, relating them to a bell-shaped curve.

STUDY TERMS

anencephalic   165

attachment   168

attachment in the making   170

autism   181

clear-cut attachment   170

critical period   169

crying   164

developmental coordination disorder   181

difficult   161

dyadic model   158

easy   160

exceptionality   179

fear   165

gender roles   177

gender typing   177

goal-corrected attachment   170

incongruity hypothesis   172

infant care   174

infant state   159

insecure-ambivalent   168

insecure-avoidant   168

insecurely attached   168

laughing   165

mother–infant bond   169

other-directed regulatory behaviors   166

personality   160

pervasive developmental disorder   181

preattachment   170

rapid eye movement (REM) sleep   159

securely attached   168

self-directed regulatory behavior   166

significant developmental motor disability   180

slow to warm up   160

smiling   165

Strange Situation   167

temperament   160

transitional objects   173

FURTHER READINGS

The following two books underline the role of family systems in influencing developmental outcomes:

Ambert, A. M. (1992). *The effect of children on parents.* New York: The Haworth Press.

White, D., & Woollett, A. (1992). *Families: A context for development.* New York: The Falmer Press.

A good summary of research and applications in temperament research is contained in:

Carey, W. B., & McDevitt, S. C. (Eds.). (1989). *Clinical and educational applications of temperament research.* Berwyn, PA: Swets North America.

There is not enough child care in North America; nor is there enough *quality* child care, says Angela Browne Miller in the first of the following three books. The other two detail changes in contemporary North American society that are having an important impact on the lives of infants:

Browne Miller, A. (1990). *The day care dilemma*. New York: Plenum.

Hernandez, D. J., & Myers, D. E. (1993). *America's children: Resources from family, government, and the economy*. New York: Russell Sage.

Hayes, C. D., Palmer, J. L., & Zaslow, M. J. (Eds.). (1990). *Who cares for America's children? Child care policy for the 1990's*. Washington, D.C.: National Academy Press.

Pogrebin's book is a provocative analysis of the role parents play in gender typing their infants:

Pogrebin, L. C. (1980). *Growing up free: Raising your child in the 80's*. New York: McGraw-Hill.

This guide provides specific, detailed descriptions of methods that can be used with exceptional children:

Noonan, M. J., & McCormick, L. (1993). *Early intervention in natural environments: Methods and procedures*. Pacific Grove, CA: Brooks/Cole.

When you think that the eyes of your childhood
dried at the sight of a piece of gingerbread and
that a plum-cake was a compensation for the
agony of parting with your mamma and sisters;
O my friend and brother, you need not be too
confident of your own fine feelings.

WILLIAM MAKEPEACE THACKERAY
Vanity Fair

EARLY CHILDHOOD

With the proliferation of day care, perhaps preschoolers no longer # PART THREE
sense so profound an agony at parting from mama. Perhaps, too, with the reduction in the size of the family, there are no sisters to bring to the eyes tears of sadness—or of joy.

Still, it's true that preschoolers often don't need more than a piece of gingerbread or a plum-cake to dry their tears. At the same time, they don't need a very serious personal crisis to make them cry.

As we see in the next two chapters, their understanding of the world is different from ours. So, too, are their emotional responses. It is as though the line between joy and sorrow has not yet been firmly drawn; it is easily crossed. Tears and laughter come more easily. I can move Jennie from gladness to tears if I take her stuffed toy from her. But now, if I give her a cookie (or a plum-cake), she smiles.

We, too, can still cry when someone takes our stuffed toys. But what will dry our grown-up tears? Where are our gingerbreads and our plum-cakes?

Physical and Cognitive Development: Early Childhood

T is the eye of childhood,
That fears a painted devil

William Shakespeare
Macbeth, II, ii

CHAPTER 7

I'm 7 years old. I'm dressed like a pirate because it's Halloween, and I'm ringing Mr. Delisle's doorbell, hoping Mrs. Delisle will answer because she always puts more stuff in our bags. My 4-year-old sister, Paulette, is standing next to me, dressed in some yukky girl-costume like a fairy. My mother made me bring her.

I have no way of knowing who's on the other side of the door. I know one of Mr. Delisle's dogs bit him on the bum a little while ago, and he's awful upset, everybody says, because he can't sit down or sleep except on his belly, which is too big to be a good way for him to sleep. I know he's real mad at his dogs. "If they come close enough, I'll bite the boogers," he told Mrs. Delisle (who then told my mother, which is how I know all this for a fact). "He's trying to think up some way of punishing them," my mother told my dad, which, again, is how I know this.

What I don't know is that the perfect punishment has accidentally occurred to Mr. Delisle, because he just happened to buy one of those disgustingly monstrous masks, which, for some twisted reason, he thought he would use to scare the living begory out of us when we came to his door. I haven't yet found out that earlier this afternoon, he put on that mask and an old buffalo coat and went out behind the dog kennel to make himself a hiding place. And when the dogs saw him the wind was wrong and they couldn't smell him, and they looked scared enough to inspire Mr. Delisle to lunge screeching toward the kennel, sending all of them yelping to the far corner—which made him pretty happy and his bum didn't burn quite so much.

So Paulette and I ring Mr. Delisle's doorbell and yell "Trick or treat," saying "treat" like it has two long syllables, praying Mrs. Delisle will be the one . . . and then Shwack! The door flies open, and there's this thing with a horrible face and long-haired skin, and it screams at us, "Death to all dogs at the hand of the painted devil!" And Paulette has a small accident right there and runs home crying.

"Her, she was scared," I tell my mom. "Me, I just drank too much softdrink."

THIS CHAPTER

In retrospect, I might have been wrong. It's likely that for both Paulette and me, and for Mr. Delisle's dogs, experience had not yet drawn its thick black line between reality and fantasy. It's a line that we adults are so careful to keep firmly in view. Preschoolers scarcely know it exists. For the first seven or eight years of life, Pearce (1977) informs us, the child often does not bother to check thinking against reality. Thinking is wishful, fantastic. It somehow assumes that reality can be changed or controlled by thoughts, that thoughts enter the real world and make of it what we wish—or, sometimes, what we fear. When

Vikan and Clausen (1993) questioned 4- to 6-year-olds, they found that children firmly believe that people can be influenced, even *controlled*, by wishful thoughts and magical behavior just as readily as by rewards or persuasion. Thus it is that a magic spell can produce a witch or a princess, a silver thread or a pot of gold; and a kiss can cure a booboo, and a mother can make a dragon smile. Thus it is, too, that a painted devil can strike terror in a child's heart.

In this chapter, we examine the early development of thinking in preschool children, tracing their astounding achievements as they begin to glimpse the logic that governs the real world—perhaps, in the process, losing some of the ability to see things through the eyes of childhood as a more adultlike vision takes over. We look, too, at preschool education and at the development of language. But first, we turn to physical growth and motor development in children ages 2 to 6.

PHYSICAL GROWTH

At birth, the fetus has been growing at a rate of about 24 centimeters and 10 kilograms (9.4 inches and 22 pounds) per year (Tanner, Whitehouse, & Takaishi, 1966). During infancy, however, there is a rapid reduction in rate of growth. As a result, between ages 2 and 6, the child gains 6 to 8 centimeters and about 2 kilograms (2 to 3 inches and 4.4 pounds) per year. As we see in Chapter 11, at adolescence there is a dramatic, but relatively brief, acceleration of growth; but by about age 16 for girls and 18 for boys, growth rates are almost zero. (See Figure 7.1 for a representation of velocity curves—or speed of growth—for weight for boys and girls.)

FIGURE 7.1
Body weight velocity curves (speed of growth) for boys and girls, from birth to age 18. The shape of the curves is much the same for height. (From Tanner, Whitehouse, Takaishi, Archives of Diseases in Childhood, *1966, vol. 41, pp. 454–471. Reprinted by permission.)*

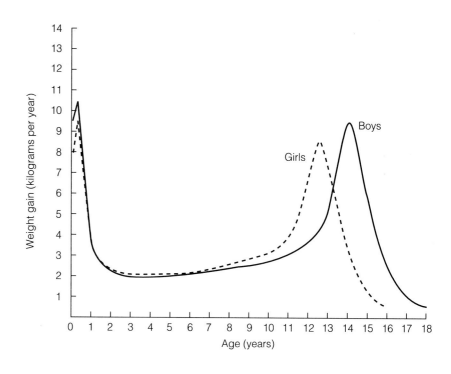

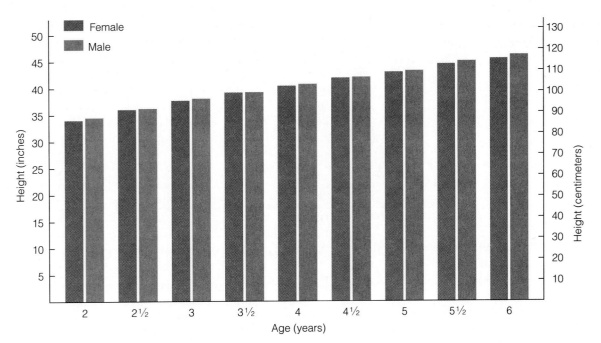

FIGURE 7.2

Height at 50th percentile for U.S. children ages 2 to 6. (Adapted from the Health Department, Milwaukee, Wisconsin; based on data by H. C. Stuart and H. V. Meredith, prepared for use in Children's Medical Center, Boston. Used by permission of the Milwaukee Health Department.)

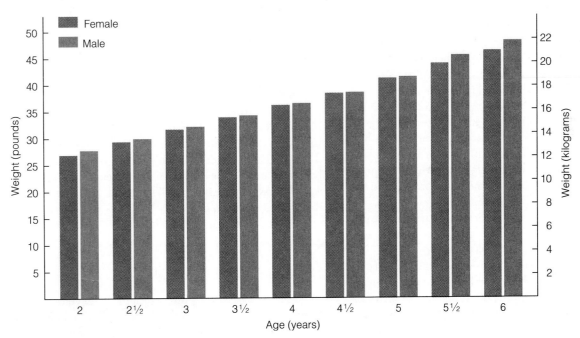

FIGURE 7.3

Weight at 50th percentile for U.S. children ages 2 to 6. (Adapted from the Health Department, Milwaukee, Wisconsin; based on data by H. C. Stuart and H. V. Meredith, prepared for use in Children's Medical Center, Boston. Used by permission of the Milwaukee Health Department.)

In spite of the deceleration in *growth rates* in infancy through the preschool period, there are nevertheless phenomenal changes that take place during this period, as a comparison of the 6-year-old with the 2-year-old shows

(see Figures 7.2 and 7.3). Not only do preschoolers gain an average of an additional 30 centimeters and 9 kilograms (about 1 foot and 20 pounds), but there are also some marked differences in rates of change for various parts of

FIGURE 7.4
Changes in form and proportion of the human body during fetal and postnatal life. (From Jensen et al., Biology, 1979, p. 233. Used with permission of the Wadsworth Publishing Company.)

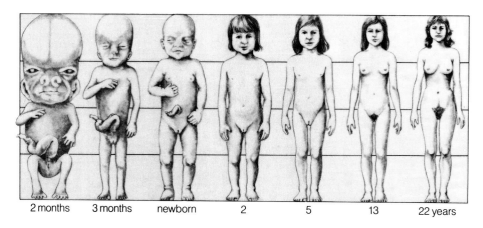

2 months   3 months   newborn   2   5   13   22 years

the body. These differences are reflected in the very different, and far more adult appearance of the 6-year-old compared with the 2-year-old. For example, the thick layers of fat that give 1-year-old infants their babyish appearance begin to disappear slowly during the second year of life and continue to recede gradually. Because these tissues grow much more slowly than other tissues, by the time children have reached age 6 their layers of fat are less than half as thick as they were at age 1.

Not only does the relative amount of fatty tissue change during the preschool years but its distribution also changes as a result of the more rapid growth of bone and muscle. The squat appearance of infants is explained by the fact that their waists are usually as large as their hips or chests. Six-year-old children, in contrast, have begun to develop waists that are smaller than their shoulders and hips. This becomes even more evident in early adolescence than at the end of the preschool period.

The relatively larger infant waists are due not only to layers of fat but also to the size of the internal organs, many of which grow at a much more rapid rate than other parts of the body. Given space limitations between the child's pelvis and diaphragm, their abdomens often protrude. This condition changes as they grow in height during the preschool years.

Other aspects of body proportions that account for the different appearance of the 6-year-old include changes in the ratio of head to body size (shown in Figure 7.4). The head of a 2-month-old fetus is approximately half the length of the entire body; at birth, it is closer to one-fourth the size of the rest of the body; and by the age of 6, it is close to one-eighth the size, which is a short step removed from the head-to-body relationship typical of the normal adult with a normal-sized head: one-tenth. Thus, from the age of 2 to 6, the head changes from approximately one fifth to one eighth of total body size—a significant enough change to be noticeable. Because of this, and because of changes in the distribution of fat and in the space that the child now has for internal organs, the 6-year-old looks remarkably like an adult; the 2-year-old looks more like a typical baby. (See At a Glance: "Preschoolers' Health Problems," and Figure 7.5.)

MOTOR DEVELOPMENT

Learning to walk is the infant's most significant motor achievement, with extremely important social and cognitive implications. Infants who can walk (or at least crawl) can not only approach those to whom they are attached, but they can also leave them to explore places they would otherwise see only from somebody's arms—or looking over the edge of some wheeled baby thing. Self-locomotion facilitates the process of becoming familiar with the world.

Infants not only learn to walk, but also practice and eventually learn to coordinate a wide range of other motor activities. By age 2, they are remarkably adept at picking up objects, stacking blocks, unlacing shoes, and a host of other actions.

In early childhood, children continue to progress in *motor development*, their locomotion becoming more certain as they lose the characteristic wide-footed stance of the toddler (from 18 months to 2½ years). As their equilibrium stabilizes and their feet move closer together, their arms and hands also move closer to their bodies. They no longer need as wide a stance to maintain their balance—nor do they always need to keep their arms out as if they were perpetually walking a rail. Still, they fall far more often than you or I.

But it doesn't hurt so much.

Developmental Timetables

Most parents are keenly interested in the developmental progress of their infants and children. They feel proud of their offspring's accomplishments and are sometimes distressed and worried when their children do not develop as rapidly as they expect—or as rapidly as someone else's children.

Here, as in all areas of human development, there are no absolute norms, no definite, preestablished levels of performance that must be reached by certain ages. Our definitions of what is normal are vague and inexact. Still, psychology and medicine provide us with indications of what we might expect; and this information may be used

PRESCHOOLERS' HEALTH PROBLEMS

Most preschoolers occasionally suffer from illness or injury serious enough to require medical attention or to keep them home. In fact, only 20 or 30 of every 100 preschoolers will *not* have an upper-respiratory infection at least once (a cold, for example), and almost one third will suffer some physical injury. Between ages 5 and 17, the rates for colds and other infections, and for digestive system problems decline; those for injuries increase. On average, rate of injury is about 30 percent higher for males than females (U.S. Bureau of the Census, 1994; see Figure 7.5).

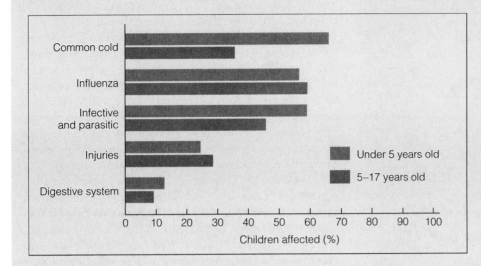

FIGURE 7.5

Preschoolers' and older children's susceptibility to injury and illness. The graph shows the percentage of children who will be affected at least once by the indicated condition, and the condition is sufficiently serious to require medical attention or staying at home. (Adapted from U.S. Bureau of the Census, 1994, p. 140.)

as benchmarks against which to evaluate our children—if we must.

Many different scales of infant and child development might be used for these purposes. As we saw, there are neonatal scales with which to assess the physiological and neurological condition of the newborn (for example, the Brazelton Neonatal Behavioral Assessment Scale or the Apgar). There are also scales to assess motor and mental development in infancy (for example, the Bayley Scales of Infant Development). And there are developmental scales that span infancy and childhood (for example, the Denver Developmental Screening Test or the Gesell Developmental Schedules). Each of these instruments typically provides simple tasks that can be presented to the infant or child or describes observations that can be made. Each also provides specific tables of norms describing what sorts of infant or child behaviors can be expected at different ages.

The *Denver Developmental Screening Test*, for example, was initially designed primarily to permit identification of infants and children suffering from developmental delays (Frankenburg et al., 1981). It has subsequently been revised and restandardized with various ethnic groups, and is now known as the *Denver II* (Frankenburg & Dodds, 1992). It provides age norms corresponding to the levels at which 25, 50, 75, and 90 percent of children are expected to demonstrate a given capability. Four different

Norms of developmental timetables tell us that most 2-year-olds cannot yet stack eight jars; nor can they stand on one foot for a whole second. But the first of these tasks can be accomplished with a little parental help. And, as for the second, well it isn't really necessary to stand on one leg in order to dance the Great Jar Tower Dance.

TABLE 7.1
Age at Which Children Accomplish Described Task

Motor Task	Approximate Ages	
	50 Percent	90 Percent
Gross		
Kicks ball forward	18.3 mos.*	23.2 mos.
Throws ball overhand	20.3 mos.	2.9 yrs.
Balances on 1 foot 1 second	2.5 yrs.	3.4 yrs.
Broad jump	2.7 yrs.	3.2 yrs.
Balances on 1 foot 5 seconds	4.3 yrs.	5.4 yrs.
Walks heel to toe	4.6 yrs.	5.7 yrs.
Fine		
Scribbles	13.2 mos.	16.3 mos.
Tower of 4 cubes	19.2 mos.	23.8 mos.
Imitates vertical line	2.4 yrs.	3.2 yrs.
Tower of 8 cubes	2.2 yrs.	3.5 yrs.
Picks longer line	3.3 yrs.	5.3 yrs.
Draws person, 3 parts	3.7 yrs.	4.6 yrs.
Draws person, 6 parts	4.6 yrs.	5.6 yrs.

* For example, 18.3 months equals 18 months and 9 days; 2.5 years equals 2 years and 6 months.

SOURCE: From the revised *Denver II* by W. K. Frankenburg and J. B. Dodds, 1992. Denver, CO: Denver Developmental Materials, Inc. Reprinted by permission of the publisher.

areas are examined by the test: language, personal-social, fine motor, and gross motor. (See Table 7.1 for examples of fine motor and gross motor tasks pertinent to early childhood.) A child is considered to be *developmentally delayed* when incapable of performing a task of which 90 percent of children of the same age are capable. Isolated developmental delays are not considered serious. But when a child is delayed on two or more tasks and in more than one area, further assessment may be required.

Developmental delays are not always evidence of genetically based problems or permanent neurological damage. Sheard (1994) reports, for example, that iron-deficient infants often perform less well on tests of intellectual and motor development. Reassuringly, however, treatment of these children with iron supplements often leads to marked improvement.

Motor and Intellectual Development

There appears to be a very close relationship between timetables for motor development and other aspects of development. In infancy, for example, learning to crawl, and eventually to walk, seems important for developing notions of depth (Bushnell & Boudreau, 1993). Similarly, the development of a variety of other motor skills in the preschool period seems to be closely related to the child's growing intelligence. In fact, motor skills that demonstrate increasing control and coordination of fine-muscle movements are often used as items on measures of intelligence. Among these, for example, are the skills required for tracing geometric figures or for copying them free-hand. Gesell (1925), whose work maps out in detail the sequential progression of children's motor development, reports that before age 2 the child is usually incapable of copying a circle or a horizontal line although the 2- to 3-year-old can do so quite easily. By the age of 4, children can also copy a cross but are unable to copy a diamond (see Figure 7.6).

The ability to draw the human figure also seems to reflect the preschooler's increasing conceptual sophistication. Thus, the preschooler's first attempts are typically crude lines with a head but no bodies or distinct limbs. In time, progressively more details and increasingly exact proportions are added. As far back as 1926, Goodenough (1926) used these observations to devise a simple intelligence test for children, the *Goodenough Draw-a-Man* test. Later, more politically correct revisions titled it the *Goodenough-Harris Drawing Test* (Harris, 1963) or the *Draw-a-Person* test (Naglieri, 1988) (see Figure 7.7). More recent evidence suggests there is a close relationship between the preschooler's drawings of human figures and cognitive development assessed in terms of Piaget's stages (discussed later in this chapter) (Chappell & Steitz, 1993).

Motor and Social Development

Most aspects of development are related to one another. Thus, motor development is related not only to the child's intellectual development, but also to social development. For example, a child's play, particularly with peers, is often influenced by motor skills because various aptitudes are called for in different games. A child who is still incapable of jumping with both feet is not likely to be invited by older children to join in a game of jump rope; a child who cannot grasp marbles skillfully may be left out of the traditional springtime marble games.* Conversely, the child who is precocious in physical and motor development is likely to be the first one asked to participate in games—indeed, may be the one to initiate them. Clearly, then, physical and motor development have an important influence on the child's social development; game playing is one important means of socialization (more about this in Chapter 8). (See Table 7.2 for a summary of some physical and motor achievements of early childhood.)

*Not always, said my grandmother. Sometimes kids just want somebody there who's gonna lose their marbles for sure. She was clearly thinking of Arthur.

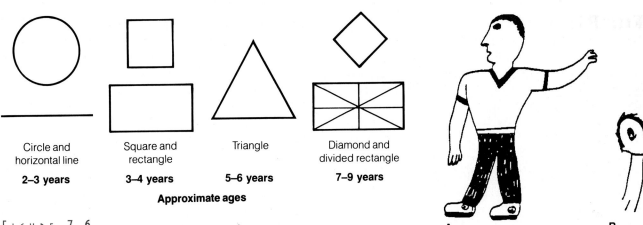

Circle and horizontal line
2–3 years

Square and rectangle
3–4 years

Triangle
5–6 years

Diamond and divided rectangle
7–9 years

Approximate ages

A

B

FIGURE 7.6

Usual order of difficulty, with very approximate ages, for copying simple geometric designs reasonably well. Because of the close relationships between motor and intellectual development in early childhood, many intelligence tests for young children include items such as these.

FIGURE 7.7

*Two examples of the Goodenough-Harris Drawing Test. Both artists were boys aged 10¾ years. The raw scores and IQ equivalents, respectively, for the drawings are **A** 41 and 110; **B** 4 and 54. The child who drew **B** also had a low Stanford-Binet IQ score. (From the Goodenough-Harris Drawing Test, as reprinted in "Children's Drawings as Measures of Intellectual Property." Copyright © 1963 by The Psychological Corporation. Reproduced by permission. All rights reserved.)*

TABLE 7.2

Physical Characteristics of the Child, Ages 2 to 5

At 2 Years Begins to	At 3 Years Begins to	At 4 Years Begins to	At 5 Years Begins to
Walk	Jump and hop on one foot	Run, jump, and climb with close adult supervision	Gain good body control
Run	Climb stairs by alternating feet on each stair	Dress self using buttons, zippers, laces, and so on	Throw and catch a ball, climb, jump, skip with good coordination
Actively explore environment	Dress and undress self somewhat	Use more sophisticated eating utensils such as knives to cut meat or spread butter	Coordinate movements to music
Sit in a chair without support	Walk a reasonably straight path on floor	Walk balance beam with ease	Put on snowpants, boots, and tie shoes
Climb stairs with help (two feet on each stair)	Walk on balance beam	Walk down stairs alone	Skip
Build block towers	Ride a tricycle	Bounce and catch ball	Jump rope, walk in a straight line
Feed self with fork and spoon	Stand on one foot for a short time	Push/pull wagon	Ride a two-wheel bike
Stand on balance beam	Catch large balls	Cut, following lines	Roller skate
Throw ball	Hop	Copy figure X	Fold paper
Catch	Gallop	Print first name	Reproduce alphabet and numbers
Jump	Kick ball		Trace
Push and pull	Hit ball		
Hang on bar	Paste		
Slide	String beads		
	Cut paper with scissors		
	Copy figures 0 and +		

SOURCE: From G. W. Maxim (1993). *The very young* (4th ed.). Columbus, OH: Merrill, p. 80. Copyright © 1993 by Macmillan College Publishing Company. Reprinted by permission of Prentice Hall, Inc.

THE PRESCHOOLER'S MIND

Fabricius and Wellman (1993) had children aged 4 to 6 judge the distances covered by different routes to the same location. Sometimes the routes were direct; at other times they were indirect; and still other times, some object placed along the route served to segment it. Many of these children insisted that the indirect and the segmented routes were shorter. Why? Perhaps, as Piaget thought, because these children focused only on one aspect of the route; or perhaps because they have difficulty representing the routes mentally.

But we do not expect our preschool children, much less our infants, to have adultlike memories or to be completely logical. We are seldom surprised when a 4-year-old is misled by appearances; we express little dismay when our 2½-year-old calls a duck a chicken. These instances of perception-dominated, and illogical thinking simply amuse us; that is what we expect of young children.

But we would be surprised if our 7-year-olds continued to think segmented routes were shorter than other identical routes or if they continued to insist on calling all reasonably shaggy-looking pigs "doggy." We expect some intellectual (or cognitive) differences between preschoolers and older children. Among cognitive skills that differentiate older children from preschoolers are those having to do with *memory*.

Infantile Amnesia

Most of us are victims of a curious phenomenon called **infantile amnesia:** We remember virtually nothing about our infancies. So powerful is infantile amnesia that Newcombe and Fox (1994) found that 9- and 10-year-old children were unable to recognize photographs of most of their preschool classmates. In contrast, adults easily remember over 90 percent of photographs of elementary school classmates even decades later.

No one knows for sure why we experience infant amnesia. It isn't simply because our infancies are so far behind us, because a 50-year-old remembers things that happened 30 years earlier but a 10-year-old remembers little of what happened only 6 years before. One theory is that parts of the infant's brain associated with memory are insufficiently mature to permit long-term remembering; another is that the infant's memory strategies are too primitive to allow the organization and associations required; still another is that there can be no memory of personal events before the infant develops a strong sense of self with which to associate them (Howe & Courage, 1993).

Our memories of early childhood are usually better than those of our infancies, but they too are full of shadows. What we retain are often global sorts of impressions, vague feelings, jumbles of emotions and events. In fact, time robs even our adult memories of crispness and clarity.

The Preschooler's Memory

Still, from the very beginning, the infant clearly has some ability to learn and to remember. But, as we saw in Chapter 5, the neonate's memory is very brief. The effects of simple conditioning procedures sometimes last only hours, or perhaps a day. Yet, the infant is not long confused about whether this is his mother's voice, or her face. Recognition of things like voices and faces is a certain sign of memory. But there are some important differences between the memories of infants and those of adults. Chief among them is that the infant does not deliberately and systematically organize, group, or elaborate material to remember it—and these three activities are the most important memory strategies of adults and older children.

Incidental Mnemonics
A number of researchers argue that the younger preschooler rarely uses systematic *memory strategies* for remembering. For example, they do not systematically rehearse (Gathercole, Adams, & Hitch, 1994), nor are they consciously aware of the possibility of using strategies (Hashimoto, 1991). Most of what the preschooler remembers is the result of what Wellman (1990) calls **incidental mnemonics.** Incidental mnemonics are not deliberate; hence they are not really strategies. They are what happens when someone pays attention, for whatever reason, and later remembers, or when someone is exposed to the same thing often enough that it becomes familiar and known. Remembering, in these cases, is not the result of a deliberate and systematic attempt to elaborate or to rehearse, but is, in a sense, involuntary.

Preschoolers' Memory Strategies
Although younger preschoolers do not appear to use or to be aware of *deliberate* and *systematic* strategies for remembering, they nevertheless do use primitive sorts of strategies. For example, Wellman (1988) asked 3-year-olds to bury a toy in a sandbox before leaving the room with the experimenter. Some of the children were asked to remember where they had buried the toy; others were asked if there was anything they would like to do before leaving, but were given no instructions about remembering. Strikingly, half the children who had been instructed to remember the toy's location *marked* it by placing a mound over the object, by marking the sand, or sometimes by placing another toy on top of it; only 20 percent of the no-instruction group did likewise (see Figure 7.8).

Marking the toy's location is an intelligent and effective strategy. As we noted, however, many of the preschooler's memory strategies are not so effective. Heisel and Ritter (1981) asked 3- and 5-year-olds to hide an object in one of 196 separate containers arranged in a 14-foot-square matrix and instructed some of them to remember where they had hidden the object. Significantly,

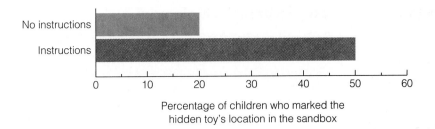

No instructions

Instructions

0   10   20   30   40   50   60

Percentage of children who marked the
hidden toy's location in the sandbox

FIGURE 7.8
Three-year-olds were asked to hide a toy in a sandbox. Half of those who were asked to try to remember where the toy was hidden (the instructions group) marked its location; only 20 percent of the no-instructions group did likewise. Preschoolers may be capable of using simple memory strategies, but often do not do so spontaneously.

many of the children in both age groups used memory strategies when they had been instructed to remember. The strategies used by the 5-year-olds were often very effective—namely, hiding the object in one of the corner locations, because these could be remembered and relocated very easily. But what is perhaps most striking is that the 3-year-olds' strategies, while every bit as consistent as those of the older children, were often very ineffective. Almost half these 3-year-olds tried to hide the object in the same location on every trial, thus demonstrating that they were using a systematic strategy; but the location was typically somewhere near the center of the array. As a result, when they were later asked to find the object, these children fared almost as poorly as those who had not used strategies.

The overuse of an inappropriate memory strategy is one of the most common mistakes made by young children trying to remember, says Wellman (1988). An important developmental change in memory strategies is a gradual reduction in the use of faulty strategies and an increase in more effective strategies.

Two things are noteworthy about the young preschooler's primitive memory strategies, says Wellman (1990): First, they seldom involve deliberate reorganization or elaboration, or even rehearsal; second, many of the preschooler's mnemonic strategies are faulty in the sense that they are misused and often do not lead to an improvement in memory. Still, older preschoolers sometimes *do* use deliberate, although not always highly effective, strategies to help them remember. The use of more effective strategies increases dramatically in elementary school.

Development of Early Memory Strategies

The preschooler's increasing ability to remember results in part from increasing familiarity with things and events. For example, Saarnio (1993) showed that the more familiar preschoolers were with certain scenes, the better they were able to remember objects in the scenes.

The development of memory skills may also depend on social interaction. (Recall from Chapter 2 that Vygotsky [1977] argues that the child's learning process is guided by interaction with adults or more advanced peers.) When Harris and Hamidullah (1993) asked mothers to teach their 4-year-olds to remember different things (like the names of four cartoon characters or the location of animals in a zoo), the mothers spontaneously used strategies. The most common strategy used was rehearsal (repeating and having children repeat). In addition, many mothers combined these verbal rehearsal strategies with nonverbal strategies such as pointing out cues (like spots on the cartoon dog whose name was "Spotty the Dog").

Ornstein, Baker-Ward, and Naus (1988) describe five stages in the early development of memory strategies:

- *Stage 1.* In the beginning, the infant doesn't deliberately use strategies to remember.

- *Stage 2.* The preschooler may occasionally use primitive strategies, but these don't always result in memory improvement.

- *Stage 3.* In the early elementary school years, children use somewhat more effective strategies, but are often distracted by irrelevant information.

- *Stage 4.* Later, strategies become increasingly effective and are applied in a variety of settings.

- *Stage 5.* Finally, as a result of repeated practice with memory strategies, their use becomes habitual and automatic.

In summary, preschoolers are clearly able to remember. But in most cases, memory results not from the deliberate use of memory strategies, but from incidental mnemonics—for example, paying attention to something or being exposed to it more than once. In contrast, the elementary school child often deliberately uses memory strategies.

One of the important differences between the older memorizer and the preschooler is that older children have acquired some understanding of the processes involved in learning and remembering. They have developed intuitive notions of themselves as information processors, capable of applying strategies and of monitoring and changing them as required. In the current jargon, they have developed some of the skills involved in **metamemory** (defined as the knowledge that children have about the processes involved in remembering). (More about the memories of older children in Chapter 9.)

TABLE 7.3

Piaget's Stages of Cognitive Development

Stage	Approximate Age	Some Major Characteristics
Sensorimotor	0–2 years	Motoric intelligence World of the here and now No language, no thought in early stages No notion of objective reality

Preoperational*
    Preconceptual
    Intuitive
	2–7 years
	2–4 years
	4–7 years
		Egocentric thought
		Reason dominated by perception
		Intuitive rather than logical solutions
		Inability to conserve

Concrete operations†	7 to 11–12 years	Ability to conserve Logic of classes and relations Understanding of number Thinking bound to concrete Development of reversibility in thought
Formal operations‡	11–12 to 14–15 years	Complete generality of thought Propositional thinking Ability to deal with the hypothetical Development of strong idealism

* Discussed in Chapter 7.

† Discussed in Chapter 9.

‡ Discussed in Chapter 11.

PIAGET'S VIEW

The infant's intelligence, as we saw in Chapter 5, is a *sensorimotor intelligence:* It involves immediate sensation and perception. The intelligence of the preschooler is more conceptual, more symbolic. It is, in Piaget's term, **preoperational**.

An **operation** is a thought characterized by some specific logical properties—a logical thought. When DeVon believes he has more gum when he rolls it into a fat ball and less when he spreads it out like a thin pancake on his sister's pillow, he is demonstrating *preoperational* (or prelogical) thinking. His thinking is not yet characterized by **reversibility**. That is, he doesn't yet understand either the possibility or the implications of *undoing* an action mentally.

Piaget divides the preoperational period (ages 2 to about 7 years) into two subperiods: The first, lasting from 2 to 4, is termed **preconceptual**; the second, from 4 to 7, is called **intuitive** (Table 7.3).

Preconceptual Thinking

Toward the end of the second year, and especially with the advent of language, infants begin to symbolize. Now they can represent their actions mentally and anticipate consequences before the action actually occurs. Also, they have begun to develop some understanding of causes—of actions as means to ends.

Preconcepts

As children begin to symbolize they develop the ability to internalize objects and events in the environment and to relate them by their common properties. Thus they develop **concepts.** But these concepts are not as complete and logical as an adult's; they are **preconcepts.** Preconcepts enable the child to make simple classifications necessary for identifying things. Thus children recognize a man because they have a building concept that tells them that a *man* is whatever walks on two legs, has hair, wears pants, and speaks in a gruff voice. By noting their characteristics, children can identify dogs, birds, elephants, and houses. What they frequently cannot do, however, is distinguish among different individuals belonging to the same species. Piaget (1951) illustrates this with his son, Laurent, who pointed out a snail to his father as they were walking. Several minutes later they came upon another snail, and the child exclaimed that here again was *the* snail. The child's failure to recognize that similar objects can belong to the same class and still be different objects—that is, they can retain an identity of their own—is an example of a preconcept. A related example is the preschooler who steadfastly continues to believe in Santa Claus, even after seeing 10 different Santas on the same day. For the child they are all identical.

There are two other striking features of the child's reasoning processes during the preconceptual period, evident in *transductive reasoning* and *syncretic reasoning*.

Transductive Reasoning

There are two main types of logical reasoning: *deduction* and *induction*. To *deduce* is to go from the general to the particular. For example, from my knowledge that mammals give birth to live young, I might deduce that a specific mammal such as a three-toed sloth gives birth to tiny live sloths. In contrast, to induce is to go from specific examples to a broader generalization. After observing a number of barn swallows build nests of a mixture of mud and a cementlike type of saliva, I might generalize that all barn swallows build similar nests.

Transductive reasoning goes not from general to particular or particular to general, but makes inferences from one particular to another—that is, from one instance to another, often based on superficial similarities. It is very much like inductive reasoning except that it is based on a single case rather than many. If I find that one red-headed person has a particularly charming personality, I might transduce that all red-headed persons will also be charm-

The preschooler's logic, says Piaget, is less than perfect: it tends to be intuitive and egocentric, and it relies on perception more than on reason. Still, it represents enormous advances over the infant's primitive understanding. Although this preschooler still suspects little about the logic that governs things like conservation of substances like sand, he has developed highly useful and completely adequate notions of quantity of sand and of ways of getting it from beach to pail—and perhaps eventually onto the floor of his mother's bedroom.

ing. Transductive reasoning can occasionally—and somewhat accidentally—lead to a correct inference; it can also lead to totally incorrect conclusions. Consider the following example:

A flies; B flies; therefore B is A.

Clearly, if A is a bird and B is also a bird, then A is a B and vice versa. If A is a plane and B is a bird, the same reasoning process leads to an incorrect conclusion. Thus it is that a young preschooler can unashamedly insist that cats are dogs and chickens are turkeys.

Syncretic Reasoning

The preschooler's classification behavior reveals **syncretic reasoning** in which different objects are grouped according to the child's limited and frequently changing rules. For example, a 2-year-old child who is placed in front of a table bearing a number of objects of different kinds and

colors and who is asked to group objects that go together might reason something like this: The blue truck goes with the red truck because they both are trucks, and this thing goes with them because it's blue and that truck is blue. Here's a ball and here's a marble and they go together, and here's a crayon that's yellow like the ball so it goes with them too.

The important point is that preschoolers' classification rules change constantly; they see little reason to use the same rule consistently. We adults, whose thinking is not so magical, do not have the same luxury.

Intuitive Thinking

The period of *intuitive thinking* begins at about age 4 and ends at approximately 7. It is termed *intuitive* because although children solve many problems correctly, they do not always do so using logic. During this period their thinking is said to be *intuitive, egocentric, perception-dominated,* and characterized by *classification errors.*

An Example of Intuitive Thinking

In one of Piaget's problems, three balls are shown to a child and then inserted into a hollow cardboard tube so that the child can no longer see them. The balls are blue, red, and yellow. At first when the tube is held vertically, the child knows clearly which ball is on top. Then the tube is turned a half rotation (180 degrees), and the child is asked which ball is now at the top. Alternatively, it may be turned a full rotation, one and one-half turns, two turns, and so on. Piaget found that as long as preschoolers could continue to imagine the position of the balls inside the tube, they could answer correctly. But they could not arrive at a rule about the relationship between odd and even numbers of turns or half turns and the location of the balls. They solved the problem through *intuitive* mental images rather than logical reasoning.

Classification Problems of the Preschooler

To demonstrate the preschooler's problems with *classification,* a Piaget-type problem presents the child with a collection of objects made up of two subclasses—for example, a handful of wooden beads of which 15 are brown and 5 are blue. The child readily admits that all are wooden beads, and the experimenter then divides the beads into the subclasses, brown and blue, and asks whether there are more brown beads or more wooden beads. The trick is obvious, you say? Not to the child at this stage of development. "There's more brown beads," the child replies, as though breaking down a class into its subparts destroys the parent class.

Preschooler Egocentricity

In one Piaget study, a girl doll and a boy doll are placed side by side on a piece of string in plain view of a child. Now the experimenter, holding one end of the string in each hand, steps behind a screen so that the dolls are hidden from the child's view. The child is asked to predict which of the dolls will appear first if the experimenter moves the string toward the right. Let us assume that the boy doll appears first. The experimenter then hides the dolls again and repeats the same question: "Which of the dolls will come out first if they are moved to the same side?" The procedure is repeated several times regardless of whether the child answers correctly. A normally intelligent child will answer correctly for every early trial. What happens in later trials is striking: The child eventually makes the opposite and clearly incorrect prediction! If asked why, one of the more common answers is that it is not fair that the same doll comes out first every time; now it is the other doll's turn. Children inject their own values, their own sense of justice, into the experimental situation, demonstrating their egocentric thought processes. The term **egocentric** is not derogatory but simply points out an excessive reliance on the thinker's individual point of view coupled with a corresponding inability to be objective.

Egocentric thought is also demonstrated by the preschooler's inability to imagine what a mountain looks like when seen from another point of view—for example, the top or bottom or another side. It is apparent too in what Piaget terms *egocentric speech*, the characteristic self-talk of the budding young linguist who repeats words and sounds to himself—much as a young prelingual infant might babble—but using real words.

Reliance on Perception

The preschooler's perception also dominates thinking, as is easily shown in Piaget's **conservation** problems (see Chapter 9). In a typical conservation of mass problem, for example, a child is shown two identical balls of modeling clay and acknowledges that there is the same amount of clay in each. One of the balls is then flattened into a thin pancake, broken into small pieces, rolled into a long snake, or otherwise deformed. The child now believes that the ball of clay that has been altered contains either more or less clay because it *looks* that way. The preoperational child relies on the appearance of the object rather than on any of the logical rules that will later govern thinking (for example, nothing has been added to or taken away from the clay, and so it must still contain an identical amount). Figure 7.9 illustrates simple tasks that can be used to demonstrate some of the important prelogical characteristics of the preschooler's thought processes.

Replications of Piaget's Work

Literally hundreds of studies have been conducted to investigate Piaget's view of the child's progression through stages of cognitive development. With a few exceptions, most have found that the sequence described by Piaget is valid, not only in European and North American countries, but in many other parts of the world as well. However, some evidence shows that Piaget's estimates of the ages of attainment are, in effect, *underestimates* for some North American and European children on specific tasks. One type of study that illustrates this point concerns Piaget's "mountain" problems.

In the original study, children observed three mountains of unequal height set on top of a table. They were allowed to walk around the display, becoming familiar with all sides of the mountains. Later they sat on one side of the table, a doll was placed on the other side, and they were asked to select photographs representing the doll's point of view. Piaget found that children in the preoperational period usually indicated that the doll would see the same things they themselves saw, a finding that he interprets as evidence of egocentricity.

When Piaget's mountain task is made simpler, the child sometimes responds quite differently. Liben (1975) asked preschoolers to describe what a white card would look like from their point of view and from the experimenter's point of view if, for example, the experimenter, but not the children, wore green-tinted glasses. A correct, nonegocentric response in this case would be that the card would look green to the experimenter. Liben found that almost half the 3-year-olds answered correctly, and most of the older children had no difficulty with the questions. Similarly, when Hughes (reported in Donaldson, 1978) presented preschoolers with a situation in which they had to determine whether a "policeman" could see a boy doll from a vantage point quite different from the child's, subjects had little difficulty determining what the policeman's point of view would actually be (Figure 7.10).

Was Piaget Wrong?

Do these studies mean that Piaget's conclusions about the preoperational child's egocentricity are invalid? The answer is no. Donaldson (1978) points out that all these studies present the child with problems that are really very different from the problem of the mountains. The child who can accurately predict whether a policeman can see into an area when the policeman is on the *opposite* side of the table from the child should not be expected to be able to describe what the physical array would look like to the policeman. Among other things, doing so would require that the child be able to reverse left and right (in other words, that the child realize the policeman's left is the child's right)—a task that is sometimes difficult even for adults, as those of us who have occasionally been surprised by our movements in mirrors can testify.

What these and related studies most clearly point out is that egocentricity and other characteristics of children's thinking are far more complex than had been suspected. Indeed, they are far more complex than Piaget himself had suspected, and it is only recently that the neo-Piagetians have begun to explore that complexity. The most striking thing about these recent investigations is their emphasis on what preoperational children *can* rather than what they *cannot* do.

FIGURE 7.9

Tasks and experiments concerned with preoperational thought.

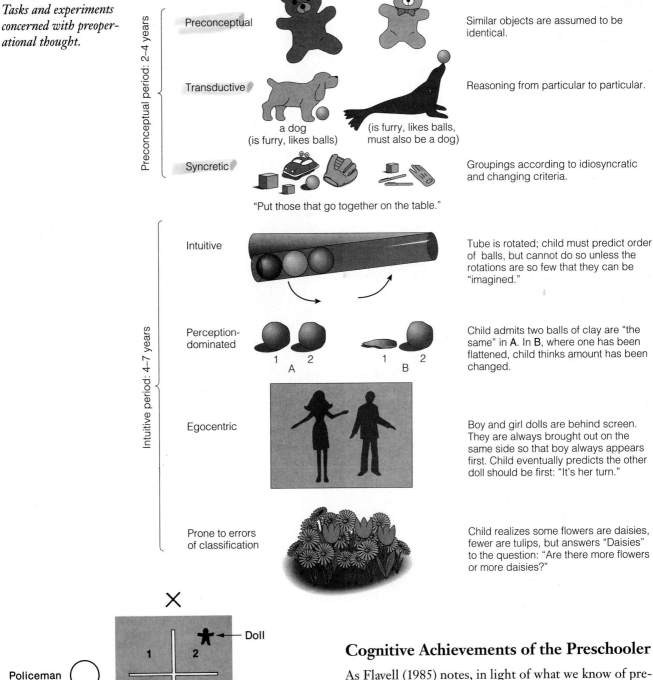

Preconceptual period: 2–4 years

Preconceptual — Similar objects are assumed to be identical.

Transductive — Reasoning from particular to particular.

a dog (is furry, likes balls)

(is furry, likes balls, must also be a dog)

Syncretic — Groupings according to idiosyncratic and changing criteria.

"Put those that go together on the table."

Intuitive period: 4–7 years

Intuitive — Tube is rotated; child must predict order of balls, but cannot do so unless the rotations are so few that they can be "imagined."

Perception-dominated — Child admits two balls of clay are "the same" in **A**. In **B**, where one has been flattened, child thinks amount has been changed.

1 2
A

1 2
B

Egocentric — Boy and girl dolls are behind screen. They are always brought out on the same side so that boy always appears first. Child eventually predicts the other doll should be first: "It's her turn."

Prone to errors of classification — Child realizes some flowers are daisies, fewer are tulips, but answers "Daisies" to the question: "Are there more flowers or more daisies?"

FIGURE 7.10

Arrangement for the Hughes experiment. Subjects had to determine whether a doll hidden in 1, 2, 3, or 4 could be seen by the policeman. In a later part of the experiment, a second policeman was placed at X. The child now had to decide where the doll would have to be hidden so as not to be seen by either policeman. Preschoolers had little trouble answering correctly.

X

Doll

Policeman

1 2
3 4

Subject

Cognitive Achievements of the Preschooler

As Flavell (1985) notes, in light of what we know of preschoolers' cognitive achievement, it is inappropriate and misleading to think of them as *pre*operational or *pre*conceptual. For example, there have been monumental advances in the child's ability to represent the world symbolically, highly evident in the use of language. Thus, when Smith (1979) asked 4-year-olds questions of the type "A basenji is a kind of dog but not a poodle. Is a basenji an animal?" many answered correctly. Similarly, many had no difficulty with questions of the form, "An abalone is a kind of food but not a plant. Is an abalone a vegetable?" These are class-inclusion questions; they require knowledge of class membership (animals include dogs; nonplants are not included among vegetables). They depend on the child's ability to reason by relating concepts. In addition, children's ability to classify and their understanding of number is quite phenomenal.

Number Concepts

There are few preschoolers who cannot count objects and who do not understand that six jellybeans is more than four. Indeed, most will tell you without prompting that six is exactly two more than four or that if you had six jellybeans to begin with and your little brother ate four of them, you would have only two left. Children *invent* their own solutions for problems of this kind, claims Aubrey (1993). As a result, they come to school with a wide range of competencies, not all of which are taken into account by the school curriculum.

Gelman (1982; Gelman & Gallistel, 1978) identifies the rather remarkable sorts of knowledge that underlie the preschooler's understanding of number. First there are *number abstraction skills* that give the child an understanding of *numerosity*—of how many things there are in a collection of, say, snails in one's pockets. Second, there are *numerical reasoning principles* that allow the child to reason about or predict the outcome of certain simple numerical operations, such as adding to or taking from. And finally, there are the principles that allow children to *count*. We adults take these principles completely for granted although they are remarkably complex and wonderfully logical. And, amazingly, the preschooler discovers and uses them without anyone needing to actually teach them.

To some extent, psychology's preoccupation with what preschool children *cannot* do has often obscured their achievements. Number abstraction and numerical reasoning skills are important and complex cognitive abilities that illustrate dramatically some of these achievements. Also, their language development is nothing short of phenomenal. In short, preschoolers are a tremendous cognitive distance from sensorimotor children.

Can their capabilities be influenced through preschool education? Should they be?

PRESCHOOL EDUCATION

These questions are not without controversy. On one side are those like Elkind (1987), who fears that we push our children so relentlessly toward competence that the hurried child misses much of childhood, or Sigel (1987), who deplores the hothouse atmosphere of many early childhood programs. There are a number of misconceptions about *preschool education*, say Canning and Lyon (1991). One is the assumption that children need to be given experiences not provided in most homes; another is the belief that structured experiences (such as learning to play the violin as a toddler or being taught a second language) will inevitably have a beneficial effect on the child's development in general. This "myth of early experience," write Canning and Lyon, has led us to forget that "the adult's role in

Among the cognitive achievements of the preschooler are remarkable advances in language and in understanding numbers, as well as a budding new ability to classify and to relate concepts. These achievements, notes Piaget, are highly dependent on the child's experiences with real objects—such as, for example, goats.

preschool environments should be to provide appropriate play opportunities and be available to children" (p. 2).

On the other side of the debate are those who reason that preschool children can benefit tremendously from formal academic instruction. Even infants can be—and should be—taught basic reading skills, says Doman (1984). Accordingly, there has been a strong trend toward providing progressively more structured educational programs at the preschool level. This trend, says Rescorla (1991), stems from psychology's emphasis on the importance of early experience, a perception of decline in achievement of North American students relative to other groups (for example, the Japanese), and parents' desire for their children to be the best. It stems, as well, from the observation that in developing countries such as India, children who are exposed to preschool education typically manifest significant intellectual advantages over those who aren't (Pandey, 1991).

There is no simple and clear resolution to this debate—which may be one reason why there are so many different forms of preschool education programs. Some are distinct—that is, they are describable in terms of specific principles and procedures. The majority, however,

In many parts of the world, preschools are rare and elitist. But in North America, they are nearly universal—in spite of ongoing debate about whether their main purpose should be academic preparation or social development.

are highly eclectic. They include kindergartens, nursery schools, preschools, play schools, intervention programs, compensatory education programs, even day-care centers (day care is discussed in Chapter 8). They are found in schools and homes, in church basements and community centers, in parks and shopping malls, in universities and technical schools, even in office buildings. Their offerings are a varied mixture dictated in part by the ages of their charges, the resources available, the wishes of parents, the restrictions and mandates of local laws and regulations, and the inclinations and capabilities of instructors and caregivers.

Preschools are a relatively universal phenomenon in much of the world. In the Philippines, for example, kindergartens are rare. In fact, almost 20 percent of children aged 6 to 11 are not enrolled in school; and one third of all children don't graduate from fourth grade (Tsuchiyama, 1992). Similarly, in Africa as well as in most other developing countries, fewer than 50 percent of all children attend primary schools; many drop out before they finish (Grant, 1993). And in most of the world's poorer countries, only a tiny percentage—those from rich families—have access to preschool education.

But in North America and much of Europe, our children have free (even compulsory) access not only to elementary and high school education, but also to a tremendous assortment of preschools. The following sections present very brief summaries of some forms of preschool education.

Nursery Schools

For many years, *nursery schools* were among the most prevalent form of preschool education. They typically take in very young preschoolers and emphasize social and emotional development. Their principal activities consist of games, dancing, singing, listening to stories, and so on—

many of the functions that are also performed by good day-care facilities. In fact, as Caldwell (1991) points out, so close are the functions of day-care facilities and of nursery schools (and other preschools) that many of today's day-care facilities are equivalent to what were once called "nursery schools" (see Chapter 8 for a discussion of day care). She coins a new term for the function of these day cares: *educare*. (See At a Glance: "Working Mothers and Preschool Children," and Figure 7.11.)

Compensatory Programs

Compensatory preschool programs are designed to make up for initial deficits in children. The best-known and most massive compensatory education program ever undertaken in the United States was **Project Head Start**, which began in 1964, and which was conceived as part of the American war on poverty. The program allocated large amounts of funds to the creation of eight-week summer programs for children from disadvantaged backgrounds. Almost three decades later, the Head Start budget has grown to almost $3 billion, and almost 800,000 preschoolers are enrolled in the program ("Bush Calls for Unprecedented Increase," 1992).

Because of the variety of approaches used in these projects, it has been difficult to assess their effectiveness. Many early studies indicated that children enrolled in Head Start programs continued to be inferior to more advantaged children who had not been exposed to such programs, and critics were quick to conclude that huge amounts of money had been squandered in poorly planned, poorly executed, and basically ineffective programs (for example, Bronfenbrenner, 1977). However, subsequent research has sometimes found quite dramatic improvements resulting from Head Start programs. Previous researchers, say Lee, Brooks-Gunn, and Schnur (1988), often failed to look at initial differences between

WORKING MOTHERS AND PRESCHOOL CHILDREN

In 1991, 53 percent of U.S. children between the ages of 3 and 5 who lived at home with their mothers had mothers who were employed. In fact, more than half of all new mothers go back to work within one year of giving birth (U.S. Bureau of the Census, 1993). The number one reason for going back to work is financial need; career development and personal enjoyment are also important reasons (Volling & Belsky, 1993). Of the more than 11 million U.S. children ages 3 to 5 in day care in 1991, over 6 million were in nursery schools and kindergartens. Only 14 percent of the 5-year-olds were not enrolled in preprimary schools.

FIGURE 7.11

Preprimary school enrollment, 1991, for U.S. children ages 3 to 5. (Adapted from U.S. Bureau of the Census, 1993, p. 156.)

groups exposed to Head Start and comparison groups. When they found that disadvantaged groups were still disadvantaged after the programs, they concluded that the programs had not worked. A study of 969 subjects conducted by Lee and associates found that although Head Start programs did not eliminate the difference between Head Start children and comparison groups, they did reduce it.

Following a review of various studies of Head Start programs, Haskins (1989) concludes that such programs have an immediate, positive impact on children. In addition, many programs also appear to have long-term benefits. Barnett (1993) reports, for example, that 25 years after a compensatory preschool program, the economic benefits to the participants (and the community) were far in excess of the costs of the program. Many of these long-term benefits are evident in "life success measures" such as, for example, reductions in teenage pregnancy, delinquency, unemployment, and reliance on welfare assistance (Barnett, 1992).

Good Compensatory Programs

One of the problems associated with Head Start, claims Zigler (1994), has to do with the types of programs used and especially with their implementation. One of the essential requirements for an effective intervention program seems to be that the *family as a child-rearing unit* be taken into account, and that an attempt be made to provide conditions that will ameliorate a negative home environment (for example, McCartney & Howley, 1992). Accordingly health, nutrition, housing, and employment need to be raised to an adequate level for intervention programs to be effective. And parents need to be involved directly in the program (White, Taylor, & Moss, 1992).

What are the *best* forms of preschool intervention? It depends, of course, on what the goals are. If we measure success in terms of preparation for academic tasks, the most effective forms of intervention are typically highly specific, "model" approaches. These are usually based on identifiable theories and characterized by well-formulated approaches and carefully developed materials. Of hun-

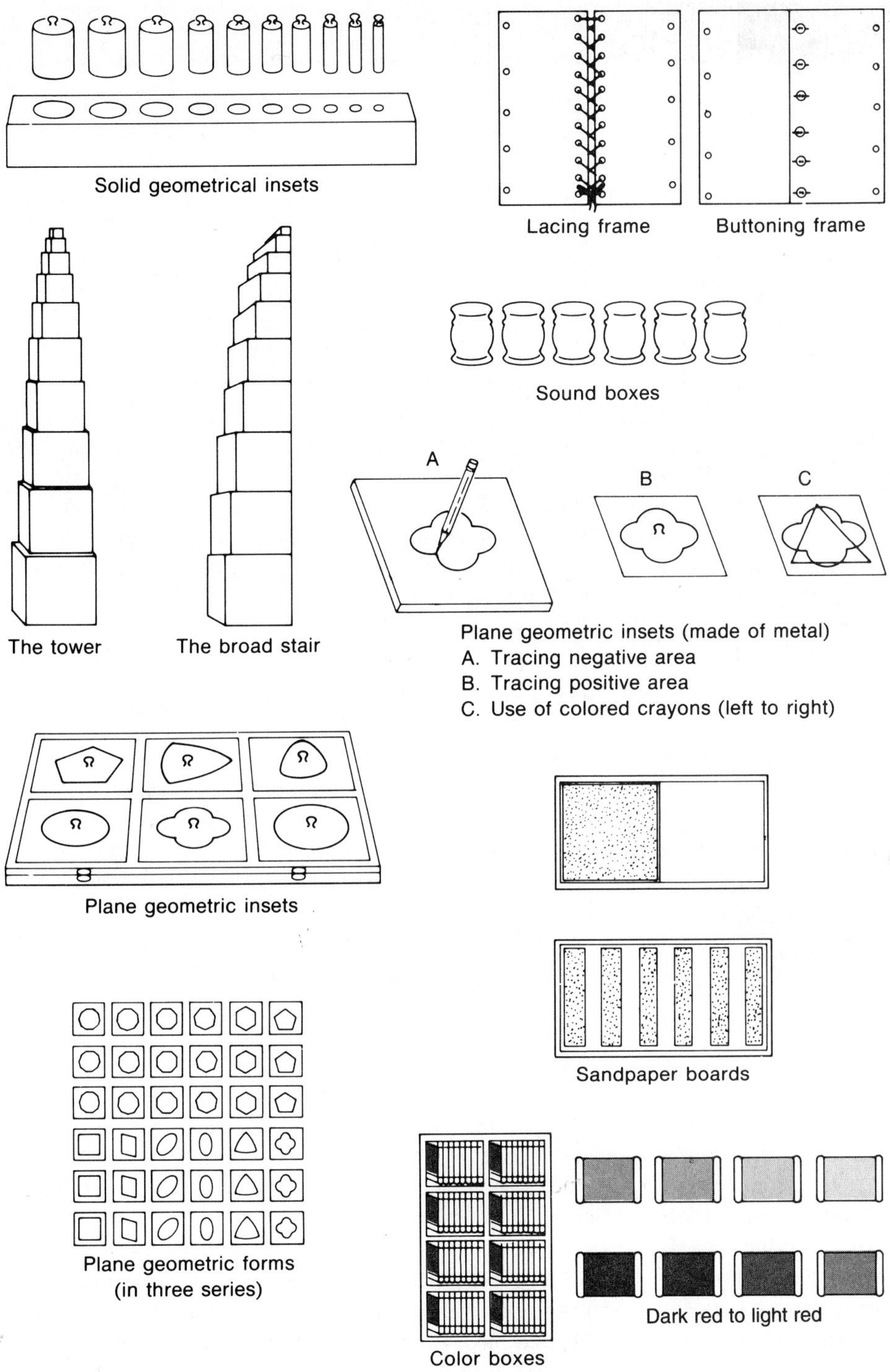

FIGURE 7.12
Some traditional Montessori materials.

Solid geometrical insets

Lacing frame

Buttoning frame

Sound boxes

The tower

The broad stair

Plane geometric insets (made of metal)
A. Tracing negative area
B. Tracing positive area
C. Use of colored crayons (left to right)

Plane geometric insets

Sandpaper boards

Plane geometric forms
(in three series)

Color boxes

Dark red to light red

dreds of different possible examples, one of the better known is the **Montessori method,** which dates back to the turn of the century (Montessori, 1912). It was initially developed for use with mentally retarded children, but has proven highly effective and popular as a general program. Unlike most preschool programs, it is designed for use in elementary and high school as well.

One of the distinctive features of the Montessori approach is the use of specially developed materials for teaching sense discriminations. Montessori believed that all learning stems from sense perception and can therefore be improved by training the senses. Among the best known of her materials are large letters of the alphabet covered with sandpaper, which are used to teach the child to read. The prescribed teaching method requires not only that children look at the letters, but also that they trace the shapes with their fingertips, saying the sound of the letter and getting a tactile sensation of it at the same time. (See Figure 7.12 for examples of some Montessori materials.)

HIROKI'S PRESCHOOL

Hiroki had seemed exceptionally intelligent and creative to some American observers in Komatsudani, a preschool on the east side of Tokyo. When they mentioned this to Fukui-sensei, the teacher, she seemed puzzled. "Hiroki's intelligence is about average," she said, "about the same as most other children." But, the observers protested, he seems gifted. He finishes his work so fast and then he entertains the children with his wonderful songs. No, protested the teacher, speed isn't the same thing as intelligence. "And his entertaining the other children," she added, "is a reflection not so much of intelligence as it is of his great need for attention" (Tobin, Wu, & Davidson, 1989, p. 24).

The teacher's response to individual talents and weaknesses might be one of the important differences between Japanese and North American preschools—a difference evident as well in the nature of the classroom activity. Whereas North American schools tend to emphasize individual activity with some group activities (such as reading), Japanese schools are characterized by far more of what the Early Childhood

Education Association of Japan labels "all-together classroom activity." Thus in Komatsudani, some of the activities on a typical day included an early-morning exercise song, during which children formed a circle and went through a series of group exercises; the end-of-exercise, go-to-your-room song, during which the teacher led the students in a running file to the classroom, each child removing shoes at the doorway; the morning song sung in unison by the children and played on an organ by Fukui-sensei, the teacher; chanted roll call attendance, followed by a group counting song; a workbook project; group lunch; a group rest period, heads on your tables; a major origami (paper-folding) group project; and a teacher-read story using *kami shihai* (a "paper show" in which the story is told in pictures on one side of cards held up by the teacher who simultaneously reads the story written on the backs of the cards) (Tobin et al., 1989).

Another difference between Japanese and North American preschools—a direct result of the greater emphasis on group activities in the Japanese preschool—is their much larger size. Government

---

Evaluations of Montessori programs have generally been quite positive, in spite of the criticism that such programs, given their highly structured nature, might stifle the child's creativity. For example, a study of the long-term effects of preschool programs found that the highest achievers in grades 6, 7, and 8 were males who had been exposed to a preschool Montessori program (Miller & Bizzell, 1983).

Kindergartens

Not long ago, *kindergartens* were usually considered an optional preschool program. Now, a majority of North American children attend kindergartens, most of which are housed in regular schools, funded in the same manner as schools, and staffed by teachers whose certification requirements are the same as those who teach at more advanced levels. In many ways, kindergartens are part of regular school. Many no longer simply prepare the child for the first-grade tasks of learning to read and write and count; they actually engage in the business of teaching these things (if the children don't already know them). One of the big differences between kindergartens and regular schools, in most (but no longer all) jurisdictions, is that kindergarteners can go home at lunch time, and stay there the rest of the afternoon; or they can stay home all morning and go to school only in the afternoon.

But perhaps we are hurrying our children too much, Elkind (1981a) warns. Perhaps we should let them slow down and be children—let them play and dream and do magical things that don't require knowing how to read

and write and count real numbers in perfect sequence. Marcon (1993), for example, reports a study in which children who attended kindergartens whose emphases were mainly social-emotional development fared as well in the long run as did children who attended more academic kindergartens. (In fact, these children were *less* likely to be retained a grade in elementary school!)

Not only are we hurrying our children, says Elkind (1987), but many parents are also *miseducating* them. These are "Gold Medal" parents whose burning ambition is to produce a star basketball or hockey player, a world-class gymnast, a violin prodigy. Or they are "College Degree" parents whose babies are destined for Harvard or MIT. For these parents, children have become symbols of parental ambitions and proof of parental success.

We have to strike a balance, Elkind (1981a) urges, between the spoiled child, who remains a child too long, and the hurried child, who does not remain a child long enough, and whose life might be plagued by "a fear of failure—of not achieving fast enough or high enough" (p. xii). (See Across Cultures: "Hiroki's Preschool.")

LANGUAGE AND THE PRESCHOOLER

Language, defined as *the use of arbitrary sounds with established and accepted referents, either real or abstract, that can be arranged in sequence to convey different meanings*, is still, as far as we know, uniquely human. When psychologist

guidelines suggest that classes should not be larger than 40 students. In one study, average size of preschools was around 34 students (Hinago, 1979).

And a final difference may be that Japanese parents are more demanding than many North American parents. Even at the preschool level, they have begun to measure the accomplishments of their children. One study reports that 71 percent of all children aged 3 to 5 can already boast of some accomplishment (swimming, ballet, gymnastics, calligraphy, violin, and so on); and 100 percent of the 5-years-olds have achieved some accomplishment (Horiuchi, 1979).

To Think About   Ohba (1979) suggests that Japanese society is characterized by a strong "my homeism," a powerful sort of family cohesiveness that finds expression in parents' strong wish that children excel, and in powerful pressures put on children to do so. Elkind (1981a) says the same is true of much of North American society where parents often push their children relentlessly, hurrying them through their childhoods. What do you think?

Language (though not communication) is, as far as we know, a uniquely human phenomenon, the purposes and functions of which are staggeringly important. Even when raised with humans and their children, non-human primates—and teddy bears—do not acquire the ability to speak.

Hayes and his wife tried to teach a chimpanzee to speak, they failed (Hayes & Hayes, 1951). It seems that the chimpanzee's vocal apparatus simply does not lend itself to *speaking* a language.

More recently, Savage-Rumbaugh and associates (1993) raised a child and an ape with the same caregiver, exposing both to the same language environment. When the child was 2 and the ape 8, both were asked to respond to 660 novel sentences. And both did about equally well, indicating that although the ape had not learned to *speak* English, it had learned to *comprehend* it.

Comprehension, most linguists agree, precedes the ability to speak. One of the major differences between apes and humans, in an evolutionary sense, Savage-Rumbaugh and associates speculate, may be that when humans raised themselves up on their hind legs to become bipedal, there followed adjustments in their vocal tract and in the soft palate. These adjustments made the production of speech sounds possible. Thus the capacity to comprehend speech might have existed some millions of years before the capacity to produce it; apes are still at that first stage.

Since the Hayes' attempt to teach a chimpanzee to speak, a succession of researchers have undertaken to teach chimpanzees American Sign Language. Its big advantage is that it does not require chimpanzees (or gorillas) to make sounds, but simply to make gestures. A number of these individuals report what seemed like remarkable success (for example, Fouts, 1987). However, critics insist that none of the chimpanzees in question have actually learned a language. Detailed examinations of videotapes of "sign-speaking" chimpanzees seems to indicate that what they have learned was simply to imitate—to associate a symbol or gesture with food, or to use some movement or gesture to make some demand associated with reinforcement (Terrace, 1985). But the debate is by no means over, and researchers continue to report the development of "communicative" or "conversational" competence among various nonhuman primates (for example Greenfield & Savage-Rumbaugh, 1993).

TABLE 7.4
Stages in Children's Development of Grammar

Stage of Development	Nature of Development	Sample Utterances
1. Prespeech (before age 1)	Crying, cooing, babbling.	"Waaah," "dadadada."
2. Sentencelike word (holophrase) (by 1 year)	The word is combined with nonverbal cues (gestures and inflections).	"Mommy." (meaning: "Would you please come here, mother?")
3. Two-word sentences (duos) (by 1½ years)	Modifiers are joined to topic words to form declarative, question, negative, and imperative structures.	"Pretty baby." (declarative) "Where Daddy?" (question) "No play." (negative) "More milk!" (imperative)
4. Multiple-word sentences (by 2 to 2½ years)	Both a subject and predicate are included in the sentence types. Grammatical morphemes are used to change meanings (*ing* or *ed*, for example).	"She's a pretty baby." (declarative) "Where Daddy is?" (question) "I no can play." (negative) "I want more milk!" (imperative) "I running." "I runned."
5. More complex grammatical changes and word categories (between 2½ and 4 years)	Elements are added, embedded, and permuted within sentences. Word classes (nouns, verbs, and prepositions) are subdivided. Clauses are put together.	"Read it, my book." (conjunction) "Where is Daddy?" (embedding) "I can't play." (permutation) "I would like *some* milk." (use of "some" with mass noun) "Take me *to* the store." (use of preposition of place)
6. Adultlike structures (after 4 years)	Complex structural distinctions made, as with "ask-tell" and "promise."	"Ask what time it is." "He promised to help her."

SOURCE: Based in part on Barbara S. Wood, *Children and Communication: Verbal and Nonverbal Language Development* (2nd ed.), p. 142 © 1981. Reprinted by permission of Prentice-Hall, Inc., Englewood Cliffs, New Jersey.

Language Development in Infancy

Infants, unlike nonhuman primates, seem remarkably well prepared to learn language—as we saw in the Chapter 5 discussion of the first three stages of language development (see Table 7.4). Thus, in the first short year of life (the prespeech stage), there is a dramatic transition from crying, gurgling, cooing, and babbling to the utterance of meaningful speech sounds. At around 1, the sentencelike word appears, accompanied by a repertoire of gestures, cries, and inflections that serve to communicate meaning. And by the age of 18 months, the infant readily uses two-word sentences (*duos*). Increasing language sophistication now makes it possible for the infant to combine words with different modifiers to ask questions, make declarations, express denial, or issue commands. The story continues here with a discussion of the remaining three stages.

Multiple-Word Sentences

At around age 2½, children move from two-word combinations to multiple-word sentences. "Allgone" becomes "Banana is gone" and eventually "The banana is gone" or "My banana is gone."

Although the child's speech continues to be somewhat telegraphic, children now make increasing use of *morphemes* to express meaning (Brown, 1973). Recall that these are the smallest units of meaning in language. They include all words, as well as grammatical endings such as

ed and *ing*, suffixes, prefixes, articles, and so on. The use of grammatical morphemes, for example, is what allows the child to transform the verbs *go* to *going*, *jump* to *jumped*, *eat* to *eated*, and *do* to *doed*.

Morphemes in the English language tend to be acquired in about the same order both by children who develop normally and by those who experience delays in language development (Paul & Alforde, 1993).

As children learn to combine words in longer expressions and to use a greater variety of morphemes to change meanings, they often become highly inventive in their use of language. Examples of inventiveness are found in the words they create as they reinvent the grammatical rules of their language and discover the meanings of its many morphemes. "Daddy unpickmeup," insisted my youngest linguist, squirming to be put down. "You already feeded me." Similarly, his 3-something-year-old sister, having learned that "pitch black" was very black, insisted that other things can be "pitch clean," "pitch empty," or "pitch big."

More Complex Changes

The power of the child's language takes a bound with the development of the ability to make meaningful transformations using *conjunction*, *embedding*, and *permutation* (Wood, 1981)—a development that occurs between the ages of 2½ and 3 or 4. Simple conjunction is illustrated by the addition or combination of two sentences. "Where?" and "We go" now becomes "Where we go?" Embedding is inserting. For example, the word *no* may be embedded in the sentence "I eat" to form a sentence with the opposite meaning: "I no eat." Permutation involves changing word order to change meaning. At first, children use intonation instead of permutation. For example, the sentence "I can go" may be a simple declaration when the "I" or the "can" is emphasized but becomes a question when "go" is emphasized. A simple permutation from "I can go" to "Can I go?" achieves the same meaning with much less ambiguity.

As children begin to show an understanding of various adult-accepted rules for transforming sentences, they also behave as though they had an implicit understanding of the grammatical function of various words and phrases. They now use nouns as nouns and not as verbs; adjectives are no longer treated as verbs; and nouns are further categorized as plural or singular. Evidence of children's understanding of this type of categorization is evident in their appropriate use of verbs and of such determiners as *that*, *the*, *those*, and *these*. For example, the child will now say "That box is empty"; an earlier error might have taken the form of "This boxes is empty."

Adultlike Structures

The further refinement and elaboration of speech requires mastery of countless subtle and intricate grammatical rules that we all use unconsciously. Some of these rules govern the arrangement of words in meaningful expressions; they specify what is (and is not) grammatically acceptable and meaningful. They tell us that "the fat mosquito" is a correctly structured phrase, but "Fat the mosquito" is not (although "Fat, the mosquito" might be). Other rules permit us to transform phrases or to combine them to create a variety of meaningful statements. Thus, there are rules that allow us to transform a passive sentence into an active one ("The dog was bitten by the man" to "The man bit the dog") or a negative to a positive ("I did not go" to "I went"). Much of this learning occurs in the first elementary grades.

EXPLANATIONS OF LANGUAGE DEVELOPMENT

Each of us uses language as if we had a relatively complete understanding of a tremendous range of grammatical rules. Yet, unless we are taught these rules formally, we can't explain them. In fact, linguists have not yet been able to work out a complete set of consistent and valid rules even for a single language.

The remarkable thing is that, in an amazingly short time, young children acquire a working knowledge of a very complex system of rules. How?

There are two principal classes of explanations for the development of language. One emphasizes the role of experience (learning); the other emphasizes the importance of biology (hereditary predispositions). Current evidence suggests that biology and experience are both important but that each, by itself, does not present an entirely adequate explanation.

The Role of Biology

Some, like Chomsky, believe that language is innate, that our brains have evolved in such a way as to make language development not only possible but almost inevitable. Rymer (1993) quotes Chomsky in an interview: "If you were to put prelinguistic children on an island, the chances are good that their language facility would soon produce a language. Maybe not in the first generation. And that when they did so, it would resemble the languages we know. You can't do the experiment because you can't subject a child to that experience" (p. 38). (However, Genie's experience *is* that experiment—a *natural* experiment—as we see below).

Others, like Piaget, argue that language arises mainly from interactions with the environment and results from the infant's being able to *abstract* and *represent* sensorimotor schemata. Piattelli-Palmarini (1994), following an extensive analysis of a debate that took place between Piaget and Chomsky in 1975, gives the nod to Chomsky. The evidence, Piattelli-Palmarini argues, strongly suggests that the human brain is "language specific"—that it is prewired for language. Furthermore Chomsky's theory of language development (and that of Lenneberg, 1969) is *critical period-based*. It argues that the critical period for learning language is before age 5 and that, almost invariably, language learning is pretty well complete by puberty.

The Evidence for Biology

There are several observations that support the hypothesis of a strong biological influence on language learning. For example, there is the fact that the earliest speech sounds of infants from very different backgrounds—even those of children whose parents are deaf—are highly similar. There is also the ease and and astounding rapidity with which children learn language, in a sense reinventing the grammar of the language as they learn, and making only a fraction of the mistakes they might be expected to make if they were learning primarily through reinforcement, imitation, and trial and error. Finally, there is the observation that many of the mistakes children do make are not imitative but appear to result from the overapplication of rules that are themselves correct.

These observations have given rise to a number of biological theories to explain language learning, the best known of which is Chomsky's (1957; 1965) theory of a **language acquisition device** (or LAD). Simplified, it attempts to account for the infant's apparent predisposition for acquiring language by assuming that we are born with some special language-learning capacity. Children behave as though they were prewired for grammar, says Chomsky. How else are we to explain the fact that they make so few errors while learning syntax?

In effect, LAD is more a metaphor than an explanation. As a metaphor, it says that infants behave *as if* they already have at their command a range of cognitive skills, of language-related predispositions. And from this observation, we might infer that there must be some innate neurological prewiring at birth. But as Rice (1989) observes, this is not a completely satisfactory explanation of how these things work. Metaphors are not machines; they are simply comparisons.

Genie's Story

Genie's story, described briefly in Chapter 3, provides another line of evidence for the Chomsky biological and critical period hypothesis. Recall that Genie was abandoned from the age of 20 months until almost 14 years. When she surfaced, she made few sounds other than a peculiar laugh. For example, when angry, she wouldn't yell or scream; instead, she would scratch or gouge her face, urinate, smear mucus on herself, or blow her nose loudly into her clothes—or all of these. Rymer speculates that because she had been prevented from making noise by her father, she had learned to turn her emotions inward. When she really needed to make a noise, she would use other things to do so like dragging a chair, banging objects, or scratching her nails on a balloon.

At first, Genie's vocabulary seemed to be increasing relatively rapidly. She would often drag people around pointing at things and asking that they be named. But, at least for the first year, her expressions remained limited to short, largely incoherent verbalizations. But a year and a half after being "found," Genie would only rarely put two words together, and almost never three. And, unlike normal children, who, after they reach the two-word-sentence stage, typically experience an explosion of rapid language learning, Genie continued to plod along. Even four years later, the kinds of sentences she would build when pushed to do so included confused combinations like "Where is may I have a penny?" or "I where is graham cracker on top shelf?" She continued to have no understanding of personal pronouns, totally confusing *I*, *me*, and *you*, never quite able to figure out who she was and who was somebody else. Nor did she ever learn to respond to "hello" with "hello," or even to understand the meaning of "thank you."

Scans of activity in Genie's brain subsequently showed that her left hemisphere remained virtually unresponsive to language (it's normally centrally involved in language functions). This is additional evidence that early experience may be essential for organizing the brain in the first place—during a critical period.

At the time of Rymer's writing, Genie had apparently regressed to a largely nonverbal existence and lived in a home for retarded adults. In the last photos Rymer saw of

her, Genie was 29, a large, bumbling person with an expression of "cowlike incomprehension" on her face, an inmate of an asylum, totally withdrawn from the world.

In support of Chomsky's theory, Curtiss (1977) writes, "Language grows like an organ. When it comes to physical growth, no one asks why—why do arms grow? Learning a language is like learning to walk, a biological imperative timed to a certain point in development. It's not an emotional process" (p. 205).

The Role of Early Experience

In spite of the role of biology in language learning, there is little doubt that there is an overwhelming amount of learning involved in making the transition from the first meaningful sound to the fluent conversations of the 6-year-old. Yet most children accomplish this learning apparently effortlessly and in much the same sequence across different cultures. Strangely, however, adults who are initially without language (because of isolation, for example) do not fare as well—as Genie's story illustrates. Similarly, adult learners who try to acquire a second language usually experience more difficulty doing so than do young children; and even if they are successful, their pronunciation will typically be characterized by a variety of errors that would not be found among those who learned the language at a younger age. There appears to be a sensitive period early in life when learning one or more languages will be easiest.

Parents as Teachers

That children acquire the speech patterns, idioms, accents, and other language characteristics of those around them makes it clear that learning is centrally involved in language acquisition. Parents and other caregivers play an important role as language models: They provide the child with models of correct language as well as of the subtle rules governing conversations and the communication of messages. In addition, parents also serve as important dispensers of reinforcement for the child's verbalizations.

In Chapter 5 we spoke of the bidirectionality of parent–child influence, noting that what a caregiver does influences the infant and, no less true, what the infant does influences the caregiver. We see evidence of bidirectionality of influence in the development of language as well. The infant's level of language comprehension and use appears to have subtle but marked effects on the behavior of parents. Bruner (1978) refers to a fine-tuning theory of mother–infant interaction—"mother" because she is more often the principal caregiver than is the father. Virtually all mothers, he notes, alter their speech patterns according to the understanding of their children. It is as though the mother becomes a teacher, not because she consciously intends to be, but because she "fine-tunes" her responses and behaviors to the immediate demands of her child. Furthermore, there is a consistency and regularity in the mother's altered speech patterns. One mother typically employed four sequential types of statements when "reading" to her young son. First she would say "Look": an attention-getting utterance. Next she would pose a standard question—"What is that?"—pause, and provide a label: "It's an X." Finally, following the child's response, she would say, "That's right." Additional evidence of fine-tuning occurred whenever the child responded earlier in the sequence. If, for example, he said "Truck" as the page turned, the mother would go immediately to her final response: "That's right."

Child-Directed Language (Motherese)

In later stages of language development, the role of the mother as sensitive, fine-tuned teacher becomes even more apparent. The language mothers employ when talking to their children—sometimes called *motherese* (or *child-directed language*)—is quite different from what they would normally use when speaking with adults. Motherese is a good example of pragmatics in language; the mother adjusts her speech to the requirements of the situation. Thus, mothers tend to use simpler, shorter, and more repetitive utterances. In other words, they *reduce* (by simplifying and repeating). On other occasions, mothers *expand* the child's expressions. A child might say, "Daddy gone," to which the mother might reply, "Yes, Daddy is gone." Moerk (1991) points out that most expansions are corrections, and that corrections of this kind are especially important in early language learning.

Studies of motherese in different languages have typically found that the most important features of mother-to-infant speech appear to be universal. For example, Grieser and Kuhl (1988) found this to be true even in a language such as Mandarin Chinese, which is very different from English in that it is *tonal* (inflection and intonation are far more meaningful). Mothers' speech in Mandarin Chinese also tends to be grammatically and semantically simpler, and pitched at a higher frequency.

There are other, perhaps more subtle, ways in which the speech of the mother (or other caregivers, as well as siblings) is influenced by the presence of infants. Thus typical caregiver speech is simpler, higher pitched, characterized by exaggerated intonation, made up of shorter sentences, and consists of a higher than normal percentage of questions. In addition, the speech of caregivers vis-à-vis their infants is almost always centered on the present and only seldom on the past or future, almost as though they knew, with Piaget, that the young infant's world is a world of the here and now. Accordingly, we would expect that most of the child's first words would deal with things that are immediate, directly perceivable, and important to the child—an expectation that is confirmed by research (Rice, 1989).

Some children are fast language learners; others are much slower. For example, one study found a difference

When interacting with their infants, parents unconsciously tend to use shorter, grammatically simpler, higher-pitched, present-tense expressions. They also ask more questions and name more objects and actions. This child-directed speech, also called motherese, *contributes to child language-learning.*

of 30 months between the fastest and the slowest learners among a sample of 128 3½-year-olds (Wells, 1985). One of the differences between the fastest and the slowest learners may be the extent and quality of the motherese to which they are exposed. Hampson and Nelson (1993) videotaped a sample of 45 toddlers and analyzed their speech and that of their mothers. They found that the mothers of the most linguistically advanced children used a higher percentage of object names in their speech—and fewer commands. Also, Pelaez-Nogueras and Gewirtz (1993) report that motherese that imitates infant's vocalizations appears to reinforce them.

In summary, there is growing evidence that the mother (or father) plays a crucial role in the development of language and that this role goes well beyond providing a suitable model of the family's language. Unconsciously, parents modify their speech and become teachers—perhaps far better teachers than they could possibly be trained to be.

The preschooler's memory is not as impressive as yours or mine; they don't yet recognize the power of strategies like organizing or elaborating or rehearsing. But, remarkably, if you ask this bespectacled young scholar either "¿Como te llamas?" or "What's your name?" he will answer without hesitation, and correctly. And if he is exposed to two language environments throughout the preschool years, by the time he is 6 he will have learned a second language far more competently than would most adults over the same period of time.

A CHANGING LANGUAGE CONTEXT

In 1982, almost 75 percent of schoolchildren in the United States were white; about 10 percent were Hispanic; and the remainder included a varied mixture of ethnic groups. Now, in California, the "minority" has become the "majority," notes Garcia (1993): 52 percent of students currently belong to "minority" categories. Projections are that by 2020, 70 percent of beginning first-grade students will belong to nonwhite groups, and the percentage of white school-age Americans will have dropped to about 50 percent while the Hispanic group will have increased to around 25 percent. The remainder will be African Americans (about 16.5 percent) and other races (Pallas, Natriello, & McDill, 1989). (See At a Glance: "Changing Demographics" and Figure 7.13.) The educational implications of these changes are considerable. In 1982, most schoolchildren spoke English—the dominant, standard, majority language. Now more than

15 percent speak a different language at home; and in over half of all cases, that language is Spanish (U.S. Bureau of the Census, 1994).

Different Views of Bilingualism

There are two views with respect to the psychological effects of bilingualism. One maintains that there is a limited amount of cognitive space available for language and that learning two or more languages places such a strain on cognitive capacity that the individual suffers. According to this view, the second language competes with the first, and, in the end, the individual is not as proficient in either language as the monolingual individual. This competitive view is based in part on early studies of bilingualism, which often concluded that bilingual children were handicapped. Not only did they perform less well on measures of ability (such as intelligence tests), but they also tended to do less well in either language.

The second view maintains that there is no competition among languages and no clear limitation of cognitive resources necessary for language learning. This view is based on research that indicates that "all other things being equal, higher degrees of bilingualism are associated with higher levels of cognitive attainment" (Hakuta & Garcia, 1989, p. 375).

Subtractive bilingualism is the term coined by Lambert (1975) to describe the negative influence of a second language. **Additive bilingualism** describes situations in which learning a second language has a positive influence on the first. And **transitional bilingualism** describes a common situation in which the dominant language replaces the minority language within a few generations.

Transitional Bilingualism

For most children whose early environment includes two languages, learning a second language does not appear to be much more complicated than learning to ride a bicycle. In the end, however, for most individuals there is a dominant or preferred language. Few individuals become what Diaz (1983) calls *balanced bilinguals*—people who are equally fluent and comfortable in both languages. That, suggests Moffatt (1991), may be because most children learn languages *sequentially* rather than simultaneously; and rarely are the two languages equally valued in the society. This may be especially true in North American societies where the dominant language is highly reinforced, but second languages often are not. As Pease-Alvarez and Hakuta (1992) put it, "Don't worry about English; they are all learning it; instead, if you are going to worry, worry about the lost potential in the attrition of the second language" (p. 5). In fact, note Hakuta and D'Andrea (1992), in many instances the bilingualism that has characterized parts of North America has been purely "transitional": Within three or four generations, the native language is completely replaced by the dominant English language.

CHANGING DEMOGRAPHICS

As recently as 1980 in the United States, the dominant language was standard English and about three quarters of all schoolchildren were white. But in some states like California, more than half of current schoolchildren have a language other than English as their first language. That percentage is expected to reach 70 within two decades—at which time it is expected that fewer than half of all schoolchildren in major urban schools throughout the United States will speak English as a first language. This will have important implications for education.

Part of the reason for these changing demographics is smaller family size among white groups (in 1992, 3.18 for white married couples, 3.62 for African Americans, and 4.02 for Hispanics.) In addition, net immigration rates continue to be much higher for nonwhite races. Projections are that by the year 2050, the percentage of the U.S. population that is white will have decreased by about one third; the Hispanic portion will have more than doubled (U.S. Bureau of the Census, 1993).

FIGURE 7.13

Rate of annual population growth from natural increases and immigration for three U.S. groups, 1989. (Adapted from U.S. Bureau of the Census, 1992, p. 14.)

Subtractive Bilingualism

Research indicates that for some minority group children, whose first language is a minority language, learning a second language may be a subtractive experience (Cummins & Swain, 1986).

Learning a second language for children who are members of a distinct minority group (such as the French-speaking in Canada and the Spanish-speaking in the United States) may be *subtractive* in the sense that they become progressively less functional and fluent in their first language as their language skills improve in the second (Pease-Alvarez & Hakuta, 1992). This does not happen because learning the second language actually interferes with learning or remembering the first, but for one of several other reasons. One is that the majority language (the second language in this case) is usually the dominant language in the media and in the community. As a result, the minority language receives little support and reinforcement outside the home. Consequently, it tends to be used in less-valued social roles and milieus.

A second explanation for the occasionally negative (subtractive) effect of learning the dominant language as a second language is that use of the minority language in the home is sometimes discouraged by parents or by the children themselves.

And third, the minority language employed in the home is sometimes not a very good model of that language. It is often characterized by idiom and colloquialism, by vocabulary impoverishment, by improper grammar, and by idiosyncratic pronunciation. And if it is not part of the children's schooling, they are unlikely to read or write in it. Thus they may develop a relatively high level of oral proficiency in the minority language while developing little competency in reading or writing it. For all of these reasons, competence in the minority language suffers; and the bilingual experience becomes subtractive.

Additive Bilingualism

However, learning a second language for children whose first language is the majority language appears to be largely an *additive* experience. Such is the case, for example, for many English-speaking children enrolled in French immersion programs in Canada and in Spanish immersion programs in the United States. The evidence seems clear that these programs can be very successful in developing linguistic skills, as well as in contributing to general academic achievement (Garcia, 1993). Although most students who go through immersion schooling don't develop as high a level of proficiency as native speakers, their language deficiencies don't seem to interfere with their use of the second language. In addition, these students typically achieve at least as well as comparable students in conventional English programs in academic subjects and on measures of social and cognitive development.

Which View Is Correct?

Do languages compete so that learning two or more languages is a subtractive experience? Or does learning a second language have a generally positive influence?

The answer is that although one language may suffer as a second is being learned, it is not because of competition between the two, but more often because of social conditions that reduce the value of one language and that provide a poor model of the language or even actively discourage its use. The current view is that a second language does *not* interfere with the first; in fact, level of proficiency and rate of learning of the second language is closely related to proficiency in the first (Hakuta & Garcia, 1989). It's important to note, too, that the higher the level of proficiency in the second language, the more likely that there will be cognitive benefits rather than deficits (Ricciardelli, 1992).

There has been a staggering amount of research on the effects of bilingual programs, says Cziko (1992). But the conclusions are neither clear nor simple. One of the problems, as Lam (1992) notes, is that some programs are exemplary, and others are not; some teachers are more effective than others; some students learn more easily.

Under the right circumstances, argue Cummins and Swain (1986), bilingual programs can be a positive experience both for minority and majority group children. Not only does a good bilingual program develop functional proficiency in a second language, but it can also strengthen the first language. Immersion programs are likely to provide an additive experience for children whose first language is the majority language, and who already have a high level of proficiency in their native language. However, for minority-group children, instruction should occur primarily in the minority language, and the majority language should be learned as a second language. French minority group children whose schooling is primarily in French, with English as a second language, not only maintain and improve their French far more than those schooled primarily in English, but they also perform as well in English (Cummins, 1986).

Bilingualism in Today's Schools

From the very beginning, North American societies have been multilingual and multicultural—although education has more often been unilingual. This has often posed problems for students and teachers—problems that, Brisk (1991) notes, were traditionally viewed as problems with *students* rather than with the educational system. As a result, in most cases schools accepted no responsibility for any problems a minority-language child might experience. Teachers simply assumed that the problem would rectify itself with exposure to traditional schooling. If it didn't . . . well, too bad, students would simply have to fail.

The current emphasis in education is for schools to accept responsibility for problems related to minority languages. A common educational response is to establish bilingual or English as a second language (ESL) programs. The main purpose of these programs, says Brisk, has been to prepare students to fit into the traditional, English-only school curriculum.

Brisk (1991) argues that as our societies become increasingly multilingual and multicultural, schools must become more responsive to the needs of students. What schools should be focused toward, say Collett and Serrano (1992), is becoming truly *inclusive*—that is, truly multicultural. Schools should not simply admit students from different backgrounds and then try to make them all the same by preparing them to fit into a traditional English-only curriculum. Serafini (1991) argues that recognizing and encouraging diversity in schools, and valuing competence in more languages than simply English, may do much to reduce racism.

The Other Side

It would be astounding were we all to agree. We don't. In the United States, powerful, well-funded, and highly vocal groups of *English Only* advocates argue that English should be designated the official language—as it has been in at least 18 states (Padilla, 1991). Many English Only (or *English First*, or *U.S. English*) members are strongly opposed to publicly funded bilingual education. In contrast, groups such as *English Plus* advocate expanding bilingual programs both for adults and for children.

The debate is tense, notes McGroarty (1992), even though in the United States bilingual education is mandated by law. U.S. courts have ruled that putting all children in English classrooms regardless of their language and cultural background does not amount to treating all children equally. In Canada, right to instruction in both official languages is guaranteed in some provinces but not others. Most notably, Quebec's Bill 101 tends to entrench the use of French only in all public sectors in the province of Quebec (Padilla, 1991).

SPEECH AND LANGUAGE PROBLEMS

We assume that by the time children reach school age, their language skills will be sufficient for them to understand and follow instructions, express interests and wants, tell stories, ask questions, carry on conversations—in short, communicate. Sadly, that is not always the case.

There are a number of different language and *speech problems*, each of which can vary tremendously in seriousness. At one extreme are children who, because of severe mental retardation, neurological damage or disease, mental disorders such as autism, or deafness, are essentially nonverbal. Their communication might consist of a few gestures or signs.

There are others whose speech is largely incomprehensible, sometimes because conceptual development is so poor that thought sequences seem illogical and speech becomes largely nonsensical, and sometimes because of speech production problems like those reflected in poor articulation, voice control problems, and stuttering.

And there are those whose language development is less advanced that normal, perhaps because of mild mental retardation or because of a learning disability reflected in language deficits. The predominant view is that these children don't learn different language forms or acquire language differently; their skills simply develop more slowly. Some of these children are of normal or above-normal intelligence and have no deficits other than their problems with language. However, because of our schools' predominantly verbal teaching and testing methods, many of these children are viewed as intellectually handicapped, and their language problems may be interpreted as the result of inferior ability rather than as the cause of poor achievement.

It is not clear what causes language problems in the absence of other handicaps. Although an impoverished and unstimulating home context may sometimes be implicated, in some cases children of apparently normal intelligence from advantaged backgrounds experience significant developmental delays or language impairments (Rice, 1989).

Speech problems and delayed language development are most common among children who have some other handicap—that is, retarded children and others suffering from motor, neurological, or mental disorders. They are relatively uncommon among the majority of children.

Early diagnosis of speech and language problems is especially important, notes Ruben (1993), because of the critical period in early childhood during which most language learning occurs. It is also important because of the significant correlations that have been found between retarded language development and subsequent behavior and emotional problems, including a greater probability of criminality (Stattin & Klackenberg-Larsson, 1993). Part of the explanation for this relationship, explain Benasich, Curtiss, and Tallal (1993), may lie in the drop in intelligence that often accompanies significant language impairment in early childhood. These children may subsequently experience far more difficulty coping both in school and in society.

LANGUAGE, THOUGHT, AND COMMUNICATION

Clearly, language is centrally involved in successful adjustment to virtually all aspects of society. Not only does language allow children to direct the behavior of others according to their wishes (as when they ask for something) but it also provides a means for acquiring information that would otherwise be inaccessible (as when they ask questions, listen to stories, or watch television). In addition, it's clear that language is closely involved in logical thought processes, although the exact nature of the relationship between the two remains uncertain.

Thinking and Language

One extreme position, the *Whorfian*, maintains that language is essential for thinking (Whorf, 1956). This position is based on the assumption that all thinking is verbal and that thought is therefore limited to what is made possible by language. There are two forms of the Whorfian hypothesis. The strongest form argues that thought *depends on* language, and that it will not occur in its absence. The weaker version maintains that language *influences* thinking.

To accept the more extreme position would be to deny that those who are prelinguistically deaf and who have not learned an alternate communication system can think. We would also have to believe that the prelinguistic infant cannot think and that, among those who have begun to develop language, thought is restricted to subjects and ideas for which the thinker has appropriate language. And we would have to believe that cows cannot think.

We don't believe all these things. So we accept, agreeing with psychologists such as Piaget and Vygotsky, that thought often precedes language. Piaget (1923), for example, points out that the development of certain logical concepts often precedes the learning of words and

Communication, although it is tremendously facilitated by language, is not entirely dependent on speaking or understanding words. Even non-human animals can communicate, as do bees telling others where the pollen is, or deer flagging potential danger. Preschoolers, too, communicate a great deal without always resorting to language. Sometimes simple gestures are all that they need.

phrases corresponding to those concepts. Words such as *bigger, smaller, farther,* and so on do not appear to be understood until the concepts they represent are themselves understood. Both Vygotsky and Piaget argue that language and thought first develop independently. Thus, there is considerable evidence of what we consider to be thought among preverbal children and nonhuman animals. But after the age of 2, language and thought become more closely related. After that age, thought becomes increasingly verbal, and language acquires the capacity to control behavior.

In brief, both research and good sense inform us that our sophisticated thought processes are inextricably bound with language—as are our belief systems, our values, our world views (Hunt & Agnoli, 1991). So convinced are we of this that attempts to bring about difficult social changes often begin with attempts to change language. Antiracist and antisexist movements are a case in point. In the first edition of this text, it was acceptable to use masculine pronouns as though all children, all psychologists, and, indeed, all significant people, were male. Speaking of one of Blaise Pascal's *Pensées,* for example, I wrote: "One of the paradoxes of human existence is that despite man's great intelligence it is impossible for him to know where he came from or where he is going" (Lefrançois, 1973, p. 351).

That this type of chauvinistic sexism is no longer acceptable in our language may eventually be reflected in its eradication from our thoughts and those of our children.

Communicating and Conversing

Language is more than a collection of sounds whose combinations refer to objects and actions and whose expression conveys our meanings. And it is more than a means for thinking and expressing our thoughts. Language is the means by which we draw information from past generations, record our own small contributions, and pass them on to generations that will come later. It is the great binding force of all cultures.

But infants and preschoolers, newly learning language, are not concerned with its great cultural contributions. Their first interest is in communicating—and the first communications are simple assertions ("that dog," "see daddy," "my ball") or requests ("milk!" "more candy"). The second concern is with conversation.

A conversation is an exchange typically involving two or more people (although some people do talk to themselves—and answer). It is generally verbal, although it can consist of a combination of gestures and verbalization, or it can consist entirely of gestures as in the case of ASL (American Sign Language). Genuine conversational exchanges begin around age 2. Initially, they are highly telegraphic, as is the child's speech; there aren't many variations possible when your sentences are limited to a single word. A short excerpt from an intelligent conversation with one of my own illustrates this:

Him: Fish.

Me: Fish?

Him: Fish!

Me: Fish? Fish swim.

Him: Fish! Fish! (The conversation becomes more complex.)

Me: There are fish in the lake. (An original thought, meant to stimulate creativity.)

Him: Fish. (Pointing, this time, in the general direction of the lake—I think.)

From this primitive, repetitive conversation, children progress to more complex expressions and begin to learn the importance of subtle cues of intonation, accentuation of words, rhythm of sentences, tone, and accompanying gestures. They learn, as well, about the implicit agreements that govern our conversations—the well-accepted rules that determine who shall speak and when, whether interruptions are permissible and how they should occur, what information must be included in our conversations if we are to be understood, and what we can assume is already known.

Thus, more or less, does the infant progress from a sound to a word, from one word to two, from an expression to a conversation, from a conversation to a book. . . .

Physical Growth

1. There is a gradual slowing of sheer physical growth after infancy. In addition, different parts of the body grow at different rates (the head grows more slowly, for example) so that a typical 6-year-old looks more like an adult (and less like an infant) than a 2-year-old does.

Motor Development

2. Among significant motor achievements of infancy are learning how to walk and to coordinate other motor activities. Motor, intellectual, and social development are very closely related.

The Preschooler's Mind

3. We remember little of personal experience of infancy and the early preschool period (*infantile amnesia*). Preschoolers' memories result largely from *incidental mnemonics* (paying attention, repeated exposure) rather than from the deliberate use of strategies (such as organizing or rehearsing). However, older preschoolers may deliberately use strategies when instructed to remember something, although these are sometimes inappropriate.

Piaget's View

4. Piaget's preoperational period includes *preconceptual thinking* (2–4: classification errors, preconcepts, and transductive and syncretic reasoning) and *intuitive thinking* (4–7: egocentricity, errors of class inclusion, and a marked reliance on perception). Piaget's developmental sequence has often been replicated although he seems to have underestimated ages of attainment in some cases. The neo-Piagetians present a somewhat more optimistic view of the preschool child, emphasizing that one of the major achievements of this period is the ability to relate one or more ideas or concepts.

5. As a result of their ability to relate concepts, preschoolers can classify and solve simple class-inclusion problems, have a remarkable understanding of number that reflects both number abstraction skills (understanding of numerosity, based on universal counting principles) and numerical reasoning (understanding of some of the effects of transformations), and have made enormous strides in language learning.

Preschool Education

6. Preschool education programs include nursery schools, day-care centers, compensatory programs, and a variety of other approaches. In general, compensatory preschool programs (Head Start, for example) have measurably positive effects on cognitive and social development, as do regular kindergartens. However, some fear that emphasis on formal instruction at the preschool level hurries children unnecessarily and robs them of their childhood.

Language and the Preschooler

7. Language—the use of arbitrary sounds with established and accepted referents, either real or abstract, that can be arranged in sequence to convey meaning—appears to be unique to humans. The child goes from one-word sentences (holophrases) to two-word sentences (duos) and then to multiple-word sentences (rather than simply to three-word sentences). Multiple-word sentences appear by age 2 to 2½ and make extensive use of grammatical morphemes such as *ing* and *ed* to convey meaning. More complex sentences and adultlike grammatical structures are typically present by age 4.

Explanations of Language Development

8. Imitation and reinforcement are not completely adequate explanations for the observation that the earliest speech sounds of all infants are very similar, that infants make few directly imitative mistakes as they learn language, and that there appears to be a critical period for language learning early in life (as Genie's story illustrates). Chomsky advances the metaphor of a language acquisition device (LAD), which suggests that children learn language as if they were neurologically predisposed to do so.

9. The mother (and other caregivers) play an important role as language teacher; she unconsciously fine-tunes her speech patterns to a level just in advance of that of her child. Thus, *motherese* is characterized by shorter sentences, more repetition, simpler and more concrete concepts, and exaggerated intonation.

A Changing Language Context

10. Changing demographics are rapidly changing the language composition of North American countries, although bilingualism is often *transitional*, lasting only three or four generations. Learning two languages may sometimes be a *subtractive* experience (especially when minority-language speakers are schooled exclusively in a more socially valued majority language), or an *additive* experience (more common when a minority language is learned as a second language in a school immersion setting).

Speech and Language Problems

11. The language sophistication of most school-age children is sufficient for them to ask and answer questions, tell stories, follow instructions, engage in conversations, and so on. However, some children experience language and speech problems ranging from complete absence of speech and comprehension to minor articulation and voice problems. These problems may be related to mental retardation, neurological damage or disease, or mental disorders, and are sometimes associated with adjustment problems in school and society.

Language, Thought, and Communication

12. Evidence suggests that language sophistication can contribute significantly to higher mental thought processes. The strong version of the Whorfian hypothesis maintains that language precedes and is necessary for thought. A weaker version is that language influences thought. Piaget and Vygotsky note evidence of thought prior to language (and in nonhuman animals). One of the major social functions of language is to enable communication through conversation.

FOCUS QUESTIONS: APPLICATIONS

1. How are motor and intellectual development related?
   - What sorts of motor skills might you use as indicators of intellectual development? Why?

2. What are the most important intellectual achievements of preschoolers?
   - Write a brief essay comparing the intellectual strengths and weaknesses of preschoolers and infants.

3. Is exposure to preschool education good, bad, or irrelevant?
   - Using library and other resources, evaluate the proposition that out-of-home care is often *not* the best alternative for preschoolers, but that it is politically unwise to say so.

4. How do children learn language?
   - Summarize the major psychological explanations for language learning.

STUDY TERMS

additive bilingualism   212

classification   199

compensatory preschool programs   203

concepts   198

conservation   200

Denver Developmental Screening Test   193

egocentric   200

growth rates   191

incidental mnemonics   196

infantile amnesia   196

intuitive   198

intuitive thinking   199

kindergartens   206

language   206

language acquisition device   209

memory   196

memory strategies   196

metamemory   197

Montessori method   205

motherese   211

motor development   192

number abstraction skills   202

numerical reasoning principles   202

nursery schools   203

operation   198

preconcepts   198

preconceptual   198

preoperational   198

preschool education   202

Project Head Start   203

reversibility   198

sensorimotor intelligence   198

speech problems   215

subtractive bilingualism   212

syncretic reasoning   199

transductive reasoning   198

transitional bilingualism   212

Whorfian hypothesis   215

A simple, layperson's description of physical growth, play, parenting, and preschools is:

Lee, C. (1990). *The growth and development of children* (4th ed.). New York: Longman.

Wellman's book is a fascinating look at how preschoolers view the world and especially at what they know about thinking and about states of mind:

Wellman, H. M. (1990). *The child's theory of mind.* Cambridge, MA: MIT Press.

The first of the next two references is a relatively complex look at the philosophical underpinnings of Piaget's theory; the second is a simpler summary of important aspects of the system:

Smith, L. (1993). *Necessary knowledge: Piagetian perspectives on constructivism.* Hillsdale, NJ: Erlbaum.

Wadsworth, B. J. (1989). *Piaget's theory of cognitive and affective development* (4th ed.). New York: Longman.

The following collection presents a brief and useful look at preschool programs, especially for children with special needs:

Gettinger, M., Elliott, S. N., & Kratochwill, T. R. (1992). *Preschool and early childhood treatment directions.* Hillsdale, NJ: Erlbaum.

Language development is described in more detail in:

Berko-Gleason, J. (Ed.). (1993). *The development of language* (3rd ed.). Columbus, OH: Merrill.

The Greenberg and Tobach book is a fascinating collection of papers dealing with language and thinking in both animals and humans:

Greenberg, G., & Tobach, E. (1987). *Cognition, language and consciousness: Integrative levels.* Hillsdale, NJ: Erlbaum.

The book by Cummins and Swain provides an account of bilingual education programs and their effects:

Cummins, J., & Swain, M. (1986). *Bilingualism in education: Aspects of theory, research and practice.* London: Taylor & Fry.

SOCIAL DEVELOPMENT: EARLY CHILDHOOD

A certain amount of timidity obviously adapts us to the world we live in, but the fear-paroxysm is surely altogether harmful to him who is its prey.

WILLIAM JAMES
Principles of Psychology

CHAPTER 8

In my memory, it's exactly one year after Mr. Delisle wore his painted devil and forever ruined my sister's love of Halloween. We decide to pass up his stingy treats because my cousin Claude has some fiendish trick we're going to play on him instead: We're going to let his dogs loose! Hot dang! "He'll never get them back unless there's a month of Saturdays," says Claude. "My dad said so, 'cause he never lets 'em out except when he goes hunting."

So when it's dark, we sneak into the Delisle yard and tie a long rope to the kennel latch and snake it back to where we can all hide on the roof of the shed, just in case the dogs decide they might like to chew on somebody other than Mr. Delisle. And, muffling our laughter, all of us pulling in turn on the rope, we ease the kennel door open.

For a minute, nothing happens, almost as if the dogs can't quite believe that the door is actually open. Then one of the braver ones goes to the entrance, stands there for a moment, and then leaps out and goes tearing down the street, and all the other dogs go barking after him. Gawd, what a marvelous trick, we all thought.

Except Mr. Delisle, he sees the loose dogs from his porch, and he doesn't even drop his popcorn; he just whistles twice, yells "Kennel!" and then he goes right back to doling out his meager treats.

Claude's father is wrong: It isn't a month of Saturdays before the dogs are all back in the kennel; it's only about as long as it takes for them to run over Paul Gaudry's two sisters—Emmy, who is not yet 3, and Priscilla, who's 7—whirl around, run over the sisters once more, and race back to the kennel, tails between their legs. Emmy's response to being run over is to sit on the sidewalk, screw her eyes shut, and put her hands over her ears. This made the dogs disappear, she later explains. Priscilla's more mature response is to scream all the way home and then tell her mother she thinks Guy and his friends are to blame—which is why I have a lot of experience cleaning dog kennels.

THIS CHAPTER

That Emmy could make a pack of barking dogs disappear simply by closing her eyes and blocking her ears is a piece of magic available to many preschoolers. Sadly, it's magic that you and I have quite forgotten.

This chapter deals with this and related topics as it looks at preschoolers' social development and at their expression and control of emotions. It looks, as well, at play, which is tremendously important to the child's social, physical, and intellectual development—and which can also be fun. The development and the implications of gender roles, which, even in the preschool period, are enormously significant, are also explored. Finally, the chapter examines the role of the family in the early socialization of the child, focusing on current issues such as separation and divorce, single-parent families, remarriage, and alternate forms of child care, paying attention to the general effects of day care and to the characteristics of high-quality care.

SOCIAL DEVELOPMENT

Preschoolers do not have the same sense of self, the same understanding of emotions (or the same control over them), or the same understanding of what is appropriate behavior and what isn't as do older children (or adults). **Socialization** (or *social learning*) is fundamental in the development of these important things. Simply defined, *socialization* is the process by which children learn behaviors appropriate for people of their gender and age. It is also through socialization that they learn and acquire the traditions, the beliefs, the values, and the customs of their groups.

What is learned through socialization is determined largely by the cultural context. Thus, in some societies, children might learn to be aggressive and fearless; in others they might be socialized to be timid and fearful—a fact

One of the important developmental tasks of the preschool period, claims Erik Erikson, is to develop a sense of initiative, of personal competence, and of autonomy. Raking the grass "all by myself, don't help me" is no trivial thing for this girl's development.

that makes our average child even more of a myth. But the processes by which socialization occurs are highly similar in different cultural groups.

Erikson's Psychosocial Stages

One well-known theory of social development is that advanced by Erik Erikson. It describes sequential stages of social development, each of which is characterized by conflicting tendencies or desires, and each of which requires the attainment of some new competence. Because of the theory's strong emphasis on social development, it is often labeled a theory of *psychosocial development*. The first three of Erikson's stages span the years from birth to around the end of the preschool period.

The first Erikson stage, **trust versus mistrust**, lasts through most of infancy. The principal task for the infant in this stage is to develop sufficient trust in the world to be able to go out and begin exploring it actively. Throughout this period, the most important influence in the infant's life is clearly the principal caregiver(s)—most often the mother.

The second stage, **autonomy versus shame and doubt,** spans the first year or so of the preschool period. At this time, children begin to discover that they are responsible for their own actions—a discovery that is closely

TABLE 8.1
Erikson's Psychosocial Stages of Preschool Development

Stage	Approximate Age	Principal Development Task
Autonomy vs. shame and doubt	18 months to 2–3 years	Developing a sense of control and mastery over actions
		Learning that one is autonomous, that intentions can be realized
		Overcoming the urge to return to the comfort of trusting parents, and especially the mother, to do all important things
Initiative vs. guilt	2–3 to 6 years	Developing a sense of self, largely through identifying with parents
		Developing a greater sense of responsibility for own actions
		Achieving progressive independence from parents

linked with the development of *intentionality.* The child's developing autonomy depends on opportunities to explore and to be independent, says Erikson (1959). Hence the need for a balance in parental control. Overprotection can lead to doubt and uncertainty. Yet, there is clearly a need to continue to protect; the young preschooler cannot be permitted unsupervised and unlimited freedom to explore.

The third stage, **initiative versus guilt,** spans the remaining preschool years. The new sense of competence required of the child involves a sense of initiative—a sense of personal agency. But there still lingers a desire to retain the comfort and security that come from allowing other people—especially parents—to maintain control and responsiblity.

In summary, according to Erikson, much of "growing up" during the preschool period involves developing a sense of an *autonomous self*—a self that is capable of forming intentions and of behaving in ways that are effective. Development is greatly facilitated by the infant's physical exploration of the environment, as well as by mushrooming language skills that make it possible to explore in other ways—as, for example, when the 4-year-old bombards caregivers with questions. The development of social competence through the preschool period also requires achieving progressive independence from parents. The overprotective parent who does not easily permit independence may make the child's progression through Erikson's stages more difficult. (See Chapter 2 for more details; see also Table 8.1.)

Social Imitation

Erikson (1968) believed that **imitation** is one of the important means by which preschool children become socialized, especially in the first two or three years of life. Later, **identification** (a process whereby children do not merely imitate models, but adopt their values and beliefs—in a sense, becoming like them) becomes more important.

One important theory of social learning based on imitation is that proposed by Albert Bandura. To summarize

Children learn a tremendous range of behaviors through imitation—behaviors like licking the spoon to test the broth. Less obvious, but perhaps far more important, imitation is also central in transmitting values and beliefs.

briefly: Bandura's theory explains the effects of modeling partly in terms of rewards and punishments, but gives a tremendously important role to the informative function of models and to the observers' understanding and interpretation of that information. It is what the observer imagines and expects that is important in learning through imitation.

Bandura describes three separate effects of imitation. There is the *modeling effect,* evident in learning new behavior; the *inhibitory and disinhibitory effects,* in which the rewards or punishment a model receives serve to bring about (disinhibit) some previously suppressed behavior or, alternately, to inhibit current behavior; and the *eliciting effect,* in which the model's behavior serves to evoke a related behavior in the observer.

Imitation-based theories of social learning are useful for explaining how children in nontechnological societies learn how to do things like set snares and traps or wield

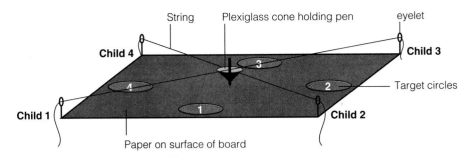

INTERACTIVE FIGURE 8.1

Cooperation board: Examine the layout of the board. Imagine that you are the child sitting in position 1; three other children occupy positions 2, 3, and 4. Each of you has grasped the string that runs from the cone at the center. You know that if you pull hard enough, the cone will slide toward you and the pen will draw a line right to your corner. The four of you are asked to draw a line through each of the target circles in order, from 1 to 4. What do you need to do to succeed? Suppose, now, that the target circles are moved so that each is placed directly under the string at the four corners of the board. To win this game, you have to pull the pen so that it traces a line through your circle. But there doesn't have to be just one winner; all four can win. Suppose, further, that you know you are the strongest one of the four, and that if you pull hard enough, no one else can win. How do you think you would have acted as a child? (Adapted from Madsen & Lancy, 1981, p. 397.)

brooms and corn-grinding stones. But most of us no longer need to learn how to operate a corn-grinding stone or lay out a trap. So what do we learn from social imitation in more complex societies?

Cooperation and Competition

Among other things, perhaps we learn important social tendencies like cooperation and competition. In fact, there is considerable research to support the belief that children are socialized to be cooperative or competitive by the predominant way of life, the mores, the traditions, of their immediate social environment. As a result, children from different ethnic groups can be remarkably different in terms of cooperation and competition.

Studies of cooperation and competition often use the four-person cooperation board developed by Madsen (Madsen & Lancy, 1981). This is simply an 18-inch paper square covered with a piece of paper set up as shown in Interactive Figure 8.1 (Madsen, 1971). Note that when a child holds each of the strings at the four corners, the pen can be made to trace a line through any or all targets, as long as participants *cooperate*; if, on the other hand, they choose to *compete*, then the strongest child will only succeed in pulling the pen to one corner. In a variation of this procedure, target circles might be drawn under the strings at each of the four corners so that a child might win (and prevent others from winning) by competing.

A Cross-Cultural Illustration

Madsen and Lancy (1981) used the cooperation board to look at competition and cooperation among two groups of Papua New Guinea children: the Imbonggu, a highly intact tribal group whose traditional way of life is based on cooperation; and the Kila-Kila, a more heterogeneous group, heavily influenced by rapid modernization and living in an urbanized setting characterized by violence and crime.

First, children, in groups of four, were simply instructed to draw a line through the numbered circles, in order, and were rewarded *as a group* for being successful (each child was given a coin). The objective was simply to determine whether children were able to cooperate when so instructed and when rewarded for doing so.

After three 1-minute trials under this "group reward" condition, subjects were then asked to write their names next to one of the circles (either to their right or left) and were told they would receive a coin each time the line passed through *their* circle. Now, in order to be successful, subjects must cooperate.

The results of the study are striking. There were no differences between the Imbonggu and Kila-Kila on the first three trials. Each of the groups improved on every trial, and by the third trial, each succeeded in crossing an average of slightly more than 12 circles. But the results on the fourth, fifth, and sixth trials, where subjects were being rewarded individually rather than as a group, are intriguing. Whereas the Imbonggu continued to improve on each of the trials—a clear sign that they continued to cooperate—the performance of the Kila-Kila foursomes deteriorated dramatically. In fact, two thirds of the Kila-Kila groups did not cross a single circle on the fourth trial; in contrast, the Imbonggu group that cooperated the least still managed to cross six circles (Figure 8.2).

These marked differences in competitive and cooperative tendencies, claim Madsen and Lancy (1981), are due

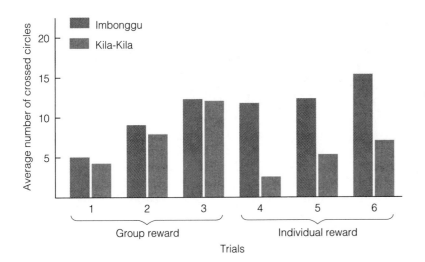

FIGURE 8.2

Differences in cooperation and competition between Imbonggu and Kila-Kila children. (Adapted from Madsen & Lancy, 1981, p. 399.)

to differences in immediate cultural contexts. Not surprisingly, similar research has found the same sorts of patterns among various other groups where the cultures are different in terms of cooperation and competition. Thus rural Mexican children have been found to be more cooperative, less competitive, than urban Mexican children—as have kibbutz Israeli children compared with urban Israeli children; Blackfoot Indians compared with urban Caucasians in Canada; urban and rural Colombians; urban and rural Maoris in New Zealand, and various other groups (Madsen & Lancy, 1981).

Observational Learning in Complex Societies

It seems clear that observational learning—social imitation—is involved in learning important cultural values and tendencies (reflected, for example, in competition and cooperation), even in heterogeneous societies such as ours. However, because our societies are so heterogeneous, the result is that some of us are gentle and cooperative, some are fiercely competitive, and others, of course, are both, depending on the situation.

One of the characteristics of highly heterogeneous societies is that the models they present are highly varied. In advanced societies, many of these are **symbolic models,** which need not be real, immediately present people. These may include characters in literature, movies, television programs; verbal and written instructions; religious beliefs; or folk heroes (such as musicians or athletes). One of the most powerful transmitters of these symbolic models may well be television (about which we say more in Chapter 10).

PRESCHOOLERS' EMOTIONS

Socialization, or social learning, Parke (1994) explains, is fundamental in the development of emotions among preschoolers. Young children, he notes, do not have as fine a control as we do over the emotions they feel—or over their expression. (They control their emotions more through behavior than through cognition;) thus can they make a pack of wild dogs disappear just by closing their eyes. And they are more easily moved to tears and to laughter than we are. Put another way, their emotions are not completely socialized.

The socialization of emotions involves at least three things: learning to interpret emotions, achieving some control over them, and learning when, where, and how displaying them is appropriate and expected.

Interpreting Emotions

Initially, the infant does not know how to interpret the feelings of others. Facial expressions of joy or sadness, for example, are meaningless for the 1-month-old infant. But sometime between the ages of 3 and 6 months, there appears a growing recognition not only that others are capable of emotional reactions, but that these can be inferred from expressions and from behavior. By the age of 9 months to 1 year, infants in ambiguous situations actively search other people's faces as though looking for a clue that might guide their own behavior. This is referred to as **social referencing.** Denham (1993) observed 28 mother–toddler pairs and found a very high correspondence between the infant's emotional responses and the mother's emotional displays. Similarly, many kindergarten students respond with obvious facial distress (sad expressions) when they hear an infant cry—clear evidence that they have learned to interpret the infant's emotional expressions (Eisenberg et al., 1993). When they see others crying, they are likely to feel sad—perhaps even to cry. And if others laugh and are happy, they, too, are more likely to be joyful.

In spite of their growing ability to interpret their emotions and those of others, preschoolers' verbal descriptions of emotions remain relatively imprecise. When Brown, Covell, and Abramovitch (1991) asked preschoolers how they would feel following a story event associated with happiness, sadness, or anger, they typically responded in terms of an intense emotion. And when, later in the story, an event occurred that would lead to a lessening of the emotion, preschoolers often thought they would feel a different emotion. If they had been sad earlier, now they would be happy. Strikingly, it seldom occurred to them that they might be *more or less* sad or happy. In contrast, older children in the same study often thought they would feel a different degree of the same emotion.

If specifically asked to describe what they think someone else is feeling, preschoolers might infer that someone feels "good" or "bad" because he or she is crying or laughing. They don't yet look for underlying causes upon which to base inferences. Yet when Boyatzis, Chazan, and Ting (1993) read brief stories describing a boy's emotion to 3½-year-old children, most had little difficulty selecting the photograph that accurately reflected the emotion in question. Interestingly, girls in this study (which also included 5-year-olds) were better than boys at identifying emotions.

Not surprisingly, early in the preschool period, children cannot readily tell the difference between emotions that are real and those that are a pretense. Thus, if someone falls but jumps up and "laughs it off" in embarrassment, the 2-year-old is likely to conclude that the person is happy. In contrast, in the same situation, the 5-year-old is likely to interpret the event more accurately, realizing that the person who has fallen is, in fact, pretending.

Regulating Emotions

Eisenberg and associates (1993) note that learning how to regulate (control) emotions, especially negative emotions like fear, has a significant bearing on the quality of the child's social interactions and adjustment. They suggest, too, that parental encouragement of the *expression* of negative emotions may be an important contributor to how well children cope with negative emotions.

As we saw in Chapter 6, even very young infants are capable of simple behaviors whose effect is to control the emotions they feel. For example, a frightened infant might close his eyes, suck his thumb, or snuggle his face in his mother's lap—an example of what Gianino and Tronick (1988) call *self-directed regulatory behaviors*. Alternatively, an infant might push away an object that is frightening her—an example of *other-directed regulatory behaviors*.*

Preschoolers, with their ever-expanding mobility and rapidly developing cognitive and social skills, become increasingly adept at avoiding situations that lead to negative emotions, and at seeking out and maintaining those associated with good feelings. But, a little like infants, their control of emotions is situational and behavioral rather than cognitive. When they hear the ice cream truck's bell, they run to get mother—or money; and when the frightening part of the story comes, they close their eyes and cover their ears. In the Brown, Covell, and Abramovitch (1991) investigation in which children were questioned following emotion-related events in stories, the younger children saw emotions as being situation-specific. Hence, to change a feeling, change the situation. A child who is sad over losing a favorite toy will nevertheless be happy when she goes to bed. Why? "Because I won't have to look for it."

In contrast, the older child's control of emotions is more cognitive. One way of not feeling sad about a lost toy, the older child insists, is not to think about it—or to think a happy thought. Most of us are more like older than younger children. And our emotions have clearer links with our cognitions (Mathews & MacLeod, 1994).

Emotional Expression

Infants are easily moved to tears or to laughter. It doesn't shame them to cry in front of strangers, nor does it ever embarrass them to laugh; they don't yet know what it is to feel foolish. But preschoolers are a little more restrained; they have begun to learn what researchers call *display rules*.

One aspect of display rules has to do with learning when and how it is appropriate to display certain emotions; another deals with understanding the emotional expressions (emotional displays) of others. Part of display rule learning involves discovering that expressed emotion does not always correspond with underlying emotion. Even young children are able to smile when they lie, or pretend it doesn't hurt when it would be embarrassing to cry.

It is not clear how preschoolers learn simple display rules such as, for example, the rule stating that if you are disappointed with a gift, you should not cry in front of the giver—not that they are always successful in doing so. Even we adults are not always able to hide our feelings. If someone gives us a rose when we fully expected a whole garden, we might find it very difficult to smile, even though our socialization is far more advanced than that of children.

Among the many activities and experiences of childhood that contribute to the socialization of the child, perhaps none is more important than play.

PLAY

Defined most simply, **play** is activity that has no long-range goal, although it might have some immediate objectives (to hop from here to there, to make a sand hill, to fly a kite). Play is what children, and grown-ups, do *for the*

---

*Emmy's closing her eyes to make Delisle's dogs disappear is an example of a *self-directed regulatory behavior*. An *other-directed regulatory behavior* would have been illustrated had she chosen to yell at them instead, which is what my grandmother said was all a person had to do with a mean-acting dog. I, who have twice been bitten, know that that is not entirely true.

fun of it. But that play has no ultimate purpose does not mean it is unimportant and useless. In fact, it is extremely important for all aspects of the child's development: social, physical, and intellectual.

Functions and Types of Play

Among animals, ethologists tell us, play has two important functions: First, it is useful in developing and exercising physical skills that might be important in hunting or escaping from predators; second, it serves to establish social position and to teach acceptable behaviors such as in the mock-fighting, rough-and-tumble play of lion cubs or chimpanzees.

In some ways, some of the functions of play among children are not very different from those among animals. **Practice play** (or **sensorimotor play**) is useful in developing and exercising physical skills, and might also contribute to social adaptation. In addition, play involving physical exploration is closely linked to attention and learning (Ruff & Saltarelli, 1993).

Pretend play (or **imaginative play**) has quite different functions. Imagining involves important cognitive abilities related to symbolizing, imitating, anticipating, and problem solving. Children's growing awareness of self and of others, and their gradual realization that we are all *thinking* beings, have their roots in play, claims McCune (1993). Not surprisingly, research reports positive correlations between play and level of cognitive development (Tamis-LeMonda & Bornstein, 1993). It also reports a close relationship between play and measures of social competence, such as are evident in friendships, for example (Park, Lay, & Ramsay, 1993). It is no surprise that play can successfully be used as a form of therapy for children experiencing learning problems, depression, socially inappropriate behavior, and a variety of other social and emotional problems (Landreth, 1993).

Practice Play

Practice play is mainly physical activity and is evident among the young of many animals (for example, a kitten chasing a ball). It involves manipulating objects or performing activities simply for the sensations that result, and is a very common form of infant play. It may consist of motor activities such as creeping, crawling, walking, running, skipping, hopping, manipulating objects and parts of one's own anatomy, and so on. It is evident in the countless solitary games of young preschoolers.

Pretend Play

Many of the preschooler's solitary games are not simply practice play, but also *pretend* play. Even infants as young as 1 can pretend, although their pretending usually takes the form of simulating common activities—for example,

TABLE 8.2
*Types of Play**

Type	Example
Practice	
Solitary	Bouncing a ball, up, down, up, down . . .
Social	Playing baseball
Pretend	
Solitary	Giving a doll pretend tea
Social	Dramatizing monsters in a group

* Note that these simple categories of play are not mutually exclusive. A single "game" or play session might involve elements of practice and pretend games, and might be solitary in some respects and social in others. Also, there are different types of social play (see Table 8.3).

pretending to eat or pretending to sleep. By age 2, however, a wide range of make-believe games becomes possible as the child learns to make objects, people, and themselves and their activities become things they actually are not. In pretend play, boys are often superheroes such as Superman (or super antiheroes such as dragons or monsters); girls are often mothers or nurses (Paley, 1984). Both practice and pretend play can be solitary (a single player) or social (at least two players). (See Table 8.2.)

Reality and Fantasy

Preschoolers are sometimes uncertain about the difference between reality and fantasy. Three-year-old Mollie wants to play a pretend game with the other nursery school children, but she knows some *pretend* bad thing is going to happen. The child is scared because, "What if the bad thing doesn't know it's pretend?" (Paley, 1986, p. 45).

"Go to sleep, Mollie," Libbie orders. "There might be something dangerous. You won't like it."

"I know it," Mollie says. "But I got a bunk bed at home and I sleep there."

"Bunk beds are too scary," Amelia says.

"Why are they?" Mollie looks worried.

"It's a monster, Mollie. Hide!" (p. 45).

But Mollie protests that there are no monsters in her house today. Still, she is unwilling to take any chances:

"I'm going to be a statue," Mollie whispers. "So he won't see me" (p. 45).

Now Frederick comes roaring in on all fours. "I'm a lion. I'm roaring," he says.

"Is he scaring you, Mollie?"

"No."

"Is anyone scaring you?"

"The bunk bed," she answers solemnly (p. 45).

Mollie, like many other 3-year-olds, can create her own ghosts and monsters; and she has developed her own ways of dealing with them. If they threaten too frighteningly, she can become a statue so they won't see her, or

The line between reality and fantasy is not as clear for the preschooler as it is in sober adulthood—and, some say, that may be one of the strengths rather than one of the weaknesses of childhood.

she can hide by the teacher—or she can, ultimately, resort to her knowledge that the monsters are pretend monsters.

But when others create monsters, Mollie can never be quite certain that they are truly *pretend pretend*. Perhaps, just perhaps, one of them might be *real pretend*.

We, of course, do not suffer from the same limitations as does Mollie (nor do most of us enjoy quite as boundless an imagination). We have somehow learned to tell the difference between fantasy and reality; we can dismiss our monsters if they frighten us. Can't we?

Daydreaming and Imaginary Playmates

One type of imaginative play that becomes increasingly prevalent as the preschooler ages is daydreaming. Unlike other types of imaginative play in which the child actively engages in fantasy, daydreaming is imagining without the activity. Daydreaming is a normal and healthy activity, engaged in by adults as well as children. Not surprisingly, however, teachers tend to perceive students with attention problems as being more prone to daydreaming than are more attentive children (Stanford & Hynd, 1994).

Daydreaming, which is a solitary form of imaginative play, sometimes gives rise to the imaginary playmate—constant companion and friend to approximately half of all preschool children. These imaginary friends, complete with names and personalities, are spoken to, played with, teased, and loved by their creators. In one study, Taylor, Cartwright, and Carlson (1993) interviewed a dozen 4-year-olds who had imaginary playmates, asking them to describe their imaginary friends—which they did quite readily. The remarkable thing is that when these children were interviewed again seven months later, their descriptions had hardly changed; they were every bit as stable as descriptions of real friends.

There is little information about the role imaginary companions might play in the preschooler's development. However, some evidence suggests that the creation of an imaginary playmate is often associated with more advanced language and social development, and may predict later creativity (Singer & Singer, 1990).

Contributions to a Theory of Mind

Pretend play, says Leslie (1988), contributes to one of the cognitive capacities that sets us apart from other species: Specifically, it eventually enables us to think about ourselves and about others as thinkers—as organisms capable of having different states of mind. When mother puts a banana in her ear and says "Hello," 4-year-old Nancy recognizes at once that the banana is a pretend telephone. But there is no confusion here between reality and fantasy; she still knows very clearly that this is a banana. What is also clear to Nancy, however, is that mother can have different *states of mind*—and that she can too. Nancy has begun to develop a **theory of mind**, says Leslie. And one important aspect of this theory is the recognition of others and of self as thinkers capable of deliberately selecting and manipulating ideas—even pretend ideas. Here, in the preschool period, is the dawning of what psychologists label **metacognition**—knowing about knowing.

Social Play

Social play is any type of play that involves interaction among two or more children. Thus, both practice and pretend play are social when they involve more than one child. Skipping rope alone in the darkness of one's basement is a solitary sensorimotor activity; skipping rope out on the playground with others turning the rope, "pepper, pepper, salt and . . . ," is a cooperative or social activity. Similarly, creating elaborate and fantastic daydreams in the solitude of one's bedroom is private imaginative play; but playing "let's pretend"—"you be the veterinamen and I'll be the dog"—is social imaginative play.

Parten (1932) describes the play behavior of preschoolers as being *solitary* or as reflecting one of five different kinds of social play distinguishable in terms of the type and amount of peer interaction involved. Although these develop sequentially, they also overlap (see Table 8.3).

TABLE 8.3
Classifications and Examples of Children's Social Play

Classification	Possible Activity
Solitary play	Child plays alone with blocks.
Primitive social play	"Peek-a-boo."
Onlooker play	Child watches others play "tag" but does not join in.
Parallel play	Two children play with trucks in sandbox, but do not interact. They play beside each other, but not together.
Associative play	Two children play with dolls, talk with each other about their dolls, lend each other diapers and dishes, but play independently, sharing neither purpose nor rules.
Cooperative play	"Let's pretend. You be a monster and I'll be the guy with the magic sword and . . ."

Solitary play

In *solitary play*, the child plays alone with toys or engages in some solitary motor activity, paying little attention to other children. Much of the child's play before the age of 2 appears to be solitary.

Primitive Social Play

Although infant play is mainly solitary, there are some primitive forms of social play that sometimes occur even before the age of 6 months. Many of these, like "peek-a-boo" games, and play that includes tickling, tossing, and related activities, typically occur with parents or older children. Some, like the "chase" games of toddlers or the "touch me and I'll touch you" game, are examples of non-solitary play among infants (Brenner & Mueller, 1982).

Onlooker Play

As the label implies, *onlooker play* consists of a child watching others play, but not participating actively. Onlooker play occurs throughout childhood. Often, the onlooker may talk with the players, perhaps even giving them advice or asking questions.

Parallel Play

In *parallel play*, children play side by side, often with similar toys, but do not interact, do not share the activities involved in the game, and do not use any mutually accepted rules. Parallel play is nevertheless social play of a primitive sort because it involves two or more children who apparently prefer to play together even if they do not interact. Some research indicates that the presence of toys often detracts from social interaction and leads to parallel or perhaps solitary play, particularly among very young children (Vandell, Wilson, & Buchanan, 1980). Not surprisingly, in the absence of toys, children are more likely to interact with each other.

Associative Play

With advancing age, children become more interested in interacting with peers and are more likely to include toys in what is termed *associative play*. This type of play involves interaction among children, even though they continue to play separately. In associative play, children sometimes share toys, but each child plays independently without mutually accepted goals or rules. Goncu (1993) reports that this type of shared play becomes increasingly common between ages 3 to 4½.

Cooperative Play

Children who play cooperatively help one another in activities that require shared goals and perhaps even a division of roles. Although most research on the preschooler's play behavior indicates that associative and *cooperative play* are not common before the age of 4 or 5, there is sometimes evidence of cooperation in the play of much younger children.

It is largely through cooperative social play that preschoolers form friendships. Not surprisingly, the best-liked children appear to be those who are most cooperative (as well as least aggressive and least difficult) (Denham & Holt, 1993). Patterns of interactions in preschool friendships appear to be quite stable (Park et al., 1993).

An important example of cooperative social play is found in the drama that children sometimes enact in their pretend play.

"You be the baby."

"I be the baby."

"I be the mother."

"You be the mother. I be the baby."

"If you're bad . . . if you wee-wee your diaper, well, you know . . ." (making an abrupt spanking gesture, but smiling broadly all the while).

Garvey (1977) found that the most common roles in dramatic play were mother–infant, mother–child, or mother–father. She found too that children often reveal their fears and worries, their hopes and aspirations, in their dramatic play. Social play of this kind is more than just fun; it provides an important opportunity for acquiring and practicing behaviors involved in social interaction, for developing cooperative behaviors, for learning how to resolve conflict, for making friends, and for fostering imagination and creativity.

Cultural Differences in Play

Play appears to be universal among all cultures, but its frequency and the forms it takes are strongly influenced by the preschooler's context (Hughes, 1990). For example, in societies where children have to assume work responsibilities at very early ages, there is less childhood play—an observation that is also often true of children who are economically and socially disadvantaged (Schwartzman, 1987). (See Across Cultures: "The Worlds of Lata Sakharam Narvankar and of Olivia Miller" on page 230.)

THE WORLDS OF LATA SAKHARAM NARVANKAR AND OF OLIVIA MILLER

Lata Sakharam Narvankar is a girl of the "sweeper class" who lives in Gujerat, India. Her life, says Rice (1972), is an unending, unchanging cycle of poverty and work. She lives in a *hutment,* an abject cluster of tenement housing—little huts made of woven palms and thatched roofs through which the sun and the rain pass freely. In Lata's world, children begin to work as soon as they can toddle. The older ones, the 4- and 5-year-olds, look after the babies. Also, they cook and clean and shop for small handfuls of food when they can. If they live where people have money, their daily work is to beg. Lata, who is 12, works as a "sweeper" in an apartment during the day—washing, cleaning, sweeping, swabbing. At night, she returns to her poverty. Without hesitation, she gives all her earnings, 21 rupees a month, to her mother. When asked what she would do if she had a lot of money, she doesn't know what to say; the possibility is so remote that she has never dreamed about it. "There are very few childhood games," writes Rice (1972), "no toys, no schooling, no entertainment. . . ." (p. 19).

Olivia Miller is the same age as Lata Sakharam Narvankar. She lives in Moose Jaw, Saskatchewan, in a comfortable middle-class house. She is expected to go to school 198 days a year; her mother also asks her to help with simple household chores on an occasional basis. And she is expected to keep her room reasonably tidy. Her room is about the size of Lata's entire *hutment,* and has far more valuable things in it than belong to all of Lata's family. In fact, there is vastly more forgotten money in Olivia's piggy bank than an entire year of Lata's wages.

And, yes, Olivia is expected to play and amuse herself, alone and with others, during most of her very abundant free time. Even much of school involves play.

To Think About Given the vastly different childhood contexts in which Olivia and Lata live, do you think many of our developmental

generalizations might apply equally to both? Which generalizations would (would not) apply? Why?

To Do Quick sketches such as these are misleading in that they omit too many details and, especially in cases such as Lata's with which we tend to be less familiar, they lead us too easily to inappropriate generalizations. As an antidote to the tendency to think of all Indian children as downtrodden, oppressed, and doomed to joyless and playless childhoods, you might consult the following book on children's play in different cultures, and especially the chapter that deals with play in the East Indian context: Roopnarine, J. L., Johnson, J. E., & Hooper, F. H. (Eds.). (1994). *Children's play in diverse cultures.* Albany, NY: State University of New York Press.

Children learn many of their first play behaviors in interaction with principal caregivers, note O'Reilly and Bornstein (1993). One would therefore expect that among the poor, many mothers would be preoccupied or busy and would devote less time to interacting with infants. Bowman (1993) reports that this expectation has been corroborated in the finding that the play of poor children is sometimes less complex and involves less advanced usage of language. (See Interactive Figure 8.4 on p. 233 for information about where British children play.)

GENDER ROLES IN EARLY CHILDHOOD

Gender is one of those visually conspicuous characteristics on which we base our judgments of people and our reactions to them, says Fiske (1993) (others are age, race, and physical appearance). In most cultures, including ours,

there are usually marked differences between the ways in which males and females are expected to think, act, and feel. The range of behaviors considered appropriate for males and females—that is, considered *masculine* or *feminine*—together with the attitudes and personality characteristics associated with each, define **gender roles.** The learning of sex-appropriate behavior is **gender typing.** Gender typing, as we saw in Chapter 6, begins from the very earliest moment when the mere fact that the child is male or female determines much of what a parent's reactions to the infant will be.

Gender Schemas

"One of the first social dimensions that children notice is sex," claim Serbin, Powlishta, and Gulko (1993, p. 1). Very early in life, they begin to develop what researchers label **gender schemas** (also sometimes termed *gender scripts*). Gender schemas are the child's knowledge about

Children begin to learn gender-typed behaviors at very young ages. But this particular behavior boys will actively renounce very shortly. However, as Robert Browning noted in Fra Lippo Lippi, *"You should not take a fellow eight years old and make him swear to never kiss the girls."*

characteristics associated with being male and female (Levy, 1993). Much of this knowledge consists of stereotypes such as those associated with common occupations or with predominant personality characteristics. Children use their gender schemas as guides for interpreting and understanding the behavior of others, as well as for directing their own behavior.

Developing Gender Schemas and Stereotypes

By the age of 2 or 3 years, children can not only correctly label people "man" or "woman" (or "boy" or "girl"), but they can also predict the sorts of activities or occupations that would be most likely for specific individuals, knowing nothing about them other than their gender. But even though children begin to discriminate between male and female very early in life—that is, they begin to develop gender schemas early—it isn't until later in the preschool period that they finally understand that gender is a permanent category that can't easily be changed (Serbin et al., 1993). At the same time, children begin to assume the role they associate with their sex. And their understanding of this role, claim Levine, Resnick, and Higgins (1993), determines and constrains much of their behavior. Because boys are not *supposed* to cry, Miguel tries hard not to. And because girls aren't supposed to like computers, Sarah ignores the thing on her brother's desk.

Two Theories

Freud suggested that boys learn to behave as "boys" and girls as "girls" at least partly through identifying with their parents and with other males and females. In his

terms, the values, the behaviors, the beliefs, and the attitudes of each sex become the child's as they are *introjected* (in a sense, borrowed) from significant people in the child's environment.

A more cognitive explanation suggests that gender typing results from the preschooler's understanding of the meaning of *gender*. Kohlberg (1966) describes three stages—three levels of understanding—that reflect the child's increasing awareness of gender:

- *Stage 1. Basic gender identity* describes the initial stage where the infant recognizes simply that he is a boy or she is a girl.
- *Stage 2. Gender stability* refers to the realization that gender is permanent and unchangeable.
- *Stage 3. Gender constancy* reflects the child's eventual understanding that superficial changes (in ways of behaving or dressing, for example) are irrelevant to basic gender.

Kohlberg argues that once children become aware of their gender identity and its meaning, they actively participate in organizing their behaviors as well as their environments to conform to sex-appropriate patterns. Thus, having decided that she is a female, a girl selects feminine toys and behaviors. And having decided that he is a male, the boy leaves the doll corner except when he raids it with his phasers and missiles or haunts it as a pretend monster. Not surprisingly, the most widely used indicators of gender typing at the preschool level are based on selection of toys and activities. In the elementary school years, more abstract measures of self-perception are possible (Boldizar, 1991).

Gender Differences and Stereotypes

There are obvious biological differences between the sexes; that there are also psychological differences is less obvious and certainly far more controversial. Nevertheless, as is shown in Chapter 12, there are some small (and declining) differences between males and females in some areas—perhaps most notably in aggressiveness, where males have the doubtful distinction of being considerably more aggressive.

That our common **stereotypes** (fixed beliefs) of masculinity and femininity are still clearly different is apparent even at very young ages. For example, Henshaw, Kelly, and Gratton (1992) asked 15 boys and 15 girls aged 8 to 9 to give an experimenter advice about whether a boy (John) and a girl (Sally) would like masculine toys (cricket bat, train set, skateboard), or feminine toys (doll, skipping-rope, baby carriage), or neutral toys as a present. Only 7 percent of the children thought John would like girls' toys; in contrast almost half thought Sally would like boys' toys.

In the same study, children were also asked whether John and Sally would like activities such as karate, football,

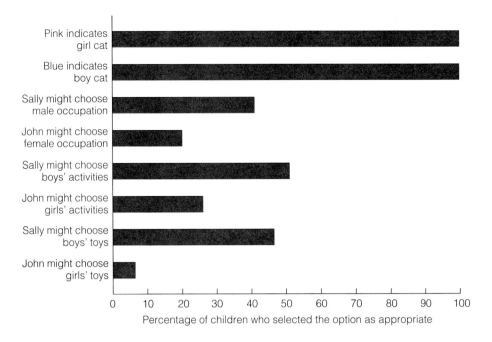

FIGURE 8.3
Children's gender stereotypes.
(Based on Henshaw, Kelly, &
Gratton, 1992.)

and climbing trees (masculine activities), or activities such as dancing, gymnastics, and skipping (feminine activities), or more neutral activities. They were also asked similar questions relating to traditionally male occupations (farmer, bus driver, judge) and those that have traditionally been female (cook, secretary, librarian). Finally, they were asked whether a stylized drawing of a cat with either a pink bow, a blue bow, or a yellow bow would be a boy or a girl cat. Results, summarized in Figure 8.3, indicate that the children clearly differentiated between masculine and feminine interests and activities. Perhaps more striking, they also reveal that boys' roles are more constrained than those of girls. That is, it is considered less likely and less appropriate that a boy be interested in a girls' toy or activity than that a girl show interest in boys' things. As Henshaw and associates (1992) put it, boy sissys are more strongly sanctioned than girl tomboys: "Girls in trousers are acceptable in a way that boys in dresses will probably never be" (p. 230). Or, in the words of one of the children who participated: "Skipping's for girls—I wouldn't skip and my friends wouldn't skip" (p. 234).

In much the same way, pink is for girls and blue is for boys, even for cats. Not a single child thought the pink cat would be a boy cat—or vice versa. Ten percent thought the yellow-ribboned cat might be male; 27 percent thought it might be female.

Sex Differences in Play
When they are only 3, Paley (1984) informs us, boys will gladly pretend to be babies, mothers, fathers, or monsters. Most are as comfortable wearing the discarded apron and the nursery school teacher's high-heeled shoes as the fire fighter's hat or the ranch hand's boots. They play in the "doll corner" as easily as do the girls. (See Interactive Figure 8.4 for information about *where* children play.)

But when preschoolers reach age 5, the atmosphere in the doll corner changes dramatically. Now when there are pretend games, the boys are monsters and superheroes; and in the pretend games of the girls, there are princesses and sisters. But these are not the only changes that come with age. In Paley's (1984) words:

> In the class described in this book, for example [a kindergarten class], you hop to get your milk if you are a boy and skip to the paper shelf if you are a girl. Boys clap out the rhythm of certain songs; girls sing louder. Boys draw furniture inside four-story haunted houses; girls put flowers in the doorways of cottages. Boys get tired of drawing pictures and begin to poke and shove; girls continue to draw. (p. xi)

Genetic Influences
Do these early differences in male/female interests and behaviors primarily reflect the influence of social context? Or are they partly biologically based?

The evidence is not entirely clear or complete, but there are strong indications that at least some male/female differences are biological. The evidence is clearest with respect to the greater aggressiveness of males than females. Males are more aggressive than females at an early age; this finding is consistent in most cultures and also for nonhuman primates; and the injection of male hormones into pregnant mothers affects the subsequent aggressiveness of female children who are in utero at the time (Jacklin, 1989; Maccoby & Jacklin, 1980).

Sociocultural Models and Expectations
We should not conclude, however, that the greater aggressiveness of males in our culture is inevitable given probable genetic differences in aggression. The influence of cultural factors cannot be discounted. For example, many

LAWNS .71
PLAYGROUNDS
PLAY EQUIPMENT
SCHOOLYARDS .65
CHILD'S OWN HOME .51
LOCAL PARKS .40
SINGLE TREES .36
THROUGH STREETS .34
PAVEMENTS .30
OTHER DWELLINGS .29
FENCES .28
FRIENDS' HOMES .25
FOOTPATHS .24
SWIMMING POOLS .19
SPORTS FIELDS .18
FLOWERS/MISC. STRUCTURES .17
PONDS & LAKES .16
SHRUBS .15
CHILD'S SCHOOL/CHILD'S FRIENDS .13
TRAFFIC/BRIDGES .11
SELF PORTRAIT/TOPOGRAPHY/DIRT & SAND .10

* * * * * *

TREE CLUSTERS/YARDS & GARDENS .09

HILLS/ASPHALT & CONCRETE/CLIMATIC CONDITIONS .08

CAR PARKS/CLIMBING TREES/WOODLAND/ABANDONED BUILDINGS .06

WILD BIRDS & INSECTS/CUL DE SACS/CULVERTED STREAMS/LOCAL SHOPS/TALL GRASS, LEAVES & WEEDS/CATS &
DOGS/BUILDING INTERIORS/SHOPPING CENTERS/COMMUNITY BUILDINGS/VEGETABLE
GARDENS/ROCKS/STREAMS/WILD ANIMALS/CHILD'S RELATIVES & OTHER ADULTS/RAILWAY LINES/BUS
STOPS/FORTS, CLUBHOUSES & CAMPS/SPORTS COURTS/VACANT BUILDING SITES/FRUITING TREES/NEIGHBORS' &
BABYSITTER'S HOUSES/SECRET HIDING PLACES/TREE HOUSES/TREE SWINGS/FISH & AQUATIC LIFE/CHILD'S
SIBLINGS/CHURCHES .05 AND LESS

Children's favorite play places: Can you recall the five favorite play places (activities) of your childhood? Robin Moore (1986) asked 48 boys and 48 girls ages 9–12 to make maps or drawings of their favorite play places and then interviewed each child. He also accompanied 24 of them to their favorite play places and interviewed their parents. How do their favorite play places and activities compare with yours? (From Moore, 1986.)

occupations requiring physical aggression and strength have traditionally been restricted to males, whereas those requiring nonaggressive, passive, nurturant behavior have been considered more appropriate for females. Hence the models society provides for children are clear.* Children see them everywhere: on television, in books, in schools, on the playground. The message is clearly that there are certain behaviors, attitudes, and interests that are appropriate—and others inappropriate—for one's sex (Henshaw et al., 1992). The same message is clear, as well, in the sorts of behaviors society reinforces in children. Male popularity, for example, depends primarily on athletic ability and toughness; female popularity depends on attractiveness, social skills, and academic achievement (Adler, Kless, & Adler, 1992).

Finally, gender role messages are evident in the way parents treat their children—how they dress them, what they expect of them, how they react to their displays of aggression or nurturance (Etaugh & Liss, 1992). In fact, the family is probably the greatest single socializing influence in the life of the preschooler.

THE CONTEMPORARY FAMILY

Our vision of the "typical" North American family is still often that of a **nuclear family**—mother, father, and one or two children—with father as breadwinner, although mother, too, might work (as opposed to an **extended**

*My grandmother liked to point out that most soldiers, police officers, wardens, and politicians who control the machinery of collective violence are men—as are most murderers, rapists, muggers, and scoundrels.

CHANGES IN THE U.S. FAMILY

The average size of the American family has declined in recent decades and is now at about 3.16 persons—a drop of a full half-child since 1960. As population has increased, the number of married couples has also increased. But whereas families with both spouses present increased by about 33 percent between 1960 and 1993, the number of male-headed families increased by a whopping 125 percent in the same period. And yet, there are still about four times more female-headed households—some 11.9 million in the United States in 1993, an increase of close to 150 percent between 1960 and 1993.

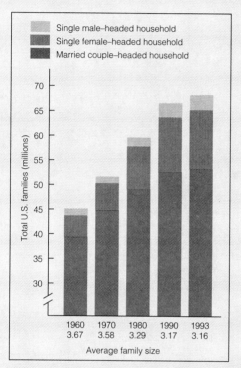

FIGURE 8.5

Changes in U.S. average family size and increases in single-parent families, 1960–1993. (From data in U.S. Bureau of the Census, 1994, p. 58.)

family, which includes many other relatives as well). But in the United States in 1993, only slightly more than half of all households consisted of married couples. Of households that had families, 52 percent of the black households were single parent, as were 31 percent of the Hispanics and 18 percent of the whites (U.S. Bureau of the Census, 1994). Hence the traditional "white, two parents, and children" definition of the North American family is no longer correct. "There is no single correct definition of what a *family* is," Fine (1993, p. 235) writes. It might be white, African-American, Hispanic, or some other mix; it might be one or two parent; it might be an intact family or a blended family ("stepfamily"); or it might be a gay or a lesbian family. The average size of the U.S. family in 1993 was 3.16—a drop of about half a child per family household since 1970. (See At a Glance: "Changes in the U.S. Family," and Figure 8.5).

Not only is the family difficult to define, but it is also very private and highly dynamic. That it is highly private means that researchers seldom have access to the most in-timate aspects of its functioning. And that it is dynamic—that is, it changes not only with the addition or loss of members but also as relationships among its members change—means that the relationships and influences within the family do not expose themselves clearly and simply to the scrutiny of the social scientist. Hence, it is difficult to research the family. There is much about which we can only speculate.

Parenting in Early Childhood

The family serves three principal functions in North American societies, claims Westman (1991): (1) it has a *sustenance* function (to provide food, shelter, clothing; (2) it has *developmental* functions (through caregiving and parenting); and (3) it has *advocacy* functions (through ensuring the child's access to education, health care, a safe environment, and so on).

In Chapter 6 we reviewed findings that the most important features of caregiving for the infant are *attentive-*

TABLE 8.4
Parenting Styles

Style	Characteristics	Examples
Permissive	Laissez-faire Nonpunitive Child responsible for own actions and decisions Autonomy more important than obedience Nondemanding	"Okay. I mean sure. Whatever you want. You decide."
Authoritarian	Dogmatic Very controlling Obedience highly valued Self-control and autonomy limited Little recourse to reasoning	"You're going to darn well study for 40 minutes right now. Then you say your prayers and go right to bed. Or else!"
Authoritative	Based on reason Permits independence but values obedience Imposes regulations, but allows discussion	"Don't you think you should study for a while before you go to bed? We'd like you to get good grades. But you know we can't let you stay up that late. It isn't good for you."

ness, *physical contact, verbal stimulation, material stimulation, responsive care*, and *absence of restrictiveness.* As infants age and as their verbal, motor, and intellectual abilities blossom, important dimensions of parenting begin to change. But parenting is no less important for older children than it is for preschoolers.

Parenting Styles

Baumrind (1967) looked at the kinds of parenting associated with three distinct groups of children: One group consisted of buoyant, friendly, self-controlled, and self-reliant children; another, of discontented and withdrawn children; and a third, of children who lacked self-reliance and self-control.

Baumrind found some consistent and striking differences among the parenting styles of the mothers and fathers of these children. Parents of children in the friendly, self-controlled, self-reliant group were significantly more controlling, demanding, and loving than parents of either of the other groups. Parents of the discontented and withdrawn children also exercised much control but were detached rather than warm and loving. And parents of the children low in self-esteem were warm but highly permissive.

On the basis of studies such as these, Baumrind identifies three different styles of parenting, each of which is characterized by different types of parental control (Baumrind, 1989): permissive, authoritarian, and authoritative.

Permissive parenting is a nonpunitive, nondirective, and nondemanding form of parental control. Permissive parents allow children to make their own decisions and to govern their own activities. They don't try to control through the exercise of the power that comes from authority, physical strength, status, or the ability to grant or withhold rewards; but they might, on occasion, try to appeal to the child's reason.

Authoritarian parenting is grounded on firm and usually clearly identified standards of conduct. These are often based on religious or political beliefs. The authoritarian parent values obedience above all, and exercises whatever power is necessary to make the child conform. Children in authoritarian homes are given no responsibility for personal decisions; nor are they involved in rational discussion of the family's standards.

Authoritative parenting falls somewhere between permissive and authoritarian control. It uses firm control, but allows for rational discussion of standards and expectations; it values obedience, but tries to promote independence. Authoritative parents, in contrast with authoritarian parents, are those whose standards derive more from reason than from religious or political beliefs (Table 8.4).

Interestingly, the parenting styles of mothers and fathers within families tend to be more alike than different. Bentley and Fox (1991) compared the responses of 52 pairs of mothers and fathers of 1- to 4-year-olds to the Fox Parenting Inventory (Fox, 1990). The scale measures three areas of parenting: *expectations* ("My child should use the toilet without help"); *discipline* ("I yell at my child for whining"); and *nurturance* ("I read to my child at bedtime"). Although mothers received higher nurturance scores than fathers, mothers and fathers did not differ on expectations or discipline.

Novice and Expert Parents

Some parents are probably better at parenting than others. In Cooke's (1991) terms, some are *novices* and some *experts.* How are the two different? Among other things, experts are better at sensing the child's needs and goals, especially in problem-solving situations; they have better general knowledge of child development and child rearing; they have consciously thought about their roles and their goals; and they foster activity that provides their children with opportunities to be self-directive. These characteristics of expert parents are most evident in *competent* children—that is, in children whose measured achievement compares favorably with that of other children.

Do Parents Make a Measurable Difference?

Do parents really matter? And if so, which of these parenting styles is best? The Freudian model says yes, parents matter a great deal because children are extremely sensitive to the emotional experiences of their early lives and especially to their relationships with their parents. And the behavioristic model says yes, too, because children are highly responsive to the rewards and punishments of their environments.

Conflicting Findings
But the research has not always been entirely clear. For example, retrospective studies (looking backward in time, often using interviews or questionnaires) with delinquent and otherwise disturbed adolescents and adults have generally found that their childhoods were marked by a variety of traumas sometimes associated with alcoholic or abusive parents, poverty, authoritarianism, rejection, and a variety of other factors. In one such study, women whose partners were alcohol-dependent reported significantly more problem behaviors among their children (Tubman, 1993). But when researchers try to predict which of a group of children will be maladjusted and which will be happy and well adjusted, they are unsuccessful about two thirds of the time (Skolnick, 1978). Indeed, some very successful, well-adjusted individuals have home environments that should place them at high risk. It seems that predicting the effects of child-rearing practices is far more difficult than explaining these effects after the fact.

Baumrind's Advice
Following extensive investigations of the relationships between behavior and characteristics of parents and the personalities of their children, Baumrind (1977; 1993) concludes that there is no one best way of rearing children. Like McClelland (1973), she argues that there are no *specific* child-rearing practices that should be advocated rather than others (about breast-feeding, toilet training, and coloring with oils, for example); but there are some general characteristics of parents, reflected in their behaviors and attitudes toward their children, that clearly have highly positive effects—and negative ones, too. She found, for example, that parents who were firm and directive were more likely to have children who would be responsible (as opposed to socially disruptive and intolerant of others) and active (as opposed to passive). But what she advocates is not authoritarian but *authoritative* parenting—parenting that is firm, but reasonable; demanding, but warm, nurturing, and loving. Better-than-adequate parenting by parents who are confident of their parenting

skills, she insists, can optimize the development of both children who are normal and those who are at risk (Baumrind, 1993).

There is evidence that Baumrind's advice is sound. Bronstein and colleagues (1993) report a number of studies that have found a link between authoritative parenting and positive child outcomes—and between lax parenting and poorer child adjustment. Similarly, Dekovic and Janssens (1992) found that children of parents who were authoritative (democratic) rather than authoritarian (restrictive) tended to have higher social status among their peers, and were more likely to engage in prosocial behavior.

Child-Care Advice
Parents do make a difference. As McCartney and Jordan (1990) note, the conclusions of parenting research have not always been clear because researchers have tended to use simple models that were not adequate for the complexity of the interactions involved. If the conclusions are to be valid and useful, they argue, researchers must adopt ecological models that not only emphasize the complexity of parenting, but that also recognize the possibility that parenting styles that are excellent for certain children in given circumstances may be quite disastrous for other children—or under different circumstances.

There are nevertheless some recognizably good—and bad—ways of parenting. "At the most simple level," says Christopherson (1988), "if the children are basically happy, the parents are probably not doing too much that is wrong" (p. 133). At a more detailed level, he offers seven guidelines for child-rearing practices (pp. 133–136):

- Behavior and relationships with others depend on the extent to which the child's basic needs are met.
- Parents need to recognize each child as a unique individual.
- The faith, honesty, confidence, and affection between the parent and child affects the quality of the parent–child relationship.
- Parents should separate the worth of a child from the behavior.
- The child should be allowed as much freedom as possible to make mistakes and discoveries, but to do so with safety, respect for the rights of others, and for the social convention.
- Parents should arrange the environment to encourage prosocial behavior.
- Parents should be ready to lend support directly or indirectly through physical or verbal guidance.

Learning How to Parent

In many close-knit and allegedly "primitive" societies, the old ones show the young ones how to parent. There is evidence that, at least to some extent, the same thing happens in our more complex, contemporary societies. Ijzen-

There are countless books, courses, and other sources of professional advice about parenting. But in the end, much of what we do as parents has been learned from our experiences with our own parents.

doorn (1993) surveyed a large number of parenting studies and found a significant amount of what is termed *intergenerational transmission of parenting styles.* It seems that we have a tendency to parent as did our own parents.

Sources of Child-Care Advice

Not all parents simply rely on their own intuition, common sense, and intelligence, or on the transmitted wisdom of their parents and grandparents. Many others turn to one or more of three major groups of commercial child-care advisors: (1) the medical profession, whose doctors and nurses readily provide advice relating to psychological as well as physical health; (2) books; and (3) parenting courses.

Parenting Courses

There are a handful of well-known and widely established parent-education courses, most of which require relatively lengthy training and practice sessions. Some of these have proven especially valuable for children with learning and behavior problems (Thompson, Grow, & Ruma, 1993).

Parenting courses are almost invariably based on a recognition of the rights of children and take into consideration their needs and desires. They treat children as important human beings and discourage punitive approaches to parental control (such as shouting, threatening, physical punishment, and anger-based behaviors), instead encouraging reasoning. The ultimate aim of most of these courses is to foster a warm, loving, and nurturant relation-

ship between parent and child. And the principal method by which each of the various techniques operates involves communication.

In short, most parent education programs encourage parents to be authoritative (firm, democratic, reasonable, respectful) rather than authoritarian (harsh, controlling, demanding, dogmatic, powerful) or permissive (laissez-faire, noncontrolling, weak); in addition, they teach specific techniques to help parents become authoritative. The major weaknesses of these programs include the fact that the solutions they provide are often too simple for the complexity of the problems with which parents must occasionally deal; they typically do not take into account important differences among children of different ages and of different sex; and they sometimes mislead parents into thinking that all answers are to be found in a single method (Brooks, 1981).

FAMILY COMPOSITION

The family, says Hoffman (1991), is a dynamic (changing) and interactive social unit. Parenting styles define one feature of this unit; so do other factors such as birth order, family size, and spacing of siblings.

Birth Order

Galton (1896) was among the first to note the effects of **birth order** when he observed that there was a preponderance of firstborn children among great British scientists. Since then, research has attributed many advantages to being the first born (or an only child). Among them are more rapid and more articulate language development, higher scores on measures of intellectual performance, higher scores on measures of achievement motivation, better academic performance, more curiosity, a higher probability of going to college, and a higher probability of being a president and, of course, a king or queen (see, for example, Gaynor & Runco, 1992).

There are a number of plausible explanations for the observed effects of birth order. Certainly, these effects are not due simply to being a firstborn, a middle, or a last-born child, but to the fact that the interactions and relationships to which the child is exposed are influenced by position in the family. What being first born means, says Albert (1980), is that the child is exposed to a family environment with a different "quality and tone"—one where the child is more likely to be perceived and treated as being "special."

Before we go running off bragging that we're first borns or only children—or complaining that we're not—we should note that the contribution of birth order to intelligence and academic achievement may, after all, be quite negligible. What appears to be important is not just whether you are firstborn or laterborn, but the size of your family as well as its spacing (Bauer, 1992).

Family Size

In general, although things may be "cheaper by the dozen," the larger the family, the more limited the advantages to the children. In fact, some investigators report lower intelligence test scores among members of larger families (for example, Zajonc, 1976). In explaining these findings, Zajonc argues that the intellectual climate in homes with large families is, on the average, less conducive to cognitive development than the climate characteristic of homes with smaller families. However, it's difficult to separate the effect of family size from the effects of social class, religion, or rural versus urban environment. Larger families are far more common among the poor, the culturally deprived, and certain ethnic minorities. When these factors are taken into account, socioeconomic status emerges as a more important predictor of intelligence and academic achievement than does family size or birth order.

Age Intervals

Family size and birth order, taken together, are important predictors of academic success, achievement, and even creativity; and the prediction becomes even more powerful if a third variable is introduced into the equation: that of *age intervals*. Simply put, children whose siblings are significantly younger or older seem to be at an advantage. Gaynor and Runco (1992) looked at the correlation between the creative abilities of 116 children who had siblings and the age interval between the children and their closest sibling. They found that larger age intervals were positively related to higher measured creativity.

In summarizing various studies that have looked at the effects of family spacing on developmental outcomes, Wagner, Schubert, and Schubert (1985) conclude: "The findings on spacing effects are astonishingly consistent. Close spacing . . . seems deleterious to intelligence and achievement [and] to good relations between children and parents" (p. 196).

The influence of age intervals, like that of birth order and family size, is probably best explained in terms of the sorts of family relationships and interactions that are most likely to result. A child whose siblings are much older or much younger, Gaynor and Runco (1992) explain, is more likely than other children to be perceived by parents as special.

We should always bear in mind that the conclusions of our social sciences are usually based on the average performance of large groups of individuals. Within these groups, there are those whose behavior does not come close to matching the predictions that social science might make based on its conclusions. Thus there are saints and geniuses whose siblings numbered in the tens and twenties, all closely spaced; and there are poltroons and oafs who were born first into tiny little families.

ONE-PARENT FAMILIES

Close to half of all American children are spending (or will spend) an average of six years in a family with only one parent. The large majority of these one-parent families, most of which are headed by mothers rather than fathers (see Figure 8.5), result from separation or divorce; a smaller proportion result from the death of a parent or from bearing children out of wedlock. Amato and Keith (1991) cite projections that parents of 38 percent of white children and 75 percent of black children in the United States will divorce before the children are 16.

Do Separation or Divorce Have Negative Effects?

There is considerable controversy over the most likely effects on children of parental separation and divorce. One large body of research seems to show clearly that the effects are primarily negative and that they are also highly general. Other recent studies present far less negative outcomes.

For example, Allison and Furstenberg's (1989) investigation of 1,197 children found that marital breakup had widespread and lasting effects evident in higher incidences of problem behaviors, increased psychological distress, and poorer academic performance. Similarly, Amato and Keith's (1991) summary of 92 individual studies (termed a *meta-analysis*) of the impact of divorce found significant negative effects on school achievement, behavior, adjustment, self-concept, and relations with both the remaining and the departed parent. In Bronstein and associates' (1993) words: "Children from divorced families are more likely to experience behavioral, social, emotional, or academic problems" (p. 268).

Age- and Sex-Related Effects of Divorce

The Amato and Keith (1991) meta-analysis concludes that the negative effects of divorce are related to the ages of the children. In almost all investigations, the most serious effects are on children in the middle age groups—mainly elementary and high school—with college students least affected. Frieman (1993) also reports that parental breakup often results in dramatic changes in classroom behavior.

Wallerstein and Kelly (1976; 1980) conducted a longitudinal investigation of age-specific effects of divorce among a group of 60 families. Their conclusion was that divorce has negative effects at all ages. Specifically, they describe the effects for the youngest group (2- to 3-year-olds) as being evident in regression manifested in loss of toilet habits, bewilderment, and clinging behavior directed toward strangers. Three- and 4-year-old preschoolers showed loss of confidence and self-esteem, and were quick to blame themselves for the departure of the father. The next age group (5- and 6-year-olds) seemed less affected developmentally, although some of the daughters tend to deny the situation and to continue expecting their fathers' return. The 7- and 8-year-olds were understandably frightened by the divorce and intensely saddened, many of them missing their fathers constantly. Many of these children also live in fear of making their mothers angry, perhaps imagining that she too might leave them. Nine- and 10-year-olds initially react with apparent acceptance, many of them trying to understand why the divorce has occurred. But their outward calm covers feelings of anger, sometimes intense hostility toward one or the other parent (or both), and shame (Wallerstein & Kelly, 1976). About half suffered from varying degrees of depression, low self-esteem, poorer school performance, and poorer relationships with peers. The adolescent group (ages 12 to 14) reveal a much deeper understanding of their parents' divorce (Springer & Wallerstein, 1983). Many adolescents were keen observers and analyzers of interactions between their parents, and were able to evaluate the situation objectively. Unlike younger children, they are much less likely to harbor feelings of guilt about the divorce or hostility toward one or both parents. However, some of these children, who initially seem to cope well, later manifest varying degrees of anger, resentment, and maladjustment—an example of what Wallerstein (1989) labeled the "sleeper" effect.

Some researchers have suggested that boys are more adversely affected by divorce than are girls, although the Amato and Keith (1991) meta-analysis indicates that sex differences are not very pronounced. Other than for the fact that boys sometimes exhibit more unhappiness or emotional distress following a divorce than do girls, there is no consistent pattern of greater negative effects for boys than girls. In short, there is no greater incidence of behavior problems, of difficulty in school, of lowered self-esteem, or of problems with parent–child relationships.

Why Divorce or Separation Might Have Negative Effects

There are several reasons why divorce might affect children negatively, explains Amato (1993). These include the absence of one of the parents, problems associated with adjusting to the remaining parent, conflict between parents, economic hardship, and generally stressful life changes. They include, as well, the child's relationship with the departing parent both before and after the divorce or separation.

Father (or Mother) Absence
Much of the research in this area has focused on, and has attributed negative consequences to, the father's absence. We might expect that father absence could affect children either because the roles traditionally filled by the father would no longer be filled (or might be filled less ade-

quately by the mother, who must also continue to carry out her own roles) or because the absence of the father has an effect on the mother, who then interacts with her children differently.

Economic Impact
The economic circumstances of the one-parent home are, on average, considerably less advantageous than those of the two-parent family. In 1991, the average income in mother-headed homes was only 60 percent that of father-headed homes (and 40 percent that of married-couple families). More telling, 46 percent of single-mother families were below the poverty level compared with only 7 percent of married couples with children (U.S. Bureau of the Census, 1994). The change from relative affluence to poverty can be especially difficult for children whose peers are more advantaged. Economic hardship also increases the risk of trouble with the law, and is associated with a higher probability of not finishing school. (See At a Glance: "Characteristics of U.S. Families," and Figures 8.6, 8.7, and 8.8.)

Family Conflict
A third explanation for the negative effects of divorce relates to stresses associated with conflict between parents, both before and during the process of separation (Thiessen, 1993). One of the most striking findings revealed in the research summarized by Amato and Keith (1991) is that children living in high-conflict but intact families fared less well than children whose parents had divorced: They manifested more adjustment difficulties, lower self-esteem, and more behavior problems. Conversely, in a study of 225 divorced fathers, Arditti and Michaelena (1994) found that those who had the most positive relationships with their wives both before and after the marital breakup also experienced better postdivorce relationships with their children.

Parental Disengagement
Peterson, Leigh, and Day (1984) present what they refer to as a "middle range theory of the potential impact of divorce." It is a theory that deals with two principal variables. The independent variable is the degree of *parental disengagement*. (An *independent variable*, recall, is a variable that, in an experiment, is manipulated by the experimenter; it is the variable that is expected to have an effect on outcomes.) The dependent variable is the child's *social competence*. (A *dependent variable*, remember, is that which is presumably affected by the independent variable.) So, the degree of parental disengagement—which ranges from varying levels of marital discord through temporary separation, long-term separation, divorce, and death—may affect the child's social competence, which is manifested in the child's ability "to engage in social relationships and possess adaptive psychological qualities" (Peterson et al., 1984, p. 4).

CHARACTERISTICS OF U.S. FAMILIES

Dramatic increases in divorce rates now mean that more than one child in four lives with only one parent; and almost 9 times out of 10, that parent is the mother (Figure 8.6). Unfortunately, the median income for mother-only families about half that for father-only families (and less than one third that for two-parent families). In addition, of the 2.2 million children who lived only with their fathers in 1992, more than half lived in homes their family owned (51.5 percent); in contrast, only 31.7 percent of children living with mothers were living in their own homes (Figures 8.7 and 8.8).

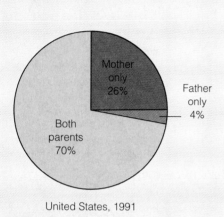

United States, 1991

FIGURE 8.6
Living arrangements of U.S. children. (From data in U.S. Bureau of the Census, 1994, p. 63.)

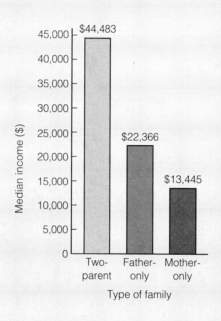

FIGURE 8.7
Median family income of mother-only, father-only, and two-parent U.S. families with children under 18, 1992. The median is the midpoint; half the families in each category earn more than the median and half earn less. (From data in U.S. Bureau of the Census, 1994, p. 471.)

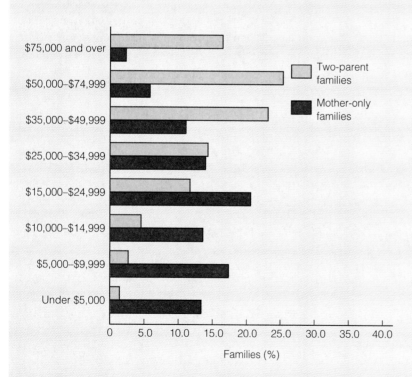

FIGURE 8.8
Percentage of two-parent and mother-only U.S. families in various income brackets, 1992. (From data in U.S. Bureau of the Census, 1994, p. 471.)

Although divorce is almost invariably a difficult time for children, its effects vary enormously depending on the age of the children, their relationship with parents both before and after the separation, and the social contexts within which they live. That these two children have each other to play with may also help a great deal.

In examining the relationship of these two variables—parental disengagement and the child's social competence—Peterson, Leigh, and Day (1984) take into account much of the wealth of research in this area and reduce it to a handful of conclusions:

- The higher the degree of disengagement, the greater the impact on the child. In other words, divorce would generally be more stressful than temporary separation. By the same token, a situation in which one of the parents breaks all ties with the child would be more stressful than one in which both parents continue to maintain close ties with the child.

- The severity of the immediate crisis brought about by the divorce is closely related to the negative impact of divorce. Children who have been abused or neglected by a parent are less likely to view the divorce as a very serious calamity, and are likely to experience a lower degree of stress.

- The more accurate the child's perception of the parents' relationship prior to marital breakup, the less negative the consequences. Those who incorrectly view their parents' relationship as "happy" immediately before separation or divorce suffer the highest stress.

- The more positive and amicable the parents' relationship following marriage breakup, the less negative the effect on the child.

- The closer the relationship between the leaving parent and the child prior to marital breakup, the more serious the effect on the child.

- Age is related to the severity of consequences in a curvilinear fashion, with the most serious consequences occurring for children between the ages of 3 and 9, and the least severe occurring before and after those ages.

Less Negative Effects of Divorce

An increasing number of researchers do not agree with the general conclusion that children of divorce are likely to suffer lasting adjustment problems. Demo (1993), for example, argues that much of the research that supports this conclusion is flawed. Among other things, much of it failed to take into consideration the predivorce status of the children involved. The Wallerstein and Kelly longitudinal study, for example, describes troubled children of various ages *following* their parents' divorce; but because there is no information concerning what these children were like *before* the divorce, it does not follow logically that their present condition was caused by the divorce. In fact, these children might have been negatively affected by parental conflict before the parents separated.

K. R. Allen (1993) and Kurdek (1993) also suggest that the general conclusion that divorce has primarily negative effects on children is based on relatively weak evidence, unsupported speculation, and an unacknowledged bias toward the traditional family structure. In fact, more recent research often fails to find significant negative effects among children following parental separation. For example, Kier and Lewis (1993) compared 38 infants and preschoolers (ages 11 to 45 months) whose parents had divorced or separated, with 38 comparable children from intact families. Their general conclusion: These infants were far more alike than different. In short, there was little evidence of children's problems resulting from the family breakup.

Resolving the Controversy

One of the remarkable findings of the Amato and Keith (1991) meta-analysis of 92 studies was that the year of the study is related to its outcome. In general, more recent investigations are finding less negative effects on children. Apparently, the impact of divorce was far stronger in the 1950s and 1960s than is now the case. Why? Perhaps because divorces were less common, less culturally acceptable, and more difficult to arrange. Consequently, both children and parents would be more likely to have to cope with disapproval, and would be provided with less support. Perhaps for these same reasons, the consequences of divorce are less severe in the United States than they are in many other countries (Amato & Keith, 1991).

A Final Word

There are several dangers implicit in interpreting studies such as these. One is that we might inadvertently stress either the negative or the positive aspects of divorce. Although divorce is often a trying time for children, living in conflict (and sometimes with physical and mental abuse) can also be very trying. At a certain point, family conflict in the intact home may have negative effects on children far greater than the potentially negative effects of divorce. When that point is reached, divorce often is the best solution, both for parents and for their children. It bears repeating that some loving single parents can effectively overcome whatever trauma might be associated with the loss of one parent, and that there are countless two-parent families in which parenting is inadequate and love is seldom if ever shown.

Most children (and parents) adapt to life in a single-parent home within two or three years of the initial disruption (Hetherington, Stanley-Hagan, & Anderson, 1989). Richards and Schmiege (1993) interviewed 71 single parents. They found that money was the number one problem for mothers; problems with the ex-spouse was a greater problem for men. Both men and women reported that parenting became easier over time. However, at about the time that adjustment to life in the one-parent family seems almost complete, remarriage often occurs. And that, too, can require major readjustments.

CHILDREN IN STEPFAMILIES

About 60 percent of all first marriages now end in divorce; and the majority of those who divorce remarry. Thus about half of all American children spend at least some time in a one-parent family and many of them also eventually become members of stepfamilies (also called *blended* families) (Pasley, Dollahite, & Ihinger-Tallman, 1993).

A *stepfamily* is the family grouping that results from the remarriage of a widowed or divorced parent and in which, consequently, only one of the two married adults in the family is the child's biological parent. More than one in every six American families with children under 18 is a stepfamily (U.S. Bureau of the Census, 1994); and projections are that this proportion may reach 50 percent by the year 2000.

Interestingly, stepfamilies are no more enduring than first marriages, with about 60 percent ending in divorce (Pill, 1990). In addition, remarriages in which there are stepchildren are more likely to dissolve than if there are no children, especially if the children are older—above 9 (Visher & Visher, 1988).

Possible Problems in Stepfamilies

Does this mean that parenting is more difficult in stepfamilies? Perhaps. Clearly, the number and complexity of relationships that can exist within a stepfamily is much greater. For example, the marriage of a man and woman who have both been married previously and who both have children can create a staggering number of new relationships involving the biological relatives of each of the stepparents, not to mention previous spouses and their parents, siblings, uncles, aunts, and cousins. In addition, there has been considerable legal ambiguity surrounding the rights and obligations of stepparents and stepchildren, especially in cases where the stepfamily breaks up (Fine & Fine, 1992).

The remarriage of the parent in a one-parent family sometimes brings new problems for a child who not only has had to cope with the initial disruption of the family through death or divorce but must now cope with another reorganization of the family. And whereas remarriage is almost invariably seen as a highly positive gain for the *parent* because it reestablishes an important relationship, it is often seen as a loss by the *child* because it implies a change in the relationship between the child and the natural parent. Many children experience feelings of abandonment following the remarriage of a parent (Fine & Kurdek, 1992).

In addition to the loss, real or imagined, of some of the biological parent's attention and perhaps affection, the stepchild must now also deal with establishing new relationships with the stepparent, with stepsiblings if there are any, and perhaps with a new set of grandparents and other relatives. Furthermore, the stepchild's role in the family often changes. This can be particularly difficult for

Although children sometimes experience problems adjusting to life in a stepfamily, the effects of stepfamilies on children are often highly positive. This stepmother hardly looks like the wicked stepmother of fairy tales.

adolescent children. Their newly developed adult roles, sometimes accelerated by the absence of the parent (for example, the boy has become "man of the house" following his biological father's departure), can be severely disrupted by the appearance of a new stepparent. Similarly, the creation of a new stepfamily can disrupt established patterns of control and discipline and sometimes lead to serious problems ("You're not my dad! I don't have to listen to you!").

Other possible problems sometimes associated with the stepfamily include sexual fantasies and inclinations between stepsiblings as well as between children and their stepparents (and resulting feelings of guilt and confusion); stepsibling rivalry and competition; ambivalence about the stepchild's role in the family; confusion over whether and how the departed parent should continue to fit into the child's life; and the need for the child to abandon the fantasy or wish that the natural parents might one day be reunited.

The Positive Side

Fortunately, the effects of stepfamilies on children are often highly positive. Pasley and colleagues (1993) report that well-functioning stepfamilies are no different from well-functioning intact families, although it's true that there is a sometimes difficult period of early adjustment. Interestingly, stepparents who have previously been parents tend to adjust more easily to the stepparenting role. Also, those who ease more slowly into the new stepparenting roles fare better than those who try to assume the role too quickly—especially with respect to control and discipline.

The fairy-tale stereotype of the stepfather or stepmother as the wicked wielder of terrible powers is, in fact, a fairy tale. Clearly, many stepparents are kind and considerate people who want to love and be loved by their stepchildren. When the initial adjustments have been made, the stepchild might, in a great many cases, be as fortunate as many in intact nuclear families.

NONPARENTAL CHILD CARE

In the old days, most North American children spent their preschool years in intimate contact with their mothers. Today an increasing number of children are cared for during the day by others. In fact, child care by someone other than a parent is now the norm for more than 50 percent of all American preschool children—a percentage that is climbing (Browne Miller, 1990). About 75 percent of mothers of preschoolers now work, and it is becoming increasingly common for many mothers to go back to work within weeks of childbirth. In 1993, 57.5 percent of U.S. women went back to work within one year of giving birth (U.S. Bureau of the Census, 1994). As a result, *infant* child care is the fastest growing type of supplemental care in the United States.

Nonparental child care takes a variety of forms ranging from situations in which families can afford to hire a private, in-the-child's-home caregiver to substitute for the mother during her absence, to institutionalized centers for large numbers of children with many caregivers. Most common, however, are private homes that look after perhaps a half-dozen youngsters—referred to as *family child care*. About half of all children are cared for by grandparents or other relatives (Hofferth, 1992). Although family child care is the most common form of early child care, most of the research in this area has focused on institutional centers.

In addition to arranged care for children, there are self-supervised or *latchkey* children, so called because their parents sometimes hang keys around their necks so they can let themselves into their homes after school. Some studies report that self-supervision is sometimes associated with more behavior problems (Vandell & Ramanan, 1991). Many find no measurable difference between self-supervised children and those who are looked after by their parents.

General Effects of Child Care

Given the proliferation of nonparental child care, it's important to ask whether it's as good for infants and preschoolers as parental care and what the characteristics of good child care are. There is no lack of research (see, for example, Hayes, Palmer, & Zaslow, 1990; Scarr & Eisenberg, 1993).

Child Care Versus Home Care

The early emphasis in much of this research was to determine whether infants and preschoolers cared for by someone other than their mother might suffer harmful consequences relating to difficulties in forming affectional bonds with their mother. In spite of this largely negative orientation, a review of several dozen early studies found few significant differences in social, intellectual, and motor development between child-care and home-care children (Bronfenbrenner, Belsky, & Steinberg, 1977). More recent research has generally corroborated these findings. As Bowman (1993) puts it, "In general, nonfamily care and education have not been found to jeopardize the development of young children" (p. 109).

Specific Effects of Child Care

Child-care research now often focuses on the characteristics of programs that seem to have the most positive effects on children, as well as on the characteristics of children for whom nonparental care is most likely to be a positive or a negative experience. For example, Phillips, McCartney, and Scarr (1987), in a study of 166 child-care children, found a significant relationship between indicators of child-care quality (such as staff–child ratio, caregiver–child interaction, equipment and supplies, and so on) and the child's social development (revealed in measures of intelligence, considerateness, sociability, task orientation, and dependence). Similarly, Caughy, DiPietro, and Strobino (1994) looked at the effects of nonparent child care among 867 5- and 6-year-old children. Children from the more impoverished homes in the sample typically fared better on later tests of reading and arithmetic, especially if they had been placed in child care before the age of 1, and also when the child care occurred in a center rather than in a private home. Children from more optimal home environments did not show the same advantages of child care.

In summary, the effects of nonparental child care are closely related to *quality* of care. Although poor quality care has sometimes been associated with poorer adjustment and social-emotional problems, especially among boys (particularly if they are temperamentally difficult) (Mott, 1991), higher quality child care has been linked with measurable advantages for children, especially for

those from disadvantaged homes. What is important to note is that the occasional negative effects of child care are almost invariably associated with *poorer quality* child care (Scarr & Eisenberg, 1993).

Finding Quality Child Care

How can parents determine what is likely to be good or bad child care? In a highly practical book, Endsley and Bradbard (1981) try to advise parents on this question. They suggest that although it is difficult to evaluate different child-care programs, those that are very bad may have a number of characteristics in common, and those that are excellent might also. Among programs to avoid are those characterized by the following:

- Unsanitary and unhealthy physical surroundings
- Obvious physical hazards
- Excessive overcrowding, both in terms of the available space and too many young children for the available supervising adults (for example, adult–child ratios that exceed 1 to 20 or, in the case of infants, 1 to 10)
- Lack of activities and materials that are interesting and challenging to young children
- Staff, usually untrained, who are at best thoughtless and insensitive and at worst reject and abuse young children
- Disregard for parent's feelings about child rearing (p. 32)

In contrast, characteristics associated with high-quality programs include:

- The financial resources to design and equip a special environment for their children
- The time, freedom, motivation, and physical energy to work with their children only for 6 to 10 hours each day
- The training necessary to organize experiences and activities to develop optimally their children's understanding of themselves and the world about them (p. 33)

Licensing requirements for establishing child-care facilities vary tremendously throughout North America, and are usually nonexistent for smaller, family-based centers (Hernandez & Myers, 1993). As a result, although there are many high-quality facilities available, there are others whose environments are of far lower quality. To evaluate these facilities, Endsley and Bradbard (1981) suggest that parents should obtain personal references and, perhaps most important, visit the centers, observe them in operation, and talk with the people in charge. Sadly, however, most of us are likely to spend more time looking, comparing, and obtaining references when buying a car than we are when finding someone to care for our children.

Social Development

1. Erikson's stage theory of social development describes the resolution of psychosocial conflicts through the development of competence. Stage 3, *initiative versus guilt*, spans the preschool period, and involves developing a sense of personal agency and accepting responsibility for one's actions. Bandura's theory of social development holds that much social learning takes place through observational learning (imitation), including acquiring such socially important characteristics as the tendency to cooperate or to compete, which are highly influenced by the individual's immediate culture.

Preschoolers' Emotions

2. Socializing emotions requires learning how to interpret feelings (sometimes using *social referencing*), achieving some control over them (through *other-* and *self-regulatory behaviors*), and learning rules of emotional display.

Play

3. Practice play may be useful for developing and exercising important physical skills, as well as for establishing social position and teaching acceptable forms of behavior. Pretend play is closely related to cognitive development and the development of the child's *theory of mind*. Social play underlies personality development and the development of social skills. Infants as young as 1 year are often capable of pretend play (for example, pretending to be asleep or pretending to eat). Later, during the preschool period, boys' pretend play often involves monsters or superheroes; girls' pretend play is often more concerned with home-related or nurturant themes. Daydreaming and imaginary playmates are forms of pretend play. Social play, which involves interaction among two or more children, may be onlooker play (looking without joining in), parallel play (playing independently side by side), associative play (playing together without sharing rules), or cooperative play (sharing of rules and goals).

Gender Roles in Early Childhood

4. Gender roles, the range of behaviors and personality traits that are considered appropriate for males and females (that are *masculine* or *feminine*) result from an interaction of genetic and contextual forces. Sex differences in childhood are evident in the tendency of boys to play more physically, in the toys they select and are given, and in the roles they assume in their pretend games (these differences are more apparent later rather than earlier in

the preschool period). A cognitive explanation for gender typing describes three stages: recognizing basic gender identity (maleness or femaleness); realizing that gender is stable, permanent, and unchangeable; and realizing that superficial changes, in dress or behavior, for example, do not alter gender.

5. Genetic influences on gender differences are especially evident in the greater aggressiveness of males. Contextual influences are reflected in the fact that most parents treat boys and girls differently—rewarding aggression, independence, and boisterousness in boys, and nurturant, affective, compliant behavior in girls.

The Contemporary Family

6. A *nuclear* family (as opposed to an *extended* family) consists of mother, father, and children, and is no longer the most common North American family. Baumrind describes parenting styles as permissive (nonpunitive, noncontrolling, nondemanding), authoritarian (dogmatic, controlling, obedience-oriented), or authoritative (firm but based on reason, nondogmatic, geared toward promoting independence but encouraging adherence to standards)—and advocates authoritative parenting. Both the psychoanalytic and the behavioristic models probably exaggerate the extent to which the child is susceptible to external influences. Three important sources of childcare advice are the medical profession, books, and parenting courses.

Family Composition

7. Firstborn and only children often have some achievement and intellectual advantages over their siblings—as do children whose siblings are much younger or older than they are. Children from larger families sometimes do less well than children from smaller families on measures of intellectual performance. These observations are due mainly to the social and economic characteristics of large and small families, and to the influence of birth order, birth interval, and family size on the relationships most likely to develop between children and their parents.

One-Parent Families

8. Some of the possible negative effects of divorce and separation on children relate to the child's age: Preschool children may view divorce as a parent leaving them because they have been "bad"; older children may experience anger and hostility, mixed with sadness; adolescents may view the situation more realistically. These effects may be due to absence of a parent, family conflict, economic

hardship, and stressful life changes, and are more serious with greater parental *disengagement*. An increasing number of more recent studies find few long-term negative effects of divorce, perhaps because it is now more common and more socially accepted.

Children in Stepfamilies

9. Stepfamilies result from the remarriage of a widowed or divorced parent. Stepchildren sometimes face problems relating to loss of some of the parent's time and affection, establishing relationships with stepfamily members, and abandoning the fantasy that the biological parents may reunite. In many cases, these potential problems are insignificant or nonexistent.

Nonparental Child Care

10. Nonparental child care does not generally have negative effects on the social, emotional, or cognitive development of children and can, in fact, have beneficial effects, especially for children from disadvantaged homes. Important factors to consider when selecting a day-care facility include staff–children ratio, physical environment, equipment and materials provided for children, financial resources, and the qualifications of staff members.

FOCUS QUESTIONS: APPLICATIONS

1. What do preschoolers understand of what others feel?

- Can you explain why young children are so easily moved to tears or to laughter?

2. What is the importance of play in early childhood?

- Write a major paper relating the different kinds of play to social, emotional, and physical development, explaining how each might contribute to the child's development.

3. To what extent are masculinity and femininity determined by early experiences?

- List and research the arguments you might use to support the proposition that gender is (is not) determined largely by heredity.

4. How important is parenting? Family size? Position in the family?

- Can you classify the parenting behavior of your own parents in terms of one of Baumrind's classifications? How differently do you suppose you might have turned out given a different style of parenting?

5. What are the effects of divorce on children?

- Using library resources, write a paper on the effects of parental death (or divorce) on children of different ages.

STUDY TERMS

associative play   229

authoritarian parenting   235

authoritative parenting   235

autonomy versus shame and doubt   222

birth order   237

cooperative play   229

display rules   226

extended family   233

gender roles   230

gender schemas   230

gender typing   230

identification   223

imaginative play   227

imitation   223

initiative versus guilt   223

metacognition   228

nuclear family   233

onlooker play   229

parallel play   229

permissive parenting   235

play   226

practice play   227

pretend play   227

psychosocial development   222

regulating emotions   226

sensorimotor play   227

social play   228

social referencing   225

socialization   222

solitary play   229

stereotypes   231

symbolic models   225

theory of mind   228

trust versus mistrust   222

Paley's books offer a fascinating, often delightful, description of life in the preschool. The first of these short books follows 3-year-old Mollie through a year of nursery school, revealing her excitement and her fears in the little dramas that are an intrinsic part of Paley's classes. The second follows the lives of a kindergarten class, providing fascinating insights into how they struggle to arrive at their own understanding of what it means to be a boy or a girl:

Paley, V. G. (1986). *Mollie is three: Growing up in school.* Chicago: University of Chicago Press.

Paley, V. G. (1984). *Boys and girls: Superheroes in the doll corner.* Chicago: University of Chicago Press.

The first of the following two books presents a brief but detailed analysis of the games children play and of the role of play in development; the second is a collection of articles dealing with the significance of social pretend play:

Hughes, F. P. (1990). *Children, play, and development.* Boston: Allyn & Bacon.

Howes, C., Unger, O., & Matheson, C. C. (Eds.). (1992). *The collaborative construction of pretend: Social pretend play functions.* New York: State University of New York Press.

The Hernandez and Myers book presents a detailed analysis of recent changes in North America that are having an important impact on child care:

Hernandez, D. J., & Myers, D. E. (1993). *America's children: Resources from family, government, and the economy.* New York: Russell Sage.

The following collection is a useful look at recent changes in nonparental child care:

Booth, A. (Ed.). (1992). *Child care in the 1990's: Trends and consequences.* Hillsdale, NJ: Erlbaum.

"Suppose there are two mobs?" suggested Mr. Snodgrass.
"Shout with the largest," replied Mr. Pickwick.

CHARLES DICKENS
Pickwick Papers

MIDDLE CHILDHOOD

PART FOUR

As we see in Chapters 9 and 10, there are more than just two mobs in middle childhood. All compete for the child's attention. "This way," the mobs clamor. "Everybody is going this way. You should go where everybody is going."

"Study!" schools say. "It's important for your future!"

"Play!" friends and peers urge. "It's heck-a-fun!"

"Watch!" television demands. "Never mind playing and studying. Watch and then run out and buy what I sell you!"

"Read!" the newsstands coax. "Look at the pretty pictures. Become a comic-book collector!"

"Caution!" parents advise. "Find some balance, my child. Study, play, watch, read. Be cautious. *And* do the dishes!"

Is the child just some piece of clay to be shaped by the strongest and the most determined hands? Or is there a *self* that emerges through childhood and into adulthood—a self that evolves from the budding consciousness of the infant, that learns intention and willfulness and the making of choices, that develops notions of worth and feelings of effectiveness, or sometimes of powerlessness?

Perhaps, Mr. Snodgrass, even if there are two very large and very loud mobs—or even a dozen of them—you should not simply shout with the largest.

If you have a self, you might first want to listen to what each has to say.

Physical and Cognitive Development: Middle Childhood

*T*he cattle . . . eat themselves up . . . into obesity.

J. Wilson
Chronicles of the North

It's not a happy image, that of cows eating themselves **CHAPTER 9** into obesity. It comes to my mind as I sit on the bench at the back of the store, sucking quietly on a Pepsi, listening to the grown-ups talk. What brings obese cows to mind is what Mr. Delisle is saying about Dennis. "He'll wind up in the circus," he tells my dad knowingly, "where people pay good money to look at guys who weigh a thousand pounds."

"Yep," adds Mr. Boutin, "He's already like a little Caterpillar."

I tell Claude what they said and right on the spot, he invents Dennis's nickname. "He's a WD9," he says, that being the only model of Caterpillar any of us has reason to know by name because Paul's uncle has one.

"WD9," we chant when Dennis waddles by on his way to and from school. "WD9," we write on his notebooks when his back is turned. "WD9," we yell at his house in the darkness, proving that we are as mean as any semi-organized gang of elementary school ruffians.

For a long time, WD9 Dennis suffers mostly in silence, accepting the taunts and the teasing tight-lipped, avoiding us whenever he can. As he becomes more clearly the object of our ridicule and sport, the last of his friends abandon him, and he takes to spending every night and most weekends shut in his house. Greatly encouraged, we redouble our efforts to shame him at every turn.

Then one day, Paul meets Dennis alone in the alley behind the Watrin house. Maybe Paul whispers, "WD9." Maybe not. Whatever, Dennis loses his sad-eyed control, grabs Paul, throws him face down in the dirt—and sits on him.

"Sat on me for an hour," Paul explains, still visibly shaken the next morning. We all act like we think this is hugely funny. Hah! Hah! But after school, as if this is something he has been meaning to do, Dennis walks up to Claude, thumps him down on his belly in the grass, and sits on him, glowering at the rest of us. We stand silently, listening to the cries of our poor leader, who's not a very big guy. Then I have to go home right away, and so do the others. And when the last of us has left, Dennis gets up and wordlessly walks away.

THIS CHAPTER

Dennis never became close friends with any of our group, although some of us used to talk about "our buddy Dennis," after his career in football. Nor was he ever forced to join a circus. Instead, he enlisted in the armed forces. But that story ends very badly. At Wainwright training camp, he stepped into a badger hole and fell, and a tank, bigger even than a WD9, ran over him.

Dennis's story is not the story of the average child in middle childhood; it's the story of a unique individual. But it, too, provides glimpses into the minds of children. The purpose of this chapter is to clarify those glimpses. It traces the continued growth of the child's mind through **middle childhood** (approximately ages 6 to 12), looking at how children know and remember, how they solve problems, how they develop notions of themselves as effective processors of information. It deals with the growth of normal intelligence, as well as with exceptionality. But first, it looks at physical development.

PHYSICAL AND MOTOR DEVELOPMENT

The physical development of many of the world's children is far from optimal—sometimes because of inadequate diet, and sometimes simply because of lack of exercise. In 35 of the world's most undeveloped countries, 50 percent of children under age 4 are significantly underweight. Not surprisingly, the mortality rate for these countries is more than 100 per 1,000 children under age 5 (Grant, 1993).

In contrast, the under 5 mortality rate for the world's most developed countries is insignificant, as is the percentage of children who are underweight. In fact, estimates are that as many as 20 percent of all North American children may be obese. These observations underline the importance of knowledge about the normal course of physical development and about the contributions of nutrition and exercise to physical and mental well-being.

Height and Weight

Although girls tend to be slightly shorter and slightly lighter than boys from birth to the end of the preschool period, the growth rates for each are almost identical. This pattern changes in middle childhood. As Figures 9.1 and 9.2 show, although the average girl is three fourths of an inch (2 cm) shorter at the age of 6, she has caught up with and surpassed the average boy by the age of 11 and is still slightly taller at the age of 12. With respect to weight, girls are close to 2 pounds (1 kg) lighter at the age of 6 and do not catch up with boys until the age of 11. Between the ages of 11 and 12, however, girls undergo a sudden spurt of weight gain that puts them 3 pounds ahead of boys in a single year. Chapter 11 points out that not until the age of 14½ do boys overtake girls in weight, and at 13½ they exceed girls in height.

Fat and Fat-Free Mass

A common way of describing the mass of the human body is in terms of parts referred to as **fat-free mass** and **fat mass.** Fat-free mass, also termed *lean body mass* and consisting mainly of bones, organs, and muscle tissue, is the most stable part of body mass. Fat mass, consisting mainly of *white adipose tissue* (fat cells), is more susceptible to the influences of diet and exercise. In the average adult male, about 85 percent of body weight is accounted for by fat-free mass and only 15 percent is fat mass. In contrast, almost 30 percent of the weight of average adult females is fat mass (Malina & Bouchard, 1991).

In infancy, fat mass is relatively high in both males and females (about 25 percent of total body weight). The pattern for boys is for a gradual reduction of percentage of fat mass through middle childhood, with a very slight increase during the growth spurt at adolescence. Following this growth spurt, there is continued slow decline until the adult ratio of about 15 percent fat mass is reached at around age 20. For girls, the reduction in proportion of fat mass is even more gradual until early adolescence, when there is again a very gradual increase until the adult ratio of close to 30 percent is reached at about age 20 (Malina & Bouchard, 1991). In general, then, girls tend to retain a higher percentage of body fat than boys, whereas muscle development is more rapid in boys (Smoll & Schutz, 1990). (Figure 11.3 in Chapter 11 shows growth curves for fat mass in males and females.)

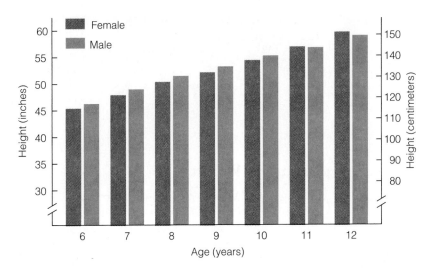

FIGURE 9.1
Height at 50th percentile for U.S. children. (From the Health Department, Milwaukee, Wisconsin; based on data by H. C. Stuart and H. V. Meredith, prepared for use in Children's Medical Center, Boston. Used by permission of the Milwaukee Health Department.)

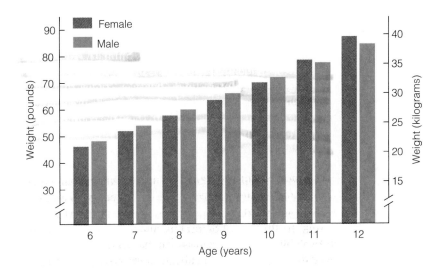

FIGURE 9.2
Weight at 50th percentile for U.S. children. (From the Health Department, Milwaukee, Wisconsin; based on data by H. C. Stuart and H. V. Meredith, prepared for use in Children's Medical Center, Boston. Used by permission of the Milwaukee Health Department.)

The Growth Spurt

Toward the end of middle childhood there occurs a sudden growth spurt in both height and weight. It is generally taken to signal the beginning of sexual maturation (and of adolescence). *On average*, this spurt begins almost two years earlier for girls than for boys. Average age of maximum rate of growth in height (termed **peak height velocity**) is 11.4 for girls and 13.4 for boys (Malina, Bouchard, & Beunen, 1988). For some, however, the growth spurt can occur years later or earlier than average. As a result, there are sometimes dramatic height differences among children of the same ages during middle childhood. This can be a source of embarrassment and worry for some children. At a time when peer approval has become among the most important things in life, it may be seen as a great misfortune to be either precocious or retarded in physical development. Nature sometimes compensates for initial discrepancies so that the early-maturing child stops growing while others catch up—or

so that the late-maturing child suddenly blossoms and rapidly overtakes the others. And sometimes it doesn't. (See Chapter 11 for a discussion of the psychological effects of early and late maturation.)

Nutrition and Health

If they are well nourished, between the ages of 6 and 12, children grow 2 to 3 inches (4.4–6.6 cm) and gain about 5 to 7 pounds (approximately 2–2.75 kg) each year. Normal gains in height are a better indicator of the long-term adequacy of the child's nutrition than are weight gains; gains in weight often reflect the shorter-term effects of nutrition.

Nutrients are found in various classes of food and drink, among the most important of which is water. It makes up slightly more than 60 percent of the body weight of children (and of adults). Also critical are carbohydrates, fats, proteins, and various minerals and vitamins. In fact, during middle childhood, the recommended daily

Children's motor coordination, agility, and strength increase dramatically through middle childhood. The skills required for this girl's participation in a strikingly complex rope skipping game are tremendously important to her self-concept and happiness.

allowances of substances like calcium and most vitamins and minerals are almost as high for children as for adults (Food and Nutrition Board, 1989).

Unfortunately, as we saw in Chapter 1, many of the world's children are not well nourished, and many millions die of starvation each year. Although starvation is uncommon in North America, malnutrition is not. Malnutrition takes one of two forms: overnutrition, often leading to obesity; and undernutrition, often reflected in the intake of foods low in protein and essential vitamins and minerals.

Obesity

The most common nutritional problem among children in North America is *obesity*, which may affect more than 20 percent of all children (Looney & Plowman, 1990). Obesity is a serious condition that is difficult to rectify. Its relationship to cardiovascular and other health problems is well known; its implications for the child's social and emotional well-being are perhaps less obvious but no less real. Not only does the severely obese child often find it difficult to participate in games and activities that are an important part of the lives of many children, but such a child may be subjected to the ridicule and ostracism that are reflected in derogatory nicknames like the one we invented for Dennis—"WD9."

Obesity in children is linked to several factors. Overeating of both fat and energy (calories) is clearly the most important: Children simply take in more than they expend in growth and activity. This, of course, does not mean that the obese child eats excessively all the time. In fact, many obese children might eat only slightly more than they require each day, but the cumulative long-term effect is obesity.

Also important is the child's genetic background: Some children are clearly more susceptible to obesity than others. Those whose parents are themselves obese are more likely to also become obese than are children of slim parents (Malina & Bouchard, 1991). Similarly, when one member of an identical twin pair is obese, the other is also more likely to be. Interestingly, however, studies of identical twins indicate that those who are genetically predisposed to being thin are much less likely to show the consequences of overeating. It's as if their bodies are programmed to burn more calories (Bouchard et al., 1990).

A third important factor in childhood obesity is inactivity. Children who lead sedentary lives, who spend much of their day watching television, are more likely to gain excess weight. Watching television is especially important in contributing to weight gain, not only because it is physically passive but also because it encourages high-calorie snack and drink consumption.

A fourth factor in obesity is the use of food as a reward—or a punishment. Children who are given "treats" for good behavior may learn to reward themselves with junk food—or to console themselves in the same way.

Although obesity is difficult to reverse, it can be prevented in most children even where genetic background predisposes the child to gaining excess weight. Two factors need to be controlled: diet and exercise. Children need to be encouraged to develop good eating habits. Care must be taken to ensure that they consume adequate amounts of proteins, vitamins, minerals, and fibers—and also that they resist the ever-present temptation of junk foods. Contrary to popular wisdom, the body does not automatically hunger for specific minerals, vitamins, or other nutrients it might lack. Even animals do not select the most nutritious meal when there are other more appealing alternatives (Galef, 1991).

Diseases and Infections

Although the development of vaccines has drastically reduced the incidence of diseases and infections among children, most nevertheless suffer occasionally from various problems. Most common are respiratory infections such as colds, although these are about half as common after age 5 as before. About 66 percent of children under 5 suffer from a cold at least once a year, but only 35 percent of those ages 5 to 17 do so (U.S. Bureau of the Census, 1994). Less common are communicable diseases such as chicken pox, mumps, mononucleosis, and measles. Very uncommon are vaccine-preventable diseases such as tetanus, poliomyelitis, pertussis (whooping cough), and smallpox. Rabies, too, is uncommon.

Motor Development

Children's strength and muscular control develops significantly during the years from 6 to 12. Early in this period, their control of large muscles is considerably better than their control over smaller muscles (an explanation for the inelegant writing of first- and second-grade children). By the end of middle childhood, control over the small muscles is much improved.

Sex Differences in Motor Performance

Changes in *locomotor skills*, agility, coordination, and physical strength vary not only by age but also show consistent differences between the sexes. These differences may be important in explaining some of the child's interests. For example, throughout middle childhood, the boy's physical strength (measured in terms of grip strength) is superior to the girl's even though the average girl is taller and heavier than the boy. Similarly, boys consistently outjump girls after the age of 7, presumably because boys have greater leg power and arm–leg coordination for jumping than do girls. Malina and Bouchard (1991) also cite evidence that boys do better than girls in tests of kicking, throwing, catching, running, and broad jumping. But girls surpass boys in a number of motor skills during middle childhood, particularly when the skills require muscular flexibility, balance, or rhythmic movements, such as those in hopscotch and rope skipping and some forms of gymnastics, as well as in the ability to balance on one foot (Morris et al., 1982).

Not surprisingly, these differences are consistent with the gender typing of these activities. That is, rope skipping and hopscotch have traditionally been more feminine than masculine; throwing balls, catching, running, and jumping are considered more masculine. In addition, the differences between boys and girls, while consistent, are seldom very great. There is typically a great deal of overlap so that in activities in which boys are better than girls, some girls are better than some boys; conversely, where girls are, on the average, better than boys, some boys are nevertheless better than some girls (Lockhart, 1980).

It is important to note that although sex differences in motor skills are usually very small during middle childhood, after adolescence the disparity increases dramatically (Smoll & Schutz, 1990), generally in favor of the males.

Notwithstanding widespread beliefs to the contrary, today's school children are not *less fit than was the case several decades ago—especially if they live in environments that allow them to participate in active games and sports such as this school soccer match.*

Explanations of Sex Differences

The extent to which sex-related differences in motor skills, both in childhood and later in adolescence, result from innate biological differences between the sexes, and the extent to which cultural norms, expectations, and experience are involved is not clear. We do know, however, that at least for some activities, proportion of adipose (fatty) tissue is closely related to performance for both boys and girls. In a comparison of the motor performance of more than 2,000 children ages 9 to 17, Smoll and Schutz (1990) found that fatness alone accounted for as much as 50 percent of the variance between males and females. Given the much greater percentage of fat mass retained by females from early childhood on, some of the observed male–female differences in motor performance are probably related to this biological difference. However, with advancing age, sex differences in motor performance are increasingly influenced by environmental factors.

It bears repeating that sex differences in motor skills are often trivial. And although some of these differences are a function of innate biological differences, social expectations and environmental opportunities also influence the activities in which youngsters become interested and proficient.

Physical Fitness

There is a widespread belief that schoolchildren are not as fit today as was the case several decades ago. The belief is based in part on the observation that as many as 20 percent of school-age children are obese. It also stems from the fact that many children spend much of their time watching television, playing and working with computers, or engaged in other relatively nonactive endeavors. And evidence does suggest that teenagers are not as active now as they were even 10 years ago (Center for Disease Control, 1992).

Does this mean that today's children are relatively unfit? No, claim Pangrazi and Corbin (1993). "Recent research suggests that they are more fit than previously reported," they explain (p. 14). Part of the confusion stems from the fact that definitions of physical fitness have changed from a concern with *performance* on various tests of speed, skill, strength, and flexibility, to a concern with more *health-related* criteria like stamina and body fat percentage. Children are only slightly fatter now than they were 20 years ago, claim Looney and Plowman (1990); more than 80 percent meet high standards of physical fitness (Corbin & Pangrazi, 1992).

Some Physical and Sensory Problems

Not all children are born with normal physical skills or sensory abilities; nor do all have the same potential to develop. Those who differ markedly from the average are termed *exceptional*.

Exceptionality is evident in all areas of human development: physical and motor, intellectual, and social-emotional. In each area, it may be positive (evident in extraordinary talents and skills), or it may be negative (apparent in deficits and disorders). Later in this chapter, we look at both the positive and negative dimensions of intellectual exceptionality in middle childhood. Here we look briefly at physical and sensory problems.

Visual Impairment

Those who can see at 20 feet what a "normal" person can see at 20 feet are said to have 20/20 (or normal) vision; those who can see at 20 feet what normal people see at 200 feet are said to have 20/200 vision and are classified as legally blind if their corrected vision in their better eye is no better than 20/200. Accordingly, many individuals who are classified as legally blind do, in fact, see; this is one reason why the term *visually impaired* is highly preferable to *blind*. Approximately half of all legally blind children can read large type or print with the help of magnification. For the special education teacher, it is especially important to determine whether a child will be able to learn to read visually or will have to learn to read by touch. For those who can read visually, the "special" qualities of education might not need to go beyond providing magnifying equipment or large type, unless there are other problems involved.

Special classrooms and special teachers for visually impaired children are much less common than they once were; many of these children are now being educated in regular classrooms, a practice termed mainstreaming (about which more is said later in this chapter). Those who must learn to read braille, however, require special equipment and teachers.

Hearing Impairment

Deafness is the inability to hear sounds clearly enough for the ordinary purposes of life. The *hard of hearing* are described as those who suffer from some hearing loss but who can function with a hearing aid and sometimes without.

A useful way of describing deafness is to distinguish between *prelinguistic* and *postlinguistic* deafness—in other words, between loss of hearing that occurs prior to learning a language and that which occurs later. Unfortunately, in 9 out of 10 deaf children, loss of hearing was congenital (present at birth) or occurred within the first two years, often resulting from infections such as **otitis media.**

Otitis media is the second most common reason why parents bring their children to doctors (the first involves upper respiratory infections). It's a middle ear disease that may be accompanied by mild to severe loss of hearing that sometimes lasts for months. Because it is highly common in infancy, when the child is acquiring language, otitis media can be associated with retarded language growth and related cognitive problems. The milder forms of otitis media, lasting only a few weeks, are often treated effectively with antibiotics. More severe, recurring (chronic) cases lead to buildup of fluid in the middle ear, which causes deafness. In these cases, treatment often involves surgically inserting tubes in the ear to allow the fluid to drain (Feagans & Proctor, 1994).

In terms of cognitive development, deafness generally presents a far more serious handicap than does visual impairment, largely because of the severe difficulties it presents for learning to understand and to speak—hence the historical, but no longer popular, expression "deaf and dumb" or "deaf-mute." There is little evidence that the visually impaired are intellectually handicapped as a result of their blindness, but the same is not true of those who are hearing impaired. The academic achievement of children who are deaf often lags behind, a problem that can be attributed largely to language deficiencies. This observation, of course, applies to the prelinguistically deaf and not to those whose loss of hearing occurred after they had already learned a language.

In addition to the academic problems associated with deafness, there are often emotional and social problems. These problems probably result from lack of social interaction, in turn resulting from impaired ability to communicate through language.

The education of the deaf generally requires specially trained teachers and most often occurs in institutions. Understandably, the principal emphasis is on the acquisition of language—usually a combination of American Sign Language (ASL), finger spelling, and speech reading (lipreading).

The education of children with only a partial hearing loss may also require special instruction, particularly if the loss is manifested in speech disorders. Although many children with partial hearing are capable of following conversations if the conversations are at close range or sufficiently loud, they often experience difficulty in distinguishing among consonants for which there are no visual clues (for example, *p-b*, *t-d*, and *f-v*). Their own speech may consequently be affected. Special education for these children can often be implemented without removing them from regular classrooms, simply by providing special instructional sessions for them. Itinerant teachers (who travel from class to class) are often used for this purpose.

Other Problems

A number of other physical problems in middle childhood sometimes require special education or services. These include diseases and conditions such as muscular dystrophy, cancer, asthma, diabetes, and the absence of one or more limbs, as well as paralysis. Some are congenital, some are caused by infections, and others result from accidents of various kinds. In many cases, serious emotional and social problems are associated with them. As Zigler and Hodapp (1991) note, the handicapped child is often a source of stress in the family—especially in those that are economically disadvantaged or headed by a single parent. As a result, some (though far from all) handicapped children may experience difficulty in being accepted by others and in developing a positive self-concept. Hence, a great deal of what special education programs, parents, and therapists can do for physically exceptional children relates to their emotional and social well-being.

The Physically Gifted

The main emphasis in exceptionality has long been on those individuals whose exceptionalities have placed them at a disadvantage. But there are exceptional individuals at the other end of the spectrum as well. Although increasing attention is being paid to cognitive giftedness, particularly as it is manifested in intellectual and creative endeavors, much less attention has been focused on systematically identifying those who possess exceptional physical skills and on providing special education programs so that these children might develop their "full human potential." Indeed, there is an increasingly noticeable lack of research on the emotional, social, and intellectual characteristics of the physically gifted and on how their development might be enhanced. But we do provide scholarships for those who are inclined toward competitive athletics.

INTELLECTUAL DEVELOPMENT: PIAGET'S VIEW

Physical and motor development are two important aspects of development through middle childhood; closely related is intellectual development, one description of which is provided by Jean Piaget in his account of **concrete operations.** Recall that the Piaget child approaches

TABLE 9.1

Piaget's Stages of Cognitive Development

Stage	Approximate Age	Some Major Characteristics
Sensorimotor	0–2 years	Motoric intelligence
		World of the here and now
		No language, no thought in early stages
		No notion of objective reality
Preoperational	2–7 years	Egocentric thought
Preconceptual	2–4 years	Reason dominated by perception
Intuitive	4–7 years	Intuitive rather than logical solutions
		Inability to conserve
Concrete operations	7 to 11–12 years	Ability to conserve
		Logic of classes and relations
		Understanding of number
		Thinking bound to concrete
		Development of reversibility in thought
Formal operations	11–12 to 14–15 years	Complete generality of thought
		Propositional thinking
		Ability to deal with the hypothetical
		Development of strong idealism

this period by way of the sensorimotor period (birth to 2 years) and two preoperational subperiods: (preconceptual thought, 2 to 4 years) and intuitive thinking (4 to 7 years) (see Table 9.1).

According to Piaget, the child's thinking toward the end of the intuitive stage is egocentric, perception-dominated, and intuitive. As a result, it is marked by contradictions and by errors of logic. With the beginning of the period of concrete thought, many of these deficiencies disappear and are replaced by more logical thinking. Recall, however, that although Piaget's descriptions serve to highlight some of the important features of preschooler thinking, they do not always do justice to the child's cognitive achievements. In addition, not only are there tremendous individual variations in performance on the various Piagetian tasks by different children of the same ages, but very minor changes in the tasks used can sometimes lead to very different responses.

The Conservations

Conservation refers to the realization that *quantities* do not change unless something has been added or taken away. In Chapter 7, for example, we described a situation in which a child is shown two equal balls of modeling clay and asked

The school child, says Piaget, discovers a new logic to guide thinking and to erase the contradictions and the confusion of earlier developmental stages. But there are important new discoveries yet to come, and tremendous individual variations in the ease and confidence with which different children master them.

A   **B**

FIGURE 9.3

*Young children typically draw fluid level in a tilted jar as shown in **A** rather than **B**—not because they have ever seen anything like **A** in the real world, but because the logic they use in their attempts to make meaning out of their experiences is not always appropriate.*

whether there is still as much clay in each after one has been flattened. The preoperational child's belief that amount has changed because the deformed ball looks different is an example of failure to *conserve*. The eventual realization that the transformed object does not have more or less substance than it previously had marks not only the acquisition of concepts of conservation but also the transition between preoperational thought and concrete operations.

Constructing Knowledge

The significance of the acquisition of conservation is not so much that children are no longer deceived by the problem but rather that they have now developed certain basic logical rules, evident in much of their thinking. That is, in the course of what Kuhn (1984) calls *meaning-making* (or what Piaget called *constructing knowledge*), the child has discovered that a certain logic governs things and relationships—that the game of knowing has rules. These rules make it possible for children to overcome many of the errors that characterized their thinking during the preoperational period. In a sense, they free the child from reliance on perception and intuition; like some of us, children can now rely on logic. Put another way, they can rely on **operations** (thought processes governed by rules of logic) rather than on **preoperations.**

Just because children now attempt to use logic in constructing knowledge does not mean that they will always respond correctly (Smith, 1993). In fact, one of the most dramatic and clearest illustrations of an incomplete logic used in the construction of knowledge occurs during the late preoperational period and leads to an incorrect answer. When a young child—say, 3 or 4 years of age—is asked to draw what the water would look like in a tilted jar, the most common response is, in Thomas and Lohaus's (1993) words, "a scribbling or the like" (p. 9). At

this early stage, children lack any clear notion of lines, water levels, and so on. But in response to the same problem, a 5- to 7-year-old brings a clever, but inappropriate logic to bear on the matter—a logic that, according to Piaget, reflects the child's understanding that the water level in a container is ordinarily parallel to the bottom of the container. The child's drawing is therefore something like that shown on the left side in Figure 9.3—rather than the correct response, which is shown on the right. As Kuhn (1984) points out, the child has never actually seen anything like the drawing on the left. Therefore, it does not reflect actual experience with the world as much as the child's attempts to make sense—to construct meaning—out of experience.

Interestingly, later investigations show that almost half of adolescents and adults also fail this water levels task (see Thomas & Lohaus, 1993). They suggest this may be because not all errors on the task are due simply to the absence or misapplication of an appropriate rule (appropriate logic). Some result from what they term *field effects*—a tendency to be misled by the appearance of the problem. Thus, among many adolescents and adults who fail the problem, the more the jar is tilted, the greater the tendency to make an error.

Rules of Logic

Part of constructing knowledge involves a gradual recognition of the logic that governs things. Three rules of logic that are discovered (or invented) during concrete operations are important for the acquisition of conservation: identity, reversibility, and compensation. Each can be illustrated by the conservation-of-quantity problem in which children must decide whether amount has changed in a deformed ball of clay. Children who answer correctly (who have acquired conservation) may be reasoning in one of three ways: Nothing has been added to or taken away from the flattened object, and it must therefore be identical to what it was (**identity**); the pancakelike shape can be reformed into the original ball, in which case the pancake and the ball must contain the same amount (**reversibility**); or the flattened object appears to have more material

1. Conservation of substance (6–7 years)

A

The experimenter presents two identical modeling clay balls. The subject admits that they have equal amounts of clay.

B

One of the balls is deformed. The subject is asked whether they still contain equal amounts.

2. Conservation of length (6–7 years)

A

Two sticks are aligned in front of the subject. The subject admits their equality.

B

One of the sticks is moved to the right. The subject is asked whether they are still the same length.

3. Conservation of number (6–7 years)

A

Two rows of counters are placed in one-to-one correspondence. The subject admits their equality.

B

One of the rows is elongated (or contracted). The subject is asked whether each row still has the same number.

4. Conservation of liquids (6–7 years)

A

Two beakers are filled to the same level with water. The subject sees that they are equal.

B

The liquid of one container is poured into a tall tube (or a flat dish). The subject is asked whether each still contains the same amount.

5. Conservation of area (9–10 years)

A

The subject and the experimenter each have identical sheets of cardboard. Wooden blocks are placed on these in identical positions. The subject agrees that each cardboard has the same amount of space remaining.

B

The experimenter scatters the blocks on one of the cardboards. The subject is asked whether each cardboard still has the same amount of space remaining.

because it is larger but its thinness makes up for its diameter (**compensation**).

Once the child has learned about identity, compensation, and reversibility, do the rules apply to all thinking? The answer is no. There are about as many different kinds of conservation as there are characteristics of objects that can vary in quantity. In addition to conservation of amount (or mass, involving liquids or solids, or discontinuous material like beads, beans, or baubles), there is conservation of number, length, area, volume, and so on. If the rules of logic that make these conservations possible were completely general, they would all be acquired at the same time. When children realize that amount of clay does not change when a ball is flattened, they should also realize

that amount of water does not change when it is poured from a tall, thin vase into a shallow, wide bowl. But, as Figure 9.4 shows, approximate ages at which the various conservations are acquired span several years.

Additional evidence that the child's rules of logic at the concrete operations stage are not completely general are found in extinction studies. In these studies, children who have already acquired a specific conservation are given evidence that their reasoning is incorrect. The argument is that if a conserver truly believes that conservation is a logical and necessary consequence, there should be strong resistance to extinction of that logic. To simplify, consider a typical extinction experiment in conservation of weight. First, subjects are presented with two identical clay balls. Conservers agree that both weigh an equal amount and continue to maintain that this is the case, even after one or both of the balls have been deformed or broken into little pieces. At this point, however, the experimenter asks that participants verify their conservation response by means of a balance scale. But it's a trick! The scale is "rigged" so that one of the balls now weighs more than the other.

In more than 25 separate extinction experiments, subjects believed evidence that contradicted their original conservation response (Miller, 1981). Young conservers (and sometimes older ones) do not always behave as if they believe these rules of logic to be necessarily true in all relevant cases. However, further questioning of subjects reveals that they don't doubt the certainty of the logical rule but are simply not always clear about when to apply the rule. Miller's (1981) research indicates that even young children realize that social rules, for example, are arbitrary and uncertain but that Piagetian rules of logic are more universal. However, the rigged balance scale presents a real-life problem rather than a problem in logic. Specifically, in this situation, children are not deciding whether the logical rule is correct (they know it is) but whether the scale is correct.

In a similar series of experiments, Winer and McGlone (1993) asked children *and college students* misleading conservation questions such as, "When do you weigh more, when you are walking or running?" Or, after presenting two equal rows of checkers in a conservation of number problem and then spreading one out, they asked, "Who has more, you or I?" Strikingly, some college students show lack of conservation in these circumstances— and even more grade 3 and 6 students do likewise. Why? Perhaps, though not likely, because we are acquiescent, suggest Winer and McGlone. Or maybe because subjects are responding to what they think the experimenter *means* rather than *says* ("She probably means 'Who *looks* like they have more?' rather than 'Who actually has more?'."). Or, most likely, this simply illustrates that both children and adults are capable of thinking at various levels of sophistication; and even after we have learned a dozen elegant rules of logic, we don't always behave as though we had.

Acceleration of Conservation

Some researchers and educators have been keenly interested in the question of whether the intellectual abilities described by Piaget can be taught. The assumption is that teaching Piagetian concepts might provide a way of speeding up the developmental process, increasing children's cognitive capabilities, and maybe even making them more intelligent. Thus, many researchers have looked at the possibility of accelerating the development of concepts of conservation—concepts that are simply defined, easy to measure, and highly significant in general cognitive development. But the results have generally

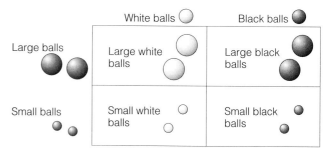

INTERACTIVE FIGURE 9.5

Suppose X comes in exactly two shapes, each of which can be either black or white. How many different X's are there? Right. There are four. The concrete operations child may have some difficulty with this simple classification problem because it's too abstract. X is not concrete enough. The problem is simpler if we ask, instead, "How many kinds of balls do we have if we have big and small black ones, and big and small white ones?" Such a problem can be used to test a child's ability to classify objects.

been mixed, with many researchers failing to bring about significant change, while others have reported some success, especially with children with delayed development (see, for example, Campbell & Ramey, 1990; Perry, Pasnak, & Holt, 1992). The evidence does not support the conclusion that development can be altered easily and significantly through short-term training programs. Conservation can be accelerated, but training programs need to be detailed and systematic, especially if the children are still some distance from acquiring conservation naturally (Furth, 1980). Whether such efforts, when successful, contribute significantly to intellectual development—or to happiness and self-esteem—remains unclear.

Classes, Seriation, and Number

During concrete operations, children not only acquire various conservations, but also acquire or improve three other abilities.

Classes

For example, they achieve the capacity to understand class inclusion and to reason about the composition and decomposition of *classes*. Ten-year-old Anna scoffs at the ridiculous simplicity of a question that asks whether there are more roses or more flowers in a bouquet of 15 roses and 5 tulips. She now understands that roses make up a subclass of the larger class, flowers. Similarly, she has little difficulty multiplying two classes in the problem "If there are blue balls and gray balls, and some are large while others are small, how many different kinds of balls are there?" (The answer is illustrated in Interactive Figure 9.5.) Tom, her 5-year-old brother, on the other hand, does not easily understand this problem. Nor can he answer the flowers

FIGURE 9.6
A test of a child's understanding of seriation. The elements of the series are presented in random order and the child is asked to arrange them in sequence of height. The top row was arranged by a 3½-year-old; the bottom, by an 8-year-old.

problem correctly. But he too, as we saw in Chapter 7, demonstrates some ability to deal with class inclusion problems when he answers the following problem correctly: "A Siamese is a cat but not an alley cat. Is a Siamese an animal?"

Seriation

A second achievement of the period of concrete operations is an understanding of **seriation** (ordering in sequence). One of Piaget's seriation tasks involves presenting the child with a series of objects—for example, a group of dolls, each a different length so that the objects can be arranged from longest to shortest. The bottom row of Figure 9.6 illustrates the arrangement desired, quickly produced by the child in concrete operations. A typical preoperational response to this problem is to place several of the dolls in order while ignoring the fact that others may fit in between those that have already been positioned. If the next doll the child selects is too short to be placed where the child intended it to be (at the upper end), it is placed without hesitation at the other end, even though it might be taller or shorter than the doll that is already positioned there. The child does not understand that if A is greater than B, and B is greater than C, then A must also be greater than C. Understanding this concept eliminates the necessity of making all the comparisons that would otherwise be necessary.

Number

Understanding this concept also makes a more complete understanding of *number* possible because the *ordinal* properties of number (their ordered sequence—first, second, third, and so on) depend on a knowledge of seriation.

Similarly, their *cardinal* properties (their quantitative properties—the fact that they represent collections of different magnitude) depend on a knowledge of classification. As we saw in Chapter 7, many preschool children already have an impressive knowledge of number, a fact Piaget largely overlooked as he searched for the limitations of preoperational versus operational thought.

A Summary of Concrete Operations

An *operation* is a thought that is characterized by rules of logic. Because children acquire conservation early in this period, and because these concepts are manifestations of operational thinking, the period is called *operational*. It is *concrete* because children's thinking deals with real objects or those they can easily imagine. Children in the concrete operations stage are bound to the real world; they don't yet have the freedom made possible by the more advanced logic of the formal operations stage: freedom to contemplate the hypothetical, to compare the ideal with the actual, to be profoundly unhappy and concerned about the discrepancy between this world and that which they imagine possible.

THE CHILD AS INFORMATION PROCESSOR

Piaget's view of the growth of mind is one approach to understanding the intellectual development of children. A second approach, one that complements rather than contradicts Piaget, is the **information-processing approach.**

It begins, as all views of the developing person must, with the observation that a newborn infant is very different from an older child—or an adult. Among other things, infants do not know that day follows night, which itself follows day; that butterflies whisper to each other when they perch on buttercups in the sunshine; or that tigers have tails. In fact, they are strangers to their very own hands and feet, strangers to the world. These things are not familiar to them. And, as Rheingold (1985) points out, the process of development is a process of becoming familiar with the world.

The difference between the newborn, who is almost totally unfamiliar with everything around, and the older child, who has learned about tigers, tautologies, and tarantulas, can be described in a number of ways. We can say, with Piaget, that the developing child, through the processes of assimilation and accommodation, has constructed a sort of reality that conforms, more or less, to certain logical rules, which, in turn, characterize and make possible a sequence of orderly stages.

Or we can say that the developing child begins with no knowledge base, few strategies for dealing with cognitive material, and no awareness of the self as a knower or as a processor of information. This approach permits us to view development as the business of acquiring a **knowledge base,** developing **cognitive strategies,** and gradually developing an awareness of self as a knower. This is an information-processing approach to cognitive development.

Accordingly, the information-processing approach looks at three things: the knowledge base and its creation; the processes and strategies by which information becomes part of the knowledge base or is retrieved from it; and the emergence of the child's awareness of self as a player of what Flavell (1985) calls the *game of cognition.* The first two of these relate to human memory because the individual's knowledge base is made up of what is in memory; and the strategies that enable the child to develop and use a knowledge base are those that permit adding things to or retrieving things from memory. The third component, the recognition of the self as a knower capable of using and evaluating strategies, involves what is termed **metacognition.** Literally, metacognition refers to *knowing about knowing.*

Components of Memory

The information-processing model views the child as a consumer and processor of information—as a little organism that sheds its ignorance as it builds up a store of memories. The most common description of this model is based on the work of Atkinson and Shiffrin (1971), which describes three types of information storage: sensory memory, short-term memory (also called *working memory*), and long-term memory. Each of these is distinguished primarily by the amount and nature of processing

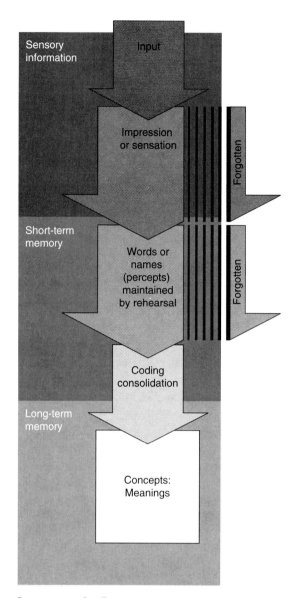

FIGURE 9.7

The three components of memory. Sensory information first enters sensory memory. From there it may go into short-term memory, where it is available as a name or word, for example, as long as it is rehearsed. Some of the material in short-term memory may then be coded for long-term storage, where it might take the form of meanings and concepts. These three components of memory do not refer to three different locations in the brain or other parts of the nervous system, but to how we remember—or, more precisely, how we study memory. (From Guy R. Lefrançois, Theories of Human Learning: Kro's Report *(3rd ed.). (Pacific Grove, CA, 1995) Copyright © 1995, 1982, 1972 by Brooks/Cole Publishing, a Division of International Thomson Publishing Inc. Reprinted by permission of the publisher.)*

that it involves. The term *processing* refers to mental activities such as sorting, analyzing, rehearsing, and summarizing (see Figure 9.7).

Sensory Memory

Sensory memory refers mainly to sensation—the momentary impressions associated with sensory stimulation. It requires virtually no cognitive processing. You cannot, at every moment, be aware of all the sights, sounds, tastes, smells, and feelings that are immediately possible—that require only that you pay attention. Hence, most of the sensory stimulation that surrounds us is not processed at all but has only a fleeting (less than 1 second) and unconscious effect on memory.

Short-Term Memory

Your ability to recall the beginning of a sentence as you read it illustrates **short-term** (or *working*) **memory.** If you can't remember the beginning of the sentence, it is usually because you aren't paying attention. In a sense, then, short-term memory is equivalent to attention span. Attention span has two main limitations: First, its capacity in adults appears to be limited to about seven items (plus or minus two; Miller, 1956); second, it seems to hold material only for seconds rather than minutes.

But these storage limitations are not as serious as they might seem. Although we seem to be able to attend to only about seven items at once, a process called **chunking** (grouping items into related units) can be used to increase memory capacity significantly. Miller (1956) illustrates chunking by reference to a change purse that can hold only seven coins. If you put seven pennies into this purse, its capacity is seven cents. However, if you fill it with seven groupings (chunks) of coins, such as nickels, dimes, or quarters, its capacity increases dramatically.

A common measure of short-term memory is to have subjects try to repeat a sequence of unrelated numbers they have just heard—a task that is used on a number of intelligence tests. Average adolescents and adults are able to repeat correctly six or seven (or sometimes even nine) digits. In contrast, 6-year-olds will typically succeed in repeating only two or so.

The child's limited working memory may be very important in explaining some aspects of cognitive development. Siegler (1989), for example, suggests that children are often unable to solve certain problems simply because they cannot keep in mind all relevant information simultaneously. And Case (Case et al., 1988) claims that the most important constraint on the child's ability to understand and solve problems is simply a limitation on short-term storage space.

Sensory memory, as we saw, does not involve cognitive processing but is a fleeting impression, almost like an echo. In contrast, short-term memory is highly dependent upon *rehearsal* or repetition. When I look up and dial a new telephone number, by the time I have finished dialing, I will usually no longer remember the number.

Long-Term Memory

But if I think I might need the number again tomorrow, there are several things I can do. One is to write it down so that I will not have to remember it. That would impose little cognitive strain. I would not have to use any of the strategies required to move material from short-term to long-term storage. Still, it would require the use of long-term memory; tomorrow I would have to remember not only that I made a note of the number but also where the note is. And I would have to remember a tremendous range of other information as well, including how to translate telephone numbers into the orderly and sequential act of dialing, how to speak and listen with a telephone, and so on. Put another way, even as habitual a behavior as using a telephone requires a tremendous knowledge base. And our knowledge base is, in effect, our **long-term memory.** It includes everything we know—about ourselves, about the world, about knowing.

Long-term memory has three important characteristics. First, it is highly stable. What you can remember today of what you learned in high school, you are relatively likely to remember tomorrow or next week, or next year.

Second, long-term memory appears to be *generative* rather than simply reproductive. That is, we remember main ideas and tend to generate (make up) details on the basis of our knowledge of **scripts**—that is, our knowledge of what goes with what, of what ordinarily follows what. Research on children's memories indicates that they, too, tend to fill in gaps according to their personal scripts. In one study, Johnson, Bransford, and Solomon (1973) presented subjects with the following short passage:

> John was trying to fix the birdhouse. He was pounding the nail when his father came out to watch him and to help him do the work.

When subjects were later shown these sentences along with others, one of which was

> John was using the hammer to fix the birdhouse when his father came out to watch and to help him do the work.

they overwhelmingly agreed that they had seen the last sentence rather than the two that they had actually seen. Note that the hammer was not even mentioned in the original text. It seems that participants recalled the central ideas of the two sentences and "generated" the hammer because hammers are what we use to pound nails. Their birdhouse-building scripts, like yours and mine, use hammers.

The third characteristic of long-term memory is that *understanding* facilitates remembering—as would be expected given that we tend to "generate" on the basis of our understanding. Paris and Lindauer (1976) asked children to remember the simple sentence "The workman

Table 9.2
Three Levels of Memory

	Sensory	Short Term	Long Term
Alternate Labels	Echoic or iconic	Primary or working	Secondary
Duration	Less than 1 second	Less than 20 seconds	Indefinite
Stability	Fleeting	Easily disrupted	Not easily disrupted
Capacity	Limited	Limited (7 ± 2 items)	Unlimited
General Characteristics	Momentary, unconscious impression	Working memory Immediate consciousness Active, maintained by rehearsal	Knowledge base Associationistic Passive The result of encoding

SOURCE: From G. R. Lefrançois. (1994). *Psychology for Teaching* (8th ed.). Belmont, CA: Wadsworth Publishing, p. 127.

dug a hole in the ground," adding "with a shovel" for half their subjects. One of the recall procedures was to present subjects with cue words (in this case, *shovel*). Significantly, the word *shovel* served equally well as a cue for children who had not seen the word in the original sentence. Clearly, the cue word would have been totally meaningless for children who did not initially understand that holes can be dug with shovels. (Some of the characteristics of these three components of memory are summarized in Table 9.2).

Types of Long-Term Memory

When the centipede was asked how it managed to walk with its many legs, it was stunned to realize it had never really thought about the problem. It just simply knew how. But, the story goes, it now began to think about it, trying to understand the process, to figure out which leg moved where, when, which next, and on and on, until, finally, the poor thing wound up totally confused and helpless, its legs wrapped in dozens of little knots.

Declarative Versus Nondeclarative Memory

There is much that we, too, know not consciously or in words, but perhaps in our muscles or maybe in some unconscious part of our nervous systems—things like how to ride a bicycle, or our unthinking reactions to things that frighten or excite us. Memories of this kind are labeled **nondeclarative memory** or **implicit memory** (simply because they can't be put into words).

In contrast, memories relating to our addresses, people's names, the meanings of words, and so on, can be put into words. Such memories make up **declarative memory,** also called **explicit memory.** The main distinction between declarative and nondeclarative memory, explain

Squire, Knowlton, and Musen (1993), is that declarative memory is *conscious* memory for facts and events; nondeclarative memory is *unconscious* memory.

Semantic Versus Episodic Memory

There appear to be at least two distinct types of declarative long-term memory, explains Tulving (1991). On the one hand, there is stable, abstract, *general knowledge* about the world—the sort of knowledge you need to understand language, for example. This type of declarative knowledge makes up **semantic memory.** In addition to this general, abstract body of long-term memories, each of us has a large store of *personal memories*—memories of things that have happened to us personally, of little episodes in our lives. These memories make up **episodic memory.** Episodic memory is *autobiographical* knowledge. (See Figure 9.8 for a summary of the different types of and labels for long-term memory).

Processes in Long-Term Memory

Three basic processes are involved in remembering: rehearsing, elaborating, and organizing.

Rehearsing

Rehearsing involves repetition and is important in maintaining information in short-term memory as well as in transferring material from short- to long-term storage. The simplest rehearsal strategy is to name the material (five, five, five, one, two, one, two) over and over again until it seems unlikely that it will escape. Most children younger than 5 do not rehearse in order to remember, and cannot easily be taught to do so (Wellman, 1990). In fact, the majority do not spontaneously rehearse until the age of 7 or 8.

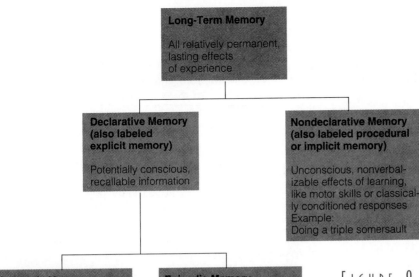

Long-Term Memory

All relatively permanent, lasting effects of experience

Declarative Memory (also labeled explicit memory)

Potentially conscious, recallable information

Nondeclarative Memory (also labeled procedural or implicit memory)

Unconscious, nonverbalizable effects of learning, like motor skills or classically conditioned responses
Example:
Doing a triple somersault

Semantic Memory

Stable, abstract knowledge that underlies language, principles, facts, strategies
Example:
Knowing that the Pyrenees separate France and Spain

Episodic Memory

Personal, autobiographical knowledge; memory of self doing things
Example:
Cycling through Roncevales in the rain

FIGURE 9.8

Different types and labels for long-term memory. Researchers describe different long-term memory systems that are distinguishable in terms of the kind of material stored in each. (From Guy R. Lefrançois, Theories of Learning: Kro's Report *(3rd ed.). (Pacific Grove, CA: Brooks/Cole, 1995), p. 263.)*

Memories that we can put into words, like how to divide numbers or our telephone numbers, define explicit (or declarative) memory. But many of the things we know are implicit (or nondeclarative). How to do the perfect double-twisting somersault is one of those implicit memories; so, too, is how to do the primitive, double-legged, twisted, frog-dive.

Elaborating

To elaborate is to extend material or add something to it to make it more memorable. For example, **elaborating** might consist of forming associations between new material and existing knowledge, or of forming mental images that go beyond (elaborate on) the actual material. Elaboration that relates to the meaning of what is being learned seems most effective. Bradshaw and Anderson (1982) had children try to recall sentences such as "The fat man read the sign." Those who elaborated this sentence to something like "The fat man read the sign warning of thin ice" significantly improved their ability to remember that the man in question was fat. Younger children do not spontaneously elaborate to improve their recall. By age 12, however, most have learned that certain strategies are better than others and have begun to use them deliberately.

Organizing

Organizing refers to grouping and relating material. Chunking material into related groups is one example of organization. Assume, for example, that you have been asked to memorize the following list as rapidly as you can: pencil, horse, pen, house, barn, cat, apartment building, bear, typewriter. Some of you will immediately notice that the list can easily be organized into three groups of related items (animals, dwellings, writing instruments) and will use this organization to help remember the items. Interestingly, young children will not spontaneously organize material the way you would. Their use of strategies is more limited than yours; they know less about knowing.

Developmental Changes in Memory

An information-processing model of memory is particularly useful for looking at the development of memory because it leads to several predictions about infant and child memory that can be tested directly. For example, we would expect that for the types of memory that involve little cognitive processing, young children might not perform very differently from older children or adults, but that where processing strategies are necessary, there would be more differences between them.

Sensory and Short-Term Memory

In general, research supports this prediction: Recall that does not depend on strategies does not appear to change very much as the child develops. For example, recognition memory, a task that does not ordinarily involve complex strategies, is highly accurate from early childhood on (Nelson, 1993). Similarly, comparisons between adults and children with respect to sensory and short-term memories—neither of which requires any strategy more elaborate than simple repetition—have found few significant differences. Apparently, short-term and sensory memory change little from childhood to adulthood because they do not require the use of elaborate or cognitively demanding strategies.

Longer-Term Memory

Recall that is highly dependent on the use of strategies should improve as the infant's recognition and understanding of strategies improves. This prediction, too, is supported by the evidence. As we saw earlier, very young children don't rehearse and organize as systematically as do older children. Paris and Lindauer (1982) note that research has found significant developmental changes in memory under at least four sets of circumstances: when the memory task requires intentional memorization, when the material is unfamiliar, when specific organizational strategies are required, and when the task requires a change in the learner's strategies.

Not surprisingly, research indicates that children become progressively better at remembering as they get older. Between the ages of 5 and 10, for example, they make progressively fewer errors in tasks that require them to identify facial photographs that they have seen for anywhere from 5 to 20 seconds (Davies, 1993). Nevertheless, they consistently make more errors on these sorts of tasks than do adults, who find facial recognition very easy.

Children as Witnesses

Questions about the accuracy and adequacy of children's memories are especially important in courts of law, where children are increasingly being called upon to testify in various cases, many of which have to do with abuse. Unfortunately, there are no simple rules by which courts can determine whether a child's testimony is reliable. Like adult witnesses, who sometimes remember things that have never happened (see Loftus, 1979), children, too, often misremember.

Davies (1993) reviewed a large number of studies that have looked at children's memories. Among other things, these studies lead to some important observations. First, the younger the child, the less the amount of information provided. Interestingly, however, the proportion of errors (of actual misinformation) stays relatively constant from childhood to adulthood. But adult recollections typically include far more detail.

Second, children are remarkably poor at judging people's ages, although they are more willing to estimate age than other physical characteristics, like weight or height. Before age 10, children seem not to be very aware of the sorts of cues that adults use for estimating age. Thus, adults can easily arrange in order photographs of a single individual taken at different ages, a task that young children typically fail.

Third, after age 6, children often perform about as well as adult witnesses in tasks that require them to identify a "criminal" from an array of photographs. A common study exposes "witnesses" to a staged event and later asks them to select a "perpetrator" from a series of photos. In seven different studies reviewed by Davies, very young children (3-year-olds) did more poorly than older children and adults. In general, however, older children and adults were about equally accurate, although accuracy ranged from very low in some studies (17 percent) to almost perfect in others.

Fourth, delays between the enactment of a crime and the testing of children's recollections do not seem to significantly reduce the accuracy of the child's memory.

In summarizing these studies, Davies (1993) stresses that the results are not entirely consistent. Although they indicate that children's memories improve with age, they also show that the elementary school child's reliability as a witness is not significantly poorer than that of an older child, or even of an adult. In Davies's (1993) words, "Thus, to use the results of studies that have simply found significant developmental effects as a reason for excluding children from giving testimony would be quite wrong" (p. 152).

Metacognition and Metamemory

In general, younger children are less capable of organizing material to facilitate their recall; in addition, they seem to be less aware of the importance of doing so (Short, Schatschneider, & Friebert, 1993). In other words, they seem to know less about knowing—to understand less about understanding. They are not reflective about themselves as knowers and seem not to have recognized the special skills that allow them to know and remember: They still lack the skills of *metacognition*—the skills that would allow them to monitor their progress, to estimate the effects of their efforts to learn, and to predict their likelihood of success in remembering. The skills of metacognition are what tell us that there are ways to organize material so that it will be easier to learn and remember, that there are rehearsal and review strategies that are more effective for one kind of learning than another, and that some kinds of learning require the deliberate application of cognitive strategies. Because memory is inseparably linked with cognition, metacognition includes what is sometimes termed *metamemory*—knowing about remembering.

Metacognitive skills seem to be largely absent in younger children. This does not mean that they use no memory or learning strategies; it simply means that they are not aware of them—that they do not consciously apply them. When Moynahan (1973) asked young children whether it would be easier to learn a categorized list of words or a random list, children below the third grade selected either list; children in the third grade were more likely to select the categorized list. Paradoxically, even when children are capable of engaging in useful memory strategies, they often do not. Hence, it may be important to teach children when and how to use the strategies, as well as the strategies themselves (Mayo, 1993).

Mulcahy (1991) points out that teachers are often not very systematic about teaching memory skills and other cognitive strategies. As a result, children are usually left to decide on their own whether a strategy should be used, what strategy, when, and how. Not surprisingly, then, they often know about a strategy but do not spontaneously use it.

Teaching Strategies

Teachers have traditionally not taught cognitive strategies systematically in schools. Instead, they simply assume that students will learn them incidentally. However, a number of programs have been designed deliberately to teach children cognitive strategies (see Royer, Cisero, & Carlo, 1993). For example, Mulcahy (1991) uses a *Socratic dialogue* question-and-answer teaching method to lead students to a recognition of their own cognitive strategies. Similarly, Collins, Brown, and Newman (1989) suggest a *cognitive apprenticeship* approach where mentors (parents, teachers, peers, siblings) serve as both models and teachers. The object is to provide learners with cognitive strategies so that they are equipped to explore, organize, discover, and learn on their own. Research makes it plain, claim Perkins, Jay, and Tishman (1993), that instruction in the skills that define metacognition can significantly improve learning and memory.

A Summary of Memory Development

Metacognition and metamemory deal with our knowledge about how we know—our awareness of ourselves as players of what Flavell calls the *game of cognition*. The object of the game of cognition is to pay attention, to learn, to remember, to retrieve from memory, and to do a variety of things such as sorting, analyzing, synthesizing, evaluating, and creating.

There is more than one way to play the game of cognition. Some people play it very badly. They learn slowly, remember inaccurately, and seem lost and clumsy when faced with tasks requiring evaluation, synthesis, or creation. Others play the game very well. Their responses are quick and accurate, their syntheses elegant, their creations startling.

Children do not play the game of cognition as well as adults. Why? Research reviewed in this section suggests at least four reasons: Children do not have (or do not use) strategies that are as effective; they lack basic knowledge about the world; their metamemory skills (their awareness of the need to monitor, to evaluate, to use strategies) are absent or less well developed; and their short-term memory capacity is more limited. These four factors, says Peverly (1991), account for the development of memory. They are the tools of intelligence.

INTELLIGENCE

"Intelligence is what the tests test," Boring (1923, p. 35) informed us. This simple definition of what is not a simple concept is useful and not entirely tongue-in-cheek. Weight is not a simple concept either. Yet to say that weight is what a scale measures is useful and accurate. A butcher need not know the scientific definition of weight to use the scales. Perhaps a psychologist or a teacher need not know what intelligence is to make use of the results of intelligence tests.

Then again, perhaps we do need to know, because there is a fundamental difference between measuring weight and measuring intelligence. We agree about weight; we know what it is. We define it precisely, and our scales measure accurately: They measure exactly what they are supposed to measure and nothing else (they are **valid**). And they measure consistently, yielding the same measurement for the same weights over and over again (they are **reliable**).

What Is Intelligence?

But we do not know exactly what *intelligence* is. Some theorists argue that it is a quality of human functioning that depends on some basic, general capacity or trait in the person—that if you have a lot of this general something (referred to as *g*), your behavior will be intelligent. In contrast to this **general factor theory**, some theorists believe that intelligence is split into several separate abilities like memory or reasoning or mathematical computation skills. This approach is labeled **special abilities theory**.

Although psychologists present a staggering array of different definitions for intelligence, most agree that it is a quality that contributes to adaptation in a real-life, practical sense. Thus, to use a lid to slide down the hill when the old sled has busted itself against a tree may be a very intelligent thing to do. Avoiding the tree in the future might be even more intelligent.

Intelligence is adaptation to real-world environments and involves selecting and shaping the environment.

Metacomponents

Executive skills involved in planning, monitoring, and evaluating cognitive activity

1

Performance components

Processes actually used in carrying out tasks, such as encoding, inductive reasoning, and remembering

2

Knowledge acquisition components

Processes used in acquiring new information, such as separating important from unimportant information (selective encoding), relating items of information (selective combination), and comparing new information with old (selective comparison)

3

Fluid and Crystallized Abilities

One view that is especially useful for our purposes combines these two approaches: It is that advanced by Cattell (1971). On the one hand, he explains, there are certain abilities that seem to underlie much of our intelligent behavior—a sort of a general factor. He labels these abilities **fluid abilities** (or *fluid intelligence*). Fluid abilities are reflected in the individual's ability to solve abstract problems and in measures of general reasoning, memory, attention span, and analysis of figures. Because these abilities are not learned, they are relatively unaffected by context.

In contrast to these basic fluid abilities is a grouping of intellectual abilities that are mainly verbal and that are highly influenced by culture, experience, and education. These **crystallized abilities** (*crystallized intelligence*) are reflected in measures of vocabulary, general information, and arithmetic skills.

Several developmental predictions can be based on the notion of fluid and crystallized intelligence. First, because fluid intelligence is independent of experience, it should remain constant throughout most of development, perhaps increasing slightly as the nervous system matures through childhood and adolescence, and maybe decreasing somewhat in old age as the nervous system ages. Second, because crystallized intelligence is highly dependent on experience, it should increase with increasing experience, perhaps right through old age. These predictions have received some support (see Chapters 15 and 17).

FIGURE 9.9

Sternberg's contextual view of intelligence, and the three components of intelligence.

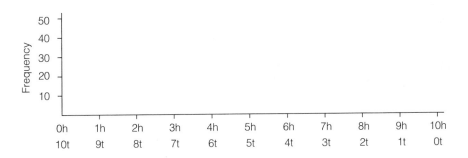

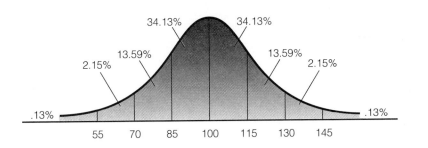

INTERACTIVE
FIGURE 9.10

On a sheet of paper, draw two axes as shown at left.

Now shake 10 coins in a cup, roll them out, count the heads and tails, and record them. Do this at least 50 times, although 500 would be better. When you are finished, plot your results. The resulting graph should be a close approximation of the figure below, which is a normal curve *depicting the theoretical distribution of IQ scores. Note that average events (an average IQ of 100; an equal number of heads and tails) are most frequent, and more unusual events (10 heads or 10 tails; IQs above 130 or below 70) are least frequent. Only 2.28 percent of the population scores above IQ 130 or below 70. Two thirds of the entire population scores between IQ 85 and 115.*

A Contextual Approach

A second view that is useful in a study of the human lifespan is that of Sternberg (1984), who sees intelligence as a quality of human functioning best defined in terms of the context in which it occurs. In this **contextual theory of intelligence,** intelligence is what makes adaptation possible, and adaptation occurs in specific contexts. Thus, certain behaviors may be highly intelligent in one context but quite unintelligent in others. In Sternberg's (1984) words, intelligence is the "purposive selection and shaping of and adaptation to real-world environments relevant to one's life" (p. 312).

How do we find out what intelligence is in a particular context? One way, according to Sternberg, is to ask people. In North American cultures, for example, people might tell you that the most intelligent individuals are those who have high practical problem-solving ability, high verbal ability, and a high level of social competence. Elsewhere, the definition might be somewhat different.

Another way of looking at intelligence, Sternberg (1985) suggests, is to look at its three major components: *metacomponents, performance components,* and *knowledge-acquisition components.*

The *metacomponents* are the cognitive strategies of which we spoke earlier. This component of intelligence includes what we have been discussing as metacognition or metamemory.

Performance components relate to actually doing—in contrast to the metacomponents, which are involved in selecting problems and procedures, responding to feedback, changing procedures, and so on. Put another way, the metacomponents of intellectual functioning define its executive functions—its decision-making functions. Perfor-mance refers simply to the execution of decisions made at the metacomponent level.

The third component, *knowledge acquisition,* refers to what is actually achieved in the process of learning. This component has to do with adaptation. Hence, it relates directly to Sternberg's contextual theory of intelligence (see Figure 9.9).

Measuring Intelligence

The principal use of intelligence tests is for prediction. An intelligence test score is, in effect, a prediction that an individual will do well (or not do well) on tasks that require intelligence.

Among the most widely used intelligence tests are the Stanford-Binet and the Wechsler. These are **individual intelligence tests;** they can be administered to only one child at a time and only by a trained tester. Hence they are quite expensive, but they yield a richer picture of intellectual functioning than do **group intelligence tests**—tests that can be administered to a large group at one time and that are commonly of a paper-and-pencil variety.

The Stanford-Binet yields scores in four areas: verbal reasoning, quantitative reasoning, abstract/visual reasoning, and short-term memory. It also provides a composite score that is described as a measure of "adaptive ability" and that can be interpreted as an Intelligence Quotient (IQ). The IQ derives its meaning from the fact that we know that the average IQ of large, unselected populations is around 100 and that it is distributed as shown in Interactive Figure 9.10. Note that approximately two thirds of all individuals have measured IQs that range between 85 and 115. Fewer than 2.5 percent score above 130 or below 70.

TABLE 9.3
The Wechsler Intelligence Scale for Children Revised (WISCR)

Verbal Scale	Performance Scale
1. *General information.* Questions relating to information most children have the opportunity to acquire. (M)*	1. *Picture completion.* Child indicates what is missing in pictures. (M)
2. *General comprehension.* Questions designed to assess child's understanding of why certain things are done as they are. (M)	2. *Picture arrangement.* Series of pictures must be arranged to tell a story. (M)
3. *Arithmetic.* Oral arithmetic problems. (M)	3. *Block design.* Child is required to copy exactly a design with colored blocks. (M)
4. *Similarities.* Child indicates how certain things are alike. (M)	4. *Object assembly.* Puzzles to be assembled by subjects. (M)
5. *Vocabulary.* Child gives meanings of words of increasing difficulty. (M)	5. *Coding.* Child pairs symbols with digits following a key. (M)
6. *Digit span.* Child repeats orally presented sequence of numbers in order and reversed. (S)	6. *Mazes.* Child traces way out of mazes with pencil. (S)
	7. *Symbol search.* Child performs symbol location task that measures mental-processing speed and visual search skills. (S)

*M = mandatory; S = supplementary.

The Wechsler Intelligence Scale for Children (3d ed., 1991), also called the WISC-III, yields a composite IQ score comparable to that obtained with the Stanford-Binet. The tests differ in several important ways, however. Most notably, the WISC-III also yields separate standardized scores for various subjects, as well as a verbal IQ and a performance IQ (in addition to the composite IQ). Deficiencies in language background are sometimes apparent in discrepancies between verbal and performance scores.

Wechsler tests are also available for adults (WAIS-R: *Wechsler Adult Intelligence Scale Revised*, ages 16 to 75), and for preschool children (WPPSI: *Wechsler Preschool and Primary Scale of Intelligence*, ages 4 to 6½). The various subtests of the WISC-III are described in Table 9.3.

Developmental Changes in IQ

A normal 6-year-old child can correctly repeat two or three digits if they are presented clearly and distinctly at a rate of approximately one per second, but would not be expected to repeat four digits in reverse order. An average 3-year-old can quickly identify legs, arms, hands, nose, and mouth on a doll, but might hesitate if asked to point to the infranasal depression. Clearly, there is a marked improvement in children's problem solving, remembering, language, reasoning, and so on. Does that mean that intelligence improves?

The answer, of course, depends on how intelligence is defined. If it's defined simply in terms of being able to *do* those things we consider to be examples of intelligent behavior (such as remembering, reasoning accurately, and expressing oneself clearly), then the answer is yes—children become more intelligent with age. But if intelligence is defined *psychometrically* (that is, in terms of how we measure it), the answer is no because measured IQ is not an absolute indicator of what or how much a child can do. Instead, it is a measure of what a child can do *compared* with other children of similar ages and experience. And

because children improve at similar rates and in similar ways, then the average child's measured intelligence does not change from year to year. By definition, it stays right around 100.

But, as we have said more than once, there is no average child; the average is merely a mathematical invention. What about the individual?

The individual, research informs us, may display a great variety of intellectual developmental patterns. As a result, measured differences between two individuals do not necessarily remain constant. For some children, measured IQ may increase over a period of years, or it may decrease, or it might go up and down like a bouncing ball. For the majority, however, measured IQ is relatively stable; it fluctuates within a range that would be expected given the imprecision of the tests. This indicates, claim Gustafsson and Undheim (1992), that the factors that underlie intelligence are relatively stable.

Misconceptions and Facts About IQ

The IQ is not always clearly understood; nor is it always used intelligently. A number of misconceptions are still common.

Misconception 1

IQ is a mysterious something possessed in lesser or greater quantities by everyone. In fact, the IQ is simply a mathematical expression based largely on an individual's ability to perform selected tasks in prescribed circumstances. It does not reveal mystical, hidden qualities that would otherwise be known only by clever psychologists who have dedicated their lives to the pursuit of the hidden truth.

Misconception 2

IQ is a constant. I have x amount, you have y, and that's that. Not so, claim Salomon, Perkins, and Globerson (1991). There is evidence that interaction with new technologies like computers and television may be *increasing* measured intelligence. And there is also striking evidence that schooling increases intelligence (Husén & Tuijnman, 1991). But even if intelligence did not change, *measures* of IQ are not constant; they can vary tremendously from one testing time to another. This might not mean, of course, that whatever underlies intelligent behavior is unstable and highly variable. It might mean, instead, that we simply cannot measure it very well.

Misconception 3

IQ tests are fair measures of all the important things. Not really. As Weinberg (1989) notes, IQ tests tell us nothing about social intelligence or about adaptation, motivation, or emotion. Nor do they reveal anything about athletic ability, creativity, self-concept, or a host of important personality variables.

Misconception 4

IQ tests are fair. Many intelligence tests are culturally biased; they penalize children whose backgrounds are different from the dominant white, middle-class majority. They are culturally biased because they are constructed with the middle-class child in mind and because they are usually standardized on samples of middle-class children. Not surprisingly, children from minority groups often do less well on these tests than their like-aged, middle-class white counterparts. However, the most recent revisions of the Wechsler and Stanford-Binet have taken this weakness into account and have used more representative norming samples. Accordingly, they are now much more **culture fair** to minorities.

Fact

IQ is related to academic and job success. In an important article, McClelland (1973) argued that intelligence tests bear very little relationship to success in life or in careers. This article had a profound influence on psychologists as well as on popular thinking, and led quickly to widespread skepticism about intelligence testing. In fact, formal intelligence testing has been abandoned in many school jurisdictions, often at the insistence of parents. But McClelland's conclusions are wrong, claim Barrett and Depinet (1991), following a detailed review of relevant research. "The evidence from these varied scientific studies leads again and again to the same conclusion: Intelligence and aptitude tests are positively related to job performance" (p. 1016).

Still, the controversy over the use and usefulness of intelligence tests will not be quickly resolved. They have weaknesses and limitations; yet they can be very useful. Unfortunately, although they are widely used, they are not always well understood. Hence, the need to urge that information derived from tests be used in a restrained and intelligent way. This means that no important decisions should be based on a single test without considering information from other important sources. And perhaps nowhere is this admonition more true than when we are dealing with exceptional children.

INTELLECTUAL EXCEPTIONALITY

Exceptionality refers to mental, physical, or social-emotional functioning that is significantly better or poorer than average. Thus there are those who are exceptionally gifted, who possess extraordinary talents; and there are those to whom nature and nurture have been less kind. Here we speak of both dimensions of intellectual exceptionality: mental retardation on the one hand, and intellectual giftedness or very high creativity on the other.

Mental Retardation

Mental retardation is a complex, multifaceted exceptionality that can vary tremendously in severity.

Definition

The most obvious feature of **mental retardation** is a general depression in the ability to learn; a second important feature involves problems in adapting. These two characteristics are reflected in the widely accepted definition of retardation presented by the American Association on Mental Retardation (AAMR):

> Mental retardation refers to significantly subaverage general intellectual functioning resulting in or associated with concurrent impairments in adaptive behavior and manifested during the developmental period. (Grossman, 1983, p. 12)

The meaning of this definition is clarified by Grossman's (1983) analysis of the key terms involved. First, *general intellectual functioning* is defined in terms of test scores on one or more of the well-known individual intelligence tests—for example, the Stanford-Binet or the Wechsler. An IQ of 70 is the accepted (and admittedly inexact) cutoff between normality and mental retardation.

Second, *impairments in adaptive behavior* are described as significant maturational deficits that are most often manifested in inability to learn or in inability to reach the levels of independence, social responsibility, and social effectiveness that would normally be expected (or in both). Failure to learn to dress oneself during the preschool period might be one indication of an impairment in adaptive behavior; failure to toilet train would be another.

Finally, the definition specifies that the deficits must be *manifested during the developmental period*—a period that extends from conception to age 18.

Identification

In practice, mental retardation is most often identified and defined by performance on intelligence tests, with some occasional, though limited, attention to adaptive behavior, a characteristic that is difficult to measure or define (Landesman & Ramey, 1989). This excessive reliance on measured intelligence is sometimes unfortunate for at least two reasons: First, measures at the lower levels of mental retardation are extremely unreliable because almost nobody in the norming samples ever scores below 50 (Reschly, 1992); second, intelligence may be reflected more accurately—and more usefully—in the individual's level of adaptation than in more abstract measures of IQ, especially for those from different cultural or language backgrounds.

The AAMR provides a detailed discussion of what is meant by "adaptive behavior" and how it might be assessed. For example, adaptation during infancy and early childhood is evident in the child's development of sensory motor skills, the ability to communicate, the appearance of self-help skills, and progressive socialization. During later childhood, children would also be expected to learn and apply basic academic skills, develop age-appropriate reasoning and judgment, and develop social skills evident in participation in group activities. During adolescence, in addition to the continued age-appropriate development in all these areas, the individual would also be expected to assume more adult roles reflected in work and social responsibilities. Various standardized inventories are available for assessing level of adaptive behaviors (see Reschly, 1990).

Prevalence

Estimates of the prevalence of mental retardation vary. The normal distribution of intelligence in the general population suggests that 2.68 percent of the population should score below IQ 70 (Reschly, 1992). But if level of adaptation is taken into account, the figure is closer to 1 percent (Patton & Polloway, 1990).

As we noted in Chapter 6, the existence of multiple developmental problems is not uncommon (Hooper, 1992). Thus, many children who are mentally retarded also manifest other developmental disorders. For example, Coulter (1993b) reports that many mentally retarded children also have cerebral palsy. And of these, about half also suffer from epileptic seizures.

Causes

The causes of mental retardation are so varied that it is almost always classified in terms of severity rather than cause. Still, researchers identify two main groups of causes: the *organic* and the *familial* (Zigler & Hodapp, 1991). Organic causes can be either *pre-* or *post*natal. They include chromosomal aberrations such as Down syndrome (see Chapter 3); maternal conditions such as rubella, malnutrition, or diabetes; drugs or chemicals; and radiation. Familial causes include unstimulating environments, inadequate genetic endowment, or a combination of both.

Although identifying causes may be very important, particularly for medicine and genetics, it is much less important for special educators and clinicians. Hence, men-tally retarded children are ordinarily described in terms of degree rather than cause of exceptionality.

Categories and Characteristics

The American Association on Mental Retardation distinguishes among four categories of retardation: *mild, moderate, severe,* and *profound.* The American Psychiatric Association makes exactly the same distinctions but allows for more overlap between categories. The categories are defined in terms of scores on intelligence tests (Figure 9.11). Overlapping categories that are of more practical use for special-needs educators distinguish among *educable, trainable,* and *custodial* retardation.

The largest proportion of intellectually handicapped children (approximately 75 percent) are only *mildly retarded.* Most of these children are not identified as being retarded until they have been in school for some time. They ordinarily develop social and language skills and experience relatively normal motor development. The majority are capable of acceptable academic achievement in elementary school. This is the group described as *educable mentally retarded* (EMR).

Children classified as *moderately retarded* compose another 20 percent of the retarded group. These children can learn to talk during the preschool period; most will also learn to walk, although their verbal and motor skills may be inferior to those of normal children. Many moderately retarded children are *mainstreamed*—that is, educated in regular schools though often with special teachers and equipment.

Severe mental retardation is usually associated with poor motor development, few communication skills (although these sometimes develop slightly later in life), and a high degree of dependence throughout life. Children who are *profoundly mentally retarded* may not learn toilet or dressing habits; in addition, many do not learn to walk.

Learning Disabilities

There are a significant number of children in schools who, in the absence of perceptible emotional or physical disturbances and without being mentally retarded, experience serious learning difficulties in one or more areas. Such children have sometimes been described as suffering from *hyperactivity, learning dysfunction, cerebral dysfunction, minimal brain damage, perceptual handicaps, dyslexia,* or *perceptual disability,* or simply as being *slow learners.* Each of these terms is relatively nonspecific, often confusing, and sometimes meaningless. In 1963, Samuel Kirk proposed a new term that would, in effect, include all of the conditions previously described by these and other labels: **learning disability.** It does not carry the stigma attached to such terms as *brain damage* or *cerebral dysfunction,* nor does it complicate our understanding with excessive categorization (Hammill, 1993).

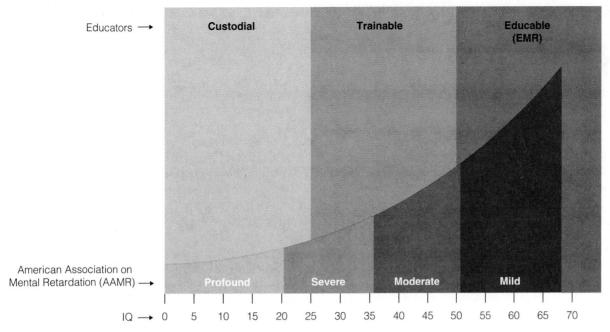

FIGURE 9.11

Two common classification schemes for mental retardation. Note that these classifications are based entirely on measured IQ. In practice, adaptive skills would also be taken into account. The AAMR classifications shown here are based on the Stanford-Binet or Cattell tests. The Wechsler Scales have a different distribution and therefore different cutoff points: 55–69 (mild); 40–54 (moderate); 25–39 (severe); below 25 (profound).

Definition

The term *learning disability* is now widely used to describe a variety of conditions. Unfortunately, these conditions are not always easily defined or identified. U.S. Public Law 94-142, which provides funding programs for special education, includes a definition of learning disabilities that serves as a guideline for the allocation of funds. However, the definition is open to several interpretations and has led to considerable controversy. Consequently, various jurisdictions have modified existing definitions and have established their own criteria for learning disabilities. None of these definitions and criteria says what a learning disability actually is; each simply stipulates behaviors and conditions considered symptomatic of the condition (Kavale, Forness, & Lorsbach, 1991). In addition, because of the very general nature of most definitions, many researchers have proposed more precise definitions for what appear to be relatively specific disabilities (for example, Cole, 1993; Stanovich, 1993).

In spite of the considerable disagreement concerning what learning disabilities are and are not—and how many there really are (Kavale, 1993), most definitions emphasize four characteristics of a learning disability:

- There is a marked disparity between expected and actual behavior, which is often apparent in an uneven pattern of academic achievement.

- While learning-disabled children do reasonably well in many subjects, there are specific subjects and areas in which they are unable to do certain things that other children do quite easily.

- Children with a learning disability typically experience problems in one of the basic psychological processes involved in language or in arithmetic. Hence, the condition is often evident in disorders of listening, thinking, talking, reading, writing, spelling, or arithmetic.

- Finally, the problems associated with learning disabilities are not the result of other problems relating to hearing, vision, or general mental retardation.

Symptoms and Identification

Initial indications of learning disabilities are typically tentative and probabilistic. The most obvious characteristic, and the one most likely to be noticed by parents and teachers, is general academic retardation. Note, however, that academic retardation does not define a learning disability, although it often occurs as a result of the child's problems with reading, writing, and other aspects of the language arts.

Other general symptoms are sometimes associated with learning disabilities. These can include inattentiveness, mood shifts, hyperactivity, and impulsiveness (see

TABLE 9.4

Some Symptoms Associated with Learning Disabilities

Inattentiveness (short attention span)

Impulsiveness

Hyperactivity

Frequent shifts in emotional mood

Impaired visual memory (difficulty in recalling shapes or words)

Motor problems (difficulty in running, hitting a ball, cutting, writing)

Disorders of speech and hearing

Specific academic difficulties (reading, writing, spelling, arithmetic)

SOURCE: Based in part on *Minimal Brain Dysfunction in Children: Terminology and Identification* (by S. D. Clements, 1966) (NINDB Monograph No. 3). Washington, DC: U.S. Department of Health & Human Services; and Edmonton (Alberta) Public School Board (1978) *Learning Disability, No. 7.*

Table 9.4). Short-term memory problems are not uncommon among those with learning disabilities (Swanson, 1993). Some research indicates, as well, that children with learning disabilities are more likely to abuse drugs than those not so classified, perhaps because of their poorer school performance and subsequent adjustment problems (Karacostas & Fisher, 1993). By the same token, adolescents with learning disabilities may be at slightly higher risk of suicide (Huntington & Bender, 1993).

A variety of tests are used in identifying the learning disabled. These are designed to provide information concerning three aspects of the student's characteristics and functioning. They measure general intelligence, examine basic psychological processes involved in learning and remembering, and look at the possibility that other factors—such as visual problems, hearing deficits, physical or health handicaps, low intelligence, or environmental disadvantages—might be involved. While the first and third of these (measuring intelligence and eliminating other defects) are relatively straightforward, the second (assessing basic psychological processes) is not. One of the problems is that there isn't widespread agreement on what these processes are. Certain tests, such as the Detroit Tests of Learning Aptitude, attempt to look at processes involved in activities such as reading and are sometimes useful for identifying specific weaknesses.

Given the problems of definition and identification involved, it is not surprising that faulty categorization is very common in this area. Now more than two of every five students receiving special education in the United States is classified as "learning disabled"—a total of almost 4 percent of the school population (Chalfant, 1989).

Categories

Relatively little is known about the origins and causes of specific learning disabilities—although brain damage or some other neurological impairment is suspected in many cases (Mercer, 1990). Various diseases and infections, malnutrition, and other environmental or genetic factors might also be involved.

Learning disabilities are most often classified according to the specific area of disability and are labeled according to whether they involve oral or written speech, comprehension or production of speech, or particular problems in spelling or arithmetic. By far the most frequently diagnosed learning disabilities are those that have to do with language—especially with reading.

A common learning disability manifested in reading problems is **developmental reading disorder**—also called *dyslexia,* or *specific reading disability* (Stanovich, 1992). The main feature of developmental reading disorder, according to the American Psychiatric Association, is impairment in recognizing words and understanding what is read. These difficulties are not related to mental retardation, physical problems such as deafness, or inadequate schooling (American Psychiatric Association, 1987). Developmental reading disorder is usually first manifested in problems associated with learning to read and may later be evident in spelling difficulties. Individuals with developmental reading disorder are typically of average measured intelligence but, in spite of ample opportunity to learn to read, are usually several years behind in reading skills. Remedial teaching can sometimes be highly effective in overcoming some of the effects of dyslexia.

The American Psychiatric Association also recognizes what is labeled **developmental arithmetic disorder** (American Psychiatric Association, 1987). Its essential feature is significant impairment in developing arithmetic skills in the absence of other problems such as mental retardation. Developmental arithmetic disorder may be evident in computational problems (difficulties in adding, subtracting, multiplying, or dividing), or in problems in processing visual or auditory information. Accordingly, reading problems are sometimes associated with arithmetic disabilities (Semrud-Clikeman & Hynd, 1992).

In addition to reading and arithmetic disorders, learning disabilities also include what are referred to as *process disorders*—that is, they are sometimes labeled in terms of a deficit in a basic psychological process. Thus, there are deficits relating to perception (some students are confused by words that sound or look alike), memory (sometimes evident in problems associated with remembering and generalizing what has been learned), and *attention span* (a condition labeled "attention deficit disorder" that is sometimes associated with restlessness, hyperactivity, low frustration tolerance, and distractibility). In practice, however, it is often difficult to separate a basic process disorder from a disorder that is manifested in a specific subject area.

Learning disabilities, as they are presently defined, are usually treated in the regular classroom. Alternately, learning disability specialists, many of whom specialize in reading or writing skills, may work with these children in the regular classroom. In a declining number of cases, they are given no special treatment.

Intellectual Giftedness

Intellectual giftedness may be apparent in two related aspects of cognitive functioning: high intelligence and high creativity. But in the same way as mental retardation is defined not only in terms of performance on an intelligence test but also in terms of adaptive behavior, intellectual giftedness, too, cannot easily be identified solely on the basis of scores on measures of intelligence or creativity. Motivational and personality factors that are associated with the full development of potential must also be taken into account.

U.S. Public Law 91-230 defines giftedness as follows:

Gifted and talented children are those identified by professionally qualified persons, who by virtue of outstanding abilities, are capable of high performance. These are children who require differentiated educational programs and/or services beyond those normally provided by the regular school programs in order to realize their contribution to society.

The law goes on to state that capacity for high performance may involve demonstrated achievement, or the potential for high achievement, in one or more of the following areas: general intellectual ability, specific academic aptitude, creative thinking, leadership ability, visual and performing arts, or psychomotor ability.

A common estimate is that somewhere between 3 and 5 percent of the school population might be considered gifted (Hallahan & Kauffman, 1991). However, special education programs are provided for nowhere near this number. This is especially true of the gifted who are culturally disadvantaged (Patton, Prillaman, & Tassel-Baska, 1990).

Among these highly gifted are the creative.

Creativity and Giftedness

Psychology offers us a wealth of definitions for **creativity,** none of them exceptionally clear or useful. One of the major problems in the area of giftedness, says Hoge (1988), has to do precisely with the definition of the qualities in question. In practice, these qualities are most often defined in terms of scores on tests: Intellectual giftedness is defined as a very high measured IQ, and high creativity is defined as an extraordinarily high score on a test designed to measure creativity. And the school administrator who must make a decision about who will be labeled "gifted" (and who, at least by implication, will be labeled "not gifted") also looks at test scores and perhaps asks teachers for their nominations. There are serious problems with this approach, claims Hoge. First, there is considerable ambiguity about the meaning of high IQ or high creativity scores; second, what is represented by these tests is often quite different from the definitions that government agencies or school jurisdictions have adopted; and third, the programs that are provided for children identified as gifted are not often matched to the specific strengths or weaknesses revealed by tests.

Identifying the Gifted and Creative

Heinzen (1991) describes three approaches to measuring creativity: *personality inventories, biographical and activity inventories,* and *behavioral measures.* Personality inventories focus on what are considered to be the characteristics of creative people (for example, openness, flexibility). Biographical and activity inventories are based on the assumption that past creative activity is the best predictor of future creativity. They look at the extent to which individuals have already *been* creative. And behavioral measures try to predict future creativity by looking at specific behaviors such as performance in school. With all of these approaches, there is, in Heinzen's (1991) words, tremendous "diversity and lack of coherence" (p. 8).

In studies of creativity, the most frequently used measures are open-ended tests that require subjects to produce a variety of different responses. These are sometimes called tests of *divergent thinking.* Individuals think divergently when they produce a number of different solutions for a single problem. In contrast, measures of intelligence typically present items that require *convergent thinking*—the production of a single correct response.

Most production measures of creativity are based on Guilford's (1950) assumption that the most important factors involved in creative ability are *fluency, flexibility,* and *originality.* Accordingly, the open-ended tasks require the production of a variety of different responses that can then be scored in terms of these factors. For example, one item asks subjects to think of as many uses as they can for a brick. Counting the total number of responses gives a measure of fluency. Flexibility is revealed in the number of shifts from one *class* of uses to another (for example, shifting from responses where bricks are used for building purposes to ones where they are used for holding objects down). Originality is revealed in the number of unusual or rare responses. Interactive Table 9.5 gives one example of a creativity item and how it might be scored.

Interestingly, when children are given tests of divergent (creative) thinking and told to be creative, their scores typically increase (Runco, 1986a). This finding has sometimes been used as a basis for arguing that children who normally score high on creativity tests simply perceive the test differently. It is significant, however, that children who improve most on measures of originality when they are asked to be creative are those who score highest on measures of giftedness in the first place.

Runco (1986b) makes the important point that while measures of creativity reflect creative potential, they do not reflect creative performance. The greatest achievers—those who eventually attain eminence in the world—are characterized by more than just high scores on measures of intelligence and creativity.

Some Characteristics of Creative and Gifted Children

Creativity appears to be relatively stable. Children who are creative as preschoolers tend to continue to be creative throughout their childhood and into adulthood. However,

Giftedness may be apparent in high intelligence and high creativity, as well as in personality characteristics. But perhaps most important for those who eventually become eminent is not only that they be highly gifted but also that their family contexts encourage and provide opportunity for the development of their special talents.

correlations between childhood and adult measures of creativity are usually considerably lower than those for intelligence (Kogan, 1983). It is not clear to what extent this results from the greater unreliability of measures of creativity and to what extent it might be due to greater fluctuations in creativity itself.

A number of studies have looked at the characteristics of creative and gifted children. None of them present a simple description of what these children are like—probably because each is unique, very different from the others. Hoge and Renzulli (1993), for example, looked at the self-concepts (the self-esteem) of gifted students in an effort to discover whether the gifted have higher evaluations of themselves. It might be reasonable to expect that they would have, argue Hoge and Renzulli, given that their accomplishments should be superior to those of more ordinary individuals. Also, if they are labeled "gifted," that too might have a positive effect on their self-concepts. But there is the possibility, they also caution, that the high expectations that are sometimes placed on the gifted might

lead them to greater feelings of frustration and dissatisfaction, and might be evident in *lower* rather than *higher* self-concepts.

Hoge and Renzulli looked at 15 different studies that compared the self-concepts of gifted and nongifted children. Their conclusions? "In general, gifted children displayed slightly higher self-concept scores than more average children" (p. 458). Not surprisingly, this finding was most evident in measures of what is termed *academic self-concept*—the children's evaluations of their academic abilities. However, a review of seven studies that had looked at the possibility that labeling a child "gifted" might increase self-esteem found no relationship between labels and self-concept.

Other research indicates that the gifted are, in fact, probably better players of what is sometimes called the *game of cognition*. Both Swanson (1992) and Cheng (1993) found that the gifted children manifest higher *metacognitive skills*. That is, they are more aware of their cognitive processes, and better at selecting and applying cognitive strategies and at evaluating their effectiveness.

An older study by Wallach and Kogan (1965) looked at the personality characteristics of highly creative children and compared them with those of children identified as being highly intelligent. Among other things, the highly intelligent but less creative students in this sample tended to be addicted to school and were well liked by teachers. In contrast, highly creative but less intelligent students were most frustrated with school and suffered most from feelings of inadequacy. The most favored group, not surprisingly, were those who were high on

		Measured intelligence	
		High	Low
Divergent thinking (creativity)	High	High control over their own behavior; capable of adultlike and childlike behavior	High internal conflict; frustration with school; feelings of inadequacy; can perform well in stress-free environment
	Low	Addicted to school; strive desperately for academic success; well liked by teachers	Somewhat bewildered by environment; defense mechanisms include intensive social or athletic activity, occasional maladjustment

FIGURE 9.12

Characteristics of children identified as high and low on measures of intelligence and creativity. (Based on studies reported by Wallach & Kogan, 1965.)

INTERVIEW

SUBJECT

Male; age 75; retired schoolteacher.
(referring to one of his sons, who is a writer)

"He was probably always different . . . well, maybe not really *different.* What I mean is you sort of knew, even when he was just little, that he was going to do something or be famous. Not that he went out of his way to get people's attention. Just that he stood out. A lot of his teachers mentioned it one time or another. And it wasn't that his marks were that much better than anyone else's or that his writing really stood out that much. I'm not sure he was even interested in writing then. But he was independent and he liked to express himself. He liked to say what he thought. And he had a tremendous sense of humor even though he didn't seem to care that much to make other people laugh. He just found all sorts of things funny."

---

both intelligence and creativity. These students were most in control of their behaviors and were capable of both adultlike and childlike behaviors. (See Figure 9.12.)

A review by McCabe (1991) suggests that IQ is a better predictor of achievement than is creativity. But the highest achievers are those who are both highly creative and highly intelligent.

A Context for Eminence

For practical purposes, there is seldom a need to separate high intelligence and high creativity. Not only is there a close relationship between the two, but programs for gifted and talented children are seldom tailored for one or the other. And studies of eminent individuals—that is, of those who have achieved fame and recognition on the basis of outstanding performance in any area—typically find that these individuals are both highly intelligent and specially gifted in a creative sense (Albert & Runco, 1986).

But eminent individuals are something other than simply highly intelligent and specially gifted. Countless individuals score extremely high on all our measures of giftedness and intelligence but never approach eminence. A follow-up of the Terman (1925) studies of genius, for example, found that very few of the original sample ever attained eminence (Oden, 1968).

What is special about those few gifted individuals who achieve eminence? Perhaps a number of personality characteristics—qualities such as high motivation and persistence—and, perhaps most important, the right family context. Family background seems to have been an important factor in the lives of a majority of those who have achieved eminence.

Albert and Runco (1986) warn that perhaps we have taken too simple and too cognitive a view of giftedness and that, as a result, we have been guilty of neglecting important personality and family variables. They suggest that seven important factors are involved in the development of eminence. If children are to become eminent, it is best that they:

- be both intelligent and creative
- develop the values, motivation, and abilities that allow them to undertake important or highly unusual work
- have a family context that encourages the development of these values and drives
- find a "fit" between talents and career demands, such that the demands of the career are sufficiently challenging to lead to eminence
- have a family that provides the right combination of experiences (that is, musical, athletic, academic, and so on)
- have a family history consistent with appropriate experiences and values (that is, grandparents, who were influenced by their parents, also influenced their children, who now influence the children of whom we speak)

BARBARA FOLLETT, MISSING PERSON

When Barbara Follett was only 4, she became fascinated by her mother's old portable typewriter. And when she had barely turned 5, she typed a long letter to her friend, Mr. Oberg. One paragraph reads:

> The goldfinches come every afternoon and eat their supper on the clump of bachelor's-buttons right on the left-hand side of the path that leads from the back door to our road. There are ten goldfinches, five males and five females. Before they eat their suppers, they sit on the clothesline and swing in the breeze. I wish you could be here to see them. (McCurdy, 1966, p. 4)

At the age of 6, she was writing poetry and long prose stories filled with the beauty of nature and with childish love and enthusiasm:

> The butterflies are coming fast now. Sometimes I sit down in a chair and suddenly I see a white Butterfly fly in circles about the potato patch; and I jump from my seat and run after it and see it alight and I tiptoe up to it, and I am just about to open my fingers to take it by the wing when away it would fly. (McCurdy, 1966, p. 22)

At the age of 9, she had finished a book, later published under the title *The House Without Windows.* It is an enchanting story of a little girl who runs away into a world of animals and meadows; later into the sea; finally into a world of eternal snows where she is utterly alone until a flurry of butterflies carries her off into invisibility. The story ends:

> She was a fairy—a wood nymph. She would be invisible forever to all mortals, save those few who have minds to believe, eyes to see. To these she is ever present, the spirit of Nature—a sprite of the meadow, a naiad of lakes, a nymph of the woods. (McCurdy, 1966, p. 67)

When Barbara Follett was 13, she published a second book consisting of a series of letters she had written while sailing. And on

Thursday, December 7, 1939, when she was only 24, she walked out of her apartment in Brookline and was never seen again.

To Think About   Barbara Follett never attended school. Professor Howard Mumford Jones, when reviewing her first book, wrote, "there seems to be no sane reason why she should ever go to one" (quoted in McCurdy, 1966, p. vii). McCurdy, in the preface to Barbara's autobiography, writes that from a study of eminent people, he has concluded that intellectual development depends on three factors: intense stimulation by loving adults, relative isolation from other children during childhood, and considerable exercise of the imagination. None of these, says he, are particularly encouraged by the public school system. What do you think? Do you think the aspects of context McCurdy describes are particularly important for creative achievement and eminence? Or do you think other factors are more important?

- be subjected to family direction consistent with the development of the gifted child's talents (rather than unrealistic, overly demanding, or uncaring)

Notice how important the family is in Runco's suggestions. In much the same way, Christian and Morgan (1993) offer numerous suggestions for *parents* of gifted children, advising them on how to cope with the interests, the energy level, the challenges of the gifted. Karges-Bone (1993), too, argues that the most important source of influence in the life of the gifted child is the family. (See Across Cultures: "Barbara Follett, Missing Person.")

Trends and Controversies in Special Education

There are a number of trends and controversies in implementing special services for exceptional children. Some of these are summarized briefly here.

Mainstreaming

First, there has been a gradual shifting of responsibility for children with special needs from special organizations and institutions to the public school systems. In part, this trend reflects a growing recognition that children who are disadvantaged should have an opportunity to lead lives as nearly normal as possible. Deinstitutionalization and non-segregation are the natural consequences of this trend; and perhaps nowhere is this more obvious than in the **mainstreaming** movement.

To mainstream is to place in regular classrooms children who might once have been placed in "special" classrooms or even in institutions. The mainstreaming movement followed the passage of U.S. Public Law 94-142 in 1975 in the United States. This law requires, among other things, that school jurisdictions provide special services for exceptional children in "the least restrictive environment" possible. Subsequently, various court decisions interpreted "the least restrictive environment" to mean the regular classroom. The effectiveness of special classrooms for mildly retarded children had been called into question, and a consensus seemed to be growing that mildly retarded children would do better in regular classrooms.

Mainstreaming remains controversial for several reasons (Chester, 1992). First, the inclusion of special needs students in the regular classroom is expensive and difficult for school administrators, particularly because the law stipulates a need for extensive, *unbiased* testing. Second, caring for special needs students sometimes presents a difficult burden for classroom teachers who are not always trained for this responsibility. Third, there is evidence that some exceptional children might fare better in segregated classrooms—or, alternatively, that the regular classroom might fare better without these students. For example, Simon (1992) argues that behaviorally disruptive children with serious aggressive tendencies might function better in segregated classrooms with specially trained teachers.

The bulk of the research indicates, however, that inclusive education can meet the needs of exceptional children and that the self-concepts of mainstreamed students are typically better than those of segregated students (Macmillan, Keogh, & Jones, 1986). As Sobsey (1993) puts it, "The majority of the research to date shows both educational and social advantages for integrated settings over segregated alternatives" (p. 1). However, he advises that in many cases, the needs of the exceptional child can best be served through *adaptive education*—that is, by providing intensive, individualized, "special" programs for these children within the regular classroom.

Labeling

A second controversy concerns the use of labels. Critics of the use of labels argue that they are unfair because (1) a disproportionate number of minority group children are labeled (and perhaps mislabeled, owing to the biased nature of many of our tests); (2) the imposition of a label changes the child's environment by affecting the child's self-concept; and (3) there is a growing tendency to view exceptional children as being quantitatively rather than qualitatively different from normal children.

In spite of these objections, labeling has definitely not been abandoned, although there has been a concerted attempt to use more euphemistic (less stigmatizing) labels, to use them more judiciously, and to avoid making labels serve as explanations. It has never been very useful to label Johnny "dyslexic" and then to say that he can't read because he's dyslexic. Here, as elsewhere, labels name and classify; they do not explain.

THE MAGICAL CHILD

"The parents of the magical child lead him into the world by example," Pearce (1977) tells us. "At seven, he is open to suggestion, able to construct the abstractions needed for moving into the world . . . he is fascinated with the world and becomes analytic. He wants to take the world apart and see what makes it tick" (p. 213).

In Piaget's terms, the child of whom we have spoken in this chapter is ready to construct a knowledge system that will lead to a mounting understanding of the world.

Or, in the language of information-processing theory, the child seeks to develop a knowledge base, to discover processes and strategies for dealing with knowledge, and to develop a sense of self as perceiver, knower, and rememberer.

As we noted, infants are not expected to know that day follows night, that butterflies whisper to each other when they perch on buttercups in the sunshine, and that there is a smooth, cold logic that can be invented to explain the mysteries of numbers and classes and series, although perhaps not the whispers of butterflies. Those are among the discoveries of later childhood.

But happily, the grand mysteries of cognition are not all solved through middle childhood. There is yet a concreteness to the child's logic, a limit to the reaches of imagination. We continue the story in Chapter 11.

MAIN POINTS

Physical and Motor Development

1. Boys are normally heavier and taller than girls throughout life, but the female growth spurt occurs earlier. Girls retain a higher percentage of fat mass than do boys throughout life. Obesity (linked to overeating, underexercising, and genetic background) is the most common childhood nutritional problem in North America. Children are more fit than is generally thought.

2. The majority of children classified legally blind (corrected vision poorer than 20/200 in the better eye)

can see well enough to read large print and to function normally in society. Hearing impairments (often congenital or associated with otitis media) have more social-emotional and academic problems associated with them, largely because of language deficits.

Intellectual Development: Piaget's View

3. *Conservation* is the realization that certain transformations do not change the quantitative features of objects, and may reflect the logic rules of *identity*, *reversibility*, and

compensation. Attempts to accelerate the acquisition of specific conservations have met with mixed success. In addition to the conservations, children acquire abilities relating to classification, seriation, and number.

The Child as Information Processor

4. Information-processing approaches to cognition look at knowledge base, strategies for dealing with cognitive material, and awareness of the self as a knower or as a processor of information. Memory (closely related to knowledge base and to cognitive strategies) may be described in terms of three components: sensory memory (the momentary effect of sense impressions), short-term memory (similar to attention span; seconds long, highly limited), and long-term memory (indefinite duration; requires cognitive processing). Long-term memory may be declarative (explicit, verbalizable) or nondeclarative (implicit, nonverbalizable). Declarative memory may be semantic (stable, abstract knowledge base) or episodic (memory for personal events). The three basic memory processes are rehearsal (repetition), elaboration (extending or adding something to material), and organization (forming associations).

5. Sensory and short-term memory, which are not highly dependent on strategies, are not very different in younger and older children, but long-term memory is superior in detail in older children and adults. However, both make about the same proportion of errors in "witness" studies. Developmental changes in long-term memory may be due to the development of processing abilities in children and to their eventual recognition of their own cognitive processes (metacognition and metamemory).

Intelligence

6. Some describe intelligence as a general factor underlying ability that determines performance in all areas; some describe it in terms of separate and distinct abilities. Cattell describes *fluid abilities* (unlearned, unaffected by culture, evident in the ability to solve abstract problems and to reason) and *crystallized abilities* (learned, highly influenced by culture, reflected in measures of vocabulary and general information). Sternberg's *contextual* theory defines intelligence in terms of how well people adapt and function in context. His three components of intelligence are *metacomponents* (metacognition and metamemory, executive functions), *performance components* (intellectual skills such as analyzing, sorting, elaborating), and the *knowledge-acquisition component* (what is achieved in the process of learning).

7. Two widely used individual (one child at a time) intelligence tests are the Stanford-Binet and the Wechsler tests. Defined psychometrically, average IQ does not change from year to year; however, the measured intelligence of any given individual before the age of 2 does not predict later intelligence as well as tests given later. Measured IQ is not a mystical, fixed, unchanging, and unmodifiable something. Intelligence tests often do not measure a variety of important things (interpersonal skills, motivation, creativity, athletic and musical ability) and are often culturally biased.

Intellectual Exceptionality

8. Mental retardation is characterized by a general depression in the ability to learn and is defined in low measured intelligence and poor childhood adaptation. It is currently classified in terms of the severity of retardation, regardless of cause (mild, moderate, severe, and profound). Learning disabilities include a wide range of specific learning problems not associated with mental retardation or other physical or emotional disturbances (performance below expectation). They are often manifested in language-related problems and are often evident in difficulties associated with learning to read or to do arithmetic (developmental reading disorder—*dyslexia*—and developmental arithmetic disorder).

9. Intellectual giftedness is manifested in exceptional intelligence, exceptional creativity, and high motivation. Creativity is often defined in terms of innovation or originality and may involve intellectual characteristics not ordinarily measured by intelligence tests. The family context is extremely important in the development of eminence.

10. Recent trends in special education include deinstitutionalization, mainstreaming, and an antilabeling movement. Each is characterized by some controversy.

FOCUS QUESTIONS: APPLICATIONS

1. What is the most common nutritional problem of childhood?

   ■ Outline what you think would be a good nutritional and physical activity program for your ideal elementary boarding schools.

2. What is Piaget's view of important intellectual changes in middle childhood?

   ■ Either (a) replicate one of Piaget's conservation problems with several children of different ages or (b) attempt to teach a specific conservation to a nonconserver.

3. What model of human memory is basic to current information-processing approaches?

   ■ Illustrate sensory, short-term, and long-term memory using examples from your own experiences.

4. What are the dimensions of intellectual exceptionality?

   ■ Write out a series of clearly documented arguments that might be used by one or the other side in a debate on the merits of mainstreaming.

STUDY TERMS

attention span   274

chunking   263

classes   260

cognitive strategies   262

compensation   258

concrete operations   257

conservation   257

constructing knowledge   258

contextual theory of intelligence   269

creativity   275

crystallized abilities   268

culture fair   271

declarative memory   264

developmental arithmetic disorder   274

developmental reading disorder   274

elaborating   265

episodic memory   264

exceptionality   256

explicit memory   264

fat-free mass   252

fat mass   252

fluid abilities   268

general factor theory   267

group intelligence tests   269

identity   258

implicit memory   264

individual intelligence tests   269

information-processing approach   261

intellectual giftedness   275

intelligence   267

knowledge base   262

learning disability   272

locomotor skills   255

long-term memory   263

mainstreaming   278

meaning-making   258

mental retardation   271

metacognition   262

middle childhood   252

nondeclarative memory   264

number   261

obesity   254

operations   258

organizing   265

otitis media   256

peak height velocity   253

preoperations   258

rehearsing   264

reliable   267

reversibility   258

scripts   263

semantic memory   264

sensory memory   263

seriation   261

short-term (or working) memory   263

special abilities theory   267

valid   267

FURTHER READINGS

The following book is a highly readable and excellent analysis of cognitive development. It looks in detail both at Piaget's theory and at current work in information processing and metacognition:

Flavell, J. H. (1985). *Cognitive development.* Englewood Cliffs, NJ: Prentice-Hall.

A detailed look at research that explores children's memories is:

Nelson, C. A. (Ed.) (1993). *Memory and affect in development: The Minnesota Symposia on Child Psychology* (Vol. 26). Hillsdale, NJ: Erlbaum.

A clear and useful account of developmental disorders in infancy and childhood is:

Hooper, S. R., Hynd, G. W., & Mattison, R. E. (Eds.). (1992). *Developmental disorders: Diagnostic criteria and clinical assessment.* Hillsdale, NJ: Erlbaum.

A thorough look at physical and motor development in children is presented in:

Malina, R. M., & Bouchard, C. (1991). *Growth, maturation, and physical activity.* Champaign, IL: Human Kinetics Books.

A provocative and practical book dealing with the development of creativity, critical thinking, and problem-solving skills is:

Fisher, R. (1990). *Teaching children to think.* Oxford: Basil Blackwell.

Social Development: Middle Childhood

A manner rude and wild
Is common at your age.

HILLAIRE BELLOC
Bad Child's Book of Beasts

My neighbor's 8-year-old CHAPTER 10
Thomas is a case in point.
"You know what that little beggar did last night?" his father asks by way of introduction, and the way he says it, you can tell maybe he'll brag a little, that he really isn't all that upset with the little beggar. "Drove across the lake," he continues.

"Drove across the lake?"

"In the boat."

"What?"

"Yep. Took the key from behind the door, fired her up, and zoomed right over to Billy's place."

"He's only 8," I says. "That's a 90-horse you got there."

"He knows how to run it," his father answers, unable to hide his pride. "Full speed all the way too. Have to hide the key now. Car key too. He's a wild one, that little beggar." It's less complaint than boast.

When I go back home, I take all the keys off their hooks by the back door—the ones for the boat and the snowmobile and the ATV. Even the one for the truck.

"All the keys are hidden in the linen drawer," I tell everybody at dinner that night.

"Why?"

I explain about 8-year-old Thomas, how wild he's turning out.

"That's an 8-year-old for you," says my 18-year-old.

This Chapter

But surely not all children are rude and wild through middle childhood. Some, of either sex, must also be polite and gentle and well behaved. Given a thousand 8-year-olds, will they be found to be more rude than polite? More wild than restrained?

This chapter presents the beginning of an answer. It looks at how children are socialized through the middle years, how they become caring and concerned individuals, and how they develop notions of who they are and of their self-worth. It examines the role of parents, peers, and friends in shaping the developmental process. It looks, too, at how important school and television are in the child's context.

Like little beggar Thomas's pranks, much of the wildness—and the rudeness—of middle childhood is playful. Sadly, some is not. There are dysfunctional families where children are neglected and abused, sometimes in shocking ways. This chapter closes with a look at child maltreatment, followed by a discussion of social-emotional exceptionality.

Social Cognition

Cognition refers to knowing; *metacognition* is knowing about knowing; and **social cognition** refers to an awareness of others as selves that, like our own selves, are also capable of feelings, motives, intentions, and so on. The purpose of social cognition, says Fiske (1993), is for people to make sense of others.

The Origins of Social Cognition

Social cognitions have their roots in the infant's realization that there are things out there that are persons and others that are nonpersons (Wellman & Gelman, 1992). At about the same time, infants begin to develop a sense of self, and to form bonds, usually to their caretakers. Thus begins the process of socialization.

But the infant's social cognitions unfold slowly and reflect many of the limitations that characterize nonsocial

cognitions. Recall how young infants and even preschoolers have difficulty adopting another person's point of view, as is illustrated by Piaget's mountains problem (in which children view a three-dimensional "mountain" display from one angle and are asked to describe what it would look like from a different angle). In much the same way, infants and preschoolers cannot easily make inferences about what other people are thinking or feeling. Still, recent research suggests that preschoolers may be far better social thinkers than had been thought.

Theories of Mind

"Current research," write Wellman and Gelman (1992), "reveals sophisticated reasoning about the mental states of self and others in 3- to 5-year-olds" (p. 351). It seems that preschoolers have already begun to develop a **theory of mind.** This implicit theory of mind is based on an understanding that others have mental states—that is, that they have thoughts, emotions, wishes, beliefs. It is essential that children have a theory of mind if they are to understand others and interact intelligently with them.

If 4-year-old Elizabeth does not have a theory of mind—that is, does not understand that her mother has her own thoughts and beliefs—then it would not occur to her to lie when her mother asks, "Did you poke that hole in your bedsheet, Elizabeth?" Intentional deception, claim Ruffman and colleagues (1993), requires that children understand not only that people can believe different things, but also that it is possible to make people believe things that are false. Three-year-olds have considerable difficulty deceiving others or understanding deception.* But the 4-year-old has no such problem—strong evidence, claim Ruffman and associates (1993), of the beginning of a theory of mind.

The roots of a theory of mind are found in the behavior of even younger children. "Children as young as 2 years old are, in some respects, quite competent social reasoners, and so they must have some kind of 'theory of mind,'" writes Perner (1991). They show awareness of others' mental states in their conversations, their play, their fighting. Two-year-olds who tease a sibling or steal a favorite toy or call each other names act as if they *know* the likely effects of their behaviors. However, this might have nothing to do with the ability to understand or to represent what the other child is feeling (Flavell, 1985). That a 4-year-old lies to her mother does not prove she understands this might affect her mother's beliefs. It's possible that she has simply learned that certain behaviors are less likely to be punished—or more likely to be considered funny.

---

*"No, I'm behind the couch!" 3-year-old Tyler yells in the middle of the hide-and-seek game when his older sister says, "I'll bet you're hiding in the bathroom again, Tyler."

TABLE 10.1
Selman's Developmental Progression in Social Cognition

Perspective-Taking Stage	Description	Typical Responses to Cat Story*
0: Egocentric (to 6 years)	"There is no perspective but mine. People feel the way I would in that situation."	"Her daddy will be happy 'cause he likes the kitten."
1: Social-informational (6–8)	"Okay, so others have a point of view too, but they would feel the way I do if they had the same information."	"He'd let her climb if he understood how she felt."
2: Self-reflective (8–10)	"Actually, we can have different points of view. There's hers and there's mine. I can see mine; she can see hers."	"He'll be mad 'cause he doesn't want her to climb trees."
3: Mutual (10–12)	"Well, maybe I can see hers and she can see mine. We can even talk about our different points of view."	"Holly and her father can talk to each other. They will understand each other. They can work it out."
4: Social and conventional (12–15+)	"Actually, within the context of discombobulism, and taking into consideration the teachings of MUMU and the charter of personal delimitations, her point of view is totally philanthropic. On the other hand . . ."	"It depends on whether her father thinks the cat's life or Shawn's feelings are more important than obedience. Besides . . . "

* Note that these reflect children's ability to *verbalize* their perspectives and their understanding of other perspectives. However, their actual behavior reflects more advanced understanding of other people's thoughts, beliefs, and feelings during the preschool period.

Role Taking and Empathy

Early investigations of the development of *empathy* (the ability to recognize and share the feelings of others) often asked children to recognize the emotion that would accurately reflect the reaction of a person in a story. In one study, for example, Selman (1980) told children the following story:

> Holly is an 8-year-old girl who likes to climb trees. She is the best tree climber in the neighborhood. One day while climbing down from a tall tree, she falls off the bottom branch but does not hurt herself. Her father sees her fall. He is upset and asks her to promise not to climb trees anymore. Holly promises.
>
> Later that day, Holly and her friends meet Shawn. Shawn's kitten is caught up in a tree and can't get down. Something has to be done right away, or the kitten may fall. Holly is the only one who climbs trees well enough to reach the kitten and get it down, but she remembers her promise to her father. (p. 36)

Children were then asked whether Holly knows how Shawn feels about the kitten; what Holly thinks her father will do if she climbs the tree; how Holly's father will feel if he knows she has climbed the tree; and what the child being questioned would do in the same situation.

Selman summarizes the development of the child's ability to understand and verbalize another person's point of view in five stages—numbered 0 to 4. These are shown in Table 10.1. In general, they describe the preschooler as largely unaware of others' states of mind, and as developing a gradually more sophisticated and abstract understanding of the thinking of others through middle childhood.

One possible conclusion from studies such as Selman's is that infants and preschoolers are largely ignorant of the states of minds of others until the age of 6 or 7—that, as Moore and Frye (1991) put it, they have not yet learned to see the world through others' eyes. However, as we saw, preschoolers' ability to deceive, and their apparent anticipation of the consequences of their behavior, indicate that they *do* have some understanding of others' mental states. But preschoolers' understanding remains limited. They cannot easily imagine themselves in someone else's mental state or verbally explain another person's behavior. For example, Bruchkowsky (1991) showed children a video in which a girl's (Mary's) dog dies. Children were later asked, "What made Mary feel sad?" A typical 4-year-old answered, "Because Harry died." "Why did that make Mary sad?" asked the experimenter. Silence.

In contrast, 6-year-olds responded immediately: "Because her dog died, and she misses him." And 10-year-olds elaborated even more: "Because her dog died, and she really loved him, and still really misses him 'cause he was her best friend" (p. 160).

Clearly, the preschooler's theory of mind is less sophisticated than that of the older child. But just as clearly, important developments have occurred in the preschooler's growing capacity to understand belief, intention, and other aspects of mind.

SELF-WORTH

The child's theory of mind, says Astington (1991), "is the understanding children have of their own and others' minds. . . . This understanding enables children to predict and explain actions by ascribing mental states . . . to themselves and to other people" (p. 158). Thus, theory of mind implies an awareness of self and of others as distinct selves.

Throughout elementary school, the most important dimension on which children evaluate their self-worth is that of physical appearance: less important are scholastic and athletic competence, acceptance by peers, and personal conduct. This girl's stunning hat, especially if her friends like it as much as she does, may contribute a great deal to her positive evaluations of self, and to her happiness.

Put another way, it implies a **self-concept. Self-worth, self-esteem,** or self-concept are all aspects of what we refer to in Chapter 2 as *self-referent* thought—thought that has to do with our **selves** (that is *self-reflective*).

Some Definitions

One aspect of *self-concept* is evaluative; it refers primarily to how we evaluate ourselves. People have *positive* self-concepts when they think well of themselves, and *negative* self-concepts when they do not think much of themselves. Terms like *self-esteem, self-worth,* or *self-appraisal* are better expressions for this meaning because they are clearly evaluative (Yost, Strube, & Bailey, 1992).

Some aspects of the self-concept are not evaluative. They have to do with abstract, cognitive notions of what the self *is* rather than with whether the self is good or bad, worthwhile or worthless, lovable or detestable, moral or immoral.

TABLE 10.2
Two Theories of the Basis of Self-Worth

Theory	Example of Reasoning Process
James: Discrepancy between actual and ideal self What I would like to be versus what I think I am	"I'm a blonde, which is what I would want to be if I had a choice. My skin is clear, and I like my eyes—nice blue. Physically, I know I'm well, pretty attractive. But I've just been pulling off C's in school, which is the pits. I want at least B's."
Cooley: Looking-glass self What I think important others think of me	"Willie asked me out. Billy asked me out. Sam looks at me as if he wants to ask me out, and he could go out with anybody in the school. I must be pretty attractive."

Two Approaches to Self-Worth

There are two major (and very old) approaches to explaining self-worth (or self-esteem): those of James and Cooley.

James's Approach
William James's (1892) approach says: My self-worth is a direct function of the difference between what I would like to be and what I think I am. The closer my actual self (as I perceive my *self*) is to my ideal self (the way I would like to be), the more I will like myself, and, hence, the higher my self-esteem.

Cooley's Approach
Cooley (1902) argues: My self-worth is a direct function of what I think others think of me; my worth is reflected in their behavior toward me (hence, his expression *looking-glass self*). If people avoid me, that is evidence that I am not very worthy; if they seek me out, the evidence is more positive. Those who are most important in serving as mirrors in whose behavior I can view my *self* are people who are most important to me (part of the *microsystem* in Bronfenbrenner's terms). Hence, for the preschooler, parents and siblings are most important; for the elementary school child, peers and teachers also become important—and perhaps coaches, mentors, tutors, religious leaders, and so on (see Table 10.2).

Measuring Self-Worth

There are a number of scales for measuring self-worth (for example, the Rosenberg Self-Esteem Scale and the Harter Self-Perception Profile for Children) (see Hagborg, 1993, for a look at the validity of these measures). These scales typically ask children questions about how well they think they perform in various areas considered important for developing notions of self-worth. For example, the Harter scale asks questions relating to five areas: athletic, scholastic, social, physical, and moral.

TABLE 10.3
Areas in Which Children Evaluate Their Self-Worth *

Area	Description
1. Scholastic competence	How competent or smart the child feels with regard to schoolwork
2. Athletic competence	How competent the child feels at sports and games requiring physical skill or athletic ability
3. Social acceptance	How popular or socially accepted the child feels with peers
4. Behavioral conduct	How adequate the child feels with regard to behaving in the way one is supposed to behave
5. Physical appearance	How good-looking the child feels, how much the child likes such characteristics as height, weight, face, hair

* Children's estimates of self-worth are based on (1) what significant other people (the microsystem) think of the child's capabilities and worth (Cooley's looking-glass theory) and (2) the extent to which the child lives up to personal ideals and aspirations (James's discrepancy between aspirations and competence theory). Both kinds of evaluations occur in the five areas described here.

SOURCE: Based on Harter, 1987.

Some Investigations of Self-Worth

In some of Harter's (1987; 1988) studies, children were asked how *important* they think it is to do well in these areas. Thus, investigators could look at the difference between actual performance (competence) and the child's wishes, and arrive at a measure relating to James's approach.

Children were also asked to what extent they felt their importance is recognized by others, how well others treat them, whether they think they are liked, admired, and respected. This line of questioning provides information relating to the regard in which others hold the child (Cooley's approach).

Finally, children were asked questions relating to a more global concept of self-worth—questions relating to how well they like themselves as people.

Use of questions such as these provides answers for a number of important questions: Are competence/aspiration-based estimates of self-worth (James's theory) or "looking-glass" estimates (Cooley's theory) actually related to general concepts of self-worth? Are discrepancies between competence and the ideal more important in one area than another (for example, are athletics more important than scholastics)? Are there developmental changes in areas of importance? Is the source of approval and social regard important?

Harter (1987) provides answers for a number of these questions based on her investigations of children in grades 3 through 8 (approximately 8 to 13 years of age). Prior to the age of 8, children do not seem to have a single, clearly defined, and measurable notion of self-worth; accordingly, younger children are not included in Harter's samples.

TABLE 10.4
Correlations Between Children's Self-Worth and Perceived Inadequacies in Specific Areas

	Elementary School (grades 3–6)	Middle School (grades 6–8)
Physical appearance	.66	.57
Social acceptance	.36	.45
Scholastic competence	.35	.36
Athletic competence	.33	.24
Behavioral conduct	.30	.26

SOURCE: "The Determinants and Mediational Role of Global Self-Worth in Children" by S. Harter, 1987. In *Contemporary Topics in Developmental Psychology* (p. 229), N. Eisenberg (Ed.), New York: John Wiley. © 1987 John Wiley & Sons, Inc. Used by permission of the publisher.

Some Important Findings

First, although children have a general estimate of personal worth, they also make individual estimates of self-worth in at least five separate areas: *scholastic competence, athletic competence, social acceptance, physical appearance,* and *behavioral conduct* (Table 10.3). In other words, some children may see themselves as athletically competent (good and worthwhile); but these same children may have decided that they were not "good" in a moral sense—or that they are not as worthwhile scholastically. There is evidence that self-concept is relatively stable, although self-esteem might increase or decrease depending primarily on the child's experiences (Block & Robins, 1993).

Second, Harter's studies indicate that the child's judgments of self-worth reflect both major sources described by James and Cooley. That is, the difference between competencies (in each of the five important areas) and the child's aspirations and desires is reflected in estimates of self-worth. At the same time, how others regard the child also has an important influence on self-esteem.

Third, not all five areas are equally important to every child. High or low competence in important areas will have a more powerful influence than competence or incompetence in less important areas. If athletics are more important than being good (behavior conduct), not being a good athlete will be more damaging to self-esteem than behaving immorally. In Harter's studies physical appearance is the most important area in determining self-worth, both for the younger (grades 3 to 6) and the older (grades 6 to 8) children. Children who see themselves as attractive are most likely to like themselves. For both these age groups, behavioral conduct (goodness of behavior in a moral sense) was least important (see Table 10.4).

Fourth, as we noted, some sources of social regard and support are more important than others. For example, it might not matter very much that some nameless fan yells disparaging remarks while 10-year-old Willie stands

FIGURE 10.1

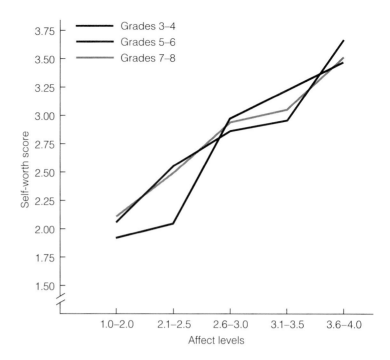

The relationship between mood and self-concept. In
Harter's study, children who were sad (low affect
level) had the lowest opinions of themselves. (From
S. Harter, "The Determinants and Mediational
Role of Global Self-Worth in Children," in Con-
temporary Topics in Developmental Psychology,
p. 234, N. Eisenberg (Ed.). © 1987 John Wiley &
Sons, Inc. Used by permission of the publisher.)

at the plate waiting for the pitch, but it might matter a great deal if his coach later makes the same remarks. In Harter's (1987) studies, the most important sources of support in determining self-worth, for both the younger and the older children, are parents and classmates, rather than friends or teachers. It is noteworthy that parents retain their importance through these years, because this contradicts a popular belief that as peers become more important, parents must become less important. It is also significant that classmates are typically more important than are friends. This may well be because classmates' opinions may be seen as more objective; the evaluation of friends, on the other hand, may be more biased.

Fifth, estimates of self-worth are closely linked with affect (emotion or mood), which, in turn, has much to do with motivation. As Harter (1988) comments, elementary school children who like themselves (who have high self-esteem) are the happiest; in contrast, those who do not think very highly of themselves are more likely to feel sad or even depressed. Also, children who are happy are most likely to feel motivated to do things; those who are sad are least likely to want to do things. Figure 10.1 depicts the relationship between mood and self-worth scores for three groups of children from grades 3 through 8. Note that for all three groups, very low affect scores (sadness bordering on depression) are associated with very low self-worth scores; conversely, high affect is associated with high measures of self-worth.

Some Implications
Some of the practical implications of self-worth are clear. To the extent that positive self-esteem is closely related to

happiness and to high motivation—and, by the same token, to social adjustment and general well-being—parents, teachers, and others who share responsibility for rearing youngsters must be concerned with far more than their cognitive development or their physical well-being. They must do what they can to ensure that the evaluation that every child places on the *self* is a positive judgment. In fact, enhancement of children's self-esteem is one of the key recommendations of most parenting programs, and may be especially important for children at risk for developmental problems (Cutright, 1992; Silvestri, Dantonio, & Eason, 1994).

Unfortunately, the causes of feelings of self-worth are not simple. They include factors over which we have limited control like scholastic competence or physical appearance. But they also include things over which we have more control—like our personal estimates of our children and our communication of love and support.

We are not alone in determining children's self-worth. Friends, classmates, teachers, and parents are all important.

FRIENDS AND PEERS

"Friendships of children," writes Berndt (1989), "appear to exist in a kind of never-never-land, a world of fun and adventure that adults rarely if ever enter and cannot fully understand" (p. 332). But science, in her careful and analytic way, asks questions whose answers might increase understanding—questions like "How do children view friendship?"

For very young children, friends are whoever happens to be there to play with. Older children understand that friendships grow over time and involve sharing, trust, respect, and mutual interests. Among this group of soccer players, there are likely to be a number of "best" friends, some of whom will remain close friends throughout their lives.

Children's Views of Friendship

For the 3- to 5-year-old, claims Selman (1980; 1981), a *friend* is merely a playmate and friendship is nothing more complex than "playing together." A friend is someone who happens to be present and who plays with the child. At this stage, children have no concept of friendship as an enduring kind of relationship. And if they are asked how friendships are formed, they are likely to say, "By playing together." If asked to describe a friend, they will speak of activities, but not of traits or characteristics ("He plays with me" or "He doesn't hit me").

Even in the preschool period, however, patterns of interactions among pairs of friends appear to be relatively stable over time. Park, Lay, and Ramsay (1993) studied 24 pairs of preschool friends (average age 46 months) and found high correlations between observations made one year apart. Pair interactions tended to be highly consistent in terms of characteristics like how happily the children played together, what strategies were used for resolving conflicts, and how well children shared.

By the age of 11 or 12, children understand that friendships develop over time and that they involve a reciprocal sharing of thoughts and feelings and a high degree of mutual trust. When asked to describe friends, they are likely to speak of qualities ("She understands people; she's so sincere") and of mutual interests ("We like a lot of the same things"). Whereas younger children assume that the best friends are those who live close by and who want to play, older children realize that the best friends are those who share interests, who are mutually supportive, who like each other. A 5-year-old assumes that to become friends it

is only necessary to play together; a 12-year-old believes that to become friends it is necessary to get to know one another.

Dimensions of Childhood Friendships

"Not having friends," writes Bullock (1994), "contributes to loneliness, low self-esteem and inability to develop social skills" (p. 95). Peer relations, she argues, are *necessary* for healthy development.

Best Friends
Strictly speaking, only one of our friends can be our *best friend;* none of the others can be more than second best. However, in common usage, *best friend* refers to a close type of friendship in which several people can be best friends all at the same time.

Most 6- to 12-year-old youngsters have more than one best friend, although that is not always apparent in the research. Berndt (1988) points out that if children are asked to name their best *friend*, they will obligingly name only one person. But if they are asked to name their best *friends*, they gladly name a number of people. And if the question is changed only slightly, and they are asked instead to indicate whether each child in their class is a best friend, a friend, or not a friend, some children will name most of the class as best friends.

Sex Differences
Most children have a number of close friends who are most often of the same age, race, and grade, who share common interests, and who are almost invariably of the

same sex. Both boys and girls usually have two or three close friends rather than just one *best* friend. And for both sexes, friendships tend to be highly mutual: If one child indicates that a second is a best friend, the second child will very likely also have chosen the first as a best friend. As Hartup (1983) notes, reciprocity is a prominent characteristic of all childhood friendships.

One of the main differences between girls' and boys' friendships is that girls' relationships tend to involve more kindness, empathy, and self-revelation (Clark & Bittle, 1992). That is, girls' friendships are often more intimate. In addition, the pattern in elementary school, notes Erwin (1993), is for boys to have more friends than girls and to play in larger groups. Furthermore, as we noted in Chapter 8, they play more aggressively and more competitively at all ages.

Importance of Friends

There is little doubt that having friends is extremely important to all normal children. Sadly, however, Bullock (1994) reports that between 6 and 11 percent of elementary school-age children have no friends. More than half the children referred for emotional or behavioral problems have no friends or have difficulty in peer interactions (Oden, 1988).

Rubin (1980) suggests that, among other things, friendships contribute significantly to the development of social skills (such as being sensitive to other people's points of view; learning the rules of conversation; learning sex- and age-appropriate behaviors). In addition, interactions with friends are involved in developing notions of self and self-worth. Friendships may also be important in developing feelings of belonging to a group, and may therefore play a crucial role in the development of notions of cultural identity. Not surprisingly, children who have no friends are at much higher risk of dropping out of school (Bullock, 1994).

It is also clear that friends have powerful influences on each other. Berndt (1988) summarizes research that has found that a child's academic performance can be positively or negatively influenced by choice of friends. Similarly, friends may serve to encourage or discourage deviant behaviors (such as delinquency or drug use).

Close friends are one source of influence on the developing child; peers are another.

Peer Groups

A **peer group** is a group of equals. Most individuals in our society have a peer group, excluding hermits, whose peers, by definition, are also isolated and therefore of little consequence to their development.

The peer group is one of the major transmitters of cultural expectations and values, particularly during middle childhood. During these years, the peer group typically consists of like-sexed children. In addition, because

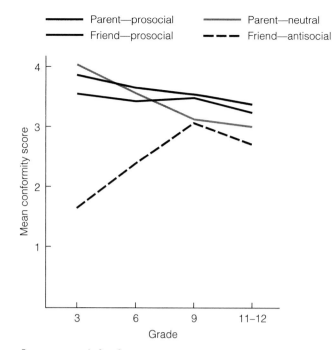

FIGURE 10.2

Changes in average conformity scores as a function of age and source of pressure. (From T. J. Berndt, "Developmental Changes in Conformity to Peers and Parents," Developmental Psychology 15, pp. 608–616. © 1979 by the American Psychological Association. Reprinted by permission of APA and the author.)

of the different abilities, capacity for understanding, and varied interests among the different ages spanning this period, the peer group usually consists of peers close in age.

Parents and Peers

In infancy and early childhood, parents have traditionally been the center of the child's life—although with increasing numbers of children in day-care facilities, the importance of peer groups during the preschool period has increased significantly in recent decades. By the beginning of middle childhood, peers have assumed tremendous significance. And as children's interests and allegiance shift gradually toward peers, there are important changes in the ways in which they interact with and conform to their parents.

In early childhood, parental authority is largely unquestioned. This does not mean that all children always obey their parents. Sometimes temptation or impulse are just too overwhelming. And sometimes, too, parents overstep the unwritten but clearly understood boundaries of authority. As Braine and colleagues (1991) note, parental authority does not extend to immoral acts; nor can it be permitted to infringe on important areas of personal jurisdiction, such as choice of friends.

In later childhood and adolescence, parental authority is subjected to more constraints, and the child's area of con-

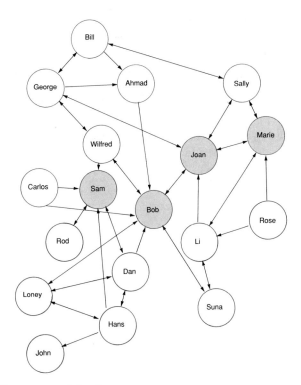

FIGURE 10.3
A sociogram of friendships in a fourth-grade classroom.

TABLE 10.5
Five Categories of Social Status

Category	Characteristics
Sociometric stars	Especially well liked by most.
Mixers	High peer interaction. Some well liked; others not.
Teacher negatives	Typically in conflict with teachers. Some are liked; others not.
Tuned out	Not involved; are ignored rather than rejected.
Sociometric rejectees	Not liked very much. Rejected rather than simply ignored.

SOURCE: Based on Gottman, 1977.

trol increases. Berndt (1979) asked 251 children in grades 3, 6, 9, and 11–12 to respond to hypothetical situations in which parents or peers urged them to do something antisocial, something prosocial, or something neutral. As expected, Berndt found that conformity to parents decreased steadily with age; and so did conformity to peers, except with regard to antisocial influences, which increased until about grade 9 (age 14), before beginning to decline again (see Figure 10.2).

Here, as in other areas of human development, relationships and interactions are complex and influence each other. Accordingly, it is misleading and overly simplified to consider parent–child relations on the one hand, and child–peer relations on the other, and to compare and contrast them as though they were isolated and unrelated. There is evidence, for example, that the kind of relationship a child has with parents is very closely related to later relationships with peers. For example, Fuligni and Eccles (1993) found that children who felt their parents did not relax their power and provide them with more opportunities for decision making as they neared adolescence were more likely to be extremely peer oriented.

There is considerable evidence that supportive parenting leads to good peer relationships. Thus, securely attached infants (see Chapter 6) are more likely to later have good relationships with peers. Similarly, authoritative-democratic (as opposed to authoritarian-restrictive) parenting is associated with the most positive peer relationships (Dekovic & Janssens, 1992).

Peer Acceptance

Peer acceptance or rejection (**sociometric status**) is typically assessed using one of two methods: *peer ratings* or *peer nominations*. In a peer-rating study, each member of a group (for example, a classroom) might be asked to rate all other members of the group in terms of how well they like them, whether they would like to play with them, how smart they are, how popular, and so on. A study using peer nominations might ask participants to name the three individuals they like best, the three they like least, the three smartest kids, and so on. Data gathered in this way can then be analyzed to provide an index of sociometric acceptance or rejection, and can sometimes be depicted pictorially in a **sociogram** (Figure 10.3). Information of this kind is sometimes useful in research that looks at the qualities associated with popularity or social isolation.

Sociometric Status

We are not all equally loved and sought after by our friends. Indeed, not all of us have friends. Some of us are *social isolates.* Social isolates are those who do not often interact with peers, or those who are seldom selected as "best friend" by anyone. These two definitions are different, says Gottman (1977). Some children are liked and accepted but do not interact much with their peers; on the other hand, some children are very low on everybody's list of "my best friends" or "who I would most like to be *with*" or "who I would most like to be *like*," but they nevertheless interact frequently with peers.

Five Levels of Social Status

In an attempt to investigate these definitions and clarify the nature of social isolation, Gottman studied 113 children in depth. His observations suggest five distinct categories of children (see Table 10.5). *Sociometric stars* are those who are consistently "especially liked." *Teacher negatives* are usually in conflict with teachers, and might be either high or low on measures of peer acceptance. *Mixers* are those who interact often with peers; they too might be high or low on measures of acceptance. The *tuned out* are those who are usually not involved with what is going on—who are tuned "out" rather than "in." The tuned out, rather than being strongly rejected, are simply ignored. And, finally, *sociometric rejectees* are those who are not only disliked by their peers, but are actively rejected by everyone. These are the children who, in childhood, are the butts of all the cruel jokes and taunts.

Qualities Related to Peer Acceptance

In general, children who are friendly and sociable, and who evaluate others positively, are more easily accepted than those who are hostile, unsociable, withdrawn, or indifferent (Rabiner, Keane, & Mackinnon-Lewis, 1993). Similarly, children who are intelligent and creative are more accepted than those who are slow learners or retarded. Size, strength, athletic prowess, and daring are particularly important characteristics for membership in boys' peer groups; maturity and social skills are more important for girls, especially as they approach adolescence. Attractiveness is important for both (Hartup, 1983).

The observation that friendly, socially competent children have more friends (have higher *status*, as the sociologists put it) raises an interesting and important question: Are the characteristics of high-status (accepted) and low-status (rejected) children the cause or the result of their status? Does a friendly child have many friends because she is friendly, or is she friendly because she has many friends? Similarly, does social rejection lead to socially incompetent behavior, or is the socially incompetent behavior present to begin with, and lead to social rejection?

A review of a large number of studies strongly suggests that popular children are popular because they are more competent socially and that unpopular children lack social skills (Newcomb, Bukowski, & Pattee, 1993). In other words, how a child interacts with others is a primary cause of social status. The most socially competent children quickly sense what is happening in an unfamiliar social situation and are able to modify their behaviors accordingly. Thus, they are less likely to engage in behaviors that are inappropriate or unexpected than are socially incompetent children. In addition, Bryant (1992) found that the most socially preferred children are those most likely to use calm approaches to resolve conflicts. In contrast, children most likely to be rejected by peers are those who react to conflict either with anger and retaliation or with avoidance.

Qualities Related to Peer Rejection

Among characteristics often associated with peer rejection are those that make the child different or that are perceived as undesirable—like high aggression. In a study of 362 8- to 11-year-olds, Pope, Bierman, and Mumma (1991) found that aggressive, hyperactive, and immature boys were likely to be rejected. Parkhurst and Asher (1992) also found that rejected students tend to be the most aggressive or, interestingly, the most submissive. In fact, a combination of aggression-submissiveness, coupled with low social competence, were most closely associated with rejection in this study of 450 elementary schoolchildren. Related to this, Juvonen (1991) reports that those who engage in behaviors others consider deviant (rule breaking, for example) are more likely to be rejected.

Consequences of Peer Acceptance and Rejection

Research indicates that the quality of children's relationships with their peers is very important for their happiness and adjustment (La Greca & Stone, 1993). Rejected children, Crick and Ladd (1993) report, are more lonely, more socially anxious, and more likely to avoid social situations.

Ollendick, Weist, and Borden (1992) ranked the sociometric status of 296 fourth graders, and, five years later, evaluated the academic performance and social adjustment of 267 of these children. Those classified as "rejected" fared significantly more poorly on both sets of measures. Similarly, Vitaro, Tremblay, and Gagnon (1992) found that preschoolers classed as "rejected" two years in a row were significantly more likely to manifest later behavior problems like fighting, withdrawal, or hyperactivity, than were children identifed as "rejected" only one of two years.

Note that although peer rejection may be associated with poorer adjustment, that is certainly not always the case. In a study of 881 children in grades 3 through 5, Parker and Asher (1993) found that many children who are *not* very popular nevertheless have very close and very satisfying friendships. There are wide individual differences in the *sociability* of different children. Not all are outgoing, talkative, expansive; many appear withdrawn and shy. We should not make the mistake of assuming that children who appear shy are also lonely and friendless. Nor should we assume that they are likely to be rejected by their peers or socially tuned out. Some of these children are extraordinarily socially competent. Many have a large number of close friendships. Some might, in fact, be among Gottman's sociometric stars. (See Across Cultures: "Koyoteru Okouchi and Lewis Pagan, Bullied.")

THE SCHOOL

Outside of the family, say Asp and Garbarino (1988), the school is the most pervasive socializing influence in the life of the child. Schools are centrally involved in teaching children much that is necessary for their effective interaction in our increasingly complex world. In fact, notes Stevenson and colleagues (1991), the influence of the school is so

KOYOTERU OKOUCHI AND LEWIS PAGAN, BULLIED

Nisho City, Japan: When he was only 10, his classmates began to taunt and bully Koyoteru Okouchi, a student at Tobu junior high school in Nisho City, central Japan. The bullying worsened rapidly, and soon the bullies began demanding that he give them money. When they thought he might refuse, they dunked him in the nearby river. After three years of bullying, they had extorted more than $10,000 from him, much of which he had stolen from his parents and grandparents after selling his books and his computer software. "If only I'd had the courage to say no," Koyoteru wrote just before he hanged himself. He was only 13. And even in his final note, he doesn't name his tormentors, speaking of them only as "the usual four" (Bullies Drive Teen to Suicide, 1994).

New York, U.S.: David Harris, age 12, is dead. Lewis Santiago Pagan is accused of killing him. Lewis is a shy, awkward, giant of a boy, already 6 feet tall and weighing more than 200 pounds at age 13. David was a puny 4 feet 5 inches; he weighed only 80 pounds. But, in spite of his size, David had joined a group of bullies who ridiculed and taunted Lewis, pulling his legs out from under him and making him fall. In the end, Lewis pulled out a large "Rambo-type" knife and stabbed David three times in the chest, killing him. "It seems that Lewis had finally had enough," said Detective Kim Royster (" 'Gentle Giant' Stabs Boy for Taunts," 1994).

As a result of incidents such as these, a number of school jurisdictions have begun to look at bullying as a serious problem that needs to be *prevented* rather than simply dealt with in response to a crisis. In Norway, for example, following the suicides of three different victims of bullying in one year, a national antibullying campaign has been established (Tattum & Herbert, 1993).

To Think About Children's lives can be dramatically affected by some apparent weakness or difference—sometimes physical, often

racial or religious. What do you suppose might be done to prevent or counter bullying?

To Consult Tattum, D., & Herbert, G. (1993). *Countering bullying: Initiatives by schools and local authorities.* Stoke-on-Trent, England: Trentham Books.

Smith, P. K., & Thompson, D. (Eds.). (1991). *Practical approaches to bullying.* London: David Fulton.

Olweus, D. (1993). *Bullying at school: What we know and what we can do. Understanding children's worlds.* Cambridge, MA: Blackwell.

---

pervasive in our societies that much of what developmental psychologists view as "normal" development is, in fact, a reflection of what children learn in schools.

Schooling and Measured Intelligence

Schools do more than socialize children and teach them important information and skills; there is evidence that they also increase measured intelligence. For example, there has been a massive increase in IQ scores in the Netherlands since the 1950s. This increase, argue Husén and Tuijnman (1991), is due to changes in context, the most important of which may be formal schooling. Similarly, Flynn (1987) found that in 14 industrialized countries, there has been an increase of about 15 IQ points in one generation.

There is additional evidence that formal schooling is closely tied to measured intelligence. For example, Ceci (1991) reviews studies that show a relationship between level of schooling (grade attained) and IQ; between missing school and declines in IQ; between delayed school entrance and lower IQ; and between increasing school attendance in an area and general increases in measured IQ. And Stevenson and associates (1991) found significant differences in cognitive development between Peruvian children who attended school and those who didn't. Perhaps more striking, they found remarkable similarities in the cognitive functioning of first graders from such diverse cultural backgrounds as Peru, Taiwan, Japan, and the United States—almost as though the experiences of first grade had already begun to wipe out what would otherwise have been highly noticeable differences.

Schooling is essential for imparting important skills and knowledge—even for increasing measured intelligence. Perhaps equally important, school experiences also contribute significantly to the development of the public personality that will characterize children throughout life.

The evidence, claim Husén and Tuijnman (1991), supports the conclusion "that not only does child IQ have an effect on schooling outcomes, but also that schooling per se has a substantial effect on IQ test scores" (p. 22).

Teacher Expectations

One illustration of how schools can affect children is found in the classical Rosenthal and Jacobson (1968a; 1968b) study of how teacher expectations can become *self-fulfilling prophecies*. The study involved administering students an intelligence test in the spring of the school year, telling teachers this was a test designed to identify academic "bloomers" (students *expected* to blossom next year), and later "accidentally" allowing teachers to see a list of likely bloomers. In fact, these bloomers were a randomly chosen group of about 20 percent of the school's population. No other treatment was undertaken.

The Self-Fulfilling Prophecy
Amazingly, many teachers observed exactly what they expected. The experimental group not only scored higher on measures of achievement than a comparable control group, but also scored higher on a general measure of intelligence.

Hundreds of replication studies have been undertaken since the original studies. Not all of them provide very clear evidence of the existence or importance of teacher expectations (see Meyer, 1985). However, there is some evidence that many teachers develop predictable patterns of expectations. These are often more positive for children from more advantaged socioeconomic backgrounds,

as well as for students who are more attractive, more articulate, who sit close to the teacher and speak clearly, and who are given the most positive labels—"learning disabled" rather than "retarded" (Rolison & Medway, 1985). Not surprisingly, even children have stereotypes about others who are labeled, and react accordingly. Miller, Clarke, and Malcarno (1991) observed 9- to 14-year-old children interacting with others described as being either "special education" students or regular students. The labels alone had a significant impact on how these children interacted.

Unfortunately, a quick overview of the results of studies such as these makes them seem far more dramatic and important than they actually are. In addition, there is a tendency to assume that negative expectations are more potent and more pervasive than are positive expectations. That is not the case.

Attribution Theory

Teacher expectations, it seems, might affect the performance of some students. Can the student's own expectations also have an effect? Attribution theory suggests yes.

An **attribution** is an assignment of cause or blame for the outcomes of our behaviors. If I think my stupidity is due to my having hit my head on a low branch when I was 10, then I *attribute* my stupidity to that event. Attribution theories look for regularities in how we attribute causes to the things that happen to us (Weiner, 1980).

We saw in Chapter 2 that children are different in how they typically assign responsibility for their successes or failures. Some accept personal responsibility for the

WHY DID YOU SUCCEED OR FAIL?

In Chapter 3, you were asked to figure out what Henry VIII didn't know that might have influenced his habit of beheading wives who failed to give him sons. Did you succeed or fail? Why? Are you one of those who characteristically accept personal responsibility for successes and failures? Or are you more likely to invoke luck, the difficulty (or easiness) of the task, or other factors over which you have no control? How do you explain your high (or low) grades to yourself? Your reasons reveal important things about your personality and achievement motivation.

External	Internal
Difficulty (task easy or too difficult)	Ability (intelligence, skill, or the lack thereof)
Luck (bad or good)	Effort (hard work, industriousness, self-discipline, or laziness, distractions, lack of time)

consequences of their behavior. They are said to have an *internal locus of control* (or to be **mastery-oriented** or persistent; Dweck, 1986). Others are more likely to attribute successes and failures to circumstances or events over which they have no control, and are described as having an *external locus of control* (in Dweck's terms, characterized by **learned helplessness** rather than by persistence). Thus, mastery-oriented children are most likely to attribute their successes to ability or effort (factors that are personal, or factors over which they at least have personal control); in contrast, helpless children are more likely to attribute their successes or failures to luck or the difficulty of the task (factors over which they have no personal control) (see Interactive Table 10.6).

How Mastery-Oriented and Helpless Children Differ

Differences between mastery-oriented and helpless children are often highly apparent. First, mastery-oriented children tend to be much more highly achievement-oriented. They undertake tasks that are more challenging, and strive harder to do well in them (Thomas, 1980).

Second, mastery-oriented and helpless children react very differently to successes and failures. When Diener and Dweck (1980) arranged a problem situation so that all children would experience an unbroken sequence of eight successes, helpless children still predicted they would not do very well if they had to repeat the eight tasks. These children found it difficult to interpret success as indicating that they are capable. Even after succeeding, they continue to underestimate future successes and overestimate future failures. In contrast, mastery-oriented children were confident they would continue to perform as well. And even when they were given a series of failure experiences, they continued to see themselves as capable and to predict future success experiences. They have higher expectations of themselves.

There appear to be some clear advantages to being mastery-oriented, especially in school. For this reason, a number of programs have been developed to change attributions. These are based on the assumption that the tendency to attribute outcomes to internal or external factors is at least partly learned, and can therefore be changed.

Schools clearly have a profound influence not only on the learning of "things," but also on social learning. Another source of profound influence on both of these classes of learning is television.

TELEVISION

For some time now, our prophets have been predicting that television will have highly negative effects on children. Some claim that television is producing a generation of passive people—inactive, lethargic, apathetic. Others argue that the violence characteristic of much of television will produce a generation of violent people. Still others fear that television has a corrupting influence through its transmission of undesirable values, including the message that immorality is often rewarded. There is also the possibility that, given the amount of the child's time it consumes, television may have a harmful effect on family relationships, on the social development of children, and on sports, reading, and other activities. Although the research evidence is incomplete, we have enough answers to partially respond to these criticisms and to present a more balanced impression of the actual influence of television on the lives of children.

Viewing Patterns

In 1950, there were about 100,000 television sets in North American homes; one year later, there were more than 1 million. Now it is no easy thing to find any home without at least one set (Gunter & McAleer, 1990). A conservative estimate is that preschoolers spend more than a third of their waking time watching television. Even 9-month-olds watch about 90 minutes of television a day (Cohen, 1993/1994). Many young children spend more time watching television than they spend in conversation with adults or siblings. In fact, by age 18, many children will have spent about 50 percent more time watching television than going to school and doing schoolwork combined. Only sleeping will have taken more time than watching television (Huston et al., 1990).

Comprehension

What children see and understand from television might be quite different from what you or I might see. Not only do they lack the experiences that we have, but their conceptual bases are more fragmented, less complete. Researchers now recognize that how children process

For many children, growing up in the developed world during the latter part of the 20th century means less contact with extended as well as immediate family members, more time alone as families become smaller and more parents work outside the home, and an enormous amount of time spent watching television. Fortunately, in spite of the violence and the questionable values sometimes characteristic of television, its effects are not entirely and always negative.

television information must be closely related to whatever effects television might have (Geiger & Newhagen, 1993).

Hayes and Casey (1992) report that preschoolers understand very little of the emotions and motives of characters—hardly surprising given their social cognitions. Accordingly, the preschooler responds to the most striking features of what is actually happening—the sights, the sounds, the action. What they don't understand, notes Evra (1990), they simply ignore. But even at the age of 5 or 6, children use fairly sophisticated cognitive skills to understand television's messages. And those with the most advanced verbal skills have a much higher level of comprehension (Jacobvitz, Wood, & Albin, 1991). With advancing age, children become progressively more sensitive to motives and more attentive to implications of actions for the characters involved.

Commercial programs for young children seem to be based on the assumption that the best way of capturing and holding the viewer's attention is through rapid action, constant change, high noise level, and slapstick violence (Huston & Wright, 1983). One very important question concerns the effects of this violence on children.

Does Television Viewing Lead to Aggression and Violence?

In much of literature that looks at the influence of television on children, the terms *violence* and *aggression* are used as though they mean exactly the same thing. In fact, they mean slightly different things

The more general of these two terms is **aggression,** which is defined as "hostile or forceful action intended to dominate or violate" (Lefrançois, 1983, p. 504). It includes a wide range of behaviors beginning with insistence, assertiveness, or perhaps intrusion and culminating in anger and violence. Thus, violence is simply an extreme form of aggressiveness. **Violence** implies physical action or movement and possible or actual harm to people or objects. It is well illustrated in television episodes where people are kicked, beaten, shot, or knifed, or where rocks and other objects are dropped on their heads from great heights. It is also evident in situations where dogs are kicked or cars are smashed.

Clearly, aggression is not always undesirable—or unavoidable. The totally nonaggressive are unlikely to achieve as many of their desires as are the more aggressive. In fact, our survival as a species, as well as that of many other animals, is very likely related to our aggressiveness. That, of course, does not necessarily mean that we still need to be as aggressive as many of us now are.

Television programming for children (and for adults) is marked by a very large number of violent images. Many of these, note Potts and Henderson (1991), have to do with injury-related events. Not only are these far more common on television than in real life, but their negative consequences are often trivialized, and they often happen in "humorous" circumstances.

Laboratory Research on the Effects of Television Violence

In an early series of studies, Bandura and his associates (Bandura, 1969; Bandura, Ross, & Ross, 1963) exposed children to violent models that were either live actors, films of real people, or films of cartoon characters. Following exposure to a violent model (typically, the model was aggressive toward an inflated rubber clown), children were given objects similar to those toward which the model had been aggressive and were observed at play through a one-way mirror. In most studies of this kind, a majority of the children who have been exposed to models of violence behave aggressively; in contrast, those who have not been exposed to violent models most often respond nonaggressively.

Although these studies have been widely interpreted as evidence that violence on television leads to violence in real life, there are at least three reasons why this kind of generalization may be unrealistic. First, the aggression displayed in an ordinary television program is directed against people rather than against inanimate objects, and children learn early in life, through socialization, that aggression against people is normally punished. Second, the experimental situation generally exposes the child to objects identical to those aggressed upon by the model, and usually immediately afterward. But a child who watches a violent scene on television is rarely presented immediately with an object (or person) similar to the one on whom the televised violence was inflicted. Third, striking a rubber clown with a mallet, kicking it, or punching it after seeing a model do so may not be a manifestation of aggression at all. The child has simply learned that these are appropriate and expected behaviors with this inanimate object.

Naturalistic Research on the Effects of Television Violence

Studies of television viewing under more natural circumstances may provide clearer information about its impact. Unfortunately, it is difficult to find children who have not been exposed to television and who can therefore serve as control groups for these studies; hence there are few of them.

One study reported by Williams and Handford (1986) looked at sports participation of children without television compared with children who had access to only one channel and others who could access four channels. Not surprisingly, they found that the greater the access to television, the less likely the children were to participate actively in sports.

A study conducted by Joy, Kimball, and Zabrack (1977) involved children in a town where television was just being introduced. Two years later, comparisons of these children with comparable children in another town that still had no television found a measurable increase in aggressive behavior among the television children. Similar results were also reported in Sweden where researchers found high positive correlations between television viewing and aggressiveness (Rosengren & Windahl, 1989). Note, however, that these studies do not prove that viewing violent television programs *causes* aggression. It may be that children who initially preferred violent programs would have been more aggressive and more prone to

delinquency than other children even if they had not been exposed to these programs.

Cross-Cultural Comparisons

A series of studies looked at the effects of television violence on aggressiveness in children from five countries: the United States, Finland, Israel, Poland, and Australia (Huesmann & Eron, 1986). Not only are these cultures very different, but television accessibility and the nature of television programming varied tremendously. For example, in the Israeli kibbutz, children watched TV for only one or two hours a week, and were almost never exposed to television violence. In contrast, American children watched 20 or more hours of television, most of it characterized by violent themes and violent acts.

The main conclusion advanced by Huesmann and Eron is essentially the same as the conclusion reached by the *Surgeon General's Report on Television and Social Behavior* more than a decade earlier: Television violence does have an adverse effect on some children. Second, the relationship between television viewing and aggression appears to be interdependent. That is, the most aggressive children tend to select the more violent television programs and to view more of them; at the same time, those who watch more violent programs tend to be more aggressive.

In conclusion, most research summaries that have looked at the relationship between aggression and television viewing reach similar conclusions: As Rosenkoetter, Huston, and Wright (1990) put it, "Most professional reviews . . . have concluded that the weight of evidence indicates that television violence does increase viewer aggression" (p. 125). But, as Evra (1990) emphasizes, the most recent studies indicate that the *long-term* impact of television violence may, in fact, be negligible.

Other Possible Negative Effects of Television

Another possible negative effect of violence on television is the instillation of *fear* in some children—an effect that, for some, may be more serious than increased aggressiveness. In fact, a survey conducted by Ridley-Johnson, Surdy, and O'Laughlin (1991) found that parents are as concerned about fear-related influences of television as about aggression-related effects.

There is a possibility, too, that television may have changed the nature of children's play. Cohen (1993/1994) notes not only that children who watch more television may participate less in sports, but also that the influence of parents and peers seems to have declined with the television generation. Television is now a primary source of information and influence, he argues. It not only reinforces models of social behavior, but creates them as well. So important is it that children and, indeed, families, often arrange their schedules (and their furniture) around television.

Positive Effects of Television

However, the potential effects of television are not all negative. Evidence shows, for example, that the language development of preschoolers can be signficantly improved with educational television (Koutsouvanou, 1993). Similarly, children who watch the news show "Channel One" in the classroom do learn more news than those who don't (Greenberg & Brand, 1993). At the same time, they are also motivated to want to buy the products they see advertised, even when they don't understand the meaning of the commercials (MacNeal, 1992).

There is evidence, too, that in the same way that television might be instrumental in undermining values such as nonviolence, family stability, cooperation, altruism, and gender equality, so too might it serve to bring about and strengthen these values. Baran, Chase, and Courtright (1979) found that cooperation could be increased in young children after exposure to an episode of "The Waltons," which dealt with cooperation in problem solving. Similarly, research with episodes from "Mister Rogers' Neighborhood" and with a number of other deliberately prosocial programs found clear evidence of improvement in prosocial behaviors such as friendliness, generosity, cooperation, creativity, empathy, racial tolerance, and others (Rosenkoetter et al., 1990). Unfortunately, however, as Cohen (1993/1994) points out, only rarely does commercial television teach these messages.

Why Is Television Influential?

Explanations of the effects of television typically rely on one or more of several explanations.

Theories of *imitation* (observational learning) suggest that children learn aggressive behaviors from observing television models performing aggressive acts (Bandura & Walters, 1963).

An *attitude-change* model suggests that constant exposure to violence might serve to desensitize children, leaving them with the impression that the aggressive acts so common on television are, in fact, trivial and socially acceptable.

Another explanation of the effects of television violence is the cognitive, *information-processing* theory advanced by Huesmann and Eron (1986). Much of our social behavior is controlled by our knowledge of what goes with what—that is, by our *scripts*—they explain. From television children learn scripts for violence. Subsequently, whenever they remember violent scenes, or fantasize them, they are rehearsing a violent script. And whenever violence is seen in a new context, or whenever a slightly different form of violence is seen in an old context, the script is elaborated. The result is that the imaginative and aggressive child who views a lot of television violence ends up with a wealth of violence scripts that detail when violence is appropriate and the precise sequence in which it is to be manifested. All that is left is for the child to retrieve these schemata and their related scripts as required.

Rock Videos, VCRs, and Video Games

Television-related technology now provides us with new sources of potential influence on children.

Rock Videos

Close to the cutting edge of television technology, and sometimes very close as well to the edge of what society's evolving tastes and morals find acceptable, are rock videos. They are very simple: Take a popular, avant-garde, rock-type song; create images to accompany the lyrics; and combine the two in a frenetic, jarring, surprising, evocative, and sometimes bizarre way. The result? A dazzling, seductive, intriguing, audiovisual experience that has transformed the music industry—and that has alarmed some parents and educators as well. Why? Because, as one commentator put it, "Some of them are sending messages that are questionable, to say the least: anti-work, anti-marriage, anti-family, pro-violence, pro-casual sex, pro-woman-as-victim" (*Television & Your Children*, 1985, p. 52).

Rock videos, says Luke (1988), have much the same faults that are found in commercial television: They are racist, sexist, violent, and highly commercialized. Although research on their effects is still rare, it is likely that they will be at least as influential as more ordinary television programs. Indeed, they might even be more influential given their technological slickness, the addictive quality of their lyrics and their rhythms, and their popularity with the teen and preteen generation. At the same time, their popularity might also be used to advantage in some circumstances, perhaps as a motivational tool in the classroom. For example, Berg and Turner (1993) report a project in which sixth-grade students created their own music videos based on great works of art as well as on their own art.

VCRs

The rapid proliferation of VCRs brings an additional worry for those concerned with the potentially harmful effects of television. Rosengren and Windahl (1989) point out that parents and society either do not have, or often don't exercise, significant control over children's selections of the video recordings that they rent for home viewing. In most areas, it is possible for children to rent videos that depict aggression and standards of morality that would not be considered acceptable on public television. Similarly, the increasing availability of quasi-private channels through home satellite systems means that increasing numbers of children may be exposed to extreme forms of violence and pornography at very young ages (Nelson, 1992). There is clearly a need for more research to ascertain the probable effects of this exposure and to identify the parameters that might interact to make some children more vulnerable than others.

Video Games

Video games have been a source of concern for some parents as well, particularly in light of their quasi-addictive qualities, and their overwhelmingly violent themes. However, Griffiths's (1991) review of relevant studies indicates that frequent players are no more maladjusted, conduct disordered, or likely to use drugs than infrequent or non-players. While some studies report greater incidence of aggressiveness among frequent players, at least half do not.

A Summary of the Television Controversy

"Television," writes Neuman (1991), "is a wonderful nemesis for those inclined to fret over the education of the young. It has been accused of robbing youngsters of childhood, reducing attention spans, and impairing children's ability to think clearly" (p. 158). She goes on to describe how television has been blamed for poor achievement, aggression, illiteracy, and so on. But, following a review of the research, she concludes, "The charges against the medium have been unwarranted" (p. 158).

That is one side of the controversy. The other side is summarized by Cohen (1993/1994): "Research data support past warnings of the potential negative effects associated with frequent television watching, especially among younger viewers" (p. 103).

An increasing number of researchers are now arguing that schools should teach children the basic skills of television literacy—skills relating to distinguishing between reality and fantasy, making wise choices among available programming, and limiting viewing and engaging in other important social and intellectual activities such as conversation, reading, and playing (Cohen, 1993/1994).

Following a review of television and its effects on children, Huston, Watkins, and Kunkel (1989) recommend federal guidelines that would ensure a minimum amount of quality children's programming and that would protect children from commercial exploitation. The long-range goal, these authors argue, should be to eliminate advertising for children. This, they believe, would have a significant impact on programming. And ultimately, it might serve to reduce violence in the contemporary family.

VIOLENCE IN THE FAMILY

There are a frightening number of crimes *against persons* in the United States each year—crimes like rape, robbery, and assault. In 1991, almost one out of every four households was touched at least once by crime. An astounding 42 percent of the offenders were friends or relatives of the victims. In addition, nearly 2 million instances of child abuse and neglect are reported each year in the United States (U.S. Bureau of the Census, 1994).

Children are surrounded by violence—in the home, on television, in school. Boulton (1993) surveyed more than 100 elementary school boys and girls. More than half reported they had engaged in at least one physical fight during the preceding year, mainly in retaliation for teasing or because of disagreements over the way games were being played. Boys engaged in more fights than girls.

Some argue that much of the violence in our society begins with violence in the home; and much of the violence in the home begins with cultural values that, at least implicitly, have maintained that it is acceptable for parents to use physical force to control and to punish their children.

Prevalence of Child Maltreatment

Reported cases of child maltreatment continue to increase—from 3.5 per 1,000 population in 1980 to 10.8 per 1,000 in 1991 (U.S. Bureau of the Census, 1993).* In 1991, nearly 2.7 million children were subjects of reported child abuse and neglect cases. Of these, nearly 1 million cases were substantiated (see At a Glance: "Child Maltreatment," and Figures 10.4 and 10.5 on page 300). However, it is not clear whether this means that child maltreatment is actually increasing or whether reporting and detection are more thorough. Still, given the difficulty of obtaining information from parents and even from doctors in cases of child abuse, this figure may represent a very conservative estimate. Murray, Henjum, and Freeze (1992) surveyed a sample of 110 college students and found that a shocking 22 percent of the women had been sexually abused as children (6 percent of the men); about three fourths had experienced physical punishment (spanking, slapping, hitting). And in Wellman's (1993) sample of 824 college students, 6 percent of the males and 13 percent of the females reported being sexually abused as children or adolescents.

In a survey of child abuse in the United States, Straus and Gelles (1986) found that 43 percent of a sample of 1,428 parents had used some form of physical violence on a child at least once during the past year (see Table 10.7 on page 301). An astounding 2.9 percent admitted to having used a knife or a gun on one of their children at least once in their lifetimes—small wonder that one out of every five murders in the United States is committed among immediate family members in their own home.

Nature of Child Maltreatment

Not all maltreatment of children involves physical violence; some also takes the form of physical neglect, emotional abuse, or sexual abuse.

Physical Abuse

Physical injury to the child is the main criterion of physical abuse. However, the distinction between what is abuse and what is permissible punishment (or attempted control) by a parent is not at all clear. As a result, many physicians, for example, are uncertain about what to report (Warner & Hansen, 1994). Similarly, a survey of 264 elementary schoolteachers and 47 principals revealed that school personnel have widely differing notions of what

---

*Note that these figures are per 1,000 *population.* Instances of abuse and neglect are about three times greater per 1,000 *children.*

CHILD MALTREATMENT

Reported instances of child abuse and neglect have risen dramatically in recent decades—from 10.1 cases per 1,000 children in 1976 to more than 30 cases per 1,000 in 1986 (the numbers in Figure 10.5 are per 1,000 *population,* and are therefore lower). A total of more than 2.8 million children were victims of reported maltreatment in 1992. Of these children, 46.5 percent were male; 52.8 percent, female (the sex was unknown in 0.7 percent of reported cases). Those perpetrating the maltreatment were male in 44.1 percent of cases and female in the other 55.9 percent. It is unclear to what extent rising rates represent an actual increase in maltreatment and to what extent they reflect increased awareness and reporting by teachers, physicians, relatives, and family acquaintances.

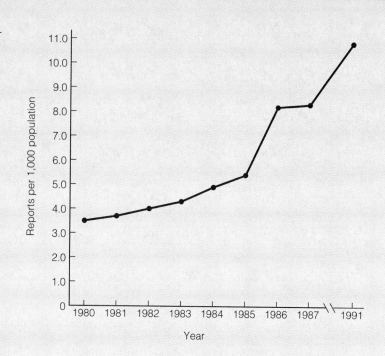

FIGURE 10.4

Reported cases of child neglect and abuse per 1,000 population, 1980 to 1991. Note that these figures would be about three times higher per 1,000 children. (Adapted from U.S. Bureau of the Census, 1992, p. 176, and 1993, p. 209.)

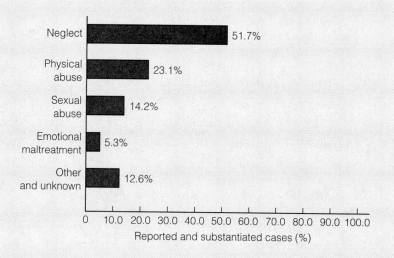

FIGURE 10.5

Child maltreatment cases, with type of maltreatment as a percentage of the 838,232 cases substantiated by child protective services in 1991. (Note that some children are classified in more than one way; hence percentages total slightly more than 100.) (Adapted from U.S. Bureau of the Census, 1994, p. 213.)

abuse is (Tite, 1993). In addition, most prefer to deal with suspected abuse informally rather than file formal complaints with the authorities.

Physical Neglect

Physical neglect involves acts of *omission* rather than *commission* and is usually evident in parents' failure to ensure that children have adequate nourishment, shelter, clothing, and health care. Physical neglect is somewhat more difficult to detect than physical abuse, but nevertheless makes up more than half of reported abuse cases (U.S. Bureau of the Census, 1994).

Emotional Abuse

Emotional abuse, sometimes referred to as *psychological abuse*, consists of parental behaviors that cause emotional and psychological harm to the child, but that are not instances of physical abuse or neglect—for example, continually shaming or ridiculing children (especially in public), isolating them, confining them in small spaces, severely verbally abusing them, depriving them of emotional contact and comfort, blaming, yelling, and other behaviors that might be classified as involving mental cruelty (Burnett, 1993). The effects of emotional abuse, unlike those of physical abuse or neglect, are often invisible. Conse-

TABLE 10.7
Violence Against Children in the United States, 1985

Type of Violence	Rate per 1,000 Children Aged 3 Through 17*
Minor violence acts	
Threw something	27
Pushed, grabbed, shoved	307
Slapped or spanked	549
Severe violence acts	
Kicked, bit, hit with fist	13
Hit, tried to hit with something	97
Beat up	6
Threatened with gun or knife	2
Used gun or knife	2
Violence indexes (cases)	
Overall violence	620
Severe violence	107
Very severe violence	19

* For two-caregiver households with at least one child 3 to 17 years of age at home.

SOURCE: Adapted from "Societal Change and Change in Family Violence from 1975 to 1985 as Revealed by Two National Surveys" by M. A. Straus and R. Gelles, 1986, *Journal of Marriage and the Family* 48, 465–479. Copyright 1986 by the National Council on Family Relations, 3989 Central Ave., N.E., Suite 550, Minneapolis, MN 55421. Reprinted by permission.

quently, instances of emotional abuse are seldom reported. However, the long-term effects of emotional abuse and neglect are sometimes more serious than those of physical abuse. They may come to light years later and may involve serious adjustment and emotional problems (Rowan, Foy, & Rodriguez, 1994).

Sexual Abuse

Sexual abuse is a form of child maltreatment in which sexual behaviors are forced upon a child. Victims of sexual abuse are primarily female and are often very young—in fact, they are sometimes still infants. Incest is often but not always involved in the sexual abuse of children.

Estimates of the prevalence of sexual abuse vary considerably. There are several reasons for this. One is the problem of definition. Sexual abuse may be defined as an unwanted sexual act involving physical contact; it may also be defined as any of a number of actions that *do not* involve physical contact (for example, a proposition or suggestion, verbal enticements, exhibitionism). Estimates vary depending on the researcher's definition. Lamb and Coakley (1993) point out that a variety of cross-gender sexual play among children may be considered sexual abuse, depending on the researcher's definition. In their survey of 128 female undergraduate students, 44 percent might be considered by some to have experienced sexual abuse. Using less global definitions, however, estimates are much lower—for example, 13 percent in the Wellman (1993) survey.

A second problem in arriving at accurate estimates has to do with the extreme social taboos that surround all forms of incest and especially father–daughter incest. Estimates of these acts have typically been based on cases reported to courts or other legal jurisdictions or that come to light in the course of mental health treatment and are probably gross underestimates.

A third problem is that many of the victims are too young to understand what is happening or to be reliable witnesses. Hence, researchers sometimes rely on relatively vague methods, such as reenactment with dolls or children's drawings, to detect possible victims of sexual abuse (Sadowski & Loesch, 1993).

Because of these problems, estimates of sexual abuse are largely meaningless. For example, Finkelhor and colleagues' (1986) survey of 10 studies found prevalence rates of sexual abuse ranging from a low of 6 percent of the sample to 62 percent. This review indicates that there are some broad characteristics that might serve to identify situations where the risk of sexual abuse is higher than normal. To begin with, girls are at considerably higher risk than are boys, although boys too are at some risk. Those who live alone with their fathers, or who live with stepfathers, are at higher risk, as are those whose mothers are employed outside the home or who are ill, disabled, battered, or alcoholics. A review by Powell (1991) found that marital dissatisfaction, poor mother–daughter relationship, social isolation of the family, a history of child abuse in the family, and violence in the home all increased the likelihood that a daughter would be sexually abused. Note, however, that these are extremely broad categories that include so many individual exceptions that their predictive value is severely limited.

The Consequences of Maltreatment

The most serious possible physical consequences of child abuse—child death—is substantially underdiagnosed, claims Kotch (1993), following an analysis of 92 cases of *fatally* injured children in New Zealand, and another 393 cases of children who were intentionally injured. Other possible physical consequences include blindness, deafness, disfiguration, and other atrocities.

Apart from these physical consequences, there are serious emotional and psychological consequences, not all of which are highly apparent. These can result perhaps as readily from physical abuse and neglect as from emotional or sexual abuse.

General Effects of Maltreatment

Abused children are often frightened, confused, and unhappy; their behaviors may range from complete social withdrawal, uncontrolled aggression, and regression to behaviors characteristic of younger children: crying, truancy,

Emotional abuse of children (shaming or ridiculing them, verbally abusing them, depriving them of emotional contact and comfort) can have effects that are more serious and longer lasting—though less immediately apparent—than those of physical abuse.

and delinquency. Reyome (1993) also reports that the school achievement of sexually abused and neglected children, on average, is significantly poorer than that of those who are not maltreated. Not surprisingly, their social relationships also suffer, as Salzinger, Feldman, and Hammer (1993) found in a comparision of 87 physically abused children with 87 nonabused children. The abused children had fewer friends and lower sociometric status, and were rated as more aggressive by their peers and more disturbed by their teachers.

Possible Effects of Sexual Abuse

Among adolescents who have been victims of sexual abuse, there is a higher than normal incidence of running away, attempted suicides, emotional disorder, and adolescent pregnancies—particularly if the father was the abuser. One investigation of 41 rural mothers who had been pregnant as teenagers found that an astounding 54 percent had been sexually abused before the age of 18 (Butler & Burton, 1990).

Kendall-Tackett, Williams, and Finkelhor (1993) reviewed 45 studies that have looked at the consequences of sexual abuse on children aged 18 or younger. About one third of the victims of abuse appeared to have no symptoms; a full two thirds did. The most commonly studied childhood symptom of sexual abuse—and perhaps one of the most common effects of sexual abuse—is *sexualized behavior*. Sexualized behavior includes sexual play with dolls, inserting objects in vaginas and anuses, excessive masturbation, seductive behavior, asking for sexual stimulation from others, and more advanced sexual knowledge than

expected. Other effects of sexual abuse include anxiety, depression, fears, poor self-esteem, and behavior problems.

Rowan, Foy, and Rodriguez (1994) provide evidence that the long-term effects of sexual abuse can be serious and persistent. Among a group of 47 adults sexually abused as children who later sought therapeutic help, 69 percent manifested symptoms of *posttraumatic stress disorder*. This condition may be apparent in symptoms such as fatigue, depression, loss of appetite, and obsessive thoughts.

The Abusive Family Context

Theories such as Bronfenbrenner's emphasize the importance of looking at the interactions within which the abused child and parent find themselves. From this perspective, child abuse may be seen as a symptom of a dysfunctional family. When Madonna, Van Scoyk, and Jones (1991) compared 30 families in which there had been reported incest with comparable but nonincest families, they found clear patterns of dysfunction in the incest families. Not only were these families typically characterized by very rigid belief systems, but one parent was generally highly dominant. In addition, these families were characterized by parental neglect and emotional unavailability of parents, and by lack of autonomy among children. There is evidence, as well, that in families where children are abused, spouse abuse is also common (McKay, 1994).

Membership in an abusive family system would be expected to have negative effects not only on the victims of abuse, but on other family members as well. Accordingly, it is perhaps not surprising that when Jean-Gilles and Crittenden (1990) compared reported abuse victims to their siblings, they found remarkable similarities between the two. Siblings were also frequently subjected to abuse (often not reported) and manifested similar behavior problems. The common view that one child in a family serves as a scapegoat and that the others are spared is largely inaccurate and misleading, claim Jean-Gilles and Crittenden. Thus, our attempts to understand, prevent, and treat child abuse and neglect need to take into consideration the entire family as a dynamic, functioning system.

Characteristics of Abusive Parents

Child maltreatment sometimes appears to be a lower-class phenomenon because parents of abused children tend to be from lower socioeconomic levels and have lower educational achievements. They are also more likely to be unemployed and on social assistance (Trickett et al., 1991). However, higher-class parents may simply be better at hiding child maltreatment. When the poor and uneducated need help, they go to the police; when the well-to-do need help, they hire professional counselors.

Many abusive parents have themselves suffered abuse as children, but only a small number of child abusers may be classified as "psychotic" or as suffering from some other personality disorder (Dubowitz, Black, & Harrington, 1993). However, many abusive parents share one or more of the following traits: limited knowledge of child rearing; low tolerance for common infant behaviors, such as crying; and misinterpretations of children's motivations for crying (Emery, 1989). An investigation of 28 abusive families found that parents in these families were less satisfied with their children, found child rearing difficult and unsatisfying, lived with more anger and conflict, and were less likely to reason with their children than simply to forbid certain behaviors (Trickett & Susman, 1988). In addition, there is evidence that drug abuse can be a major contributing factor in child abuse and neglect (Blau et al., 1994).

Who Is Maltreated?

In 1992, almost 14 percent of all abused children were under age 1; one quarter were between 2 and 5, and 35 percent were 10 or older. Fifty-three percent of the total were female (U.S. Bureau of the Census, 1994).

Among the factors that contribute to the likelihood of an infant's being abused are prematurity, the presence of deformities, being a twin, being born to a mother who has often been pregnant, and being born to a very busy or depressed mother. In addition, there is some evidence that infants of difficult temperament (who adjust to change less easily, who cry more, whose routines are less predictable) are more often victims of abuse. Thus, children who are abused are sometimes characterized by extreme irritability, feeding problems, excessive crying, and other behaviors that are annoying to parents (Ammerman, 1990). Not surprisingly, toddlers and preschool children who are abused also often manifest a variety of behavior problems, the most common of which include excessive crying and aggressiveness. However, these may often be the consequences, rather than the causes, of abuse. Not surprisingly, attempts to identify children who are most at risk for abuse on the basis of their temperaments and early behaviors have not been very successful (Berthier et al., 1993).

In the United States, there is an overrepresentation of nonwhite children among those abused. This higher incidence appears to be related to a variety of socioeconomic factors, including poverty, lower educational levels of parents, larger families, and a higher likelihood of having a father substitute in the home.

What Can Be Done?

Although it is unlikely that child abuse can be completely eliminated—particularly because physical force is a widely accepted child-rearing technique in contemporary societies and also because of the privacy of the family—a number of things can still be done. Gaudin (1993) suggests several approaches that might reduce the frequency and seriousness of child abuse. These include direct interventions to remedy neglect and abuse, family-focused interventions to prevent recurrence, efforts to strengthen and preserve functional families, group approaches involving both victims and perpetrators, and legal intervention where necessary.

Some prevention strategies have tried to discover ways of predicting which parents or children are most likely to be involved in child abuse so that something can be done before the problem occurs. Unfortunately, although abused children have a number of characteristics in common, many of these characteristics are also found among nonabused children (Berthier et al., 1993). Similarly, although we know that certain racial, economic, and social factors are involved in child abuse, we cannot reliably predict who is most likely to be abused (or abusive). Prevention based on prediction remains difficult, costly, and susceptible to the error of false identification (Jordan, 1993).

Other preventive strategies that might be highly effective in the long term include Jordan's (1993) suggestion that parents and communities be more closely involved in both prevention and remediation. Specific programs, such as the "Talking about Touching" program for use with young children, can increase children's knowledge about abuse and also can suggest ways of avoiding it (Madak & Berg, 1992).

Emery (1989) describes two types of intervention that might be used. The first is apprehension and punishment of abusers; the second includes social programs and therapy, often involving the entire family. Baxter and Beer (1990) suggest that school personnel also need to be involved. In particular, they need assistance in dealing with immediate problems relating to child maltreatment; and they need training in identifying instances of abuse and neglect and in understanding the legal and psychological implications of their involvement. There is a need, too, argues Moriarty (1990), for screening procedures and pre-employment testing to ensure that potential child molesters and abusers are not employed in situations in which children are easy victims. Unfortunately, this is very difficult because there is no clear personality profile that easily identifies potential child maltreaters—other than perhaps criminal conviction or psychiatric diagnosis in the case of pedophiles.

Neither the problem nor its solution is simple.

SOCIAL-EMOTIONAL EXCEPTIONALITY

Among the possible consequences of child maltreatment are a variety of adjustment and behavioral problems. These problems tend to be both varied and highly individualistic; they are not easily classified or even defined. Many of the problems result from the interactions of a variety of other factors.

Terms that are frequently used synonymously to refer to children with problems in this area are *behavior disordered*, *emotionally disturbed*, and *socially maladjusted*. Each of these terms describes children who are troubled and who may also cause trouble for parents, teachers, peers, and others (Kovacs, 1989).

Note that the labels describing social and emotional problems are only descriptions, not explanations. Children who are diagnosed as having "attention deficit hyperactivity disorder" are so labeled because they display a common set of behavioral and emotional symptoms; but the label serves in no way to explain these behaviors and symptoms.

Problems associated with defining and identifying social-emotional maladjustment are far more difficult than those relating to physical exceptionality. Whereas reasonably competent individuals can usually arrive at an agreed-on diagnosis of visual or hearing impairments, the same does not hold for the common social-emotional problems such as autism, childhood depression, or attention deficit disorders.

Prevalence, Classifications, and Contributing Factors

Estimates of the prevalence of *emotional* or *behavior disorders* (the terms are used interchangeably in this section) vary considerably depending on the criteria used for identification and on whether estimates include mild as well as severe instances of disturbance. Tuma (1989) reports data indicating that about 15 to 19 percent of U.S. children and adolescents suffer from problems requiring some form of mental health services.

Classifications

Classifying emotional disturbances in childhood presents a number of special difficulties. First, because many childhood disorders are characteristically different from adult behaviors, models of adult affective disorders are not always appropriate. For example, a number of behaviors that might be symptoms of underlying disorders in adults are relatively common in younger children: Uncontrollable laughter—or temper tantrums—are common and expected in childhood; but among adults, these behaviors might seem bizarre and might be a symptom of some underlying disorder (Kazdin, 1989).

Second, for some behaviors, developmental changes have to be taken into account. One example is that of apparent problems that become less frequent and less serious with increasing maturity. Lying, for example, is quite common among 6-year-old boys, but becomes far less frequent by adolescence. A second example is that of behavioral and emotional problems that are manifested in different symptoms as the child ages. Kazdin (1989) illustrates this by reference to the youngster who initially threatens and shoves other children who are in his way, but whose aggressive behavior will later take other forms more appropriate for his age—for example, fighting or using weapons.

Finally, there are disorders that are primarily childhood problems; others are more common in adulthood. For example, hyperactivity (discussed in the next section) appears to be primarily a childhood disorder, although there is now evidence that many children do not "outgrow" it (Henker & Whalen, 1989). In contrast, serious affective (emotional) disorders such as depression and mania were long thought to be adult rather than childhood disorders. We now know, however, that although children rarely suffer the manic disorders, they do suffer depression (Kovacs, 1989).

Contributing Factors

The factors that contribute to the development of behavior disorders vary a great deal as well. These are often classified in one of two ways: genetic-congenital and social-psychological. Possible genetic and congenital causes include chromosome abnormalities, maternal malnutrition, maternal infections, and birth injury. Social-psychological contributing factors include neglect, maltreatment, malnutrition, head injuries, and diseases and illnesses, as well as conditions within the family, like stress associated with conflict. In addition, poverty, parental abuse, parental rejection, physical handicaps, age, sex, and racial and religious discrimination have been implicated (Kazdin, 1989). Also, there is evidence that cognitive problems such as mental retardation or learning disabilities are sometimes related to behavior problems (Cole, Usher, & Cargo, 1993).

Risk and Resilience

Given adequate knowledge of the child's biological history and environment, it is sometimes possible to identify

Table 10.8
DSM-III-R Diagnostic Criteria for Attention Deficit Hyperactivity Disorder

A. A disturbance of at least 6 months during which at least 8 of the following are present:*

1. Often fidgets with hands or feet or squirms in seat (in adolescents, may be limited to subjective feelings of restlessness)
2. Has difficulty remaining seated when required to do so
3. Is easily distracted by extraneous stimuli
4. Has difficulty awaiting turn in games or group situations
5. Often blurts out answers to questions before they have been completed
6. Has difficulty following through on instructions from others (not due to oppositional behavior or failure of comprehension), for example, fails to finish chores
7. Has difficulty sustaining attention in tasks or play activities
8. Often shifts from one uncompleted activity to another
9. Has difficulty playing quietly
10. Often talks excessively
11. Often interrupts or intrudes on others; for example, butts into other children's games
12. Often does not seem to listen to what is being said to him or her
13. Often loses things necessary for tasks or activities at school or at home (such as toys, pencils, books, assignments)
14. Often engages in physically dangerous activities without considering possible consequences (not for the purpose of thrill-seeking); for example, runs into street without looking

B. Onset before the age of 7.

C. Does not meet the criteria for a Pervasive Developmental Disorder.

* A criterion is considered to be met only if the behavior is considerably more frequent than that of most people of the same mental age. The items are listed in descending order of discriminating power based on data from a national field trial of the *DSM-III-R* criteria for Disruptive Behavior Disorders.

SOURCE: Adapted from *Diagnostic and Statistical Manual of Mental Disorders* (3d ed., rev.) (pp. 53–54), 1987. Copyright © 1987 American Psychiatric Association. Reprinted with permission.

children who may be described as being at greater psychiatric risk than others. Werner (1993) describes a number of risk factors: birth problems, poverty, and family environments marked by alcoholism, mental illness, or conflict. Each of these has been linked with subsequent emotional and behavior problems in children. Significantly, however, many children whose backgrounds include one or even all of these characteristics nevertheless grow up to be well adjusted, socially competent individuals. Werner describes these children as *resilient* or *invulnerable*. His research on a number of high-risk infants who turned out well suggests that resilient infants share a number of common characteristics. For example, as infants, most seem to be characterized by easy temperaments. They are outgoing, adjust quickly to change, cry little, establish eating and sleeping routines, and are alert and responsive. As elementary school students, they concentrate well and are active and sociable. And perhaps most important, their environments typically include some clear

source of support that helps them withstand stress. Support often takes the form of substitute parents (perhaps grandparents or older siblings), as well as close friends.

Attention Deficit Hyperactivity Disorder

Estimates are that as many as 3 percent of current elementary schoolchildren suffer from varying degrees of hyperactivity (American Psychiatric Association, 1987). Of these, a significant number also suffer from attention problems, and are classified as having **attention deficit hyperactivity disorder (ADHD)**. Attention problems can also exist without hyperactivity. Many ADHD children experience considerable difficulty adjusting to school and home and are considered to have relatively serious problems (Zentall, 1993).

In general, ADHD is marked by excessive general activity for the child's age (often taking the form of incessant and haphazard climbing, crawling, or running); difficulty in sustaining attention and apparent forgetfulness; and impulsivity (tendency to react quickly, difficulty taking turns, low frustration tolerance). The criteria described by the APA also stipulate that the duration of the child's hyperactivity be at least six months.

Diagnosis

Diagnoses of hyperactivity (or hyperkinesis) are sometimes—perhaps even often—made inappropriately by parents and teachers who are confronted by children who are restless and who find it difficult to do the quiet things that adults sometimes demand. Strictly speaking, attention deficit hyperactivity disorder as defined by the American Psychiatric Association (1987) requires the presence of at least 8 of the 14 criteria presented in Table 10.8. The onset of the disorder needs to occur before the age of 7 to differentiate it from disorders that might arise as reactions to stressful events or illness.

Clearly, not all children suffering from this disorder will display the same combination and seriousness of symptoms. However, given the fact that the condition appears easy to diagnose (it is defined largely in terms of observable behaviors) and that it can therefore easily be overdiagnosed, extreme caution should be exercised before applying the label to any child.

Treatment

The most common treatment for a child diagnosed as having an attention deficit disorder with hyperactivity involves the use of stimulant drugs such as dextroamphetamine (Dexadrine) and methylphenidate (Ritalin). This might seem strange given that stimulants ordinarily increase activity and the ADHD child already suffers from excessive activity. However, these drugs appear to have what is termed a *paradoxical effect* on children. That is, they appear to sedate rather than stimulate (Swanson et al., 1991). Some evidence suggests that they are about twice as effective as behavior modification (primarily the use of rewards)

Attention deficit hyperactivity disorder (ADHD) is sometimes inappropriately diagnosed by parents and teachers in response to children's normal restlessness or to learning problems related to other causes. Although the boy shown here has been diagnosed as having ADHD, the disorder is not readily apparent on the playground or in the park—where high levels of physical activity are normally expected. It is more evident in school where sustaining attention often requires curtailing physical activity.

in controlling problem behavior in many ADHD children, as well as in improving academic achievement (Pelham et al., 1993).

Pelham and colleagues (1990) conducted an experiment in which 17 boys classified as ADHD played baseball. Some of the boys were medicated with Ritalin; others had received a placebo. And, in this *double-blind* experiment (see Chapter 1), neither the examiners nor the participants knew who the experimental subjects were. Behaviors examined included the effectiveness of the boys' judgments when batting, their batting skill during the game, their performance on game-related drills, and their ongoing awareness of the status of the game. Results indicated that boys treated with Ritalin performed better and were more clearly focused on the game than the placebo-treated group.

Although the use of stimulants to treat ADHD children is often associated with preventing continued achievement declines in school (Weber, Frankenberger, & Heilman, 1992), as well as with increasing the manageability of the children in question, it remains a controversial treatment. These drugs can also have some negative side effects such as weight loss, growth retardation, and mood changes (Henker & Whalen, 1989).

Causes

The causes of ADHD are unclear although the fact that between 80 and 90 percent more males than females are hyperactive suggests that it is at least partly genetic. There

is evidence that it is largely a maturational problem involving the central nervous system. Not only is the activity level of hyperactive children often similar to that typical of children four or five years younger, but many hyperactive children—though not all—seem to outgrow their symptoms after adolescence (Henker & Whalen, 1989).

Other explanations for hyperactivity have sometimes implicated neurological impairment or brain damage and dietary or vitamin-linked causes. However, the evidence for either of these causes is weak (Erickson, 1992). There is some suggestion, too, that between 5 and 10 percent of hyperactive children react badly to certain food dyes and that these children might therefore be helped through dietary means (Ross, 1980).

Other Behavior Disorders

There are a number of other, sometimes serious, behavior disorders of childhood and adolescence, not all of which can easily be classified. Many of these are problems of socialization, seen in aggressive, hostile, and essentially antisocial behavior—as in, for example, extreme noncompliance (labeled *oppositional defiant disorder* by the APA). Alternatively, conduct disorders might be evident in withdrawal, social isolation, or extreme shyness. Not surprisingly, aggressive and hostile behaviors (delinquency, vandalism, and so on) are likely to be dealt with—or at least punished. Social isolation and extreme shyness are much more likely to be ignored.

Other social disorders may be manifested in lying, stealing, inability to form close relationships with others, temper tantrums, disobedience and insolence, extremely negative self-concepts, and related behaviors and attitudes.

Anorexia nervosa is another disorder that might be classified as a conduct or behavior disorder. It involves drastic changes in eating habits, leading to serious—sometimes fatal—weight loss. Because it affects adolescents far more often than any other age group, it is discussed in Chapter 11.

Treatment of children exhibiting conduct and personality disorders depends largely on the severity of the disturbance. In cases of moderate or mild disturbance, teachers and parents can often cope adequately; with the occasional help of professional personnel, they can sometimes do much more than cope. More severe disturbances may require therapeutic and sometimes judicial intervention.

Stress in Childhood

Many of the emotional and behavioral problems of childhood, and perhaps a number of the physical problems as well, are related to something we call *stress*—a difficult concept that everybody understands at least intuitively.

Stress Defined

In the physical sciences, stress is a force that is exerted on a body, sometimes causing deformation or breakage. In psychology, **stress** is a nonphysical force that is exerted on an individual, sometimes causing negative change. Skinner and Wellborn (1994) suggest that there are two approaches to defining stress. One is concerned with stimuli; the other with responses. Stimuli are said to be stressful when they make excessive demands on the individual; responses are stressful when they are accompanied by the physiological changes of high arousal such as increased heart rate, perspiration, trembling, and so on.

The Effects of Stress

Lazarus (1993) classifies stress in terms of the severity of its effects. Thus, there is *harm*, which implies actual damage; *threat*, which implies the possibility of damage; and *challenge*, which implies demands that can be met.

This classification recognizes that stress is clearly not always negative. Challenge, and even threat, may lead to what are essentially adaptive physiological responses. In such cases, stress prepares the individual for action. The sudden shot of adrenaline and the acceleration of heart rate when we are threatened or challenged increase the effectiveness of our running, our fighting, or our speech-making.

But under other circumstances, we may have an overload of stress and suffer harm. The implications of this overload vary from one individual to another, but are clearly not limited to adults. As we saw in Chapter 6, infants and preschoolers can suffer profound distress at the loss of a parent or sometimes even as a result of temporary separation from a parent. The effects may be apparent in sleeping or eating disturbances, as well as in a general listlessness that may border on depression (Honig, 1993).

Among children, the effects of stress might include physical complaints (such as stomach pains, sometimes caused by ulcers, or asthma) or emotional problems (such as persistent fears, high anxiety, or even depression) (Johnson, 1986).

Stress in Childhood

Many of the things that children fear, notes Kupetz (1993), are a source of considerable stress for them. She warns that parents often trivialize these fears because they judge them by adult standards ("Don't be silly, Guy, there's nothing in the closet. Hey, you guys, did you hear what Guy's scared of now?"). Parents need to realize that children's fears are real, and they need to help them reduce the stressors in their lives.

Fears are just one source of childhood stress; Elkind (1981a) describes several others, many of which are more common to this generation of children than they were to earlier generations. They relate to *stimulus* or *demand* overloads. There is, for example, *responsibility overload*, in which young children whose parents work are made responsible for tasks like looking after younger siblings, buying groceries, preparing meals, cleaning the house, and so on. There is *change overload*, in which children from mobile families are shunted rapidly from one community to another, transferred from school to school, and left with a sequence of caregivers. *Emotional overload* may result when children are exposed to emotion-laden situations that impact directly on their lives, but over which they have little control (parents quarreling, for example). Finally, there is *information overload*, resulting largely from the tremendous amount of information to which television exposes the child. Add to all these potential sources of stress the sometimes exorbitant achievement demands that are placed on the child by school, parents, and society. "Hurry," they all say to Elkind's (1981a) *hurried child*. "Hurry! Grow up! There isn't much time!"

Clearly, not all children are exposed to the same stressful situations; nor will all react the same way. Some children remain unperturbed in the face of events that might prove disastrous for others. Nevertheless, psychology provides a number of ways of assessing stress in the lives of children or at least of determining potential for stress. Many of these are based on the assumption that all major changes in a person's life are potentially stressful and that, although most individuals can cope with a limited number of changes, there eventually comes a breaking point. Accordingly, these stress scales simply ask individuals to identify all major changes they have recently experienced. Some changes are clearly more important than others (the death of a parent compared with changing schools, for example). Values are assigned accordingly. Table 10.9 is one example of this approach for children.

TABLE 10.9
*Stressful Events in Children's Lives**

Life-Change Event	Points	Life-Change Event	Points
Parent dies	100	Changes responsibilities at home	29
Parents divorce	73	Older brother or sister leaves home	29
Parents separate	65	Trouble with grandparents	29
Parent travels as part of job	63	Outstanding personal achievement	28
Close family member dies	63	Moves to another city	26
Personal illness or injury	53	Moves to another part of town	26
Parent remarries	50	Receives or loses a pet	25
Parent fired from job	47	Changes personal habits	24
Parents reconcile	45	Trouble with teacher	24
Mother goes to work	45	Change in hours with baby-sitter or at day-care center	20
Change in health of a family member	44	Moves to a new house	20
Mother becomes pregnant	40	Changes to a new school	20
School difficulties	39	Changes play habits	19
Birth of a sibling	39	Vacations with family	19
School readjustment (new teacher or class)	39	Changes friends	18
Change in family's financial condition	38	Attends summer camp	17
Injury or illness of a close friend	37	Changes sleeping habits	16
Starts a new (or changes) an extracurricular activity (music lessons, Brownies, and so forth)	36	Change in number of family get-togethers	15
Change in number of fights with siblings	35	Changes eating habits	15
Threatened by violence at school	31	Changes amount of TV viewing	13
Theft of personal possessions	30	Birthday party	12
		Punished for not "telling the truth"	11

* If scores for a 1-year period total ≤150, stress exposure is average; if between 150 and 300, there is a higher probability of stress-related symptoms; above 300, serious consequences are even more probable.

SOURCE: From *The Hurried Child* (pp. 162–163) by David Elkind. © 1988. Reading, MA: Addison-Wesley Publishing Co., Inc. Adapted with permission of the publisher.

Social-Emotional Giftedness

Here, as elsewhere, exceptionality has two dimensions: the disadvantaged, among whom are the autistic, the depressed, the hyperactive, and those exhibiting personality and conduct disorders; and the advantaged, to whom we have paid little special attention.

Among the advantaged are the *resilient*, sometimes labeled "superkids" or "invulnerables." In Werner's (1993) study of at-risk children, for example, about one third of the children whose early background and family environments placed them at high risk for emotional and behavioral problems nevertheless grew up to be apparently strong, well-adjusted individuals. (That 129 children, fully two thirds of the original sample, developed serious learning or behavior problems in elementary school, manifested delinquent behavior in adolescence, or experienced mental health problems at some point in development is also highly significant.)

Recall that the resilient children in Werner's investigation were characterized by highly adaptable, easy-to-get-along-with temperaments, that they later became sociable, outgoing youngsters, and that most had some significant source of close personal support in their environments (for example, an older sibling or some surrogate parent). And in the end, not only did some of these children appear to be invulnerable to the emotional and behavioral disorders that would surely claim a large number of other children in the same circumstances, but they also seemed to thrive on early adversity and to emerge unscathed and in some ways superior. The importance of understanding why some children survive and even thrive in high-risk situations and why others do not is related directly to the possibility of "inoculating" children against risk or of ameliorating risk for those who are most vulnerable, suggests Anthony (1975). Perhaps exposure to a certain amount of adversity may be crucial for the development of resistance to disturbance. At the same time, exposure to too many stresses may have just the opposite effect. It may be that there is a particular combination of personality characteristics or genetic predispositions that, in interaction with a stressful environment, produces a highly adjusted healthy person. The critical problem is to identify this combination of characteristics and environment in an effort to maximize the development of human potential. The emphasis is dramatically different from that which focuses on identifying and treating disorders.

Exceptional social and emotional competence may be seen not only in those who survive high risk but also in exceptional individuals whose early lives and biological history present no unusual psychological threats. Among these socially gifted children may well be found the leaders of tomorrow. Perhaps we should provide "special" education not only for those with handicaps but for the socially gifted as well.

Social Cognition

1. *Social cognition* refers to an awareness of ourselves and of others as being capable of feelings, motives, intentions, and so on. Its development implies that the child has begun to develop a theory of mind. Selman's five stages of role taking reflect the child's ability to verbalize other perspectives: *egocentric* (to age 6: one point of view), *social-informational* (6–8: my view is correct, others less informed), *self-reflective* (8–10: people are aware only of their views), *mutual* (10–12: people recognize and talk about each other's views), and *social and conventional* (12–15+: abstract recognition of different views).

Self-Worth

2. *Self-worth* refers to personal evaluations of the self. James viewed self-worth in terms of the discrepancy between the real individual and aspirations; Cooley argued that self-worth reflects how we think others evaluate us. After age 8, children can make global assessments of self-worth and separate evaluations in five areas: scholastic, athletic, physical appearance, social acceptance, and morality. The most important sources of information in determining the child's self-worth stem from parents and classmates (rather than from friends or teachers). High self-worth is associated with happiness; low self-worth, with sadness and depression. In turn, these moods are linked with motivation.

Friends and Peers

3. For preschoolers, friendship is playing together; in middle childhood, friendships involve enduring, reciprocal relationships. Most children have more than one "best" friend. Friends and peers are critical for positive self-concepts and for learning sex-appropriate values and attitudes.

4. Social competence contributes to high status; social incompetence contributes to lower status. Five categories of social status determined through sociometry are: *sociometric stars* (especially well liked), *mixers* (high interaction), *teacher negatives* (conflict with teachers), *tuned out* (uninvolved; ignored rather than rejected), and *sociometric rejectees* (not liked). High social competence is reflected in the child's ability to sense what is happening in social groups, in a high degree of responsiveness to others, and in an understanding that relationships develop slowly over time.

The School

5. The school is a powerful socializing and intellectual influence. Teacher expectations may affect student performance, as might the student's tendency to be *mastery-oriented* (accepting personal responsibility for outcomes, attributing them to intelligence or effort, for example) or *helpless* (accepting no responsibility, attributing outcomes to things like luck or task difficulty).

Television

6. Young children spend approximately one third of their waking hours watching television, but do not comprehend all they see. There is evidence of a relationship between television viewing and aggression. Prosocial television themes can have positive effects. An information-processing explanation for the effects of television maintains that children encode violence (represent it mentally), rehearse and elaborate it in fantasy (the result of seeing variations of it in different television programs), and then retrieve it along with relevant scripts (routines detailing the sequence in which the violence is to be perpetrated) when they are moved to aggression.

Violence in the Family

7. Violence touches many North American homes each year, some of it in the form of child abuse, which may be *physical abuse* (punching, kicking, beating), *physical neglect* (failure to provide food, clothing, shelter, health care), *emotional abuse* (habitual ridicule, scolding, ostracism), or *sexual abuse* (sexual behaviors forced upon the child). Any of these forms of abuse can have serious and long-lasting physical and psychological consequences. Many infants are included among abused children (more probable if the infant is premature, deformed, or irritable, or if the mother is overworked, often pregnant, or depressed). Nonwhites are overrepresented among this group in the United States. The abusive family context may include

abusers who are disturbed in a clinical sense (although often they are not); individuals who were themselves abused when young; restrictive, authoritarian parenting; and parental emotional unavailability. It is difficult to predict who is most likely to be abused or who is most likely to abuse. Some programs for preventing child abuse and treating its consequences suggest changing attitudes toward the use of physical punishment.

Social-Emotional Exceptionality

8. The causes of emotional disorders include predisposing factors (genetics and environmental conditions, such as parental abuse) and precipitating factors (specific environmental events, such as the death of a parent or serious illness). Knowledge of a child's biological and environmental history sometimes makes it possible to identify those who run a higher risk of emotional disturbance.

9. *Attention deficit hyperactivity disorder* (ADHD, often simply called *hyperactivity*) is characterized by excessive activity and deficits in attention span without evidence of brain damage or neurological dysfunction. Hyperactive children frequently present behavior problems for teachers and are sometimes treated with stimulant drugs. Other behavior disorders are manifested in socialization problems: extreme defiance (*oppositional defiance disorder*); misbehaviors such as lying, stealing, delinquency, and aggression; social withdrawal and excessive shyness; and eating disorders.

10. Stress among children can result from many sources including fears, responsibility overload, change overload, emotional overload, school-related stress, and information overload. Scales that look at major events in children's lives are sometimes useful in identifying the possibility of stress-related problems. Some children are more resistant to stress (*resilient*) than others.

1. What do children know of the states of minds of others?

   - Pretend you are 8. Write down what you know and believe about the feelings and thoughts of others. Label it your "theory of mind."

2. What is self-esteem and why might it be important?

   - Consult the literature or, better yet, a handful of elementary schoolchildren, and make a list of the features of their *selves* that are most important to them.

3. What role do friendships play in a child's development? How important are friends and peers?

   - List five categories of social status, and identify some of the important characteristics/behaviors that might contribute to each.

4. Does television have a primarily negative, positive, or neutral effect on children?

   - Prepare one (or both) sides of a debate on the positive/negative effects of television viewing on young children.

5. How prevalent and how serious is child abuse?

   - Identify some of the factors that contribute to child abuse and neglect. Based on these factors, develop an intervention/prevention program.

STUDY TERMS

The Frye and Moore book presents an intriguing account of children's development of intuitive theories of mind; the collection edited by Gauvain and Cole contains a wide-ranging collection of fascinating articles on various aspects of development from birth through adolescence:

Frye, D., & Moore, C. (Eds.). (1991). *Children's theories of mind: Mental states and social understanding.* Hillsdale, NJ: Erlbaum.

Gauvain, M., & Cole, M. (Eds.). (1993). *Readings on the development of children.* New York: W. H. Freeman.

A detailed analysis of the dimensions and importance of childhood friendships is:

Erwin, P. (1993). *Friendship and peer relationships in children.* New York: John Wiley.

A brief, simple, and useful analysis of child-rearing practices that might contribute to child maltreatment is:

Sabatino, D. A. (1991). *A fine line: When discipline becomes child abuse.* Blue Ridge Summit, PA: TAB Books.

The much-studied impact of television on the lives of children is reviewed in:

Gunter, B., & McAleer, J. L. (1990). *Children and television. The one-eyed monster?* New York: Routledge.

Evra, J. V. (1990). *Television and child development.* Hillsdale, NJ: Erlbaum.

The following collection presents articles that look in depth at child abuse and neglect, at the characteristics of victims and perpetrators, and at programs designed to prevent its occurrence or to treat its effects:

Ammerman, R. T., & Hersen, M. (Eds.). (1990). *Children at risk: An evaluation of factors contributing to child abuse and neglect.* New York: Plenum.

A clear but comprehensive look at childhood behavior disorders is presented in:

Erickson, M. T. (1992). *Behavior disorders of children and adolescents* (2d ed.). Englewood Cliffs, NJ: Prentice-Hall.

Youth is the time to go flashing from one end of the world to the other both in mind and body; to try the manners of different nations; to hear the chimes at midnight; to see sunrise in town and country; to be converted at a revival; to circumnavigate the metaphysics, write halting verses, run a mile to see a fire, and wait all day long in the theatre to applaud "Hernani."

ROBERT LOUIS STEVENSON
Virginibus Puerisque

ADOLESCENCE

There is little of revivals and fires, or of theaters and sunrises, in the two chapters that summarize the adolescent experience—although there is something of scarification, circumcision, and the taboos of primitive rites of passage. There is also a good deal about one of the most important developmental tasks of this period: the selection and formation of an identity. It is in adolescence that we struggle to decide who we are, and that we begin to flesh out the dream of who we will be.

In these chapters, there is much, too, about newly expanding powers of mind and body—powers that make it possible to go flashing from one end of the world to the other, trying different manners, hearing chimes, and being converted at revivals—powers that make it possible to write halting verses, mostly about love.

PART FIVE

FOCUS QUESTIONS

1. Is adolescence a universal phenomenon, or is it largely cultural?
2. What are the universal biological features of adolescence?
3. What are the most common eating disorders of adolescence?
4. What is adolescent egocentrism?
5. Is being good or bad a fundamental part of our personalities?

OUTLINE

Physical and Cognitive Development: Adolescence

*T*hey always take a new name, and are supposed by the initiation process to become new beings in the magic wood.

Mary Kingsley
West Africa

"We won't cut ourselves up like they do," Ronald

CHAPTER 11

Gaudry is explaining, pointing to one of the photographs in Mr. Delisle's book. It's a picture of a newly circumcised African male. For some reason none of us can understand, he's looking at the camera with a smile as wide as his whole face.

"Never know, the knife might slip." How droll. We laugh in our new adolescent voices. "We'll do the other things instead," Ronald says, unfolding a piece of paper. "I made a list up direct from the book." None of the rest of us has read the book, but we believe him. He's written out the first thing on his list in big red letters: "CHICKEN BLOOD." Then there's other stuff like "RAILROAD TRACKS" and "BIG FISH" and about seven other things.

We're in the basement of Ronald's house later that night. Paul, who's been appointed to bring the chicken because his uncle has a chicken farm, pulls out a plastic bag. In it, there's a chicken. It's dead and already cleaned, which isn't what Ronald had in mind at all. "How the heck we gonna get blood out of that?" he asks.

"There's already some in the bag," says Paul, which we all agree there is, and we pour it into a little glass, Paul squeezing the chicken so as to get more juice from it. But no one can quite bring himself to take the first sip until it occurs to Ronald that it would surely taste a lot better if it were cut with a little of his dad's whiskey—which isn't really whiskey at all, just homebrew with burnt sugar in it so that it'll have that light whiskey color and the police won't know any better if they just happen to see a bottle of it some time.

So Ronald cuts the chicken's blood with a good slosh of hot whiskey and, being our leader, says, "I'll go first." Then he tells us his new name, which is an important part of the whole thing. "Hawkface," is what he wants to be called. Then, a little like a hawk, he screws up his face and takes the first sip, yelling, "To the manhood of Hawkface," as he does so—and almost immediately turns green and becomes so sick we have to call his mother from upstairs, who takes him straight to the doctor.*

"I think it's just the flu," the doctor says, "but if it isn't, it's one of those growing-up things adolescents go through."

THIS CHAPTER

This chapter looks at some of the important "growing-up things" adolescents go through—things like the momentous physical changes that mark the transition from childhood to adolescence. These changes have tremendous implications for social development (covered in the next chapter). It also discusses some of the implications of early and late maturation, and some of the physical concerns of adolescence that may be manifested in eating disorders. Later sections in the chapter deal with the growth of logic and with egocentrism in adolescence. The chapter concludes with a discussion of moral development and behavior. But first it looks at the transition to adulthood and at some of the chicken-blood-and-whiskey-type rites that sometimes accompany this transition.

ADOLESCENCE AS TRANSITION

Adolescence is the transition between childhood and adulthood—the period during which the child has achieved sexual maturity but has not yet taken on the roles and responsibilities, or the rights, that accompany full adult status.

In contemporary industrialized countries, adolescence is relatively easily defined, say Schlegel and Barry (1991): It spans the period of the teen years. But in preindustrial societies, it is not always clear that the period even exists.

*To this day, we call him "Chicken" or "Chickenface"—never "Hawk-face."

Primitive Transitions

In some preindustrial societies, like the African tribes in Mr. Delisle's book, passage from childhood to adulthood is clearly marked by ritual and ceremony collectively termed **rites of passage**. Interestingly, even in totally unrelated societies, these rites often have several common features. Most rites of passage involve four steps: First, is *separation*, a period during which the child is separated from the group. A common **taboo** (forbidden behavior) during this period is that of brother–sister or mother–son contact.

Second, prior to becoming an adult, children are trained in behaviors expected of adults. Sometimes this involves teaching through telling. Or it might involve showing the child by example.

The third step is the **initiation** itself—the actual rituals that mark passage from childhood to adulthood. These ceremonies are often accompanied by feasting. They are a time of celebration; but they are also usually a time of pain and suffering. Thus many initiation ceremonies include fasting, scarification (the inflicting of wounds with resulting scars), and circumcision.

The final step of the passage rite is **induction** (absorption into the tribe). Inductees now know, without any doubt, that they are full-fledged, adult members of their social group.

Rites of passage can serve a number of useful functions. They impart a sense of adult responsibility to children, and they lessen the ambiguity that might otherwise exist between childhood and adulthood. In addition, many primitive rites reinforce certain important taboos such as those having to do with incest. Bloch and Niederhoffer (1958) suggest this may be the main reason for separating boys and girls, as well as parents and their opposite-sexed children, prior to initiation.

Another important function of a passage rite is that it creates a strong psychological bond between the initiate and the tribe, as well as among initiates. At the same time, it helps to sever bonds between the child and the immediate family. It is as if initiates are being told that they now belong to the tribe and not the family, that they can look to it for support and strength, but that they must also defend and protect it. (See Across Cultures: "Kumkleseem—Son of Hanni, Wife of Swamas.")

Contemporary Transitions and Rites

These nonindustrialized societies do not have a long period of adolescence as we know it. There is only childhood, the passage, and adulthood. They are sometimes referred to as **discontinuous societies** because they provide a clear break between important developmental stages.

We, on the other hand, live in **continuous societies.** We do not have clear boundaries between developmental stages—no *formal* rites of passage. Our young ones are ex-

KUMKLESEEM—SON OF HANNI, THE WIFE OF SWAMAS

When Kumkleseem approached manhood, everyone waited to see what would happen. A boy sees things with the eyes of a child, things that men can no longer see. But the child must die, say the old ones, so that the man can be born and walk in the world that other men have made. "The boy says 'I.' The man says 'We!' and this word that the man speaks is the word of his greatest magic" (O'Hagan, 1979, p. 38).

Toward the end of his childhood, Kumkleseem did all the things that boys must do if they are to be men. Whenever the camp moved, he waited until it was far out of sight before running after it. In this way, his legs would become hard and his breath long, and he would never be left behind. And every day, he walked into the ice-cold river and the people beat him with willow sticks when he came out. When the nights grew cold, he lay outside all night, naked and with no robe, sometimes holding his hands in the flowing water through the night. But even when he had become the fastest runner and the best hunter, he was still not a man, for he had not yet gone alone to a place of his own choosing and fasted and prayed for the vision that would reveal to him the shape and texture of his life as a man.

And so one night Kumkleseem walked out into the awesome valley where men of his tribe do not walk for fear their voices will be taken and they will be left only with the voices of coyotes. For 12 days he was gone and when he returned, lean and hard from his fasting, he sat by the fire and would not eat until he had spoken.

"You have come far," said Tis-Kwinit.

"I have gone far," Kumkleseem answered, telling them then of the voices he had heard, the things he had seen after he had walked four days and then sat four days, looking and listening while the mountains pressed in on him at night so that he could not move his elbows. "On

the ninth day I turned back the way I had come. Now I am here," he finished.

"What you say is good," said Tzalas. And Kumkleseem was a man.

To Think About   What purposes might be served by beliefs and behaviors such as these? How universally valid do you think our conceptions of adolescence are?

SOURCE: Based partly on O'Hagan, H. (1979). "Tay John." In D. Gutteridge (Ed.), *Rites of passage*. Toronto: McClelland & Stewart.

empted from the separation, the training, the initiation, and the induction. Instead, they are put through a period labeled "adolescence"—a period of life G. Stanley Hall (1916) described as the most troubled, the most stressful, and the most difficult of all stages of development. According to Hall's theory, all adolescents go through a period of **sturm und drang** (storm and stress). He believed that because this period of upheaval and turmoil is biologically based, it is largely inevitable, and it must also be common to all cultures. We now know that this view is fundamentally incorrect and misleading, and that this developmental period is not tumultuous for the majority of adolescents.

In contemporary Western culture, there have not been formal rites of passage (except, perhaps, the Bar Mitzvah or the Bat Mitzvah, in which the Jewish boy or girl becomes an adult at the age of 13 through religious ceremony, and the "coming-out" party in certain social groups). Our "rites" of passage have historically been in-

definite and confusing. They have included a wide range of events that can span many years: getting a driver's license, being old enough to vote or to drink, losing virginity, beginning work, growing (or trying to grow) a mustache, starting to date, and graduating from high school.

There are writers who claim that secondary schools now serve as *rites de passage* similar to the traditional rites of many nonindustrialized societies. They have all the same characteristics, Fasick (1988) argues. They exemplify *separation* (children are segregated into schools), *training* (the adolescent is formally socialized for the responsibilities of adult life), and the high school graduation is an *initiation* and *induction* ceremony. Fasick suggests that this ceremony is almost universal for much of the middle and working class; for many adolescents, it clearly marks passage from the world of childhood to a world of adult responsibilities.

There are a relatively large number of writers who now suggest that formal rites of passage might not only

Adolescence, as a biological phenomenon defined in terms of a period of rapid sexual maturation, is universal (although it occurs at different ages among different groups). But as a psychological phenomenon, sometimes marked by a prolonged period of readjustment, it appears to be highly culture-specific.

In many non-industrialized societies, the passage from childhood to adulthood is unmistakably marked by rites and ceremonies. Our contemporary societies are somewhat less clear about the passage. Thus even after graduation from high school, which is often considered to be one of the clearest signs of passage from childhood, there are many who will not adopt the roles and responsibilities of adulthood for a long time.

be very useful for psychological and social reasons, but that adolescents may have a strong need (or at least a strong desire) to take part in such rituals (Christie & Dinham, 1991; Gill, 1992). Butler (1993) argues, for example, that because they lack institutionally approved rites of passage, many adolescent college students use alcohol as a rite of passage. He suggests that colleges and universities should look at implementing approved rites of passage. Similarly, Redding and Dowling (1992) point out that many adolescent girls and their families are developing rites of passage that mark progress through college (dances, parties, graduation dinners, presents).

    In the United States, there are now an increasing number of African-American rites of passage programs, many of them linked to specific schools and communities. Warfield-Coppock (1992) describes 20 such programs. These are typically organized and supervised programs that include training in life skills and social skills, as well as social events. Some also include opportunities for vol-

unteer community service (Trotter, 1991). Their goal is often to foster greater cultural awareness, to enhance the development of self-esteem, and to ease the transition from childhood to adulthood.

PHYSICAL AND BIOLOGICAL CHANGES

As a psychological phenomenon, adolescence may not be common to all cultures; but the biological changes of this period are universal (Montemayor & Flannery, 1990).

    Biologically, adolescence is the period from the onset of puberty to adulthood. **Puberty** signifies sexual maturity; **pubescence** refers to the changes that result in sexual maturity. These changes occur in late childhood or early adolescence. Although adulthood is not easily defined, age 20 is a convenient, although arbitrary, beginning point. The beginning of adolescence is even more variable and occurs at different ages for the sexes, but age 12 is often used as an approximation.

Physical Changes

Only during infancy do humans experience a more rapid period of postnatal growth than they do at adolescence.

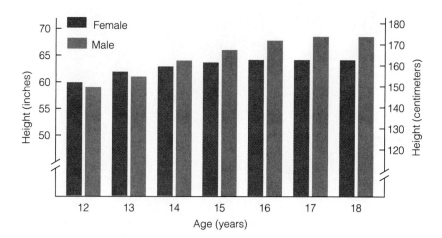

FIGURE 11.1

Height at 50th percentile for U.S. children. (From the Health Department, Milwaukee, Wisconsin; based on data by H. C. Stuart and H. V. Meredith, prepared for use in Children's Medical Center, Boston. Used by permission of the Milwaukee Health Department.)

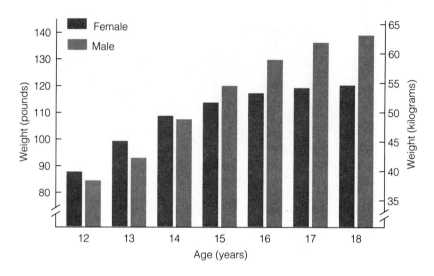

FIGURE 11.2

Weight at 50th percentile for U.S. children. (From the Health Department, Milwaukee, Wisconsin; based on data by H. C. Stuart and H. V. Meredith, prepared for use in Children's Medical Center, Boston. Used by permission of the Milwaukee Health Department.)

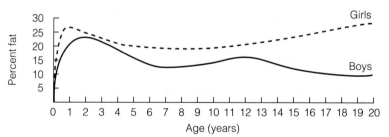

FIGURE 11.3

Growth curve for fat mass in boys and girls. Distinct average sex differences in ratio of fat-free to fat mass may account for many of the observed sex differences in motor performance. (Adapted from Malina & Bouchard, 1991.)

Height and Weight

The rapid changes in height and weight characteristic of pubescence begin before the age of 12 and are shown in Chapter 9 (Figures 9.1 and 9.2). Figures 11.1 and 11.2 show average height and weight changes for boys and girls from 12 to 18. On average, by the age of 11½ girls surpass boys in height and maintain a slight advantage until 13½. Girls outweigh boys at approximately 11, but by 14½ boys catch up to and surpass girls.

An additional physical change, of particular significance to boys, is a rapid increase in the length of limbs. As a result, many boys acquire the gangling appearance often associated with early adolescence, exaggerated by the fact that their rate of purchasing clothes is often considerably behind the rate at which they outgrow them.

Body Composition

As we saw in Chapter 9, the body composition of boys and girls is different throughout childhood, with boys having relatively more **fat-free mass** and less **fat mass;** the two, taken together, determine body weight. During the adolescent growth spurt, boys' proportion of fat decreases even more because fat-free mass grows at a faster rate than does fat mass. This is not the case for girls, however, so that average sex differences in proportion of body weight due to fat mass are magnified (see Figure 11.3).

With the physical growth spurt of adolescence, there is a rapid increase in muscular strength and motor capacity, especially for boys. This is less true for girls, partly because their fat to fat-free ratio tends to increase more than that of boys. There is little research to clarify changes in the ability to stand on one's head, although the inclination to do so may lessen dramatically with the increased maturity of the adolescent.

Strength and Motor Performance

Changes in muscular strength, aerobic performance, and motor capacity also reflect the physical growth spurt, especially in boys. Malina and Bouchard (1991) report a high, positive correlation between the maturity level of adolescent boys and their performance in running, jumping, and throwing, as well as in measures of strength. Thus, boys who mature earlier tend to be stronger and faster, and to perform better in sports. In contrast, girls' motor performance does not appear to be closely related to maturity status, so that younger, less mature girls frequently outperform more mature girls. One explanation for this is that with increasing maturity, the girl develops a higher proportion of fat relative to fat-free mass. As a result, sex differences in many areas of motor performance increase in favor of males (Beunen & Malina, 1988). This is especially evident in competitive athletics, where male records almost invariably surpass those of girls.

Pubescence: Sexual Changes

Pubescence refers to all the changes that lead to sexual maturity. These changes, which are universal, are precipitated by a dramatic increase in hormones produced by the adrenal glands, the hypothalamus, and the gonads (testes

in boys and ovaries in females) (Dubas & Petersen, 1993). Most signs of pubescence are well known. Among the first in both boys and girls is the appearance of pigmented pubic hair, which is straight initially but becomes characteristically kinky during the later stages of pubescence. At about the same time as pubic hair begins to appear, the boy's testes begin to enlarge, as do the girl's breasts. The girl then experiences rapid physical growth, her first menstrual period (menarche, a relatively late event in pubescence), the growth of axillary (armpit) hair, the continued enlargement of her breasts, and a slight lowering of her voice. The boy's voice changes much more dramatically than the girl's, and he, too, grows rapidly, particularly in height and length of limbs. Boys also acquire the capacity to ejaculate semen, grow axillary hair, and eventually develop a beard.

The changes of pubescence that relate directly to the production of offspring involve **primary sexual characteristics.** These include changes in the **ovaries** (organs that produce ova in the girl) and the **testes** (organs that produce sperm in the boy) so that these organs are now capable of producing mature ova and sperm.

Changes that accompany the maturation of the sex organs but that are not directly related to reproduction are said to involve **secondary sexual characteristics.** The ap-

Sequence	Physiological Event*
1	Beginning of adolescent growth spurt
2	Appearance of unpigmented pubic down
3	Breast elevation ("bud" stage)
4	Appearance of pigmented, kinky pubic hair
5	Increase in size of vagina, clitoris, and uterus
6	Decline in rate of physical growth
7	Menarche
8	Development of axillary (armpit) hair; continued enlargement of breasts; slight lowering of the voice
9	Increase in production of oil; increased perspiration; possible acne

* The first of these changes may occur as young as age 7¼; the last may not be completed before age 16. Average age of menarche is 12.

TABLE 11.2
*Normal Sequence of Sexual
Maturation for North American Boys*

Sequence	Physiological Event*
1	Appearance of unpigmented pubic down; growth of testes and scrotum (sac containing testes)
2	Beginning of adolescent growth spurt
3	Enlargement of penis
4	Appearance of pigmented, kinky pubic hair
5	Lowering of voice; appearance of "down" on upper lip
6	First ejaculations occur
7	Decline in rate of physical growth
8	Development of axillary (armpit) hair; growth of facial hair
9	Increase in production of oil; increased perspiration; possible acne
10	Growth of chest hair

* The first of these changes may occur as young as age 9½; the last may not be completed before age 18. Average age of first ejaculation is 12 to 14.

pearance of facial hair in the boy and the development of breasts in the girl, voice changes, and the growth of axillary and pubic hair are all secondary sexual characteristics.

The ages at which primary and secondary sexual characteristics develop vary a great deal, but the sequence of their appearance is more predictable—although not entirely fixed. Tables 11.1 and 11.2 summarize that sequence.

Puberty: Sexual Maturity

Puberty is sexual maturity—the ability to make babies. However, it is very difficult to determine exactly when a person becomes fertile. Although research has often used the girl's first menstrual period (**menarche**) as an indicator, a girl is frequently infertile for about a year after her first menstruation, so that the menarche is not an accurate index of puberty; nevertheless it is a useful indication of impending sexual maturity (Malina, 1990).

It is almost impossible to arrive at a clear index of sexual maturity for boys, although first ejaculation (**spermarche**) is sometimes taken as a sign comparable to menarche. However, the probability that a boy can become a father immediately after first ejaculation is low—although not zero—as the concentration of sperm in the semen remains very low for the first year or so.

Age of Puberty

The average age for puberty in North America is about 12 for girls and 14 for boys, immediately following the period of most rapid growth (the growth spurt). Consequently, the age of puberty may be established by determining the period during which the person grew rapidly.

The period of rapid growth may begin as young as 8.7 for girls compared with 10.3 for boys (Malina, 1990). However, there is a wide age range. Some girls may not reach sexual maturity until age 16; some boys, not until age 18 (Dubas & Petersen, 1993). And in other parts of the world, sexual maturity may occur much earlier or much later. For example, in New Guinea, menarche occurs at ages ranging from an average of 15.5 to 18.4. Similarly, among a large sample of Nigerian boys, spermarche occurred at an average age of 14.3 (Adegoke, 1993).

Early and Late Maturation

Like the average child, the average adolescent whose growth is depicted in Figures 11.1 and 11.2 is an abstraction, an invention designed to simplify a very complex subject. Hence, although the average adolescent matures at about 12 or 14 depending on sex, some mature considerably earlier and some considerably later. The timing of this event may be very important to the child.

Effects for Boys

The research indicates quite consistently that early maturation may be a definite advantage for boys. Early-maturing boys are typically better adjusted, more popular, more confident, more aggressive, and more successful in heterosexual relationships. In addition, they appear to have more positive self-concepts (about which more is said in the next chapter). In contrast, adolescent boys who mature later than average are, as a group, more restless, more attention-seeking, less confident, and have less positive self-concepts (Crockett & Petersen, 1987).

Effects for Girls

Findings are less consistent for girls. However, most studies indicate that on measures of adjustment, early-maturing girls are at a disadvantage—in contrast to early-maturing boys. Dubas and Petersen (1993) summarize the main findings: Early-maturing girls are more likely to have poorer self-concepts, to feel depressed, to date earlier but also to engage in more disapproved behavior, such as getting drunk and skipping school, and to be concerned about their body weight. On average, early-maturing girls weigh more than girls who mature later, and are more likely to develop long-lasting eating problems (Brooks-Gunn, 1988).

A number of studies indicate that early-maturing girls are initially at a disadvantage, a finding that directly contradicts the results of similar studies conducted with boys (Siegel, 1982). Stattin and Magnusson (1990) found higher incidence of sexually precocious behavior and violations of social norms among early-maturing girls. Similarly, Simmons and Blyth (1987) report more conduct problems in school among early maturers, and lower academic success. In later adolescence, however, these disadvantages have often disappeared. Thus, it appears that the effects of early and late maturation in girls depends on their ages. Early maturation is a disadvantage in the very early grades (fifth or sixth), when most girls have not yet begun to mature and when the early-maturing girl is likely to find herself excluded from peer group activities. Also, given the fact that girls are on the average two years in advance of boys in physical maturation, the early-maturing girl may well be four or more years in advance of like-aged boys—which might not contribute positively to her social life. At a later age, however, when most of her age-grade mates have also begun to mature, the early-maturing girl may suddenly find herself in a more advantageous position. Her greater maturity is now something to be admired.

An Ecological Interpretation

As Petersen (1988) notes, pubertal change is most stressful when it puts the adolescent out of step with peers, especially if the change is not interpreted as desirable. And the consequences of maturational timing are most clearly understood in terms of their effects on relationships and interactions that are important to the adolescent. Thus, early maturation may enhance peer relations for boys largely because the boys often excel in activities and abilities that are highly prized in the adolescent peer culture. Not only are they larger and stronger and therefore more likely to be better athletes, but they are also more socially mature and hence more likely to lead in heterosexual activities. Furthermore, evidence suggests that relations with parents are better for early-maturing boys and for late-maturing girls (Savin-Williams & Small, 1986).

From an ecological perspective, what we know of the implications of maturational timetables presents an excellent example of child characteristics interacting with each

TABLE 11.3
Personal Concerns of Adolescents

Concern	Percentage Indicating "A Great Deal" or "Quite a Bit" of Concern
What am I going to do when I finish school?	68
Finances (40 percent of respondents worked part-time)	54
School concerns	50
Time (not enough time to do the things they want)	48
Appearance	44
What is the purpose of life?	44
Boredom	43
Height or weight	43
Loneliness	35
Feelings of inferiority (poor self-image)	29
Sex	28
Parents' marriage	20

SOURCE: From *The Emerging Generation: An Inside Look at Canada's Teenagers,* by R. W. Bibby and D. C. Posterski. © 1985, Irwin Publishing, Inc. Adapted by permission from Table 4.1, p. 60.

other (specifically, degree of sexual maturity interacting with age) to determine important elements of the child's ecology (namely, the nature of interaction with parents and peers). But we should note that the child's ecology is unique to that child. Thus, although there may be some general advantages or disadvantages associated with the timing of pubescence, there are many individual exceptions to our generalizations. Not all early-maturing boys and girls are characterized by the same advantages or disadvantages of early maturation; nor are all those who mature later affected in the same way.

Some Concerns of Adolescents

In Harter's (1990) studies of the self, physical appearance is one of the most important factors in determining self-worth. Hence, it is not surprising to find that almost half of all teenagers list their appearance as one of their major concerns. One of the items most frequently mentioned as the greatest worry for both adolescent boys and girls is the presence of blackheads or pimples ("zits"). Acne is a pervasive problem for many teenagers, a large number of whom consult physicians in search of relief. Treatments sometimes involve dietary change (to diets lower in fat content), the use of special soaps and lotions, abrasive cleaners, drugs, and even abrasion of the skin to stimulate new skin growth (Martin, 1991/1992).

In a survey of 3,600 Canadian adolescents from 150 different schools, the adolescent's greatest worry con-

Rapid physical changes during adolescence, sometimes apparent in changing body shape, skin eruptions, obesity, and physical awkwardness, may be a source of concern for some adolescents. However some changes can often be a source of pride and of increasing feelings of self-worth.

cerned life beyond graduation—"What am I going to do after high school?"—a problem that affected approximately two thirds of all respondents. Other important concerns had to do with money, achievement in school, boredom, loneliness, and the parents' marriage (see Table 11.3). Almost half indicated that their physical appearance is a matter of considerable concern, and about the same number were worried about their height or weight (Bibby & Posterski, 1985). Unfortunately, these concerns are sometimes evident in some serious eating disorders.

NUTRITION AND EATING DISORDERS

Most adolescents, especially if they are very active physically, expend a large number of calories each day. Some, however, take in more than they need; others take in fewer.

Obesity

Obesity, the most common nutritional problem among both children and adolescents, affects up to a quarter of all North American teenagers (Whitney & Hamilton, 1984). Although obesity in infancy is not a good indicator of obesity in later life, obesity in childhood and adolescence is (Malina & Bouchard, 1991).

The increased medical risks for cardiovascular disease that obesity poses are serious and well known; its psychological risks are less apparent. However, there is little doubt that obesity can contribute to peer rejection, to negative peer interactions, to low self-esteem, and to un-

happiness (Baum & Forehand, 1984). It is also associated with poorer performance in school, although it isn't clear whether this is because obese adolescents are subject to discrimination, because they are expected to do less well, because they avoid participation, because teachers involve them less, because they lack self-esteem or independence, or for other reasons (Morrill et al., 1991).

About 25 percent of the variation in fat distribution among individuals is genetic, explain Malina and Bouchard (1991); another important influence has to do with lifestyle. Among children, for example, obesity is often associated with a combination of high-fat foods and low physical activity (Muecke, Simons-Morton, & Huang, 1992). Contrary to what might be expected, psychology has not found that any particular combination of personality characteristics, family structure, or child-rearing pattern is highly predictive of obesity (Burgard, 1993; Crawford & Shapiro, 1991). Put most simply, other than for rare glandular and metabolic problems, and in spite of genetic contributions, obesity in adolescents—and others—is caused by taking in more calories than are expended. Weight reduction can therefore be achieved by consuming fewer calories and by expending more.

Unfortunately, the problem is not so simple. Its alleviation requires nutritional information that not all adolescents have or are interested in acquiring; and it requires changing habits that are not only self-rewarding but encouraged by the media, and that are consequently extraordinarily persistent. And the problem is compounded by the fact that weight levels that Western societies consider ideal, both esthetically and for health reasons, may not be "reasonable weight levels" for those who are severely obese (Brownell & Wadden, 1992). Because these "ideal" weights seem unattainable, they discourage rather than encourage weight loss. As a result, obesity continues to be a very significant North American problem, and its alleviation, a major industry.

Strangely, despite the prevalence of obesity, contemporary Western societies place tremendous emphasis on physical attractiveness, which, especially among girls, is clearly defined as *thinness*.

Anorexia Nervosa

Translated literally, **anorexia nervosa** means "loss of appetite as a result of nerves." It describes a complex and only partly understood condition that may be increasing in frequency.

Definition

Anorexia is defined medically as involving a loss of at least 15 to 25 percent of "ideal" body weight, this loss not being due to any detectable illness. The American Psychiatric Association (1987) definition includes intense fear of gaining weight, disturbance in body image, and significant weight loss as criteria (Wilson & Walsh, 1991).

Anorexia nervosa almost always begins with a deliberate desire to be thin and consequent dieting, and ends in a condition in which the patient seems unwilling or unable to eat normally. Many affected females cease menstruating relatively early following initial dieting, and many become excessively active and continue to engage in strenuous exercise programs even after their physical conditions have deteriorated significantly (Warah, 1993). In the absence of medical intervention, anorexia nervosa can be fatal.

Prevalence

Estimates of the prevalence of anorexia vary considerably depending on the criteria used (Martin, 1993). Although surveys often find that only about 1 percent of the population is *severely* anorexic, when estimates of anorexia are based just on eating attitudes and habits, estimates are much higher. For example, in a study of 191 athletes, Stoutjesdyk and Jevne (1993) found that 10.6 percent of the females and 4.6 percent of the males scored in the "anorexic" range on a test of eating attitudes. Similarly, in a study of more than 1,250 13- to 19-year-old adolescents, Lachenmeyer and Muni-Brander (1988) found that a full 13 percent of the girls reported significantly restricting their diets and scored very high on measures of eating attitudes and behaviors linked with anorexia. Although not every one of these "restricters" (see At a Glance: "Eating Disorders Among Adolescents," and Figure 11.4) meets the strict criteria for a diagnosis of anorexia, each is at risk.

Although anorexia continues to be far more common among girls than boys, there are indications that eating disorders are now much more frequent among adolescent boys than had previously been suspected. Significantly, in the Lachenmeyer and Muni-Brander survey, 6.3 percent

Distortion of body image is a common symptom of anorexia nervosa. Many very thin anorexic women, looking into perfectly good mirrors, consistently overestimate their body size.

of the males in a lower socioeconomic sample (primarily black and Hispanic students) and 3.4 percent of a higher socioeconomic sample (primarily white) were also "restricters." These rates for males are much higher than have traditionally been reported.

Causes

The causes of anorexia nervosa are neither simple, nor well understood, probably because there are a variety of possible contributing factors. Endocrine imbalances are sometimes, although infrequently, involved, and there is some indication as well that the disease may be genetically linked (Holland et al., 1984). In general, however, the condition is thought to be primarily psychological. It has sometimes been associated with depression (Nagel & Jones, 1992). In addition, its onset among adolescent girls often coincides with the beginning of dating—perhaps because the girl's appearance becomes more important to her at that time (Smolak, Levine, & Gralen, 1993). Some speculate that anorexic individuals are typically those who do not feel that they are in control of their lives, but who discover that they *can* control their body weight; in the

EATING DISORDERS AMONG ADOLESCENTS

An investigation by Penner, Thompson, and Coovert (1991) indicates that very thin, anorexic women consistently overestimate their body size, whereas average-size, nonanorexic women do not. Anorexia, severely restricted eating, is just one of the eating disorders that relates to our current cultural emphasis on being thin. Bulimia—alternating food binges with severe dieting and self-induced vomiting and diarrhea—is perhaps three or four times more common than anorexia (Figure 11.4).

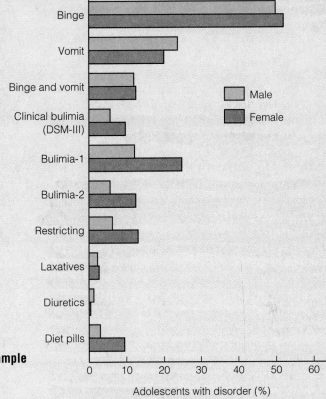

A   Study 1—Low Socioeconomic Sample

FIGURE 11.4

*Prevalence rates for eating disorders among adolescents. The low-socioeconomic sample (**A**) consisted of 328 females and 384 males; the high-socioeconomic sample (**B**) consisted of 314 females and 235 males. Note that clinical bulimics meet all DSM-III criteria for bulimia; Bulimia-1 individuals meet all criteria except one; and Bulimia-2 individuals meet all criteria except two. (Data from Lachenmeyer & Muni-Brander, 1988.)*

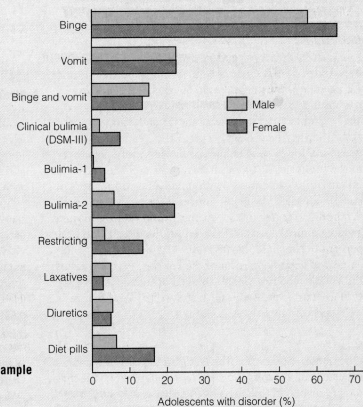

B   Study 2—High Socioeconomic Sample

end, control becomes an obsession. Others suggest that lack of positive self-image coupled with the emphasis that society places on thinness (particularly among females) may be manifested in anorexia in those cases where the person attempts to obtain approval by dieting.

Bulimia Nervosa

Whereas anorexia nervosa is characterized by not eating (in spite of the fact that some anorexics occasionally do go on eating binges), **bulimia nervosa** (or simply *bulimia*) involves recurrent episodes of binge eating.

Definition

The American Psychiatric Association (1987) describes bulimia nervosa in terms of *recurrent* episodes of binge eating (rapid consumption of large amounts of food in a short time). Other criteria for a diagnosis of bulimia nervosa include a feeling of lack of control over eating behavior; regular episodes of self-induced vomiting, use of laxatives or diuretics, strict dieting or fasting, or vigorous exercise; a minimum average of two binge-eating episodes per week; and persistent overconcern with body shape and weight.

Typically, foods consumed during a binge are high calorie and are eaten inconspicuously. Abdominal pain is a common result, as are frequent weight fluctuations. Other possible medical consequences of bulimia nervosa are listed in Table 11.4. Unlike anorexia, bulimia does not usually present an immediate threat to life—although its eventual medical consequences can be quite serious.

Prevalence

Bulimia is a more common eating disorder than anorexia. In a study of 544 female college students, between 1 and 4.2 percent of the sample could be classified as anorexic; a frightening 6.5 to 18 percent were bulimic (Pope et al., 1984). Similarly, in the Lachenmeyer and Muni-Brander (1988) survey mentioned earlier, 7.6 percent of the total *nonclinical* lower socioeconomic sample, and 4.7 percent of the higher socioeconomic sample met *all* the criteria for a clinical diagnosis of bulimia! The proportion of males who are clinically bulimic is higher than expected: 5.7 percent of the males in the lower socioeconomic group, compared with 9.7 percent of the females; and 2.1 percent of the males in the higher socioeconomic group compared with 7.6 percent of the females. Percentages of the sample who occasionally binged or induced vomiting, or both, and who used laxatives, diuretics, and diet pills were also very high.

Causes

One important contributing factor in the increasing incidence of bulimia nervosa is the tremendous emphasis that society places on thinness. Not surprisingly, among characteristics that most clearly differentiate bulimic girls from those who are nonbulimic are a greater desire to be thin, a

TABLE 11.4
Possible Medical Consequences of Bulimia Nervosa

Dehydration.

Constipation.

Abnormal heartbeat, atrial flutter, fibrillation.

Increased susceptibility to cold.

Menstrual irregularities.

Abdominal distention.

Excessive weight fluctuations.

Dehydration and fluid shifts, sometimes resulting in headaches and fainting. Problem more serious if diuretics are used or if bulimia follows prolonged fasting.

Electrolyte imbalance, aggravated by laxative or diuretic use, as well as by repeated vomiting.

Hypoglycemic symptoms.

Malnutrition-related problems (might include cardiovascular, kidney, gastrointestinal, or blood problems as well as insomnia).

Dental/oral problems sometimes associated with loss of enamel as a result of frequent exposure to stomach acidity during vomiting episodes. Other possible gum, salivary duct, and tongue problems associated with emesis (vomiting).

Specific gastrointestinal difficulties, sometimes associated with ipecac abuse. Prolonged use can lead to cardiac problems and death.

Laxative-related problems, which vary depending on the nature of the laxative abused.

Insomnia resulting from malnutrition, nocturnal binges, or underlying depression.

Various neurological and endocrine problems.

SOURCE: Based on Goode, 1985, and Brown, 1991.

higher degree of dissatisfaction with their bodies, and chronic dieting. In addition, bulimic females are more likely to see themselves as being overweight and tend to be significantly more depressed (Ledoux, Choquet, & Manfredi, 1993). Miller, McCluskey-Fawcett, and Irving (1993) report that adolescents who were sexually abused are at higher risk of being bulimic. So, too, are those whose parents have the highest frequency of addictive problems (alcoholism, drug use, overeating, and gambling), as well as those who are most inclined toward *perfectionism* (Brouwers & Wiggum, 1993). In line with this view, Polivy and Herman (1985) suggest that part of the explanation for bulimia may lie in the fact that dieting promotes the adoption of cognitive rather than physiological controls over eating. The high-control, perfectionistic individual *decides* when to eat and when not to, and ignores physiological indicators of hunger. And perhaps the binges that follow dieting are partly facilitated by the awareness (cognition) that the individual can control the effects of the binge through a purge and through continued dieting, as well as by the fact that the individual has learned to ignore the physiological signals that ordinarily control food intake.

Some Treatments

Anorexia nervosa and bulimia are frightening and baffling conditions for parents. Anorexia is especially frightening because it can be fatal; and it is baffling and frustrating because it may seem to parents that the anorexic adolescent deliberately and totally unreasonably refuses to eat. And neither pleas nor threats are likely to work. What is?

Because anorexia and bulimia are not, in most instances, primarily biological or organic disorders, their treatment is often complex and difficult. There are no drugs or simple surgical procedures that can easily cure these conditions. In some extreme instances, patients respond favorably to antidepressant drugs; at other times, it is necessary to force-feed them to save their lives. Generally, however, successful treatments have typically involved one of several forms of psychotherapy. Among these, what is termed **cognitive-behavior therapy**—the use of reinforcement and/or punishment combined with more *rational* approaches—has sometimes been dramatically effective (Wilson & Fairburn, 1993). For example, Wilfley and associates (1993) significantly reduced binge eating among 56 bulimic women using *group* cognitive-behavioral therapy. Similarly, Agras and colleagues (1994) reduced binge eating in bulimic women using *individual* cognitive-behavioral therapy, as well as a combination of antidepressant medication with the therapy.

There are some who argue that one of the main causes of anorexia and bulimia is dieting, and that to treat these disorders effectively, it is necessary to treat dieting.

And perhaps to treat dieting, it is necessary to change the social and cultural conditions that have placed such a tremendous value on thinness.

ADOLESCENT INTELLECTUAL DEVELOPMENT

Jean Piaget's view of intellectual development begins with a description of infants *assimilating* aspects of the environment, *accommodating* to others, *equilibrating* (balancing) the two processes, and constructing progressively more advanced views of reality. In time the infant succeeded in separating self from world, in representing aspects of the world symbolically, and in dealing with knowledge in increasingly logical ways. And by the end of concrete operations, the child understood the logical necessity of conservation, could solve a variety of problems, and could classify, seriate, and deal with number at a surprisingly sophisticated level.

In the following sections, we continue our examination of intellectual development, looking first at Piaget's contributions and then at information-processing approaches.

Piaget's View: Formal Operations

Some of the important distinctions between concrete and **formal operations** are illustrated in children's responses to the following Inhelder and Piaget (1958) problem.

FIGURE 11.5

All possible combinations of the four test tubes to which the fifth can be added. The experiment requires the subject to discover the combination(s) that will yield a yellow liquid when potassium iodide is added. The correct solutions have a light gray background.

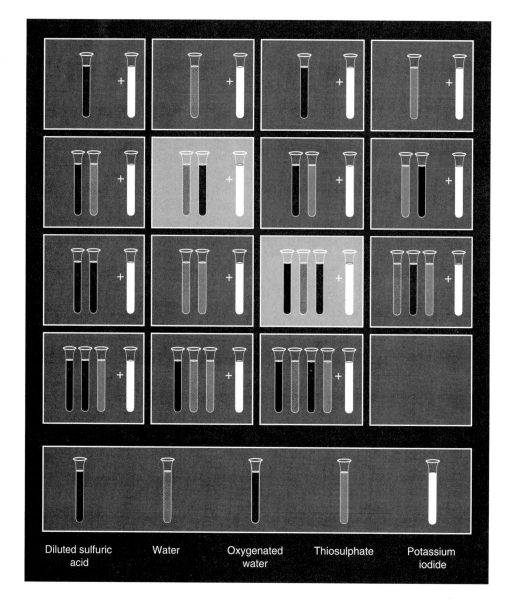

| Diluted sulfuric acid | Water | Oxygenated water | Thiosulphate | Potassium iodide |

A Piagetian Problem

Participants are presented with five test tubes that contain different unidentified chemicals; a combination of these chemicals will result in a yellow liquid. This phenomenon is demonstrated for participants so they know that one special tube, which is kept apart, is the catalyst for the desired reaction. What they are asked to do is discover which combination of the other four tubes is the correct one. They are allowed to experiment as necessary to solve the problem.

Typical 10-year-olds begin by combining two of the chemicals, then two more, then again two. If, by chance, they arrive at a correct solution, they exclaim, "There, those two! That's the solution." But if they are asked whether they can find any other solutions, their strategy changes little. They continue to combine pairs of liquids, or even three or four at once. Their behavior is unsystematic, and if they are unlucky or not persistent enough, they may be incapable of discovering even one correct combination.

Intelligent 15-year-olds behave quite differently. As illustrated in Figure 11.5, they can solve the problem by systematically combining the tubes by twos, threes, and finally all four, yielding all possible combinations. In the end, there will be no doubt in their minds that they have found all correct combinations.

Formal Versus Concrete Thinking

In this experiment, there are clues to some of the important differences between the child's thinking during the stage of concrete operations and thinking characterized by formal operations.

First, 10-year-olds begin their solution by attempting actual combinations; their hypotheses are real behaviors. In contrast, the bright 15-year-old begins by *imagining* all the possibilities and then tries them. There is a fundamental difference in the orientations. The first reflects the *concrete* nature of the child's thought; the second reflects the adolescent's ability to deal with the *hypothetical*.

Second, the experiment illustrates the *logical* capacity of the adolescent's thinking. Because 10-year-olds consider every combination as a separate and unrelated hypothesis and because they arrive at these combinations in a haphazard way, they are likely to overlook possibilities in the process. In contrast, adolescents first consider the range of all possible combinations. The concrete logic that was sufficient to deal with classes and seriation is replaced by what Piaget terms the *logic of propositions*. This form of logic is a much more powerful tool for dealing with the hypothetical—with statements that need not relate to reality but are simply characterized by the possibility that they can be true or untrue (in fact, this is the definition of a proposition: a verbal statement that can be true or false).

Implications of Formal Thinking

The adolescent's newly acquired capability to deal with the hypothetical might not be very obvious, or perhaps even very important, if it were manifested only in problems of chemistry and physics. But formal operations extend well beyond the realms of science. They are apparent in new preoccupations with understanding the self as an abstraction (Harter, 1990), in an egocentric reliance on logic (Lapsley, 1990), and in an intense new idealism. Children can now contemplate states of affairs that do not exist; they can compare the ideal to the actual; they can become profoundly distressed at the failure of preceding generations to avoid the confusion that they observe around them; and they can be puzzled by some of the profound questions that have always tormented philosophers. It is precisely the adolescent's ability to deal with the hypothetical that made it possible for 44 percent of the subjects in Bibby and Posterski's (1985) study to claim that they were very concerned about the purpose and meaning of life. Such questions do not often suggest themselves to the 10-year-old.

With the idealism of formal operations, there also comes a belief in the omnipotence of thought. The egocentrism of adolescence (which we discuss later in this chapter) can be seen in the belief that reason and logic provide all the answers and in an apparent inability to adopt the point of view that admits that we do not have all the answers, and that even if we did, social, political, and other human realities sometimes oppose their implementation. It is this unshakable belief in the power of thought that may underlie the adolescent's absolutely insistent political, social, and religious arguments with parents and others.

An Information-Processing View

Piaget's stage-bound description of intellectual development, although it provides many important insights into cognitive functioning, is not always an accurate description of the child's capabilities. Ironically, whereas Piaget seems to have *under*estimated the cognitive achievements of infants and preschoolers, he may have *over*estimated

The information-processing approach to cognitive development looks at the individual's knowledge base, development of strategies for processing information, and self awareness as a processor of information. The skills reflected in this girl's playing of the flute are based on years of experience and practice that have enriched her knowledge base, gradually transforming her from novice into expert.

those of the adolescent. There is evidence, for example, that the abstract and logical thinking of formal operations, which is not ordinarily present at the beginning of formal operations (at age 11 or 12), is often not even present among adults.

A complementary approach to understanding intellectual development falls under the general heading of *information processing*. As we saw in Chapter 9, information-processing theories are concerned with three important aspects of cognition: the acquisition of a knowledge base, the development of information-processing strategies, and the development of metacognitive skills.

To review briefly, the knowledge base consists of all the concepts, ideas, information, and so on that we have in memory. Infants begin life with very little knowledge base. The knowledge base derives from the individual's experiences; schools do a great deal to expand and organize the knowledge base.

Information-processing strategies are the procedures involved in learning and remembering. They include strategies such as organizing and rehearsing.

Metacognitive skills relate to information the knower has about the processes of knowing and remembering, and to awareness of the self as an information processor. As metacognitive skills increase, so too does the child's ability to analyze performance, to predict the likelihood of success, to change strategies, to evaluate, and to monitor.

An information-processing view of development describes how each of these three aspects of information processing (knowledge base, processing skills, and meta-cognitive skills) change with age and experience.

Changes in Knowledge Base

Knowledge base grows with increasing experience and exposure to schooling. Anderson (1980) describes how children progress from being *novices* in all areas to being *experts* in at least some areas—especially in certain games, in aspects of social interaction, in certain levels and classes of school subjects, and perhaps in hobby-related or cultural pursuits. One of the important differences between experts and novices has to do with knowledge base. But the difference is not simply that experts know more (have more content in their knowledge bases), but also that they have formed more associations among the things they know. Their knowledge is richer in the sense that it suggests more relationships. The artist who is an expert in color does not understand the color blue in the same way I, a novice, might. My pitiful understanding permits me to relate blue to robin eggs, morning skies, and northern lakes; the expert might relate it to these as well, but might also break it down into a dozen hues whose subtlety and associations have no meaning for me. More than this, the expert might well understand blue as a wavelength, might understand its relationships to other waves of different lengths, and might have a sense of its crispness or fragility that quite escapes me.

Changes in Processing

If development is a process of shedding some of the novice's ignorance and acquiring increasing expertise, then it follows that expertise involves more than changes in knowledge base—that it must also involve changes in information-processing capacity. Among other things, information-processing capacity depends on the availability of appropriate strategies—and it depends on attention span.

That attention span increases with age is clear. Intelligence tests such as the Stanford-Binet, for example, require that subjects try to recall sequences of digits presented at 1-second intervals. Whereas a preschool child might correctly recall a string of two or three digits, an adolescent might easily recall six or seven.

Changes in the availability of appropriate strategies are not as easily investigated, partly because it is not always simple to identify a strategy and determine whether it is present. However, Piaget's investigations of concrete and formal operations suggest that the strategies available to older adolescents are substantially different, and consider-ably more powerful, than those available to the younger child. For example, Demetriou, Efklides, and Papadaki (1993) show how the strategies that adolescents use become progressively more systematic and specialized, enabling them to do things like form hypotheses, design experiments, and even build models and theories. In addition, adolescents have more ready-made solutions for problems. Thus, there are many Piagetian tasks that present real problems for a younger child but that can be solved almost from memory by an older child. A 6-year-old might need to "figure out" whether there is still the same amount of material in a deformed object; the adolescent need not "figure."

Metacognitive Change

One additional important area of developmental change in information processing involves the child's understanding of the self as a processor of information and an increasing understanding of the processes of cognition. As we saw in Chapter 9, metacognitive skills seem to be largely absent in young children, but are clearly present in older children and adolescents.

In summary, information-processing views of cognitive development describe changes in three areas: content (knowledge base increases in terms of specific knowledge as well as in terms of relations and associations among items of information); processing capacities (increases in memory and attention capacities, and in the availability of more sophisticated strategies); and metacognitive changes (increasing awareness of self as information processor, and increasing ability to monitor, evaluate, and control ongoing cognitive activities). These changes make more of an expert of the adolescent. But they do not eliminate the adolescent's egocentrism.

ADOLESCENT EGOCENTRISM

In Piagetian theory, *egocentrism* is not a derogatory term as it might be in ordinary usage. It refers less to a *selfishness* than to a cognitive and emotional *self-centeredness* and is apparent in children's inability to be completely objective in their understanding of the world and in their interactions with others. During sensorimotor development, for example, infants are egocentric in that they cannot easily differentiate between self and the physical world: Objects exist only when they are being looked at, tasted, felt, or smelled—a rather extreme egocentrism. And in the preschool period there is evidence of egocentricism in the children's centeredness on the perceptual features of objects when they respond incorrectly to conservation problems.

The egocentrism of the adolescent is not as extreme or naive as that of the infant. It is characterized by an inability to differentiate between objects and events that are

The concept of the adolescent's imaginary audience is a recognition of the adolescent's self-consciousness and egocentricity—a recognition of the fact that many adolescents act as though they think others are always watching and judging them. Whether this girl thinks her imaginary audience is shocked and disgusted, mildly amused, or very impressed at how much pizza she can put in her mouth at one time might have important implications for her behavior.

of concern to others and those of concern to the adolescent. As Jahnke and Blanchard-Fields (1993) note, it's a sort of confusion between the adolescent's thoughts and the thoughts of others. **Adolescent egocentrism** is sometimes apparent in behaviors that seem to be motivated by the adolescent's belief that everybody is watching and is terribly concerned—that there is, in other words, an *imaginary audience* that is always passing judgment. It is also apparent in the adolescent's private conviction that he or she is special—a conviction that defines the *personal fable*. These two concepts—the imaginary audience and the personal fable—are the two main dimensions of adolescent egocentrism (Elkind, 1967).

The Imaginary Audience

The adolescent's **imaginary audience** is a hypothetical collection of all who might be concerned with the adolescent's self and behavior. It is the *they* in expressions such as "They say . . ." or "They predict . . ." Social psychologists inform us that each of us behaves as though "they" are

watching and care. But the imaginary audiences of most adults are less important than those of adolescents. According to Elkind (1967), it is because of this imaginary audience to which the adolescent is continually reacting that young adolescents are often very self-conscious. It is also because of this same audience that many become so concerned with their hair, clothing, and other aspects of their physical appearance. It is as though adolescents believe that others are as deeply concerned about them as they themselves are and that these others constantly judge them.

Measuring the Imaginary Audience

How does research investigate beliefs such as these? How can psychology locate an imaginary audience?

The answer is with one of several instruments such as Elkind and Bowen's (1979) *Imaginary Audience Scale* (IAS) or Enright and colleagues' (1980) *Adolescent Egocentrism-Sociocentrism Scale*. The IAS, for example, is based on the assumption that individuals who act as though an imaginary audience is watching them will be *self-conscious*. Accordingly, the scale is really a measure of self-consciousness. Items for the IAS were selected from a pool of suggestions given by students who were asked to describe situations they might find embarrassing. The final scale consists of 12 items, the first 4 of which are reproduced in Interactive Table 11.5.

A number of investigations using the IAS or the Enright scale have found considerable variability in the ages at which children become egocentric (Jahnke & Blanchard-Fields, 1993). However, the evidence seems clear that egocentrism is an important phenomenon of adolescence. And although it typically declines following early adolescence, when Peterson and Roscoe (1991) gave the IAS to female college freshmen, they found that their scores were even higher than those of young adolescents. They reason that being placed in a new social environment results in a greater self-protectiveness and consequently a greater self-consciousness.

Implications of the Imaginary Audience

Understanding adolescent self-consciousness might not only do a great deal to clarify the adolescent experience for us, but might also have a number of practical implications. For example, Elkind (1981b) suggests it might contribute in important ways to our understanding of vandalism, teenage pregnancy, drug abuse, and other related behaviors. And, interestingly, measures of self-consciousness have been found to be among the best predictors of whether sexually active, unmarried adolescent girls use contraception (Green, Johnson, & Kaplan, 1992; Johnson & Green, 1993). One of the important motives that might underly these decisions may relate directly to what the adolescent expects the reaction of the imaginary audience to be. Teachers, parents, counselors, and friends are all members of that audience. Mine is made up mainly of popes and presidents.

THE IMAGINARY AUDIENCE SCALE (IAS)

Instructions: Please read the following stories carefully and assume that the events actually happened to you. Place a check next to the answer that best describes what you would do or feel in the real situation.

1. You have looked forward to the most exciting dress-up party of the year. You arrive after an hour's drive from home. Just as the party is beginning, you notice a grease spot on your trousers or skirt. (There is no way to borrow clothes from anyone.) Would you stay or go home?

___ Go home.

___ Stay, even though I'd feel uncomfortable.

___ Stay, because the grease spot wouldn't bother me.

2. Let's say some adult visitors came to your school and you were asked to tell them a little bit about yourself.

___ I would like that.

___ I would not like that.

___ I wouldn't care.

3. It is Friday afternoon and you have just had your hair cut in preparation for the wedding of a relative that weekend. The barber or hairdresser did a terrible job and your hair looks awful. To make it worse, that night is the most important basketball game of the season and you really want to see it, but there is no way you can keep your head covered without people asking questions. Would you stay home or go to the game anyway?

___ Go to the game and not worry about my hair.

___ Go to the game and sit where people won't notice me very much.

___ Stay home.

4. If you went to a party where you did not know most of the kids, would you wonder what they were thinking about you?

___ I wouldn't think about it.

___ I would wonder about that a lot.

___ I would wonder about that a little.

SOURCE: From D. Elkind and R. Bowen, "Imaginary Audience Behavior in Children and Adolescents," *Developmental Psychology* 15 (1), pp. 38–44. Copyright 1979 by the American Psychological Association. Reprinted by permission.

The Personal Fable

Adolescent egocentrism is reflected not only in the imaginary audience but also in the elaboration of fantasies, called **personal fables.** Not surprisingly, the adolescent is the hero in these fables. The fantasies have a number of identifying themes, the most common of which are "I am *special.*" "Eagles and gods do not do untidy things upon me." "I will not get pregnant." "I will not become addicted to these drugs I take only for recreation." "Mom, you just don't understand what real love is." "Neither do you, Dad!"

One of the characteristics of the personal fable is a sense of invulnerability. Unfortunately, it is often sadly inappropriate, as is evident in the fact that adolescents—especially males—have the highest accident rate of all age groups except those over 65 (U.S. Bureau of the Census, 1994).

Elements of the personal fable run through the lives of most of us. We believe that we are somewhat unique—just a little special. But these beliefs appear to be greatly exaggerated in adolescents and may partially account for their casual attitude with regard to taking risks.

Reckless Adolescent Behavior

Adolescents—especially males—engage in a variety of reckless behaviors, many of which have potentially devastating consequences (see At a Glance: "Adolescent Risks and Violent Death," and Table 11.6).

Manifestations of Adolescent Recklessness

Where I live, automobile insurance rates for a 16-year-old, accident-free male driver are about four times higher than they are for *moi*. Why? Not because I am technically a better driver, but simply because more 16-year-olds drive at high speed when sober, and even more of them drive at high speed when drunk. Over one third of all drunk drivers involved in fatal accidents are aged 16 to 24. Yet this age group represents fewer than one fifth of all licensed drivers (U.S. Bureau of the Census, 1994).

About 50 percent more sexually active teenage girls than sexually active 25- to 44-year-olds do not use contraception. And over 1 million unmarried teenagers become pregnant in the United States each year (U.S. Bureau of the Census, 1994).

ADOLESCENT RISKS AND VIOLENT DEATH

"We have reason to worry about our young people," write Lavery and colleagues (1993). "Adolescents are at high risk for accidental injury, violence, and the initiation of lifestyles and habits which present long-term health risks" (p. 277). Their risk-taking behavior is manifested in drug abuse, dangerous hobbies, and automobile and other accidents, and is especially evident in the incidence of violent death among white adolescent males. Violent death among blacks is more common than among whites but does not reveal the same pattern of higher incidence in adolescence. This might be because death among blacks involves a higher proportion of homicides, which continue at a high rate after adolescence, and perhaps because of more limited access to automobiles. For both blacks and whites, violent death is considerably lower for females than for males (Table 11.6).

TABLE 11.6

1991 U.S. Death Rates (per 100,000) by Age for Accidents, Suicides, and Homicides Combined

Age	White		Black	
	Male	Female	Male	Female
15–24	104.2	31.2	231.9	37.0
25–34	94.2	24.7	213.8	47.7
35–44	78.5	23.5	171.8	40.0
45–54	72.9	25.2	132.4	33.1
55–64	75.6	26.6	124.7	32.5
65 and older	147.4	79.6	182.2	78.6

SOURCE: U.S. Bureau of the Census, 1994, p. 100.

Adolescents have the highest rate of illegal drug use of any age group (Arnett, 1992). In 1990, 40 percent of all serious crimes in the United States were committed by those under 18 (U.S. Bureau of the Census, 1994).

Why Adolescents Take Risks

The adolescent's reckless behaviors, explains Arnett (1992), involve doing things that the adolescent recognizes as dangerous, but the adolescent deliberately underestimates the danger and ignores precautions that could be taken. When Beyth-Marom and colleagues (1993) asked adult and adolescent subjects to describe the possible consequences of high-risk behaviors like drinking and driving, their responses were remarkably similar. Adolescents *know* the risks involved in their behaviors; they can anticipate their possible outcomes as clearly as can adults. But they consistently underestimate risks associated with activities in which they themselves engage. Benthin,

Behaving morally requires four things: recognizing a problem; evaluating it in terms of personal values; deciding what ought to be done; and acting. One of the characteristics of adolescence, says Piaget, is a new-found idealism linked with the adolescent's ability to imagine a better world—and a willingness to get one's hand's dirty trying to improve it.

Slovic, and Severson (1993) had adolescents rate perceived risks and benefits of 30 high-risk activities like smoking, drug use, drinking, and sex. Not only did participants perceive lower risks for their own high-risk behaviors, but they also perceived greater benefits. And, strikingly, they consistently overestimated the extent to which their peers engaged in the same activities.

Adolescents' tendency to underestimate the probability of bad outcomes for themselves is one factor that explains risk taking, claims Arnett (1992). Another is their personal fable of invulnerability—their frequently expressed belief that "It won't happen to me." A third is the personality trait labeled "sensation-seeking," which may be related to levels of sex hormones. Sensation seeking implies a desire to take risks for the sensations involved. Driving motorcycles, water skiing, and using drugs have all been shown to be related to high scores on the sensation-seeking scale. Fourth, a wealth of research suggests that peer influences contribute to the likelihood of reckless behavior (Arnett, 1992). Finally, some high-risk-takers are adolescents who score high on measures of social maladjustment (Lavery et al., 1993).

The Cautious Adolescent

Although adolescence is a period of greater apparent recklessness than any other period of life, it would be misleading not to emphasize that the majority of adolescents are

not reckless. In 1992, more than 6.7 million American 16- to 19-year-olds worked—and more than 10 million were in school—and school, for a lot of them, is serious, non-reckless work. It is also worth noting that in a 1992 survey, 96 percent of all 12- to 17-year-olds did not use marijuana, 98.6 percent had never used crack, and more than half did not use alcohol (U.S. Bureau of the Census, 1994).

Clearly, the adolescent is not totally unrestrained, reckless, and immoral.

MORAL DEVELOPMENT

Morality involves interactions between people in which questions of trust, ethics, values, and rights are involved. Most of us believe implicitly that some people are good and others less good—that goodness or evil is an intrinsic part of what we are—of ourselves. When we judge people morally "good" or "bad," says Kohlberg (1964), we might be referring to any one of three things: their ability to resist temptation, the amount of guilt that accompanies failure to resist temptation, or the individual's evaluation of the morality of a given act based on some personal standard of good or evil. These dimensions of morality are not necessarily very closely related. A person may repeatedly violate some accepted code of conduct—behave immorally, in other words—and yet feel a great deal of guilt. A second may engage in exactly the same behavior and feel

Some view morality as a cognitive phenomenon in that it involves making judgments about right and wrong as well as about actions that ought to be taken. Guidance for moral judgment and action is sometimes found in religions or in the behavior of others. Some, like this woman, look for moral advice in the written word.

TABLE 11.7
Components of Moral Behavior
Illustrated by the Kitty Genovese Murder

Moral Behavior Requires	Possible Reasons for Not Intervening
Moral sensitivity (recognition of a moral problem)	Failure to recognize seriousness of situation ("It's only a lover's quarrel.")
Moral judgment (deciding what *ought* to be done)	Inability to devise a plan of behavior compatible with ideals and values ("How can I save her life without endangering mine?")
Moral values (conscience; ideals; that which guides moral action)	Individual's values run counter to helping someone in this situation ("If he wants to kill her, hey, it's up to him.")
Moral action (implementing moral or immoral behavior)	Unable to implement the plan the individual might have devised ("I should restrain the attacker physically, but I'm not strong enough.")

no guilt. Yet both may judge the act equally evil. Who is most moral?

Morality as a Cognitive Phenomenon

Carroll and Rest (1982) suggest that there are four steps involved in behaving morally: First, moral behavior requires recognizing a moral problem and being sensitive to the fact that someone's welfare is involved. Second, it is necessary to make a judgment about what is right and wrong—about what ought to be done in a given situation. Third, the individual needs to make a plan of action that takes into account relevant ideals and values. Finally, the plan must be put into action.

It is entirely possible, Carroll and Rest argue, to fail to act morally because of a deficiency in only one of these components. Research on bystander intervention, stimulated by the now-famous murder of Kitty Genovese, is a case in point (Latané & Darley, 1970). Kitty was a New Yorker who, returning home from work at 3 o'clock one morning, was set upon by a maniac and murdered. The murder took an entire half hour to complete and was watched by at least 38 of Kitty's neighbors, most of them

from their windows. No one tried to help her; no one yelled at the murderer; no one even called the police. Table 11.7 shows how the behavior of the bystanders might be interpreted in light of Carroll and Rest's analysis of what is required for moral behavior.

Piaget's Approach

Carroll and Rest's view of morality, which follows closely the work of Kohlberg (1969; 1980) and Piaget (1932), is clearly based on the individual's *cognition* (understanding) of a situation. Not surprisingly, research indicates that moral reasoning and behavior are closely linked with metacognition (for example, Swanson & Hill, 1993).

Piaget's description of moral development is also a cognitive one. He investigated children's morality by telling them stories and asking them to *judge* how good or bad the characters were—essentially a cognitive activity. In one story, for example, a child accidentally breaks 15 cups, and another deliberately breaks a single cup. Is one worse than the other?

Younger children, notes Piaget, judge guilt by the apparent consequences of the act: The child who has broken the largest number of cups or who has stolen the greatest quantity of goods or the largest amount of money is more evil than the one who deliberately broke only one cup, stole just a few things, or took just a little money. Later, children's judgment becomes more adultlike. They are more likely to consider the intentions and motives behind the act.

Piaget's Two Stages of Moral Development
Based on children's responses to these stories, Piaget identified two broad stages in the evolution of morality. In the first stage, lasting until about age 8 or 10, children respond in terms of the immediate consequences of

KOHLBERG'S LEVELS OF MORALITY

Kohlberg identified levels of moral judgment in children by describing to them situations involving a moral dilemma. One example is the story of Heinz, which can be paraphrased as follows: Heinz's wife was dying of cancer. One special drug might save her, a drug recently discovered by a local druggist. The druggist could make the drug for about $200 but was selling it for 10 times that amount. So Heinz went to everyone he knew to try to borrow the $2,000 he needed, but he could only scrape together $1,000. "My wife's dying," he told the druggist, asking him to sell the drug cheaper or let him pay later. But the druggist refused. Desperate, Heinz broke into the drug store to steal the drug for his wife. Should Heinz have done that? Why? (Kohlberg, 1969, p. 379)

Level I Preconventional	Stage 1: Punishment and obedience orientation	"If he steals the drug, he might go to jail." (Punishment.)
	Stage 2: Naive instrumental hedonism	"He can steal the drug and save his wife, and he'll be with her when he gets out of jail." (Act motivated by its hedonistic consequences for the actor.)
Level II Conventional	Stage 3: "Good-boy, nice-girl" morality	"People will understand if you steal the drug to save your wife, but they'll think you're cruel and a coward if you don't." (Reactions of others and the effects of the act on social relationships become important.)
	Stage 4: Law-and-order orientation	"It is the husband's duty to save his wife even if he feels guilty afterward for stealing the drug." (Institutions, law, duty, honor, and guilt motivate behavior.)
Level III Postconventional	Stage 5: Morality of social contract	"The husband has a right to the drug even if he can't pay now. If the druggist won't charge it, the government should look after it." (Democratic laws guarantee individual rights; contracts are mutually beneficial.)
	Stage 6: Universal ethical*	"Although it is legally wrong to steal, the husband would be morally wrong not to steal to save his wife. A life is more precious than financial gain." (Conscience is individual. Laws are socially useful but not sacrosanct.)

* None of Kohlberg's subjects ever reached Stage 6. However, it is still described as a "potential" stage. Kohlberg suggests that moral martyrs like Jesus or Martin Luther King, Jr., exemplify this level.

SOURCE: Based on Kohlberg, 1969 and 1980.

behavior, manifesting a morality that is governed by the principles of pain and pleasure. Thus, good behaviors are those that have pleasant consequences; bad actions have unpleasant consequences. Accordingly, the child responds primarily to outside authority, because authority is the main source of reinforcement and punishment. Piaget labels this first stage of moral development **heteronomy.**

In the second stage, beginning at around 11 or so, morality comes to be governed more and more by principles and ideals. As a result, moral judgments become more individual and more autonomous; hence Piaget's label, **autonomy,** for the second stage.

Kohlberg's Stages

Kohlberg (1969; 1980), whose research closely follows Piaget's pioneering investigations, studied moral development by posing moral dilemmas to groups of children, as well as to adolescents and adults. These dilemmas took the form of stories, one of which is paraphrased and illustrated in Interactive Table 11.8.

Children's responses suggest three levels in the development of moral judgments, each consisting of two stages of moral orientation (shown in Table 11.8). The three levels are sequential, although succeeding levels never entirely replace preceding ones, making it almost impossible to assign ages to them.

Preconventional

At the **preconventional level,** the child believes that evil behavior is that which is likely to be punished, and good behavior is based on obedience or the avoidance of the evil of disobedience (Stage 1). Similarly, the child's judgments tend to be **hedonistic:** Good is that which is pleasant, and evil is that which has undesirable consequences (Stage 2).

Conventional

The second level, a morality of **conventional** role conformity, reflects the increasing importance of peer and social relations. Thus, moral behavior is behavior that receives wide approval from significant people—parents, teachers, peers, and society at large (Stage 3). Similarly, conforming to law becomes important for maintaining adults' approval (Stage 4).

Postconventional

At the highest level, the **postconventional,** the individual begins to view morality in terms of individual rights and as ideals and principles that have value as rules or laws, apart from their influence on approval (Stage 5). Stage 5 moral judgments are rare even among adults; and Stage 6 judgments, based on fundamental ethical principles, even rarer. Colby and Kohlberg (1984) suggest that there is some doubt as to whether Stage 6 should even be included as a stage in moral development.

A Seventh Stage?

But Kohlberg (1984) also spoke of the possibility of a seventh stage—a mystical, contemplative, religious stage—a metaphorical stage in which, through the "logic of contemplation and mystical logic . . . we all know that the deepest feeling is love and the ultimate reality is life" (Hague, 1991, p. 283).

Research on the Views of Piaget and Kohlberg

Some researchers present evidence that contradicts Kohlberg's belief that stages of moral development parallel cognitive development and that they are universal. For example, Kurtines and Grief (1974) and Fishkin, Keniston, and Mackinnon (1973) found few advances in moral reasoning among older children and found that subjects often operated at different stages depending on the specifics of the moral questions to which they were responding. Subsequently, a reanalysis of Kohlberg's original data using new scoring procedures found that progression through the stages takes much longer than had at first been thought (Colby & Kohlberg, 1984). The reanalysis also indicated that postconventional morality is the exception rather than the rule even among adults. Specifically, 10-year-olds were typically either in Stage 2 or still in transition between Stages 1 and 2; young adolescents (ages 13 to 14) were primarily still in transition between Stages 2 and 3; and late adolescents as well as early adults were mainly in Stage 3. Only one of every eight adults in this sample operated at a postconventional level.

Most of the research now agrees that although progress through the higher stages may be possible with the development of formal operational thinking in adolescence, it typically remains *potential* rather than actual. As Lapsley (1990) notes, adolescence is not marked by principled moral reasoning, contrary to what we might expect given the adolescent's newly developed ability to deal with abstractions and principles. Most young adolescents reason at a preconventional, Stage 2 level (a self-serving, hedonistic morality) or at a conventional, Stage 3 level (emphasis on conforming, being good, doing the expected). In fact, Stage 3 reasoning is not very common until the age of 16 to 18, but it is more likely in adulthood.

More Recent Findings and Conclusions

Some researchers suggest that Kohlberg's moral dilemmas are perhaps too verbal and too abstract for children. They require that the child understand and keep in mind very complex situations involving a number of actors; they require the manipulation of a variety of factors and circumstances; and often they don't provide enough information (but if they did, they would be even more complex). As a result, it appears that the Kohlberg dilemmas underestimate children's moral reasoning. When questions are made simpler, or when children and adolescents are observed in naturalistic settings, researchers sometimes find evidence of very sophisticated moral reasoning at very young ages.

Children as young as 6 or 7 are likely to consider the actor's intentions in judging the severity of an act, report Darley and Shultz (1990). Also, they often take into account other factors, such as whether an authority permits the act to occur (Tisak, 1993). Thus, children will judge an act more harshly if it intentionally causes harm, or if the consequences could have been foreseen, than if the action's harm is unintentional and could not have been expected. Similarly, preschoolers, like older children, readily differentiate between lies and the truth, and judge lies as being less moral than the truth (Bussey, 1992). Says Buzzelli (1992), even preschoolers are not really "premoral." "As early as the second year of life, children begin to use standards in evaluating their own behavior and the behavior of others" (p. 48).

In some ways, then, the moral judgments of children are somewhat similar to those of adolescents and adults. But, as Kohlberg's (1980) research shows, their verbalized understanding of right and wrong is really quite different.

Gilligan's Approach: Gender Differences

Gilligan (1982) advances two principal criticisms of Kohlberg's work: one is that all his subjects were male; the other is that the moral dilemmas that he used were typically irrelevant to the lives of his subjects. A person's response to an abstract or hypothetical moral dilemma ("What would you do if you had to choose between letting your partner die or spending the rest of your life in jail?") might be quite different from that person's actual behavior in the case of a *real*, rather than hypothetical, dilemma.

Female Morality

Gilligan reasoned that subjects' apparent stages of moral reasoning might seem *higher* in the case of an abstract and impersonal moral dilemma like Heinz's problem (Interactive Table 11.8) than they would be in the case of a real, immediate dilemma. Following this line of reasoning, she examined morality by interviewing 29 women while they were currently facing the moral dilemma of needing to make a decision about having an abortion.

Based on her analysis of the women's reasons for having or not having an abortion, Gilligan describes three stages in female moral development. In the first stage, the woman is moved primarily by selfish concerns ("This is what I want . . . what I need . . . what I should do . . . what would be best for me"). In the second stage, the woman progresses through a period of increasing recognition of responsibility to others. And the final stage reflects a morality of "nonviolence." At this stage, the woman's decision is based on her desire to do the greatest good both for self and for others.

Gilligan's View of Male–Female Differences

If Gilligan's description of female moral development is accurate, it reflects a number of important differences between male and female morality. In contrast with Kohlberg's description of male moral progression from what are initially hedonistic (pain–pleasure) concerns toward a conventional, rule-regulated morality, Gilligan describes female morality as a progression from initial selfishness toward a recognition of social responsibility. Boys are perhaps more concerned with law and order than the personally meaningful dimensions of morality. Women's is a morality of *caring* rather than of *abstract justice* (Stander & Jensen, 1993).

Nunner-Winkler (1984) elaborates Gilligan's position by reference to Kant's (1797/1977) distinction between *negative* and *positive* moral duties: Negative duties are illustrated in rules such as "Do not kill" and "Do not steal." These rules are absolute and clear; you follow them, or you do not. In contrast, positive duties are openended. They are reflected in rules such as "Be kind" and "Be compassionate." There are no boundaries or limits on positive duties. They don't specify how kind, to whom, how often, when.

Negative duties, says Nunner-Winkler, reflect the justice orientation of males; females feel more obliged than males to fulfill positive duties, which relate more closely to caring and compassion.

Other Research on Male–Female Differences

Do women and men see the world differently, and make different moral judgments? Some research says yes. Stimpson and colleagues (1991) asked college students to rate 18 adjectives having to do with "interpersonal sensitivity" and "caring." Females consistently rated these adjectives higher in terms of goodness than did males. Similarly, Eisenberg and associates (1991) found that girls' prosocial reasoning was higher than boys in late childhood and adolescence.

But other research finds less clear evidence of sex differences in morality. Muss (1988) reviewed a number of studies and concluded that the distinctions between male and female morality are not very clear. He reasons that if Gilligan's descriptions are correct, it follows that females should, on average, be more altruistic, more empathetic, more concerned with human relations; in contrast, males should be less altruistic. But research on altruism, cooperation, and other forms of prosocial behavior has not found these differences. Note, however, that these findings do not invalidate Gilligan's basic conclusions. It may well be that males and females are equally altruistic, but their altruism might stem from fundamentally different orientations, reflecting very different moralities. Females may, as Gilligan suggests, be altruistic because of their concern

for humanity; males may be just as altruistic because of their adherence to principles and ideals that stress the injustice of being unkind.

One of the important contributions of Gilligan's approach is that it underlines the need to be aware of the possibility that many of our theories and conclusions in human development are not equally applicable to males and females. In Gilligan's (1982) words, the sexes speak *in a different voice*. Neither voice is louder or better; they are simply different.

Implications of Research on Moral Development

Some of the most important implications of research on morality relate to the observation that individuals who operate at the lowest levels (hedonistic) are more likely to be delinquent than those who operate at higher levels. As Gibbs (1987) notes, the delinquent's behavior generally reflects immature moral reasoning and egocentricity. Individuals who operate at higher levels of morality are more likely to be honest and to behave in a generally moral way. Similarly, altruism in children is highly related to level of moral development (Eisenberg, Miller, & Shell, 1991). Even the political choices of adolescents appear to be related to moral development (Thoma, 1993).

Can moral reasoning and behavior be improved?

School Influences

There is considerable evidence that moral judgments and behaviors can be influenced by specific programs in schools (Damon & Colby, 1987). Specific techniques used in these programs include simply discussing moral dilemmas, evaluating the ethical implications of human behavior, role-playing situations involving specific moral dilemmas, modeling procedures, and direct teaching. For example, Stoll and Beller (1993) report that by using a combination of approaches they succeeded in bringing about significant behavior change in a group of student athletes over a three-year period (evident in a decline in fighting, increased caring for others, better classroom behavior, and even an improvement in grades).

A comprehensive program designed to increase prosocial behavior among elementary schoolchildren is described by Battistich and colleagues (1991). This program included activities in the school as well as in the home. Activities were geared toward developing prosocial values and interpersonal understanding, and made extensive use of cooperative learning and discussion of rationales for rules and reasons underlying moral behaviors. The authors report that after five years, program children engage in more spontaneous prosocial behavior in the classroom, have improved perspective-taking skills, and are better at resolving conflicts. They caution, however, that differences between program children and other comparable children are slight and often inconsistent. In addition, it isn't always easy to measure the effects of programs such as this.

Family Influences

In addition to what schools and educators might attempt to do, the values and behaviors of parents are highly instrumental in determining the values of their children (Johnson & McGillicuddy-Delisi, 1983).

Research reveals a clear relationship between parenting styles and children's morality. Specifically, the internalization of moral rules is fostered by two things: (1) the frequent use of discipline that points out the harmful consequences of the child's behavior for others; and (2) frequent expression of parental affection (Hoffman, 1979). Most forms of parental discipline, Hoffman argues, contain elements of "power assertion" and "love-withdrawal." That is, discipline usually involves at least the suggestion of the possibility of loss of parental love as well as something like deprivation of privileges, threats, or physical punishment. The main purpose of this "power assertion," according to Hoffman, is to get the child to stop misbehaving and pay attention. From the point of view of the child's developing morality, however, what is most important is that there now be an accompanying verbal component. The purpose of this verbal component is to influence the child cognitively and emotionally—perhaps by bringing about feelings of guilt or of empathy, and by enabling the child to foresee consequences. The verbal component might simply admonish ("Don't do that"); ideally, however, it should go beyond the admonishment to describe the consequences ("Don't do that because . . ." or "If you do that, the cat might . . .").

The future of this world depends on the morality of our children.

MAIN POINTS

Adolescence as Transition

1.   In many nonindustrialized (discontinuous) societies, passage from childhood to adulthood is marked by rites of passage, often distinguished by separation, training, initiation (sometimes with scarification and circumcision), and induction into the tribe. Continuous societies have no formal rites of passage (there are some experimental programs in some schools and communities), although some writers claim that secondary schools serve a similar purpose.

Physical and Biological Changes

2.   There is a spurt in rate of height and weight increase during adolescence, which occurs about two years earlier for girls than for boys. Boys retain relatively less fat mass and, on average, outperform girls on measures of strength, speed, and endurance, although not in rhythmic activities. The changes of *pubescence* (in primary sexual characteristics, directly related to reproduction; and in secondary sexual characteristics, not directly related to reproduction) lead to *puberty* (sexual maturity).

3.   Early maturation is often advantageous for boys but less so for girls. Pubertal change is most stressful when it puts the adolescent out of step with peers, especially if it is not seen as desirable. Common adolescent concerns include worries about such things as the future, finances, school, appearance, feelings of inferiority, loneliness, the purpose of life, sex, the stability of the parents' marriage, and lack of time.

Nutrition and Eating Disorders

4.   Because of rapid muscular and skeletal growth, adolescents require large amounts of protein and minerals such as calcium. Most also expend a relatively large number of calories, but obesity is still the most common nutritional problem of adolescents in North America.

5.   Anorexia involves significant weight loss, refusal to maintain weight, and distorted body image. Bulimia is defined in terms of recurrent episodes of binge eating (often followed by "purges") that are accompanied by the realization that the behavior is not normal and by feelings of guilt or self-deprecation. Both anorexia and bulimia are most common among adolescent girls (10 times more girls than boys), are probably associated with our sociocultural emphasis on thinness, and can sometimes be treated with antidepressant drugs or with interventions like cognitive-behavioral therapy.

Adolescent Intellectual Development

6.   The intellectual development of the adolescent may culminate in thought that is potentially completely logical, is inferential, deals with the hypothetical as well as with the concrete, and is systematic. Formal operations make possible a type of intense idealism that may be reflected in adolescent frustration or rebellion, as well as in more advanced levels of moral orientation.

7.   Information-processing views of development are concerned with the acquisition of a knowledge base (grows with experience and schooling), the development of information-

processing strategies (becomes better and more appropriate with advancing age), and the development of metacognitive skills (increasing understanding of personal processes involved in learning and remembering).

Adolescent Egocentrism

8. Adolescent egocentrism describes a self-centeredness that leads adolescents to believe that others are highly interested in their thoughts and behaviors (a *self-consciousness*). It is evident in the *imaginary audience* (an imagined collection of people assumed to be concerned with the adolescent) and the *personal fable* (feelings of invulnerability and uniqueness). Adolescents' greater propensity for taking high risks may be linked to their sense of invulnerability and uniqueness.

Moral Development

9. Carroll and Rest describe four components of moral behavior: (1) recognizing a moral problem (*moral sensitivity*), (2) deciding what ought to be done (*moral judgment*), (3) devising a plan of action according to ideals (*moral values*), and (4) implementing the plan (*moral action*). Failure to act morally may be the result of a deficiency in any one of these four components.

10. Piaget describes morality as progressing from a stage of *heteronomy* (to age 9 or 12; responds to external rewards and punishments) to eventual *autonomy* (after age 10 or so; self-determined principles and ideals). Kohlberg describes progression through three levels, each with two stages: *preconventional* (concerned with self—pain, pleasure, obedience, punishment), *conventional* (concerned with the group, with being liked, with conforming to law), and *postconventional* (concerned with abstract principles, ethics, social contracts). The last level is rare, even among adults; most operate at the conventional level ("I'll be a good boy/girl so you will like me; I'll obey the law because it's the law").

11. Gilligan's work suggests that men and women differ in their moral development—that men become progressively more concerned with law and order whereas women respond more to social relationships and to the social consequences of behavior. Various programs using indoctrination, role playing, and modeling have been successful in increasing levels of moral judgment and, sometimes, moral behavior in students. Parental discipline that points out the harmful consequences of the child's behavior for others, and the frequent expression of parental affection, are also important.

FOCUS QUESTIONS: APPLICATIONS

1. Is adolescence a universal phenomenon, or is it largely cultural?
   - Using anthropological studies of puberty rites in other cultures, discuss the notion that adolescence is a culture-bound phenomenon.

2. What are the universal biological features of adolescence?
   - Describe the main physiological changes of pubescence for males and females. Why might the timing of these changes be important?

3. What are the most common eating disorders of adolescence?

   - List the principal criteria of these eating disorders.

4. What is adolescent egocentrism?
   - Define the concepts *imaginary audience* and *personal fable* and illustrate how these might affect adolescent behavior.

5. Is being good or bad a fundamental part of our personalities?
   - Make up a brief story illustrating a moral dilemma and ask several people to select the most desirable response and to justify it. Analyze their responses in terms of Kohlberg's levels and stages.

STUDY TERMS

adolescence   316

adolescent egocentrism   331

adolescent recklessness   332

anorexia nervosa   324

autonomy   336

bulimia nervosa   326

cognitive-behavior therapy   327

continuous societies   316

conventional level   336

discontinuous societies   316

fat mass   319

fat-free mass   319

FURTHER READINGS

An excellent account of contemporary adolescence, viewed against the backdrop of historical changes in adolescence, is provided by:

Kett, J. F. (1977). *Rites of passage: Adolescence in America, 1790 to the present.* New York: Basic Books.

The first of the following two books is a useful collection of chapters dealing with the transition from childhood to early adolescence. Especially pertinent to this chapter are Malina's chapter on physical growth and performance, Eisenberg's chapter on morality and prosocial development, and Lapsley's account of social/cognitive development. The second book describes eating disorders, provides case examples of them, and describes an approach toward treating them:

Montemayor, R., Adams, G. R., & Gullotta, T. P. (Eds.). (1990). *From childhood to adolescence: A transitional period?* (Vol. 2). (*Advances in adolescent development*). Newbury Park, CA: Sage.

Burton, E. (1993). *Eating disorders: Personal construct therapy and change.* New York: John Wiley.

Sugar's book provides a detailed look at the biological and psychological changes experienced by adolescent girls, and examines a wide range of other topics such as the role of the family, delinquency among adolescent girls, and adolescent motherhood:

Sugar, M. (Ed.). (1993). *Female adolescent development.* New York: Brunner/Mazel.

A useful collection of articles that describes various approaches and programs for fostering moral development is:

Kurtines, W. M., & Gewirtz, J. L. (Eds.). (1991). *Handbook of moral behavior and development.* (Vol. 3). (*Application.*) Hillsdale, NJ: Erlbaum.

SOCIAL DEVELOPMENT: ADOLESCENCE

*J*t's all that the young can do for the old, to shock them and keep them up to date.

GEORGE BERNARD SHAW
Fanny's First Play

CHAPTER 12

"When I tell you what J. J. went and done this time," Mr. Delisle announces solemnly to my parents, "you gonna be shocked." He's sitting at the kitchen table with my mom and dad, his hands wrapped around a mug of coffee that's been boiled on the woodstove. They're having one of those grown-up conversations, voices quiet and serious, us supposed to be in bed and out of earshot. Through the crack, I can see the lines of thin blue smoke from the crinkled roll-yer-owns my dad and Mr. Delisle are smoking.

"Always just trying to shock everybody," he continues. "I know the type." Which he probably does, given what his family's like. J. J.'s one of my cousins, so I'm paying attention. One of my wild cousins. Just a couple of months ago, J. J., who's 15, talked Paul and another guy into stealing the police chief's car and driving it into my grandmother's chicken coop— where it stayed all night with the windows open, which the chickens thought was just fine, but not the chief.

Another time, J. J. got a bunch of us to dig out the sand from under the wheels of Mr. Westlock's Ford where it was parked behind the dunes along the lake, so that in the end, even Bouchard's tractor had trouble pulling it out. Mr. Westlock, who was our school principal, was somewhere out in the dunes at the time; so was Miss Ryan, who was, for a short while, secretary at the school. Mr. Westlock said he'd never forgive J. J.

But what Mr. Delisle says next stuns me breathless. "J. J.'s pregnant," he says. "Knocked up. Bread's in the oven." I can't believe it. I always thought J. J.'s wildness was a male kind of wildness—loud and tough—and certainly not feminine enough to become pregnant, for crying out loud.

THIS CHAPTER

It wasn't so much because J. J.'s pregnancy was unexpected that we were shocked; it was because we were products of our families, of our religion, of our close-knit peer system—all of which had conspired to produce a generation of adolescents and adults whose values condemned premarital intercourse, and whose morality was profoundly offended and scandalized by teenage pregnancy. We felt shame for my cousin. Had we been products of another context, we might have reacted very differently.

This chapter looks at adolescent social development, not only in the North American context, but also in other more universal contexts. It deals with the evolution of the self, with emerging gender roles, with sexual beliefs and behaviors, and with some manifestastions of adolescent turmoil and rebellion.

Keep in mind that change is fundamental through the entire lifespan. Our attitudes and our values are not fixed immutably, bound always to reflect the social, religious, political, educational, and family contexts from which we emerged at adolescence.

Even I would no longer be surprised or shocked by my cousin's pregnancy.

Contexts might be seen as exercising an equalizing influence. The pressure of a single ecology tends to produce individuals with similar values and attitudes. Clearly, however, we don't all turn out the same. Not a single one of us is average in every respect. Our selves and our identities are solely our own. Still, they, too, reflect our contexts.

SELF AND IDENTITY

The **self** is crucially important to a study of adolescence—as it is to all of psychology. In fact, Banaji and Prentice (1994) report that in the six years immediately preceding 1993, more than 5,000 articles have been published on the self.

The self is a difficult and complex concept, not easily defined. In one sense, the self is the *essence* of a person—that which makes the person unique. Thus *personality*, which consists of all our traits and characteristics, is the external manifestation of self.

The term **identity** is often used synonymously with *self*. For example, in Erikson's writings on adolescence, *identity* means individuals' own notions about who they are—their *self-definition*. One of the important tasks of adolescence is to develop a strong sense of identity—that is, of *self*.

The Self in Adolescence

In Chapter 10 we spoke of the evaluative aspects of self in childhood, often termed *self-worth* (or *self-esteem*). Self-worth is a reflection of how well one likes oneself in general, and reflects the individual's evaluations of different aspects of the self such as athletic, scholastic, social, physical, and behavioral (Harter, 1983). For those who think being a good athlete is most important for being liked, evaluations of their worth as athletes contributes significantly in determining general feelings of self-worth.

In adolescence, the evaluation of self becomes more cognitive, say Byrne and Shavelson (1987). It is based on a more objective (rather than emotional) understanding of who and what the self is—rather than mainly on how well adolescents like themselves or how competent they think they are in important areas.

Self-Image and the Offer Questionnaire

The term *self-image* is used extensively in adolescent research. It means something very similar to *self-esteem* or *self-worth*. Thus the *Offer Self-Image Questionnaire*, a widely used instrument for assessing self-image, has teenagers report on their attitudes toward and feelings about themselves in a number of different areas (Offer, Ostrov, & Howard, 1981).

Offer's Facets of Self
Like Harter (1983), Offer assumes that the adolescent has a multiplicity of selves that can be considered and evaluated separately:

- *Psychological self.* Reflects adolescents' emotions, their conceptions of their bodies, and their ability to control impulses.

- *Social self.* Consists of adolescents' perceptions of their relationships with others, as well as their morals and their goals.

- *Sexual self.* Reflects attitudes and feelings about sexual experiences and behavior.

- *Familial self.* Consists of adolescents' feelings and attitudes toward parents and other members of their family.

- *Coping self.* Reflects psychological adjustment and how effectively the adolescent functions in the outside world.

The Offer questionnaire investigates these five facets of self by presenting adolescents with a series of statements (for example, "Being together with other people

One of the most important aspects of adolescent development is the development of high self-esteem. Teenagers who like themselves tend, also, to be liked by others. And those who are liked by others tend to have positive self-images.

TABLE 12.1
Facets of Self in the Offer Self-Image Questionnaire

Important Aspects of Self	Relevant Self-Evaluative Questions
Psychological self	Do I like my body? Am I in control of myself? What are my wishes? My feelings? My fantasies?
Social self	Am I friendly? Outgoing? Do people like me? What kind of morals do I have? What are my aspirations? Am I a loner?
Sexual self	How do I feel about sex? What do I think of pornography? Am I sexually attracted to others? Sexually attractive to them? Comfortable with my sexuality?
Familial self	How do I feel about my parents? Home? Siblings? Other relatives? Do I prefer to stay home? Do people at home like me? Need me? Want me?
Coping self	How effective am I? How well do I cope with what others demand? What school demands? What I demand? Am I well adjusted? Reasonably happy? How decisive am I?

gives me a good feeling") and having them select one of six alternatives relating to how well the statement describes them (ranging from *describes me very well* to *does not describe me at all*). (See Table 12.1.) Each descriptor in the questionnaire is worded both positively and negatively.

The Offer questionnaire was developed more than 20 years ago (scoring procedures have changed since then) and has now been given to tens of thousands of adolescents. Results provide important data concerning the adolescent experience.

In a massive study, appropriate translations of the Offer Self-Image Questionnaire were administered to 5,938 adolescents in 10 different countries (Australia, Bangladesh, Hungary, Israel, Italy, Japan, Taiwan, Turkey, former West Germany, and the United States) (Offer et al., 1988). One of the objectives was to compare adolescents' self-images in each of these countries, and arrive at a better understanding of what is universal about adolescence in today's world and what might be specific to given cultural contexts. Adolescents included in the study were

TABLE 12.2
*Sexual Self: Sample Items Showing Consistent Cross-National Differences Across Age and Gender**

Item	Percent Endorsement								
	Australia	*Bangladesh*	*Hungary*	*Israel*	*Italy*	*Taiwan*	*Turkey*	*United States*	*West Germany*
Dirty jokes are fun at times.	82	33	39	78	69	43	19	78	69
I think that girls/boys find me attractive.	53	63	58	68	55	41	59	73	63
Sexually I am way behind.	20	26	11	10	7	33	19	24	11
Thinking or talking about sex scares me.	7	50	13	6	7	27	22	10	6
Sexual experiences give me pleasure.	67	44	65	72	67	22	49	74	67
Having a girl-/boyfriend is important to me.	69	77	68	75	76	52	74	73	82

* Items presented (1) were on a scale on which at least one country was consistently high (or low) in all four age-by-gender cells and (2) were consistently high (or low) for that country for that scale. Consistently high (or low) was defined in terms of being in the upper (or lower) third of nine countries in all four age-by-gender cells. Percentages shown are the average percent endorsement for that item for the country across four age-by-gender cells.

SOURCE: From *The Teenage World: Adolescents' Self-Image in Ten Countries* by D. Offer, E. Ostrov, K. Howard, and R. Atkinson, 1988, New York: Plenum. Reprinted by permission of the author and publisher.

both male and female, classified into two age groups: younger (ages 13–15) and older (ages 16–19).

The Universal Adolescent

What is similar about adolescence in these 10 countries? A surprising number of things. The *"universal adolescent,"* to use Offer and associates' phrase, resembles most other adolescents in some ways with respect to each of the major facets of self-image:

- *Psychological.* The universal adolescent is usually happy and optimistic, and enjoys being alive.

- *Social.* The universal adolescent enjoys the company of others, is caring and compassionate, and places great value on school, education, and preparation for adult work.

- *Sexual.* The universal adolescent is confident about the sexual self, and willing to talk and think about sex.

- *Familial.* The universal adolescent expresses strongly positive feelings toward parents, a high degree of satisfaction with home lives, and good feelings about relationships at home.

- *Coping.* The universal adolescent expresses confidence in his or her ability to deal with life, and feels talented and able to make decisions.

The Context-Bound Adolescent

But there are differences, too, across these cultures. Adolescents from Bangladesh, for example, were consistently lower on impulse control. Forty-two percent of the Ben-

gali (Bangladesh) adolescents reported they were constantly afraid; many admitted feeling inferior to other people, as well as feeling sadder, lonelier, and more vulnerable. Why? Context seems the most plausible explanation. This was the poorest of the countries sampled. Lack of economic opportunities and adequate medical care, coupled with widespread disease and starvation, might well lead to feelings of vulnerability and fear.

Other cross-national differences included the very high value placed on vocational and educational goals by American adolescents and the very low value placed on them by Hungarian and Israeli teenagers—probably because vocational choice is a complex and important developmental task for American adolescents. For most Israeli and Hungarian adolescents, choices are more limited or are largely predetermined by society.

Not surprisingly, there were marked differences in the sexual attitudes of adolescents from some countries. In particular, Turkish and Taiwanese adolescents reported extremely conservative sexual attitudes and behaviors—clear evidence of the extent to which such attitudes are influenced by cultures (see Table 12.2). Similarly, Israeli adolescents reported the most positive family relationships, again not very surprising given the emphasis on family and community.

Sturm und Drang?

G. Stanley Hall believed that adolescence is a period of **sturm und drang** (storm and stress) for most adolescents in all cultures because the mood swings, the irritability, the conflict of this period are related directly to a dramatic in-

Contrary to some earlier beliefs, the identity crises of adolescence are not invariably marked by "storm and stress." Many explore life's alternatives and reach adult commitments with little apparent turmoil and conflict.

Stress and Life Change

A number of researchers have suggested that one of the main reasons for higher **stress** during this period is that adolescents experience more significant changes in their lives than do younger children (Mullis et al., 1993). To investigate this belief, Larson and Ham (1993) gave questionnaires to 483 fifth to ninth graders and their parents to obtain a measure of life events. They also obtained a measure of students' emotions by having them rate their moods at various times. There were two especially important findings: (1) Young adolescents experienced significantly more life-change events than preadolescents, many of them family based (getting along worse with parents; someone going to the hospital; someone in the family being in trouble with the law). In addition, they experienced more school-based changes (disciplinary action; changing schools; being suspended), as well as relationship-based changes (breaking up with a girl- or boyfriend), and other events like being sick or being cut from a sports team. And (2) young adolescents reported significantly more *negative affect* than preadolescents. Larson and Ham (1993) conclude: "Higher rates of daily distress experienced in adolescence may be partly attributed to the greater number of negative life events encountered" (p. 130). This pattern of negative affect in response to negative life experiences, they add, "is not the universal storm and stress described by early theorists" (p. 138). "But it is experienced by a substantial minority and it does suggest that for some early adolescence is a pivotal point in the development of positive versus negative adjustment to daily life" (p. 138).

The Development of Identity

The notion that one of the most important aspects of all development is the development of a sense of personal identity is shared by many psychologists, including Erik Erikson (discussed in Chapter 2). Recall that the fifth of

crease in sex hormones. But when Buchanan, Eccles, and Becker (1992) examined the research, they found this supposition to be untrue. Adolescents are not victims of raging hormones, they claim; in fact, nonbiological, contextual factors are more important influences on adolescent moods and behavior than are hormones. Not surprisingly, if the Offer and associates (1988) cross-national study were to be summarized in a single paragraph, it might read something like this: Contrary to what has been a popular view of adolescence since G. Stanley Hall's pronouncements about the storm and stress of this period, adolescence throughout the world is predominantly a positive, nonturbulent, energetic, growth-filled period.

At the same time, approximately 15 percent of North American adolescents describe themselves as anxious, depressed, confused, and emotionally empty (Offer, Ostrov, & Howard, 1984). This percentage is, in fact, significantly higher than for preadolescents.

Erikson's eight developmental stages is termed *identity versus role diffusion*. By the term *identity*, Erikson (1968) means a sort of *wholeness* that derives from the past but that also includes future goals and plans. The primary developmental crisis facing the adolescent, says Erikson, is the conflict between accepting, choosing, or discovering an identity and the diffusion of the adolescent's energies resulting from conflict and doubt concerning choice of identities. As Nightingale and Wolverton (1993) note, adolescents don't often have carefully prepared, socially approved, and highly appreciated roles in contemporary industrialized societies. As a result, they are left to struggle alone with the problems of establishing these roles—in other words, with the problems of developing an identity.

Resolution of adolescents' identity crises can take a variety of forms—the most common of which is the selection of an identity that conforms to societal norms and to individuals' expectations of themselves. Erikson points out that one of the major social functions of prolonged adolescence is simply to serve as a breathing space (an **adolescent moratorium,** in his terms) during which adolescents can experiment with different roles in their quest for identity. He is not particularly alarmed that some of these roles constitute what he terms *negative identities* (delinquency and other forms of rebellion, for example), because in most cases they are temporary, eventually giving way to more acceptable and happier identities.

Erikson's description of this developmental stage has been clarified by Marcia's investigations of the development of identity in adolescence (Kroger, 1993a; Marcia 1966; 1993). Building on Erikson's work, Marcia identifies four distinct types of identity status on the basis of whether the adolescent has undergone (or is currently undergoing) a crisis and on whether a commitment has been made to a specific identity.

Identity Diffusion

Adolescents in a state of *identity diffusion* are characterized by a total lack of commitment, as well as no experience with an identity crisis. These are individuals whose political, social, and religious beliefs are ambiguous or nonexistent, and who have no vocational aspirations. Individuals who have not developed a mature sense of identity by late adolescence are sometimes recognizable as full-time fun seekers (what Marcia calls "playboys") or as disturbed individuals characterized by high anxiety, low self-esteem, and lack of self-confidence (Marcia, 1980).

Foreclosure

Foreclosure is a strong commitment to an identity without having experienced a crisis. Foreclosure is clearly illustrated in instances where political, religious, and vocational decisions have been made for the adolescent and are accepted without question. This is often the case, for example, in close-knit religious or political communities where the roles and the beliefs of each individual are determined

by others. It is also the case when adolescents simply allow parents or, sometimes, peers to make important identity-related decisions for them. These adolescents do not go through an identity crisis. Their most striking characteristics appear to be high adherence to authoritarian values (obedience and respect of authority) (Marcia, 1980).

Moratorium Individuals

According to Erikson, one of the important functions of adolescence is to serve as a time during which it is not essential to be fully committed to one lifestyle, one vocation, one set of beliefs—a *moratorium* during which the adolescent can explore the tremendous variety of alternatives that might be available. Moratorium adolescents have vague, changing commitments; in this sense, they are in crisis. But it is a useful crisis for most adolescents, because in the absence of a moratorium during which to explore, there is a danger of premature commitment (as in the case of *foreclosure*) or of continuing lack of commitment (as in identity diffusion).*

Identity Achieved

Adolescents who have experienced a crisis (a moratorium) and made a choice (a commitment) are described as *identity achieved*. And among the choices that are most important for identity formation, notes Kroger (1993b), are those that have to do with occupation or career. Marcia (1980) reports that adolescents who have achieved an

---

*Some, like Côté and Levine (1988), point out that the negative aspects of adopting a "ready-made" identity have been unfairly emphasized. On the positive side, some of the "foreclosed" choices that adolescents adopt are admirable. My grandmother agreed. "Look at Cecile," she said, as proof. When adolescence had barely struck, Cecile, J. J.'s sister, decided to become a nun—which she has been ever since. J. J. has since been many things, but never a nun.

Dependence on parents decreases during the teen years; and allegiance to peers increases. The lad with the pointed hair is not imitating his father's coiffure.

(See Table 12.3.)

TABLE 12.3
*Marcia's Descriptions of Identity Status in Terms of Crisis and Commitment**

Status	Characteristics
Identity diffusion	No crisis; no commitment (ambiguous belief systems; no vocational commitment)
Foreclosure	No crisis; strong commitment (commitment predetermined by political, social, or religious affiliation)
Moratorium	Crisis; no commitment (period of exploration of alternatives)
Identity achieved	Crisis finished; commitment made

* A *crisis* is defined as a period of active and conscious decision making during which various alternatives are examined and evaluated. *Commitment* is acceptance of a combination of political, social, religious, or vocational alternatives.

TABLE 12.4
Three Stages of Socialization

Stages	Time Frame	Conflict
High dependence on parents	Early childhood	Low
Decreasing dependence on parents and increasing independence	Late childhood–early adolescence	Increasing
High independence	Late adolescence–early adulthood	Decreasing

identity are more independent, respond better to stress, have more realistic goals, and have higher self-esteem than adolescents in any of the other three categories. However, he also emphasizes that identities are never static and absolutely permanent. Even when the adolescent appears to have achieved an identity, further changes often occur. For example, some college students move in and out of identity crises before finally achieving a final commitment. And, as we will see in Chapter 13, the Peter Pans among us may never resolve our identity crises. (See Table 12.3.)

SOCIAL DEVELOPMENT IN CONTEXT

The development of self and identity do not occur in a vacuum, but rather in a specific social context—a social ecology describable in terms of a wealth of interactions and influences. And at every age throughout childhood and adolescence, peers and parents are a fundamental part of this context.

Parent–Adolescent Relationships

Developmental psychologists generally agree that one of the things that happens throughout childhood and especially at adolescence is an *emotional distancing* of child from parents (Grotevant, 1994). Thus, at the risk of oversimplifying, we can describe the socialization of the adolescent in terms of three stages based on changing roles of parents and peers (see Table 12.4). The first, a preadolescent stage, is marked by the child's high social, emotional, and physical dependence on parents, and is characterized by low conflict. The second, spanning early adolescence, involves increasing independence—that is, increasing *emotional distancing*—and often increasing conflict as well. And the third, beginning in later adolescence, is marked by declining conflict and the achievement of relative independence.

In spite of the near universality of the adolescent's emotional distancing from parents, it would be misleading to assume that adolescents and parents eventually end up far apart emotionally. The expression *emotional distancing* as a description of changing adolescent–parent relationships is accurate and useful only as an indication of adolescent emotional dependence on parents *relative to* that characteristic of the preadolescent. In fact, adolescents and parents typically remain very closely attached emotionally. This attachment, Grotevant (1994) explains, serves as a *buffer* for adolescents, protecting them from some of the stresses and anxieties of growing up and adjusting to a complex world.

Parenting Adolescents

Much of parenting involves protecting children from their own immaturity. For young children, whose immaturity is clearly reflected in their dependence, this role poses little conflict. But for adolescents, whose immaturity is less (and who, in most cases, do not recognize their immaturity), parenting is a far more difficult function.

Other important parental responsibilities vis-à-vis adolescents, says Alvy (1987), include providing basic resources and care, guiding and supporting development (providing opportunities for intellectual, social, emotional, and spiritual growth; fostering self-esteem), and advocacy (supporting and helping adolescents in relation to institutions or groups such as schools and employers).

There are several reasons, suggest Small and Eastman (1991), why rearing adolescents in contemporary society might be more difficult and might lead to more conflict than in the past. First, the period of adolescence has increased significantly in all industrialized countries. Hurrelmann (1990) notes that most adolescents attend schools and postsecondary institutions through their teen years and beyond, and many remain economically dependent on the family for all or much of that time. This has led to greater uncertainty about the responsibilities of parents. Parents have also become confused about how best to prepare adolescents for entry into an increasingly complicated and rapidly changing world with competing sources of information and values. There are also more dangers about which to worry—high-risk and potentially harmful activities, substances, and influences, such as drugs and radical cults. Finally, increases in family breakup and increased mobility of family members have led to an erosion of the family, so that parents of adolescents have fewer sources of advice or support.

Partly because of the responsibilities and difficulties of parenting adolescents, and partly because of the changing roles and relationships of parents and adolescents, this period frequently involves conflict.

Parent–Adolescent Conflict

Several decades ago, the predominant view was that conflict was the main characteristic of parent–adolescent relationships. As Kaplan (1984) put it, "The irrevocable giving-up of the love relationships of childhood entails an extended and painful emotional struggle" (p. 141). The more current view, however, is that although *parent–adolescent conflict* is not uncommon, parents continue to have a significant influence on the thinking and behavior of their adolescents. Interestingly, the greatest conflict occurs in early adolescence (during puberty) and often declines in later adolescence. The reasons for this, suggest Paikoff and Brooks-Gunn (1991), is that conflict typically arises because the changing needs and interests of the adolescent require a readjustment in the family system. Once this adjustment has been made, conflict declines.

Part of the "turbulence on the home front," say Bibby and Posterski (1992), relates to the adolescent's increasing allegiance to peers. In their survey of nearly 4,000 adolescents, freedom and friendship ranked first and second in terms of importance; family life was a distant ninth (see Interactive Figure 12.1).

Peer Groups

"Adolescents have an urgent need to belong," says Drummond (1991, p. 283). Not only do the peer group and friends satisfy emotional needs, but they are an important source of information and opportunity for socialization. The adolescent peer group is, in many ways, like a separate culture that eases transition from childhood to adulthood.

Adolescent peer groups vary in size, interests, social backgrounds, and structure. They might consist of two or three like-sexed persons (buddies, pals, best friends), larger groups of like-sexed individuals, or couples. Yet another type of peer group comprises persons of both sexes who "hang out" together. In addition, there are gangs, close-knit groups of individuals distinguished by their conflict with authority (more about gangs later). Most adolescents belong to several groups at the same time. Indeed, friends (who are typically part of the peer groups) are the adolescent's most common source of enjoyment (Bibby & Posterski, 1992).

A number of distinctly different peer groups appear to be common to most contemporary high schools. For example, Brown and colleagues (1993) studied 3,781 students in six different U.S. high schools in an effort to identify their peer group affiliations. They were also interested in determining the extent to which parents are a source of influence in the lives of contemporary adoles-

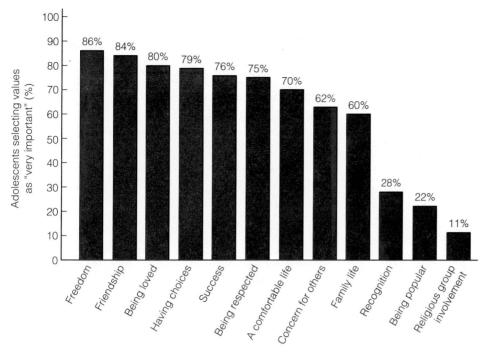

INTERACTIVE FIGURE 12.1

Percentage of Canadian adolescents selecting each value as "very important." Most of us go through life without thinking very much about our values, without trying to sort them out. Our values are reflected in what we choose to do and in how we behave rather than in conscious decisions we make about what is important and what isn't. They are more concrete than abstract. Yet there might be some benefit in contemplating abstract values, both in terms of self-knowledge and in terms of guiding our real-life choices. One way of doing this is to rank values such as those given here in terms of their personal importance. Do so, and then compare your ranking with that of the nearly 4,000 adolescents whose responses are represented in Figure 12.1. (From Bibby & Posterski, 1992, p. 15.)

Having friends and being loved were two of the three most important things in the lives of the nearly 4,000 adolescents studied by Bibby and Posterski; freedom was the other. Not surprisingly, acceptance by peers and the development of close relationships are among adolescents' greatest sources of joy and self-esteem.

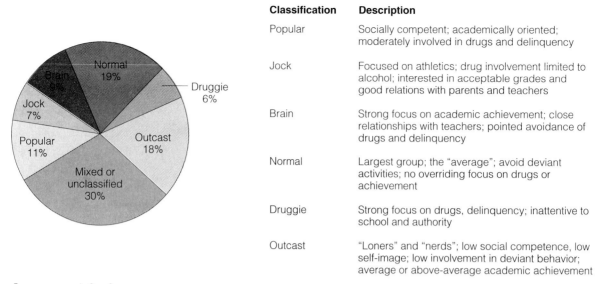

Classification	Description
Popular	Socially competent; academically oriented; moderately involved in drugs and delinquency
Jock	Focused on athletics; drug involvement limited to alcohol; interested in acceptable grades and good relations with parents and teachers
Brain	Strong focus on academic achievement; close relationships with teachers; pointed avoidance of drugs and delinquency
Normal	Largest group; the "average"; avoid deviant activities; no overriding focus on drugs or achievement
Druggie	Strong focus on drugs, delinquency; inattentive to school and authority
Outcast	"Loners" and "nerds"; low social competence, low self-image; low involvement in deviant behavior; average or above-average academic achievement

FIGURE 12.2

"Crowds" in the typical U.S. high school. These six groups accounted for 70 percent of the 3,781 students who were rated in a study of six high schools. (Based on Brown et al., 1993.)

cents. On the basis of their research, they identified six distinct peer groups (or "crowds") in these schools.

All schools, Brown and colleagues (1993) note, have an "elite" peer group composed of two distinct crowds. On the one hand are the "jocks," consisting of students committed to athletics and not overly focused on academics, but who are nevertheless interested in pleasing teachers and in getting acceptable grades. Their interest in drugs is generally limited to alcohol. Also among the elite group are the "populars," who are more strongly committed to academics than the jocks, but who are also "moderately" interested in drug use and in delinquent behavior.

At the opposite end of the scale in terms of social status are a group labeled "outcasts" and made up of "loners" and "nerds"—children who are socially awkward and inept, and whose social status is very low. Other fringe groups include some smaller groups described by Brown and associates (1993) as more "alienated." They include "druggies," "greasers," and others who are heavily involved in drug use or delinquency, and who are often rebellious in school and society. Their values and behavior stand in sharp contrast to those of the "brains" or "eggheads" who are strongly focused on academic achievement, who value close relationships with parents and authority, and who carefully avoid drugs and delinquency. Their social standing is "marginal."

Finally, the largest peer group is composed of "normals." Brown and colleagues (1993) note that these children tend to avoid deviant activities but are not clearly or strongly enough focused on any other activity to be identified as belonging to another distinct group (see Figure 12.2).

INTERVIEW

SUBJECT
Female; age 14; ninth grade. (concerning friends)

"I have quite a lot of good friends. Lana is probably my best friend. And Sherri. The three of us always sit together in school and we go roller skating. Jackie used to be with us too, but now she's going around with Phil. He's a hunk!

I have lots of other friends at band and at school, too. I think that's one of the most important things in life, is your friends. I would always be willing to do whatever I can for my friends and I'm sure they would for me, too. That's what being friends is about."

Perhaps the most revealing finding of the Brown investigation is that parents play a critical role in determining their children's most likely peer affiliations. Not only are parents instrumental in shaping their children's social skills and values, but they also exercise considerable influence over peer choice through their selection of neighborhoods in which to live as well as through their selection of schools, school programs, and leisure activities (such as sports). Brown and colleagues (1993) report that some specific parenting practices—such as monitoring the adolescent's activities, encouraging achievement (academic or athletic), and being involved in joint decision making with the adolescent—are closely reflected in adolescent behav-

Gender roles define patterns of behavior commonly associated with being male or female. Our gender-role stereotypes see males as aggressive, boisterous, and physical—and females as more passive, gentler, more home oriented. Increasingly, however, our gender-based stereotypes need revising. For example, we do not, in our stereotyped images, see young teenagers like this 12-year-old girl and 14-year-old boy, holding hands and sliding in the mud just for the pure joy of it.

iors and values, especially with regard to things like academic achievement and drug use.

The influence of parents on adolescents may also be evident in the observation that "brains" tended to be overrepresented among children living in intact families, and that children from stepfamilies or one-parent families were underrepresented among "brains" but overrepresented among "druggies." As Brown and associates (1993) put it, "Parenting practices and family background characteristics cannot determine a teenager's crowd affiliation, but their influence should not be discounted."

GENDER AND GENDER ROLES

Probably the most salient of all human characteristics are those that indicate membership in one of two categories: male or female. At one level, these are biological categories, easily identified and defined. But at another level,

they are psychological and sociological, and less clearly defined. They are evident in the sometimes dramatic (and sometimes very subtle) differences in the behaviors that are expected of males and females—hence that are considered masculine or feminine. These differences in behavior, together with the attitudes and personality characteristics associated with them, are what define **gender roles** (sex roles). **Gender** refers specifically to the psychological characteristics typically associated with biological sex. Thus there are two sexes, male and female, and two corresponding genders, masculine and feminine. Bem (1974) also argues that there are individuals who share relatively equally the characteristics of both genders, and labels these individuals **androgynous.** The learning of sex-appropriate behavior (of gender roles) is referred to as **gender typing.** Explanations of gender typing are presented in Chapter 8.

Common Gender-Role Stereotypes

Very early in life, children begin to learn about the behaviors their culture finds acceptable and desirable for their sex. For example, in North America, boys might learn to play with toy trucks and guns, to be interested in wrestling and play fighting, and to engage in boisterous, loud sports. Girls might learn to play with dolls and houses, to be interested in arts and books, and to like to cook and sew. These, and many other activities and interests, are parts of the **sexual stereotypes** that characterize our societies.

Sexual stereotypes are preconceived, typically unquestioned beliefs about male–female differences. In some cases, they are superficial and trivial; in others, they are more fundamental. Some might reflect basic, undeniable anatomical differences; others are influenced more by context. In general, North American gender roles associate the male figure with active, work-oriented, and positively evaluated activities and the female figure with more passive, home-oriented, and less positively evaluated roles (Long, 1991). Boys and girls still have little difficulty in identifying personality characteristics that are stereotypically masculine or feminine.

Gender-Role Preference

Not only do children agree as to what boys and girls should be like, but also they agree that masculine characteristics are more desirable. "If you woke up tomorrow and discovered that you were a girl, how would your life be different?" Tavris and Baumgartner (1983) asked a group of American boys. "Terrible," "A catastrophe," "I would immediately commit suicide" were some typical answers. But when girls were posed the same question—that is, what would happen if they discovered they had become a boy?—they responded quite differently: "Great," "Now I can do what I want," "Now I can be happy." Patterns of responses were clear: Girls often responded positively to the "change-sex" question; boys did so extremely rarely.

This difference was evident in children as young as age 8 and as old as age 17. Sexual stereotypes appear to be learned very young and to be very pervasive.

Five years later, Intons-Peterson (1988) asked the same question of 11-, 14-, and 18-year-old Swedish and American adolescents to see if there had been any measurable changes in the intervening years. Her expectation was that gender stereotypes would not be as marked in Sweden as in the United States and that male and female reactions to the sex-change question would not reflect as decided a preference for the male sex (because of the Swedish government's explicit, family-based social program aimed at equalizing the sexes).

As expected, the male gender in the United States was still associated with the "hard-driving, macho image of lore" (Intons-Peterson, 1988); females were seen as less aggressive, gentler. And although these differences were also apparent in the Swedish samples, they were not as extreme. Swedish samples were more likely to view women as capable and effective and men as being emotional and tender.

Responses to the sex-change question were essentially identical to what they had been in 1983. Although a majority of females were content with their gender, most responded in terms of the positive aspects of becoming male. They wrote that they would now enjoy athletics more, that they would travel and stay out later at night, that they would study less but think more about a career. They also felt that they would be more aggressive and less emotional, that they would be less concerned about their appearance, and that they would need to become interested in fighting and in "showing off."

Most males still responded very negatively to the thought of becoming female. They saw themselves becoming burdened by menstruation, and concerned with contraception and pregnancy. They expected to be more passive, weaker, and restricted more to indoor activities. They thought, too, that they would become more interested in permanent sexual relationships and more emotional.

Interestingly, these *gender differences* are more apparent for the 18-year-olds than for the younger group, especially in Sweden. This might be evidence that attempts to eradicate sex stereotypes and to achieve greater gender equality are beginning to have an effect.

Gender Differences

Gender stereotypes reflect widely held beliefs about gender—in other words, they reveal our prevalent sexual stereotypes. Some of these beliefs may well be accurate, and others not.

Biological Differences

There are obvious biological and physical differences related to anatomical sex. We know that males are taller and heavier than females (except for a brief period in late childhood), and that females mature approximately two years earlier than males. Other biological differences include the fact that, beginning from puberty, male blood pressure is higher than that of females; female heart rate is between two and six beats higher than that of males; fat-free mass in males is relatively higher than in females, as is metabolic rate; and among males, physical energy is greater, recuperative time is less, and muscle fatigue is slower.

In many ways, however, males are the weaker sex—even from the very beginning. About 50 percent more sperm bear the male (Y) than the female (X) sex chromosome, but there aren't 150 male infants born for every 100 females because the male sperm is more fragile. And so it continues throughout life. At birth, there are about 105 males for every 100 females, but males are more vulnerable to most infections and diseases, so that by adolescence, numbers of males and females surviving are approximately equal; by age 65, there are almost 150 females living for every 100 males (U.S. Bureau of the Census, 1994).

Not only are males more fragile and less long-lived, but they are also more prone to learning, speech, and behavior disorders, greatly overrepresented among the retarded and the mentally disordered, and more prone to bed-wetting, night terrors, and hyperactivity (Shepherd-Look, 1982).

Psychological Differences

Biological differences between the sexes are generally clear and agreed upon (although, even here, there are many exceptions). Psychological differences are far less obvious and far more controversial.

In an early review and summary of much of the important research in this area, Maccoby and Jacklin (1974) had concluded that there are clear differences between the sexes in four areas: verbal ability (favoring females); visual/spatial ability (favoring males); mathematical ability (favoring males); and aggressiveness (lower among females).

But at least some of these gender differences no longer seem as clear in the mid-1990s as they did in 1974—evidence perhaps that because they resulted mainly from socialization processes, they reflected a cultural context that has changed dramatically in the last several decades.

Verbal Ability

For example, the once-apparent greater verbal ability of females relative to males no longer appears very general, is usually very small, and is not apparent at early ages (Shepherd-Look, 1982). In fact, in a large-scale survey of performance in high school (and beyond), Marsh (1989) found no significant differences between boys and girls on measures of verbal performance. Girls in this sample were somewhat more likely than boys to take further English courses; but they were no less likely to take mathematics courses.

Visual/Spatial Ability

Males often do better than females in tests of visual/spatial ability after early adolescence. Tests of spatial ability require that the subject visualize three-dimensional objects and be able to rotate or otherwise manipulate them mentally. As Chipman (1988) notes, there isn't a great deal of information about the importance of spatial ability, although some researchers argue that this gender difference may be related to differences in mathematics achievement (Pearson & Ferguson, 1989).

Mathematics and Science

There is some evidence that males perform better than females in mathematical skills *from adolescence onward* (Randhawa, 1991), as well as in science (Erickson & Farkas, 1991). Differences are most evident at the highest levels of mathematics achievement where males consistently outnumber females. Hedges and Friedman (1993) report that there are about twice as many males as females in the top 5 percent in tests of mathematical ability—and about six times more in the top 1 percent. Interestingly, gender differences in mathematics and science are negligible in the earlier years. Hence, the fact that females do not continue to do as well may be explained by culturally determined interest and motivational factors (Kaiser-Messmer, 1993).

Significantly, in the same way that gender differences in verbal performance have declined and, in many instances, completely disappeared, so too have differences in mathematics performance. Hyde, Fennema, and Lamon (1990) did a meta-analysis of 100 studies in this area, involving more than 3 million subjects. Their conclusion? Girls actually show a slight superiority in mathematical computation in elementary and junior high school; but differences in favor of males emerge in high school, and are most evident in problem solving.

Aggression

As we saw in Chapter 8, males are *generally* more aggressive than females. Following yet another meta-analysis (there has been a great deal of interest, and consequently of research, in this area), Hyde and Linn (1986) conclude that males are, *on average*, more aggressive both physically and verbally. This gender difference is assumed to have a biological as well as a cultural basis. But even if aggressiveness is related to anatomy and to hormones (hence to genes), it does not follow that observed gender differences would continue to exist in the same form in different sociocultural contexts.

In conclusion, studies of gender differences in academic achievement reveal some small and declining differences largely explainable in terms of culturally based interests and opportunities. They do not provide data that would be sufficient for making inferences about specific individuals. Linn and Hyde (1989) point out that gender differences in height and strength are far more significant and far more stable. Interestingly, so are gender differences in career accessibility and in earning power—as well as in social attitudes toward careers and roles most appropriate for males and females (Morinaga et al., 1993). Other than perhaps for aggressiveness, not only are psychological gender differences very small, but they may not be very important. Perhaps it would be far more useful to try to understand how interests and abilities develop and interact.

SEX

Sex is an area of profound preoccupation for many adolescents[*]—an area that consumes a great deal of their time and energy.

In psychology, sex is many things. To begin with, of course, it is simply a category—male or female—that is usually easily defined by some obvious biological differences. But it is also a psychoanalytic term; according to Freud, sex is the source of energy that motivates all of us from birth to death. *Sex* is more than a psychoanalytic term or a biological dichotomy. It can mean (as it does in this section) nothing more or less complicated than the physical union between male and female, or variations thereof, or the wish thereto, or the fantasy thereof.

Sexual Beliefs and Behavior

There have been some major changes in sexual attitudes and behavior in recent decades. These are reflected in three areas, says Zani (1991): standards, attitudes toward sexual behavior, and age of sexual initiation.

The Double Standard

The old *sexual double standard* has largely crumbled. This standard said, basically, "Boys will be boys, but girls, well, they should behave." In the 1950s, when Kinsey and his associates (1948; 1953) first began to research sexual activity, the standard was in full force. At that time, most males reported experiencing orgasm before marriage, but only 30 percent of females reported doing so. By the mid-1960s, incidence of premarital intercourse among females had risen to about 40 percent—still some distance shy of males' reported 60 percent (Packard, 1968). By the 1980s, however, percentages were about equal at around 75 or 80 (Darling, Kallen, & Van Dusen, 1984); and by the 1990s, females' percentages had increased even more to around 80 to 85 percent (Chase-Lansdale & Brooks-Gunn, 1994) (see Figure 12.3).

Attitudes

Recent decades have seen dramatic changes in *attitudes* toward sexuality. These are reflected not only in the demise of the double standard, but also in an increased openness

---

[*]"Humph! Grown-ups too!" said my grandmother, when she first read this. "Take your Uncle Renald, for example...." But that's another story.

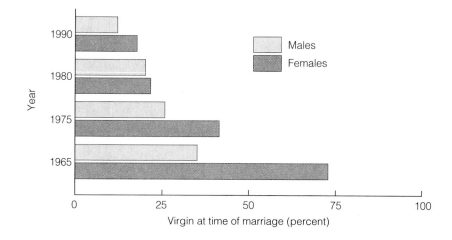

FIGURE 12.3

One manifestation of the sexual revolution: the decline in approximate percentage of people who claim to be virgins at the time of marriage—a more dramatic change for females than for males.

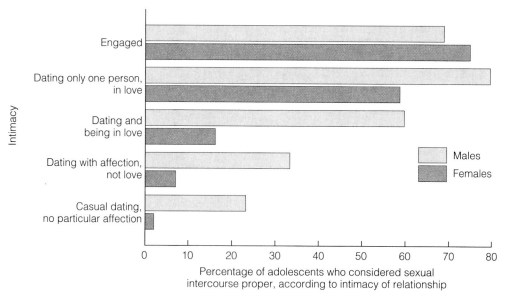

FIGURE 12.4

Percentage of a sample of 238 primarily Roman Catholic adolescents who considered sexual intercourse proper, according to intimacy of relationship. (Based on data from Roche & Ramsbey, 1993.)

about sexuality and in a wider acceptance of premarital sex. This does not mean that sex has become totally casual and matter-of-fact among today's adolescents. In fact, the vast majority of teenagers do not think it is appropriate to have intercourse when dating casually, but more than half believe it proper when in love and dating only one person (Roche & Ramsbey, 1993) (Figure 12.4). For the majority of adolescents, the critical factor is whether the partners have a caring and committed relationship. The new standard holds that sexual activity is permitted for both sexes providing there is affection between partners (Table 12.5). However, male attitudes toward premarital sex among casual acquaintances continue to be more liberal than those of females (Wilson & Medora, 1990).

Age of Initiation

Average age of sexual initiation has declined in recent decades. A study of more than 600 Italian adolescents found that about one third of the girls and one quarter of the boys had had sexual intercourse before age 15 (Zani, 1991). Brooks-Gunn and Furstenberg (1989) report similar findings for the United States, but note that it is not uncommon for teenagers to have sex at 14 or 15 and then not to repeat the activity for another year or more.

Among the most obvious antecedents of sexual activity are the biological changes of pubescence. Changes in hormone levels affect sexual arousal directly; in addition, changes in secondary sexual characteristics, such as breast enlargement in the girl or lowering of the boy's voice, may

TABLE 12.5

What Adolescents Consider Appropriate Dating Behavior*

"If two people on a date like each other, do you think it is all right for them to"	Percentage		
	Male	*Female*	*Total*
Hold hands			
Yes, first date	92	91	92
Yes, after a few dates	7	9	8
No	1	0	0
Kiss			
Yes, first date	84	80	82
Yes, after a few dates	16	19	18
No	0	1	0
Neck			
Yes, first date	59	42	50
Yes, after a few dates	38	52	45
No	3	6	5
Pet			
Yes, first date	42	16	28
Yes, after a few dates	50	63	56
No	8	20	15
Have sexual relations			
Yes, first date	19	3	11
Yes, after a few dates	51	33	42
No	29	59	44
If they love each other	1	5	3

* Based on a survey of 3,600 high school students, aged 15 to 19.

SOURCE: From *The Emerging Generation: An Inside Look at Canada's Teenagers,* by R. W. Bibby and D. C. Posterski, 1985, Irwin Publishing, Inc.. Reprinted by permission from Table 5.1, p. 76.

serve as important sexually linked stimuli. Other important factors linked to age of first sexual intercourse include a number of specific events and behaviors, including parental divorce, drug use, and age of dating (Dorius, Heaton, & Steffan, 1993). Peers also influence whether or not an adolescent is likely to engage in sexual intercourse. Significantly, adolescents typically overestimate the amount of sexual activity engaged in by their peers, and underestimate the age of first intercourse (Roche & Ramsbey, 1993; Zani, 1991). (See Figure 12.5.)

Masturbation

The most common form of sexual outlet for adolescent males and females is **masturbation.** Although contemporary attitudes toward masturbation are that it is normal, pleasurable, and harmless, some adolescents continue to feel guilty and ashamed about masturbating. Males masturbate more frequently than females, and often have more liberal attitudes toward the acceptability of masturbation; college experience tends to have a liberating effect on women's attitudes toward masturbation (Davidson & Darling, 1988).

For males, first ejaculation (spermarche), sometimes through a nocturnal emission or through masturbation or intercourse, is usually the first sign of pubescence. But unlike the girl's menarche, it is often a secretive affair. In Adegoke's (1993) sample of Nigerian boys, only half told someone—usually a friend—about their first ejaculation. Sixty percent of these boys were not prepared for the event. Zani (1991) notes that because of males' reluctance to admit ignorance or innocence in sexual matters, most do not seek information.

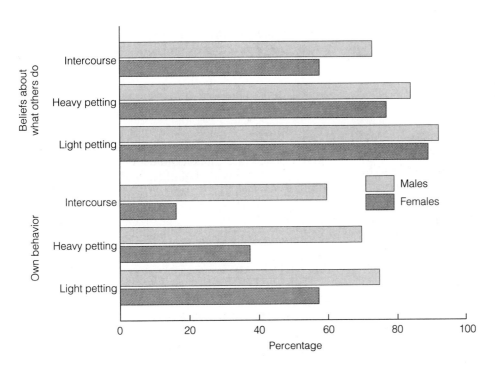

FIGURE 12.5

Teenagers' reported sexual behavior and their beliefs about what others do when dating and in love. (Based on data from Roche & Ramsbey, 1993.)

BIRTHS TO UNMARRIED TEENAGERS

In the United States, an increasing number of infants are being born to unmarried women. In 1970, about 1 in 10 births was to an unmarried mother (10.7 percent); by 1989, the proportion had risen to almost 1 in 4 (27 percent). In 1991, nearly one third of all births to unmarried women were to adolescents aged 15 to 19—some 357,500 infants. This figure represents about one third of all teenage pregnancies. The others are births to married teenagers or are pregnancies terminated by abortion or other fetal loss (see Figures 12.6 and 12.7).

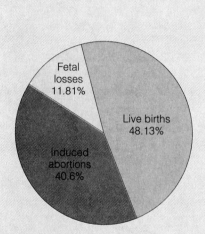

FIGURE 12.6

Pregnancy outcomes for U.S. teenagers (aged 19 or less), 1988. (Based on U.S. Bureau of the Census, 1994, p. 84.)

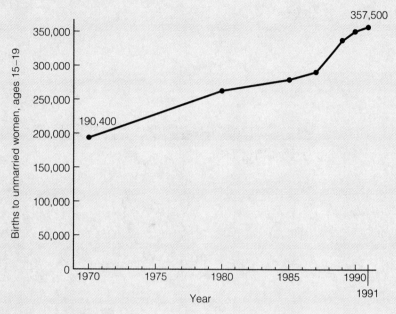

FIGURE 12.7

Births to unmarried mothers aged 15 to 19, 1970–1991. (Based on U.S. Bureau of the Census, 1994, p. 80.)

Adolescent Pregnancy

Estimates suggest that there are as many as 12 million sexually active teenagers in the United States—7 million males and 5 million females. Of the 5 million or so sexually active females, approximately 1 million become pregnant each year (see At a Glance: "Births to Unmarried Teenagers," and Figures 12.6 and 12.7). The teenage birthrate in the United States accounts for 12.5 percent of all births; it also accounts for 26 percent of all abortions (U.S. Bureau of the Census, 1994; see Figure 12.8). Who gets pregnant? Why? What are the outcomes and implications of teenage pregnancy?

Who Gets Pregnant

It's important to note that although teenage pregnancies, by definition, involve teen mothers, it is misleading and inaccurate to treat the situation as though it were solely a teen problem. In fact, notes Males (1993a), in 69 percent of all teenage births where the mother is a teenager, the father is an adult. Even in cases where mothers are younger than 15, more than half of the fathers are adults.

Teenage pregnancies are not restricted to any particular social, economic, religious, or ethnic group. However, in the United States, pregnancies are more common among black than white teenagers. In 1989, 23.1 percent of all births to black mothers were to teenagers; 10.7 percent of white births were to teenagers. For mothers of Hispanic origin, 16.7 percent of births were to teenage mothers (U.S. Bureau of the Census, 1994).

Teenage pregnancies are also more common in economically depressed areas (Donnelly & Voydanoff, 1991). Compared with married mothers of the same age, socioeconomic status, and religious background, unmarried teenage mothers often have lower educational and occupational status, more often come from broken homes, and have more difficulty with opposite-sex relationships (Danilewitz & Skuy, 1990).

Why?

The vast majority of teenage pregnancies are unplanned. Among reasons for the increasing rates of teenage pregnancy, note Black and DeBlassie (1985), are changes in so-

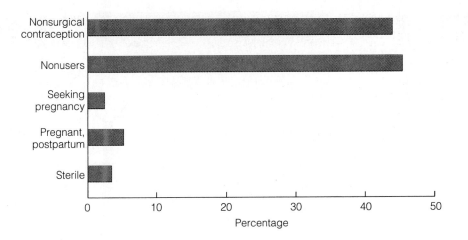

FIGURE 12.8
Reproductive status of U.S. women, ages 15 to 24, 1988. (Based on U.S. Bureau of the Census, 1994, p. 84.)

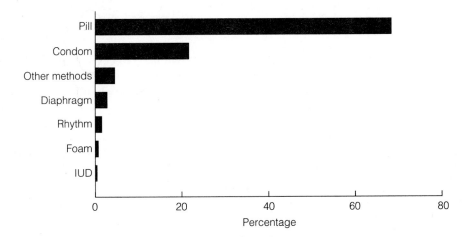

FIGURE 12.9
Choice of contraceptive method by the 43.5 percent of U.S. women, ages 15 to 24, who used nonsurgical contraception in 1988. (Based on U.S. Bureau of the Census, 1994, p. 84.)

cial attitudes toward sexual activity and toward pregnancy. Pregnancy no longer brings shame and humiliation; accordingly, there is less pressure, both on boys and girls, to prevent conception.

Second, there are a raft of psychological factors that might motivate sexual intercourse, leading to pregnancy: loneliness and alienation that are often part of life in socially and economically depressed surroundings; the girl's wish to "get back" at overprotective parents; the boy's wish to establish the "macho" image that some male societies still reinforce. Not surprisingly, girls from poorer families are more likely to become pregnant (Males, 1993b), as are those from rigid, authoritarian families (Romig & Bakken, 1990).

Third, there is the adolescent's egocentrism—the personal fable that stresses the special invulnerability of the teenager and that is premised on the belief that "It won't happen to me." This, coupled with the adolescent's sensation-seeking tendencies may account for some teenage pregnancies (Arnett, 1992). Johnson and Green (1993) found that the more mature (cognitively, as well as in terms of age and grade) and the less egocentric the female teenager, the more likely she was to use contraception.

Fourth, and perhaps most important, the majority of pregnancies occur accidentally and as a consequence of ignorance or misinformation concerning sex and contraception. More than half of all teenagers do not use contraception at the time of first intercourse, and perhaps a third continue to use none later (Arnett, 1992). Significantly, approximately half of all pregnancies occur within six months of first intercourse. Many teenagers do not know where to get birth control information. And of those who have adequate information, many are only intermittently sexually active. For them, the cost of the safest birth control methods makes their use prohibitive. In addition, use of an IUD (intrauterine device), oral contraceptives, or of a diaphragm requires the cooperation of a physician. As a result, of those who do employ contraception, many are forced to use the least reliable methods: withdrawal, rhythm (attempting to time intercourse to coincide with the woman's cyclical periods of infertility), and condoms. Brooks-Gunn and Furstenberg (1989) argue that we need to know much more about teenage sexual activity and attitudes toward condoms in order to encourage their use (see Figures 12.8 and 12.9).

Implications

Pregnancy for an unmarried teenager is often a serious problem. As Chase-Lansdale and Brooks-Gunn (1994) put it, "Normative developmental sequences and life transitions are irrevocably altered or delayed, and risks to healthy development in multiple domains occur" (p. 208). Many teenage pregnancies result in a dramatic disruption of the mother's educational and career plans. There are also much higher health risks with teenage pregnancy and delivery, both for mother and infant. Moreover, the economic and social conditions under which the majority of teenage mothers are forced to live, and the emotional stresses associated with these conditions, as well as with child rearing, can be a heavy burden. Not surprisingly, divorce rates for teenage marriages are much higher than for marriages that occur later.

In addition to disadvantages of teenage pregnancy for the mother, there are also disadvantages for their offspring. Donnelly and Voydanoff (1991) summarize these as follows: "Children [of unmarried adolescent mothers] are more likely than those of older mothers to experience a number of difficulties as they grow and develop. These difficulties include poverty and its associated problems, physical problems, lower educational attainments, problem behaviors, maltreatment and the increased likelihood of becoming adolescent parents" (p. 404).

Teenage parents, note Passino and colleagues (1993), tend to be less socially competent than their nonpregnant peers. They also manifest higher levels of stress, and are less sensitive to the needs of their infants. Although the economic disadvantages of teenage childbearing often disappear over time, as Furstenberg, Brooks-Gunn, and Chase-Lansdale (1989) put it, "The children of teenage mothers however, are distinctly worse off throughout childhood than the offspring of older childbearers" (p. 313).

The implications of teenage parenthood are clearly more direct and more applicable for mothers and children than for fathers, a great many of whom are not involved in any pregnancy-related decisions or in child rearing later—and the majority of whom are not teenagers (Males, 1993b). However, school dropout rates are higher for teenage fathers even when they do not marry the mother (Marsiglio, 1986).

However, these observations and conclusions do not apply to all teenage parents. Many are sensitive, caring, and competent parents. Sadly, the probability that this will be the case, given their relative immaturity and lack of experience and information, is not overwhelmingly high.

What to Do?

Not all teenage mothers are economically disadvantaged, have inadequate job skills, and raise children who experience developmental problems. Still, as Roosa (1991) puts it, "The vast majority of adolescent mothers and their children would benefit by postponing early pregnancies."

Given the staggering economic, psychological, and social costs of adolescent parenthood, the United States Public Health Service has, since 1981, funded a variety of pregnancy prevention programs. The majority of these are offered in junior high schools through sex and family-

life education programs. Their objectives are to decrease adolescent pregnancy by changing sexual attitudes and sexual behavior. For legal, and sometimes moral, reasons, many are *abstinence* programs that do not permit discussion of contraception or abortion (Jorgensen, 1991). Others offer free access to contraception, provide information about sexuality and contraception, and attempt to influence sexual attitudes and to expand adolescents' life options (Chase-Lansdale & Brooks-Gunn, 1994).

Sex education and pregnancy prevention programs in schools remain controversial; even more controversial is the move by a number of school jurisdictions to provide condom dispensers for students. There are parents who fear that sex education and easy access to contraception may serve to increase adolescent sexual behavior and to foster values that run counter to those of the family and the community. Because of this, and because of the danger of sexually transmitted diseases, many parents advocate sexual abstinence programs (see Hess, 1990). However, adolescents are not always highly motivated to participate in such courses, especially when what the programs teach contradicts their values and their behaviors.

Many pregnancy prevention programs have not been based on systematic research or knowledge about the antecedents of pregnancy; and most have not involved the adolescent's family and peer systems. Not surprisingly, most have not proven highly effective (Males, 1993b). However, indications are that with more sensitive and careful program development and evaluation, and with further refinement of preventive strategies, program results can be positive (Haynes, 1993; Smith, 1994). Such programs need to take into account the realities of contemporary life—realities that, for example, not only condone but encourage sexual intercourse and that include adult men having sex with teenage girls. Given these realities, abstinence programs may be too simplistic (and too unrealistic) argue Brick and Roffman (1993). When

Christopher and Roosa (1990) investigated the effects of an adolescent pregnancy prevention program that focused on self-esteem and resisting peer pressure, and that taught that sex should occur only after marriage, program dropout rates were very high. Nor was there any evidence that the program was effective in reducing sexual activity.

Brooks-Gunn and Furstenberg (1989) report that sex education programs are rare in elementary school, although the vast majority of parents and school jurisdictions support them in high school. They report, as well, that the fear that these programs might increase sexual activity does not appear to be warranted.

Homosexuality

Homosexual experiences during adolescence do not appear to be very common. Evidence suggests that approximately 1 out of every 10 adolescent boys, and perhaps half that number of girls, have isolated sexual experiences with someone of the same sex, usually during early adolescence (Dreyer, 1982). Estimates of the number of these who subsequently adopt a homosexual or bisexual lifestyle are extremely unreliable, but are probably considerable less than the 8 or 9 percent who have had adolescent homosexual experiences. In Michael and colleagues' (1994) comprehensive survey of the sexual behaviors of 3,432 randomly selected adults, only 2.8 percent of men and 1.4 percent of women claimed to be homosexual or bisexual. That homosexual groups have become more visible and more outspoken in recent decades may account for the popular perception that their numbers have increased.

Causes of homosexuality are not known although there are a variety of theories: genetic, social learning, hormonal. And it is extremely difficult, in most cases impossible, to alter sexual preference.

Sexually Transmitted Diseases

There are more than two dozen known *sexually transmitted diseases* (*STDs*, also known as *venereal diseases*). Among the most common are chlamydia, gonorrhea, and herpes. Less common are syphilis and AIDS, although both of these are increasing. There are now about twice as many reported cases of syphilis in the United States each year than there were in 1980 (113,000 cases in 1992; U.S. Bureau of the Census, 1994). Significantly, STD rates are more than twice as high among teenage girls than would be predicted on the basis of rates among teenage boys. The reason for this, suggests Males (1993b), is the high rate of intercourse between adult males and teenage females.

Chlamydia

Chlamydia is currently the most common of the STDs ("Sleeping with the Enemy," 1991). It was rarely seen until very recent years and still goes largely undetected. Estimates are that as many as 1 of every 10 sexually active women has chlamydia—twice as many as have gonorrhea.

It is now one of the leading causes of infertility among women (Gibbons, 1991). In the majority of women, chlamydia presents no symptoms in its early stages (approximately 80 percent); this is also the case for about 20 percent of infected men. In later stages, abdominal pain may cause the victim to seek medical help, but by then the woman is often infertile. Chlamydia can be treated easily and effectively with antibiotics.

Gonorrhea

Gonorrhea has declined dramatically since 1980 when there were more than 1 million cases reported in the United States; but is still a highly common STD at about 501,000 reported cases in the United States in 1992 (U.S. Bureau of the Census, 1994). Symptoms in the male usually include a discharge from the penis and pain during urination. Symptoms in the female are more subtle and often go unnoticed. The disease can usually be treated simply and effectively with penicillin and related drugs. Like some other sexually transmitted diseases, it can sometimes be prevented through the use of a condom or simply by washing the genitals thoroughly after intercourse.

Genital Herpes

Herpes is caused by a virus and remains incurable, although the virus can remain inactive for long periods of time. An estimated 500,000 new cases are reported each year. The disease is believed to be contagious only when lesions are present (like tiny cold sores, commonly found on the penis and scrotum in males, and on the vulva, vagina, and cervix in females).

AIDS

AIDS (**acquired immune deficiency syndrome**) is a sexually transmitted disease caused by the human immunodeficiency virus (HIV)—an organism that appears to mutate rapidly, thereby increasing the difficulty of treating it (Alcamo, 1993). At present, it is incurable and fatal. It is transmitted through the exchange of body fluids, principally blood and semen. Largely for that reason, AIDS has been found primarily among four high-risk groups: intravenous drug users who often share needles; homosexual males who engage in anal intercourse; hemophiliacs who have been exposed to the virus through blood transfusions; and certain groups of Haitians who engage in rituals involving blood exchange. As of 1992, 244,939 cases had been reported in the United States; of these, 166,467 had died (U.S. Bureau of the Census, 1994; see Figure 12.10).

Because there may be as much as a 10-year lag between exposure to the virus and development of symptoms, reported cases reflect what was happening 10 years ago. The World Health Organization predicts that worldwide, 4 million women will have died of AIDS by the year 2000 ("AIDS Will Kill 4M Women by 2000: WHO," 1993). At present, there are about seven times more male than female cases of AIDS in the United States, and

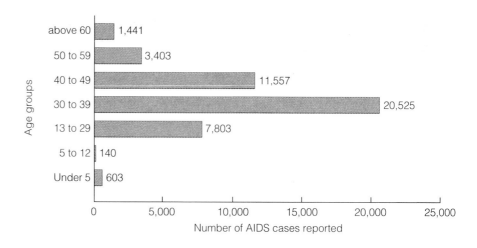

FIGURE 12.10

Number of AIDS cases reported in the United States in 1992. Total number of cases was 45,472. Of these, 86 percent were male, 35 percent were blacks, and 15 percent were Hispanics. Highest number of cases were reported in California (18.8 percent) and New York (18.5 percent); lowest were in Oregon (0.6 percent) and Arizona (0.8 percent). (Based on U.S. Bureau of the Census, 1994, p. 139.)

homosexual as well as drug-related transmission are most common. However, heterosexual transmission is the norm throughout most of the world, and is expected to become more common in North America as well ("Sleeping with the Enemy," 1991).

Adolescents appear to be relatively well informed about AIDS and how it is transmitted (Lamport & Andre, 1993); and as many as one third claim they have changed their sexual behavior because of fear of AIDS. That means, however, that two thirds have not. There is some indication that sexual activity—especially unprotected sexual activity—among homosexual males has declined in the wake of widespread accounts of increases in the incidence of AIDS and other STDs (Stall, Coates, & Hoff, 1988).

Other STDs

Among other STDs is **acute pelvic inflammatory disease,** a complication that can result from diseases such as gonorrhea or chlamydia. It is a major health problem, affecting more than 1 million U.S. women a year (Quan, 1994). Resulting inflammation of the cervix and Fallopian tubes can lead to infertility or tubal pregnancies, especially following repeated infections. In one study of 1,309 women who had been diagnosed as having acute pelvic inflammatory disease, 12.1 percent were found to be infertile. Of the others who did become pregnant, 7.8 percent had tubal pregnancies (Westrom, 1994).

Genital warts are also sexually transmitted. They are caused by a virus and affect about 1 million people in the United States each year. They are not usually dangerous, and can be removed. Sexual transmission is also the leading cause of hepatitis B, which accounts for about 5,000 deaths in the United States each year ("Sleeping with the Enemy," 1991).

ADOLESCENT TURMOIL

A large majority of adolescents pass exuberantly through the teen years, enjoying their increased powers of mind and body, successfully overcoming or avoiding the turmoil

that besets their less fortunate peers. But for others, perhaps some 15 percent who describe themselves as anxious or confused or depressed (Offer, Ostrov, & Howard, 1984), adolescence can be a turbulent and troubled time. Clearly, then, the turmoil topics—delinquency, gangs, drugs, suicide—relate only to the minority. But they are an important minority.

Delinquency

Delinquency is a legal rather than a scientific category. A *delinquent* is a juvenile who has been apprehended and convicted for transgression of established legal rather than moral laws. Adults in similar situations are criminals rather than delinquents.

When delinquency is defined in this manner, surveys of its prevalence can be based directly on police and legal records. These records indicate a tremendous increase in the delinquency rate in recent decades. There are now more crimes committed by adolescents and younger children than by people over 25 (U.S. Bureau of the Census, 1994). However, many of the offenses for which juveniles are apprehended and brought to court are status offenses such as truancy, running away, sexual promiscuity, underage drinking, or driving without a license (see At a Glance: "Gangs, Violence, and Delinquency," and Table 12.6).

A number of factors appear to be related to delinquency, but because most of the studies that have investigated delinquency simply indicate correlations, it is impossible to identify its specific causes. Age, for example, is related to delinquency; but we have no evidence that it *causes* delinquency. Other related but not necessarily causal factors include social class, intelligence, peers, parents, personality, and sex.

Social Class

Research on the relationship between social class and delinquency is ambiguous and inconclusive. Although the lower classes, as well as some racial subgroups, are greatly overrepresented among delinquent groups, it is by no means clear that there are, in fact, many more delinquents

GANGS, VIOLENCE, AND DELINQUENCY

Random and unprovoked violence, sometimes perpetrated by gangs and sometimes by individuals, is as frightening as it is unpredictable. Violence that is not random, but that is based on allegiance to ideology and on hatred of identifiable groups (as is the case for some racist groups), is no less terrifying. Although the number of delinquency cases dealt with by U.S. courts has not changed very much in recent years (in the United States, 1.05 million cases in 1975 and 1.338 million in 1991), incidence of *violent* juvenile offenses in the United States increased from 57,000 cases in 1982 to 103,000 cases in 1991. With respect to violent offenses, males outnumber females by approximately 7 to 1. As a result, more than 80 percent of all juveniles held in custody in 1991 were male.

TABLE 12.6
Number and Types of Delinquency Cases Disposed of by U.S. Juvenile Courts in 1991

All delinquency offenses	1,338,000
Violent offenses	103,000
Criminal homicide	3,000
Forcible rape	5,000
Robbery	30,000
Aggravated assault	66,000
Property offenses	577,000
Burglary	149,000
Larceny	351,000
Motor vehicle theft	70,000
Arson	7,000
Delinquency offenses	658,000
Simple assault	130,000
Vandalism	103,000
Drug law violations	59,000
Obstruction of justice	79,000
Other*	286,000

* Includes such offenses as stolen property offenses, trespassing, weapons offenses, other sex offenses, liquor law violations, disorderly conduct, and miscellaneous offenses.

SOURCE: Adapted from U.S. Bureau of the Census, 1994, p. 213.

among these groups. Because of the nature of law enforcement systems, their often unconscious prejudices, and their consequently greater likelihood of recognizing and apprehending delinquents among minority and lower-class groups, it is hardly surprising that more of these adolescents are classified as delinquents. At the same time, to the extent that delinquency is a form of rebellion that is sometimes motivated by the desire for material possession, it is reasonable to expect that more of the poorer adolescents would be delinquent. Furthermore, lower-class parents tend to look to the police for help with their children; middle-class parents go to therapists.

Intelligence

There is a large body of evidence linking delinquency with lower than average measured intelligence (Binder, 1988). However, this should not be taken as direct evidence that lower intelligence causes delinquency. Quay (1987) notes that much of this difference in measured intelligence may be accounted for in terms of lower verbal ability. This puts children at a disadvantage in social interaction as well as in school. Consequently, they are more likely to get into trouble with teachers, school administrators, parents, and perhaps friends as well.

Peers

Peer groups, particularly in the form of gangs, can also contribute to delinquent behavior. Like other peer groups, the delinquent gang reinforces its dominant values and also serves as a model for translating these values into actual behaviors. Correctional institutes for juveniles, which are comprised primarily of delinquent peer groups, may be one example of the influence of peers on delinquent behavior. Not surprisingly, more than half of all admissions to most correctional institutions are, in fact, readmissions.

A study reported by Claes and Simard (1992) indicates that delinquent adolescents are more likely to make friends outside of school than are nondelinquents. Not surprisingly, they are also more likely to commit antisocial acts with their friends.

Parents

The father is perhaps the most influential parent with respect to juvenile delinquency. Fathers of delinquent boys are often more severe, more punitive, more prone to alcoholism, more rejecting, and more likely to have engaged in delinquent behavior themselves. At the same time, many parents of delinquent adolescents are likely not to have monitored or disciplined their children closely while they were growing up (Patterson, DeBaryshe, & Ramsey, 1989). Not surprisingly, children of adolescent mothers are more likely to engage in delinquent behaviors (Chase-Lansdale & Brooks-Gunn, 1994).

There is evidence, too, that father absence may be related to delinquency (Amato & Keith, 1991). Some speculate that father absence may contribute to delinquency in

Gangs are social groups that organize themselves spontaneously and whose defining characteristic is found in conflict with other groups or with established society. They tend to encourage delinquent values and behaviors.

sons, perhaps by failure to provide adequate male models, perhaps as a function of protest against female domination, or perhaps simply because of inadequate supervision. Girls, too, appear to be more prone to delinquency in father-absent homes or where the mother is viewed as cold and rejecting (Kroupa, 1988).

Personality

Many studies have looked at the possibility that delinquency is at least partly a function of the individual's personality characteristics. Results are generally inconclusive although there is some evidence that high impulsivity (low impulse control), high need for stimulation (danger-seeking orientation), and low self-esteem are related to delinquency (Binder, 1988). With respect to low self-esteem, we noted earlier that delinquents typically think less well of themselves than do nondelinquent adolescents.

Sex

The incidence of delinquency is about four times higher among boys than girls. This may be partly explained by the male's greater aggressiveness. Traditionally, delinquency among males has involved more aggressive transgressions, whereas girls were apprehended more often for sexually promiscuous behavior, shoplifting, and related activities. Evidence indicates this pattern is now changing, as more girls become involved in aggressive delinquent acts, including breaking and entering, car theft, and even assault. Drug-related offenses also account for an increasing number of detentions. Interestingly, in a study of female delinquency, Caspi and colleagues (1993) found highest risk for delinquency among girls who matured earliest. Early-maturing girls were far more likely to know—and be friends with—delinquent boys than was the case for girls who matured later.

In summary, a complex set of psychological and social forces impinge on the potential delinquent, although no single factor can reliably predict delinquent behavior. Social class, age, sex, home background, intelligence, personality, relationship with the father, and peer influences are all implicated, but these, alone or in combination, cannot give a complete picture. Clearly, many adolescents from the most deprived of backgrounds are not delinquents, and many from apparently superior environments are.

Adolescent Gangs

Sociologists define a *gang* as a group that forms spontaneously, that interacts on a face-to-face basis, and that becomes aware of its group membership through conflict with some other group or, perhaps more often, with some representatives of established society. A gang may consist of different numbers of individuals from a wide variety of backgrounds and locales, although it typically includes a fairly homogeneous group of people who at least live close to one another and who often attend the same school. But most important, a group does not become a gang until it comes into conflict with something external. It is hardly surprising, then, that the word *gang* has always been closely associated with juvenile delinquency, truancy, rebelliousness, and other disturbing behaviors.

Lasley (1992) reports that gangs are primarily composed of adolescents. As gang members age, they typically drop out and are replaced by younger members. Hence, many gang members are school-aged and, as a result, gangs pose a real danger in some schools. Burke (1991) describes how wearing highly prized clothing (like certain sports jackets) can place an individual in danger, and how some high school girls participate in gang activities, often

WAR AND PEACE IN SCHOOLS

School One: On a recent morning at a central city high school in New York City, a 15-year-old boy walked up to two of his schoolmates, pulled out a 38-caliber pistol, and shot one in the head and the other in the chest; both died. A friend of one of the dead boys, very upset, called another friend to tell him what had happened. As he spoke to him on the phone, he heard a clicking sound. "What's that noise?" he asked. "I'm playing Russian roulette," said the other. And then Bang! He lost the game and became the third violent student death in that school that morning (Knox, Laske, & Tromanhauser, 1992).

Perhaps as many as 20 percent of all high school students in the United States carry weapons to school; a quarter of these claim to carry guns. Many of those who carry weapons are members of gangs that consist mainly of racial minority groups. Many attend schools in deteriorating city centers and live in an atmosphere of crime and poverty. They see schools not as a neutral place for learning but just as another piece of turf over which to fight.

School Two: "Does anyone carry weapons in your school?" I ask a handful of teenagers, all students at a large suburban high school. Ray, whose parents are both doctors, is an outstanding student (90+ average) in a special advanced academic program. He plays the cello, enjoys badminton, hockey, and football, and swims and wrestles. His ambition is to go into medicine, specializing in general practice. "I don't know anyone who would have a weapon in this school," he says. "That, like, would suck, man."

To Think About   Schools, which are such an important part of the growing person's context, can vary tremendously in the sorts of experiences they provide and the values they encourage. There are some who fear that violence and gangs are rapidly growing phenomena in North America, not only in urban but also in more rural centers. What, do you suppose, should or can be done?

To Consult   Knox, G. W., Laske, D. L., & Tromanhauser, E. D. (1992). *Schools under siege.* Dubuque, IA: Kendall/Hunt.

Lal, S. R., Lal, D., & Achilles, C. M. (1993). *Handbook on gangs in schools: Strategies to reduce gang-related activities.* Thousand Oaks, CA: Corwin.

by hiding gang members' drugs and weapons in their school lockers.

Of special current concern are gangs whose members engage in violent behaviors often simply because of an apparent taste for violence and mayhem. Some British soccer riots and the occasional school-holiday violence seen in some North American resort areas are examples of this kind of violence. Also of concern is gang violence premised on fundamental beliefs and principles that are focused against specific groups or institutions. Here in Edmonton, for example, two members of a group identifying themselves as neo-Nazi skinheads beat up and blinded a 60-year-old man who had, more than a decade earlier, expressed anti-Nazi views ("The 'Scene' and the

Skinheads," 1990). Their admitted philosophy is clearly racist; their dream is of an all-white society; their music is counterculture, frenetic, and anarchistic; their dress, hairstyles, and makeup are intended to shock and outrage; and violence is their modus operandi.

Violence among delinquent gangs is often an expression of a new identity that gang members adopt. Adolescents who join small, highly cohesive, counterculture groups are provided with a set of beliefs and principles that are sometimes very well articulated. Their allegiance to the gang is not only a rejection of family, school, and larger cultural values, but is also an embracing of the values and of the individuals in their new community. (See Across Cultures: "War and Peace in Schools.")

TABLE 12.7
Classification of the Most Frequently Abused Drugs

Class	Examples
Narcotics	Opium
	Morphine
	Heroin
	Codeine
	Methadone
Sedatives (downers)	Barbiturates (Phenobarbital, Seconal, Nembutal)
	Tranquilizers (Valium, Librium, Vivol)
	Alcohol
Stimulants (uppers)	Cocaine
	Crack
	Amphetamines (Benzedrine, Dexedrine, Methedrine)
Hallucinogens (psychoactive, psychotropic, psychedelic, psychomimetic)	LSD
	PCP
	Mescaline
	Psilocybin
	Marijuana
Inhalants	Glue
	Paint thinner
	Aerosol sprays
	Solvents
Unclassified (or sometimes classified as stimulant)	Nicotine
"Designer" drugs	Any of a combination of chemicals and drugs, often manufactured by amateur chemists

But not all adolescents who are dissatisfied, disillusioned, or in need of the community of groups join them in protest. A significant number of the severely dissatisfied drop out of society. Lest another stereotype be fostered, we must point out that the methods of dropping out described here are undertaken by both the adventurous and the timid, the weak and the strong, the deluded and the rational—and frequently they are not attempts to drop out but merely attempts to intensify the experience of living.

Drugs

Drug use is an almost inescapable fact of contemporary life. **Drugs** are with us constantly in the guise of coffee, tea, headache tablets, cocktails, and in thousands of other forms. People have known about drugs for centuries, although they have not always known the chemical components of the substances they ate, drank, chewed, applied to wounds, inhaled, put in ears, or otherwise used on their persons.

The most commonly abused drugs in North America are classified in Table 12.7. The U.S. Bureau of the Census (1994) reports declines between 1974 and 1992 in use of hallucinogens, tranquilizers, marijuana, and even cigarettes. However, there are some indications that alcohol use and abuse has increased during this time. The United States has the highest rates of illegal drug use among industrialized nations (Newcomb & Bentler, 1989). (See At a Glance: "Changing Patterns of Drug Use," and Figure 12.11.)

Some Definitions

The American Psychiatric Association distinguishes among a number of drug-use terms. **Drug abuse** refers primarily to the *recreational* use of drugs, and is not considered a disorder unless it impairs social or occupational functioning. **Drug dependence** is a disorder ordinarily resulting from the repeated use of drugs, and manifested in a strong desire to continue taking the drug—either for the pleasant sensations that might result or to escape feelings of withdrawal.

The APA distinguishes between **physiological dependence**, commonly called *addiction*, where the desire to continue taking the drug is at least partly organically based (for example, not taking it will lead to unpleasant physiological reactions), and **psychological dependence**, sometimes called *habituation*, where the desire to continue taking the drug has to do mainly with its psychological rather than its physiological effects. **Drug tolerance** refers to changes that occur in the user so that with the passage of time, more and more of the drug is required to produce the desired effect.

Widiger and Smith (1994) make the important point that there are no infallible rules for identifying clearly when drug use is a problem for a given individual. A forthcoming revision of the APA's *Diagnostic and Statistical Manual* (*DSM-IV*) recognizes that drug use and abuse exist on a continuum marked by increasing lack of control (*dyscontrol* is the termed employed). To some extent, whether or not drug use is *abuse* depends on the drug, the organism, and the context. Thus, use of certain drugs that are toxic or that are likely to have serious adverse consequences is probably abuse; use of drugs by young children or adolescents may be abuse because of the possibility that drug use will interfere with important aspects of development and adjustment; and use of drugs in inappropriate contexts (at work, in school) is also more likely to be abuse.

Who Uses Drugs?

Researchers have sometimes assumed that there is a drug-use continuum that reflects psychological health and adjustment: At the most positive extreme is the drug abstainer; at the most negative extreme, the frequent drug user or the addict; and in between are infrequent users who occasionally experiment with drugs. However, a longitudinal study conducted by Shedler and Block (1990) contradicts this view. The study looked at psychological

CHANGING PATTERNS OF DRUG USE

In the 1960s, social prophets loudly trumpeted their fears that drugs were taking over the lives of adolescents, that coming decades would witness drug-related social upheavals and political catastrophes that could scarcely be imagined. But recent decades have seen a decline in the use of drugs in most categories.

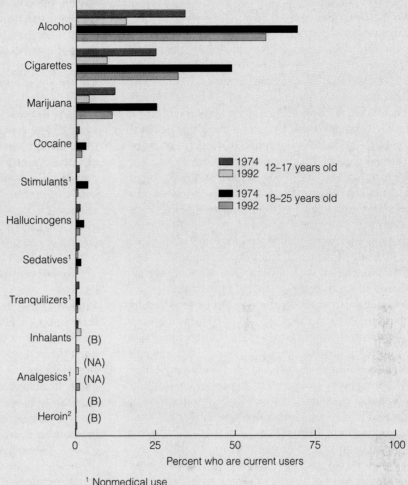

FIGURE 12.11

Changing patterns of drug use in the United States, 1974–1992. (Based on U.S. Bureau of the Census, 1994, p. 141.)

[1] Nonmedical use
[2] Figures are not available for both age groups
B Base too small to meet statistical standards for reliability of a derived figure
NA Not available

characteristics of children from preschool through age 18. At age 18, children were identified as drug abstainers, drug experimenters, and drug users. As expected, drug users were found to be the least well adjusted, the most impulsive, and the most likely to suffer from emotional problems. But the abstainers were not the best adjusted of the three groups; the drug experimenters were. In Shedler and Block's (1990) words, "The picture of the abstainer that emerges is of a relatively tense, overcontrolled, emotionally constricted individual who is somewhat socially isolated and lacking in interpersonal skills" (p. 618).

In the Shedler and Block study, children who later became frequent drug users were often identifiable by a complex set of common characteristics even as young as age 7. Often, these children did not get along as well with

their peers, were less advanced in moral judgments, were more impulsive, displayed less self-reliance, had lower self-esteem, and were more prone to emotional distress. At age 11, these children continued to be more emotional, less attentive, and less cooperative, and reacted poorly to stressful situations. In short, frequent drug users often appear to have been relatively maladjusted as children. Low self-esteem is perhaps the single personality variable that is most often implicated in drug abuse.

There also appear to be gender differences in drug user characteristics. Male drug users are often more aggressive or more shy as children; females are more likely to show symptoms of emotional disorders like depression, to have attempted suicide, to have been abused as children, and to have a family history of drug abuse (Toray et al.,

1991). For both males and females, father alcoholism is also a strong predictor of drug abuse (Chassin, Rogosch, & Barrera, 1991).

Reasons for Drug Use

Experimentation with drugs is primarily an adolescent phenomenon. And when teenagers are asked about their decisions to use or not to use drugs, they seldom refer to morality, social convention, or even parents or the law. Even non–drug users claim that the decision is a matter of personal choice dictated by prudence and not by morality. And perhaps the most important factor in making that personal decision is the individual's perception of dangers associated with a drug. Frequent drug users are most likely to discount a drug's harmfulness (Nucci, Guerra, & Lee, 1991).

The reasons for drug use are many and complex, and are not to be found solely in the personality characteristics of the frequent drug user. As we saw, personality characteristics and environmental factors such as father alcoholism or maltreatment as a child may be implicated. The fact that children of alcoholics may be as much as four times more likely to become alcoholics than children of nonalcoholics also suggests the possibility of a genetic contribution (Marlatt et al., 1988). However, the meaning of this relationship is not entirely clear. It might mean that there are genetically determined physiological (chemical/hormonal/metabolic) characteristics that make one person more susceptible than another to alcoholism. It might also mean that the social and economic implications of being raised in the home of an alcoholic parent are conducive to alcoholism. Or both.

One of the most important influences in the adolescent's decision to use drugs relates to the influence of peers. Dinges and Oetting (1993) surveyed more than 100,000 junior high and high school students. Among other things, they found that adolescents who used a specific drug almost invariably had friends who also used the same drug. In their words, "Drug-using friends are a necessary condition in the evolution of drug use" (p. 263). Swaim and colleagues (1993) report similar results with samples of American Indian adolescents.

Reasons for first *using* (and not necessarily eventually *abusing*) drugs often have to do with a simple urge to experiment (Pearl, Bryan, & Herzog, 1990). However, those who subscribe to the **gateway drug-use theory** believe that early use of drugs like alcohol and nicotine serves, in a sense, as a gateway to the use of other drugs (Pentz, 1994). Rarely does the adolescent begin with drugs like cocaine or heroin. This doesn't mean, however, that most adolescents who use these gateway drugs will become drug abusers. In fact, the vast majority will not. Newcomb and Bentler (1989) argue that there is little evidence to support the belief that experimentation with drugs presents a significant danger to later health and psychological well-being.

Use of drugs is most likely to become misuse, Franklin (1985) suggests, among individuals with poor self-esteem who also experience the strong pressures of a peer drug culture, and who are not reared in a growth-fostering environment (parental neglect, abuse, alcoholism; poverty; inadequate schooling; and so on). The type of drugs experimented with is also very important. Some drugs have a higher potential for physiological and psychological dependence than others (heroin and free-base cocaine, or crack, for example). In addition, genetics may well be involved in the nature and intensity of the individual's reaction.

The fact that there are genetic, social, and personality variables that appear to be related to the likelihood of drug use and abuse should be interpreted with caution. The evidence does not warrant the conclusion that these inevitably *cause* drug abuse. Nor, as experience clearly shows, does the apparent absence of these factors guarantee that a given adolescent is safe. As Polson and Newton (1984) point out, one of the most common refrains heard when parents are first confronted with the fact of their child's drug use is, "Not my kid, couldn't happen to my kid."

Sadly, perhaps, it could.

Implications of Teenage Drug Use

It is clearly unrealistic to expect that adolescents will not experiment with drugs. As Newcomb and Bentler (1989) note, the vast majority will have puffed on a cigarette or sipped somebody's alcoholic drink well before adolescence. In adolescence, not to drink occasionally—and perhaps not to smoke cigarettes or try marijuana—would, in many instances, not be socially *normal*. Society's focus, these authors claim, should be on *delaying* drug experimentation for as long as possible to allow for the development of social and intellectual adaptive skills. The emphasis should perhaps be less on preventing *use* than on preventing *abuse*.

The short-term implications of drug abuse among adolescents are sometimes painfully obvious. Alcohol, for example, is implicated in a staggering number of fatal, teenage automobile accidents. Less dramatic, but no less real, drug abuse may be reflected in poorer school achievement, dropping out of school, failure to adjust to the career and social demands required for transition to young adulthood, deviance, and criminality. Watts and Wright (1990) report very high correlations between use of alcohol, tobacco, marijuana, and other illegal drugs and delinquency. In their study of black, white, and Mexican-American adolescents, frequent drug use was the best predictor of both minor and violent delinquency.

The long-term implications of teenage drug abuse have been examined by Newcomb and Bentler (1988), who looked at seven different aspects of the lives of young adults (including family formation, stability, criminality, mental health, and social integration). They found that teenagers who had used large amounts of drugs were more likely to have left school early and to have consolidated family and career plans earlier. Those who had used a variety of drugs had often adopted adult roles less suc-

The most commonly used drug among North American teenagers is alcohol. It is a physiologically addictive drug that, with prolonged excessive use, can have serious health consequences. One of its main effects is to suppress inhibition. Thus, it has made this young man far more willing to sing for what he assumes is an adoring public. Unfortunately it has not made him a better singer.

cessfully; their attempted careers and marriages were more likely to have failed.

The long-term medical consequences of drugs such as nicotine and alcohol have also been extensively researched and are well known. In the following sections we look at these and at some other commonly used drugs.

Marijuana

Marijuana, whose active ingredient is **tetrahydrocannabinol (THC),** is derived from hemp, a tall annual plant appearing in male and female forms. It is variously known as hashish, bhang, grass, ganja, charas, marijuana, muta, grefa, muggles, pot, reefer, gauge, stick, Acapulco Gold, Panama Red, Panama Gold, Thai stick, jive, Indian, Jamaican, tea, and dope. It is ordinarily smoked although it can also be eaten or drunk. Its main psychological effect is a pleasant emotional state. If taken in sufficient doses and in sufficiently pure forms, it may evoke the same types of hallucinogenic reactions sometimes associated with stronger drugs like LSD (Cox et al., 1983).

Whether marijuana is physically addictive remains controversial. Gold (1989) suggests it may be addictive following prolonged use; others believe it has not been shown to be addictive or especially harmful (Royal College of Psychiatrists, 1987). In one study in which 382 habitual marijuana users participated in a program designed to help them stop, many experienced considerable difficulty and distress (Stephens, Roffman, & Simpson, 1993).

The physiological effects of marijuana use depend largely on the dosages and the frequency of use. Minor cardiovascular changes (increased heart rate, for example) are common even with very low doses. The respiratory system may be adversely affected with prolonged use and heavier doses (marijuana produces more tars than tobacco, and these contain a higher concentration of certain cancer-causing agents) (Cox et al., 1983).

The fear that marijuana is the first step toward heroin addiction has generally been discounted. There is no evidence that marijuana users develop tolerance to marijuana as users do to some other drugs like heroin. Hence, the marijuana user does not need to go to more powerful drugs to continue to achieve the same "high." Nor is there any evidence that using marijuana leads to a psychological craving for heroin.

LSD

D-lysergic acid diethylamide tartrate, or **LSD-25**, is the most powerful hallucinogen known. Because it is a synthetic chemical, it can be made by anyone who has the materials, the equipment, and the knowledge. The most common street name for LSD-25 is acid; others are barrels, California sunshine, blotters, cubes, domes, flats, wedges, purple haze, jellybeans, bluecaps, frogs, microdots, and window panes. Its use appears to have declined recently (U.S. Bureau of the Census, 1994).

LSD-25 (ordinarily referred to simply as LSD) is usually taken orally, commonly in the form of a white, odorless, and tasteless powder. Its effects vary widely from one person to another, as well as from one occasion to another for the same person. The predominant characteristic of an LSD experience (called an "acid trip") is the augmented intensity of sensory perceptions. On occasion, an acid trip is accompanied by hallucinations, some of which may be mild whereas others may be sufficiently frightening to lead to serious mental disturbance in the subject even after the immediate effects of the drug have worn off.

Alcohol

Alcohol, the most commonly used and abused drug in contemporary society, is a central nervous system depressant. In relatively moderate doses, its primary effect is to suppress inhibition, which is why many individuals who

TABLE 12.8
Students Reporting Drinking with Friends

Age	"Never" (%)	"Sometimes" (%)	"Usually" (%)	"Always" (%)	At Least "Sometimes" (total %)	Total Number of Students
12	72	24	2	2	28	163
13	62	29	6	3	38	142
14	34	37	23	6	66	242
15	20	42	28	10	80	208
16	13	35	35	17	87	249
17	12	41	33	14	88	219

SOURCE: Brown & Finn, 1982, p. 15.

have consumed alcohol behave as though they had taken a stimulant. In less moderate doses, the individual progresses from being "high" or "tipsy" to intoxication. Literally, to be intoxicated is to be poisoned. Behavioral symptoms of varying degrees of intoxication may include impaired muscular control, delayed reflexive reactions, loss of coordination and balance, impaired vision, uncertain speech, faintness, nausea, amnesia (blackouts), and, in extreme cases, paralysis of heart and lung muscles sometimes leading to death (Reid & Carpenter, 1990).

Alcohol is physiologically addictive, although prolonged or excessive consumption is generally required before symptoms of physical addiction are present. Signs of psychological dependency (a strong desire to continue taking the drug) may appear considerably sooner. One of the major physiological effects of alcohol is its contribution to cirrhosis of the liver—one of the 10 leading causes of death in the United States. In addition, it is implicated in more than half of all motor vehicle deaths, a large number of which involve adolescents (Beatty, 1991).

Alcohol consumption among adolescents is widespread. Most surveys report that extremely few teenagers have not tried alcohol at least once (Newcomb & Bentler, 1989). Close to 20 percent of adolescents aged 14 to 17 are considered problem drinkers (see Table 12.8).

Why do adolescents drink? There are clearly many reasons, including social pressure, experimentation, insecurity, and other personal problems, as well as simply for the sensation of being "tipsy," "high," or "drunk." Why do adolescents want to get drunk? To feel good, have fun, celebrate, let off steam, cheer up, forget worries, feel less shy, and impress friends, they claim (Brown & Finn, 1982). But when they are asked what their actual behaviors and feelings are when they are drunk, although a large number do "feel good" and "laugh a lot," a significant number fall asleep, feel unhappy, cry, damage property, and get into fights—and approximately one third at all age levels occasionally get sick.

When is alcohol consumption by adolescents deviant or a problem? Is it a problem only when the adolescent gets into trouble? Does it become a problem when alcohol consumption becomes habitual or excessive or when it interferes with normal social or physical functioning? Or is it always a problem because the behavior is generally illegal? There are no easy answers.

Cocaine

Cocaine is ordinarily a white powder derived from coca leaves. Also known as coke, big "C," snow, gold dust, star dust, flake, Bernice, or Corine, it is most commonly inhaled vigorously through the nostrils, although it can also be injected. Cocaine is sometimes purified to produce *freebase* cocaine, which has a more profound effect on the user. Some users mix it with heroin and inject it intravenously (called a *speedball*).

In moderate doses, the primary effect of cocaine, like that of other stimulants, is one of euphoria and high energy. In higher doses, it can lead to hallucinations and sometimes convulsions. For some decades it was widely believed that cocaine is nonaddictive and largely harmless. It is now considered to be extremely dangerous (Cheung, Erickson, & Landau, 1991). Indications are that it may be as addictive as heroin (Ringwalt & Palmer, 1989).

Cocaine use has increased dramatically among high school populations, especially in its freebase (**crack** or "rock") form (U.S. Bureau of the Census, 1994). Next to marijuana, it is the most widely used *illegal* drug in North America.

Crack appears to be particularly attractive to adolescents for several reasons. First, it is far cheaper than cocaine. Second, its effects are almost instantaneous and intensely euphoric. And third, so much glamour and misinformation has surrounded the so-called recreational use of cocaine that many adolescents think there is nothing to fear.

Crack is easily and quickly manufactured by *cooking down* ordinary powdered cocaine with bicarbonate of soda

TABLE 12.9
Symptoms of Drug Use and/or Abuse

Drug	Signs and Early Symptoms	Long-Term Symptoms
Narcotics	Medicinal breath	Loss of appetite
	Traces of white powder around nostrils (heroin is sometimes inhaled)	Constipation
	Red or raw nostrils	
	Needle marks or scars on arms	
	Long sleeves (or other clothing) at inappropriate times	
	Physical evidence may include cough syrup bottles, syringes, cotton swabs, and spoon or cap for heating heroin	
Sedatives	Symptoms of alcohol consumption with or without odor	Withdrawal symptoms when discontinued
	Poor coordination and speech	Possible convulsions
	Drowsiness	
	Loss of interest in activity	
Stimulants	Excessive activity	Loss of appetite
	Irascibility	Possible hallucinations and psychotic reactions
	Argumentativeness	
	Nervousness	
	Pupil dilation	
	Dry mouth and nose with bad breath	
	Chapped, dry lips	
	Scratching or rubbing of nose	
	Long periods without sleep	
	Loss of appetite	
	Mood shifts	
	Changes in friends	
	"Hangover" symptoms	
Hallucinogens, marijuana	Odor on breath and clothing	None definite
	Animated behavior or its opposite	
LSD, PCP, MDA, STP	Bizarre behavior	Possible contribution to psychoses
	Panic	Recurrence of experiences after immediate effects of drug
	Disorientation	
Inhalants	Odor of glue, solvent, or related substance	Disorientation
	Redness and watering of eyes	Brain damage
	Appearance of alcoholic intoxication	
	Physical evidence of plastic bags, rags, glue, or solvent containers	

(or mixing it with some petroleum product like ammonia). Small pieces of the resulting off-white, rocklike, mouldy-smelling solid are then chopped up and smoked, usually in a waterpipe. The euphoric effect or "rush" occurs within 5 to 10 seconds and is far more intense than that associated with inhaling ordinary cocaine—the reason being that the concentrations of cocaine that reach the brain are many times higher than is the case with inhalation. Consequently, there is a far higher risk of overdosing with crack, of experiencing convulsions, or even of dying. Many users of crack experience an overwhelming compulsion to use it again as soon as possible, even after using it only once. The use of crack is also associated with psychological changes, the most common of which involve strong feelings of paranoia. Many users also become violent (Washton, 1989), and some commit suicide.

Other Drugs

Other drugs used by some adolescents include various hallucinogens such as STP and MDA (methyl amphetamines), PCP (phencyclidene), inhalants, various barbiturates and other milder tranquilizers, and a range of new molecular variations of these and other chemicals, sometimes collectively labeled "designer drugs." Of these, alcohol is still the drug of choice, both among adolescents and adults (see Table 12.9 for some symptoms of drug use and abuse).

ADOLESCENT SUICIDE

Adolescent suicide rates have risen dramatically in the past several decades. In the United States, the rise reflects an enormous increase for males but not for females. Males typically use more violent and more final methods such as guns (65 percent of all male suicides compared with 40 percent of female suicides); female methods are more passive and protracted and sometimes less successful (for example, poison: 36.8 percent of female suicides compared with 13.3 percent of male suicides).

FIGURE 12.12

Changes in suicide rates for U.S. adolescents, 1970–1991. (Based on U.S. Bureau of Census, 1994, p. 101.)

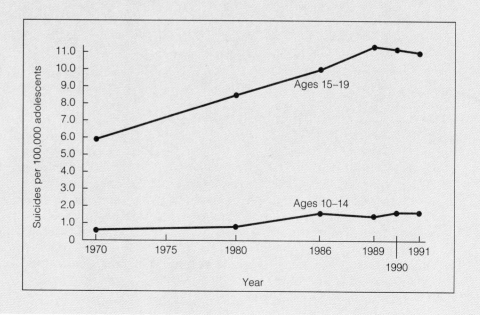

Suicide

Suicide, the deliberate taking of one's life, is final—an end that is sought when individuals can see only two choices: life as it is now or death. Evidently, they prefer to die.

Suicide is not a pleasant topic—it so violently contradicts our implicit belief in the goodness of life. Consequently, a powerful social stigma is associated with the act, and the event is often covered over both by the information media and by the attending physician. As a result, we know only of suicides of people whom we have known (and sometimes not even then), or of particularly prominent persons (not always those either), or of people who commit the act so flagrantly that it compels attention.

There are relatively few scientific investigations of suicide, its causes, and the personalities of those who deliberately choose their time and method of departure. Do children commit suicide? How often? How about adolescents, disillusioned idealists that they are, caught up in the stress and turmoil of the transition to adulthood? Here are some facts.

Rate

The suicide rate in the United States is 12.4 per 100,000. Few children under the age of 15 commit suicide. Suicide rates increase slowly from adolescence, and then more rapidly after age 65 (U.S. Bureau of the Census, 1993). The most dramatic recent increase in suicide rates is among those aged 15 to 19, where suicide rates nearly doubled between 1970 and 1990 (U.S. Bureau of the Census, 1994; see At a Glance: "Adolescent Suicide," and Figure 12.12).

Sex Differences

Among adolescents, far more girls than boys attempt suicide, but about four times more of the boys are successful. More than 24,000 males aged 15 to 19 committed suicide in the United States in 1990, compared with slightly more than 6,000 like-aged females. Some have argued that this is because the boys who attempt suicide are more serious about wanting to die than are the girls. It may also be because the more violent and instantaneous methods employed by males (for example, guns) do not provide much opportunity for help. In contrast, the slower and more passive methods most often employed by females (such as pills) often allow time for rescue.

Psychological Explanations

There are many psychological explanations for suicide. For example, there are biological theories (suicide is due to bad genes, psychiatric disorders, biochemical changes of adolescence, and the like); psychoanalytic theories (suicidal adolescents are those whose unconscious death wish is exaggerated by deficient ego development during this critical period); psychological stress theory (suicide results from a perceived inability to cope with stress associated with rapid and demanding life changes); sociological theories (social norms sometimes sanction suicide by providing the adolescent with the opportunity to die for the group; alternately, groups sometimes exclude the adolescent thus causing depression and leading to suicide); social learning theories (suicidal behavior is suggested by the behaviors and attitudes of friends, family, or other important people); and ecological theory (individual, environmental, and social factors contribute to suicidal tendencies).

Henry and associates (1993) suggest that of these, the most useful may be the ecological approach. Not only does it take into account most of the explanations included in other theories, but it provides a way to understand how suicide might result from the combined effects of a variety of factors. Thus, reasons for adolescent suicide can include a range of family-based problems (Bronfenbrenner's microsystem), such as death in the family, parental abuse or alcohol use, suicide by other family members, and inability to satisfy parental expectations. They can also include wider social problems (meso-, exo-, or macrosystems). For example, Henry and colleagues (1993) report that suicide rates are about 10 times higher among Native American youth, perhaps partly because of economic, social, and even cultural factors associated with hopelessness. In the same way, certain characteristics of contemporary societies—such as high mobility, family instability, lack of intergenerational cohesiveness, poor economic conditions, high unemployment, and expensive and sometimes inaccessible postsecondary education—might all contribute to a greater likelihood of suicide (de Jong, 1992; Stack, 1993).

Individual Explanations

Although adolescent suicide might result from the combined effects of these various factors, it is often precipitated by a single event such as the death of a parent or friend, fear of pregnancy, rejection by a close friend, or arrest. Meneese, Yutrzenka, and Vitale (1992) found that the best predictors of adolescent suicide for males are depression and lack of family cohesiveness; for females, the best predictors are depression and level of anxiety (as a personality characteristic). In a study by Neiger and Hopkins (1988), depression and family relationships were also found to be strong predictors of suicide, as were alcohol and drug use, failure in school, and a recent serious loss. Shreve and Kunkel (1991) suggest that the *shame* that accompanies these conditions may be the determining motive.

Adolescent suicide, like most adult suicides, rarely occurs without advance warning. The most common warning is one or more unsuccessful attempts at suicide. Other warning signs include statements such as "I wish I were dead," "Nobody would miss me if I weren't here," and "I wish I'd never been born."

Suicide is still the solution of an isolated few. Most of us choose to wait for death and hope that it will be a long time in coming. And for most adolescents, life is only occasionally turbulent and stressful; for most, it abounds with joy and excitement.

The vast majority of adolescents are not delinquent, don't belong to gangs, and are not drug addicts. Many are simply happy, normal—sometimes exuberant—teenagers.

ANOTHER NOTE

Suicide would not have been a very pleasant note upon which to end this chapter. Nor would it have been very realistic. Indeed, closing the chapter with the "turmoil topics," as we have, is misleading. As Astroth (1993) points out, adolescents today have lower rates of suicide, drug abuse, unwed pregnancies, and drunk driving than do young and middle-aged adults.

It bears repeating that the adolescents whose lives are described among these last pages are not our "average" adolescents. Our average adolescents are more joyful than sad, more exuberant than depressed, more confident than self-deprecating. They like order more than chaos, purpose more than dissipation—and junk food more than drugs.

And they laugh and smile a lot more than they cry.

That's a better note upon which to end.

Self and Identity

1. Global self-worth (or self-esteem) reflects how well one likes oneself. Self-evaluations are possible in different areas (for example, the Offer categories of psychological, social, familial, coping, and sexual). Adolescence is not generally a period of storm and stress. Rather, the universal adolescent is generally happy and optimistic; caring, concerned, and sociable; confident and open about sexual matters; and strongly positive toward the family. Context also leads to some systematic differences among adolescents from different cultures.

2. According to Erikson, the major developmental task of adolescence is to develop a sense of identity. Marcia describes four possible identity statuses: *identity diffusion* (early adolescence: no commitment and no identity crisis); *foreclosure* (strong commitment to an imposed identity); *moratorium individuals* (adolescents actively exploring alternative identities; vague, changing commitments); and *identity achieved* (commitment following the crisis of the moratorium).

Social Development in Context

3. Social development progresses from a stage of relative dependence on the parents to a stage of relative independence. The role of parents in adolescence is to provide resources, protect adolescents, guide their development, and serve as advocates for them. Increasing allegiance to peers does not necessarily entail a high degree of parent–adolescent conflict. The majority of teenagers have good relations with their parents, although one of the developmental tasks of this period involves increasing independence from parents.

4. The adolescent's acceptance by peers is profoundly important for social and psychological well-being. High-status (well-liked) children tend to be happier, more cheerful, more active, and more successful. Peer groups in schools often sort themselves into "crowds" on the basis of principal interests and behaviors (populars, jocks, brains, normals, druggies, and outcasts).

Gender and Gender Roles

5. Gender refers to characteristics associated with biological sex (masculine or feminine). Stereotypes view the male gender as dominant and active, and the female gender as more passive and nurturant. Responses to the "sex-change" question reveal predominantly positive evaluations of the male role and negative evaluations of the female role—by both males and females.

6. Some gender differences are biological, evident in the greater fragility of the males (higher mortality). Gender differences in mathematics and spatial ability (favoring males) and in verbal ability (favoring females) are small, not usually apparent prior to adolescence, and best explained in terms of culturally determined interests and opportunities rather than in terms of genetically ordained differences.

Sex

7. The sexual revolution among adolescents is evident in an increase in sexual activity (greater among females than males) and a lowering of the age of first intercourse. Almost half of young adolescents consider sexual relations permissible if partners have been together a number of times and have developed a caring relationship. Approximately 20 percent of sexually active teenage girls become pregnant each year, and almost half give birth. About 40 percent undergo abortions. Teenage parenthood is often associated with disadvantages to both mother (interruption of normal developmental progression) and infant (higher infant mortality, child neglect, developmental problems among children).

8. The most common sexually transmitted diseases are gonorrhea, herpes, and chlamydia; syphilis and AIDS are rarer. Gonorrhea, chlamydia, and syphilis can be cured with drugs; herpes can sometimes be controlled, but it cannot be cured; AIDS is incurable and fatal.

Adolescent Turmoil

9. Delinquency is a legal category defined by juvenile apprehension and conviction of a legal transgression, and associated with social class, sex, self-esteem, intelligence, home, and peer influences (such as gang membership). Gangs, many of which are violent, are cohesive groups defined by confrontation with authority.

10. Incidence of drug use among adolescents appears to have leveled off in recent years, except for use of cocaine. Alcohol is still the drug of choice, nicotine is second, and marijuana is a close third. Drug abuse refers to the recreational use of drugs in which use impairs normal functioning. Drug dependence (physiological or psychological) is manifested in a strong desire to continue taking a drug. Reasons for drug abuse include a complex set of genetic and social-environment factors. Predictors of the likelihood of drug abuse among teenagers include drug use among peers or parents; delinquency; stressful life changes; parental neglect, abuse, or abandonment; and low self-esteem.

11. Suicide is uncommon, although its frequency among adolescents has more than doubled in recent decades. More girls than boys attempt suicide, but fewer are successful. Although adolescent suicides are often precipitated by a single event (such as the death of a friend, pregnancy, parental divorce, or arrest), few occur without warning.

12. For most adolescents, life is only occasionally turbulent and stressful; most of the time, it abounds with joy and excitement.

FOCUS QUESTIONS: APPLICATIONS

1. Is adolescence typically a time of strife and conflict?
   - Using library resources, examine the proposition that adolescence is a period of sturm und drang.

2. How important are parents and peers throughout adolescence?
   - Plan and write up a proposal for a study that would allow you to determine some aspects of the relative importance of parents and peers during adolescence.

3. Are there real and important psychological differences between the sexes?
   - Do an informal survey of the person on the street (or around your dinner table) to determine what some views are regarding male–female differences with respect to qualities such as intelligence, aggression, and so on. Compare these opinions with scientific conclusions.

4. What are the principal sexual beliefs and behaviors of adolescents?
   - As a major term paper, summarize recent literature on the sexual beliefs and behaviors of teenagers.

5. How common and serious are adolescent delinquency, drug abuse, and suicide?
   - Develop a drug abuse prevention program that reflects each of the factors potentially involved in drug abuse.

STUDY TERMS

acute pelvic inflammatory disease 362

adolescent moratorium 348

adolescent pregnancy 358

AIDS 361

androgynous 353

chlamydia 361

crack 370

D-lysergic acid diethylamide tartrate (or LSD-25) 369

delinquency 362

drug abuse 366

drug dependence 366

drug tolerance 366

drugs 366

emotional distancing 349

foreclosure 348

gang 364

gateway drug-use theory 368

gender 353

gender differences 354

gender roles 353

gender typing 353

gender-role preference 353

gonorrhea 361

herpes 361

identity 344

identity achieved 348

identity diffusion 348

masturbation 357

moratorium 348

parent–adolescent conflict 350

peer group 350

physiological dependence 366

psychological dependence 366

self 344

self-esteem 344

self-image 344

self-worth 344

sex 355

sexual double standard 355

sexual stereotypes 353

sexually transmitted diseases (STDs) 361

stress 347

sturm und drang 346

tetrahydrocannabinol (THC) 369

universal adolescent 346

GROWING TOGETHER

The middle years of our lives span the second of the three great stages that make up *The Lifespan*'s photo album. These are our growing together years, the years during which our relationships with others do much to mold the shapes of our lives, giving them joy and purpose.

The transition from the growing up of childhood to the growing together of adulthood is sometimes difficult and uncertain. Unlike more tribal, nonindustrialized people, we seldom mark our passage with feasting and rituals—although we sometimes look to graduations and weddings as signs that we too have grown up.

Edward, second from the right. Hot Dang!

Tekla's wedding chair dance. Guess who's in the front.

Jill and her first Scottish husband. Hah! Hah!

$\mathcal{A}$dulthood brings no developmental task more important than that of establishing and nourishing relationships—with marriage or non-marriage partners, with children, with parents, with friends, with workmates, perhaps with dogs, horses, birds, and trees…

Yes, it did so move!

Todd and Emma before the kids!

One more and we'll need a new car.

Eighteen captains, and 'twas a cold crossing indeed.

Rio with Becky, dreaming of their next big win.

Not all of adulthood need to be tied only to serious things like work and family. There is much to be said for learning how to use our leisure—perhaps even for relearning how to play as we did when we knew we would never need to grow up, ever.

*I*f we can no longer remember to play as we did when we were children, perhaps we can now come to know some of the other faces of play.

Dang if it ain't a white-breasted kite!

Let her rip, Curt!

Offer and associates presented a self-image questionnaire to nearly 6,000 teenagers in 10 different countries. The result is a fascinating look at the thoughts and attitudes of teenagers around the world:

Offer, D. O., Ostrov, E., Howard, K., & Atkinson, R. (1988). *The teenage world: Adolescents' self-image in ten countries.* New York: Plenum.

The following two books present a detailed look at identity in adolescence. The first is an insightful collection that looks at the development of identity; the second contains fascinating interviews with some of the principal researchers and theorists in this area:

Adams, G. R., Gullotta, T. P., & Montemayor, R. (Eds.). (1992). *Adolescent identity formation* (Vol. 4). Newbury Park, CA: Sage.

Kroger, J. (1993). Ego identity: An overview. In J. Kroger (Ed.), *Discussions on ego identity.* Hillsdale, NJ: Erlbaum.

Gender stereotypes are widely held beliefs about male–female characteristics and differences. The first of the following two references presents a balanced view of some of the gender differences that psychology has actually found; the second looks at gender from a feminist perspective:

Halpern, D. F. (1986). *Sex differences in cognitive abilities.* Hillsdale, NJ: Erlbaum.

Hare-Mustin, R. T., & Marecek, J. (Eds.). (1990). *Making a difference: Psychology and the construction of gender.* New Haven, CN: Yale University Press.

This volume is a collection of articles that look at the incidence, methods, and reasons relating to adolescent suicide:

Whitaker, L. C., & Slimak, R. E. (Eds.). (1990). *College student suicide.* New York: Haworth.

Sing on! sing on! I would be drunk with life,
Drunk with the trampled vintage of my youth.

OSCAR WILDE
The Burden of Itys

EARLY ADULTHOOD

It's not always an easy thing to grow up, to leave one's childish toys and become an adult. There # PART SIX

are important psychosocial tasks to be accomplished first, the psychologists tell us in their peculiar jargon. As we see in the next two chapters, there are competencies to be acquired, crises to be conquered, old attitudes and old ways of thinking to be discarded. There are mature commitments to be made to careers, to friends and spouses and family, perhaps even to dogs and horses and other beasts. There is intimacy to be explored and earned and given.

These are the trappings of adulthood, not of adolescence and childhood. The things of childhood and adolescence must be left behind, trampled in the dust of childish years where wild oats were once sown.

If we do grow up, will our trampling of the vintage of our youth leave us with a wine so sweet it will make us want to sing with joy through our young adulthood?

Or will it leave us with only a vinegar to pucker our lips and furrow our brows and snatch the song from our hearts?

FOCUS QUESTIONS

1. Is early adulthood a period of physical growth, decline, or stability?

2. What is normal (and average) sexual behavior and responsiveness for young adults?

3. How do people select careers? Why is work important?

4. Is the thinking of the young adult different from that of children and adolescents?

OUTLINE

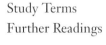

Physical and Cognitive Development: Early Adulthood

Peter: "Would you send me to school?"
Mrs. Darling (obligingly): "Yes."
Peter: "And then to an office?"
Mrs. Darling: "Very soon."
Peter (passionately): "I don't want to go to school and learn solemn things. No one is going to catch me lady, and make me a man. I want always to be a little boy and to have fun."

James Barrie
Peter Pan

Armand Delisle, like Peter Pan, decided one day he would rather not grow up. "I'm never gonna grow up," he informed his mother in his sweet little voice, crinkling his nose in that so-cute way of his. "I'm always gonna be your little boy."

CHAPTER 13

"Yeah, right," she said. "Now go out and feed the chickens." But she should have taken him more seriously because Armand, unlike the rest of us who merely flirted with the enchantment of not growing up, developed an unshakable devotion to the idea. He meant what he said. As a result, he didn't have to take school very seriously. So he played more sports than anyone else; and he also missed more school, mostly for hunting or fishing. Mr. Delisle tried quite often to straighten him out but it didn't help. And Mrs. Delisle . . . well, she kept him feeding the chickens whenever he happened to be around at the right time.

The rest of us eventually left, went on to other other things, mastering the developmental tasks of early adulthood right and left—getting jobs, cars, marriages, careers, children, mortgages. . . .

Armand is 40-something now. He still lives at home with his parents. He sometimes says he's looking after the farm, but really, the hired man does that. Mostly he fishes and hunts and looks for people who want to play golf or go to Europe.

THIS CHAPTER

Kiley (1983) speculates that increasing numbers of young people, like Armand Delisle, are unwilling to grow up. These individuals suffer from the **Peter Pan syndrome.** They are unwilling or unable to accept the ordinary responsibilities that come with increasing maturity. Accordingly, they are reluctant to make career decisions, to become economically independent, or, even more, to become emotionally independent and to accept responsibility for others. They are also anxious and lonely because they don't relate well to others who have matured more normally.

But most of us cannot stay little boys and girls and just have fun. We have to go off and learn solemn things. And we have to feed the chickens.

This chapter describes some of what is involved in "growing up"—that is, in making the transition from childhood to adulthood. It deals with the first major stage of adulthood, imaginatively termed *early adulthood* (20 to 40–45); *middle adulthood* (40–45 to 65–70) and *later adulthood* (65–70 onward) follow in *The Lifespan.* Thus, this chapter looks at physical development, health, sexual behavior and reproduction, work and careers, and cognitive change. Keep in mind, however, that many of the important activities and events of adulthood can occur at any age.

EARLY ADULTHOOD

As we saw in Chapter 11, adolescence is generally considered to begin with pubescence (changes leading to sexual maturity) and to end with adulthood. Unfortunately, for those of us who would like things to be simple, both of these events can occur at very different times for individuals of the same sex and do occur about two years apart for individuals of different sexes. Thus adolescence, as a transition period, has rather fuzzy boundaries.

Some writers describe another developmental period in late adolescence and early adulthood that is often labeled **youth.** Coleman (1974) defines youth as the period from age 14 to age 24—because nobody can be called an adult prior to the age of 14 and nobody can still be classed a child after the age of 24. That, of course, is not to say that all 14-year-olds are childish and all 24-year-olds mature—witness our Peter Pans. Our definitions are only definitions; they do not alter the exceptions that reality provides.

Early adulthood includes the years between the end of adolescence (or, sometimes, the end of youth) and about

Early adulthood stretches across a wide reach of years—from the end of adolescence to the beginning of middle age at about age 45. Thus this mother and daughter are both young adults, although each is at a different end of that span.

age 40 or 45—which signals the beginning of middle adulthood. However, the period is better understood in terms of the physical, intellectual, and social changes that occur rather than simply in terms of having attained a given age. One approach to understanding these changes is to look at some of the important developmental tasks of this period.

Developmental Tasks

Developmental tasks are sequential milestones that reflect the acquisition of some major new competence, or the occurrence of a social event with important psychological consequences. Some developmental tasks arise from physical maturation; others are more closely tied to social demands and expectations. For example, maturation-related developmental tasks of infancy include learning to walk and talk; two developmental tasks of childhood that are more culturally based are learning how to get along with peers and developing basic skills in reading, writing, and arithmetic. These are achievements with immediate and obviously important consequences for children.

Most of the developmental tasks of adolescence and early adulthood have consequences that are not as imme-

HAVIGHURST'S DEVELOPMENTAL TASKS

Developmental tasks are important social and psychological milestones in human development. Note that they are highly contextual—that is, they vary from one context to another. In contexts where accomplishing a task is seen as highly important (or essential), failure to do so may be linked with considerable distress and unhappiness. However, societies such as ours tolerate and encourage such a wide range of lifestyles and values that failure to accomplish one or more tasks may be inconsequential. How many of the tasks of adolescence—and young adulthood—have you now accomplished? Which of those that remain are important to you?

Period	Tasks	Period	Tasks
Adolescence	1. Developing conceptual and problem-solving skills	Young adulthood	1. Courting and selecting a mate
	2. Achieving more mature relationships with male and female peers		2. Learning to live happily with partner
	3. Developing an ethical system to guide behavior		3. Starting a family and assuming parent role
	4. Striving toward socially responsible behavior		4. Rearing children
	5. Accepting the changing physique and using the body effectively		5. Assuming home management responsibilities
	6. Preparing for an economically viable career		6. Beginning career or occupation
	7. Achieving emotional independence from parents		7. Assuming appropriate civic responsibilities
	8. Preparing for marriage and family life		8. Establishing a social network

diate, that are more future oriented (Nurmi, 1991). Many of the tasks that are set for adolescents by teachers, parents, and social contexts have to do with expectations and goals for the future. Even the adoption of an identity is future oriented insofar as it involves commitment to career, lifestyle, and values.

The developmental tasks of early adulthood, too, are transitional and future oriented: Most of them are important in terms of their future implications for career and family. And as adolescents age into young adulthood, Nurmi (1991) informs us, they become even more future oriented. Havighurst and Coleman each describe two somewhat different sets of developmental tasks characteristic of early adulthood.

Havighurst's Tasks of Early Adulthood

Robert *Havighurst*'s (1972) tasks for adolescence and young adulthood are shown in Interactive Table 13.1. (Later stages are shown in Tables 15.1 and 18.2.) These have to do primarily with establishing a family, a career, and a place in the community—all future-oriented activities. They include things such as courting and selecting a mate, learning to live happily with a partner, starting a family and assuming a parental role, and rearing children (topics that we cover in the next chapter). They include, as well, beginning a career or an occupation (a topic covered in the final sections of this chapter).

There are two important things to keep in mind when looking at developmental tasks. First, they are highly culture specific. They reflect competencies and achievements that are important and relevant primarily in North American societies, as well as in many industrialized societies elsewhere. However, many of these developmental tasks would be totally irrelevant in other societies.

Second, although developmental tasks describe what is common and expected in a given context, failure to achieve a developmental task, or achieving it earlier or later than expected, is not evidence of abnormality. Clearly, not all young adults want a mate. Similarly, some cannot, some will not, and some should not have children. Nor do all need to select and develop a career.

Coleman's Transitional Tasks

According to *Coleman*, a successful transition between childhood and adulthood requires meeting two classes of developmental objectives. The first concerns the individual's own capacities and abilities, and is referred to as *self-centered;* the second has to do with how the individual relates to others and is termed *other-centered* (see Table 13.2).

Self-centered objectives have to do with the development of skills required for achieving economic independence. They include skills relating to specific occupations or careers, which might be acquired through postsecondary schooling, or through the cultivation of some special talent such as that of a musician or singer, for example. They also include skills relating to the management of one's own affairs—for example, handling financial matters and resisting the lure of easy credit. Less obvious, but perhaps no less important, are tasks such as finding and looking after a living space, arranging for utilities, cooking, making decisions about leisure time, and on, and on. And a third self-centered objective has to do with acquiring the skills that are required to be an intelligent consumer, not so much of goods as of the "cultural riches of civilization" (Coleman, 1974, p. 4).

A final self-centered skill required for effective participation in adult society is the ability to engage in

TABLE 13.2
Skills Required for Effective Transition to Adulthood

Self-Centered Skills	Useful For
Work and occupational skills	Attaining economic independence
Self-management skills	Making reasonable decisions in the face of wide choice
Consumer skills	Learning how to use and enjoy culture as well as goods
Concentrated involvement skills	Succeeding in undertakings; making significant contributions in many areas

Other-Centered Skills	Useful For
Social interaction skills	Effective commerce in a variety of situations with different people
Skills relating to management of others	Assuming responsibility for those who are dependent
Cooperative skills	Engaging in joint endeavors

SOURCE: Based on Coleman, 1974.

Our continuous societies don't tell us very clearly when adolescence ends and adulthood begins. But, taken together, events such as graduation, getting a driver's license, obtaining permanent employment, getting married—even voting—are important signs of having grown up.

concentrated activity. That is, a completely successful transition to adulthood requires individuals to dedicate themselves to certain endeavors, unlike Peter Pan. In many cases, these endeavors will be job-related; in other cases, they might relate to community activities, specific hobbies, religious beliefs, or political interests. Coleman suggests that the greatest of human achievements in all areas are usually the result of such concentrated activity.

Among *other-centered* objectives, Coleman lists three types of experiences that contribute significantly to the adoption of mature social roles. These include the opportunity to interact with a variety of individuals from many different social classes, races, age groups, religions, and occupations; experience in situations where the individual is responsible for others; and experience in activities where the outcomes depend on the cooperation of a number of individuals.

Acquiring these skills should facilitate the transition to adulthood, and result in better-adjusted and happier adults.

The Transition

When does childhood finally become adulthood? There is no simple, widely accepted answer. In general, however, the beginning of adulthood coincides roughly with attaining economic and emotional independence from the family. Accordingly, the most common manifestations of independence are finding some means of financial support (obtaining a job, for example) and establishing a new home, sometimes alone but very often with a friend or a mate.

One result of today's complex, technological societies has been to prolong the transition to adulthood. Simply

achieving puberty no longer provides the child with the skills required for optimal participation in adult life. In the days of our grandparents, being able to make babies might have been sufficient qualification for admission to the rank of adulthood. Today, however, a great many of us are required to spend an increasing amount of time learning the skills—the "solemn things"—that we are likely to need later. And during this time, whether we are in college, in the military, unemployed, or elsewhere, we are likely to be neither child nor adult but somewhere in between.

We should note again, however, that this swiftly brushed picture of the transition to early adulthood paints only one of several possible scenes. Growing up today does not always entail a prolongation of adolescence—a period of what some term *youth*. There are many who still enter the work force during adolescence. And among these, many become adult in all significant ways far before others of identical age. Similarly, even in the time of our great-grandparents and beyond, during a period when we imagine life to have consisted largely of idyllic meanderings through pastoral scenes, many people prolonged their adolescence for long periods, unable or perhaps simply unwilling to become adult. Then, as today, there were some people who knew very clearly that we do not all have

Early adulthood sees the peak of our lives in terms of physical strength, stamina, and endurance, as well as intellectual capacity. This camp counselor can not only run faster than his charges, throw a ball farther, and chop more wood, but inside the binder on his lap he has hidden inventions that will amaze and astound them.

to become adults (in terms of work roles, responsibilities, and attitudes toward self, others, and life in general). There are those who can dream and play—like children—through the entire lifespan. Let others feed the chickens.*

PHYSICAL DEVELOPMENT

One of the reasons developmental psychology has traditionally been concerned with children and not with adults is simply that children change a great deal—sometimes very rapidly and dramatically; changes among adults are usually less dramatic and less uniform. Hence, the temptation is to think of adulthood as a *plateau*—a resting state following development and preceding decline. It is worth emphasizing again that contemporary models of lifespan development recognize that change occurs throughout the entire lifespan.

*"Your Uncle Albert was like that," said my grandmother. "When he wouldn't work on the farm and your grandpa sent him away, he just went straight into the army because he thought that would be a lot of fun and somebody would look after him. Then he married Rose so she'd look after him. And when she got tired of that and left him, he just went straight to jail, 'cause there, they look after people too. And you can bet if he hadn't been run over by the truck, there'd still be somebody looking after him."

In the area of physical development, adulthood clearly is not a plateau. Although change might not be as predictable or as dramatic as it was in earlier years, there are still some small mountains to climb and a few slopes to descend.

Performance

From childhood through adolescence, there is measurable improvement in various aspects of motor performance. For example, both boys and girls can run about 4 yards (3.64 meters) per second at the age of 4. By age 12, their speed has increased to about 6 yards (5.41 meters) per second. For boys, running speed continues to increase, reaching about 7 yards (6.37 meters) per second by age 17; but for girls, there is a slight decline after age 12 (Espenschade & Eckert, 1980). Haywood (1986) reports similar findings for motor tasks like throwing or vertical jumping. The pattern is of gradual improvement through childhood and into adolescence for males, with an earlier plateau and occasional slight decline for girls, closely correlated with the adolescent girl's increase in relative proportion of fat mass. Interestingly, this plateau is less apparent in more recent measures, probably because of increased female participation in sports (Haywood, 1986). It is also not apparent among competitive male or female athletes—evidence, says Haywood, of the social and practice factors involved in motor performance.

Not surprisingly, the best adult performers on measures of strength and speed are those who were also the best performers as adolescents, report Lefevre and associates (1993), following a longitudinal study of 173 Flemish boys during adolescence and again at age 30. Interestingly, however, other things being equal, late-maturing boys, compared with early-maturing boys, appeared to have a distinct advantage as adults (although, of course, not as adolescents).

Note that measures such as those of running speed and of distance an object is thrown are *quantitative*. *Qualitative* assessment of motor performance is difficult and inexact, but is sometimes accomplished using super-slow-motion pictures. These permit motor sequences to be analyzed and judged on different qualitative dimensions. When motor performance is evaluated *qualitatively*, especially for complex and highly practiced skills, the developmental pattern observed is slightly different. Whereas quantitative measures tend to peak and plateau in the early twenties, motor skills required for high-level performance in sports such as basketball, hockey, and football, for example, continue to improve into adulthood.

Flexibility

Improvements in motor performance after adolescence are highly dependent on practice. Perhaps nowhere is this more evident than in measures of range of joint motion (flexibility). In fact, without training, flexibility begins to decline at about the age of 12. Decline is gradual and often goes unnoticed, but, in the absence of training, continues through early adulthood. But with continued exercise, says Ward (1994), the rate of decline for most measures of fitness, including flexibility, slows significantly. In fact, 60-year-old master athletes can often outperform 30-year-olds who are customarily inactive. Rontoyannis (1992) reports the case of a 79-year-old elite long-distance runner whose performance and physiology remain very close to that of other runners who are half a century younger.

Athough exercise *slows* the rate of decline in flexibility, it does not completely *prevent* it. Flexibility often diminishes even for athletes and others who work physically, simply because few sports and occupations require a full range of motion in all joints. For example, the 79-year-old runner studied by Rontoyannis (1992) had lost considerable joint flexibility relative to younger runners although he could perform as well as many of them. Loss of flexibility is not nearly as apparent in the case of gymnasts and dancers whose training is directed toward maintaining flexibility, and who typically retain a high range of motion in all joints through early adulthood. Flexibility can be maintained through training, and perhaps increased through appropriate exercises, even when these are begun very late in life.

Declining flexibility results largely from the fact that certain motions are not generally required in ordinary life.

TABLE 13.3
Age Ranges: Peak Athletic Achievement

	Age Range (years)
Professional football players	22–26
Professional prizefighters	25–26
Professional hockey players	26
Professional tennis players	25–29
Leading chess contestants	29–33
Professional golfers	31–36
World billiards record holders	31–36

SOURCE: From *Age and Achievement* by H. C. Lehman, 1953, Princeton, NJ: Princeton University Press. Copyright 1953, © 1981 by the American Philosophical Society. Reprinted by permission of the publisher.

As a result, the individual is often unaware that range of joint movement is gradually decreasing. When it becomes most apparent—for example, in the shorter steps and reduced pelvic rotations of older walkers—it is often dismissed as one of the inevitable consequences of aging. But it may not be completely inevitable given continued high-flexing activity throughout life.

Strength and Stamina

Early adulthood is potentially the peak of our physical development in terms of speed, strength, coordination, and endurance, as well as in terms of general health. If we remain fit and active during our twenties and early thirties, we can lift more, run faster, throw farther, work longer, climb higher, and crawl lower than at any other time in our lives. It is not surprising that Lehman's (1953) studies of the ages at which people were most likely to achieve in a variety of fields found that the twenties and sometimes the early thirties were periods of highest achievement for sports requiring strength, stamina, and coordination (see Table 13.3).

The evidence is clear, Ward (1994) adds, that exercise need not be vigorous or difficult to maintain fitness and flexibility, but that moderate exercise, provided it occurs for three or four 30-minute periods a week, can be just as effective. However, the evidence also suggests that many young adults do not exercise and as a result, manifest low levels of physical fitness. Pierce and colleagues (1992), who evaluated the fitness levels of 258 male and female college students, report finding relatively low levels of cardiovascular fitness, an indication of a lack of physical activity. Interestingly, however, strength measures for these students remained high.

In a similar study, Glenmark and colleagues (1994) evaluated 55 men and 26 women at the age of 16 and again at the age of 27, looking at both exercise levels and various measures of strength. They, too, found relatively high levels of strength in early adulthood, *regardless of physical activity level*. Strangely, it seems that there is relatively little correlation between physical exercise and muscle strength, especially for men.

The normal developmental pattern with respect to physical strength sees a very gradual decline following the peak years. This decline is often not particularly noticeable until the forties and is most apparent with respect to back and leg strength.

In addition to a gradual loss of strength following the peak in early adulthood, there is a more noticeable loss of stamina, usually related to poorer aerobic functioning (heart–lung efficiency). Few 40-year-olds can still compete with younger individuals in athletic events and sports requiring strength and endurance (marathons or hockey, for example). For this reason, in the same way that competitions in childhood are made more fair by assigning competitors to age-determined classes, so adult competitions are sometimes separated into age classes. But whereas the older age groups typically outperform the younger groups in childhood, the opposite is true in adulthood. Masters' class (over 40) marathons are won with slower times than the open classes.

It is important to note that here, as elsewhere, many of the changes and declines of age are neither dramatic nor inevitable. Thus, declines in physical endurance and strength before the age of 50 are scarcely noticeable so that early adulthood is best described as a period of *stability* rather than one of decline. And with proper exercise and training, many individuals are able to continue performing physically at high levels well into old age—witness Rontoyannis's (1992) 79-year-old long-distance runner.

The Senses

There are no dramatic age-related changes in the functioning of our senses through early adulthood: All our senses continue to function about as well at the end of early adulthood as they did at the beginning.

However, there are a number of more subtle changes. Their effects are generally felt so gradually that they are seldom noticed as they are occurring. Morioka and associates (1990) looked at vision and hearing among more than a thousand normal individuals aged 5 to 24. Both visual accommodation and hearing declined systematically, but very slowly, with age. It seems that the lens in the eye is subject to the effects of aging almost from birth, becoming progressively less flexible and changing its shape so that most individuals become increasingly farsighted as they age.

Hearing, like vision, changes only slightly in early adulthood but, on average, begins to decline in the thirties and accelerates after middle age (Belsky, 1990). Losses

that do occur are typically more common for men than for women. Hearing losses in early adulthood are most often the consequence of environmental factors, such as prolonged exposure to noisy environments, rather than the effects of age.

Changes in touch sensitivity, as well as in taste and smell, are not apparent in early adulthood.

HEALTH

In the same way that early adulthood is characterized by the peak of physical strength and endurance, as well as of sensory capacity, so is it characterized by the peak of physical health. In particular, many of the infections of childhood become far less common in early adulthood and remain so throughout life. With increasing age, however, there is increased susceptibility to chronic (recurring) medical complaints, such as back and spine problems, heart ailments, and so on. Whereas the leading causes of death among young adults are accidents, heart disease and cancer are the leading causes of death among men after age 45 and among women after age 35 (U.S. Bureau of the Census, 1994). In this connection, there have been some dramatic changes in the most common causes of death during the last several decades. In 1940, the leading cause of death was pneumonia and influenza, followed closely by tuberculosis. Fifty years later, influenza and pneumonia accounted for fewer than one twentieth as many deaths as heart disease and cancer, which now lead the list. And in 1992, tuberculosis accounted for only 1 of every 200,000 deaths in the United States (U.S. Bureau of the Census, 1994).

The majority of adults (over 80 percent) consider themselves to be in "good-to-excellent" health in early adulthood (Bayer, Whissell-Buechy, & Honzik, 1981). Toward the end of this period, however, there is a gradual increase in the number who suffer from a variety of complaints, and a corresponding increase in the number who become more concerned with exercise and health (Hooker & Kaus, 1994). Among women, the most common complaints relate to the *reproductive system*. These may involve attempts to become pregnant, pregnancy itself, problems relating to menstruation, ovarian cysts and tumors, and infections. Among men, the most common complaints relate to the digestive system; men have three times the incidence of stomach ulcers that women do.

Another sex difference with respect to adult health is that women generally report more illnesses than do men. Ironically, their life expectancies continue to be significantly higher. Some theorize that women are more sensitive to their bodies and perhaps less likely to dismiss symptoms as inconsequential. Accordingly, they are more likely to seek medical help and thus to report more illnesses. Also, they are more likely to receive assistance when it will be most effective.

Active lifestyles are characteristic of an increasing number of young adults. Such lifestyles not only contribute to increased health and happiness, but are also an important way of meeting people—which might be the reason for the empty seat.

Exercise and Lifestyle

Participate! Play tennis! Play racquetball! Play squash! Dance! Join a spa! Take an exercise class! Skate! Ski! Swim! Run! Jog! At least walk.

Literally millions of adults, many of whom have engaged in virtually no unnecessary physical activity since high school or college—and perhaps not even then—embark on *exercise* programs in early or middle adulthood. And many undertake these programs with the same dedication and determination that they bring to their careers—and perhaps to other aspects of their lives. Why? Simply, to be happy and healthy. That is, after all, what most of us want. Exercise, we are told, will make us healthier, may enable us to live longer, and should make us trimmer, more fit, and perhaps even more attractive, given our contemporary cultural standards of physical attractiveness.

How valid are these claims? Research leaves little doubt that exercise contributes significantly to good health. Numerous studies of cardiovascular fitness have repeatedly found higher levels of fitness and lower incidence of coronary heart disease among those who exercise regularly than among those whose lives are more sedentary (Ward, 1994). In addition, exercise is important in reducing the percentage of body fat and in increasing muscle and bone density (Sambrook, Kelly, & Eisman, 1993).

But does exercise make us happier? Does it affect us psychologically? Blumenthal and associates (1982) say yes. They investigated the effects of exercise on a group of 16 subjects, aged 25 to 61, who had registered for a 10-week adult fitness program. At the beginning of the program, all subjects were administered a battery of three psycho-

logical tests to assess mood, anxiety, and some general aspects of everyday functioning, such as sleep patterns and social habits. A control group, consisting of healthy but sedentary individuals of similar age, was also administered these same tests.

The exercise program for the 16 experimental subjects consisted of a 10-minute routine of stretching exercises, followed by 45 minutes of walking or running, three times a week over a period of 10 weeks. All exercise periods were under medical supervision. Control-group members continued as before, without any regular exercise program.

At the end of the 10-week period, individuals in both the experimental and the control groups were again administered the three psychological instruments. The results are clear and striking. Whereas the groups had initially been similar on each of these instruments, the experimental group now felt less tension, fatigue, depression, and confusion, and experienced significant reductions in immediate and general anxiety. And, as expected, physiological measures indicated significant improvements in the experimental groups.

Apparently, adults who are inactive but basically healthy can increase their well-being, as well as their sense of well-being, through exercise.

Drugs and Stress

Whereas exercise generally has a positive effect on health and well-being, recreational drugs and excessive **stress** typically do not. Of the drugs used by young adults, alcohol and nicotine are by far the most common. In fact, they are the two that show only slight decline after age 25; marijuana, cocaine, stimulants, and all others show a marked decline (U.S. Bureau of the Census, 1994). The health consequences of nicotine use and heavy alcohol consumption are well known.

Some Consequences of Stress

The effects of stress on the health of the young adult are not as clear as those of drugs such as alcohol and nicotine. This is largely because stress is far more difficult to define and measure than is alcohol or nicotine use. In addition, its effects are more subtle and may involve a greater number of systems. Interestingly, one of the effects of stress seems to be an increased probability of abusing alcohol and drugs (Labouvie, 1990).

As we saw in Chapter 10, stress may be defined in terms of stimuli that make excessive demands on the individual, or in terms of responses that are accompanied by the physiological changes of high arousal. We saw, too, that in some ways a stress response is an adaptive response. The physiological changes of arousal—the sudden spurt of adrenaline, for example—are useful in mobilizing the individual's systems for responding. However, prolonged exposure to stress can eventually lead to a "stress overload" and to a consequent breakdown of the adaptive response.

Excessive stress in childhood is sometimes evident in sleeping or eating disturbances, depression, and a variety of physical complaints. The consequences of stress for adults are perhaps not very different from those in children. Thus, stress is linked to several physical complaints that sometimes appear in early adulthood, including gastrointestinal problems such as ulcers, heart problems, and high blood pressure (Longstreth & Wolde-Tsadik, 1993).

In general, high stress is often associated with anxiety, and high anxiety is one of the most common of all psychiatric symptoms. There is evidence that stress in adulthood can interact with other stressors to which the individual might have been exposed in childhood, increasing the probability of psychiatric disorder and of drug and alcohol abuse. For example, Landerman, George, and Blazer (1991), who studied a sample of 3,801 adults, found that those who had recently been exposed to stress *and* who had, as children, been exposed to stress associated with parental mental illness or divorce, were now more likely to suffer from depression and were more vulnerable to alcohol abuse.

Individual Responses to Stress

Not all adults respond to stressful events in the same way. Psychology and medicine have sometimes found it useful to distinguish between two types of individuals, identifiable largely in terms of the level of stress that seems to permeate their lives. These types, well popularized in literature, are labeled "Type A" and "Type B" (Friedman & Rosenman, 1974).

Type A individuals are hard-driving, aggressive, ambitious, impatient, and competitive (Smith, 1994). These are individuals who drive themselves mercilessly, who sense most keenly the unrelenting pressures of time and the urgency of their lives. In contrast, *Type B* individuals are slow, relaxed, easygoing. They speak more softly, tend to impose few deadlines on themselves, and do not, in general, respond to life with the same sense of urgency that drives Type A's.

Type A and B individuals are often identified by means of the Jenkins Activity Survey, which asks questions such as "Do people sometimes tell you that you eat too fast?" or "Do the people with whom you work see you as being aggressive and achievement oriented?" (Jenkins, Zyzanski, & Rosenman, 1971). Researchers have found that about 40 percent of the population is Type A; the remainder is Type B. Clearly, however, the types are less a dichotomy than a continuum: Some Type A individuals would manifest extremes of Type A behavior and others would be only slightly different from Type B individuals.

The medical profession has found this typology particularly useful because of an apparent relationship between Type A behavior and coronary problems (Deary et al., 1994). Some studies indicate that Type A individuals are approximately twice as likely as Type B individuals to suffer fatal heart attacks ("Down with Type A!" 1983). Small wonder that being a Type A individual has sometimes been accorded the same weight as a contributor to coronary problems as high blood pressure, high cholesterol level, smoking, and obesity. However, subsequent research has not always found as high a relationship between Type A behavior and coronary problems as did earlier research. But what this research has been finding is that certain components of the Type A personality are more important than others in contributing to health problems. In particular, Type A individuals who are hostile and angry seem to be more prone to coronary-problems than Type A's who are simply highly achievement oriented, aggressive, and fast-paced (Deary et al., 1994).

Smith (1994) suggests that, at least to some extent, Type A personalities may be physiologically based. Nevertheless, it is worth noting that through training in relaxation, and with proper motivation, Type A individuals can become more like Type B's (Ovcharchyn, Johnson, & Petzel, 1981). At the very least, such individuals might learn to relax sufficiently so that they can effectively rid themselves of the damaging effects of stress, although they continue to be hard-driving Type A's in the workplace.

Sources of Stress

Sources of stress in everyday life might include a variety of frustrations, demands, and conflicts having to do with social relationships, spouse and children, career, and so on. They might also include significant events or changes. Several theorists suggest that *all* change is stressful—even

SOCIAL READJUSTMENT RATING SCALE

Major, and even minor, changes can be sources of stress. Some theorists suggest that *all* change is stressful, and that its effects are cumulative. You can obtain a rough estimate of the stress in your own life using the scale reproduced here. Simply total the life-change unit values associated with each of the life events you have experienced during the past 12 months. Scores of 150 or less are associated with continued health and happiness; scores above 300 are sometimes associated with later problems. However, these generalizations are based on averages, and do not reflect countless individual exceptions. Some people are remarkably resistant to stress; others buckle more easily.

Rank	Life Event	Mean Value (life-change units)	Rank	Life Event	Mean Value (life-change units)
1	Death of spouse	100	23	Son or daughter leaving home	29
2	Divorce	73	24	Trouble with in-laws	29
3	Marital separation	65	25	Outstanding personal achievement	28
4	Jail term	63	26	Wife begins or stops work	26
5	Death of close family member	63	27	Begin or end school	26
6	Personal injury or illness	53	28	Change in living conditions	25
7	Marriage	50	29	Revision of personal habits	24
8	Fired at work	47	30	Trouble with boss	23
9	Marital reconciliation	45	31	Change in work hours or conditions	20
10	Retirement	45	32	Change in residence	20
11	Change in health of family member	44	33	Change in schools	20
12	Pregnancy	40	34	Change in recreation	19
13	Sex difficulties	39	35	Change in church activities	19
14	Gain of new family member	39	36	Change in social activities	18
15	Business readjustment	39	37	Mortgage or loan less than $10,000	17
16	Change in financial state	38	38	Change in sleeping habits	16
17	Death of close friend	37	39	Change in number of family get-togethers	15
18	Change to different line of work	36	40	Change in eating habits	15
19	Change in number of arguments with spouse	35	41	Vacation	13
20	Mortgage over $10,000	31	42	Christmas	12
21	Foreclosure of mortgage or loan	30	43	Minor violations of the law	11
22	Change in responsibilities at work	29			

SOURCE: From "The Social Readjustment Rating Scale" by T. H. Holmes and R. H. Rahe, 1967, *Journal of Psychosomatic Research* 11, pp. 213–218. Elsevier Science Ltd., Pergamon Imprint, Oxford, England. Reprinted with permission of the publisher.

pleasant changes such as going on vacation. In Chapter 10, there is a scale of potential changes in the lives of children ranked in terms of their probable stressful impact. Interactive Table 13.4 presents a similar scale for adults. In an early study involving 400 subjects, Rahe (1972) reported that those who claimed scores of 150 or lower in the preceding year were likely to remain healthy; those whose scores were above 300 were much more likely to develop physical as well as mental problems.

SEX AND REPRODUCTION

The most dramatic changes in the reproductive system throughout the entire lifespan are those that occur in adolescence. It is then, as we saw in Chapter 11, that profound hormonal changes trigger the well-known series of developments that define pubescence and that lead eventually to puberty (sexual maturity). Within approximately a year of the girl's first menstrual period and the boy's first ejaculation of semen (although sometimes sooner), each is capable of becoming a parent.

Normal Sexual Responses

The normal sexual response in both males and females is often described as a four-stage event: excitement, plateau, orgasm, and resolution (Masters & Johnson, 1966). *Excitement* is a preparatory phase leading to sexual arousal. Major changes that mark the excitement phase in females include vaginal lubrication and expansion and distension of the vagina; in males, excitement is characterized by erection of the penis.

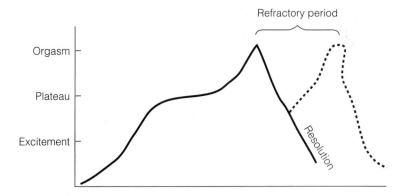

FIGURE 13.1
Male sexual response. (Based on Masters & Johnson, 1966.)

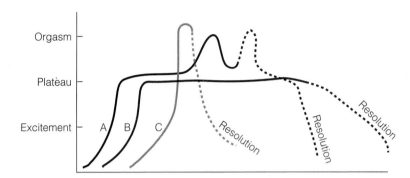

FIGURE 13.2

Three female sexual response cycles. (Based on Masters & Johnson, 1966.)

The *plateau* is a period of continuing sexual arousal following initial excitement, but preceding orgasm. Among women, the plateau entails continued swelling of the vagina, some changes in the labia ("lips" surrounding vaginal opening), breast enlargement and sometimes nipple erection, increased heart rate and blood pressure, and occasionally a flushing of chest, neck, and face. Among men, the plateau is marked by a maintenance of the erection, enlargement of the testes, occasional nipple erection, and a sharp increase in pulse rate, blood pressure, and respiration rate.

The orgasmic phase in women entails between 5 and 15 contractions of the outer third of the vagina, some uterine contractions, some muscle spasms, and a marked increase in respiration. *Orgasm* in men may involve explosive contractions of the urethra as sperm is emitted (*seminal emission* or *ejaculation*), muscle spasms, rapid increase in respiration rate, and maximum heart and blood pressure levels. However, in many cases, especially among older men, orgasm does not necessarily involve seminal emission (Gibson, 1992). The two events are confused, says Gibson, because they ordinarily occur together among younger men.

In both males and females, *resolution* involves a rapid return to a preexcitement state.

There are two important differences between male and female response patterns. First, immediately following the male orgasm, there is a period, termed *refractory*, during which the male is incapable of a second orgasm.

This period may be as short as a few minutes or as long as several hours. (See Figure 13.1.)

Second, whereas the usual male pattern of sexual response is a single excitement-plateau-orgasm-resolution cycle, there are three common patterns of female sexual response. The first (A in Figure 13.2) involves excitement, the plateau, an ensuing orgasm, and the possibility of one or more subsequent orgasms (without recycling through the excitement phase), followed by the resolution after the final orgasm. The second (B) is marked by a longer plateau and a slower resolution, but no orgasm. And the third (C) is a faster response cycle that goes relatively directly from excitement to orgasm and returns equally rapidly to a normal state.

In both men and women, the entire sexual response cycle is typically accompanied by physical sensations that vary from mildly to intensely pleasurable. In light of this, and given its biological significance, it is little wonder that sexuality is among the most important of human motivations and behaviors.

Adult Sexual Behavior in the United States

Following a series of 90-minute interviews with 3,432 randomly selected adults aged 18 to 59, Michael and associates (1994) report on some of the sexual practices of American men and women. Among their findings:

- Only 3 percent of all respondents claimed to have had five or more sex partners during the preceding year. The vast majority, more than 80 percent, reported having only one partner, or none.

- The majority of married people (75 percent of the men and 85 percent of the women) claim they are faithful to their spouses.

- On average, American males report they have had six sex partners during their lifetimes; women report they have had two.

- Forty-one percent of married couples have sex at least twice a week.

- Married people and couples who live together have sex more often than single people.

- Seventy-five percent of married women and 95 percent of married men report always or almost always having an orgasm during sex.

The results of this survey, the authors point out, indicate that most people are not having sex as often as had been thought, and that they are doing so primarily with their spouses or partners with whom they live.

There are two kinds of problems that can interfere with sexual responsiveness and reproduction: sexual dysfunctions and infertility.

Sexual Dysfunctions

Sexual disturbances of various kinds are often temporary and appear to be relatively common. But because of the secrecy that surrounds these issues, most people who suffer from these dysfunctions think that they are rare and experience needless anxiety. In one longitudinal survey that consisted of four interviews of a sample of young adults over a 10-year period (between ages 20 and 30), one out of two of the females and one out of three of the males reported sexual disturbances (Ernst, Foldenyi & Angst, 1993).

The most common **sexual dysfunction** among men who consult sex therapists is **erectile dysfunction** (*impotence*)—the inability to achieve or to maintain an erection. This condition is more common with increasing age. In as many as 50 percent of all cases, it may have physical or medical origins; in others, its roots are more psychological. Among its possible causes are certain drugs (Fleischhacker et al., 1994), as well as anxiety and depression (Holzapfel, 1993).

Premature ejaculation—the inability to control ejaculation—is a relatively common sexual dysfunction among men in early adulthood, but becomes less common with increasing age (Gibson, 1992).

Retarded ejaculation—essentially the opposite of premature ejaculation—is characterized by an inability to achieve orgasm during sexual intercourse. In many cases, retarded ejaculation is situational—that is, it is manifested in some situations, but not others. Evidence suggests that stress and anxiety are often involved.

Female sexual dysfunctions include inability to derive pleasure from sexual intercourse; *vaginismus*, or involuntary contractions of the vagina that make intercourse painful or impossible; and inability to achieve orgasm. Inability to achieve orgasm is not viewed as a problem unless the woman expects that she *should* experience one. As we saw, a female sexual response cycle without an orgasm is common and pleasurable for many women.

Hypoactive sexual desire is yet another sexual dysfunction that appears to be highly common, but that is not easily defined or treated (Trudel, Ravart, & Matte, 1993). Put simply, hypoactive sexual desire is manifested by a lower than normal interest in sexual activity. It affects both males and females, but appears to be more prevalent among females. Katz, Frazer, and Wilson (1993) report that there has been a significant increase in lack of sexual desire among young adults in recent years. Their data suggest that much of it is related to higher general sexual anxiety associated with fear of AIDS.

All of these sexual dysfunctions can be treated, sometimes by means of psychological-sexual therapy, sometimes medically. Of them, only severe vaginismus, retarded ejaculation, and impotence are likely to result in infertility—the inability to produce children.

Infertility

With puberty, most men and women not only acquire the capacity to respond sexually, but also develop strong urges to do so. There appear to be few major changes in these urges or in the capacity to respond through early adulthood—although frequency of sexual intercourse declines rapidly within the first few years of marriage (see Chapter 14). Some evidence indicates that men might, on the average, be slightly less easily aroused toward the end of early adulthood, and achieve orgasm more slowly. At the same time, through early adulthood, women apparently become more capable of achieving orgasm during intercourse (Gibson, 1992).

Biologically, women and men are capable of producing healthy infants throughout early adulthood. As we saw in Chapter 3, however, the probability of genetic and birth complications increases with advancing age of both parents, but especially the mother.

Infertility, however, is a relatively common problem among both men and women. Among women, it is most often due to blocked Fallopian tubes, the blockage usually resulting from infections such as chlamydia and acute pelvic inflammatory disease (Quan, 1994). In addition, fertility in women drops slowly from the age of 20. One reason is that ovulation, which may initially occur regularly, sometimes becomes less predictable as menstrual cycles become less regular. Nor does ovulation always occur with every cycle. Thus, on the average, even when they are fertile, older women do not become pregnant as easily as younger women.

Infertility in women is also sometimes associated with alterations in the menstrual cycle, or complete cessation of menstruation (*amenorrhea*) as a result of strenuous exercise. This is essentially an adaptive response to metabolic stress in the body, notes Bonen (1994). This type of infertility is temporary, however, and usually reverses with a change in exercise patterns.

Fertility among men also decreases very gradually through early adulthood, largely because of a decrement in the production of sperm. However, this decrement is very slight before middle age—most men in very late adulthood still produce sperm. However, the number of viable sperm produced by elderly men is ordinarily too small to make conception very likely. In a small number of cases (about 1 percent), infertility among men is related to tumors on the testes, to brain tumors, or to other uncommon medical problems (Jarow, 1994).

It's important to note that decreasing fertility among men and women in early adulthood is not a *primary* aging process—that is, it is not an inevitable consequence of age. In fact, the principal causes of changes in fertility rate during this period are infections and diseases. And although these become more probable with advancing age, they are not a result of aging.

As is discussed in Chapter 14, many women are now having children somewhat later than in the past. Although the overall birthrate has scarcely risen in North America in recent decades, the number of first births to women over the age of 30 has increased by more than 35 percent (U.S. Bureau of the Census, 1994). One reason for this is that recent decades have seen some profound changes in female work and career patterns.

WORK AND CAREERS

One of the most important developmental tasks in making a successful transition from youth to adulthood is finding some sort of "adult" employment. But finding employment is far more than simply a mundane developmental task; it is fundamentally important to who and what we are. And the ease with which we make the transition from nonwork to work, either at the beginning of our adult years or at the end (or, perhaps, even in the middle) is fundamentally important to our well-being.

Employment: Some Definitions

Although terms such as *career, vocation, job,* and *occupation* are often used interchangeably, their precise meanings are somewhat different. The narrowest of these terms is **job,** which refers to the specific tasks or duties that the worker performs. Thus, one of the jobs undertaken by a caretaker might be to empty wastebaskets. In much the same way, there are jobs associated with being a lawyer or a dentist—specific tasks that are part of the individual's work responsibilities.

Occupation is a more general term than job; it refers to a broad employment classification such as accounting, clerking, selling, being a mechanic, and so on. Occupations are categories of work that cover a variety of related jobs.

The term **career** is far broader than either occupation or job. It does not refer to any specific occupation or employment but to an entire range of related occupations. Thus, a career will often span an entire lifetime of work and may include a host of related occupations (each with its own jobs). A career in food services, for example, might include such occupations as busboy, waiter, bartender, food manager, convention manager, and chain food-services supervisor. It is possible, of course, to have more than one career in a single lifetime.

In its strictest sense, the term **vocation** refers to a "calling" and has traditionally been restricted to the clergy and to certain white-collar professions. Thus, one can have a vocation for the ministry, a vocation for medicine, or a vocation for the law; it is less appropriate to refer to a laborer's or a secretary's vocation.

In this text, as in many other contexts, **work** is often used as a general term to include all manner of occupations, careers, professions, jobs, and vocations.

Why Work?

Work serves a variety of economic, social, and psychological purposes. Its economic functions include what we usually mean when we speak of "making a living"—that is, they have to do with the satisfaction of physical needs. In industrialized societies such as ours, however, the economic benefits of work often go considerably beyond putting a chicken (or a zucchini, for those who prefer) in our pots. Many people can put a dozen or more chickens in their pots. That's one sign of "success."

The social purposes of work are reflected in opportunities for social interaction and the development of friendships. More than this, work provides people with status and responsibility, and gives them reasons for feeling important and wanted.

The psychological purposes of work, closely related to its social purposes, have a lot to do with the development of confidence and self-esteem. It is through working and earning that people achieve a sense of self-worth and satisfaction. More than this, it is from our work that many of us derive important aspects of our identities. It is no accident that many of us answer the question "What do you do for a living?" with "I am a(n) _____ ." In a sense, we *are* what we do.

Changes in Work Opportunities

In recent decades, there have been some startling changes in the nature of the work people do in Western societies. We went very rapidly from societies that were primarily agricultural to societies that were increasingly industrial. Now we have entered a third phase—that of the technological society. The technological society mechanizes

Rapidly developing technological societies present increasingly frequent changes in work opportunities. There is little guarantee that the book-building in which these two are engaged will not have been replaced by some new, computer-driven job—maybe next week.

production and services; it thrives on the collection, storage, analysis, and dissemination of information; and it creates a vast array of new jobs while at the same time eliminating a great many others. In addition, it requires a far more educated work force than was the case a scant few decades ago (Hansen, 1993).

Coupled with the rapid industrialization of society, there are some continuing demographic trends. The population of the entire industrialized Western world is rapidly aging. This means that there will be proportionally fewer children and young adults in coming decades, and proportionally more middle-aged and older adults. These changes are reflected very clearly in the fact that the most rapidly growing occupational categories are health-care related.

Job Trends

Today's high-tech society presents an incredible array of jobs, an increasing number of which have replaced unskilled, low-education occupations. Furthermore, the nature of these jobs is in a constant state of flux, as are the markets that provide employment. For example, since 1976, there has been an increase of more than 50 percent in technical and related occupations, as well as in managerial and administrative jobs—and similar increases in professional specialities and in marketing. During the same period, service occupations increased by only 28 percent, and manufacturing and labor jobs by only 3 percent; meanwhile, forestry, farming, and fishing occupations declined by 8 percent (Silvestri & Lukasiewicz, 1989).

INTERVIEW

SUBJECT

Male; age 24; single; high school dropout; varied history of short-term employment, primarily as laborer for construction firms.

QUESTION

"What do you want out of life? What do you dream of being or doing? Say, when you're 40 or so."

"Well, I sure wouldn't want to be doing what I'm doing now. And I won't be. No way, Jose! Maybe I'll win the lottery. . . . What would I do then? Heck, nothing. Drink beer and party. Have a good time."

Forecasts of future occupations have been controversial and unreliable, notes Bailey (1991). On the one hand are those who argue that rapid technological advances leading to increasing automation will greatly reduce the demand for unskilled, low-level employment, and that most of the jobs created in the future will require education and training beyond the high school level (Johnston & Packer, 1987). On the other hand are those who note that modern technology is increasingly successful in reducing the need for trained and educated workers, and that the ultimate effect of this is that *less* rather than more education will be required of many workers in the fu-

PROJECTED JOB TRENDS, 1990–2005

There are hundreds of jobs today that did not exist a mere one or two decades ago. Yet the fastest-growing job markets are those that have existed for centuries. Five of the jobs projected to grow fastest by the year 2005, for example, are health-care related—a direct result of our aging population coupled with advances in medical knowledge and technology. The most rapidly declining job markets have to do with equipment and electronic manufacturing and assembling, and stenographers—a result of the use of computers in the workplace. Retail salespersons is the single largest job category at present, and is projected to be the largest in 2005; second is general managers and top executives (U.S. Bureau of the Census, 1993).

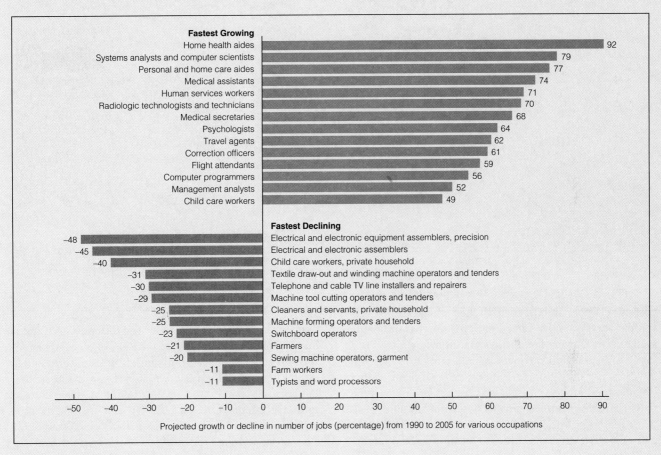

FIGURE 13.3

Fastest-growing and fastest-declining jobs: moderate estimates, 1990–2005. (Based on U.S. Bureau of the Census, 1993, p. 408.)

ture—witness the "dumbing-down" of cashier jobs as one example, where electronic bar-code readers automatically enter prices; or the use of icons of tiny hamburgers, fries, or sodas on multikeyed, computerized registers, so that fast-food employees need not even know how to read or recognize numbers (let alone add or subtract).

Our best guess, says Bailey, is that there will be a gradual increase in the need for highly educated workers, although lower-skill occupations such as sales, janitorial and cleaning work, and food or beverage service occupations are projected to have a very large absolute growth (see At a Glance: "Projected Job Trends, 1990–2005," and Figure 13.3). And the need for upgrading within occupations will become greater as workers are forced to keep up with rapidly changing technology.

Other Job Changes

Other important changes in employment include the fact that more than half of all adult women are now in the work force (U.S. Bureau of the Census, 1994); an increase in

A JOB–PERSON MATCHING MODEL
BASED ON HOLLAND'S COPING STYLES

You who have recently made (or may soon make) a career decision might find it interesting to examine the goodness-of-fit between your characteristics and interests and the decision you have made (may make). If you have a realistic notion of your characteristics and interests (shown in column 2), you can assess your type (column 1) and see whether what you plan to do is anything like the corresponding list in column 3. If the match seems strained, don't be alarmed; perhaps you don't know yourself very well. Besides, global matching models of this kind are not sufficiently sensitive to slot everybody into the very best of all possible careers; and, for many, there may be a very wide range of *nearly best* of all possible careers.

Type	Characteristics and Interests	Recommended Job Settings	Type	Characteristics and Interests	Recommended Job Settings
Realistic	Concrete	Gas station	Social	Extroverted	Social work
	Mechanically oriented	Construction		Socially concerned	Teaching
	Motor activity	Labor		High verbal ability	Counseling
		Skilled trade		High affiliative needs	
		Farm	Enterprising	Domineering	Leadership roles
Intellectual	Abstract	Research		Adventurous	Planning roles
	Creative	Academics		Impulsive	Real estate development
	Introverted			Extroverted	
Artistic	Subjective	Performing arts	Conventional	Unimaginative	Accounting
	Creative	Visual arts		High self-control	Banking
	Intuitive			Want social approval	Business/clerical
	Emotional			Systematic	

part-time work; significantly higher educational levels among workers; and a reduction in the number of people available for lower-paying jobs. In addition, there is a vastly increased job turnover rate and much higher job mobility, not only among different occupations within a single career but also among different careers. How is the young adult (or adolescent) to choose from among so many careers? Or the older adult, for that matter? Do we naturally drift toward a career? Do our personal talents and interests urge us gently down the right paths? Or should we be guided? And if we are to be guided, how should it be done?

Theories of Career Choice

There are two general groups of theories that have influenced much of the thinking in career guidance. One is based on the notion that individuals and jobs should be matched with respect to the individual's interests and talents and the job's requirements. This approach is sometimes referred to as *job–person matching*. The other emphasizes the development of career-related abilities rather than simple job-interest matching and includes what are termed *developmental models of guidance*. A third *family-based model* combines aspects of these two basic models, but pays more attention to the individual's context.

Job–Person Matching

Guidance counselors who adopt the **job–person matching** model attempt to identify talents that are essential for specific occupations, administer batteries of tests to discover talents, and then try to match the two. The matching generally takes into account the individual's interests as well as talents. One well-known example of this trait-interest, job-matching approach is that of *Holland* (1992), who developed the Holland Vocational Preference Inventory. It identifies six specific combinations of traits and interests, labeled "coping styles": *realistic, intellectual, social, conventional, enterprising,* and *artistic*. These styles, and recommended occupations, are summarized in Interactive Table 13.5.

Trait–interest matching approaches to career guidance have proved highly useful and continue to be widely used both in schools and in placement and employment offices (Holland, 1994). Computer-assisted career guidance (CACG) systems are widely used to match individuals with careers, to suggest alternatives, or to permit exploration of various careers. There are a large number of such systems available (Sampson & Reardon, 1990; Sampson, Reardon, & Lenz, 1991).

Developmental Career Models

Developmental career models are concerned less with matching jobs and persons than with understanding and

TABLE 13.6
Ginzberg's Developmental Guidance Model

Stage	Approximate Ages	Major Career Events
Fantasy	To 10 or 12	Unrealistic notions of career possibilities; child wants to be a president, an astronaut, a ballerina, an actress, a famous explorer, a cowboy.
Tentative	10–12 to about 16	Growing awareness of requirements of different careers; increasing realization of personal interests and capabilities; keener awareness of the status and rewards associated with different careers.
Realistic	Late adolescence through early adulthood and even later	Involves beginnings of career decisions through active *exploration* of alternatives; commitment to a clear career choice (*crystallization*); undertaking series of activities necessary for implementing choice (*specification*). For many individuals, the process of career evaluation continues through life, and different career choices may be made in midladder.

facilitating the chronological development of career decisions. These models typically view career choices as beginning in childhood and as involving a gradual, decision-making process. Among the best known of developmental guidance models are those advanced by *Ginzberg* (1972) and *Super* (1990; 1994). Ginzberg's model describes three sequential preadult stages in career development: the *fantasy period*, the *tentative period*, and the *realistic period* (see Table 13.6).

The fantasy period lasts until approximately age 10 or 12 and is often characterized by highly unrealistic notions of career choice. This is the stage during which children want to be astronauts, baseball players, physicians, or presidents.

During the tentative period (ages 11 to 16), adolescents gradually become aware of the requirements of different careers, as well as of their own personal interests and capabilities. Slowly and tentatively, they begin to think about matches between their interests and abilities and the various career opportunities that might be open to them. They also become increasingly aware of the values and rewards attached to different occupations, and they evaluate these as well.

The realistic period begins about age 17 and involves the beginnings of career decisions. However, final decisions might be some distance in the future, particularly in view of the extent to which postsecondary education extends adolescence and often postpones the need to enter the work world. Even after a career choice has been made, it will remain tentative for some time.

Ginzberg speaks of three substages within the realistic period. The first, *exploration*, consists of actively investigating, and even trying out, some of the various options. Exploration often occurs when first entering the job market or in the early years of college or other postsecondary education. The individual then moves from exploration to *crystallization*, which entails a relatively firm commitment to a career. The final stage, *specification*, involves doing the things required to implement the career decision.

According to Ginzberg's developmental model, career evaluation occurs first in early adulthood and often

INTERVIEW

SUBJECT

Male; age 46; divorced; no children; involved in film business.

QUESTION

"How or why did you become a _____? And is this the type of work (career) that you think you would have chosen when you were in high school?"

"Sure. When I was in high school we had a communications course and everybody made little 8-millimeter films. I guess I had some talent which the teacher recognized. I'll never forget that teacher. It's probably because of him that I went into this business. I mean, it wasn't just an accident. I decided this is what I wanted, and I've been working at it ever since. I haven't done everything I want to yet, but it's shaping up. It's a lot of work and learning and contacts. This is a tough business, but I wouldn't want to be anything else."

continues through much of the remainder of the lifespan. Increasingly, when people's evaluations of their careers reveal less satisfaction and happiness than had been anticipated, alternate career decisions are made; this can occur at almost any time throughout the lifespan. As is discussed later, middle-of-the-lifespan career choices are made not only by women returning to the work force after raising children or entering it for the first time, but also by men who might already have devoted many of their working years to climbing the ladders of a career whose summits they no longer wish to reach—or whose slopes they find too steep or too unrewarding.

A Lifespan Career Model

Most approaches to career exploration and development have several assumptions in common, say Grotevant and Cooper (1988); and these assumptions are not always valid. They assume, for example, that the young adult will leave

TABLE 13.7
Super's Lifespan Career Development Model

Stage	Age Range	Substages	Major Possible Occurrences
Birth/Growth	0 to 14	Fantasy Interest Capacity Tentative	Initially unrealistic notions of career choice; eventual recognition of own interests and capacities; more realistic tentative choices
Exploration	14 to 25	Trial transition Implementing Specifying Crystallizing	Beginnings of career decisions; exploration of alternatives; preparation for career; eventual commitment
Establishment	25 to 40	Stabilization Advancement or frustration	Continued development and stabilization of career; resolution of occasional crises
Maintenance	45 to 60	Innovation, stagnation, or updating	Possible career changes ("recycling"); possible skills/knowledge improvement; possible stagnation
Decline	60 to death	Deceleration Disengagement	Retirement; career change; postretirement career; life management

---

INTERVIEW

SUBJECT

Male; age 26; single; recent university graduate; permanent employment with government department.

QUESTION

"What do you want out of life?
What do you dream of being or doing? Say, when you're 40 or so."

"You're sure this is going to be anonymous? . . . Okay. What I'd really like, I guess, is a good administrative position in this department or in another one. It doesn't really matter. As long as I'm in charge. Of people and decisions. I know I've got the right background, and if I play my cards right I should be assistant director by the time I'm 35. I'll be in line for a supervisor's job by next summer. But there's lots of politics, and if it doesn't work out—like if I don't go as fast as I think I should—then I'd move. Transfer to another department, or maybe even run for politics. If the situation looks right. I don't want to waste my time and run if it doesn't look like I can win. Here you have to be in the right party. But mostly I think I can make a heck of a good career here if I play my cards right."

INTERVIEW

SUBJECT

Female; age 48; widowed; two children, both independent; manager of a cleaning business.

QUESTION

"How or why did you become a _____? And is this the type of work (career) that you think you would have chosen when you were in high school?"

"Not bloody likely (laughter). I mean, working my fingers to the bone like this (laugh). I would of been a princess like that, what's her name, Grace Kelly. Married a prince if I could of. But I married this guy when I got pregnant and I never found no prince. Just this guy who cleaned rugs and stuff. Till he got a heart attack. That's how come."

---

home to establish a commitment to work—and to intimacy as well. But in many industrialized societies, it has become increasingly common to delay leaving home—or to return after initially leaving—so that career plans and intimate relationships are sometimes highly developed before the young adult leaves. And even after the young adult leaves, the family continues to be an important source of influence on careers.

Many career development models also assume that adolescents and young adults have a relatively unlimited number of options from which to select a career. While this may be true for some, it does not take into consideration the various constraints, such as economic opportunity, employment availability, gender, race, and intelligence, that sometimes restrict career choice.

These models also assume that career exploration begins late in adolescence, that career choice and development progress in a linear and irreversible fashion, and that the process is complete with the adoption of a career. But, say Grotevant and Cooper (1988), career exploration may start in early childhood, may involve a variety of abandoned choices that require starting over again, and in many

SHASHI KANTA, DREAMER

"I want to become a doctor. Indian medicine is sweeter, western medicine is bitter," says Shashi Kanta, a 15-year-old girl whose father is principal of a school in Anangpur where they live. Her father interrupts the interview and says in English, which Shashi doesn't understand, "It is impossible for a village teacher to educate his children as doctors. It's too expensive" (Rice, 1972, p. 121).

"We are Banyas," Shashi continues, explaining how, because they are members of a business caste, they do not mix with some of the lower castes like the sweepers (a caste whose principal occupation is to look after other people's houses). Because the caste system is officially frowned upon by the government, the castes are often mixed in the schools, although there are still some schools where the lower castes are not allowed to come inside. Instead, they sit on the verandah and listen to the lessons through the windows. "I believe in a democratic way of life," says Shashi, "but I couldn't marry someone from another class." She explains how her father will find her a husband. In her village, girls marry at the age of 10 or 12, but because she will go to university to become a doctor, her father will wait until she is 23 or 24 before finding her a husband.

"It is a dream, this wanting to be a doctor," says her father in English so that Shashi does not know what he says. "All my children are dreamers. We must face the facts. It is a tragedy. It is too expensive" (Rice, 1972, p. 124).

To Think About   Among the important developmental tasks of early adulthood are those relating to selecting and preparing for both a career and a lifestyle. And in more than 90 percent of all cases in North America, the lifestyle involves marriage—at least once. Consider how different your decisions, and options, in early adulthood might be in a culture such as Shashi's.

---

cases is a lifelong process. Hence the need for a career exploration model that takes into account the influence of interactive contextual factors such as the family, the social environment, and the individual's characteristics.

Super's career developmental model extends over most of the lifespan and takes into account the possibility of "recycling"—that is, of starting over again at various stages of career development (Freeman, 1993). It describes five lifespan stages in the development of a career (described in Table 13.7). These are much like Ginzberg's descriptions for the early stages, but extend into early and middle adulthood.

Work Selection

It would be naive and misleading to suggest that most of us make our career choices following well-reasoned decisions based on what we know of our interests and abilities—that each of us undertakes a careful examination of available careers and a thoughtful analysis of their requirements as well as of their potential contributions to our eventual growth and satisfaction. In fact, many of us select our careers (or are selected for them) in very different ways. Among other things, the occupations of our parents, our sex, our socioeconomic status, and other personal and contextual factors may each contribute significantly to what we eventually become.

Fortune, too, may play a role. It might provide a variety of chance happenings that mold great chunks of our lives. A father dies and leaves his child a business, a farm, or a family to look after; a teenage girl becomes pregnant; a dedicated young doctor marries into great wealth. Events such as these can profoundly influence the course of an individual's career, as can the simple availability of jobs. For those who attempt to enter the labor market directly from high school, or even before completing high school, the first job obtained is likely to be the one that is first available. And in many cases, the individual's eventual career may be related to this first accidental job.

Socioeconomic background also influences choice of careers, with people from higher levels being most likely to obtain postsecondary education or training, and consequently being most likely to select professional, white-collar, and high-technology occupations. People from lower levels are more likely to be found in blue-collar occupations. (See Across Cultures: "Shashi Kanta, Dreamer.")

Career Self-Efficacy Expectations

Also very important in determining choice of career are the individual's expectations of performing competently and

Work that reflects personal interests, that is challenging, and that provides adequate income is most likely to lead to job satisfaction. It may also be very important that employment provide workers with leisure—with time in which to study or travel, to build and grow, or perhaps just to fish and dream.

successfully—a notion that in today's jargon is labeled **career self-efficacy expectations.** Other things being equal, individuals are most likely to select careers in which they have high expectations of being competent and successful—hence high perceptions of self-efficacy. Self-efficacy expectations appear to be tied to a number of factors, not the least important of which is previous achievement (Kelly, 1993). Gender, too, has much to do with career choice and with self-efficacy expectations. Despite rapidly changing social conditions, stereotypes of appropriate male–female career divisions are still prevalent and may limit the number of choices girls think they have and affect their estimates of the likelihood of succeeding in these careers. Not surprisingly, women in nontraditional careers tend to have high notions of self-efficacy (Read, 1994). Similarly, career-women in the kibbutz, compared to more traditional non-career women, see themselves as more independent and emotionally stable and also manifest higher levels of self-esteem (Lobel, Agami-Rozenblat, & Bempechat, 1993). In this connection, it's interesting to note that males often have lower self-efficacy expectations when considering cross-gender careers than do females in the same situation (Gillespie & Hillman, 1993). In other words, females are more likely to expect to be competent in male-typed careers than males are in female-typed careers.

Job Satisfaction

Not many decades ago, the primary motivations for work were money, perhaps security, and often duty. And the emphasis was on being a successful, productive worker. But, as Kuder (1977) notes, it is no longer sufficient just to have a job; we also want to be happy in our work and to

feel that our contributions are worthwhile. In Terkel's (1972) words, work is "a search for daily meaning as well as daily bread, for recognition as well as cash, for astonishment rather than torpor; in short, for a sort of life rather than a Monday through Friday sort of dying. Perhaps immortality, too, is part of the quest" (p. xiii).

How Happy Are Workers, and Why?

How satisfied and happy are most of us with what we do? Here, as in the more general areas of satisfaction with their lives, few adults are willing to describe themselves as very dissatisfied or very unhappy (see Chapter 16). In a widescale study of workers, Dawis (1992) found that at least three quarters of all workers at any age level describe themselves as being satisfied with their jobs and happy. Interestingly, however, if given an opportunity, about half of them would change their occupations.

There is evidence, too, that the longer people stay in a job, the more likely they are to like it. In a survey regarding job satisfaction conducted by Quinn, Staines, and McCullough (1974), for example, 75 percent of those under the age of 21 describe themselves as happy; 84 percent of those between 20 and 30 and an amazing 90 percent of those above 30 also describe themselves as happy.

Why do we become progressively more happy with our jobs? In addition to the fact that work gives meaning to a great many lives and that we therefore *want* to be satisfied, perhaps finding it difficult to admit even to ourselves that we might not be, there are at least three reasons why people might become happier with their work as they age. The first and most obvious is that those who are truly unhappy with their careers will often change them early in their lives. The second is that it is possible to grow to love (or at least accept) a career that at first seems unpleasant. And third, as we age, many of us might modify our original dream, dropping our aspirations, lowering our estimates of what our contributions and rewards should be; perhaps we become satisfied with less as it becomes clearer that we are unlikely to be given more.

Clausen (1981) identifies three factors that appear to be closely related to the satisfaction workers experience with their occupations. Most important is the extent to which the job reflects personal interests. Also crucial is the extent to which it requires full use of the worker's capabilities and provides an opportunity to develop ideas. Finally, income also contributes to job satisfaction. It is revealing that although each of these factors was important for both white- and blue-collar workers in Clausen's sample, more than half of the blue-collar workers also indicated that job security was extremely important. In contrast, fewer than 20 percent of those in white-collar occupations thought job security was critical. Clausen speculates that this might be because a common characteristic of white-collar occupations is that job permanence or security is seldom an issue. Such is not the case for blue-collar occupations, particularly during economic recessions.

Fast Trackers and Dead Enders

Not all people are bound to succeed, as *success* is commonly defined in the economically driven corporate world. Not all will climb the high ladders of corporate achievement to accumulate great power and status, to become, as Kanter (1981) puts it, "fast trackers." Many more will simply be "dead enders"—those who never reach the summits toward which the "fast trackers" climb so rapidly. Dead enders, Kanter tells us, include those who initially enter occupations that have low ceilings, those who are in high-ceiling employment but who fail somewhere along the line, and those who simply take the wrong paths. Low-ceiling jobs are those that do not ordinarily lead to advancement; they include many labor and clerical jobs. High-ceiling occupations include opportunities for advancement. Dead enders in low-ceiling employment are relatively satisfied; those in high-ceiling employment but who fail to climb upward are among the least satisfied. And those who simply climb the wrong ladders in the beginning find themselves at an intermediate level of satisfaction. There are, of course, other definitions of success. And "dead ender," because of its negative connotations, is not a good label for all those who enter low-ceiling occupations. There are sources of job satisfaction that have absolutely nothing to do with climbing corporate ladders.

COGNITIVE CHANGE

Our predominant models of human development have historically assumed that most of the major developmental changes occur early in the lifespan, that after infancy, childhood, and adolescence, we are characterized more by stability than by change. However, the current lifespan view of human development has largely rejected this model in favor of the belief that there are some important positive changes that occur throughout the lifespan. This model insists that much of development is not complete at adolescence and that the human being remains highly changeable throughout much of life. It maintains that the principal characteristic of adult human development is *change* rather than *stability*.

The evidence that might clarify this issue, notes Alwin (1994), is not entirely clear. However, much of it points to the likelihood that characteristics such as intelligence are far more stable than changing. This, of course, does not mean that change is not possible and does not occur; what it means, in effect, is that the *rate* of change slows very dramatically in adulthood.

Still, some aspects of intellectual functioning seem to change in systematic and predictable ways. Different theorists describe this change in different ways.

Riegel's Dialectical Thinking

Klaus *Riegel* (1970; 1972; 1976), for example, suggests that thinking becomes more *dialectical* with age. *Webster's Third New International Dictionary* defines *dialectics* as "the process of self-development or unfolding (as of an action, event, idea, ideology, movement, or institution) through the stages of thesis, antithesis, and synthesis. . . ." It further defines *dialectical* as being "marked by a dynamic internal tension, conflict, and interconnectedness of its parts or elements." Dialectical thinking, notes the Oxford English Dictionary, relates to a series of contradictions and their solutions—to conflict and change.

Dialectical thinking, says Klaus Riegel, is evident in the adult's increasing recognition of conflict, of contradiction and uncertainty. He argues that our conventional views of development as a series of stages or plateaus characterized by a state of balance or equilibrium are incorrect and misleading. According to Riegel, lifespan human development is best viewed as sequences of conflicts, crises, or contradictions and their continued resolution. The concept of *dialectics* is implicit in the view that conflicts or crises arise from contradictory actions and reactions—the classical situation of a thesis leading to an antithesis and finally being resolved in a synthesis.

More specifically, dialectical thinking is evident in the individual's recognition, acceptance, and resolution of conflicts. For example, a young adult's sexual maturity might lead toward behaviors that are culturally problematic. From this lack of synchrony between desires and opportunities, conflict arises, and conflict is the root of dialectical processes. Resolution of conflicts may lead to new developments, new behaviors, new ways of thinking. And when the reorganization is sufficiently dramatic, says Riegel, we might be tempted to recognize a *stage* or a

Adolescents and young adults strive to be logical thinkers, says Piaget, searching for correct, reason-driven solutions for the world's problems. But with age, thinking becomes more pragmatic, more attuned to contradictions, more relativistic, more tolerant of ambiguity. These differences are often apparent in the discussions and arguments of older and younger adults—even at friendly family picnics.

plateau. But a dialectical view does not emphasize the plateau or the equilibrium—as does Piaget's theory, for example. Instead, it views development as a continuous process because the organism and society are never static. Change is constant, and complete synchrony is rare and fleeting.

Riegel (1973a) proposes a fifth Piagetian stage—a *dialectical stage.* In this fifth stage, there are no clear plateaus—no levels of cognitive accomplishment clearly evident in the ability to solve a new class of problems. Instead, there is a renewed realization that development occurs on different levels, that it is replete with contradictions, that not all problems and conflicts can be permanently resolved, that it is appropriate to change one's beliefs and to accept contradiction and uncertainty. "The developmental and aging processes . . . are founded upon the ability to tolerate contradictions and insufficiencies in action and thought," Riegel informs us (1973b, p. 482).

Basseches's Dialectical Schemata

In close agreement with Riegel is Basseches (1986), who argues that the thought processes that our cognitive and developmental theories have described are not nearly as relevant for adults as they are for children and adolescents. Cognitive development continues after adolescence, Basseches insists, and much of it is dialectical. Dialectical thought, in Basseches's (1984) words, "represents a development beyond Piaget's formal operations stage. . . . [It]

describes a more epistemologically powerful way of making sense of the world" (p. 15).

What the dialectical view of development provides is the recognition that there are no static levels—no stages—toward which the individual strives and that, once reached, represent the culmination of that age's developmental progress. The adult dialectical thinker struggles to create meaning and order, but is always aware of conflict—of thesis and antithesis. Unlike Piaget's formal operations adolescent (or adult) who sees logic as omnipotent, the dialectical thinker recognizes that logic cannot solve all of life's problems. In fact, the most important problems in life are those that demand the application of values and the examination of alternatives.

Basseches proposes that through early adulthood, cognitive growth, to the extent that it occurs, may take the form of **dialectical schemata.** These schemata are patterns of thought that are involved in dialectical thinking. Some of these schemata, for example, draw the thinker's attention to relationships and interactions, some have to do with change and movement, and some deal with form or pattern. All relate to the recognition and resolution of conflict.

Basseches proposes that dialectical thinking is a uniquely adult form of reasoning that places the adult in the world of changing systems, and that allows the application of thought and of values to an analysis and interpretation of these systems. In the same way as concrete operations made it possible for the schoolchild to reason

about real classes and objects, so dialectical operations make it possible for the adult to reason about social and political systems, interpersonal relationships, and so on. But, even as formal operations remain a potential stage for many adolescents, so too does dialectical thought remain merely potential for many adults.

In summary, dialectical thinking is a mode of thinking that involves recognition of ambiguities and contradictions, *and* increasing tolerance of these. Unlike formal reasoning, which is highly constrained in the sense that it is limited by rules of logic, dialectical thinking is more intuitive, more subject to value judgments. Formal reasoning, claims Basseches, is rarely used in the real world, although it might occasionally be used in science or in a formal testing situation—or perhaps to confirm the results of intuition. Dialectical thought, on the other hand, can be applied to problems relating to intimate personal interactions, artistic activities, business transactions, the sciences, and so on.

Labouvie-Vief's Pragmatic Wisdom

Much adult reasoning, *Labouvie-Vief* (1980) argues, occurs in very different contexts than does child and adolescent reasoning. Reasoning that involves the manipulation of classes or the consideration of all possible alternatives might be entirely appropriate for many of the problems that children face, especially in schools. But these ways of thinking are not very suitable or useful for many of the sit-

uations that the adult faces. Because of the realities of adult responsibilities, because of the practical demands of certain contexts, and because of ethical constraints, the reasoning that evolves in adulthood is different from the reasoning of the preadult. It is, in Labouvie-Vief's (1980) words, a form of reasoning that is "marked by specialization, concrete pragmatics, and pressures towards social system stability" (p. 141). As a result, in adult thought, there is often a trade-off between the most scientific or most logically correct of possible alternatives and a desire for social stability—or for the most ethical alternative. It is as though age and experience grant adults a kind of wisdom—a dialectical wisdom—that allows them to factor more variables into their problem-solving activities than formal operations allow (Labouvie-Vief & Lawrence, 1985).

A Summary

Riegel, Basseches, Labouvie-Vief, and others who are concerned with the cognitive processes of adults present a compelling argument that the logic of systems such as Piaget's do not adequately describe the thinking of adults (Stevens-Long, 1990). They argue that with adulthood there may come an increasing recognition of ambiguity and contradiction, greater tolerance for these, and the learning of new dialectical schemata. These schemata are ways of thinking that allow the ongoing resolution of problems, but that bring into play a variety of important considerations other than simple logic—for example, ethics, feasibility, social implications, and so on.

Although it is still too early to evaluate the impact and the usefulness of these ideas, their emphasis on aspects of development that have largely been ignored may lead to important insights about changes in thinking through the lifespan. These notions might also do much to resolve what has been an ongoing controversy about the nature of age-related changes in intellectual ability.

Sternberg's Theory of Adult Intelligence

There are those who have believed that one of the inevitable consequences of aging is a marked decline in intellectual functioning; others insist that this decline has been greatly exaggerated, that it does not involve most areas of cognitive functioning, and that even where it is apparent, it is trivial into very old age. (This controversy and its resolution are covered in Chapters 15 and 17.)

Robert *Sternberg* describes some aspects of adult intelligence that are different from those of adolescents and children. In Chapter 9, we spoke of Sternberg's *contextual* theory of intelligence. This theory maintains that behavior is intelligent if it is adaptive in the context in which it occurs. In some contexts, it might be intelligent to fight when confronted by an enemy (if, for example, *not* fighting would lead to a great loss, or even death); in other situations, *not* fighting might be far more intelligent (if, for example, fighting would almost certainly mean losing or dying—or both).

Sternberg's theory of intelligence is not only contextual, but also *componential*. As we saw in Chapter 9, the theory describes intelligence in terms of three major components: metacomponents (cognitive skills having to do with recognizing a problem, selecting a strategy for its solution, and monitoring cognitive activity), performance components (skills actually used in solving problems), and knowledge-acquisition components (relating to what is actually learned or decided).

There is a third aspect to Sternberg's explicit theory of intelligence—hence his label **triarchic theory of intelligence.** The first two arches of this theory are the componential theory and the contextual theory; the third is *experiential*. It deals primarily with the application in new situations of what has been learned through experience. (See Table 13.8.) Experiential intelligence describes a *practical* kind of intelligence, in contrast to definitions of intelligence that emphasize *rationality* (Sternberg, 1993). Hence, it is a dimension of intelligence that is highly dependent on the individual's exposure to a variety of situations. Accordingly, experiential intelligence is likely to be greater in adults than in children.

Sternberg and Berg (1987) asked a sample of 152 adults to list behaviors that they thought might characterize extremely intelligent and extremely unintelligent 30-, 50-, and 70-year-olds. Subsequently, they asked a second sample to rate the importance of the factors identified by the first sample. Later, a third sample was asked to rate the

TABLE 13.8

Main Aspects of Intelligence According to Explicit (Triarchic) Theory

I. Componential Subtheory
   A. Metacomponents
      1. Recognizing existence of a problem
      2. Defining nature of the problem
      3. Selecting lower-order components to solve problem
      4. Selecting strategy into which to combine components
      5. Selecting a mental representation upon which strategy acts
      6. Allocating mental resources
      7. Solution monitoring
      8. Utilizing external feedback
   B. Performance Components (partial list)
      1. Encoding stimuli
      2. Inferring relations between stimuli
      3. Mapping higher-order relations between relations
      4. Applying old relations to new stimulus domains
      5. Comparing stimuli
      6. Justifying selected solutions
      7. Responding to stimuli
   C. Knowledge-Acquisition Components
      1. Selective encoding of information
      2. Selective combination of information
      3. Selective comparison of new to old information
II. Experiential Subtheory
   A. Dealing with relative novelty
   B. Automatizing information processing
III. Contextual Subtheory
   A. Adaptation to environment
   B. Shaping of environment
   C. Selection of environment

SOURCE: From "What Are Theories of Adult Intellectual Development Theories Of?" (p. 11), by R. Sternberg and C. Berg, 1987. In *Cognitive Functioning and Social Structure Over the Life Course*, C. Schooler and K. W. Schaie (Eds.). Reprinted by permission of Ablex Publishing Corporation.

likelihood of intelligent and unintelligent 30-, 50-, and 70-year-olds engaging in the behaviors ranked in the second study.

There were two striking findings from this investigation: First, people seem to have clear and remarkably consistent notions of what intelligence is; and second, these notions vary systematically according to the age for which the judgment is being made. All groups typically placed greater weight on the more conventional indicators of intelligence for the younger age group; and the majority agreed that social and contextual features of intelligence—those that relate to the everyday requirements of living—are more important for the 70-year-olds.

Conventional measures of intelligence typically tap a number of processes and capabilities that compose what

Sternberg has labeled the "componental aspect of intelligence"; they do not ordinarily sample behaviors that might reflect contextual intelligence or the application of experience in novel but real situations. Says Sternberg (1992), these tests are inadequate; they don't reflect current research and thinking in the field. And they may be unfair to those whose intelligence is more practical and more intuitive. If the dialectical theorists are correct, such tests are unfair to adults.

Researchers have now begun to identify a number of important cognitive changes that occur with age and that appear to lend support to those who argue that thought processes are dialectical—or at least *different*, perhaps in the sense that they are more pragmatic. Additional evidence suggests that adults emphasize different aspects of intelligence in their behavior.

We look at these topics again in Chapter 15.

A CONTEXTUAL REMINDER

This chapter is clearly rooted in the Western industrialized world, as, of course, is most of this book. That is probably as it should be because I am of that world; and most of you are as well. But it is worth repeating once more that much of what we have to say about human development reflects the contexts in which we live and work. Thus, what we believe about the vigor and health of young adulthood, the excellent functioning of the senses, the benefits of exercise, and the relative absence of disease may well be true and important in our Western industrialized world, but not the least bit true in Sierra Leone where the average life expectancy is 43 (Grant, 1993). There, the normal course of physical development is quite different.

Similarly, we can make grand pronouncements about how work must not only put chickens in our pots but also fill our souls with a sense of value and purpose. But these assertions would mean nothing if we were speaking of natives of the Amazon basin. These people have no careers comparable to ours; they have no corporate ladders to climb—or from which to fall. What they have is a compelling need to go out into the jungle every day of their lives and gather enough food to survive yet another season.

Do you suppose their thoughts are dialectic? Do you think they struggle to balance pragmatics and morals in the resolution of issues of profound social and economic importance?

Or is their thinking different, their intelligence more *of their context?*

MAIN POINTS

Early Adulthood

1. The Peter Pan syndrome describes people who have not finished growing up in that they have refused or avoided completing the important developmental tasks (according to Havighurst, sequential milestones that reflect the acquisition of important competencies and responsibilities such as establishing a family and a career) of youth (ages 14 to 24, according to Coleman).

2. Transition to adulthood, says Coleman, requires "self-centered" competencies (for example, relating to economic independence), and "other-centered" capabilities (having to do with social interaction and social responsibility).

Physical Development

3. Adulthood is not a plateau according to our current models. Motor performance among males, measured quantitatively (speed of running, distance throwing) usually improves through childhood and adolescence and peaks in early adulthood; among females, there is sometimes a plateau or decline after puberty, associated with limited practice. Qualitative measures show continued improvement of motor performance into adulthood. In the absence of training, flexibility declines gradually from about age 12, but can be maintained and even improved into adulthood with training.

4. There are no dramatic age-related changes in the functioning of the senses through early adulthood, but there are subtle changes in the flexibility of the eyes' lenses, and gradual, mostly noise-induced hearing loss, especially in men.

Health

5. In early adulthood, there is a decreased susceptibility to common infections, but a somewhat greater incidence of chronic complaints. Exercise contributes in important ways to physical *and* psychological well-being. Accidents are the principal cause of death prior to age 45, and heart disease and cancer after age 45. Stress is implicated in physical complaints (ulcers, hypertension, cardiovascular problems) as well as in psychological complaints (Type A individuals, who are aggressive and hard-driving, are more likely to suffer from coronary heart disease than Type B's, who are more easygoing and relaxed).

Sex and Reproduction

6. The human sexual response cycles through excitement (preparation), plateau (mounting arousal), orgasm, and resolution. Sexual dysfunctions in the male include premature ejaculation, retarded ejaculation, and erectile dysfunction; in the female, hypoactive sex drive, inability to attain orgasm or pleasure from sexual intercourse, and vaginismus. Infertility increases gradually through early adulthood. The most common causes are blocked Fallopian tubes in the female (often due to acute pelvic inflammatory disease) and low sperm count in men.

Work and Careers

7. Work serves economic, social, and psychological functions. *Jobs* are specific tasks or duties; *occupation* is a broad employment classification (such as being a mechanic); *career* refers to a range of related occupations; *vocation* refers to a "calling" (like to the ministry).

8. Health-care related jobs are projected to be among the fastest growing; manufacturing and assembling jobs, the fastest declining. A job–person matching approach to career choice (Holland) tries to match individual interests and talents with work requirements; developmental guidance models (Ginzberg, Super) describe sequential stages of exploration and preparation for a career (Ginzberg lists three: *fantasy, tentative, realistic*). In practice, career selection is highly influenced by family and other contextual influences, career self-efficacy expectations (anticipations of being competent and successful), and other factors such as race, sex, and economics. Fortune also plays a role.

9. We ask not only that our jobs fill our bellies but also that they make us happy. Job satisfaction is related to personal interest in the work, the extent to which it requires use of the individual's capabilities, income, and job security.

Cognitive Change

10. Riegel, Basseches, and Labouvie-Vief suggest that with adulthood there may come an increasing recognition and tolerance of ambiguity, conflict, and contradiction, and the learning of new (dialectical) ways of thinking that allow the ongoing resolution of problems, but that bring into play a variety of important considerations other than simple logic—for example, ethics, feasibility, and social implications.

11. Sternberg's triarchic view of intelligence is *componential* (intelligence consists of metacomponents, performance components, and knowledge-acquisition components), *contextual* (intelligence is adaptive in a specific context), and *experiential* (intelligence may be manifested in the application of old learning to new situations). Indications are that contextual and experiential intelligence become more important as individuals age.

A Contextual Reminder

12. Our observations and conclusions are context specific.

FOCUS QUESTIONS: APPLICATIONS

1. Is early adulthood a period of physical growth, decline, or stability?

- Describe some of the normal changes in strength, stamina, and flexibility that occur in early adulthood. Explain how exercise can affect these changes.

2. What is normal (and average) sexual behavior and responsiveness for young adults?

- Using library resources, summarize some of the most common sexual dysfunctions.

3. How do people select careers? Why is work important?

- Can you find examples of *career development* and of *person–interest matching* among your career-related activities or those of people you know?

4. Is the thinking of the young adult different from that of children and adolescents?

- Using your own examples, explain and illustrate what is meant by *dialectical thinking*.

STUDY TERMS

FURTHER READINGS

In the following chapter, Alwin explores in detail the stability of intellectual and personality characteristics throughout the lifespan, and concludes that there is perhaps more stability than change in these areas:

Alwin, D. F. (1994). Aging, personality, and social change: The stability of individual differences over the adult life span. In D. L. Featherman, R. M. Lerner, & M. Perlmutter (Eds.), *Lifespan development and behavior* (Vol. 12). Hillsdale, NJ: Erlbaum.

The first of the following two books presents a detailed and comprehensive look at career education and vocational guidance, which should be of particular value for those who are concerned with career education at different stages in the lifespan. The second is a collection of articles that attempt to integrate different theories of career development:

Drummond, R. J., & Ryan, C. W. (1995). *Career counseling: A developmental approach.* Englewood Cliffs, NJ: Prentice-Hall.

Savikas, M. L., & Lent, R. W. (Eds.). (1994). *Convergence in career development theories.* Palo Alto, CA: CPP Books.

Dialectical thinking and other forms of postadolescent thought are examined in:

Stevens-Long, J. (1990). Adult development: Theories past and future. In R. A. Nemiroff & C. A. Colarusso (Eds.), *New dimensions in adult development.* New York: Basic Books.

Those interested in the surprising sexual habits of Americans might want to consult:

Michael, R. T., Gagnon, J. H., Laumann, E. O., & Kolata, G. (1994). *Sex in America: A definitive survey.* New York: Little, Brown.

Because of the computer, says Papert, today's children have new, self-directed methods of accessing knowledge. The impact on the thinking of tomorrow's adult may be considerable:

Papert, S. (1993). *The children's machine: Rethinking school in the age of the computer.* New York: Basic Books.

SOCIAL DEVELOPMENT:
EARLY ADULTHOOD

A marriage on board of a king's ship, by the captain, duly entered in the log-book, is considered valid.

MARRYAT
Forster (1832)

"It doesn't really have to be a ship's captain," says Claude. "Like it could be a general or something. Or maybe a foreman."

CHAPTER 14

"Yeah," Paul agrees.

"So for sure I could do it and it would be legal as could be," Claude continues, " 'cause I'm the president," which is what we have decided he is and sometimes some of us even call him Prez when we happen to think to do it.

"So ask her then," says Armand, and Claude asks Bella, telling her, like we planned, that we're just practicing for a play. She goes right along with the idea and next thing you know, there she is standing next to Armand, whose idea it is in the first place. The plan is simple. He's gonna marry Bella Bouchard, and when he's tired of her, he'll get divorced.*

The marriage part works fine, Claude saying all the right things as solemn as you please, Armand folding up and putting away the marriage document, handwritten by Paul and witnessed by every one of us. Then he

---

*Armand had also read, in *Penny Cyclopedia of the Society for the Diffusion of Useful Knowledge* (published by C. Knight, London, 1837): "By the Mohammedan law a man may divorce his wife orally and without any ceremony. He may divorce her twice, and take her again without her consent; but if he divorce her a third time . . . he cannot receive her again until she has been married and divorced by another husband." So he knew from the very beginning that he'd be able to divorce Bella with no more fuss than he had married her.

leaves with his new bride, the two walking side by side down the alley, Armand showing Bella where it says, in the book, how a ship's captain could marry two people and Claude was really our captain and that was a log book she has signed so now they really are married so the church wouldn't be upset at all if, you know . . .

But Bella hauls off and punches him in the side of the nose, which we later decide is probably as good a divorce as the oral one Armand had held in reserve.

THIS CHAPTER

Armand would never admit he was heartbroken, preferring instead to laugh with us at what a huge joke this had all been. But when he turned 20, without a moment's hesitation, he actually did marry Bella Bouchard for real. "I always loved ya," he told her.

Love, McAdams (1984) informs us, and *power* are the two basic themes that seem to be common in all our lives. These themes surface repeatedly in the fantasies and dreams in which we are the larger-than-life heroes. The love theme is revealed in our concern with personal relationships and in our need to be liked and wanted. The power theme manifests itself in our wish that others recognize our strength and leadership.

The importance of these themes, McAdams tells us, is that they reveal two of our most important motives. First, we are driven by an intimacy motive, revealed in our "preference for close, warm, communicative exchange with another" (p. 166). Second, we respond to a power motive, evident in a desire to establish or maintain impact, control, or influence over others, and apparent, as well, in our strivings for prestige and recognition.

As Kegan (1982) put it, in the cognitive sphere, we strive to make sense of the world—to construct meaning. And in the social sphere, we strive to become meaningful. In becoming meaningful, we achieve both intimacy and power. What these two motives have in common is that they deal with human relationships. Adult socialization and relationships are the topics of this chapter.

Socialization begins in infancy and continues through childhood and into adulthood. With adulthood come new roles, new statuses, new expectations. The child who has read comic books now reads journals; the adolescent who has written poetry now writes legal briefs. And those whose socialization has gone awry, note Elkin and Handel (1989), may end up in a *resocialization* context, such as a prison or a mental institution.

Continued social adjustment requires that we remain socially malleable into old age—not only because of the changing requirements of our adult roles, but also because

we continue to meet new people, change old relationships, and form new ones throughout our lives.

We look at relationships in this chapter, beginning with a discussion of Erikson's view of social development in early adulthood; then we turn to the complex and sometimes perplexing topic of love; finally, we focus on contemporary lifestyles, marriage, and the family.

PSYCHOSOCIAL DEVELOPMENT: ERIKSON

Recall from Chapter 2 that *Erikson*'s theory describes a series of eight stages through which individuals progress as they develop (Erikson, 1959; 1987) (see Figure 14.1). Each of these stages involves the resolution of an important conflict that arises out of the individual's social interaction—hence the label "psychosocial theory." Progression from one stage to the next requires the resolution of this conflict, an achievement that evolves through the development of a new competence. But the conflicts specific to each stage are never completely resolved during that stage; they continue, in one form or another, throughout life. As we develop and grow, our social environments change, and as a result, so do our most important conflicts.

With the advent of adulthood, the adult is faced with a series of new social demands that require additional adjustments. These, too, may be viewed in terms of competing tendencies—crises that will be resolved through the development of new competencies. Erikson describes three developmental stages that span adulthood and old age: (1) *intimacy and solidarity versus isolation*, (2) generativity versus self-absorption, and (3) integrity versus despair (the last two of these are discussed in Chapters 16 and 18, respectively).

Intimacy Versus Isolation

Erikson believed that the search for identity does not always end with puberty but may continue through adolescence and beyond—a view that has been supported by Côté and Levine's (1992) survey of 623 university professors.

Relationships with the Opposite Sex

One of the principal ways in which adolescents and young adults achieve a sense of personal identity and self-worth is through feelings of intimacy with others. According to Erikson (1980), for the majority of young adults, although not for all, the intimacy they seek will come through a relationship with someone of the opposite sex. But here, as in other stages of the lifespan, there is a conflict—in this case, a conflict between the need to make a commitment and an unwillingness to do so. The individual has an urge to remain independent, to retain a hard-won sense of per-

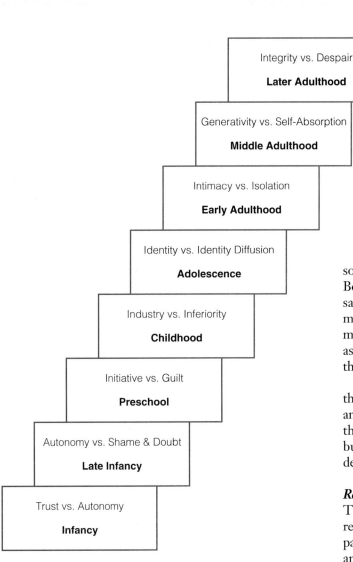

Integrity vs. Despair
Later Adulthood

Generativity vs. Self-Absorption
Middle Adulthood

Intimacy vs. Isolation
Early Adulthood

Identity vs. Identity Diffusion
Adolescence

Industry vs. Inferiority
Childhood

Initiative vs. Guilt
Preschool

Autonomy vs. Shame & Doubt
Late Infancy

Trust vs. Autonomy
Infancy

FIGURE 14.1
Overview of Erikson's psychosocial theory.

sonal identity; in addition, there is a fear of commitment. Both of these mitigate against intimacy. As a consequence, says Erikson, many young adults enter into sexually intimate relationships that involve little emotional commitment. Erikson and Hall (1983) describe these relationships as primarily "genital" (phallic or vaginal), and claim that they may lead to feelings of extreme isolation.

The culmination of this developmental period, and the resolution of the conflict between a need for intimacy and a drive for independence, is to be found in a balance that permits the commitment and the mutuality of love, but that also allows the individual to retain an independent identity.

Relationships with Parents

The young adult's search for intimacy and independence requires a redefinition and realignment of relationships with parents. As we saw, this process begins in early adolescence and is sometimes marked by conflict—although conflict is not the main characteristic of most parent–adolescent relationships.

Miller and Lane (1991) note that the adolescent's happiness is more closely related to the quality of the parental relationship than the peer relationship. Adolescents who describe their relationships with parents as supportive and emotionally warm have a higher sense of well-being than those who see themselves in conflict. Might this also be the case for young adults?

Miller and Lane presented questionnaires to 72 college undergraduates in an attempt to discover the nature and importance of their relationships with their parents. One of their clearest findings is that these students, both male and female, felt closer to their mothers and spent more time with them than with their fathers. Both parents appeared to have considerable emotional influence on their young adult children. "Adolescents achieve autonomy by asserting themselves in a context of close and supportive relations with parents," claim Miller and Lane, "rather than by distancing themselves from them" (p. 180). In early adulthood, close parental relationships continue to be important; but the development of a close relationship with someone else is also very important.

Even after young adults have gone beyond the family to find intimacy—and perhaps passion and commitment too—parents continue to have considerable influence on their emotional lives. They remain an important source of support and help in times of need; and a reason for joy and laughter.

One of the new developmental competencies that Erikson describes as being characteristic of early adulthood is that of becoming generative—an achievement that might be evident in work roles, in community responsibilities, and in producing and caring for children. Does this mean that the person who has two jobs—or twin girls—is twice as developmentally competent?

According to Erikson, the crowning achievement of early adulthood is most often found in marriage and child rearing. This view has been criticized and is often rejected. There are many individuals who lead happy, well-adjusted lives, but who do not express their need for intimacy in a lifelong marital commitment. And although Erikson describes a social pattern that is still relatively common, it is perhaps no longer as common in the late 20th century as it was in the middle of the century.

Research on Erikson's Model

Although a theory such as Erikson's cannot easily be tested, several studies have attempted to confirm some of its most important beliefs. Among these, a longitudinal study conducted by Vaillant and Milofsky (1980) involved a sample of 94 male college students and a second sample of 392 noncollege, inner-city residents (first selected as a control group in Glueck and Glueck's 1950 study of juvenile delinquency). Snarey (1993) also followed up 240 sub-

jects from the Glueck and Glueck study, interviewing them at ages 14, 25, 31, and 47.

One of the objectives of these studies was to determine which of Erikson's developmental stages most accurately described individual subjects. For example, assignment to Stage 4 (industry versus inferiority) would reflect the extent to which the subject "did things beside and with others" and would be determined by summing scores assigned for doing home chores, adjusting to school academically, and participating in extracurricular jobs and related tasks. Assignment to Stage 5 required that the subject have achieved some sense of identity, most often evident in the fact that he would now be self-supporting and relatively independent of the family. Stage 6 (intimacy), as defined by Erikson, requires that the subject be involved in a long-lasting and interdependent relationship. For the men in this study, cohorts of the early to mid-1920s, this relationship typically involved marriage.

Vaillant and Milofsky introduce an additional stage between Erikson's sixth and seventh (appropriately num-

TABLE 14.1
Several Items from Rubin's Loving and Liking Scales*

Loving-Scale Items

1. I feel that I can confide in _____ about virtually everything.
2. If I could never be with _____, I would feel miserable.
3. One of my primary concerns is _____'s welfare.

Liking-Scale Items

1. I think that _____ is unusually well adjusted.
2. I would highly recommend _____ for a responsible job.
3. _____ is the sort of person whom I myself would like to be.

*   Each scale is ranked 1 to 9 to indicate degree of agreement.

SOURCE: From "Measurement of Romantic Love" by Z. Rubin, 1970, *Journal of Personality and Social Psychology* 16, pp. 265–273. Copyright 1970 by the American Psychological Association. Reprinted by permission of the author.

bered Stage 6a), termed *career consolidation versus self-absorption*. Erikson had originally believed that career consolidation occurred during the fifth stage (identity formation), an observation that might have been more accurate in an early sociocultural context in which career decisions were often made earlier than they are now. Assignment to the seventh stage, generativity, was based on evidence of the individual's having assumed responsibility for others. The most common indication of generativity in this study involved caring for adolescents, as well as various wider community involvements.

Once the results of the questionnaires and interviews had been sorted, Vaillant and Milofsky looked at three hypotheses, each of which was supported by their observations. First, they predicted that because Erikson's model is open-ended, people should reach the various stages at different ages. In their data, for example, although between 30 and 40 percent of the middle-aged men (around age 47) could be described as *generative*, almost 20 percent were still struggling with the identity issues of adolescence.

Second, if the model is to be useful and generalizable, it should be relatively independent of social class and education. In fact, social-class membership and educational level were not related to the subject's developmental level. Although there were very marked contrasts between the two major groups involved in this study (a juvenile delinquency sample on the one hand, raised in an inner-city high-crime, low-status area; and a college sample on the other), approximately equal proportions of each of these groups were assigned to each stage at any given age.

Third, because the model is developmental, progression through each of the stages should be sequential. That is, an individual should not reach Stage 6 or 7 before having achieved Stage 4 or 5. As expected, progression through the stages appeared to be remarkably sequential. Achieving identity and being self-supporting seemed to be a requirement for developing a committed and intimate relationship. By the same token, intimacy seemed to precede career consolidation, which, in turn, preceded generativity.

Snarey (1993) also reports strong support for Erikson's theory, especially in his conclusion that parents, and particularly fathers, play a critical role in their children's development.

It's important to note that because Erikson's theory is an open-ended model, aging does not in any way guarantee the achievement of psychosexual maturity. The term *stage*, which Erikson uses to describe sequential developmental achievements, is metaphorical rather than literal. These are less *stages* than organized and somewhat predictable *changes* in commitments and relationships. Accordingly, terms such as *developmental level* or *developmental task* would probably be more appropriate.

The single most important developmental task of early adulthood, Erikson tells us, is to achieve intimacy. By intimacy, he means something very close to what others call love.

LOVE AND MATE SELECTION

Freud (1935) put it very simply: There are two things that are essential to be a healthy adult: **love** and work; Erikson (1987) agreed.

Love was the province of the poet long before science claimed it. And even now, poets may know more about love than does science. Still, with its penchant for measurement and investigation, science provides us with ways of measuring, if not of completely understanding, love. Rubin's (1970) *Loving and Liking Scales* attempt to provide a way of separating interpersonal attraction into two categories (see Table 14.1). The scales are based on the assumption that those who like each other sense that they have things in common, evaluate each other positively, and appreciate each other's company. But loving is not simply more of liking, according to Rubin. Loving involves three components: deep caring, strong attachment, and intimacy. Love implies a degree of emotional interdependence, a quality of exclusiveness and absorption. If you simply like someone, that person does not dominate your thoughts and your dreams; nor are you concerned that someone else might also like the same person. Love, on the other hand, often brings with it a measure of fierce possessiveness and the possibility of jealousy and pain— perhaps the possibility of ecstasy as well.

A Model of Love

Interpersonal attraction is no simple thing, Sternberg (1986) informs us. There are at least eight varieties of it including nonlove, romantic love, liking, fatuous love, infatuation, companionship, empty love, and consummate love

STERNBERG'S MODEL OF LOVE

Do you have a main relationship? Is it love? How can you tell for sure? One way, says Rubin, is to use scales with items such as those in Table 14.1, which attempt to separate loving from merely liking. Another way is to analyze the dimensions of your relationship. The Sternberg model describes eight possible relationships, each of which is defined in terms of the balance among passion (physical attraction), intimacy (affection, mutual disclosure), and commitment (conscious decision to love, to share, to be together). Does your main relationship fit one of these categories?

Relationship	Balance of Components	Possible Attitude
Nonlove	No passion, no intimacy, no commitment	"Who? I didn't notice him."
Infatuation	Passion; no intimacy or commitment	"I just want to be with him—physically, you know."
Liking	Intimacy; no passion or commitment	"She's nice to talk to."
Romantic love	Passion and intimacy; no commitment	"He's for me; he's the one! At least for the time being."
Companionate love	Intimacy and commitment; no passion	"She's like a sister! We're in it for the long haul."
Fatuous love	Commitment and passion; no intimacy	"I need him . . . can't leave. But I need to talk to you."
Empty love	Commitment; no passion or intimacy	"We'll stick it out. But just because of the kids."
Consummate love	Intimacy, passion, and commitment	"I want him. I like him. I'm his. Forever."

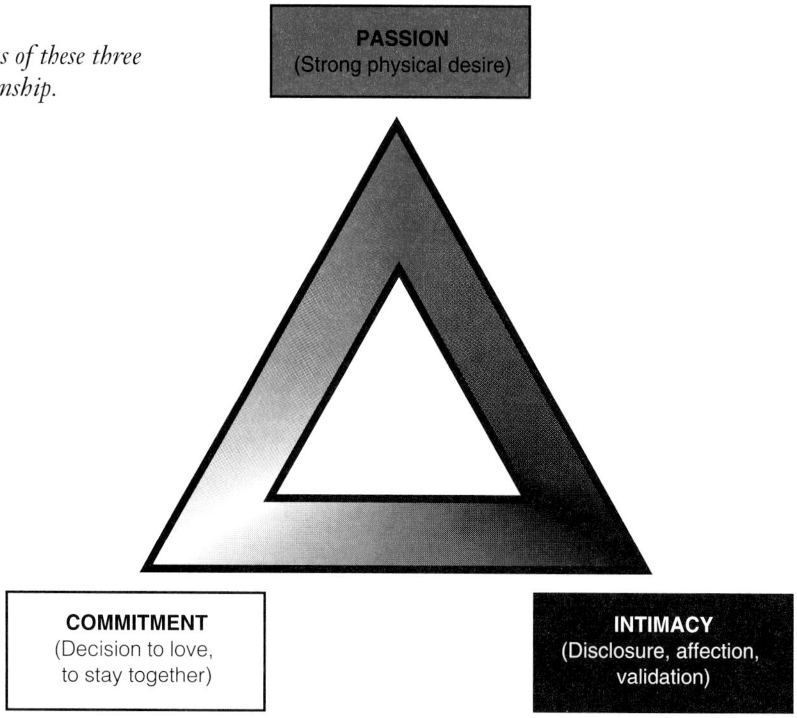

FIGURE 14.2

Sternberg's triangle of love. Different combinations of these three components determine the nature of the love relationship.

PASSION
(Strong physical desire)

COMMITMENT
(Decision to love, to stay together)

INTIMACY
(Disclosure, affection, validation)

(see Interactive Table 14.2). What differentiates these states from one another is the combination of **intimacy, passion,** and **commitment** involved in each. Accordingly, Sternberg, who, as we saw in Chapter 13, has presented us with a triarchic theory of intelligence, has also given us a **triangular theory of love.** But the triangle in this theory is not the classical male–male–female or female–female–male love triangle. It is the intimacy–passion–commitment triangle (see Figure 14.2).

In this model, intimacy refers to emotions that bring people closer together—emotions such as respect, affection, and support. Feelings of intimacy are what lead two people to want to share things, perhaps to disclose personal, private things.

Passion is a strong, sometimes almost overwhelming, desire to be with another person. Passion is often, although not always, sexual. Sternberg suggests that passion is a feeling that builds rapidly, but then gradually subsides.

In trying to explain how this thing called love begins, psychology points its finger at physical attraction, similarity, and propinquity (physical proximity). And in trying to describe its dimensions, it looks at the balance among intimacy, passion, and commitment. But always, it speaks only in generalities. Thus, concerning the love that makes these twins laugh, it says much less than might a poet.

Commitment implies a decision-making process, and may involve either a short-term or a long-term decision. On a short-term basis, commitment requires making the decision that one is in love. From a long-term point of view, commitment involves deciding to cultivate and maintain the loving relationship. In practice, this often implies a decision to share living arrangements and sometimes the raising of a family, either in marriage or otherwise.

Sternberg's (1986) theory of love holds that it is the particular combination of these three components—intimacy, passion, and commitment—that determines the nature of the relationship. As Interactive Table 14.2 shows, for example, empty love involves commitment but is devoid of passion or of intimacy ("By $%#$, we'll stay together until the children are gone. Then adios!") Consummate love, on the other hand, has all three components. And, interestingly, so does high creativity, says Pyryt (1993). Eminent creative achievers, he claims, are those whose relationship with their work shows evidence of the same sort of intimacy, passion, and commitment that are characteristic of consummate love.

There is a pattern to the development of many relationships, Sternberg suggests. Thus two individuals might begin with nonlove—no passion, commitment, or intimacy. In time, as intimacy grows, nonlove might give way to infatuation, which has passion but no commitment or intimacy—or perhaps to romantic love, which now adds

intimacy but is still short of commitment. Eventually, consummate love might evolve as commitment is brought into the relationship. And perhaps the end result will be marriage or some other long-term commitment, reflecting the resolution of the crisis Erikson describes for early adulthood.

But even consummate love is not a static, unchanging thing. Sternberg (1986) points out that passion is usually very high early in a consummate relationship. But with the passage of time, it diminishes; at the same time, however, commitment and intimacy might increase. Sternberg suggests that intimacy and commitment are generally viewed as being more important for a lasting love relationship than is passion. However, the breakdown of a marriage, notes Roberts (1992), most often stems from emotional problems linked directly to romantic love and sexual attraction—evidence of their importance in a lasting relationship.

The Rules of Attraction

How does this thing called love begin? And when it has happened, how does one know that it is true love and not puppy love? A romance and not a crush? An *amour* and not an infatuation?

It begins, social psychologists tell us, with interpersonal attraction; and interpersonal attraction seems to be

THE DOWRIES OF MARIA GONÇALES AND SHUDHRA OF SHAHJAHAPUR

As was the custom in the 17th century, when the parents of Maria Gonçales of São Paulo arranged for her marriage after carefully selecting the family into which she would marry, they also settled on a dowry price. Dowries in São Paulo, as in most countries of the world where such practices were followed, were given to both the husband and the daughter, or sometimes just to the husband or his family. Dowry marriages were typically arranged by parents, and the purpose of the dowry was to help the young couple start out. In Brazil, daughters' dowries were often much larger than the inheritance that a son would receive, sometimes being a very large fraction of the father's entire estate. In addition, sons were often expected to contribute to the dowry, as might, too, uncles and other relatives. So when Maria Gonçales married, her dowry included not only her eventual and complete share of her father's estate (termed her *legítima*), but also one chest; one tablecloth and six napkins; six silver spoons; six plates; two towels; eight scythes; eight hoes; eight wedges; 10 head of cattle; one horse and saddle; and at least 16 Indians. Her brother received far fewer household items—only three pigs and just five Indians (Nazzari, 1991).

When Shudhra of Shahjahapur married—some 300 years later, on an entirely different continent, and in a very different culture—the customs were strikingly similar. Not only was her marriage arranged, but the dowry price was settled on beforehand. It included not only that her mother, her only surviving parent, pay for all the expensive rituals and rites, but that she also spend many thousands of rupees on jewelry, clothes, furniture, utensils, and household articles, and then perhaps 25 percent as many rupees again on gifts of cash and objects for the groom's parents and other relatives. But Shudhra's husband was not happy with the dowry. It was not everything that he had been promised. And so, seven days after the marriage, he arranged to have Shudhra

killed. "He wanted a scooter," explained Shudhra's distraught mother. "I had promised one and I wanted to give it also. But my means were limited. Besides the expenditure at the marriage of my daughter had gone much beyond my expectations" (Kumari, 1989, p. 70).

To Think About   Dowry victims, such as Shudhra, are apparently a relatively common phenomenon even in today's India (Kumari, 1989). Some writers claim that the practice is evidence of strongly male-dominated cultures. But Nazzari (1991) interprets the dowry system in Brazil as a practice that favors daughters over sons. Are there similar practices, implicit or explicit, in your society? Do you think a dowry system might work for you? What might be some of its advantages (disadvantages)?

strongly influenced by three things: physical attraction, similarity, and proximity. The first of these, physical attractiveness, is important in determining whether people want to see each other again after they have met.

Similarity and physical proximity (often referred to as *propinquity* in social psychology) are related variables. People who are in close proximity are typically those who attend the same schools, churches, or colleges, or who go to the same country clubs, bars, or bingo parlors. By the same token, people who go to the same schools, churches, and other places are likely to be similar in a lot of important ways. Accordingly, there is a high tendency for individuals to select mates from very similar backgrounds and who are, therefore, very similar in social class, race, age, education, and religious background. (See Across Cultures: "The Dowries of Maria Gonçales and Shudhra of Shahjahapur.")

Selecting a Mate

Physical attraction, propinquity, and similarity. Put the three together and *voilà*, a potential mate!

Perhaps. But often, it isn't quite so simple. You see, there are dozens, perhaps hundreds, of potential candidates who might all, at one time or another, be sufficiently attractive, sufficiently near, and sufficiently similar to become a potential mate for any given person—well, perhaps not *any* given person but *many* given persons.

When South (1991) surveyed 2,000 adults, he found that mate selection is highly influenced by the perceived characteristics of the potential mate. Men placed high value on physical attractiveness and on youthfulness of women; in contrast, women placed higher value on the potential mates' employment stability and earnings. But mate selection followed by marriage is not the only choice, although it is the most common.

Basic lifestyle choices that young adults make (or allow circumstances to make for them) include singlehood, homosexuality, cohabitation, marriage, or one of a variety of communal living arrangements. Of these, marriage is by far the most common, although numbers of unmarried couples, approximately one third of whom have children, have increased dramatically in the last two decades.

CHOICES OF LIFESTYLE

At some point, usually in early adulthood or even before (although sometimes much later), many young adults make a very basic lifestyle choice: to marry or not to marry. By the age of 65, more than 95 percent of all adults have been married at least once (U.S. Bureau of the Census, 1994). This figure is very similar to what it was in 1970. The most striking change between 1970 and 1992 is a sharp increase in the age at which people first marry.

Cohabitation, homosexuality, singlehood (with or without children), and a variety of communal living arrangements are among the other lifestyles young adults might select. We look briefly at each of these before turning to the most common adult lifestyle: marriage.

Cohabitation

Cohabitation, living together without being married, was a rare and scandalous occurrence a mere handful of decades ago. For today's cohorts, it is neither rare nor scandalous.

Incidence

In 1970, there were 523,000 unmarried couples living together in the United States—196,000 of whom had children under age 15. This represented only 1.2 percent of all couples—about 1 family out of 100. By 1993, 1 family out of every 16 was unmarried (6 percent of all couples), more than 3.5 million unmarried couples. And more than 1.2 million of them had children under 15 (U.S. Bureau of the Census, 1994).

Throughout much of Europe, the number of unmarried cohabiting couples has increased even more rapidly than it has in North America. In Sweden, more than one out of every eight couples is not married, and close to 40 percent of all infants are born to unmarried couples.

INTERVIEW

SUBJECT

Female; age 31; never married; university education; successful career in a helping profession. (concerning a recently ended relationship with a man with whom she had been living)

"I read an article that described a couple making love. They both liked different music, so she would listen to one thing on headphones and he would listen to something else. Sometimes making . . . well, not even making love with him reminded me of that article. It was like we both wanted to be listening to something else. We were so different we never heard or saw the same things even when we were together. . . .

I don't think I will get married now. At least not for a while. I'm not saying no, period. I might like to have a child someday. But I guess it wouldn't really matter if I was married or not."

Reasons

Couples live together without marrying for several reasons. Among college students, for example, it has become increasingly common to share accommodations for financial reasons. Sexual relations might or might not be part of the arrangement. Among couples whose relations are intimate, cohabitation is sometimes preferred over marriage because the legal obligations are different, partners want intimacy and passion without long-term commitment, or marriage is simply being delayed. In many cases, cohabitation serves as a sort of "trial marriage" during which couples explore their compatibility and assess the rewards that each is likely to obtain from a permanent relationship. Few cohabiting couples view their arrangement as long-term and permanent. Most plan either to eventually marry the person with whom they currently live or to marry someone else. In fact, however, perhaps as many as two thirds of all cohabiting couples do *not* marry each other. Some evidence indicates that white, cohabiting American women are somewhat more likely to marry their partners if they become pregnant; among black women, pregnancy does not increase the likelihood of marriage (Manning, 1993).

Who Cohabits?

Cohabitation, note Schoen and Weinick (1993), is a distinctly different lifestyle than marriage. Among other things, cohabitors are somewhat less likely to select partners who are highly similar in terms of age, religion, or race—all important variables in mate selection for marriage. At the same time, they are more likely to select those with a similar educational background.

Very generally, those who cohabit have a tendency to be somewhat younger than those who marry. They are also, on average, less religious (in terms of church attendance, for example) and somewhat more unconventional, particularly in terms of family-related values (Demaris & MacDonald, 1993). In the United States, more blacks than whites and more individuals from large population centers than from smaller or more rural areas cohabit. Education and employment levels tend to be lower among men who cohabit than among married men. Interestingly, the opposite is true for women. Cohabitant women tend to be better educated and are more often employed than married women.

Other important differences between cohabiting and married couples include the observation that there is usually less commitment in cohabitation. That is, unmarried couples typically do not have the same personal commitment to continuing the relationship over the long term or to maintaining it through difficulty; also, unmarried couples usually do not have the same impediments to terminating the relationship. Often, there are few possessions that need to be divided or disposed of, no continuing financial obligations, and no ongoing responsibilities for children. But that, of course, is not always the case.

Cohabitation and Later Marriage

As noted, the majority of those who cohabit view their relationship as temporary. Most intend to eventually marry, although not necessarily to marry the person with whom they are living.

The research is impressively unanimous in indicating that cohabitation is *not* especially good preparation for later marriage. For example, Thomson and Colella (1992) found that couples who had cohabited before marriage reported poorer quality marriages, viewed marriage less favorably, and were more likely to divorce. Similarly, Stets (1993) found that prior cohabitation with someone *other than* the current spouse had an especially negative effect on the current marriage.

One possible reason why cohabitation might be associated with less marital satisfaction or stability later is that those who cohabit tend to be more unconventional and to have less traditional views of the family. However, Demaris and MacDonald (1993) found that these factors were largely unrelated to later marital instability.

Another possibility is that some of those who cohabit are more inclined to want to explore relationships, less reluctant to do so, and more willing to make and to change commitments.

Common-Law Relationships

In some jurisdictions, cohabitation has legal status and can, therefore, entail the same sorts of legal responsibilities that are more explicit in conventional marriage. Where cohabitation defines a legally recognized union of partners, it is termed a *common-law marriage*. Common-law marriages apparently originated on the frontier, where ministers, priests, rabbis, and ships' captains were scarce, and where couples were often forced to exchange "marriage" vows, sometimes in the presence of witnesses but often in private as well. Subsequently, these common-law marriages were upheld as being valid in the courts.* The result is that, to this day, if it can be established that a couple intend to live together with the same commitments as a married couple, theirs may be a legal, common-law marriage.

A word of caution is appropriate at this point. There is a danger, when summarizing research of this nature, to mistakenly assume that what is generally true must also be true in individual cases. That, of course, is clearly not the case. For example, to say that unmarried couples are, on the average, younger than married couples is not to deny the fact that there are 50-, 60-, and even 90-year-old couples living together but unmarried. Similarly, to say that unmarried couples typically do not share the same kind and degree of commitment as do married couples is not to deny the fact that there are many couples who are firmly committed to their relationship but who have decided not to marry. It would be highly misleading to suggest that the characteristics of those who cohabit and the possible consequences of cohabitation are as simple as they might appear in this handful of paragraphs. Here, as in so many other areas where social scientists ferret, there are too many exceptions to count.

---

*Which is exactly what Armand Delisle tried to tell Bella Bouchard at the beginning of their relationship (and at the beginning of this chapter). Much later, at the time of the dissolution of their subsequent relationship, she listened quite happily to the judge's brief discourse on legal contracts and responsibilities as he so very neatly severed Armand from a sizable chunk of his past accumulations. "What hurt the most," said Armand, "was losing the damn pension. I wish the heck I'd let it go after she punched me in the nose that first time."

Homosexuality

Several lifestyles are available to those whose sexual preferences are directed toward members of their own sex (*homo*sexual) rather than toward members of the opposite sex (*hetero*sexual). Here, as elsewhere, however, things are seldom simply an either/or proposition; there are degrees of attraction to one or both sexes.

Estimates of the number of people who are considered to be homosexual vary a great deal and tend to be highly unreliable. In a widescale survey in the United States, 2.8 percent of the male respondents and 1.4 percent of the female respondents claimed to be gay or bisexual; about 8 percent of the men and 4 percent of the women had had at least one homosexual experience (Michael et al., 1994).

Homosexuality is still viewed with fear and prejudice by many, and those who are homosexual are not always treated equitably. Even on university campuses, for example, there are numerous instances of violations of homosexual students' rights to free assembly, access to university services, and so on (Liddell & Douvanis, 1994). Many still view homosexuality as deviant and unnatural, although it has been deleted from the American Psychiatric Association's manual of mental disorders. In spite of this, there are continuing efforts to reorient the sexuality of homosexuals. Haldeman (1994), following an extensive review of the sexual reorientation literature, reports that there is little evidence that any of these treatments are effective.

Indications are that perhaps fewer than half of homosexual men live as couples, whereas approximately three quarters of lesbians are coupled (Harry, 1983). Research on the nature of homosexual couples reveals that, contrary to a popular stereotype, it is uncommon for one partner to adopt the "feminine" role and the other the "masculine" (Bell & Weinberg, 1978).

In addition to obvious differences in sexual orientation, there are several notable differences between homosexual and heterosexual couples. First, most of the literature indicates that couple relationships among homosexuals, especially among gay males, tend to involve younger individuals and not to last as long. Harry (1983) cautions, however, that many of these studies might have underrepresented older and longer-lasting relationships by drawing most of their samples from gay bars and gay associations, both of which tend to be frequented by younger people.

A second difference concerns sexual exclusivity. Whereas contemporary standards within marriage stress the importance of sexual fidelity, this appears to have been less the case among gay men and women (Peplau, 1981). However, fear of AIDS seems to have reduced promiscuity among gay males, a fact that has resulted in a decline in the number of other sexually transmitted diseases in the gay population (Lamanna & Riedmann, 1988).

Approximately 25 percent of gay men and 33 percent of gay women have been or are married. Of these, many have children. Gay fathers who leave their wives very seldom gain custody of their children. However, some do, and a number establish gay stepfamilies with a male partner. Crosbie-Burnett and Helmbrecht (1993) studied 48 such families. They report that happiness in such families was closely tied to the extent to which the gay stepfather was included in family activities and child-rearing decisions. Relationships of gay fathers with their children often remain close and caring even after the children have been told of their father's sexual orientation. The same appears to be true of lesbian mothers, far more of whom retain custody of their children after they have divorced and established a homosexual couple relationship.

Homosexual relationships may differ from heterosexual relationships in important ways, but the need to love and be loved is common to all people regardless of sexual orientation.

Singlehood

Single adults include not only those who have never married but also those who are divorced, separated, or widowed. There is strong evidence that each of these categories is growing. The age of marriage has increased dramatically in the last several decades, thereby prolonging the period of singlehood before marriage. In 1960, only 30 percent of women ages 20 to 24 had not yet married, but by 1980, that figure had risen to 50 percent; by 1992, it had reached 65.7 percent (U.S. Bureau of the Census, 1994). As we saw previously, the number of unmarried couples living together in the United States increased sixfold between 1970 and 1993. In addition, during that period, the number of one-parent families also increased dramatically. Almost one out of every four children (24 percent) under the age of 18 is now in a one-parent home—more than twice as many as in 1970 (U.S. Bureau of the Census, 1994).

Never-Marrieds

Close to 5 percent of the population never marries (95 percent do at least once) (U.S. Bureau of the Census, 1994). The never-marrieds make up the largest group of singles, accounting for almost 20 percent (see At a Glance: "The Never-Marrieds," and Figure 14.3).

Among the never-marrieds are those who have deliberately chosen never to marry, those who have temporarily postponed marriage for one reason or another, and those who have been unsuccessful in finding a mate. Accordingly, several social factors have contributed to the increasing number of never-marrieds, as well as to the rising age of first marriage. Among them are the greater number of women going to college and beginning careers before marriage; expanding career opportunities for women; more women than men at the "most marriageable age"; the increasing divorce rate, which, for some, has reduced the appeal of marriage; the widespread

THE NEVER-MARRIEDS

Singlehood includes adults who have never married, as well as the widowed, separated, and divorced. Numbers of the separated and divorced have increased dramatically in recent decades, as have numbers of older widows. But in 1992, by the age of 65, just as many people had been married at least once as had been the case in 1970. The big change is that age of first marriage had risen dramatically. For example, in 1970, by the age of 29, about 80 percent of all males and 90 percent of all females had been married. By 1992, these figures had been reduced to about 52 percent for males and 67 percent for females.

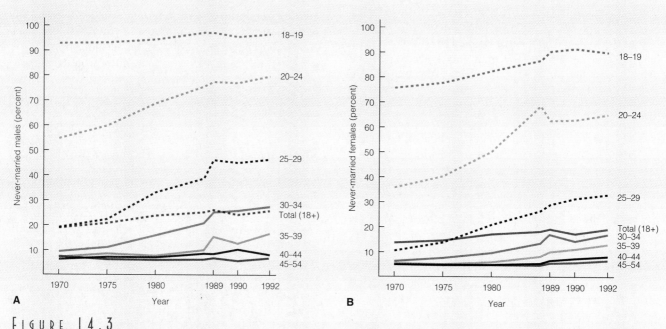

FIGURE 14.3

Percentage of **A** *males and* **B** *females over 18 who have never married, by age. (Based on U.S. Bureau of the Census, 1993, p. 53.)*

acceptability of cohabitation; and the increasing availability of birth control methods.

One of the important implications of these social changes is that many of the never-marrieds who have deliberately postponed marriage, often for an education or a career, and who see their singlehood as temporary, may end up in a state of involuntary, rather than voluntary, singlehood. This may be especially true of women whose increasing age and increasing educational, social, or professional status may serve to dramatically reduce the number of men who are likely to be suitable mates.

We should hasten to point out that unlike a character in a novel by Jane Austen, who exclaims, "Lord, how ashamed I should be of not being married before three and twenty!" today's generation typically sees no shame in singlehood. Indeed, among men it is not uncommon to take pride in being *"le gai bachelor"*; and perhaps these attitudes are becoming increasingly common among women as well.

The Separated and Divorced

As we have seen, there are many among the never-married who are voluntarily single, either temporarily or permanently. The singlehood characteristic of the separated and divorced, although it may well result from a deliberate and completely voluntary decision to end a marriage, was initially unplanned and may not be quite so voluntary.

Chances of a marriage ending in separation or divorce have increased dramatically in recent decades. More than one in three marriages now end in divorce; indications are that this proportion may soon reach 50 percent (O'Leary & Smith, 1991). The majority of those who divorce, however, will remarry. More men remarry than women, and they tend to remarry sooner after divorce (five out of six men and three out of four women typically remarry within three years). Obviously, divorce does not disillusion those who have already been married. And happiness ratings are about the same for people in a second marriage as for

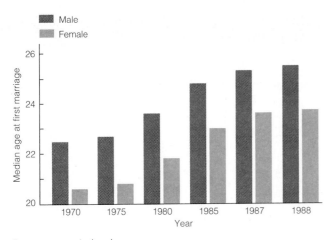

FIGURE 14.4

Median age of first marriage for men and women in the United States. (Based on U.S. Bureau of the Census, 1994, p. 103.)

comparable people in their first. However, people who have divorced and remarried often report more happiness in their second than in their first marriage (Benson-von der Ohe, 1984).

Because more divorced men than women remarry, because they do so sooner, and because men die sooner than women, there are more separated, divorced, widowed, and never-married women than men in all age groups, but especially at the upper age levels.

Cold statistics do not reveal the potential emotional impact of divorce. In Chapter 8, we looked at this impact on children, more than one of every four (30.2 percent) of whom are currently living with only one parent—85.6 percent of them with the mother (U.S. Bureau of the Census, 1994). We noted, among other things, that there are large individual variations in the extent to which children are chagrined or disturbed by their parents' divorce; these differences are sometimes related to the child's age and sex.

There are large variations in adult reactions to divorce as well. For women, the effects of divorce often include substantial, and sometimes very serious, reductions in income. In 1992, the median income of a female-headed home in the United States was $17,221; that of a male-headed single-parent home was about 60 percent higher at $27,821; and median income in the two-parent home was $42,064 (U.S. Bureau of the Census, 1994).

In addition to having to cope with reduced income, divorced women must adjust to different living arrangements, establish new social relationships, and sometimes assume a new work role in addition to the old homemaker role (Fine & Fine, 1992). Remarriage also brings a need for new adjustments, and typically also leads to a reduction in support from the ex-husband (Hill, 1992).

The lives of men are often changed less by divorce than those of women, particularly if they continue in the same work roles. But men, too, need to adjust to new living arrangements and a continued need for intimacy. It is worth noting that studies of happiness typically find that married men are happier than those who are not married, and among the least happy are those who are divorced (Campbell, 1981).

Clearly, however, divorce is not inevitably difficult and traumatic for everyone. And, as we noted in Chapter 8, there are conflict-ridden and unhappy marital relationships in which the partners involved, and the children, may be far better off in different situations.

Communes

Communes are yet another possible lifestyle. But unlike most other choices, this one does not necessarily exclude any other lifestyle. Communes are, by definition, *communities*—joint, cooperative attempts to carve a happy or useful lifestyle. Although they present a lifestyle that is different from, and hence an alternative to, the lifestyles we have looked at thus far, they are compatible with any of them. Thus, there are communes for conventionally married couples, as well as for people involved in group marriages; there are homosexual and heterosexual communes, religious and political communes, utopian communes, and all manner of other possible communal arrangements. Some communes are established so that members can do their own, presumably unconventional, "thing"; others function primarily to pool individual resources as a means of coping more effectively with society. And still others result from fundamental religious beliefs that can more easily be encouraged and practiced in relative isolation from society.

MARRIAGE

Although we have a choice of many lifestyles, marriage is the choice of the vast majority. It is perhaps notable, however, that we choose it somewhat later than did our parents—and they later than theirs. The median age of first marriage for men is 25.5, and for women it is 23.7 (U.S. Bureau of the Census, 1994) (Figure 14.4).

In most Western industrialized societies, there is only one officially approved form of marriage: that where each partner is entitled to only one other partner—**monogamy.** Having more than one wife or husband is illegal in North America and is termed *bigamy* by the courts. **Polygamy** is a more general expression for the same state of affairs. It includes *polygyny*, where the man is permitted to have more than one wife, and *polyandry*, where a wife is permitted more than one husband. Murdock (1957) looked at 554 of the world's societies and found that only 24 percent

CHANGES IN MARRIAGE

Marriage is as popular an institution as ever, but recent years have seen significant changes. Both men and women are now marrying about three years later than they were two decades ago. In addition, fewer marriages are the first marriage for either partner (more are re-

marriages). Interestingly, for marriages that end in divorce (approximately half), the median duration has not changed in almost two decades—it is still about seven years. (Does this prove the existence of the seven-year itch?)

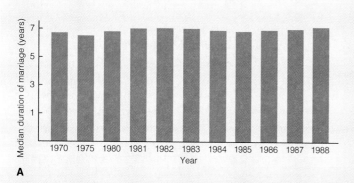

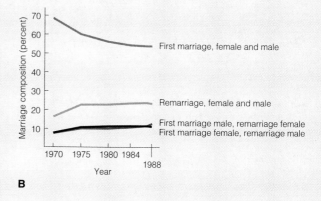

FIGURE 14.5

A *Median duration of first marriage, and* **B** *changes in composition of first and subsequent marriages, 1970–1988. (Based on U.S. Bureau of the Census, 1994, pp. 102, 103.)*

TABLE 14.3
Common Forms of Marriage Among 554 of the World's Societies

Type of Marriage	Number of Societies	Percentage
Monogamy	135	24
Polygamy	419	76
Polyandry	4	1
Polygyny	415	75

SOURCE: Based on data reported in "World Ethnographic Sample" by S. P. Murdock, 1957, *American Anthropologist* 59, pp. 664–688. Reprinted by permission of the American Anthropological Association.

sanctioned only monogamy. The vast majority (75 percent) permit polygyny; only 1 percent permit polyandry (see Table 14.3). Note, however, that even in those societies that permit one or more forms of polygamy, these are typically the exception rather than the rule. Often only the old and the wealthy can afford more than one wife (or husband). Often, too, only the very highly placed in the social hierarchy are permitted polygamy. Even today, however, in certain African countries such as Transkei, polygyny is not uncommon (Cherian, 1990).

Although contemporary Western societies do not permit polygamy, they do permit what Mead (1970) calls *serial monogamy:* We are free to marry, divorce, and remarry an unlimited number of times. (See At a Glance: "Changes in Marriage," and Figure 14.5.) In addition, various group-sex arrangements, mate swapping, open marriages, and other forms of sexual and emotional permissiveness, while not a dominant part of the current social mainstream, are nevertheless not altogether uncommon.

Premarital Sex

Indications are clear that monogamy is not what it used to be. This is particularly true for the many women whose roles were determined largely by the well-known double standard that was rampant until recently and that still rears its head on occasion in various male bastions: "Boys will be boys, you know." It went without saying that "girls will not be girls; if they must be anything, they will be angels." As we saw in Chapter 12, approximately as many women as men are now nonvirgins when they marry (see Figure 12.3, Chapter 12).

Contrary to some popular predictions, however, the sexual revolution did not translate itself into widespread, indiscriminate, totally recreational sex, although there is clearly more of this type of sexual activity now than there was when my grandfather sowed his particular species of oats. True, the sexual revolution of these past decades does

TABLE 14.4
Alternative Nonexclusive Marital Lifestyles

Type	Characteristics
Open marriage	Major concern is with the independence and growth of individual partners and the development of mutually accepted rules governing the relationship
Extramarital sex	Mostly nonconsensual, secretive, clandestine "sexual affairs" that tend to be of short duration
Nonsexual extramarital relationships	More open, nonsexual opposite-sex relationships involving dinners and movies, for example; apparently widely approved by college populations
Sexually open marriage	An open arrangement designed to permit sexual adventuring by either or both partners with other individuals in independent relationships that do not threaten the marriage
Swinging	Concerned with recreational sex rather than with relationships and often involves groups and mate swapping
Group marriage	An uncommon alternative usually involving four adults (two spouse pairs)

SOURCE: Based on "'Open' Marriage and Multilateral Relationships: The Emergence of Nonexclusive Models of the Marital Relationship" by D. L. Weis, 1983. In *Contemporary Families and Alternative Lifestyles: Handbook on Research and Theory* (pp. 194–215), E. D. Macklin and R. H. Rubin (Eds.), 1983, Beverly Hills, CA: Sage. Used by permission of the publisher.

manifest itself in greater sexual permissiveness. But it is a permissiveness that, with some notable exceptions, insists on affection. And even when dating and in love, 40 percent of the males and more than 80 percent of the females in Roche and Ramsbey's study of 268 college students did *not* engage in sexual intercourse (see Figure 12.5, Chapter 12). In addition, incidence of premarital sex among this sample had dropped significantly for girls in the preceding five years, although this was not the case for boys. Among girls, high self-esteem and positive attitudes toward school and family are closely related to the decision not to engage in premarital sex (Plotnick, 1992).

Extramarital Sex

Among the several alternatives to the traditional marital relationship are a number that propose sexual nonexclusivity—that condone extramarital sexual relations (see Table 14.4). Although extramarital sex (*adultery*, if a spade is to be called a shovel) is apparently not entirely uncommon, most societies discourage its practice, often on the grounds that it threatens the family unit. There is ample evidence, however, of a powerful double standard here, as there is with respect to premarital sex. In Japan and in many European countries, it is quite acceptable for a man to have a mistress, providing he is reasonably discreet about the affair and continues to meet his familial obliga-

tions. The same behavior is far less easily tolerated among married women and, indeed, is often grounds for punishment or divorce; such is seldom the case when the man is the adulterer.

A recent survey of more than 3,000 men and women in the United States reveals that extramarital sex is not overwhelmingly common. In this survey, 85 percent of the married women and 75 percent of the married men reported they were faithful to their spouses (Michael et al., 1994).

Types of Marriage Relationships

We know that about half of all new marriages now end in divorce (see At a Glance: "Marriage and Divorce," and Figure 14.6). We know, too, that some spouses, even if they remain married all their lives, will not always be sexually faithful. But we also know that married people describe their lives in more satisfactory terms and see themselves as being happier than those who remain single (or who are separated, divorced, or widowed).

To describe a marriage as being either "good" or "bad" is usually oversimplistic. There can be much that is good and much that is bad in any marriage. But it might be helpful to know what a "good" marriage can be like. Lavee and Olson (1993) provide us with some answers. They studied 8,385 marriages, analyzing them in terms of nine major dimensions such as personality issues, communication, conflict resolution, financial management, sexual relationships, and relationships with children, family, and friends. Subsequently, they identified seven different types of relationships, each of which reflects different values and emphases with respect to the nine dimensions studied.

At one extreme is the *vitalized couple*, in which each of the spouses expresses a high degree of satisfaction with all aspects of the marriage. At the other is the *devitalized* couple, in which both are dissatisfied with all aspects of the marriage. *Financially focused* couples are bound by material and financial goals in relationships marked by dissatisfaction with all aspects of the marriage except the financial. The *conflicted couple* shows dissatisfaction with the couple-related issues (communication, personality, conflict resolution), but higher satisfaction with external issues like leisure time activities. In contrast, the *harmonious marriage* is characterized by high accord with respect to couple-related issues but less agreement regarding external activities. *Traditional couples* experience considerable stress with interspousal relationships, but share high satisfaction with respect to family and religious values. And *balanced couples* are generally satisfied with most aspects of their marriage in spite of some problems in different areas.

In the Lavee and Olson (1993) study, 40 percent of the more than 8,000 couples could be described as *devitalized* (high dissatisfaction with all aspects of the marriage) and

MARRIAGE AND DIVORCE

Divorce rates in the United States more than doubled between 1960 and 1975, and have remained relatively constant since then, at about 4.8 per 1,000 population. At present, about half of all marriages end in divorce. The majority of those who divorce remarry, about half of them within five years. Although marriage rates have declined slightly in very recent years, marriage is still more common than divorce.

FIGURE 14.6

A *Marriage rate and* **B** *divorce rate per 1,000 population. (From U.S. Department of Health and Human Services, 1989, p. 4; and U.S. Bureau of the Census, 1994, p. 102.)*

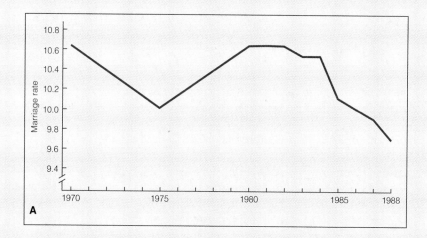

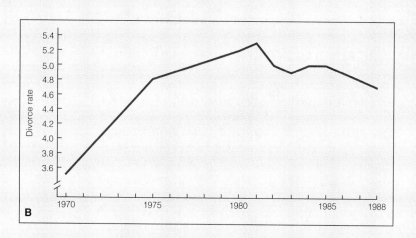

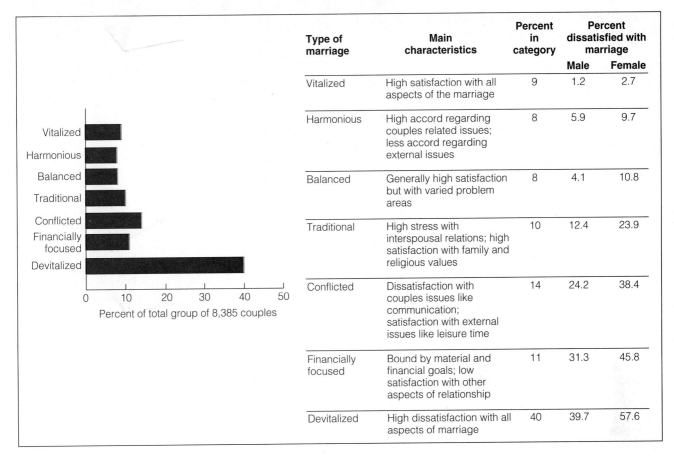

Type of marriage	Main characteristics	Percent in category	Percent dissatisfied with marriage	
			Male	Female
Vitalized	High satisfaction with all aspects of the marriage	9	1.2	2.7
Harmonious	High accord regarding couples related issues; less accord regarding external issues	8	5.9	9.7
Balanced	Generally high satisfaction but with varied problem areas	8	4.1	10.8
Traditional	High stress with interspousal relations; high satisfaction with family and religious values	10	12.4	23.9
Conflicted	Dissatisfaction with couples issues like communication; satisfaction with external issues like leisure time	14	24.2	38.4
Financially focused	Bound by material and financial goals; low satisfaction with other aspects of relationship	11	31.3	45.8
Devitalized	High dissatisfaction with all aspects of marriage	40	39.7	57.6

FIGURE 14.7
Lavee and Olson's seven types of marriage. (Based on Lavee & Olson, 1993.)

only 9 percent as *vitalized* (high satisfaction with all aspects of the relationship). Membership in other categories was relatively evenly distributed (see Figure 14.7).

These seven types of marriages describe the nature of the relationships that are possible between husband and wife, but they do not describe whether a marriage is good or bad. In fact, note Lavee and Olson, happy (and unhappy) families can differ a great deal. Some happy couples might be happy with all aspects of their marriage (in this study, only about 9 percent were, however); and some might be quite dissatisfied with certain aspects of their relationship, but nevertheless describe themselves as generally happy. Thus, even among the most happy of marriages (the *vitalized*), almost one quarter of the women and 16 percent of the men admitted to having considered divorce. It is perhaps equally significant, however, that among the least happy couples (those in *devitalized* relationships), 25 percent of the women and 37 percent of the men claimed that they had *not* considered divorce. Hence, each of these different types of relationships can be characteristic of an enduring marriage.

Marital Discord
But each can also be marked by considerable marital discord, which can be an extremely serious problem, say O'Leary and Smith (1991). Not only do difficulties with relationships cause great distress and unhappiness among married couples, as well as among their children, but they are the most important factor in many suicides. Relationship problems are also involved in a large number of family homicides.

The reasons for marital discord are complex and varied. O'Leary and Smith (1991) review a number of studies suggesting that marriage partners tend to select each other for similarity of personality traits, values, goals, and other important characteristics. Apparently, a basic wisdom guides this selection process, because degree of similarity is predictive of marital adjustment and satisfaction; by the same token, dissimilarity may be associated with marital discord.

Also related to marital discord are certain personality variables associated with depression and emotional instability—characteristics such as impulsivity, fearfulness, poor social adjustment, and what is termed *dysphoria*, which means a general unhappiness (Beach & O'Leary, 1993). In addition, those who initially hold nontraditional views about marriage and family life are more likely to be *less* satisfied with their marriages (Lye & Biblarz, 1993).

Research indicates that marital dissatisfaction tends to increase over the early years of marriage as partners are required to make difficult adjustments, and perhaps to reassess their expectations of continuing, idealized romantic love (Belsky & Rovine, 1990). Not surprisingly, about one third of all divorces occur within the first four years of marriage (U.S. Bureau of the Census, 1994).

Marital discord is often characterized by misunderstanding among partners, poor communication, misinterpretation of actions and intentions, and limited engagement in shared activities (Zuo, 1992). A large number of marriage enhancement programs have arisen to remedy these conditions and restore harmony to discordant marriages. Many of these, note O'Leary and Smith (1991), have not been systematically investigated and may have no beneficial effects. However, others have been shown to be effective for some couples.

Marital Satisfaction

The simple longevity of a marriage may be a poor indicator of marital satisfaction. Indeed, a great many abjectly miserable marriages endure; and a number of perfectly contented marriages may end too abruptly.

We ask a great deal of our marriages. Our forebears asked mostly that marriage bring them a workable, child-rearing arrangement with a clear division of duties and responsibility. Now we expect marriage to make us happy; we think happiness is our right. And if it does not come sooner, we seldom wait for it to come later. We simply try again.

But are the married happier? More satisfied? The evidence suggests yes. When compared with unmarried individuals, married people at all ages report higher levels of satisfaction and happiness. Coombs (1991) reviewed 130 studies of the relationship between marriage and well-being. He concludes, "Married men and women are generally happier and less stressed than the unmarried" (p. 97).

Happiness in marriage does not appear to be a static, unchanging thing. Although some studies find little relationship between length of marriage and measures of marital happiness, most studies indicate that there is a curvilinear relationship between the two. Couples tend to report highest levels of satisfaction in the early, prechildbearing years of marriage, least satisfaction through the childbearing years, and a return to higher levels of satisfaction in later years (see Figure 14.8). The lowest point with respect to marital happiness, report Vaillant and Vaillant (1993) following a 40-year study of 169 college men and their wives, is approximately 20 years into the marriage. Researchers have hypothesized that the presence of children puts considerable strain on a couple. And 20

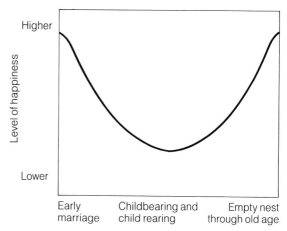

FIGURE 14.8

Graphic representation of U-shaped curvilinear relationship between level of marital happiness and stage in family life cycle. Note that the lower levels of reported happiness through the child-rearing years do not indicate unhappiness. Note, too, that happiness is highly individualistic and highly varied. Clearly, not all marriages follow this idealized pattern.

years into the marriage coincides with the teen-rearing years. The requirements associated with raising children, and especially teenagers, make tremendous demands on the time and energy of parents. In addition, this is often the time when career demands on the father are greatest. As a result, time for interaction between spouses and for leisure activities becomes scarce.

In spite of the fact that marital happiness often declines in midmarriage, absolute levels of happiness, as we saw earlier, tend to be higher for the married than for the single, although perhaps not markedly so. And happiness, of course, is relative and highly individualistic. It does not allow itself to be easily measured.

Who Among the Married Are Happiest?

Skolnick (1981) provides some insights into who among the married might be happier and why, following intensive interviews with 232 members of the Oakland Guidance Study and the Berkeley Guidance Study. In this study, several social factors appeared to be closely related to marital satisfaction. For women, the most important of these was age at first marriage. In general, the older the woman, the more likely she is to be happily married later on. That teenage marriages break up twice as frequently as older marriages is additional corroboration of this finding. For men, the social variable most highly related to marital satisfaction is occupation, with socioeconomic status, a closely related variable, being almost equally important. In general, executives and professionals tend to be more happily married than other men. And for both men and women, amount of education is positively related to marital satisfaction, as is socioeconomic status and absence

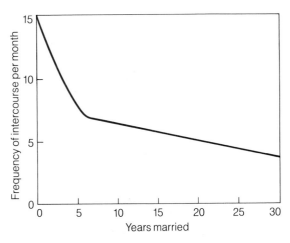

FIGURE 14.9

Average frequency of intercourse per month according to years of marriage. (Based on L. A. Westoff and C. F. Westoff, From Now to Zero, 1971. Reprinted by permission of Little, Brown & Co., Inc.)

of children. Contrary to what might be expected, couples who are voluntarily childless report higher levels of happiness than couples with children (Somers, 1993).

Skolnick also looked at the contribution of personality variables to marital happiness. Like most other researchers, she found that opposites do not attract and complement each other or live happy lives because the strengths of one make up for the weaknesses of the other. Quite the contrary, similar people are attracted to each other. Indeed, the more similar members of a pair were, the more likely they were to report high marital satisfaction. This was particularly true of cognitive variables such as intelligence and impulsiveness or reflectiveness. It is also true of social characteristics. Couples in which both members share some major social characteristic (for example, both are highly aggressive or highly sociable) tend to live in greater harmony than those in which each is the opposite of the other.

Finally, Skolnick (1981) reports that those marriages that were rated most satisfactory were typically those in which spouses liked, admired, and respected each other. In contrast, spouses who had discordant personalities, who were critical of each other, and who saw their relationship as utilitarian (rather than as personally close) were more likely to have unhappy marriages.

Sex, too, appears to be related to marital happiness, with both men and women selecting it as one of their favorite activities—and many singling out unsatisfactory sexual relations as the reason for unhappy marriages. On average, frequency of sexual intercourse is highest for the first few years after marriage and then declines rapidly for the next few years. Subsequent average declines are more gradual (see Figure 14.9). Initial declines probably have more to do with the woman becoming pregnant and with

the resulting pressures, time constraints, and lack of privacy associated with child rearing than with declining sexual interest. Most evidence suggests, in fact, that males do not experience a noticeable reduction in sexual interest until well into middle age; and 40 percent of married couples claim they have sex at least twice a week (Michael et al., 1994). Women, too, report little reduction in sexual interest or, indeed, in sexual responsiveness through the bulk of their adult years. Solnick and Corby (1983) report that some women are still capable of orgasm well into their seventies and eighties.

THE FAMILY

A marriage is simply the legal union of two individuals. Its social function, however, goes considerably beyond these two individuals; it makes possible the *family*, of which, historically, there have been two types. The one most common in Western societies consists of parents and their immediate children, and is termed **nuclear.** That which is most prevalent throughout the world includes grandparents and assorted other relatives in addition to children and their parents, and is termed **extended.**

Some widely held notions about what "proper" or "ideal" families are like are based directly on a no-longer entirely realistic belief that North American families are nearly all nuclear, mother–father–children families—or, ideally, should be. This image, note White and Woollett (1992), is widely portrayed on television. But it is a misleading image because of some dramatic and well-known changes in the family. Among other things, the North American nuclear family is much shorter-lived (about half of all first marriages end in divorce, and that, in an average of about seven years); far more couples cohabit without marrying; there has been a sharp increase in one-parent families; and increasing numbers of children are being raised in stepfamilies.

In spite of these changes, the nuclear family is still the most prevalent child-rearing unit in North America. Whereas in 1970, 85 percent of American children lived with both parents, in 1992, the percentage was still 73 (79 percent of whites, 67 percent of Hispanics, and 38 percent of blacks; U.S. Bureau of the Census, 1994). Hence the following discussion of the family is based primarily on a description of systematic changes in the intact nuclear family with the coming and leaving of children, and with the aging of parents. Bear in mind, however, that this is a description of only one of North America's many families.

The Life-Cycle Approach: Duvall

A family may be thought of as having a *life cycle*—a beginning, a growing and changing, and eventually an ending. The **family life-cycle** concept provides a useful basis for describing the family and its functions. One example of

*Duvall's eight stages of the family
life cycle: At which stage of the cycle
is your parents' family? Your family,
if you are married? What are the
tasks and responsibilities of those
stages? (From Duvall, 1977, p. 148.
Based on data from the U.S. Bureau
of the Census and from the National
Center for Health Statistics,
Washington, DC.)*

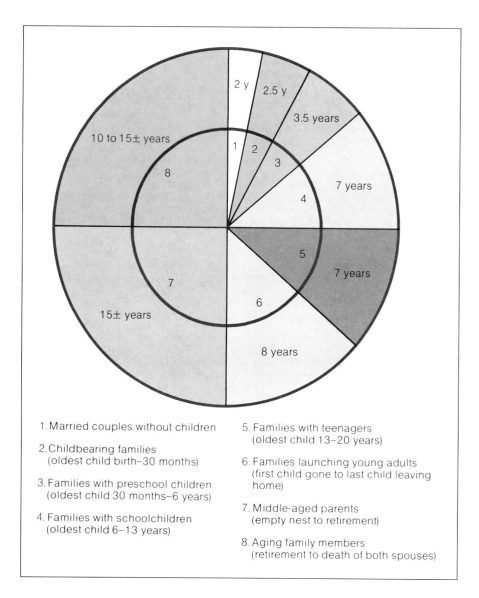

1. Married couples without children

2. Childbearing families
   (oldest child birth–30 months)

3. Families with preschool children
   (oldest child 30 months–6 years)

4. Families with schoolchildren
   (oldest child 6–13 years)

5. Families with teenagers
   (oldest child 13–20 years)

6. Families launching young adults
   (first child gone to last child leaving
   home)

7. Middle-aged parents
   (empty nest to retirement)

8. Aging family members
   (retirement to death of both spouses)

this approach, described here, is provided by Duvall (1977). He identifies eight sequential stages in the evolution of the family. These stages often overlap and can also be very different for different families. In the main, however, they describe a relatively common progression identifiable in terms of a series of important developmental tasks, most of which relate to child rearing (Interactive Figure 14.10). Keep in mind, however, that the family cycle described here applies primarily to "traditional" first-marriage, child-rearing families. In addition, this approach neglects the many important influences on the family other than children—such as careers, as well as relationships with parents, friends, siblings, and spouse. Also, it concentrates on the influence of the first, and thus oldest, child, and ignores the impact of other children (Vinovskis, 1988). However, other approaches that include more factors become too complex to be very practical.

The first five of Duvall's eight stages span the period of early adulthood, and are described briefly here. The sixth and seventh last through middle adulthood and are discussed in Chapter 16; the eighth stage is covered in Chapter 18.

Stage 1: To Have Children?

Most families begin as a childless couple, a period that, in Duvall's model, lasts for approximately two years. In fact, however, when Duvall developed his model, the largest number of births occurred to women between ages 20 and 24; but in 1991, women had more children between the ages of 25 and 29 than at any other period—and women aged 30 to 34 had almost as many (see At a Glance: "Changing Birthrates and Age of Childbearing," and Figure 14.11). Hence the first stage (sometimes called the *honeymoon* stage) might now last much longer.

The first stage often brings with it three important sets of developmental tasks: those having to do with selecting and developing a career (or finding and keeping a job); those relating to sexual fulfillment and the develop-

CHANGING BIRTHRATES
AND AGE OF CHILDBEARING

Since 1970, the average age at first marriage has increased by about three years. In addition, as increasing numbers of women have entered the workplace, some have delayed having children; others have decided not to have any. As a result, overall birthrate in the United States has

dropped by about 20 percent in the last two decades (from 87.9 per 1,000 women between ages 15 and 44 in 1970 to 69.6 in 1991). As is shown in Figure 14.11, the peak childbearing years in 1970 were between 20 and 24; in 1991, they were between 25 and 29.

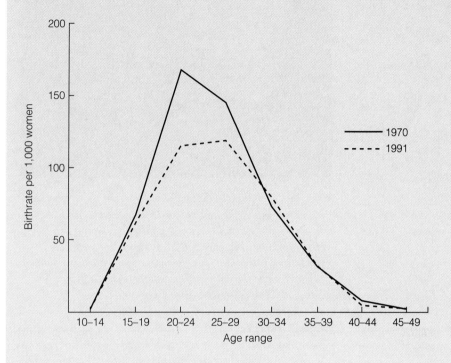

FIGURE 14.11
Birthrate per 1,000 women ages 10 to 49, 1970–1991. (Based on U.S. Bureau of the Census, 1994, p. 76.)

ment of a harmonious marriage; and those relating to whether and when to have children, a decision that is often more complicated in families in which both partners have careers. As Wilk (1986) points out, in the dual-career family, the decision to start a family (or not to do so) will be affected by at least four groups of considerations. The first two of these, lifestyle and career issues, are most relevant to women who work. The other two, marriage and psychological issues, affect all potential parents.

Lifestyle issues involve questions relating to how the presence of children might change the partners' activities, the impact of potential reduction of income coupled with the costs associated with child rearing, and decisions that have been made or are being made by important reference groups such as friends and co-workers.

Career issues relate to whether the wife is satisfied with her career and her future career prospects, and whether the development of her career can survive one or more interruptions. The transition to a parenting role is sometimes more difficult for dual-career families, and especially for mothers in these families (Romanin & Over,

1993). Marriage issues have to do with how happy each of the partners is with their marriage, how stable they think it is, and how they think it will respond to the introduction of children. As we noted earlier, the family is a dynamic system. It changes as its composition changes; and it changes, as well, in response to changes in its larger context. It is, in the jargon of this age, an *ecological* system, composed of complex and ever-changing relationships that give it a life of its own. The strength and viability of this system, its likely effects on children, and the likely effects of children on it, are all important factors—not only for dual-career families but also for others.

Psychological factors that are important in making a childbearing decision affect all potential mothers—and all potential fathers as well. They have to do with individual values and preferences, and are related to a host of other variables, the most important of which might be the potential parents' relationships with their own parents when they were children. There are some who do not *want* children for personal reasons. (Wilk's [1986] decision-making model is summarized in Figure 14.12.)

PREMARITAL DISCUSSION OF INTENTIONS

↓

FEMININE INTRAPSYCHIC DETERMINANTS

Relationship to mother
Relationship to father
Feminine identification
Personality characteristics:
flexibility
interdependence

MARRIAGE DETERMINANTS

Stability
Satisfaction with support from spouse
Stress management system

CAREER DETERMINANTS

Level of responsibility
Degree of career change viewed as acceptable
Satisfaction with career

LIFE-STYLE DETERMINANTS

Financial issues
Childfree relationship
Reference groups

↓

CHILDBEARING DECISION

FIGURE 14.12
A dual-career childbearing decision model. (From C. A. Wilk, Career Women and Childbearing. *© 1986 Van Nostrand Reinhold. Used by permission.)*

Current lifespan models of the family life cycle recognize that among the most profound and predictable changes in the development of the family are those relating to having and raising children. Not only will his family exert tremendous influence on this infant, but the infant's presence and personality will shape the nature of his family—even affecting how mother and father relate to each other.

There are those for whom the question is difficult; sometimes it is simply put off as a result. There are some, too, who do not ask or answer the question, but who simply let nature or luck answer it for them. And there are others for whom the answer is so clear that they scarcely need to ask themselves the question.

Stages 2–5: Child Rearing

The next 20 years of Duvall's family life cycle are the childbearing and child-rearing years. Keep in mind, however, that this stage now often occurs much later than was recently the case. And for those who do not have children, it simply doesn't happen.

Stage 2: Infancy

The infancy stage of the life cycle begins with the birth of the first child and lasts approximately two and a half years. Much of the literature that deals with this period, note Seltzer and Ryff (1994), deals with the effects of parents and parenting on infants rather than on parents. A lifespan view of the family life cycle changes that focus. It recognizes, for example, that this is a period of very rapid changes and adjustments in the family, which bring a variety of demands for both mother and father. Among other things, the mother is called upon to develop and clarify her roles as mother, wife, and person; she needs to learn how to care for and cope with infants and young preschoolers; she needs to maintain a satisfying relationship with her husband; and she must, through all this, nevertheless maintain some sense of personal autonomy. The father, too, is required to make numerous adjustments, including reconciling conflicting conceptions of his role as father, accepting new responsibilities for parenting, conforming to changes in schedules, coping with the reduced time and attention that the wife can now devote to him, and maintaining a satisfying marital relationship and a sense of autonomy and self-worth. Not surprisingly, evidence reported by Seltzer and Ryff (1994) suggests that parents whose infants were characterized by "easy" rather

The family cycle brings with it a series of changing developmental tasks. Some relate to coping with and caring for children; others have to do with maintaining satisfying relationships with spouse, friends, and others, while at the same time developing and maintaining a sense of personal autonomy. Happy, "easy" children such as this little tyke make it far easier to adjust to parenthood.

than "difficult" temperaments adjust more easily to parenthood and see it as a more positive experience.

Stage 3: Preschool

As the first child reaches the preschool age, the family enters the third stage of Duvall's family life cycle. It begins when the first child is 2, ends with school age (6), and brings with it a continuation of most of the developmental tasks that were first introduced in the preceding stage. Few of these tasks are ever completely resolved during any one phase of the cycle. Indeed, such important tasks as maintaining a sense of autonomy and worth while striving for the development of a mutually satisfying and happy marriage continue from the beginning to the very end of the family life cycle. In addition, the presence of preschoolers in the family brings additional demands for income, space, equipment, time, and attention, as well as a new set of child-rearing responsibilities and problems. And to complicate matters, only those families with a single child can be described as being in only one developmental phase at one time. For many families, there is considerable overlap among stages as additional children are born.

Stage 4: Preteen School Years

The fourth stage, much longer than any of the first three, spans the preteen school years of the oldest child (6 to 13). It brings three important developmental tasks, none of which is exclusive to this developmental phase, but all of which are fundamentally important to the happy and effective functioning of the family: providing for children's special as well as ordinary needs; enjoying life with children; and encouraging children's growth. Although these

tasks are difficult and demanding, most parents raise their children without a great deal of deliberation or guidance, relying primarily on intuition, folk wisdom, and their recollection of the child-rearing techniques of their parents. Interestingly, a study of 454 couples indicates that parents who had more socialization experiences related to child rearing (for example, babysitting, teaching, being a camp counselor, looking after siblings, or taking parenting courses) were happier parents who more easily made the transition to parenthood (Gage & Hendrickson Christensen, 1991).

Stage 5: Teen Years

The fifth phase in the family life cycle spans the teen years of the oldest child (13 to 20) and brings with it the occasional parenting problems of adolescence. These present many family developmental tasks, including working out possible financial problems, reallocating the sharing of responsibilities, bridging the communication gap between generations, and, all the while, continuing to maintain the marriage relationship. Seltzer and Ryff (1994) cite evidence that parents who have strong commitments to their occupations are less likely to experience conflict and stress related to the increasing independence of their adolescents.

An Evaluation of the Life-Cycle Approach

It is important to keep in mind that life-cycle approaches such as Duvall's describe common patterns in *traditional* families. However, increasing numbers of families are no longer traditional. As a result, many of the important events that serve as transitions from one stage to another in the evolution of the family now occur much later than they once did, or don't occur at all. Not only are young adults getting married at later ages, but also many are delaying the start of a family. And, increasing numbers of adult children continue to live with their parents. In fact, Aquilino (1990) reports that about 45 percent of parents ages 45 to 54 who have adult children have an adult child living at home.

Approaches such as this also tend to oversimplify very complex and highly dynamic relationships. They are based on assumptions that might not always be correct—for example, that families with more than one child go through the same sorts of changes as families with only one child. Nor can they take into account the impact of family crises such as death and divorce; and they say little about the vast number of families that do not fit the traditional mold of working father and homemaking mother. Divorce, one-parent families, career mothers, and a variety of other family situations that have become increasingly common in recent decades present different sets of problems and tasks. In spite of this, however, we should not forget that no matter the nature of their families, children still progress in similar ways through their infancies and childhoods, into their adolescence, and finally into the world. And it is children who, after all, define the very existence and nature of the family.

FAMILY VIOLENCE

Prophets and others who specialize in gloom and related states have been warning us for some time that violence is rapidly becoming a way of life in contemporary societies. And perhaps they are correct. Although the U.S. Bureau of the Census (1994) data indicate that the percentage of households touched by crime was lower in 1992 than in 1981 (22.6 percent compared with 30 percent), rates for many violent crimes have increased (Figure 14.13). In particular, sexual violence seems to have increased dramatically in recent decades (Figure 14.14).

Although it might be tempting to assume that violence typically involves strangers and that surrounding ourselves with friends and family will therefore protect us, that, sadly, does not appear to be the case. Indeed, more than 25 percent of all assaults and homicides that are reported to police involve members of the same family; and 42 percent of all crime victims know the perpetrator. More than half of all rapes, crimes that most of us attribute to disturbed strangers in dark parking lots, are committed by acquaintances or relatives—or "dates." One third of all female murder victims are killed by boyfriends or husbands (U.S. Bureau of the Census, 1994). As Gelles (1978) puts it, "We have discovered that violence between family members, rather than being a minor pattern of behavior, or a behavior that is rare and dysfunctional, is a patterned and normal aspect of interaction between fam-

ily members" (p. 169). In a national survey, Resnick, Kilpatrick, and Dansky (1993) found that more than a third of American women had been exposed to some violent, traumatic event (such as sexual assault or homicide) involving themselves or some close friend at some time in their lives.

Violence in the family takes a variety of forms. It is clearly evident in the observation that the majority of parents admit to using physical force to punish children, and is even more dramatically apparent in instances of child abuse (discussed in Chapter 10). In 1992, almost 2.9 million children were involved in reported instances of child abuse and neglect; of these, more than 990,000 were substantiated by authorities (U.S. Bureau of the Census, 1994).

Family violence is present, as well, in countless episodes of aggression among siblings. Indeed, violence among siblings seems to be highly prevalent among young children, although it diminishes rapidly with increasing age. In a sample of 2,143 families, Straus (1980b) found that 74 percent of all 3- to 4-year-old children who had siblings occasionally resorted to some form of physical aggression in their interactions. Thirty-six percent of those ages 15 to 17 behaved in similar fashion.

Interspousal Violence

Violence in the family is also apparent in instances of wife and husband beating, as well as in the verbal aggression that Stets (1990) found almost invariably accompanies physical violence. And surprisingly, the latter is almost as common as the former. In Straus and Gelles's (1986) investigation of American families, 3.8 percent of all husbands admitted to activities that the authors define as wife beating. These activities include kicking, biting, hitting with the fist or some other object, threatening with a knife or a gun, or actually using a knife or a gun. And an amazing 4.6 percent of all wives admitted to similar activities with respect to their husbands. However, Straus cautions that wife beating tends to be hidden and secretive more often than is husband beating, and that wives are, in fact, far more often victims than are husbands.

The picture presented by surveys such as these is probably only a partial sketch, given the privacy of the family. Its affairs are not easily accessible to social science or to law enforcement agencies. In addition, our prevailing attitudes concerning the right of parents to punish their children physically, the normality of siblings fighting, and, yes, even the right of a husband to beat his wife tend to obscure the prevalence and seriousness of violence in the family.

Why do some husbands beat their wives? There is no simple answer. Some, probably a minority, might be classified as suffering from a psychological disorder. In one study involving 100 battered wives, 25 percent of the husbands had received psychiatric help in the past. And, according to the wives, many more were in need of such

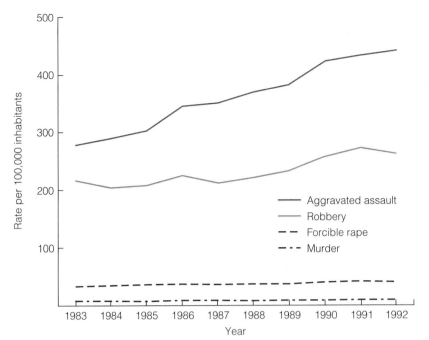

FIGURE 14.13
Increases in rates of selected crimes in the United States, 1983–1992. (Based on U.S. Bureau of the Census, 1994, p. 198.)

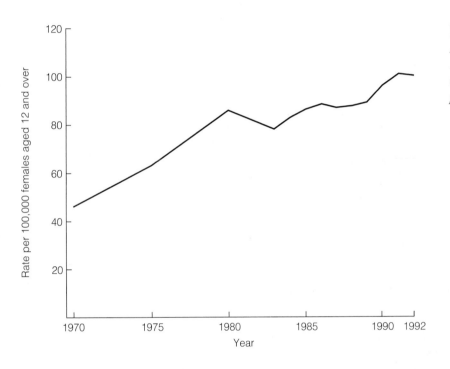

FIGURE 14.14
Rate of forcible rape, 1970–1992. Rate per 100,000 females aged 12 and over. (Based on U.S. Bureau of the Census, 1994, p. 202.)

help (Gayford, 1978). Many of these husbands came to their marriages with a history of violence. Many had been physically abused and beaten as children. And compared with the general population, more of them were chronically unemployed and poorly educated.

Other factors that contribute to violence in the family include the high incidence of violence in society, cultural attitudes that accept violence as a legitimate reaction in certain situations, and our predominantly sexist attitudes toward the roles of husband and wife in contemporary marriage. These and other contributing factors are summarized in Figure 14.15.

Sexual Assault and Acquaintance Rape

One form of violence that is not restricted to the family, but that is pertinent there as well, is sexual assault. Sexual assault can range from sexual innuendo and unwanted suggestions to forcible rape. It is an increasingly common problem with a range of sometimes extremely negative consequences.

Rape is ordinarily defined as forcible sexual intercourse with someone *other* than a spouse (Gelles, 1979). In 1992, 100.5 out of every 100,000 American women over the age of 12 were subjected to attempted or actual

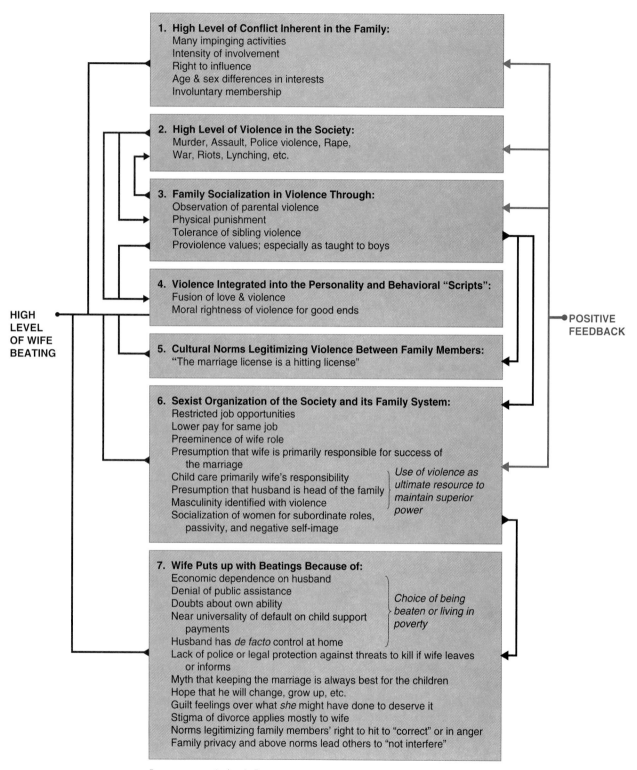

HIGH LEVEL OF WIFE BEATING

1. **High Level of Conflict Inherent in the Family:**
   Many impinging activities
   Intensity of involvement
   Right to influence
   Age & sex differences in interests
   Involuntary membership

2. **High Level of Violence in the Society:**
   Murder, Assault, Police violence, Rape,
   War, Riots, Lynching, etc.

3. **Family Socialization in Violence Through:**
   Observation of parental violence
   Physical punishment
   Tolerance of sibling violence
   Proviolence values; especially as taught to boys

4. **Violence Integrated into the Personality and Behavioral "Scripts":**
   Fusion of love & violence
   Moral rightness of violence for good ends

5. **Cultural Norms Legitimizing Violence Between Family Members:**
   "The marriage license is a hitting license"

6. **Sexist Organization of the Society and its Family System:**
   Restricted job opportunities
   Lower pay for same job
   Preeminence of wife role
   Presumption that wife is primarily responsible for success of
       the marriage
   Child care primarily wife's responsibility
   Presumption that husband is head of the family   } Use of violence as
   Masculinity identified with violence   ultimate resource to
   Socialization of women for subordinate roles,   maintain superior
       passivity, and negative self-image   power

7. **Wife Puts up with Beatings Because of:**
   Economic dependence on husband
   Denial of public assistance
   Doubts about own ability
   Near universality of default on child support   Choice of being
       payments   beaten or living in
   Husband has *de facto* control at home   poverty
   Lack of police or legal protection against threats to kill if wife leaves
       or informs
   Myth that keeping the marriage is always best for the children
   Hope that he will change, grow up, etc.
   Guilt feelings over what *she* might have done to deserve it
   Stigma of divorce applies mostly to wife
   Norms legitimizing family members' right to hit to "correct" or in anger
   Family privacy and above norms lead others to "not interfere"

POSITIVE FEEDBACK

FIGURE 14.15

*Some of the factors accounting for the high incidence of wife
beating (solid lines) and positive feedback loops maintaining
the system (colored lines). (From Straus, 1980a. Used by
permission of the University of Minnesota Press.)*

forcible rape—a total of more than 109,000 incidents. This represents an increase of more than 180 percent since 1970, when the rate per 100,000 women was 46.3 (U.S. Bureau of the Census, 1994).

Note that the legal definition of rape specifically excludes the wife as victim. In this definition is an implicit acceptance of a husband's right to use physical force on his wife—and an explanation for the reluctance of law enforcement agencies to charge husbands with assault when wives are victims. English common law maintains that a man is still king in his castle, however humble that castle might be.

In many jurisdictions, then, it is legally impossible for a man to rape his wife—although he might well be guilty of sexual violence variously labeled "sexual aggression," "sexual coercion," or "sexual victimization." It is not legally impossible for a friend, a date, or an acquaintance to rape his partner. In fact, such behaviors are shockingly common, and are often termed *courtship violence*, *date rape*, or *acquaintance rape*.

Acquaintance Rape on Campus

Ward and associates (1991) speak of four different kinds of rape that occur on college and university campuses (and elsewhere, too, of course): (1) the *stranger* incident in which the perpetrator attacks an unknown victim, (2) the *party* incident in which victim and perpetrator know each other from a single social function during or after which the assault occurs, (3) the *acquaintance* incident in which the man and woman know each other casually, and (4) the *date* incident in which the man and woman have an ongoing relationship.

Prevalence of sexual assault on college campuses is difficult to ascertain, as it is elsewhere. There are problems of definition, as well as problems having to do with underreporting. Koss (1988) found that only 58 percent of rape victims reported the incident to anyone at all; a mere 5 percent went to the police. Many women are uncertain or ambiguous about the seriousness of the incident; and many think that little or nothing can be done.

In one survey of 531 college women, Finley and Corty (1993) found that one out of every six women had experienced some sort of sexual assault the preceding year. Other reports indicate that about one third of college women experience unwanted sexual contact in any given year (for example, De Keseredy, Schwartz, & Tait, 1993; Ward et al., 1991). The Ward and associates survey involved 524 women and 337 men on a college campus. Thirty-four percent of the women in this group had experienced unwanted sexual contact (kissing, fondling, or touching in a sexual way); 20 percent had been subjected to attempted sexual intercourse; and 10 percent had experienced unwanted completed sexual intercourse. The majority of these episodes occurred with an acquaintance at a party; about three quarters involved alcohol use by the male and one half involved alcohol use by the female; and

TABLE 14.5
Characteristics of "Most Serious" Sexual Incidents

	Type of Experience		
	Contact (N = 176)	Attempted Intercourse (N = 102)	Intercourse (N = 50)
Location			
Dorm	32%	41%	50%
Fraternity	28	10	8
Apartment	29	43	36
Other	11	6	6
Occasion			
Date	9%	8%	14%
Party	68	65	57
Other	24	27	29
Alcohol Use			
Male use	80%	77%	76%
Female use	57	54	65
Relationship			
Stranger	18%	9%	12%
Acquaintance/friend	66	57	47
Boyfriend	14	30	33
Other	2	5	8
Male Tactics			
Just did it	77%	62%	46%
Verbal	15	28	33
Force	8	10	21
Female Response*			
Too frightened	6%	6%	20%
Said no	76	91	70
Cried	5	9	22
Struggled/fought	17	16	28
Other protests	17	7	12
What Resulted*			
Physical injury	0%	3%	10%
Psychological injury	18	30	51
Required counseling	2	2	8
Who Was Told*			
No one	23%	30%	41%
Roommate	41	38	25
Close friend	59	54	41
Counselor	<1	<1	4

* Percentages do not add to 100 because of multiple responses.

SOURCE: From Ward, S. K., Chapman, K., Cohn, E., White, S., & Williams, K. (1991). Acquaintance rape and the college social scene. *Family Relations* 40, 65–71. Copyright 1991 by the National Council on Family Relations. Reprinted by permission.

in almost half the cases of unwanted intercourse, no one was told later (see Table 14.5).

It is perhaps striking that, in this sample, men's recollections of sexual incidents were dramatically different from the women's. Only 9 percent of the men recalled having sexual contact with an unwilling woman, and another 9 percent claimed they had attempted intercourse with an unwilling partner (women reported 34 and 20 percent, respectively); a mere 3 percent of men admitted they had actually completed intercourse (women reported 10 percent).

Attitudes Toward Sexual Violence

Other research indicates that many students don't view date rape as a particularly serious problem. In one survey of 172 college men and women, only about half thought date rape was a problem; and very few believed it was a *major* problem (Walton, 1994). Even among college students, males are more likely than females to assign responsibility for date rape to the victim, believing that the woman probably wanted to have sex, and that she should have foreseen the man's actions (Proite, Dannells, & Benton, 1993). In this sense, sexual assault is a form of violence that reflects an attitude of male dominance and female passivity, and an implicit assumption of the male's rights to sexual satisfaction under certain circumstances. That these attitudes are slowly changing is reflected in what is termed *rape shield law*, which prohibits that the victim's sexual history or apparently promiscuous behaviors be used against her (Julian, 1993).

Many campuses organize and support workshops designed to increase student awareness of sexual violence, as well as to reduce male callousness toward date rape and to debunk the myths that still surround sexual aggression. These often result in significant attitude changes among males, report Szymanski, Devlin, and Chrisler (1993). Interestingly, male students who live in coeducational residences and fraternities typically have less traditional views of gender and are less accepting of rape myths (Schaeffer & Nelson, 1993).

THE CONTINUING EVOLUTION OF SELF

Family violence and sexual assault would not have been a happy topic with which to end this chapter. It is shocking and distressing to consider that more than 3 million men and women and more than 2 million children in the United States are victims of *severe* violence each year. The topic smacks too much of power and too little of love.

Love and power are the two themes that run through our dreams. They are the themes that unify the stories of our lives, that give purpose and direction to our actions. It is through expressions of love and power that we achieve meaning—that we become meaningful. Being meaningful is the essence of Kegan's (1982) view of the evolution of the self.

Kegan describes five stages in the evolution of the self—five major transformations in the relationships that link individuals and their contexts. The first, the age of the *impulsive self*, describes a self that is embedded in im-

Kegan describes five great stages in the continuing evolution of self. The infant shown here is still at the age of the impulsive self, driven by basic needs and urges, unfettered by more adult-like notions of reality. His father's self is an interindividual self, defined mainly in relationships with others—including relationships with the infant. But even in the adult, there remain elements of each of the earlier selves: impulsive, imperial, interpersonal, and institutional.

pulses and perceptions. This is the self of Piaget's sensorimotor and preoperational child. But the correspondence to these periods is only conceptual, not chronological. There are many adults whose selves do not evolve beyond this level, and whose preoccupations throughout life remain fixed at the level of gratification of impulses.

The second self, the *imperial self*, struggles to take over the power and the control that were previously held by parents. The imperial self strives toward the development of personal competence and the achievement of personal control. Much energy is directed toward gaining power and becoming self-sufficient. Developmentally, this self corresponds to Piaget's period of concrete operations and to Erikson's initiative versus guilt. The imperial self's making derives from relationships with school, family, and peers.

As the self continues to evolve, the imperial self gradually transforms into the *interpersonal self*—a self that recognizes the mutuality of relationships and searches for reciprocity. Whereas the imperial self is oriented toward power and control, the interpersonal self orients itself around inner feelings and interpersonal relationships. Self-definition—being meaningful—is no longer expressed simply in competence and control but is now found in the feelings others have toward the self.

The self of the transition through adolescence to young adulthood is the *institutional self*. It is a self that is embedded in culture, work, and love. In Erikson's view, it is a self that creates its meaning through the selection and cultivation of a personal identity.

The self of early adulthood is a more *interindividual self*—a self oriented toward adult relationships. It is the interindividual self that searches for the special combination of passion, intimacy, and commitment that make up consummate love.

The interindividual self of the young adult, like all of Kegan's other selves, is all that has come before it. At every stage, we retain elements of the selves that we have been. Thus, the interindividual self continues to develop the abilities and the competencies that admission to the public world of adulthood demand; at the same time, it retains an orientation toward independence and reciprocal interpersonal relationships. And through all of young adulthood, as through all of life, the self struggles to remain meaningful—to mean something.

If we are loved and have power, do we not mean something?

Psychosocial Development: Erikson

1. According to Erikson's psychosocial theory of stages characterized by basic conflicts and their resolution, the young adult struggles with *intimacy versus isolation* as relationships with parents and peers change. During this period, the young adult strives to achieve intimacy, often through a reciprocated love relationship with someone of the opposite sex.

Love and Mate Selection

2. Liking implies positive evaluation; loving implies absorption, attachment, and intimacy (a capacity for pain as well as ecstasy). Sternberg's model describes eight varieties of love (or nonlove), identifiable on the basis of combinations of *passion* (strong physical desire), *intimacy* (affection, disclosure), and *commitment* (a decision to be in love, to stay together). Important antecedents of interpersonal attraction (which underlies love) include physical attractiveness, similarity, and propinquity (physical proximity).

Choices of Lifestyle

3. One basic lifestyle choice is to marry or not to marry. Nonmarried lifestyles include singlehood, cohabitation, homosexual relationships, or one of a variety of communes. Singlehood includes the never-married (voluntarily or not), the divorced or separated, and the widowed. More than one in three marriages ends in divorce, but the majority of the divorced remarry. The emotional, social, and economic impact of divorce is sometimes severe (especially the economic impact for women).

Marriage

4. Marriage is the lifestyle choice of about 95 percent of people. Social standards governing premarital sex have moved from condoning total abstinence, through the period of the double standard (which lingers still), to a period of sexual permissiveness especially where there is affection between partners. Some (though few) marriages tolerate (or even encourage) extramarital sexual encounters.

5. Enduring marriages may be *vitalized* (high general satisfaction); *devitalized* (high general dissatisfaction); *financially focused* (high dissatisfaction except for financial issues); *conflicted* (continual conflict regarding couple issues; satisfaction with more external issues); *harmonious* (satisfaction regarding couple issues but not external issues); *traditional* (general dissatisfaction except for family and religious issues); or *balanced* (general satisfaction with some problem areas).

6. Factors contributing to marital satisfaction among women include age at first marriage (later is better), education, and socioeconomic status. Among men, occupation, socioeconomic status, and education contribute to marital satisfaction. The more alike (and the more sexually compatible) two people are, the more likely they are to describe their marriage as happy. Frequency of sexual intercourse is highest for several years immediately following marriage.

The Family

7. The family can be described in terms of a life cycle with eight task-defined stages: the initial childless years (important tasks center on whether or not to have children, and other career and self-related developmental tasks); the first child; the phase of the preschool child; a school-aged phase (seven years); a teenager phase (seven years); a "launching" phase (eight years); the empty nest to retirement period (15 years); and a retirement-until-death phase. Although this life-cycle approach is useful, it does not apply to nontraditional, increasingly common family groupings (like single-parent families). Nor is it sensitive to differences related to family occupations, social status, attitudes, family size, and so on.

Family Violence

8. Incidence of many types of violent crimes continues to increase, almost half of them perpetrated by acquaintances or relatives of the victim. It is evident in interspousal violence, child abuse, and sexual assault, including date rape. Prevailing social attitudes about the permissibility of physical punishment and stereotypes of male dominance contribute to violence in the family.

The Continuing Evolution of Self

9. Kegan's five selves, in order of their evolution, are *impulsive* (concerned with gratification of impulses), *imperial* (oriented toward developing personal competence and achieving control), *interpersonal* (concerned with reciprocal relationships), *institutional* (embedded in work, love, and culture), and *interindividual* (oriented toward adult relationships).

FOCUS QUESTIONS: APPLICATIONS

1. What are the main challenges of early adulthood?

- Assess the extent to which you have met (or are currently working on) each of the developmental tasks for early adulthood described by Havighurst.

2. What sorts of lifestyle choices are most common among today's young adults? How have these changed in recent years?

- Summarize Sternberg's model of love. As a personal exercise, you might want to assess one or more of your relationships in terms of the balance among the three principal components of love.

3. What kinds of changes have there been in the family?

- Consult library resources and marshal arguments to support (or refute) the contention that the sexual double standard has largely been eroded.

4. How common is family violence?

- Develop an intervention program that might be applied in an attempt to reduce family violence.

STUDY TERMS

balanced couples   423

bigamy   421

commitment   414

conflicted couple   423

courtship violence   435

devitalized couple   423

Erikson   410

extended family   427

family life cycle   427

financially focused couples   423

harmonious marriage   423

imperial self   436

impulsive self   436

institutional self   437

interindividual self   437

interpersonal self   437

intimacy   414

intimacy and solidarity versus isolation   410

love   413

monogamy   421

nuclear family   427

passion   414

polyandry   421

polygamy   421

polygyny   421

traditional couples   423

triangular theory of love   414

vitalized couple   423

The following short book presents a thoughtful look at interactions in the family, including discussions of topics such as child abuse, stress in the family, and how couples adjust to parenthood:

White, D., & Woollett, A. (1992). *Families: A context for development.* New York: Falmer Press.

Much of our family-oriented research looks at the effects of parents and parenting on children. The following book looks specifically at the effects of children on parents:

Ambert, A. M. (1992). *The effect of children on parents.* New York: Haworth.

Berner's book is a highly readable account of some of the second-generation effects of divorce: What sort of parents are those whose own parents were divorced?

Berner, R. T. (1992). *Parents whose parents were divorced.* New York: Haworth.

The following volume is a highly respected collection of chapters dealing with different aspects of lifespan development. Of particular relevance to Chapter 14 is the following contribution, which reviews research dealing specifically with parenting:

Seltzer, M. M., & Ryff, C. D. (1994). Parenting across the lifespan: The normative and nonnormative cases. In D. L. Featherman, R. M. Lerner, & M. Perlmutter (Eds.), *Lifespan development and behavior* (Vol. 12). Hillsdale, NJ: Erlbaum.

Women sit or move to and fro, some old, some young.
The young are beautiful—but the old are more beautiful than the young.

WALT WHITMAN
Beautiful Women

MIDDLE ADULTHOOD

PART SEVEN

Are the old really more beautiful than the young? Almost everything that we see and hear in this century's youth-worshiping context would have us think not. "Think young!" "Feel young!" "Be young!" we are told. When your face begins to fall, you must lift it. Cream and rejuvenate your wrinkles. Restretch your sagging skin. Color your graying hair. Starve yourself if that's what is needed to maintain your hips and your belly. Dance and drink and sing all night even if you would rather dream by the fire.

We struggle so desperately to delay or hide the signals of aging. We do not mature gracefully.

Yet, as we see in Chapters 15 and 16, the middle-aged have more of almost everything we work so hard to achieve—hence more of everything we value. On average, it is the middle-aged who have the most money, the greatest number of possessions, the most power, perhaps even the most love.

In many ways, middle adulthood is the very peak of life's mountain.

But how steep is the downhill side?

PHYSICAL AND COGNITIVE DEVELOPMENT: MIDDLE ADULTHOOD

*T*o youth I have but three words of counsel—work, work, work.

OTTO VON BISMARCK

CHAPTER 15

"Get to work," my grandpa says tiredly to my Uncle Robert, using only one of Bismarck's three words of counsel.

"Sure," he says, and off he goes to where he's supposed to be picking stones, except everybody, even my grandfather, knows that our Uncle Robert isn't going to do any work. He never does. So we follow him because he always gives us something—like money, when he's got it—to do his work for him.

It's August, I remember, hot as a winded mare, and there's this big pile of rocks to throw onto the stone boat, but Robert's got his pockets sucked dry from last Saturday night.

"So what do you want, then, this time?" he asks, "'cause I got not a cent left."

"I got an idea," says Claude, and you can tell he's been thinking a lot about this idea.

"Spit it out, man."

"Saturday," Claude blurts out.

"Wha' d'you mean, Saturday?"

"What you done Saturday," Claude says. "You fix it so's me and Guy . . . Next Saturday, you fix it so's we go with you and everything."

I wouldn't have gone. I swear it. I don't even know for sure if we're dealing with what I think we might be dealing with because Claude was 2 years older than me, and never explained it all that clearly. Anyway, Uncle Robert turns down the deal and won't negotiate a new one. And about a week later, he packs up and moves out.

"I'm not going to work," he explains, "I'm just going to where the action is." Two months later, he moves into jail. But that's another story.

THIS CHAPTER

My Uncle Robert never, in all his "preretirement" years, had anything that looked like a job for more than a week or so at a time. He was a lot like the guy in Jerome K. Jerome's *Three Men in a Boat* who declared, "I like work; it fascinates me. I can sit and look at it for hours. I love to keep it by me: the idea of getting rid of it nearly breaks my heart."

But in the middle years that this chapter spans, work is more likely to break people's hearts when they don't get it—or when they lose it. In fact, work is one of the most important things in the lives of most adults. Accordingly, it is one of the topics of this chapter.

In addition, the chapter deals with the physical changes of this period—changes in appearance, in the senses, in organ functioning, and in general health as well as major changes in the reproductive system, particularly in women. It looks, as well, at cognitive changes and at the controversy over whether some aspects of intellectual functioning suffer from the ravages of age. In its final sections, it looks at the changing workplace and at the role of careers in the lives of men and women. Finally, it turns to leisure.

MIDDLE ADULTHOOD

To keep things clear and simple, **middle adulthood** is defined as the two-decade span from the age of 40 or 45 to around 60 or 65. Unfortunately, however, age does not tell us very much about the social and emotional lives of most adults—nor even all that much about their physical lives. Here, as elsewhere in the lifespan, there are those we think of as being old before their time; and there are

TABLE 15.1
Havighurst's Developmental Tasks

Challenges in Middle Adulthood

- Assisting children in the transition from home to world
- Developing adult leisure activities
- Relating to spouse as a person
- Reaching adult social and civic responsibility
- Maintaining satisfactory career performance
- Adjusting to physiological changes of middle age
- Adjusting to aging parents

those we consider young for their age. In general, however, the very old think of the middle-aged as young; and the very young think of the 40-year-old as very old.

And those who are middle-aged? How do they see themselves and their lives?

The answer depends, of course, on the individual. For those whose identities are closely bound to their physical selves, the advent of the middle years can be a source of consternation and perhaps even grief. As is discussed in this chapter, there are, in the middle years, some subtle but largely inevitable and irreversible changes in the body—changes that, given our contemporary definitions of physical attractiveness, are often viewed as negative. But for those whose identities—whose personal meaningfulness—stems more from relationships, from knowledge and intelligence, from cultural competence and success, and from the power that results, the middle years can be a source of profound happiness.

For most adults, the middle years are very busy years. From a career point of view, these are often the most productive and the most successful years of adulthood. Middle-aged workers, on average, already earn and possess more than younger workers, continue to earn and accumulate more, have more competence, and wield more power.

From a social point of view, middle adulthood often involves more close interpersonal relationships than any other period in the lifespan—relationships with aging parents, with children and grandchildren, with siblings and co-workers, and with half a lifetime's worth of friends and acquaintances.

But it is also in the middle years that something happens to our perceptions of time—something initially quite subtle, but nevertheless significant. Our psychological perceptions of time are tied to our ages; they are also very personal. For the very young, days last forever. As Wordsworth put it in "To a Butterfly," "Sweet childish days, that were as long as twenty days are now." But as we get older, the opposite happens, and 20 days now seem no longer than one used to be. And when we reach a point close to the middle of life, Neugarten (1968) tells us, our

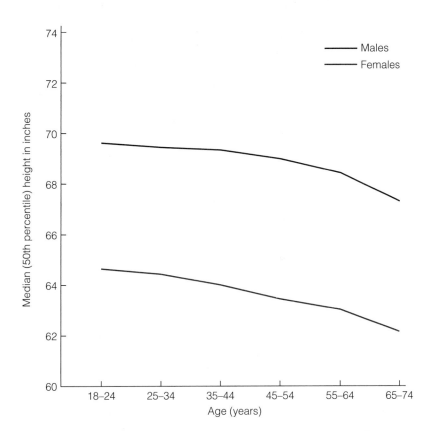

FIGURE 15.1
Decrements in adult median height for men and women. (Based on U.S. Bureau of the Census, 1993, p. 141.)

perception of time changes in yet another way: We stop thinking in terms of how long we have lived; now we begin to think in terms of how much time we have left.

And if there is much we still want to do, perhaps we must now run a little faster. But alas, we tire more easily. Besides, the days have shrunk.

Do they lengthen again in old age? We look at this question in Chapter 18.

Some Tasks of Middle Adulthood

Havighurst describes developmental tasks as culturally determined responsibilities that represent competencies or achievements important for happiness and adjustment. There are a different series of such tasks at every stage of the lifespan, he informs us (see Chapters 2 and 13). Those that are important for middle adulthood are summarized in Table 15.1. They include problems of adjusting to physiological changes, as well as to work and leisure; these are the subjects of this chapter. In addition, Havighurst's developmental tasks for the middle years deal with relationships with children, parents, spouse, and the community; these are the focus of Chapter 16.

PHYSICAL CHANGES

Aging is a linear, time-bound, biological process. Some of its consequences, like loss of hair or hair pigmentation, are clearly visible; others, like reduction in the efficiency of various organs, are not so obvious.

Appearance

Although the normal changes in appearance that occur in the middle years typically bear little relationship either to health or physical functioning, for those whose meaning is closely bound to their physical selves, they can be tremendously important.

Our cultural standards of beauty and attractiveness, closely tied to physical appearance, dictate that peak attractiveness will generally occur during early adulthood. This is particularly true for females and is evident in the physical appearance of the models employed by the advertising industry. It is also evident in the enormous salaries that many of these models command before age 25; witness as well the period of peak income for movie actresses and models, which has traditionally been near the beginning of early adulthood, or between ages 23 and 27—although there are indications that this has changed somewhat in recent years. Men, whose attractiveness (or ugliness) seems, for cultural reasons, not to be so close to the skin, have typically fared somewhat better as older models and actors.

Physical changes that account for our progressively changing appearance are highly varied and initially very subtle. The most obvious are changes in height and weight. After the late teens or early twenties, height does not generally increase. However, after the age of 45 (sometimes earlier and sometimes later), there are frequently decrements in height. On the average, lifetime decrements are greater for women, at about 4.9 centimeters (almost 2 inches), than for men at 2.0 centimeters (about 3/4 inch). Thus, as Figure 15.1 shows, the median height of American

FIGURE 15.2
*Relative amounts of body fat by age and sex.
(From Novak, 1972, p. 440. Reprinted by
permission of the Gerontological Society of
America.)*

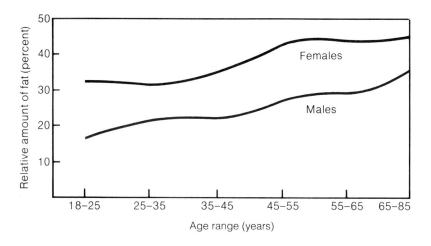

men aged 18 to 24 is about 177 centimeters (just under 5 feet 10 inches), and that of men aged 45 to 54 is closer to 175 centimeters (about 5 feet 9 inches). Median height for women aged 18 to 24 is under 164 centimeters (slightly less than 5 feet 4.5 inches), but at age 45 to 54, median height has dropped to around 161.5 centimeters (5 feet 3.6 inches).

Although changes in height are usually so gradual that they are not often detected, changes in weight are often far less subtle. Recall that by age 20, about 30 percent of the body weight of females, and 15 percent of the weight of males, is fat mass (Malina & Bouchard, 1991). Figure 15.2 presents the results of a study that looked at relative distributions of fat among 520 adults (215 males, 305 females) between the ages of 18 and 85. Note that by the middle years, percentage of fat has increased to about 40 for females and close to 30 for males. Fatty accumulations also tend to be distributed differently in men and women. Typically, excess fat first finds its way around the middles of men; it is more likely to be deposited on the hips among women.

With the increase of fat mass relative to fat-free mass in both men and women, there is a loss of about 40 percent of muscle and about 30 percent of muscle strength between ages 20 and 70 (Rogers & Evans, 1993). However, weight and aerobic training through middle and older age can change this "normal" pattern of muscle atrophy dramatically. Loss of muscle and of strength, note Rogers and Evans, need not be considered an inevitable consequence of aging.

Other physical changes that contribute to the adult's changing appearance include loss of skin elasticity, thinning of hair, loss of flexibility in joints, gradual recession of gums (hence the expression "long in the tooth"), and the appearance of longer, stiffer hair in the eyebrows, ears, and nose (Spence, 1989). In addition, even among adults who remain trim, there is a gradual thickening of the torso but an eventual thinning of the legs and arms. It is partly for this reason that a skinny old person does not look like a skinny young person.

Although most of the physical changes of the middle years are very gradual and seldom dramatic while they are occurring, we resist them with incredible passion and vigor, especially early in the middle years. We have made a cult of being and looking youthful. Americans spend an estimated $10 billion plus a year for lotions, creams, potions, herbs, toupees, dyes, tonics, salves, pigments, tinctures, and unguents designed to make them at least *look* young—not to mention the countless billions more spent on other chemical, surgical, or natural cosmetic aids and on various exercise, weight-reducing, and rebuilding and repair programs for aging bodies.

There are, of course, extremely wide individual variations, not only in the speed with which we age physically but also in the ways we age. Some of us will lose all our hair; the hair of others will turn snowy white. And some, like my paternal great-grandfather, will retain a thick head of raven-black hair right into their tenth decade of life.

The Senses

Like most of our physical systems, our senses are subject to the influences of time. Vision, for example, is best at around age 20 and typically remains relatively constant until age 40. Because of gradual thickening of the lens, loss of lens elasticity, and increased lens density, most individuals become more farsighted beginning in middle age. There is also a gradual loss of light-sensitive cells in the eye beginning around midlife, which might account for some loss of visual acuity (Curcio et al., 1994). In one longitudinal study of aging, it was found that by the age of 50, 88 percent of the women and all of the men had at least one pair of eyeglasses (Bayer, Whissell-Buechy, & Honzik, 1981). **Glaucoma** (increased pressure in the eye that can cause blindness if not treated), and **cataracts** (clouding of the lens caused by fibers) are also associated with aging. Both become more common after age 50 (Spence, 1989).

Physical and sensory changes throughout adulthood are gradual and almost imperceptible. But slowly our hair recedes and fades, our skin loses elasticity and gains wrinkles, our joints become less flexible, and our stamina and endurance decline. And eventually there comes a day when we require glasses—perhaps even more than one pair. For those whose sense of self-worth is closely tied to their physical selves, these changes can be difficult.

INTERVIEW

SUBJECT
Male; age 33; first marriage;
two children; university education; professional career.

QUESTION
"When do you think the 'prime of life' is?"

"The prime of life. It depends exactly what you mean . . .

Okay. Well, generally, the prime of life is right at the peak. I'd say it probably goes from the time you're grown up and finished with education—20 or 25 maybe—right up until you're 'over the hill,' and I suppose for most people that wouldn't happen for quite a long time. Retirement, maybe. Sixty or sixty-five . . . Well, if I had to narrow it down to just five years, I'd say maybe around . . . well it depends. My physical prime is different. Probably from 25 to 30. But intellectually and in my work, I haven't reached my prime yet. Maybe around 45 years."

Hearing losses are also very gradual during the early years of adulthood but are typically more severe for men than for women. **Presbycusis** is the term used for hearing losses associated with age. It is most apparent in an inability to hear high-pitched sounds. Bayer, Whissell-Buechy, and Honzik (1981) report that hearing complaints at the age of 30 are very few (2 percent of the men and none of the women in the sample). By the age of 42, however, while very few women had experienced noticeable hearing loss, 14 percent of the men had—a figure that had risen to 32 percent by the age of 50.

Changes in the ability to taste appear to be very slight until later adulthood, although by the age of 50, some individuals are less sensitive to spices, salts, and sugars—a fact that most are not likely to have noticed. Loss of taste sensitivity is common during adulthood—a condition that might be linked to heavy drinking and smoking as well as to the excessive use of salt. In later adulthood, loss of taste sensitivity often leads individuals to flavor their foods with quantities of salt and pepper that children would find almost unpalatable.

Health and Organ Function

Although health generally continues to be good through the middle years, there is a gradual decline in the efficiency of most major organ systems. For example, beginning in early adulthood, the volume of blood the heart pumps declines very slowly. At the same time, there is frequently a gradual accumulation of plaque on the insides of blood vessels (**atherosclerosis**) and a progressive thickening and hardening of artery walls (**arteriosclerosis**). This increases blood pressure and also increases the probability of a *stroke* (caused by the blockage of blood flow to part of the brain) and heart attack (the result of a blockage of blood flow to the heart muscle). (See At a Glance: "Health in the Middle Years," and Figures 15.3 and 15.4.)

Other organs that become less efficient through the middle years include lungs, stomach, and liver. The lungs, for example, take in progressively less air with each breath as the person ages. This is mainly because the amount of

HEALTH IN THE MIDDLE YEARS

During the midlife years, there is a gradual decline in strength and stamina, as well as in the functioning of the senses. But for most adults, health continues to be relatively good through the middle years. In fact, there is a marked decline in susceptibility to many acute conditions, such as infections and colds. However, there is an increase in chronic conditions, such as arthritis and heart disease (Figures 15.3 and 15.4).

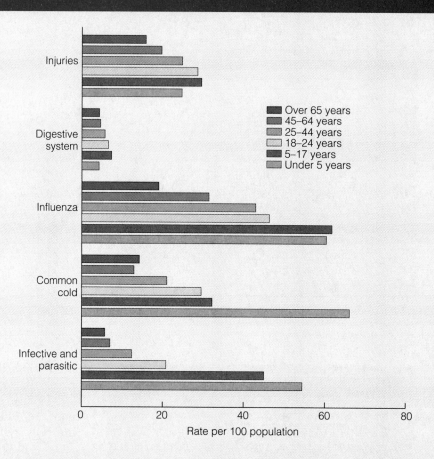

FIGURE 15.3
Decline in rate of acute conditions with advancing age. (Based on U.S. Bureau of the Census, 1994, p.140.)

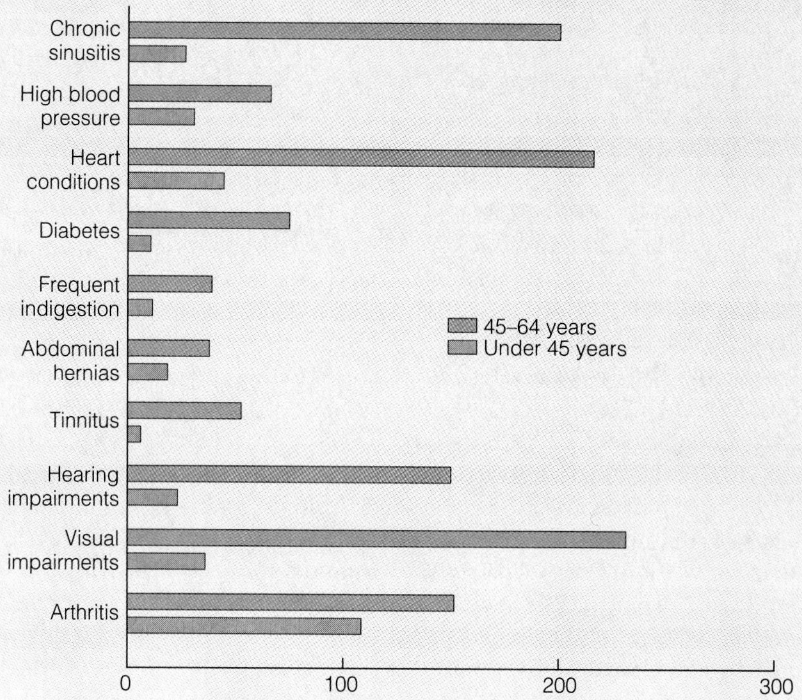

FIGURE 15.4
Increase in rate of chronic conditions with advancing age. (Based on U.S. Bureau of the Census, 1994, p.140.)

air that remains in the lungs after expelling a breath increases. Part of the reduced lung efficiency of older people is due to loss of lung tissue elasticity, as well as to increasing rib cage stiffness (Johnson, Badr, & Dempsey, 1994). As a result of declines in lung efficiency, middle-aged adults suffer from more pulmonary chronic complaints such as emphysema and tuberculosis.

Various diseases to which individuals become more susceptible with age include cancer, arthritis, hypertension (high blood pressure), and **osteoporosis,** a thinning and weakening of the bones. Women are much more prone to this latter condition than are men. And although it does not commonly become serious until later adulthood, it often begins in midlife or earlier. A diet rich in calcium (low-fat milk products, vegetables such as broccoli and turnips, and seafood products such as sardines and salmon), as well as in protein and vitamin D can help prevent osteoporosis or reduce its seriousness (Allen, 1993). So can exercise, which contributes to bone growth and strength. In one study of 111 women, regular exercise contributed significantly to reducing the development of osteoporosis (Brodigan, 1992).

In addition to exercise, hormone replacement therapy (HRT) is sometimes recommended after menopause (discussed shortly) or after a woman's ovaries have been surgically removed. However, estrogen therapy is somewhat controversial, given its link with a higher incidence of cancer. As a result, an increasing number of women, notes Wilbush (1994), resist the advice of their physicians with respect to hormone therapy. However, the evidence suggests that although risk of cancer does increase with long-term estrogen replacement, there also results a dramatic reduction in fatal heart disease—as well as a reduction in hip and other bone fractures. On the basis of a number of longitudinal studies, Gorsky and colleagues (1994) have calculated that if 10,000 women aged 50 were to be placed on estrogen replacement therapy, by age 75, 574 deaths would have been prevented and an additional 3,951 years would have been added to their lives.

Diet and Exercise

Not all middle-aged persons experience the same declines in organ functioning; nor are all equally susceptible to various diseases and infections. Genes continue to be extremely important influences on health at all stages in the lifespan. We know that susceptibility to many forms of heart disease, as well as to cancer—the two leading causes of death in the middle years—is partly inherited. At the same time, however, exercise and diet can each play a significant role in preventing disease and in delaying the effects of age. Obesity, for example, is clearly implicated in heart disease. There is evidence, too, that certain cholesterols contribute to atherosclerosis, that alcohol is a prime cause of cirrhosis of the liver, and that excessive salt intake is related to heart disease. And not only does cigarette

Physical exercise can do much to keep joints flexible, bodies trim, cardiovascular functioning optimal, and bone loss in check. Perhaps as important, physical fitness is closely related to feelings of positive self-worth and happiness. Being able to keep up with your younger friend doesn't hurt either.

smoking contribute to emphysema, to lung cancer, and to other forms of cancer, but it also contributes negatively to bone density. Hopper and Seeman (1994) studied 21 pairs of identical twins, one of whom had smoked at least five years more than the other. Their conclusion: Women who smoke a pack of cigarettes a day through their adulthood will, on average, have 5 to 19 percent less bone density at menopause.

Exercise, for its part, can do a great deal to keep the middle-aged strong and healthy. Research has repeatedly found that those who exercise regularly are more fit and less prone to coronary heart disease (Ward, 1994). This is largely because exercise increases cardiac output, improves circulation and decreases fatty accumulation in blood vessel walls, helps keep arteries and veins flexible, prevents obesity, and increases muscle and bone density (Sambrook, Kelly, & Eisman, 1993). And, as we saw in Chapter 13, exercise can also contribute significantly to a general sense of well-being.

The Climacteric and Menopause

One area of physical change that is important for understanding the adult years involves changes in the sex glands and is popularly referred to as the *change of life* or, more properly, the **climacteric.** The term originates from two Greek words meaning "critical time" and "rung" (as of a ladder). Use of the expression is perhaps unfortunate; it implies too strongly that the rung is critical—that it might break or not be reached, or cause pain and suffering.

A Physiological Event

Among women, the climacteric involves **menopause,** the cessation of menstruation. Among men, the climacteric is more subtle, which has led to some debate concerning whether it is fruitful or even appropriate to speak of a male climacteric or change of life.

The secretion of the sex hormones by the ovaries (primarily estrogen) and the testes (primarily testosterone) is among the most important changes of pubescence (see Chapter 11). These hormones are closely involved in the development of secondary sexual characteristics (breasts, facial hair, voice changes, and so on), as well as in sexual interest and behavior. Their production continues, relatively unabated, from puberty through early adulthood. But by the late thirties or early forties among women, and perhaps by the early fifties for men, the production of sex hormones begins to decrease. Among men, this decrease is often very gradual and not easily noticed.

Among women, changes in production of sex hormones are considerably less gradual and far more noticeable and are linked with the woman's declining store of ova. Women are born with about 800,000 immature ova. By puberty, half of these have died; and by the early forties, few—if any—are left. Only about 300 or so will ordinarily mature and be potentially fertilizable in the woman's lifetime.

Among the first signs of menopause in women are changes in menstrual pattern: irregularity, skipping of menstrual periods, or noticeably reduced discharge during menstruation. Eventually, menstruation stops entirely.

Nonphysiological Symptoms

Strictly speaking, menopause is a biological event with discernible causes and clear biological effects—specifically, cessation of ovulation and menstruation, and consequent permanent infertility. The changes of menopause can affect most of the body's organs, notes Hargarten (1994), and lead to any of a variety of psychological symptoms. For example, menopause is sometimes accompanied by "hot flashes," dizziness, headaches, mood fluctuations, tremors, and weakness (Hargarten, 1994). In as many as one third of all women, these symptoms are serious enough to cause the women to consult a physician, and are medically labeled the **climacteric syndrome** (Porcile et al., 1994). One of the occasional symptoms of this climacteric syndrome is depression, which increases during the climacteric (Coleman, 1993).

Interestingly, in many countries of the world, incidence of climacteric syndrome is much lower than in the West. Datan, Rodeheaver, and Hughes (1987) report, for example, that among five different Israeli subcultures, where loss of fertility is a welcome event, the psychological consequence of menopause is typically positive. Similarly, Haines, Chung, and Leung (1994) found significantly fewer acute menopausal symptoms among a sample of Chinese women in Hong Kong.

Beyene (1989), who studied menopause among Mayan and Greek peasant women, also found evidence that many of its symptoms are context specific. For example, the most common menopausal symptom among the Greek women was hot flashes. Cold sweats, insomnia, and irritability were also relatively common; depression was rare, but did occur occasionally. In contrast, none of the Mayan women experienced any of these symptoms. About one third of them experienced headaches and dizziness (more than 40 percent of the Greek women reported these symptoms); and about one fifth experienced hemorrhaging (12 percent of the Greek women reported hemorrhaging).

These differences, claims Beyene, cannot be accounted for solely in terms of role changes or cultural expectations, given marked similarities among the peasant women in their attitudes toward menopause and in the social implications of the event. In other areas such as diet and childbearing patterns, however, the women were very different. Mayan women typically had protein-deficient diets, consisting primarily of corn and very rarely of meat or eggs; Greek women ate meat and cheese, and a variety of legumes. Also, more than half of the Mayan women had five or more children (one in five had eight or more); more than 60 percent of the Greek women had two children or fewer. More cross-cultural studies are needed to clarify the role of these and other variables, says Beyene.

Treatment

Where problems accompanying menopause are sufficiently serious, they are sometimes treated with **estrogen replacement therapy (ERT)**. In effect, this therapy serves to replace some of the estrogen that is no longer being produced after menopause. As we saw, ERT is also sometimes used in an attempt to reduce the risk and seriousness of osteoporosis. For example, Porcile and colleagues (1994) used an oral contraceptive containing low levels of estrogen with 30 women at menopause. They found a clear reduction of the symptoms of climacteric syndrome. In addition, exercise is one of the important treatments for climacteric syndrome. Hargarten (1994) reports that exercise can reduce most of its symptoms.

Symptoms similar to those that occasionally accompany menopause have sometimes been reported by men, although there is little evidence that they might be tied to hormonal changes that are common to most men. In fact, hormonal changes among men are seldom sufficient to lead to infertility, although they often do lead to a reduction in the number of viable sperm that are produced. It may be significant that when Solstad and Garde (1992) investigated men's beliefs about a male climacteric, the proportion of men who believed in the reality of the phenomenon decreased with advancing age. However, this might reflect the fact that a relatively large number experienced no symptoms. And that 18 percent of the 51-year-old men in the sample thought they had experienced (or were experiencing) the climacteric may also be revealing. Solstad and Garde (1992) conclude that the male climacteric is simply a general label for a variety of nonspecific, unexplained physical complaints.

Sexuality

Janus and Janus (1993) report that more than 80 percent of men and almost 70 percent of women aged 39 to 50 claim to have sex at least weekly. These figures are almost identical to those for younger adults. And the numbers among 39- to 50-year-olds who claim to have sex daily (15 percent of men and 10 percent of women) are also almost identical to those for younger age groups. Apparently, sexual interest and behavior among men and women changes little with the advent of the middle years. However, there are often some slight changes in sexual functioning. For example, although women continue to be interested in sex and capable of orgasm, there is often some reduction in vaginal lubrication following arousal. Among men, changes in sexual functioning are gradual and vary a great deal from one individual to another. It may now take longer, and more direct penile stimulation, for the man to achieve an erection, both before and after intercourse, and the erection might not always be as firm as it was some decades ago. In addition, ejaculation will typically be less forceful, and will not necessarily occur with every orgasm (Gibson, 1992).

Unfortunately, these highly common changes are seldom discussed openly and are often interpreted as evidence of rapidly declining sexual prowess—an event that can lead to considerable anxiety concerning sexual performance and that is often implicated in the man's resulting impotence. In fact, the process of aging does not entail the loss of ability to perform sexually.

COGNITIVE CHANGES

Many of the physical changes of aging are obvious. We can see the wrinkles and the sags, the graying and the thickening, the bending and the slowing. Cognitive changes, however, are not so obvious. Do they even occur? We have had little difficulty in answering this question with respect to childhood and adolescence when, at every succeeding age, we could detect increases in comprehension and reasoning, and in the ability to analyze, synthesize, and solve problems. The task is not so simple with respect to adults and has led to considerable controversy. Does cognitive ability—like strength, vision, and the elasticity of our skin—reach a peak in early or middle adulthood, enter a period of stability, and then begin a downhill slide—slow and imperceptible at first but gradually more rapid until, in the words of Shakespeare, we reach again our "second childishness"? Or does it continue to grow so that, when we are finally old, we might also be truly wise?

Does IQ Change with Age?

At first glance, it might not seem very difficult to answer these questions. After all, if cognitive ability is reflected in measured IQ, all we should need to do is administer appropriate tests to the appropriate people, and *voilà*, an answer: Intelligence increases fantastically with age; intelligence decreases with age; intelligence doesn't change; or intelligence changes this way to begin with, then that way, and then that way.

What do the experts tell us? Some of them suggest that some intellectual decline with age is inevitable (for example, Horn & Donaldson, 1976). Others argue strongly that the belief that intellectual decline with age is inevitable is largely a myth (Schaie, 1994).

The Evidence

It turns out that the questions are not so simple, and the evidence is not so clear. And much of the controversy stems from the fact that the complexity of the question and the inadequacy of the evidence have not always been recognized.

While some measures of intellectual functioning sometimes begin to decline very slowly toward the end of middle age, measures that reflect the accumulated effects of experience (what Cattell labels crystallized abilities) often continue to increase through middle adulthood. There is very little that this mature horticulturalist doesn't know about plants.

FIGURE 15.5

Mean scores on two subtests of the Primary Mental Abilities Test. Note that this is cross-sectional data, meaning that each group consisted of different people tested at the same point in time (hence, different cohorts—that is, people born in different historical periods). (Based on "Variability in Cognitive Function in the Elderly: Implications for Social Participation" by K. W. Schaie, December 1986. Paper presented at the Symposium on Phenotypic Variation in Populations: Relevance to Risk Assessment. Upton, NY: Brookhaven National Laboratory.)

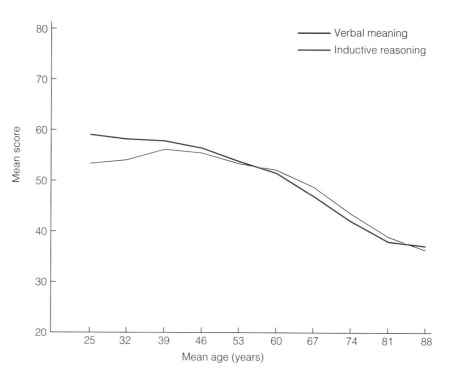

Cross-Sectional Studies

The first studies that looked at age-related changes in intelligence were typically **cross-sectional**; they compared the performance of groups of individuals of different ages. Almost invariably, when the intelligence test scores of older subjects were compared with those of adolescents or young adults, the adults did less well (Schaie, 1986). On general intelligence tests such as the Stanford-Binet and the WAIS (Wechsler Adult Intelligence Scale), the highest scores are almost always obtained by adolescents (or young adults), with progressively lower scores for older age groups. The same is also true of measures of specific mental abilities such as knowledge of verbal meaning, inductive reasoning, number concepts, and so on (see Figure 15.5).

But the meanings of these findings are not quite so clear-cut. For one thing, patterns of decline are not consistent across all abilities. Some abilities (for example, verbal ones) decline less than others (inductive reasoning, for example) (Bromley, 1990). And, more important, cross-sectional studies cannot take into account the influence of cohort variables. Recall that a **cohort** is a group of individuals born within the same time period. In effect, what a cross-sectional study does is compare different cohorts. When it compares 70-year-olds to 20-year-olds in 1995, it is comparing a group of individuals born in 1925 with one born in 1975. Clearly, these cohorts have been exposed to dramatically different environmental influences. Among other things, individuals born in 1925 have spent consid-

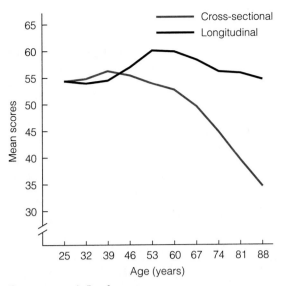

FIGURE 15.6

Comparison of cross-sectional and longitudinal age differences for verbal meaning. (Adapted from Schaie, 1986. Used by permission of Brookhaven National Laboratory.)

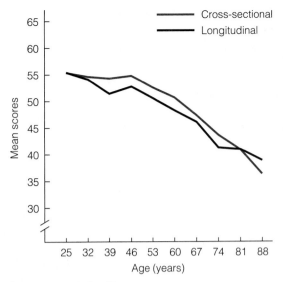

FIGURE 15.7

Comparison of cross-sectional and longitudinal age differences for spatial orientation. (Adapted from Schaie, 1986. Used by permission of Brookhaven National Laboratory.)

erably less time in school, were not exposed to television and computers in their childhood, are often totally unfamiliar with the types of items in most intelligence tests, may never have been exposed to electronically scored answer sheets with their fine print and their demand for careful eye–hand coordination, and might be quite intimidated by the entire testing procedure. Thus, the older cohort's lower scores in cross-sectional studies (such as are illustrated in Figure 15.5) might not result from a natural decline in intelligence with age but might simply reflect the historical disadvantages experienced by that cohort.

Longitudinal Studies

Longitudinal studies do not share this weakness. Recall that a longitudinal study compares the performance of the *same* individuals at different times. For example, a study that presents intelligence tests to a group of 20-year-olds in 1955 and presents the same test to the same individuals in 1975 and again in 1995 is longitudinal. It provides far better data for reaching conclusions about changes that are age-related rather than specific to cohort variables (Schaie, 1988). However, their findings might be valid for only one cohort.

Sequential Studies

As we saw in Chapter 1,* **sequential designs** combine elements of longitudinal and cross-sectional studies and avoid some of the disadvantages of each. One good example is Schaie's (1983c; 1994) investigation of intelligence,

---

*"Who remembers Chapter 1 when they get to Chapter 15?" my grandmother used to say. "Sometimes you got to repeat things." So I do. Briefly.

a 35-year longitudinal study (the Seattle Longitudinal Study), with intelligence testing of all subjects at seven-year intervals and the addition of new samples at each of the testing times. Subjects ranged in age from 25 to 88. Thus the study permitted comparison of different cohorts (cross-sectional) as well as the investigation of each of four cohorts over the 35-year period. The results of the cross-sectional part of the study were as expected: There appears to be an age-related decline in performance on the different subtests of the Primary Mental Abilities Test, two of which are shown in Figure 15.5. However, when different cohorts are compared with each other, it becomes apparent that the earlier-born cohorts *are* at a general disadvantage—strong evidence that at least part of the decline in intellectual functioning is due to cohort-related influences (such as schooling) rather than to age. And this possibility is further supported by the results of the longitudinal part of the investigation. Vastly simplified, these results show very little decline within cohorts over the 28-year period prior to the age of 67! In fact, for some abilities such as verbal meanings, performance continues to increase slightly after age 25; at age 88, individuals still perform as well as at age 25 (see Figure 15.6). But for other abilities such as spatial orientation, there is, in fact, some decline (see Figure 15.7).

A Conclusion

Most researchers now agree that the current evidence supports two conclusions (for example, Alwin, 1994; Perlmutter, 1994):

- There is a decline in some measures of intellectual capacity or performance with age.

- Some measures of intellectual capacity are stable or continue to increase through early and middle adulthood and sometimes even into old age.

It is instructive and revealing to look at the nature of the abilities that remain stable or continue to increase, and those that decline. In general, it seems that those capacities that depend on underlying physiological mechanisms—on a smoothly functioning nervous system, for example—are most likely to decline with age. These capacities define what Cattell calls **fluid intelligence.** Fluid abilities don't improve with experience but seem to depend more on some underlying, basic capacity. They are reflected in general reasoning, memory, attention span, and analysis of figures.

Capacities that depend more on experience are most likely to remain stable or even to increase. After all, why shouldn't general information, vocabulary, and the other legacies of experience not continue to increase with growing experience? These capacities define **crystallized intelligence;** they are reflected in measures of vocabulary, general information, and arithmetic skills.

Our reasoning suggests that fluid abilities, which depend on a smoothly functioning nervous system, should decline with age; by the same token, crystallized abilities, which depend on experience, should remain stable or perhaps increase. That, in fact, is the case, as is shown in Figures 15.8 and 15.9.

Decline and Stability

Alwin (1994) points out that although it is generally true that some capacities decline with age while others might increase slightly, intellectual performance through the middle years (and sometimes well into old age) is marked more by *stability* than by anything else. In addition, patterns of intellectual changes can be very different for different individuals. For example, for some individuals in the Berkeley Growth Studies, there were significant increases in measured IQ between ages 17 and 18, and again between ages 36 and 48 (Honzik, 1984). As might be expected, these increases are related primarily to better performance on crystallized (culture-influenced) measures. Not surprisingly, the people most likely to continue to perform well or even to improve their performance as they age are those whose spouses were significantly more intelligent than they themselves were to begin with (in terms of measured IQ). There appears to be little doubt that continued intellectual stimulation and opportunity to stretch the capacities that define intelligence are closely related to maintaining or improving peak performance. It is worth noting, as well, that those who experienced the greatest intellectual declines in the Berkeley studies often were heavy drinkers or those who had suffered some illness.

Most researchers do not deny that decline is frequently observed with advancing age (Zelinski, Gilewski, & Schaie, 1993). However, the majority maintain that belief in its inevitability and irreversibility is not warranted.

As Bromley (1990) notes, the reasons for decline may often be physical factors such as reduced oxygen supply to the brain—which may in turn be due to reversible conditions such as illnesses, stress, or even lack of exercise. The most sensible conclusion at this point is an optimistic one. Decline in important areas such as verbal ability, reasoning, and numerical skills is usually inconsequential until well into the sixties. Given appropriate environmental stimulation, not only will many cognitive abilities not decrease with age, but some may actually continue to *increase* well into old age (Schaie, 1993). Wisdom, which we discuss in Chapter 17 (along with other aspects of cognitive change), may be a case in point.

Thinking in Middle Adulthood

As we saw in Chapter 13, current views of adult thinking have changed remarkably in recent decades. We know that adults continue to learn through much of the lifespan, both formally and incidentally (Rossing, 1991). It is inevitable that this learning should be reflected in their thinking.

Researchers such as Labouvie-Vief and Basseches argue that the problems that adults face, and the circumstances of their lives, exercise a profound influence on their cognitive processes. The formal logic of a Piagetian system might be suitable in an academic setting, or perhaps even for the adolescent who has not yet learned that there are reasons why logic is not always the only—or even the best—approach. Real-life problems often require *experience* and *intuition* as much as logic, and their solutions need to reflect practical realities (*pragmatics*).

Basseches (1984) suggests that a uniquely adult form of reasoning evolves through early adulthood and into the middle years. It is a form of thinking that is *dialectical.* Not only are adult **dialectical thinkers** more sensitive to contradictions—and more tolerant of them—but they have learned a series of procedures (*dialectical schemata*) for dealing with them. Thus they have an ability to reason about political and social systems, as well as about interpersonal relationships, that is not commonly found in younger individuals. And perhaps that is why, for many adults, the middle years are the most creative of the entire lifespan.

Creativity in the Middle Years

Perhaps the most convincing evidence of the middle-aged person's continuing intellectual competence is found in creative performance.* Among the first studies in this area

---

*"Which clearly doesn't end in middle age," snorted my grandmother. "Look at Monet and Michelangelo and Picasso. They all painted when they were in their eighties and nineties. And Grandma Moses was 100 when she did her last painting, and Freud wrote a book when he was 83. And look at Mr. Delisle, why don't you, and that poem he wrote me last spring."

"But it's not evidence you need," she added. "It's respect."

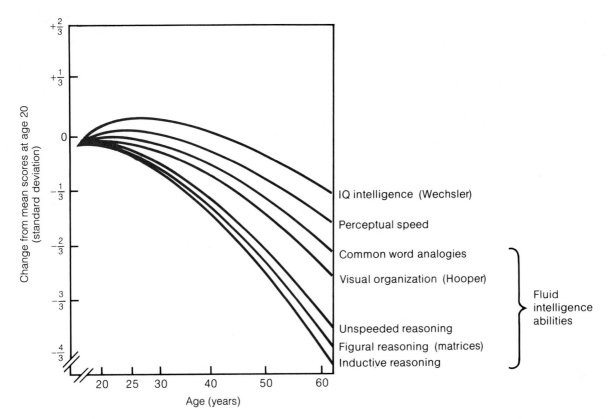

FIGURE 15.8

Smoothed curves summarizing several studies on aging and fluid intelligence. (From Horn & Donaldson in Brim & Kagan, 1980, p. 469.)

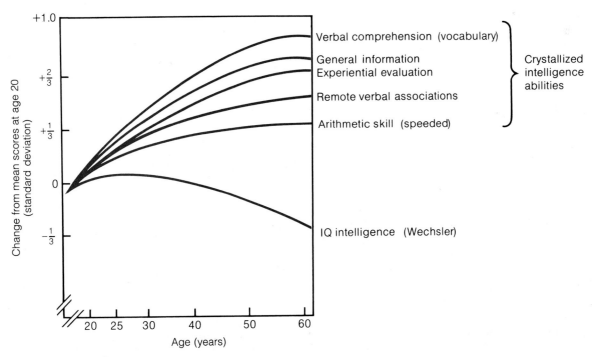

FIGURE 15.9

Smoothed curves summarizing several studies on aging and crystallized intelligence. (From Horn & Donaldson in Brim & Kagan, 1980, p. 471.)

TABLE 15.2
Creative Output by Decade for Men Living to Age 79 or More

Area	Number of Men	Number of Works	Decade					
			20s	*30s*	*40s*	*50s*	*60s*	*70s*
Scholarship								
History	46	615	3	19	19	22	24	20
Philosophy	42	225	3	17	20	18	22	20
Scholarship	43	326	6	17	21	21	16	19
Sciences								
Biology	32	3,456	5	22	24	19	17	13
Botany	49	1,889	4	15	22	22	22	15
Chemistry	24	2,420	11	21	24	19	12	13
Geology	40	2,672	3	13	22	28	19	14
Invention	44	646	2	10	17	18	32	21
Mathematics	36	3,104	8	20	20	18	19	15
Arts								
Architecture	44	1,148	7	24	29	25	10	4
Chamber music	35	109	15	21	17	20	18	9
Drama	25	803	10	27	29	21	9	3
Librettos	38	164	8	21	30	22	15	4
Novels	32	494	5	19	18	28	23	7
Operas	176	476	8	30	31	16	10	5
Poetry	46	402	11	21	26	16	16	10

SOURCE: From "Creative Productivity Between the Ages of 20 and 80" by W. Dennis, 1966, *Journal of Gerontology* 21, pp. 1–18. Reprinted by permission of the publisher.

were Lehman's (1953) estimates of the age ranges during which peak creativity, leadership, and achievement occurred. He found that the peak in most areas (the sciences, mathematics, music) occurred in the thirties, except for the writing of novels and other books (excluding poetry), which peaked in the forties. Achievement in athletics peaks much earlier, generally during the twenties.

Later analyses revealed that Lehman's studies had used some questionable procedures (including failing to take subject mortality into account) and that his estimates of ages of peak performance were therefore biased toward the younger age groups. The problem was that many creative people in his samples didn't live long enough to show that it's possible to be creative in old age. When Dennis (1966) replicated the Lehman study, including in his sample only men who lived at least until the age of 79, he found that the age of peak achievement in most areas is substantially higher than Lehman had estimated (see Table 15.2). In fact, peak production seldom occurs before the forties, and sometimes even the fifties and sixties. And in many areas, it continues well into the seventies.

When peak production declines during the middle years, this does not always mean that the capacity for creative production has also declined. Diamond (1986) points out that many highly successful adults find their creative

output reduced precisely because of their success. In many fields, those who are the highest producers are also those who are most likely to be promoted. Administrative responsibilities might then severely reduce the individual's output. Furthermore, assessing creative potential solely on the basis of measurable production is misleading. As Sasser-Coen (1993) argues, creativity in the second half of life is often evident in *qualitative* improvements rather than in quantity of production.

In many areas, creative production is based not only on the special predispositions and talents that make up the creative personality (see Chapter 9) but also on a large store of relevant information and experience. Dennis's finding that creative output in most areas seldom peaks before the middle years should come as no surprise. In fact, there are some who believe that creativity in later life is unique in that it is based not only on talent but also on wisdom (Hildebrand, 1990).

WORK

Not only are the middle years the most creatively productive, they are also the most productive in the area of careers and jobs. Middle-aged adults hold more administrative and high-level positions than younger workers, and they earn more. In general, they are more competent.

In Chapter 13, we discussed the nature and rewards of work, changes in attitudes toward work as well as in employment opportunities, and processes involved in selecting and preparing for careers. As we saw, there have been major changes in employment opportunities in recent decades. No one has been more affected by these changes than women.

Women in the Workplace

Between 1900 and 1970, the percentage of adult women working for a salary in North America more than doubled (from 20 to 45 percent; Sheppard, 1976). By 1993, about 58 percent of women between 18 and 44 were employed (U.S. Bureau of the Census, 1994) (see At a Glance: "U. S. Women in the Work Force," and Figures 15.10 and 15.11). Figure 15.12 shows the relative distribution of the U.S. work force in 1992 by age, sex, and marital status. Not surprisingly, the period of peak employment for females—especially for married females—occurs somewhat later than that for men (ages 35 to 44 rather than 25 to 34). It coincides with children being older or leaving home.

Male–Female Differences at Work

Fewer women than men work for a salary—69 percent of all women between 25 and 64 in 1991, compared with over 89 percent of all men (U.S. Bureau of the Census, 1993). As mentioned previously, typical female occupations are not yet on a par with male occupations in terms of status, prestige, or income. For example, 97 percent of receptionists, 99 percent of secretaries, 92 percent of teachers' aides, and 87 percent of telephone operators are women. In contrast, women make up only 4 percent of airplane pilots and navigators, 4 percent of mechanics, 2 percent of the construction trades, and 12 percent of administrative supervisors (U.S. Bureau of the Census, 1994).

Average income for females is about 65 percent that of males. In 1991, women with four years of college earned about as much as men who had only completed high school (U.S. Bureau of the Census, 1993). Those with high school diplomas earned less than men who had never gone to high school (see At a Glance: "Inequity in the Workplace," and Figures 15.13 and 15.14 on page 460).

Social Changes

In my grandmother's era, women who continued their education or who took one of various job-training courses often claimed that they were doing so in order "to have something to fall back on later." These women typically assumed that they would get married and raise children while the husband earned their bread. Having to "fall back" was something that would happen only in the wake

Among male–female differences in the work place are differences in income, in job status, in administrative positions, and in the nature of the jobs that are most typically male or female. But profound social changes are rapidly reducing and eliminating these differences. This man answering the phone and booking appointments for his boss while she conducts an important board meeting is a situation that would have been relatively unlikely a handful of decades ago.

of some great misfortune like illness or death of the husband or, heaven forbid, separation or divorce.

Not so any longer. Changing social conditions are reflected not only in the increasing numbers of women who have entered the work force but also in the fact that the expected family pattern, where the man works outside the home and the woman inside, describes fewer than 20 percent of all contemporary American families. Approximately 59 percent of two-parent families also have two wage earners (U.S. Bureau of the Census, 1993). Increasing numbers of families have deliberately chosen not to have children. Furthermore, single-parent families headed by a woman are now as common as the more traditional two-parent family, where the man is the sole wage earner.

U.S. WOMEN IN THE WORK FORCE

At the turn of the century, fewer than 20 percent of American women were in the work force. By midcentury, the percentage had almost doubled, and by 1993, it had nearly tripled. During this time, the percentage of men in the work force hardly changed. However, between 1960 and 1993 the percentage of *married* men in the work force *declined* from 89.2 to 77.3. During the same period of time, the percentage of married women working *increased* from 31.9 to 59.4 (Figures 15.10 and 15.11).

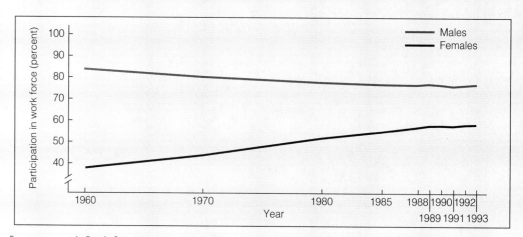

FIGURE 15.10

Increase in percentage of women in U.S. work force, 1960–1993. (From U.S. Bureau of the Census, 1993, p. 395 and 1994, p. 395.)

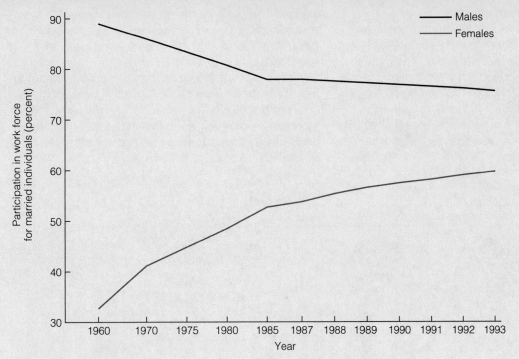

FIGURE 15.11

Changes in U.S. work force participation for married men and women, 1960–1993. (From U.S. Bureau of the Census, 1994, p. 401.)

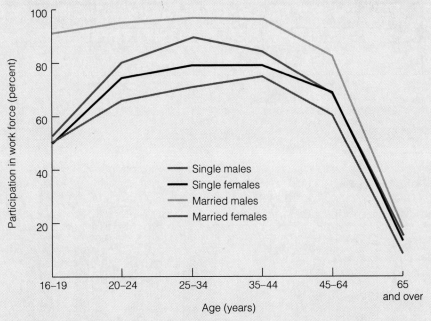

FIGURE 15.12

Work force participation rates by age, sex, and marital status in the United States, 1993. (From U.S. Bureau of the Census, 1994, p. 401.)

INEQUITY IN THE WORKPLACE

Despite dramatic changes in the workplace, certain forms of employment are still primarily male, and others female. In the United States in 1992, for example, almost 12 million precision production jobs (mechanics, construction trades, repairs) were held by males, and only about 1 million by females. In contrast, nearly 15 million clerical, support, and receptionist positions were held by females, and only about 3 million by males. In the United States, the average income of female workers in 1991 was only 65 percent that of males. The ratio of female–male earnings for all full-time workers in Canada in 1987 was also

65 percent. Gains since 1967 have been small (see Figure 15.13); and a woman with four years of college can still expect to earn less than a man with no more than a secondary school education (see Figure 15.14).

In spite of these continuing inequities in the workplace, there have been some dramatic changes in recent decades—changes not only in the number of women working, but also changes in the nature of the work they do. Rogers (1993) reports that there has been a literal explosion of job classifications for women, and that many of the more sexist job titles have now disappeared.

FIGURE 15.13

Changes in ratio of female-to-male earnings in Canada, 1967–1990. (Based on Statistics Canada, 1992, p. 12.)

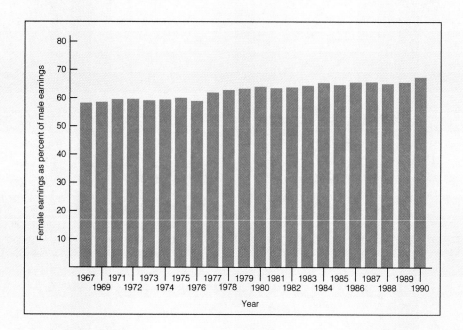

FIGURE 15.14

U.S. male and female earnings by educational attainment in 1991. (Based on U.S. Bureau of the Census, 1993, p. 467.)

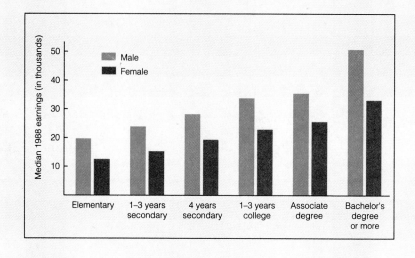

TAKASHI WAGATSUMA AND HIROSHI KOYAMA GET MARRIED

When Takashi Wagatsuma was ready to get married, he followed the traditional Japanese customs for the pure *miai* marriage. This required a formal introduction, an approved meeting or *miai,* and the posing of the question by both his parents and hers. The *miai* marriage is recognizable by four themes, says Blood (1967): observing traditional formalities, relying on the initiative of others, absence of premarital interaction, and lack of love. As Takashi later put it: "Ours was a pure *miai* marriage and a very rational one. I must confess that in the marriage decision there was, to a certain extent, a calculating, self-interested aspect. I thought that after the calculation, affection for her would naturally arise in me" (Blood, 1967, p. 20).

When Hiroshi Koyama of Kyoto wanted to get married, he followed none of the traditional procedures. For him, there were no go-betweens, no arranged meeting or *miai,* no formal exchange of presents (the *yuino*). He met his future bride "through the mere chance of working together." "My case may safely be called a pure love match," claimed Hiroshi. "During the whole process of arranging for marriage no interference broke in from the parents or friends" (Blood, 1967, p. 21).

Omiai, arranged marriages, are still very common in Japan, accounting for more than one third of all marriages. And when Blood (1967) compared such marriages with *love* marriages, he found that both husbands and wives tended to be more satisfied with arranged marriages, especially with respect to what Blood refers to as the *structural* aspects of marriage—things like the respect husband and wife have for each other and how well each performs expected duties. Only with respect to the more *dynamic* aspects of marriage, such as sexual satisfaction and companionship, was there a very slight difference in favor of love marriages.

To Think About A Japanese man, speaking about differences between traditional Japanese marriages and American marriages, comments that there are many things in marriage more important than sexual or emotional passion—things like the household and the honor of the family, duty and respect, work, and, yes, deep companionship. He finds it sad that Americans have so little in their lives that they need so much from their marriage—and must, therefore, almost always be disappointed: "Americans are highly unrealistic about marriage: They expect too much from that single relationship" (Hamabata, 1990, p. 124). What do you think?

Clearly, there have been some profound changes in the American family. (See Across Cultures: "Takashi Wagatsuma and Hiroshi Koyama Get Married.")

Dual Careers

Families with two wage earners now appear to be the norm rather than the exception. However, a two-earner family is not necessarily a **dual-career family.** A career, as we saw, is defined by a relatively systematic progression through a series of related occupations. Unlike a simple job, a career demands commitment and loyalty; typically, it requires a greater investment of time and energy.

A dual-career family is one in which both the husband and the wife have separate careers and the career of neither is sacrificed for the other—or for the family. Among college populations, the notion of a dual-career family has apparently become increasingly popular. In one survey, more than 80 percent of both male and female college stu-

dents indicated they were interested in having a dual-career family (Nadelson & Nadelson, 1980).

Surveys of dual-career couples reveal that they often share several common characteristics. Typically, for example, the husband and the wife have very similar values, possess relatively high-level job skills, are self-reliant and independent, and have high incomes. It is also quite common for these couples either not to have children or to have small families, which are typically started only after the wife has already established her career (Hertz, 1986).

Double Careers

Dual-career families sometimes entail unique sets of problems. One of the most common affects the wife rather than the husband, and results from the fact that many wives not only are members of a dual-career partnership but also are involved in a **double career** (also referred to as a *double-track career*). The difference between a dual career and a double career is simple: Dual careers exist

Voluntary changes of career do not have the same psychological implications as involuntary changes. It's the best time of my life, says this former accountant who has sold his practice to set up a business that caters to family and company picnics.

where two people develop separate and individual careers; a double career exists when a *single* person assumes the responsibilities of two careers at the same time.

Double careers are common among wives who are responsible for their careers outside the home and who must also assume responsibility for a tremendous range of home-related tasks: cooking, cleaning, supervising, child rearing, and so on. What is perhaps surprising is that most college students and, indeed, most young couples believe strongly that if both husband and wife are to have individual careers, each should share domestic responsibilities equally. Ironically, however, this is not often the case in practice. In a survey of 287 fully employed, married women, Pina and Bengtson (1993) found marked inequity in division of household chores. Similarly, Demo and Acock (1993) found that among all family groupings in a sample of 2,528 families (stepfamilies, single-parent families, and two-parent families), women did between two and three times more housework than their spouses or cohabiting mates. In light of this, it's hardly surprising that Ward (1993) found that working outside the home does not seem to contribute to the woman's marital happiness.

One of the possible results of the tremendous burden of responsibilities that the double-tracked woman carries is **burnout**—a term used to describe a situation in which the individual no longer feels able to cope. Ways of preventing burnout, or of relieving its effects, might include abandoning or postponing one spouse's career, enlisting the husband's help with domestic duties (difficult in practice), making children increasingly responsible for their own care, or hiring domestic help or "nannies."

Many of the problems of double-career women relate not only to inequities in allocation of domestic duties, but have to do as well with child care. Often there are problems associated with availability of care, its cost, and its quality (Neugebauer, 1994). In addition, as Joshi and Davies (1992) have documented, women who work *and* have children not only bear the cost of looking after and raising these children, but also suffer considerable lifetime losses of earning relative to women who have never interrupted their working careers to have children.

Career Changes

Career changes in midlife, notes Levinson (1981), are not uncommon. These often result from the reevaluation of dreams that sometimes occurs in the forties, and from the individual's changing views of life and of the self. Increasingly, however, career changes occur not only at midlife but throughout the individual's working career. Drummond and Ryan (1995) note that employment longevity is rapidly declining, and that more employers are now hiring workers on a job or contract rather than a career basis. Of the top 10 occupations in terms of average tenure of workers in 1991, seven lasted for an average of only 15 years. And the average tenure for all workers in all occupations was 6.5 years (U.S. Bureau of the Census, 1993).

Voluntary Career Changes

Clearly, not all career changes are voluntary. But for those that are, there are many reasons people might choose to change careers. Midlife changes and reevaluations (dis-

Involuntary career changes—like getting fired, for example—can be highly devastating not only because of their economic implications, but also because of their blow to the individual's feelings of worth and competence. The love and sympathy of a good dog may help.

cussed in the next chapter) are one reason. Often, men abandon careers that have demanded too much time and energy, and that have not allowed enough time for family and other personal concerns. These might be abandoned in favor of more gentle, less aggressive pursuits, suggests Levinson. In contrast, at midlife many women become more career-oriented, more aggressive, more interested in exploring their strengths and talents, and in testing their limits in different settings (Sheehy, 1981). Their career changes might be motivated accordingly.

Technological changes present another reason for voluntarily making career changes. Sometimes these lead to restlessness about the permanence and value of present careers. Alternatively, these changes can open up exciting new fields and, rather than chasing people from careers, might attract them instead.

Another relatively common reason for voluntary midlife career changes is the emptying of the family nest. When the little ones have flitted away, the parents are freed. They now have less reason to fear the risks that might come with career changes. In addition, mothers who have interrupted their schooling or their careers to raise children can now resume the interrupted activity. If the mother begins to earn a second family income, the resulting reduction in the financial risk involved will sometimes lead to the father's changing careers.

Not surprisingly, studies that have looked at the characteristics of people who voluntarily decide to change careers have often found these people to be more self-reliant, somewhat more willing to take risks, and generally characterized by feelings of control and power, of

what is now termed **career self-efficacy.** (Mathieu, Sowa, & Niles, 1993). This is not to say, however, that all people who change careers are more in control, more self-reliant, and more characterized by feelings of self-efficacy. Some who make career changes are marked more by fluctuating and unstable interests, a high fear of failure, and emotional problems than by high feelings of competence.

Involuntary Career Changes

From a psychological point of view, people who deliberately choose to change careers may be in a much better position than those whose career changes are involuntary. As my cousin Luke could easily testify, should he be willing, there are five reasons for making an involuntary career change, and he experienced them all.

To begin with, he was fired. A career change resulting from being fired is perhaps the most difficult to cope with and often gives rise to a reaction not unlike the grief that might follow the loss of a loved one (Jones, 1979).

A second reason for involuntary career change is the loss of a career because of changes in the workplace. If all the oil fields dry up, many oil-related careers are involuntarily disrupted. This, Luke insisted, happened to him!

Third, some careers are of short duration by their very nature. These "early-leaver" careers include most professional sports and certain high-risk and highly demanding occupations. Luke had a brief but incredibly successful career as a chicken sexer until age, some three months later, lessened his tactile sensitivity and forced him into an early retirement.

Although our cultures have traditionally emphasized work over leisure, increasing industrialization and technological advance may result in increasing leisure—and in a belated recognition of its importance. A hole in one—well, even in four or five—can do a great deal for self-esteem and happiness.

Fourth, involuntary career changes are sometimes necessitated by illness or injury. In Luke's case, an assortment of temporary injuries forced yet another involuntary switch in careers.

And fifth, of course, is mandatory retirement. In some cases, retirement, whether mandatory or not, is quite voluntary; in many, however, it isn't. "I didn't want to quit, no way," Luke is reported to have said. "But what the heck. Elizabeth's got a good job anyway. D'you wanna go fishing?"

In 1992 more than 8 million people were unemployed in the United States; 2.6 percent were without work for 15 weeks or more (U.S. Bureau of the Census, 1993). Among those in the American work force who were unemployed but looking for work, unemployment lasted about two to three months (Wegmann, 1991). It took about three weeks longer for men to be reemployed than it did for women, with younger groups (16–24) being unemployed for shorter periods of time than older groups (25–44). Not surprisingly, given more limited work op-

portunities, unemployment periods were longer for college graduates than for high school dropouts—or high school graduates. Possible reactions to prolonged unemployment include marital problems, depression, suicidal tendencies, and low self-esteem (Hurst & Shepard, 1986).

Others simply enjoy the enforced leisure.

LEISURE

Is work the most important thing in our lives? Do we, as we struggle to grasp the slippery rungs of corporate, academic, social, and financial success, sometimes become addicted to this thing called work? Do those who no longer stop to smell the roses even remember that roses are out there?

There *are* roses out there. We need only the leisure to notice. Leisure, Aristotle claimed, is the purpose of everything else we do. *Leisure* may be defined as discretionary time—time during which we have no obligation to do anything specific, time that we spend as we choose.

Lu and Argyle (1994) investigated the relationships between leisure activities and general happiness among a group of 114 subjects. Sixty-eight percent of this group reported they were committed to some kind of leisure activity. Interestingly, those with higher self-esteem tended to devote their leisure to voluntary work; those marked by high levels of cooperativeness were more likely to join clubs; and those who were somewhat more neurotic were most likely to select private hobbies.

Perhaps the most important finding of the Lu and Argyle study is that commitment to leisure activities is closely related to happiness. Yet our culture remains somewhat ambivalent about leisure; it is not entirely certain how to treat it. The work ethic that drove our forebears, and that still drives sizable numbers of us, sees virtue and grace in work but sees little value in leisure. Accordingly, we continue to be socialized to work but not to play. We are taught a thousand subtle tricks for navigating through the courses of our work lives, but we are seldom given any advice about how to play. Indeed, we are seldom even told that we should play, or why.

But we should. Leisure can not only make us happier, but it also helps relieve the effects of stress—effects that can sometimes be very damaging. And what we do with leisure, like what we do with work, can have a tremendous impact on our self-esteem. In fact, leisure activities can sometimes provide us with *identity* in much the same way as work might. For example, Luke, for a brief period, did not simply cut the tops off tall trees, he *was*, you better believe it, a lumberjack! But even while he was being a lumberjack, there were times when he would swell with rushes of well-being when someone would say about him, "That Luke there, he's quite a poker player."

Although our cultures have traditionally emphasized work far more than leisure—and, in fact, often continue to define leisure as time off work—there are signs of ongoing change. Current emphases in an increasing number of career guidance and counseling programs are no longer on setting goals and making whatever sacrifices are necessary to obtain them in the distant future—after which come the gold watch and the phases of retirement. Instead, people are urged to find occupations that are pleasant and satisfying for them. More than this, these occupations must not only involve rewarding activities but also provide people with the income and, far more importantly, with the leisure required for a truly high-quality life.

If we learn to make the most of our leisure activities, then there is a very good chance that work will not be the only important thing in our lives when, and if, we reach for our gold watches and our pension checks. Not only will we have smelled so many more roses, now dead, but we may have learned where the new ones grow.

Middle Adulthood

1. Middle adulthood is a two-decade period from around 40 or 45 to 60 or 65. Relevant developmental tasks include emptying the nest, maintaining a career, adjusting to the physiological changes of middle age, and maintaining changing relationships with children, spouse, and parents.

Physical Changes

2. Physical changes of middle age include cessation of growth in height (a slight decrement in later years), the accumulation of fatty tissue, loss of skin elasticity, thinning of hair, stiffening of joints, loss of muscle tone, and reduction in muscle tissue. Sensory changes include a gradual reduction in visual acuity, greater farsightedness, and a gradual loss of hearing ability, particularly for higher tones.

3. Major organ systems slowly become less efficient after early adulthood. Signs of arteriosclerosis (hardening of artery walls) are common, and people become more susceptible to heart disease, cancer, arthritis, cirrhosis, hypertension, and osteoporosis, but less susceptible to acute infections. Diet and exercise can contribute significantly to reducing and delaying some of the effects of aging.

4. By the late thirties or early forties for women, and perhaps by the fifties for men, the sex glands' production of hormones decreases, leading to the *climacteric* or "change of life" (not dramatic among men; cessation of menstruation, or *menopause*, among women). Menopause is sometimes accompanied by physical symptoms ("hot flashes," trembling, dizziness, and headaches) that are occasionally treated with hormone replacements. Sexual interest and functioning are ordinarily maintained after the climacteric (some reduction in vaginal lubrication for women; slower sexual arousal for men).

Cognitive Changes

5. Cross-sectional studies find cohort-related evidence of intellectual decline with age. Longitudinal studies show that abilities dependent on experience (*crystallized* verbal and numerical abilities, for example) tend not to decline. In contrast, abilities less dependent on experience (*fluid*, like reasoning or attention span) do not fare as well. Significant gains in measured IQ have been observed well into middle age.

6. Middle-aged thinking profits from the greater experience of adults, their increased sensitivity to contradictions, and their responsiveness to social, political, and economic realities. Peak years for creative output in fields where production depends on information and experience are the middle-age years. In areas that require physical strength and stamina (athletics) or culturally defined physical attractiveness (modeling), peak performance occurs at younger ages.

Work

7. The percentage of adult women who work has more than doubled in this century. More than half of two-parent families have two wage earners. Some involve *dual careers* (husband and wife have independent, equal careers); many involve *double careers* (inequitable division of home-making, child-rearing responsibilities so that one partner, usually the wife, juggles two careers). Women's occupations still tend to be lower than men's in status and income, and still reflect many old stereotypes.

8. Children in homes where both parents work are not at a measurable disadvantage. Voluntary career changes throughout the lifespan may occur in response to the occasional crises of the middle years or because of changes in the work context (such as technological changes) or the individual (for example, emptying of the family nest). Involuntary changes can be related to being fired, external changes in the workplace, advancing age for "early-leaver" careers, illness or injury, or mandatory retirement.

Leisure

9. Leisure, discretionary time, is important for psychological health and happiness and, like work, can contribute significantly to our identities and to our feelings of worth. Besides, if we smell no roses before we retire, the ones we could have smelled will be gone, and we may not have learned where the new ones grow.

FOCUS QUESTIONS: APPLICATIONS

1. What are the principal physical and sensory changes of middle age?

- As a major term paper, write a well-researched piece on the various benefits of exercise.

2. What is the climacteric? How is it related to the midlife crisis?

- Prepare a series of arguments supporting or refuting the proposition that the symptoms of menopause are largely culturally based.

3. Does measured intelligence change with age? Does it decline in middle or old age?

- Distinguish between fluid and crystallized intellectual abilities and explain how and why each is most likely to change with age.

4. What sorts of gender changes have occurred in the workplace and in child care in recent decades?

- Explore the psychological consequences of voluntary versus involuntary career changes.

STUDY TERMS

arteriosclerosis   447

atherosclerosis   447

burnout   462

career self-efficacy   463

cataracts   446

climacteric   450

climacteric syndrome   450

cohort   452

cross-sectional studies   452

crystallized intelligence   454

dialectical thinkers   454

double career   461

dual-career family   461

estrogen replacement therapy (ERT)   451

fluid intelligence   454

glaucoma   446

leisure   464

longitudinal studies   453

menopause   450

middle adulthood   444

osteoporosis   449

presbycusis   447

sequential designs   453

stroke   447

Those interested in a technical account of the physiological changes of aging might consult:

> Spence, A. P. (1989). *Biology of human aging*. Englewood Cliffs, NJ: Prentice-Hall.

Beyene's book is a fascinating account and comparison of the lives, roles, and reactions to menopause of peasant Mayan and Greek women:

> Beyene, Y. (1989). *From menarche to menopause: Reproductive lives of peasant women in two cultures*. New York: State University of New York Press.

The Alwin article in the first of the following two collections is a look at stability and change in important personality variables (including intellectual functioning) throughout the lifespan. The Perlmutter chapter in the second collection looks primarily at cognitive skills in adulthood:

> Featherman, D. L., Lerner, R. M., & Perlmutter, M. (Eds.). (1994). *Lifespan development and behavior* (Vol. 12). Hillsdale, NJ: Erlbaum.

> Fisher, C. B., & Lerner, R. M. (Eds.). (1994). *Applied developmental psychology*. New York: McGraw-Hill.

The following book looks at career counseling at each of the major stages of the lifespan, including young and middle adulthood as well as older adults:

> Drummond, R. J., & Ryan, C. W. (1995). *Career counseling: A developmental approach*. Englewood Cliffs, NJ: Prentice-Hall.

SOCIAL DEVELOPMENT: MIDDLE ADULTHOOD

*Spring still makes spring in the mind
When sixty years are told.*

RALPH WALDO EMERSON
The World Soul

"Speaking of spring," says my grandmother disgust- **CHAPTER 16** edly, pointing her cane in the direction of Lalonde's house, "there's no fool like an old fool." She adjusts the cane across her lap and continues, "You know what happened to him the first time?" But it's one of those rhetorical questions that I don't have to answer because she's going to tell me the story in any case—as if I haven't already heard all the different versions.

The basic story is simple: When he was about 20, Eddy Lalonde was crazy in love with Emma Carpenter. They'd had a steaming, gawking-at-the-moon-and-stuff kind of courtship for about half a year when, the story goes, Eddy jokingly suggested that maybe Emma shouldn't always say, "I love you too," whenever Eddy said it first; and she maybe shouldn't always reassure him that she would never look at another man whenever he swore on his father's bald head that he, Edward Joseph Lalonde, would sure as the devil never look at another woman in his entire life or hope to die.

"Pretend like you've got a lover or something," said Eddy, suddenly inspired, "which'll make me jealous and then we can make up and everything." Depending on who's weaving it, the story takes different twists at this point, but the gist of most versions is that a little while later, Emma confessed to Eddy that she had a lover. "Heh, heh," he is reported to have laughed. "Gawd, I felt jealous there for a minute."

"I really do," said Emma.

"I know you're joking," said Eddy. "You don't really have to."

"But I do," said Emma. "He's hiding behind the garage, waiting for you to leave."

"I should go see?" asked Eddy. "Is that part of the game?"

"It's no game," said Emma.

"Well played," said Eddy. "You almost had me convinced."

And the lovers went back to holding hands and looking at the moon. But when Eddy left that night, just to be absolutely sure, he detoured around the back of the garage.

And bumped smack into Ronald Latham who, some say, had been taking a shortcut to his mother's place. Others tell the other version, the one that Father Paradis later worked into his sermon on the great sins.

Eddy came out with a couple of black eyes, a split lip, and a sore jaw. Ronald wound up with a sore stomach—and, about three weeks later, he also got Emma.

"Now that poor fool who's been nursing a busted heart for 40 years has got himself turned north to south over that Gillis woman who's young enough to be his daughter!" harrumphs my grandmother. "The poor fool's got spring on the brain."

THIS CHAPTER

Is spring in the mind of a 60-year-old the same color as the spring of earlier years? Or is it colored by the seasons that have passed?

You see, the seasons of our lives follow each other, nose to tail, in a straight line. In childhood, when all our seasons stretch unbroken before us, we know that they—and we—will last forever. Even as adolescents, our own special egocentrism, our fable of invulnerability, convinces us that our own personal winters will never come.

But somewhere in the middle years, Neugarten (1968) tells us, there is a change in our perception of personal time. Age is no longer simply a question of how long we have lived, but more a question of how much—or how little—there is still to come. And our youthful myth of immortality and invulnerability crumbles.

Perhaps middle age is only the autumn of our lives; but our springs and summers are gone. Still, as we see in Chapters 17 and 18, our winters might yet be our very best seasons.

Chapter 16 begins with a look at some of the theories that try to clarify the seasons of our adult lives, and especially the stages and transitions of the middle adult years (40 or 45 to about 60 or 65). It deals in turn with theories described by Erikson, Peck, Levinson, Sheehy, and Gould; and then it asks the question: Is there a period in our middle years when, overwhelmed by existential anguish, we struggle more desperately with the meaningfulness of our lives? Is there, in the popular jargon, a midlife crisis? Was my grandmother's old fool, Eddy, having one—and resolving it with the Gillis woman?

The chapter looks at these questions, and examines as well the importance of relationships with spouse, with children, with aging parents, and with friends. Then, it examines personality changes in middle adulthood; and finally, it presents a recipe for happiness and satisfaction.

DESCRIPTIONS OF MIDDLE ADULTHOOD

Our intuitive notions about the life cycle, says Nanpon (1991), agree remarkably well with those of the experts—except that younger people tend to view the later stages of life as occurring at earlier ages. He asked 100 beginning psychology students to trace a "life" line across a sheet of paper, mark it off into major life stages with specific age boundaries, label each of these stages, and describe the key characteristics of each. Students were free to describe as many or as few stages as they wished.

Most students described the expected preadult stages: infancy, the preschool period, preadolescence, and adolescence. Many described adulthood as beginning at 18, and a large number thought age 25 represented a significant transition to life as a couple (or its equivalent). The next important transition was age 40, which students saw as the beginning of a transition between adulthood and old age. For a remarkable number (25 of the 100), age 50 was seen as the end of professional life and the beginning of old age. Another 48 thought old age began later, at about age 60.

Our intuitive notions of stages of the life cycle, says Nanpon, are typically tied to important sociocultural events—for example, access to school, voting or drinking age, average ages of marriage and retirement. Erikson's theory, too, is tied to social and cultural demands.

Generativity Versus Self-Absorption: Erikson

Erikson's theory of psychosocial development describes crises and conflicts at every developmental stage. These arise mainly from social demands placed on the individ-

FIGURE 16.1
Erikson's theory revised. Peck defines seven additional adult developmental tasks during the last two stages of Erikson's scheme.

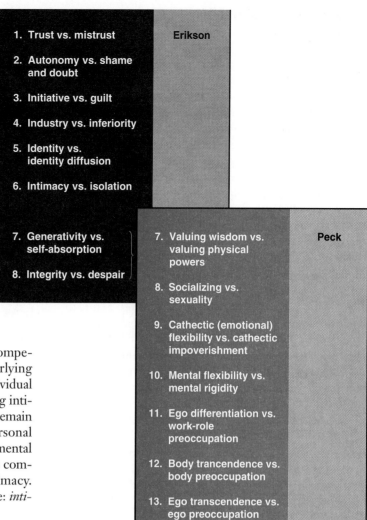

Erikson

1. Trust vs. mistrust
2. Autonomy vs. shame and doubt
3. Initiative vs. guilt
4. Industry vs. inferiority
5. Identity vs. identity diffusion
6. Intimacy vs. isolation
7. Generativity vs. self-absorption
8. Integrity vs. despair

Peck

7. Valuing wisdom vs. valuing physical powers
8. Socializing vs. sexuality
9. Cathectic (emotional) flexibility vs. cathectic impoverishment
10. Mental flexibility vs. mental rigidity
11. Ego differentiation vs. work-role preoccupation
12. Body trancendence vs. body preoccupation
13. Ego transcendence vs. ego preoccupation

ual. Progress at each stage requires acquiring a competence or an attitude that resolves the conflict underlying the crisis. In early adulthood, for example, the individual confronts the profoundly important task of achieving intimacy and, at the same time, overcoming an urge to remain independent, to retain the autonomy and the personal identity that have been achieved in earlier developmental stages. These urges make it difficult to achieve the commitment that is required for genuine, mutual intimacy. Hence the conflict; and hence, too, the stage's name: *intimacy versus isolation.*

In the *middle adult years*, individuals are faced with a new developmental task and a new crisis: *generativity versus self-absorption.* With increasing maturity, the adult needs to establish the sorts of caring and work relationships that will benefit the world and the community—that is, to be generative or productive rather than absorbed in self. **Generativity** can be evident in different areas. One is work. As we note in Chapter 13, for many, work is far more than a means of earning a living or of "killing time." It can be a way of *being* someone, a means of self-discovery and self-expression, an essential aspect of feeling worthwhile, as well as a means of contributing to family and society in significant ways.

Another way of expressing generativity is through the establishment of a family—by producing children and acting as a parent. Note, again, Erikson's continuing emphasis on the individual's relationship to the sociocultural environment.

As in all of Erickson's stages, there is a crisis, a conflict here. Generativity requires a concern for others. People are generative when they rear and guide their children or the children of others, when they contribute to the community through political, social, or economic involvement, and when they contribute through their work. But even the most selfless and the most generative of individ-

uals are occasionally tempted to look inward at themselves. There is an urge to become preoccupied with things that affect the self—things such as health, the accumulation of money, the enjoyment of life. Resolution of the crisis does not require abandoning all thoughts of self, but rather achieving a balance between self-interests and the interests of others.

Elaborating Erikson: Peck

Although Erikson's description is valid and useful, argues Peck (1968), the fact that he covers the entire last 40 or 50 years of life in only two stages provides too little detail to account for some of the critical issues during those years. He suggests there are several additional crises related primarily to the physical and mental changes of adulthood, as well as to some of the more common social changes. These crises describe an additional seven stages, the first four of which are applicable primarily to middle age; the last three relate to old age (see Figure 16.1).

Valuing Wisdom Versus Valuing Physical Powers

Middle age is marked by a gradual decline in stamina, elasticity, muscle tone, and other components of strength, endurance, and athletic prowess. These physical changes make it progressively more difficult for laborers to toil without pain, for professional athletes to continue participating in their sports, or for fathers to beat their sons at racquet sports or Indian leg wrestling. As these changes occur, it becomes more important for individuals to place greater emphasis on nonphysical activities. The athlete must develop other competencies; the laborer must work differently or change employment; and the father might consider less physically demanding sports, such as billiards or darts, or more cerebral competitions, such as chess or poker—hence the label for this particular psychosocial conflict.

Socializing Versus Sexuality

Hormonal changes through middle age often result in changes in sexual interest, behavior, or capability. And some of the important interpersonal relationships that characterize early adulthood, and that might initially have had a strong sexual component, change accordingly. Friendship, trust, emotional and moral support, companionship, and other dimensions of social relationships may become more important as sexuality becomes less so.

Emotional Flexibility Versus Emotional Impoverishment

Social, as well as physical, changes in the middle years also require adaptation and change. The third of Peck's stages illustrates this: Through middle age (sometimes much earlier and sometimes much later), many of our emotional ties are strained or ruptured for any of a variety of reasons: People die, children leave home, couples separate and get divorced, careers end, and dogs run away. Adjusting to these emotional changes often requires considerable emotional flexibility.

Mental Flexibility Versus Mental Rigidity

In the same way that changes in our emotional lives require us to be able to form new relationships and sometimes to forget old ones, so a variety of social and cultural changes require us to accept new ideas and sometimes to reject old ones. Hence the need for mental flexibility. We cannot always rely on old beliefs and opinions or on old attitudes. (The last three of Peck's stages correspond to Erikson's final stage; all are discussed in Chapter 18.)

Theories such as those of Erikson and Peck do not lend themselves easily to specific age-related predictions for any given individual. Nor can they easily be validated experimentally. However, in a sample of adults aged 22 to 72, McAdams, St. Aubin, and Logan (1993) found evidence of higher *generativity* among the middle-aged group than among younger adults. They defined genera-

INTERVIEW

SUBJECT

Male; age 46; divorced; no children; involved in film business.

QUESTION

"Do you think you experienced a midlife transition or crisis?"

"Do I? I have a couple every week. Seriously, though, sure. Doesn't everybody? I mean, there was a period, there, just about the time I turned 40, when I figured—I guess I just wasn't that certain anymore. Here I was, 40, I'd been divorced for about three years, and I was feeling an awful lot of pressure about deciding if I was ever going to get married again and about whether I was going to have kids. I mean, at 40 it didn't seem like I had forever left anymore, and whatever I was going to do I better get on and do it. And then I thought, 'What the heck, Bob, you're doing exactly what you want to do, so go with the flow.' Maybe that's my philosophy. 'Go with the flow.'"

tivity in terms of the individual's concerns, behaviors, and commitments that are aimed at providing for the next generation. They found, too, that the most generative individuals tended also to be the happiest.

One of the principal contributions of these approaches lies in the insights they provide for understanding the concerns and preoccupations of adults. That, too, is the principal usefulness of the two descriptions we consider next: Levinson's seasons and Sheehy's passages.

Seasons of a Man's Life: Levinson

In a widely read book, Levinson (1978) attempts to organize the lives of 40 men around universal themes and changes. The book is based on 5 to 10 separate, in-depth interviews with each man. Following these interviews, Levinson advanced a description of adult development, an account of the *seasons of a man's life*. Like Erikson's and Peck's accounts, this description deals primarily with psychological and social change, and their relationship to one another.

Levinson (1981) suggests that the human lifespan divides itself roughly into five major eras or ages: preadulthood (birth to 22); early adulthood (17 to 45); middle adulthood (40 to 65); late adulthood (60 to 85); and late late adulthood (80 to death). Within these eras, he identifies a sequence of stages that appear to be common to each of the 40 subjects. These are described here and summarized in Figure 16.2.

Early Adulthood

Each of Levinson's stages involves a major developmental task. For example, the transition into early adulthood re-

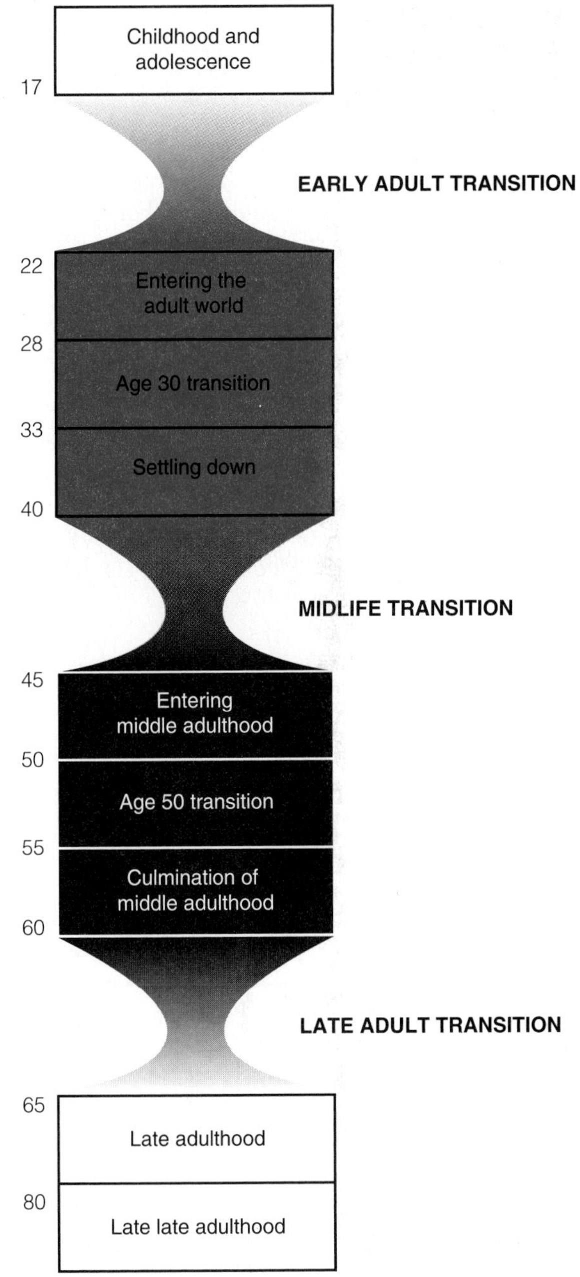

FIGURE 16.2
Levinson's description of major developmental periods through early and middle adulthood. (From D. J. Levinson, The Seasons of a Man's Life. *Copyright © 1978 by Daniel J. Levinson. Reprinted by permission of Alfred A. Knopf, Inc.)*

quires separating from the family and establishing a separate identity; entering the adult world involves exploring career roles as well as establishing stable adult roles.

Of major significance toward the end of this period—at around age 30—is the adoption of what Levinson refers to as a "dream." **Levinson's dream** is an idealized fantasy

INTERVIEW

SUBJECT

Female; age 48; widowed; two children, both independent; manager of a cleaning business.

QUESTION

"Do you think you experienced a midlife transition or crisis?"

"What the heck is that? My whole life is a bloody crisis! . . . I get'cha, but the answer is no, I never had no crisis like that. I was too bloody busy bringin' up the kids and tryin' to make ends meet—which they never did. If my husband hadn't of died, I might've had enough time. No, I'm afraid I can't help you there at all."

that includes the goals and aspirations of the dreamer. In one sense, the dream is a tentative blueprint for the dreamer's life. In Levinson's (1978) words:

> These are neither night dreams nor casual daydreams. A "dream" of this kind is more formed than a pure fantasy, yet less articulated than a fully thought-out plan. . . . In its primordial form, the Dream is a vague sense of self-in-adult-world. It has the quality of a vision, an imagined possibility that generates excitement and vitality. (p. 91)

The majority of men's dreams have to do with occupations. Some men also include marriage and family goals in their dreams, or sometimes personal growth or spiritual goals (Gooden & Toye, 1984). Women's dreams are more likely to involve marriage and family goals (Roberts & Newton, 1990).

Individuals often reexamine career and lifestyle choices during early adulthood, and especially during the *age 30 transition,* and reevaluate them in terms of the dream. Divorce and career changes sometimes result.

The next period, *settling down* (late thirties), is marked by major efforts to lay the groundwork for accomplishing the dream in all-important areas: career-related, social, economic, political, family-related, and so on.

The Midlife Transition

Probably the most highly popularized of all adult developmental stages is the *midlife transition*—often referred to as the **midlife crisis.** The main developmental task of this period is to come to grips with successes and failures relative to the dream. Otherwise, suggests Tamir (1982), the dream may continue to exercise the same power it held when the dreamer had more time, energy, and perhaps opportunity to achieve it.

Drebing and Gooden (1991) looked at the importance of the dream in the lives of 68 men ages 36 to 55. They found that 78 percent of these men had formed a dream in early adulthood. Of the men who had developed a dream (primarily occupational in nature), 38 percent claimed to have been largely successful in fulfilling it while 10 percent had failed. Others were in the process of trying to alter their dreams, either by changing them or by adding to them.

The most important findings from this study have to do with the importance of the dream's outcome to the individual's sense of well-being. The most depressed, anxious, and purposeless individuals in this sample (that is, those who most clearly were experiencing a crisis) were those who had never developed a dream. And those who had failed in their dreams were also significantly more depressed and anxious, and had lower scores on a measure of *purpose in life* than those who had been successful in their dreams. Interestingly, those who were still pursuing dreams, often modified from earlier aspirations, were characterized by higher levels of emotional well-being.

The urgency of the need to reexamine the dream in midlife is aggravated by the fundamental change that now occurs in the individual's perception of time. As Neugarten (1968) described it, people change from a perspective of "time from birth" (age, in other words) to one preoccupied with "time until death." Any of a variety of what Levinson calls "marker events" can contribute dramatically to this change in time perspective: death of parents, children leaving home, death of friends and age peers, sickness, and so on. Following these and other less dramatic events (such as being beaten at tennis or golf by one's son), individuals become progressively more conscious of their own mortality and of the idea that there may not be enough time to achieve the dream. For many, it now becomes fundamentally important to modify the dream—to change commitments and lifestyles and to emphasize those aspects of life that might have been neglected. For some men, the result is a resolution to spend more time with family and friends—and perhaps less with work and career. For others, it might involve a complete abdication of earlier responsibilities and commitments—and new commitments to what are sometimes dramatically different lifestyles.

Entering Middle Adulthood

Individuals enter middle adulthood at about age 45. Some bring with them renewed commitment to family and career; others, following the crises of the preceding period, enter middle adulthood with new lifestyles. All, according to Levinson (1978), experience fundamental change following the midlife transition, even if they continue in the same external roles. Detailed examinations of the lives of his subjects leads him to observe that there are typically changes in relationships with work, family, and others—sometimes for better and sometimes for worse. Thus there is tremendous variation in the extent to which men find their lives satisfactory during this period.

Age 50 Transition

Levinson (1986) provides only a quick sketch of developmental phases after the age of 45. He suggests that at about age 50, another period of transition involves tasks very similar to those of the midlife transition: namely, to reexamine accomplishments and relationships in relation to the dream espoused in early adulthood. For those who have accomplished this task inadequately in their early forties, there may be a crisis similar to that of the midlife; for others, the period may be relatively free of turmoil.

Culmination of Middle Adulthood

Following this period of transition, there is a relatively stable "settled" period during which the individual's career will begin to wind down. In a final period of transition, bridging middle and late adulthood, the key tasks will involve reconciling the dream with reality, accepting again the notion of one's own mortality, and preparing for what are sometimes drastic changes brought about by retirement and all that it entails.

Seasons of a Woman's Life: Levinson

Critics of Levinson's work suggested that the *seasons of a woman's life* don't necessarily follow the same cycles as those of a man. In response, Levinson (1990) undertook detailed interviews with a group of 45 women in much the same way as he originally had with the 40 men. And, in general, he found that women go through similar stages as do men, but with a number of important differences.

Gender-Based Dreams

For example, the dreams of Levinson's men tended to focus primarily on their work and careers. But the women's dreams embraced family as well as careers. In general, the women tended to be less career-oriented than the men, less driven to climb corporate ladders or accumulate the visible, material trappings of success. Levinson terms this phenomenon *gender-splitting*. He claims that gender-splitting is a powerful and probably universal phenomenon, evident in the fact that most women placed *more* weight on the family than on the career aspect of the dream.

The dreams of women, notes Levinson, are more complex than those of men. Not only do they reflect career as well as family aspirations, but they are subject to rapidly changing social conditions that impact more on women than on men—changes in work opportunities, in the stability of the family, in gender stereotypes, and so on. As a result, women's dreams are more subject to revision and change than are those of men. And fewer women are completely happy with the outcomes of their dreams.

Career Transition

A second important developmental difference between adult men and women, notes Levinson, is that women tend to complete their preparation for a career, and to begin their careers, later than men. Whereas most men are well into the beginnings of their careers by the age 30 transition, many women are just starting their preparation at that point. In addition, for many men, a special relationship with a respected *mentor* is an important part of preparation for and development of a career. However, relatively few women in Levinson's sample had mentors—perhaps because there are fewer available.

In summary, Levinson's account of the adult lifespan describes major tasks during developmental phases that last between five and seven years. The tasks typically involve making important choices about family, lifestyle, and career. In an overly simplified sense, for men, the primary preoccupation during early adulthood revolves around work: climbing the ladder, being recognized, achieving success, being somebody in the community. For many women, the dream includes establishing a home and starting a family as well as a career.

Between ages 40 and 45, the individual confronts his or her dreams and evaluates life in relation to earlier goals and ambitions. This confrontation often translates itself into a crisis ("Where am I going? What do I want out of life? What is really important?"). Subsequently, the dream may change and different things may become more important.

Sheehy's (1976) journalistic account of the lives of 115 men and women also describes a developmental progression very much like that described by Levinson—but with a number of important differences.

Sheehy's Passages

Sheehy (1976; 1981), a journalist, suggests that the word *crisis* is often interpreted too seriously. It hints of impending catastrophe, of calamity just around the corner. For this reason, *crisis* is not entirely appropriate to describe most of the events that characterize the adult lifespan—hence her substitution of the term *passages*. Sheehy's passages are very similar to Levinson's stages, but the labels have been changed (see Interactive Table 16.1).

It is in her description of entry into middle adulthood, the *deadline decade*, that Sheehy departs most significantly from Levinson. This phase, corresponding to Levinson's midlife transition, is accorded a longer age span by Sheehy (ages 35–45, compared with 38–43), in recognition of the possibility that midlife crises can occur much later or much earlier than Levinson had thought.

Male–Female Differences at Midlife

A second important observation made by Sheehy is that although the general developmental pattern for men and women is highly similar, the midlife passage often occurs considerably earlier for women—frequently at about age 35 (compared to 40 or 45 for men). Even more important, resolution of this crisis sometimes takes a dramatically different form for men than for women.

Highly simplified, Levinson's view is that men spend much of their early twenties deciding on a "life structure," commit themselves to career and life-plan decisions

TABLE 16.2
Gould's Transformations

Age	Major False Assumptions	Major Tasks
16–22	"My parents will always be my parents. I'll always believe in them."	Move away from home; abandon idea that parents are always right.
22–28	"If I want to succeed, I need to do things the way my parents do." "If I make mistakes and need rescuing, they'll rescue me."	Become independent; explore adult roles; abandon idea that things will always turn out right if done in the manner of parents.
28–34	"Life is pretty straightforward, especially if you're on the right track. There aren't too many contradictions."	Explore aspects of inner self; become more sensitive to emotions; begin to realize inner contradictions.
34–45	"I have all the time I need. I am doing the right thing."	Recognize and accept idea of one's own mortality; develop strong sense of personal responsibility; reassess values and priorities.

during their thirties, and then subject their lives to profound reexamination at about age 40. The result is a midlife crisis of varying severity, the resolution of which is often seen in the man's subsequently greater concern with family and self than with aggressive, achievement-related goals.

In contrast to this general male pattern, says Sheehy, not only do women begin their reexamination of goals and priorities considerably earlier, but their resolutions often take a different twist. Whereas many men become more passive, more oriented toward *feeling*—perhaps more "feminine"—many women become more active, more aggressive—perhaps a little more "masculine" (Hyde, Krajnik, & Skuldt-Niederberger, 1991). As Gutmann (1990) puts it, resolution of the midlife crisis often sees a "return of the repressed." Specifically, the man's repressed femininity and the woman's repressed masculinity begin to assert themselves in a gradual movement toward the greater **androgyny** (combination of masculine and feminine characteristics) that is often part of old age.

As Sheehy notes, one of the ways in which couples can sometimes resolve their midlife dilemmas and find new excitement and meaning in the next decades is to "renegotiate" traditional roles. Perhaps the wife can contribute salary and vacations to the family—and the husband can provide nurturance, laundered clothing, and pot roasts.

The *freestyle fifties* is characterized by individuals who have accepted who they are. Transition through the *selective sixties* frequently involves a new recognition of what is most important in life—friends, family, loving, caring, sharing. These attitudes carry on into the *thoughtful seventies*, when individuals are in an excellent position to contemplate important philosophical, religious, social, and political abstractions—and on into the *proud-to-be eighties*, when some individuals find new vigor and pride in existence. In Sheehy's (1981) words: "The approach of the final passage transforms the grains in the hour-glass to the dust of gold and cinnamon—precious enough to be spent well and to be savored in the smallest ways" (p. 53).

Gould's Transformations

Gould's transformations provide yet another description of adult development. Gould (1972; 1978) studied a large sample of more than 500 men and women between the ages of 16 and 60. What was most unusual about his sample, however, was that members were outpatients at a psychiatric clinic (at the University of California, Los Angeles) involved in group therapy. Subjects in this sample were divided into different groups according to age and were interviewed by psychiatrists, who attempted to uncover feelings and statements that would be most characteristic of each age group. In this way, Gould hoped to arrive at a sequential description of important changes in the adult lifespan. Following these initial interviews, questionnaires were sent to a sample of 524 individuals who were not psychiatric patients. These questionnaires were based primarily on patients' statements that appeared to be characteristic of specific age groups. This aspect of the study was intended simply to corroborate initial findings and to establish that the patient population was not fundamentally different from a nonpatient population.

Gould's description of adult development is summarized in Table 16.2. At first glance, it appears to be very similar to that advanced by Levinson and Sheehy. Thus early preoccupations center on separating from the family and establishing an adult identity (work, family, social responsibility); crises occur about age 30 and again at 40, the latter being tied to a recognition of mortality and a sense of urgency with respect to goals.

Closer examination reveals that Gould's transformations present a different emphasis from that of Levinson's seasons or Sheehy's passages. Gould, a psychiatrist, is concerned less with the individual's relationship to work, career, dreams, and family, and more with the person's *self-consciousness*—that is, with the individual's understanding of the self and with the gradual transformations that change a child's consciousness into an adult's consciousness. Thus development is described through developmental tasks that involve getting rid of the false, "childish" assumptions of early years and replacing them with more adult assumptions. For example, between ages 16 and 22, the principal false (or immature) assumption that dominates the individual's life concerns the rightness of parents: "I'll always want to be with my parents and believe in them—and they can always rescue me if I need help." Accordingly, the major developmental task of this early period is that of leaving home—but not simply in a physical sense. To really "leave" home is to discard these false assumptions concerning the rightness and potency of parents and to accept that parents can be wrong. We do this *intellectually*, says Gould (1990), long before we are successful in doing it emotionally.

In a similar fashion, progress through the lifespan requires shedding a variety of other false assumptions and adopting ones that are more realistic (see Table 16.2). The result, according to Gould, is greater self-understanding and greater self-acceptance.

Is There a Midlife Crisis?

Popular literature, rather than psychological research, may be largely responsible for the currency of the expression *midlife crisis* or *midlife identity crisis*. Unfortunately, books such as Levinson's and Sheehy's are not based on the kind of investigation that science demands. But they are nevertheless intriguing and suggestive, and sometimes they can lead to important insights. Still, what does science say about the midlife crisis?

Costa and McCrae (1980) looked at *distress* among men ages 30 to 70, assuming that distress is an emotion that would accompany a serious midlife crisis. In this study, however, distress did not peak in the middle years; in fact, it was higher for younger than for older adults. Similarly, Long and Porter (1984) report that for many women, the changes that occur at midlife (children leaving home, perhaps resuming a career) are often liberating. Although these changes require major readjustments, the eagerness with which many women embrace them hardly connotes a crisis.

These two studies, however, do not establish that the concept of a midlife crisis is invalid, but suggest, instead, that the notion of a *universal* crisis at this stage is probably inappropriate. Farrell and Rosenberg (1981) developed a questionnaire designed to assess the presence of conflict and crisis in midlife—a "midlife crisis scale." This scale ranks responses to statements such as "I find myself wondering what I really want in life." When they administered this scale to groups of younger and older men, they found some degree of dissatisfaction and conflict in more than half their respondents, but only 12 percent could be classified as having genuine midlife crises.

The best answer to the question "Is there a midlife crisis?" is simply that yes, there is, but it isn't universal. Medicine, for example, recognizes its existence as a collection of midlife symptoms of distress. Ellman (1992) describes various ways of treating these symptoms. And Waskel (1992; Waskel & Coleman, 1991) shows how midlife crises are often tied to individuals' concerns about dying.

Most researchers agree that the middle years involve major transitions that require change if the individual is to cope and remain reasonably happy. During this period, the increasing frailness of aging parents, or their death, underline for the middle-aged their own potential frailty, and their own inevitable mortality. Sometimes the realization leads to a difficult adjustment—and sometimes to a crisis. However, there are important transitions throughout the lifespan, and major adjustments to be made at all levels. Furthermore, crises are tied less to age than they are to events. Hence, crises that occur in midlife for some might occur much earlier or much later for others.

In summary, it is misleading to refer to the midlife as a period of universal crisis. However, it is not misleading to suggest that at some point in middle adulthood, many individuals will reevaluate their lives, and some will suffer frustration and regret at the outcome. For some, the situation may evolve into a crisis; for others, it may be interpreted as simply another opportunity for growth.

FAMILY RELATIONSHIPS

Of all the stages in the span of our lives, the middle years have the potential for the greatest number of different family relationships. A middle-aged couple can have relatively young children, or children who are themselves on the threshold of the middle years. They can have grandchildren who are infants and some who are old enough to have given them great-grandchildren. They can have parents who are still in the upper reaches of middle adulthood, or parents who are very old. Add to this all the possibilities of aunts and uncles, cousins and nephews and nieces, brothers and sisters, in-laws, and so on and the web of possible relationships can become enormously tangled.

Or they can be brilliantly simple. Clearly, there are many individuals who have no children and few, if any, family connections. Their midlife experiences might be vastly different from those described here.

Relationships with Children

For those whose lives include families and children, two stages of Duvall's eight-stage description of the family life cycle are directly pertinent: the **launching phase** and the **empty nest phase** (see Figure 14.10). Keep in mind, however, that because Duvall's approach describes the

Contrary to what we might expect, for married couples the period of the "empty nest"—that is, the period immediately following what Duvall terms the "launching phase"—is among the happiest of the stages of the family life cycle.

most common child-rearing patterns in traditional families, it does not take into consideration the possibility that the major events and tasks that define the stages might occur much later, or sometimes earlier, in many families. Nor is it suitable for cultural contexts different from ours. In addition, there is a tendency to oversimplify when discussing complex relationships within simple stages. At the same time, however, the simplification is sometimes an advantage, providing a way to organize and understand facts.

Launching

The **launching phase,** the sixth in Duvall's cycle of the family, begins with the first child's leaving home and ends when the youngest child departs, an average of about eight years. Hence, during the launching phase, there are often adolescents still in the home, and the problems and challenges of parenting adolescents continue. One of these challenges has to do with resolving conflict with teenagers while continuing to maintain a rewarding and smoothly functioning marital relationship. Following a longitudinal study of parenting, Vuchinich, Vuchinich, and Wood (1993) report that parental agreement is important for solving a family's problems. Interestingly, however, when agreement is so strong that it is seen as a *coalition*, it may have the opposite effect. This, they suggest, is because strong parental coalitions may frustrate the adolescent's need to develop autonomy.

Other challenges and problems brought about by the launching phase include the need to rearrange physical facilities and resources, additional expenses relating to the launching (college or wedding expenses, for example), and

reassigning responsibilities among grown and growing children. Clearly, the launching phase will be longer, more expensive, and perhaps more difficult in those families in which there are many children, and in which the space between the oldest and youngest child is greatest. In addition, given that the U.S. National Survey of Families and Households reports that the level of support given children (both economic and social) often declines very little until the thirties, some of the responsibilities of the launching phase may last many years (Cooney & Uhlenberg, 1992).

The Empty Nest

The **empty nest phase,** the seventh in the family life cycle, begins with the launching of the last child and lasts perhaps 15 or more years. The average age of the mother at the beginning of this stage is about 52 (54 for the average father). Although the family continues to function as an important social unit and to encourage the development of autonomy among its sons and daughters, its primary developmental tasks shift away from children and refocus on the husband and wife. Among these tasks are those that relate to maintaining a sense of well-being, developing and enjoying career responsibilities, dealing with aging parents, and establishing and maintaining a useful or enjoyable position in the community.

Although folklore has often associated the departure of children with unhappiness and even depression among parents, especially among mothers, remarkably consistent research findings contradict this belief. As an example, Rollins and Feldman (1981) looked at marital satisfaction through Duvall's stages among 850 couples. Like other researchers, they found that the majority (around 80 percent) of husbands and wives thought their marriages were "going well" either all or most of the time. But they also found that happiness and satisfaction tend to be highest in the first stage of the cycle (prior to the advent of children) and begin to decline with the first child, reaching a low at about the time that the oldest child is entering adolescence. By the time of the empty nest stage, happiness and satisfaction again begin to increase, and continue to do so until the retirement years (see Figure 16.3). Not surprisingly, many parents look forward to their children's leaving and establishing their own independent lives as adults. And many are distressed when, because of economic and employment conditions, their adult children either do *not* empty the nest as expected or return after having left (Glick & Lin, 1986).

An earlier study of 1,746 couples conducted by Nock (1979) had concluded that the most happily married couples are those *without* children, whether they are couples who have not yet had children, couples who will never have children, or couples whose children have already left home. In addition, childless couples are least likely to contemplate divorce. Connidis and McMullin (1993) showed that the relationships are somewhat more complex than this.

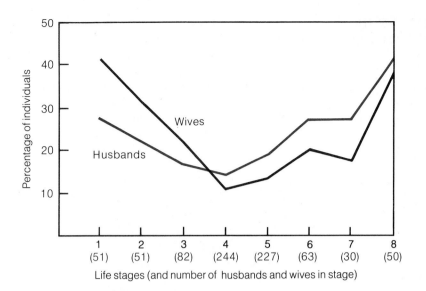

FIGURE 16.3
Percentage of individuals at each stage of the family life cycle (from stage 1, "beginning families," to stage 8, "retirement") reporting their marriage was going well "all the time." (Figures in parentheses indicate the number of husbands and wives in each stage. There was a total of 1,589 cases.) (From Rollins & Feldman, 1981, p. 308. Used by permission of Columbia University Press.)

Increasing life expectancy means that more middle-aged parents and their children are likely to know parents and grandparents for very long periods of time—which can be a source of tremendous joy and comfort. It can also present some middle-aged parents with the challenge of caring both for children and for aging parents at the same time.

Specifically, it isn't simply the fact of having or not having children that is important, but rather how *close* parents and children are. Not surprisingly, those who are closest are happiest. Similarly, those who are childless *by choice* are happier than those who are childless by circumstance.

In summary, in the majority of cases, both mothers and fathers evaluate the nest-emptying experience positively more often than negatively (Borland, 1982). Typically, relationships with children who have left home remain close and positive, and parents continue to support their children and to advise them on all kinds of subjects ranging from careers to child rearing. In fact, when children and their parents interact and advise one another, most of the advice flows from parent to child no matter whether the children are 20 or 50 (Cohler & Grunebaum, 1981).

Relationships with Aging Parents

For most of us, the realization that our parents are not the strongest and the wisest people in the whole world is a reluctant discovery. In childhood, we have little doubt about what father and mother are, and what they can do. Even through adolescence, when logic and experience should teach us better, we remain convinced that in at least some ways, our parents are still the biggest and the best. And so it continues through early adulthood.

But finally there comes a day, usually some time in the middle years, when we look at our parents and make the shocking discovery that our childhood convictions were an illusion. It is a sobering and sometimes distressing realization. Midlife brings with it not only the problems of adjusting to the changes that age brings our parents, but also often brings the stress of looking after them—and eventually the challenge of adjusting to the death of one or both of them.

Given the dramatic increase in life expectancy in recent decades, there are now proportionally more older

WENG FU'S SON

In the street of Wang's Broken Tea Cup, Weng Fu, the beggar, stood and shouted thunderously, "Who'll buy? Who'll buy? What young man wishes to buy a father?" Young men gathered around, making sport of Weng Fu. A richly dressed youth held out some money and Weng Fu reached for it. But it was only a jest; the youth closed his hand on the money before the beggar could grasp it, and ran off laughing. Weng Fu lurched after him, reaching for the money. Someone stuck out a foot and tripped the old beggar, who fell into the mud.

Ah Tzu, an orphan, tugged at the beggar's rags to help him rise. "Will you buy me for a father?" asked the beggar. "Certainly," answered the boy, "where is your house?" So Weng Fu took the boy to a house with straw so thin for a roof that it would stop no rain, and with holes in the walls. "Give me all your money," said the beggar, "that I might eat, and while I am gone, braid me some sandals." And the beggar left, returning later with a silver tray laden with wonderful food. "You haven't finished the sandals," said he. "Work while I eat." And the beggar ate at great length, making loud noises of appreciation while Ah Tzu finished the sandals. "Now," said Weng Fu, "there is a bean cake in the cupboard which you may eat." Ah Tzu got from the cupboard a single dried-up bean cake. "But I am still hungry," said the beggar, "give me half the cake." And he took three fourths of the dried-up cake, leaving only a small corner that had been chewed by mice.

For three days, Ah Tzu stayed in the beggar's house, protecting it, serving his new father, guarding his jewels, and beating away thieves. Then the house caught fire and the two had to flee. But at the door, Weng Fu turned and said to Ah Tzu, "There is a brick on the floor in the far corner of the house; get it for me." Ah Tzu did so, risking his life for a worthless brick. "Ah," said his new father, "I have lost my ribbon. Go now to the emperor and ask him for one of his discarded queue ribbons for Weng Fu, the beggar." Ah Tzu did so, even though he knew he would receive nothing from the emperor but a rope for his own neck. Trem-

bling like a leaf, he knelt in front of the emperor and made his request. "No, my son, I shan't give you a ribbon for old Weng Fu. He no longer exists," said the emperor—who was also Weng Fu. Having no children, he had gone out as a beggar to find someone pious enough, obedient enough, to be his beloved son and heir. (Based on Chrisman, 1968.)

To Think About   This is one of hundreds of stories told to Chinese children, stressing the value of *filial piety*. Among important cultural values reflected in stories of filial devotion, says Wu (1981), are the beliefs that (1) from the earliest age, children should show great devotion to their parents; (2) parents' welfare comes before that of children; (3) children should be obedient and try to make their parents' lives pleasant and comfortable no matter what.

Are there similar values in your culture? Are cultural values important? How? Why?

adults than there have ever been (U.S. Bureau of the Census, 1994). This may be a source of joy for middle-aged adults. But it can also be a source of frustration and anxiety and depression as well, report Spitz and colleagues (1994), when the middle-aged child assumes the responsibility of caring for an aging parent.

In North America, aging adults do not commonly move in with their children unless financial need or health problems compel them to do so—although they often move closer to them. It is the parent generation, and not the children, who most insist on independence, says Shanas (1980). However, as parents become more frail, there is a greater need for children to provide assistance and support—sometimes financial, often emotional and physical. Not surprisingly, the closer the relationship between parent and child has been in the past, the more likely the now-adult child is to care for aging parents (Whitbeck, Hoyt, & Huck, 1984). Also, daughters are

more likely than sons to provide this care although, as Lee, Dwyer, and Coward (1993) discovered, this is so primarily because far more aging mothers than fathers are in need of care (fathers don't live so long). Same-gender care, they point out, is the rule rather than the exception. Thus, when it is fathers who need to be cared for, sons are more likely to assume the responsibility.

Adjusting to the death of a parent is a sometimes difficult developmental task that is often accompanied by intense grief and sometimes depression (Moss, Moss, & Rubinstein, 1993). If the care has been prolonged, and especially if the aged parent has been seriously ill or physically or mentally incompetent, grief often lessens rapidly following death (Collins et al., 1994). Parental death, interestingly, is one possible cause of marital strife in the middle years (Guttman, 1991). (See Across Cultures: "Weng Fu's Son.")

MARRIAGE AND DIVORCE

Taking into account population increases, wedding bells ring about as often now as they did in the days of our grandparents. In any given year, around 10 or 11 marriages take place for every 1,000 people. But when our grandparents or great-grandparents agreed to marry and remain married "until death do us part," they were far less likely to break the agreement. In 1910, there was less than 1 divorce per 1,000 population; 85 years later, that number had increased by a factor of more than 5. Median age of divorce for men is now about 35.1; for women, it's 32.6 (U.S. Bureau of the Census, 1994). Because half of all divorces occur after these ages, a relatively large number occur in the middle years (Figure 16.4).

FIGURE 16.4

Changes in marriage, divorce, and birthrates per 1,000 population, 1910–1992. (From U.S. Bureau of the Census, 1994, p. 75.)

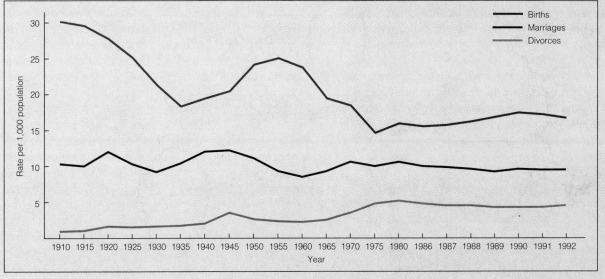

Relationships with Spouse

The middle years, notes Maltas (1992), are the prime of life, a time of joy and plenty; but there is often "trouble in paradise." The "trouble" of which Maltas speaks is marital strife, a relatively common midlife occurrence.

Marital Disruption

Marital disruption affects all stages of the lifespan. In Chapter 6, we looked at its implications for infants and young children; in Chapter 8, we examined how children of different ages react to the separation of their parents; and in Chapter 14, we looked at the effects of divorce on husbands and wives. We noted there that currently about 50 percent of all marriages end in divorce, and that the vast majority of those who divorce will also remarry, most within three years. (See At a Glance: "Marriage and Divorce," and Figure 16.4.)

Research suggests that divorce in middle age can be difficult for both the husband and the wife. In general, the longer the couple has been married, the more difficult the adjustment. Lingering unhappiness, bitterness, and even depression are not uncommon (Maltas, 1992).

Divorce is often more difficult for middle-aged women than for men, for several reasons. The fact that men often receive more emotional and psychological support outside the home, particularly in a one-wage-earner family, may make it easier for men to make the transition out of a marital relationship. In addition, women are more

Although divorce has become enormously more common in recent decades, marriage continues to be as popular as it ever was. About 95 percent of all Americans marry at least once. Some do it over and over again.

likely than men to suffer economic hardship following divorce. And perhaps most important, the chances of finding someone suitable for an intimate relationship or for remarriage are lower for middle-aged women than men. For one thing, by middle age, more men than women have died, so that the total pool of men has been reduced; for another, our contemporary standards of physical attractiveness penalize women more than men (Bogolub, 1991). Not surprisingly, middle-aged men tend to remarry younger women.

Remarriage

Among the adjustments and changes that are sometimes required following *remarriage* in middle age are those having to do with the marital relationship itself. Often, difficult interpersonal adjustments are required of two individuals who have had half a lifetime to establish their own habits and expectations. In addition, there may be the need to establish relationships with an entirely new set of in-laws, as well as perhaps stepchildren.

We should note, however, that these adjustments and changes are not necessarily problems, although they can be challenges. And divorce in middle age is not always traumatic. In addition, remarriage and the creation of *stepfamilies* has some definite benefits. For example, whereas divorce often brings economic hardship, remarriage generally eliminates that hardship. Furstenberg (1987) reports that remarried women are about as well off as women in their first marriage. They are about as likely to work, and no more likely to consider their economic situation a problem. At the same time, on the average, remarried women are far better off economically than those who have not remarried.

In addition to the possible economic benefits of remarriage, there are clearly some emotional benefits. Not surprisingly, remarried men and women consider themselves to be happier than do those who are divorced. In fact, the happiness ratings of remarried couples is about the same as that of those who are still in their first marriage (Glenn & Weaver, 1977).

Stepparenting

Remarriage where one or both of the partners have children from a previous marriage can sometimes lead to complicated patterns of relationships among members of the resulting stepfamily—and which can become even more complicated with the pregnancy of the wife (Dimmock, 1992). Such families, notes Dietz-Omar (1991), often remain *evolving* rather than *established* families for a prolonged period of time, and are sometimes marked by less cohesion and satisfaction among their members. For example, Furstenberg and Spanier (1984) found that remarried parents frequently do not consider stepchildren part of their family system. Similarly, stepchildren tend not to consider the stepparent part of their family. And even with the passage of time, this situation often remains unchanged. When members of stepfamilies were asked for their subjective impressions of family life, both parents and children who were members of stepfamilies had somewhat more negative evaluations than those who belonged to intact nuclear families. Stepfamilies are seen as less relaxed and less close, and as more tense, complex, and disorganized, than traditional families (Fursternberg, 1987; see Figure 16.5).

In spite of these findings, on the whole, both children and parents have positive evaluations of life in a stepfamily. And when the stepfamily consists of their biological mother and a stepfather (rather than their biological father and a stepmother), stepchildren rate their stepfami-

Quality of family life

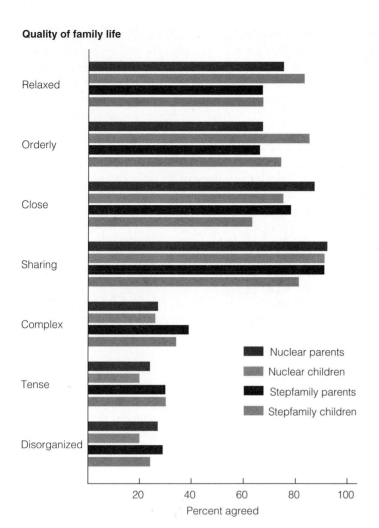

FIGURE 16.5

Percentage of parents and children who agreed that their family life conformed with the listed descriptions in the preceding few months. (From Furstenberg, 1987, p. 50. Reprinted by permission of The Guilford Press.)

lies about as positively as do children with both biological mother and father.

The stepfamilies that result from remarriages in middle age, if they include children at all, are more likely to include older rather than younger children. Even when older children have been living with one of the partners prior to the remarriage, it is not uncommon for them to move out at the time of remarriage. Giles-Sims (1987) reports a number of case studies that illustrate this pattern, and that illustrate, as well, that the greatest amount of adjustment occurs during the first year or two of the new marriage. These first years are a time of negotiation and bargaining; they are a time for establishing roles and defining norms.

But ultimately, as we have seen, the majority of those who have remarried will rate their lives as "very happy."

STABILITY AND CHANGE IN MIDDLE AGE

We are *persons;* our **personality** characteristics are what make us what we are. As personalities, we can be described in terms of several characteristics, or traits. Some people are bold and assertive; others are retiring and submissive. Some are anxious; others, secure. Some are depressive; others, optimistic; conservative or experimenting; emotional or stable; trusting or suspicious; relaxed or tense; practical or imaginative; and on and on.

One way to simplify the study of human personality is to group related traits together into what are sometimes called *types.* This is what Costa and McCrae (1978) did, resulting in what they label the **NEO typology:** *N* for neuroticism, *E* for extraversion, and *O* for openness. These three *types* include most of the personality variables that would be of interest to those doing research on personality changes throughout the lifespan. Neuroticism, for example, includes such traits as anxiety and depression. And a common belief has been that many older people become more depressed with age. Extraversion includes traits such as those sometimes labeled "sensation seeking" (adventurousness) and "activity." Again, we have often assumed that both adventurousness and activity decline with age. And openness refers primarily to the individual's receptivity to new experiences and might also be reflected in measures of dogmatism, rigidity, and authoritarianism.

An important question in the study of the development of personality concerns the extent to which people change with age. Is the cheerful, outgoing 20-year-old likely to be a cheerful, outgoing 60-year-old? Are there major developmental changes in personality traits that occur with age, and if so, are these changes consistent and predictable?

Cross-Sectional Research

In a widely reported study of aging, Neugarten (1964) studied groups totaling more than 1,000 subjects aged 40 to 90, trying to identify general patterns of personality change. As we saw earlier, Neugarten observed a tendency for men and women to alter their dominant approaches to life in middle adulthood: Males became less aggressive, more passive, more concerned with emotions and with internal states—in short, they became somewhat more "feminine." In contrast, women often became more aggressive, more active, and more concerned with achieving personal goals (Helson & Wink, 1992).

A similar study, also conducted by Neugarten (1968), looked at the *self-concepts* of 100 middle-aged men and women. All these individuals were highly articulate, well-educated, successful business and professional leaders. Interviews revealed that most felt that middle age is "the prime of life." As one of the subjects put it, "There is a difference between wanting to *feel* young and wanting to *be* young" (Neugarten & Datan, 1981, p. 281). Although subjects would have liked to retain the appearance and the vigor of youth, most would have been reluctant to give up the competence, confidence, power, and other rewards that had come with maturity.

Middle age, Neugarten informs us, is characterized by a tremendous increase in self-awareness and introspection and by greatly heightened self-understanding. Accordingly, the prevalent theme of these middle years is the reassessment of self. And, as we saw, the result of this reassessment often takes the form of greater femininity for males and greater masculinity for females. Gutmann (1990) suggests that one of the reasons for this change lies in the fact that the roles that men and women play with respect to child rearing during their early adulthood require that women be unaggressive and nurturant if they are to be good mothers, and that men be aggressive and active if they are to be successful breadwinners. Following midlife, when men and women are finally freed from parenting roles, they are able to concentrate on those aspects of their personalities that had previously been repressed.

Two important points must be noted here. First, these patterns of personality change are far from universal, and they are not usually very dramatic. In other words, most men do not become highly (or even noticeably) feminine after age 55, and most women do not become dramatically more aggressive. In fact, in an important longitudinal study of personality changes (discussed in more detail shortly), Costa, McCrae, and Arenberg (1983) point out that although there were declines in masculinity scores for

their male subjects, these were so slight that at current rates of decline it would take 136 years for an "average" 75-year-old man to reach the average masculine score of the women in the sample!

Second, to the extent that this slight change in gender roles after the midlife is due to the different roles played by men and women, it follows that changing conceptions of gender roles with respect to parenting, economic support of families, and decision making may do a great deal to lessen personality differences that now exist between younger males and females. In the end, it may be far less likely that males will become less aggressive or females more active and aggressive. In other words, the changes in male and female personality characteristics in middle adulthood described by Neugarten might well be cohort specific rather than age-related. This, of course, makes them no less real or important, but might significantly alter our explanations and our understanding.

Longitudinal Research

Although a number of cross-sectional studies, such as the Neugarten studies described here, report some small but relatively consistent changes in personality with age, these studies do not warrant the conclusion that change is a function of age. It bears repeating that cross-sectional studies cannot separate the effects of age from those of the cohort.

Using data from the Baltimore Longitudinal Study, Costa, McCrae, and Arenberg (1983; McCrae & Costa, 1987) performed a series of studies employing sophisticated sequential designs (see Chapter 1). These designs allow researchers to separate age effects from those related only to the specific cohorts being examined, as well as from the effects of time of testing.

A variety of personality tests were employed in the Baltimore study, with testing occurring every one or two years after 1958, and including samples spanning all age decades between 20 and 80.

The results of these studies can be summarized very simply: For almost all the personality scales used, there is no consistent change related to age. In fact, not only is there no consistent change, but there is firm evidence of considerable stability through the entire age range for all important traits that make up the NEO model (neuroticism, extraversion, and openness to experience), plus two new traits—conscientiousness and agreeableness. Two exceptions are scores on the general activity and masculinity scales of the Guilford-Zimmerman Temperament Survey. As we noted earlier, masculinity scores tend to decline for males and increase for females. Similarly, measures of general activity level also tend to decline with age. However, changes on both these scales tend to be very small.

McCrae and Costa (1984), following their extensive sequential investigation of personality change, conclude that there is overwhelming evidence for stability of per-

Most adults see themselves as relatively satisfied and happy—although some are less so than others. Among the happiest are those who are healthy, who have adequate income, and who have positive self-concepts. And, other things being equal (are they ever?), the married are happier than the single, widowed, or divorced.

sonality traits. As Alwin (1994) puts it, "The general conclusion in the literature is that personality traits increase in relative stability in young adulthood and grow to high levels of stability in adulthood" (p. 159). This does not mean, of course, that there is no possibility of significant personality change throughout the lifespan. Quite the contrary. Here, as elsewhere, our conclusions apply to a mythical average person rather than to the individual. And we do know that there are sometimes remarkable and dramatic changes. Miserable, cranky individuals sometimes become very agreeable; some very agreeable people sometimes become quite unbearable. These changes might be brought about by some major event in a person's life such as a near-death experience, the loss of a loved one, or the winning of a lottery; or they might simply be the result of sheer personal effort.

But the research does indicate that there is a very strong likelihood that those who are happy-go-lucky, extraverted, and agreeable as young adults will also be agreeable, outgoing middle-aged adults; and they are likely to continue to be sociable and agreeable as very old people. And those who are introverted and anxious as youngsters are also more likely to be tense and withdrawn as oldsters.

HAPPINESS AND SATISFACTION

"Taking all things together, how would you say things are these days—would you say you are very happy, pretty happy, or not too happy?" (Campbell, 1981, p. 27). When this question was first asked in a psychological survey in 1957, more than one person in three described themselves as being "very happy"; one in 10 were "not too happy." The remaining 54 percent thought they were "pretty happy." But by 1972, only one in four people selected "very happy," a finding that seems strange in view of the tremendous growth in prosperity between 1957 and 1972, and the concomitant rise in the standard of living. Is happiness inversely related to owning two cars and having quail and other exotic meats in many pots? Does it increase or decrease with age? Who is most likely to be happy?

These are fundamentally important questions to each of us, for it is happiness, in any of its many disguises, for which we all strive.*

---

*"I struggle for happiness, too," said my grandmother. "But I'll have mine after my lifespan instead of right now, like you."

Are the Satisfied Happy?

Contrary to what we might have expected, **satisfaction** and **happiness** are different. Nor do they always go hand in hand. Satisfaction is a relatively stable dimension. If I am satisfied with my job, my spouse, or my life in general today, I am still likely to be satisfied tomorrow, next month, and perhaps even next year. In this context, to be satisfied is to confess either to the fulfillment of one's goals and aspirations or to a resignation to the way things are.

Happiness, on the other hand, is more subject to the fluctuations of mood. It is a personal, highly subjective feeling, easily sensed and interpreted by each of us but not always easily communicated to others. Nor can it readily be tied to satisfaction. Campbell, Converse, and Rodgers (1976) found that although "completely satisfied" individuals most often saw themselves as being "very happy," many were only "pretty happy." And a large number of individuals were dissatisfied with the major domains of life, such as job, health, housing, and marriage, but nevertheless felt "pretty happy" or even "very happy."

Who Is Happiest?

Who are the happiest people? The rich or the poor? The married or the single? The young or the old? Some tentative answers are available, following extensive interview studies reported by Campbell and associates. These studies involved randomly selected samples representative of the entire population of the United States. The samples ranged in size from 2,164 to 3,692 individuals and totaled more than 12,000 subjects. Interviews were conducted on five separate samples, and provide information about satisfaction with various important dimensions of life, self-estimates of happiness, and detailed information about sex, age, marital status, and so on.

A word of caution is appropriate at the outset. The results of studies such as these have to be interpreted tentatively, primarily because of the highly subjective nature of some of the questions involved. Not only might there be systematic differences in the ways in which different groups interpret the questions, but there might be systematic biases in the ways in which people choose to respond.

Health
Not surprisingly, health is among the most important of all variables in predicting whether people will describe themselves as being happy. Those who suffer serious or chronic health problems are most likely to be unhappy or even depressed. Not surprisingly, health concerns are among the important causes of suicide.

Age
Age-related changes in satisfaction and happiness are somewhat difficult to separate from those associated with major personal events, particularly because many of these events (marriage, childbearing and child rearing, career

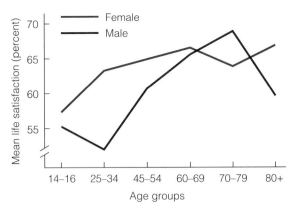

FIGURE 16.6

Differences in life satisfaction by age and group. (From Morganti et al., 1988, p. 50. Reprinted by permission of Baywood Publishing Company and John Morganti.)

advancement, and retirement) are closely tied to chronological age. Thus, it is difficult to determine whether our popular notions of youth as a time of carefree abandonment and happiness and of old age as a period of contentment and serenity are accurate portrayals of age-related changes.

Campbell's (1981) research, as well as other studies reviewed by him, indicates that there has been a systematic change in professed happiness of young people since the early 1970s. Fewer of them report a high level of happiness. The same is not true of older people. As Campbell (1981, p. 176) put it, "In 1978 . . . the young people were less positive than any of the older generations except the very old." Campbell suggests that social, political, and other cohort-specific environmental variables might well account for these observations.

Among the most surprising findings, at least on the surface, is the observation that adolescents and young adults are also typically less *satisfied* than older people (Morganti et al., 1988) (see Figure 16.6). But, as Campbell (1981) explains, this finding is perhaps not so surprising when one considers the possibility that younger adults may be dissatisfied not because their lives are objectively less satisfying than those of older adults but because they have not yet resigned themselves to not fulfilling all their dreams and aspirations. In contrast, adults past middle age might well have resigned themselves to the objective realities of their lives, feeling less able to make significant changes in them.

Marriage and Children
Other intriguing findings from the Campbell studies are that single women are happier than single men, married people are typically happier than the unmarried (single, widowed, or divorced), divorced women are less happy than divorced men, childless couples are as happy as couples with children, and couples whose children have left

home continue to report high levels of satisfaction and happiness. As we saw, the empty nest does not always lead to unhappiness.

Other Contributors to Happiness

In a study of 162 women, Kopp and Ruzicka (1993) discovered that the more roles a woman is called upon to assume, the happier she is likely to be. In this study, women who occupied two or more of the roles of partner, mother, and out-of-home employment were happier than women who had only one role. This finding might seem counterintuitive, but is supported by other research that indicates that work involvement is positively related to happiness.

Another intriguing but totally unexplained finding is that television watching in general is associated with lower levels of happiness, but watching television *soaps* is *positively* correlated with happiness (Lu & Argyle, 1993)!

A Recipe

If psychology were to be so bold as to attempt to provide us with a recipe for happiness, it would first look at what have been found to be the most consistent correlates of reported happiness. From the Berkeley Guidance Study, we learn that there are several conditions in early adulthood (specifically, age 30) that serve as good predictors of happiness at age 70 (Mussen, Honzik, & Eichorn, 1982). For women, these include satisfaction with their marriages (compatibility with their husbands) and satisfaction with their husbands' jobs. For men, the most important early predictors of later happiness are health, stamina, energy level, their wives' emotional stability, job satisfaction, and marital compatibility.

From the Campbell research, psychology would conclude that health and marriage are important for happiness. Research reported by Markides and Martin (1979) agrees; health, income, and activity level are three common correlates of happiness. The Sears (Sears & Barbee,

---

INTERACTIVE TABLE 16.3

A TENTATIVE RECIPE FOR HAPPINESS IN ADULTHOOD

Satisfaction is a relatively stable feeling associated with the extent to which our goals and aspirations are fulfilled; happiness is more subject to fluctuations linked to current events in our lives. What sorts of things are most closely associated with happiness in your life? Does your list correspond with that which psychology provides in this tentative recipe for happiness?

Most Important Ingredient	Other Important Ingredients
Health	Work involvement
	Marriage
	Emotionally stable spouse
	Adequate income
	Stamina
	Energy level
	Friendship
	Positive self-concept
	High personal autonomy
	Television soaps

SOURCE: Gleaned from scattered pieces of psychological research.

1977) longitudinal study would add that for men, working into the sixties and maintaining an intact marriage are important for happiness; and for women, working and being married are also important. The Morganti and associates (1988) study found that satisfaction increases with age (until very old age), and that it is highly correlated with health, self-concept, and personal autonomy (control). (See Interactive Table 16.3.)

Psychology's recipe for happiness might include all the foregoing and might add, as well, that we should try to die at least as early as our spouses. But psychology would not dare be so bold or so flippant.

MAIN POINTS

Descriptions of Middle Adulthood

1. Erikson describes the conflict of the middle years as one of *generativity* (being productive in work, community, family) *versus self-absorption* (temptation to become self-absorbed). Peck elaborates Erikson's last two major stages, adding for middle adulthood *valuing wisdom versus valuing physical powers*, *socializing versus sexuality*, *emotional flexibility versus emotional impoverishment*, and *mental flexibility versus mental rigidity*.

2. Levinson describes several developmental phases, each with important tasks (such as leaving home and making lifestyle decisions) in the early and middle adulthood *seasons* of our lives. Between these phases are important transition periods (ages 20, 30, 40, 50, and so on), the most highly popularized of which is the *midlife transition*, which entails a serious reexamination of the individual's life, particularly in relation to the "dream." Women's dreams are different from men's (concerned with both career and family), reflecting *gender-splitting*.

3. Sheehy's lifespan *passages* give the midlife crisis a wider age range (30 to 50), place it earlier for women than for men, and recognize that resolution of the midlife crisis often results in a "turning inward" among men and the opposite among women. Happiness, she argues, is associated with age (older is better), love (married people are happier), and enjoyment of work.

4. Gould describes several *transformations* whereby a childish consciousness, characterized by false and immature assumptions (particularly concerning parents), is gradually replaced by a more adult consciousness.

5. Research suggests that midlife crises are tied more to events than to age and that the majority of individuals do *not* have a full-blown crisis during middle age. But some do.

Family Relationships

6. Middle age in Duvall's family life cycle includes the *launching phase* (from first to last child leaving home) and the *empty nest phase* (from last child leaving to retirement). Relationships with departed children tend to remain close, and the empty nest does not ordinarily lead to serious unhappiness. Relationships of middle-aged individuals with their aging parents also tend to be warm, and often require caring for them, and adjusting to their dying.

7. Divorce in middle age is less common than at earlier ages and is often harder for women. Remarriage is more common for men than for women after a middle-age divorce (diminishing pool of men). Remarriages in the middle years bring substantial emotional, and sometimes economic, benefits, but may require major readjustments, especially if children are involved. Neither stepparents nor stepchildren easily accept stepkin emotionally as an integral part of their family.

Stability and Change in Middle Age

8. Some research suggests that males and females become less gender typed and more androgynous through middle age. The magnitude of these changes is very small. Longitudinal investigations of personality change using sequential designs support the hypothesis that there is far more stability than change with age.

Happiness and Satisfaction

9. Satisfaction relates to the extent to which various objective aspects of our lives correspond with our goals and aspirations. Happiness is an emotional state, susceptible to fluctuations of mood. Married individuals report more happiness than those who are alone (single, widowed, or divorced); childless couples report as much happiness as those with children; couples whose children have left home (the empty nest) do not, as a result, report lower levels of happiness; and perceived health is closely related to happiness. But psychology does not yet have a complete recipe for happiness.

FOCUS QUESTIONS: APPLICATIONS

1. What are the major transitions and periods of stability of middle adulthood?

- Summarize Erikson's description of the major psychosocial conflicts and challenges of middle age, and relate them to Levinson's description of the seasons of a person's life.

2. Do relationships with friends and family become less important with age?

- Using library resources, answer the question: Is there a midlife crisis?

3. Is personality pretty well established by adolescence? Or does it continue to change in adulthood?

- Explain why cross-sectional and longitudinal research might lead to different conclusions. Use examples from studies of personality or intellectual change in adulthood.

4. Who is most likely to be happy?

- Write out a life plan based on a recipe for happiness, taking into consideration each of the factors that has been shown to contribute to happiness.

STUDY TERMS

androgyny   476

deadline decade   475

empty nest phase   477

freestyle fifties   476

generativity   471

generativity versus self-absorption   471

Gould's transformations   476

happiness   486

launching phase   477

Levinson's dream   473

marital disruption   481

GROWING OLD

The final age in *The Lifespan*'s photo album spans the years of growing old. In these years, we begin to shed some of the urgency that might have driven us through earlier years. Now a gentler peacefulness, a more tranquil rhythm, color the comings and goings of our days. Still, for many there is a great deal yet to be done.

With the coming of the growing old years, many dedicate themselves with renewed vigor to hobbies and interests, some old, some new. Others race about the globe, seeing and doing things about which, earlier, they had scarcely had time to dream

Amy with her Indian water buffalo.

Me (in the middle) and my new "friends" Beth and Viktor.

*A*t each of the ages of our lifespan, there is room—and need—for play. Is the play of the very old so different from that of the very young?

Mabel always liked pink.

And it wasn't even New Year's. Just another Cruise Night!

Ride the sucker, Bill!

Grandma Jones when she was 87.

Some of the elderly seek solitary activities; yet few disengage completely from more social interests. For most, personal relationships—with spouse, family, friends, even pets—are the most important things in life.

Grandpa Kaplan when he was 82.

Aunt Clara says she's watching for her ship to come in.

Another of Grandma's blankets.

*I*n the first ages of our lives, when we rest, we often dream of things we have yet to do. And in the last ages of our lives, we rest again. And perhaps now we dream and reminisce of things we have done.

FURTHER READINGS

Belsky's book is a straightforward account of important changes that occur in adulthood and old age. Especially relevant for this chapter are sections on personality changes and the family:

Belsky, J. K. (1990). *The psychology of aging* (2d ed.). Pacific Grove, CA: Brooks/Cole.

Probably the best sources of additional information with respect to descriptions of the lifespan are original books written by Levinson, Sheehy, and Gould. Jacobs's much shorter account is based on the lives of women and provides some interesting insights into female adult development:

Gould, R. L. (1978). *Transformations: Growth and change in adult life*. New York: Simon & Schuster.

Jacobs, R. H. (1979). *Life after youth*. Boston: Beacon Press.

Levinson, D. J. (1978). *The seasons of a man's life*. New York: Knopf.

Sheehy, G. (1976). *Passages: Predictable crises of adult life*. New York: Dutton.

Sheehy, G. (1981). *Pathfinders*. New York: Morrow.

The classic studies of satisfaction and happiness in the United States, conducted by Campbell and his associates beginning in 1957, are summarized in:

Campbell, A. (1981). *The sense of well-being in America: Recent patterns and trends*. New York: McGraw-Hill.

The years like great black oxen tread the world,
And God, the herdsman goads them on behind,
And I am broken by their passing feet.

WILLIAM BUTLER YEATS
The Countess Cathleen

LATE ADULTHOOD

In our youths, we scarcely know there are great black oxen that **PART EIGHT**
tread the world. We believe we are alone, gifted and special, with our paths stretching out forever before us. In those carefree years, we know with the certainty of youth that there will always be roses along the way, and that we will always know to smell them.

But even then, if we allow ourselves to think of it, we realize that the great black oxen march relentlessly and that they will catch up to us one day. Even as children, if we look to the horizon, we can see their shadows. It is inescapable.

They are not malevolent, God's great beasts. It is not that they have singled us out, you and I, that they have decided it is us upon whose bones they will tread. But they cannot slow down, the oxen of our years; and we can go no faster.

In Part Eight, the breaths of God's great black oxen are hot upon the backs of our subjects. But the bones that are broken in these chapters are accidental. And it would be a mistake to think that the beasts that age brings rumbling behind us always bring pain and fear. There is much of late adulthood that is hopeful and wonderfully happy.

When, as old men and old women, our years have finally caught up with us and the beasts are no longer simply shadows, perhaps they will have become our friends. Maybe then we will see that they do not care to chew on our roses.

In the end, they will break our bones, God's great black oxen. But that won't be until Part Nine.

Physical and Cognitive Development: Late Adulthood

"You are old, Father William," the young man said,
"And your hair has become very white; and yet you incessantly stand on
your head—
Do you think, at your age, it is right?"

Lewis Carroll
Alice in Wonderland

CHAPTER 17

"Help me, Guy," she says. "Prop me up in the corner so's I don't fall down." I wrap my hands around her gray-socked ankles and ease her feet back, planting one against either wall. My grandpa's coveralls, which she has put on not because she needs a work-out suit but more to preserve her modesty, slip down past her bony knees, exposing her blue-veined shanks.

"Hey," I say, "I'll get the hammer and nail your feet smack to the wall so's you don't fall down!" Gawd, what a sense of humor! But my grandmother doesn't laugh; this is serious. Her *Digest* lies open on the table and I can see the title of the article she had just read: "Shrink Your Varicose Veins!" it promises, "And Increase Your Intelligence," the subtitle adds, as a less consequential side benefit of standing on your head 10 minutes a day.

"Okay," says she, "beat it. I'll find my own way down." I look at her for a minute, her inverted face framed by the thick green cushion under her head, her features all upside-down slack, her wrinkles drooping unexpectedly toward her forehead. I can't tell whether she's smiling or grimacing in pain, or whether it's just gravity pulling her lips in the wrong direction.

"Beat it," she croaks again. "Okay," I say, and I go out thinking I'm going to go across the road to where I can watch the barn swallows building their mud-and-spit nest against the beam on the church porch—and I run smack into Father Paradis half-way to the gate.

"Your grandmother home?" he asks.

"Sure, go on in," I say, gawd forgive me, which he does. And then I hear what I imagine is my grandmother finding a very quick way down (good thing I didn't actually nail her feet), and Father Paradis, all embarrassed, excusing himself, saying "I'll come back later," and he passes me even before I reach the gate.

"Is there something wrong with your grandmother?" he asks. "She's standing on her head."

THIS CHAPTER

We don't expect our old people to stand on their heads.

Nor do we expect our youth to sit in rocking chairs, reminiscing about the good old days. We expect that people will act their ages. And we have certain widely held beliefs about what is appropriate behavior for different ages.

Unfortunately, the expectations our society has for old people are sometimes inaccurate, and prejudicial. Negative expectations of this kind that are based solely on age define **ageism.** Ageism is the first topic in this chapter.

The chapter looks as well at important changes in the demographics of old age, brought about by dramatic increases in life expectancy (although not in lifespan). It discusses various explanations for why we age, and examines some of the important physical changes that are part of the aging process. Finally, it looks at intellectual changes in old age, and at the growth of wisdom.

AGEISM

"How old are you?" Few questions are more important to any of us when we first meet someone. Of course, it isn't always proper to ask; there are many for whom age is very private.

But if we do ask and find out how old someone is, what have we actually discovered? A great deal, most of us think, for we all have definite opinions about what people of different ages *should* be like. We know, for example, that children should be immature and impulsive; that adolescents should be moody and sometimes rebellious; that young adults should be adventurous, bold, and energetic;

that middle-aged adults should be responsible, controlled, and strong; that older adults should be cautious, rigid, and narrow-minded; and that the very old should not be totally competent in all areas. Armed with these tidbits of folk knowledge, we glibly judge people to be "old" or "young" for their age. And, in fact, our judgments are probably often accurate and useful. At other times, however, our age-based expectations are inaccurate and highly prejudiced. *Ageism* is the term used to describe *negative* attitudes toward a group that are based solely on age.

Examples of Ageism

Ageism is most common with respect to old age, which is often described by the young in terms such as "used up," "ready to die," "narrow-minded," "prejudiced," "worn," and "incompetent." When Ng, Giles, and Moody (1991) asked people what kind of information they would ask of a driver involved in an automobile accident so that they might assign responsibility, they found that responses were highly dependent on the *age* of the driver—but not the sex. Younger drivers would be asked about their driving conduct (Had they been drinking? Had they been in previous accidents? How fast were they going?). But older drivers would be asked about their *competence* (How was their vision? Their health? Were they licensed to drive? Were they mentally capable? Were they physically capable?). Implicit in these questions are negative age-related stereotypes of the old.

Social Treatment and Media Portrayal

Negative attitudes such as these are sometimes manifested in age discrimination, in which older and younger people are treated differently simply on the basis of age. For example, medical treatment of the elderly often reflects ageism. Not only do the medical professions assign a lower priority to research dealing with diseases associated with aging, but expensive medical screening such as that undertaken for cancer is more likely to be provided for the young than the old, even though there is far more cancer in those above age 65 (Derby, 1991). Similarly, the care of the aged is often inferior to that provided for a younger person in the same circumstances, often because medical personnel don't understand the changes of aging very well (Bader, 1994).

Another example of ageism may be found in immigration policies, which have traditionally favored the young and which, earlier in U.S. history, allowed parents to bring their children from foreign countries but often did not permit them to bring their parents. Similarly, ageism is illustrated in age-based mandatory retirement. And it is evident in the negative media portrayals of the old as doddering, feebleminded, wrinkled, and laughable men and women, standing weakly and foolishly on the last of their worn legs.

Child-Directed Speech

Ageism is evident as well in the speech that is often used when communicating with the elderly, speech that is highly reminiscent of that of mothers to their infants. Thus, speech directed to the old is often higher-pitched, sentences are shorter, ideas are presented in their simplest forms and are often repeated, delivery is slower and more careful, and there is more use of body language such as widening of the eyes and exaggerated gestures and expressions. This type of speech, say Bunce and Harrison (1991), reflects a view of the elderly as helpless and incompetent. In addition, it communicates lowered expectations and fosters negative stereotypes that might lead to lower self-esteem on the part of the elderly, withdrawal from social interaction, and poorer performance (Giles et al., 1992). Many among the elderly find child-directed speech degrading. However, there is evidence that with some of the very old, clear and very simple communication might be associated with better performance (Bunce & Harrison, 1991).

Ageism and Other Negative Attitudes

Ageism describes negative attitudes that are prejudicial because they are based on age alone. Attitudes that are based on fact, even though they might be negative, do not illustrate ageism. Thus the sometimes gloomy pictures that we have of social, physical, and psychological changes in very old age might, to some extent, be fact—negative and uncomfortable fact, to be sure, but fact nevertheless. And social policies that appear to favor the young might often be based not on a stereotyped and prejudiced ageism but on the sometimes painful recognition that the elderly present much greater risks of decline in all areas. Indeed, they are at much greater risk of death, and it would be a pointless exercise in wishful thinking to behave as if this were not the case.

Ward (1979) suggests that one of the reasons why ageism might appear to be more prevalent now is that it is only recently that the old have become numerous. In addition, attitudes toward the old sometimes reflect environmental, economic, political, and social conditions. For example, in harsh and demanding environments, where survival is at a premium, the old quickly become a burden. And, in the same way that children who were an economic burden were sometimes killed during the Middle Ages, there are societies in which the elderly were also killed or customarily committed suicide (Mowat, 1952; Simmons, 1960).

Lest this paint too cynical a picture, let me hasten to point out that many people are not guilty of ageism. Nor, as is made clear in this chapter, does everything suddenly become gloomy with the advent of old age. The rapidly growing proportion of old people in contemporary society is having a profound effect on public opinion as well as on social policy. The middle-aged and the elderly are increasingly breaking traditional age barriers. Many go back to school, begin new careers, marry for the first time, or devote themselves to dramatically new lifestyles at ages that would have been considered far too advanced only a few decades ago. People such as Segovia, Picasso, Grandma Moses, or Freud, all of whom played music, painted, or wrote into their eighties, nineties, or even, in Grandma Moses's case, at age 100, do much to relieve us of lingering age-related negative stereotypes.

LATE ADULTHOOD: WHO AND HOW MANY?

When does old age actually begin? Most of us think of age 65 as the boundary between middle and old age, perhaps because 65 has been a common retirement age. In addition, Social Security and pension programs for the aged, as well as the various concessions that some public and private entities grant the "elderly" are typically for those aged 65 and above.* In fact, however, variability among individuals is at least as great at age 65 as it is at any other time in the lifespan. It is important to keep in mind that there are 65-year-olds whose interests, activities, and vitality are comparable to those of an average 50-year-old. And, of course, there are some who are "old before their time."

---

*"That's not true any more," complained my grandmother. "Used to be you had to be 65 to get stuff like that. But now they got stuff for people who're only 55, or sometimes just 50, like deals in stores and traveling and condominiums." She cocked her head and pointed her cane dangerously toward me, adding in her cynical, sly way: "But it's not that you guys are getting old younger. It's that the marketing people who run the world know where the numbers and the money are. So there!"

THE DEMOGRAPHICS OF AGING

The demography of old age has changed dramatically in the last 30 years. Between 1960 and 1992, the number of people age 65 and older in the United States increased from 16.7 to 32.3 million, an increase from 9.2 to 12.7 percent of the total population (Figure 17.1). The greatest percentage increase occurred at the upper levels: The percentage of those age 85 and older more than tripled. Because of increased longevity, percentages of those widowed declined during that period; but the percentage of those divorced more than doubled (Figure 17.2).

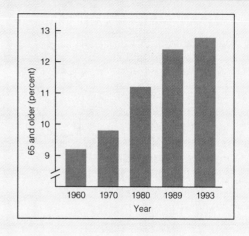

FIGURE 17.1

Percentage of total population age 65 and older. (Based on U.S. Bureau of the Census, 1991, p. 13, and 1994, p. 47.)

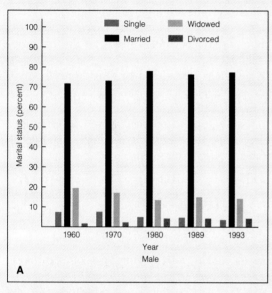

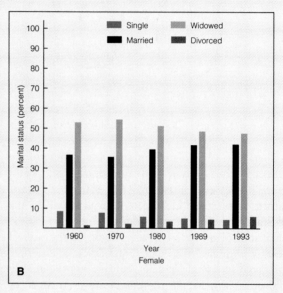

FIGURE 17.2

*Marital status of **A** males and **B** females, age 65 to 74. (Based on U.S. Bureau of the Census, 1991, p. 37, and 1994, p. 47.)*

Dividing Up Old Age

Although it is convenient and simple to group all those above age 65 in a single category, we should also bear in mind that there is a tremendous spread of years between a 65-year-old and an 85- or 90-year-old. As a result, says Fisher (1993), a single stage of adulthood is totally inadequate if we are to understand the changes and the complexity of this phase of life. And, given that so many people are living so much longer, dividing up old age and recognizing the possibilities makes increasing sense. Fisher interviewed 74 people aged 60 or more and identified five distinct possible phases of older adulthood. These are described in the next chapter, which deals with the social and emotional changes of this period.

Neugarten (1978), too, suggests that it might be fruitful to divide old age into periods. She describes two major categories: The "young-old," roughly between ages 55 and 75, are those who are still highly active physically, mentally, and socially (although they may be retired from their main careers). The "old-old" are those for whom physical activity is more limited and among whom the effects of decline have become more apparent and more rapid.

These unimaginative and somewhat clumsy labels reflect our lack of more common terms with which to discuss the elderly, and are another indication of how we have historically had little interest in aging. Unfortunately, being called "old-old" or even "young-old" may not be looked on with great favor by those who are now often labeled "seniors" or "senior citizens."

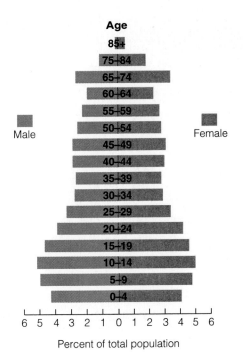

FIGURE 17.3

Age–sex population pyramid for the United States: 1970. (Based on U.S. Bureau of the Census, 1994, p. 14.)

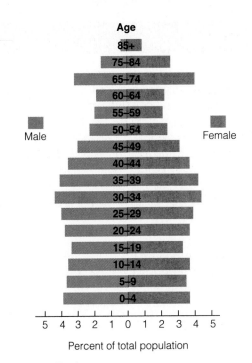

FIGURE 17.4

Age–sex population pyramid for the United States: 1992. (Based on U.S. Bureau of the Census, 1994, p. 14.)

Changing Demographics

Numbers of older people have increased dramatically, both in absolute terms and as a proportion of the overall population. For example, while the population of the United States increased almost two and a half times during the first six decades of this century, the number of people over the age of 65 increased by a factor of more than 5. This tremendous increase is due in part to a high birthrate early in the century, as well as to immigration policies that increased the number of young people in North America. Initially, therefore, there were relatively few old people. Dramatic increases resulted not only because the children of the high-birthrate group had grown up but also because medical advances, as well as changes in nutrition, have contributed to our increased life expectancies. The net result was that, by 1992, about one in eight people in the United States was 65 or more—over 31 million individuals (see At a Glance: "The Demographics of Aging," and Figures 17.1 and 17.2). And the percentage continues to increase. Projections are that by the year 2000, almost 14 percent of the population will be over 65; that percentage is expected to increase to 20 percent by the year 2030 (U.S. Bureau of the Census, 1993). At present, the fastest growing age group in the United States is above age 80.

One of the reasons for predicting a continued increase in the proportion of older people is the effect of the population bulge created by the postwar baby boom (evident in Figure 17.3). As this bulge moves into old age, the numbers of old people relative to younger people will increase

dramatically (Figure 17.4). The net effect is increased even more by declining birthrates. As a result, the age-population pyramids shown in Figures 17.3 and 17.4 are not pyramids at all—as they would be if birthrates remained relatively constant and if deaths occurred primarily from "natural" causes (rather than as a result of wars or other events that kill primarily within selected age groups).

LIFESPAN AND LIFE EXPECTANCY

In North America, life expectancy has increased by almost one quarter of a century in little more than three quarters of a century. At the turn of the century, the average individual did not live 50 years; now we can reasonably expect to live to about age 76—less if we are male, more if we are female. Table 17.1 presents life-expectancy data for 16 countries. Note the tremendous variation for different countries. In addition, in most of these countries, there is a wide discrepancy between male and female longevity. In Canada and the United States, for example, women live an average of between seven and eight years longer than men, a fact that is partly explained in terms of the greater susceptibility of men to stress-related disease (heart disease, for example) and to their traditionally less restrained lifestyles (more automobile accidents, for example) (see At a Glance: "Male and Female Longevities," and Figure

MALE AND FEMALE LONGEVITIES

From the very beginning, men are more fragile than women. There are about twice as many male as female sperm produced, but only about 105 males are born for every 100 females. And because more male than female infants die—and more male children and adolescents also die, numbers are about equal at adulthood. By the time men and women reach the age of 65, there are approximately three women alive for every two men. In the past half-century, life expectancy has increased by some 10 years for both men and women, but has remained approximately seven years longer for women than for men.

FIGURE 17.5

Life expectancy for women and men in the United States, 1940–1992, with projections for 2010. (From U.S. Department of Health and Human Services, 1988, p. 4, and U.S. Bureau of the Census, 1994, p. 87.)

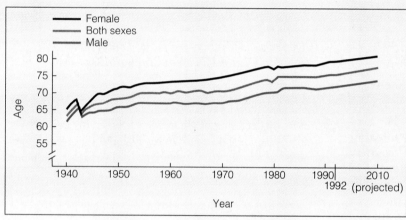

17.5). But part of the explanation must also lie elsewhere, because male infants and children are also more likely to die than are female infants and children. Although approximately 105 males are born for every 100 females, the numbers of each still alive are equal by early adulthood. And by age 65, fewer than 70 males are still alive for every 100 females. Above age 85, there are more than 250 females for every 100 males (Figure 17.6). Social and cultural sex biases may have favored males; nature has been less kind.

Theories of Biological Aging

Although improved nutrition and medical care have given us 25 more years than our late-19th-century predecessors, our **lifespans** (the maximum length of life in the absence of disease or accident) still remain virtually identical to what they have always been. If we live until age 65, our

life expectancy (the average anticipated years of life) is another 15.2 years for males and 19.1 for females (U.S. Bureau of the Census, 1994)—only a few years more than it was almost a century ago. In other words, while it is now far more likely that we will reach old age (approximately two thirds of us can expect to reach age 70), the very oldest among us will, in the end, live no longer than the very oldest who lived a long time ago. If disease, accident, or boredom do not claim us, old age surely will.

Genetic Theory

Although we do not yet know exactly why we age, there are several theories of biological aging. A **genetic theory of aging** holds, for example, that cells are programmed to die—that, in other words, the limits to life are biological and are inherent in the cells of which we are composed or in the protein matter that binds the cells (collagen) (Koli & Keski-Oja, 1992). When tissue cultures are raised in

TABLE 17.1
Life Expectancies at Birth in Selected Countries

Country	Life Expectancy at Birth (years)
Sierra Leone	42
Uganda	43
Bangladesh	52
Indonesia	62
Nicaragua	65
Costa Rica	70
USSR (former)	70
Poland	71
China	72
United States	75
United Kingdom	76
Germany	76
France	77
Spain	77
Australia	77
Canada	77

SOURCE: From Grant, 1993, pp. 68–69, and U.S. Bureau of the Census, 1994, p. 88.

FIGURE 17.6

Changing ratio of females to males in the United States above age 65, 1992. (Based on U.S. Bureau of the Census, 1994, p. 47.)

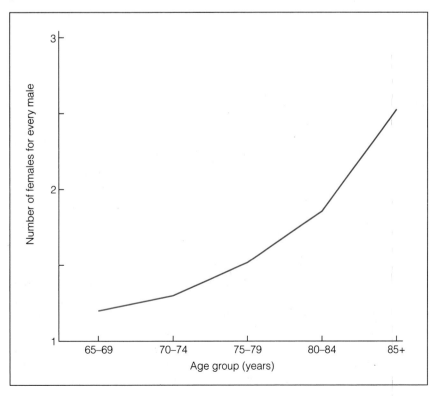

the laboratory, these cultures initially regenerate and multiply at a high rate. But eventually, they begin to atrophy and finally die. What is perhaps most striking about this observation is that while cultures based on human embryonic lung tissue regenerate perhaps 15 times before dying (more if the donor is younger, less if older), cultures from animals with shorter lives regenerate correspondingly fewer times. In fact, there is an almost perfect relationship between the normal lifespan of organisms and the number of times that cultures derived from their tissue will regenerate (Brouwer, 1990). Only certain defective, usually cancerous, cells regenerate indefinitely.

Cell Malfunction Theories

There are several other theories of aging that also relate directly to body cells. **Cell error theory** suggests that, with the passage of time, certain changes occur in DNA material so that the cell eventually ceases to function. These changes are seen as *errors* rather than as genetically preprogrammed occurrences. DNA damage, notes Simic (1992), can be detected through urinalysis and can be tempered through reduction of calorie intake.

The **toxin theory of cell malfunction** maintains that there is a gradual buildup of foreign material in the cell. Although much of this material is poisonous, initially it is present in insufficient quantities and does not affect cell function. With the passage of time, however, it continues to accumulate until the cell dies. One of the consequences is a reduced ability to combat infections and disease (Koli & Keski-Oja, 1992).

The **free-radical theory** argues that portions of cells sometimes become detached during normal metabolic processes. Many of these "free radicals" are highly unstable chemical compounds that may interact with various enzymes and proteins in the body and significantly affect the cell's ability to function normally (Harman, 1993).

A last cell-related theory is **cross-linking theory,** which describes a process whereby bonds ("cross-links") form between molecules or parts thereof, changing the properties of the component cells and altering their functioning.

Organ and System Theories

In addition to these genetic and cell-based theories of biological aging, other theories speculate that various body systems undergo age-related changes that eventually lead to their breakdown or malfunction. Such theories sometimes argue that aging results from reductions in the efficiency of body systems that control temperature, blood-sugar level, and so on (Davies, 1990). Perhaps best known among these theories is that involving our immune systems. These are the systems in our bodies designed to guard against foreign invaders. They protect us from cancer, for example, as well as from a variety of infections. With advancing age, however, not only do our immune systems weaken so that they can less effectively protect us from infection and disease, but they also sometimes make errors and interpret some of our own cells as invaders. This process, known as **autoimmunity,** leads to the production of antibodies that may attack the body itself. Autoimmunity is thought to be involved in some diseases of aging, such as rheumatoid arthritis (Luqmani, Gordon, & Bacon, 1994).

Aging, says Harman (1993), is essentially the accumulation of changes that accompany age. Some of these changes are due to the environment and to disease; others are related to inborn processes of aging. Furthermore, the causes underlying the changes of age interact with each other; hence the importance of a variety of explanations (see Table 17.2).

Longevity in North America

Harman (1993) suggests that by optimizing the environment and controlling and treating disease, it might be possible to add as much as five years to life expectancy. As far as science knows, however, our lifespans are the upper biological limits of our lives. And our life *expectancies* will seldom reach the limit of our *spans.* Some of us will die sooner, others later. Why these differences in longevity?

Several factors contribute to longevity. As we see in Table 17.1, culture, or at least some of the complex of variables associated with it, is one such factor; and as Figure 17.5 shows, sex is another. Women live longer than men, whites longer than blacks, and Americans longer than Ugandans, *on average.* Some of the reasons for this are clearly environmental and relate to nutrition, medical care,

TABLE 17.2

Theoretical Explanations for Why We Will Die in Any Case

Theory	Explanation
Genetic	Cells are preprogrammed to die.
Cell error	Cellular changes lead to cells becoming nonfunctional as a result of errors that occur in DNA material over time.
Toxin	The gradual buildup of foreign material in the cells eventually becomes toxic and the cell dies.
Free-radical	Portions of cells become detached, interact with various chemicals and enzymes, and eventually impede the cells' ability to function normally.
Cross-linking	Bonds form among cells, changing their properties and altering their functioning.
Immune system breakdown	Immune system weakens with age and provides less protection against viral and bacterial invasion or, in a process known as autoimmunity, loses the ability to recognize foreign invaders and begins to attack the system it previously protected.

health habits, and various vices and virtues having to do with lifestyle—exercising, drinking, smoking, and so on. Other reasons for longevity are genetic and relate to inherited susceptibility to various diseases, as well as to other genetically linked strengths and weaknesses.

A variety of other factors have also been found to be linked to longevity. These include physical condition (overweight individuals have shorter life expectancies; those who exercise are more likely to live longer), nature of occupation (people whose jobs require little physical activity live less long on the average), locale (rural people live longer than those in urban environments), wars (life expectancies of those actively engaged in such contests are understandably less), and religious calling (nuns live longer than monks; other things being equal, both live longer than you and I). In addition, the unmarried tend not to live as long as those who are married, and professional athletes have life expectancies that are several years longer than those of nonathletes (Rahman, 1993; Sarna et al., 1993). These and other factors are summarized in Interactive Table 17.3.

So should we all become athletic monks and nuns, and move to the country? Perhaps not, because the most important factors in determining a long life are those over which we have no control—namely, genetic factors, the environments of our grandmothers and of our mothers before and during pregnancy, and our own experiences in early childhood. Sadly, we can far more easily shorten our lives than lengthen them. That is, the good that we might do by *not* smoking or drinking is not likely to equal, in terms of years, the bad that we might do were we to smoke

A RECIPE FOR LONGEVITY

How long can you expect to live? On average, the U.S. Bureau of the Census (1994) tells us, if you are a white American female age 20, about 60.3 more years (55.3 years if black). If you are a white American male age 20, your average life expectancy is another 54.0 years (46.7 if black). But some of us will live longer; others will die sooner. Sex and race are only two of the factors that influence longevity. You cannot control your sex or race; and you have only limited control over the possibility of accidental death. But perhaps you can control some of the other factors associated with longevity, listed here.

You may live longer if:

1. You are female.
2. Your ancestors lived long lives.
3. You are a large tortoise and not a housefly.
4. You remain physically active well into old age.
5. You are highly educated.
6. Your employment is high-status.
7. You continue to be employed well into old age.
8. You are a monk or a nun.
9. You are married or cohabit full-time.
10. You exercise moderately on a regular basis.
11. You drink moderately and do not smoke.
12. You avoid wars, accidents, and homicidal maniacs.
13. Your job requires physical activity.
14. You are not overweight.
15. You sleep less than nine hours per night.
16. There is no incidence of cardiovascular disease, cancer, chronic bronchitis, or thyroid disorders among your close relatives.
17. You live in the country rather than in the city.
18. You undergo regular medical examinations.

Life expectancy at birth for North American males is now around 72; for females, it's about 79. Certain lifestyle factors (like smoking and drinking, or exercising and avoiding wars) can affect longevity. But factors over which we have little control are perhaps most influential in determining how long we live. Thus, the long lives of these 94-year-old identical twin dentists may well reflect the effects of genetics and of early nutrition and care.

and drink. And perhaps living a long time is not very important. We have to be concerned with the quality of our lives as well as with their length.

Longevity Elsewhere

In most parts of the world, only two or three people out of every 100,000 live to be 100; one in 1 million reach 105; and only one in 40 million live to be 110 (Hayflick, 1975). Occasionally, however, the popular press tantalizes us with visions of healthy old people, sometimes 120 or more years of age, living in some faraway place. There are at least three such groups of people: the Vilcabambans in Ecuador, the Hunzukuts in the Karakoram Range of Kashmir, and the Abkhasians in parts of the Caucasus of the Georgian Republic of the former Soviet Union. Scientists have visited each of these parts of the world, interviewed the inhabitants, and attempted to determine what they might have in common (Leaf, 1973). They found, for example, that some long-lived individuals smoked and drank rum and never bathed; others climbed up and down mountains and bathed in ice-cold streams. Some ate chicken but no pork or other fatty meats; others ate mutton and goat; still others were largely vegetarian. Most were illiterate, medical care was primitive or nonexistent, and infant mortality was high.

Unfortunately, none of this information is very valuable because scientists were unable to verify the ages of the older people in these societies. None had valid birth records, and many of the older people seemed to systematically exaggerate their ages by as many as 40 years (Hayflick, 1975).

Models of Aging

Although there is no proof that people in these cultures live longer than North Americans or western Europeans, their aging nevertheless appears to be very different. Old Abkhasians, for example, are vigorous and strong, and never completely retire. In addition, they continue to walk up and down the mountain slopes, to swim in icy streams, and sometimes to father children at remarkable ages (Benet, 1976).

Why do the Abkhasians age so well? There are two plausible reasons, says Benet. One is genetic: Those who have survived in the harshness of the mountain country may have served to select for a better genetic pool. The other is social-environmental: Among other things, the Abkhasian culture stresses the importance of physical work but sees no virtue in overexertion; the common diet consists primarily of fruit, vegetables, and meat; and it expresses different attitudes toward aging in that individuals do not retire or lose status with age.

In contrast, in the Western world, little is asked of the individual for the first 20 or so years of life; a contribution is expected during the middle 30 or 35 years; and after age 60 or 65, little more is expected. This *discontinuity* between productive and nonproductive life, is, in effect, a clear social signal that differentiates between being useful and being useless, between being culturally valued and not being valued, between being wanted and not being wanted.

It is highly revealing that in societies such as ours, like Jack Benny, we are more likely to claim we are 39 than 79 when we find ourselves somewhere in between. It is also revealing that "looking one's age" is considered negative (as in "He's sure been looking his age lately"). Many people only reluctantly allow themselves to look their age, resorting to facelifts, skin tonics, hair transplants, and the hundreds of other means that our culture defines as cosmetic improvement.

Still, many people genuinely look forward to aging. Perhaps, as the proportion of the aged continues to increase, many more will do so.

PHYSICAL CHANGES

The lifespan view of human development recognizes that change occurs at all stages. But it recognizes, too, that many, though by no means all, of the physical, social, and cognitive changes of the final stage involve decline. The technical term for this period of decline is **senescence.** Senescence can begin at very different ages for different individuals, and the losses it entails are not always dramatic or rapid. In addition, manifestations of aging are not identical for all individuals. Some results of aging are nearly universal and are sometimes referred to as **primary aging.** Loss or atrophy of brain cells is one primary change of senescence, as is gradual loss of cells from all organ systems (Booth, Weeden, & Tseng, 1994). Various forms of

Signs of aging are clear in changes in our skin as it becomes less elastic, thinner, dotted with brown splotches, wrinkled and creased—changes that can be accelerated by a lifetime of exposure to the elements.

degeneration are also part of senescence. One example is the loss of calcium in bones, leading to osteoporosis. Another is arteriosclerosis—a gradual hardening of the arteries—which begins very early in life and becomes progressively more serious, although its severity varies greatly among different individuals.

Appearance

Most of the physical changes characteristic of old age begin well back in middle age and progress slowly through the remainder of the lifespan. For example, as we saw in Chapter 13, both strength and endurance peak in early adulthood (through the twenties and sometimes early thirties), and begin to decline very slowly from that point. In the same way, height usually reaches its maximum in early adulthood and begins to decline very slowly after age 45, partly because of tendons that shrink and harden, feet that become flatter, a spinal column that shortens, and muscles that have begun to atrophy. The combined result of these changes can often be seen in the characteristically stooped posture of the very old.

Among the many changes that contribute to the appearance of age, perhaps none are more apparent than

The performance of senior athletes can exceed that of non-athletes who are 30 years younger. Exercise and training can do a great deal to maintain and even improve muscular strength and endurance, flexibility, and stamina well into late adulthood.

those that occur in the skin, on the face, and on the head. Our skins are truly marvelous things. Indeed, it is difficult to imagine a better wrapping for our bodies—totally flexible, self-regenerating and self-repairing, sensitive to heat and cold as well as to pain, highly elastic, porous yet impervious to wind and rain, and totally washable. But with age, these wrappings become thinner and far less elastic, and are often flecked with little splotches of brown pigment (popularly called "liver spots") as well as with warts, bristly hairs, and the blackish bruises of tiny leaks in blood vessels. As fatty cells die, old skin is no longer sufficiently elastic to cover the loss; it sags and droops under our arms and chins, and it creases and wrinkles. And the wrinkles of the very old are quite different from those of the middle-aged. No longer do they follow the contours of muscles that have repeatedly stretched the skin in the same way—the laugh lines on the cheek, the "crow's feet" at the corners of the eyes, and the frown lines on the forehead. The wrinkles of the very old are an almost random arrangement of tiny little creases running in all directions be-

tween larger crevices. But these are the wrinkles of the very old; there is a long space of time between the appearance of our first wrinkles and the wizening of very old age.

Other physical changes that have begun in middle age (or earlier) also continue. Hair becomes thinner or loses pigment; wear on remaining teeth (if any still remain) becomes more apparent, and gums continue to recede. Thus the caricature of the "old codger" might be either "toothless" or "long in the tooth."

The timing and the exact manifestations of these changes are sometimes very different in different individuals. Nutrition and physical activity can affect their appearance, as can genetic background.

Fitness and Exercise

When older adults were asked to throw tennis balls as hard and as well as they could, investigators found that they threw with about the same motions and velocities as 9- or 10-year-old children (Williams, Haywood, & Vansant, 1991). Clearly, with age, there is ordinarily a steady decline in flexibility, strength, stamina, and various aspects of physical performance. This decline is related not only to the gradual deterioration of muscles but also to the shortening and stiffening of tendons and ligaments, to the weakening of bones, to loss of aerobic capacity, and to loss of motor neurons (Booth et al., 1994). The important point, however, is that much of this decline does not result from primary aging processes. Hence, much of it is avoidable, and some is reversible.

In the absence of sustained training, for example, flexibility declines gradually from about age 12. But when Voorrips and colleagues (1993) tested 50 elderly women, they found that those who were more physically active had significantly greater flexibility, as well as better scores on most measures of physical performance.

Evidence of the benefits of fitness and exercise are perhaps most dramatic in the case of older athletes. Many elderly master athletes, notes Ward (1994), perform better on measures than do sedentary men who are 30 years younger—and perform enormously better than the elderly who are also sedentary. For example, many older adults cannot perform a single sit-up, or a modified push-up; yet competitors at a Seniors' Games event, which included such activities as track and field, tennis, swimming, golf, softball, and horseshoes, performed at levels far beyond expectation, often exceeding performance levels of groups 10 to 30 years younger (O'Brien & Conger, 1991). In fact, 70-year-old male athletes demonstrated higher grip strength than 60 percent of 17- to 19-year-olds. And 70-year-old women were as flexible as teenagers. The authors conclude, "Seniors who are physically active in late life are advantaged in terms of strength, muscular endurance, and joint flexibility into their years beyond age seventy" (p. 78). It is also worth noting that these athletes were remarkably positive about life: They had plans and goals for the future, and they felt useful, important, and wanted.

In addition to the benefits exercise has for physical fitness, it also has clear and significant positive effects on health. Among other things, it strengthens bones and muscles, reducing the risk of falling and breaking bones (Pendergast, Fisher, & Calkins, 1993); it improves cardiopulmonary functioning (Green & Crouse, 1993); it improves circulation and abates the risk of arteriosclerosis (Seals et al., 1994); and it may even improve functioning of the immune system (Nieman & Henson, 1994).

Health

Because of demographic changes in the industrialized world, most evident in the rapidly increasing proportion of the very old, there is tremendous interest in the consequences of aging, and especially in the burden these elderly might place on medical systems (Mosley, 1994). We noted earlier that susceptibility to diseases changes from childhood through middle adulthood. Whereas the young are more susceptible to acute infections (colds, for example), those who are older suffer more from chronic complaints (back problems, heart disease). This pattern continues into old age. In addition, whereas the old are perhaps less susceptible to acute infections, they experience greater difficulty in coping with them. Upper respiratory infections are not often fatal among children, but they sometimes are among the very old.

The most common chronic conditions in people above the age of 65 include arthritis, hypertension, hearing impairment, heart conditions, visual impairments, and arteriosclerosis. Other diseases to which the elderly are susceptible include *Parkinson's disease*, which is linked to a deficiency in the neurotransmitter dopamine and which is often characterized by coarse tremors, generalized weakness, slow movement, sleep disturbances, and sometimes depression; cancer; kidney and urinary problems; and acute brain syndrome, which may be characterized by confusion, speech disturbances, hysteria, paranoia, or other symptoms of mental disturbance, but which, to the extent that it is acute (as opposed to *chronic*, or recurring), will generally respond to treatment. *Acute brain syndrome* often results from drug overdoses, toxic drug combinations, or excessive ingestion of alcohol. The elderly are particularly susceptible to acute brain syndrome, not only because of age-related changes in the brain and nervous system but also because many elderly people take an alarming number and variety of prescription drugs.

In addition, the elderly, as we saw, are more susceptible to osteoporosis. Hence the bones of the old are more brittle than those of the young. This, combined with an approximately fourfold increase in the likelihood of falling, means that their bones are far more likely to break (Pendergast et al., 1993). And, unfortunately, they mend more slowly and with more difficulty. Finally, Alzheimer's disease, discussed next, is an important disease of old age.

There is a danger, when listing the possible ailments of the aged, that we will confound aging with disease.

Some diseases become more common with age; but they are not caused by age, and are therefore not an inevitable consequence of aging. Our focus, claims Butler (1989), should be on the extraordinary potential of the elderly.

Alzheimer's Disease

Alzheimer's disease is a brain disorder first identified by Dr. Alois Alzheimer in 1906. It occurs more in older than younger individuals, but may occur in people as young as 40 or as old as 80 or more. Estimates are that it might affect as many as 2 percent of individuals over the age of 65 and 5 percent of those over 75. Physiologically, it involves a tangling and plaquing of nerve fibers visible under microscopic examination of the brain, as well as a gradual shrinking of the brain (Wisniewski, Silverman, & Wegiel, 1994). Until recently, Alzheimer's could be conclusively diagnosed only following a neurological examination after death. Now, however, it has been discovered that those with Alzheimer's are extraordinarily sensitive to eyedrops commonly used by ophthalmologists to dilate the pupil. Whereas the pupils of normal patients typically dilate about 4 percent, those with Alzheimer's dilate at least 13 percent (Gorman, 1994).

Among the earliest symptoms of Alzheimer's is progressive loss of memory. Individuals suffering from the disorder gradually forget all sorts of information, including how to do things they have done all their lives. They can become confused and disorganized, easily lost—even in their own homes—and bewildered. Perhaps even more frightening, in the early stages of the disease (which can run over an 8- to 20-year course), they are often fully aware of what is happening to them. Eventually, they may not recognize people they have always known, and in advanced cases, they may lose all sense of their own personal identity. Affected individuals eventually revert to a speechless childishness; it is necessary to feed them, dress them, sit them on the toilet, and lead them around by the hand.

It appears that Alzheimer's may have a variety of causes, some of which may interact with each other. For example, some cases of Alzheimer's appear to be genetic and have been associated with a specific DNA mutation (Wallace, 1994). Other possibilities include viruses (perhaps contracted in childhood but inactive or ineffectual until old age); metals (higher concentrations of zinc and aluminum have been found in the brains of some Alzheimer's victims [Goudsmit, Neijmeijer-Leloux, & Swaab, 1992]); defects in brain neurotransmitter substances; and malfunctions of the immune system.

Alzheimer's remains a progressive and irreversible condition. There are several potential treatments including diet control of aluminum, attempts to reduce aluminum concentrations in victims, and the delivery of neurotransmitter substances to patients' brains by means of tiny pumps and plastic tubes that are surgically implanted. In addition, the emerging research on the genetic basis of some manifestations of Alzheimer's suggests the possibility of identifying those who are at risk, perhaps

One of the main sensory changes associated with old age is hearing loss, a problem that is more severe and more common for men than for women. The consequences of hearing loss, especially when it leads to social withdrawal, can be quite serious. Fortunately, advances in hearing-aid technology can sometimes compensate for hearing loss.

even before birth (Post, 1994)—a possibility that entails difficult ethical questions, particularly because the disease is seldom manifested until old age.

Lest this brief examination of the health consequences of aging paint too grim a picture, let me hasten to point out that although some 86 percent of the elderly suffer from one or more major conditions, the majority do not consider their health to be a very serious problem. Remarkably few are bedridden, dependent, or hospitalized.

Sensory Changes

As we saw in Chapter 15, beginning in early adulthood, there are very gradual changes in most of the sensory systems.

Vision

Virtually all individuals require at least one pair of prescription eyeglasses by the end of middle age, with men generally requiring them at younger ages than women. The most common problem is farsightedness, which is related to decreasing elasticity and thickening of the lens, and its consequent inability to focus clearly on nearby objects. The lens also becomes less transparent with age. Peripheral vision, depth perception, color vision, and adaptation to the dark also become poorer, and sensitivity to glare increases (Perlmutter, 1994). In addition, the vast majority of all people over 70 have at least the beginning of cataracts. However, most of these vision problems can

be corrected with surgery, although over half of the blind are found among the elderly. Blindness often results from glaucoma—increased pressure in the eyeball.

In spite of these potential problems, the vast majority of old people function very well with glasses.

Hearing

One of the major sensory changes associated with aging is presbycusis, the loss of hearing due to aging. This loss is often associated with changes in the inner ear, including the loss of hair cells, which are closely involved in translating vibrations into nerve impulses, and also the loss of nerve cells along auditory pathways. Symptoms of presbycusis often begin in midlife and become more serious after the age of 60. They are more common for men than for women and are most evident in decreased sensitivity to higher tones and in difficulty in discriminating among different sounds (Macrae, 1991). It is partly for this reason that older people sometimes find it very difficult to follow conversations when there is background noise (other conversations, radio or television, or children playing, for example). The desire that many older people have for quiet environments may well be related not to an aversion to noise so much as to a desire to follow normal conversation without strain.

The psychological consequences of a hearing loss can be quite serious. Elderly people whose impairment is severe enough to seriously limit the ability to understand speech may be prevented from enjoying such pastimes as playing cards, watching television, attending movies and concerts, and so on. Even more serious, hearing-impaired elders may deliberately avoid social interaction and also suffer loss of self-esteem. The result may be loneliness and depression.

The physical changes that lead to hearing loss among the elderly can sometimes be corrected simply by removing earwax, or occasionally through surgery. In other cases, they are irreversible and irremediable. However, the hearing system is only one of the components involved in communication. Fortunately, something can often be done about other components: The acoustic signal, for example, can be amplified and sometimes clarified by means of a hearing device; and the environment can be altered to eliminate background noise. Something as simple as placing furniture so that speakers must face each other can be highly helpful. And the speaker can take pains to speak loudly (without shouting), to face the listener with mouth and lips in full view and uncovered, and to enunciate clearly and distinctly.

Other Senses

Many older people frequently find that food does not taste as good as it once did. Some use far more salt, pepper, and other spices than they did when younger, because both smell and taste become less acute in old age. In fact, in one study, subjects over 65 were about 10 times less sensitive to odors than subjects between 18 and 26 (Murphy et

Society is uncertain about the sexuality of the very old, preferring to think of them as affectionate, perhaps, but essentially sexless. Yet research shows that the majority, providing they have partners, continue to be sexually active. These newlyweds are 84 and 76.

al., 1991). This diminishment is due to a combination of loss of nerve cells, changes in parts of the brain related to smell and taste, and the cumulative effects of lifestyle factors such as drinking alcohol, smoking, and perhaps eating spicy foods.

Reaction Time and Attention Span

Late adulthood comprises a substantial portion of the lifespan; it can last more than 30 years. As a result, it is highly misleading to make general statements about capacities and declines of this period as if they were common to the entire period. It is extremely important to keep in mind that the sensory losses and the physical changes that we have described thus far may be undetectable at the very beginning of late adulthood, and often occur so gradually that they are not easily noticed until very late in life—if at all.

Changes in reaction time and attention span are no different. Although it has long been established that reaction time slows significantly in late adulthood, it is not true that all elderly people are markedly slower than younger people. On the average, however, people over 65 do not react as rapidly, either physically or mentally (Botwinick, 1984). That is, they do not reach conclusions or make decisions as rapidly; nor do they respond as quickly. And evidence suggests, as well, that for some of the elderly, there is a reduction in attention span, especially when what is being attended to needs to be thought about (Perlmutter, 1994).

As we see later in this chapter, slower reaction time and attention problems are one explanation for the poorer performance of the very old on timed cognitive measures. It is also part of the explanation for their worsening per-

formance in sports that require rapid reactions (tennis, for example). And it explains in part why older people have proportionally more traffic accidents. But there are, of course, other explanations for the poorer performance of some of the elderly. These include changes in both physical functioning and sensory abilities.

Sexuality

One of the myths that we have long entertained with respect to the old is that they are essentially sexless—affectionate and emotional, perhaps, but generally devoid of either the desire or the ability for sexual expression. It bears repeating that this view *is* a myth. In one study of more than 4,000 men and women above age 50, the vast majority reported that they were sexually active. Even after the age of 70, two of every three women and four of every five men continued to be sexually active (Brecher, 1984; Figure 17.7). And the majority of women who are sexually inactive simply lack sexual partners, most often because their partners have died (Gibson, 1992).

There are, nevertheless, some differences in sexual responsiveness between the young and the old. In the female, for example, after the climacteric there is a gradual shrinking and loss of elasticity in the uterus, a thinning of the walls of the vagina, and a loss of fatty tissue and elasticity surrounding the vagina. In addition, lubrication may occur more slowly and be less plentiful. As a result, some women may experience pain and irritation during intercourse. However, these changes are much less noticeable in some women than in others. Furthermore, in most women, the clitoris remains sensitive to stimulation, so that the vast majority of women who were capable of orgasm when younger will not lose this capability.

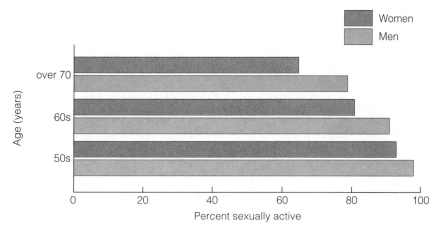

FIGURE 17.7
Change in sexual activity with age. (Based on Brecher, 1984, p. 313.)

Among men, there is a higher incidence of erectile impotence with advancing age. This condition may be related less to age than to other factors such as heart or circulatory disease, diabetes, or certain types of surgery or medication (Gibson, 1992). In addition, older men often require more time and stimulation to achieve an erection, tend to be less active sexually than younger men, and may experience less intense orgasms.

Although sexual activity, defined in terms of intercourse or orgasm, clearly declines with advancing age, there is little evidence that sexual interest does likewise. When the definition of sexual activity is broadened to include a variety of activities such as caressing and holding, it becomes clear that sexuality can continue to be important throughout the upper reaches of the lifespan. We should note, however, that sexual behavior is a highly private matter for many, and perhaps even more so for the cohorts that have thus far reached old age. In addition, among these cohorts, extramarital sexual activity has not been widely accepted. Because the majority of very old women are not married but the majority of very old men are, opportunities for sexuality in old age may be limited for many women and less so for men. Succeeding cohorts may tell a different story.

COGNITIVE CHANGES

Although the physical changes of late adulthood are extremely important, perhaps equally important for daily functioning is the individual's ability to maintain an adequate level of functioning in the cognitive resources involved in remembering, thinking, and problem solving.

Memory

We are, in effect, what we remember. To lose one's memory is also to lose one's identity. But loss of one's identity through memory loss is relatively rare, although it is sometimes the eventual outcome of Alzheimer's disease.

Less extreme losses of memory, however, may not be uncommon with age. Indeed, one of our stereotypes of old age is the belief that old people have considerable difficulty learning new things and remembering recent events. Another related belief is that old people can remember things that happened long ago better than things that happened recently. We examine the validity of some of these beliefs in the following sections.

Divisions of Memory

Remembering, as we saw in Chapter 9, may be described in terms of **short-term memory,** which is much like attention span, or **long-term memory,** which includes all our knowledge base. In addition, long-term memory consists of **declarative memory** (conscious or explicit memory), which includes **semantic memory** (stable, abstract knowledge) and **episodic memory** (autobiographical memory). Long-term memory may also be **nondeclarative memory** (nonverbalizable or implicit) (see Chapter 9 and Figure 17.8 for more clarification).

Short-Term Memory

One of the most common measures of short-term memory, also common in many intelligence tests, is the *digit-span test:* Numbers are read out at 1-second intervals and the testee tries to remember as many as possible. A 5-year-old child might recall three or four numbers; a young adult will remember about seven; a middle-aged adult will also remember seven or so. Between 60 and 80, however, there is an average loss of one or two digits. This is not a very significant decrement, and may not be especially important for cognitive functioning (Poon, 1985). In addition, it may be due to slower processing of information rather than to an actual memory impairment (Cunningham, 1989).

Nondeclarative Memory

Implicit, nonverbalizable knowledge like how to ride a bicycle or how to read and write is largely unaffected by age. Even motor skills that have not been practiced for years

FIGURE 17.8
A model of memory.

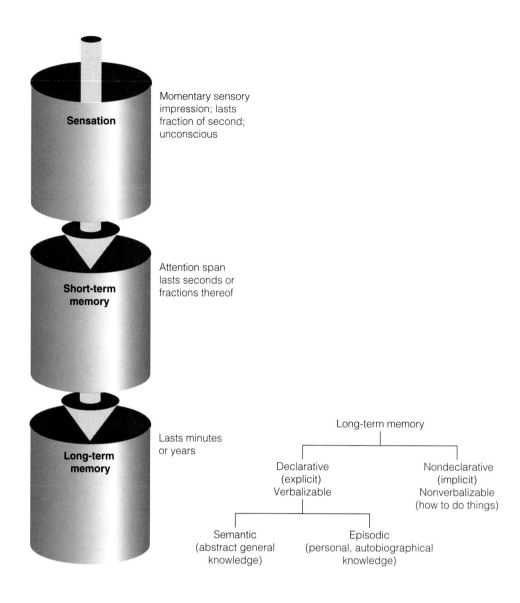

Sensation

Momentary sensory impression; lasts fraction of second; unconscious

Short-term memory

Attention span lasts seconds or fractions thereof

Long-term memory

Lasts minutes or years

Long-term memory

Declarative (explicit) Verbalizable

Nondeclarative (implicit) Nonverbalizable (how to do things)

Semantic (abstract general knowledge)

Episodic (personal, autobiographical knowledge)

are not ordinarily forgotten, even if the coordination, balance, and strength to execute them are not always available (Perlmutter, 1994).

Episodic and Semantic Memory

Semantic memory (abstract, verbalizable, general knowledge) is highly dependent on experience. Consequently, it, too, shows few age-related declines until well into old age. In fact, notes Perlmutter (1994), it can sometimes give the older person an advantage, or at least a way of compensating for slower reaction time or slower decision making.

Episodic memory (personal, autobiographical knowledge of individual experiences) is not nearly as resistant to the effects of aging. This is true for younger adults (try to remember the presents you received last Christmas, for example), and even more so for the elderly.

Some measures of long-term memory are more sensitive than others, that is, they are more likely to provide evidence of memory. For example, *recognition recall*, in which the task is simply one of recognizing, is easier than *free recall*, in which the task is one of generating a correct recollection from memory. Measures of recognition often show little decline with age, but such is not the case for free recall. In one study, Bahrick, Bahrick, and Wittlinger (1975) found virtually no changes in the ability of individuals to recognize the names and photographs of those with whom they went to high school, whether they were tested 1.3 months or almost 50 years after leaving school. During the entire span, recognition hovered around 90 percent. But when the task is changed so that individuals are asked to *recall* rather than *recognize* those with whom they went to school, the rate drops dramatically (see Interactive Figure 17.9).

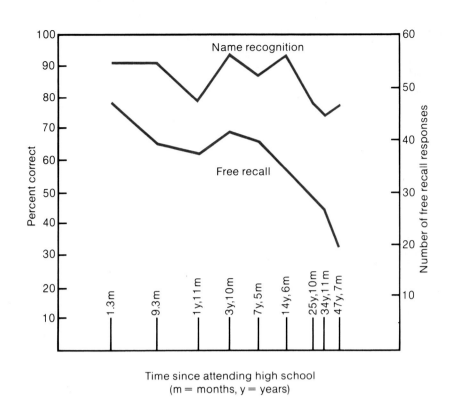

INTERACTIVE FIGURE 17.9
Free recall and name recognition as a function of age. How many of the names of your 12th-grade classmates can you recall and write down at this moment? Of your 8th-grade classmates? How many of those you have forgotten do you suppose you would recognize if you were shown a list of names that included them? The graph depicts the results of a study in which subjects who had left school between 1.3 months and 50 years earlier were asked either to recall the names of their former classmates or to recognize them from lists. (From Bahrick, Bahrick, & Wittlinger, 1975, pp. 62, 66. Reprinted by permission of The American Psychological Association and H. P. Bahrick.)

Some Conclusions

The most important conclusions warranted by the evidence are the following:

- Short-term memory is not dramatically affected by the passage of time, although attention span (short-term memory span), which is normally somewhere around seven plus or minus two items, declines at an average of perhaps one item per decade after age 60.

- Episodic memory losses are evident from early adulthood on, but become more apparent in old age; nondeclarative and semantic memory are more resistant to aging.

- There are important changes in the brain that probably underlie memory loss in old age. By age 90, the brain weighs about 10 percent less, largely because of loss of neurons (Spence, 1989). This reduction in brain mass is related to declining speed of responding in the elderly.

Note that observed memory declines are seldom very noticeable before age 70 or beyond. Furthermore, the greatest differences between older and younger subjects generally relates to *timed recall of unfamiliar material*, and may underestimate the elderly person's memory because of a tendency to respond more slowly. Not surprisingly, age differences in long-term memory are not nearly as apparent when the materials are highly meaningful and relevant to people's lives (Ratner, Padgett, & Bushey, 1988).

> ### INTERVIEW
>
> #### SUBJECT
> Male; age 75; retired schoolteacher.
>
> #### QUESTION
> "Do you notice any difference in how well you remember things now compared to, say, 20 or 30 years ago?"
>
> "No. To be quite honest, I don't really. Maybe little things once in a while but nothing really important. Everybody forgets some things no matter how old they are. I think if I've forgotten more than, say, somebody your age, it's just because I've had that much more time to forget. What I mean is the saying that your memory goes when you get older isn't right. Your memory doesn't get poorer—except maybe if you're really old. What happens is that you forget a lot of things that happened 20 or 30 years ago. And when you're 50 or 60, the same thing happens. Everybody forgets what happened a long time ago no matter what their age unless it's something important. Then you remember it no matter how old you are. That's what I think."

The general pattern of declining memory in old age is not universal; there are many older people who maintain remarkable cognitive skills throughout life. It is continuing potential we should emphasize, says Perlmutter (1988), and not deficits.

Intelligence

Maintaining a high level of cognitive resources is essential, note Poon and colleagues (1992), for successful, independent adaptation to old age. Among our important cognitive resources are memory and intelligence. Some important aspects of memory, as we saw, are not highly affected by aging. Is this also the case with other aspects of intelligence?

Decline or Stability

Research reviewed in Chapter 15 leads to several observations and conclusions:

- Cross-sectional comparisons of intellectual performance have typically found far more striking evidence of intellectual decline than longitudinal studies, which suggests that cohort (or generational) influences may be involved. To the extent that this is correct, it is likely that the next generations will show even less decline in measured intelligence.

- Longitudinal studies of changes in intelligence find little general decline in performance before age 67. For some specific abilities, there is little measurable decline prior to the ninth decade of life (Schaie, 1994).

- Intellectual abilities that are most likely to decline in old age are those that Cattell termed **fluid abilities.** Declines are most apparent in timed tasks such as code-substitution, reaction time, and inspection time in analysis of figures (Nettelbeck & Rabbitt, 1992). Functioning well on these tasks is highly dependent on intact physiological systems but relatively independent of experience. Hence, their decline may be associated with physiological changes such as loss of neurons in the brain and reduced delivery of oxygen to the brain (Spence, 1989).

- Abilities that are least likely to decline and that may, in fact, continue to improve well into old age are the **crystallized abilities.** These are highly dependent on culture and experience, and are evident in verbal and numerical skills. Thus older people sometimes do less well on the *performance* scales of the Wechsler tests; these require motor coordination, speed, dexterity, and spatial-visual abilities. In contrast, they continue to do as well and sometimes even better on the *verbal* scales of the Wechsler tests (vocabulary, information, comprehension) (Bromley, 1990). These scales deal with familiar, rather than unfamiliar, items and do not reward speed (or punish slowness) as do the performance scales.

- At very advanced ages, most measures of intellectual performance, including those of crystallized abilities, show decline. Poon and colleagues (1992) gave a series of tests to a sample of 165 people aged between 60 and 100. All of these subjects, including

the *centenarians*—the 100-year-olds—lived in private homes and were independent or semi-independent. As Figure 17.10 shows, there is decline in all areas between ages 60 and 100—except in a measure of problem solving. This measure dealt with practical questions highly relevant to day-to-day adaptation: what to do in the case of electrical failure; child-care questions; how to deal with prank telephone calls; banking questions; and so on. It is highly significant that the elderly in this sample not only maintained their practical, problem-solving abilities, but actually improved them.

In summary, there is some decline in intellectual performance with advancing age *on the average*. It must be stressed, however, that decline is not usually significant until near age 70 or beyond and that it is not universal in two senses: First, it does not affect all aspects of intellectual functioning equally; second, it does not affect all individuals equally.

IQ Fluctuations and Terminal Drop

When summarizing research of this kind, there is always the danger of mistakenly assuming that what is generally true should apply to all "normal" people. Not so. There are, in fact, 30-year-olds who experience measurable and sometimes very rapid and highly significant declines in intellectual functioning. In the same way, there are 60-, 70-, and 80-year-old people who also experience declines in intellectual functioning. Is age the cause, always and inevitably, in the case of the older people? The simple answer is no. There is evidence, for example, that intellectual decline can occur throughout the lifespan as a result of illness (Belsky, 1990). Because the elderly are more at risk of chronic illness than the young, observed differences in intellectual performance might conceivably be related to illness, or perhaps to drugs taken to counteract the illness, rather than to age itself.

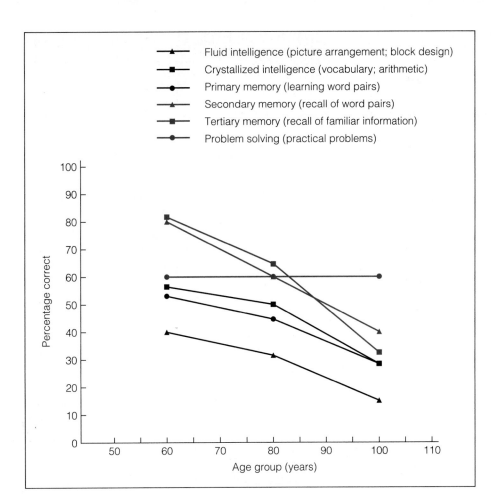

Legend:
- ▲ Fluid intelligence (picture arrangement; block design)
- ■ Crystallized intelligence (vocabulary; arithmetic)
- ● Primary memory (learning word pairs)
- ▲ Secondary memory (recall of word pairs)
- ■ Tertiary memory (recall of familiar information)
- ● Problem solving (practical problems)

One curious observation based on studies of intellectual change in old age concerns the phenomenon labeled **terminal drop,** first labeled by Kleemeier (1962) after he noticed that among subjects who died during the course of his longitudinal study, there were many whose measured intelligence started to drop sharply not long before death. Subsequently, other researchers noticed much the same thing: Many people experience a sudden drop in intellectual performance one or two years prior to dying (Riegel & Riegel, 1972). This finding has sometimes been explained in terms of a general decline in functioning that might be associated with poorer health preceding death. Thus, sudden declines in IQ scores might be an early indication of a physical change and impending illness.

Not all cognitive declines are *terminal* in the sense that they herald death (Bromley, 1990). Some may simply reflect the older person's deliberate *disengagement* from life. As Lapierre, Bouffard, and Bastin (1992/1993) discovered, the aspirations of the very old tend to be directed toward issues having to do with self-preservation; aspirations related to the outside world and to self-development are more characteristic of those not quite so old. One manifestation of this disengagement or turning inward might be a drastic reduction in motivation to do well on measures of intelligence.

Problem Finding and Intuition

Strikingly, however, as Poon and associates (1992) found, even the very old often continue to do remarkably well on measures of practical problem-solving ability. Yet, they often don't do nearly as well on more abstract problems. Why?

One possibility is that they approach problems at a more concrete, less abstract level. In the game 20 Questions, for example, adolescents and middle-aged adults typically ask general, abstract questions that allow them to eliminate large numbers of alternatives at once ("Is it alive?" "Is it vegetable?"); in contrast, the very young and the very old are more likely to ask very specific questions to test concrete hypotheses immediately ("Is it my baseball cap?" "Is it my gold star?"). In Bromley's (1990) words, "Old subjects tend to pay attention to irrelevant information, to miss or forget the point of the exercise, to let personal experience substitute for logical reasoning" (p. 198).

Mythical Thinking: Mythos

These findings do not necessarily mean that older persons are less capable of abstract and rational thought than adolescents. They might mean, instead, that older adults simply approach problems differently, and with very different motivation. As we saw in Chapter 15, the thinking of older adults may be more pragmatic and more attuned to social and economic realities. As a result, abstract questions might not seem very meaningful or important to them. Hence, when older adults are faced with abstract formal reasoning tasks, they tend to personalize them (Datan et al., 1987). Instead of applying the logico-deductive system that would lead directly to the correct solution, they rely on more personal and intuitive ways of thinking. Labouvie-Vief (1986) labels this approach **mythos** (for mythical, as opposed to *logos* for logic). Mythos is a form of thinking that is subjective, personal, and intuitive. But it is not, she insists, inferior to a formal, logical approach; it is simply different. The two types of thinking coexist, and in some adults, they reach a balance. In others, perhaps, there is an imbalance—an overreliance on intuition and pragmatics, and an underreliance on logic. It is as if the pendulum has now swung fully from the other extreme that once characterized adolescence, in which the thinker believed in the omnipotence of logic.

Competence of the Elderly

Applying the cold rules of logic in solving a game of 20 Questions or a problem in algebra reflects one kind of competence; but it's the sort of competence that may not be very relevant to the life of the very old. The competence they require is that which allows them to use phones, to understand how and when to take medication, to look after personal finances, to shop, to keep house, and to understand a television guide. And, report Willis and Schaie (1994), a remarkable percentage of the elderly are fully competent in these important areas.

Life, perhaps a little like school, is full of problems that require solutions and that demand decisions. But the problems presented to us in school are well defined and conform nicely to the methods of solution that we have been carefully taught. They have reassuringly simple answers, unique solutions that fit and that earn check marks and gold stars and smiles and hugs and pretty rainbows.

Many of life's problems are not so simple. Nobody presents them to us clearly defined; nobody teaches us the precise and appropriate methods for solving them; they have no simple, unique solutions; they tend to be long-term problems requiring long-term decisions, rather than short-term problems with immediately available solutions. Life's problems are open-ended and context-bound. Problems of human relationships, of history, of politics, of economics, cannot neatly be factored and solved. And there isn't always someone there to give us our gold stars and our hugs or to stamp neat check marks onto our life's work.

In many ways, adulthood requires a different kind of thinking—not a schoolchild's thinking, which accepts teacher-determined problems and applies prelearned strategies in an attempt to reach *the* correct solution, but thinking that is concerned more with identifying problems, with deciding which ones are in need of solution,

For many, new learning enriches the years of later adulthood. Many adult education programs specialize in high-interest courses; others are designed to be more practical and sometimes lead to second careers. This intense lady may well throw such a fine mess of pots that they will beg her to sell them at the Saturday market.

and with determining which solutions are pragmatic and ethical. Although older persons might not play the game of 20 Questions at as abstract and complex a level as the young adult, their solutions to real-life problems might be just as effective.

Learning in Adulthood

The reality of eventual decline in the performance of physical and intellectual tasks cannot be denied. However, in most cases, these declines do not significantly affect the older person's ability to adjust to changes or to cope with the demands of everyday life throughout most of late adulthood. For most individuals, learning can, and does, continue throughout the lifespan. In fact, it is possible to significantly improve the memories of older people through systematic training programs. However, as Kruse, Lindenberger, and Baltes (1993) found in a study of memory training, even with very intensive training, elderly subjects are often unable to reach the levels that younger subjects reached after only a few training sessions.

Increasingly, older people are going back to school after retirement. As a result, adult education programs are proliferating. Many of these specialize in high-interest courses, responding to the fact that many older people take courses primarily out of personal interest. For many, retirement means that they can finally do what they have wanted to do for a long time.

Wisdom is a special combination of patience, intelligence, kindness, and practical decision-making capacity more often associated with the old than with the young. It rests not so much on logic as on an ability to draw from life's lessons and to balance alternatives in the face of uncertainty. It is not a quality possessed by all the old; nor is it guaranteed by great intelligence. Thus Einstein was considered brilliant but was not often described as wise—although he well might have been. The puppet thinks so.

There are others, too, who undertake programs for more practical reasons, who see potential economic benefit from learning. For example, it is increasingly common for a retired person to take courses in order to launch a cottage industry—market gardening, hydroponics, ceramics, freelance accounting, writing, and on and on. Second careers often begin in middle adulthood, but there are some that begin in late adulthood as well.

Learning programs that are geared to the very old need to consider some of the possible differences between the old and the young. For example, the learning environment needs to be comfortable, well lighted, and free from distracting background noises. The stimuli used should consider the probability that some learners will have hearing or vision losses. Accordingly, speech should be clear, distinct, and unhurried; printed materials should be non-glossy (to reduce glare), and typefaces should be bold and high-contrast; and steps should be taken to ensure that the material presented is interesting, personally relevant, and not overly demanding. It is a social failing that our culture, unlike that of the Chinese (Ho, 1983), does not encourage

reverence for the elderly. The old can contribute a great deal to society—witness Picasso, Segovia, and George Burns. Even if they do not paint, play, act, write, or grow orchids, the elderly are perhaps much wiser.

WISDOM

Wisdom is a particular quality of human behavior and understanding that has long been associated with old age. This quality appears to combine the types of intuition, emotion, and knowledge that are not easily available to those whose experiences span only a few years. Thus it is that we believe the ancients—the old ones—to be wise.

Perlmutter (1994) defines wisdom as a combination of intellectual, emotional, and behavioral characteristics that are apparent in "exceptional knowledge and understanding of life matters, unusual judgment and communication skills, and extraordinary social sensitivity and interpersonal skill" (p. 123).

Wisdom is not a highly obvious and easily measured human characteristic, which might account for its relative absence in psychological literature. Peck (1968), in his elaboration of Erikson's theory, is one of the few developmental theorists to mention wisdom specifically as an age-related characteristic. According to Peck, as physical strength and endurance decline, one of the important developmental tasks that faces the adult is that of valuing wisdom rather than physical powers. But what, precisely, is wisdom? How does it develop? And does it truly belong only to the old?

Some Philosophical Conceptions

Psychology suggests a few tentative answers for these questions, but in the main, biblical history and ancient philosophy deal most thoroughly with wisdom. Clayton and Birren (1980) present a review of some of the important literature. Among other things, they note that although wisdom is universally acknowledged as a quality most commonly found in older persons, Eastern and Western beliefs concerning how it is most likely to be acquired differ somewhat.

In the West, there have been three paths to wisdom—all of which need to be followed if the individual is to be truly wise. The first is that of formal education, which historically emphasized the ability to make intelligent judgments and thoroughly reasoned decisions. The second path involved listening to and learning from parents or other important and influential mentors. The third path to wisdom is that of faith—in some ways a far easier path than the first two: Some individuals are simply chosen to be wise. These people are given wisdom in the same way that others are given long noses or curly hair.

Eastern conceptions concerning paths to wisdom are somewhat different. In the main, these are tied to religion,

SHYAM NARAYAM TIDORI, GURU

"When I met Shyam Narayam Tidori," writes Edward Rice (1972), "I felt for the first time in my life that I was in the presence of an ancient man. He is a guru, a spiritual guide" (p. 35).

"We are gurus," Shyam informs Rice, "that is priests and teachers, my father and his father and my brothers and I, as far back as anyone can remember." Why? Because they are Brahmins, the caste of priests, gurus by heredity. "We are the face of Brahman, the Absolute, the One Reality which is the Ground and Principle of all beings," says Shyam. He explains that his special devotion is to the Lord God Shiva, the benevolent God, an idol in the temple to which he goes morning and night. In the morning, he offers the Lord God Shiva leaves from the bel tree and pours water on the idol; in the evening, he places lighted lamps around its feet. It is part of *kharma,* part of the balance of good and evil. Life is an almost endless series of cycles of which there are more than 8 million. When a man dies, his soul simply goes into another womb. Which womb, fish, animal, bird, depends on whether his *kharma* is good or bad. And when the soul has accumulated enough good deeds, it then goes to heaven, a place that it will never want to leave. But without a guru, no man can ever hope to attain salvation, or *mukti.*

So spoke Shyam Narayam Tidori, guru. He was only 17.

To Think About Even at age 17, Shyam Narayam Tidori already had disciples, young men he had initiated into the secrets of Hinduism, men into whose ear he had whispered the secret mantra, the sacred verse that they would never, in their entire lives, reveal to anyone else.

In the Western world, we tend to think of wisdom as something achieved only by those who are intellectually gifted, who have studied

much, who have lived a long time, and who convince others by their words and behaviors that they possess some rare qualities of judgment and decision making. Can a 17-year-old, like Shyam Narayam Tidori, be truly wise?

but unlike the Western belief that having faith might be sufficient to be granted wisdom, most Asian religions require great sacrifice and dedication on the part of those who would be wise. These religions often prescribe specific behaviors and regimens, such as meditation or fasting, that must be followed by those who are disciples of wisdom. Most have in common the belief that wisdom (often referred to as *enlightenment*) requires long periods in the presence of a master teacher.

Both Western and Eastern conceptions of wisdom view it as a type of knowledge that leads to a greater understanding of reality (of life, its meaning and purpose, and so on). And if the descriptions of its development provided by East and West are accurate, it is unlikely that the young will be very wise. (See Across Cultures: "Shyam Narayam Tidori, Guru.")

Psychological Conceptions

Historical views of wisdom, notes Assmann (1994), range from a conception of wisdom as a problem-solving capacity applied to practical problems, to ill-defined notions of cosmic consciousness or religious salvation. Our implicit views of wisdom, perhaps closer to current psychological views, say four things about wisdom. Specifically, those who are wise

- know more than other people
- know things at a greater depth than others
- know things that other people can't understand
- know what is good for them and for others

Wisdom and Age

Clayton and Birren (1980) looked at how wisdom is seen by individuals of different ages and at whether it is typically associated with the elderly. They presented 21-year-olds, 49-year-olds, and 70-year-olds with 15 terms that might be considered to be related to wisdom (for example, *intuitive, pragmatic, understanding, gentle, sense of humor,* and so on). These were presented in 105 pairs, and subjects were asked to judge how similar each pair was. (For example, are *wise* and *aged* highly similar? Are *experienced* and *knowledgeable* alike?) In general, this study revealed that most subjects tend to associate wisdom with age—although older subjects were not very likely to see themselves as being wise.

Why might the old be wiser than the young? Perhaps, suggests Basseches (1984), because the old do not always apply the straightforward rules of logical, deductive thought to the solution of real-life problems. Instead, their thinking is *dialectic*. Their wisdom stems from the ability to recognize contradictions and to deal with them, from their understanding that knowledge is relative rather than absolute, that reality abounds with contradictions, and that the most effective kind of thinking is contextual—that is, it arises from the practical, real-life circumstances that surround contradictions.

Interestingly, these characteristics of dialectical thinking are very similar to Dittmann-Kohli and Baltes's (1986) description of what is involved in the ability to make wise decisions. Specifically, they suggest that wise decision making requires (1) some level of skill or expertise relevant to the problem at hand, (2) emphasis on the practical aspects of solutions, (3) a related emphasis on the problem's context, (4) a recognition of uncertainty, and (5) relativism in judgment and behavior. In other words, wisdom is a sort of marriage between knowledge and a pragmatic or practical intelligence. Dittmann-Kohli and Baltes suggest that as a result of the wisdom that older people acquire, they are better able to resolve complex interpersonal problems.

It is perhaps significant that, historically, positions of greatest responsibility requiring fundamentally important decisions are seldom entrusted to the young. With some notable exceptions, presidents, popes, emperors, and kings and queens have generally been older rather than younger. Lehman (1953) found that even in industry and commerce, the peak age for leadership was above 65. Perhaps even more significant, Dennis (1966) reports that maximum creative output in the fields of history and philosophy occurs in the sixties, seventies, and beyond. And there are countless examples of outstanding achievement in art, music, literature, and psychology by individuals well into old age.

THE IMPLICATIONS OF PHYSICAL AND COGNITIVE CHANGE

Although it might be somewhat distressing to contemplate the increasing probability of decline with age, most of us will in the end cope successfully and even happily with aging—should we be lucky enough to live that long. We are, after all, human, and part of being human is being resilient, remembering the good things, and always having hope. There is little evidence that age robs us of any of these qualities.

There are other reasons, too, why the aged might cope successfully with whatever declines and losses they experience. To begin with, changes often occur so slowly that it is often possible to adapt to them without making any major adjustments. In addition, other people of the same age also experience similar changes, and that, presumably, makes life easier. Even more dramatic and perhaps more personal changes that might initially appear to be totally devastating (knowledge of a serious health problem or death of a spouse, for example) can usually be adapted to. It is important to keep in mind that physical and cognitive decline is only one feature of the lives of the very old. Increasing wisdom and peaceful reflectiveness may be others. As the studies of life satisfaction that we review in the next chapter clearly show, happiness and joy can continue to come from many sources.

Ageism

1. The elderly are often the object of *ageism* (negative prejudices that are based solely on age), evident in media portrayals, in expected behaviors, and in child-directed speech.

Late Adulthood: Who and How Many?

2. Old age is socially defined as beginning at age 65. The proportion of people over 65 in the United States has increased fivefold in this century, while the entire population has slightly more than doubled.

Lifespan and Life Expectancy

3. Life expectancies (but not lifespans) have increased nearly 50 percent since the turn of this century. In the industrialized world, women can expect to live about eight years longer than men. Aging may be due to a combination of genetic factors (lifespan limits are programmed in cells), cell malfunctions (cell errors, toxins, free radicals, or cross-linked cells hamper normal cell functioning), or immune system defects. Longevity is related to sex, race, mobility, education, occupation, employment, locale, heredity, and other factors such as cultural expectations, attitudes toward aging, and lifestyle.

Physical Changes

4. *Senescence* describes biological decline as a function of age. Among nearly universal characteristics of aging are arteriosclerosis and increased susceptibility to cancer, arthritis, and acute brain syndrome. Visible physical changes of age include loss of skin elasticity and consequent wrinkling, loss of hair or hair pigmentation, and loss of teeth or recession of gums, and loss of strength, stamina, and flexibility, much of which can be prevented or moderated through exercise. The elderly are less susceptible to acute infections but more prone to chronic conditions (arthritis, hearing losses, heart disease, visual impairment, and arteriosclerosis), as well as to diseases like Alzheimer's (brain deterioration characterized by memory loss, disorientation, and eventual death).

5. The elderly become more farsighted, may suffer hearing loss and reduced taste and smell sensitivity, and may not react as quickly mentally or physically. Age-related changes in sexual functioning among women include diminished lubrication and loss of vaginal elasticity; in males, changes include greater time for achieving an erection and orgasm, and decline in the force of ejaculation and the intensity of orgasm. Old age brings some decline in sexual interest and activity, but in most cases, sexual activity can continue well into old age.

Cognitive Changes

6. Short-term memory is not dramatically altered by the passage of time, although its capacity may slowly diminish. Procedural (how to do things) and semantic (abstract knowledge) memory are quite resilient; episodic (autobiographical) memory suffers. Declines are most apparent under timed conditions with nonmeaningful material.

7. Age differences in intellectual performance in cross-sectional studies reflect cohort differences (for example, those related to education). Longitudinal studies find little general decline before age 67, with most of the decline in fluid abilities (attention span, speeded abstract tasks); crystallized abilities (dependent on experience) sometimes continue to increase in old age. Declines on measures of intelligence might reflect problems of performance rather than lack of competence. Just prior to dying, measured IQ sometimes drops (*terminal drop*), perhaps because of health problems or *disengagement*.

8. Older adults often do not do as well as younger individuals on tasks requiring abstract reasoning. Labouvie-Vief describes the thinking of older adults as more intuitive and more personal (*mythos*) rather than formal and logical (*logos*). Adult learning is a fast-growing field of education that reflects well the capabilities, interests, and enthusiasm of many older people.

Wisdom

9. Wisdom is one of the positive qualities we typically associate with old age. The characteristics of dialectical thinking (openness to contradiction, recognition of the relative nature of knowledge, emphasis on context and pragmatics, acceptance of uncertainty) are closely related to what psychologists think of as wise decision making.

The Implications of Physical and Cognitive Change

10. Elderly adults, on average, adjust well to aging. The majority continue to experience joy and happiness in their lives.

FOCUS QUESTIONS: APPLICATIONS

1. What is ageism? How does it affect the elderly?

- How many examples of ageism can you find in a single issue of your local newspaper?

2. How are lifespan and life expectancy different? Can either be changed?

- Write out a series of recommendations that might increase life expectancy. Among these recommendations for increased *quantity* of life, are there some whose cost might be too high in terms of reduced *quality* of life?

3. What are some of the most common physical changes in late adulthood?

- Summarize some of the apparent benefits of exercise in late adulthood.

4. What are some of the most common intellectual changes in late adulthood?

- Prepare a series of research-based arguments to support (refute) the proposition that there is significant intellectual decline in late adulthood.

acute brain syndrome   504

ageism   494

Alzheimer's disease   504

autoimmunity   500

cell error theory   499

centenarians   510

cross-linking theory   500

crystallized abilities   510

declarative memory   507

episodic memory   507

fluid abilities   510

free recall   508

free-radical theory   500

genetic theory of aging   498

life expectancy   498

lifespans   498

long-term memory   507

mythos   512

nondeclarative memory   507

Parkinson's disease   504

primary aging   502

recognition recall   508

semantic memory   507

senescence   502

short-term memory   507

terminal drop   511

toxin theory of cell malfunction   499

wisdom   513

A far more complete account of aging than can be contained in a single chapter may be found in the following book:

Belsky, J. K. (1990). *The psychology of aging* (2d ed.). Pacific Grove, CA: Brooks/Cole.

Those interested in the problems facing elderly women and adjustments sometimes required of them might consult the following highly readable collection of chapters:

Rosenthal, E. R. (Ed.). (1990). *Women, aging, and ageism.* New York: Harrington Park Press.

The following two collections are especially valuable sources of recent thinking in a variety of areas touched on in this chapter:

Magnusson, D., & Casaer, P. (Eds.). *Longitudinal research on individual development: Present status and future perspectives.* Cambridge: Cambridge University Press.

Featherman, D. L., Lerner, R. M., & Perlmutter, M. (Eds.) (1992). *Life-span development and behavior* (Vol. 12). Hillsdale, NJ: Erlbaum.

The following is a straightforward description of the physiological changes in sexual interest and functioning that occur among the elderly, and a candid look at their sexual lives. It is especially valuable for those who counsel the elderly:

Gibson, H. B. (1992). *The emotional and sexual lives of older people: A manual for professionals.* New York: Chapman and Hall.

SOCIAL DEVELOPMENT:
LATE ADULTHOOD

*O*ld age is no such uncomfortable thing if one gives oneself up to it with a good grace, and don't drag it about "To midnight dances and the public show."

HORACE WALPOLE
Letter

"There's two kinds of old folks," says my grand-mother, as she hoists another sack of potatoes up onto her shoulder. "There's those who don't much like to sit still as long as they got the strength, God willing, and they'll keep doing their share and more." She trudges through the garden toward the house, her feet sinking into the sandy brown dirt, leaving indistinct prints between the rows. When she reaches the back of the house, she dumps the potatoes emphatically down the chute.

CHAPTER 18

"So what if they want to go dancing once in a while?" she asks, almost angry. It's me she's asking, but it's not me she wants an answer from, because I'm not the one who said anything. It's my mother who said, sort of as a joke I thought, "You're pretty old to go to dances, don't you think?"

"The other kind," my grandmother continues just a little scornfully, shaking the dust out of the empty potato sack, "is like Old Man Boutin who'd just as soon eat and sleep, and rock on the porch a little if the weather's warm and there's no mosquitos." She slings the empty sack over her shoulder and heads back out across the garden, toward where my mother's digging the big, red-skinned Norlands out of the ground.

"Me," says my grandmother in a voice so there's no doubt everybody hears her, "my only rocking's gonna be on the freakin' dance floor."

THIS CHAPTER

For many, old age is a time of withdrawal and rocking chairs; for others, "midnight dances and the public show" are more appealing, and digging potatoes is sort of fun just because you can, by gosh, still do it.

Is one preferable to the other? Does one imply more successful aging? These are two of the questions this chapter addresses. It also looks at the *life review*, the process of examining and evaluating the course of one's life and of coming to terms with the future. It examines, as well, the impact of retirement from work, the continued development of important relationships with others, and alternative living arrangements for the elderly. It concludes with a discussion of satisfaction and happiness.

VIEWS OF DEVELOPMENT IN LATE ADULTHOOD

One of the alternatives to satisfaction and happiness is despair, the possibility of which looms ever larger with the progressive shortening of our spans.

Integrity Versus Despair: Erikson

The fundamental conflict between despair and a sense of integrity, a conviction that life has been useful and worthwhile, is the essence of Erikson's final stage of the life cycle: *integrity versus despair*. What the elderly need to do, says Erikson, is integrate the experiences of a lifetime, make sense of them, and achieve a feeling of acceptance and contentment. The alternative to a sense of integrity is despair. Feelings of integrity and satisfaction result from a positive evaluation of one's life and an acceptance of its final outcome as natural and inevitable, note Botella and Feixas (1992/1993); in contrast, despair is characterized by regret over the past, by the frustration that accompanies the realization that it is now too late to do anything further, and by fear of aging. As we saw, fear of aging, which can be tapped by various scales (see Lasher & Faulkender, 1993), is not uncommon even among young adults.

Erikson, now more than 80 years old and still active, speaks of two new insights regarding the upper end of the lifespan. The first is his realization that the elderly are far more creative, far more *generative*, than he had thought; the second is the recognition that increased life expectancy may require a reexamination of the entire lifespan, but especially of the upper end of the lifespan (Erikson, Erikson, & Kivnick, 1986).

Peck's Elaboration of Erikson

As we saw in Chapter 16, Peck (1968) believed that Erikson's description of psychosocial conflicts in adulthood did not do justice to the variety of important events that can occur during this period. Accordingly, he describes three stages that span late adulthood. He believes that successful resolution of the conflicts that characterize each is important for adjustment and happiness in old age.

Ego Differentiation Versus Work-Role Preoccupation
According to our current models, development does not end with middle age but continues well into old age. With retirement, for example, it often becomes necessary to develop new interests—to shift one's preoccupations from work and career to other aspects of living. And as children leave home, the concerns of parenting must be abandoned, but they need to be replaced if the individual is to maintain a sense of integrity and worth.

Body Transcendence Versus Body Preoccupation
One of the prices we sometimes pay for our longer lives is a longer period during which we suffer aches, pains, and disabilities of greater or lesser severity. As these become more evident, there is a tendency to become preoccupied with affairs of the body. Resolution of the resulting psychosocial conflict requires that the individual's preoccupations transcend the flesh.

Ego Transcendence Versus Ego Preoccupation
In the same way as the aging individual must transcend preoccupation with bodily aches and pains, so there is a need to transcend a concomitant preoccupation with the inevitability of death. Those who fear death unduly must also fear life, for one is surely the price we pay for the other.

Fisher's Five Periods of Older Adulthood

To obtain greater insights into the experience of older adulthood, Fisher (1993) conducted detailed interviews with 74 people aged 60 or more. Analysis of information from these interviews suggests it might be useful to describe the upper lifespan in terms of five distinct periods.

1. Continuity with Middle Age
For many of Fisher's interviewees, old age and retirement don't bring very sudden or dramatic changes in attitudes, but are marked, instead, by a continuation of many of the preoccupations and behaviors of middle age. This continuity, notes Fisher, may be apparent in that leisure activities (traveling, playing golf, fishing) are now substituted for work activities, and everything else carries on much as it was. It may also be apparent in that the material problems (saving for a trip, buying a new car, paying the rent) and other preoccupations of life continue relatively unchanged for a period of time.

2. Early Transition
Often, however, some major event, either voluntary or involuntary, eventually precipitates a transition. Most common among Fisher's interviewees were things like the death of a spouse, an important change in health, or the need to relocate. For example, for many people, moving

TABLE 18.1
Fisher's Five Periods of Older Adulthood

Period	Characteristics
1. Continuity with middle age	Retirement plans pursued
	Middle-age lifestyle continued
	Other activities substituted for work
2. Early transition	Involuntary transitional events
	Voluntary transitional events
	End of continuity with middle age
3. Revised lifestyle	Adaptation to changes of early transition
	Stable lifestyle appropriate to older adulthood
	Socialization realized through age-group affiliations
4. Later transition	Loss of health and mobility
	Need for assistance and/or care
	Loss of autonomy
5. Final period	Adaptation to changes of later transition
	Stable lifestyle appropriate to level of dependency
	Sense of finitude, mortality

SOURCE: Based on Fisher, 1993, p. 81.

5. Final Period

With the fourth period's loss of health, independence, or mobility, and the increased need for assistance, there is a need for new adjustments, and a need to develop new goals and activities consistent with the individual's capabilities and interests. With these adjustments, there is a new period of stability. And for many in Fisher's sample, this was a time of new challenges, new interests, and new growth. It is also a time during which the inevitability of death and decline forces a recognition of mortality and leads to a new sense of resignation and acceptance.

Although these five periods, which are summarized in Table 18.1, are sequential, they are clearly tied to major life events rather than to age. Thus those who continue to be healthy, independent, and active into their eighties and nineties might retain a continuity with middle age far longer than others, and might never be forced to revise their lifestyles in the way that others who suffer serious health losses do. For some in Fisher's sample, for example, continuity with middle age extended into the seventies; in contrast, others in their early seventies were already well into the final period.

THE LIFE REVIEW

Resolving the various psychosocial conflicts of old age that Erikson and Peck describe, or adjusting to the transitions of which Fisher speaks, requires less the development of new competencies or new social skills than changes in attitudes. And one of the most important tools in bringing about these changes is what Butler (1963) labels a **life review.**

Personal Narratives

"We tell ourselves stories in order to live," Didion (1979, p. 11) informs us. These stories, called **personal narratives,** are stories about our own lives. They result from our attempts to weave the different events of our lives into a single meaningful, sensible story. This story integrates past and present events, and includes a vision of the future. According to McAdams (1984), its principal character is the self and its main themes are love and power.

One of the functions of these personal narratives, claims Cohler (1982), is to provide us with a sense of stability and consistency—a feeling of continuity that spans the course of our lives. In a sense, it is as though we tell ourselves stories of our lives, giving them beginning, middle, and end, providing them with an orderliness and predictability that real life usually lacks. Through these stories, we come to understand *our* selves in relation to *other* selves (Taylor, 1989).

But we do not simply construct the story of our lives, as though it were ours to invent. Instead, we recall important episodes, we reminisce about them, perhaps we review and evaluate them. These processes, according to a

from a house to an apartment following retirement is the first step in a major early transition. Early transitions mark a definite break with middle age, notes Fisher, and are often accompanied by a sense of loss and sadness.

3. Revised Lifestyle

The early transitions of the second period require major readjustments, and often result in a revision of the person's lifestyle. If, for example, period 2 transitions were precipitated by the death of a spouse with whom the person previously traveled, traveling might now involve organized tours with like-aged people. If the transition were precipitated by ill health, there might be important changes in the person's leisure activities.

For many, adaptations during this period are highly positive; for others, less so. The end result is typically a relatively stable lifestyle, sometimes marked by highly predictable, effective, and satisfying routines.

4. Later Transition

In Fisher's sample of 74 elderly individuals, later transitions of old age are tied mainly to health losses, often accompanied by loss of mobility and sometimes loss of some independence as well. Understandably, few individuals expect the precipitating event and deliberately prepare for it. That is, the elderly who are financially independent typically don't move into retirement communities or into children's or other relatives' homes until illness and inability to live independently force them to.

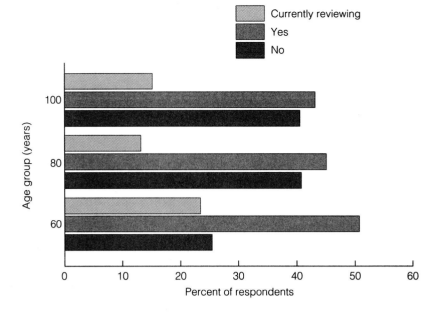

FIGURE 18.1
*Percentage of 60-, 80-, and 100-year-olds
who have conducted a life review. (Based on
Merriam, 1993, p. 170.)*

Currently reviewing
Yes
No

growing number of theorists, are extremely important at
all stages of the lifespan, but especially in later adulthood
when the personal narrative often takes the form of a *life
review.*

Personal Narratives of the Elderly

The personal narratives that the elderly construct often
take the form of an ongoing review and evaluation of their
lives. They involve more reminiscing and more nostalgia
than might a story constructed by a younger person. And,
not surprisingly, they may not reach as far into the future.

There is an important difference between reminiscence and the life review. *Reminiscence* is a passive activity,
made up largely of daydreams and odd tidbits of nostalgic
memories. The old, we are told, are more prone to reminiscing than are the young (Berman, 1992/1993). The *life
review,* in contrast, is more active, more dynamic. It, too,
is based on the past, but it requires more than simple recall and idle enjoyment of scattered memories; it demands
a concerted attempt to analyze and evaluate past experiences. And one of its important features is that it brings to
mind unresolved conflicts. A principal purpose of the life
review is to resolve these conflicts or to arrive at some acceptance of them.

Life Review Through the Lifespan

Life reviews can occur throughout the lifespan, note
Webster and Young (1988). They are most likely to be
triggered by specific crises and events in one's life—for
example, the death of a spouse, the loss of employment, or
a life-threatening illness. Accordingly, most major transitions in life (such as those described by Levinson and
Sheehy) might trigger a life review. Reviewing the past,
Webster and Young argue, provides the substance and the
motivation for making changes in the present and ultimately exercising some control over the future.

In late adulthood, conducting a life review is a highly
positive event, contrary to the notion that reminiscing and
daydreaming by the old might be a sign of withdrawal and
might be unhealthy. Haight (1991) reviewed 97 studies of
reminiscing published between 1960 and 1990. Of these,
only seven reported that reminiscing might be associated
with negative outcomes. Similarly, Fry (1991) found that
reminiscing among the old is essentially a pleasant and
positive activity associated more with a sense of psychological well-being than with negative feelings such as frustration, despair, regret, or loneliness.

With advancing age, the life review becomes more urgent and more universal—perhaps because of the person's
need to achieve a sense of meaningfulness and integrity.
This feeling of integrity, and a concomitant conquering of
despair, result from a positive evaluation of the past—as
well as the future. This doesn't mean, however, that all
adults engage in a life-review process. Merriam studied
centenarians, 80-year-olds, and 60-year-olds. Although the
number of individuals who had engaged in a life review increased after age 60, more than half claimed not to have
done so. The sample of 289 is admittedly somewhat biased, however, in that all of these individuals had to be relatively independent (cognitively intact and community
dwelling). To the extent that a life review is often precipitated by some important life change, individuals who have
lost some degree of independence may be more likely to
have conducted a life review (see Figure 18.1).

Satisfaction and the Life Review

It is worth emphasizing that the life review is not characteristically negative. Nor does the fact that many older
people engage in reminiscing and reviewing their lives
mean that they are invariably turned inward and toward
the past. In fact, many do not reminisce any more than

The life review is common among the old. It takes the form of reminiscing about past experiences, evaluating earlier deeds and misdeeds, and resolving or simply accepting old conflicts. The life review is essentially a positive process associated more with a sense of psychological well-being than with despair, frustration, or regret. Nor does it consume all that much time; there is usually more than enough for sitting on the bench and staring at the photographers.

younger adults, and many are remarkably future oriented. For example, among O'Brien and Conger's (1991) sample of senior athletes, 73 percent of the women and 80 percent of the men claimed that they were indeed very much looking forward to the future. The most common themes among the things to which they looked forward included continuing relationships with family and friends, and doing or seeing new things. Many of them had clear future goals. For men, these often included sports and competition, physical fitness, and traveling and adventuring. For women, hobbies, volunteer work, physical activity, and traveling were all part of future plans.

One of the important features of a life review is evaluation of the rightness of past behaviors, of moral and ethical issues, of the advisability or inadvisability of certain decisions in terms of their implications for the lives of others as well as for the self. Often, as Coleman (1986) notes, behaviors that might have seemed traumatic, immoral, or inadvisable in the context in which they occurred, will, in the present context, seem trivial. Thus, the life review gives the older person an opportunity to reevaluate incidents that might have been a source of guilt and unhappiness; the result might be the elimination of guilt and the restoration of a measure of happiness. And contrary to what we might think, there is little about their past lives that most older adults would change. When DeGenova

(1992) asked 122 retired persons what they would do differently if they had their lives to lead over again, the one area in which the largest number of people would have made changes was in education. Men would have spent more time pursuing education, often for career reasons; and women would have spent more time improving their intellects, often for personal reasons. On the whole, however, most of the elderly are happy with their choices—although not all retire gladly from work.

RETIREMENT

Retirement is a 20th-century phenomenon, a luxury made possible by a rapidly increasing standard of living, extraordinarily high productivity, and a relatively large surplus of labor. It was not always this way. Before this century, **retirement,** most often defined in terms of leaving full-time work and receiving a pension, was almost unknown. Although people might have stopped working when they were too old or not well enough to continue, there were no pensions (Ransom, Sutch, & Williamson, 1993). Significantly, the number of people below poverty level in the United States is now about half of what it was in 1970 (14.5 percent in 1991; 24.6 percent in 1970), and has remained relatively constant since 1980 (U.S. Bureau of the

FIGURE 18.2
Percentage of people below the poverty line in the United States. (Based on U.S. Bureau of the Census, 1994, p. 476.)

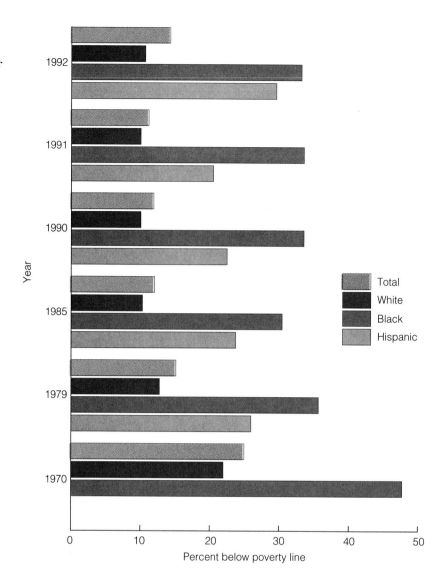

Census, 1994; Figure 18.2). However, poverty levels among blacks and Hispanics remain very high.

Our prevailing attitude is now that retirement is everybody's right—that it is not a luxury that should be available only to the select few, but that it is society's duty to look after all who have worked long enough. We earn our pensions and, by gar, we deserve them!

The Future

The next century might bring changes again. For example, there are current signs of changing employment patterns where redundancy or economics force "early" retirement (Coleman, 1992). In addition, dramatically declining birthrates, coupled with the fact that the population bulge associated with the last of the big baby booms is rapidly approaching retirement age, mean that ultimately there will be fewer workers and far more retirees—hence fewer people to produce the goods and pay the taxes that maintain complex Western societies. This, along with a third crucial factor, inflation, may bring our

dream of the easy and well-fed retirement to its knees. Consider, for example, that if the annual inflation rate were 12 percent, the purchasing power of an unindexed pension would be reduced by approximately 90 percent in a mere 20 years. At lower inflation rates, it simply takes longer. And when pensions are indexed (adjusted yearly according to increases in the cost of living), the amount of money required to maintain them simply increases at the same rate as the purchasing power would otherwise have decreased. The effects of inflation on retired individuals are compounded by the fact that, at retirement, average income drops significantly (Figure 18.3).

Attitudes Toward and Effects of Retirement

Atchley's (1989) investigations of retirement suggest that people generally have positive attitudes toward retiring, particularly if they have looked forward to it, have planned it, and expect to have adequate income. Apparently, the higher the person's expected retirement income, the more

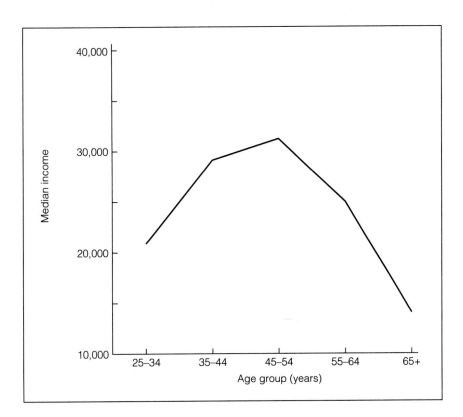

FIGURE 18.3
Median U.S. income, 1992, for different age groups. (Based on U.S. Bureau of the Census, 1994, p. 473.)

likely that retirement will be viewed positively. Similarly, people with higher levels of education often look forward to retiring. Negative attitudes toward retirement are most common among those who are forced to retire but who would prefer to continue working (Laczko, 1989).

Attitude toward retirement is an important predictor of later satisfaction; so is social support. Robbins, Lee, and Han (1994) report that those whose social networks are most supportive of retirement are more likely to experience high quality of leisure time and more life satisfaction. Nevertheless, as many as one third of all retirees experience some difficulty in making the postwork transition (Jensen-Scott, 1993). In an in-depth study of 17 new retirees, Theriault (1994) found that retirement led to significant increases in measures of anxiety.

In spite of this, and contrary to earlier findings and speculation, the overall effect of retirement on happiness and health is positive. Kelly and Westcott's (1991) case studies of 25 recent retirees found the vast majority of these "ordinary" retirees to be happy in their retirement. "On the whole," they write, "retirement is now going as well or better than expected" (p. 84). Retirees especially enjoy their sense of freedom, and the time to do what they want.

Atchley (1989) found that retirement is most likely to be a positive experience under four sets of circumstances: (1) retirement is voluntary rather than forced; (2) work is not the only or even the most important thing for the individual; (3) both health and income are adequate to permit the enjoyment of increased leisure; and (4) the retirement has been prepared for and planned.

TABLE 18.2

Atchley's Phases of Retirement*

Phase	My Cousin Luke's Response
Preretirement	"It's gonna be great living out there on the coast, fishing, visiting the kids, playing . . ."
Honeymoon	"Let's go, Elizabeth! We never had time to see much and now we're gonna cruise right around the old ball. Just got to get me my check cashed. Love it!"
Rest and relaxation	"No meetings for me, no canvasing, no causes. Nosiree, Elizabeth, I'm bloody retired and I'm just gonna put my feet up there next to yours."
Disenchantment	"Sure I think your camp cooking is as good as your mother's was, Elizabeth. But the fishing isn't what it used to be."
Reorientation	"Hey, they've got an opening for a night watchman out there at the underwear factory."
Routine	"What's today? Monday? We always get our groceries Monday."
Termination	"Enough of this being retired and independent guff, Lizzie. Let's go terrorize our kids."

* These are not always sequential, nor are they universal. Only a small number go through the disenchantment and reorientation phases. Many go directly from the honeymoon to the retirement routine.

Phases of Retirement

Atchley (1982, 1985) describes retirement in terms of seven sequential phases, several of which appear to be optional—that is, experienced by some but not all retirees (see Table 18.2). Although these phases are sequential, they cannot, of course, be tied to chronological ages, not only because retirement occurs at different ages for different individuals but also because some will spend more time than others in a given phase. What Atchley's seven phases represent, in effect, are the various processes involved in taking on the role of the retired person, carrying it out, and eventually giving it up. They emphasize strongly that retirement is a *process* rather than a final state.

Preretirement

Prior to retirement, the individual begins to consider its occurrence and to prepare for it. As the time of retirement approaches, more time and energy are devoted to elaborating sequences of fantasies about what life will be like after work. People who worry about retirement at this stage are usually concerned more with health and income than with the prospect of abandoning work.

Honeymoon

For the first period following retirement, many individuals go through a period of intense and usually joyful activity. As Long (1989) notes, retirement is not just the end of paid employment and a time to grow old; rather, it is a time for new leisure pursuits. This is the time when retirees do all those things they never had time to do. Many go through this period with newfound vigor and zest. But like most honeymoons, this one seldom lasts forever. Money, time, energy—all may eventually run out. In addition, as Gibson (1992) points out, married couples often experience new problems following retirement. Some of these may relate to the new roles that each might have to develop with respect to home-related tasks, increased contact, and perhaps uncertainty about how to deal with each other during this transitional period.

Rest and Relaxation

When the honeymoon is over, it's time to settle down. Atchley (1982) observed that many people go through a period of low activity following retirement. This period is usually temporary and is often followed by a return to higher levels of activity. In this context, activity includes participation in religious and political organizations, community involvements, hobbies, volunteer work, recreational activities, exercise, and so on. For the retirees studied by Kelly and Westcott (1991), family-related activities were highly common. The general picture, claim Kelly and Westcott, is one of continuity—doing the kinds of things that were done before retirement.

Disenchantment

Among the retirement phases not experienced by the majority of retirees, but still common enough to merit attention, is a period of disenchantment that sometimes follows the honeymoon and settling-down phases. Disenchantment is most common among those who fantasized most unrealistically about what retirement would be like and

who were subsequently most disappointed. In addition, poor health or loss of a spouse are the most common causes of dissatisfaction in retirement among those who have adequate income (Richardson & Kilty, 1991).

Reorientation

When disenchantment occurs, its resolution generally requires a phase of reorientation, during which the person reexamines life, explores available options, and begins to develop new commitments. Some individuals reorient themselves by going back to work, where that is possible. Others embark on entirely new careers. Eisler (1984) argues that new careers (or the resumption of old ones) for the retired and elderly are important for maintaining their independence and sense of worth. He cautions that we have largely ignored careers in old age because of the tendency to view all people over the age of 65 as retired and no longer involved in careers. In fact, however, in many cases retirement is an artifact of the places we work. Self-employed individuals, while they may not be rewarded with gold watches and pensions at the age of 60 or 65, might well continue to work with much of the same commitment and dedication, and perhaps more wisdom and grace, than they did when younger.

Routine

Routines involve predictable, orderly ways of doing things. Many older adults seem to develop an increasing need for routines; many also come to dislike disruptions of routine (Reich & Zautra, 1991). Accordingly, one of the eventual characteristics of most happy retirements is the establishment of routines. This does not mean that the retired life does not allow for change or for excitement, but it does indicate that it tends to be stable rather than unpredictable. Atchley (1985) reports that many individuals go directly to this phase from the honeymoon phase. For these individuals, there is no brief period of rest sandwiched between periods of higher activity, no disenchantment requiring reorientation. Instead, the transition from preretirement to the stable and generally satisfying routines of retirement is smooth.

Termination

The retirement role, as described by Atchley, does not invariably continue through the remainder of the lifespan but is sometimes interrupted by illness and perhaps by eventual loss of independence. In these cases, the individual takes on different, more dependent, roles (those of the sick or disabled, for example).

These phases should be viewed as broad descriptions of very general patterns through retirement. They provide a useful way of looking at retirement as an active and ongoing process that requires a series of new adjustments and that, like all adjustments, can have happy or less happy outcomes.

Successful Aging

Day (1991) summarizes a large number of studies that have looked at human aging and that have tried to define what is meant by "successful" aging. She identifies three different groups of variables that these studies have looked at: developmental (such as those described by Erikson, like wisdom and generativity), psychological (like optimism and satisfaction), and environmental (like longevity and continued independence).

In its simplest sense, to age successfully is to age in relative contentment and happiness. That must surely be an almost universal goal. And to age unsuccessfully might be to age in misery and despair—and perhaps alone and in poverty as well. As our sensationalist media often remind us, some of the elderly struggle desperately for survival on meager incomes. And a few do eat foods that the more affluent feed their pets, and do sometimes freeze in unheated dwellings. Fortunately, however, poverty afflicts only a minority. But that this minority even exists is a sad reflection on our humanity.

Attempts to understand and explain the lives and the activities of those who appear to age successfully have led to two somewhat different points of view concerning the most likely course for the aged: **disengagement theory** and **activity theory.**

Disengagement Theory

Disengagement theory is based on the notion that as people age, they progressively *disengage*, withdrawing from social, physical, and emotional interaction with the world. And while this process is largely voluntary, it is also two-sided. Not only does the aging person gradually give up active social roles and narrow the sphere of emotional commitment, but society begins to withdraw its engagement with the aging person. This happens in several ways, the most obvious relating to the ways in which society often encourages—or even legislates—retirement from work and sometimes from other commitments as well.

One of the basic premises of disengagement theory is that withdrawal is not only natural but desirable. The predominant argument is that with declining physical and mental powers, the elderly find it increasingly difficult to continue to engage successfully in work-related activities, as well as in social, emotional, or political involvements. Consequently, they look forward to withdrawing and experience greater satisfaction and happiness if they are permitted to do so. Disengagement, notes Manning (1993), is one of the ways in which the elderly learn to cope with age-related loss.

Much of the research that has looked at disengagement theory has found that disengagement is often an accurate description of what happens in old age. However, disengagement is not often descriptive of the entire period of old age, but usually of the later years (Fry, 1992).

And it often involves less disengagement than strict interpretation of the theory might indicate. That is, although most individuals will have withdrawn from work and from many other involvements by the time they are 75 or 80, few will have completely withdrawn from important emotional commitments. Many will continue to fulfill crucial social roles as wives and husbands; some will be actively engaged in productive activities, such as looking after grandchildren or raising geraniums and chickens and growing potatoes; and many will be active in religious, political, and community organizations. We should note, too, that societies that do not have marked discontinuities between adulthood and old age do *not* require or encourage disengagement.

Activity Theory

In fact, these societies encourage continued involvement and activity in all areas; as such, they exemplify *activity theory*, which is, in some important ways, the opposite of disengagement theory. Although it recognizes that a great deal of social and psychological disengagement does occur among older people, activity theory stresses that life satisfaction is highly dependent upon continued active involvement. According to this theory, those who age "best" are those who maintain the highest level of social, emotional, and physical involvement.

Among the variety of studies that have attempted to evaluate these opposing points of view, the majority indicate that continued involvement is often associated with satisfaction in later life. Stevens (1993), for example, questioned 108 older adults and found that continued involvement with the family and with significant others, as well as involvement in the community, produced a sense of usefulness that was highly correlated with satisfaction in later life. Similarly, Myers (1993) reports that the social breakdown and negative adjustment of many older people, especially in institutions, can often be halted and perhaps reversed by *empowering* the elderly—that is, by giving them control over their own lives, by keeping them physically and psychologically well, and by changing attitudes of caregivers who tend to view them as helpless and powerless.

Disengagement or Activity?

In conclusion, some degree of disengagement is usually characteristic of aging. At the same time, however, there is considerable evidence that continued involvement might contribute significantly to satisfaction, happiness, and health—witness the remarkable optimism and future orientation of O'Brien and Conger's (1991) sample of senior athletes. In fact, it isn't as though the elderly must make a choice between full disengagement or full activity. As Fry (1992) points out, disengagement occurs at various levels. Thus, some may disengage *socially* as a means of finding time for contemplation and personal growth.

Some of the elderly disengage from social, emotional, and political involvement. Others, like this Delaware grandmother who still cares to tell of the magic of the symbols, remain actively engaged—and perhaps happier.

Others may also turn inward to contemplate and review their lives, but without disengaging the least bit socially. And, of course, the vast majority will eventually disengage economically, but not necessarily socially, or in terms of their interest in and concern about the larger community.

There are some, like my grandmother, who crave involvement, responsibility, and activity; and there are others, like Old Man Boutin, who prefer the contentment of solitary rocking chairs.

SOCIAL RELATIONSHIPS IN LATE ADULTHOOD

It is important to stress once more that the age span with which we deal in this chapter stretches across many years and is marked by tremendous variation in abilities, interests, activities, and family relationships. Any generalizations that we might make must always be tempered by the awareness that the average older adult, to whom our generalizations are meant to apply, is probably even scarcer than the average child. The life circumstances of older adults vary tremendously from one individual to another. In addition, these circumstances often change, sometimes dramatically, from the beginning to the end of this possibly lengthy period. As a result, the combination of family relationships, living arrangements, financial strength, health, and involvement of an older person might be quite unique to that person.

Still, we cannot say very much about unique individuals in a text such as this; we can only speak generally. (See Table 18.3 for a general description of developmental tasks of late adulthood.)

TABLE 18.3
Havighurst's Developmental Tasks in Late Adulthood

1. Adjusting to physical changes
2. Adjusting to retirement and to changes in income
3. Establishing satisfactory living arrangements
4. Learning to live with spouse in retirement
5. Adjusting to death of spouse
6. Forming affiliations with aging peers
7. Adopting flexible social roles

Common sense and research both agree that, in general, family relationships are usually the most important of all social relationships throughout the entire lifespan; they continue to be tremendously important to the very end.

Relationships with Children

Following a survey of 432 retired married couples, Warnes (1985) reports that one of the clearest findings is that, other than for their own marital relationship, the most important social relationships for the vast majority of these couples are with their children. This survey, which looked at how geographical distances separating older parents from their children affect parent–child relationships, found that about one in five parents would have liked to live closer to their children. Being closer would have made visiting easier and perhaps more frequent (see At a Glance: "Contact Between Elderly Parents and Their Children," and Figure 18.4).

CONTACT BETWEEN ELDERLY
PARENTS AND THEIR CHILDREN

The most important relationships for most older people, other than for those they might have with a spouse, are those with their children. In the United States, more than half of those age 65 or older live within a half hour of their children; almost half see or talk to their children every day. As they age, elderly parents tend to move *closer* to, rather than farther from, their children. In one British survey, 42 percent of older adults who had children lived with them.

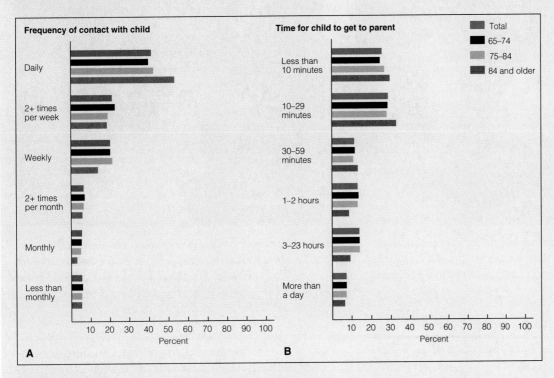

FIGURE 18.4

A *Frequency of contact and* **B** *proximity between persons age 65 and older and their children, by age. (From U.S. Bureau of the Census, 1988, p. 36.)*

It is highly revealing, too, that whereas fewer than 5 percent of the very old live in institutions, far more live with their children. Gibson (1992), for example, reports a British study in which 3.7 percent of the elderly lived in institutions but a full 42 percent lived with their children. Another 40 percent lived less than a half hour away. Kelly and Westcott (1991) found that retirees plan much of their lives around trips to visit children and other family. For those with children, the immediate family is usually the center of their social world.

Manifestations of the complex of relationships that exist between older parents and their children include such things as the exchange of gifts, services (mowing lawns, doing tax returns), advice, and financial help. These, of course, do not always flow in only one direction, particu-larly if the parents are not yet very old. As Tomlin and Passman (1991) found, for example, grandmothers are an important source of child-rearing advice for mothers.

As parents age, relationships with their children also change. One of the outcomes of increased longevity is a larger population of very old people who suffer from a variety of physical and mental disorders. As a result, children are increasingly being called upon to provide assistance to their frail parents. Malonebeach and Zarit (1991) report that children, and especially daughters, are now providing more care for their parents than ever be-fore—an undertaking that, in their words, can be "expensive to the caregiver socially, psychologically, physically, and financially" (p. 103).

The most important relationships for the very old are those with their spouses and other partners—if they are still alive. Second are their relationships with their children and grandchildren.

Relationships with Grandchildren

Clearly, however, only a small percentage of late adults are very old and in need of special care. In fact, late adults are often the ones who care for their grandchildren. For many children, their grandparents' home is a special and very safe place, almost like another home; and grandparents are a source of love and support—a little like another set of parents. Some grandparents take their grandchildren in regularly, or go to their homes, so that their daughters or daughters-in-law can work. Tomlin and Passman (1989) report that under these circumstances, children respond to grandmothers very much as they would to mothers (for example, in a strange situation). This is what Neugarten and Weinstein (1964) term the *surrogate-parent role*, one of five distinct styles of grandparenting. Others include the *fun-seeking grandparent role* (indulgent playmate), the *grandparent-as-distant-figure role* (benevolent but uninvolved), the *reservoir-of-family-wisdom role* (important, traditional source of advice), and the *formal grandparenting style* (interested, emotionally attached, but not directly involved).

The formal style appears to be the most common style of grandparenting in North America. It's an approach that pays strict attention to the widely accepted rule that grandparents should not interfere in the upbringing of their grandchildren, that they should be very careful not to offer advice or criticism. The formal grand-

The most common role of grandparents vis-à-vis their grandchildren is a formal role where there is no involvement in parenting but nevertheless emotional involvement; others, like the grandfather shown here, gladly accept the role of surrogate-parent while the grandchild's parents work.

parenting role permits buying presents on suitable occasions (birthdays and Christmas) and infrequent and irregular babysitting or holiday visits. It also permits the establishment of very warm, loving relationships between grandparents and grandchildren. But it does not permit the type of control, guidance, or decision making that parents are called upon to make. In this model, parents do all the parenting; grandparents do the grandparenting. (See At a Glance: "Grandparenting Styles," and Figure 18.5.)

Studies of the relationship between children and their grandparents typically reveal very close ties (Hodgson, 1992). This can be both a source of happiness, and a source of problems for grandparents. As Gibson (1992) points out, grandparents strongly attached to their grandchildren may experience distress at not being granted sufficient contact with them. This is especially true in situations in which parents divorce and custody of the children remains with the unrelated parent (Myers & Perrin, 1993).

Relationships with Spouse

One of the clearest predictors of satisfaction and happiness in old age is a life that includes a spouse or, in an increasing number of cases, cohabitation with an intimate friend. As we saw in Chapter 16, marital satisfaction be-

GRANDPARENTING STYLES

The roles of grandparents are not clearly defined in North American society and may take a variety of styles. These grandparenting styles are influenced by the grandparents' personalities, as well as by geography, health, finances, personalities of the grandchildren, and the ages of both grandchildren and grandparents. Perhaps the most important influence in determining the nature of grandparenting styles is the explicit or implicit wishes of the parents. Grandparenting roles are complex and dynamic, and they change with circumstances.

Formal
Not involved in parenting; emotionally involved, loving grandparents

Fun-seeking
Indulgent grandparents; assume playmate role

Distant figure
Uninvolved; very little close contact

Parental surrogate
Assume role of parent, usually so mother can work

Reservoir of family wisdom
Powerful patriarch or matriarch of extended family

10 20 30 40 50
Percent (approximate)

FIGURE 18.5

Styles of grandparenting as identified by Neugarten and Weinstein (1964).

gins to increase at around the empty nest phase; it apparently continues to do so into old age (Atchley, 1992). In a general way, the pattern of rising and falling marital happiness, notes Cox (1988), conforms with a couples opportunity for shared time—which is often curvilinear. Thus, spouses tend to spend a great deal of time doing things together early in the marriage, share less time alone with the advent of children and increasing work pressures, and again begin to share more activities as children leave home and one or both partners retire.

Sexual activity typically continues to be an important part of a couple's relationship through the older years (Gibson, 1992). Among elderly people who do not continue to engage in sex, the most important reason is simply lack of a partner, a situation that is far more common among women than men. Remarriage and cohabitation in old age have become more frequent in recent years, partly explaining the fact that fewer older persons now live with their children (Cox, 1988).

Relationships with Friends

Contrary to our popular stereotype of the elderly person as often lonely, most older people have one or more close friends and do not consider themselves very lonely. Friends satisfy many needs in late adulthood. They might provide intimacy, an opportunity for shared leisure activity, or cognitive stimulation. They can be a source of excitement and joy (Adams, 1986). They can be important confidants and serve to help control and relieve the tensions and stresses of everyday life.

One of the best predictors of happiness and satisfaction in old age is a life that includes a spouse or some other intimate cohabiting friend. Not surprisingly, as increasing numbers of the very old remain independent for longer periods of time, more are getting remarried at later ages, often following the death of a spouse.

THE WIDOWED ELDERLY

In 1992, 63.4 percent of the total male population were married, 2.8 percent were widowed, and 7.6 percent were divorced. Among females, 59.2 percent were married, 11.5 percent widowed, and 10.1 percent divorced. Given the longer life expectancies of women, the number of

widows increases far more dramatically with age than does the number of widowers. In 1992, 22.6 percent of men over the age of 75 were widowed, while 63.8 percent of women in the same age bracket were widows.

FIGURE 18.6

Widowhood relative to age and sex in the United States, 1992. (Based on U.S. Bureau of the Census, 1994, p. 56.)

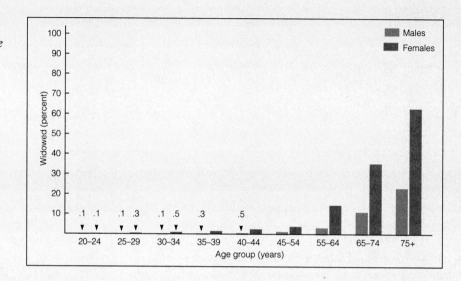

Although the elderly do not ordinarily make many new friends, relationships with existing friends become more rather than less important with the passage of time. Even among a sample of adults aged 85 or more, the majority continued to be in very close contact with their friends (Johnson & Troll, 1994). And when Flanagan (1982) asked 70-year-olds to list things that most contributed to an "excellent" quality of life, friends, spouse, and children were almost always at the top of the list.

In an intergenerational study that looked at young adult women, their mothers, and their grandmothers, social support for all three groups came from friends as well as close family members (Levitt, Weber, & Guacci, 1993). Interestingly, however, the older generation tended to include more family members among their sources of social support than did the younger generation.

Friendships among the elderly are especially important for women, because they are far more likely than men to lose their spouses. Whereas 80 percent of all men are still married between the ages of 65 and 74, only 54 percent of the women are; above age 74, percentages of those married have dropped to 71 for men and only 27 for women (U.S. Bureau of the Census, 1994).

Widowhood

The much higher percentage of *widows* than *widowers* is due to the greater fragility of the male and a life expectancy that, at present, is about eight years shorter. As a result, by age 65, there are already about 50 percent more women than men—and the ratio becomes increasingly unbalanced at higher age levels (U.S. Bureau of the Census, 1994). In Barer's (1994) sample of 150 very old community-dwelling men and women (average ages 88.1 for the men, 89.2 for the women), more than half the men were still married and living with their spouse. In contrast, only 10 percent of the women were still married.

In 1993, there were 11.2 million widows (age 15 or more) in the United States but only some 2.5 million widowers in the same age range. The chance of a woman being a widow, and therefore involuntarily single, at the age of 65 is almost one in two; by age 85, it is more than three in four (U.S. Bureau of the Census, 1994). (See At a Glance: "The Widowed Elderly," and Figure 18.6).

Society does not prepare us well for widowhood; we don't often speak openly of the possible deaths of those near to us. Some research indicates that the impact of the

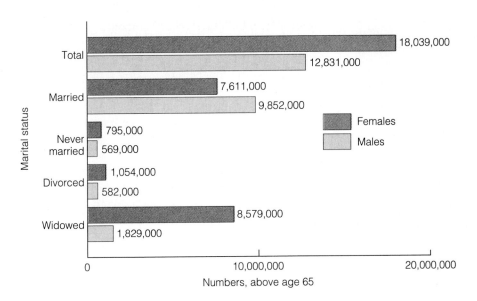

FIGURE 18.7
*Marital status of the U.S.
population above age 65, 1993.
(Based on U.S. Bureau of the
Census, 1994, p. 56.)*

Chart labels:
- Total: 18,039,000 (Females); 12,831,000 (Males)
- Married: 7,611,000 (Females); 9,852,000 (Males)
- Never married: 795,000 (Females); 569,000 (Males)
- Divorced: 1,054,000 (Females); 582,000 (Males)
- Widowed: 8,579,000 (Females); 1,829,000 (Males)

Legend: ■ Females ▨ Males

Y-axis: Marital status
X-axis: Numbers, above age 65 (0, 10,000,000, 20,000,000)

death of a spouse is more severe for younger than older survivors, perhaps because with age we are exposed to increasing numbers of people who are widowed—and perhaps, too, because as we grow older, we are more likely to confront the possibility, at least privately, and to begin to prepare for it (DiGiulio, 1992). Research indicates that the impact is, in fact, sufficiently severe that it may reduce the life expectancy of the surviving spouse, especially for men (Gibson, 1992).

One of the relatively common outcomes of loss of a spouse is depression that is serious enough to require treatment and sometimes hospitalization. However, in the majority of cases, the depression is of relatively short duration (Robinson & Fleming, 1992).

Even in the absence of serious depression, after the initial period of mourning that follows the death of a spouse, there are often periods of loneliness and sorrow that can sometimes last for a very long time. One of the problems often associated with widowhood, apart from the resulting grief and loneliness, is the need to redefine the self. This is especially true for widows whose identity has centered on being a wife. Resolution of the resulting conflicts often takes the form of investing more energy in work or in social organizations, or becoming more involved with friends and family (Pellman, 1992). For women who do not have many friends before widowhood and who are not involved in outside work, these transitions are often difficult.

Not surprisingly, studies of satisfaction and happiness often report less positive emotions among the widowed. In the Kelly and Westcott (1991) interviews with 25 retirees, only nine expressed disappointment and unhappiness with retirement. Of these, four were widowed and two were divorced. Two others had serious health problems, and one had a conflict-ridden, unhappy marriage.

With the passage of time, many widows and widowers adjust quite happily to their new circumstances. And for some, remarriage is sometimes the solution. Unfortunately, given the far greater number of women than men who are widowed, the option of remarriage is not available to many women.

CARE OF THE VERY OLD

One of the fears of many elderly married women, notes Gibson (1992), is that they will be left alone in their later years. The fear is not unfounded given the rate at which men die. In 1993, for example, there were about 5 million more women than men above age 65 in the United States. And because a much larger proportion of the men still had wives, there were about 8 million more widowed and divorced women than widowed and divorced men (U.S. Bureau of the Census, 1994; Figure 18.7).

Family Care

Most elderly adults in North America live in their homes and care for themselves. And, not surprisingly, older adults who continue to live independently and to care for themselves have higher self-esteem and a higher sense of satisfaction with life (Bunce & Harrison, 1991). Most are anxious not to become dependent (O'Bryant, 1991).

In shared households, the majority of which consist of husband and wife, it is not uncommon that one partner will assume most of the caregiving functions. Contrary to our popular stereotype, which holds that caregiving is undertaken almost exclusively by females, in about one quarter of all cases the caregivers are male—usually the husband, but sometimes a son or other relative. Arber and

The majority of elderly adults in North America live in their own homes or apartments and care for themselves. A small percentage of the elderly live in special care facilities of various kinds. And some, like this grandmother, live with their children and grandchildren—a situation that has become rarer with the increasing mobility of the family and with governments and employers accepting more responsibility for financial and social assistance to the elderly.

Gilbert (1989) note that female caregivers often assume their responsibilities as a result of a deliberate decision, perhaps motivated by social expectations (for example, a daughter looking after aging parents). In contrast, men usually come into the caregiving role by virtue of living arrangements rather than as a result of a deliberate decision (for example, a husband looking after an ailing wife, or an unmarried son who has not left the parental home gradually assuming a caregiving role). Other things being equal, there is a slightly greater tendency for children to care for the like-sexed parent (Lee et al., 1993).

In many cultures (such as the Chinese), notions of *filial responsibility* (or *filial piety*) dictate that children will look after their parents in their old age (Ho, 1983). Even in Western cultures, there is a strong social expectation that offspring will make every effort to meet their parents' needs. And, in fact, that is generally what occurs (Zarit & Reid, 1994). Specific manifestations of filial re-

sponsibility might take the form of shopping with (or for) parents, escorting them to various events, helping them with daily tasks, perhaps sharing living arrangements with them, and caring for them or making arrangements for their care when necessary.

Although adult children continue to provide primary support for aging parents, certain contemporary trends have made this more difficult and perhaps less likely in some cases. Pensions and other forms of social assistance for the elderly constitute one such trend; increasing urbanization and increasing family mobility are others. As governments and other institutions accept more responsibility for the financial well-being of the aged, children's financial responsibilities for their parents are increasingly becoming the exception rather than the rule. In addition, many families are so widely scattered that adult children are quite incapable of assuming day-to-day filial responsibilities. Moreover, even when geography is not a problem, many adult children are physically, emotionally, or economically unable to provide long-term care for their parents.

Care Facilities for the Elderly

When the elderly are unable to care for themselves and the burden of their care has become too overwhelming for their spouse, children, or friends, they may be cared for in one of a number of *care facilities for the elderly.* There are a number of such facilities, the most common being hospitals and nursing homes. In general, only the *very* old live permanently in these facilities. The majority are there because of physical or mental impairments. In spite of this, in many cases the institutionalized person feels abandoned and alone, and the family suffers from feelings of guilt.

There is some evidence of "excess institutionalization"—that is, individuals who are inappropriately given over to the permanent care of a facility. Large-scale surveys, based on the functional capabilities of the institutionalized elderly, suggest that this might occur in 10 to 18 percent of cases (Lawton, 1981). This is less likely to happen for individuals who have a spouse or children.

There is also some evidence of *elder abuse* in some care facilities. Abuse of the elderly, like child abuse, may be physical or emotional, and often involves *neglect* as well as overt actions (Shiferaw, Mittelmark, & Hofford, 1994). Adult abuse often reflects a form of ageism in which the very old are seen as helpless and burdensome. Pietrukowicz and Johnson (1991) suggest that mistreatment of the elderly in care facilities is often linked to the impersonal and largely negative view that caregivers might have of their elderly residents—a condition that is worse in commercial care facilities where resident-to-staff ratios are high. They report that something as simple as including a brief life biography in each resident's medical chart can contribute significantly to staffs' positive perceptions of the elderly in their care.

Other Alternatives

In recent years, the provision of alternatives to institutional care for the elderly has been emphasized. These alternatives include providing community-based assistance for the elderly in private homes. Such assistance might take the form of home visitations by personnel with expertise in the care of the old, or perhaps the delivery of hot meals on a regular basis. It might also include visits by community volunteers, who sometimes simply talk with the elderly but who might also assist them with chores such as shopping and might occasionally take them outside the home to various athletic and cultural events.

The variety of other alternatives to institutionalization includes the many housing projects that are designed specifically for the elderly. Some of these are government assisted; others are private. They include apartment- or motel-type projects as well as single-unit, detached dwellings. Some are designed to provide a wide range of services, including residential medical care, much as a nursing home might; others do little more than bring elderly people together, where they can live independently but in close community. One of the things that is especially important to the elderly, both in their own homes and in other alternatives, is security. Also important for many is access to nature (Talbot & Kaplan, 1991).

Numerous studies have been designed to assess whether communities designed specifically for the elderly are as satisfactory for them as simply living in a "normal" community, which is where more than 90 percent of those over age 65 live. These studies have typically presented a relatively positive picture in terms of the degree to which residents feel satisfied with their housing, with the social interaction available to them, and with their participation in various activities (Lawton, 1981). Among the advantages of retirement communities is that they increase the availability and proximity of peers, thereby providing opportunities for new friendships to develop. In addition, they tend to increase social participation and delay disengagement.

Although most of the elderly would prefer to remain independent, or to move in with relatives if they cannot remain independent, the need for other alternatives is increasing rapidly. This demand is occurring not only because the absolute number of elderly people is increasing dramatically but also because of medical advances that now make it possible for individuals to live longer following the onset of a variety of chronic disorders. Many of these alternatives can perhaps fill the gap between independence and institutionalization and, in the process, make the lives of the very old far happier.

HAPPINESS IN OLD AGE

Early in this chapter, we looked at two theories of aging: *Disengagement* theory describes a process of gradual withdrawal from active involvement and a transition to the passive existence exemplified perhaps by the rocking chair; *activity* theory describes continued involvement in social, economic, political, religious, or other areas, and might be exemplified by the life of the older person who writes a personal narrative or who chases fish with a grandchild. And who will be happier? The old person in the solitary rocking chair or the one writing biographies or catching fish?

Either one might be happy, or both might be unhappy, suggests research. It may be a platitude, but it is no less true to say that it depends very much on the individual and on that person's dreams and accomplishments. Some people seek rocking chairs in old age because they are satisfied that they have done their life's work, and they wish to rest; others want to remain active, and do so. And both might be very content.

But there are also those who find themselves in their rocking chairs not by choice but because age has put them there, and they now lack the abilities or the strength required to continue their activities. And there are those who remain active but who labor with a sense of frustration, not only because of the insufficient time they have left but also because they recognize the meaninglessness of their lives. Both of these might be unhappy.

Factors Linked to Happiness

At all stages of the life cycle, health is closely associated with happiness. It becomes an even more critical factor with the physical decline and increased susceptibility to disease of old age. Not surprisingly, health is often the single most important determinant of adjustment and happiness, or depression, in old age (Belsky, 1990). (See Across Cultures: "Mrs. Smith and Mrs. Crawford.")

Income is also related to a sense of well-being in old age, perhaps partly because of the feeling of security that comes with having enough money and partly because those who are healthy and who have sufficient money are more easily able to remain actively involved (Kelly & Westcott, 1991).

Another factor that appears to be related to happiness is educational level (Dillard, Campbell, & Chisolm, 1984). Again this may be related to the opportunities that education provides for continued involvement in interesting activities, such as reading or doing crossword puzzles, sometimes well beyond the time that physical strength, energy, or general well-being allow more physical involvements. It is noteworthy that in DeGenova's (1992) study, in response to the question "What would you do differently if . . . ?" participants most regretted not having spent more time on education and intellectual self-improvement.

There are several personality characteristics that also appear to contribute to happiness. Costa and McCrae (1984), in a longitudinal investigation of psychological well-being, identified three such characteristics: emotional stability, objectivity, and friendliness. Those high on measures of emotional stability are, by definition, less

MRS. SMITH AND MRS. CRAWFORD

Mrs. Smith, age 84, is a widow who lives alone in a rented set of rooms. She sleeps not in a bedroom, but on a davenport in the main room. With an income below $5,000 per year, she is one of America's poor—the 1 out of every 15 people above age 65 who live below the poverty level (for blacks, the proportion is closer to 1 in 4; for whites, it is less than 1 in 20; U.S. Bureau of the Census, 1994). Not only is she poor, but she is abandoned, isolated, in poor health, depressed, and highly dependent on others for shopping, meals, laundry, housework, managing her finances, and so on. When asked what she does, she answered, "I don't do anything" (Day, 1991, p. 247). Her eyesight is too poor to allow her to do any of the things she likes. In the past year, she has visited no one, gone nowhere, and had no friends or relatives visit. Asked what she expects of the future, she replied, "I don't think I'll be here in a couple of years. I hope I am not" (p. 247).

Mrs. Crawford, age 88, is confined to a wheelchair and is entirely dependent on her husband for household chores and cooking, as well as for personal care. In spite of this, she is profoundly contented. Her kitchen is filled with her books and music, and she banters lightheartedly and pleasantly with her husband. She is happy and optimistic about the future (Day, 1991).

To Think About Both Mrs. Crawford and Mrs. Smith are very dependent on others for their care. But one is highly satisfied and the other, defeated and unhappy. Their situations underline, once more,

how poorly our generalizations apply to individuals identified only on the basis of age. One reason why Mrs. Crawford and Mrs. Smith have such different evaluations of their lives, explains Day (1991), relates to the social supports that Mrs. Crawford has and that Mrs. Smith lacks. Can you think of any other contextual reasons for contentment or discontentment in old age? Can you think of noncontextual reasons (for example, personality variables)?

Happiness in very old age, psychology tells us, is linked with good health, income, educational level, emotional stability, and close friendships. And a good joke now and again doesn't hurt either.

likely to suffer serious depression. Those who are characterized by objectivity rather than subjectivity are less concerned with internal states, perhaps less preoccupied with declining capacities, and, by the same token, more likely to be involved in external activities. And those high on friendliness are more likely to have more friends and to satisfy continuing needs for intimacy. The presence of close friends can be tremendously important in maintaining happiness, even in the face of serious and tragic events such as the death of a spouse or serious illness (Lowenthal & Haven, 1981).

In conclusion, we cannot easily say that old age is a happier or a sadder time than any other in the lifespan. For some, it may indeed be happier, or at least as happy; for others, it might be much sadder. But whether it brings sorrow, joy, or simple resignation, it will also bring new roles and new problems, and it requires a whole new set of adjustments. Perhaps none of these adjustments is more difficult or painful than the need to face the certainty of death. We look at this topic in Chapter 19.

MAIN POINTS

Views of Development in Late Adulthood

1. Erikson's late adulthood stage, *integrity versus despair*, requires a positive evaluation of life and a decision that its final outcome is natural, inevitable, and acceptable. Peck details three psychosocial conflicts that compose the final Erikson stage: *ego differentiation versus work-role preoccupation* (need to shift preoccupations from career to self at retirement), *body transcendence versus body preoccupation* (danger of becoming preoccupied with declining physical and mental powers), and *ego transcendence versus ego preoccupation* (an acceptance of death).

2. Fisher describes five stages in late adulthood; these stages exemplify stability following transitions: (1) continuity with middle age; (2) early transition; (3) revised lifestyle; (4) later transition; and (5) final period.

The Life Review

3. Personal narratives are sensible stories of our lives that give them continuity and purpose. The life review is an active process wherein the personal narrative of the older adult involves reminiscing, evaluating, resolving old conflicts, and coming to terms with the finality of life.

Retirement

4. Retirement is a 20th-century phenomenon made possible by a high standard of living, high worker productivity, and a surplus of labor. Attitudes toward retirement are important predictors of satisfaction and healthy adjustment after retirement. Retirement is most likely to be positive if it is voluntary rather than forced, if work is not the only thing in the person's life, if health and income are sufficient to permit the enjoyment of newly created leisure time, and if retirement has been planned.

5. Atchley describes several phases of retirement: *pre-retirement* (fantasies about retirement), *honeymoon* (vigorous doing of things not done before), *rest and relaxation* (a quiet period), *disenchantment* (a relatively rare period of disillusionment), *reorientation* (coming to terms with disenchantment), *routine* (establishing satisfying routines), and *termination* (withdrawal from the retirement role).

Successful Aging

6. Most of the elderly cope with the processes of aging and continue to find contentment and joy in their lives. Disengagement theory suggests that, with failing physical and mental capabilities, the elderly seek to withdraw from active social roles and that they should be allowed, perhaps encouraged, to do so. Activity theory argues that continued social, physical, and emotional involvement is important to physical and emotional well-being.

Social Relationships in Late Adulthood

7. Family relationships are ordinarily the most important of all social relationships throughout the entire lifespan—and other than that with a spouse, the most important are with children. Grandparents can play different roles: surrogate parent (caring for children), fun-seeking (indulgent playmate), distant figure (occasional gifts), reservoir-of-family-wisdom (patriarch or matriarch of extended family), and formal (nonintrusive but emotionally involved).

8. Marriages tend to become happier with the empty nest and remain happy and sexually active into old age. Among women, decline in sexual activity is most often due to lack of a suitable partner. In late adulthood, close friends serve important roles relating to intimacy, social and intellectual stimulation, confiding, relieving stress, and providing support during crises.

Care of the Very Old

9. Filial responsibility is a common feature of most family systems, often evident in children caring for their aging parents. A small percentage of the very old, often as a last resort or for medical reasons, are in special care facilities like nursing homes. Increasing numbers also live in communities designed for the elderly. Various forms of community-based assistance sometimes make it possible for the somewhat-dependent elderly to continue to live in their homes with relative independence.

Happiness in Old Age

10. Both disengagement and continued activity may be associated with happiness or unhappiness. Health, income, friendships, and personality variables appear to be important factors for happiness in late adulthood.

FOCUS QUESTIONS: APPLICATIONS

1. What is a life review? How does it relate to the personal narrative and to reminiscing?

- Do a systematic review of your own life to this stage. Now project some years into the future and try to imagine what your life review might look like when you're 70 or 80 or 90. Do you want to make any changes?

2. Is successful, well-adjusted aging most likely to be associated with continued social, emotional, and community involvement? Or is it more likely to come to those who have disengaged?

- Summarize the conditions under which retirement is most likely to be a positive transition. Explain why these factors might be important.

3. What are the best options for the care of the very old?

- As a term project, using library resources, do a newspaper-type exposé of elder abuse in institutions.

4. What factors are most closely linked with happiness in old age?

- Write out a recipe that your grandparents (or somebody else's) might follow for greater happiness. Now write out a recipe that younger adults might follow to increase their chances for happiness in old age. How different are your two recipes?

STUDY TERMS

activity theory   527

body transcendence versus body preoccupation   520

care facilities for the elderly   534

disenchantment   526

disengagement theory   527

ego differentiation versus work-role preoccupation   520

ego transcendence versus ego preoccupation   520

elder abuse   534

filial responsibility (or filial piety)   534

Fisher's five periods of older adulthood   520

formal grandparenting style   530

fun-seeking grandparent   530

grandparent-as-distant-figure role   530

honeymoon   526

integrity versus despair   520

life review   521

personal narratives   521

phases of retirement   525

preretirement   526

reminiscence   522

reorientation   526

reservoir-of-family-wisdom role   530

rest and relaxation   526

retirement   523

routine   526

surrogate-parent role   530

termination   526

widowers   532

widows   532

The entire first issue of the 38th volume of the *International Journal of Aging and Human Development* is devoted to examining social, personality, and cultural diversity among the very old (above age 85):

International Journal of Aging and Human Development. (1994). Vol 38, No. 1.

In the following book, Gibson provides a clear and candid look at sexuality in the lives of older adults. The book also deals with family relationships, health, and social problems of aging:

Gibson, H. B. (1992). *The emotional and sexual lives of older people: A manual for professionals.* New York: Chapman and Hall.

The following collection provides an insightful look at some of the social and political realities of old age in contemporary society. Especially relevant to this chapter are sections dealing with pensions, retirement, and the care of the aged:

Schaie, K. W., & Achenbaum, W. A. (Eds.). (1993). *Societal impact on aging: Historical perspectives.* New York: Springer.

Day's book looks at the experience of aging among women in contemporary industrialized societies, and provides fascinating case descriptions of some of the paths that aging can take.

Day, A. T. (1991). *Remarkable survivors: Insights into successful aging among women.* Washington, DC: The Urban Institute Press.

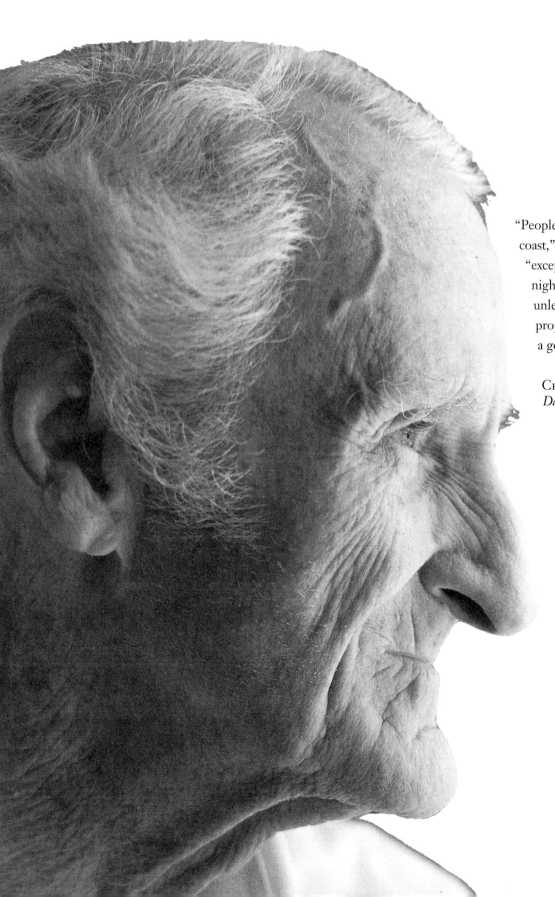

"People can't die, along the
coast," said Mr. Peggotty,
"except when the tide's pretty
nigh out. They can't be born,
unless it's pretty nigh in—not
properly born, till flood. He's
a going out with the tide."

Charles Dickens
David Copperfield

THE END

A book is a little like a life: It has a be-   # PART NINE
ginning, a middle, and an end. And some-
times it seems to have a willfulness, a vitality, that are reminiscent of life.

But if it has life, then it must also have death. Because one is surely the price
to be paid for the other. Much as we would like not to think so, they are two
sides of the same coin, are they not? Is there ever one without the other?

Sadly, the tide is nigh out for this book. There remains only one last chapter in this, the final section.

Throughout this book, the coin of life has lain faceup on the table of our
reason. Now, in this final chapter, we must pick it up, turn it, and look at
the other side.

CHAPTER 19   Dying

DYING

*D*o not go gentle into that good night,
Old age should burn and rave at close of day;
Rage, rage against the dying of the light.

DYLAN THOMAS
Do Not Go Gentle

Old man! 'Tis not so difficult to die.

LORD BYRON
Manfred

CHAPTER 19

It's late summer and Mouche, Marc Voisin's dirty-yellow dog, has cornered a bear in the raspberries and foolishly insists on snarling at its heels. We watch from the other side of the fence, close enough to the barn that we can run for it if we have to. Finally annoyed, the bear turns suddenly and clouts Mouche up the side of the head. Then, as if bewildered by what he's done, or maybe simply no longer hungry for raspberries, he trundles off across the pasture and into the trees. The boss cow, the one we call Imelda, stares balefully at the bear as he waddles past.*

We find Mouche lying there among the raspberry canes. "I think he's dead," Marc announces gravely.

"How can you tell?" I ask.

"My dad showed me," he answers. "Wait." And off he runs, leaving me alone among the raspberry canes. I wait a long time, looking at Mouche but not quite daring to touch him; I'm not absolutely certain that death isn't catching, it being my first close experience with the phenomenon.

---

*Parts of Imelda's story are told in G. R. Lefrançois. *Psychology for teaching: A bear faces the future*, 8th edition. 1994. Belmont, CA: Wadsworth.

When Marc comes back, he's carrying a small mirror, which he holds in front of the dog's nostrils. "If he's still alive, it'll cloud over," Marc says. "That's what my dad showed me."

Mouche is dead, which we now prove. Then we prove we're still alive by repeatedly clouding the mirror. And for a few months after that, I always carry a small mirror around with me in case I should ever need it—until the day Robert Gaudry trips me and I fall into the river and break my mirror and maybe almost drown and die, but I wouldn't have had my mirror anymore to prove it.

THIS CHAPTER

Science doesn't need a mirror to prove death (although it might sometimes be useful to prove life); it has other ways.

Science's understanding of death and dying are the subject of this chapter. It looks at what death is and at how medicine and common sense define it. It examines developmental changes in our beliefs about dying. It traces the stages that death may take. And it deals with the effects of death on those who are left to mourn.

And in the end, the chapter turns and looks once more at the themes that were presented at the very beginning of the text—themes that underlie our study and understanding of development throughout the lifespan.

DEATH

Dying is a highly personal thing. For some, perhaps it is not so difficult a thing, but there are many who burn and rave and rage at its coming. My grandfather tried to go more gently and with a little humor. Having probably read a translation of Viscount Henry John Temple Palmerston's famous last words,* he paraphrased them for my grandmother: "Die?" he is reported to have said, "That's the last thing I'm gonna do!" Which he then did.

That, of course, is the problem with dying. Once we have done it, we can no longer write textbooks—or even letters—about it. We take its secrets to our graves.

But science has ways to pry the dusty grave, ways to define, analyze, and measure even this most private, unique, and ultimate of all events.

Some Definitions

Not very many years ago, if someone stopped breathing, or the heart stopped beating, everybody agreed that that person was dead. Doctors noted, as well, that the pupils

*Viscount Palmerston's last words were, allegedly, "Die, my dear Doctor, that's the last thing I shall do!"

dilated when someone died, that being the reason, in so many movies, the possibly dead person's eyelids are lifted by someone who then peers intently at the eyeball. Other changes that characterize death include eventual rigor mortis (stiffening of the corpse) and relaxation of the sphincter muscle.

Now, however, there is a new concept of **death** in the medical professions: that of neurological, or brain, death. When the dying person's heart and lungs stop functioning, the brain is quickly deprived of oxygen, and electrical activity of the brain, detected by means of an electroencephalogram (EEG), eventually stops. Death is said to have occurred following complete cessation of brain activity for a certain period of time. However, recent medical advances now make it possible to restart heart and lung action or to substitute for their normal functioning by means of life-sustaining equipment. In fact, it is now possible to keep some people alive in the physiological sense—that is, their bodies consume and process nutrients and oxygen, and eliminate wastes—even though they have suffered irreparable brain damage as a result of temporary cessation of heart and lung activity. Defining death in such circumstances presents serious medical and ethical problems.

Bereavement is the term used to describe the loss suffered by those who are friends and relatives of the person who has died. The bereaved are those left behind—those from whom something has been taken. Bereavement is typically accompanied by **grief**—the bereaved person's emotional reaction to the loss. Grief reactions may include feelings of anger, guilt, anxiety, depression, or preoccupation with thoughts of the deceased. In addition, grief reactions sometimes include physical components such as shortness of breath, dizziness, heart palpitations, loss of appetite, sighing, and so on. As we saw in Chapter 18, there is also a slight reduction in life expectancy for the widowed person for a few years immediately following death of the spouse (we look at grief in more detail later in this chapter). The term **mourning,** which describes external manifestations of grief, is often used to indicate a period of time during which the bereaved person grieves.

NOTIONS OF DEATH THROUGH THE LIFESPAN

Throughout many of the world's cultures, the most common attitudes toward death are fear and denial (McLennan, Akande, & Bates, 1993). We do not resign ourselves easily to the inevitability of our ends.

Distancing and Denying Death

We deny death in countless ways. We seldom speak seriously about it—and we speak of it in a personal way even less often. Nor are we willing to admit our fear of dying,

Fear of dying, of no longer existing, is expressed in a search for immortality. To this end, the ancient Egyptians built pyramids and invented mummification. Now we resort to lines carved in stone to preserve a memory of the dead.

says Belsky (1990); somehow, it embarrasses us. When death does come, we often pretend that it is an accident—especially if it came before the end of what we expect will be a normal lifespan. We use expressions such as *untimely* or *sudden* or *unexpected* to describe it. And we invent euphemisms to replace the harsh reality of the words *dead* or *died*: "Passed away," we say, or "dearly departed," or "departed loved ones," or "gone beyond," or "passed on."

Contemporary society distances itself from death not only in its language, but also in the way funerals are generally handled. For example, it has become rare for the deceased to be kept at home, or even in churches, for a brief period of mourning. In North America, the vast majority of all funerals now occur in funeral parlors, with brief periods of visitation by family members and friends.

Our denial of death is evident as well in the limited training that many medical schools provide physicians and other health personnel with respect to death and dying. For example, when Rappaport and Witzke (1993) questioned 106 medical students whose practical training had required them to care for a terminally ill patient, they found that most considered themselves poorly prepared for the undertaking. In addition, 41 percent had never been present when a physician had attended a dying patient; 35 percent had never discussed attending a dying patient with a physician; 73 percent had never witnessed hospital staff advising relatives regarding negative outcomes of surgery; and 85 percent had never been present when family members were advised of a patient's death. As Gloth (1994) notes, the medical profession pays relatively little formal attention to the process of dying and to how to care for terminally ill patients.

The process of dying, itself, is often very private. Many hospitals go to great lengths to isolate patients who are expected to die, and then remove the bodies as unob-

trusively as possible. Unless we have been in wars, or have witnessed automobile accidents or other similar events, most of us have not had a great deal of exposure to human death and dying. For many, all there has been is a brief glimpse of the deceased in a well-lined casket. Ironically, under these circumstances, the dead are carefully arranged to look as lifelike as possible.

Given our society's widespread denial and avoidance of death, what do children—to say nothing of adolescents and adults at all stages of adulthood—know of dying?

Children's Understanding of Death

Many children's first real exposure to death comes when a family pet dies. But for most, there is a great deal of secondhand exposure to death and dying in the media. Television is especially prone to presenting vivid and dramatic portrayals of death—especially of violent death. Its depictions of grief and remorse are considerably more rare.

Do children, as a result of personal and vicarious experience, understand death?

Early research and theorizing indicated that they typically know very little. Very young children (ages 3 to 4), reported Nagy (1948), don't understand the finality of death. And older children (ages 5 to 9), tend to *personify* it, turning death into a "bogeyman," a "witch," or some other wicked something that is capable of taking people away. Only after age 10 or so do children begin to understand that the end of life is a biological process, that its cause lies within the body rather than with some outside force.

Perhaps because of widespread media exposure to dying, even very young children now seem to have a clearer understanding of the biological finality of death. For example, Mahon (1993) interviewed 58 children (ages 5 to 14), half of whom had experienced a sibling's death approximately one year earlier. Although having experienced a recent death in the family did not seem to increase children's understanding of death, almost half of the 5-year-olds, 60 percent of the 6- to 8-year-olds, 90 percent of the 10-year-olds, and *all* of the older children already had an accurate concept of death.

The fact that some young children's answers to questions about death and dying reveal a limited awareness of what dying is does not mean that they do not understand or respond to loss. The ability to verbalize an understanding of death presupposes some relatively advanced cognitive and language skills. Perhaps because infants and young children do not yet possess these skills, their cognitive understanding of death seems undeveloped. In fact, their distress at losing a parent, for example, provides overwhelming behavioral evidence indicating that loss does have profound meaning for them (Bloom-Feshbach & Bloom-Feshbach, 1987).

As children become older and more sophisticated intellectually, their verbalized understanding of death becomes progressively more adult. But for most of them, thoughts of death are remote and abstract. There is little reason to be concerned with dying when the future stretches ahead seemingly forever.

Kastenbaum (1985) suggests that people's understandings of death at any age may have as much, or more, to do with their life experiences than with their age. Thus, although active, healthy children do not ordinarily think very much about death, and do not necessarily develop very sophisticated notions of what it means, those who are terminally ill seem to have an understanding of dying that goes well beyond their years. Bluebond-Langner (1977) reports that terminally ill children understand the inevitability and the absolute finality of death even in early childhood. The time orientation of these children changes dramatically, notes Bluebond-Langner. As death nears, conversations about the distant future disappear from their speech. Now the future that concerns them is very immediate—the next birthday, Christmas, Easter. Some children pay a lot of attention to these upcoming events, almost as though trying to rush them, to make them more real and immediate by talking about them.

Adolescent Notions of Death

Although adolescents understand clearly the finality, the inevitability, and the unpredictability of death, their views are often colored by the personal fables they have developed. These fables stress adolescents' specialness, the concern others have for them, and their invulnerability. It might follow from this that they would not be very concerned about dying. Yet some evidence indicates that thoughts of dying and accompanying fears are common in adolescence. This may be at least partly due to the fact that violent and unexpected deaths occur quite frequently in adolescence, especially among males.

Kastenbaum (1985) notes that some studies have reported little concern about death among adolescents, whereas others have suggested that adolescents are extremely preoccupied with and worried about death. The contradiction may be at least partly due to the reluctance of adolescents (and others) to talk about dying. Talking about death in a personal way, admitting fears and concerns, requires, in a very real sense, an admission of what we are socialized to deny at every turn. We do not easily admit that death is something that might happen to us personally—either in adolescence or later; for most, the thought is very frightening. So we repress it and tell each other that it is wise to smell the roses.

Deep down, that, too, may be an admission of fear of death.

Notions of Death in Early and Middle Adulthood

Through adulthood, many events generally conspire to emphasize the transitory nature of living. These include the sometimes painful observation that with every passing decade, more and more of our friends, acquaintances, and relatives die. In addition, many adults experience the loss of their parents or observe signs of aging and impending loss. And, as Kalish (1981) notes, because we all know that parents are supposed to die before children, we perhaps fear death less while our parents still live—and more after they die.

With passing years, the inevitability of death becomes clearer and we begin to think in terms of the number of years we have yet to live rather than of the time we have lived (Neugarten, 1968). This change in time orientation is one aspect of the midlife crisis described in Chapter 16.

Views of Death in Late Adulthood

How do old people feel about dying? Reassuringly, they often report less fear of death than at earlier ages. Kalish (1981) suggests several reasons this might be so. In the first place, the elderly have usually had far more experience with death than younger people, and many of these experiences have involved close friends, relatives, perhaps even a spouse. They have therefore been repeatedly compelled to think about death. In addition, progressive changes in their own bodies, often accompanied by one or more diseases, continue to emphasize that their own end is imminent, forcing them to adjust gradually to thoughts of dying. "Whereas death is accidental in other stages," notes Assmann (1994), "it becomes existential in old age" (p. 215).

Kalish (1981) also suggests that our knowledge of what normal life expectancy is has led us to accept a lifespan of 70 or so years as one over which we have few legitimate complaints. But if we should live so long, then life expectancy tables tell us we can expect to live another

AGE-BASED LIFE EXPECTANCIES

In 1991, the average life expectancy in the United States for all races and sexes combined was 75.4 years—a full 12.7 years longer than in 1940 (U.S. Bureau of the Census, 1994). When we are young, Neugarten says, we think in terms of how old we are—how long we have lived. But starting in midlife, we begin to think more about how long we have left to live. Reassuringly, the longer we have lived, the longer we can expect to live—up to a point. Thus, although our life expectancy at birth might be 75, if we actually reach the age of 75, we can reasonably expect to live 10.9 more years (12.0 if we are white and female; 9.4 if white and male. Corresponding life expectancies for 75-year-old black females and males are 11.2 and 8.6, respectively).

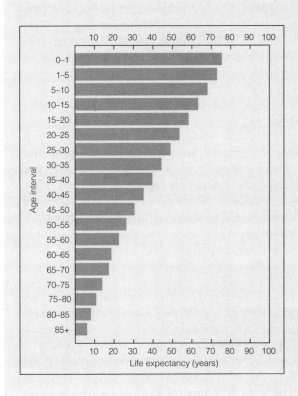

FIGURE 19.1

Average life expectancy in the United States, 1991, for individuals of given age. (Based on U.S. Bureau of the Census, 1994, p. 88.)

13.9 years (U.S. Bureau of the Census, 1994; see At a Glance: "Age-Based Life Expectancies," and Figure 19.1).

Fear of Dying

It would be misleading to imply that fear of dying gradually diminishes and finally vanishes altogether in old age. Although the majority of adults do not report a morbid fear of death, death anxiety is found at all age levels including late adulthood (Seigle, 1993). We no longer believe in the bogeyman that we invented in our childish minds, the one we feared might come one dark night and get our parents—or, worse yet, us. Yet, if we think about it, the bogeyman still lurks there in the shadows, and deep down we know that we are never completely safe.

It is not a happy thought. Say what we will, few of us are not afraid of dying; few of us can remain perfectly calm at the thought of the bogeyman—which is why we keep him in the shadows.

There are at least seven reasons why we might fear death, claim Schultz and Ewen (1988):

- Fear of physical suffering and pain
- Fear of the impact of death on those left behind
- Fear of the deaths of those we love

The elderly spend more time thinking about dying than do those who are younger. But they also report less fear of death—perhaps because they have seen more of it; and maybe because their declining physical powers have led them to confront their own mortality and they have succeeded in overcoming the despair that can result.

- Fear of eternal punishment
- Fear of not achieving important goals
- Fear of humiliation and cowardice
- Fear of not existing

This last source of fear, fear of not existing, may be what has driven so many to search for some form of immortality. Arnett (1991) describes how the kings of ancient Assyria tried to achieve a form of immortality by emphasizing the continuity and importance of the family tree, and especially of the males in this line. Each king took great pains to remember the achievements and glories of past kings, to praise their names—expecting, in turn, that succeeding kings would do the same for them. Thus could kings buy a hint of immortality in the memories of generations to come.

Ego Integrity

Freud is said to have become increasingly preoccupied with dying in his later years. "On March 13 of this year," he writes, "I quite suddenly took a step into real old age. Since then the thought of death has not left me. Some-times I have the impression that seven of my internal organs are fighting to have the honor of bringing my life to an end" (quoted in Jones, 1957, p. 78). In spite of his constant thoughts of death, however, Freud was reportedly not overwhelmed or depressed at the prospect of dying. "Still, I have not succumbed to this hypochondria," he continues, "but view it quite coolly . . ." (p. 79).

Our reactions to dying, says Bromley (1990), are highly individual. They include calm acceptance, grim determination to fight, or profound depression. One of the important developmental tasks of late adulthood, according to Erikson, is to confront our mortality while still maintaining a sense of integrity, a feeling that life has been worthwhile. Those who have truly achieved integrity do not fear death.

Not everyone resolves the crisis in the same way, or equally effectively. To realize the inevitability of our ends is not necessarily to become reconciled to death. There are some who, in Dylan Thomas's words, "Do not go gentle into that good night" but instead "Rage, rage against the dying of the light."

DYING

Psychologists have divided much of our lifespans into stages. There is nothing magical about these stages, nor is there anything intrinsically correct about them. They are simply inventions that simplify our understanding and that sometimes lead to important theoretical and practical insights.

Stages of Dying

Must we also die in stages? Some theorists suggest that this might sometimes be the case. Clearly, we need not resort to stages to understand the immediate and senseless finality of a gun, a bomb, or a plane crash. But perhaps a stage approach might be useful for understanding the process of dying when the person knows that death is near. (See At a Glance: "Common Causes of Death," and Figures 19.2 and 19.3 on pp. 550–551.)

Elisabeth Kübler-Ross (1969; 1974) describes five stages through which a patient progresses after learning of a terminal illness. In the first, *denial*, the patient often rejects the diagnosis and its implications: "This can't happen to me. There must be some mistake." Denial is sometimes followed by *anger*: "Why me? It shouldn't be me." The third stage, *bargaining*, is characterized by the patient's attempts to look after unfinished business (with God, for example), promising to do well in exchange for a longer life or less suffering. The fourth stage, *depression*, frequently follows. Finally, the patient may arrive at an *acceptance* of death. (See Table 19.1.)

Kübler-Ross's main concerns have been with the needs of the dying and with those who are left to mourn.

TABLE 19.1
Kübler-Ross's Sequential Stages of Dying

Stage	Illustration
Denial	"Not me! I don't believe it! There must be a mistake!"
Anger	"Why me? Lots of people smoked more than I did, and look at them! It isn't fair!"
Bargaining	"Okay, I might die. Just let me live a little longer so I can wrap up the business and see my new grandson."
Depression	"Yes, it's happening. There's nothing I can do. I wish I had died a long time ago."
Acceptance	"Let it happen. It's okay. I'm not interested in anything anymore. I'm not unhappy, just tired."

Accordingly, much of her work deals less with a description of stages of dying than with advice concerning practical questions related to dying: When should a patient be told? Who should do the telling? How can we reduce fear of death? Nevertheless, her description of the stages of dying has had a tremendous impact on the various professions that deal with death.

Some have criticized Kübler-Ross's stages, claiming that they are a highly subjective interpretation of the process of dying, and that many people do not pass through these five stages in the order prescribed. Some alternate between different stages, vacillating between acceptance and denial, sometimes depressed and other times resigned. Moreover, Kübler-Ross's stages do not recognize that one of the recurring emotions characterizing many of the terminally ill is *hope*. Still, her description provides a useful way of looking at dying. Claxton (1993) notes that many terminally ill cancer patients do appear to go through emotional stages very much like those described by Kübler-Ross, and suggests that health-care workers' knowledge of these stages might enable them to help patients express their emotions and achieve some degree of acceptance.

Life's Trajectories

Kübler-Ross's stages are one way of understanding the process of dying; trajectories are a second. A *trajectory* implies something quite different from a stage. Stages are like steps, small plateaus that must be successively scaled. They imply a marked degree of discontinuity. Hence, each stage can be labeled differently, and each can be compared and contrasted with preceding and succeeding stages. One of the main values of stages is that they tell us very specific and sometimes very important things about people at each plateau or level. And sometimes they tell us things about the process of getting from one stage to another as well.

A trajectory is a continuous path. It has a beginning and an end, and it can usually be described as ascending or descending (or sometimes both). But it is not described in

steps or stages. A missile's path or the flight of a baseball represent trajectories; a journey from my basement to my kitchen represents stages.

Our lives, as we have seen repeatedly throughout this book, can be conceived of in terms of stages, as can our dying. They can also be thought of in terms of trajectories. These are, after all, only metaphors. Neither conception need be evaluated in terms of correctness; it need only provide insight.

Pattison (1977) defines the **life trajectory** as the expected span of life. It is our life's trajectory about which we construct personal narratives and in which we are the incomparable heroes. And it is also our life's trajectory about which we reminisce, analyze, and evaluate when, in old age, we conduct our life review.

Dying Trajectories

When, either in old age or sometime earlier, something happens that informs us that the end of our span is imminent, our life trajectories become **dying trajectories.** The phrase *dying trajectory* is used in medicine and psychology to refer to the speed of dying. For example, *expected swift death* describes a trajectory often found in emergency wards; *expected temporary recovery* is another possible trajectory. *Expected lingering while dying* describes a trajectory that is sometimes characteristic of diseases such as cancer. Such trajectories, note Muzzin and colleagues (1994), often span many years (half of those with cancer survive more than five years), and present serious adjustment problems for the individuals concerned. Many of these relate to how relationships with others are negatively affected by a dying trajectory.

Belsky (1990) points out that misdiagnosed trajectories or trajectories that change during the patient's illness can have serious implications for both the patient and his or her relatives. Patients who linger far longer than expected might occasionally be given less care than required because they have been expected to die. And going from an "expected to die within weeks" to "in temporary remission" complicates the process of accepting death as well as that of advance grieving undertaken by survivors.

Reactions to Knowledge of Imminent Dying

Pattison (1977) describes three phases that characterize our personal trajectories when we discover (because of illness or accident, for example) that we will die sooner than we had hoped or expected. The first, the *acute crisis phase*, begins with knowledge of impending death and is often marked by extreme anxiety and depression. It is during this phase that the denial and perhaps the anger of which Kübler-Ross speaks are most likely.

The *chronic phase* involves gradual adjustment to the thought of dying. Most professionals in this field now advocate that the certainty of impending death should not be denied—that there should be open communication among family members and spouse. Longer dying trajectories

COMMON CAUSES OF DEATH

In 1991, about 87 percent of all deaths in the United States were assigned to 10 leading causes. Of these, heart disease remains the most common killer, especially among men; cancer (malignant neoplasms) is second. For many of these diseases, there is some indication of reduced death rates in recent years. Between 1970 and 1992, deaths from atherosclerosis declined from 15.6 to 6.3 per 100,000. Deaths from heart disease have also been declining since 1950; those due to liver disease and cirrhosis have declined since 1979. However, between 1985 and 1991, there were increases in deaths from AIDS and pulmonary diseases.

FIGURE 19.2

A *Causes of death for U.S. males, 1991.* **B** *Causes of death for U.S. females, 1991.* **C** *Causes of death for those ages 75–84. (Based on U.S. Bureau of the Census, 1994, p. 96.)*

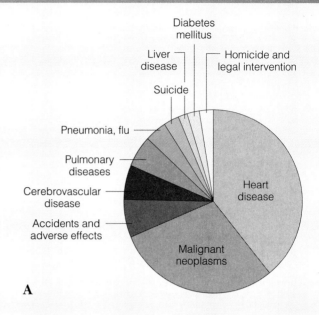

A

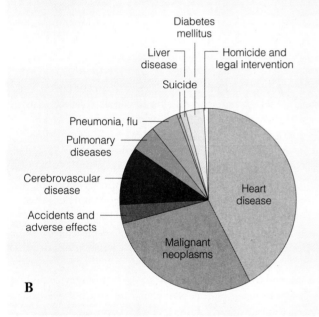

B

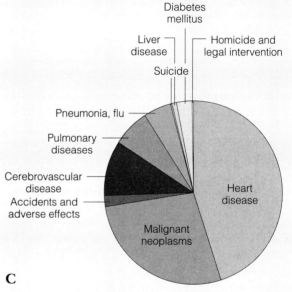

C

provide more time for the dying person to adjust and to die with some measure of acceptance; perhaps as important, they provide survivors with an opportunity to grieve in advance and to begin to make their own adjustments.

The final portion of our dying trajectories, the *terminal phase*, follows final acceptance of the inevitability of dying.

Like stages, trajectories do not describe patterns or movements that are common to everyone. Both leave little room for individual differences. Not all of us go through stages or phases in this order and with these emotions. Dying is a highly individualistic process.

So is living.

Terminal Care

In much the same way that most people try to avoid thinking about their personal deaths, so too do most try to avoid the death of others. In fact, even those in the medical professions are sometimes guilty of trying to distance themselves from death. Not only does medical training often pay little attention to death and dying, but the care afforded those who are most likely to die is often inferior to that afforded others. Mills, Davies, and Macrae (1994) analyzed the care given 50 dying patients in 13 wards of four large teaching hospitals. Among other things, they found that often little effort was made to provide for pa-

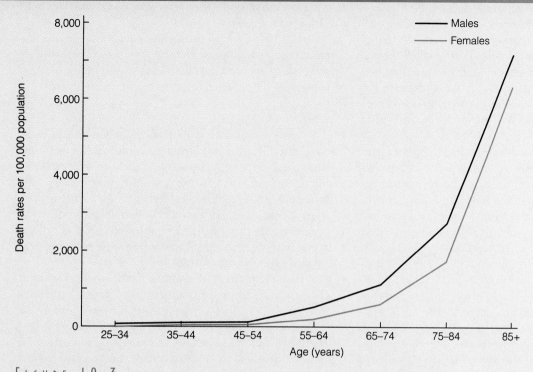

FIGURE 19.3

Heart disease, age, and sex: Death rate from heart disease per 100,000 population. (Based on U.S. Bureau of the Census, 1994, p. 96.)

tient comfort (providing water, encouraging them to eat, brushing their teeth). In addition, contact between nursing staff and dying patients tended to be minimal, and the patient's isolation tended to increase as death become more imminent.

Palliative Care and Hospices

Palliative care, a medical specialization concerned specifically with the needs of the terminally ill, is aimed toward easing the physical and psychological distress of those who are dying. Palliative care units are often found in conventional hospitals, but may also be found in facilities set up specifically to care for those who are dying. The palliative

care and hospice movement, notes Dudgeon (1994), arose specifically because the needs of terminal patients were not being met by the established health-care system.

A **hospice** might be a medical or housing facility specifically dedicated to the care of the terminally ill; or it might be the terminally ill patient's own home. In the past 10 years, notes Hohl (1994), home health care has grown dramatically. This is partly because of a rapidly aging population, and also because of an overburdened and expensive medical system. Home health care now includes such elements of care as IV (intravenous) therapy, changing dressings, and physical therapy. When the home is used as a hospice—that is, as a place to die in dignity—hospice workers, who are trained medical personnel, usually visit the home daily—as might psychological, occupational, physical, and other therapists (Smith & Yuen, 1994).

Palliative care in out-of-home hospices reflects a new sensitivity to death and dying. It is a movement that is characterized by a "hands-on" type of care, very similar to that which a terminally ill person might receive in a private home. Such care is intended only for short-term patients with *expected-to-die-soon* trajectories. In one survey of 405 hospice patients, average survival time following admission was 29 days (Christakis, 1994).

When dying patients are brought into a separate hospice facility, members of their families are ordinarily expected to provide much of the needed care, sometimes being required to remain in the hospice with the terminally ill person on a full-time basis. As a result, about half of all hospice patients are male, although they make up a much smaller proportion of the population. Also, because of the cost, hospice care is available to only a small proportion of the terminally ill. Hospices provide medical attention, including pain-relieving drugs, but they do not ordinarily use any life-prolonging measures. Their goals are not only to ease the process of dying for the person involved but also to ease the process for friends and relatives. As a result, many of them also include elements of spirituality, and sometimes of religion as well.

The hospice movement is not without critics. Because it shifts the burden of medical care for the terminally ill from hospital facilities, where care is very expensive, to the home, where care is relatively inexpensive, there is a danger that hospices may become dumping grounds for certain patients who require a lot of medically uncomplicated care. However, the fact that hospice care is restricted to those diagnosed as terminally ill reduces this risk somewhat. By the same token, restricting hospices in this way makes them inappropriate for many of the dying. Only if both the patient and the patient's family have completely accepted the inevitability of death is the patient eligible for hospice care. Accordingly, entering a hospice requires giving up whatever vestige of hope might have been left. And even at the very end—even after complete acceptance of the inevitability of imminent death—there is always room for a little hope.

We can always hope for a miracle, for those who believe in such things; or for a happy day or a happy hour; or maybe for just one last sniff of the rose.

Euthanasia

In November 1994, Robert Latimer was convicted of murder for killing his severely disabled daughter. In some ways, this case (which is under appeal) is similar to that of the Rambergs' who, 50 years earlier, killed their 2-year-old son, Victor. Victor was suffering from terminal, inoperable cancer, and screamed in pain, day and night. In the end, the parents ran a hose from the automobile exhaust into Victor's room. Although they described clearly what they had done, the jury refused to convict them (Toneguzzi, 1994).

Popularly referred to as *mercy killing*, **euthanasia** encompasses a complicated and controversial collection of issues, which are presented here starkly, with little evaluative comment; our consciences make their own comments.

Definitions

The term *euthanasia* is of Greek origin and means, literally, "good death." A distinction is often made between *passive* and *active* euthanasia. *Active euthanasia* involves deliberately doing certain things to shorten life, such as administering a lethal injection or removing a patient from life-support systems. *Passive euthanasia* involves not doing certain things that might have prolonged life and is illustrated in those instances in which heart surgery is not performed or blood transfusions are not given.

Holland is the only country in the world that, as of this writing, fully accepts euthanasia. Certain guidelines govern its use. Most important is that two conditions be met: The patient must be terminally ill, suffering hopelessly, and with no possibility of a cure; and there must be repeated requests for assisted suicide. Euthanasia has now been practiced in Holland for more than 10 years, but still remains highly controversial.

The Controversy

Some physicians, for example, absolutely refuse to perform euthanasia under any circumstance (often for religious reasons) (Harvey, 1994). Some fear that legalizing voluntary euthanasia may quickly lead to *involuntary* euthanasia. There are apparently several hundred cases in Holland every year in which the conditions for euthanasia have not been clearly met but in which the patient's life is ended in any case (Saunders, 1994). Others caution that the terminally ill patient's spoken thoughts about dying, and even their requests for assistance in so doing, do not necessarily reflect a sustained desire for assisted suicide or euthanasia (Block & Billings, 1994). After a review of the situation in Holland, the Board of Trustees of the American Medical Association strongly recommended that euthanasia and physician-assisted suicide be rejected by the American Medical Association (anonymous, 1994).

On the other hand, there are others who argue that terminally ill patients have a right to refuse medical care, and that their decisions should be respected and supported (Cain et al., 1990). Suicide is very common among the elderly, notes Carpenter (1993), in spite of the fact that public opinion is predominantly negative. He argues that the elderly have a right to what he labels "ethical" suicide, unobstructed suicide following a rational decision based on the "wisdom" of old age. Similarly, Humphry (1992) argues that although "old age" should never be sufficient

ADVANCE DIRECTIVE
Living Will and Health Care Proxy

Death is a part of life. It is a reality like birth, growth and aging. I am using this advance directive to convey my wishes about medical care to my doctors and other people looking after me at the end of my life. It is called an advance directive because it gives instructions in advance about what I want to happen to me in the future. It expresses my wishes about medical treatment that might keep me alive. I want this to be legally binding.

If I cannot make or communicate decisions about my medical care, those around me should rely on this document for instructions about measures that could keep me alive.

I do not want medical treatment (including feeding and water by tube) that will keep me alive if:
- I am unconscious and there is no reasonable prospect that I will ever be conscious again (even if I am not going to die soon in my medical condition), <u>or</u>
- I am near death from an illness or injury with no reasonable prospect of recovery.

I do want medicine and other care to make me more comfortable and to take care of pain and suffering. I want this even if the pain medicine makes me die sooner.

I want to give some extra instructions: *[Here list any special instructions, e.g., some people fear being kept alive after a debilitating stroke. If you have wishes about this, or any other conditions, please write them here.]*

The legal language in the box that follows is a health care proxy. It gives another person the power to make medical decisions for me.

I name _____, who lives at _____
_____, phone number _____,

to make medical decisions for me if I cannot make them myself. This person is called a health care "surrogate," "agent," "proxy," or "attorney in fact." This power of attorney shall become effective when I become incapable of making or communicating decisions about my medical care. This means that this document stays legal when and if I lose the power to speak for myself, for instance, if I am in a coma or have Alzheimer's disease.

My health care proxy has power to tell others what my advance directive means. This person also has power to make decisions for me, based either on what I would have wanted, or, if this is not known, on what he or she thinks is best for me.

If my first choice health care proxy cannot or decides not to act for me, I name _____
_____, address _____,
phone number _____, as my second choice.

(over, please)

LWGEN

I have discussed my wishes with my health care proxy, and with my second choice if I have chosen to appoint a second person. My proxy(ies) has(have) agreed to act for me.

I have thought about this advance directive carefully. I know what it means and want to sign it. I have chosen two witnesses, neither of whom is a member of my family, nor will inherit from me when I die. My witnesses are not the same people as those I named as my health care proxies. I understand that this form should be notarized if I use the box to name (a) health care proxy(ies).

Signature _____

Date _____

Address _____

Witness' signature _____

Witness' printed name _____

Address _____

Witness' signature _____

Witness' printed name _____

Address _____

Notary [to be used if proxy is appointed] _____

Drafted and Distributed by Choice In Dying, Inc—the National Council for the right to Die. Choice In Dying is a National not-for-profit organization which works for the rights of patients at the end of life. In addition to this generic advance directive, Choice In Dying distributes advance directives that conform to each state's specific legal requirements and maintains a national Living Will Registry for completed documents.

CHOICE IN DYING INC.—
the national council for the right to die
(formerly Concern for Dying/Society for the Right to Die)
200 Varick Street, New York, NY 10014 (212) 366-5540

5/92

FIGURE 19.4
A living will. (Reprinted with permission from Choice in Dying, 200 Varick Street, New York, NY 10014.)

grounds for legal suicide, the presence of an irreversible, pain-causing, terminal illness should be.

The Living Will

Do we have a moral or a legal right to decide when we, or others, shall die? Do conditions such as severe and irreversible pain, coupled with inevitable and imminent death, justify euthanasia? Is passive euthanasia less objectionable than active euthanasia? Are there significant ethical or biological issues that clearly separate suicide, euthanasia, and perhaps even abortion?

These questions are far easier to ask than to answer. But for those whose answers are clear and who believe they would want to choose death under certain circumstances, the Euthanasia Education Council provides a document that can be used to formalize these wishes. It is called a *living will* and is reproduced in Figure 19.4. This is merely a sample form. State-specific forms are available, free of charge, from Choice in Dying.

BEREAVEMENT AND GRIEVING

Bereavement, as we saw earlier, is the loss of something or someone important. *Grief* is an intense emotional reaction to bereavement. *Mourning* is what is done as a result of grief—for example, crying, praying, or, as at some Irish wakes, singing and drinking, and perhaps even fighting and dancing, in addition to crying and praying.

In some cultures and in some religions, length of mourning is predetermined. Often, too, certain ritual behaviors are undertaken by the bereaved. Some of these behaviors, like wearing the black colors of "widow's weeds" or sprinkling ashes on one's head, may serve as external symbols of loss. They are also a sign of homage for the deceased. But perhaps even more importantly, they provide a ritualized and acceptable way of displaying grief, and they may accelerate the eventual acceptance of the loss. (See Across Cultures: "Makoto Moriuchi's Father's Ghost.")

MAKOTO MORIUCHI'S FATHER'S GHOST

When Hozumi, a Japanese nobleman, saw Shakespeare's *Hamlet* for the first time, he was somewhat taken aback at Hamlet's reaction of fear when faced with his father's ghost, victim of a "foul and most unnatural murder." "Ghost scenes are not uncommon in Japanese theatres," he writes, "and when the ghost appears to the parents, sons, daughters, friends or lovers, those who meet never show signs of dread, but those of joy for the meeting" (quoted in Hamabata, 1990, p. 54).

In Japan, explains Hamabata, the dead and their ancestors are as much a part of the household, of the *ie*, as the living. And although the dead are transformed, through stages observed by regular and formal ritual, from spirits of the newly deceased (*shiryoo*) to new-buddhas (*nii-botoke*), then to buddhas (*hotoke*), and finally to ancestors-cum-gods (*senzo*), they are not forgotten. Among the many ceremonies that remember the dead is the *obon,* an annual four-day series of rituals during which the spirits of the dead are welcomed back to their households. On the first day of the *obon*, the living of the family go to the temple graveyard, clean the tombstones, offer flowers and food, and, in the evening, lead the spirits of the dead back to their homes with a lantern bearing the family's crest. And, four days later, they lead them back to the temple, or they light a fire to guide them on their journey from the living to the dead.

This, the *obon,* is only one of many rituals involving care of the dead. Makoto Moriuchi, for example, has a cabinet in a corner of his large dining room. In the cabinet is a photograph of Mr. Moriuchi, his dead father. Also there are candles and flowers and other objects such as, for example, a brass container with cooked rice in it, a dish of fruit, and a miniature bottle of Johnnie Walker Black Label scotch. "Father likes to drink," explained Makoto, after he had introduced his guest to his father—always speaking in the present tense (Hamabata, 1990, p. 61).

Forty-nine days after Mr. Moriuchi's death, a special traditional ceremony took place wherein his remains were placed in the household tomb. This marked the transformation of his spirit from the world of the newly-dead to that of the new-buddha. And it also marked a change in the relationship between members of the family and Mr. Moriuchi. In

Hamabata's (1990) words, these ceremonies "did not eliminate Mr. Moriuchi from their lives. Instead, they opened the way for Mr. Moriuchi's continued presence in the household" (p. 67). The ghost of Mr. Moriuchi lives.

To Think About   These few short paragraphs cannot do justice to the richness and meaning of these ceremonies and beliefs. But they outline attitudes and customs very different from those prevalent in North America, where quickly forgetting the dead is often seen as a mark of strength and adjustment. What advantages (if any) do you think one system might have over the other? How might these different attitudes and beliefs be reflected in our attitudes toward our own dying, as well as toward the death of others?

Effects of Bereavement

Bereavement appears to have both long-term and relatively short-term effects.

Short-Term Effects

There is considerable variation in the ways in which different people express grief, as well as in the length of time required for recovery. However, there are a number of symptoms and behaviors that appear to be quite general following the death of someone close. Among these are physiological signs of distress such as crying, eating and sleeping disturbances, and other physical symptoms such as constriction of the throat, heart palpitations, trembling, and sighing. Also, many who are recently bereaved are constantly preoccupied with the image of the dead person, almost as though it were a hallucination. Some hear the dead person's voice, or think they have caught glimpses of the deceased among crowds. Others feel a sort of presence, and become fearful that they are losing their minds. Still others become obsessed with details of the dead person's last days or hours. In addition, there may be feelings of guilt about things that were done or not done for the deceased.

Long-Term Effects

Most of the short-term effects of bereavement disappear slowly and are typically gone within the first year. However, Byrne and Raphael (1994) found that about 50 percent of a sample of widowed, elderly men continued to

Depression following bereavement is quite common but doesn't usually last as long as depression following other causes. Recovery from bereavement is sometimes faster among those who mourn openly than among those who deny and hide their grief.

manifest recurring symptoms of severe grief 13 months after their bereavement. Among possible long-term effects of bereavement are physical complaints and sometimes even decreased life expectancy (Gibson, 1992). Other studies suggest that severe depression requiring medical or psychiatric attention is more common following bereavement (Zisook et al., 1994). Depression after bereavement, however, is not ordinarily as severe as depression resulting from other causes, and usually responds to treatment. And five years following bereavement, there is no longer higher incidence of illness or of mortality.

The long-term effects of bereavement vary considerably from one person to another, depending partly on individual personality characteristics and partly on the nature of the bereavement. Loss of a child is especially difficult for parents (Tamer, Tamer, & Warey, 1991). In contrast, loss of an elderly parent is more easily accepted.

Anticipatory Grief

In addition, loss that is anticipated typically leads to less severe and shorter-duration grief reactions, a fact sometimes attributed to what is termed *anticipatory grief*. Anticipatory grief relates to the grief reactions people experience in the time between learning that someone is terminally ill and the actual death. Anticipatory grief can be very profound, and is often accompanied by many of the physiological and psychological symptoms that follow actual bereavement. However, some evidence suggests that anticipatory grief can sometimes temper the severity

of the grief reaction following death and reduce the length of the grieving period (Byrne & Raphael, 1994).

Many theorists believe that working through grief (often referred to as *grief work*) is extremely important to recovering from bereavement and to subsequent happiness and well-being. Unfortunately, however, there are no easy recipes for alleviating the pain and agony of the bereaved. And although formal periods of mourning that are dictated and sanctioned by society sometimes appear helpful, there are those who argue that grief work may *not* be very important for adjustment to death. For example, Stroebe (1992/1993) argues that there is little evidence to support the notion that grief work is necessary or even very important. She points out that different cultures have many ways of coping with loss. Perhaps we can learn something from them.

FINAL THEMES

Dying and grieving are not happy notes upon which to end a chapter—or a book; birth would have been happier. Unfortunately, however, the chronology of our lives inevitably runs in a womb-to-tomb direction. And *The Lifespan* has been structured along that same chronology.

But this isn't real life; it's just a book. We can end where and how we please. If we wanted to, we could slap a birth right onto the tail end of this tale, pretend life is a huge cycle, and start all over again, full of joy and hope.

Instead, we end not with a new birth but with a brief summary of the most important themes that have run through this book, giving it continuity. These themes, which define the lifespan perspective, are presented as an introduction in Chapter 1. Here, they are a summary.

- *Development is continuous.* It isn't something that happens only to infants, children, and perhaps adolescents, and then ceases with adulthood. There are important positive changes throughout the entire lifespan. Sadly, there are negative changes, too.

- *Maturity is relative.* Human development does not eventually culminate in a predetermined, final state of maturity. Hence, the developmental psychologist is interested as much in the *processes* of development as in states of competence. Our competencies are relative; they do not always endure. A mature and fully competent 2-year-old can pull my baseball cap over her ears, but cannot tie her shoes; a mature 10-year-old can tie his shoes, but cannot solve an abstract problem of Boolean algebra; a mature 65-year-old may solve the problem in Boolean algebra, but will be hard-pressed to explain the final and absolute meaning of existence.

- *Development is contextual.* What we become and how we think, feel, and act are bound to the contexts from which we have emerged and in which we continue to interact. The conclusions of developmental psychology need to be interpreted in light of what we know of the lives and the cultures of those whose behaviors led to the conclusions. Intelligence in North America presupposes the ability to acquire high levels of facility with symbolic systems such as written language; elsewhere, intelligence might be more closely related to the ability to recognize slug tracks in the sand.

- *Developmental influences are bidirectional.* We are part of our contexts; we carry them around with us. They shape us; we shape them. Jessica's parents bought her a set of encyclopedias—which helped her prove to them (and others) that she was as intelligent as they suspected. That they suspected she was intelligent influenced them to buy the books in

the first place. Her behavior influenced their suspicions, which influenced their behavior, which influenced her . . .

- *Heredity and environment interact throughout the lifespan.* Gene–environment interactions affect all aspects of human functioning: physical, social, and intellectual. Alone, neither explains very much at all.

- *There is no average person.* Each of us is unique, very special, quite wonderful.

And perhaps even after our mirrors no longer cloud over, we may still continue to be very special and wonderful.

Perhaps God's great black oxen will not trample our bones after all. Maybe when they reach us, they will pause for a moment so that we might scramble onto their broad backs. And then they will carry us through eternity, stopping as often as we wish so that we can smell the new roses.

MAIN POINTS

Death

1. Neurological, or brain, death signifies cessation of electrical activity in the brain. *Bereavement* describes a loss; *grief* is an intense emotional reaction to bereavement; and *mourning* describes the things people do when they are grieving.

Notions of Death Through the Lifespan

2. Our culture tends to distance and deny death (through euphemisms and avoidance of contact or care). Very young children often do not completely understand the finality of death, although media exposure has made them considerably more sophisticated. With advancing age, declining health and other events conspire to make us more conscious of our mortality. Fear of death appears at all stages of life.

Dying

3. Kübler-Ross describes five possible stages of dying (for those who know death is imminent): *denial* ("not me"), *anger* ("why me?"), *bargaining* ("let me suffer less and I will . . ."), *depression*, and *acceptance*. Not all people go through these stages and in this order.

4. Our life trajectories are our expected spans of life. When something happens to inform us that our trajectories will end, our perspectives change from life trajectory to dying trajectory. Medically, the phrase *dying trajectory* refers to the speed with which a person is expected to die.

5. *Palliative care* for the terminally ill is designed to ease their dying as well as to make things easier for the

bereaved. *Hospice care* is short-term care for the terminally ill outside a hospital setting, sometimes in the patient's home or in centers designed specifically for that purpose.

6. *Euthanasia*, popularly called *mercy killing*, is a controversial procedure that can be either passive (not doing something that would prolong life) or active (deliberately doing something to shorten life). Under certain conditions, it is completely legal in Holland.

Bereavement and Grieving

7. Grief can result in a wide range of short-term symptoms and behaviors (appetite loss, sleep disturbances, crying); longer-term effects of bereavement can include psychological and physical problems, sometimes evident in serious depression. For some, experiencing grief (grief work) may be important for mental and psychological well-being. Sometimes *anticipatory grief* (profound grief that results when the bereaved first learns about the impending death) may reduce the length and severity of subsequent grieving.

Final Themes

8. Development is continuous from birth until death. Maturity is always relative rather than absolute. At all stages, context exerts a profound, bidirectional influence on the person. Nature and nurture interact throughout life. Ultimately, there is no average person.

9. There are always new roses.

1. What do children understand of death? And adolescents? And you?

    ▪ How many examples of death denial and distancing can you find that relate to your cultural context? What sorts of arguments might you advance to support (or refute) the proposition that distancing and denying death is socially and psychologically healthy?

2. What are some possible stages of dying?

    ▪ Why might it be inappropriate and unwise to assume that all dying is best described in terms of stages?

3. What is euthanasia? Is it legal?

    ▪ Using current library resources, research the history of euthanasia in Holland, paying particular attention to the laws governing its application, and to alleged instances of violations of these laws.

4. How inevitable is grief following bereavement? Is it important to grieve?

    ▪ Some theorists suggest that the value of grief work has been exaggerated. Can you find good evidence to support or contradict this belief?

STUDY TERMS

acceptance 548

active euthanasia 552

anger 548

anticipatory grief 555

bargaining 548

bereavement 544

death 544

denial 548

depression 548

dying trajectories 549

euthanasia 552

grief 544

hospice 551

life trajectory 549

living will 553

mourning 544

palliative care 551

passive euthanasia 552

stages of dying 548

FURTHER READINGS

A classic layperson's book on death and dying is the one by Kübler-Ross:

> Kübler-Ross, E. (1969). *On death and dying.* New York: Macmillan.

Irish provides an enlightening look at how different cultures react to bereavement in:

> Irish, D. P. (1993). *Ethnic variations in dying, death, and grief: Diversity in universality.* Washington, DC: Hemisphere.

The following is a useful guide intended specifically for those involved in helping children cope with death and dying:

> Ward, B. (1993). *Good grief: Exploring feelings, loss, and death with under elevens: A holistic approach.* London: Jessica Kingsley.

GLOSSARY

This glossary defines the most important terms and expressions used in this text. They are boldfaced throughout the text and most are listed as study terms at the end of each chapter. In each case, the meaning given corresponds to the text usage. (The number after each definition indicates the page on which the term is first discussed.) For more complete definitions, consult a standard psychological dictionary.

Abortion A miscarriage occurring usually before the 20th week of pregnancy when the fetus normally weighs less than 1 pound. 112

Accommodation The modification of an activity or an ability that the child already has in order to conform to environmental demands. Piaget's description of development holds that assimilation and accommodation are the means by which an individual interacts with and adapts to the world. 47

Acquired immune deficiency syndrome (AIDS) An incurable and fatal disease, transmitted through the exchange of body fluids. 101

Active vocabulary Consists of words the child actually uses. (See *passive vocabulary*.) 148

Activity theory A theory of aging based on the belief that successful aging is more likely among those who remain most involved in world and community affairs. (See *disengagement theory*.) 527

Acute pelvic inflammatory disease A sexually transmitted disease that frequently results from other STDs such as gonorrhea. Also termed *salpingitis* or *endometritis*, pelvic inflammatory disease affects about 1 million women a year and is often associated with infertility and tubal pregnancies. 362

Adaptation Changes in an organism in response to the environment. Such changes are assumed to facilitate interaction with the environment. Adaptation plays a central role in Piaget's theory. 47

Additive bilingualism Phrase used to describe situations in which learning a second language has a positive effect on the first, as well as on general psychological functioning. (See *subtractive bilingualism*.) 212

Adolescence A general term for the period from the onset of puberty to adulthood and typically including the teenage years. 316

Adolescent egocentrism A cognitive and emotional self-centeredness characteristic of the adolescent, resulting from a confusion of the thoughts of the self with those of others. Evident in the imaginary audience and the personal fable. (See *imaginary audience* and *personal fable*.) 331

Adolescent moratorium Erikson's term for the social function of the hiatus between childhood and adulthood. The adolescent period is a moratorium in that it provides the child with a period of time during which to experiment with various identities. 348

Affiliation A positive emotional relationship. Affiliative behavior is evident in behavior designed to make friends and includes talking, smiling, and playing with others. Affiliation implies a weaker relationship than does attachment. 172

AFP test A screening test designed to detect the likelihood of a fetal neural tube defect by revealing the presence of alphafetoprotein in the mother's blood. 75

Afterbirth The placenta and other membranes that are expelled from the uterus following childbirth. 109

Ageism Negative stereotyped prejudice based on age; common with respect to the elderly. 494

Aggression Forceful actions intended to dominate or intimidate, including actions such as insisting, asserting, intruding, or being angry or even violent. (See *violence*.) 296

Alzheimer's disease A disease associated with old age (but also occurring as young as 40), marked by progressive loss of memory and of brain function and eventual death. 504

Amniocentesis A procedure in which amniotic fluid is removed by a hollow needle from around the fetus in a pregnant woman. Subsequent analysis of this fluid may reveal chromosomal aberrations (Down syndrome, for example) and other fetal problems. 78

Amniotic fluid A clear or straw-colored fluid in which the fetus develops in the uterus. 78

Amniotic sac The sac, filled with amniotic fluid, in which the fetus develops in the uterus. 109

Anal stage The second of Freud's psychosexual stages of development, beginning at approximately 8 months and lasting until around 18 months. It is characterized by the child's preoccupation with physical anal activities. 34

Androgynous Characterized by a balance of masculine and feminine characteristics. 353

Anencephalic A condition involving missing parts or all of the brain. 165

Anorexia nervosa A medical condition not due to any detectable illness, primarily affecting adolescent girls, and involving a loss of 15 to 25 percent of ideal body weight and subsequent refusal or inability to eat normally. 324

Anoxia A condition in which there is an insufficient supply of oxygen to the brain. 115

Arousal A term with both physiological and psychological meaning. Physiologically, arousal refers to changes in heart rate, respiration, brain activity, and so on. Psychologically, it refers to corresponding changes in alertness or vigilance. 45

Arteriosclerosis Thickening and hardening of artery walls; associated with aging. (See *atherosclerosis*.) 447

Artificial insemination A breeding procedure often used in animal husbandry and sometimes with humans. The procedure eliminates the need for a physical union between male and female. 67

Assimilation The act of incorporating objects or aspects of objects to previously learned activities. To assimilate is, in a sense, to ingest or to use something that is previously learned; more simply, it is the exercise of previously learned responses. 47

Association Relates to associationism, a term employed almost synonymously with stimulus–response learning. Associationism refers to the formation of associations or links between stimuli, between responses, or between stimuli and responses. 40

Atherosclerosis The gradual accumulation of plaque (fatty deposits) on the insides of blood vessels. (See *arteriosclerosis*.) 447

Attention deficit hyperactivity disorder (ADHD) A disorder marked by excessive general activity relative to the child's age, attention problems, high impulsivity, and low frustration tolerance. 305

Attribution An assignment of cause or blame for the outcomes of our behaviors. Our attributions are important influences on our behavior. 294

Authoritarian parenting A highly controlling, dogmatic, obedience-oriented parenting style in which there is little recourse to reasoning and no acceptance of the child's autonomy. 235

Authoritative parenting A moderately controlling parenting style in which value is placed on independence and reasoning, but in which parents impose some regulations and controls. 235

Autism A serious childhood mental disorder that is usually apparent by age 3 and that is characterized by social unresponsiveness, poor or nonexistent communication skills, and bizarre behavior. 181

Autoimmunity A malfunction in the body's disease-fighting capabilities whereby the body's own benign cells are identified as harmful and thus attacked. Autoimmunity is thought to be involved in some age-related diseases. 500

Autonomy Piaget's label for the second stage of moral development, marked by a reliance on internal standards as guides for behaving and for judging morality. (See *heteronomy*.) 336

Autonomy versus shame and doubt The second Erikson stage, about ages 18 months to 2 or 3, when the preschooler faces the challenge of developing a sense of mastery and control (autonomy) and giving up some of the security of relying on parents. 222

Autosome Any chromosome in mature sperm and ova other than the sex chromosome. Each of these cells therefore contains 22 autosomes. 68

Babbling The relatively meaningless sounds that young infants make or repeat. 150

Babinski reflex A reflex present in the newborn child but disappearing later in life. When infants' feet are tickled in the center of their soles, the toes fan outward. Normal adults curl their toes inward. 95

Baby tossing The medieval practice of tossing infants from one player to another in a bizarre game; the object was to throw accurately and *not* drop the baby. Someone usually lost. 14

Basic need An unlearned physiological requirement of the human organism. Specifically, the need for food, drink, and sex. 56

Behavior modification A general term for the application of behavioristic principles (primarily those of operant conditioning) in systematic and deliberate attempts to change behavior. 43

Behavioristic theory A general term for those theories of learning that are primarily concerned with the observable components of behavior (stimuli and responses). Such theories are labeled S–R learning theories and are exemplified in classical and operant conditioning. 39

Bereavement A term used to describe the loss suffered by friends and relatives of a person who has died. 544

Bidirectionality Describes the reciprocal effects on one another of people or people and their environment. 7

Birth order The position that a child occupies in a family (for example, first-, second-, or third-born). 237

Breech birth An abnormal presentation of the fetus at birth with the buttocks first rather than the head first. 109

Bulimia nervosa Significant overconcern over body shape and weight, manifested in recurrent episodes of binge eating often accompanied by self-induced vomiting, use of laxatives or diuretics, strict fasting, or vigorous exercise. 326

Burnout A general term used to describe the effects of stress associated with job overload. Often expressed in a feeling of not being able to cope. 462

Canalization Waddington's term to describe the extent to which genetically determined characteristics are resistant to environmental influences. A highly canalized trait (such as hair color) remains unchanged in the face of most environmental influences; less canalized characteristics (such as manifested intelligence) are highly influenced by the environment. 70

Career A broad term including a range of related occupations or jobs that often span an entire working lifetime. (See *job, work, occupation*.) 393

Career self-efficacy The individual's expectations of success and competence in a career. Closely tied to sex, previous achievement, interests, and experience. 400

Cataracts A clouding of the eye caused by fibrous growth over the eyeball. Associated with aging and surgically correctable. 446

Cell error theory A theory of aging based on the notion that with the passage of time, certain changes occur in DNA material causing the cell to malfunction or to cease functioning. 499

Cephalocaudal Referring to the direction of development, beginning with the head and proceeding outward toward the tail. Early infant development is cephalocaudal because children acquire control over their heads before gaining control over their limbs. 96

Cerebral palsy Label for a collection of congenital motor problems associated with brain damage and manifested in motor problems of varying severity, and occasionally in other problems such as convulsions or behavior disorders. (See *significant developmental motor disability*.) 180

Cervix The small circular opening to the womb (uterus) that dilates considerably during birth to allow passage of the child. 109

Cesarean delivery A common surgical procedure in which the fetus is delivered by means of an incision in the mother's abdomen and uterus. 110

Chorion biopsy A procedure in which samples of the membrane lining the uterus are used to permit prenatal diagnosis of potential birth defects. 78

Chromosomal disorders Abnormalities, inconsistencies, or deformities in chromosomes, sometimes involving absent or extra chromosomes. 75

Chromosome A microscopic body in the nucleus of all human and plant cells containing genes—the carriers of heredity. Each mature human sex cell (sperm or ovum) contains 23 chromosomes, each containing countless numbers of genes. 68

Chunking A type of memory strategy (cognitive strategy) whereby related items are grouped into more easily remembered "chunks" (for example, a prefix and four digits for a phone number rather than seven unrelated numbers). 263

Classical conditioning Also called learning through stimulus substitution, it involves the repeated pairing of two stimuli so that a previously neutral (conditioned) stimulus eventually elicits the same (conditioned) response that was previously evoked by the first (unconditioned) stimulus. Pavlov was the first to describe this type of conditioning. 40

Climacteric Popularly called the "change of life" that accompanies middle age. It involves reduced reproductive capabilities in both men and women and culminates in menopause for women. (See *menopause*.) 450

Climacteric syndrome Medical label for symptoms that sometimes accompany the climacteric. Might include dizziness, hot flashes, headaches, mood fluctuations, and general weakness. 450

Cognition To cognize is to know. Hence, cognition refers to knowing, understanding, problem solving, and related intellectual processes. 47

Cognitive Descriptive of mental processes such as thinking, knowing, and remembering. Cognitive theories attempt to explain intellectual development and functioning. 47

Cognitive strategies Procedures, knowledge, and information that relate to the processes involved in learning and remembering rather than to the content of what is learned. Cognitive strategies are used to identify problems, select approaches to their solution, monitor progress, and use feedback. Cognitive strategies are closely related to metacognition and metamemory. 262

Cognitive-behavior therapy A therapeutic approach that combines the use of reinforcement and/or punishment (behavioristic techniques) with more reason-based approaches. 327

Cohort A group of individuals born within the same specific period of time. For example, the 1920s cohort includes those born between 1920 and 1929. 20

Commitment The decision-making aspect of Sternberg's theory of love. Involves *deciding* that one is in love and deciding what to do as a consequence. (See *passion; intimacy; triangular theory of love*.) 414

Communication   The transmission of messages. Communication does not require language, although it is greatly facilitated by it. Nonhuman animals communicate even though they do not possess language.   147

Compensation   A logical rule stating that certain changes can compensate for opposing changes, thereby negating their effects. For example, as a square object becomes thinner, it also becomes longer; increases in length compensate for decreases in width. These changes combine to negate any actual changes in the object's mass.   258

Compensatory preschool programs   Preschool education programs whose purpose is to make up for early disadvantages in the lives of some children. The best known of these programs in the United States is Project Head Start. (See *Project Head Start.*)   203

Concept   A collection of perceptual experiences or ideas related by virtue of their common properties.   198

Conception   The beginning of human and other animal life. Also called fertilization, conception occurs with the union of a sperm cell with an egg cell.   67

Conceptualization   The forming of concepts (ideas or meanings). An intellectual process leading to thinking and understanding.   135

Concrete operations   The third of Piaget's four major stages, lasting from age 7 or 8 to approximately 11 or 12, and characterized primarily by the child's ability to deal with concrete problems and objects, or objects and problems easily imagined in a concrete sense.   48

Conditioned response   A response that is elicited by a conditioned stimulus. In some obvious ways, a conditioned response resembles its corresponding unconditioned response, although they are not identical.   40

Conditioned stimulus   A stimulus that either does not elicit any response or initially elicits a global orienting response. As a result of being paired with an unconditioned stimulus and its response, the conditioned stimulus comes to elicit the same response. For example, a stimulus that is always present at the time of a fear reaction may become a conditioned stimulus for fear.   40

Conditioning   A term that describes a simple type of learning. (See also *classical conditioning; operant conditioning.*)   40

Conscience   An internalized set of rules governing an individual's behavior.   34

Conservation   A Piagetian term implying that certain quantitative attributes of objects remain unchanged unless something is added to or taken away from them. Mass, number, area, and volume are capable of being conserved.   200

Constructivism   A psychological-philosophical orientation that views the central problem in explaining cognitive development as one of understanding how the mind succeeds in inventing (constructing) relationships among objects and events.   49

Contextual model   A developmental model that emphasizes the importance of environmental variables such as culture, cohort, family, and historical events. This model maintains that in order to explain and understand human development, the context in which development occurs must be considered.   32

Contextual theory of intelligence   The label for Sternberg's belief that intelligence involves adaptation in real-life contexts (in contrast with the view that intelligence is best measured by means of abstract timed questions and problems).   269

Continuous society   A society that does not clearly mark passage from one period of life to another. (See *discontinuous society.*)   316

Control group   A group of subjects who are not experimented with but who are used as comparisons to an experimental group to ascertain whether an experimental procedure affected the experimental group.   18

Conventional   Kohlberg's second level of morality, reflecting a desire to establish and maintain good relations with others (law and order; obedience).   336

Correlational study   A study that looks at the relationship (correlation) between two or more variables—for example, home background and delinquency, or achievement and intelligence.   18

Crack   Name given to the drug that results when cocaine is "cooked down" with bicarbonate of soda to produce freebase cocaine (also called rock). It is usually smoked rather than snorted and produces a much stronger and more immediate rush than cocaine.   370

Creativity   Generally refers to the capacity of individuals to produce novel or original answers or products. The term *creative* is an adjective that may be used to describe people, products, or processes.   275

Critical period   The period during which an appropriate stimulus must be presented to an organism for imprinting to occur.   50

Cross-linking theory   Describes an aging process whereby unexpected bonds form between body cells, altering the functioning of the cells.   500

Cross-sectional study   A technique in the investigation of human development that involves observing and comparing different subjects at different age levels. For example, a cross-sectional study might compare 4- and 6-year-olds by observing two different groups of children at the same time, one group consisting of 4-year-old children and the other of 6-year-old children. A longitudinal study would require that the same children be examined at age 4 and again at age 6.   19

Crystallized abilities   Cattell's term for intellectual abilities that are highly dependent on experience (verbal and computational skills and general information, for example). These abilities may continue to improve well into old age. (See also *fluid abilities*.) 268

Culture fair A general label for intelligence tests that are less heavily biased in favor of the cultural groups for which the tests were initially designed and on which they have been normed—in other words, tests that are more fair to certain cultures. 271

Cyclic movements Expression used to describe the infant's spontaneous, regularly recurring, motor movements. 134

Death Cessation of vital functioning. Medically, death is usually defined in terms of cessation of brain activity. 544

Declarative memory Explicit, conscious long-term memory, in contrast with implicit (or nondeclarative) memory. Declarative memory may be either semantic or episodic. (See *semantic memory*; *episodic memory*.) 264

Defense mechanism A relatively irrational and sometimes unhealthy method used by people to compensate for their inability to satisfy basic desires and to overcome the anxiety accompanying this inability. 35

Deferred imitation Imitating people or events in their absence. Deferred imitation is assumed by Piaget to be critical to developing language. 145

Dependent variable The variable that may or may not be affected by manipulations of the independent variable in an experimental situation. 17

Development The total process whereby individuals adapt to their environment. Development includes growth, maturation, and learning. 7

Developmental arithmetic disorder A learning disability evident in specific problems in developing arithmetic skills in the absence of other problems such as mental retardation. 274

Developmental career model An approach to career guidance that attempts to prepare individuals for career choice by facilitating a sequence of decisions and personal preparations related to a career. (See *job–person matching*.) 396

Developmental coordination disorder A childhood motor skills disorder not associated with brain damage or cerebral palsy, often evident in difficulties in learning or in carrying out motor tasks. 181

Developmental psychology The study of changes in the behavior and thinking of human beings over time. 6

Developmental reading disorder A learning disability manifested in reading problems of varying severity—sometimes evident in spelling difficulties. Also labeled "dyslexia" or "specific reading disability." 274

Developmental task A social, cultural, or physical milestone that requires the development of new capabilities or the assumption of new responsibilities at a given developmental stage. Accomplishing a developmental task leads to adjustment and happiness; failure to do so may lead to unhappiness and difficulty with later tasks. 38

Developmental theory A body of psychological theories concerned with the development of children from birth to maturity. 39

Diabetes An insulin deficiency disease, some forms of which are associated with a recessive gene. 75

Dialectical schemata Basseches's expression for ways of thinking dialectically. For example, dialectical schemata might focus attention on relationships, on moral questions, on sources of conflict and agreement. Dialectical schemata are geared toward the recognition and resolution of conflict. (See *dialectical thinking*.) 402

Dialectical thinking According to Riegel, thinking that recognizes, accepts, and attempts to resolve conflicts. Dialectical thinking is thought to be more characteristic of adults than of children or adolescents. 401

Diary description As a method of child study, it involves recording sequential descriptions of a child's behavior at predetermined intervals (daily or weekly, for example). Sometimes useful for arriving at a better understanding of general developmental patterns. 17

Dilation and curettage (D & C) A surgical procedure that involves scraping the walls of the uterus. It is occasionally necessary after birth if all of the placenta has not been expelled. 110

Discontinuous society A society that clearly marks passage from one developmental stage to another. Many nonindustrialized societies are labeled "discontinuous" because of their childhood-to-adulthood rites of passage. (See *continuous society*.) 316

Disengagement theory A theory of aging that holds that it is normal and useful for the elderly to disengage themselves from community and other involvements. (See *activity theory*.) 527

Disinhibitory effect See *inhibitory-disinhibitory effect*. 43

Disorganized/disoriented Describes infants whose attachment behaviors toward caregivers are confused, unclear, and sometimes contradictory. 168

Dizygotic Resulting from two separate eggs and forming fraternal (nonidentical) twins. 83

DNA (deoxyribonucleic acid) A substance assumed to be the basis of all life, consisting of four chemical bases arranged in an extremely large number of combinations. The two strands of the DNA molecule that compose genes are arranged in the form of a double spiral (helix). These double strands are capable of replicating themselves as well as crossing over from one strand of the spiral to the other and forming new combinations of their genetic material. The nuclei of all cells contain DNA molecules. 67

Dominant gene The gene (carrier of heredity) that takes precedence over all other related genes in genetically determined traits. Because all genes in the fertilized egg occur in pairs (one from the male and one from the female), a dominant gene as one member of the pair of genes means that the related hereditary characteristic will be present in the individual. 69

Double-blind procedure An experimental method in which experimenters collecting or analyzing data do not know which subjects are members of experimental or control groups. Double-blind procedures are used as a safeguard against experimenter bias. 23

Double career Expression that describes a situation in which the individual assumes responsibility for two careers simultaneously. Common among mothers who have both an out-of-home and a family-based career. (See *dual-career family*.) 461

Double helix The natural state of DNA molecules. Essentially, two spiralling, intertwining chains of corresponding molecules. 68

Down syndrome The most common chromosomal birth defect, related to the presence of an extra 21st chromosome (technically labeled Trisomy 21) and sometimes evident in mild to severe mental retardation. 75

Drug abuse The recreational use of drugs. The APA considers drug abuse a disorder when it impairs functioning. 366

Drug dependence A strong, sometimes overwhelming desire to continue taking a drug. (See also *physiological dependence; psychological dependence*.) 366

Drug tolerance A change resulting from drug use in which the user requires more frequent or stronger doses of the drug to maintain its initial effects. 366

Drugs Chemical substances that have marked physiological effects on living organisms. 366

Dual-career family A family in which both husband and wife develop separate, equally important careers, neither being sacrificed for the other—or for the family. (See *double career*.) 461

Dying trajectories An expression used in reference to the process of dying. Dying trajectories are temporal—that is, described in terms of time (for example, expected swift death, expected lingering while dying, or expected temporary recovery). 549

Dyslexia A form of learning disability manifested in reading problems of varying severity. Dyslexia may be evident in spelling errors that are erratic rather than consistent. 272

Early adulthood Arbitrarily defined in this text as the period from the end of adolescence to about age 40 or 45. 382

Ecological systems theory Label for Bronfenbrenner's theory, which is based on the notion that understanding human development requires understanding the interactions that occur between individuals and their contexts (their ecologies). 53

Ecology The study of the interrelationships between organisms and their environment. In developmental psychology, ecology relates to the social context in which behavior and development occur. 7

Egg cell See *ovum*. 67

Ego The second stage of the human personality, according to Freud. It is the rational, reality-oriented level of human personality that develops as the child becomes aware of what the environment makes possible and impossible, thereby serving as a damper to the id. The id tends toward immediate gratification of impulses as they are felt, whereas the ego imposes restrictions that are based on environmental reality. 33

Egocentric Adjective based on Latin words for *self* (ego) and *center*. Literally, it describes a self-centered behavior, attitude, or personality characteristic. Although egocentrism often has negative connotations of selfishness, it is simply descriptive when applied to the child's perception of the world. For example, egocentric perception is characterized by an inability to assume an objective point of view. 200

Egocentric speech Vygotsky's intermediate stage of language development, common between ages 3 and 7, during which children often talk to themselves in an apparent effort to control their own behavior. (See *inner speech; social speech*.) 52

Elaborating A long-term memory process involving changing or adding to material, or making associations to make remembering easier. (See *organizing; rehearsing*.) 265

Electra complex A Freudian development stage during which a girl's unconscious sexual feelings toward her father lead to jealousy of her mother. (See *Oedipus complex*.) 35

Elicited response A response brought about by a stimulus. The expression is synonymous with the term *respondent*. 41

Eliciting effect That type of imitative behavior in which the observer does not copy the model's responses but simply behaves in a related manner. 44

Embryo stage The second stage of prenatal development, lasting from the end of the second through the eighth week after conception. 93

Emitted response A response not elicited by a known stimulus but simply by the organism. An emitted response is an operant. 41

Empty nest phase The seventh stage in Duvall's family life cycle, beginning when the last child leaves home, and lasting about 15 years. 477

Environment The significant aspects of an individual's surroundings. Includes all experiences and events that influence the child's development. 64

Epigenesis The developmental unfolding of genetically influenced characteristics. 71

Epilepsy A seizure disorder, sometimes genetic in origin, varying in severity, often treatable or controllable with drugs. 181

Episiotomy A small cut made in the vagina to facilitate the birth of a child. An episiotomy prevents the tearing of membranes and ensures that once the cut has been sutured, healing will be rapid and complete. 109

Episodic memory A type of declarative, autobiographical (conscious, long-term) memory consisting of knowlege about personal experiences, tied to specific times and places. (See *semantic memory*.) 264

Equilibration A Piagetian term for the process by which we maintain a balance between assimilation (using old learning) and accommodation (changing behavior; learning new things). Equilibration is essential for adaptation and cognitive growth. 142

Erectile dysfunction A male sexual disfunction, also termed *impotence*. The inability to achieve or maintain an erection. 392

Estrogen replacement therapy (ERT) A medical treatment in which women whose production of hormones has declined or ceased—often because of menopause or surgical removal of the ovaries—are given estrogen. ERT has been found to reduce risk of osteoporosis but remains controversial given a possible link with cancer. 451

Ethologists Scientists who study the behavior of animals in their natural habitats. 50

Eugenics A form of genetic engineering that selects specific individuals for reproduction. Although widely accepted and practiced with animals, as applied to humans, the concept raises many serious moral and ethical questions. 81

Euthanasia Deliberate ending of another's life for reasons of compassion. Also called mercy killing or assisted suicide. 552

Event sampling A method of child study in which specific behaviors are observed and recorded and unrelated behaviors are ignored. 17

Exceptionality A category used to describe physical, social, or intellectual abilities and performance that are significantly above or below average. 179

Exosystem Interactions between a system in which the child is involved (microsystem) and another system that does not ordinarily include the child (father's relationships with employers, for example). 53

Experiment A procedure for scientific investigation that requires manipulation of some aspects of the environment to determine the effects of this manipulation. 17

Experimental group A group of subjects who undergo experimental manipulation. The group to which something is done in order to observe its effects. 17

Explicit memory See *declarative memory*. 264

Extended family A large family group consisting of parents, children, grandparents, and sometimes uncles, aunts, cousins, and so on. 233

Fallopian tube One of two tubes that link the ovaries and the uterus. Fertilization (conception) ordinarily occurs in the fallopian tubes. From there, the fertilized egg cell moves into the uterus and attaches to the uterine wall. 93

Family life cycle A sociological term referring to the stages through which typical families progress (for example, early marriage, raising children, raising adolescents, postchildren, and dissolution). 427

Fat mass Made up mostly of white adipose tissue (fat cells). Accounts for an average of about 30 percent of body weight in adult females and about 15 percent in adult males. 252

Fat-free mass The major constituent of the human body, consisting largely of organs, muscles, and bone (which, in turn, consist primarily of water). 252

Feral children Those raised by animals in the wild and away from human contact. 65

Fertilized ovum The first stage of prenatal development, beginning at fertilization and ending at the end of the second week. 93

Fetal alcohol syndrome (FAS) A pattern of birth defects associated with alcohol consumption by pregnant women. FAS symptoms include mental retardation, retarded physical growth, and facial and cranial deformities. 98

Fetoscopy A surgical procedure that allows the physician to see the fetus while obtaining tissue samples to determine its status. 78

Fetus stage The final stage of prenatal development, which begins at the end of the eighth week after conception and lasts until the baby's birth. 93

Fluid abilities Cattell's term for intellectual abilities that seem to underlie much of our intelligent behavior and that are not highly affected by experience (general reasoning, attention span, memory for numbers). Fluid abilities are more likely to decline in old age than are crystallized abilities. (See also *crystallized abilities*.) 268

Forceps Clamplike instruments that may sometimes be used in a baby's delivery. 115

Formal operations The last of Piaget's four major stages, beginning around the age of 11 or 12 and lasting until about 14 or 15. It is characterized by the child's increasing ability to use logical thought processes. 48

Fragile X syndrome A sex-linked, primarily male disorder that is often manifested in mental retardation. Susceptibility increases with the mother's age. 76

Fraternal twins Twins whose genetic origins are two separate eggs. Such twins are as genetically dissimilar as average siblings. (See also *dizygotic*.) 83

Free-radical theory Argues that portions of cells sometimes become detached, becoming "free radicals" that significantly affect the cell's ability to function normally, and that account for some of the components of aging. 500

Galvanic skin response (GSR) A measure of the skin's electrical conductivity. With increases in emotional reaction (arousal), conductivity increases; hence, GSR measures may be considered indexes of arousal or emotion. 132

Gametes Mature sex cells. In humans, the egg cell (ovum) and the sperm cell. 67

Gateway drug-use theory The observation that certain drugs such as tobacco, alcohol, and marijuana are typically used first (usually in the order mentioned) before other "stronger" drugs, in a sense serving as a gateway to use of other drugs. 368

Gender The characteristics typically associated with biological sex. Thus there are two genders, masculine and feminine, corresponding with the two sexes, male and female. 353

Gender roles Attitudes, personality characteristics, behavior, and other qualities associated with being male or female in a specific culture. Gender roles are the groupings of qualities that define masculine and feminine. Because they are largely culturally defined, gender roles may be quite different in different cultures. 177

Gender typing Learning behavior appropriate to the sex of the individual. The term refers specifically to the acquisition of masculine behavior by a boy and feminine behavior by a girl. 177

Gene A carrier of heredity. Each of the 23 chromosomes contributed by the sperm cell and the ovum at conception is believed to contain 50,000 to 100,000 genes. 69

General factor theory A theory of intelligence based on the assumption that there is a basic underlying quality of intellectual functioning that determines intelligence in all areas. This quality is sometimes termed *g*. 267

Generalizability The extent to which conclusions, rules, and principles are applicable to new situations—in short, their generality. 22

Generativity According to Erikson, the major developmental task of middle age. Generativity is expressed in the sorts of acts and commitments that are productive and that benefit society—that are *generative* rather than *self-absorbed*. 471

Genetic theory of aging Holds that the biological limits of life are programmed into cells and that, once they have reproduced a predetermined number of times, they die. 498

Genetics The science that studies heredity. 67

Genital stage The last of Freud's stages of psychosexual development, beginning around age 11 and lasting until around 18. It is characterized by involvement with normal adult modes of sexual gratification. 35

Genitalia A general term referring to sex organs. 95

Genome One set of single chromosomes with the genes they contain; considered an organism's genetic map. 72

Germinal stage Another label for the prenatal developmental period of the fertilized ovum, the first stage of intrauterine growth. (See *fertilized ovum*.) 93

Gestation period The time between conception and birth (typically 266 days for humans). 92

Glaucoma A medical condition defined in terms of increased pressure in the eye that is associated with age; if untreated, glaucoma can damage vision and even lead to blindness. 446

Grief An emotional reaction to loss. Grief reactions are sometimes accompanied by both physical and psychological symptoms (shortness of breath, heart palpitations, sighing, loss of appetite, and so on, as well as anxiety, depression, anger, and guilt). 544

Group intelligence test An intelligence test, generally of the paper-and-pencil variety, that can be administered to large groups of individuals at a time. 269

Growth In the study of children, a term that ordinarily refers to physical changes that are primarily quantitative because they involve addition rather than transformation. 7

Happiness A personal, highly subjective feeling of well-being, of contentment. The term has shorter-term connotations than satisfaction and is more subject to mood. (See *satisfaction*.) 486

Head-turning reflex   A reflex elicited in infants by stroking the cheek or the corner of the mouth. Infants turn their heads toward the side being stimulated. 132

Hedonistic   Relating to the pain–pleasure principle— to the tendency to seek pleasure and avoid pain. 336

Heredity   The transmission of physical and personality characteristics and predispositions from parent to offspring. 64

Herpes   An incurable sexually transmitted viral disease whose symptoms usually include sometimes painful or itchy lesions in the genital area. 100

Heteronomy   Piaget's label for the first stage of moral development, marked by reliance on outside authority. (See *autonomy.*) 336

Heterozygous   Refers to the presence of different genes with respect to a single trait. One of these genes is dominant and the other is recessive. 73

Holophrase   Term used to describe a single word in early infant speech, the meaning of which is global and imprecise, including a wide range of actions, objects, or events. 151

Homozygous   Refers to an individual's genetic makeup. Individuals are homozygous with respect to a particular trait if they possess identical genes for that trait. 73

Hospice   A facility established to provide care for the terminally ill. May be part of a hospital, in a private home, or a separate institution. (See *palliative care.*) 551

Humanism   A philosophical and psychological orientation primarily concerned with the worth of humans as individuals and with processes that augment their human qualities. (See *self-actualization.*) 55

Huntington's disease   An inherited neurological disorder characterized by neural degeneration typically beginning between the ages of 20 and 40, and usually leading to death. 72

Hypothesis   A prediction based on partial evidence of some effect, process, or phenomenon that must be experimentally verified. 17

Id   One of the three levels of the human personality, according to Freudian theory. The id is defined as all the instinctual urges to which humans are heir; it is the level of personality that contains human motives. A newborn child's personality, according to Freud, is all id. 33

Identical twins   Twins whose genetic origin is a single egg. Such twins are genetically identical. (See *monozygotic.*) 83

Identification   A general term referring to the process of assuming the goals, ambitions, mannerisms, and so on of another person—of identifying with that person. (See *imitation.*) 223

Identity   A term with several meanings. (1) A logical rule specifying that certain activities leave objects or situations unchanged. (2) In Erikson's theory, a term closely related to *self.* To achieve identity is to arrive at a clear notion of who one is. It includes the goals, values, and beliefs to which the individual is committed. (3) Often used synonymously with the term *self,* identity refers to the individual's self-definition, a personal sense of who and what one is. One of the important tasks of adolescence is to select and develop a strong sense of identity. 36

Imaginary audience   One manifestation of adolescent egocentrism. A reflection of the adolescent belief that a wide range of individuals are always aware of the adolescent's behavior and are very concerned about it. 331

Imaginative play   Activities that include make-believe games; these are particularly prevalent during the preschool years. 227

Imitation   The complex process of learning through observation of a model. 43

Immature birth   A miscarriage occurring sometime between the 20th and 28th weeks of pregnancy and resulting in the birth of a fetus weighing between 1 and 2 pounds. 120

Implicit memory   See *nondeclarative memory.* 264

Imprinting   An instinctlike type of learning that occurs shortly after birth in certain species and that is seen in the "following" behavior of young ducks and geese. 50

In utero   A Latin term meaning inside the uterus. 94

Incidental mnemonics   The young preschooler's *accidental* rather than deliberate and systematic memory aids. Includes such things as paying attention and repeated exposure. 196

Incongruity hypothesis   The supposition that infant fear reactions result from a discrepancy between reality and what the infant has learned to expect. 172

Independent variable   The variable in an experiment that can be manipulated to observe its effects on other variables. 17

Individual intelligence test   An intelligence test, like the Wechsler or the Stanford-Binet, that can be administered to only one individual at a time. 269

Induction   As an aspect of rites of passage, acceptance into adult status. 316

Infancy   A period of development that begins a few weeks after birth and lasts until approximately the age of 2. 9

Infant state   An expression used to describe the general, current condition of an infant—for example, sleeping, crying, drowsy, or alert. 159

Infantile amnesia   A generally unexplained but apparently universal human phenomenon evident in the fact that most people do not remember events of infancy or of the early preschool period. 196

Information-processing approach A psychological orientation that attempts to explain cognitive processes such as remembering, decision making, or problem solving. This orientation is primarily concerned with how information is acquired and stored (acquisition of a knowledge base), as well as the development of both cognitive strategies and notions of the self as a processor of information (metacognition). 261

Inhibitory-disinhibitory effect Imitative behavior that results in either the suppression (inhibition) or appearance (disinhibition) of previously acquired deviant behavior. 43

Initiation Ceremonies and rituals that, in some societies, mark entry into adulthood. 316

Initiative versus guilt The third of Erikson's stages (2 or 3 to 6 years), marked by a developing sense of self and of responsibility, and a greater independence from parents. 223

Inner speech Vygotsky's final stage in the development of speech, attained at around age 7, and characterized by silent "self-talk," the *stream-of-consciousness* flow of verbalizations that give direction and substance to our thinking and behavior. Inner speech is involved in all higher mental functioning. (See *egocentric speech; social speech.*) 52

Insecure-ambivalent Describes infants who are profoundly upset when the principal caregiver leaves and who often display anger when that person returns. 168

Insecure-avoidant Describes infants who are anxiously attached to a caregiver, who show little signs of distress when that person leaves, and who initially avoid reestablishing contact when the person returns. 168

Intimacy In Sternberg's theory of love, refers to emotions that lead two people to want to share things, perhaps to disclose personal, private things. (See *passion; commitment; triangular theory of love.*) 414

Intuitive A substage of Piaget's preoperational period, lasting from age 4 to about 7 or 8, marked by problem solutions more intuitive than logical, and characterized by excessive reliance on perception. 198

Job Specific task or duty associated with one's work or employment. (See *career; occupation.*) 393

Job–person matching Theories of career choice that advocate matching people with careers on the basis of the person's characteristics and interests and the principal requirements of the job. (See *developmental career model.*) 396

Knowledge base All that is in memory. Information-processing approaches to learning and development look at the nature of the knowledge base, its creation, strategies for adding material to, or retrieving from, the knowledge base, and the knower's awareness of self as knower. 262

Labor The process during which the fetus, placenta, and other membranes are separated from the mother's body and expelled. The termination of labor usually is birth. 107

Language Complex arrangements of arbitrary sounds that have accepted referents and can therefore be used for communication among humans. 147

Language acquisition device (LAD) A label used by Chomsky to describe the neurological something that corresponds to grammar and which children are assumed to have in their brains as they learn language. 209

Lanugo Downy, soft hair that covers the fetus. Lanugo grows over most of the child's body sometime after the fifth month of pregnancy and is usually shed during the seventh month. However, some lanugo is often present at birth, especially on the infant's back. 95

Latency stage The fourth of Freud's stages of psychosexual development, characterized by both the development of the superego (conscience) and loss of interest in sexual gratification. This stage is assumed to last from ages 6 to 11. 35

Launching phase The sixth of Duvall's eight stages of the family life cycle, spanning the years from the leaving of the first child to the leaving of the last. 477

Learned helplessness Personality characteristic evident in a tendency to attribute outcomes to causes over which the person has no control. (See *mastery-oriented.*) 295

Learning Changes in behavior resulting from experience rather than from the maturational process. 7

Learning disability Significant impairment in a specific skill or ability in the absence of mental retardation (a general depression in ability to learn). 272

Levinson's dream In Levinson's description, a sort of fantasy developed in early adulthood, including the individual's goals and aspirations. Successes and failures are later measured against the dream. 473

Libido A general Freudian term denoting sexual urges. The libido is assumed to be the source of energy for sexual urges. Freud considered these urges the most important force in human motivation. 33

Life expectancy The expected duration of a human life. An average of the ages at which individuals die. 498

Life review A dynamic process whereby an individual remembers, analyzes, and evaluates past experiences in an effort to resolve and accept personal conflicts. The life review is common in late adulthood but may occur throughout life. (See *personal narrative.*) 521

Life trajectory The expected span of life. (See *dying trajectory*.) 549

Lifespan The total length of an individual life; not an expectancy, but the maximum attainable in the absence of accident and disease. 498

Lifespan developmental psychology The area of psychology concerned with the development of individuals from conception to death—that is, with the entire lifespan. 6

Longitudinal study A research technique in the study of child development that observes the same subjects over a period of time. 19

Long-term memory A type of memory whereby with continued rehearsal and recoding of sensory input (processing in terms of meaning, for example), material will be available for recall over a longer period of time (minutes to years). 263

Love The poets may grasp this one more clearly than the scientists. A strong, interpersonal attraction, says science. A combination of passion, intimacy, and commitment. 413

LSD-25 (d-lysergic acid diethylamide tartrate) A particularly powerful hallucinogenic drug, this inexpensive, easily made synthetic chemical can sometimes have profound influences on human perception. In everyday parlance, it is often called acid. 369

Lymphoid system Includes all lymph tissues in the body (for example, in lymph glands, the tonsils, the thymus, the intestine). These produce a yellowish liquid, lymph, involved in the individual's immunological system. 127

Macrosystem All interactive social systems that define a culture or subculture. 53

Mainstreaming The practice of placing students in need of special services in regular classrooms rather than segregating them. Also called *inclusive* education. 278

Marker genes A length of DNA material that seems to be identical in all individuals with a specific characteristic. 72

Mastery-oriented A personality characteristic marked by a tendency to attribute the outcomes of behavior to factors under personal control. (See *learned helplessness*.) 295

Masturbation The self-stimulation of one's genitals for sexual gratification 357.

Maturation A term used to describe changes in human development that are relatively independent of the environment. 7

Mature birth The birth of an infant between the 37th and 42d weeks of pregnancy. 112

Mechanistic model A model of human development based on the belief that it is useful to view human beings in terms of their reactive, machinelike characteristics. 31

Meiosis The division of a single sex cell into two separate cells, each consisting of 23 chromosomes rather than 23 pairs of chromosomes. Meiosis therefore results in cells that are completely different, whereas mitosis results in identical cells. 68

Menarche A girl's first menstrual period, an event that transpires during pubescence. 22

Mendelian genetics The study of heredity through an examination of the characteristics of parents and offspring. (See *molecular genetics*.) 72

Menopause The cessation of menstruation in women. Menopause may begin in the early forties or late thirties and usually is complete around age 50. (See *climacteric*.) 67

Menses A monthly discharge of blood and tissue from the womb of a mature female. The term refers to menstruation. 92

Mental retardation A global term referring to the mental state of individuals whose intellectual development is significantly slower than that of normal individuals and whose ability to adapt to their environment is therefore limited. 271

Mesosystem Interactions among two or more microsystems (for example, family and school). 53

Metacognition Knowledge about knowing. As we grow and learn, we develop notions of ourselves as learners. Accordingly, we develop strategies that recognize our limitations and that allow us to monitor our progress and take advantage of our efforts. 228

Metamemory The knowledge that we develop about our own memory processes—knowledge about how to remember rather than simply about our memories. 197

Metaneed Maslow's term for a "higher" need. In contrast to a basic need, a metaneed is concerned not with physiological but with psychological functions. It includes the need to know truth, beauty, justice, and to self-actualize. 56

Microsystem Defined by immediate, face-to-face interactions, where everybody affects everybody (for example, child and parent). 53

Middle adulthood Arbitrarily defined in this text as the period from about age 40 or 45 to around age 65 or so. 444

Middle childhood An arbitrary division in the sequence of development beginning somewhere around age 6 and ending at approximately 12. 252

Midlife crisis A popular expression for the potential emotional turmoil that sometimes occurs in middle age with the individual's growing recognition of mortality and with the realization that the dreams of younger years may never be achieved. 473

Mitosis The division of a cell into two identical cells. Mitosis occurs in body cells rather than in sex cells. 68

Model A pattern for behavior that can be copied by someone else. (See also *symbolic models*.) Alternatively, a model is a representation, usually abstract, of some phenomenon or system. Thus we might have a model of the universe or a model of some aspects of behavior. 31

Modeling effect Imitative behavior involving the learning of a novel response. 43

Molecular genetics The study of genetics based on the structure of chromosomes. (See *Mendelian genetics*.) 72

Monogamy The practice of being married to one person at a time. (See *polygamy*.) 421

Monozygotic Twins resulting from the division of a single fertilized egg. The process results in identical twins. 83

Montessori method A compensatory preschool education program developed for use with children with mental handicaps but also adapted for use with normal children both at the preschool and post-preschool level. Makes extensive use of specially prepared materials designed to train the senses. 205

Morality The ethical aspect of human behavior. Morality is intimately bound to the development of an awareness of acceptable and unacceptable behaviors. It is therefore linked to what is often called conscience. (See *conscience*.) 334

Moro reflex The generalized startle reaction of a newborn infant. It characteristically involves throwing out the arms and feet symmetrically and then bringing them back in toward the center of the body. 132

Morpheme Combination of phonemes that make up the meaningful units of a language. 147

Mother–infant bond Expression for a biological and physiological process involved in the very early formation of emotional links between mother and infant. 169

Mourning The external manifestations of grief. Many cultures and religions have prescribed periods of mourning—periods during which the bereaved are expected to show their grief. 544

Muscular dystrophy (MD) A degenerative muscular disorder, most forms of which are genetic, usually manifested in an inability to walk and sometimes fatal. 74

Mutagen Substance capable of causing changes in genetic material. (See *teratogen*.) 96

Mythos Labouvie-Vief's label for the *mythical* (as opposed to logical) thinking of old age. Thinking that is subjective, personal, pragmatic, and intuitive. 512

Naive theory A general term for folk beliefs in psychology. Also referred to as *commonsense* or *implicit* theories, naive theories typically have no scientific basis. 30

Natural childbirth Also called *prepared childbirth*, refers to the process of giving birth without anesthetics. 114

Nature–nurture controversy A long-standing psychological argument over whether genetics (nature) or environment (nurture) is more responsible for determining development. 16

Negative reinforcement A stimulus that increases the probability of a response when the stimulus is removed from the situation. A negative reinforcer is usually an unpleasant or noxious stimulus that is removed when the desired response occurs. 42

NEO typology Costa and McCrae's analysis of personality into three types: neuroticism (anxiety, depression), extraversion (sensation seeking, adventurousness), and openness (dogmatism, rigidity, authoritarianism). 483

Neonatal abstinence syndrome Neonatal symptoms associated with narcotics use by the mother that has resulted in the newborn also being addicted. Severe cases may be fatal. 99

Neonate A newborn infant. Newborns typically lose weight immediately after birth, but regain it within two weeks. The neonate period terminates when birth weight is regained. 109

Neural tube defects Spinal cord defects often linked with recessive genes, sometimes evident in failure of the spine to close (spina bifida), or in absence of portions of the brain. 74

Nominal fallacy The assumption that naming something explains it. 30

Nondeclarative memory Also termed *implicit* or *procedural* memory, refers to unconscious, nonverbalizable effects of experience such as might be manifested in acquired motor skills or in classical conditioning. (See *declarative memory*; *semantic memory*; *episodic memory*.) 264

Norm An average or standard way of behaving. Cultural norms, for example, refer to the behaviors expected of individuals who are members of that culture. 134

Normal curve A mathematical function represented in the form of a symmetrical bell-shaped curve that illustrates how a large number of naturally occurring or chance events are distributed. 70

Nuclear family A family consisting of a mother, a father, and their offspring. 233

Observational learning   Learning through imitation. 43

Occupation   A relatively broad employment classification such as secretary or accountant. (See *job; work; career*.) 393

Oedipus complex   A Freudian stage of development during which a boy unconsciously has sexual desires for his mother and a consequent resentment of his father. (See *Electra complex*.) 35

Ontogeny   Systematic changes that occur in the lives of individuals. Changes that define lifespan development. (See *phylogeny*.) 15

Operant   The label used by Skinner to describe a response not elicited by any known or obvious stimulus. Most significant human behaviors appear to be operant. Such behaviors as writing a letter or going for a walk are operants if no known specific stimulus elicits them. 41

Operant conditioning   A type of learning involving an increased probability of a response occurring as a result of reinforcement. Much of B. F. Skinner's experimental work investigates the principles of operant conditioning. 41

Operation   Piaget's term for mental activity. An operation is a thought process characterized by certain rules of logic. Preoperations are more intuitive and egocentric and less logical. 48

Oral stage   Freud's first stage of psychosexual development, lasting from birth to approximately 8 months of age. The oral stage is characterized by preoccupation with the immediate gratification of desires. This is accomplished primarily with the mouth, by sucking, biting, swallowing, playing with the lips, and so on. 34

Organismic model   This model in human development assumes that it is useful to view people as active rather than simply reactive, as more like biological organisms than machines. 31

Organizing   A memory strategy involving grouping and relating material to maintain it in long-term memory. (See *elaborating; rehearsing*.) 265

Orienting response   The initial response of humans and other animals to novel stimulation. Also called the orienting reflex or orientation reaction. Components of the orienting response include changes in EEG patterns, respiration rate, heart rate, and conductivity of the skin to electricity. 132

Osteoporosis   A thinning and weakening of the bones, often associated with aging, and more common in women than in men. 449

Otitis media   A highly common childhood disease of the middle ear, sometimes accompanied by prolonged hearing loss, the main medical symptom of which is fluid in the middle ear. May be associated with language problems. 256

Ovary   A female organ (most women have two) that produces ova (egg cells). 93

Ovum (plural *ova*)   The sex cell produced by a mature female approximately once every 28 days. When mature, it consists of 23 chromosomes as opposed to all other human body cells (somatoplasm), which consist of 23 pairs of chromosomes. It is often referred to as an egg cell.   67

Palliative care   Care of the terminally ill, designed primarily to ease their physical and psychological distress. Specifically, the kind of care provided in hospices. (See *hospice*.) 551

Palmar reflex   The grasping reflex that a newborn infant exhibits when an object is placed in its hand. 133

Passion   In Sternberg's theory of love, a strong, often sexual, sometimes almost overwhelming, desire to be with another person. (See *commitment; intimacy; triangular theory of love*.) 414

Passive vocabulary   Consists of all the words the child understands. Not all of these words will actually be used in the child's speech. (See *active vocabulary*.) 148

Peak height velocity   Period during which stature (height) is increasing at the highest rate. Occurs during the adolescent growth spurt and coincides, approximately, with sexual maturation. 253

Peer group   A group of equals. Peer groups may be social groups, age groups, intellectual groups, or work groups. When the term applies to young children, it typically refers to age and grade mates. 290

Perception   Reaction to and interpretation of physical stimulation (sensation). A conceptual process, dependent on the activity of the brain. 135

Permissive parenting   A parenting style that may be characterized as laissez-faire. Permissive parents are nonpunitive and undemanding. Their children are autonomous rather than obedient, and thus are responsible for their own decisions and actions. 235

Personal fable   The belief that we are unique, special, and right. This belief is sometimes exaggerated in adolescence as a function of adolescent egocentrism. 332

Personal narrative   The stories we tell ourselves of our own lives, that give them a sense of stability and continuity. Includes reminiscences as well as goals. In later life, personal narratives may become more evaluative, taking the form of a life review. (See *life review*.) 521

Personality   The set of characteristics that we typically manifest in our interactions with others. It includes all the abilities, predispositions, habits, and other qualities that make each of us different. 160

Pervasive developmental disorder   A disorder first manifested in infancy or childhood, evident in delayed or abnormal development especially in social skills, communication, and emotional maturity. May take the form of autism or childhood schizophrenia. 181

Peter Pan syndrome   Label for an unwillingness to grow up as adults, evident in a reluctance to accept the responsibilities that normally come with increasing age. 382

Phallic stage   The third stage in Freud's theory of psychosexual development, beginning at 18 months and lasting to approximately 6 years of age. During this stage, children become concerned with their genitals and may show evidence of the much-discussed Oedipus and Electra complexes. 35

Phenomenology   An approach concerned primarily with how individuals view their own world. Its basic assumption is that each individual perceives and reacts to the world in a unique manner, and that it is this phenomenological world view that is important in understanding the individual's behavior. 55

Phenylketonuria (PKU)   A genetic disorder associated with the presence of two recessive genes. 74

Phoneme   The simplest unit of language, consisting of a single sound, such as a vowel. 147

Phonology   One of the four major components of language. Phonology has to do with the sounds (phonemes) of a language. 147

Phylogeny   Changes that occur in a species over generations. Evolutionary changes. (See *ontogeny*.) 15

Physiological dependence   Also known as addiction. The desire to continue using a drug for organic or physiological reasons, and involving unpleasant reactions when the drug is not taken. 366

Placenta   A flat, thick membrane attached to the inside of the uterus and to the developing fetus during pregnancy. The placenta connects the mother and the fetus by the umbilical cord. 94

Play   May be defined as activities that have no goal other than the enjoyment derived from them. 226

Polygamy   Forms of marriage that permit a husband to have more than one wife (polygyny) or a wife to have more than one husband (polyandry) at the same time. 421

Positive reinforcement   A stimulus that increases the probability of a response recurring as a result of being added to a situation after the response has occurred. It usually takes the form of a pleasant stimulus (reward) that results from a specific response. 42

Postconventional   Kohlberg's third level of morality, reflecting an understanding of social contract and more individualistic principles of morality. 336

Postmature birth   The birth of an infant after the 42d week of pregnancy. 112

Postpartum depression   A form of depression that affects about 10 percent of all women beginning shortly after childbirth. In some cases, postpartum depression can be serious and dangerous, but usually ameliorates and disappears with time. 115

Practice play   See *sensorimotor play*. 227

Pragmatics   One of four components of language, relating to the practical aspects of language. Pragmatics includes all the implicit rules that govern when and how speakers interact in conversation, as well as the subtle rules of intonation, accent, emphasis, and other variations that give rise to different meanings. 147

Preconcept   The label given to the preconceptual child's incomplete understanding of concept, resulting from an inability to classify. 198

Preconceptual   Piaget's label for the first subphase of the preoperational period, spanning ages 2 to 4, characterized by an excessive reliance on perception and egocentricity. 198

Preconventional   The first of Kohlberg's three stages of moral development, based on hedonistic or obedience-oriented judgments. 336

Pregnancy   The condition of a woman who has had an ovum (egg cell) fertilized and who, nature willing, will eventually give birth. 92

Premature birth   The birth of a baby between the 29th and 36th weeks of pregnancy. A premature baby weighs between 2 and 5½ pounds (1,000 to 2,499 grams). 112

Prenatal development   The period of development beginning at conception and ending at birth. That period lasts approximately nine calendar months in the human female (266 days). Chickens develop considerably faster. 92

Preoperation   Piaget's label for a thought that is not limited by ordinary rules of logic. Preoperations tend to be unstable, idiosyncratic, perception dominated, and egocentric. 198

Preoperational thought   The second of Piaget's four major stages, lasting from about 2 to 7 or 8 years. It consists of two substages: intuitive thinking and preconceptual thinking. 48

Presbycusis   Most common cause of hearing loss with age, associated with degeneration of auditory system. Most evident in loss of ability to hear higher tones. 447

Pretend play   See *imaginative play*. 227

Primary aging   Nearly universal changes associated with advancing age, such as loss or atrophy of brain cells or loss of bone calcium. 502

Primary circular reaction   An expression used by Piaget to describe a simple reflex activity such as thumb-sucking. 144

Primary sexual characteristics   Sexual characteristics directly associated with reproduction (for example, ovaries and testes).   320

Project Head Start   A large-scale, federally funded preschool program in the United States conceived as part of the war on poverty. It is designed to overcome some of the disadvantages associated with economic and social deprivation in early life and, in a sense, to give children a head start.   203

Prolapsed cord   A condition that sometimes occurs during birth when the infant's umbilical cord becomes lodged between the body and the birth canal, thereby cutting off the supply of oxygen. This may result in brain damage of varying severity, depending on the length of time until delivery following prolapsing of the cord.   115

Proteins   Molecules made up of chains of one or more amino acids. In a sense, proteins are the basis of organic life.   67

Proximodistal   Literally, from near to far. Refers to a developmental progression in which central organs develop before external limbs, and the infant acquires control over muscles close to the center of the body before acquiring control over those that are more peripheral.   96

Psychoanalytic   General label for Freudian theory. Also used to describe clinical or therapeutic procedures based on Freudian ideas, and especially on ideas related to the subconscious.   32

Psycholinguist   Those who study the relationship between language (linguistics) and development, thinking, learning, and behaving (psychology).   147

Psychological dependence   Drug dependence in which the desire to continue taking a drug is related primarily to its psychological rather than its physical effects (for example, a strong sense of well-being).   366

Psychology   The science that examines human behavior (and that of animals as well).   6

Psychosexual   A term used to describe psychological phenomena based on sexuality. Freud's theories are psychosexual in that they attribute development to sexually based forces and motives.   34

Psychosocial   Pertaining to events or behaviors that relate to the social aspects of development. Erikson's theory is psychosocial in that it deals with the resolution of social crises and the development of social competencies (independence or identity, for example).   36

Puberty   Sexual maturity following pubescence.   67

Pubescence   Changes that occur in late childhood or early adolescence and that result in sexual maturity. In boys, these changes include enlargement of the testes, growth of axillary hair, deepening of the voice, and the ability to ejaculate semen. In girls, pubescence is characterized by rapid physical growth, occurrence of the first menstrual period (menarche), a slight lowering of the voice, and enlargement and development of the breasts.   127

Punishment   Involves either the presentation of an unpleasant stimulus (punishment I or *castigation*) or the withdrawal of a pleasant stimulus (punishment II or *penalty*) as a consequence of behavior. Punishment should not be confused with negative reinforcement because punishment does not increase the probability of a response occurring; rather, it is intended to have the opposite result.   42

Pupillary reflex   An involuntary change in the size of the pupil as a function of brightness; it is present in the neonate.   136

Quickening   The name given to the first movements of the fetus in utero. Quickening does not occur until after the fifth month of pregnancy.   92

Rapid eye movement (REM) sleep   A stage of sleep characterized by rapid eye movements. Most of our dreaming occurs during REM sleep, which accounts for approximately 25 percent of an adult's sleep time and as much as 50 percent of an infant's.   159

Recessive gene   A gene whose characteristics are not manifest in the offspring unless it is paired with another recessive gene. When a recessive gene is paired with a dominant gene, the characteristics of the dominant gene will be manifest.   69

Rehearsing   A memory process involving repetition, important in maintaining information in short-term memory and in transferring it to long-term memory. (See *elaborating; organizing*.)   264

Reinforcement   The effect of a reinforcer. Specifically, to increase the probability of a response recurring.   42

Reinforcer   A reinforcing stimulus. A consequence, such as a reward, that increases the probability of a behavior recurring.   42

Reliable   A measure is reliable to the extent that it measures accurately whatever it measures.   267

Respondent   A response elicited by a specific known stimulus, used by Skinner to contrast with operant.   41

Response   Any organic, muscular, glandular, or psychic reaction resulting from stimulation.   39

Retirement   Permanent leaving of full-time work, often with a pension, and sometimes mandatory at a given age.   523

Reversibility   A logical property manifested in the ability to reverse or undo activity in either an empirical or conceptual sense. An idea is said to be reversible when a child can unthink it and realizes that certain logical consequences follow from doing so.   198

Reward An object, stimulus, event, or outcome that is perceived as pleasant and may therefore be reinforcing. 42

Rites of passage A collective term for the ceremonies and rites that accompany transition from one stage to another within a culture. The most dramatic examples of rites of passage include the initiation or puberty rites of some "primitive" cultures. 316

Rooting reflex A neonatal reflex manifested, for example, in the infant's attempts to find a breast. 132

Rubber band hypothesis Stern's comparison of human intelligence to a rubber band, the original length of which is genetically determined but the final length of which is affected by the environmental forces that stretch it. 86

Satisfaction A relatively stable dimension related to the fulfillment of one's expectations or aspirations or to a resignation to the way things are. (See *happiness*.) 486

Scheme (also **schema** or **schemata**) The label used by Piaget to describe a unit in cognitive structure. In one sense, a scheme is an activity together with its structural connotations. In another sense, a scheme may be thought of as an idea or a concept. It usually labels a specific activity: the looking scheme, the grasping scheme, the sucking scheme. 47

Script A term used to describe our knowledge of what goes with what and in what sequence. Scripts are a part of cognitive structure that deals with the routine and the predictable. 263

Secondary circular reaction Infant responses that are circular in the sense that the response serves as a stimulus for its own repetition and secondary because the responses do not center on the child's body, as do primary circular reactions. 144

Secondary sexual characteristics Sex-linked features not directly linked with reproduction (for example, facial hair or breast development). 320

Securely attached Describes infants who are strongly and positively attached to a caregiver, who are distressed when that person leaves, and who quickly reestablish contact when the person returns. 168

Self The concept that an individual has of himself or herself. Notions of the self are often closely allied with individuals' beliefs about how others perceive them. 344

Self-actualization The process or act of becoming oneself, developing one's potential, achieving an awareness of one's identity, fulfilling oneself. The term *actualization* is central to humanistic psychology. 56

Self-concept The concept that an individual has of him- or herself. Notions of the self are often closely allied with individuals' beliefs about how others perceive them. 37

Self-efficacy Personal estimates of our effectiveness in dealing with the world. 45

Self-esteem See *self-worth*. 286

Self-referent Pertaining to the self. Self-referent thought is thought that concerns our own mental processes (for example, thoughts that evaluate our abilities or that monitor our progress in solving problems). 45

Self-worth The desire to be held in high esteem by others and to maintain a high opinion of one's own behavior and person. 286

Semantic memory A type of declarative (conscious, long-term) memory consisting of stable knowledge about the world, principles, rules and procedures, and other verbalizable aspects of knowledge, including language. (See *episodic memory*.) 264

Semantics The component of language that relates to meaning or significance of sounds. 147

Senescence Technically, the period in later adulthood marked by physical and cognitive decline. It begins at different ages for different individuals, and is not always characterized by very dramatic changes. 502

Sensation The physical effect of stimulation. A physiological process dependent on activity of the senses. 135

Sensitive period A period during which specific experiences have their most pronounced effects—for example, the first 6 months of life during which the infant forms strong attachment bonds to the mother or caregiver. 50

Sensorimotor period The first stage of development in Piaget's classification. It lasts from birth to approximately age 2 and is so called because children understand their world primarily through their activities toward it and sensations of it. 48

Sensorimotor play (also called **practice play**) Activity involving the manipulation of objects or execution of activities simply for the sensations that are produced. (See *play*.) 227

Sensory memory The simple sensory recognition of stimuli (also called short-term sensory memory). Sensory memory requires no cognitive processing and does not involve conscious awareness or attention. 263

Sequential designs Research strategies that involve taking a sequence of samples at different times of measurement in order to reduce or eliminate biases that may result from confounding the effects of the age of subjects, the time of testing, and the cohort to which subjects belong. 21

Seriation   The ordering of objects according to one or more empirical properties. To seriate is essentially to place in order. 261

Sex chromosome   A chromosome contained in sperm cells and ova that is responsible for determining the sex of offspring. Sex chromosomes produced by the female are of one variety (X); those produced by the male are either X or Y. At fertilization (the union of sperm and ovum), an XX pairing will result in a girl, and an XY pairing will result in a boy. The sperm cell is essentially responsible for determining the offspring's sex. 68

Sex roles   See *gender roles*. 177

Sexual abuse   A form of maltreatment in which the victim is forced—physically or by virtue of the abuser's status and power—to submit to sexual behaviors (ranging from talking, looking, or touching to actual intercourse or other sexual acts). Children are often victims of sexual abuse. 301

Sexual dysfunction   Impediments to participation in or enjoyment of sexual intercourse. Includes impotence, premature ejaculation, and vaginismus (painful contractions of the vagina). 392

Sexual stereotype   A preconceived belief about gender differences and gender roles. 353

Short-term memory   A type of memory in which material is available for recall for a matter of seconds. Short-term memory primarily involves rehearsal rather than more in-depth processing. It defines our immediate consciousness or awareness. 263

Siblings   Offspring whose parents are the same; brothers and sisters. 83

Sickle-cell anemia   A blood-cell disorder associated with a recessive gene, far more common among blacks than whites. 73

Significant developmental motor disability   A collection of symptoms manifested early in life, evident primarily in motor problems, associated with brain damage, and commonly labeled "cerebral palsy." Can vary in severity from barely detectable to severe paralysis. (See *cerebral palsy*.) 180

Social cognition   The realization that others have feelings, motives, intentions, and so on; knowledge of the emotions of others. 284

Social play   Activity that involves interaction between two or more children and frequently takes the form of games with more or less precisely defined rules. 228

Social referencing   The act of looking at how others respond to a social situation as a guide for one's own reactions. 225

Social speech   In Vygotsky's theorizing, the most primitive stage of language development, evident before age 3, during which the child expresses simple thoughts and emotions out loud. The function of social speech is to control the behavior of others. (See *egocentric speech; inner speech*.) 52

Socialization   The complex process of learning those behaviors that are appropriate within a given culture as well as those that are less appropriate. The primary agents of socialization are home, school, and peer groups. 222

Sociobiology   The systematic study of the biological basis of all social behavior. 51

Sociogram   A pictorial or graphic representation of the social structure of a group. 291

Sociometry   A measurement procedure used extensively in sociological studies. It attempts to determine patterns of likes and dislikes in groups; it also plots group structure. 291

Special abilities theory   A theory of intelligence based on the assumption that intelligence consists of several separate factors (for example, numerical, verbal, memory) rather than a single underlying factor common to performance in all areas. (See *general factor theory*.) 267

Specimen description   As a method of child study, it involves recording detailed, specific instances of a child's behavior. Useful for in-depth studies of individual children. 17

Spermarche   A boy's first ejaculation. Often a nocturnal event. (See *menarche*.) 321

Sperm cell   The sex cell produced by a mature male. Like egg cells (ova), sperm cells consist of 23 chromosomes rather than 23 pairs of chromosomes. 67

Stage   An identifiable phase in the development of human beings. Developmental theories such as Piaget's are referred to as stage theories because they describe behavior at different developmental levels. 16

Stereotype   Denotes a fixed, firm, relatively unexamined belief typically generalized to a class of superficially similar situations or individuals. 231

Stethoscope   A medical instrument that amplifies the sound of a heartbeat. 92

Stimulus (plural *stimuli*)   Any change in the physical environment capable of exciting a sense organ. 39

Strange Situation   Label for Ainsworth's widely used approach for investigating infant–caregiver attachment, based on the infant's reaction to separation and reunion with the caregiver. (See *securely attached*.) 167

Stress   A force exerted on an individual often related to change or to high environmental demands; sometimes associated with high arousal. 307

Sturm und drang   Literally, storm and stress (German). G. Stanley Hall's expression to describe what he thought was the confusion, the turmoil, the stresses, the difficulties of the adolescent period. 317

Subtractive bilingualism   Phrase used to describe a situation where learning a second language has a generally negative effect often evident in lower proficiency in both languages. (See *additive bilingualism*.) 212

Sucking reflex   The automatic sucking response of a newborn child when the mouth is stimulated. Nipples are particularly appropriate for eliciting the sucking reflex. 95

Sudden infant death syndrome (SIDS)   Unexplained and unexpected infant death. The leading cause of infant death between ages 1 month and 1 year. (Not really a cause, because it is unknown; SIDS is simply a label.) 130

Superego   The third level of personality according to Freud. It defines the moral or ethical aspects of personality and, like the ego, is in constant conflict with the id. 34

Symbolic   The final stage in the development of a child's representation of the world. The term may be used to describe a representation of the world through arbitrary symbols. Symbolic representation includes language, as well as theoretical or hypothetical systems. 43

Symbolic models   Nonhuman models such as movies, television programs, verbal and written instructions, or religious, literary, musical, or folk heroes. 43

Syncretic reasoning   A type of semilogical reasoning characteristic of the classification behavior of the very young preschooler. In syncretic reasoning, objects are grouped according to egocentric criteria. These criteria change from object to object. In other words, children do not classify on the basis of a single dimension but change dimensions as they classify. 199

Syntax   Part of the grammar of a language that consists of the set of implicit or explicit rules that govern the combination of words that compose a language. 147

Taboo   A prohibition imposed by social custom or as a protective measure. 316

Tay–Sachs disease   A fatal genetic enzyme disorder that can be detected before birth, but that cannot yet be prevented or cured. 74

Temperament   The biological basis of personality—its hereditary components. 160

Teratogen   An external influence (as opposed to an inherited genetic influence) such as a virus or a drug that is capable of producing defects in a fetus. 96

Terminal drop   A label for the observed decline in measured intelligence that sometimes occurs a year or two before a person's death. 511

Tertiary circular reaction   An infant's response that is circular in the sense that the response serves as the stimulus for its own repetition, although the repeated response is not identical to the first response. This last characteristic, the altered response, distinguishes a tertiary from a secondary circular reaction. 144

Testes   Organs, of which there are two, that produce sperm in males. 320

Tetrahydrocannabinol (THC)   The active ingredient in marijuana and related substances (hashish, bhang). 369

Theory   In its simplest sense, an explanation of observations. Theories emphasize which facts (observations) are important for understanding and which relationships among facts are most important. 30

Theory of mind   The child's loosely organized notions about the nature of thinking, imagining, remembering, learning, and other mental processes. The child's understanding of the "mind" and of mental states, and the realization that these exist in both self and others. 228

Time sampling   A method of child observation in which behavior is observed during specific time intervals, frequently with the aim of recording instances or frequency of specific behaviors. 17

Time-lag study   A research design in which subjects of the same age but belonging to different cohorts are compared (for example, 40-year-olds in 1985 are compared with other cohorts of 40-year-olds in 1990 and 1995). 21

Toxin theory of cell malfunction   Recognizes that a gradual buildup of foreign material in body cells may eventually lead to their death and is one of the explanations for aging. 499

Transductive reasoning   The type of semilogical reasoning that proceeds from particular to particular rather than from particular to general or from general to particular. One example of transductive reasoning is the following: (1) Cows give milk, (2) goats give milk, (3) therefore, goats are cows. 198

Transitional bilingualism   Describes a situation in which a minority language is gradually replaced by the dominant language, essentially disappearing within a few generations. 212

Transitional objects   A general term for objects such as blankets and bears that are temporary objects of attachment and affection for some children while they are in transition between high dependence on parents and growing personal independence. 173

Transverse presentation   A crosswise presentation of the fetus at birth. 109

Triangular theory of love   Sternberg's notion that love consists of a particular combination of passion, commitment, and intimacy, and can take a variety of different forms depending on the presence or absence of each of these. (See *commitment; intimacy; passion*.) 414

Triarchic theory of intelligence   Sternberg's notion that intelligence can usefully be viewed in terms of three parts (three arches): the contextual (intelligence defined in terms of its immediate context), the componential (meta-, performance, and knowledge-acquisition components of intelligent behavior), and the experiential (a practical, experienced-based intelligence). 404

Trust versus mistrust   The first of Erikson's stages (to age 2), marked by a conflict between the infant's need to develop trust and an urge to remain dependent. 222

Ultrasound   A diagnostic technique in medicine whereby high-frequency sound waves are used to provide images of internal body structures. Ultrasound recordings are used extensively to evaluate the condition of the fetus. 78

Umbilical cord   A long, thick cord attached to what will be the child's navel at one end and to the placenta at the other. It transmits nourishment and oxygen to the growing fetus from the mother and carries away waste material from the fetus. 94

Unconditioned response   A response elicited by an unconditioned stimulus. 40

Unconditioned stimulus   A stimulus that elicits a response prior to learning. All stimuli capable of eliciting reflexive behaviors are examples of unconditioned stimuli. For example, food is an unconditioned stimulus for the response of salivation. 40

Uterus   The organ in which the embryo or fetus is contained and nourished during pregnancy; also called the womb. 93

Valid   A measure is said to be valid to the extent that it measures what it is intended to measure. (See *reliable*.) 267

Variable   A property, measurement, or characteristic that is susceptible to variation. In psychological experimentation, qualities of human beings such as intelligence and creativity are referred to as variables. (See *dependent variable; independent variable*.) 17

Vegetative reflex   A reflex pertaining to the intake of food (for example, swallowing and sucking). 132

Version   Turning the fetus manually to assist delivery. 109

Violence   An extreme form of aggressiveness, implying physical action and real or possible physical harm to people or objects. (See *aggression*.) 296

Vocation   Refers to a "calling" and is usually restricted to a religious occupation, although it is also sometimes used to refer to certain white-collar careers such as law or medicine. (See *work; job; occupation; career*.) 393

Wisdom   A quality of human personality and behavior reflected in knowledge that is wide-ranging and deep, not easily accessible, and directed toward goodness. Often associated with old age. 513

Work   Activities engaged in for gain rather than primarily for the pleasure derived from them. A general term that includes jobs, occupations, and careers. 393

Youth   Label sometimes used for a transition period spanning the adolescent years and extending to about age 24. 382

Zone of proximal development   Vygotsky's phrase for the individual's current potential for further intellectual development—a capacity not ordinarily measured by conventional intelligence tests. He suggests that hints and questions might help in assessing this zone. 52

References

Abramson, L. (1991). Facial expressivity in failure to thrive and normal infants: Implications for their capacity to engage in the world. *Merrill-Palmer Quarterly, 37,* 159–182.

Adams, R. E., Jr., & Passman, R. H. (1981). The effects of preparing two-year-olds for brief separations from their mothers. *Child Development, 52,* 1068–1070.

Adams, R. E., Jr., & Passman, R. H. (1983). Explaining to young children about an upcoming separation from their mother: When do I tell them? *Journal of Applied Developmental Psychology, 4,* 35–42.

Adams, R. G. (1986). Friendship and aging. *Generations, 10,* 40–43.

Adegoke, A. A. (1993). The experience of spermarche (The age of onset of sperm emission) among selected adolescent boys in Nigeria. *Journal of Youth and Adolescence, 22,* 201–209.

Adler, P. A., Kless, S. J., & Adler, P. (1992). Socialization to gender roles: Popularity among elementary school boys and girls. *Sociology of Education, 65,* 169–187.

Agras, W. S., Rossiter, E. M., Arnow, B., Schneider, J. A., Telch, C. F., Raeburn, S. D., Bruce, B., Perl, M., & Koran, L. M. (1992). Pharmacologic and cognitive-behavioral treatment for bulimia nervosa: A controlled comparison. *American Journal of Psychiatry, 149,* 82–87.

AIDS kids beat odds against survival. (1994, April 17). *Edmonton Journal,* p. C7.

The AIDS threat: Who's at risk? (1988, March 14). *Newsweek,* pp. 42–52.

AIDS will kill 4M women by 2000: WHO. (1993, Sept. 8). *Edmonton Journal,* p. A12.

Ainsworth, M. D. S., Blehar, M. C., Waters, E., & Wall, S. (1978). *Patterns of attachment.* Hillsdale, NJ: Erlbaum.

Albert, R. S., & Runco, M. A. (1986). The achievement of eminence: A model based on a longitudinal study of exceptionally gifted boys and their families. In R. J. Sternberg & J. E. Davidson (Eds.), *Conceptions of giftedness.* New York: Cambridge University Press.

Alcamo, I. E. (1993). A vaccine for AIDS. *American Biology Teacher, 55,* 198–202.

Alcock, J. (1984). *Animal behavior: An evolutionary approach* (3rd ed.). Sunderland, MA: Sinauer.

Allen, K. R. (1993). The dispassionate discourse of children's adjustment to divorce. *Journal of Marriage and the Family, 55,* 46–50.

Allen, S. H. (1993). Primary osteoporosis. Methods to combat bone loss that accompanies aging. *Postgraduate Medicine, 93,* 43–46, 49–50, 53–55.

Allison, P. D., & Furstenberg, F. F., Jr. (1989). How marital dissolution affects children: Variations by age and sex. *Developmental Psychology, 25,* 540–549.

Alvy, K. T. (1987). *Parent training: A social necessity.* Studio City, CA: Center for the Improvement of Child Caring.

Alwin, D. F. (1994). Aging, personality, and social change: The stability of individual differences over the adult life span. In D. L. Featherman, R. M. Lerner, & M. Perlmutter (Eds.), *Lifespan development and behavior* (Vol. 12). Hillsdale, NJ: Erlbaum.

Amato, P. R. (1993). Children's adjustment to divorce: Theories, hypotheses, and empirical support. *Journal of Marriage and the Family, 55,* 23–38.

Amato, P. R., & Keith, B. (1991). Parental divorce and the well-being of children: A meta-analysis. *Psychological Bulletin, 110,* 26–46.

Ambert, A. M. (1992). *The effect of children on parents.* New York: Haworth.

American Psychiatric Association. (1987). *Diagnostic and statistical manual of mental disorders* (3rd ed., rev.). Washington, DC: American Psychiatric Association.

Ammerman, R. T. (1990). Predisposing child factors. In R. T. Ammerman & M. Hersen (Eds.), *Children at risk: An evaluation of factors contributing to child abuse and neglect.* New York: Plenum.

Anderson, J. R. (1980). *Cognitive psychology and its applications.* San Francisco: Freeman.

Anisfeld, M. (1991). Review: Neonatal imitation. *Developmental Review, 11,* 60–97.

Anonymous. (1994). Report of the Board of Trustees of the American Medical Association. Euthanasia/physician-assisted suicide: Lessons in the Dutch experience. *Issues in Law and Medicine, 10,* 81–90.

Anthony, E. J. (Ed.). (1975). *Exploration in child psychiatry.* New York: Plenum.

Antonarakis, S. E. (1991). Parental origin of the extra chromosome in trisomy 21 as indicated by analysis of

DNA polymorphisms. Down Syndrome Collaborative Group. *New England Journal of Medicine, 324,* 872–876.

Aquilino, W. S. (1990). The likelihood of parent-adult child coresidence: Effects of family structure and parental characteristics. *Journal of Marriage and the Family, 52,* 405–419.

Arber, S., & Gilbert, G. N. (1989). Transitions in caring: Gender, life course and the care of the elderly. In B. Bytheway, T. Keil, P. Allatt, & A. Bryman (Eds.), *Becoming and being old: Sociological approaches to later life.* London: Sage.

Arditti, J. A., & Michaelena, K. (1994). Fathers' perspectives of their co-parental relationships postdivorce: Implications for family practice and legal reform. *Family Relations, 43,* 61–67.

Ariès, P. (1962). *Centuries of childhood: A social history of family life* (R. Baldick, Trans.). New York: Knopf. (Original work published 1960.)

Armen, J. C. (1974). *Gazelle boy.* New York: Universe Books. (Translated by S. Hardman from *L'enfant sauvage du grand désert.* Neuchâtel: Delachaux & Niestlé.)

Arnett, J. (1992). Reckless behavior in adolescence: A developmental perspective. *Developmental Review, 12,* 339–373.

Arnett, W. S. (1991). Growing old in the cradle: Old age and immortality among the kings of ancient Assyria. *International Journal of Aging and Human Development, 32,* 135–141.

Aslin, R. N. (1987). Visual and auditory development in infancy. In J. D. Osofsky (Ed.), *Handbook of infant development.* New York: John Wiley.

Aslin, R. N., Pisoni, D. P., & Jusczyk, P. W. (1983). Auditory development and speech perception in infancy. In M. H. Haith & J. J. Campos (Eds.), *Handbook of child psychology* (Vol. 2): *Infancy and developmental psychology.* New York: John Wiley.

Aslin, R. N., & Smith, L. B. (1988). Perceptual development. *Annual Review of Psychology, 39,* 435–473.

Asp, E., & Garbarino, J. (1988). Integrative processes at school and in the community. In T. D. Yawkey & J. E. Johnson (Eds.), *Integrative processes and socialization: Early to middle childhood.* Hillsdale, NJ: Erlbaum.

Assmann, A. (1994). Wholesome knowledge: Concepts of wisdom in a historical and cross-cultural perspective. In D. L. Featherman, R. M. Lerner, & M. Perlmutter (Eds.), *Life-span development and behavior* (Vol. 12). Hillsdale, NJ: Erlbaum.

Astington, J. W. (1991). Intention in the child's theory of mind. In D. Frye & C. Moore (Eds.), *Children's theories of mind: Mental states and social understanding.* Hillsdale, NJ: Erlbaum.

Astroth, K. A. (1993). Are youth at risk? Reevaluating the deficit model of youth development. *Journal of Extension, 31,* 22–25.

Atchley, R. C. (1982). Retirement: Leaving the world of work. *Annals of the American Academy of Political and Social Sciences, 464,* 120–131.

Atchley, R. C. (1985). *Social forces and aging: An introduction to social gerontology* (4th ed.). Belmont, CA: Wadsworth.

Atchley, R. C. (1989). *A continuity theory of aging. Gerontologist, 29,* 183–190.

Atchley, R. C. (1992). What do social theories of aging offer counselors? *Counseling Psychologist, 20,* 336–340.

Atkinson, R. C., & Shiffrin, R. M. (1971). The control of short-term memory. *Scientific American, 225,* 82–90.

Aubrey, C. (1993). An investigation of the mathematical knowledge and competencies which young children bring into school. *British Educational Research Journal, 19,* 27–41.

Babies without dads: Single women turning to artificial insemination. (1992, Jan. 16). *Edmonton Journal,* p. B9.

Bäckström, K. (1992). Children's rights and early childhood education. *International Journal of Early Childhood, 24,* 22–27.

Bader, J. E. (1994). Essential lessons of gerontology and geriatrics. *Journal of the American Optometric Association, 65,* 58–62.

Bahrick, H. P., Bahrick, P. O., & Wittlinger, R. P. (1975). Fifty years of memory for names and faces: A cross-sectional approach. *Journal of Experimental Psychology: General, 104,* 54–75.

Bailey, T. (1991). Jobs of the future and the education they will require: Evidence from occupational forecasts. *Educational Researcher, 20,* 11–20.

Baillargeon, R. (1987). Object permanence in 3½- and 4½-month-old infants. *Developmental Psychology, 23,* 655–664.

Baillargeon, R. (1992). The object concept revisited. In *Visual perception and cognition in infancy: Carnegie-Mellon symposia on cognition* (Vol. 23). Hillsdale, NJ: Erlbaum.

Baird sounds off at Snell. (1994, Oct. 20). *Gateway,* p. 3.

Bajaj, J. S., Misra, A., Rajalakshmi, M., & Madan, R. (1993). Environmental release of chemicals and reproductive ecology. *Environmental Health Perspectives, 2,* 125–130.

Baker, D. P. (1993). Compared to Japan, the U.S. is a low achiever . . . really: New evidence and comment on Westbury. *Educational Researcher, 22,* 18–20.

Baker, R. L., & Mednick, B. R. (1984). *Influences on human development: A longitudinal perspective.* Boston: Kluwer-Nijhoff.

Bakwin, H. (1949). Psychologic aspects of pediatrics. *Journal of Pediatrics, 35,* 512–521.

Balke, E. (1992). Children's rights and the world summit for children. *International Journal of Early Childhood, 24,* 2–7.

Baltes, M. M., & Silverberg, S. B. (1994). The dynamics between dependency and autonomy: Illustrations across the lifespan. In D. L. Featherman, R. M. Lerner, & M. Perlmutter (Eds.), *Life-span development and behavior* (Vol. 12). Hillsdale, NJ: Erlbaum.

Banaji, M. R., & Prentice, D. A. (1994). The self in adolescence. *Annual Review of Psychology, 45,* 297–332.

Bandura, A. (1969). *Principles of behavior modification.* New York: Holt, Rinehart & Winston.

Bandura, A. (1977). *Social learning theory.* Englewood Cliffs, NJ: Prentice-Hall.

Bandura, A. (1981). Self-referent thought: A developmental analysis of self-efficacy. In J. H. Flavell & L. Ross (Eds.), *Social cognitive development: Frontiers and possible futures.* Cambridge: Cambridge University Press.

Bandura, A. (1986). *Social foundations of thought and action: A social cognitive theory.* Englewood Cliffs, NJ: Prentice-Hall.

Bandura, A. (1993). Perceived self-efficacy in cognitive development and functioning. *Educational Psychologist, 28,* 117–148.

Bandura, A., Ross, D., & Ross, S. A. (1963). Vicarious reinforcement and imitative learning. *Journal of Abnormal and Social Psychology, 67,* 601–607.

Bandura, A., & Walters, R. (1963). *Social learning and personality development.* New York: Holt, Rinehart & Winston.

Banks, M. S. (1980). The development of visual accommodation during early infancy. *Child Development, 51,* 646–666.

Baran, S. I., Chase, L. I., & Courtright, J. A. (1979). Television drama as a facilitator of prosocial behavior: "The Waltons." *Journal of Broadcasting, 23,* 277–285.

Barer, B. M. (1994). Men and women aging differently. *International Journal of Aging and Human Development, 38,* 29–40.

Barnett, W. S. (1992). Benefits of compensatory preschool education. *Journal of Human Resources, 27,* 279–312.

Barnett, W. S. (1993). Benefit-cost analysis of preschool education: Findings from a 25-year follow-up. *American Journal of Orthopsychiatry, 63,* 500–508.

Barrett, G. V., & Depinet, R. L. (1991). A reconsideration of testing for competence rather than for intelligence. *American Psychologist, 46,* 1012–1024.

Bartoshuk, L. M., & Beauchamp, G. K. (1994). Chemical senses. *Annual Review of Psychology, 45,* 419–449.

Basseches, M. (1984). *Dialectical thinking and adult development.* Norwood, NJ: Ablex.

Basseches, M. (1986). Comments on social cognition in adulthood: A dialectical perspective. *Educational Gerontology, 12,* 327–334.

Bates, E., Thal, D., Whitesell, K., Fenson, L., & Oakes, L. (1989). Integrating language and gesture in infancy. *Developmental Psychology, 25,* 1004–1019.

Bates, J. E. (1989). Concepts and measures of temperament. In G. A. Kohnstamm, J. E. Bates, & M. K. Rothbart (Eds.), *Temperament in Childhood.* New York: John Wiley.

Battistich, V., Watson, M., Solomon, D. I., Schaps, E., & Solomon, J. (1991). The child development project: A comprehensive program for the development of prosocial character. In W. M. Kurtines & J. L. Gewirtz (Eds.), *Handbook of moral behavior and development* (Vol. 3: Application). Hillsdale, NJ: Erlbaum.

Bauer, K. L. (1992). Birth order: How it affects children. *PTA Today, 17,* 13–15.

Baum, C. G., & Forehand, R. (1984). Social factors associated with adolescent obesity. *Journal of Pediatric Psychology, 9,* 293–302.

Baumrind, D. (1967). Child care practices anteceding three patterns of pre-school behavior. *Genetic Psychology Monographs, 75,* 43–88.

Baumrind, D. (1977). Some thoughts about child rearing. In S. Cohen & T. J. Comiskey (Eds.), *Child development: Contemporary perspectives.* Itasca, IL: F. E. Peacock.

Baumrind, D. (1989). Rearing competent children. In W. Damon (Ed.), *Child development today and tomorrow.* San Francisco: Jossey-Bass.

Baumrind, D. (1993). The average expectable environment is not good enough: A response to Scarr. *Child Development, 64,* 1299–1317.

Baxter, G., & Beer, J. (1990). Educational needs of school personnel regarding child abuse and/or neglect. *Psychological Reports, 67,* 75–80.

Bayer, L. M., Whissell-Buechy, D., & Honzik, M. P. (1981). Health in the middle years. In D. H. Eichorn, J. A. Clausen, N. Haan, M. P. Honzik, & P. H. Mussen (Eds.), *Present and past in middle life.* New York: Academic Press.

Beach, S. R. H., & O'Leary, K. D. (1993). Dysphoria and marital discord: Are dysphoric individuals at risk for marital maladjustment? *Journal of Marital and Family Therapy, 19,* 355–368.

Beatty, P. (1991). Foreword. *The Journal of Drug Issues, 21,* 1–7.

Beauchamp, G. K., Cowart, B. J., & Schmidt, H. J. (1991). Development of chemosensory sensitivity and preference. In T. V. Getchell, R. L. Doty, J. B. Snow, & L. M. Bartoshuk (Eds.), *Smell and taste in health and disease.* New York: Raven.

Beckwith, L., & Rodning, C. (1991). Intellectual functioning in children born preterm: Recent research. In L. Okagaki & R. J. Sternberg (Eds.), *Directors of development: Influences on the development of children's thinking.* Hillsdale, NJ: Erlbaum.

Beckwith, R. T. (1991). The language of emotion, the emotions, and nominalist bootstrapping. In D. Frye & C. Moore (Eds.), *Children's theories of mind: Mental states and social understanding.* Hillsdale, NJ: Erlbaum.

Bell, A., & Weinberg, M. (1978). *Homosexuality: A study of diversity among men and women.* New York: Simon & Schuster.

Belmont, J. M. (1989). Cognitive strategies and strategic learning: The socio-instructional approach. *American Psychologist, 44,* 142–148.

Belsky, J. (1981). Early human experience: A family perspective. *Developmental Psychology, 17,* 3–23.

Belsky, J. K. (1990). *The psychology of aging: Theory, research, and interventions* (2nd ed.). Pacific Grove, CA: Brooks/Cole.

Belsky, J., Lerner, R. M., & Spanier, G. B. (1984). *The child in the family.* Reading, MA: Addison-Wesley.

Belsky, J., & Rovine, M. (1990). Patterns of marital change across the transition to parenthood: Pregnancy to three years postpartum. *Journal of Marriage and the Family, 52,* 5–20.

Belsky, J., & Rovine, M. J. (1988). Nonmaternal care in the first year of life and the security of infant-parent attachment. *Child Development, 59,* 156–167.

Bem, S. L. (1974). The measurement of psychological androgyny. *Journal of Consulting and Clinical Psychology, 42,* 155–162.

Benasich, A. A., Curtiss, S., & Tallal, P. (1993). Language, learning, and behavioral disturbances in childhood: A longitudinal perspective. *Journal of the American Academy of Child and Adolescent Psychiatry, 32,* 585–594.

Benet, S. (1976). *How to live to be 100.* New York: Dial.

Benson-von der Ohe, E. (1984). First and second marriages: The first three years of married life. In S. A. Mednick, M. Harway, & K. M. Finello (Eds.), *Handbook of longitudinal research* (Vol. 2): *Teenage and adult cohorts.* New York: Praeger.

Benthin, A., Slovic, P., & Severson, H. (1993). A psychometric study of adolescent risk perception. *Journal of Adolescence, 16,* 153–168.

Bentley, K. S., & Fox, R. A. (1991). Mothers and fathers of young children: Comparison of parenting styles. *Psychological Reports, 69,* 320–322.

Berg, B., & Turner, D. (1993). MTV unleashed: Sixth graders create music videos based on works of art. *Techtrends, 38,* 28–31.

Berg, W. K., & Berg, K. M. (1987). Psychophysiological development in infancy: State, startle, and attention. In J. D. Osofsky (Ed.), *Handbook of infant development* (2nd ed.). New York: John Wiley.

Bergman, L. R. (1993). Some methodological issues in longitudinal research: Looking ahead. In D. Magnusson & P. Casaer (Eds.), *Longitudinal research on individual development: Present status and future perspectives.* Cambridge: Cambridge University Press.

Berland, M. (1991). Genital herpes and childbirth. *Revue Francaise de Gynécologie et D'Obstétrique, 86,* 639–643.

Berman, H. J. (1992/1993). Joyce Carol Oates's "A theory of Knowledge." *International Journal of Aging and Human Development, 36,* 293–302.

Berndt, T. J. (1979). Developmental changes in conformity to peers and parents. *Developmental Psychology, 15,* 608–616.

Berndt, T. J. (1988). The nature and significance of children's relationships. In R. Vasta (Ed.), *Annals of child development* (Vol. 5). Greenwich, CT: JAI Press.

Berndt, T. J. (1989). Friendships in childhood and adolescence. In W. Damon (Ed.), *Child development today and tomorrow.* San Francisco: Jossey-Bass.

Berndt, T. J., Cheung, P. C., Lau, S., Hau, K. T., & Lew, W. J. F. (1993). Perceptions of parenting in Mainland China, Taiwan, and Hong Kong: Sex differences and societal differences. *Developmental Psychology, 29,* 156–164.

Bertenthal, B. I., & Campos, J. J. (1990). A systems approach to the organizing effects of self-produced locomotion during infancy. In C. Rovee-Collier & L. P. Lipsitt (Eds.), *Advances in infancy research* (Vol. 6). Norwood, NJ: Ablex.

Berthier, M., Oriot, D., Bonneau, D., Chevrel, J., Magnin, G., & Garnier, P. (1993). Failure to prevent physical child abuse despite detection of risk factors at birth and social work follow-up. *Child Abuse and Neglect, 17,* 691–692.

Beunen, G., & Malina, R. M. (1988). Growth and physical performance relative to the timing of the adolescent spurt. *Exercise and Sport Sciences Review, 16,* 503–540.

Beyene, Y. (1989). *From menarche to menopause: Reproductive lives of peasant women in two cultures.* New York: State University of New York Press.

Beyth-Marom, R., Austin, L., Fischhoff, B., Palmgren, C., & Jacobs-Quadrel, M. (1993). Perceived consequences of risky behaviors: Adults and adolescents. *Developmental Psychology, 29,* 549–563.

Bibby, R. W., & Posterski, D. C. (1985). *The emerging generation: An inside look at Canada's teenagers.* Toronto: Irwin.

Bibby, R. W., & Posterski, D. C. (1992). *Teen trends: A nation in motion.* Toronto: Stoddart Publishing Co.

Bijou, S. W. (1989). Psychological linguistics: Implications for a theory of initial development and a method for research. In H. W. Reese (Ed.), *Advances in child development and behavior.* New York: Academic Press.

Binder, A. (1988). Juvenile delinquency. *Annual Review of Psychology, 39,* 253–282.

Bishop, J. E., & Waldholz, M. (1990). *Genome: The story of the most astonishing scientific adventure of our time— the attempt to map all the genes in the human body.* New York: Simon & Schuster.

Black, C., & DeBlassie, R. R. (1985). Adolescent pregnancy: Contributing factors, consequences, treatment, and plausible solutions. *Adolescence, 78,* 281–290.

Blake, J., & de Boysson-Bardies, B. (1992). Patterns in babbling: A cross-linguistic study. *Journal of Child Language, 19,* 51–74.

Blau, G. M., Whewell, M. C., Gullotta, T. P., & Bloom, M. (1994). The prevention and treatment of child abuse in households of substance abusers: A research demonstration progress report. *Child Welfare, 73,* 83–94.

Bleeker, S. (1970). *The Zulu of South Africa: Cattlemen, farmers, and warriors.* New York: Morrow.

Bloch, H. A., & Niederhoffer, A. (1958). *The gang: A study of adolescent behavior.* New York: Philosophical Library.

Block, J., & Robins, R. W. (1993). A longitudinal study of consistency and change in self-esteem from early adolescence to early adulthood. *Child Development, 64,* 909–923.

Block, S. D., & Billings, J. A. (1994). Patient requests to hasten death. Evaluation and management in terminal care. *Archives of Internal Medicine, 154,* 2039–2047.

Blood, R. O. (1967). *Love match and arranged marriage: A Tokyo-Detroit comparison.* New York: The Free Press.

Bloom-Feshbach, J., & Bloom-Feshbach, S. (1987). *The psychology of separation and loss: Perspectives on development, life transitions, and clinical practice.* San Francisco: Jossey-Bass.

Bluebond-Langner, M. (1977). Meanings of death to children. In H. Feifel (Ed.), *New meanings of death.* New York: McGraw-Hill.

Blum, K., Noble, E. P., Sheridan, P. J., Montgomery, A., Ritchie, T., Jagadeeswaran, P., Nogami, H., Briggs, A. H., & Cohn, J. B. (1990). Allelic association of human dopamine D$_2$ receptor gene in alcoholism. *Journal of the American Medical Association, 263,* 2055–2060.

Blumenthal, J. A., Sanders Williams, R., Needels, T. L., & Wallace, A. G. (1982). Psychological changes accompany aerobic exercise in healthy middle-aged adults. *Psychosomatic Medicine, 44,* 529–536.

Bogolub, E. B. (1991). Women and mid-life divorce: Some practical issues. *Social Work, 36,* 428–433.

Boldizar, J. P. (1991). Assessing sex typing and androgyny in children: The Children's Sex Role Inventory. *Developmental Psychology, 27,* 505–515.

Bonen, A. (1994). Exercise-induced menstrual cycle changes. A functional, temporary adaptation to metabolic stress. *Sports Medicine, 17,* 373–392.

Boodman, S. (1994, Oct. 8). "Miracle" babies face physical, intellectual disabilities—study. *Edmonton Journal,* p. E2.

Booth, F. W., Weeden, S. H., & Tseng, B. S. (1994). Effect of aging on human skeletal muscle and motor function. *Medicine and Science in Sports and Exercise, 26,* 556–560.

Boring, E. G. (1923). Intelligence as the tests test it. *New Republic, 35,* 35–37.

Borland, D. C. (1982). A cohort analysis approach to the empty-nest syndrome among three ethnic groups of women: A theoretical position. *Journal of Marriage and the Family, 11,* 117–128.

Bornstein, M. H., & Marks, L. E. (1982, January). Color revisionism. *Psychology Today, 16,* pp. 64–72.

Botella, L., & Feixas, G. (1992/1993). The autobiographical group: A tool for the reconstruction of past life experience with the aged. *International Journal of Aging and Human Development, 36,* 303–319.

Botwinick, J. (1984). *Aging and behavior* (3rd ed.). New York: Springer-Verlag.

Bouchard, C., Shephard, R. J., Stephens, T., Sutton, J. R., & McPherson, B. D. (Eds). (1990). *Exercise, fitness, and health: A consensus of current knowledge.* Champaign, IL: Human Kinetics Books.

Bouchard, T. J., Jr., & McGue, M. (1981). Familial studies of intelligence: A review. *Science, 212,* 1055–1059.

Boulton, M. J. (1993). Proximate causes of aggressive fighting in middle-school children. *British Journal of Educational Psychology, 63,* 231–244.

Bower, T. G. R. (1989). *The rational infant: Learning in infancy.* New York: W. H. Freeman.

Bowlby, J. (1958). The nature of the child's tie to his mother. *International Journal of Psychoanalysis, 39,* 350–373.

Bowlby, J. (1969). *Attachment and loss* (Vol. 1): *Attachment.* New York: Basic Books.

Bowlby, J. (1979). *The making and breaking of affectional bonds.* London: Tavistock Publications.

Bowlby, J. (1980). *Attachment and loss* (Vol. 3): *Loss, sadness and depression.* New York: Basic Books.

Bowlby, J. (1982). *Attachment and loss* (Vol. 1): *Attachment* (2nd ed.). London: Hogarth Press.

Bowman, B. (1993). Early childhood education. In L. Darling-Hammond (Ed.), *Review of Research in Education* (Vol. 19). Washington, DC: American Educational Research Association.

Bowman, J. M. (1990). Maternal blood group immunization. In R. D. Eden, F. H. Boehm, & M. Haire (Eds.), *Assessment and care of the fetus: Physiological, clinical, and medicolegal principles.* Norwalk, CT: Appleton & Lange.

Boyatzis, C. J., Chazan, E., & Ting, C. Z. (1993). Preschool children's decoding of facial emotions. *Journal of Genetic Psychology, 154,* 375–382.

Boyd, G. A. (1976). *Developmental processes in the child's acquisition of syntax: Linguistics in the elementary school.* Itasca, IL: F. E. Peacock.

Boyles, M., & Tilman, R. (1993). Thorstein Veblen, Edward O. Wilson, and Sociobiology: An interpretation. *Journal of Economic Issues, 27,* 1195–1218.

Bradshaw, G. L., & Anderson, J. R. (1982). Elaborative encoding as an explanation of levels of processing. *Journal of Verbal Learning and Verbal Behavior, 21,* 165–174.

Braine, L. G., Pomerantz, E., Lorber, D., & Krantz, D. H. (1991). Conflicts with authority: Children's feelings, actions, and justifications. *Developmental Psychology, 27,* 829–840.

Bramham, D. (1994, April 16). Putting pain in punishment. *Edmonton Journal,* p. G3.

Brazelton, T. B. (1973). *Neonatal behavior assessment scale.* Philadelphia: Lippincott.

Brazelton, T. B. (1990). Saving the bathwater. *Child Development, 61,* 1661–1671.

Brazelton, T. B., Nugent, J. K., & Lester, B. M. (1987). Neonatal behavioral assessment scale. In J. D. Osofsky (Ed.), *Handbook of infant development.* New York: John Wiley.

Brecher, E. M. and the editors of Consumer Reports books. (1984). *Love, sex and aging: A Consumers Union Report.* Boston: Little, Brown.

Brendt, R. L., & Beckman, D. A. (1990). Teratology. In R. D. Eden, F. H. Boehm, & M. Haire (Eds.), *Assessment and care of the fetus: Physiological, clinical, and medicolegal principles.* Norwalk, CT: Appleton & Lange.

Brenner, J., & Mueller, E. (1982). Shared meaning in boy toddler's peer relations. *Child Development, 53,* 380–391.

Bretherton, I. (1991). Intentional communication and the development of an understanding of mind. In D. Frye & C. Moore (Eds.), *Children's theories of mind: Mental states and social understanding.* Hillsdale, NJ: Erlbaum.

Brick, P., & Roffman, D. M. (1993). "Abstinence, no buts" is simplistic. *Educational Leadership, 51,* 90–92.

Bridges, L. J., Connell, J. P., & Belsky, J. (1988). Similarities and differences in infant-mother and infant-father interaction in the strange situation: A component process analysis. *Developmental Psychology, 24,* 92–100.

Brisk, M. E. (1991). Toward multilingual and multicultural mainstream education. *Journal of Education, 173,* 114–129.

Brodigan, D. E. (1992). Osteoporosis. The effects of exercise variables. *Melpomene Journal, 11,* 16–22.

Brody, J. (1988, September). Cocaine: Litany of fetal risks grows. *New York Times,* pp. C1, C8.

Bromley, D. B. (1990). *Behavioural gerontology: Central issues in the psychology of ageing.* New York: John Wiley.

Bronfenbrenner, U. (1977, May). Nobody home: The erosion of the American family. *Psychology Today,* pp. 41–47.

Bronfenbrenner, U. (1989). Ecological systems theory. In R. Vasta (Ed.), *Annals of child development* (Vol. 6). Greenwich, CT: JAI Press.

Bronfenbrenner, U., Belsky, J., & Steinberg, L. (1977). Daycare in context: An ecological perspective on research and public policy. In *Policy issues in daycare.* Washington, DC: U.S. Department of Health & Human Services.

Bronson, G. W. (1972). Infants' reactions to unfamiliar persons and novel objects. *Monographs of the Society for Research in Child Development, 37*(3).

Bronstein, P., Clauson, J., Stoll, M. F., & Abrams, C. L. (1993). Parenting behavior and children's social, psychological, and academic adjustment in diverse family structures. *Family Relations, 42,* 268–276.

Brooks, J. B. (1981). *The process of parenting.* Palo Alto, CA: Mayfield.

Brooks-Gunn, J. (1988). Antecedents and consequences of variations in girls' maturational timing. *Journal of Adolescent Health Care, 9,* 365–373.

Brooks-Gunn, J., & Furstenberg, F. F., Jr. (1989). Adolescent sexual behavior. *American Psychologist, 44,* 249–257.

Brouwer, A. (1990). The nature of ageing. In M. A. Horan & A. Brouwer (Eds.), *Gerontology: Approaches to biomedical and clinical research.* London: Edward Arnold.

Brouwers, M., & Wiggum, C. D. (1993). Bulimia and perfectionism: Developing the courage to be imperfect. *Journal of Mental Health Counseling, 15,* 141–149.

Brown, B. B., Mounts, N., Lamborn, S. D., & Steinberg, L. (1993). Parenting practices and peer group affiliation in adolescence. *Child Development, 64,* 467–482.

Brown, J., & Finn, P. (1982). Drinking to get drunk: Findings of a survey of junior and senior high school students. *Journal of Alcohol and Drug Education, 27,* 13–25.

Brown, J. L. (1964). States in newborn infants. *Merrill-Palmer Quarterly, 10,* 313–327.

Brown, K., Covell, K., & Abramovitch, R. (1991). Time course and control of emotion: Age differences in understanding and recognition. *Merrill-Palmer Quarterly, 37,* 273–287.

Brown, M. H. (1991). Innovations in the treatment of bulimia: Transpersonal psychology, relaxation, imagination, hypnosis, myth, and ritual. *Journal of Humanistic Education and Development, 30,* 50–60.

Brown, R. (1973). *A first language: The early stages.* Cambridge, MA: Harvard University Press.

Browne Miller, A. (1990). *The day care dilemma: Critical concerns for American families.* New York: Plenum.

Brownell, K. D., & Wadden, T. A. (1992). Etiology and treatment of obesity: Understanding a serious, prevalent, and refractory disorder. *Journal of Consulting and Clinical Psychology, 60,* 505–517.

Bruchkowsky, M. (1991). The development of empathic cognition in middle and early childhood. In R. Case, et al. (Eds.), *The mind's staircase: Exploring the conceptual underpinnings of children's thought and knowledge.* Hillsdale, NJ: Erlbaum.

Bruner, J. S. (1978, September). Learning the mother tongue. *Human Nature,* pp. 43–49.

Bruner, J. S. (1983). *Child's talk.* New York: Norton.

Bruner, J. S. (1986). *Actual minds, possible worlds.* Cambridge, MA: Harvard University Press.

Bryant, B. K. (1992). Conflict resolution strategies in relation to children's peer relations. *Journal of Applied Developmental Psychology, 13,* 35–50.

Buchanan, C. M., Eccles, J. S., & Becker, J. B. (1992). Are adolescents the victims of raging hormones: Evidence for activational effects of hormones on moods and behavior at adolescence. *Psychological Bulletin, 111,* 62–107.

Buchholz, E. S., & Korn-Bursztyn, C. (1993). Children of adolescent mothers: Are they at risk for abuse? *Adolescence, 28,* 361–382.

Bullies drive teen to suicide. (1994, Dec. 6). *Edmonton Sun,* p. 24.

Bullinger, A. (1985). The sensorimotor nature of the infant visual system: Cognitive problems. In V. L. Shulman, L. C. R. Restaino-Baumann, & L. Butler (Eds.), *The future of Piagetian theory: The neo-Piagetians* (pp. 19–32). New York: Plenum.

Bullock, J. R. (1993). Children's loneliness and their relationships with family and peers. *Family Relations, 42,* 46–49.

Bullock, J. R. (1994). Children without friends: Who are they and how can teachers help? *Childhood Education, 69,* 92–96.

Bunce, V. L., & Harrison, D. W. (1991). Child- or adult-directed speech and esteem: Effects on performance and arousal in elderly adults. *International Journal of Aging and Human Development, 32,* 125–134.

Burgard, D. (1993). Psychological theory seeks to define obesity. *Obesity and Health, 7,* 25–27, 37.

Burke, J. (1991). Teenagers, clothes, and gang violence. *Educational Leadership, 49,* 11–13.

Burnett, B. B. (1993). The psychological abuse of latency age children: A survey. *Child Abuse and Neglect: The International Journal, 17,* 441–454.

Bush calls for unprecedented increase in Head Start program. (1992, Jan. 22). *The Monterey Herald,* p. A3.

Bushnell, E. W., & Boudreau, J. P. (1993). Motor development and the mind: The potential role of motor abilities as a determinant of aspects of perceptual development. *Child Development, 64,* 1005–1021.

Buss, A. H., & Plomin, R. (1985). *Temperament: Early developing personality traits.* Hillsdale, NJ: Erlbaum.

Bussey, K. (1992). Lying and truthfulness: Children's definitions, standards, and evaluative reactions. *Child Development, 63,* 129–137.

Butler, E. R. (1993). Alcohol use by college students: A rites or passage ritual. *Naspa Journal, 31,* 48–55.

Butler, J. R., & Burton, L. M. (1990). Rethinking teenage childbearing: Is sexual abuse a missing link? *Family Relations, 39,* 73–80.

Butler, R. N. (1963). The life review: An interpretation of reminiscence in the aged. *Psychiatry, 26,* 65–76.

Butler, R. N. (1989). Productive aging. In V. L. Bengtson & K. W. Schaie (Eds.), *The course of later life: Research and reflections*. New York: Springer.

Buzzelli, C. A. (1992). Young children's moral understanding: Learning about right and wrong. *Young Children, 47,* 48–53.

Byczkowski, J. Z., Gearhart, J. M., & Fisher, J. W. (1994). "Occupational" exposure of infants to toxic chemicals via breast milk. *Nutrition, 10,* 43–48.

Byrne, B. M., & Shavelson, R. J. (1987). Adolescent self-concept: Testing the assumption of equivalent structure across gender. *American Educational Research Journal, 24,* 365–385.

Byrne, G. J., & Raphael, B. (1994). A longitudinal study of bereavement phenomena in recently widowed elderly men. *Psychological Medicine, 24,* 411–421.

Cain, J., Stacy, L., Jusenius, K., & Figge, D. (1990). The quality of dying: Financial, psychological, and ethical dilemmas. *Obstetrics and Gynecology, 76,* 149–152.

Cairns, R. B., Gariépy, J. L., & Hood, K. E. (1990). Development, microevolution, and social behavior. *Psychological Review, 97,* 49–65.

Caldwell, B. (1991). Educare: New product, new future. *Journal of Developmental and Behavioral Pediatrics, 12,* 199–205.

Caldwell, B. M. (1989). Achieving rights for children: Role of the early childhood profession. *Childhood Education, 66,* 4–7.

Caldwell, J. C. (1986). Routes to low mortality in poor countries. *Population and Development Review, 12,* 171–214.

Campbell, A. (1981). *The sense of well being in America: Recent patterns and trends.* New York: McGraw-Hill.

Campbell, A., Converse, P. E., & Rodgers, W. L. (1976). *The quality of American life: Perceptions, evaluations, and satisfactions.* New York: Russell Sage.

Campbell, F. A., & Ramey, C. T. (1990). The relationship between Piagetian cognitive development, mental test performance, and academic achievement in high-risk students with and without early educational intervention. *Intelligence, 14,* 293–308.

Campbell, S. B., & Cohn, J. F. (1991). Prevalence and correlates of postpartum depression in first-time mothers. *Journal of Abnormal Psychology, 100,* 594–599.

Canning, P. M., & Lyon, M. E. (1991). Misconceptions about early child care, education and intervention. *Journal of Child and Youth Care, 5,* 1–10.

Carey, W. B. (1989). Introduction: Basic issues. In W. B. Carey & S. C. McDevitt (Eds.), *Clinical and educational applications of temperament research.* Berwyn, PA: Swets North America.

Carpenter, B. D. (1993). A review and new look at ethical suicide in advanced age. *Gerontologist, 33,* 359–365.

Carroll, J. C., & Rest, J. R. (1982). Moral development. In B. B. Wolman et al. (Eds.), *Handbook of developmental psychology.* Englewood Cliffs, NJ: Prentice-Hall.

Case, R. (1991). Stages in the development of the young child's first sense of self. *Developmental Review, 11,* 210–230.

Case, R., Hayward, S., Lewis, M., & Hurst, P. (1988). Toward a neo-Piagetian theory of cognitive and emotional development. *Developmental Review, 8,* 1–51.

Caspi, A., Lynam, D., Moffitt, T. E., & Silva, P. A. (1993). Unraveling girls' delinquency: Biological, dispositional, and contextual contributions to adolescent misbehavior. *Developmental Psychology, 29,* 19–30.

Cattell, R. B. (1971). *Abilities: Their structure, growth, and action.* Boston: Houghton Mifflin.

Caughy, M. O., DiPietro, J. A., & Strobino, D. M. (1994). Day care participation as a protective factor in the cognitive development of low-income children. *Child Development, 65,* 457–471.

Ceci, S. J. (1991). How much does schooling influence general intelligence and its cognitive components? A reassessment of the evidence. *Developmental Psychology, 27,* 703–722.

Center for Disease Control. (1992). Vigorous physical activity among high school students—United States, 1990. *Morbidity and Mortality Weekly Report, 41,* 33–36.

Chalfant, J. C. (1989). Learning disabilities: Policy issues and promising approaches. *American Psychologist, 44,* 392–398.

Chappell, P. A., & Steitz, J. A. (1993). Young children's human figure drawings and cognitive development. *Perceptual and Motor Skills, 76,* 611–617.

Chase-Lansdale, P. L., & Brooks-Gunn, J. (1994). Correlates of adolescent pregnancy and parenthood. In C. B. Fisher & R. M. Lerner (Eds.), *Applied developmental psychology.* New York: McGraw-Hill.

Chasnoff, I. J. (1986/1987). Cocaine and pregnancy. *Childbirth Educator,* 37-42.

Chassin, L., Rogosch, F., & Barrera, M. (1991). Substance use and symptomatology among adolescent children of alcoholics. *Journal of Abnormal Psychology, 4,* 449–463.

Cheng, Pui-wan. (1993). Metacognition and giftedness. *Gifted Child Quarterly, 37,* 105–112.

Cherian, V. I. (1990). Academic achievement of children from monogamous and polygynous families. *Journal of Social Psychology, 130,* 117–119.

Chess, S., & Thomas, A. (1989). Temperament and its functional significance. In S. I. Greenspan & G. H. Pollock (Eds.), *The course of life: Vol II early childhood.* Madison, CT: International Universities Press.

Chester, R. D. (1992). Views from the mainstream: Learning disabled students as perceived by regular education classroom teachers and by non-learning disabled secondary students. *Canadian Journal of School Psychology, 8,* 93–102.

Cheung, Y. W., Erickson, P. G., & Landau, T. C. (1991). Experience of crack use: Findings from a community-based sample in Toronto. *Journal of Drug Issues, 21,* 121–140.

Chez, R. A., & Chervenak, J. L. (1990). Nutrition in pregnancy. In R. D. Eden, F. H. Boehm, & M. Haire (Eds.), *Assessment and care of the fetus: Physiological, clinical, and medicolegal principles.* Norwalk, CT: Appleton & Lange.

Chipman, S. F. (1988). Far too sexy a topic. *Educational Researcher, 17,* 46–49.

Chomsky, N. (1957). *Syntactic structures.* The Hague: Mouton.

Chomsky, N. (1965). *Aspects of the theory of syntax.* Cambridge, MA: MIT Press.

Chrisman, A. B. (1968). *Shen of the sea: Chinese stories for children.* New York: Dutton.

Christakis, N. A. (1994). Timing of referral of terminally ill patients to an outpatient hospice. *Journal of General Internal Medicine, 9,* 314–320.

Christian, L., & Morgan, G. H. (1993). Roses are red, violets are blue, my child is gifted and my family's a zoo. *Gifted Child Today, 16,* 14–17.

Christie, N. G., & Dinham, S. M. (1991). Institutional and external influences on social integration in the freshman year. *Journal of Higher Education, 62,* 412–436.

Christopher, F. S., & Roosa, M. W. (1990). An evaluation of an adolescent pregnancy prevention program: Is "Just say no" enough? *Family Relations, 39,* 68–72.

Christopherson, V. A. (1988). The family as a socialization context. In T. D. Yawkey & J. E. Johnson (Eds.), *Integrative processes and socialization: Early to middle childhood.* Hillsdale, NJ: Erlbaum.

Churchill, J. A. (1965). The relationship between intelligence and birth weight in twins. *Neurology, 15,* 341–347.

Ciesielski, K. T., & Knight, J. E. (1994). Cerebellar abnormality in autism: A nonspecific effect of early brain damage? *Acta Neurobiologiae Experimentalis, 54,* 151–154.

Claes, M., & Simard, R. (1992). Friendship characteristics of delinquent adolescents. *International Journal of Adolescence and Youth, 3,* 287–301.

Clark, M. L., & Bittle, M. L. (1992). Friendship expectations and the evaluation of present friendships in middle childhood and early adolescence. *Child Study Journal, 22,* 115–135.

Clarke-Stewart, K. A. (1989). Infant day care: Maligned or malignant? *American Psychologist, 44,* 266–273.

Clausen, J. A. (1981). Men's occupational careers in the middle years. In D. H. Eichorn, J. A. Clausen, N. Haan, M. P. Honzik, & P. H. Mussen (Eds.), *Present and past in middle life.* New York: Academic Press.

Claxton, J. W. (1993). Paving the way to acceptance. Psychological adaptation to death and dying in cancer. *Professional Nurse, 8,* 206–211.

Clayton, V. P., & Birren, J. E. (1980). The development of wisdom across the life span: A reexamination of an ancient topic. In P. B. Baltes & O. G. Brim, Jr. (Eds.), *Life-span development and behavior* (Vol. 3). New York: Academic Press.

Cobb, P. (1994). Constructivism in mathematics and science education. *Educational Researcher, 23,* 4.

Cohen, S. (1993/1994). Television in the lives of children and their families. *Childhood Education, 70,* 103–104.

Cohler, B. J. (1982). Personal narrative and lifecourse. In P. B. Baltes & O. G. Brim, Jr. (Eds.), *Life-span development and behavior* (Vol. 4, pp. 205–241). New York: Academic Press.

Cohler, B. J., & Grunebaum, H. V. (1981). *Mothers, grandmothers and daughters: Personality and childcare in three-generation families.* New York: John Wiley.

Colborn, T., vom Saal, F. S., & Soto, A. M. (1993). Developmental effects of endocrine-disrupting chemicals in wildlife and humans. *Environmental Health Perspectives, 101,* 378–384.

Colby, A., & Kohlberg, L. (1984). Invariant sequence and internal consistency in moral judgment stages. In W. M. Kertines & J. L. Gewirtz (Eds.), *Morality, moral behavior, and moral development* (pp. 41–51). New York: John Wiley.

Cole, P. G. (1993). A critical analysis of Siegel's case for revision of the learning disability construct. *International Journal of Disability, Development and Education, 40,* 5–21.

Cole, P. M., Usher, B. A., & Cargo, A. P. (1993). Cognitive risk and its association with risk for disruptive behavior disorder in preschoolers. *Journal of Clinical Child Psychology, 22,* 154–164.

Coleman, A. (1992). Coping with change: Focus on "retirement." *International Review of Education, 38,* 438–443.

Coleman, J. S. (1974). *Youth: Transition to adulthood.* Chicago: University of Chicago Press.

Coleman, P. G. (1986). *Aging and reminiscence processes: Social and clinical implications.* New York: John Wiley.

Coleman, P. M. (1993). Depression during the female climacteric period. *Journal of Advanced Nursing, 18,* 1540–1546.

Collett, J., & Serrano, B. (1992). Stirring it up: The inclusive classroom. *New Directions for Teaching and Learning, 49,* 35–48.

Collins, A., Brown, J. S., & Newman, S. E. (1989). Cognitive apprenticeship: Teaching the craft of reading, writing, and mathematics. In L. B. Resnick (Ed.), *Knowing, learning, and instruction: Essays in honor of Robert Glaser.* Hillsdale, NJ: Erlbaum.

Collins, C., Stommel, M., Wang, S., & Given, C. W. (1994). Caregiving transitions: Changes in depression among family caregivers of relatives with dementia. *Nursing Research, 43,* 220–225.

Collins, N. L., Dunkel-Schetter, C., Lobel, M., & Scrimshaw, S. C. (1993). Social support in pregnancy: Psychosocial correlates of birth outcomes and postpartum depression. *Journal of Personality and Social Psychology, 65,* 1243–1258.

Collins, W. A., & Gunnar, M. R. (1990). Social and personality development. *Annual Review of Psychology, 41,* 387–416.

Collins, W. A., & Russell, G. (1991). Mother–child and father–child relationships in middle childhood and adolescence: A developmental analysis. *Developmental Review, 11,* 99–136.

Connidis, I. A., & McMullin, J. A. (1993). To have or have not: Parent status and the subjective well-being of older men and women. *Gerontologist, 33,* 630–636.

Cooke, B. (1991). Family life education. *Family Relations, 40,* 3–13.

Cooley, C. H. (1902). *Human nature and the social order.* New York: Scribner's.

Coombs, R. H. (1991). Marital status and personal well-being: A literature review. *Family Relations, 40,* 97–102.

Cooney, T. M., & Uhlenberg, P. (1992). Support from parents over the life course: The adult child's perspective. *Social Forces, 71,* 63–84.

Corbin, C. B., & Pangrazi, R. P. (1992). Are American children and youth fit? *Research Quarterly for Exercise and Sport, 62,* 96–106.

Correy, J. F., Newman, N. M., Collins, J. A., Burrows, E. A., Burrows, R. F., Curran, J. T. (1992). Use of prescription drugs in the first trimester and congenital malformations. *Australian & New Zealand Journal of Obstetrics & Gynaecology, 31,* 340–344.

Costa, P. T., Jr., & McCrae, R. R. (1978). Objective personality assessment. In M. Storandt, I. C. Siegler, & M. F. Elias (Eds.), *The clinical psychology of aging.* New York: Plenum.

Costa, P. T., Jr., & McCrae, R. R. (1980). Still stable after all these years: Personality as a key to some issues in aging. In P. B. Baltes & O. G. Brim (Eds.), *Life-span development and behavior* (Vol. 3). New York: Academic Press.

Costa, P. T., Jr., & McCrae, R. R. (1984). Personality as a lifelong determinant of well being. In C. Z. Malatesta & C. E. Izard (Eds.), *Emotion in adult development* (pp. 141–158). Beverly Hills, CA: Sage.

Costa, P. T., Jr., McCrae, R. R., & Arenberg, D. (1983). Recent longitudinal research on personality and aging. In K. W. Schaie (Ed.), *Longitudinal studies of adult psychological development* (pp. 222–265). New York: Guilford Press.

Costello, P. M., Beasley, M. G., Tillotson, S. L., & Smith, I. (1994). Intelligence in mild atypical phenylketonuria. *European Journal of Pediatrics, 153,* 260–263.

Côté, J. E., & Levine, C. (1988). A critical examination of the ego identity status paradigm. *Developmental Review, 8,* 147–184.

Côté, J. E., & Levine, C. G. (1992). The genesis of the humanistic academic: A second test of Erikson's theory of ego identity formation. *Youth and Society, 23,* 387–410.

Coulter, D. (1993a, Oct. 25). Alberta students lag behind Asians in math: North American youths spend too much time on sports, socializing, study shows. *Edmonton Journal,* p. A5.

Coulter, D. L. (1993b). Epilepsy and mental retardation: An overview. *American Journal on Mental Retardation, 98,* 1–11.

Court to decide right of surrogate mother. (1992, Jan. 24). *Monterey Herald,* p. A8.

Coustan, D. R. (1990). Diabetes mellitus. In R. D. Eden, F. H. Boehm, & M. Haire (Eds.), *Assessment and care of the fetus: Physiological, clinical, and medicolegal principles.* Norwalk, CT: Appleton & Lange.

Cowen, E. L., Work, W. C., Hightower, A. D., Wyman, P. A., Parker, G. R., & Lotyczewski, B. S. (1991). Toward the development of a measure of perceived self-efficacy in children. *Journal of Clinical Child Psychology, 20,* 169–178.

Cox, H. G. (1988). *Later life: The realities of aging* (2nd ed.). Englewood Cliffs, NJ: Prentice-Hall.

Cox, T. C., Jacobs, M. R., Leblanc, A. E., & Marshman, J. A. (1983). *Drugs and drug abuse: A reference test.* Toronto: Addiction Research Foundation.

Crawford, M. A. (1993). The role of essential fatty acids in neural development: Implications for perinatal nutrition. *American Journal of Clinical Nutrition, 57,* 703s–709s.

Crawford, M. A., Doyle, W., Leaf, A., Leighfield, M., Ghebremeskel, K., & Phylactos, A. (1993). Nutrition and neurodevelopmental disorders. *Nutrition and Health, 9,* 81–97.

Crawford, P. B., & Shapiro, L. R. (1991). How obesity develops: A new look at nature and nurture. *Obesity and Health, 5,* 40–41.

Creasy, R. K. (1990). Preterm labor. In R. D. Eden, F. H. Boehm, & M. Haire (Eds.), *Assessment and care of the fetus: Physiological, clinical, and medicolegal principles.* Norwalk, CT: Appleton & Lange.

Crick, N. R., & Ladd, G. W. (1993). Children's perceptions of their peer experiences: Attributions, loneliness, social anxiety, and social avoidance. *Developmental Psychology, 29,* 244–254.

Crockett, L. J., & Petersen, A. C. (1987). Pubertal status and psychosocial development: Findings from the early adolescence study. In R. M. Lerner & T. T. Foch (Eds.), *Biological-psychosocial interactions in early adolescence: A life-span perspective.* Hillsdale, NJ: Erlbaum.

Crosbie-Burnett, M., & Helmbrecht, L. (1993). A descriptive empirical study of gay male stepfamilies. *Family Relations, 42,* 256–262.

Crowell, J. A., & Feldman, S. S. (1991). Mothers' working models of attachment relationships and mother and child behavior during separation and reunion. *Developmental Psychology, 27,* 597–605.

Culbertson, J. L. (1991). Child advocacy and clinical child psychology. *Journal of Clinical Child Psychology, 20,* 7–10.

Cummins, J. (1986). Empowering minority students: A framework for intervention. *Harvard Educational Review, 56,* 18–36.

Cummins, J., & Swain, M. (1986). *Bilingualism in education: Aspects of theory, research and practice.* London: Taylor & Fry.

Cunningham, W. R. (1989). Intellectual abilities, speed of response, and aging. In V. L. Bengtson & K. W. Schaie (Eds.), *The course of later life: Research and reflections.* New York: Springer.

Curcio, C. A., Millican, C. L., Allen, K. A., & Kalina, R. E. (1994). Aging of the human photoreceptor mosaic: Evidence for selective vulnerability of rods in central retina. *Investigative Ophthalmology and Visual Science, 34,* 3278–3296.

Curtiss, S. (1977). *Genie: A psycholinguistic study of a modern-day wild child.* New York: Academic Press.

Curtius, H. C., Endres, W., & Blau, N. (1994). Effect of high-protein meal plus aspartame ingestion on plasma phenylalanine concentrations in obligate heterozygotes for phenylketonuria. *Metabolism: Clinical and Experimental, 43,* 413–416.

Cutright, M. C. (1992). Self-esteem: The key to a child's success and happiness. *PTA Today, 17,* 5–6.

Cutting, W. A. (1994). Breast-feeding and HIV—a balance of risks. *Journal of Tropical Pediatrics, 40,* 6–11.

Cziko, G. A. (1992). The evaluation of bilingual education. *Educational Researcher, 21,* 10–15.

Dalton, K. (1980). *Depression after childbirth.* Oxford: Oxford University Press.

Damon, W., & Colby, A. (1987). Social influence and moral change. In W. M. Kurtines & J. L. Gewirtz (Eds.), *Moral development through social interaction.* New York: John Wiley.

Danilewitz, D., & Skuy, M. (1990). A psychoeducational profile of the unmarried mother. *International Journal of Adolescence and Youth, 2,* 175–184.

Darley, J. M., & Shultz, T. R. (1990). Moral rules: Their content and acquisition. *Annual Review of Psychology, 41,* 525–556.

Darling, C. A., Kallen, D. J., & Van Dusen, J. E. (1984). Sex in transition, 1900–1980. *Journal of Youth and Adolescence, 13,* 385–394.

Darwin, C. (1877). A biographical sketch of an infant. *Mind, 2,* 285–294.

Datan, N., Rodeheaver, D., & Hughes, F. (1987). Adult development and aging. *Annual Review of Psychology, 38,* 153–180.

Davidson, J. K., Sr., & Darling, C. A. (1988). Changing autoerotic attitudes and practices among college females: A two-year follow-up study. *Adolescence, 23,* 773–792.

Davies, G. M. (1993). Children's memory for other people: An integrative review. In C. A. Nelson (Ed.), *Memory and affect in development: The Minnesota Symposia on Child Psychology* (Vol. 26). Hillsdale, NJ: Erlbaum.

Davies, I. (1990). A physiological approach to ageing. In M. A. Horan & A. Brouwer (Eds.), *Gerontology: Approaches to biomedical and clinical research.* London: Edward Arnold.

Dawis, R. V. (1992). The individual differences tradition in counseling psychology. *Journal of Counseling Psychology, 39,* 7–19.

Day, A. T. (1991). *Remarkable survivors: Insights into successful aging among women.* Washington, DC: The Urban Institute Press.

de Jong, M. L. (1992). Attachment, individuation, and risk of suicide in late adolescence. *Journal of Youth and Adolescence, 21,* 357–373.

De Keseredy, W. S., Schwartz, M. D., & Tait, K. (1993). Sexual assault and stranger aggression on a Canadian university campus. *Sex Roles: A Journal of Research, 28,* 263–277.

de Saint-Hilaire P. (1992). Prenatal diagnosis of trisomy 21: Limits of chorionic villi sampling. *Revue Francaise de Gynecologie et D'Obstetrique, 87,* 527–532.

Deary, I. J., Fowkes, F. G., Donnan, P. T., & Housley, E. (1994). Hostile personality and risks of peripheral arterial disease in the general population. *Psychosomatic Medicine, 56,* 197–202.

DeCasper, A. J., & Fifer, W. P. (1980). Of human bonding: Newborns prefer their mother's voices. *Science, 208,* 1174–1176.

DeGenova, M. K. (1992). If you had your life to live over again: What would you do differently? *International Journal of Aging and Human Development, 34,* 135–143.

Dekovic, M., & Janssens, J. M. (1992). Parents' child-rearing style and child's sociometric status. *Developmental Psychology, 28,* 925–932.

DeLong, G. R. (1993). Effects of nutrition on brain development in humans. *American Journal of Clinical Nutrition, 57,* 286s–290s.

Demaris, A., & MacDonald, W. (1993). Premarital cohabitation and marital instability: A test of the unconventionality hypothesis. *Journal of Marriage and the Family, 55,* 399–407.

DeMause, L. (1974). The evolution of childhood. In L. DeMause (Ed.), *The History of Childhood.* New York: Psychohistory Press.

DeMause, L. (1975, April). Our forebears made childhood a nightmare. *Psychology Today,* pp. 85–88.

Demetriou, A., Efklides, A., & Papadaki, M. (1993). Structure and development of causal-experimental thought: From early adolescence to youth. *Developmental Psychology, 29,* 480–497.

Demo, D. H. (1993). The relentless search for effects of divorce: Forging new trails or tumbling down the beaten path. *Journal of Marriage and the Family, 55,* 42–45.

Demo, D. H., & Acock, A. C. (1993). Family diversity and the division of domestic labor: How much have things really changed? *Family Relations, 42,* 323–331.

Denham, S. A. (1993). Maternal emotional responsiveness and toddlers' social-emotional competence. *Journal of Child Psychology and Psychiatry and Allied Disciplines, 34,* 715–728.

Denham, S. A., & Holt, R. W. (1993). Preschooler's likability as cause or consequence of their social behavior. *Developmental Psychology, 29,* 271–275.

Dennis, W. (1951). A further analysis of reports of wild children. *Child Development, 22,* 153–158.

Dennis, W. (1966). Creative productivity between the ages of 20 and 80. *Journal of Gerontology, 21,* 1–18.

Derby, S. E. (1991). Ageism in cancer care of the elderly. *Oncology Nursing Forum, 18,* 921–926.

Deuel, R. K. (1992). Motor skill disorders. In S. R. Hooper, G. W. Hynd, & R. E. Mattison (Eds.), *Developmental disorders: Diagnostic criteria and clinical assessment.* Hillsdale, NJ: Erlbaum.

deVries, M. W. (1989). Difficult temperament: A universal and culturally embedded concept. In W. B. Carey & S. C. McDevitt (Eds.), *Clinical and educational applications of temperament research.* Berwyn, PA: Swets North America.

deVries, M. W., & Sameroff, A. J. (1984). Culture and temperament: Influences on infant temperament in three East African societies. *American Journal of Orthopsychiatry, 54,* 83–96.

Dewey, D. (1993). Error analysis of limb and orofacial praxis in children with developmental motor deficits. *Brain and Cognition, 23,* 203-221.

Diamond, A. M. (1986). The life-cycle research productivity of mathematicians and scientists. *Journal of Gerontology, 41,* 520–525.

Diaz, R. M. (1983). Thought and two languages: The impact of bilingualism on cognitive development. In E. W. Gordon (Ed.), *Review of research in education* (Vol. 10). Washington, DC: American Educational Research Association.

Dick-Read, G. (1972). *Childbirth without fear: The original approach to natural childbirth* (4th ed.) (H. Wessel & H. F. Ellis, Eds.). New York: Harper & Row.

Didion, J. (1979). *The white album.* New York: Simon & Schuster.

Diener, C. I., & Dweck, C. S. (1980). An analysis of learned helplessness: II. The processing of success. *Journal of Personality and Social Psychology, 39,* 940–952.

Dietz-Omar, M. (1991). Couple adaptation in stepfamilies and traditional nuclear families during pregnancy. *Nursing Practice, 4,* 6–10.

DiGiulio, J. F. (1992). Early widowhood: An atypical transition. *Journal of Mental Health Counseling, 14,* 97–109.

Dill, F., & McGillivray, B. (1992). Chromosome anomalies. In J. M. Friedman, F. J. Dill, M. R. Hayden, & B. C. McGillivray (Eds.), *Genetics.* Baltimore: Williams & Wilkins.

Dillard, J. M., Campbell, N. J., & Chisolm, G. B. (1984). Correlates of life satisfaction of aged persons. *Psychological Reports, 54,* 977–978.

Dimmock, B. (1992). Stepfamilies. "A child of our own." *Health Visitor, 65,* 368–370.

Dinges, M. M., & Oetting, E. R. (1993). Similarity in drug use patterns between adolescents and their friends. *Adolescence, 28,* 253–266.

Dittmann-Kohli, F., & Baltes, P. B. (1986). Towards a neo-functionalist conception of adult intellectual development: Wisdom as a prototypical case of intellectual growth. In C. Alexander & E. Langer (Eds.), *Beyond formal operations: Alternative endpoints to human development.* New York: Oxford University Press.

Doman, G. J. (1984). *How to multiply your baby's intelligence.* Garden City, NY: Doubleday.

Donaldson, M. (1978). *Children's minds.* London: Fontana/Croom Helm.

Donate-Bartfield, E., & Passman, R. H. (1985). Attentiveness of mothers and fathers to their baby's cries. *Infant Behavior and Development, 8,* 385–393.

Donders, G. G., Desmyter, J., De Wet, D. H., & Van Assche, F. A. (1993). The association of gonorrhoea and syphilis with premature birth and low birthweight. *Genitourinary Medicine, 69,* 98–101.

Donnelly, B. W., & Voydanoff, P. (1991). Factors associated with releasing for adoption among adolescent mothers. *Family Relations, 40,* 404–410.

Dorius, G. L., Heaton, T. B., & Steffan, P. (1993). Adolescent life events and their association with the onset of sexual intercourse. *Youth and Society, 25,* 3–23.

Down with Type A! (1983, January). *Health,* pp. 14–15.

Drebing, C. E., & Gooden, W. E. (1991). The impact of the dream on mental health functioning in the male midlife transition. *International Journal of Aging and Human Development, 32,* 277–287.

Dreyer, P. H. (1982). Sexuality during adolescence. In B. B. Wolman (Ed.), *Handbook of developmental psychology.* Englewood Cliffs, NJ: Prentice-Hall.

Driver, R., Asoko, H., Leach, J., Mortimer, E., & Scott, P. (1994). Constructing scientific knowledge in the classroom. *Educational Researcher, 23,* 5–12.

Drummond, R. J., & Ryan, C. W. (1995). *Career counseling: A developmental approach.* Englewood Cliffs, NJ: Prentice-Hall.

Drummond, W. J. (1991). Adolescent relationships in a period of change: A New Zealand perspective. *International Journal of Adolescence and Youth, 2,* 275–286.

Dubas, J. S., & Petersen, A. C. (1993). Female pubertal development. In M. Sugar (Ed.), *Female adolescent development.* New York: Brunner/Mazel.

Dubowitz, H., Black, M., & Harrington, D. (1993). A follow-up study of behavior problems associated with child sexual abuse. *Child Abuse and Neglect: The International Journal, 17,* 743–754.

Dudgeon, D. J. (1994). Physician/nursing roles and perspectives in relationship to delivery of palliative care. *Annals of the Academy of Medicine, Singapore, 23,* 249–251.

Duvall, E. M. (1977). *Marriage and family development* (5th ed.). New York: Harper & Row.

Dweck, C. S. (1975). The role of expectations and attributions in the alleviation of learned helplessness. *Journal of Personality and Social Psychology, 31,* 674–685.

Dweck, C. S. (1986). Motivational processes affecting learning. *American Psychologist, 41,* 1040–1048.

Echenne, B., Humbertclaude, V., Rivier, F., Malafosse, A., & Cheminal, R. (1994). Benign infantile epilepsy with autosomal dominant inheritance. *Brain and Development, 16,* 108–111.

Eden, R. D., Blanco, J. D., Tomasi, A., & Gall, S. A. (1990). Maternal-fetal infection. In R. D. Eden, F. H. Boehm, & M. Haire (Eds.), *Assessment and care of the fetus: Physiological, clinical, and medicolegal principles.* Norwalk, CT: Appleton & Lange.

Eilers, R. E., & Oller, D. K. (1988). Precursors to speech. In R. Vasta (Ed.), *Annals of child development* (Vol. 5). Greenwich, CT: JAI Press.

Eisenberg, N., Fabes, R. A., Carlo, G., & Karbon, M. (1992). Emotional responsivity to others: Behavioral correlates and socialization antecedents. *New Directions for Child Development, 55,* 57–73.

Eisenberg, N., Fabes, R. A., Carlo, G., Speer, A. L., Switzer, G., Karbon, M., & Troyer, D. (1993). The relations of empathy-related emotions and maternal practices to children's comforting behavior. *Journal of Experimental Child Psychology, 55,* 131–150.

Eisenberg, N., Miller, P. A., & Shell, R. (1991). Prosocial development in adolescence: A longitudinal study. *Developmental Psychology, 27,* 849–858.

Eisenberg, N., Miller, P. A., Shell, R., McNalley, S., & Shea, C. (1991). Prosocial development in adolescence: A longitudinal study. *Developmental Psychology, 27,* 849–857.

Eisler, T. A. (1984). Career impact on independence of the elderly. In W. H. Quinn & G. A. Hughston (Eds.), *Independent aging: Family and social systems perspectives* (pp. 256–264). Rockville, MD: Aspen.

Elder, G. H., Jr. (1979). Historical change in life patterns and personality. In P. B. Baltes & O. G. Brim, Jr. (Eds.), *Life-span development and behavior* (Vol. 2). New York: Academic Press.

Elder, G. H., Jr., Nguyen, T. Van, & Caspi, A. (1985). Linking family hardship to children's lives. *Child Development, 56,* 361–375.

Elkin, F., & Handel, G. (1989). *The child and society: The process of socialization* (5th ed.). New York: Random House.

Elkind, D. (1967). Egocentrism in adolescence. *Child Development, 38,* 1025–1034.

Elkind, D. (1981a). *The hurried child: Growing up too fast too soon.* Reading, MA: Addison-Wesley.

Elkind, D. (1981b). Understanding the young adolescent. In L. D. Steinberg (Ed.), *The life cycle: Readings in human development.* New York: Columbia University Press.

Elkind, D. (1987). *Miseducation: Preschoolers at risk.* New York: Knopf.

Elkind, D., & Bowen, R. (1979). Imaginary audience behavior in children and adolescents. *Developmental Psychology, 15*(1), 38–44.

Ellman, J. P. (1992). A treatment approach for patients in midlife. *Canadian Journal of Psychiatry, 37,* 564–566.

Emery, A. E., & Mueller, R. F. (1992). *Elements of medical genetics* (8th ed.). Edinburgh & London: Churchill Livingstone.

Emery, R. E. (1989). Family violence. *American Psychologist, 44,* 321–328.

Endsley, R. C., & Bradbard, M. R. (1981). *Quality day care: A handbook of choices for parents and caregivers.* Englewood Cliffs, NJ: Prentice-Hall.

Enright, R., Shukla, D., & Lapsley, D. (1980). Adolescent egocentrism-sociocentrism in early and late adolescence. *Adolescence, 14,* 687–695.

Erickson, G., & Farkas, S. (1991). Prior experience and gender differences in science achievement. *Alberta Journal of Educational Research, 37,* 225–239.

Erickson, M. T. (1987). *Behavior disorders of children and adolescents.* Englewood Cliffs, NJ: Prentice-Hall.

Erickson, M. T. (1992). *Behavior disorders of children and adolescents* (2nd ed.). Englewood Cliffs, NJ: Prentice-Hall.

Erikson, E. H. (1956). The problems of ego identity. *Journal of the American Psychoanalytic Association, 4,* 56–121.

Erikson, E. H. (1959). Identity and the life cycle: Selected papers. *Psychological Issue Monograph Series, I* (No. 1). New York: International Universities Press.

Erikson, E. H. (1961). The roots of virtue. In J. Huxley (Ed.), *The humanist frame.* New York: Harper & Row.

Erikson, E. H. (1968). *Identity, youth and crisis.* New York: Norton.

Erikson, E. H. (1980). *Themes of work and love in adulthood.* Cambridge, MA: Harvard University Press.

Erikson, E. H. (1987). *A way of looking at things: Selected papers from 1930 to 1980.* New York: Norton.

Erikson, E. H., Erikson, J. M., & Kivnick, H. G. (1986). *Vital involvement in old age.* New York: Norton.

Erikson, E., & Hall, E. A. (1983, June). A conversation with Erik Erikson. *Psychology Today, 17,* pp. 22–30.

Ernst, C., & Angst, J. (1983). *Birth order: Its influence on personality.* New York: Springer-Verlag.

Ernst, C., Foldenyi, M., & Angst, J. (1993). The Zurich Study: XXI. Sexual dysfunctions and disturbances in young adults. Data of a longitudinal epidemiological study. *European Archives of Psychiatry and Clinical Neuroscience, 243,* 179–188.

Erwin, P. (1993). *Friendship and peer relationships in children.* New York: John Wiley.

Espenschade, A. S., & Eckert, H. D. (1980). *Motor development* (2nd ed.). Columbus, OH: Charles E. Merrill.

Etaugh, C., & Liss, M. B. (1992). Home, school, and playroom: Training grounds for adult gender roles. *Sex roles: A Journal of Research, 26,* 129–147.

Ethical standards for research with children. (1973). *SRCD Newsletter,* Winter, 3–4.

Evans, R. I. (1989). *Albert Bandura: The man and his ideas—a dialogue.* New York: Praeger.

Evra, J. V. (1990). *Television and child development.* Hillsdale, NJ: Erlbaum.

Eysenck, H. J., & Kamin, L. (1981). *Intelligence: The battle for the mind.* London: Macmillan.

Fabricius, W. V., & Wellman, H. M. (1993). Two roads diverged: Young children's ability to judge distance. *Child Development, 64,* 399–419.

Fantz, R. L. (1963). Pattern vision in newborn infants. *Science, 140,* 269–297.

Farbman, A. I. (1994). The cellular basis of olfaction. *Endeavour, 18,* 2–8.

Farrell, M. P., & Rosenberg, S. D. (1981). *Men at midlife.* Boston: Auburn House.

Fasick, F. A. (1988). Patterns of formal education in high school as Rites de Passage. *Adolescence, 23,* 457–471.

Feagans, L. V., & Proctor, A. (1994). The effects of mild illness in infancy on later development: The sample case of the effects of otitis media (middle ear effusion). In C. B. Fisher & R. M. Lerner (Eds.), *Applied developmental psychology.* New York: McGraw-Hill.

Fernald, A., & Mazzie, C. (1991). Prosody and focus in speech to infants and adults. *Developmental Psychology, 27,* 209–221.

Filiano, J. J., & Kinney, H. C. (1994). A perspective on neuropathologic findings in victims of the sudden infant death syndrome: The triple-risk model. *Biology of the Neonate, 65,* 194–197.

Fine, M. A. (1993). Current approaches to understanding family diversity: An overview of the special issue. *Family Relations, 42,* 235–237.

Fine, M. A., & Fine, D. R. (1992). Recent changes in laws affecting stepfamilies: Suggestions for legal reform. *Family Relations, 41,* 334–340.

Fine, M. A., & Kurdek, L. A. (1992). The adjustment of adolescents in stepfather and stepmother families. *Journal of Marriage and the Family, 54,* 725–736.

Finkelhor, D., et al. (1986). *A sourcebook on child sexual abuse.* Beverly Hills, CA: Sage.

Finley, C., & Corty, E. (1993). Rape on campus: The prevalence of sexual assault while enrolled in college. *Journal of College Student Development, 34,* 113–117.

Fischer, K. W., & Silvern, L. (1985). Stages and individual differences in cognitive development. *Annual Review of Psychology, 36,* 613–648.

Fisher, C. B., & Lerner, R. M. (1994). Foundations of applied developmental psychology. In C. B. Fisher & R. M. Lerner (Eds.), *Applied developmental psychology.* New York: McGraw-Hill.

Fisher, J. C. (1993). A framework for describing developmental change among older adults. *Adult Education Quarterly, 43,* 76–89.

Fishkin, J., Keniston, K., & MacKinnon, C. (1973). Moral reasoning and political ideology. *Journal of Personality and Social Psychology, 27,* 109–119.

Fiske, S. T. (1993). Social cognition and social perception. *Annual Review of Psychology, 44,* 155–194.

Flanagan, J. C. (1982). *New insights to improve the quality of life at age 70.* Palo Alto, CA: American Institutes for Research.

Flavell, J. H. (1985). *Cognitive development* (2nd ed.). Englewood Cliffs, NJ: Prentice-Hall.

Fleischhacker, W. W., Meise, U., Gunther, V., & Kurz, M. (1994). Compliance with antipsychotic drug treatment: Influence of side effects. *Acta Psychiatrica Scandinavica, Supplementum, 382,* 11–15.

Fleming, P. J. (1994). Understanding and preventing sudden infant death syndrome. *Current Opinion in Pediatrics, 6,* 158–162.

Flynn, J. R. (1987). Massive IQ gains in 14 nations: What IQ tests really measure. *Psychological Bulletin, 17,* 171–191.

Fogel, A., Toda, S., & Kawai, M. (1988). Mother-infant face-to-face interaction in Japan and the United States: A laboratory comparison using 3-month-old infants. *Developmental Psychology, 3,* 398–406.

Fong, L., & Wilgosh, L. (1992). Children with autism and their families: A literature review. *Canadian Journal of Special Education, 8,* 43–54.

Food and Nutrition Board, Subcommittee on the Tenth Edition of the RDAs. (1989). *Recommended dietary allowances* (10th ed.). Washington, DC: National Academy Press.

Food and Nutrition Board. (1990). *Nutrition during pregnancy.* Washington, DC: National Academy Press.

Fouts, R. S. (1987). Chimpanzee signing and emergent levels. In G. Greenberg & E. Tobach (Eds.), *Cognition, language and consciousness: Integrative levels.* Hillsdale, NJ: Erlbaum.

Fox, N. A., Kimmerly, N. L., & Schafer, W. D. (1991). Attachment to mother/attachment to father: A meta-analysis. *Child Development, 62,* 210–225.

Fox, R. A. (1990). *Assessing parenting of young children.* Bethesda, MD: National Center for Nursing Research of the National Institutes of Health. (Contract 1 RO1 NRO1609O1A1.)

Frankenburg, W. K., & Dodds, J. B. (1992). *Denver II* (2nd ed.). *Training Manual.* Denver: Denver Developmental Materials.

Frankenburg, W. K., Fandal, A. W., Sciarillo, W., & Burgess, D. (1981). The newly abbreviated and revised Denver Developmental Screening Test. *Journal of Pediatrics, 99,* 995–999.

Franklin, J. T. (1985). Alternative education as substance abuse prevention. *Journal of Alcohol and Drug Education, 30,* 12–23.

Freeman, S. C. (1993). Donald Super: A perspective on career development. *Journal of Career Development, 19,* 255–264.

Freud, S. (1935). *A general introduction to psychoanalysis* (rev. ed.). (J. Riviere, Trans.). New York: Liveright.

Fried, P. A. (1986). Marijuana and human pregnancy. In I. J. Chasnoff (Ed.), *Drug use in pregnancy: Mother and child.* Boston: MTP Press.

Friedman, J. M. (1992). Teratogenesis and mutagenesis. In J. M. Friedman, F. J. Dill, M. R. Hayden, & B. C. McGillivray (Eds.), *Genetics.* Baltimore: Williams & Wilkins.

Friedman, J. M., Dill, F., & Hayden, M. R. (1992). Nature of genetic material. In J. M. Friedman, F. J. Dill, M. R. Hayden, & B. C. McGillivray (Eds.), *Genetics.* Baltimore: Williams & Wilkins.

Friedman, J. M., Dill, F. J., Hayden, M. R., & McGillivray, B. C. (1992). *Genetics.* Baltimore: Williams & Wilkins.

Friedman, J. M., & McGillivray, B. (1992). Genetic paradigms in human disease. In J. M. Friedman, F. J. Dill, M. R. Hayden, & B. C. McGillivray (Eds.), *Genetics.* Baltimore: Williams & Wilkins.

Friedman, M., & Rosenman, R. H. (1974). *Type A behavior and your heart.* Greenwich, CT: Fawcett.

Frieman, B. B. (1993). Separation and divorce: Children want their teachers to know—Meeting the needs of preschool and primary school children. *Young Children, 48,* 58–63.

Friendly, D. S. (1993). Development of vision in infants and young children. *Pediatric Clinics of North America, 40,* 693–703.

Fry, P. S. (1991). Individual differences in reminiscence among older adults: Predictors of frequency and pleasantness ratings of reminiscence activity. *International Journal of Aging and Human Development, 33,* 311–326.

Fry, P. S. (1992). Major social theories of aging and their implications for counseling concepts and practice: A critical review. *Counseling Psychologist, 20,* 246–329.

Frye, D. (1991). The origins of intention in infancy. In D. Frye & C. Moore (Eds.), *Children's theories of mind: Mental states and social understanding.* Hillsdale, NJ: Erlbaum.

Fuligni, A. J., & Eccles, J. S. (1993). Perceived parent–child relationships and early adolescents' orientation toward peers. *Developmental Psychology, 29,* 622–632.

Fundaro, C., Solinas, A., Martino, A. M., Genovese, O., Noia, G., Conte, G. L., & Segni, G. (1994). Neonatal abstinence syndrome and maternal toxicological profile. *Minerva Pediatrica, 46,* 83–88.

Furstenberg, F. F., Jr. (1987). The new extended family: The experience of children and parents after remarriage. In K. Pasley and M. Ihinger-Tallman (Eds.), *Remarriage and stepparenting: Current research and theory.* New York: Guilford Press.

Furstenberg, F. F., Jr., Brooks-Gunn, J., & Chase-Lansdale, L. (1989). Teenaged pregnancy and childbearing. *American Psychologist, 44,* 313–320.

Furstenberg, F. F., Jr., & Spanier, G. B. (1984). *Recycling the family: Remarriage after divorce.* Beverly Hills, CA: Sage.

Furth, H. G. (1980). Piagetian perspectives. In J. Sants (Ed.), *Developmental psychology and society.* London: Macmillan.

Gage, M. G., & Hendrickson Christenson, D. (1991). Parental role socialization and the transition to parenthood. *Family Relations, 40,* 332–337.

Galef, B. G., Jr. (1991). A contrarian view of the wisdom of the body as it relates to dietary self-selection. *Psychological Review, 98,* 218–223.

Galton, F. (1896). *Hereditary genius: An enquiry into its law and consequences.* London: Macmillan.

Gamble, T. J., & Zigler, E. (1986). Effects of infant day care: Another look at the evidence. *American Journal of Orthopsychiatry, 56,* 26–42.

Garcia, E. E. (1993). Language, culture, and education. In L. Darling-Hammond (Ed.), *Review of Research in Education* (Vol. 19). Washington, DC: American Educational Research Association.

Garvey, C. (1977). *Play.* Cambridge, MA: Harvard University Press.

Gathercole, S. E., Adams, A. M., & Hitch, G. J. (1994). Do young children rehearse? An individual-difference analysis. *Memory and Cognition, 22,* 201–207.

Gaudin, J. M., Jr. (1993). *Child neglect: A guide for intervention. The User Manual Series.* National Center on Child Abuse and Neglect. Washington, DC: Westover Consultants.

Gauoncz, L., & Kodákzopeljic, J. (1991). Exposure to two languages in the preschool period: Metalinguistic development and the acquisition of reading. *Journal of Multilingual and Multicultural Development, 12,* 137–142.

Gavin, C. E., Kates, B., Hoffman, G. E., & Rodier, P. M. (1994). Changes in the reproductive system following acute prenatal exposure to ethanol or methylazoxymethanol in the rat: I. Effects on immunoreactive LHRN cell number. *Teratology, 49,* 13–19.

Gayford, J. J. (1978). Battered wives. In J. P. Martin (Ed.), *Violence and the family.* New York: John Wiley.

Gaynor, J. L. R., & Runco, M. A. (1992). Family size, birth-order, age-interval, and the creativity of children. *Journal of Creative Behavior, 26,* 108–118.

Geiger, S., & Newhagen, J. (1993). Revealing the black box: Information processing and media effects. *Journal of Communication, 43,* 42–50.

Gelles, R. J. (1978). Violence in the American family. In J. P. Martin (Ed.), *Violence and the family.* New York: John Wiley.

Gelles, R. J. (1979). *Family violence.* Beverly Hills, CA: Sage.

Gelman, R. (1982). Basic numerical abilities. In R. J. Sternberg (Ed.), *Advances in the psychology of human intelligence* (Vol. 1). Hillsdale, NJ: Erlbaum.

Gelman, R., & Gallistel, C. R. (1978). *The young child's understanding of number.* Cambridge, MA: Harvard University Press.

"Gentle giant" stabs boy for taunts. (1994, Dec. 6). *Edmonton Sun,* p. 24.

Gesell, A. (1925). *The mental growth of the preschool child.* New York: Macmillan.

Gewirtz, J. L. (1965). The course of infant smiling in four child-rearing environments in Israel. In B. M. Foss (Ed.), *Determinants of infant behavior III.* London: Methuen.

Gianino, A., & Tronick, E. Z. (1988). The mutual regulation model: The infant's self and interactive regulation coping and defense. In T. Field, P. McCabe, & N. Schneiderman (Eds.), *Stress and coping.* Hillsdale, NJ: Erlbaum.

Gibbons, W. (1991). Clueing in on chlamydia. *Science News, 139*, 250–252.

Gibbs, J. C. (1987). Social processes in delinquency: The need to facilitate empathy as well as socio-moral reasoning. In W. M. Kurtines & J. L. Gewirtz (Eds.), *Moral development through social interaction.* New York: John Wiley.

Gibson, E. J., & Walk, R. D. (1960). The "visual cliff." *Scientific American, 202*, 64–71.

Gibson, H. B. (1992). *The emotional and sexual lives of older people: A manual for professionals.* New York: Chapman and Hall.

Giles, H., Coupland, N., Coupland, J., Williams, A., & Nussbaum, J. (1992). Intergenerational talk and communication with older people. *International Journal of Aging and Human Development, 34*, 271–297.

Giles-Sims, J. (1987). Social exchange in remarried families. In K. Pasley & M. Ihinger-Tallman (Eds.), *Remarriage and stepparenting: Current research and theory.* New York: Guilford Press.

Gill, W. (1992). Helping African American males: The cure. *Negro Educational Review, 43*, 31–36.

Gillespie, D., & Hillman, S. B. (1993). *Impact of self-efficacy expectations on adolescent career choice.* Paper presented at the Annual Meeting of the American Psychological Association, Toronto, August 20–24, 1993.

Gilligan, C. (1982). *In a different voice: Psychological theory and women's development.* Cambridge, MA: Harvard University Press.

Ginzberg, E. (1972). Toward a theory of occupational choice: A restatement. *Vocational Guidance Quarterly, 20*, 169–176.

Glenmark, B., Hedberg, G., Kaijser, L., & Jansson, E. (1994). Muscle strength from adolescence to adulthood—relationship to muscle fibre types. *European Journal of Applied Physiology and Occupational Physiology, 68*, 9–19.

Glenn, N., & Weaver, C. (1977). The marital happiness of remarried divorced persons. *Journal of Marriage and the Family, 39*, 331–337.

Glick, P. C., & Lin, S. L. (1986). More young adults are living with their parents: Who are they? *Journal of Marriage and the Family, 42*, 19–30.

Gloth, F. M. III. (1994). Hospice: The most important thing you didn't learn in medical school. *Maryland Medical Journal, 43*, 511–513.

Glueck, S., & Glueck, E. (1950). *Unravelling juvenile delinquency.* New York: The Commonwealth Fund.

Gold, M. S. (1989). *Drugs of abuse: A comprehensive series for clinicians* (Vol. 1) *Marijuana.* New York: Plenum.

Goldberg, S. (1983). Parent–infant bonding: Another look. *Child Development, 54*, 1355–1382.

Goldsmith, J. (1990). *Childbirth wisdom: From the world's oldest societies.* Brookline, MA: East West Health Books.

Goldsmith, J. P. (1990). Neonatal morbidity. In R. D. Eden, F. H. Boehm, & M. Haire (Eds.), *Assessment and care of the fetus: Physiological, clinical, and medico-legal principles.* Norwalk, CT: Appleton & Lange.

Goncu, A. (1993). Development of intersubjectivity in the dyadic play of preschoolers. *Early Childhood Research Quarterly, 8*, 99–116.

Goode, E. T. (1985). Medical aspects of the bulimic syndrome and bulimarexia. *Transactional Analysis Journal, 15*, 4–11.

Gooden, W., & Toye, R. (1984). Occupational dream, relation to parents and depression in the early adult transition. *Journal of Clinical Psychology, 4*, 945–954.

Goodenough, F. (1926). *Measurement of intelligence by drawings.* New York: Harcourt, Brace & World.

Gorman, C. (1994, Nov. 12). An eye on Alzheimer's. *Time, 144* p. 71.

Gorsky, R. D., Koplan, J. P., Peterson, H. B., & Thacker, S. B. (1994). Relative risks and benefits of long-term estrogen replacement therapy: A decision analysis. *Obstetrics and Gynecology, 83*, 161–166.

Gottesman, I. I. (1974). Developmental genetics and ontogenetic psychology: Overdue detente and propositions from a matchmaker. In A. Pick (Ed.), *Minnesota Symposia on Psychology* (Vol. 12) (pp. 55–180).

Gottesman, I. I., & Shields, J. (1982). *The schizophrenic puzzle.* New York: Cambridge University Press.

Gottlieb, G. (1992). *Individual development and evolution: The genesis of novel behavior.* Oxford: Oxford University Press.

Gottman, J. M. (1977). Toward a definition of social isolation in children. *Child Development, 48*, 513–517.

Goudsmit, E., Neijmeijer-Leloux, A., & Swaab, D. F. (1992). The human hypothalamo-neurohypophyseal system in relation to development, aging and Alzheimer's disease. *Progress in Brain Research, 93*, 237–247.

Gould, R. L. (1972). The phases of adult life: A study in developmental psychology. *American Journal of Psychiatry, 129*, 521–531.

Gould, R. L. (1978). *Transformations: Growth and change in adult life.* New York: Simon & Schuster.

Gould, R. L. (1990). Clinical lessons from adult development theory. In R. A. Nemiroff & C. A. Colarusso (Eds.), *New dimensions in adult development.* New York: Basic Books.

Gould, S. J. (1981). *The mismeasure of man.* New York: Norton.

Graham, M. V. (1993). Parental sensitivity to infant cues: Similarities and differences between mothers and fathers. *Journal of Pediatric Nursing, 8,* 376–384.

Grant, J. P. [Executive Director of the United Nation's Children's Fund (UNICEF)] (1986). *The state of the world's children: 1986.* New York: Oxford University Press.

Grant, J. P. (1992). *The state of the world's children: 1992.* New York: Oxford University Press.

Grant, J. P. (1993). *The state of the world's children:1993.* New York: Oxford University Press.

Grattan, M. P., DeVos, E., Levy, J. & McClintock, M. K. (1992). Asymmetric action in the human newborn: Sex differences in patterns of organization. *Child Development, 63,* 273–289.

Green, J. S., & Crouse, S. F. (1993). Endurance training, cardiovascular function and the aged. *Sports Medicine, 16,* 331–341.

Green, V., Johnson, S. A., & Kaplan, D. (1992). Predictors of adolescent female decision making regarding contraceptive usage. *Adolescence, 27,* 613–632.

Greenberg, B. S., & Brand, J. E. (1993). Television news and advertising in schools: The "Channel One" controversy. *Journal of Communication, 43,* 143–151.

Greenfield, P. M., & Savage-Rumbaugh, E. S. (1993). Comparing communicative competence in child and chimp: The pragmatics of repetition. *Journal of Child Language, 20,* 1–26.

Greer, J. V. (1991). A child is a child is a child. *Exceptional Children, 57,* 198–199.

Grieser, D. L., & Kuhl, P. K. (1988). Maternal speech to infants in a tonal language: Support for universal prosodic features in motherese. *Developmental Psychology, 24,* 14–20.

Griffiths, M. D. (1991). Amusement machine playing in childhood and adolescence: A comparative analysis of video games and fruit machines. *Journal of Adolescence, 14,* 53–73.

Grossman, J. J. (Ed.). (1983). *Manual on terminology and classification in mental retardation, 1983 revision.* Washington, DC: American Association on Mental Deficiency.

Grotevant, H. D. (1994). Assessment of parent–adolescent relationships. In C. B. Fisher & R. M. Lerner (Eds.), *Applied developmental psychology.* New York: McGraw-Hill.

Grotevant, H. D., & Cooper, C. R. (1988). The role of family experience in career exploration: A life-span perspective. In P. B. Baltes, D. L. Featherman, & R. M. Lerner (Eds.), *Life-span development and behavior* (Vol. 8). Hillsdale, NJ: Erlbaum.

Guilford, J. P. (1950). Creativity. *American Psychologist, 5,* 444–454.

Gunnar, M. R., Larson, M. C., Hertsgaard, L., Harris, M. L., & Brodersen, L. (1992). The stressfulness of separation among nine-month-old infants: Effects of social context variables and infant temperament. *Child Development, 63,* 290–303.

Gunter, B., & McAleer, J. L. (1990). *Children and television. The one-eyed monster?* New York: Routledge.

Gustafson, G. E., & Harris, K. L. (1990). Women's responses to young infants' cries. *Developmental Psychology, 26,* 144–152.

Gustafsson, J. E., & Undheim, J. O. (1992). Stability and change in broad and narrow factors of intelligence from ages 12 to 15. *Journal of Educational Psychology, 84,* 141–149.

Gutmann, D. (1990). Psychological development and pathology in later adulthood. In R. A. Nemiroff & C. A. Colarusso (Eds.), *New dimensions in adult development.* New York: Basic Books.

Guttman, H. A. (1991). Parental death as a precipitant of marital conflict in middle age. *Journal of Marital and Family Therapy, 17,* 81–87.

Hack, M., Breslau, N., Aram, D., Weissman, B., Klein, N., & Borawski-Clark, E. (1992). The effect of very low birth weight and social risk on neurocognitive abilities at school age. *Journal of Developmental and Behavioral Pediatrics, 13,* 412–420.

Hack, M., Taylor, H. G., Klein, N., Eiben, R., Schatschneider, C., & Mercuri-Minich, N. (1994). School-age outcomes in children with birth weights under 750 g. *New England Journal of Medicine, 331,* 753–759.

Hack, M., Weissman, B., Breslau, N., Klein, N., Borawski-Clark, E., & Fanaroff, A. A. (1993). Health of very low birth weight children during their first eight years. *Journal of Pediatrics, 122,* 887–892.

Hagborg, W. J. (1993). The Rosenberg Self-Esteem Scale and Harter's Self-Perception Profile for Adolescents: A concurrent validity study. *Psychology in the Schools, 30,* 132–136.

Hagopian, L. P., Fisher, W. W., & Legacy, S. M. (1994). Schedule effects of noncontingent reinforcement on attention-maintained destructive behavior in identical quadruplets. *Journal of Applied Behavior Analysis,* 317–325.

Hague, W. J. (1991). Kohlberg's legacy—More than ideas: An essay review. *The Alberta Journal of Educational Research, 37,* 277–294.

Haight, B. K. (1991). Reminiscing: The state of the art as a basis for practice. *International Journal of Aging and Human Development, 33,* 1–32.

Haines, C. J., Chung, T. K., & Leung, D. H. (1994). A prospective study of the frequency of acute menopausal symptoms in Hong Kong Chinese women. *Maturitas, 18,* 175–181.

Haith, M. M. (1980). *Rules that babies look by: The organization of newborn visual activity.* Hillsdale, NJ: Erlbaum.

Haith, M. M. (1991). *Setting a path for the '90s: Some goals and challenges. Infant sensory and perceptual development.* Paper presented at the Biennial Meeting of the Society for Research in Child Development, Seattle, April 18–20.

Hakuta, K., & D'Andrea, D. (1992). Some properties of bilingual maintenance and loss in Mexican background high-school students. *Applied Linguistics, 13,* 72–99.

Hakuta, K., & Garcia, E. E. (1989). Bilingualism and education. *American Psychologist, 44,* 374–379.

Haldeman, D. C. (1994). The practice and ethics of sexual orientation conversion therapy. *Journal of Consulting and Clinical Psychology, 62,* 221–227.

Hall, G. S. (1891). The contents of children's minds on entering school. *Pediatric Seminars, 1,* 139–173.

Hall, G. S. (1922). Senescence: The last half of life. New York: Appleton-Century-Crofts.

Hall, G. Stanley. (1916). *Adolescence* (2 vols.). New York: Appleton-Century-Crofts.

Hallahan, D. P., & Kauffman, J. M. (1991). *Exceptional children: Introduction to special education.* Englewood Cliffs, NJ: Prentice Hall.

Halle, P. A., de Boysson-Bardies, B., & Vihman, M. M. (1991). Beginnings of prosodic organization: Intonation and duration patterns of disyllables produced by Japanese and French infants. *Language and Speech, 34,* 299–318.

Hamabata, M. M. (1990). *Crested kimono: Power and love in the Japanese business family.* Ithaca, NY: Cornell University Press.

Hammill, D. D. (1993). A brief look at the learning disabilities movement in the United States. *Journal of Learning Disabilities, 26,* 295–310.

Hampson, J., & Nelson, K. (1993). The relation of maternal language to variation in rate and style of language acquisition. *Journal of Child Language, 20,* 313–342.

Handyside, A. H. (1991). Preimplantation diagnosis by DNA amplification. In M. Chapman, G. Grudzinskas, & T. Chard (Eds.), *The embryo: Normal and abnormal development and growth.* New York: Springer-Verlag.

Hanna, E., & Meltzoff, A. N. (1993). Peer imitation by toddlers in laboratory, home, and day-care contexts: Implications for social learning and memory. *Developmental Psychology, 29,* 701–710.

Hansen, L. S. (1993). Career development trends and issues in the United States. *Journal of Career Development, 20,* 7–24.

Hargarten, K. M. (1994). Menopause. How exercise mitigates symptoms. *Physician and Sports Medicine, 22,* 48–50, 53–56.

Harlow, H. F. (1958). The nature of love. *American Psychologist, 12,* 673–685.

Harlow, H. F. (1959). Love in infant monkeys. *Scientific American, 200,* 68–74.

Harman, D. (1993). Free radical involvement in aging. Pathophysiology and therapeutic implications. *Drugs and Aging, 3,* 60–80.

Harris, D. (1963). *Children's drawings as measures of intellectual maturity.* New York: Harcourt, Brace & World.

Harris, Y. R., & Hamidullah, J. (1993). Maternal and child utilization of memory strategies. *Current Psychology: Research and Reviews, 12,* 81–94.

Harrison, L. (1985). Effects of early supplemental stimulation programs for premature infants: Review of the literature. *Maternal-Child Nursing Journal, 14,* 69–90.

Harry, J. (1983). Gay male and lesbian relationships. In E. D. Macklin & R. H. Rubin (Eds.), *Contemporary families and alternative lifestyles: Handbook on research and theory* (pp. 216–233). Beverly Hills, CA: Sage.

Harter, S. (1983). Developmental perspectives on the self-system. In P. H. Mussen (Ed.), *Handbook of child psychology* (4th ed.) (Vol. 4): *Socialization, personality, and social development* (E. M. Hetherington, Ed.). New York: John Wiley.

Harter, S. (1987). The determinants and mediational role of global self-worth in children. In N. Eisenberg (Ed.), *Contemporary topics in developmental psychology.* New York: John Wiley.

Harter, S. (1988). Developmental processes in the construction of self. In T. D. Yawkey & J. E. Johnson (Eds.), *Integrative processes and socialization: Early to middle childhood.* Hillsdale, NJ: Erlbaum.

Harter, S. (1990). Processes underlying adolescent self-concept formation. In R. Montemayor, G. R. Adams, & T. P. Gullotta (Eds.), *From childhood to adolescence: A transitional period? (Advances in adolescent development,* Vol. 2). Newbury Park, CA: Sage.

Hartup, W. W. (1983). Peer relations. In P. H. Mussen (Ed.), *Handbook of child psychology* (4th ed.) (Vol. 4): *Socialization, personality, and social development* (pp. 103–196). (E. M. Hetherington, Ed.). New York: John Wiley.

Harvey, B. (1994, Nov. 20). Mercy Killing. *Edmonton Journal,* p. C1.

Hashimoto, N. (1991). Memory development in early childhood: Encoding process in a spatial task. *Journal of Genetic Psychology, 152,* 101–117.

Haskins, R. (1989). Beyond metaphor: The efficacy of early childhood education. *American Psychologist, 44,* 274–282.

Havighurst, R. J. (1972). *Developmental tasks and education.* New York: D. McKay.

Havighurst, R. J. (1979). *Developmental tasks and education* (4th ed.). New York: D. McKay.

Hawley, T. L. (1993). *Maternal cocaine addiction: Correlates and consequences.* Paper presented at the Biennial Meeting of the Society for Research in Child Development, New Orleans, March 25–28.

Hay, D. F., Stimson, C. A., & Castle, J. (1991). A meeting of minds in infancy: Imitation and desire. In D. Frye & C. Moore (Eds.), *Children's theories of mind: Mental states and social understanding.* Hillsdale, NJ: Erlbaum.

Hayden, M. R. (1992). DNA diagnosis. In J. M. Friedman, F. J. Dill, M. R. Hayden, & B. C. McGillivray (Eds.), *Genetics.* Baltimore: Williams & Wilkins.

Hayes, C. D., Palmer, J. L., & Zaslow, M. J. (Eds.). (1990). *Who cares for America's children? Child care policy for the 1990's.* Washington, DC: National Academy Press.

Hayes, D. S., & Casey, D. M. (1992). Young children and television: The retention of emotional reactions. *Child Development, 63,* 1423–1436.

Hayes, K. J., & Hayes, C. (1951). Intellectual development of a home-raised chimpanzee. *Proceedings of the American Philosophical Society, 95,* 105–109.

Hayflick, L. (1975, September). Why grow old? *Stanford Magazine,* pp. 36–43.

Haynes, N. M. (1993). Reducing the risk of teen parenthood: An approach that works. *Nassp Bulletin, 77,* 36–40.

Haywood, K. M. (1986). *Life span motor development.* Champaign, IL: Human Kinetics.

Hazelwood, M. E., Brown, J. K., Rowe, P. J., & Salter, P. M. (1994). The use of therapeutic electrical stimulation in the treatment of hemiplegic cerebral palsy. *Developmental Medicine and Child Neurology, 36,* 661–673.

Hazen, N. L., & Lockman, J. J. (1989). Skill and context. In J. J. Lockman & N. L. Hazen (Eds.), *Action in social context: Perspectives on early development.* New York: Plenum.

Hebb, D. O. (1966). *A textbook of psychology* (2nd ed.). Philadelphia: Saunders.

Hedges, L. V., & Friedman, L. (1993). Gender differences in variability in intellectual abilities: A reanalysis of Feingold's results. *Review of Educational Research, 63,* 94–105.

Heinzen, T. E. (1991). A paradigm for research in creativity. *The Creative Child and Adult Quarterly, 16,* 164–174.

Heisel, B. E., & Ritter, K. (1981). Young children's storage behavior in a memory for location task. *Journal of Experimental Child Psychology, 31,* 250–364.

Helson, R., & Wink, P. (1992). Personality change in women from the early 40's to the early 50's. *Psychology and Aging, 7,* 46–55.

Henker, B., & Whalen, C. K. (1989). Hyperactivity and attention deficits. *American Psychologist, 44,* 216–223.

Henry, C. S., Stephenson, A. L., Hanson, M. F., & Hargett, W. (1993). Adolescent suicide and families: An ecological approach. *Adolescence, 28,* 291–308.

Henshaw, A., Kelly, J., & Gratton, C. (1992). Skipping's for girls: Children's perceptions of gender roles and gender preferences. *Educational Research, 34,* 229–235.

Hernandez, D. J., & Myers, D. E. (1993). *America's children: Resources from family, government, and the economy.* New York: Russell Sage.

Hertz, R. (1986). *More equal than others: Women and men in dual-career marriages.* Berkeley: University of California Press.

Hess, G. C. (1990). Sexual abstinence, a revived option for teenagers. *Modern Psychology, 1,* 19–21.

Hetherington, E. M., Stanley-Hagen, M., & Anderson, E. R. (1989). Marital transitions: A child's perspective. *American Psychologist, 44,* 303–312.

Hildebrand, H. P. (1990). The other side of the wall: A psychoanalytic study of creativity in later life. In R. A. Nemiroff & C. A. Colarusso (Eds.), *New dimensions in adult development.* New York: Basic Books.

Hill, M. S. (1992). The role of economic resources and remarriage in financial assistance for children of divorce. *Journal of Family Issues, 13,* 158–178.

Hillman, L. S. (1991). Theories and research. In C. A. Corr, H. Fuller, C. A. Barnickol, & D. M. Corr (Eds.), *Sudden Infant Death Syndrome: Who can help and how.* New York: Springer.

Hinago, T. (1979). What are the characteristics of the method of early childhood education and care in Japan? In Early Childhood Education Association of Japan (Ed.), *Early childhood education and care in Japan.* Tokyo, Japan: Child Honsha.

Hinde, R. A. (1983). Ethology and child development. In P. H. Mussen (Ed.), *Handbook of child psychology* (4th ed.) (Vol. 2): *Infancy and developmental psychobiology* (pp. 27–94) (M. M. Haith & J. J. Campos, Eds.). New York: John Wiley.

Ho, D. (1983). Asian concepts in behavioral science. *Bulletin of the Hong Kong Psychological Society, 10*, 41–49.

Ho, D. Y. F. (1987). Fatherhood in Chinese culture. In M. E. Lamb (Ed.), *The father's role: Cross-cultural perspectives.* Hillsdale, NJ: Erlbaum.

Hodapp, R. M., & Mueller, E. (1982). Early social development. In B. B. Wolman et al. (Eds.), *Handbook of developmental psychology.* Englewood Cliffs, NJ: Prentice-Hall.

Hodgson, L. G. (1992). Adult grandchildren and their grandparents: The enduring bond. *International Journal of Aging and Human Development, 34,* 209–225.

Hofer, M. A. (1981). *The roots of human behavior: An introduction to the psychobiology of early development.* San Francisco: Freeman.

Hofferth, S. L. (1992). The demand for and supply of child care in the 1990s. In A. Booth (Ed.), *Child care in the 1990's: Trends and consequences.* Hillsdale, NJ: Erlbaum.

Hoffman, L. W. (1991). The influence of the family environment on personality: Accounting for sibling differences. *Psychological Bulletin, 110,* 187–203.

Hoffman, M. L. (1979). Development of moral thought, feeling, and behavior. *American Psychologist, 34,* 958–966.

Hoge, R. D. (1988). Issues in the definition and measurement of the giftedness construct. *Educational Researcher, 17,* 12–66.

Hoge, R. D., & Renzulli, J. S. (1993). Exploring the link between giftedness and self-concept. *Review of Educational Research, 63,* 449–465.

Hohl, D. (1994). Patient satisfaction in home care/hospice. *Nursing Management, 25,* 52–54.

Holland, A. J., Hall, A., Murray, R., Russell, G. F. M., & Crisp, A. H. (1984). Anorexia nervosa: A study of 34 twin pairs and one set of triplets. *British Journal of Psychiatry, 145,* 414–419.

Holland, J. L. (1992). *Making vocational choices* (2nd ed.). Odessa, FL: Psychological Assessment Resources.

Holland, J. L. (1994). Separate but unequal is better. In M. L. Savikas & R. W. Lent (Eds.), *Convergence in career development theories.* Palo Alto, CA: CPP Books.

Holzapfel, S. (1993). Sexual medicine in family practice, Part 2: Treating sexual dysfunction. *Canadian Family Physician, 39,* 618–620.

Honig, A. S. (1993). Mental health for babies: What do theory and research teach us? *Young Children, 48,* 69–76.

Honzik, M. P. (1984). Life-span development. *Annual Review of Psychology, 35,* 309–331.

Hooker, K., & Kaus, C. R. (1994). Health-related possible selves in young and middle adulthood. *Psychology and Aging, 9,* 126–133.

Hooper, S. R. (1992). The classification of developmental disorders: An overview. In S. R. Hooper, G. W. Hynd, & R. E. Mattison (Eds.), *Developmental disorders: Diagnostic criteria and clinical assessment.* Hillsdale, NJ: Erlbaum.

Hopper, J. L., & Seeman, E. (1994). The bone density of female twins discordant for tobacco use. *New England Journal of Medicine, 330,* 387–392.

Horiuchi, Y. (1979). What kind of accomplishments do Japanese children have? In Early Childhood Education Association of Japan (Ed.), *Early childhood education and care in Japan.* Tokyo, Japan: Child Honsha.

Horn, J. L., & Donaldson, G. (1976). On the myth of intellectual decline in adulthood. *American Psychologist, 31,* 701–717.

Horn, J. L., & Donaldson, G. (1980). Cognitive development in adulthood. In O. G. Brim, Jr., & J. Kagan (Eds.), *Constancy and change in human development.* Cambridge, MA: Harvard University Press.

Horn, J. M. (1983). The Texas adoption project. *Child Development, 54,* 268–275.

Howe, M. L., & Courage, M. L. (1993). On resolving the enigma of infantile amnesia. *Psychological Bulletin, 113,* 305–326.

Howes, C., & Segal, J. (1993). Children's relationships with alternative caregivers: The special case of maltreated children removed from their homes. *Journal of Applied Developmental Psychology, 14,* 71–81.

Huesmann, L. R., & Eron, L. D. (1986). The development of aggression in children of different cultures: Psychological processes and exposure to violence. In L. R. Huesmann & L. D. Eron (Eds.), *Television and the aggressive child: A cross-national comparison.* Hillsdale, NJ: Erlbaum.

Hughes, F. P. (1990). *Children, play, and development.* Boston: Allyn & Bacon.

Humphry, D. (1992). Rational suicide among the elderly. *Suicide and life-threatening behavior, 22,* 125–129.

Hunt, C. E. (1991). Sudden infant death syndrome: The neurobehavioral perspective. *Journal of Applied Developmental Psychology, 12,* 185–188.

Hunt, E., & Agnoli, F. (1991). The Whorfian hypothesis: A cognitive psychology perspective. *Psychological Review, 98,* 377–389.

Huntington, D. D., & Bender, W. N. (1993). Adolescents with learning disabilities at risk? Emotional well-being, depression, suicide. *Journal of Learning Disabilities, 26,* 159–166.

Hurrelmann, K. (1990). Parents, peers, teachers and other significant partners in adolescence. *International Journal of Adolescence and Youth, 2,* 211–236.

Hurst, J., & Shepard, J. (1986). The dynamics of plant closings: An extended emotional roller coaster ride. *Journal of Counseling and Development, 64,* 401–405.

Husén, T., & Tuijnman, A. (1991). The contribution of formal schooling to the increase in intellectual capital. *Educational Researcher, 20,* 17–25.

Huston, A. C., Watkins, B. Q., & Kunkel, D. (1989). Public policy and children's television. *American Psychologist, 44,* 424–433.

Huston, A. C., & Wright, J. C. (1983). Children's processing of television: The informative functions of formal features. In J. Bryant & D. R. Anderson (Eds.), *Children's understanding of television: Research on attention and comprehension* (pp. 35–68). New York: Academic Press.

Huston, A. C., Wright, J. C., Rice, M. L., Kerkman, D., & St. Peters, M. (1990). Development of television viewing patterns in early childhood: A longitudinal investigation. *Developmental Psychology, 26,* 409–420.

Hutchinson, J. (1991). What crack does to babies. *American Educator, 15,* 31–32.

Hyde, J. S., Fennema, E., & Lamon, S. J. (1990). Gender differences in mathematics performance: A meta-analysis. *Psychological Bulletin, 107,* 139–155.

Hyde, J. S., Krajnik, M., & Skuldt-Niederberger, K. (1991). Androgyny across the life span: A replication and longitudinal follow-up. *Developmental Psychology, 27,* 516–519.

Hyde, S., & Linn, M. C. (1986). *The psychology of gender: Advances through meta-analysis.* Baltimore: Johns Hopkins University Press.

Iffy, L., Apuzzio, J. J., Mitra, S., Evans, H., Ganesh, V., & Zentay, Z. (1994). Rates of cesarean section and perinatal outcome. Perinatal mortality. *Acta Obstetricia et Gynecologica Scandinavica, 73,* 225–230.

Ijzendoorn, M. H. Van (1993). Intergenerational transmission of parenting: A review of studies in nonclinical populations. *Developmental Review, 12,* 76–99.

Ingram, D. (1991). A historical observation on "Why 'Mama' and 'Papa'?" *Journal of Child Language, 18,* 711–713.

Inhelder, B., & Piaget, J. (1958). *The growth of logical thinking from childhood to adolescence.* New York: Basic Books.

Intons-Peterson, M. J. (1988). *Gender concepts of Swedish and American youth.* Hillsdale, NJ: Erlbaum.

Isabell, B. J., & McKee, L. (1980). Society's cradle: An anthropological perspective on the socialization of cognition. In J. Sants (Ed.), *Developmental psychology and society.* London: Macmillan.

Izard, C. E., & Malatesta, C. Z. (1987). Perspectives on emotional development I: Differential emotions theory of early emotional development. In J. D. Osofsky (Ed.), *Handbook of infant development* (2nd ed.). New York: John Wiley.

Jacklin, C. N. (1989). Female and male: Issues of gender. *American Psychologist, 44,* 127–133.

Jackson, J. F. (1993). Multiple caregiving among African Americans and infant attachment: The need for an emic approach. *Human Development, 36,* 87–102.

Jacobson, J. L., & Jacobson, S. W. (1990). Methodological issues in human behavioral teratology. In C. Rovee-Collier & L. P. Lipsitt (Eds.), *Advances in infancy research* (Vol. 6). Norwood, NJ: Ablex.

Jacobson, J. L., & Wille, D. E. (1984). Influence of attachment and separation experience on separation distress at 18 months. *Developmental Psychology, 20,* 477–484.

Jacobson, S. W., Fein, G. G., Jacobson, J. L., Schwartz, P. M., & Dowler, J. K. (1985). Neonatal correlates of exposure to smoking, caffeine, and alcohol. *Infant and Behavior Development, 7,* 253–265.

Jacobvitz, R. S., Wood, M. R., & Albin, K. (1991). Cognitive skills and young children's comprehension of television. *Journal of Applied Developmental Psychology, 12,* 219–235.

Jacopini, G. A., D'Amico, R., Frontali, M., & Vivona, G. (1992). Attitudes of persons at risk and their partners toward predictive testing. In G. Evers-Kiebooms, J. P. Fryns, J. J. Cassiman, & H. Van den Berghe (Eds.), *Psychosocial aspects of genetic counseling.* New York: John Wiley.

Jahnke, H. C., & Blanchard-Fields, F. (1993). A test of two models of adolescent egocentrism. *Journal of Youth and Adolescence, 22,* 313–326.

James, W. (1892). *Psychology: The briefer course.* New York: Henry Holt.

Janus, S., & Janus, C. (1993). *The Janus report on sexual behavior.* New York: John Wiley.

Jarow, J. P. (1994). Life-threatening conditions associated with male infertility. *Urologic Clinics of North America, 21,* 409–415.

Jean-Gilles, M., & Crittenden, P. M. (1990). Maltreating families: A look at siblings. *Family Relations, 39,* 323–329.

Jenkins, C. D., Zyzanski, S. J., & Rosenman, R. H. (1971). Progress toward validation of a computer-scored test of the type A coronary-prone behavior pattern. *Psychosomatic Medicine, 33,* 192–202.

Jensen, W. A., Heinrich, B., Wake, D. B., Wake, M. H., & Wolfe, S. L. (1979). *Biology.* Belmont, CA: Wadsworth.

Jensen-Scott, R. L. (1993). Counseling to promote retirement adjustment. *Career Development Quarterly, 41,* 257–267.

Johnson, B. D., Badr, M. S., & Dempsey, J. A. (1994). Impact of the aging pulmonary system on the response to exercise. *Clinics in Chest Medicine, 15,* 229–246.

Johnson, C. L., & Troll, L. E. (1994). Constraints and facilitators to friendships in late late life. *Gerontologist, 34,* 79–87.

Johnson, J. E., & McGillicuddy-Delisi, A. (1983). Family environment factors and children's knowledge of rules and conventions. *Child Development, 54,* 218–226.

Johnson, J. H. (1986). *Life events as stressors in childhood and adolescence.* Beverly Hills, CA: Sage.

Johnson, M. K., Bransford, J. D., & Solomon, S. (1973). Memory for tacit implications of sentences. *Journal of Experimental Psychology, 98,* 203–205.

Johnson, S. A., & Green, V. (1993). Female adolescent contraceptive decision making and risk taking. *Adolescence, 28,* 81–96.

Johnston, W. B., & Packer, A. B. (1987). *Workforce 2000: Work and workers for the 21st century.* Indianapolis, IN: Hudson Institute.

Jones, M. C. (1957). The later careers of boys who are early- or late-maturing. *Child Development, 28,* 113–128.

Jones, W. H. (1979). Grief and involuntary career change: Its implications for counseling. *Vocational Guidance Quarterly, 27,* 196–201.

Jordan, N. H. (1993). Sexual abuse prevention programs in early childhood education: A caveat. *Young Children, 48,* 76–79.

Jorgensen, S. R. (1991). Project taking charge: An evaluation of an adolescent pregnancy prevention program. *Family Relations, 40,* 373–380.

Joshi, H., & Davies, H. (1992). Day care in Europe and mothers' foregone earnings. *International Labor Review, 131,* 561–579.

Joy, L. A., Kimball, M., & Zabrack, M. L. (1977, June). *Television exposure and children's aggressive behavior.* Paper presented at the annual meeting of the Canadian Psychological Association, Vancouver, British Columbia.

Julian, F. H. (1993). Date and acquaintance rape: The legal point of view. Part 2: Reform of rape laws and alternatives to criminal prosecution. *College Student Affairs Journal, 12,* 9–17.

Juvonen, J. (1991). Deviance, perceived responsibility, and negative peer reactions. *Developmental Psychology, 27,* 672–681.

Kagan, J. (1992). Yesterday's premises, tomorrow's promises. *Developmental Psychology, 28,* 990–997.

Kagan, J., & Snidman, N. (1991). Temperamental factors in human development. *American Psychologist, 46,* 856–862.

Kagan, J. S. (1976). Emergent themes in human development. *American Scientist, 64,* 186–196.

Kaiser-Messmer, G. (1993). Results of an empirical study into gender differences in attitudes towards mathematics. *Educational Studies in Mathematics, 25,* 209–233.

Kaitz, M., Meschulach-Sarfaty, O., Auerbach, J., & Eidelman, A. (1988). A reexamination of newborns' ability to imitate facial expressions. *Developmental Psychology, 24,* 3–7.

Kalanin, J., Takarada, Y., Kagawa, S., Yamashita, K., Ohtsuka, N., & Matsuoka, A. (1994). Gypsy phenylketonuria: A point mutation of the phenylalanine hydroxylase gene in Gypsy families from Slovakia. *American Journal of Medical Genetics, 49,* 235–239.

Kalish, R. A. (1981). *Death, grief, and caring relationships.* Pacific Grove, CA: Brooks/Cole.

Kant, I. (1977). *Die metaphysic der sitten.* Frankfurt: Suhrkamp. (Originally published in 1797.)

Kanter, R. M. (1981). *Men and women of the corporation.* New York: Basic Books.

Kaplan, L. J. (1984). *Adolescence: The farewell to childhood.* New York: Simon & Schuster.

Kaplan, P. S., Fox, K. B., & Huckeby, E. R. (1992). Faces as reinforcers: Effects of pairing condition and facial expression. *Developmental Psychobiology, 25,* 299–312.

Karacostas, D. D., & Fisher, G. L. (1993). Chemical dependency in students with and without learning disabilities. *Journal of Learning Disabilities, 26,* 491–495.

Karges-Bone, L. (1993). Parenting the gifted young scientist: Mrs. Wizard at home. *Gifted Child Today, 16,* 55–59.

Kasof, J. (1993). Sex bias in the naming of stimulus persons. *Psychological Bulletin, 113,* 140–163.

Kastenbaum, R. (1985). Dying and death: A lifespan approach. In J. E. Birren & K. W. Schaie (Eds.), *Handbook of the psychology of aging* (2nd ed.). New York: Van Nostrand Reinhold.

Katz, R. C., Frazer, N., & Wilson, L. (1993). Sexual fears are increasing. *Psychological Reports, 73,* 476–478.

Kaufman, H. H., Bodensteiner, J., Burkart, B., Gutmann, L., Kopitnik, T., Hochberg, V., Loy, N., Cox-Ganser, J., & Hobbs, G. (1994). Treatment of spastic gait in cerebral palsy. *West Virginia Medical Journal, 90,* 190–192.

Kavale, K. A. (1993). How many learning disabilities are there? A commentary on Stanovich's "Dysrationalia:

A new specific learning disability." *Journal of Learning Disabilities, 26,* 520–523.

Kavale, K. A., Forness, S. R., & Lorsbach, T. C. (1991). Definition for definitions of learning disabilities. *Journal of Learning Disabilities, 14,* 257–266.

Kazdin, A. E. (1989). Developmental psychopathology: Current research, issues, and directions. *American Psychologist, 44,* 180–187.

Kegan, R. (1982). *The evolving self: Problem and process in human development.* Cambridge, MA: Harvard University Press.

Kelly, J. R., & Westcott, G. (1991). Ordinary retirement: Commonalities and continuity. *International Journal of Aging and Human Development, 32,* 81–89.

Kelly, K. R. (1993). The relation of gender and academic achievement to career self-efficacy and interests. *Gifted Child Quarterly, 37,* 59–64.

Kendall-Tackett, K. A., Williams, L. M., & Finkelhor, D. (1993). Impact of sexual abuse on children: A review and synthesis of recent empirical studies. *Psychological Bulletin, 113,* 164–180.

Kessen, W. (1965). *The child.* New York: John Wiley.

Kier, C., & Lewis, D. (1993). *Does parental marital separation affect infants?* Paper presented at the Biennial Meeting of the Society for Research in Child Development, New Orleans, March 25–28.

Kiley, D. (1983). *The Peter Pan Syndrome: Men who have never grown up.* New York: Dodd, Mead.

Kinsey, A. C., Pomeroy, W. B., & Martin, C. E. (1948). *Sexual behavior in the human male.* Philadelphia: W. B. Saunders.

Kinsey, A. C, Pomeroy, W. B., Martin, C. E., & Gebhard, P. H. (1953). *Sexual behavior in the human female.* Philadelphia: W. B. Saunders.

Klaus, M., & Kennell, J. (1976). *Maternal–infant bonding.* St. Louis: C. V. Mosby.

Klaus, M., & Kennell, J. (1983). *Bonding: The beginnings of parent–infant attachment* (rev. ed.). St. Louis: C. V. Mosby. (Originally published as *Maternal–infant bonding.*)

Klaus, M., Kreger, N., McAlpine, W., Steffa, M., & Kennell, J. (1972). Maternal attachment: Importance of the first post-partum days. *New England Journal of Medicine, 286,* 460–463.

Kleemeier, R. (1962). Intellectual changes in the senium. *Proceedings of the Social Section of the American Statistical Association, 1,* 290–295.

Kloza, E. M. (1990). Low MSAFP and new biochemical markers for Down syndrome: Implications for genetic counselors. In B. A. Fine, E. Gettig, K. Greendale, B. Leopold, & N .W. Paul (Eds.), *Strategies in genetic counseling: Reproductive genetics and new tech-*

nologies. White Plains, NY: March of Dimes Birth Defects Foundation.

Knox, G. W., Laske, D. L., & Tromanhauser, E. D. (1992). *Schools under siege.* Dubuque, IA: Kendall/Hunt.

Knuppel, R. A., & Angel, J. L. (1990). Diagnosis of fetal-maternal hemorrhage. In R. D. Eden, F. H. Boehm, & M. Haire (Eds.), *Assessment and care of the fetus: Physiological, clinical, and medicolegal principles.* Norwalk, CT: Appleton & Lange.

Kogan, N. (1983). Stylistic variation in childhood and adolescence: Creativity, metaphor, and cognitive style. In P. H. Mussen (Ed.), *Handbook of child psychology* (4th ed.) (Vol. 3): *Cognitive development* (pp. 630–706) (J. H. Flavell & E. M. Markman, Eds.). New York: John Wiley.

Kohlberg, L. A. (1964). Development of moral character and moral ideology. In M. L. Hoffman & L. W. Hoffman (Eds.), *Review of child development research* (Vol. 1). New York: Russell Sage.

Kohlberg, L. A. (1966). Cognitive-development analysis of children's sex-role concepts and attitudes. In E. Maccoby (Ed.), *The development of sex differences.* Stanford, CA: Stanford University Press.

Kohlberg, L. A. (1969). Stage and sequence: The cognitive developmental approach to socialization. In D. Gosslin (Ed.), *Handbook of socialization theory and research.* Chicago: Rand McNally.

Kohlberg, L. A. (1980). *The meaning and measurement of moral development.* Worcester, MA: Clark University Press.

Koli, K., & Keski-Oja, J. (1992). Cellular senescence. *Annals of Medicine, 24,* 313–318.

Kondro, W. (1992). Canada: Controversy over Royal Commission on Reproductive Technologies. *Lancet, 340,* 1214–1215.

Konner, M. (1982). Biological aspects of the mother–infant bond. In C. Parks & J. Stevenson-Hinde (Eds.), *The place of attachment in human behavior.* New York: Basic Books.

Kopp, N., Denoroy, L., Eymin, C., Gay, N., Richard, F., Awano, K., Gilly, R., & Jordan, D. (1994). Studies of neuroregulators in the brain stem of SIDS. *Biology of the Neonate, 65,* 189–193.

Kopp, R. G., & Ruzicka, M. F. (1993). Women's multiple roles and psychological well-being. *Psychological Reports, 72,* 1351–1354.

Koss, M. (1988). Hidden rape: Sexual aggression and victimization in a national sample of students in higher education. In A. Burgess (Ed.), *Rape and sexual assault* (Vol. 2). New York: Garland.

Kotch, J. B. (1993). Morbidity and death due to child abuse in New Zealand. *Child Abuse and Neglect: The International Journal, 17,* 233–247.

Koutsouvanou, E. (1993). Television and child language development. *International Journal of Early Childhood, 25,* 27–32.

Kovacs, M. (1989). Affective disorders in children and adolescents. *American Psychologist, 44,* 209–215.

Kozulin, A. (1990). *Vygotsky's psychology: A biography of ideas.* New York: Harvester Wheatsheaf.

Kroger, J. (1993a). Ego identity: An overview. In J. Kroger (Ed.), *Discussions on ego identity.* Hillsdale, NJ: Erlbaum.

Kroger, J. (1993b). The role of historical context in the identity formation process of late adolescence. *Youth and Society, 24,* 363–376.

Kroupa, S. E. (1988). Perceived parental acceptance and female juvenile delinquency. *Adolescence, 23,* 143–155.

Kruse, A., Lindenberger, U., & Baltes, P. B. (1993). Longitudinal research on human aging: The power of combining real-time, microgenetic, and simulation approaches. In D. Magnusson & P. Casaer (Eds.), *Longitudinal research on individual development: Present status and future perspectives.* Cambridge: Cambridge University Press.

Kruyer, H., Miranda, M., Volpini, V., & Estivill, X. (1994). Carrier detection and microsatellite analysis of Duchenne and Becker muscular dystrophy in Spanish families. *Prenatal Diagnosis, 14,* 123–130.

Kübler-Ross, E. (1969). *On death and dying.* New York: Macmillan.

Kübler-Ross, E. (1974). *Questions and answers on death and dying.* New York: Macmillan.

Kuder, F. (1977). *Activity, interests, and occupational choice.* Chicago: Science Research Associates.

Kuhn, D. (1984). Cognitive development. In M. H. Bornstein & M. E. Lamb (Eds.), *Developmental psychology: An advanced textbook* (pp. 133–180). Hillsdale, NJ: Erlbaum.

Kuhn, T. S. (1970). *The structure of scientific revolutions* (2d ed., enl.). Chicago: University of Chicago Press.

Kumari, R. (1989). *Brides are not for burning: Dowry victims in India.* Kalkaji, New Delhi: Radiant Publishers.

Kumin, L. (1994). Intelligibility of speech in children with Down syndrome in natural settings: Parents' perspective. *Perceptual and Motor Skills, 78,* 307–313.

Kupetz, B. N. (1993). Reducing stress in your child's life. *PTA Today, 18,* 10–12.

Kurdek, L. A. (1993). Issues in proposing a general model of the effects of divorce on children. *Journal of Marriage and the Family, 55,* 39–41.

Kurtines, W., & Grief, E. B. (1974). The development of moral thought: Review and evaluation of Kohlberg's approach. *Psychological Bulletin, 81,* 453–470.

Kuzyk, B. (1993, Sept. 2). Breast-feeding is best for babies. *Edmonton Sun,* p. 38.

La Greca, A. M., & Stone, W. L. (1993). Social anxiety scale for children revised: Factor structure and concurrent validity. *Journal of Clinical Child Psychology, 22,* 17–27.

Labouvie, E. W. (1990). Personality and alcohol and marijuana use: Patterns of convergence in young adulthood. *International Journal of Addictions, 25,* 237–252.

Labouvie-Vief, G. (1980). Beyond formal operations: Uses and limits of pure logic in life-span development. *Human Development, 23,* 141–161.

Labouvie-Vief, G. (1986). Modes of knowledge and the organization of development. In M. L. Commons, L. Kohlberg, F. A. Richards, & J. Sinnott (Eds.), *Beyond formal operations 3: Models and methods in the study of adult and adolescent thought.* New York: Praeger.

Labouvie-Vief, G., & Lawrence, R. (1985). Object knowledge, personal knowledge, and processes of equilibration in adult cognition. *Human Development, 28,* 25–39.

Lachenmeyer, J. R., & Muni-Brander, P. (1988). Eating disorders in a nonclinical adolescent population: Implications for treatment. *Adolescence, 23*(90), 303–312.

Laczko, F. (1989). Between work and retirement: Becoming "old" in the 1980's. In B. Bytheway, T. Keil, P. Allatt, & A. Bryman (Eds.), *Becoming and being old: Sociological approaches to later life.* London: Sage.

Lal, S. R., Lal, D., & Achilles, C. M. (1993). *Handbook on gangs in schools: Strategies to reduce gang-related activities.* Thousand Oaks, CA: Corwin.

Lam, T. C. L. (1992). Review of practices and problems in the evaluation of bilingual education. *Review of Educational Research, 62,* 181–203.

Lamanna, M. A., & Riedmann, A. (1988). *Marriages and families: Making choices and facing change* (3rd ed.). Belmont, CA: Wadsworth.

Lamb, M. E. (1980). The development of parent–infant attachment in the first two years of life. In F. A. Pedersen (Ed.), *The father–infant relationship: Observational studies in the family setting.* New York: Holt, Rinehart & Winston.

Lamb, M. E. (Ed.). (1987). *The father's role: Cross-cultural perspectives.* Hillsdale, NJ: Erlbaum.

Lamb, S., & Coakley, M. (1993). "Normal" childhood sexual play and games: Differentiating play from abuse. *Child Abuse and Neglect: The International Journal, 17,* 515–526.

Lambert, W. E. (1975). Culture and language as factors in learning and education. In A. Wolfgang (Ed.), *Education of immigrant students.* Toronto: Ontario Institute for Studies in Education.

Lamport, L. L., & Andre, T. (1993). AIDS knowledge and sexual responsibility. *Youth and Society, 25,* 38–61.

Landerman, R., George, L. K., & Blazer, D. G. (1991). Adult vulnerability for psychiatric disorders: Interactive effects of negative childhood experiences and recent stress. *Journal of Nervous and Mental Disease, 179,* 656–663.

Landesman, S., & Ramey, C. (1989). Developmental psychology and mental retardation: Integrating scientific principles with treatment practices. *American Psychologist, 44,* 409–415.

Landreth, G. L. (1993). Child-centered play therapy. *Elementary school guidance and counseling, 28,* 17–29.

Lane, H. (1977). *The wild boy of Aveyron.* London: Allen & Unwin.

Langlois, J. H., Ritter, J. M., Roggman, L. A., & Vaughn, L. S. (1991). Facial diversity and infant preferences for attractive faces. *Developmental Psychology, 27,* 79–84.

Langlois, J. H., & Roggman, L. A. (1990). Attractive faces are only average. *Psychological Science, 1,* 115–121.

Langlois, J. H., Roggman, L. A., & Rieser-Danner, L. A. (1990). Infants' differential social responses to attractive and unattractive faces. *Developmental Psychology, 26,* 153–159.

Lapierre, S., Bouffard, L., & Bastin, E. (1992/1993). Motivational goal objects in later life. *International Journal of Aging and Human Development, 36,* 279–292.

Lapsley, D. K. (1990). Continuity and discontinuity in adolescent social cognitive development. In R. Montemayor, G. R. Adams, & T. P. Gullotta (Eds.), *From childhood to adolescence: A transitional period? (Advances in Adolescent Development,* Vol. 2). Newbury Park, CA: Sage.

Larson, R., & Ham, M. (1993). Stress and "Storm and Stress" in early adolescence: The relationship of negative events with dysphoric affect. *Developmental Psychology, 29,* 130–140.

Lasher, K. P., & Faulkender, P. J. (1993). Measurement of aging anxiety: Development of the Anxiety about Aging Scale. *International Journal of Aging and Human Development, 37,* 247–259.

Lasley, J. R. (1992). Age, social context, and street gang membership: Are "youth" gangs becoming "adult" gangs? *Youth and Society, 23,* 434–451.

Latané, R., & Darley, J. M. (1970). *The unresponsive bystander: Why doesn't he help?* New York: Appleton-Century-Crofts.

Lavee, Y., & Olson, D. H. (1993). Seven types of marriage: Empirical typology based on ENRICH. *Journal of Marital and Family Therapy, 19,* 325–340.

Lavery, B., Siegel, A. W., Cousins, J. H., & Rubovits, D. S. (1993). Adolescent risk-taking: An analysis of problem behaviors in problem children. *Journal of Experimental Child Psychology, 55,* 277–294.

Lawton, M. P. (1981). Community supports for the aged. *Journal of Social Issues, 37,* 102–115.

Lazarus, R. S. (1993). From psychological stress to the emotions: A history of changing outlooks. *Annual Review of Psychology, 44,* 1–21.

Leaf, A. (1973, September). Getting old. *Scientific American, 299,* 44–53.

Leboyer, F. (1975). *Birth without violence.* New York: Random House.

Ledoux, S., Choquet, M., & Manfredi, R. (1993). Associated factors for self-reported binge eating among male and female adolescents. *Journal of Adolescence, 16,* 75–91.

Lee, G. R., Dwyer, J. W., & Coward, R. T. (1993). Gender differences in parent care: Demographic factors and same-gender preferences. *Journal of Gerontology, 48,* S9–S16.

Lee, K. (1992). Pattern of night waking and crying of Korean infants from 3 months to 2 years old and its relation with various factors. *Journal of Developmental and Behavioral Pediatrics, 13,* 326–330.

Lee, V. E., Brooks-Gunn, J., & Schnur, E. (1988). Does Head Start work? A 1-year follow-up comparison of disadvantaged children attending Head Start, no preschool, and other preschool programs. *Developmental Psychology, 24,* 210–222.

Lefevre, J., Beunen, G., Steens, G., Claessens, A., & Renson, R. (1993). Motor performance during adolescence and age thirty as related to age at peak height velocity. *Annals of Human Biology, 17,* 423–435.

Lefrançois, G. R. (1973). *Of children.* Belmont, CA: Wadsworth.

Lefrançois, G. R. (1983). *Psychology* (2nd ed.). Belmont, CA: Wadsworth.

Legerstee, M. (1991). Changes in the quality of infant sounds as a function of social and nonsocial stimulation. *First Language, 11,* 327–343.

Lehman, H. C. (1953). *Age and achievement.* Princeton, NJ: Princeton University Press.

Lenneberg, E. H. (1969). On explaining language. *Science, 164,* 635–643.

Leon, M. (1992). The neurobiology of learning. *Annual Review of Psychology, 43,* 377–398.

Lerner, J. V., & Abrams, L. A. (1994). Developmental correlates of maternal employment influences on children. In C. B. Fisher & R. M. Lerner (Eds.), *Applied developmental psychology*. New York: McGraw-Hill.

Lerner, R. M. (1991). Changing organism-context relations as the basic process of development: A developmental contextual perspective. *Developmental Psychology, 27*, 27–32.

Lerner, R. M. (1993). The demise of the nature-nurture dichotomy. *Human Development, 36*, 119–124.

Lerner, R. M., Lerner, J. V., Winelle, M., Hooker, K., Lenez, K., et al. (1986). Children and adolescents in their contexts: Tests of the goodness of fit model. In R. Plomin & J. Dunn (Eds.), *The study of temperament: Changes, continuities and challenges*. Hillsdale, NJ: Erlbaum.

Lerner, R. M., Miller, J. R., Knott, J. H., Kenneth, E. C., Bynum, T. S., Hoopfer, L. C., McKinney, M. H., Abrams, A., Hula, R. C., & Terry, P. A. (1992). Integrating scholarship and outreach in human development research, policy, and service: A developmental contextual perspective. In D. L. Featherman, R. M. Lerner, & M. Perlmutter (Eds.), *Lifespan development and behavior* (Vol. 12). Hillsdale, NJ: Erlbaum.

Leslie, A. M. (1988). Some implications of pretense for mechanisms underlying the child's theory of mind. In J. W. Astington, P. L. Harris, & D. R. Olson (Eds.), *Developing theories of mind*. New York: Cambridge University Press.

Leventhal, E. A., Levanthal, H., & Shacham, S. (1989). Active coping reduces reports of pain from childbirth. *Journal of Consulting and Clinical Psychology, 57*, 365–371.

Levine, J. M., Resnick, L. B., & Higgins, E. T. (1993). Social foundations of cognition. *Annual Review of Psychology, 44*, 585–612.

Levine, R. A. (1987). Women's schooling, patterns of fertility, and child survival. *Educational Researcher, 16*, 21–27.

Levinson, D. (1990). *The seasons of a woman's life: Implications for women and men*. Paper presented at the Annual Meeting of the American Psychological Association, Boston.

Levinson, D. J. (1978). *The seasons of a man's life*. New York: Knopf.

Levinson, D. J. (1981). The midlife transition: A period in adult psychosocial development. In L. D. Steinberg (Ed.), *The life cycle: Readings in human development*. New York: Columbia University Press.

Levitt, A. G., & Utman, J. G. (1992). From babbling towards the sound systems of English and French: A longitudinal two-case study. *Journal of Child Language, 19*, 19–49.

Levitt, M. J., Guacci, N., & Coffman, S. (1993). Social network relations in infancy: An observational study. *Merrill-Palmer Quarterly, 39*, 233–251.

Levitt, M. J., Weber, R. A., & Guacci, N. (1993). Convoys of social support: An intergenerational analysis. *Psychology and Aging, 8*, 323–326.

Levy, G. D. (1993). Introduction: An integrated collection on early gender-role development. *Developmental Review, 13*, 123–125.

Lévy-Leboyer, C., & Duron, Y. (1991). Global change: New challenges for psychology. *International Journal of Psychology, 26*, 575–583.

Liben, L. (1975, April). *Perspective-taking skills in young children: Seeing the world through rose-colored glasses*. Paper presented at the meeting of the Society for Research in Child Development, Denver.

Liddell, D. L., & Douvanis, C. J. (1994). The social and legal status of gay and lesbian students: An update for colleges and universities. *Naspa Journal, 31*, 121–129.

Lieberman, A. B. (1987). *Giving birth*. New York: St. Martin's Press.

Liggins, G. C. (1988). The onset of labor: An historical review. In C. T. Jones (Ed.), *Research in perinatal medicine (VII): Fetal and neonatal development*. Ithaca, NY: Perinatology Press.

Linn, M. C., & Hyde, J. S. (1989). Gender, mathematics, and science. *Educational Researcher, 18*, 17–27.

Liu, D. T. (1991). Introduction and historical perspectives. In D. T. Liu (Ed.), *A practical guide to chorion villus sampling*. New York: Oxford University Press.

Lobel, T. E., Agami-Rozenblat, O., & Bempechat, J. (1993). Personality correlates of career choice in the kibbutz: A comparison between career and noncareer women. *Sex Roles: A Journal of Research, 29*, 359–370.

Locke, J. (1699). *Some thoughts concerning education* (4th ed.). London: A. & J. Churchills.

Locke, J. L. (1992). Thirty years of research on developmental neurolinguistics. *Pediatric Neurology, 8*, 245–250.

Lockhart, A. S. (1980). Motor learning and motor development during infancy and childhood. In C. B. Corbin (Ed.), *A textbook of motor development*. Dubuque, IA: Brown.

Loehlin, J. C. (1985). Fitting heredity-environment models jointly to twin and adoption data from the California Psychological Inventory. *Behavior Genetics, 15*, 199–221.

Loehlin, J. C., Willerman, L., & Horn, J. M. (1988). Human behavior genetics. *Annual Review of Psychology, 39*, 101–133.

Loftus, E. F. (1979). *Eyewitness testimony*. Cambridge, MA: Harvard University Press.

Logli, P. A. (1994). We must criminalize fetal neglect. In G. E. McCuen (Ed.), *Born hooked: Poisoned in the womb* (2nd ed.). Hudson, WI: Gary McCuen Publications.

Long, J. (1989). A part to play: Men experiencing leisure through retirement. In B. Bytheway, T. Keil, P. Allatt, & A. Bryman (Eds.), *Becoming and being old: Sociological approaches to later life.* London: Sage.

Long, J., & Porter, K. L. (1984). Multiple roles of midlife women: A case for new directions in theory, research, and policy. In G. Baruch & J. Brooks-Gunn (Eds.), *Women in midlife.* New York: Plenum.

Long, V. O. (1991). Gender role conditioning and women's self-concept. *Journal of Humanistic Education and Development, 30,* 19–29.

Longstreth, G. F., & Wolde-Tsadik, G. (1993). Irritable bowel-type symptoms in HMO examinees. Prevalence, demographics, and clinical correlates. *Digestive Diseases and Sciences, 38,* 1581–1589.

Lookabaugh, S. L., & Fu, V. R. (1992). Children's use of inanimate transitional objects in coping with hassles. *Journal of Genetic Psychology, 153,* 37–46.

Looney, M. A., & Plowman, S. A. (1990). Passing rates of American children and youth on the FITNESSGRAM criterion-referenced physical fitness standards. *Research Quarterly for Exercise and Sport, 61,* 215–223.

Lorenz, K. (1952). *King Solomon's ring.* London: Methuen.

Lowenthal, M. F., & Haven, C. (1981). Interaction and adaptation: Intimacy as a critical variable. In L. D. Steinberg (Ed.), *The life cycle: Readings in human development.* New York: Columbia University Press.

Lu, L., & Argyle, M. (1993). TV watching, soap opera and happiness. *Kaohsiung Journal of Medical Sciences, 9,* 501–507.

Lu, L., & Argyle, M. (1994). Leisure satisfaction and happiness as a function of leisure activity. *Kaohsiung Journal of Medical Sciences, 10,* 89–96.

Luke, C. (1988). *Television and your child: A guide for concerned parents.* Toronto: Kagan & Woo.

Luqmani, R., Gordon, C., & Bacon, P. (1994) Clinical pharmacology and modification of autoimmunity and inflammation in rheumatoid disease. *Drugs, 47,* 259–285.

Luyendijk, W., & Treffers, P. D. (1992). The smile in anencephalic infants. *Clinical Neurology and Neurosurgery,* 1994 Supplement, S113–S117.

Lye, D. N., & Biblarz, T. J. (1993). The effects of attitudes toward family life and gender roles on marital satisfaction. *Journal of Family Issues, 14,* 157–188.

Lyne, J., & Howe, H. F. (1990). The rhetoric of expertise: E. O. Wilson and sociobiology. *The Quarterly Journal of Speech, 76,* 134–152.

Maccoby, E. E., & Jacklin, C. N. (1974). *The psychology of sex differences.* Stanford, CA: Stanford University Press.

Maccoby, E. E., & Jacklin, C. N. (1980). Sex differences in aggression: A rejoinder and reprise. *Child Development, 51,* 964–980.

Mack, J. (1980). *Zulus.* London: Macdonald Educational.

Macmillan, D. L., Keogh, B. K., & Jones, R. L. (1986). Special educational research on mildly handicapped learners. In M. C. Wittrock (Ed.), *Handbook of research on teaching* (3rd ed.) (pp. 686–724). New York: Macmillan.

MacNeal, J. U. (1992). *Kids as customers.* New York: Lexington Books.

Macrae, J. H. (1991). Presbycusis and noise-induced permanent threshold shift. *Journal of the Acoustical Society of America, 90,* 2513–2516.

Madak, P. R., & Berg, D. H. (1992). The prevention of sexual abuse: An evaluation of "Talking about Touching." *Canadian Journal of Counselling, 26,* 29–40.

Madonna, P. G., Van Scoyk, S., & Jones, D. P. (1991). Family interactions within incest and nonincest families. *American Journal of Psychiatry, 148,* 46–49.

Madsen, M. C. (1971). Developmental and cross-cultural differences in the cooperation and competitive behavior of young children. *Journal of Cross-Cultural Psychology, 2,* 365–371.

Madsen, M. C., & Lancy, D. F. (1981). Cooperative and competitive behavior: Experiments related to ethnic identity and urbanization in Papua New Guinea. *Journal of Cross-Cultural Psychology, 12,* 389–409.

Mahon, M. M. (1993). Children's concept of death and sibling death from trauma. *Journal of Pediatric Nursing, 8,* 335–344.

Mahoney, M. J. (1991). *Human change processes: The scientific foundations of psychotherapy.* New York: Basic Books.

Main, M., & Cassidy, J. (1988). Categories of response to reunion with the parent at age 6: Predictable from infant attachment classifications and stable over a 1-month period. *Developmental Psychology, 24,* 415–426.

Males, M. (1993a). Schools, society, and "teen" pregnancy. *Phi Delta Kappan, 74,* 566–568.

Males, M. (1993b). School-age pregnancy: Why hasn't prevention worked? *Journal of School Health, 63,* 429–432.

Malina, R. M. (1990). Physical growth and performance during the transitional years (9 to 16). In R. Montemayor, G. R. Adams, & T. P. Gullotta (Eds.), *From childhood to adolescence: A transitional period? (Advances in Adolescent Development,* Vol. 2). Newbury Park, CA: Sage.

Malina, R. M., & Bouchard, C. (1991). *Growth, maturation, and physical activity.* Champaign, IL: Human Kinetics Books.

Malina, R. M., Bouchard, C., & Beunen, G. (1988). Human growth: Selected aspects of current research on well-nourished children. *Annual Review of Anthropology, 17*, 187–219.

Malonebeach, E. E., & Zarit, S. H. (1991). Current research issues in caregiving to the elderly. *International Journal of Aging and Human Development, 32*, 103–114.

Maltas, C. (1992). Trouble in paradise: Marital crises of midlife. *Psychiatry, 55*, 122–131.

Mandich, M., Simons, C. J., Ritchie, S., Schmidt, D., & Mullett, M. (1994). Motor development, infantile reactions and postural responses of preterm, at-risk infants. *Developmental Medicine and Child Neurology, 36*, 397–405.

Mandler, J. M. (1984). Representation and recall in infancy. In M. Moscovitch (Ed.), *Infant memory*. New York: Plenum.

Manning, G. F. (1993). Loss and renewal in old age: Some literary models. *Canadian Journal on Aging, 12*, 469–484.

Manning, W. D. (1993). Marriage and cohabitation following premarital conception. *Journal of Marriage and the Family, 55*, 839–850.

Marcia, J. E. (1966). Development and validation of ego-identity status. *Journal of Personality and Social Psychology, 3*, 551–558.

Marcia, J. E. (1980). Identity in adolescence. In J. Adelson (Ed.), *Handbook of adolescent psychology*. New York: John Wiley.

Marcia, J. E. (1993). The relational roots of identity. In J. Kroger (Ed.), *Discussions on ego identity*. Hillsdale, NJ: Erlbaum.

Marcon, R. A. (1993). Socioemotional versus academic emphasis: Impact on kindergartners' development and achievement. *Early Child Development and Care, 96*, 81–91.

Markides, K., & Martin, H. (1979). A causal model of life satisfaction among the elderly. *Journal of Gerontology, 34*, 86–93.

Marlatt, G. A., Baer, J. S., Donovan, D. M., & Kivlahan, D. R. (1988). Addictive behaviors: Etiology and treatment. *Annual Review of Psychology, 39*, 223–252.

Marsh, H. W. (1989). Sex differences in the development of verbal and mathematics constructs: The high school and beyond study. *American Educational Research Journal, 26*, 191–225.

Marsiglio, W. (1986). Teenage fatherhood: High school accreditation and educational attainment. In A. B. Elster & M. E. Lamb (Eds.), *Adolescent fatherhood*. Hillsdale, NJ: Erlbaum.

Martin, M. E. (1993). Prevalence of eating disorders such as anorexia and bulimia nervosa among the college population. *College Student Affairs Journal, 12*, 77–80.

Martin, N., & Jardine, R. (1986). Eysenck's contributions to behaviour genetics. In S. Modgil & C. Modgil (Eds.), *Hans Eysenck: Consensus and controversy*. Philadelphia: Falmer.

Martin, P. (1991/1992). Zapping those zits: Helping teens handle acne. *PTA Today, 17*, 20–21.

Maslow, A. H. (1970). *Motivation and personality* (2nd ed.). New York: Harper & Row.

Masters, W. H., & Johnson, V. E. (1966). *Human sexual response*. London: Churchill.

Masur, E. F. (1993). Transitions in representational ability: Infants' verbal, vocal, and action imitation during the second year. *Merrill-Palmer Quarterly, 39*, 437–455.

Mathews, A., & MacLeod, C. (1994). Cognitive approaches to emotion and emotional disorders. *Annual Review of Psychology, 45*, 25–50.

Mathieu, P. S., Sowa, C. J., & Niles, S. G. (1993). Differences in career self-efficacy among women. *Journal of Career Development, 19*, 187–196.

Mayberry, L. J., & Affonso, D. D. (1993). Infant temperament and postpartum depression: A review. *Health Care for Women International, 14*, 201–211.

Mayer, N. K., & Tronick, E. Z. (1985). Mother's turn-giving signals and infant turn-taking in mother–infant interaction. In T. M. Field & N. A. Fox (Eds.), *Social perception in infants*. Norwood, NJ: Ablex.

Mayo, K. E. (1993). Learning strategy instruction: Exploring the potential of metacognition. *Reading Improvement, 30*, 130–133.

McAdams, D. P. (1984). Love, power, and images of the self. In C. Z. Malatesta & C. E. Izard (Eds.), *Emotion in adult development* (pp. 159–174). Beverly Hills, CA: Sage.

McAdams, D. P., St. Aubin, E. D., & Logan, R. L. (1993). Generativity among young, midlife, and older adults. *Psychology and Aging, 8*, 221–230.

McCabe, M. P. (1991). Influence of creativity and intelligence on academic performance. *The Journal of Creative Behavior, 25*, 116–122.

McCartney, K., Bernieri, F., & Harris, M. J. (1990). Growing up and growing apart: A developmental meta-analysis of twin studies. *Psychological Bulletin, 107*, 226–237.

McCartney, K., & Howley, E. (1992). Parents as instruments of intervention in home-based preschool programs. In L. Okagaki & R. J. Sternberg (Eds.), *Directors of development: Influences on the development of children's thinking*. Hillsdale, NJ: Erlbaum.

McCartney, K., & Jordan, E. (1990). Parallels between research on child care and research on school effects. *Educational Researcher, 19*, 21–27.

McClelland, D. C. (1973). Testing for competence rather than for "intelligence." *American Psychologist, 28*, 1–14.

McCrae, R. R., & Costa, P. T. (1984). *Emerging lives: Enduring predispositions.* Boston: Little, Brown.

McCrae, R. R., & Costa, P. T. (1987). Validations of the five factor model of personality across instruments and observers. *Journal of Personality and Social Psychology, 52,* 81–90.

McCune, L. (1993). The development of play as the development of consciousness. *New Directions for Child Development, 59,* 67–79.

McCurdy, H. G. (in collaboration with Helen Follett) (Eds.). (1966). *Barbara: The unconscious autobiography of a child genius.* Chapel Hill, NC: University of North Carolina Press.

McGraw, M. B. (1943). *The neuromuscular maturation of the human infant.* New York: Columbia University Press.

McGroarty, M. (1992). The societal context of bilingual education. *Educational Researcher, 21,* 7–9, 24.

McKay, M. M. (1994). The link between domestic violence and child abuse: Assessment and treatment considerations. *Child Welfare, 73,* 29–39.

McKusick, V. A. (1992). *Mendelian inheritance in man* (10th ed.). Baltimore: Johns Hopkins University Press.

McLaughlin, C. R., Hull, J. G., Edwards, W. H., Cramer, C. P., & Dewey, W. L. (1993). Neonatal pain: A comprehensive survey of attitudes and practices. *Journal of Pain and Symptom Management, 8,* 7–16.

McLennan, J., Akande, A., & Bates, G. W. (1993). Death anxiety and death denial: Nigerian and Australian students' metaphors of personal death. *Journal of Psychology, 127,* 399–407.

Mead, M. (1970). Marriage in two steps. In H. A. Otto (Ed.), *The family in search of a future.* New York: Appleton-Century-Crofts.

Medoff-Cooper, B., Carey, W. B., & McDevitt, S. C. (1993). The Early Infancy Temperament Questionnaire. *Journal of Developmental and Behavioral Pediatrics, 14,* 230–235.

Meltzoff, A. N., & Moore, M. K. (1989). Imitation in newborn infants: Exploring the range of gestures imitated and the underlying mechanisms. *Developmental Psychology, 25,* 954–962.

Meneese, W. B., Yutrzenka, B. A., & Vitale, P. (1992). An analysis of adolescent suicidal ideation. *Current Psychology: Research & Reviews, 11,* 51–58.

Mercer, C. D. (1990). Learning disabilities. In N. G. Haring & L. McCormick (Eds.), *Exceptional children and youth* (5th ed.). Columbus, Ohio: Merrill.

Mercer, J. R. (1973). *Labeling the mentally retarded.* Berkeley: University of California Press.

Mercer, M. E., Courage, M. L., & Adams, R. J. (1991). Contrast/color card procedure: A new test of young infants' color vision. *Optometry & Vision Science, 68,* 522–532.

Merriam, S. B. (1993). Butler's life review: How universal is it? *International Journal of Aging and Human Development, 37,* 163–175.

Mesibov, G. B., & Van Bourgondien, M. E. (1992). Autism. In S. R. Hooper, G. W. Hynd, & R. E. Mattison (Eds.), *Developmental disorders: Diagnostic criteria and clinical assessment.* Hillsdale, NJ: Erlbaum.

Meyer, W. J. (1985). Summary, integration, and prospective. In J. B. Dusek (Ed.), *Teacher expectancies.* Hillsdale, NJ: Erlbaum.

Michael, R. T., Gagnon, J. H., Laumann, E. O., & Kolata, G. (1994). *Sex in America: A definitive survey.* New York: Little Brown.

Miller, B. D. (1981). *The endangered sex: Neglect of female children in rural North India.* Ithaca, NY: Cornell University Press.

Miller, C. E., Edwards, J. G., Shipley, C. F., & Best, R. B. (1990). Assessment of routine amniocentesis for unexplained maternal serum alpha-fetoprotein elevations. In B. A. Fine, E. Getting, K. Greendale, B. Leopold, & N. W. Paul (Eds.), *Strategies in genetic counseling: Reproductive genetics and new technologies.* White Plains, NY: March of Dimes Birth Defects Foundation.

Miller, C. T., Clarke, R. T., & Malcarno, V. L. (1991). Expectations and social interactions of children with and without mental retardation. *Journal of Special Education, 24,* 54–72.

Miller, D. A., McCluskey-Fawcett, K., & Irving, L. M. (1993). The relationship between childhood sexual abuse and subsequent onset of bulimia nervosa. *Child Abuse & Neglect: The International Journal, 17,* 305–314.

Miller, G. A. (1956). The magical number seven, plus or minus two: Some limits on our capacity for processing information. *Psychological Review, 63,* 81–97.

Miller, J. B., & Lane, M. (1991). Relations between young adults and their parents. *Journal of Adolescence, 14,* 179–194.

Miller, L. B., & Bizzell, R. P. (1983). Long-term effects of four preschool programs: sixth, seventh, and eighth grades. *Child Development, 54,* 727–741.

Miller, P. H. (1993). *Theories of developmental psychology* (3rd ed.). New York: W. H. Freeman.

Miller, S. A. (1981, April). *Certainty and necessity in the understanding of Piagetian concepts.* Paper presented at the Society for Research in Child Development Meetings, Boston.

Mills, M., Davies, H. T., & Macrae, W. A. (1994). Care of dying patients in hospital. *British Medical Journal, 309*, 583–586.

Miyawaki, K., Strange, W., Verbrugge, K., Liberman, A. M., Jenkins, J. J., & Fujimura, O. (1975). An effect of linguistic experience: The discrimination of [r] and [l] by native speakers of Japanese and English. *Perception & Psychophysics, 18*, 331–340.

Moerk, E. L. (1991). Positive evidence for negative evidence. *First Language, 11*, 219–251.

Moffatt, S. (1991). Becoming bilingual in the classroom: Code choice in school. *Language and Education: An International Journal, 5*, 55–71.

Moffitt, A. R. (1971). Consonant cue perception by 20–24 week old infants. *Child Development, 42*, 717–731.

Mom, 60, delivers healthy girl. (1994, Feb. 22, Jerusalem, AP). *Edmonton Sun*, p. 18.

Montemayor, R., & Flannery, D. J. (1990). Making the transition from childhood to early adolescence. In R. Montemayor, G. R. Adams, & T. P. Gullotta (Eds.), *From childhood to adolescence: A transitional period? (Advances in Adolescent Development*, Vol. 2). Newbury Park, CA: Sage.

Montessori, M. (1912). *The Montessori method.* New York: Frederick A. Stokes.

Moore, C., & Frye, D. (1991). The acquisition and utility of theories of mind. In D. Frye & C. Moore (Eds.), *Children's theories of mind: Mental states and social understanding.* Hillsdale, NJ: Erlbaum.

Moore, R. C. (1986). *Childhood's domain: Play and place in child development.* London: Croom Helm.

Morgane, P. J., Austin-LaFrance, R., Bronzino, J., Tonkiss, J., Diaz-Cintra, S., Cintra, L., Kemper, T., & Galler, J. R. (1993). Prenatal malnutrition and development of the brain. *Neuroscience & Biobehavioral Reviews, 17*, 91–128.

Morganti, J. B., Nehrke, M. F., Hulicka, I. M., & Cataldo, J. R. (1988). Life-span differences in life satisfaction, self-concept, and locus of control. *International Journal of Aging and Human Development, 26*, 45–56.

Moriarty, A. (1990). Deterring the molester and abuser. Pre-employment testing for child and youth care workers. *Child and Youth Care Quarterly, 18*, 59–65.

Morinaga, Y., Frieze, I., & Ferligoj, A. (1993). Career plans and gender-role attitudes of college students in the United States, Japan, and Slovenia. *Sex Roles: A Journal of Research, 29*, 317–334.

Morioka, I., Shiraishi, T., Nishimura, K., Kuroda, M., Kuriyama, Y., Matsui, K., Matsumoto, K., & Takeda, S. (1990). Age variation in the upper limit of hearing and amplitude of eye accommodation in childhood and adolescence. *Annals of Human Biology, 17*, 235–243.

Morrill, C. M., Leach, J. N., Shreeve, W. C., Radenaugh, M. R., & Linder, K. (1991). Teenage obesity. An academic issue. *International Journal of Adolescence and Youth, 2*, 245–250.

Morris, A. M., Williams, J. M., Atwater, A. E., & Wilmore, J. H. (1982). Age and sex differences in motor performance of 3 through 6 year old children. *Research Quarterly for Exercise and Sport, 534*, 214–221.

Morton, J., & Johnson, M. H. (1991). CONSPEC and CONLERN: A two-process theory of infant face recognition. *Psychological Review, 98*, 164–181.

Moseley, M. J. (1990). Mother–child interaction with preschool language-delayed children: Structuring conversations. *Journal of Communication Disorders, 23*, 187–203.

Mosley, W. H. (1994). Population change, health planning and human resource development in the health sector. *World Health Statistics Quarter—Rapport Trimestriel de Statistiques Sanitaires Mondiales, 47*, 26–30.

Moss, M. S., Moss, S. Z., & Rubinstein, R. (1993). Impact of elderly mother's death on middle age daughters. *International Journal of Aging and Human Development, 37*, 1–22.

Mott, F. L. (1991). Developmental effects of infant care: The mediating role of gender and health. *Journal of Social Issues, 47*, 139–158.

Mowat, F. (1952). *People of the deer.* Boston: Little, Brown.

Moynahan, E. D. (1973). The development of knowledge concerning the effect of categorization upon free recall. *Child Development, 44*, 238–245.

Muecke, L., Simons-Morton, B., & Huang, I. W. (1992). Is childhood obesity associated with high-fat foods and low physical activity? *Journal of School Health, 62*, 19–23.

Mulcahy, B. F. (1991). Developing autonomous learners. *Alberta Journal of Educational Research, 37*, 385–397.

Mullin, J. B. (1992). Children prenatally exposed to cocaine and crack: Implications for schools. *B.C. Journal of Special Education, 16*, 282–289.

Mullis, R. L., Youngs, G. A., Jr., Mullis, A. K., & Rathge, R. W. (1993). Adolescent stress: Issues of measurement. *Adolescence, 28*, 280–290.

Murdock, G. P. (1957). World ethnographic sample. *American Anthropologist, 59*, 676–688.

Murphy, C., Cain, W. S., Gilmore, M. M., & Skinner, R. B. (1991). Sensory and semantic factors in recognition memory for odors and graphic stimuli: Elderly versus young persons. *American Journal of Psychology, 104*, 161–192.

Murray, J., Henjum, R., & Freeze, R. (1992). Analysis of male and female experiences with abuse in family of origin. *Canadian Journal of Special Education, 8*, 90–100.

Muss, R. E. (1988). Carol Gilligan's theory of sex differences in the development of moral reasoning during adolescence. *Adolescence, 23,* 229–243.

Mussen, P. H., Honzik, M. P., & Eichorn, D. H. (1982). Early adult antecedents of life satisfaction at age 70. *Journal of Gerontology, 37,* 316–322.

Muzzin, L. J., Anderson, N. J., Figueredo, A. T., & Gudelis, S. O. (1994). The experience of cancer. *Social Science and Medicine, 38,* 1201–1208.

Myers, J. E. (1993). Personal empowerment. *Aging International, 20,* 3–4, 6–8.

Myers, J. E., & Perrin, N. (1993). Grandparents affected by parental divorce: A population at risk? *Journal of Counseling and Development, 71,* 62–66.

Nadelson, C. C., & Nadelson, T. (1980). Dual-career marriages: Benefits and costs. In F. Pepitone-Rockwell (Ed.), *Dual-career couples.* Beverly Hills, CA: Sage.

Nagel, K. L., & Jones, K. H. (1992). Predisposition factors in anorexia nervosa. *Adolescence, 27,* 381–386.

Naglieri, J. A. (1988). *DAP; draw a person: A quantitative scoring system.* New York: Harcourt Brace Jovanovich.

Nagy, M. H. (1948). The child's theories concerning death. *Journal of Genetic Psychology, 73,* 3–27.

Nanpon, H. (1991). Les âges de la vie: La représentation des âges de l'existence par un groupe de jeunes étudiants. *Enfance, 45,* 205–219.

Nazzari, M. (1991). *Disappearance of the dowry: Women, families, and social change in São Paulo, Brazil (1600–1900).* Stanford, CA: Stanford University Press.

Nehlig, A., & Debry, G. (1994). Consequences on the newborn of chronic maternal consumption of coffee during gestation and lactation: A review. *Journal of the American College of Nutrition, 13,* 6–21.

Neiger, B. L., & Hopkins, R. W. (1988). Adolescent suicide: Character traits of high-risk teenagers. *Adolescence, 23,* 468–475.

Nelson, K. (1993). Events, narratives, memory: What develops? In C. A. Nelson (Ed.), *Memory and affect in development: The Minnesota Symposia on Child Psychology* (Vol. 26). Hillsdale, NJ: Erlbaum.

Nelson, M. (1992). Cable TV: The re-regulation, re-wiring, and re-education of America. *Computers in Libraries, 12,* 40–42.

Nesselroade, J. R., & Baltes, P. B. (1984). Sequential strategies and the role of cohort effects in behavioral development: Adolescent personality (1970–72) as a sample case. In S. A. Mednick, M. Harway, & K. M. Finello (Eds.), *Handbook of longitudinal research* (Vol. 1): *Birth and childhood cohorts* (pp. 55–87). New York: Holt, Rinehart & Winston.

Nettelbeck, T., & Rabbitt, P. M. A. (1992). Aging, cognitive performance, and mental speed. *Intelligence, 16,* 189–205.

Neugarten, B. L. (1964). *Personality in middle and late life.* New York: Lieber-Atherton.

Neugarten, B. L. (Ed.). (1968). *Middle age and aging: A reader in social psychology.* Chicago: University of Chicago Press.

Neugarten, B. L. (1978). The wise of the young-old. In R. Gross, B. Gross, & S. Seidman (Eds.), *The new old: Struggling for decent aging.* New York: Doubleday-Anchor.

Neugarten, B. L., & Datan, N. (1981). The subjective experience of middle age. In L. D. Steinberg (Ed.), *The life cycle: Readings in human development.* New York: Columbia University Press.

Neugarten, B. L., & Weinstein, K. K. (1964). The changing American grandparents. *Journal of Marriage and the Family, 26,* 199–204.

Neugebauer, R. (1994). Impressive growth projected for centers into the 21st century. *Child Care Information Exchange, 95,* 80–87.

Neuman, S. B. (1991). *Literacy in the television age: The myth of the TV effect.* Norwood, NJ: Ablex.

Newcomb, A. F., Bukowski, W. M., & Pattee, L. (1993). Children's peer relations: A meta-analytic review of popular, rejected, neglected, controversial, and average sociometric status. *Psychological Bulletin, 113,* 99–128.

Newcomb, M. D., & Bentler, P. M. (1988). *Consequences of adolescent drug use: Impact on the lives of young adults.* Newbury Park, CA: Sage.

Newcomb, M. D., & Bentler, P. M. (1989). Substance use and abuse among children and teenagers. *American Psychologist, 44,* 242–248.

Newcombe, N., & Fox, N. A. (1994). Infantile amnesia: Through a glass darkly. *Child Development, 65,* 31–40.

Newman, L. F., & Buka, S. L. (1991). Clipped wings: The fullest look yet at how prenatal exposure to drugs, alcohol, and nicotine hobbles children's learning. *American Educator, 15,* 27–30, 33, 42.

Ng, S. H., Giles, H., & Moody, J. (1991). Information-seeking triggered by age. *International Journal of Aging and Human Development, 33,* 269–277.

Ngubane, H. (1986). *Zulus of southern Africa.* East Sussex, England: Wayland.

Nicolopoulou, A. (1993). Play, cognitive development, and the social world: Piaget, Vygotsky, and beyond. *Human Development, 36,* 1–23.

Nieman, D. C., & Henson, D. A. (1994). Role of endurance exercise in immune senescence. *Medicine and Science in Sports and Exercise, 26,* 172–181.

Nightingale, E. O., & Wolverton, L. (1993). Adolescent rolelessness in modern society. *Teacher's College Record, 94,* 472–486.

Nock, S. L. (1979). The family life cycle: Empirical or conceptual tool? *Journal of Marriage and the Family, 41,* 15–26.

Norcia, A. M., & Tyler, C. W. (1985). Spatial frequency sweep VEP: Visual acuity during the first year of life. *Vision Research, 25,* 1399–1408.

Novak, L. (1972). Aging, total body potassium, fat-free mass, and cell mass in males and females between ages 18 and 85 years. *Journal of Gerontology, 27,* 438–443.

Nozza, R. J., Miller, S. L., Rossman, R. N., & Bond, L. C. (1990a). Reliability and validity of infant speech–sound discrimination-in-noise thresholds. *Journal of Speech and Hearing Research, 34,* 643–650.

Nozza, R. J., Rossman, R. N., Bond, L. C., & Miller, S. L. (1990b). Infant speech–sound discrimination in noise. *Journal of the Acoustical Society of America, 87,* 339–350.

Nucci, L., Guerra, N., & Lee, J. (1991). Adolescent judgments of the personal, prudential, and normative aspects of drug use. *Developmental Psychology, 27,* 841–848.

Nunner-Winkler, G. (1984). Two moralities? A critical discussion of an ethic of care and responsibility versus an ethic of rights and justice. In W. M. Kurtines & J. L. Gewirtz (Eds.), *Morality, moral behavior, and moral development.* New York: John Wiley.

Nurmi, J. E. (1991). How do adolescents see their future? A review of the development of future orientation and planning. *Developmental Review, 11,* 1–59.

Oatley, K., & Jenkins, J. M. (1992). Human emotions: Function and dysfunction. *Annual Review of Psychology, 32,* 55–85.

Oberklaid, F., Sanson, A., Pedlow, R., Prior, M. (1993). Predicting preschool behavior problems from temperament and other variables in infancy. *Pediatrics, 91,* 113–120.

O'Brien, S. J., & Conger, P. R. (1991). No time to look back: Approaching the finish line of life's course. *International Journal of Aging and Human Development, 33,* 75–87.

O'Bryant, S. L. (1991). Older widows and independent lifestyles. *International Journal of Aging and Human Development, 32,* 41–51.

Oden, M. (1968). The fulfillment of promise: 40-year follow-up of the Terman gifted group. In R. S. Albert (Ed.) (1983). *Genius and eminence: The social psychology of creativity and exceptional achievement.* New York: Oxford University Press.

Oden, S. (1988). Alternative perspectives on children's peer relationships. In T. D. Yawkey & J. E. Johnson (Eds.), *Integrative processes and socialization: Early to middle childhood.* Hillsdale, NJ: Erlbaum.

Offer, D. O., Ostrov, E., & Howard, K. (1981). *The adolescent: A psychological self-portrait.* New York: Basic Books.

Offer, D. O., Ostrov, E., & Howard, K. (1984). *Patterns of adolescent self-image.* San Francisco: Jossey-Bass.

Offer, D. O., Ostrov, E., Howard, H., & Atkinson, R. (1988). *The teenage world: Adolescents' self-image in ten countries.* New York: Plenum.

Offner, S. (1992). A plain English map of the human chromosomes. *The American Biology Teacher, 54,* 87.

Offner, S. (1993). A revised map of the human chromosomes. *The American Biology Teacher, 55,* 406–410.

O'Hagan, H. (1979). Tay John. In D. Gutteridge (Ed.), *Rites of passage.* Toronto: McClelland & Stewart.

Ohba, M. (1979). What are the characteristics of the way of living in Japan? In Early Childhood Education Association of Japan (Ed.), *Early childhood education and care in Japan.* Tokyo, Japan: Child Honsha.

O'Leary, K. D., & Smith, D. A. (1991). Marital interactions. *Annual Review of Psychology, 42,* 191–212.

Ollendick, T. H., Weist, M. D., & Borden, M. C. (1992). Sociometric status and academic, behavioral, and psychological adjustment: A five-year longitudinal study. *Journal of Consulting and Clinical Psychology, 60,* 80–87.

O'Reilly, A. W., & Bornstein, M. H. (1993). Caregiver–child interaction in play. *New Directions for Child Development, 59,* 55–66.

Olweus, D. (1993). *Bullying at school: What we know and what we can do. Understanding children's worlds.* Cambridge, MA: Blackwell.

Ornstein, P. A., Baker-Ward, L., & Naus, M. J. (1988). The development of mnemonic skill. In F. E. Weinert & M. Perlmutter (Eds.), *Memory development: Universal changes and individual differences.* Hillsdale, NJ: Erlbaum.

Osterling, J., & Dawson, G. (1994). Early recognition of children with autism: A study of first birthday home videotapes. *Journal of Autism and Developmental Disorders, 24,* 247–257.

Ovcharchyn, C. A., Johnson, H. H., & Petzel, T. P. (1981). Type A behavior, academic aspirations, and academic success. *Journal of Personality, 49,* 248–256.

Ozturk, M., & Ozturk, O. M. (1990). Thumbsucking and falling asleep. *Turkish Journal of Pediatrics, 32,* 161–174.

Packard, V. (1968). *The sexual wilderness.* New York: Pocket Books.

Padilla, A. M. (1991). English only vs. bilingual education: Ensuring a language-competent society. *Journal of Education, 173*, 38–51.

Paikoff, R. L., & Brooks-Gunn, J. (1991). Do parent–child relationships change during puberty? *Psychological Bulletin, 110*, 47–66.

Paley, V. G. (1984). *Boys and girls: Superheroes in the doll corner*. Chicago: University of Chicago Press.

Paley, V. G. (1986). *Mollie is three: Growing up in school*. Chicago: University of Chicago Press.

Pallas, A. M., Natriello, G., & McDill, E. L. (1989). The changing nature of the disadvantaged population: Current dimensions and future trends. *Educational Researcher, 18*, 16–22.

Palmlund, I., Apfel, R., Buitendijk, S., Cabau, A., & Forsberg, J. G. (1993). Effects of diethylstilbestrol (DES) medication during pregnancy: From a symposium at the 10th International Congress of ISPOG. *Journal of Psychosomatic Obstetrics and Gynecology, 14*, 71–89.

Palo, P., & Erkkola, R. (1993). Risk factors and deliveries associated with preterm, severely small for gestational age fetuses. *American Journal of Perinatology, 10*, 88–91.

Pandey, H. (1991). Impact of preschool education component in Integrated Child Development Services programme on the cognitive development of children. *Journal of Tropical Pediatrics, 37*, 235–239.

Pangrazi, R. P., & Corbin, C. B. (1993). Physical fitness: Questions teachers ask. *Journal of Physical Education, Recreation & Dance, 64*, 14–19.

Pape, K. E., Kirsch, S. E., Galil, A., White, M. A., & Chipman, M. (1994). Neuromuscular approach to the motor deficits of cerebral palsy: A pilot study. *Journal of Pediatric Orthopaedics, 13*, 628–633.

Paris, S. G., & Lindauer, B. K. (1976). The role of inference in children's comprehension and memory for sentences. *Cognitive Psychology, 8*, 217–227.

Paris, S. G., & Lindauer, B. K. (1982). Cognitive development in infancy. In B. B. Wolman et al. (Eds.), *Handbook of developmental psychology*. Englewood Cliffs, NJ: Prentice-Hall.

Park, K. A., Lay, K. L., & Ramsay, L. (1993). Individual differences and developmental changes in preschoolers' friendships. *Developmental Psychology, 29*, 264–270.

Parke, R. D. (1994). Progress, paradigms, and unresolved problems: A commentary on recent advances in our understanding of children's emotions. *Merrill-Palmer Quarterly, 40*, 157–169.

Parker, J. G., & Asher, S. R. (1993). Friendship and friendship quality in middle childhood: Links with peer group acceptance and feelings of loneliness and social dissatisfaction. *Developmental Psychology, 29*, 611–621.

Parkhurst, J. T., & Asher, S. R. (1992). Rejection in middle school: Subgroup differences in behavior, loneliness, and interpersonal concerns. *Developmental Psychology, 28*, 231–241.

Parten, M. B. (1932). Social participation among preschool children. *Journal of Abnormal Social Psychology, 27*, 243–270.

Pasley, K., Dollahite, D. C., & Ihinger-Tallman, M. (1993). Bridging the gap: Clinical applications of research findings on the spouse and stepparent roles in remarriage. *Family Relations, 42*, 315–322.

Passino, A. W., Whitman, T. L., Borkowski, J. G., Schellenbach, C. J., Maxwell, S. E., Keogh, D., & Rellinger, E. (1993). Personal adjustment during pregnancy and adolescent parenting. *Adolescence, 28*, 67–79.

Passman, R. H. (1987). Attachments to inanimate objects: Are children who have security blankets insecure? *Journal of Consulting and Clinical Psychology, 55*, 825–830.

Passman, R. H., & Adams, R. E. (1982). Preferences for mothers and security blankets and their effectiveness as reinforcers for young children's behaviors. *Journal of Child Psychology and Psychiatry, 23*, 223–236.

Passman, R. H., & Halonen, J. S. (1979). A developmental survey of young children's attachments to inanimate objects. *The Journal of Genetic Psychology, 134*, 165–178.

Passman, R. H., & Weisberg, P. (1975). Mothers and blankets as agents for promoting play and exploration by young children in a novel environment: The effects of social and nonsocial attachment objects. *Developmental Psychology, 11*, 170–177.

Patel, B. D. (1994). The fragile X syndrome. *British Journal of Clinical Practice, 48*, 42–44.

Patterson, G., DeBaryshe, B., & Ramsey, E. (1989). A developmental perspective on antisocial behavior. *American Psychologist, 44*, 329–335.

Pattison, E. M. (1977). *The experience of dying*. Englewood Cliffs, NJ: Prentice-Hall.

Patton, J. M., Prillaman, D., & Tassel-Baska, J. V. (1990). The nature and extent of programs for the disadvantaged gifted in the United States and territories. *Gifted Child Quarterly, 34*, 94–96.

Patton, J. R., & Polloway, E. A. (1990). Mild mental retardation. In N. G. Haring & L. McCormick (Eds.), *Exceptional children and youth* (5th ed.). Columbus, OH: Charles E. Merrill.

Paul, R., & Alforde, S. (1993). Grammatical morpheme acquisition in 4-year-olds with normal, impaired, and late-developing language. *Journal of Speech and Hearing Research, 36*, 1271–1275.

Pavlov, I. P. (1927). *Conditional reflexes*. London: Oxford University Press.

Pawlik, K. (1991). The psychology of global environmental change: Some basic data and an agenda for cooperative international research. *International Journal of Psychology, 26,* 547–563.

Pearce, J. C. (1977). *Magical child: Rediscovering nature's plan for our children*. New York: Bantam Books.

Pearl, R., Bryan, T., & Herzog, A. (1990). Resisting or acquiescing to peer pressure to engage in misconduct: Adolescents' expectations of probable consequences. *Journal of Youth and Adolescence, 19,* 43–55.

Pearson, J. L., & Ferguson, L. R. (1989). Gender differences in patterns of spatial ability, environmental cognition, and math and English achievement in late adolescence. *Adolescence, 24,* 421–431.

Pease-Alvarez, L., & Hakuta, K. (1992). Enriching our views of bilingualism and bilingual education. *Educational Researcher, 2,* 4–6.

Peck, R. C. (1968). Psychological developments in the second half of life. In B. L. Neugarten (Ed.), *Middle age and aging*. Chicago: University of Chicago Press.

Pelaez-Nogueras, M., & Gewirtz, J. L. (1993). *Mothers' contingent imitation increases infant vocalizations*. Paper presented at the Biennial Meeting of the Society for Research in Child Development, New Orleans, March 25–28.

Pelham, W. E., Jr., Carlson, C., Sams, S. E., Vallano, G., Dixon, M. J., & Hoza, B. (1993). Separate and combined effects of methylphenidate and behavior modification on boys with attention deficit-hyperactivity disorder in the classroom. *Journal of Consulting & Clinical Psychology, 61,* 506–515.

Pelham, W. E., Jr., McBurnett, K., Harper, G. W., Milich, R., Murphy, D. A., Clinton, J., & Thiele, C. (1990). Methylphenidate and baseball playing in ADHD children: Who's on first? *Journal of Consulting and Clinical Psychology, 58,* 130–133.

Pellman, J. (1992). Widowhood in elderly women: Exploring its relationship to community integration, hassles, stress, social support, and social support seeking. *International Journal of Aging and Human Development, 35,* 253–264.

Pendergast, D. R., Fisher, N. M., & Calkins, E. (1993). Cardiovascular, neuromuscular, and metabolic alterations with age leading to frailty. *Journal of Gerontology, 48,* 61–67.

Penner, L. A., Thompson, J. K., & Coovert, D. L. (1991). Size overestimation among anorexics: Much ado about very little? *Journal of Abnormal Psychology, 100,* 90–93.

Pentz, M. A. (1994). Primary prevention of adolescent drug abuse. In C. B. Fisher & R. M. Lerner (Eds.), *Applied developmental psychology*. New York: McGraw-Hill.

Peplau, L. A. (1981). What homosexuals want in relationships. *Psychology Today, 15,* pp. 28–38.

Pergament, E. (1990). Reproductive genetics in the 21st century: Fact and fantasy. In B. A. Fine, E. Getting, K. Greendale, B. Leopold, & N. W. Paul (Eds.), *Strategies in genetic counseling: Reproductive genetics and new technologies*. White Plains, NY: March of Dimes Birth Defects Foundation.

Perkins, D., Jay, E., & Tishman, S. (1993). Introduction: New conceptions of thinking. *Educational Psychologist, 28,* 1–5.

Perlmutter, M. (1980). Development of memory in the preschool years. In R. Greene & T. D. Yawkey (Eds.), *Childhood development*. Westport, CT: Technomic.

Perlmutter, M. (1988). Cognitive potential throughout life. In J. E. Birren & V. L. Bengtson (Eds.), *Emergent theories of aging*. New York: Springer.

Perlmutter, M. (1994). Cognitive skills within the context of adult development and old age. In C. B. Fisher & R. M. Lerner (Eds.), *Applied developmental psychology*. New York: McGraw-Hill.

Perner, J. (1991). On representing that: The asymmetry between belief and desire in children's theory of mind. In D. Frye & C. Moore (Eds.), *Children's theories of mind: Mental states and social understanding*. Hillsdale, NJ: Erlbaum.

Perry, P., Pasnak, R., & Holt, R. W. (1992). Instruction on concrete operations for children who are mildly mentally retarded. *Education and Training in Mental Retardation, 27,* 273–281.

Peters, H., & Theorell, C. J. (1991). Fetal and neonatal effects of maternal cocaine use. *Journal of Obstetric, Gynecologic, and Neonatal Nursing, 20,* 121–126.

Petersen, A. C. (1988). Adolescent development. *Annual Review of Psychology, 39,* 583–607.

Peterson, G. W., Leigh, G. K, & Day, R. D. (1984). Family stress theory and the impact of divorce on children. *Journal of Divorce, 7,* 1–20.

Peterson, K. L., & Roscoe, B. (1991). Imaginary audience behavior in older adolescent females. *Adolescence, 26,* 195–200.

Peverly, S. T. (1991). Problems with the knowledge-based explanation of memory and development. *Review of Educational Research, 61,* 71–93.

Phares, V. (1992). Where's poppa? The relative lack of attention to the role of fathers in child and adolescent psychopathology. *American Psychologist, 47,* 656–664.

Phillips, D., McCartney, K., & Scarr, S. (1987). Child-care quality and children's social development. *Developmental Psychology, 23,* 537–543.

Piaget, J. (1923). *Le langage et la pensée chez l'enfant.* London: Kegan Paul.

Piaget, J. (1932). *The moral judgment of the child.* London: Routledge & Kegan Paul.

Piaget, J. (1951). *Play, dreams and imitation in childhood.* New York: Norton.

Piaget, J. (1954). *The construction of reality in the child.* New York: Basic Books.

Piaget, J. (1961). The genetic approach to the psychology of thought. *Journal of Educational Psychology, 52,* 275–281.

Piaget, J., & Garcia, R. (1991). *Toward a logic of meanings*. Hillsdale, NJ: Erlbaum.

Pianta, R. C., & Ball, R. M. (1993). Maternal social support as a predictor of child adjustment in kindergarten. *Journal of Applied Developmental Psychology, 14,* 107–120.

Piattelli-Palmarini, M. (1994). Ever since language and learning: Afterthoughts on Piaget-Chomsky debate. *Cognition, 50,* 315–346.

Pierce, E. F., Butterworth, S. W., Lynn, T. D., O'Shea, J., & Hammer, W. G. (1992). Fitness profiles and activity patterns of entering college students. *Journal of American College Health, 41,* 59–62.

Pietrukowicz, M. E., & Johnson, M. M. S. (1991). Using life histories to individualize nursing home staff attitudes toward residents. *Gerontologist, 31,* 102–106.

Pill, C. J. (1990). Stepfamilies: Redefining the family. *Family Relations, 39,* 186–193.

Pina, D. L., & Bengtson, V. L. (1993). The division of household labor and wives' happiness: Ideology, employment, and perceptions of support. *Journal of Marriage and the Family, 55,* 901–912.

Pinchbeck, I., & Hewitt, M. (1973). *Children in English society* (Vol. 1). London: Routledge & Kegan Paul.

Pines, M. (1966). *Revolution in learning: The years from birth to six.* New York: Harper & Row.

Pinyerd, B. J. (1994). Infant cries: Physiology and assessment. *Neonatal Network, 13,* 15–20.

Pipp, S., & Haith, M. M. (1984). Infant visual responses: Which metric predicts best? *Journal of Experimental Child Psychology, 38,* 373–399.

Plomin, R. (1987). Developmental behavioral genetics and infancy. In J. D. Osofsky (Ed.), *Handbook of infant development* (2nd ed.). New York: John Wiley.

Plomin, R. (1989). Environment and genes: Determinants of behavior. *American Psychologist, 44,* 105–111.

Plomin, R., Reiss, D., Hetherington, E. M., & Howe, G. W. (1994). Nature and nurture: Genetic contributions to measures of family environment. *Developmental Psychology, 30,* 32–43.

Plotnick, R. D. (1992). The effects of attitudes on teenage premarital pregnancy and its resolution. *American Sociological Review, 57,* 800–811.

Pogrebin, L. C. (1980). *Growing up free: Raising your child in the 80's.* New York: McGraw-Hill.

Pogue-Geile, M. F., & Rose, R. J. (1985). Developmental genetic studies of adult personality. *Developmental Psychology, 21,* 547–557.

Polivy, J., & Herman, C. P. (1985). Dieting and binging: A causal analysis. *American Psychologist, 40,* 193–201.

Polson, B., & Newton, M. (1984). *Not my kid: A family's guide to kids and drugs.* New York: Arbor House.

Poon, L. W. (1985). Differences in human memory with aging: Nature, causes, and clinical implications. In J. E. Birren & K. W. Schaie (Eds.), *Handbook of the psychology of aging* (2nd ed.). New York: Van Nostrand Reinhold.

Poon, L. W., Messner, S., Martin, P., Noble, C. A., Clayton, G. M., & Johnson, M. A. (1992). The influences of cognitive resources on adaptation and old age. *International Journal of Aging and Human Development, 34,* 31–46.

Pope, A. W., Bierman, K. L., & Mumma, G. H. (1991). Aggression, hyperactivity, and inattention-immaturity: Behavior dimensions associated with peer rejection in elementary school boys. *Developmental Psychology, 27,* 663–671.

Pope, H. G., Hudson, J. I., Jurgelun-Todd, D., & Hudson, M. S. (1984). Prevalence of anorexia nervosa and bulimia in three student populations. *International Journal of Eating Disorders, 2,* 75–85.

Porcile, A., Gallardo, E., Onetto, P., & Schachter, D. (1994). Very low estrogen-desogestrel contraceptive in perimenopausal hormonal replacement. *Maturitas, 18,* 93–103.

Porter, R. H., Makin, J. W., Davis, L. B., & Christensen, K. M. (1991). An assessment of the salient olfactory environment of formula-fed infants. *Physiology and Behavior, 50,* 907–911.

Post, S. G. (1994). Genetics, ethics, and Alzheimer disease. *Journal of the American Geriatrics Society, 42,* 782–786.

Potts, R., & Henderson, J. (1991). The dangerous world of television: A content analysis of physical injuries in children's television programming. *Children's Environments Quarterly, 8,* 7–14.

Powell, M. B. (1991). Investigating and reporting child sexual abuse: Review and recommendations for clinical practice. *Australian Psychologist, 26,* 77–83.

Preemies' diet seen key to progress. (1988, Feb. 1). *Edmonton Journal*, p. C1.

Preyer, W. (1888/1889). *The mind of the child* (2 vols.). New York: Appleton-Century-Crofts. (First published in German, 1882.)

Proite, R., Dannells, M., & Benton, S. L. (1993). Gender, sex-role stereotypes, and the attribution of responsibility for date and acquaintance rape. *Journal of College Student Development, 34*, 411–417.

Pyryt, M. C. (1993). The three faces of creativity revisited: Intimacy, passion, and commitment. *Gifted Education International, 9*, 22–23.

Quaid, K. A., & Morris, M. (1993). Reluctance to undergo predictive testing: The case of Huntington disease. *American Journal of Medical Genetics, 45*, 41–45.

Quan, M. (1994). Pelvic inflammatory disease: Diagnosis and management. *Journal of the American Board of Family Practice, 7*, 110–123.

Quay, H. C. (1987). Intelligence. In H. C. Quay (Ed.), *Handbook of juvenile delinquency* (pp. 106–117). New York: John Wiley.

Quinn, R. P., Staines, G. L., & McCullough, M. (1974). Job satisfaction: Is there a trend? *U.S. Department of Labor, Manpower Research Monograph No. 30.* Washington, DC: U.S. Government Printing Office.

Rabiner, D. L., Keane, S. P., & Mackinnon-Lewis, C. (1993). Children's beliefs about familiar and unfamiliar peers in relation to their sociometric status. *Developmental Psychology, 29*, 236–243.

Rahe, R. H. (1972). Subjects' recent life changes and their near-future illness susceptibility. In Z. J. Lipowski (Ed.), *Advances in psychosomatic medicine* (Vol. 8): *Psychosocial aspects of physical illness*. Basel, Switzerland: S. Karger.

Rahman, O. (1993). Excess mortality for the unmarried in rural Bangladesh. *International Journal of Epidemiology, 22*, 445–456.

Randhawa, B. S. (1991). Gender differences in academic achievement: A closer look at mathematics. *Alberta Journal of Educational Research, 37*, 241–257.

Ranney, M. D. (1991). SIDS and parents. In C. A. Corr, H. Fuller, C. A. Barnickol, & D. M. Corr (Eds.), *Sudden Infant Death Syndrome: Who can help and how*. New York: Springer.

Ransom, R. L., Sutch, R., & Williamson, S. H. (1993). Inventing pensions: The origins of the company-provided pension in the United States, 1900–1940. In K. W. Schaie & W. A. Achenbaum (Eds.), *Societal impact on aging: Historical perspectives*. New York: Springer.

Rappaport, W., & Witzke, D. (1993). Education about death and dying during the clinical years of medical school. *Surgery, 113*, 163–165.

Ratner, H. H., Padgett, R. J., & Bushey, N. (1988). Old and young adults' recall of events. *Developmental Psychology, 24*, 664–671.

Ray, William J. (1993). *Methods toward a science of behavior and experience*. Pacific Grove: Brooks/Cole.

Rayna, S., Sinclair, H., & Stambak, M. (1989). Infants and physics. In H. Sinclair, M. Stambak, I. Lézine, S. Rayna, & M. Verba (Eds.), *Infants and objects: The creativity of cognitive development*. New York: Academic Press.

Read, B. K. (1994). Motivation factors in technical college women's selection of nontraditional careers. *Journal of Career Development, 20*, 239–258.

Recommended dietary allowances (9th ed.). (1980). Washington, DC: National Academy of Sciences.

Redding, N. P., & Dowling, W. D. (1992). Rites of passage among women reentering higher education. *Adult Education Quarterly, 42*, 221–236.

Reich, J. W., & Zautra, A. J. (1991). Analyzing the trait of routinization in older adults. *International Journal of Aging and Human Development, 32*, 161–180.

Reid, L. D., & Carpenter, D. J. (1990). Alcohol-abuse and alcoholism. In L. D. Reid (Ed.), *Opioids, bulimia, and alcohol abuse & alcoholism*. New York: Springer-Verlag.

Reissland, N. (1988). Neonatal imitation in the first hour of life: Observations in rural Nepal. *Developmental Psychology, 24*, 464–469.

Reschly, D. J. (1990). Adaptive behavior. In A. Thomas & J. Grimes (Eds.), *Best practices in school psychology* (2nd ed.). Washington, DC: National Association of School Psychologists.

Reschly, D. J. (1992). Mental retardation: Conceptual foundations, definitional criteria, and diagnostic operations. In S. R. Hooper, G. W. Hynd, & R. E. Mattison (Eds.), *Developmental disorders: Diagnostic criteria and clinical assessment*. Hillsdale, NJ: Erlbaum.

Rescorla, L. (1991). Early academics: Introduction to the debate. *New Directions for Child Development, 53*, 5–11.

Resnick, H. S., Kilpatrick, D. G., & Dansky, B. S. (1993). Prevalence of civilian trauma and posttraumatic stress disorder in a representative national sample of women. *Journal of Consulting and Clinical Psychology, 61*, 984–991.

Reyome, N. D. (1993). A comparison of the school performance of sexually abused, neglected and non-maltreated children. *Child Study Journal, 23*, 17–38.

Rheingold, H. L. (1985). Development as the acquisition of familiarity. *Annual Review of Psychology, 36*, 1–17.

Ricciardelli, L. A. (1992). Bilingualism and cognitive development in relation to threshold theory. *Journal of Psycholinguistic Research, 21*, 301–316.

Ricciuti, H. N. (1991). Malnutrition and cognitive development: Research-policy linkages and current research directions. In L. Okagaki & R. J. Sternberg (Eds.), *Directors of development: Influences on the development of children's thinking*. Hillsdale, NJ: Erlbaum.

Ricco, R. B. (1993). Revising the logic of operations as a relevance logic: From hypothesis testing to explanation. *Human Development, 36,* 125–146.

Rice, B. (1982, February). The Hawthorne defect: Persistence of a flawed theory. *Psychology Today,* pp. 71–74.

Rice, E. (1972). *Mother India's children*. New York: Friendship Press.

Rice, M. L. (1989). Children's language acquisition. *American Psychologist, 44,* 149–156.

Richards, L. N., & Schmeige, C. J. (1993). Problems and strengths of single-parent families: Implications for practice and policy. *Family Relations, 42,* 277–285.

Richardson, V., & Kilty, K. M. (1991). Adjustment to retirement: Continuity vs. discontinuity. *International Journal of Aging and Human Development, 33,* 151–169.

Ridley-Johnson, R., Surdy, T., & O'Laughlin, E. (1991). Parent survey on television violence viewing: Fear, aggression, and sex differences. *Journal of Applied Developmental Psychology, 12,* 63–71.

Riegel, K. F. (1970). The language acquisition process: A reinterpretation of selected research findings. In L. R. Goulet & P. B. Baltes (Eds.), *Life-span developmental psychology: Research and theory*. New York: Academic Press.

Riegel, K. F. (1972). Influence of economic and political ideologies on the development of developmental psychology. *Psychological Bulletin, 78,* 129–141.

Riegel, K. F. (1973a). Dialectic operations: The final period of cognitive development. *Human Development, 16,* 346–370.

Riegel, K. F. (1973b). Language and cognition: Some life-span developmental issues. *Gerontologist, 13,* 478–482.

Riegel, K. F. (1976). The dialectics of human development. *American Psychologist, 31,* 689–700.

Riegel, K. F., & Riegel, R. M. (1972). Development, drop, and death. *Developmental Psychology, 6,* 306–319.

Ringwalt, C. L., & Palmer, J. H. (1989). Cocaine and crack users compared. *Adolescence, 24,* 851–859.

Ritts, V., Patterson, M. L., & Tubbs, M. E. (1992). Expectations, impressions, and judgments of physically attractive students: A review. *Review of Educational Research, 62,* 413–426.

Robbins, S. B., Lee, R. M., & Han, T. T. M. (1994). Goal continuity as a mediator of early retirement adjustment: Testing a multidimensional model. *Journal of Counseling Psychology, 41,* 18–26.

Roberts, P., & Newton, P. (1990). Levinsonian studies of women's adult development. *Psychology and Aging, 2,* 154–163.

Roberts, T. W. (1992). Sexual attraction and romantic love: Forgotten variables in marital therapy. *Journal of Marital and Family Therapy, 18,* 357–364.

Robertson, S. S. (1993a). Mechanism and function of cyclicity in spontaneous movement. In W. P. Smotherman & S. R. Robinson (Eds.), *Behavior of the fetus*. Caldwell, NJ: Telford.

Robertson, S. S. (1993b). Oscillation and complexity in early infant behavior. *Child Development, 64,* 1022–1035.

Robinson, P. J., & Fleming, S. (1992). Depressotypic cognitive patterns in major depression and conjugal bereavement. *Omega—Journal of Death and Dying, 25,* 291–305.

Robinson, S. (1989). Caring for childbearing women: The interrelationship between midwifery and medical responsibilities. In S. Robinson & A. M. Thomson (Eds.), *Midwives, research and childbirth* (Vol. 1). New York: Chapman & Hall.

Roche, J. P., & Ramsbey, T. W. (1993). Premarital sexuality: A five-year follow-up study of attitudes and behavior by dating stage. *Adolescence, 28,* 67–80.

Roethlisberger, S. J., & Dickson, W. J. (1939). *Management and the worker*. Cambridge, MA: Harvard University Press.

Rogers, C. R. (1951). *Client-centered therapy: Its current practice, its implications, and theory*. Boston: Houghton Mifflin.

Rogers, M. A., & Evans, W. J. (1993). Changes in skeletal muscle with aging: Effects of exercise training. *Exercise and Sport Sciences Reviews, 21,* 65–102.

Rogers, M. N. (1993). Are we on equal terms yet? Subject headings concerning women in "LCSH," 1975–1991. *Library Resources and Technical Services, 37,* 181–196.

Rolison, M. A., & Medway, F. J. (1985). Teachers' expectations and attributions for student achievement: Effects of label, performance, pattern, and special education intervention. *American Educational Research Journal, 22,* 561–573.

Rollins, B. C., & Feldman, H. (1981). Marital satisfaction over the family life cycle. In L. D. Steinberg (Ed.), *The life cycle: Readings in human development*. New York: Columbia University Press.

Romanin, S., & Over, R. (1993). Australian academics: Career patterns, work roles, and family life-cycle commitments of men and women. *Higher Education, 26,* 411–429.

Romig, C. A., & Bakken, L. (1990). Teens at risk for pregnancy: The role of ego development and family processes. *Journal of Adolescence, 13,* 195–199.

Rontoyannis, G. P. (1992). Sixty-three years of competitive sport activity. Case study. *Journal of Sports Medicine and Physical Fitness, 32*, 332–339.

Roopnarine, J. L., Johnson, J. E., & Hooper, F. H. (Eds.). (1994). *Children's play in diverse cultures.* Albany: State University of New York Press.

Roosa, M. W. (1991). Adolescent pregnancy programs collection: An introduction. *Family Relations, 40*, 370–372.

Rose, N. C., Palomaki, G. E., Haddow, J. E., Goodman, D. B., & Mennuti, M. T. (1994). Maternal serum alpha-fetoprotein screening for chromosomal abnormalities: A prospective study in women aged 35 and older. *American Journal of Obstetrics and Gynecology, 170*, 1073–1078.

Rosenak, D., Diamant, Y. Z., Yaffe, H., & Hornstein, E. (1990). Cocaine: Maternal use during pregnancy and its effect on the mother, the fetus, and the infant. *Obstetrical and Gynecological Survey, 45*, 348–357.

Rosengren, K. E., & Windahl, S. (1989). *Media matter: TV use in childhood and adolescence.* Norwood, NJ: Ablex.

Rosenkoetter, L. I., Huston, A. C., & Wright, J. C. (1990). Television and the moral judgment of the young child. *Journal of Applied Developmental Psychology, 11*, 123–137.

Rosenthal, E. R. (Ed.). (1990). *Women, aging, and ageism.* New York: Harrington Park Press.

Rosenthal, R., & Jacobson, L. (1968a). *Pygmalion in the classroom: Teacher expectations and pupils' intellectual development.* New York: Holt, Rinehart & Winston.

Rosenthal, R., & Jacobson, L. (1968b). Teacher expectations for the disadvantaged. *Scientific American, 218*, 19–23.

Ross, A. O. (1980). *Psychological disorders of children: A behavioral approach to theory, research, and therapy* (2nd ed.). New York: McGraw-Hill.

Ross, G., Lipper, E. G., & Auld, P. A. (1991). Educational status and school-related abilities of very low birth weight premature children. *Pediatrics, 88*, 1125–1134.

Rossing, B. E. (1991). Patterns of informal incidental learning: Insights from community action. *International Journal of Lifelong Education, 10*, 45–60.

Rothbart, M. K., & Ahadi, S. A. (1994). Temperament and the development of personality. *Journal of Abnormal Psychology, 103*, 55–66.

Rothstein E. (1980, Oct. 9). The scar of Sigmund Freud. *New York Review of Books*, pp. 14–20.

Rousseau, J. J. (1911). *Emile, or on education* (B. Foxley, Trans.). London: Dent. (Originally published 1762.)

Rovee-Collier, C. K. (1987). Learning and memory in infancy. In J. D. Osofsky (Ed.), *Handbook of infant development.* New York: John Wiley.

Rowan, A. B., Foy, D. W., & Rodriguez, N. (1994). Post-traumatic Stress Disorder in a clinical sample of adults sexually abused as children. *Child Abuse and Neglect: The International Journal, 18*, 151–161.

Royal College of Psychiatrists (1987). *Drug scenes: A report on drugs and drug dependence by the Royal College of Psychiatrists.* London: Gaskell Press.

Royer, J. M., Cisero, C. A., & Carlo, M. S. (1993). Techniques and procedures for assessing cognitive skills. *Review of Educational Research, 63*, 201–243.

Ruben, R. J. (1993). Communication disorders in children: A challenge for health care. *Preventive Medicine, 22*, 585–588.

Rubin, J. D., Ferencz, C., & Loffredo, C. (1993). Use of prescription and non-prescription drugs in pregnancy. The Baltimore-Washington Infant Study Group. *Journal of Clinical Epidemiology, 46*, 581–589.

Rubin, J. Z., Provenzano, J. J., & Luria, Z. (1974). The eye of the beholder: Parents' views on sex of newborns. *American Journal of Orthopsychiatry, 44*, 512–519.

Rubin, Z. (1970). Measurement of romantic love. *Journal of Personality and Social Psychology, 16*, 265–273.

Rubin, Z. (1980). *Children's friendships.* Cambridge, MA: Harvard University Press.

Ruff, H. A., & Saltarelli, L. M. (1993). Exploratory play with objects: Basic cognitive processes and individual differences. *New Directions for Child Development, 59*, 5–16.

Ruffman, T., Olson, D. R., Ash, T., & Keenan, T. (1993). The ABCs of deception: Do young children understand deception in the same way as adults? *Developmental Psychology, 29*, 74–87.

Runco, M. A. (1986a). Flexibility and originality in children's divergent thinking. *The Journal of Psychology, 120*, 345–352.

Runco, M. A. (1986b). Maximal performance on divergent thinking tests by gifted, talented, and nongifted children. *Psychology in the Schools, 23*, 308–315.

Rushforth, J. A., & Levene, M. I. (1994). Behavioural response to pain in healthy neonates. *Archives of Disease in Childhood, 70*, F174–F176.

Ryall, R. G., Staples, A. J., Robertson, E. F., & Pollard, A. C. (1992). Improved performance in a prenatal screening programme for Down's syndrome incorporating serum-free HCG subunit analyses. *Prenatal Diagnosis, 12*, 251–261.

Rymer, R. (1993). *Genie: A scientific tragedy.* New York: Harper Perennial.

Saarnio, D. A. (1993). Scene memory in young children. *Merrill-Palmer Quarterly, 39*, 196–212.

Sadowski, P. M., & Loesch, L. C. (1993). Using children's drawings to detect potential child sexual abuse.

Elementary School Guidance and Counseling, 28, 115–123.

Sagan, C. (1977). *The dragons of Eden.* New York: Ballantine Books.

Sagi, A., Ijzendoorn, M. H. Van, & Koren-Karie, N. (1991). Primary appraisal of the strange situation: A cross-cultural analysis of preseparation episodes. *Developmental Psychology, 27,* 587–596.

Sagov, S. E., Feinbloom, R. I., Spindel, P., & Brodsky, A. (1984). *Home births: A practitioner's guide to birth outside the hospital.* Rockville, MD: Aspen Systems Corporation.

Saidla, D. D. (1992). Children's rights regarding physical abuse. *Journal of Humanistic Education and Development, 31,* 73–83.

Salomon, G., Perkins, D. N., & Globerson, T. (1991). Partners in cognition: Extending human intelligence with intelligent technologies. *Educational Researcher, 20,* 2–9.

Salzinger, S., Feldman, R. S., & Hammer, M. (1993). The effects of physical abuse on children's social relationships. *Child Development, 64,* 169–187.

Sambrook, P., Kelly, P., & Eisman, J. (1993). Bone mass and ageing. *Baillieres Clinical Rheumatology, 7,* 445–457.

Sampson, J. P., Jr., & Reardon, R. C. (1990). Evaluating computer-assisted career guidance systems: Synthesis and implications. *Journal of Career Development, 17,* 143–149.

Sampson, J. P., Jr., Reardon, R. C., & Lenz, J. G. (1991). Computer-assisted career guidance: Improving the design and use of systems. *Journal of Career Development, 17,* 185–190.

Sarna, S., Sahi, T., Koskenvuo, M., & Kaprio, J. (1993). Increased life expectancy of world class male athletes. *Medicine and Science in Sports and Exercise, 25,* 237–244.

Sasser-Coen, J. R. (1993). Qualitative changes in creativity in the second half of life: A life-span developmental perspective. *Journal of Creative Behavior, 27,* 18–27.

Saunders, C. (1994). Euthanasia—Definition, dangers and alternatives. *Annals of the Academy of Medicine, Singapore, 23,* 300–303.

Savage-Rumbaugh, E. S., Murphy, J., Sevcik, R. A., Brakke, K. E., Williams, S. L., & Rumbaugh, D. M. (1993). Language comprehension in ape and child. *Monographs of the Society for Research in Child Development, 58,* 1–222.

Savin-Williams, R. C., & Small, S. A. (1986). The timing of puberty and its relationship to adolescent and parent perceptions of family interactions. *Developmental Psychology, 22,* 342–347.

Scarr, S., & Eisenberg, M. (1993). Child care research: Issues, perspectives, and results. *Annual Review of Psychology, 44,* 613–644.

The "Scene" and the Skinheads. (1990, Nov. 18). *Edmonton Journal,* p. E1.

Schaeffer, A. M., & Nelson, E. S. (1993). Rape-supportive attitudes: Effects of on-campus residence and education. *Journal of College Student Development, 34,* 175–179.

Schaffer, H. R. (1966). The onset of fear of strangers and the incongruity hypothesis. *Journal of Child Psychology and Psychiatry, 7,* 95–106.

Schaffer, H. R. (1984). *The child's entry into a social world.* New York: Academic Press.

Schaie, K. W. (1965). A general model for the study of developmental problems. *Psychological Bulletin, 64,* 92–107.

Schaie, K. W. (Ed.). (1983a). *Longitudinal studies of adult psychological development.* New York: Guilford Press.

Schaie, K. W. (1983b). The Seattle Longitudinal Study: A 21-year exploration of psychometric intelligence in adulthood. In K. W. Schaie (Ed.), *Longitudinal studies of adult psychological development* (pp. 64–135). New York: Guilford Press.

Schaie, K. W. (1983c). What can we learn from the longitudinal study of adult psychological development? In K. W. Schaie (Ed.), *Longitudinal studies of adult psychological development* (pp. 1–19). New York: Guilford Press.

Schaie, K. W. (1986, December). *Variability in cognitive function in the elderly: Implications for social participation.* Paper presented at the Symposium on Phenotypic Variation in Populations: Relevance to Risk Assessment. Brookhaven National Laboratory, Upton, New York.

Schaie, K. W. (1988). Internal validity threats in studies of adult cognitive development. In M. L. Howe & C. J. Brainerd (Eds.), *Cognitive development in adulthood: Progress in cognitive development research.* New York: Springer-Verlag.

Schaie, K. W. (1993). The Seattle Longitudinal Study: A thirty-five-year inquiry of adult intellectual development. *Zeitschrift fur Gerontologie, 26,* 129–137.

Schaie, K. W. (1994). The course of adult intellectual development. *American Psychologist, 49,* 304–313.

Scher, J., & Dix, C. (1983). *Will my baby be normal? Everything you need to know about pregnancy.* New York: Dial Press.

Schlegel, A., & Barry, H., III (1991). *Adolescence: An anthropological inquiry.* New York: The Free Press.

Schneider-Rosen, K., Braunwald, K. G., Carlson, V., & Cicchetti, D. (1985). Current perspectives in attachment theory: Illustration from the study of maltreated infants. In I. Bretherton & E. Waters (Eds.), *Growing points of attachment theory and research (Monographs of the Society for Research in Child Development, 50,* No. 209).

Schoen, R., & Weinick, R. M. (1993). Partner choice in marriages and cohabitations. *Journal of Marriage and the Family, 55,* 404–414.

Schultz, R., & Ewen, R. B. (1988). *Adult development and aging: Myths and emerging realities.* New York: Macmillan.

Schwartzman, H. B. (1987). A cross-cultural perspective on child-structured play activities and materials. In A. W. Gottfried & C. C. Brown (Eds.), *Play interactions: The contribution of play materials and parental involvement to children's development.* Lexington, MA: D. C. Heath.

Seals, D. R., Taylor, J. A., Ng, A. V., & Esler, M. D. (1994). Exercise and aging: Autonomic control of the circulation. *Medicine and Science in Sports and Exercise, 26,* 568–576.

Sears, P. S., & Barbee, A. H. (1977). Care and life satisfactions among Terman's gifted women. In J. C. Stanley, W. C. George, and C. H. Solano (Eds.), *The gifted and the creative: A fifty-year perspective.* Baltimore: Johns Hopkins University Press.

Seigle, S. P. (1993). On death and dying. *Connecticut Medicine, 57,* 69–71.

Selman, R. L. (1980). *The growth of interpersonal understanding.* New York: Academic Press.

Selman, R. L. (1981). The child as friendship philosopher. In S. R. Asher & J. M. Gottman (Eds.), *The development of children's friendships.* New York: Cambridge University Press.

Seltzer, M. M., & Ryff, C. D. (1994). Parenting across the life-span: The normative and nonnormative cases. In D. L. Featherman, R. M. Lerner, & M. Perlmutter (Eds.), *Lifespan development and behavior* (Vol. 12). Hillsdale, NJ: Erlbaum.

Semrud-Clikeman, M., & Hynd, G. W. (1992). Developmental arithmetic disorder. In S. R. Hooper, G. W. Hynd, & R. E. Mattison (Eds.), *Developmental disorders: Diagnostic criteria and clinical assessment.* Hillsdale, NJ: Erlbaum.

Serafini, S. (1991). Multiculturalism in the schools of Canada: Presentation to the fourth conference of CCMIE. *Multiculturalism, 14,* 12–14.

Serbin, L. A., Powlishta, K. K., & Gulko, J. (1993). The development of sex typing in middle childhood. *Monographs of the Society for Research in Child Development, 58,* No. 2.

Shanas, E. (1980). Older people and their families: The new pioneers. *Journal of Marriage and the Family, 42,* 9–15.

Shanklin, D. R., & Hodin, J. (1979). *Maternal nutrition and child health.* Springfield, IL: Charles C Thomas.

Sheard, N. F. (1994). Iron deficiency and infant development. *Nutrition Reviews, 52,* 137–140.

Shedler, J., & Block, J. (1990). Adolescent drug use and psychological health: A longitudinal inquiry. *American Psychologist, 45,* 612–630.

Sheehy, G. (1976). *Passages: Predictable crises of adult life.* New York: E. P. Dutton.

Sheehy, G. (1981). *Pathfinders.* New York: Morrow.

Shepherd-Look, D. L. (1982). Sex differentiation and the development of sex roles. In B. B. Wolman et al. (Eds.), *Handbook of developmental psychology.* Englewood Cliffs, NJ: Prentice-Hall.

Sheppard, H. (1976). Work and retirement. In R. Binstock & E. Shanas (Eds.), *Handbook of aging and the social sciences.* New York: Van Nostrand Reinhold.

Sherman, M., & Key, C. B. (1932). The intelligence of isolated mountain children. *Child Development, 3,* 279–290.

Shiferaw, B., Mittelmark, M. B., & Hofford, J . L. (1994). The investigation and outcome of reported cases of elder abuse: The Forsyth County Aging Study. *Gerontologist, 34,* 123–125.

Short, E. J., Schatschneider, C. W., Friebert, S. E. (1993). Relationship Between Memory and Metamemory Performance: A Comparison of Specific and General Strategy Knowledge. *Journal of Educational Psychology, 85,* 412–423.

Shortening the time between the bench and the bedside. (1993, Nov. 21). *University of Alberta Folio,* p. 4.

Shreeve, D. F. (1991). Elective mutism: Origins of stranger anxiety and selective attention. *Bulletin of the Menninger Clinic, 55,* 491–504.

Shreve, B. W., & Kunkel, M. A. (1991). Self-psychology, shame, and adolescent suicide: Theoretical and practical considerations. *Journal of Counseling and Development, 69,* 305–311.

Siegel, A. W., & White, S. H. (1982). The child study movement: Early growth and development of the symbolized child. In H. W. Reese (Ed.), *Advances in child development and behavior* (Vol. 17). New York: Academic Press.

Siegel, O. (1982). Personality development in adolescence. In B. B. Wolman et al. (Eds.), *Handbook of developmental psychology.* Englewood Cliffs, NJ: Prentice-Hall.

Siegler, R. S. (1989). Mechanisms of cognitive development. *Annual Review of Psychology, 40,* 353–379.

Sigel, I. E. (1987). Does Hothousing rob children of their childhood? *Early Childhood Research Quarterly, 2,* 211–225.

Silverstein, F. S., & Johnston, M. V. (1990). Neurological assessment of children: The damaged child. In R. D. Eden, F. H. Boehm, & M. Haire (Eds.), *Assessment and care of the fetus: Physiological, clinical, and medicolegal principles.* Norwalk, CT: Appleton & Lange.

Silverstein, L. B. (1991). Transforming the debate about child care and maternal employment. *American Psychologist, 46,* 1025–1032.

Silvestri, G. T., & Lukasiewicz, J. M. (1989). Projections of occupational employment: 1988–2000. *Monthly Labor Review, 112,* 42–65.

Silvestri, L., Dantonio, M., & Eason, S. (1994). Enhancement of self-esteem in at-risk elementary students. *Journal of Health Education, 25,* 30–36.

Simic, M. G. (1992). The rate of DNA damage and aging. *EXS, 62,* 20–30.

Simmons, L. (1960). Aging in preindustrial societies. In C. Tibbitts (Ed.), *Handbook of social gerontology.* Chicago: University of Chicago Press.

Simmons, R. G., & Blyth, D. (1987). *Moving into adolescence: The impact of pubertal change and school context.* New York: Aldine & Gruyter.

Simon, L. (1992). Mainstreaming: Is it in the best interests of all children? *B.C. Journal of Special Education, 16,* 131–138.

Simpson, J. L. (1991). Aetiology of pregnancy failure. In M. Chapman, G. Grudzinskas, & T. Chard (Eds.), *The embryo: Normal and abnormal development and growth.* New York: Springer-Verlag.

Singer, D. G., & Singer, J. L. (1990). *The house of make-believe: Children's play and developing imagination.* Cambridge, MA: Harvard University Press.

Singh, J. A., & Zingg, R. N. (1942). *Wolf-children and feral man.* New York: Harper & Row.

Skinner, B. F. (1953). *Science and human behavior.* New York: Macmillan.

Skinner, B. F. (1957). *Verbal behavior.* Englewood Cliffs, NJ: Prentice-Hall.

Skinner, B. F. (1961). *Cumulative record* (rev. ed.). New York: Appleton-Century-Crofts.

Skinner, E. A., & Wellborn, J. G. (1994). Coping during childhood and adolescence: A motivational perspective. In D. L. Featherman, R. M. Lerner, & M. Perlmutter (Eds.), *Lifespan development and behavior* (Vol. 12). Hillsdale, NJ: Erlbaum.

Skolnick, A. (1978, February). The myth of the vulnerable child. *Psychology Today,* pp. 56–60, 65.

Skolnick, A. (1981). Married lives: Longitudinal perspectives on marriage. In D. H. Eichorn, J. A. Clausen, N. Haan, M. P. Honzik, & P. H. Mussen (Eds.), *Present and past in middle life.* New York: Academic Press.

Sleeping with the enemy. (1991, Dec. 9). *Newsweek,* 58–59.

Small, S. A., & Eastman, G. (1991). Rearing adolescents in contemporary society: A conceptual framework for understanding the responsibilities and needs of parents. *Family Relations, 40,* 455–462.

Smith, C. L. (1979). Children's understanding of natural language hierarchies. *Journal of Experimental Child Psychology, 27,* 437–458.

Smith, C. V., Satt, B., Phelan, J. P., & Paul, R. H. (1990). Intrauterine sound levels: Intrapartum assessment with an intrauterine microphone. *American Journal of Perinatology, 7,* 312–315.

Smith, D. F. (1994). Type A personalities tend to have low platelet monoamine oxidase activity. *Acta Psychiatrica Scandinavica, 89,* 88–91.

Smith, L. (1993). *Necessary knowledge: Piagetian perspectives on constructivism.* Hillsdale, NJ: Erlbaum.

Smith, M. A. B. (1994). Teen incentives program: Evaluation of a health promotion model for adolescent pregnancy prevention. *Journal of Health Education, 25,* 24–29.

Smith, M., & Yuen, K. (1994). Palliative care in the home. The GP/home hospice team. *Australian Family Physician, 23,* 1260–1265.

Smith, P. K., & Thompson, D. (Eds.). (1991). *Practical approaches to bullying.* London: David Fulton.

Smolak, L., Levine, M. P., & Gralen, S. (1993). The impact of puberty and dating on eating problems among middle school girls. *Journal of Youth and Adolescence, 22,* 355–368.

Smoll, F. L., & Schutz, R. W. (1990). Quantifying gender differences in physical performance: A developmental perspective. *Developmental Psychology, 26,* 360–369.

Snarey, J. (1993). *How fathers care for the next generation: A four-decade study.* Cambridge, MA: Harvard University Press.

Snyderman, M., & Rothman, S. (1987). Survey of expert opinion on intelligence and aptitude testing. *American Psychologist, 42,* 137–144.

Sobsey, D. (1993). Integration outcomes: Theoretical models and empirical investigations. *Developmental Disabilities Bulletin, 21,* 1–14.

Solnick, R. E., & Corby, N. (1983). Human sexuality and aging. In D. S. Woodruff & J. E. Birren (Eds.), *Aging: Scientific perspectives and social issues* (2nd ed.) (pp. 202–224). Pacific Grove, CA: Brooks/Cole.

Solstad, K., & Garde, K. (1992). Middle-aged Danish men's ideas of a male climacteric—and of the female climacteric. *Maturitas, 15,* 7–16.

Somers, M. D. (1993). A comparison of voluntarily child-free adults and parents. *Journal of Marriage and the Family, 55,* 643–650.

South, S. J. (1991). Sociodemographic differentials in mate selection preferences. *Journal of Marriage and the Family, 53,* 928–940.

Sparks, S. P., Jovanovic-Peterson, L., & Peterson, C. M. (1993). Blood glucose rise following prenatal vitamins in gestational diabetes. *Journal of the American College of Nutrition, 12,* 543–546.

Spellacy, W. N., Miller, S. J., & Winegar, A. (1986). Pregnancy after 40 years of age. *Obstetrics and Gynecology, 68,* 452–454.

Spence, A. P. (1989). *Biology of human aging.* Englewood Cliffs, NJ: Prentice-Hall.

Sperling, L. S., Henriksen, T. B., Ulrichsen, H. J., Hedegard, M., Moller, H., Hansen, V., Ovlisen, B., & Secher, N. J. (1994). Indications for cesarean section in singleton pregnancies in two Danish counties with different cesarean section rates. *Acta Obstetricia et Gynecologica Scandinavica, 73,* 129–135.

Spigset, O. (1994). Anaesthetic agents and excretion in breast milk. *Acta Anaesthesiologica Scandinavica, 38,* 94–103.

Spitz, G., Logan, J. R., Joseph, G., & Lee, E. (1994). Middle generation roles and the well-being of men and women. *Journal of Gerontology, 49,* S107–S116.

Springer, C., & Wallerstein, J. S. (1983). Young adolescents' responses to their parents' divorces. In L. A. Kurdek (Ed.), *Children and divorce: New directions for child development* (pp. 15–28). San Francisco: Jossey-Bass.

Squire, L. R., Knowlton, B., & Musen, G. (1993). The structure and organization of memory. *Annual Review of Psychology, 44,* 453–495.

Sroufe, L., & Waters, E. (1976). The ontogenesis of smiling and laughter: A perspective on the organization of development in infancy. *Psychological Review, 83,* 173–189.

Stack, S. (1993). The media and suicide: A nonadditive model, 1968–1980. *Suicide and Life-Threatening Behavior, 23,* 63–66.

Stall, R. D., Coates, T. J., & Hoff, C. (1988). Behavioral risk reduction for HIV infection among gay and bisexual men. *American Psychologist, 43,* 878–885.

Stambak, M., Sinclair, H., Verba, M., Moreno, L., & Rayna, S. (1989). Infants and logic. In H. Sinclair, M. Stambak, I. Lézine, S. Rayna, & M. Verba (Eds.), *Infants and objects: The creativity of cognitive development.* New York: Academic Press.

Stander, V., & Jensen, L. (1993). The relationship of value orientation to moral cognition: Gender and cultural differences in the United States and China explored. *Journal of Cross-Cultural Psychology, 24,* 42–52.

Stanford, L. D., & Hynd, G. W. (1994). Congruence of behavioral symptomatology in children with ADD/H, ADD/WO, and learning disabilities. *Journal of Learning Disabilities, 27,* 243–253.

Stanovich, K. E. (1992). Developmental reading disorder. In S. R. Hooper, G. W. Hynd, & R. E. Mattison (Eds.), *Developmental disorders: Diagnostic criteria and clinical assessment.* Hillsdale, NJ: Erlbaum.

Stanovich, K. E. (1993). Dysrationalia: A new specific learning disability. *Journal of Learning Disabilities, 26,* 501–515.

Stanton, W. R. (1993). A cognitive developmental framework. *Current Psychology: Research and Reviews, 12,* 26–45.

Statistics Canada (1992). *Earnings of men and women: 1990.* Ottawa: Minister of Industry, Science and Technology.

Stattin, H., & Klackenberg-Larsson, I. (1993). Early language and intelligence development and their relationship to future criminal behavior. *Journal of Abnormal Psychology, 102,* 369–378.

Stattin, H., & Magnusson, D. (1990). *Pubertal maturation in female development.* Hillsdale, NJ: Erlbaum.

Steenbarger, B. N. (1991). All the world is not a stage: Emerging contextualist themes in counseling and development. *Journal of Counseling and Development, 70,* 288–296.

Stephens, R. S., Roffman, R. A., & Simpson, E. E. (1993). Adult marijuana users seeking treatment. *Journal of Consulting and Clinical Psychology, 61,* 1100–1104.

Stern, C. (1956). Hereditary factors affecting adoption. In *A Study of Adoption Practices* (Vol. 2). New York: Child Welfare League of America.

Stern, P. C. (1992). Psychological dimensions of global environmental change. *Annual Review of Psychology, 43,* 269–302.

Sternberg, R. J. (1984). A contextualist view of the nature of intelligence. *International Journal of Psychology, 19,* 307–334.

Sternberg, R. J. (1985). *Beyond IQ: A triarchic theory of human intelligence.* New York: Cambridge University Press.

Sternberg, R. J. (1986). A triangular theory of love. *Psychological Review, 93,* 119–135.

Sternberg, R. J. (1991). Directors of development: A play in an unknown number of acts. In L. Okagaki & R. J. Sternberg (Eds.), *Directors of development: Influences on the development of children's thinking.* Hillsdale, NJ: Erlbaum.

Sternberg, R. J. (1992). Ability tests, measurements, and markets. *Journal of Educational Psychology, 84,* 134–140.

Sternberg, R. J. (1993). Would you rather take orders from Kirk or Spock? The relation between rational thinking and intelligence. *Journal of Learning Disabilities, 26,* 516–519.

Sternberg, R. J., & Berg, C. (1987). What are theories of adult intellectual development theories of? In C. Schooler & K. W. Schaie (Eds.), *Cognitive functioning* and social structure over the life course. Norwood, NJ: Ablex.

Stets, J. E. (1990). Verbal and physical aggression in marriage. *Journal of Marriage and the Family, 52,* 501–514.

Stets, J. E. (1993). The link between past and present intimate relationships. *Journal of Family Issues, 14,* 236–260.

Stevens, E. S. (1993). Making sense of usefulness: An avenue toward satisfaction in later life. *International Journal of Aging and Human Development, 37,* 315–325.

Stevens-Long, J. (1990). Adult development: Theories past and future. In R. A. Nemiroff & C. A. Colarusso (Eds.), *New dimensions in adult development.* New York: Basic Books.

Stevenson, H. W., Chen, C., Lee, S. Y., & Fuligni, A. J. (1991). Schooling, culture, and cognitive development. In L. Okagaki & R. J. Sternberg (Eds.), *Directors of development: Influences on the development of children's thinking.* Hillsdale, NJ: Erlbaum.

Stier, D. M., Leventhal, J. M., Berg, A. T., Johnson, L., & Mezger, J. (1993). Are children born to young mothers at increased risk of maltreatment? *Pediatrics, 91,* 642–648.

Stifter, C. A., & Fox, N. A. (1990). Infant reactivity: Physiological correlates of newborn and 5-month temperament. *Developmental Psychology, 26,* 582–588.

Stimpson, D., Neff, W., Jensen, L. C., & Newby, T. (1991). The caring morality and gender differences. *Psychological Reports, 69,* 407–414.

Stockman, J. A., III. (1990). Fetal hematology. In R. D. Eden, F. H. Boehm, & M. Haire (Eds.), *Assessment and care of the fetus: Physiological, clinical, and medicolegal principles.* Norwalk, CT: Appleton & Lange.

Stoll, S. K., & Beller, J. M. (1993). *The effect of a longitudinal teaching methodology and classroom environment on both cognitive and behavioral moral development.* Paper presented at the Annual Meeting of the American Alliance for Health, Physical Education, Recreation and Dance, Washington, DC, March 24–28.

Stoutjesdyk, D., & Jevne, R. (1993). Eating disorders among high performance athletes. *Journal of Youth and Adolescence, 22,* 271–279.

Straus, M. A. (1980a). The marriage license as a hitting license: Evidence from popular culture, law, and social science. In M. A. Straus & G. T. Hotaling (Eds.), *The social causes of husband–wife violence.* Minneapolis: University of Minnesota Press.

Straus, M. A. (1980b). Wife-beating: How common and why? In M. A. Straus & G. T. Hotaling (Eds.), *The social causes of husband–wife violence.* Minneapolis: University of Minnesota Press.

Straus, M. A., & Gelles, R. (1986). Societal change and change in family violence from 1975 to 1985 as revealed by two national surveys. *Journal of Marriage and the Family, 48,* 465–479.

Streissguth, A. P., Landesman-Dwyer, S., Martin, J. C., & Smith, D. W. (1980). Teratogen effects of alcohol in humans and laboratory animals. *Science, 209,* 353–361.

Strelau, J. (1989). Temperament risk factors in children and adolescents as studied in Eastern Europe. In W. B. Carey & S. C. McDevitt (Eds.), *Clinical and educational applications of temperament research.* Berwyn, PA: Swets North America.

Stroebe, M. (1992/1993). Coping with bereavement: A review of the grief work hypothesis. *Omega—Journal of Death and Dying, 26,* 19–42.

Sullivan, R. M., Taborsky-Barba, S., Mendoza, R., Itano, A., Leon, M., Cotman, C. W., Payne, T. F., & Lott, I. (1991). Olfactory classical conditioning in neonates. *Pediatrics, 87,* 511–518.

Super, D. (1990). A life-span life-space approach to career development. In D. Brown & L. Brooks (Eds.), *Career choice and development* (2nd ed.). San Francisco: Jossey-Bass.

Super, D. (1994). A life span, life space perspective on convergence. In M. L. Savikas & R. W. Lent (Eds.), *Convergence in career development theories.* Palo Alto, CA: CPP Books.

Suzuki, K. (1994). Molecular genetics of Tay–Sachs and related disorders: A personal account. *Journal of Neuropathology & Experimental Neurology, 53,* 344–350.

Swaim, R. C., Oetting, E. R., Thurman, P. J., Beauvais, F., & Edwards, R. W. (1993). American Indian adolescent drug use and socialization characteristics: A cross-cultural comparison. *Journal of Cross-Cultural Psychology, 24,* 53–70.

Swain, I. U., Zelazo, P. R., & Clifton, R. K. (1993). Newborn infants memory for speech sounds retained over 24 hours. *Developmental Psychology, 29,* 312–323.

Swanson, H. L. (1992). The relationship between metacognition and problem solving in gifted children. *Roeper Review, 15,* 43–48.

Swanson, H. L. (1993). Working memory in learning disability subgroups. *Journal of Experimental Child Psychology, 56,* 87–114.

Swanson, H. L., & Hill, G. (1993). Metacognitive aspects of moral reasoning and behavior. *Adolescence, 28,* 711–736.

Swanson, J. M., Cantwell, D., Lerner, M., McBurnett, K., & Hanna, G. (1991). Effects of stimulant medication on learning in children with ADHD. *Journal of Learning Disabilities, 24,* 219–230.

Szymanski, L. A., Devlin, A. S., & Chrisler, J. C. (1993). Gender role and attitudes toward rape in male and female college students. *Sex Roles: A Journal of Research, 29,* 37–57.

Talbot, J. F., & Kaplan, R. (1991). The benefits of nearby nature for elderly apartment residents. *International Journal of Aging and Human Development, 33,* 119–130.

Tamer, S. K., Tamer, U., & Warey, P. (1991). The dying child and overt parental behavior. *Indian Pediatrics, 28,* 1497–1501.

Tamir, L. (1982). *Men in their forties: The transition to middle age.* New York: Springer.

Tamis-LeMonda, C. S., & Bornstein, M. H. (1993). Play and its relations to other mental functions in the child. *New Directions in Child Development, 59,* 17–28.

Tanner, J. M., Whitehouse, R. H., & Takaishi, M. (1966). Standards from birth to maturity for height, weight, height velocity, and weight velocity: British Children 1965—I. *Archives of Disease in Childhood, 41,* 454–471.

Tattum, D., & Herbert, G. (1993). *Countering bullying: Initiatives by schools and local authorities.* Stoke-on-Trent, England: Trentham Books.

Tavris, C., & Baumgartner, A. I. (1983, February). How would your life be different if you'd been born a boy? *Redbook,* p. 99.

Taylor, C. (1989). *Sources of the self.* Cambridge, MA: Harvard University Press.

Taylor, M., Cartwright, B. S., & Carlson, S. M. (1993). A developmental investigation of children's imaginary companions. *Developmental Psychology, 29,* 276–285.

Television and your children. (1985). Ontario, Canada: TV Ontario, The Ontario Educational Communications Authority.

Tennyson, S. A., Pereyra, P. M., & Becker, L. E. (1994). The development of the diaphragm in infants with sudden infant death syndrome. *Early Human Development, 37,* 1–8.

Terkel, S. (1972). *Working.* New York: Random House.

Terman, L. M., assisted by B. T. Baldwin et al. (1925). *Genetic studies of genius* (Vol. 1). Stanford, CA: Stanford University Press.

Termine, N. T., & Izard, C. E. (1988). Infants' responses to their mothers' expressions of joy and sadness. *Developmental Psychology, 24,* 223–229.

Terrace, H. S. (1985). In the beginning was the "Name." *American Psychologist, 40,* 1011–1028.

Theriault, J. (1994). Retirement as a psychosocial transition: Process of adaptation to change. *International Journal of Aging and Human Development, 38,* 153–170.

Thiessen, I. (1993). The impact of divorce on children. *Early Childhood Development and Care, 96,* 19–26.

Thoma, S. J. (1993). The relationship between political preference and moral judgment development in late adolescence. *Merrill-Palmer Quarterly, 39,* 359–374.

Thomas, A., & Chess, S. (1977). *Temperament and development.* New York: Brunner/Mazel.

Thomas, A., & Chess, S. (1981). The role of temperament in the contribution of individuals to their development. In R. M. Lerner & N. A. Busch-Rossnagel (Eds.), *Individuals as producers of their development.* New York: Academic Press.

Thomas, A., Chess, S., & Birch, H. G. (1968). *Temperament and behavior disorders in children.* New York: New York University Press.

Thomas, A., Chess, S., & Birch, H. G. (1970). The origin of personality. *Scientific American, 223,* 102–109.

Thomas, A., Chess, S., & Korn, S. J. (1982). The reality of difficult temperament. *Merrill-Palmer Quarterly, 28,* 1–20.

Thomas, H., & Lohaus, A. (1993). Modeling growth and individual differences in spatial tasks. *Monographs of the Society for Research in Child Development, 58,* (237, 9).

Thomas, J. W. (1980). Agency and achievement: Self-management and self-regard. *Review of Educational Research, 50,* 213–240.

Thomas, R. M. (1992). *Comparing theories of child development* (3rd ed.). Belmont, CA: Wadsworth.

Thompson, R. J., Jr., Gil, K. M., & Abrams, M. R. (1992). Stress, coping, and psychological adjustment of adults with sickle cell disease. *Journal of Consulting & Clinical Psychology, 60,* 33–40.

Thompson, R. W., Grow, C. R., & Ruma, P. R. (1993). Evaluation of a practical parenting program with middle- and low-income families. *Family Relations, 42,* 21–25.

Thomson, E., & Colella, U. (1992). Cohabitation and marital stability: Quality or commitment. *Journal of Marriage and the Family, 54,* 259–267.

Thorp, J. A., Meyer, B. A., Cohen, G. R., Yeast, Y. D., & Hu, D. (1994). Epidural analgesia in labor and cesarean delivery for dystocia. *Obstetrical and Gynecological Survey, 49,* 362–369.

Thorpe, W. H. (1963). *Learning and instinct in animals* (2nd ed.). London: Methuen.

Tierney, J. (1988). Not to worry. *Hippocrates,* January/February, pp. 29–36.

Tisak, M. S. (1993). Preschool children's judgments of moral and personal events involving physical harm and property damage. *Merrill-Palmer Quarterly, 39,* 375–390.

Tite, R. (1993). How teachers define and respond to child abuse: The distinction between theoretical and reportable cases. *Child Abuse and Neglect: The International Journal, 17*, 591–603.

Tobin, J. J., Wu, D. Y. H., & Davidson, D. H. (1989). *Preschool in three cultures: Japan, China, and the United States*. New Haven, CT: Yale University Press.

Tomlin, A. M., & Passman, R. H. (1989). Grandmothers' responsibility in raising two-year-olds facilitates their grandchildren's adaptive behavior: A preliminary intrafamilial investigation of mothers' and maternal grandmothers' effects. *Psychology and Aging, 4,* 119–121.

Tomlin, A. M., & Passman, R. H. (1991). Grandmothers' advice about disciplining grandchildren: Is it accepted by mothers, and does its rejection influence grandmothers' subsequent guidance? *Psychology and Aging, 6*, 182–189.

Toneguzzi, M. (1994, Nov. 20). Jury refused to convict couple who killed son. *Edmonton Journal,* p. C2.

Toray, T., Coughlin, C., Vuchinich, S., & Patricelli, P. (1991). Gender differences associated with adolescent substance abuse: Comparisons and implications for treatment. *Family Relations, 40*, 338–344.

Tough curbs urged for reproductive medicine. (1993, Nov. 30). *Edmonton Journal,* p. A1.

Trehub, S. E., Schneider, B. A., Thorpe, L. A., & Judge, P. (1991). Observational measures of auditory sensitivity in early infancy. *Developmental Psychology, 27,* 40–49.

Trickett, P. K., Aber, J. L., Carlson, V., & Cicchetti, D. (1991). Relationship of socioeconomic status to the etiology and developmental sequelae of physical child abuse. *Developmental Psychology, 27*, 148–158.

Trickett, P. K., & Susman, E. J. (1988). Parental perceptions of child-rearing practices in physically abusive and nonabusive families. *Developmental Psychology, 24,* 270–276.

Trofatter, K. F., Jr. (1990). Fetal immunology. In R. D. Eden, F. H. Boehm, & M. Haire (Eds.), *Assessment and care of the fetus: Physiological, clinical, and medicolegal principles.* Norwalk, CT: Appleton & Lange.

Tronick, E. Z. (1989). Emotions and emotional communication in infants. *American Psychologist, 44,* 112–119.

Trotter, A. (1991). Rites of passage. *Executive Educator, 13,* 48–49.

Trudel, G., Ravart, M., & Matte, B. (1993). The use of the multiaxial diagnostic system for sexual dysfunctions in the assessment of hypoactive sexual desire. *Journal of Sex and Marital Therapy, 19,* 123–130.

Tryon, R. C. (1940). Genetic differences in maze learning in rats. *Yearbook of the National Society for Studies in Education, 39,* 111–119.

Tsuchiyama, B. (1992). Philippines OMEP kindergartens for poor children. *International Journal of Early Childhood Education, 24,* 56–64.

Tubman, J. G. (1993). Family risk factors, parental alcohol use, and problem behaviors among school-age children. *Family Relations, 42,* 81–86.

Tudge, J. R. H., & Winterhoff, P. A. (1993). Vygotsky, Piaget, and Bandura: Perspectives on the relations between the social world and cognitive development. *Human Development, 36,* 61–81.

Tulving, E. (1991). Concepts in human memory. In L. R. Squire, N. M. Weinberger, G. Lynch, & J. L. McGaugh (Eds.), *Memory: Organization and locus of change.* New York: Oxford University Press.

Tuma, J. M. (1989). Mental health services for children. *American Psychologist, 44,* 188–195.

Turgi, P. A. (1992). Children's rights in America: The needs and actions. *Journal of Humanistic Education and Development, 31,* 53–63.

Turkey baster used to help make baby. (1993, April 21). *Edmonton Sun,* p. 28.

Turkheimer, E. (1991). Individual and group differences in adoption studies of IQ. *Psychological Bulletin, 110,* 392–405.

Turner, B. L., II, Clark, W. C., Kates, R. W., Richards, J. F., Mathews, J. T., et al. (Eds.). (1991). *The earth as transformed by human action.* New York: Cambridge University Press.

U.S. Bureau of the Census. (1988). *Statistical abstracts of the United States, 1987* (108th ed.). Washington, DC: U.S. Government Printing Office.

U.S. Bureau of the Census. (1991). *Statistical abstracts of the United States, 1991* (111th ed.). Washington, DC: U.S. Government Printing Office.

U.S. Bureau of the Census. (1992). *Statistical abstracts of the United States, 1992* (112th ed.). Washington, DC: U.S. Government Printing Office.

U.S. Bureau of the Census. (1993). *Statistical abstracts of the United States, 1993* (113th ed.). Washington, DC: U.S. Government Printing Office.

U.S. Bureau of the Census. (1994). *Statistical abstracts of the United States, 1994* (114th ed.). Washington, DC: U.S. Government Printing Office.

U.S. Department of Commerce, Bureau of the Census. (1980). *Social indicators III: Selected data on social conditions and trends in the United States.* Washington, DC: U.S. Government Printing Office.

U.S. Department of Health and Human Services. (1988, September). *Monthly vital statistics report* (Vol. 37, no. 6). Public Health Service. Centers for Disease Control. Washington, DC: U.S. Government Printing Office.

U.S. Department of Health and Human Services. (1989, February). *Monthly vital statistics report* (Vol. 37, no. 11). Public Health Service. Centers for Disease Control. Washington, DC: U.S. Government Printing Office.

Udani, P. M. (1992). Protein energy malnutrition (PEM), brain and various facets of child development. *Indian Journal of Pediatrics, 59,* 165–186.

Vaillant, C. O., & Vaillant, G. E. (1993). Is the U-Curve of marital satisfaction an illusion? A 40-year study of marriage. *Journal of Marriage and the Family, 55,* 230–239.

Vaillant, G. E., & Milofsky, E. (1980). Natural history of male psychological health: IX. Empirical evidence for Erikson's model of the life cycle. *The American Journal of Psychiatry, 137,* 1348–1359.

Valdes-Dapena, M. A. (1991). The phenomenon of sudden infant death syndrome and its challenges. In C. A. Corr, H. Fuller, C. A. Barnickol, & D. M. Corr (Eds.), *Sudden infant death syndrome: Who can help and how.* New York: Springer.

Valsiner, J. (1987). *Culture and the development of children's action: A cultural-historical theory of developmental psychology.* New York: John Wiley.

Vandell, D. L., & Ramanan, J. (1991). Children of the National Longitudinal Survey of Youth: Choices in after-school care and child development. *Developmental Psychology, 27,* 637–643.

Vandell, D. L., Wilson, K. S., & Buchanan, N. R. (1980). Peer interaction in the first year of life: An examination of its structure, content, and sensitivity to toys. *Child Development, 51,* 481–488.

Vikan, A., & Clausen, S. E. (1993). Freud, Piaget, or neither? Beliefs in controlling others by wishful thinking and magical behavior in young children. *Journal of Genetic Psychology, 154,* 297–314.

Vinovskis, M. A. (1988). The historian and the life course: Reflections on recent approaches to the study of American family life in the past. In P. B. Baltes, D. L. Featherman, & R. M. Lerner (Eds.), *Life-span development and behavior* (Vol. 8). Hillsdale, NJ: Erlbaum.

Visher, E. B., & Visher, J. S. (1988). *Old loyalties, new ties.* New York: Brunner/Mazel.

Vitaro, F., Tremblay, R. E., & Gagnon, C. (1992). Peer rejection from kindergarten to grade 2: Outcomes, correlates, and prediction. *Merrill-Palmer Quarterly, 38,* 382–400.

Volling, B. L., & Belsky, J. (1993). Maternal employment: Parent, infant, and contextual characteristics related to maternal employment decisions in the first year of infancy. *Family Relations, 42,* 4–12.

Voorrips, L. E., Lemmink, K. A., van Heuvelen, M. J., Bult, P., & van Staveren, W. A. (1993). The physical condition of elderly women differing in habitual physical activity. *Medicine and Science in Sports and Exercise, 25,* 1152–1157.

Vorhees, C. V., & Mollnow, E. (1987). Behavioral teratogenesis: Long-term influences on behavior from early exposure to environmental agents. In J. D. Osofsky (Ed.), *Handbook of infant development.* New York: John Wiley.

Voss, S. (1992). The usage of pregnancy tests in one health district. *British Journal of Obstetrics and Gynaecology, 99,* 1000–1003.

Vostanis, P., Harrington, R., Prendergast, M., & Farndon, P. (1994). Case reports of autism with interstitial deletion of chromosome 17 (p11.2 p11.2) and monosomy of chromosome 5 (5pter → 5p15.3). *Psychiatric Genetics, 4,* 109–111.

Vuchinich, S., Vuchinich, R., & Wood, B. (1993). The interparental relationship and family problem solving with preadolescent males. *Child Development, 64,* 1389–1400.

Vygotsky, L. S. (1977). *Mind in society: The development of higher psychological processes.* Cambridge, MA: Harvard University Press.

Vygotsky, L. S. (1986). *Thought and language* (translated and revised by A. Kozulin). Cambridge, MA: MIT Press.

Waddington, C. H. (1975). *The evolution of an evolutionist.* Edinburgh: Edinburgh University Press.

Wadsworth, B. J. (1989). *Piaget's theory of cognitive and affective development* (4th ed.). New York: Longman.

Wagner, M. E., Schubert, H. J. P., & Schubert, D. S. P. (1985). Effects of sibling spacing on intelligence, interfamilial relations, psychosocial characteristics, and mental and physical health. *Advances in Child Development and Behavior, 19,* 149–206.

Wallace, D. C. (1994). Mitochondrial DNA sequence variation in human evolution and disease. *Proceedings of the National Academy of Sciences of the United States of America, 91,* 8739–8746.

Wallach, M. A., & Kogan, N. (1965). *Modes of thinking in young children: A study of the creativity–intelligence distinction.* New York: Holt, Rinehart & Winston.

Wallerstein, J. S. (1989, Jan. 23). Children after divorce: Wounds that don't heal. *The New York Times Magazine,* pp. 19–21, 41–44.

Wallerstein, J. S., & Kelly, J. B. (1976). The effects of parental divorce: Experiences of the child in later latency. *American Journal of Orthopsychiatry, 46,* 256–269.

Wallerstein, J. S., & Kelly, J. B. (1980). *Surviving the breakup: How children and parents cope with divorce.* London: Grant McIntyre.

Walton, S. J. (1994). Date rape: New liability for colleges and universities. *Naspa Journal, 31*, 195–200.

Wang, I. Y., & Fraser, I. S. (1994). Reproductive function and contraception in the postpartum period. *Obstetrical and Gynecological Survey, 49*, 56–63.

Warah, A. (1993). Overactivity and boundary setting in anorexia nervosa: An existential perspective. *Journal of Adolescence, 16*, 93–100.

Ward, J. (1994). Exercise and the older person. *Australian Family Physician, 23*, 642–645.

Ward, R. A. (1979). *The aging experience: An introduction to social gerontology.* Philadelphia: Lippincott.

Ward, R. A. (1993). Marital happiness and household equity in later life. *Journal of Marriage and the Family, 55*, 427–438.

Ward, S. K., Chapman, K., Cohn, E., White, S., & Williams, K. (1991). Acquaintance rape and the college social scene. *Family Relations, 40*, 65–71.

Warfield-Coppock, N. (1992). The rites of passage movement: A resurgence of African-centered practices for socializing African American youth. *Journal of Negro Education, 61*, 471–482.

Warner, J. E., & Hansen, D. J. (1994). The identification and reporting of physical abuse by physicians: A review and implications for research. *Child Abuse and Neglect: The International Journal, 18*, 11–25.

Warnes, A. M. (1985). Microlocational issues in housing for the elderly. In G. L. Maddox & E. W. Busse (Eds.), *Aging: The universal human experience.* New York: Springer.

Washton, A. M. (1989). Cocaine addiction: Treatment, recovery, and relapse prevention. New York: Norton.

Waskel, S. A. (1992). Intensity of midlife crisis on responses to the Death Concern Scale. *Journal of Psychology, 126*, 147–154.

Waskel, S. A., & Coleman, J. (1991). Correlations of temperament types, intensity of crisis at midlife with scores on a death scale. *Psychological Reports, 68*, 1187–1190.

Waters, E., Hay, D., & Richters, J. (1986). Infant–parent attachment and the origins of prosocial and antisocial behavior. In D. Olweus, J. Block, & M. Radke-Yarrow (Eds.), *Development of antisocial and prosocial behavior: Research, theories, and issues.* New York: Academic Press.

Watson, J. B. (1914). *Behavior: An introduction to comparative psychology.* New York: Holt, Rinehart & Winston.

Watson, J. B. (1930). *Behaviorism* (2nd ed.). Chicago: University of Chicago Press.

Watson, J. B., & Rayner, R. (1920). Conditioned emotional reactions. *Journal of Experimental Psychology, 3*, 1–14.

Watson, P. (1994, Dec. 14). Somali crowd cheers each stone as Islamic justice dispatches rapist. *Edmonton Journal*, p. A1, A16.

Watts, W. D., & Wright, L. S. (1990). The relationship of alcohol, tobacco, marijuana, and other illegal drug use to delinquency among Mexican-American, black, and white adolescent males. *Adolescence, 25*, 171–181.

Weber, K. S., Frankenberg, W., & Heilman, K. (1992). The effects of Ritalin on the academic achievement of children diagnosed with attention-deficit hyperactivity disorder. *Developmental Disabilities Bulletin, 20*, 49–68.

Webster, J. D., & Young, R. A. (1988). Process variables of the life review: Counseling implications. *International Journal of Aging and Human Development, 26*, 315–323.

Wegmann, R. (1991). How long does unemployment last? *The Career Development Quarterly, 40*, 71–81.

Weinberg, R. (1989). Intelligence and IQ. *American Psychologist, 44*, 98–104.

Weiner, B. (1980). *Human motivation.* New York: Holt, Rinehart & Winston.

Weisfeld, G. E. (1982). The nature–nurture issue and the integrating concept of function. In B. B. Wolman et al. (Eds.), *Handbook of developmental psychology.* Englewood Cliffs, NJ: Prentice-Hall.

Weisskopf, M. (1987). Lead astray: The poisoning of America. *Discovery, 8*, 76–77.

Wellman, H. M. (1988). The early development of memory strategies. In F. E. Weinert & M. Perlmutter (Eds.), *Memory development: Universal changes and individual differences.* Hillsdale, NJ: Erlbaum.

Wellman, H. M. (1990). *The child's theory of mind.* Cambridge, MA: MIT Press.

Wellman, H. M., & Gelman, S. A. (1992). Cognitive development: Foundational theories of core domains. *Annual Review of Psychology, 43*, 337–375.

Wellman, M. M. (1993). Child sexual abuse and gender differences: Attitudes and prevalence. *Child Abuse and Neglect: The International Journal, 17*, 539–547.

Wells, G. (1985). *Language development in the pre-school years.* Cambridge: Cambridge University Press.

Werner, E. E. (1993). Children of the garden island. In M. Gauvain & M. Cole (Eds.), *Readings on the development of children.* New York: W. H. Freeman.

Westbury, I. (1992). Comparing American and Japanese achievement: Is the United States really a low achiever? *Educational Researcher, 21*, 18–24.

Westbury, I., Ethington, C., Sosniak, L., & Baker, D. (Eds.). (1993). *In search of more effective mathematics education: Examining data from the IEA Second International Mathematics Study.* Norwood, NJ: Ablex.

Westman, J. C. (1991). Introduction. In J. C. Westman (Ed.), *Who speaks for the children?* Sarasota, FL: Professional Resource Exchange, Inc.

Westrom, L. V. (1994). Sexually transmitted diseases and infertility. *Sexually Transmitted Diseases, 21*, S32–S37.

Whiffen, V. E., & Gotlib, I. H. (1993). Comparison of postpartum and nonpostpartum depression: Clinical presentation, psychiatric history, and psychosocial functioning. *Journal of Personality and Social Psychology, 61*, 485–494.

Whitbeck, L., Hoyt, D. R., & Huck, S. M. (1984). Early family relationships, intergenerational solidarity, and support provided to parents by their adult children. *Journal of Gerontology, 49*, s85–s94.

White, D., & Woollett, A. (1992). *Families: A context for development.* New York: Falmer Press.

White, K. R., Taylor, M. J., & Moss, V. D. (1992). Does research support claims about the benefits of involving parents in early intervention programs? *Review of Educational Research, 62*, 91–125.

Whitney, E. N., & Hamilton, E. M. N. (1984). *Understanding nutrition* (3rd ed.). St. Paul, MN: West.

Whorf, B. L. (1956). *Language, thought and reality.* New York: John Wiley.

Widiger, T. A., & Smith, G. T. (1994). Substance use disorder: Abuse, dependence and dyscontrol. *Addiction, 89*, 267–282.

Widstrom, A. M., & Thingstrom-Paulsson, J. (1993). The position of the tongue during rooting reflexes elicited in newborn infants before the first suckle. *Acta Paediatrica, 82*, 281–283.

Wiebe, E., & Wiebe, A. (1994). Fragile X syndrome. *Canadian Family Physician, 40*, 290–295.

Wiggins, J. S., & Pincus, A. L. (1992). Personality: Structure and assessment. *Annual Review of Psychology, 43*, 473–504.

Wilbush, J. (1994). Confrontation in the climacteric. *Journal of the Royal Society of Medicine, 87*, 342–347.

Wilfley, D. E., Agras, W. S., Telch, C. F., Rossiter, E. M., Schneider, J. A., Cole, A. G., Sifford, L. A., & Raeburn, S. D. (1993). Group cognitive-behavioral therapy and group interpersonal psychotherapy for the nonpurging bulimic individual: A controlled comparison. *Journal of Consulting & Clinical Psychology, 61*, 296–305.

Wilk, C. A. (1986). *Career women and childbearing: A psychological analysis of the decision process.* New York: Van Nostrand Reinhold.

Willerman, L. (1979). Effects of families on intellectual development. *American Psychologist, 34*, 923–929.

Williams, K., Haywood, K., & Vansant, A. (1991). Throwing patterns of older adults: A follow-up investigation. *International Journal of Aging and Human Development, 33*, 279–294.

Williams, T. H., & Handford, A. G. (1986). Television and other leisure activities. In T. H. Williams (Ed.), *The impact of television: A natural experiment in three communities.* Orlando, FL: Academic Press.

Willinger, M., Hoffman, H. J., & Hartford, R. B. (1994). Infant sleep position and risk for sudden infant death syndrome. *Pediatrics, 93*, 814–819.

Willis, S. L., & Schaie, K. W. (1994). Assessing everyday competence in the elderly. In C. B. Fisher & R. M. Lerner (Eds.), *Applied developmental psychology.* New York: McGraw-Hill.

Wills, C. (1993). Scientific goals of the human genome project. *National Forum: Phi Kappa Phi Journal, 73*, 9–11.

Wilson, D. S. (1994). Adaptive genetic variation and human evolutionary psychology. *Ethology and Sociobiology, 15*, 219–225.

Wilson, E. O. (1975). *Sociobiology: The new synthesis.* Cambridge, MA: Belknap.

Wilson, E. O. (1976). Academic vigilantism and the political significance of sociobiology. *Bio-science, 183*, 187–190.

Wilson, G. T., & Fairburn, C. G. (1993). Cognitive treatments for eating disorders. *Journal of Consulting and Clinical Psychology, 61*, 261–269.

Wilson, G. T., & Walsh, B. T. (1991). Eating disorders in DSM-IV. *Journal of Developmental Psychology, 100*, 362–365.

Wilson, M. E., Hall, E. O., & White, M. A. (1994). Family dynamics and infant temperament in Danish families. *Scandinavian Journal of Caring Sciences, 8*, 9–15.

Wilson, S. M., & Medora, N. P. (1990). Gender comparisons of college students' attitudes toward sexual behavior. *Adolescence, 25*, 15–29.

Winer, G. A., & McGlone, C. (1993). On the uncertainty of conservation: Responses to misleading conservation questions. *Developmental Psychology, 29*, 760–769.

Wingerson, L. (1990). *Mapping our genes: The genome project and the future of medicine.* New York: Dutton.

Winnicott, D. W. (1971). *Playing and reality.* New York: Basic Books.

Wisniewski, H. M., Silverman, W., & Wegiel, J. (1994). Ageing, Alzheimer disease and mental retardation. *Journal of Intellectual Disability Research, 38*, 233–239.

Wolf-Schein, E. G. (1992). On the association between the fragile X chromosome, mental handicap, and autistic disorder. *Developmental Disabilities Bulletin, 20*, 13–30.

Wolff, P. H. (1963). Observations of the early development of smiling. In B. M. Foss (Ed.), *Determinants of infant behavior 2.* London: Methuen.

Wolff, P. H. (1966). The causes, controls, and organization of behavior in the neonate. *Psychological Issues, 5*(1)(Whole No. 17), 1–105.

Wolff, P. H. (1969). The natural history of crying and other vocalizations in early infancy. In B. Foss (Ed.), *Determinants of infant behavior 4.* London: Methuen.

Wolke, D., Gray, P., & Meyer, R. (1994). Excessive infant crying: A controlled study of mothers helping mothers. *Pediatrics, 94,* 322–333.

Wolman, W. L., Chalmers, B., Hofmeyr, F. J., & Nikodem, V. C. (1993). Postpartum depression and companionship in the clinical birth environment. *American Journal of Obstetrics & Gynecology, 168,* 1388–1393.

Wood, B. S. (1981). *Children and communication: Verbal and nonverbal language development.* (2nd ed.). Englewood Cliffs, NJ: Prentice-Hall.

Wright, H. F. (1960). Observational child study. In P. H. Mussen (Ed.), *Handbook of research methods in child development.* New York: John Wiley.

Wu, D. Y. H. (1981). Child abuse in Taiwan. In J. E. Korbin (Ed.), *Child abuse and neglect: Cross-cultural perspectives.* Berkeley: University of California Press.

Yarrow, L. J., & Goodwin, M. S. (1973). The immediate impact of separation: Reactions of infants to a change in mother figures. In L. J. Stone, H. T. Smith, & L. B. Murphy (Eds.), *The competent infant: Research and commentary.* New York: Basic Books.

Yost, J. H., Strube, M. J., & Bailey, J. R. (1992). The construction of the self: An evolutionary view. *Current Psychology: Research & Reviews, 11,* 110–121.

Young, I. D. (1991). Genetic counselling. In D. T. Liu (Ed.), *A practical guide to chorion villus sampling.* New York: Oxford University Press.

Zajonc, R. B. (1976). Family configuration and intelligence. *Science, 192,* 227–236.

Zani, B. (1991). Male and female patterns in the discovery of sexuality during adolescence. *Journal of Adolescence, 14,* 163–178.

Zarit, S. H., & Reid, J. D. (1994). Family caregiving and the older family. In C. B. Fisher & R. M. Lerner (Eds.), *Applied developmental psychology.* New York: McGraw-Hill.

Zelinski, E. M., Gilewski, M. J., & Schaie, K. W. (1993). Individual differences in cross-sectional and 3-year longitudinal memory performance across the adult life span. *Psychology and Aging, 8,* 176–186.

Zentall, S. S. (1993). Research on the educational implications of attention deficit hyperactivity disorder. *Exceptional Children, 60,* 143–153.

Zigler, E. (1994). Reshaping early childhood intervention to be a more effective weapon against poverty. *American Journal of Community Psychology, 22,* 37–47.

Zigler, E., & Freedman, J. (1987). Early experience, malleability, and Head Start. In J. J. Gallagher & C. T. Ramey (Eds.), *The malleability of children.* Baltimore: Brookes.

Zigler, E., & Hodapp, R. M. (1991). Behavioral functioning in individuals with mental retardation. *Annual Review of Psychology, 42,* 29–50.

Zisook, S., Shuchter, S. R., Sledge, P. A., Paulus, M., & Judd, L. L. (1994). The spectrum of depressive phenomena after spousal bereavement. *Journal of Clinical Psychiatry, 55,* 29–36.

Zuckerman, B., & Bresnahan, K. (1991). Developmental and behavioral consequences of prenatal drug and alcohol exposure. *Pediatric Clinics of North America, 38,* 1387–1406.

Zuo, J. (1992). The reciprocal relationship between marital interaction and marital happiness: A three-wave study. *Journal of Marriage and the Family, 54,* 870–878.

PHOTO CREDITS

p. ix Angela Mann; p. x (top) Martha Branch; p. x (bottom) Debby Kramer; p. xi (top) Lori Lawrence; p. xi (bottom) Claude Desplan; p. xii Karen Garrison; p. xiii Angela Mann; p. xiv (top) Cloyce Wall; p. xiv (bottom) Roberta Broyer; p. xv Cecilia Mantecon; p. xvi (top) Roberta Broyer; p. xvi (bottom) Michael Blanpied; pp. xvii & xviii (top) Marcia Montague; p. xviii (bottom) Bill Ralph; p. xix Guy Lefrançois; p. xx (top) Jeanne Woodward; p. xx (bottom) Laurie Campbell; p. xxi Judith Ogus; p. xxii (l) Angela Mann; p. xxii (r) Karen Garrison; p. xxii (top) Angela Mann; p. xxiii Tekla Weber; p. xxiv (top) Angela Mann; p. xxv Judith Ogus; p. xxvi (top) Patricia Waldo; p. xxvi (bottom) Karen Garrison; p. xxvii Brandon Carson; p. 2 Mike Muckley/Photophile; p. 4 Brian Berry; p. 8 Mary Cassatt, Women Admiring a Child, pastel, 1897, Gift of Edward Chandler Walker, © 1987 The Detroit Institute of Arts; p. 9 (l) Courtesy of the Huntington Library; p. 9 (r) The Bettmann Archive; p. 10 UPI/Bettmann; p. 11 Robert Brenner/PhotoEdit; p. 13 Mira Roytman; p. 19 (l) courtesy of Norbert Meroux; p. 19 (r) Norbert Meroux; p. 23 John Bergez; p. 28 Elizabeth Crews/Stock, Boston; p. 30 Wide World Photos; p. 33 Marti Wall; p. 36 Tekla Weber; p. 43 Jim Mahoney/The Image Works; p. 44 Reuters/Bettmann; p. 48 Karen Garrison; p. 51 Nita Winter; p. 62 James Carroll/Stock, Boston; p. 64 Robert Kauser; p. 65 UPI/Bettmann; p. 69 Catherine Linberg; p. 70 Ann Butler; p. 75 The National Foundation for the March of Dimes; p. 76 Milwaukee Public Museum; p. 82 Ira Berger/Woodfin Camp & Associates; pp. 90 & 94 Carnegie Institute of Washington, Department of Embryology, Davis Division; p. 100 Peter Hendrie/The Image Bank; p. 103 Alon Reininger/Woodfin Camp & Associates; p. 107 Brandon Carson; pp. 109 & 110 Pat Waldo; p. 114 Karen Garrison; p. 116 Bill Aron/Jeroboam; *Color Insert I: p. 1 (top l) Laurie Campbell; p. 1 (top r) Tekla Weber; p. 1 (bottom r) Angela Mann; p. 1 (bottom l) Tekla Weber; p. 2 (l) Cecilia Mantecon; p. 2 (top r) Tekla Weber; p. 2 (bottom r) Gail Baker Woods; p. 3 (top l) Carolyn Deacy; p. 3 (middle r) Pat Waldo; p. 3 (bottom l) G. Menzie/Photophile; p. 3 (bottom r) Brian Berry; p. 4 (top) Carolyn Deacy; p. 4 (bottom r) John Bergez; p. 4 (bottom l) Angela Mann;* p. 122 Angela Mann; p. 124 Claude Desplan; pp. 128, 129, & 134 Tekla Weber; p. 135 Hickman Archives; p. 136 (l) Topham/The Image Works; p. 136 (r) courtesy of William Vandivert, *Scientific American*, April 1960; p. 137 Spelvin Archives; p. 140 Julie Davis; p. 142 Brandon Carson; p. 146 Marvin E. Newman/The Image Bank; p. 149 Rohn Engh/The Image Works; p. 156 Jill Reinemann; p. 159 Danièle Desplan; p. 160 Karen Garrison; p. 162 Guy Lefrançois; p. 164 Cecilia Mantecon; p. 167 Harlow Primate Laboratory, University of Wisconsin; p. 169 D. Ogust/The Image Works; p. 170 Roberta Broyer; p. 172 Ann Butler; p. 175 Jill Jacobson; p. 176 Robert Kauser; p. 177 Angela Mann; p. 178 Pamela J. Zilly/The Image Bank; p. 179 Sabra Home; p. 180 B. Wells/The ImageWorks; p. 186 Bob Kramer/Stock, Boston; p. 188 Elizabeth Crews/Stock, Boston; p. 193 Angela Mann; p. 199 Stephen Rapley; p. 202 Matthew Lyle; p. 203 Nita Winter; p. 204 Peter Menzel; p. 207 (top) UPI/Bettmann Newsphotos; p. 207 (bottom) Pat Waldo; p. 211 Antman/The Image Works; p. 212 Roberta Broyer; p. 213 Elizabeth Crews/The Image Works; p. 216 Brian Berry; p. 220 Michael Dwyer/Stock, Boston; p. 222 Michael Blanpied; p. 223 Cecilia Mantecon; p. 228 Karen Hunt; p. 230 The Bettmann Archive; p. 231 Karen Hunt; p. 234 Jane Scherr/Jeroboam; pp. 237 & 241 Tekla Weber; p. 242 Diana Tejo; p. 248 Frank Siteman/Stock, Boston; p. 250 John Lei/Stock, Boston; p. 254 Christopher Brown/Stock, Boston; p. 255 Pat Waldo; p. 258 Nita Winter; pp. 265 & 268 Roberta Broyer; p. 276 Alan Venable; p. 278 Alain Choisnet/The Image Bank; p. 282 Roger Holden/Photophile; p. 286 Pat Waldo; p. 289 Suzanne Astier; p. 293 Giuliano Colliva/Image Bank; p. 294 Elizabeth Crews/Stock, Boston; p. 296 Michael Weisbrot/Stock, Boston; p. 302 Patricia Hollander Gross/Stock, Boston; p. 306 Adriane Bosworth; p. 312 Jim Whitmer/Stock, Boston; p. 314 Marcia Montague; p. 317 The Bettmann Archive; p. 318 (l) Carol Carreon; p. 318 (r) Carolyn Deacy; p. 320 Margrete Lyons; p. 323 Cleo Photography/PhotoEdit; p. 324 Tony Freeman/PhotoEdit; p. 327 Margrete Lyons; p. 329 Laurie Campbell; p. 331 Margrete Lyons; p. 333 Alan Carey/The ImageWorks; p. 334 Peter Menzel/Stock, Boston; p. 335 Margrete Lyons; p. 342 S. Dawson/Photophile; p. 345 Nita Winter;

Eichorn, D. H., 487
Eilers, R. E., 150
Eisenberg, M., 244
Eisenberg, N., 225, 226, 338
Eisler, T. A., 526
Eisman, J., 388, 449
Ejaculation, 391
Elaborating, 265
Elder, G. H., Jr., 85, 86, 138
Elder abuse, 534
Electra complex, 35
Eliciting effect, 44, 223
Elkin, F., 410
Elkind, D., 202, 206, 307, 331, 332
Ellman, J. P., 477
Embedding, 208–209
Embryo stage of prenatal development, 93, 94–95
Emery, A. E., 67, 72, 76, 77, 78, 79, 84
Emery, R. E., 303
Emotional abuse, 300–301
Emotional distancing, 350
Emotional sounds, 150
Emotions
    early childhood, 225–226
    infancy, 164–166
    and prenatal development, 101
    See also Social development
Emotive influence, 45–46
Empathy, 285
Empty nest phase, 477, 478–479
Enactive influence, 45, 46
Endres, W., 74
Endsley, R. C., 244
English Only, 214
English Plus, 214
Environment. *See* Contextual model of development
Epidural analgesia, 112
Epigenesis, 71
Epigenetic landscape, 71
Epilepsy, 181
Episiotomy, 109
Episodic memory, 264, 508
Equilibration, 141–142
Erectile dysfunction, 392
Erickson, G., 355
Erickson, M. T., 181, 306
Erickson, P. G., 370
Erikson, Erik. *See* Psychosocial theory (Erikson)
Erikson, J. M., 520
Erkkola, R., 112
Ernst, C., 83, 392
Eron, L. D., 297, 298
Erwin, P., 290
Espenschade, A. S., 385
Estrogen replacement therapy (ERT), 451
Etaugh, C., 233
Ethical Standards for Research with Children (APA), 24
Ethics, 24, 80
Ethology, 50, 54, 168
Eugenics, 80–81
Euthanasia, 552–553
Evans, R. I., 45
Evans, W. J., 446
Event sampling, 17
Evra, J. V., 296, 297
Ewen, R. B., 547
Exceptionality
    infancy, 178–182
    language development, 215
    middle childhood, 256–257, 271–279, 304–309
Excitement, 390
Exercise, 386–387, 388, 393, 449, 503–504
Exosystem, 53, 86
Experimental groups, 17–18
Experimenter bias, 23

Experiments, 17–18
Explicit memory, 264
Extended family, 233–234, 427
Extinguishing, 42
Eysenck, H. J., 85

Fabricius, W. V., 196
Failure to thrive (FTT), 168–169
Fairburn, C. G., 327
Fallopian tubes, 93
Family
    dual-career, 461–462
    and early childhood social development, 233–234, 237–243
    and infant social development, 158–159
    life cycle, 427–432
    middle adulthood, 477–483
    and moral development, 339
    single-parent, 13, 238–242
    stepfamilies, 242–243, 482–483
    violence in, 432–433
    See also Parenting
Family child care, 243
Fantz, R. L., 135, 137
Farbman, A. I., 139
Farkas, S., 355
Farrell, M. P., 477
Fasick, F. A., 317
Fat and fat-free mass, 252, 319, 446
Fathers
    adolescence, 363–364
    infancy, 171–172
    See also Family; Parenting
Faulkender, P. J., 520
Feagans, L. V., 256
Fear, 165–166, 297
Feixas, G., 520
Feldman, H., 478, 479
Feldman, R. S., 302
Feldman, S. S., 173
Female infanticide, 10
Fennema, E., 355
Feral children, 64–66, 210
Ferencz, C., 96
Ferguson, L. R., 355
Fertilization, 93
Fertilized ovum stage of prenatal development, 93–94
Fetal alcohol syndrome (FAS), 98–99
Fetal diagnosis, 77–78
Fetal erythroblastosis, 105
Fetoscopy, 78
Fetus stage of prenatal development, 93, 95–96
Field effects, 258
Fifer, W. P., 139
Filial piety, 480, 534
Filiano, J. J., 132
Fine, D. R., 242, 421
Fine, M. A., 234, 242, 421
Finkelhor, D., 301, 302
Finley, C., 435
Finn, P., 370
Fischer, K. W., 31, 32
Fisher, C. B., 32
Fisher, G. L., 274
Fisher, J. C., 496, 520–521
Fisher, J. W., 127
Fisher, N. M., 504
Fisher, W. W., 182
Fishkin, J., 337
Fiske, S. T., 230, 284
Flanagan, J. C., 532
Flannery, D. J., 318
Flavell, J. H., 126, 201, 262, 267, 284
Fleischhacker, W. W., 392
Fleming, P. J., 131, 132

Fleming, S., 533
Fluid intelligence, 268, 454, 455
Flynn, J. R., 293
Fogel, A., 169
Foldenyi, M., 392
Fong, L., 182
Forceps, 115
Foreclosure, 348
Forehand, R., 323
Formal operations stage of cognitive development, 48, 327–329
Forness, S. R., 273
Fouts, R. S., 207
Fox, K. B., 165
Fox, N. A., 162, 172, 196
Fox, R. A., 235
Foy, D. W., 301, 302
Fragile X syndrome, 76–77
Frankenberger, W., 306
Frankenburg, W. K., 193
Franklin, J. T., 368
Fraser, I. S., 127
Fraternal twins, 83
Frazer, N., 392
Freedman, J., 83
Freeman, S. C., 399
Free-radical theory of aging, 500
Free recall, 508
Freeze, R., 299
Freudian slips, 33
Freudian theory, 32–36, 171
Freud, Sigmund, 548. *See also* Freudian theory
Friebert, S. E., 266
Fried, P. A., 99
Friedman, J. M., 69, 72, 75, 76, 96, 97, 99, 100
Friedman, L., 355
Friedman, M., 389
Frieman, B. B., 238
Friendly, D. S., 135
Friendship, 288–292, 531–532
Frye, D., 144, 285
Fry, P. S., 522, 527
Fu, V. R., 173, 174
Fuligni, A. J., 291
Furstenberg, F. F., Jr., 238, 356, 359–360, 361, 482, 483
Furth, H. G., 260

Gage, M. G., 431
Gagnon, C., 292
Galef, B. G., Jr., 254
Gallistel, C. R., 202
Galton, F., 237
Galton, Francis, 81
Galvanic skin response (GSR), 132
Gamble, T. J., 176
Gametes, 67
Gangs, 350, 363, 364–366
Garbarino, J., 292
Garcia, E. E., 212, 214
Garcia, R., 48
Garde, K., 451
Gariépy, J. L., 81
Garvey, C., 229
Gateway drug-use theory, 368
Gathercole, S. E., 196
Gaudin, J. M., Jr., 303
Gavin, C. E., 98
Gayford, J. J., 433
Gaynor, J. L. R., 237, 238
Gaze, 149, 169
Gearhart, J. M., 127
Geiger, S., 296
Gelles, R., 299, 432, 433
Gelman, R., 202
Gelman, S. A., 30, 31, 49, 142, 143, 169, 170, 284

Organizing, 265–266
Orgasm, 391
Orienting response, 132
Ornstein, P. A., 197
Orofacial praxis, 181
Osteoporosis, 449
Osterling, J., 182
Ostrov, E., 344, 345, 347, 362
Other-directed regulatory behaviors, 166, 226
Otis media, 256
Ovaries, 93, 320
Ovcharchyn, C. A., 389
Over, R., 429
Ovum, 67
Ozturk, M., 173
Ozturk, O. M., 173

Packard, V., 355
Packer, A. B., 394
Padgett, R. J., 509
Padilla, A. M., 214, 215
Paikoff, R. L., 350
Pain cry, 165
Pain sensitivity, 139
Paley, V. G., 227, 232
Pallas, A. M., 212
Palliative care, 551
Palmar reflex, 133
Palmer, J. H., 370
Palmer, J. L., 244
Palmlund, I., 96
Palo, P., 112
Pandey, H., 202
Pangrazi, R. P., 256
Papadaki, M., 330
Pape, K. E., 181
Paradoxical effects, 305
Parallel play, 229
Parental disengagement, 239
Parenting
    adolescence, 349–350, 363–364, 431
    child maltreatment, 299–304
    early adulthood, 411–412
    early childhood, 210–211, 234–237, 431
    in family life cycle, 428–431
    and happiness, 486–487
    infancy, 158–159, 162–163, 166–172, 176–177, 430–431
    and late adulthood, 528–529
    and middle adulthood, 477–479
    middle childhood, 290–291, 431
    and psychosocial development, 36–37
    stepparenting, 482–483
    See also Family; specific topics
Paris, S. G., 263, 266
Park, K. A., 227, 229, 289
Parke, R. D., 225
Parker, J. G., 292
Parkhurst, J. T., 292
Parten, M. B., 228
Pasley, K., 242, 243
Pasnak, R., 260
Passino, A. W., 360
Passion, 414–415
Passive vocabulary, 148
Passman, R. H., 165, 173, 174, 529, 530
Patel, B. D., 76
Pattee, L., 292
Patterson, G., 363
Patterson, M. L., 86
Pattison, E. M., 549–550
Patton, J. M., 275
Patton, J. R., 272
Paul, R., 208

Pavlov, Ivan, 40
Pawlik, K., 25
PCBs. See Polychlorinated biphenyls
Peak height velocity, 253
Pearce, J. C., 190, 279
Pearl, R., 368
Pearson, J. L., 355
Pease-Alvarez, L., 212, 213
Peck, R. C., 471–472, 513, 520
Peer groups, 290–291, 350–353
    and delinquency, 363
    and drug use, 368
Pelaez-Nogueras, M., 211
Pelham, W. E., Jr., 306
Pellman, J., 533
Pendergast, D. R., 504
Penner, L. A., 325
Pentz, M. A., 368
Peplau, L. A., 419
Perception, 135
Pereyra, P. M., 131
Perfectionism, 326
Pergament, E., 80
Perkins, D., 267
Perkins, D. N., 270
Perlmutter, M., 141, 453, 505, 506, 508, 509, 513
Permissive parenting, 235
Permutation, 208, 209
Perner, J., 284
Perrin, N., 530
Perry, P., 260
Personal fables, 332
Personality
    and delinquency, 364
    and gene–context interaction, 84
    and happiness, 535, 537
    middle adulthood, 483–485
    vs. temperament, 160
Personal narratives, 521–522
Persuasory influence, 45, 46
Pervasive developmental disorders, 181
Peter Pan syndrome, 382
Peters, H., 99
Petersen, A. C., 320, 321, 322
Peterson, C. M., 100
Peterson, G. W., 239, 241
Peterson, K. L., 331
Petzel, T. P., 389
Peverly, S. T., 267
Phallic stage of psychosexual development, 35
Phares, V., 172
Phenomenology, 55
Phenotype, 70
Phenylketonuria (PKU), 74
Phillips, D., 244
Phonemes, 147
Phonology, 147
Physical abuse, 299–300
Physical development
    adolescence, 318–327
    early adulthood, 385–387
    early childhood, 190–195
    infancy, 129–130
    late adulthood, 502–507
    middle adulthood, 445–451
    middle childhood, 252–257
Physical neglect, 300
Physiological dependence, 366
Piaget, Jean, 15. See also Piagetian theory
Piagetian theory, 47–49
    adolescence, 327–329, 330
    early adulthood, 402
    early childhood, 198–201, 209, 215–216
    infancy, 48, 134, 141–142

middle childhood, 257–261
moral development, 335–336
as organismic model, 32
Pianta, R. C., 171
Piattelli-Palmarini, M., 209
Pierce, E. F., 386
Pietrukowicz, M. E., 534
Pill, C. J., 242
Pina, D. L., 462
Pinchbeck, I., 8
Pincus, A. L., 160
Pines, Maya, 140
Pinyerd, B. J., 164
Pipp, S., 136
Pisoni, D. P., 139
PKU. See Phenylketonuria
Placenta, 94
Plateau, 391
Play, 226–230, 232, 233
Plomin, R., 70, 80, 84, 85, 160, 162
Plotnick, R. D., 423
Plowman, S. A., 254, 256
Pogrebin, L. C., 178
Pogue-Geile, M. F., 84
Polivy, J., 326
Polloway, E. A., 272
Polson, B., 368
Polychlorinated biphenyls (PCBs), 98
Polygamy, 421–422
Poon, L. W., 507, 510, 511
Pope, A. W., 292
Porcile, A., 450, 451
Porter, K. L., 477
Porter, R. H., 139
Positive reinforcement, 42
Pospartum depression, 115
Postconventional moral level, 336
Posterski, D. C., 323, 329, 350, 351
Postmature birth, 112
Post, S. G., 505
Posttraumatic stress disorder, 302
Potts, R., 296
Poverty. See Socioeconomic status
Powell, M. B., 301
Powlishta, K. K., 230
Practice play, 227
Pragmatics, 147–148
Preconceptual thinking, 198–199
Preconventional moral level, 336
Pregnancy, 92. See also Prenatal development
Preimplantation diagnosis, 78
Premature ejaculation, 392
Prematurity, 112, 115–118
Prenatal development, 91–106
    and alcohol, 98–99
    and caffeine, 98
    and chemicals, 97–98
    chromosomal disorders, 75–77
    and drug use, 96–97, 99–100
    genetic defects, 72–75
    and maternal age, 76, 101, 103
    and maternal emotions, 101
    and maternal health, 100–101, 102
    and maternal nutrition, 103–104
    and nicotine, 98
    pregnancy detection, 92
    and prematurity, 116
    Rh(D) immunization, 104–106
    and social class, 104
    stages of, 92–96
Prentice, D. A., 344
Preoperational thought stage of cognitive development, 48, 198–201, 258
Prepared childbirth, 113–115

Schatschneider, C. W., 266
Schemata, 47, 141
Schizophrenia, 84
Schlegel, A., 316
Schmidt, H. J., 139
Schmiege, C. J., 242
Schneider-Rosen, K., 171
Schnur, E., 203
Schoen, R., 418
Schools, 292–295, 338–339
　　gangs in, 364–365
　　See also Education
Schubert, D. S. P., 238
Schubert, H. J. P., 238
Schultz, R., 547
Schutz, R. W., 252, 255
Schwartzman, H. B., 229
Schwartz, M. D., 435
Scripts, 263
Seals, D. R., 504
Sears, P. S., 487
Secondary circular reactions, 144
Secondary sexual characteristics, 320–321
Securely attached infants, 168, 171, 176
Seeman, E., 449
Segal, J., 171
Seigle, S. P., 547
Self-actualization, 56
Self-concept, 37, 286
　　adolescence, 321, 344–347
　　early adulthood, 436–437
　　middle childhood, 285–288
Self-consciousness, 476–477
Self-directed regulatory behaviors, 166, 226
Self-efficacy, 44–46, 399–400
Self-esteem. *See* Self-worth
Self-fulfilling prophecies, 294
Self-image. *See* Self-concept
Self-referent thought, 45, 286
Self-worth, 285–288
Selman, R. L., 285, 289
Seltzer, M. M., 430, 431
Semantic memory, 264, 508
Semantics, 147
Seminal emission, 391
Semrud-Clikeman, M., 274
Sensation, 135
Sensitive period, 50
Sensorimotor play, 227
Sensorimotor stage of cognitive development, 48, 134, 143–145
Sensory memory, 262, 263, 266
Separation anxiety, 172–174
Separation protest, 172
Sequential studies, 21–22, 453
Serafini, S., 214
Serbin, L. A., 230, 231
Serial monogamy, 422
Seriation, 261
Serrano, B., 214
Severson, H., 334
Sex chromosomes, 68–69
Sex differences. *See* Gender differences
Sex roles. *See* Gender roles
Sexual abuse, 301, 302
Sexual assault, 433, 435–436
Sexual double standard, 355, 423
Sexual dysfunctions, 392
Sexuality
　　adolescence, 320–322, 332, 355–362
　　early adulthood, 390–393
　　extramarital, 423
　　in Freudian theory, 33
　　late adulthood, 506–507

middle adulthood, 451
　　premarital, 422–423
Sexually transmitted diseases (STDs), 361–362, 392
Sexual stereotypes. *See* Gender roles
Shacham, S., 114
Shanas, E., 480
Shanklin, D. R., 104
Shapiro, L. R., 323
Shavelson, R. J., 344
Sheard, N. F., 194
Shedler, J., 366, 367
Sheehy, G., 463, 475–476, 522
Shell, R., 338
Shepard, J., 464
Shepherd-Look, D. L., 354
Sheppard, H., 457
Sherman, M., 82
Shields, J., 84
Shiferaw, B., 534
Shiffrin, R. M., 262
Short, E. J., 266
Short-term memory, 262, 263, 266, 507
Shreeve, D. F., 172
Shreve, B. W., 373
Shultz, T. R., 337
Siblings, 83
Sickle-cell anemia, 73–74
SIDS (Sudden infant death syndrome), 99, 130–132
Siegel, A. W., 8
Siegel, O., 322
Siegler, R. S., 263
Sigel, I. E., 202
Significant developmental motor disability, 180–181
Silverman, W., 504
Silvern, L., 31
Silverstein, F. S., 77
Silverstein, L. B., 176
Silvestri, G. T., 394
Silvestri, L., 288
Simard, R., 363
Simic, M. G., 499
Simmons, L., 495
Simmons, R. G., 322
Simon, L., 279
Simons-Morton, B., 323
Simple representation, 148
Simpson, E. E., 369
Simpson, J. L., 97
Sinclair, H., 144
Singer, D. G., 228
Singer, J. L., 228
Singh, J. A., 65
Singlehood, 419–421. *See also* Single-parent families
Single-parent families, 13, 238–242, 457
Skinner, B. F., 15, 16, 40, 41
Skinner, E. A., 307
Skolnick, A., 236, 426, 427
Skuldt-Niederberger, K., 476
Skuy, M., 358
Slovic, P., 334
Small, S. A., 322, 350
Small-for-gestational age (SGA) infants, 112, 115
Smell, 139, 505–506
Smiling, 165
Smith, C. L., 201
Smith, C. V., 139
Smith, D. A., 420, 425, 426
Smith, D. F., 389
Smith, G. T., 366
Smith, L., 47, 49, 136, 258
Smith, M., 360, 551–552
Smolak, L., 324
Smoll, F. L., 252, 255
Snarey, J., 412, 413

Snidman, N., 162
Snyderman, M., 86
Social class. *See* Socioeconomic status
Social cognition, 284–285
Social development
　　adolescence, 344–374
　　early adulthood, 409–437
　　early childhood, 194, 221–244
　　infancy, 157–178
　　late adulthood, 519–537
　　middle adulthood, 469–487
　　middle childhood, 283–309
Social learning theory. *See* Imitation
Social play, 228–229
Social referencing, 225
Sociobiology, 51, 54
Socioeconomic status
　　and delinquency, 362–363
　　and divorce, 239
　　and eating disorders, 326
　　late adulthood, 523–524
　　and prenatal development, 104
　　and psychosocial stages, 413
　　and teenage pregnancy, 358, 359
Sociometric status, 291–292
Socratic dialogue, 267
Solitary play, 229
Solnick, R. E., 427
Solomon, S., 263
Solstad, K., 451
Somers, M. D., 427
Soto, A. M., 98
South, S. J., 416
Sowa, C. J., 463
Spanier, G. B., 176, 482
Sparks, S. P., 100
Spasticity, 181
Special abilities theory of intelligence, 267
Specimen descriptions, 17
Spellacy, W. N., 101
Spence, A. P., 446, 509, 510
Sperling, L. S., 112
Spermarche, 321, 357
Sperm cell, 67
Spigset, O., 127
Spina bifida, 74
Spitz, G., 480
Springer, C., 239
Squire, L. R., 264
Sroufe, L., 165
Stack, S., 373
Stages of development, 16, 39. *See also specific topics and theories*
Staines, G. L., 400
Stall, R. D., 362
Stambak, M., 142, 144
Stander, V., 338
Stanford-Binet intelligence tests, 269
Stanford, L. D., 228
Stanley-Hagan, M., 242
Stanovich, K. E., 273, 274
Stanton, W. R., 47
Stattin, H., 215, 322
St. Aubin, E. D., 472
STDs (Sexually transmitted diseases), 361–362
Steenbarger, B. N., 32
Steffan, P., 357
Steinberg, L., 244
Steitz, J. A., 194
Stepfamilies, 242–243, 482–483
Stephens, R. S., 369
Stereotypes, 231, 353. *See also* Gender roles
Stern, C., 86
Stern, P. C., 25